FUNDAMENTALS OF CORPORATE FINANCE

FUNDAMENTALS OF CORPORATE FINANCE

David Hillier, Stephen Ross,
Randolph Westerfield, Bradford Jordan

Fourth European Edition

Fundamentals of Corporate Finance: Fourth European Edition
David Hillier, Stephen Ross, Randolph Westerfield, Bradford Jordan
ISBN-13 9781526848628
ISBN-10 1526848627

Published by McGraw Hill
8th Floor
338 Euston Road
London
NW1 3BH
Telephone: +44 (0) 203 429 3400
Website: www.mheducation.co.uk

British Library Cataloguing in Publication Data
A catalogue record for this book is available from the British Library

Library of Congress Cataloguing in Publication Data
The Library of Congress data for this book has been applied for from the Library of Congress

Portfolio Managers: Sabrina Farrugia and Lucy Wheeler
Content Developers: Georgia Martin and Maggie du Randt
Content Product Manager: Ali Davis
Marketing Manager: Vee Suchak

Text design by Kamae Design, Oxford
Cover design by Adam Renvoize
Printed and bound in Beirut, Lebanon by Arab Printing Press

Fundamentals of Corporate Finance Copyright © 2009 by McGraw Hill

Adaptation Copyright © 2022 by McGraw Hill (UK) Limited

Published by arrangement with McGraw Hill LLC

ALL RIGHTS RESERVED. NO PART OF THIS BOOK MAY BE REPRODUCED OR TRANSMITTED IN ANY FORM OR BY ANY MEANS, ELECTRONIC OR MECHANICAL, INCLUDING PHOTOCOPYING, RECORDING OR BY INFORMATION STORAGE AND RETRIEVAL SYSTEMS, WITHOUT PERMISSION IN WRITING FROM MCGRAW HILL.

Fictitious names of companies, products, people, characters and/or data that may be used herein (in case studies or in examples) are not intended to represent any real individual, company, product or event.

ISBN-13 9781526848628
ISBN-10 1526848627
eISBN-13 9781526848635

© 2022. Exclusive rights by McGraw Hill for manufacture and export. This book cannot be re-exported from the country to which it is sold by McGraw Hill.

DEDICATION

To my brother, Joe (1954–2019).

BRIEF TABLE OF CONTENTS

Dedication	v
Preface	xi
Guided Tour	xii
About the Authors	xvii
Acknowledgements	xviii

PART ONE: OVERVIEW OF CORPORATE FINANCE

1	Introduction to Corporate Finance	2
2	Corporate Governance	18
3	Financial Statement Analysis	42

PART TWO: VALUATION OF FUTURE CASH FLOWS

4	Introduction to Valuation: The Time Value of Money	70
5	Discounted Cash Flow Valuation	91
6	Bond Valuation	126
7	Equity Valuation	159

PART THREE: CAPITAL BUDGETING

8	Net Present Value and Other Investment Criteria	186
9	Making Capital Investment Decisions	223
10	Project Analysis and Evaluation	257

PART FOUR: RISK AND RETURN

11	Some Lessons from Recent Capital Market History	289
12	Return, Risk and the Security Market Line	317

PART FIVE: COST OF CAPITAL AND LONG-TERM FINANCIAL POLICY

13	Cost of Capital	353
14	Raising Capital	383
15	Financial Leverage and Capital Structure Policy	414
16	Dividends and Payout Policy	452

PART SIX: TOPICS IN CORPORATE FINANCE

17	Short-Term Financial Planning and Management	479
18	International Corporate Finance	520
19	Behavioural Finance	552
20	Financial Risk Management	571
21	Options and Corporate Finance	595
22	Mergers and Acquisitions	631

Appendix A: Mathematical Tables	660
Appendix B: Key Equations	670
Appendix 3A: Financial Planning	677
Appendix 6A: The Term Structure of Interest Rates, Spot Rates and Yield to Maturity	696
Index	706

DETAILED TABLE OF CONTENTS

Dedication	v
Preface	xi
Guided Tour	xii
About the Authors	xvii
Acknowledgements	xviii

PART ONE OVERVIEW OF CORPORATE FINANCE

1 Introduction to Corporate Finance — 2
- 1.1 Corporate Finance and the Financial Manager — 3
- 1.2 The Goal of Financial Management — 6
- 1.3 Financial Markets and the Corporation — 9
- 1.4 The Economic Environment — 12
- 1.5 Corporate Finance in Action: The Case of Alphabet Inc. — 13

2 Corporate Governance — 18
- 2.1 Forms of Business Organization — 19
- 2.2 The Agency Problem and Control of the Corporation — 24
- 2.3 International Corporate Governance — 31
- 2.4 Bringing It All Together — 36

3 Financial Statement Analysis — 42
- 3.1 The Annual Report — 43
- 3.2 Ratio Analysis — 52
- 3.3 The Du Pont Identity — 59
- 3.4 Using Financial Statement Information — 60

PART TWO VALUATION OF FUTURE CASH FLOWS

4 Introduction to Valuation: The Time Value of Money — 70
- 4.1 Future Value and Compounding — 71
- 4.2 Present Value and Discounting — 77
- 4.3 More about Present and Future Values — 80

5 Discounted Cash Flow Valuation — 91
- 5.1 Future and Present Values of Multiple Cash Flows — 92
- 5.2 Valuing Level Cash Flows: Annuities and Perpetuities — 98
- 5.3 Comparing Rates: The Effect of Compounding — 105
- 5.4 Loan Types and Loan Amortization — 110

6 Bond Valuation — 126
- 6.1 Bonds and Bond Valuation — 127
- 6.2 More about Bond Features — 134
- 6.3 Bond Ratings — 139
- 6.4 Some Different Types of Bond — 141
- 6.5 Bond Markets — 143
- 6.6 Inflation and Interest Rates — 145
- 6.7 Determinants of Bond Yields — 148

7 Equity Valuation — 159
- 7.1 Share Valuation — 160
- 7.2 Some Features of Ordinary and Preference Shares — 172
- 7.3 The Stock Markets — 173
- 7.4 Firm Valuation — 174

PART THREE CAPITAL BUDGETING

8 Net Present Value and Other Investment Criteria — 186
- 8.1 Net Present Value — 187
- 8.2 The Payback Rule — 191
- 8.3 The Discounted Payback — 194
- 8.4 The Average Accounting Return — 197
- 8.5 The Internal Rate of Return — 198
- 8.6 The Profitability Index — 209
- 8.7 The Practice of Capital Budgeting — 210

9 Making Capital Investment Decisions — 223
- 9.1 Project Cash Flows: A First Look — 224
- 9.2 Incremental Cash Flows — 225
- 9.3 Pro Forma Financial Statements and Project Cash Flows — 227
- 9.4 More about Project Cash Flow — 230
- 9.5 Alternative Definitions of Operating Cash Flow — 238
- 9.6 Some Special Cases of Discounted Cash Flow Analysis — 240

10 Project Analysis and Evaluation — 257
- 10.1 Evaluating NPV Estimates — 258
- 10.2 Scenario and Other What-If Analyses — 259
- 10.3 Break-Even Analysis — 265
- 10.4 Operating Cash Flow, Sales Volume and Break-Even — 270
- 10.5 Operating Leverage — 275
- 10.6 Capital Rationing — 277

PART FOUR RISK AND RETURN

11 Some Lessons from Recent Capital Market History — 289
- 11.1 Returns — 290
- 11.2 The Historical Record — 294
- 11.3 Average Returns: The First Lesson — 296
- 11.4 The Variability of Returns: The Second Lesson — 299
- 11.5 More about Average Returns — 303
- 11.6 Capital Market Efficiency — 306

12 Return, Risk and the Security Market Line — 317
- 12.1 Expected Returns and Variances — 318
- 12.2 Portfolios — 322
- 12.3 Announcements, Surprises and Expected Returns — 325
- 12.4 Risk: Systematic and Unsystematic — 327
- 12.5 Diversification and Portfolio Risk — 328
- 12.6 Systematic Risk and Beta — 331
- 12.7 The Security Market Line — 334
- 12.8 The SML and the Cost of Capital: A Preview — 342

PART FIVE COST OF CAPITAL AND LONG-TERM FINANCIAL POLICY

13 Cost of Capital — 353
- 13.1 The Cost of Capital: Some Preliminaries — 354
- 13.2 The Cost of Equity — 355
- 13.3 The Costs of Debt and Preference Shares — 359
- 13.4 The Weighted Average Cost of Capital — 361
- 13.5 Divisional and Project Costs of Capital — 367
- Online Supplement – Flotation Costs and the Weighted Average Cost of Capital — 371

14 Raising Capital — 383
- 14.1 The Financing Life Cycle of a Firm: Early-Stage Financing and Venture Capital — 384
- 14.2 Selling Securities to the Public: The Basic Procedure — 388
- 14.3 Alternative Issue Methods — 389
- 14.4 Underwriters — 390
- 14.5 IPOs and Underpricing — 393
- 14.6 New Equity Sales and the Value of the Firm — 396
- 14.7 The Costs of Issuing Securities — 397
- 14.8 Rights — 398
- 14.9 Dilution — 402
- 14.10 Issuing Long-Term Debt — 404
- 14.11 Bank Loans — 405
- 14.12 Lease Financing — 406

15 Financial Leverage and Capital Structure Policy — 414
- 15.1 The Capital Structure Question — 415
- 15.2 The Effect of Financial Leverage — 416
- 15.3 Capital Structure and the Cost of Equity Capital — 421
- 15.4 M&M Propositions I and II with Corporate Taxes — 425
- 15.5 Bankruptcy Costs — 430
- 15.6 Optimal Capital Structure — 433
- 15.7 The Pie Again — 437
- 15.8 Signalling — 439
- 15.9 The Pecking-Order Theory — 440
- 15.10 Observed Capital Structures — 441
- 15.11 A Quick Look at the Bankruptcy Process — 443

16 Dividends and Payout Policy — 452
- 16.1 Cash Dividends and Dividend Payment — 453
- 16.2 Does Dividend Policy Matter? — 456
- 16.3 Real-World Factors Favouring a Low-Dividend Payout — 458
- 16.4 Real-World Factors Favouring a High-Dividend Payout — 459
- 16.5 A Resolution of Real-World Factors? — 460
- 16.6 Share Repurchases: An Alternative to Cash Dividends — 462
- 16.7 What We Know and Do Not Know about Dividend and Payout Policies — 465
- 16.8 Stock Dividends and Stock Splits — 468

PART SIX TOPICS IN CORPORATE FINANCE

17 Short-Term Financial Planning and Management — 479
- 17.1 Reasons for Holding Cash — 480
- 17.2 Managing Short-Term Capital — 481
- 17.3 Investing Idle Cash — 485
- 17.4 Determining the Target Cash Balance — 487
- 17.5 Credit and Receivables — 494
- 17.6 Terms of the Sale — 495
- 17.7 Analysing Credit Policy — 499
- 17.8 Optimal Credit Policy — 501
- 17.9 Credit Analysis — 503
- 17.10 Collection Policy — 505
- 17.11 Inventory Management — 506
- 17.12 Inventory Management Techniques — 507

18 International Corporate Finance — 520
- 18.1 Terminology — 521
- 18.2 Foreign Exchange Markets and Exchange Rates — 522

18.3	Purchasing Power Parity	527
18.4	Interest Rate Parity, Unbiased Forward Rates and the International Fisher Effect	530
18.5	International Capital Budgeting	534
18.6	Exchange Rate Risk	536
18.7	Political Risk	539
18.8	Islamic Corporate Finance	541
18.9	Brexit and International Corporate Finance	545

19 Behavioural Finance — 552

19.1	Introduction to Behavioural Finance	553
19.2	Biases	553
19.3	Framing Effects	555
19.4	Heuristics	558
19.5	Behavioural Finance and Market Efficiency	561

20 Financial Risk Management — 571

20.1	Hedging and Price Volatility	572
20.2	Managing Financial Risk	573
20.3	Hedging with Forward Contracts	577
20.4	Hedging with Futures Contracts	580
20.5	Hedging with Swap Contracts	582
20.6	Hedging with Option Contracts	585

21 Options and Corporate Finance — 595

21.1	Options: The Basics	596
21.2	Put-Call Parity	599
21.3	Fundamentals of Option Valuation	602
21.4	An Option Pricing Model	607
21.5	The Black-Scholes Option Pricing Model	609
21.6	Option Applications: Employee Share Options	614
21.7	Option Applications: Equity as a Call Option on the Firm's Assets	617
21.8	Option Applications: Capital Budgeting	618

22 Mergers and Acquisitions — 631

22.1	The Legal Forms of Acquisition	632
22.2	Accounting and Tax Considerations	635
22.3	Gains From Acquisitions	635
22.4	Some Financial Side-Effects of Acquisitions	641
22.5	The Cost of an Acquisition	643
22.6	Valuation of Mergers in Practice	645
22.7	Defensive Tactics	646
22.8	Some Evidence on Restructurings: Do M&A Pay?	650
22.9	Divestitures and Restructurings	651

Appendix A: Mathematical Tables	660
Appendix B: Key Equations	670
Appendix 3A: Financial Planning	677
Appendix 6A: The Term Structure of Interest Rates, Spot Rates and Yield to Maturity	696
Index	706

PREFACE

Fundamentals of Corporate Finance is the fourth in a group of quality finance textbooks for international readers that spans *Financial Markets and Corporate Strategy* through *Corporate Finance* to the present text. All four books take a student from having virtually no knowledge of Corporate Finance to a doctoral level of understanding.

I have been teaching and practising Finance for nearly 30 years, and I fully understand the need for textbooks to be targeted to different reader groups. *Fundamentals of Corporate Finance* is no different in that regard. The book introduces non-specialist students to the key concepts in Corporate Finance in a clear and concise manner and a manageable number of chapters. The text is ideal for one- or two-semester courses. Drawing from comprehensive reviewer feedback, focus sessions, and innovations in *Corporate Finance* and *Financial Markets and Corporate Strategy*, I have extensively revised *Fundamentals of Corporate Finance* to be at the forefront of European Corporate Finance thought and practice.

The field of Corporate Finance is always changing. In this new edition, every chapter has been thoroughly updated to reflect the newest developments in the economic environment and academic research. I have also focused on providing more real-life examples of the concepts covered in the text, to ensure that readers can put the flesh of practice to the bones of theory.

Other improvements include:

- New real-world cases in each chapter, 'Real World Insights', illustrating the main concepts in the context of real corporate events.
- A stronger focus on sustainability, environmental, societal and governance issues and how these relate to corporate finance.
- The text is adapted to reflect the outcome of the UK's exit from the European Union (Brexit) and the resulting impact on businesses operating in both areas.
- New coverage of fintech and related topics, such as bitcoin, peer to peer lending and technology regulation.
- A closer alignment to ACCA, ICAEW and CIMA Financial Management syllabi.
- All the material is updated to reflect new published research and data since the previous edition.
- An updated recommended reading section in every chapter increases links to academic literature.
- Updated end-of-chapter sections with many brand new practice questions and problems, organized by level of difficulty.

Fundamentals of Corporate Finance captures current thinking in Corporate Finance and expresses it in a highly intuitive and accessible way. I've thoroughly enjoyed writing the chapters and sincerely hope you have the same enjoyment reading them.

David Hillier

GUIDED TOUR

In addition to illustrating pertinent concepts and presenting up-to-date coverage, *Fundamentals of Corporate Finance* strives to present the material in a way that makes it coherent and easy to understand. To meet the varied needs of its intended audience, *Fundamentals of Corporate Finance* is rich in valuable learning tools and support:

UNDERSTANDING AND APPLICATION

- Each chapter opens with a set of **learning objectives,** summarizing what knowledge, skills or understanding you will acquire from each chapter.

> **LEARNING OBJECTIVES**
> After studying this chapter, you should understand:
> **LO1** Dividend types, and how dividends are paid.
> **LO2** The issues surrounding dividend policy decisions.
> **LO3** The difference between cash and stock dividends.

- **Key terms** are printed in bold type and defined within the margin for easy location and identification.

> **date of record**
> The date by which a holder must be on record to be designated to receive a dividend.
>
> the equity is said to trade 'with dividend' or 'cum dividend'. Afterwards, the equity trades 'ex-dividend'.
> The ex-dividend date convention removes any ambiguity about who is entitled to the dividend. Because the dividend is valuable, the share price will be affected when the equity goes 'ex'. We examine this effect in a moment.
> 3. **Date of record:** Based on its records, the corporation prepares a list on 30 January of all individuals believed to be shareholders. These are the *holders of record*, and 30 January is the date of record (or record date). The word *believed* is important here. If you buy the equity just before this date, the corporation's records may not

- **Real World Insight** boxes which use real companies to show how they have applied corporate finance theories and concepts to their businesses and business decisions.

> **REAL WORLD INSIGHTS**
> In 2021, the First Abu Dhabi Bank (FAB) issued a five-year $500 million *sukuk* with payments set to provide a yield of 1.411 per cent. This was the first *sukuk* issue in 2021 denominated in dollars, and it attracted orders of $1.5 billion, amounting to three times the available bonds on offer. The buyers consisted of high quality international and domestic institutions, with 53 per cent of orders going to international investors. Islamic investors made up 76 per cent of the buyers and came from across the world.

- New **Sustainability in Finance** boxes provide insights into how sustainability and corporate finance can be interconnected.

> **SUSTAINABILITY IN FINANCE**
> The weighted cost of capital for renewable energy significantly varies across the European Union, amounting to 3.5 per cent in Germany and 12 per cent in Greece. These are the findings of the 'DiaCore project', funded by the Executive Agency for Small and Medium Enterprises (EASME). The research was led by Ecofys, Fraunhofer ISI, eclareon, EPU-NTUA, TU Wien and LEI. The project team is the first to estimate the costs of capital for onshore wind energy projects across the 27 EU Member States.

- Each chapter ends with a **mini case** that focuses on common situations. Each case presents a new scenario, data and a dilemma. Several case questions reinforce the material learned in that chapter.

> **MINI CASE**
> **CREDIT POLICY AT SCHWARZWALD AG**
> Dagmar Bamberger, the president of Schwarzwald AG, has been exploring ways of improving the company's financial performance. Schwarzwald manufactures and sells office equipment to retailers. The company's growth has been relatively slow in recent years, but with an expansion in the economy it appears that sales may increase more quickly in the future. Dagmar has asked Johann Rüstow, the company's treasurer, to examine Schwarzwald's credit policy to see whether a different credit policy could help increase profitability.

- Boxed **examples** using both real and hypothetical companies are integrated throughout the chapters. Each example illustrates an intuitive or mathematical application in a step-by-step format.

> **EXAMPLE 17.1**
> **CALCULATING THE REPURCHASE PRICE OF A REPO**
> Your firm requires £100 million over the next 30 days to manage a potential cash shortage from supply chain investments. Your treasury department has decided the appropriate instrument is a repo and sold £100 million of 30-day UK treasury bills to a multinational bank. The repo rate is 1.9 per cent per annum. How much is due in 30 days?

MASTERY OF MATHEMATICS

- Each chapter provides a number of **figures and tables** to help you visualize the material being covered.

- Variables and acronyms you will encounter throughout chapters are listed in **key notation** boxes at the start of the chapter.

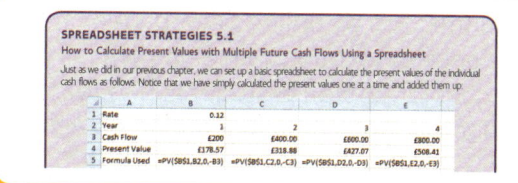

- **Spreadsheet strategies** introduce you to Microsoft Excel and help you to improve your Excel spreadsheet skills. This feature appears in self-contained sections and shows you how to set up spreadsheets and analyse common financial problems.

- When **maths equations** first appear in full, they are numbered for ease of reference and understanding.

PRACTICE AND PROFICIENCY

- Each chapter ends with **questions and problems,** graded by difficulty, to comprehensively test your knowledge of the chapter. These questions are also integrated into our digital learning and teaching environment **Connect**®.

- Chapter sections are intentionally kept short to promote a step-by-step, building-block approach to learning. Most sections are followed by a series of short **concept questions,** highlighting the key ideas presented.

- **Chapter review and self-test problems** allow you to test your abilities in solving key problems related to the chapter content, and provide instant reinforcement.

- **Summary and Conclusions** briefly review and reinforce the main topics covered in each chapter, to ensure you have acquired a solid understanding of the key topics.

Transform learning with Connect®

Boost grades, stimulate engagement and deliver an amazing course

Connect® is an online platform that integrates the science of learning with award-winning adaptive technology, to offer students and teachers a more effective teaching and learning experience.

 Connect increases my students' knowledge and has made my teaching more effective

University of Birmingham Business School, UK

The Three Pillars of Connect®

Flexible and high quality content tailored to your course

Using a combination of your content with McGraw-Hill and OER resources customise your course with the support of our dedicated academic and implementation consultants

Detailed reporting and analytics

Monitor progress and improve efficiency with detailed Connect® reports. Students and teachers can use real-time performance measurement tools to monitor learning and focus on the gaps that require more attention.

Ease of set-up and continuous support

McGraw-Hill offers comprehensive service, support and training - face-to-face, online or over the phone - throughout every phase of working with us to ensure easy set-up and access to the platform.

Bring theory to life **within Connect**®

Students can **test and apply their knowledge** with our engaging excercises and activities within Connect®

Discover the features on offer for your discipline on the next page!

Connect® for Economics

We have a wide selection of interactive excercises and activites on hand to help students gain valuable practice applying key concepts to real-world scenarios. Featured below are our Application-Based Activities and Graphing Tools.

Application-Based Activities

The Connect Application-Based Activities (ABAs) provide students valuable practice using problem solving skills to apply their knowledge to realistic scenarios. Students' progress from understanding basic concepts to using their knowledge to analyse complex scenarios and solve problems.

Available ABAs:

1. Basics of Money
2. Demand and Supply
3. Econ Production and Cost
4. Externalities
5. Fiscal Policy and Multipliers
6. Government Intervention
7. International Trade
8. Labour Market Indicators and Unemployment
9. Oligopoly
10. Opportunity, Cost, Specialization and Trade
11. Perfect Competition
12. Price Discrimination
13. Prisoner's Dilemma
14. Real and Nominal GDP
15. Reserves and Monetary Policy
16. Savings and Lending Version
17. Types of Elasticity

Graphing Tools

A series of basic and complex graphic questions are available within Connect® to aid students in their practice and development. These questions enable students to develop their graphical ability along with their calculating and plotting data skills.

Each question is auto-graded, available throughout the assignable content and are accompanied by immediate feedback to help guide students through the task.

Smarter studying with

The **SmartBook®** and **Smartbook 2.0®** tool integrated within **Connect®** maximizes learning by helping students study more efficiently, highlighting the most important points in the chapter, asking verification questions and indicating additional resources.

More Personalised

SmartBook® and Smartbook 2.0® constantly adapts to students' needs, creating a personalised learning experience.

More Productive

SmartBook® and Smartbook 2.0® creates an extremely productive learning experience, focusing students' attention on the concepts they need to learn.

More Prepared

SmartBook® and Smartbook 2.0® helps students prepare for lessons, allowing you to use class time more dynamically

> I liked the idea of continuous assessment online as it helped me to keep track of student performance while it freed up my time spent marking and meant I could focus on my research
>
> Alejandra Ramos, Trinity College Dublin, Ireland

The ReadAnywhere App

To help you study anywhere, anytime! Gain mobile freedom to access your eBook anywhere, even offline, on your smartphone or tablet.

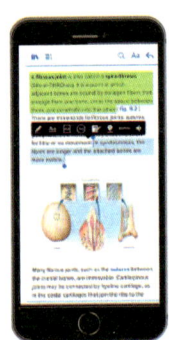

You can:
- Read offline and data-free by downloading the entire text or only the chapters you need
- Never lose an assignment, a note, or your place. ReadAnywhere includes the same functionality as the eBook offered in Connect® with auto-sync across both platforms
- Start studying anytime, anywhere

Available on:

ABOUT THE AUTHORS

David Hillier is a Professor of Finance, Executive Dean of Strathclyde Business School, and Associate Principal of the University of Strathclyde. Professor Hillier has published a wide range of peer-reviewed academic articles on corporate governance, corporate finance, insider trading, asset pricing, precious metals, auditing, and market microstructure. His research has attracted an ANBAR citation and best paper prize from one of the top finance and management journals in South East Asia. He has served on the editorial board for many of the world's top finance journals. Professor Hillier is an established teacher of executive programmes and has conducted courses for a variety of professional clients, including the World Bank and the UK National Health Service. He has extensive practical experience leading a large organization and has been awarded Public Sector Director of Year by the Institute of Directors Scotland, and received the 'Outstanding Contribution by a Business Leader' accolade by Inspiring City Awards. Professor Hillier is a council member of the Confederation of British Industry Scotland (CBI), and sits on the boards of Skills Development Scotland and Enable Scotland. He is co-author of *Corporate Finance, Fourth European Edition* (McGraw-Hill, 2020) and *Financial Markets and Corporate Strategy, Second European Edition* (McGraw-Hill, 2011).

Stephen A. Ross was the Franco Modigliani Professor of Finance and Economics at the MIT Sloan School of Management.

Randolph W. Westerfield is Dean Emeritus of the University of Southern California's Marshall School of Business and is the Charles B. Thornton Professor of Finance.

Bradford D. Jordan is Visiting Scholar at Warrington College of Business, University of Florida.

ACKNOWLEDGEMENTS

Just as in all other areas of life, the global Covid-19 pandemic had a massive impact on writing this fourth edition of *Fundamentals of Corporate Finance*. In my day job as Associate Principal of the University of Strathclyde and Executive Dean of Strathclyde Business School, I was forced to juggle the unprecedented disruption brought on by social distancing and other restrictions on everyday life, with ensuring the safety of our staff and students. This was at the same time as maintaining the education and research quality of the School, and managing the financial resources of my part of the university and meeting my responsibilities as a board member on external organizations. I wouldn't have completed the text without the help of family, friends and colleagues who collectively worked with me over the past twelve months in all my various roles. Teamwork has never been more important and to everyone (too numerous to mention) who has travelled the journey with me, thank you.

A project as large as *Fundamentals of Corporate Finance* involves more than just writing and before I started working with McGraw-Hill, I never truly understood just how much goes into getting a book off the ground. As a result, I would like to thank the following (large) group of individuals who have all contributed in some way to the book.

First, thanks go to Georgia Martin, Lucy Wheeler, Zoe Osman, Ali Davis and Sabrina Farrugia of McGraw-Hill who were absolutely crucial to every stage of development. I would also like to thank all the people who have worked on *Fundamentals* behind the scenes and who rarely get a mention in a textbook. I would like to thank Elaine Bingham (copyeditor) Lynn Brown (proofreader) and Jim Henderson (indexer). Finally, I would also like to thank the army of McGraw-Hill academic consultants who enthusiastically trundle the halls of academe and engage with Finance academics trying to sell my books. Truth be told, I think of you guys many times a year (but especially in February and August!).

This is now my twelfth year of writing Finance textbooks and I'm sure my colleagues, friends and family are becoming heartily sick of me thanking them. However, I can't ignore the fact that their goodwill has given me the space and support that allows me to undertake this work. Thanks especially to my family. Thank you to my beautiful wife, Mary-Jo, and my children, Benjy, Danny, Con, Maria, Patrick and Saoirse, for putting up with me and my eccentric ways. A final mention must go to my very special grandson, Thomas, who brings much joy and noise to my quiet life.

David Hillier, 15 January 2021

The authors and publishers would like to pay special thanks to all those who participated in the text's development:

Fergal O'Brien, *University of Limerick*, Ireland
Dirk-Jan Janssen, *Radboud University Nijmegen*, the Netherlands
Stuart Farquhar, *University of Wolverhampton*, UK
Handy Tan, *Anglia Ruskin University*, UK
Rachel Sopp, *Surrey Business School*, UK
Peter van der Meer, *Avans Hogeschool*, the Netherlands
Atle Guttormsen, *Norwegian University of Life Sciences*, Norway
Bjarne Florentsen, *Copenhagen Business School*, Denmark

Every effort has been made to trace and acknowledge ownership of copyright and to clear permission for material reproduced in this book. The publishers will be pleased to make suitable arrangements to clear permission with any copyright holders whom it has not been possible to contact.

Let us help make our **content** your **solution**

At McGraw-Hill Education our aim is to help lecturers to find the most suitable content for their needs delivered to their students in the most appropriate way. Our **custom publishing solutions** offer the ideal combination of content delivered in the way which best suits lecturer and students.

Our custom publishing programme offers lecturers the opportunity to select just the chapters or sections of material they wish to deliver to their students from a database called CREATE™ at

www.mcgrawhillcreate.co.uk

CREATE™ contains over two million pages of content from:

- textbooks
- professional books
- case books – Harvard Articles, Insead, Ivey, Darden, Thunderbird and BusinessWeek
- Taking Sides – debate materials

Across the following imprints:

- McGraw-Hill Education
- Open University Press
- Harvard Business Publishing
- US and European material

There is also the option to include additional material authored by lecturers in the custom product – this does not necessarily have to be in English.

We will take care of everything from start to finish in the process of developing and delivering a custom product to ensure that lecturers and students receive exactly the material needed in the most suitable way.

With a **Custom Publishing Solution,** students enjoy the best selection of material deemed to be the most suitable for learning everything they need for their courses – something of real value to support their learning. Teachers are able to use exactly the material they want, in the way they want, to support their teaching on the course.

Please contact your **local McGraw-Hill Education representative** with any questions or alternatively contact: custom.publishing@mheducation.com.

PART ONE

OVERVIEW OF CORPORATE FINANCE

1 Introduction to Corporate Finance — 2

2 Corporate Governance — 18

3 Financial Statement Analysis — 42

CHAPTER 1
INTRODUCTION TO CORPORATE FINANCE

> **LEARNING OBJECTIVES**
>
> After studying this chapter, you should understand:
>
> **LO1** The basic types of financial management decision and the role of the financial manager.
> **LO2** The goal of financial management.
> **LO3** How financial markets work and the reason they exist.
> **LO4** The role of sustainability and ethics in finance.

RECENT YEARS have illustrated the highly integrated nature of financial markets and the international corporate environment. The UK referendum on the country's future within the European Union in June 2016 seems a long time ago. For four years under the Trump administration, the United States shifted to a more protectionist positioning and sought to reset long-standing trade relations with all developed economies, including the UK and Europe. Climate change impacted many industries, with some (such as energy and manufacturing) being particularly affected; and health issues (most notably the global disruption to the international corporate supply chain from the coronavirus, Covid-19) have shown how fragile the international financial system is to systemic events.

During any challenging period, only the most flexible and well-run companies will be successful, and periods of change will lead to new opportunities for the entrepreneurial firm. Financial managers have a responsibility to be exceptionally careful when managing their company's assets, spotting suitable investments and raising financing. Unlike bull market economies where profitable business opportunities are common, and money is not in short supply, the business radar must be acutely sensitive to those projects that add value.

However, there is good news. New financial technologies are allowing firms to use big data with machine learning and artificial intelligence tools are being developed to price assets more sensitively and manage risk much better than before. This will lead to new opportunities and avenues to improve firm value.

The goal of this text is to allow the reader an insight into the methods, techniques and strategies to add value to firms in the present-day environment. We will consider the investment decision, how it is financed, and the various approaches to ensuring a company has the necessary liquidity to optimally run its affairs. We will also discuss the appropriate mix of debt and equity, and asset valuation methods in some detail. This takes us into issues involving corporate goals and the functioning of financial markets, both of which we introduce in this chapter.

To begin our study of modern corporate finance we address two central issues. First, what is corporate finance, and what is the role of the financial manager in the corporation? Second, what is the goal of financial management? While firms must now consider other objectives related to sustainability and the environment, share price valuation is still an exceptionally important issue. We consequently take a brief look at the financial markets and their impact on corporate decision-making.

1.1 CORPORATE FINANCE AND THE FINANCIAL MANAGER

In this section, we discuss where the financial manager fits in the corporation. We start by defining *corporate finance* and the financial manager's job.

WHAT IS CORPORATE FINANCE?

Imagine that you were to start your own business. No matter what type you started, you would have to answer the following three questions in some form or another:

1. What long-term investments should you make? That is, what lines of business will you be in, and what sorts of buildings, machinery and equipment will you need?
2. Where will you get the long-term financing to pay for your investment? Will you bring in other owners, or will you borrow the money?
3. How will you manage your everyday financial activities, such as collecting from customers and paying suppliers?

These are not the only questions by any means, but they are among the most important. Corporate finance, broadly speaking, is the study of ways to answer these three questions. Accordingly, we'll be looking at each of them in the chapters ahead.

THE FINANCIAL MANAGER

A striking feature of large corporations is that the owners (also known as shareholders) are not usually directly involved in making business decisions, particularly on a day-to-day basis. Instead, the corporation employs managers to represent the owners' interests and make decisions on their behalf. In a large corporation, the financial manager would be in charge of answering the three questions we raised in the preceding section.

The financial management function is usually associated with a top officer of the firm, such as a finance director (FD) or chief financial officer (CFO). Figure 1.1 is a simplified organizational chart that highlights the finance activity in a large firm. As shown, the finance director co-ordinates the activities of the treasurer and the controller. The controller's office handles cost and financial accounting, tax payments and management information systems. The treasurer's office is responsible for managing the firm's cash and credit, financial planning, and capital expenditures.

You may be wondering what the difference is between the finance and accounting functions in a firm. The accounting function takes all the financial information and data that arise as a result of ongoing business activities. It presents this in ways that allow management to assess the performance and risk of their firm (financial accounting) and make informed decisions on future corporate activity (management accounting). To ensure all firms provide comparable information, there are generally accepted accounting standards. In the UK and European Union, all firms listed on a stock exchange must follow International Accounting Standards (IAS), as set by the International Accounting Standards Board (IASB).

FIGURE 1.1

A sample simplified organizational chart

The finance function of the firm is related to the three general questions raised earlier, and the chapters ahead deal primarily with these issues. However, although our study bears mostly on activities associated with the finance function, we also discuss the accounting function whenever it is required to better understand the decisions made by corporations.

FINANCIAL MANAGEMENT DECISIONS

As the preceding discussion suggests, the financial manager must be concerned with three basic types of question. We consider these in greater detail next.

Capital Budgeting

The first question concerns the firm's long-term investments. The process of planning and managing a firm's long-term investments is called **capital budgeting**. In capital budgeting, the financial manager identifies investment opportunities that are worth more to the firm than they cost to acquire. Loosely speaking, this means the value of the cash flow generated by an asset exceeds the cost of that asset.

The types of investment opportunity typically considered depends on the nature of a firm's business. For example, a large retailer, like Tesco, opening another superstore, or Apple developing a new type of tablet computer, are both important capital budgeting decisions. Some decisions, such as the type of computer system to purchase, might not depend so much on a particular line of business.

Regardless of the specific nature of an opportunity under consideration, financial managers must be concerned not only with how much cash they expect to receive, but also with when they expect to receive it, and how likely they are to receive it. Evaluating the *size, timing* and *risk* of future cash flows is the essence of capital budgeting. In fact, as we shall see in the chapters ahead, whenever we evaluate a

> **capital budgeting**
> the process of planning and managing a firm's long-term investments.

business decision, the size, timing and risk of the cash flows will be by far the most important things we shall consider.

Capital Structure

The second question for the financial manager concerns ways in which the firm obtains and manages the long-term financing it needs to support its long-term investments. A firm's **capital structure** (or financial structure) is the specific mixture of **long-term debt** and **equity** the firm uses to finance its operations. The financial manager has two concerns in this area. First, how much should the firm borrow? That is, what mixture of debt and equity is best? The mixture chosen will affect both the risk and the value of the firm. Second, what are the least expensive sources of funds for the firm?

If we picture the firm as a pie, then the firm's capital structure determines how that pie is sliced – in other words, what percentage of the firm's cash flow goes to creditors and what percentage goes to shareholders. Firms have a great deal of flexibility in choosing a financial structure. The question of whether one structure is better than any other for a particular firm is the heart of the capital structure issue.

In addition to deciding on the financing mix, the financial manager has to decide exactly how and where to raise the money. The expenses associated with raising long-term financing can be considerable, so different possibilities must be carefully evaluated. Also, corporations borrow money from a variety of lenders in a number of different, and sometimes exotic, ways. Choosing among lenders and among loan types is another job handled by the financial manager.

> **capital structure**
> the mixture of long-term debt and equity maintained by a firm.

> **long-term debt**
> long-term borrowing by the firm (longer than year) to finance its long-term investments.

Working Capital Management

The third question concerns **working capital** management. The term *working capital* refers to a firm's short-term assets, such as inventory, and its short-term liabilities, such as money owed to suppliers. Managing the firm's working capital is a day-to-day activity which ensures that the firm has sufficient resources to continue its operations and avoid costly interruptions. This involves a number of activities related to the firm's receipt and disbursement of cash.

Some questions about working capital that must be answered are the following:

1. How much cash and inventory should we keep on hand?
2. Should we sell on credit? If so, what terms will we offer, and to whom will we extend them?
3. How will we obtain any needed short-term financing? Will we purchase on credit, or will we borrow in the short term and pay cash? If we borrow in the short term, how and where should we do it?

These are just a small sample of the issues that arise in managing a firm's working capital.

> **equity**
> the amount of money raised by the firm that comes from the owners' (shareholders') investment.

> **working capital**
> a firm's short-term assets and liabilities.

Conclusion

The three areas of corporate financial management we have described – capital budgeting, capital structure and working capital management – are very broad categories. Each includes a rich variety of topics, and we have indicated only a few questions that arise in different areas. The chapters ahead contain greater detail.

> **CONCEPT QUESTIONS**
>
> **1.1a** What is the capital budgeting decision?
> **1.1b** What do you call the specific mixture of long-term debt and equity that a firm chooses to use?
> **1.1c** Into what category of financial management does cash management fall?

1.2 THE GOAL OF FINANCIAL MANAGEMENT

Assuming that we restrict ourselves to for-profit businesses, the main goal of financial management is to make money or add value for the owners. This goal is a little vague, of course, so we examine some different ways of formulating it to come up with a more precise definition. Such a definition is important because it leads to an objective basis for making and evaluating financial decisions.

POSSIBLE GOALS

If we were to consider possible financial goals, we might come up with some ideas like the following:

- Survive.
- Avoid financial distress and bankruptcy.
- Beat the competition.
- Maximize sales or market share.
- Minimize costs.
- Maximize profits.
- Maintain steady earnings growth.
- Improve society.
- Positively impact the environment.

These are only a few of the goals we could list. Furthermore, each of these possibilities presents problems as a goal for the financial manager.

For example, it's easy to increase market share or unit sales: all we have to do is lower our prices or relax our credit terms. Similarly, we can always cut costs simply by doing away with things such as research and development. We can avoid bankruptcy by never borrowing any money or never taking any risks, and so on. However, it is not clear that any of these actions are in the shareholders' best interests.

Profit maximization would probably be the most commonly cited goal, but even this is not a precise objective. Do we mean profits this year? If so, we should note that actions such as deferring maintenance, letting inventories run down, and taking other short-run cost-cutting measures will tend to increase profits now, but these activities aren't necessarily desirable.

The goal of maximizing profits may refer to some sort of 'long-run' or 'average' profits, but it's still unclear exactly what this means. First, do we mean something like accounting net income or earnings per share? As we shall see in more detail in the next chapter, these accounting numbers may have little to do with what is good or bad for the firm. Second, what do we mean by the long run? As John Maynard Keynes, a famous economist, once remarked, in the long run we're all dead! More to the point, this goal doesn't tell us what the appropriate trade-off is between current and future profits.

The goals we've listed here are all different, but they tend to fall into two classes. The first of these relates to profitability. The goals involving sales, market share and cost control all relate, at least potentially, to different ways of earning or increasing profits. The goals in the second group, involving bankruptcy avoidance, stability and safety, relate in some way to controlling risk. Unfortunately, these two types of goal are somewhat contradictory. The pursuit of profit normally involves some element of risk, so it isn't really possible to maximize both safety and profit. What we need, therefore, is a goal that encompasses both factors.

Finally, notice that the last two goals listed relate to the environment and society. Sustainability and climate change have become hot topics and many companies have embraced environment-related goals as objectives.

> **REAL WORLD INSIGHTS**
>
> How does a company maximize revenue at the same time as keeping down costs and ensuring its share price is performing well? This is the difficulty that faces all publicly listed firms, whether they are small domestic companies or massive multinationals. After its public listing, Facebook saw its share price collapse by more than

50 per cent. Pressure mounted on the firm to increase revenues from mobile technology amid fears that it wasn't able to monetize the incredible user base it has across the world. The basic model of Facebook had to change and the firm introduced a new algorithm for its user posts that prioritized the visibility of paid messages over unpaid ones. This forced companies to spend more on advertising, which in turn improved the company's finances. Facebook is continually looking at ways to improve its revenues further. New Facebook technology prioritizes greater visual content over written words because of the immediacy of photos, especially on smaller mobile devices where user growth is strongest. These innovations have only one purpose: to maximize firm value and increase Facebook's share price.

AN APPROPRIATE GOAL

The financial manager in a corporation makes decisions for the shareholders of the firm. Given this, instead of listing possible goals for the financial manager, we really need to answer a more fundamental question: from the shareholders' point of view, what is a good financial management decision?

If we assume that shareholders buy shares of a company's equity because they seek to gain financially, then the answer is obvious: good decisions increase the value of the equity, and poor decisions decrease the value of the equity.

Given our observations, it follows that the financial manager acts in the shareholders' best interests by making decisions that increase the value of the equity. The appropriate goal for the financial manager can thus be stated quite easily:

> The goal of financial management is to maximize the current value per share of the existing equity.

The goal of maximizing the value of the equity avoids the problems associated with the different goals we listed earlier. There is no ambiguity in the criterion, and there is no short-run versus long-run issue. We explicitly mean that our goal is to maximize the *current* share value.

If this goal seems a little strong or one-dimensional to you, keep in mind that the shareholders in a firm are residual owners. By this we mean that they are entitled only to what is left after employees, suppliers and creditors (and anyone else with a legitimate claim) are paid their due. If any of these groups go unpaid, the shareholders get nothing. So, if the shareholders are winning in the sense that the leftover, residual portion is growing, it must be true that everyone else is winning also.

Because the goal of financial management is to maximize the value of the equity, we need to learn how to identify investments and financing arrangements that impact favourably on the value of the equity. This is precisely what we shall be studying. In fact, we could have defined *corporate finance* as the study of the relationship between business decisions and the value of the equity in the business.

A MORE GENERAL GOAL

Given our goal as stated in the preceding section (to maximize the value of the equity), an obvious question comes up: what is the appropriate goal when the firm has no traded equity? Corporations are certainly not the only type of business, and the equity in many corporations rarely changes hands, so it's difficult to say what the value per share is at any given time.

As long as we are dealing with for-profit businesses, only a slight modification is needed. The total value of the equity in a corporation is simply equal to the value of the owners' equity. Therefore a more general way of stating our goal is as follows: maximize the market value of the existing owners' equity.

With this in mind, it doesn't matter what form the business takes. Good financial decisions increase the market value of the owners' equity, and poor financial decisions decrease it. In fact, although we focus on public corporations in the chapters ahead, the principles we develop apply to all forms of business. Many of them even apply to the not-for-profit sector.

Finally, our goal does not imply that the financial manager should take illegal or unethical actions in the hope of increasing the value of the equity in the firm. What we mean is that the financial manager best serves the owners of the business by identifying goods and services that add value to the firm because they are desired and valued in the free marketplace.

> **EXAMPLE 1.1**
>
> ## CORE VALUES
>
> Every corporation will have a number of goals and objectives that contribute to the main financial management goal of increasing shareholder wealth. Some strategic goals of firms taken directly from their websites include:
>
> 1. An unfailing focus on health and safety.
> 2. Maximize the strength of the company's assets.
> 3. Focused strategy.
> 4. Simplify management structures and minimize differences among divisions.
> 5. Much greater focus on transparency and maximizing firm value.
> 6. Ensure every staff member carries out their business with integrity, commitment and loyalty.
>
> Is each goal consistent with maximizing shareholder wealth? If not, why not, and does this mean that there are other objectives not related to shareholder value? Note: Do not worry about some of the terms that you don't understand above. All will become clear in time!

THE TRIPLE BOTTOM LINE

Shareholder value maximization (the profit objective) has attracted criticism because it appears to ignore other important factors, such as employees (the social objective) and sustainability (the environment objective).

> **Triple bottom line**
> the concept that corporate objectives should focus equally on society, the environment and profit.

Since companies consist of people and use the planet's resources, they have a responsibility not only to shareholders but to society as well. The **triple bottom line** brings this argument to the centre of corporate decision-making by asking companies to maximize not just shareholder value, but to also measure its contribution to society and the environment.

A key issue with the triple bottom line is the difficulty in accurately measuring in monetary terms the effect a company has on society and the environment. For example, how would you measure the triple bottom line of a fracking company that extracts gas from underground shale formations? Fracking has been in existence since the 1990s but the long-term environmental effects are still unknown. To value the environmental and social costs of fracking would require assumptions, many of which are controversial and lack agreement.

Until we have designed a valuation paradigm that effectively incorporates all aspects of a company's operations, shareholder wealth maximization is the best option. In addition, assuming that shareholders value society and the environment in the same way as the general population, the goal of shareholder wealth maximization will necessarily capture societal and environmental objectives.

Consequently, the financial manager best serves shareholders (the business owners) by making decisions that are valued by shareholders, who in turn reflect the broader societal and environmental concerns of the general population. Shareholder wealth maximization is therefore consistent with the triple bottom line approach (assuming shareholders have the same objectives and concerns as the general population).

SUSTAINABILITY IN FINANCE

A challenge facing many companies is how to successfully implement the triple bottom line framework in a company that has focused solely on profit maximization. Another way to consider the triple bottom line is to think about the objectives of a company under the headings, 'People, Planet, Profit'.

1. **People.** How can you get the most out of your company's workforce? What investments can you make to create value for shareholders through improving the human capital of your workers and operations that affect the welfare and productivity of your people? How do you measure success?

2. **Planet.** What activities does your firm engage in that maximizes its positive impact on the environment and sustainable operations? How do you measure success?
3. **Profit.** What can your firm do to maximize its financial profit?

In a 2018 *Harvard Business Review* article, '25 years ago I coined the phrase, "triple bottom line": Here's why it's time to rethink it', the originator of the term, John Elkington, argued that when firms are under pressure, the 'people' and 'planet' objectives are dominated by the 'profit' objective. Firms must find some ways to hardwire the triple bottom line framework into its corporate objectives.

Our advice is to set annual key performance indicators (KPIs) with quantitative metrics agreed upon by the major stakeholders (shareholders, employees, etc.). Performance-related components of executive remuneration would be tied to these KPIs at the end of the financial year.

This approach has been shown to work in a wide variety of settings and ensures all three components of the triple bottom line are of equal importance.

CONCEPT QUESTIONS

1.2a What is the goal of financial management?
1.2b What are some shortcomings of the goal of profit maximization?
1.2c What are sensible KPI measures of the triple bottom line?

1.3 FINANCIAL MARKETS AND THE CORPORATION

In most countries, financial markets play a fundamental role in the operations of large corporations. Even if a firm is not traded on a stock exchange, the stock market is important because it can inform management of the performance of their competitors, suppliers, customers and the economy as a whole. The primary advantage of financial markets is that they facilitate the flow of money from those that have surplus cash to those that need financing.

CASH FLOWS TO AND FROM THE FIRM

The interplay between the corporation and financial markets is illustrated in Figure 1.2. The arrows in the figure trace the passage of cash from the financial markets to the firm, and from the firm back to the financial markets. Suppose we start with the firm selling shares of equity and borrowing money to raise cash. Cash flows to the firm from the financial markets (A). The firm invests the cash in assets (B). These can be short term (current) or long term (non-current), and they generate cash (C), some of which goes to pay corporate taxes (D). After taxes are paid, some of this cash flow is reinvested in the firm (E). The rest goes back to the financial markets as cash paid to creditors and shareholders (F).

The financial markets are not funded just by corporations paying cash to creditors or shareholders. The savings of households (G) also find their way into the financial markets. For example, whenever your salary goes into your bank account, whenever you pay insurance on your car, house or computers, and every time you pay your pension premium, this money will end up in the financial markets. This happens because the financial institutions (H) you pay your money to use it to invest in the financial markets. The difference between what financial institutions earn in the financial markets and what they have to pay you (in terms of monthly interest, random insurance payouts, and pensions) is their profit.

A financial market, like any market, is just a way of bringing buyers and sellers together. In financial markets, it is debt and equity securities that are bought and sold. Financial markets differ in detail, however. The most important differences concern the types of security that are traded, how trading is conducted and who the buyers and sellers are. Some of these differences are discussed next.

FIGURE 1.2 Cash flows between the firm, the financial markets and the economy

PRIMARY VERSUS SECONDARY MARKETS

Financial markets function as both primary and secondary markets for debt and equity securities. The term *primary market* refers to the original sale of securities by governments and corporations. The *secondary markets* are those in which these securities are bought and sold after the original sale. Equities are, of course, issued solely by corporations. Debt securities are issued by both governments and corporations. In the discussion that follows, we focus on corporate securities only.

Primary Markets

In a primary market transaction, the corporation is the seller and the transaction raises money for the corporation. Corporations engage in two types of primary market transaction: public offerings and private placements. A public offering, as the name suggests, involves selling securities to the general public, whereas a private placement is a negotiated sale involving a specific buyer.

By law, public offerings of debt and equity must be registered with the securities regulator in the country where the offerings are made. For example, in the UK this is the Financial Conduct Authority, and in the Netherlands it is the Authority for Financial Markets (Autoriteit Financiële Markten). Registration requires the firm to disclose a great deal of information before selling any securities. The accounting, legal and selling costs of public offerings can be considerable.

Partly to avoid the various regulatory requirements and the expense of public offerings, debt and equity are often sold privately to large financial institutions such as life insurance companies or mutual funds. Such private placements do not normally have to be registered with securities regulators, and do not require the involvement of underwriters (investment banks that specialize in selling securities to the public).

Secondary Markets

A secondary market transaction involves one owner or creditor selling to another. Therefore the secondary markets provide the means for transferring ownership of corporate securities. Although a corporation is directly involved only in a primary market transaction (when it sells securities to raise cash), the secondary markets are still critical to large corporations. The reason is that investors are much more willing to purchase securities in a primary market transaction when they know that those securities can later be resold if desired.

Dealer versus Auction Markets

There are two kinds of secondary market: *auction* markets and *dealer* markets. Generally speaking, dealers buy and sell for themselves, at their own risk. A car dealer, for example, buys and sells automobiles.

In contrast, brokers and agents match buyers and sellers, but they do not actually own the commodity that is bought or sold. A real estate agent, for example, does not normally buy and sell houses.

Dealer markets in equities and long-term debt are called *over-the-counter* (OTC) markets. Most trading in debt securities takes place over the counter. The expression *over the counter* refers to days of old when securities were literally bought and sold at counters in offices around the country. Today, a significant fraction of the market for equities and almost all of the market for long-term debt have no central location; the many dealers are connected electronically.

Auction markets differ from dealer markets in two ways. First, an auction market or exchange has a physical location (such as Paternoster Square for the London Stock Exchange). Second, in a dealer market, most of the buying and selling is done by the dealer. The primary purpose of an auction market, on the other hand, is to match those who wish to sell with those who wish to buy. Dealers play a limited role.

Trading in Corporate Securities

The equity shares of most large firms trade in organized auction markets. The largest such market in the world is NYSE Euronext, followed by NASDAQ, Tokyo and London. Other European exchanges include the Deutsche Börse, the BME Spanish Exchanges, the SIX Swiss Exchange, and the NASDAQ OMX Nordic Exchange. Because of globalization, financial markets have reached the point where trading in many investments never stops; it just travels around the world.

Listing

Securities that trade on an organized exchange are said to be *listed* on that exchange. To be listed, firms must meet certain minimum criteria concerning, for example, asset size and number of shareholders. These criteria differ from one exchange to another.

Considering the London Stock Exchange as an illustrative case, the listing requirements are extensive. To be listed on the LSE a company must satisfy past track record requirements, must have a minimum market value and number of publicly held shares, excellent future prospects, audited accounting information for three full years and appropriate corporate governance, and must follow international accounting standards.

> **REAL WORLD INSIGHTS**
>
> In many countries, a new type of trading platform giving small and medium-sized enterprises access to alternative sources of finance has emerged. Peer-to-peer trading platforms are used by small companies to borrow without going through the normal stock exchange listing requirements. International investors (i.e. not solely located in one country) lend to a company using an electronic platform without the need to go through a financial intermediary. Although there are lower transaction costs with these platforms, investors must undertake their own research into the company, which takes time and money.
>
> For borrowers, the cost of borrowing is likely to be lower because they don't need to pay fees to a bank. However, the amount firms can borrow tends to be small (e.g. a maximum of £5 million) and the borrowing period is short (normally up to five years). Each platform is different and there is no consistency across platforms.
>
> Given its recent emergence, peer-to-peer investing is not regulated in many countries and investors use this medium at their own risk. With the development of new financial technologies, such as blockchain, expect to see many more investing platforms in the future using not just standard currencies like euros and sterling, but cryptocurrencies, such as bitcoin and etherium.

> **CONCEPT QUESTIONS**
>
> **1.3a** What is a dealer market? How do dealer and auction markets differ?
> **1.3b** What does OTC stand for? The London Stock Exchange has a large OTC market for smaller equities and an auction market for its biggest equities. Why do you think this is the case?
> **1.3c** What are the advantages and disadvantages of using peer-to-peer trading platforms?

1.4 THE ECONOMIC ENVIRONMENT

The economic environment in which companies are operating is probably the most difficult for over fifty years. The Covid-19 pandemic that began in 2020 led to an economic shutdown in almost every developed country, followed by social distancing measures that severely curtailed the operations of many businesses.

In this context, individual country governments and regional trading blocs, such as the European Union, introduced new measures and economic policies to support businesses through this challenging period. We categorize these measures into three main groups: fiscal policy, monetary policy, and exchange rate policy. In this section, we will briefly review each of the groups and their effect on businesses.

Taken together, fiscal, monetary, and exchange rate policy is collectively known as macroeconomic policy.

MACROECONOMIC POLICY

Macroeconomic policy is concerned with government decisions that impact the economic environment. In a well-governed economy, productivity is growing, price levels are under control (not growing too fast or falling), almost everyone is in a job, and imports are roughly equal to exports.

It is not possible to guarantee this happening at any single point of time and so governments pull economic levers to achieve their objectives. The four main levers are:

Fiscal Policy

The use of fiscal variables including government spending and taxes. High taxation will theoretically reduce consumer and corporate spending, thereby providing more money for the government to spend on infrastructure.

Monetary Policy

The use of monetary variables including interest rates and money supply. High interest rates make it more expensive to borrow and better to save. More money supply will increase price inflation.

Exchange Rate Policy

The management of exchange rates to improve country trade competitiveness. Relatively low exchange rates will make exports cheaper in foreign countries and imports more expensive. Relatively high exchange rates will do the opposite. Governments can have fixed exchange rates, where the domestic currency is fixed against a benchmark such as the US dollar. Floating exchange rates fluctuate in response to demand and supply of a country's currency. If demand increases, the exchange rate will strengthen and if demand falls, the currency will weaken. Exchange rates are covered in much more detail in Chapter 18.

Foreign Trade Policy

The use of trade barriers and import controls to manage the cost of imports and exports. If a country believes that a foreign country is selling its goods too cheaply, it may introduce barriers or quotas on the goods.

These levers are not the only ones a government can use to influence the performance of an economy, but they are the main ones. Within this environment, companies must adapt, thrive, and take advantage of the opportunities presented in its own country and in others in which it operates.

EUROPEAN MONETARY UNION

The European monetary union represents the agreement among a number of European Union member countries to combine their individual currencies into one basket currency. There are three components to the European monetary union:

1. The euro. A common currency to all members of European monetary union.
2. European Central Bank (ECB). The ECB is the economic bloc's central bank. As a central bank, the ECB issues the euro, and is the lender of last resort.
3. Centralized monetary policy. The ECB is responsible for the unified monetary and exchange policy of the group of countries that have adopted the euro.

1.5 CORPORATE FINANCE IN ACTION: THE CASE OF ALPHABET INC.

The verb 'to google' is defined in *Webster's New Millennium™ Dictionary of English* as 'to search for information on the Internet'. This integration into everyday language is just one signal of the exceptional success of the Internet search engine that was started in 1996 by two Stanford PhD students, Sergey Brin and Larry Page. Alphabet Inc., which is the new name of the company that runs Google, is now worth in excess of $709 billion. During Google's massive growth, its management had to consider and deal with many issues, all of which are covered in this textbook over the next 21 chapters.

EARLY DAYS

The foundation of any new business is the product or service idea. Through their research, Brin and Page believed they had a more efficient model of searching through Internet pages than the search engines that existed in 1996. Armed only with this idea and a few working algorithms, they approached several potential investors and successfully attracted $100,000 from one of the founders of Sun Microsystems to develop their business concept. Within a year they had received a further $25 million from venture capitalists. To receive this financing, Brin and Page would have used accounting and finance information to create a business plan and cash flow forecast, from which potential investors were able to arrive at a valuation of the future company. Valuation of companies and projects is covered in Part Two of this text.

THE GOOGLE SHARE ISSUE

By 2004 Google had been so successful with its business model that it needed significant injections of cash to capture the emerging business opportunities that were becoming available. The company had two basic options. It could borrow the money (through a bank loan or public debt markets) or issue equity (through the equity markets). In the end, it chose to raise all the money in the form of equity financing. At the time of the issue, Google had no long-term debt. There are a number of reasons for this, and there are many factors to take into consideration when a firm chooses its own debt-to-equity mix, which is also known as its capital structure. Capital structure is covered in Part Three of the textbook.

The Google share issue was highly unusual in that it was organized wholly over the Internet. However, several fundamental issues had to be decided. First, what should the value of the new shares be? How risky are the shares? These questions are of huge importance to investors who are planning to invest their cash in any new investment. Assessing the risk of investments is covered in Part Four, and the process of issuing new securities is reviewed in Part Five.

GOOGLE BECOMES ALPHABET

Although Google is known as an Internet search firm, its success and size make it quite similar to other large firms in more capital-intensive industries. Google changed its name to Alphabet to reflect the change in the company's business. With so many acquisitions (over 200 since 2001), Google had ceased to be a simple search engine platform but a conglomerate of distinct businesses, admittedly with the search engine at the core of operations. The change in name to Alphabet Inc., reflects this change because it symbolizes the collection of letters in the alphabet similar to the company's collection of individual businesses.

As of 2021, Alphabet had over 127,000 employees and total assets worth $276 billion. Like all other firms, Alphabet needs to ensure it has enough liquidity and cash available to pay off its creditors. Short-term financial planning is therefore crucial to its continued existence. This is covered in Part Six of the text.

Finally, Alphabet (as Google) bought YouTube ($1.65 billion), DoubleClick ($3.1 billion), AdMob ($750 million), and Motorola Mobility ($12.5 billion). Its operations span many countries, making its global reach enormous. It is in the top two largest companies in the world and will continue to evolve and develop in the future. The final part of this textbook deals with international corporate finance, and the salient decisions involved in this area. These are extremely important to all companies, and not just Alphabet.

SO WHAT IS CORPORATE FINANCE?

Many people who think of corporate finance tend to consider valuation as being most important. Others think of risk assessment, while many think that capital structure should be emphasized. Hopefully, this section shows that, for a business to be truly successful, the management of a firm and its shareholders must have a solid understanding of all corporate finance areas, and not just one or two topics. Alphabet is a success, not just because it had a fantastic business idea, but also because it understands the fundamental basis of good business and corporate finance.

SUMMARY AND CONCLUSIONS

This chapter introduced you to some of the basic ideas in corporate finance:

1. Corporate finance has three main areas of concern:
   (a) Capital budgeting: what long-term investments should the firm take?
   (b) Capital structure: where will the firm get the long-term financing to pay for its investments? In other words, what mixture of debt and equity should the firm use to fund operations?
   (c) Working capital management: how should the firm manage its everyday financial activities?
2. The goal of financial management in a for-profit business is to make decisions that increase the market value of the equity. The triple bottom line is a useful framework to broaden corporate objectives to embrace environmental and social concerns.
3. The advantages of the corporate form are enhanced by the existence of financial markets. Financial markets function as both primary and secondary markets for corporate securities, and can be organized as either dealer or auction markets.

Of the topics we've discussed thus far, the most important is the goal of financial management: maximizing the value of the equity. Throughout the text we shall be analysing many different financial decisions, but we shall always ask the same question: how does the decision under consideration affect the value of the company's equity?

CHAPTER REVIEW AND SELF-TEST PROBLEMS

1.1 You have set up a new social media site that collates user recipes from around the Internet into a MORB (Massive Open Recipe Book). The company's advertising revenues have started to grow at an alarming rate and you have decided that a new financial manager must now be hired. What will be the main activities of your financial manager?

1.2 Your financial manager has informed you that in order to grow the firm, you must raise new capital. What are the main options open to the firm? Explain how cash flows will circulate between your company and its investors.

1.3 You have been reading in the media that the Government is demanding that companies pay taxes. However, your financial manager has approached you with a legal tax vehicle that results in very little tax being paid by the firm. Should you enter into this scheme? What are the issues a company should consider when paying tax?

SOLUTIONS

1.1 The financial manager should be concerned with how the company makes new investment decisions and whether they add value to the firm. She should also consider the different avenues for raising financing for the company's operations and the appropriate mix between the various funding types. Finally, the financial manager should ensure that the company has an appropriate level of cash and inventory on hand for operations.

1.2 A firm can either borrow money (via a bank loan or debt issue) or give up part ownership (via equity). Cash comes from investors and is used by the firm's operations to generate additional cash. This is then transferred back to investors or retained in the firm for future investment.

1.3 This is an ethical decision that all firms must make. By minimizing tax, you are increasing the funds available to give to investors or retain for future investments. However, there is a moral obligation on firms to pay taxes and contribute to society.

QUESTIONS AND PROBLEMS

1.1 Triple Bottom Line Do you consider the triple bottom line to be important to a firm's management? Explain.

1.2 Goal of the Firm Evaluate the following statement: Managers should not focus on the current equity value because doing so will lead to an overemphasis on short-term profits at the expense of long-term profits.

1.3 Corporate Finance Your grandmother sees you reading a fantastic book called *Fundamentals of Corporate Finance*. She asks you, 'What does corporate finance mean?' Explain to her in a way that doesn't send her to sleep.

1.4 Financing Goals Small firms tend to raise funds from private investors and venture capitalists. As these firms grow larger, they focus more on raising capital from the organized capital markets. Explain why this occurs.

1.5 Financial Management Goals You have read the first chapter of this textbook and have taken over a company that you now discover is losing £100,000 a week. At the rate things are going, the company won't have any cash left in 6 months to pay its creditors. What are your goals as a financial manager? Is this consistent with what you have read in this chapter? Explain.

1.6 Dealer versus Auction Markets Explain the difference between dealer and auction markets. Why do you think both types of market exist? Is there one type of market that is the best? Explain.

1.7 Corporate Cash Flows Strang plc raised £2 million in equity financing last year. This year, they were able to earn a net 10 per cent on these funds. The company pays a 23 per cent tax on earnings and has a 75 per cent pay-out ratio. How much money did it pay in taxes and dividends? How much did it retain for future operations? Note: taxes are always paid before dividends.

1.8 Not-for-Profit Firm Goals Suppose you were the financial manager of a not-for-profit business (a not-for-profit hospital, perhaps). What kinds of goals do you think would be appropriate?

1.9 Triple Bottom Line for Energy Firms How would an energy firm implement the triple bottom line framework if it has only pursued profit maximization in the past?

1.10 Triple Bottom Line for Private Firms Would it be more difficult if you are in charge of a private firm and wish to implement the triple bottom line framework? Explain.

1.11 Corporate Case Study Alphabet is special in many ways because of the firm's meteoric success and now dominant position in the world. Extend the case study on Alphabet by looking at the title of each chapter and then identifying a similar event or news story about the firm that captures the material covered by the chapter.

1.12 Ethics and Firm Goals Can our goal of maximizing equity value conflict with other goals in the context of the triple bottom line framework? Think of some specific examples to illustrate your answer.

1.13 Financial Management Goals You have been the manager of a small company for 20 years and have become great friends with your employees. In the last month, new Norwegian owners have bought out the company's founding owner and have told you that they need to cut costs in order to maximize the value of the company. One of the things they suggest is to lay off 40 per cent of the workforce. However, you believe that the workforce is the company's greatest asset. On what basis do you argue against the new owners' opinions?

1.14 Life Cycle of Firms Choose any company from your country and develop a chronology of the firm's life cycle, from the business start-up, through initial expansion, to stock exchange listing, and then (if applicable) death through merger, acquisition or insolvency. For each stage, explain the company's evolution through the eyes of a financial manager.

MINI CASE

CORPORATE FINANCE INFORMATION ON THE WEB

A skill any financial manager must have is to be able to find and understand financial and corporate information. Choose any two companies from your country. Visit the website of each company and find the investor relations page. This will show all information relating to corporate relations and financial performance.

QUESTIONS

1. For each firm, find the value of the company's total assets. Which firm is the biggest? Why?
2. Visit the Yahoo! Finance website and find the share price of each firm. What does the share price history tell you about each company? How has the share price behaved over the past three years? Can you identify any events that had a major effect on each firm's share price?
3. Check each company's website for its sustainability goals. Do any of the firms follow the triple bottom line framework? If yes, explain how it measures performance within the framework. If no, how would each company implement the triple bottom line framework and what would be appropriate KPIs used for each component?
4. On Yahoo! Finance read the news for each company. What does the news tell you about the future fortunes of each company?
5. Combining all the information, which company do you think is the best investment? Explain.

ADDITIONAL READING

The field of corporate finance is enormous and evolves in conjunction with events in the global business environment. An interesting paper for readers who wish to delve further is given below. Admittedly, the paper was written in 2000, but the discussion is still highly relevant today. Furthermore, as you will discover in later chapters, corporate finance research has progressed a lot in the years since the paper was published.

1. Zingales, L. (2000). In search of new foundations. *Journal of Finance*, 55(4), 1623–1653.

One question that has been approached in a very interesting way is 'What is more important? The business plan or the managers who carry it out?' This is examined in the following paper:

2. Kaplan, S., Sensoy, B., & Stromberg, P. (2009). Should investors bet on the jockey or the horse? Evidence from the evolution of firms from early business plans to public companies. *Journal of Finance, 64*, 75–115.

Finally, if you wish to understand more about the triple bottom line framework, check out the following papers:

3. Alhaddi, H. (2015). Triple bottom line and sustainability: A literature review. *Business and Management Studies, 1*(2), 6–10.

4. Elkington, J. (2013). Enter the triple bottom line. In *The triple bottom line* (pp. 23–38). Routledge.

5. Elkington, J. (2018). 25 years ago I coined the phrase 'triple bottom line': Here's why it's time to rethink it. *Harvard Business Review,* 25 June.

6. Hussain, N., Rigoni, U., & Orij, R. P. (2018). Corporate governance and sustainability performance: Analysis of triple bottom line performance. *Journal of Business Ethics, 149*(2), 411–432.

CHAPTER 2
CORPORATE GOVERNANCE

> **LEARNING OBJECTIVES**
> After studying this chapter, you should understand:
> **LO1** The financial implications of the different forms of business organization.
> **LO2** The conflicts of interest that can arise between managers and owners.
> **LO3** The institutional governance factors that influence corporate behaviour.

CORPORATE GOVERNANCE is concerned with how firms manage themselves, and the way in which their performance is monitored by stakeholders. When shareholders hire professional managers to run their company, it is important to ensure that business decisions maximize shareholder wealth, and not the personal wealth of managers. Ways in which this can be encouraged are by reducing the power of board members, appointing experienced independent non-executive directors to the company's board, and creating independent subcommittees to deal with executive remuneration, auditing and senior appointments.

Most countries revise their corporate governance codes every five years or so, the last big wave of changes being in response to the 2007 financial crisis. Even though firms had very strong and structured corporate governance systems prior to the Global Financial Crisis, this did little to reduce the risky behaviour of managers.

Why, when banks appeared to be well-governed, did they behave so irresponsibly? Does it mean that corporate governance is irrelevant? Does it mean that the corporate governance principles that Western companies follow are wrong? Over just a brief period, corporate governance has become one of the most important topics in corporate finance, and this chapter will explore some of the issues relating to the area.

To begin our study of corporate governance, it is important to understand the different ways in which companies are structured, and the pressures that management face in making business decisions.

2.1 FORMS OF BUSINESS ORGANIZATION

Large European firms, such as BP, Renault and Vodafone, are almost all organized as corporations. We examine the three different legal forms of business organization – sole trader (also known as sole proprietorship), partnership and corporation – to see why this is so. Each form has distinct advantages and disadvantages for the life of the business, the ability of the business to raise cash, and how it is taxed. A key observation is that, as a firm grows, the advantages of the corporate form may come to outweigh the disadvantages.

SOLE TRADER

A **sole trader** business is owned by one person. This is the simplest type of business to start and is the least regulated form of organization. Depending on where you live, you might be able to start a sole trader company by doing little more than getting a business licence and opening your doors. For this reason, there are substantially more sole traders than any other type of business, and many businesses that later become large corporations start out as sole traders.

> **sole trader**
> a business owned by a single individual.

The owner of a sole trader keeps all the profits. That's good news. The bad news is that the owner has *unlimited liability* for business debts. This means that creditors can look beyond business assets to the proprietor's personal assets for payment. Similarly, there is no distinction between personal and business income, so all business income is taxed as personal income.

The life of a sole trader is limited to the owner's lifespan, and the amount of equity that can be raised is limited to the amount of the owner's personal wealth. This limitation often means that the business is unable to exploit new opportunities, because of insufficient capital. Ownership of a sole trader business may be difficult to transfer because it requires the sale of the entire business to a new owner.

Sole traders tend to be exceptionally small, and these firms are normally called *micro-companies* or *micro-enterprises* (between one and nine employees). Although tiny, they are by far the dominant business form in Europe, constituting over 93 per cent of all firms in the region (source: Eurostat). Figure 2.1 presents a breakdown of small and medium enterprises (SME, up to 249 employees) by country.

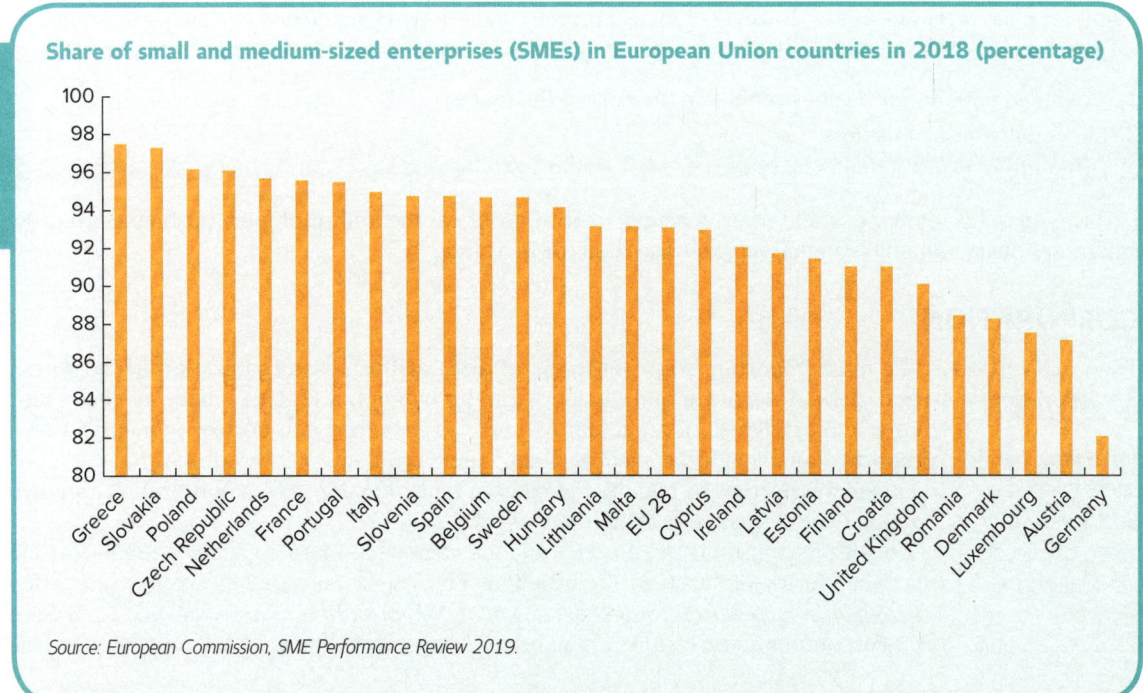

FIGURE 2.1 Share of small and medium-sized enterprises (SMEs) in European Union countries in 2018 (percentage)

Source: European Commission, SME Performance Review 2019.

According to the European Commission, there were over 25.1 million SMEs in the European Union in 2019 and by far the largest group was micro-enterprises, which numbered 23.3 million firms.

PARTNERSHIP

A **partnership** is similar to a sole trader business, except that there are two or more owners (partners). In a *general partnership*, all the partners share in gains or losses, and all have unlimited liability for *all* partnership debts, not just some particular share. The way partnership gains (and losses) are divided is described in the *partnership agreement*. This agreement can be an informal oral agreement, such as 'Let's start a lawnmowing business', or a lengthy, formal written document.

> **partnership**
> a business formed by two or more individuals or entities.

In a *limited partnership*, one or more *general partners* will run the business and have unlimited liability, but there will be one or more *limited partners* who will not actively participate in the business. A limited partner's liability for business debts is limited to the amount that the partner contributes to the partnership. This form of organization is common in law and accounting firms.

The advantages and disadvantages of a partnership are basically the same as those of a sole proprietorship. Partnerships based on a relatively informal agreement are easy and inexpensive to form. General partners have unlimited liability for partnership debts, and the partnership terminates when a general partner wishes to sell out or dies. All income is taxed as personal income to the partners, and the amount of equity that can be raised is limited to the partners' combined wealth. Ownership of a general partnership is not easily transferred, because a transfer requires that a new partnership be formed. A limited partner's interest can be sold without dissolving the partnership, but it may be difficult to find a buyer.

Because a partner in a general partnership can be held responsible for all partnership debts, it is very important to have a written agreement. Failure to spell out the rights and duties of the partners frequently leads to misunderstandings later on. Also, if you are a limited partner, you must not become deeply involved in business decisions unless you are willing to assume the obligations of a general partner. The reason is that, if things go badly, you may be deemed to be a general partner even though you say you are a limited partner.

There are notable differences in the definition of partnerships across Europe. The UK has a limited liability partnership (LLP), whereby the partnership is deemed to be an independent corporate body that can continue to exist if one or more partners leave the firm. Partners can also sign a partnership agreement that collectively takes on the responsibility for the overall firm, but bears no liability for any other partners' actions. The German Partnerschaftsgesellschaft (PartG) is similar to a limited liability partnership except that it is not a corporate entity. However, it owns property under its own name and can sue or be sued.

Based on our discussion, the primary disadvantages of sole trader businesses and partnerships are:

1. Unlimited liability for business debts on the part of the owners
2. Limited life of the business
3. Difficulty of transferring ownership.

These three disadvantages add up to a single, central problem: the ability of such businesses to grow can be seriously limited by an inability to raise cash for investment.

CORPORATION

The **corporation** is the most important form (in terms of size) of business organization in the world. A corporation is a legal 'person' separate and distinct from its owners, and it has many of the rights, duties and privileges of an actual person. Corporations can borrow money and own property, can sue and be sued, and can enter into contracts. A corporation can even be a general partner or a limited partner in a partnership, and a corporation can own equity in another corporation.

> **corporation**
> a business created as a distinct legal entity composed of one or more individuals or entities.

Not surprisingly, starting a corporation is somewhat more complicated than starting the other forms of business organization. Forming a corporation involves preparing *articles of incorporation* (or a charter) and a *memorandum of association*. The articles of incorporation must contain a number of things, including the corporation's name, its intended life (which can be forever), its business purpose, and the number of shares that can be issued. This information must normally be supplied to the country in which the firm will be incorporated. For most legal purposes the corporation is a 'resident' of that country.

The memorandum of association consists of rules describing how the corporation regulates its existence. For example, the memorandum describes how directors are elected. This may be a simple statement of a few rules and procedures, or it may be quite extensive for a large corporation. The memorandum may be amended or extended from time to time by the shareholders.

In a large corporation, the shareholders and managers are usually separate groups. In Europe, there are two main ways in which directors of a company are elected. In **single-tier board** countries, such as the United Kingdom, Ireland and Sweden (and also the US), the shareholders elect the board of directors, who then select the managers. In **two-tier board** countries, such as Denmark, Germany and the Netherlands, there are two boards. The executive board manages the day-to-day operations of the company and reports to the supervisory board which monitors the executive board's performance. The supervisory board will normally consist of representatives of major shareholders, creditors and employee groups. In both systems, managers are charged with running the corporation's affairs in the shareholders' interests. In principle, shareholders control the corporation, because they elect the directors either directly or through a supervisory board.

As a result of the separation of ownership and management, the corporate form has several advantages. Ownership (represented by shares of equity) can be readily transferred, and the life of the corporation is therefore not limited. The corporation borrows money in its own name. As a result, the shareholders in a corporation have limited liability for corporate debts. The most they can lose is what they have invested.

The relative ease of transferring ownership, the limited liability for business debts, and the unlimited life of the business, are why the corporate form is superior for raising cash. If a corporation needs new equity, for example, it can sell new shares and attract new investors. Apple is an example. Apple was a pioneer in the personal computer business. As demand for its products exploded, Apple had to convert to a corporation to raise the capital needed to fund growth and new product development. The number of owners can be huge: larger corporations have many thousands or even millions of shareholders. For example, in 2021, Royal Dutch Shell plc had several million shareholders and about 3.7 billion shares outstanding. In such cases, ownership can change continuously without affecting the continuity of the business.

The corporate form has a significant disadvantage. Because a corporation is a legal person, it must pay taxes. Moreover, money paid out to shareholders in the form of dividends is taxed again as income to those shareholders. This is *double taxation*, meaning that corporate profits are taxed twice: at the corporate level when they are earned, and again at the personal level when they are paid out. Fortunately, in many countries, including the UK, shareholders are given a partial or full tax credit, which they can offset against the double tax that is levied on their dividends.

As the discussion in this section illustrates, the need of large businesses for outside investors and creditors is such that the corporate form will generally be the best for such firms. We focus on corporations in the chapters ahead because of the importance of the corporate form in the European and world economies. Also, a few important financial management issues, such as dividend policy, are unique to corporations. However, businesses of all types and sizes need financial management, so the majority of the subjects we discuss relate to any form of business.

> **single-tier board**
> a corporate board that consists of appointed executive and non-executive directors who collectively make strategic decisions for the company.

> **two-tier board**
> a corporate structure that consists of two boards of directors: the executive or management board, and the supervisory or non-executive board of directors. The management board runs the firm's day-to-day operations and provides general direction. The supervisory board oversees the management board and must approve strategic business decisions.

A CORPORATION BY ANY OTHER NAME . . .

The corporate form of organization has many variations around the world. The exact laws and regulations differ from country to country, of course, but the essential features of public ownership and limited liability remain. These firms are often called *joint-stock companies*, *public limited companies* or *limited liability companies*, depending on the specific nature of the firm and the country of origin.

Table 2.1 gives the names of a number of corporate abbreviations, the countries in which they are used, a translation of the abbreviation and a description of its meaning.

TABLE 2.1

International corporations

Type of corporation	Country of origin	In original language	Description
Pty Ltd.	Australia	Proprietary Limited	Private limited
Limited	Australia	Limited	Publicly listed
AG	Austria, Germany	Aktiengesellschaft	Publicly listed
GmbH	Austria, Germany	Gesellschaft mit Beschränkter Haftung	Private limited
NV	Belgium, Netherlands	Naamloze Venootschap	Publicly listed
BV	Belgium, Netherlands	Besloten Vennootschap	Private limited
SA	Belgium, France, Luxembourg, Portugal, Spain	Société Anonyme/ Sociedade Anónima	Publicly listed
AD	Bulgaria	акционерно дружество	Publicly listed
OOD	Bulgaria	дружествосограниченаотговорност	Private limited
股份有限公司	China Mainland	股份有限公司	Publicly listed
有限公司	China Mainland	有限公司	Private limited
ApS	Denmark	Anpartsselkab	Private limited
A/S	Denmark	Aktieselskab	Publicly listed
SE	European Union	Societas Europaea	Publicly listed
Oy	Finland	Osakeyhtiö	Private limited
Oyj	Finland	Julkinen Osakeyhtiö	Publicly listed
AB	Finland, Sweden	Aktiebolag	Private limited
Abp	Finland	Publikt Aktiebolag	Publicly listed
SARL	France, Luxembourg	Société à Responsibilité Limitée	Private limited
Ltd	Hong Kong	Limited	Private/public
Pvt. Ltd	India	Private Limited Company	Private limited
Plc	India, Ireland, Thailand, UK	Public Limited Company	Publicly listed
S.r.l.	Italy	Società a Responsabilità Limitata	Private limited
S.p.A.	Italy	Società per Azioni	Publicly listed
AS	Norway	Aksjeselskap	Private limited
ASA	Norway	Allmennaksjeselskap	Publicly listed
OOO	Russia	Обществосограниченной ответственностью	Private limited
AO	Russia	Акционерное общество	Publicly listed
(Pty) Ltd	South Africa	Privaat Maatskappy	Private limited
LTD	South Africa	Publieke Maatskappy	Publicly listed
S.L.	Spain	Sociedad Limitada	Private limited
Ltd	Ireland, UK, US	Limited	Private limited
Inc., Corp.	US	Incorporated, Corporation	Publicly listed

NON-PROFIT ORGANIZATIONS

Non-profit organizations normally exist for a specific purpose tied to social, environmental or religious objectives. A non-profit organization won't make a profit, but instead, earns a surplus on its activities. All surpluses are reinvested in the organization to ensure its objectives are achieved.

Examples of non-profit organizations are charities, such as Oxfam and Médecins Sans Frontières.

Funding is a particular issue for non-profit organizations. There are no owners or shareholders in a non-profit organization, and in some countries, a non-profit organization is also known as a non-stock corporation because of this reason. The governance of a non-profit organization is led by the *trustees* or *board of directors*, who are appointed individuals with a legal responsibility to ensure the organization is run in a legally compliant way and for the purposes set out in the articles of incorporation. A non-profit's management may or may not be paid a salary, and the non-profit will not pay corporation tax.

External funds can only be generated through donations, sponsorship, government funding, borrowing, and revenues from activities.

Apart from the differences outlined above, non-profit organizations make the same finance decisions as for-profit corporations. They must make investments, raise financing and ensure there is enough cash available for short-term operations. Non-profits can merge with other non-profits and their operations may or may not be international in nature.

SUSTAINABILITY IN FINANCE

The Wellcome Trust is a non-profit organization whose purpose is to improve public health by funding primary research into a very large number of health projects. One of the Trust's major concerns is preparing the world for the next major pandemic, such as the Coronavirus, COVID-19. Examples of its activities are:

- Funding research to develop new vaccines against dangerous viruses
- Carrying out surveys on attitudes to health and vaccines
- Investing in projects to train health workers around the world
- Ethical health research
- Providing scholarships for research leaders in emerging markets.

The Wellcome Trust was set up in 1936 and is registered as a charity. It has an investment portfolio worth £26.8 billion, with an annual budget of around £5 billion. The Trust has a constitution, articles of association and a memorandum of association, all of which can be downloaded from its website, www.wellcome.ac.uk.

The Trust's board of governors (10 people) are ultimately responsible for all of the organization's activities. The stated objectives of the governors are to ensure that the Trust:

- fulfils its mission by adopting the right long-term strategy and priorities
- upholds high standards in the way it is run and the way the Trust conducts itself
- is true to its organizational principles in its activities
- has a high-quality culture that reflects its principles
- has the right people in place to deliver the Trust's mission, both within Wellcome and externally in the activities it supports.

The Wellcome Trust has an executive team, chaired by its chief executive officer and this reports directly to the board of governors. The executive team is responsible for the day-to-day management of the Trust.

CONCEPT QUESTIONS

2.1a What are the three forms of business organization?
2.1b What are the primary advantages and disadvantages of sole owner firms and partnerships?
2.1c What is the difference between a general and a limited partnership?
2.1d Why is the corporate form superior when it comes to raising cash?

2.2 THE AGENCY PROBLEM AND CONTROL OF THE CORPORATION

We've seen that the financial manager acts in the best interests of the shareholders by taking actions that increase the value of the company's equity. However, in many large corporations, particularly in the UK, Ireland and the US, ownership can be spread over a huge number of shareholders. This dispersion of ownership arguably means that management effectively controls the firm. In this case, will management necessarily act in the best interests of the shareholders? Put another way, might not management pursue its own goals at the shareholders' expense?

A different type of problem exists in many European firms. Whereas large British and American firms have a dispersed ownership structure, many businesses in mainland Europe have a dominant shareholder with a very large ownership stake. Primarily, these shareholders are family groups, banks or governments. In firms with a dominant shareholder, it is possible that corporate objectives will be directed by only one individual or group at the expense of other, smaller, shareholders. In this case, managers are acting in the interests of only a subset of the company's owners.

The issues we have discussed above are caused by what we call *agency relationships*. In the following pages, we briefly consider some of the arguments relating to this issue.

TYPE I AGENCY RELATIONSHIPS

The relationship between shareholders and management is called a *type I agency relationship*. Such a relationship exists whenever someone (the principal) hires another (the agent) to represent his or her interests. For example, you might hire someone (an agent) to sell a car you own while you are away at university. In all such relationships, there is a possibility there may be a conflict of interest between the principal and the agent. Such a conflict is called a **type I agency problem**.

> **type I agency problem**
> the possibility of conflict of interest between the shareholders and management of a firm.

Suppose you hire someone to sell your car and agree to pay that person a flat fee when he or she sells the car. The agent's incentive, in this case, is to make the sale, not necessarily to get you the best price. If you offer a commission of, say, 10 per cent of the sales price instead of a flat fee, then this problem might not exist. This example illustrates that the way in which an agent is compensated is one factor that affects agency problems.

MANAGEMENT GOALS

To see how management and shareholder interests might differ, imagine that the firm is considering a new investment. The new investment is expected to impact favourably on the share value, but it is also a relatively risky venture. The owners of the firm will wish to make the investment (because the share value will rise), but management may not, because there is the possibility that things will turn out badly, and management jobs will be lost. If management does not make the investment, then the shareholders may lose a valuable opportunity. This is one example of a type I agency cost.

In general, the term *agency cost* refers to the cost of the conflict of interest between shareholders and management (we shall consider later another agency relationship between controlling and minority shareholders). These costs can be indirect or direct. An indirect agency cost is a lost opportunity, such as the one we have just described.

Direct agency costs come in two forms. The first type is a corporate expenditure that benefits management but costs the shareholders. Perhaps the purchase of a luxurious and unneeded corporate jet would fall under this heading. The second type of direct agency cost is an expense that comes from the need to monitor management actions. Paying outside auditors to assess the accuracy of financial statement information could be one example.

It is sometimes argued that left to themselves, managers would tend to maximize the amount of resources over which they have control or, more generally, corporate power or wealth. This goal could lead to an overemphasis on corporate size or growth. For example, cases in which management are accused of overpaying to buy up another company just to increase the business size or to demonstrate corporate power are not uncommon. Obviously, if overpayment does take place, such a purchase does not benefit the shareholders of the purchasing company.

Our discussion indicates that management may tend to over-emphasize organizational survival to protect job security. Also, management may dislike outside interference, so independence and corporate self-sufficiency may be important goals.

DO MANAGERS ACT IN THE SHAREHOLDERS' INTERESTS?

Whether managers will, in fact, act in the best interests of shareholders depends on two factors. First, how closely are management goals aligned with shareholder goals? This question relates, at least in part, to the way managers are compensated. Second, can managers be replaced if they do not pursue shareholder goals? This issue relates to control of the firm. As we shall discuss, there are a number of reasons to think that, even in the largest firms, management has a significant incentive to act in the interests of shareholders.

REAL WORLD INSIGHTS

Matters are moving very fast with respect to shareholder activism, especially in Europe and the UK. One of the biggest changes is with respect to the Norwegian sovereign wealth fund, which invests Norway's savings from oil reserves in companies throughout the world and is worth nearly $900 billion. They gave notice in 2016 that their big focus over the coming years was managerial compensation and the levels of pay attracted by senior managers. The fund had already raised its level of engagement by voting at all of their investments' annual general meetings.

Similarly, a recent UK poll found a third of all fund investors wanted more information on the voting of fund managers at annual general meetings. Fourteen per cent wanted funds to go further and provide up-to-date and proactive information on how the funds vote on investors' behalf. Research has shown that when funds engage with managers, several things happen: operating performance goes up, profitability improves, and the way in which boards make decisions becomes more accountable and transparent.

Source: YouGov.co.uk

Managerial Compensation

Management will frequently have a significant economic incentive to increase share value, for two reasons. First, managerial compensation, particularly at the top, is usually tied to financial performance in general, and often to share value in particular. For example, managers are frequently given the option to buy equity at a bargain price. The more the equity is worth, the more valuable this option is. In fact, options are often used to motivate employees of all types, not just top managers. In the UK, workers who invest in employee share schemes for young start-up firms can pay tax on any gains at lower rates. In addition, a company like Alphabet Inc. (Google) issues new share options to all of its employees, thereby giving its workforce a significant stake in its share price, and achieving a better alignment of employee and shareholder interests. Many other corporations, large and small, have similar policies.

The second incentive managers have relates to job prospects. Better performers within the firm will tend to get promoted. More generally, managers who are successful in pursuing shareholder goals will be in greater demand in the labour market, and thus command higher salaries.

In fact, managers who are successful in pursuing shareholder goals can reap enormous rewards. Figure 2.2 presents a breakdown of total CEO remuneration by country for a sample of European firms in 2018. UK executives have the highest pay in Europe and it is almost double that of chief executives of Belgian and Scandinavian firms.

FIGURE 2.2 Total CEO remuneration 2018, STOXX EUROPE 600 companies

Source: Vlerick Business School, 2019, 'Figures and Trends in Executive Rewards'.

Total remuneration consists of a number of elements. Figure 2.3 presents a breakdown of executive remuneration into four different components for various European countries. Long-term incentives represent stock and option based compensation and short-term incentives are annual bonuses and performance awards. Guaranteed allowances include pension contributions and private health care. European executive pay structure is broadly similar across countries with base salary the largest component followed by short-term incentive awards.

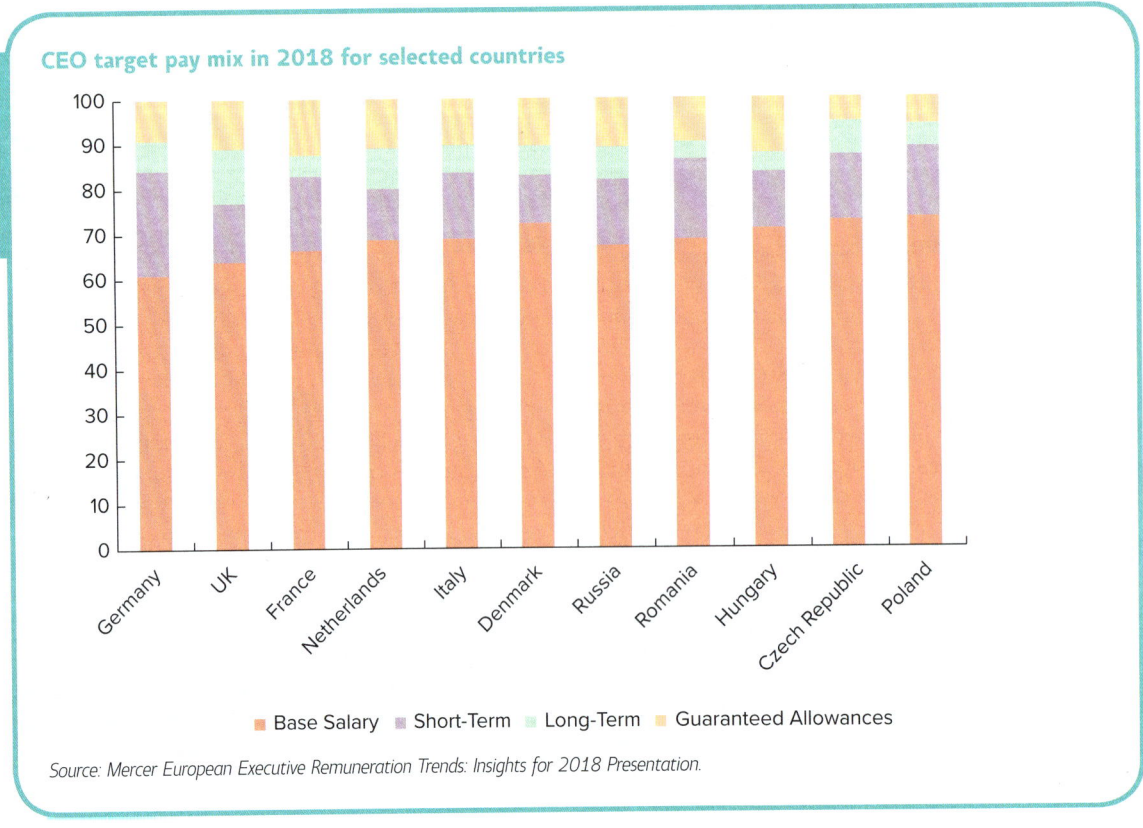

FIGURE 2.3 CEO target pay mix in 2018 for selected countries

Source: Mercer European Executive Remuneration Trends: Insights for 2018 Presentation.

Information about executive compensation, along with lots of other information, can be easily found on the Web for almost any public company or even celebrity.

Control of the Firm

Control of the firm ultimately rests with shareholders. They elect the board of directors, who in turn hire and fire managers. The fact that shareholders control the corporation was made abundantly clear by Steve Jobs' experience at Apple. Even though he was a founder of the corporation, and was largely responsible for its most successful products, there came a time when shareholders, through their elected directors, decided that Apple would be better off without him, so out he went. Of course, he was later rehired and helped turn Apple around with great new products such as the iPod, iPhone and iPad.

Shareholder Rights

The conceptual structure of the corporation assumes that shareholders elect directors, who in turn hire managers to carry out their directives. Shareholders, therefore, control the corporation through the right to elect the directors. In countries with single-tier boards only shareholders have this right, and in two-tier board countries the supervisory board undertakes this task.

In two-tier board systems the supervisory board (which consists of the main shareholder representatives, major creditors, and employee representatives) chooses the executive board of directors. In companies with single-tier boards directors are elected each year at an annual meeting. Although there are exceptions (discussed next), the general idea is 'one share, one vote' (*not* one *shareholder*, one vote). Directors are elected at an annual shareholders' meeting by a vote of the holders of a majority of shares who are present and entitled to vote. However, the exact mechanism for electing directors differs across companies. The most important difference is whether shares must be voted cumulatively or voted straight.

To illustrate the two different voting procedures, imagine that a corporation has two shareholders: Smith with 20 shares and Jones with 80 shares. Both want to be a director. Jones does not want Smith, however. We assume there are a total of four directors to be elected.

The effect of **cumulative voting** is to permit minority participation. If cumulative voting is permitted, the total number of votes that each shareholder may cast is determined first. This is usually calculated as the number of shares (owned or controlled) multiplied by the number of directors to be elected.

> **cumulative voting**
> a procedure in which a shareholder may cast all votes for one member of the board of directors.

With cumulative voting, the directors are elected all at once. In our example this means that the top four vote-getters will be the new directors. A shareholder can distribute votes however he or she wishes.

Will Smith get a seat on the board? If we ignore the possibility of a five-way tie, then the answer is yes. Smith will cast $20 \times 4 = 80$ votes, and Jones will cast $80 \times 4 = 320$ votes. If Smith gives all his votes to himself, he is assured of a directorship. The reason is that Jones can't divide 320 votes among four candidates in such a way as to give all of them more than 80 votes, so Smith will finish fourth at worst.

In general, if there are N directors up for election, then $1/(N + 1)$ per cent of the shares plus one share will guarantee you a seat. In our current example this is $1/(4 + 1) = 20\%$. So the more seats that are up for election at one time, the easier (and cheaper) it is to win one.

With **straight voting** the directors are elected one at a time. Each time, Smith can cast 20 votes and Jones can cast 80. As a consequence, Jones will elect all of the candidates. The only way to guarantee a seat is to own 50 per cent plus one share. This also guarantees that you will win every seat, so it's really all or nothing.

> **straight voting**
> a procedure in which a shareholder may cast all votes for each member of the board of directors.

As we've illustrated, straight voting can 'freeze out' minority shareholders: that is why many companies have mandatory cumulative voting. In companies where cumulative voting is mandatory, devices have been worked out to minimize its impact.

One such device is to stagger the voting for the board of directors. With staggered elections, only a fraction of the directorships are up for election at a particular time. Thus if only two directors are up for election at any one time, it will take $1/(2 + 1) = 33.33$ per cent of the equity plus one share to guarantee a seat.

Overall, staggering has two basic effects:

1. Staggering makes it more difficult for a minority to elect a director when there is cumulative voting, because there are fewer directors to be elected at one time.

2. Staggering makes takeover attempts less likely to be successful, because it makes it more difficult to vote in a majority of new directors.

We should note that staggering may serve a beneficial purpose. It provides 'institutional memory' – that is, continuity on the board of directors. This may be important for corporations with significant long-range plans and projects.

EXAMPLE 2.1

BUYING THE ELECTION

Shares in Sole SpA sell for €20 each, and feature cumulative voting. There are 10,000 shares outstanding. If three directors are up for election, how much does it cost to ensure yourself a seat on the board?

The question here is how many shares of equity it will take to get a seat. The answer is 2,501, so the cost is 2,501 × €20 = €50,020. Why 2,501? Because there is no way the remaining 7,499 votes can be divided among three people to give all of them more than 2,501 votes. For example, suppose two people receive 2,502 votes and the first two seats. A third person can receive at most 10,000 − 2,502 − 2,502 − 2,501 = 2,495, so the third seat is yours.

Proxy Voting

A **proxy** is the grant of authority by a shareholder to someone else to vote his or her shares. For convenience, much of the voting in large public corporations is actually done by proxy.

> **proxy**
> a grant of authority by a shareholder allowing another individual to vote his or her shares.

As we have seen, with straight voting each share of equity has one vote. The owner of 10,000 shares has 10,000 votes. Large companies have hundreds of thousands or even millions of shareholders. In single-tier board environments shareholders can come to the annual meeting and vote in person, or they can transfer their right to vote to another party.

Obviously, management always tries to get as many proxies as possible transferred to it. However, if shareholders are not satisfied with management, an 'outside' group of shareholders can try to obtain votes via proxy. They can vote by proxy in an attempt to replace management by electing enough directors. The resulting battle is called a *proxy fight*.

Classes of Shares

Some firms have more than one class of ordinary equity. Often the classes are created with unequal voting rights. Alphabet (formerly Google), for example, has two classes of shares. The co-founders, Larry Page and Sergey Brin, own Class B shares, which have 10 votes for each share. Other shareholders have Class A shares, which are entitled to one vote per share. So, although the founders only own 5.7 per cent of Alphabet, they have 57 per cent of the voting power.

A primary reason for creating dual or multiple classes of equity has to do with control of the firm. If such shares exist, management of a firm can raise equity capital by issuing non-voting or limited-voting shares while maintaining control.

The subject of unequal voting rights is controversial, and the idea of one share, one vote has a strong following and a long history. Interestingly, however, shares with unequal voting rights are quite common in the United Kingdom and elsewhere around the world.

Other Rights

The value of a share of equity in a corporation is directly related to the general rights of shareholders. In addition to the right to vote for directors, shareholders usually have the following rights:

1. The right to share proportionally in dividends paid.
2. The right to share proportionally in assets remaining after liabilities have been paid in a liquidation.
3. The right to vote on shareholder matters of great importance, such as a merger. Voting is usually done at the annual meeting or a special meeting.

In addition, shareholders sometimes have the right to share proportionally in any new equity sold. This is called the *pre-emptive right*.

Essentially, a pre-emptive right means that a company that wishes to sell equity must first offer it to the existing shareholders before offering it to the general public. The purpose is to give shareholders the opportunity to protect their proportionate ownership in the corporation.

Dividends

A distinctive feature of corporations is that they have shares of equity on which they are authorized by law to pay dividends to their shareholders. **Dividends** paid to shareholders represent a return on the capital directly or indirectly contributed to the corporation by the shareholders. The payment of dividends is at the discretion of the board of directors.

> **dividends**
> payments by a corporation to shareholders, made in either cash or shares.

Some important characteristics of dividends include the following:

- Unless a dividend is declared by the board of directors of a corporation, it is not a liability of the corporation. A corporation cannot default on an undeclared dividend. As a consequence, corporations cannot become bankrupt because of non-payment of dividends. The amount of the dividend and even whether it is paid are decisions based on the business judgement of the board of directors.
- The payment of dividends by the corporation is not a business expense. Dividends are not deductible for corporate tax purposes. In short, dividends are paid out of the corporation's after-tax profits.
- Dividends received by individual shareholders are taxable.

There is a common belief that shareholders prefer companies to issue dividends, because it imposes a form of discipline on incumbent managers. If a company has high levels of cash, managers may invest in projects that will not normally be chosen simply because they can. By transferring the company's cash to shareholders through dividends, managers have less scope to squander resources.

The discussion so far has concerned the agency relationship between professional managers and outside shareholders. We shall now discuss a different type of agency relationship, which is more subtle and complex, and is known as a type II agency relationship. A type II agency relationship exists between shareholders who own a significant amount of a company's shares (controlling shareholders) and other shareholders who own only a small proportional amount (minority shareholders).

TYPE II AGENCY RELATIONSHIPS

The relationship between a dominant or controlling shareholder and other shareholders who have a small proportional ownership stake is known as a *type II agency relationship*. Such a relationship exists whenever a company has a concentrated ownership structure, which is common in many countries. When an investor owns a large percentage of a company's shares, they have the ability to remove or install a board of directors through their voting power. This means that, indirectly, they can make the firm's objectives aligned to their own personal objectives, which may not be the same as that of other shareholders with a smaller proportionate stake. This is the **type II agency problem**.

> **type II agency problem**
> the possibility of conflict of interest between controlling and minority shareholders.

It may seem strange that one set of shareholders can have a different objective from that of a different set of shareholders in the same company. Surely all shareholders want to maximize the value of their firm? Agency theory recognizes that everyone has personal objectives, and these may not be congruent with other groups in an organization. Thus, for example, a dominant shareholder may benefit more from having one of her firms trading at advantageous prices with another firm she owns. This is known as a *related party transaction*.

Alternatively, a controlling shareholder may need cash for an investment in, for example, company A, and wish to take the cash from company B through an extraordinary dividend. This will obviously not be in the interests of company B's other shareholders, but in aggregate the action may be more profitable for the controlling shareholder of company B if it stands to make more money from an investment in company A.

REAL WORLD INSIGHTS

The ownership structure of multinational oil firm Tullow Oil plc is presented below.

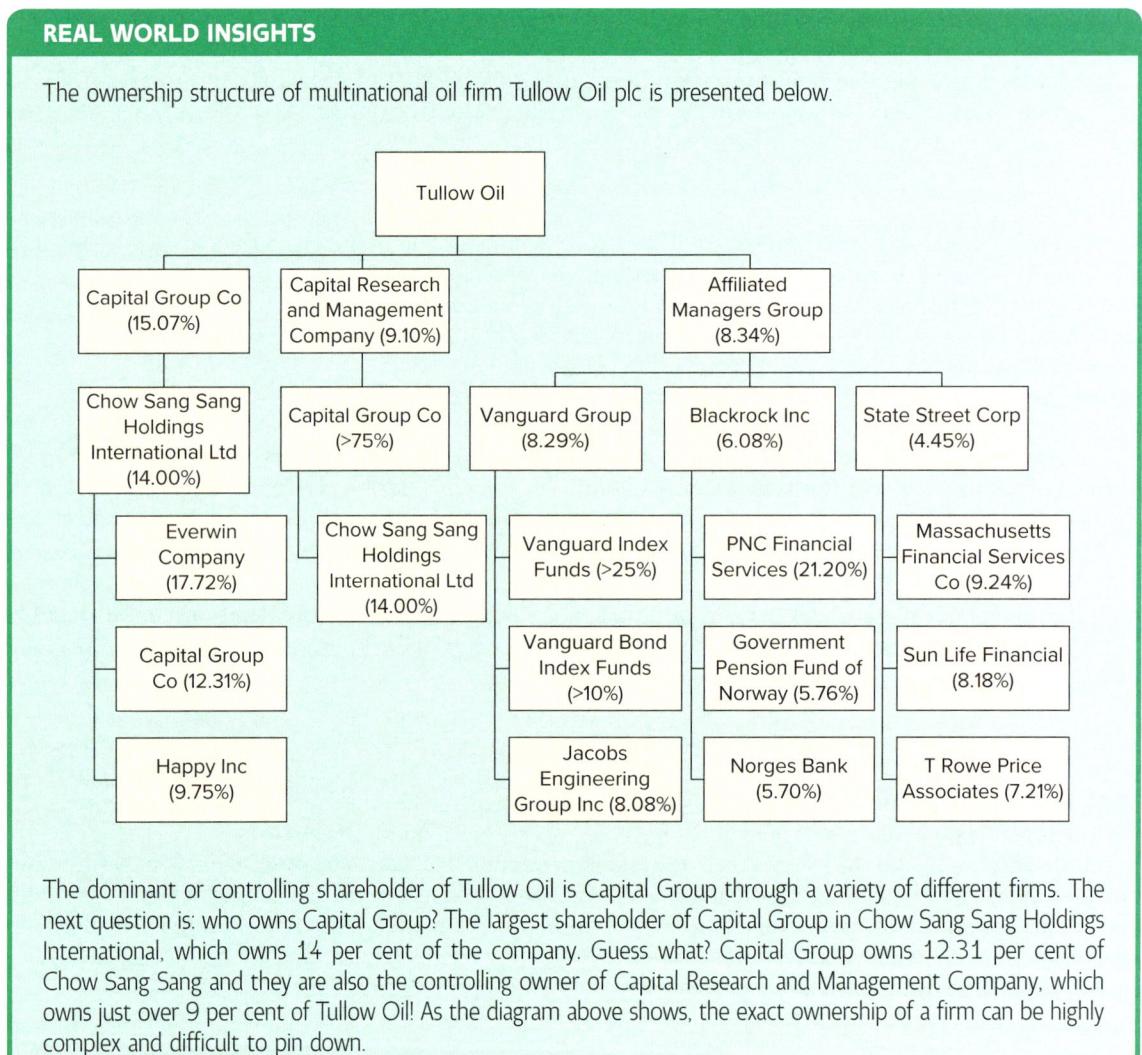

The dominant or controlling shareholder of Tullow Oil is Capital Group through a variety of different firms. The next question is: who owns Capital Group? The largest shareholder of Capital Group in Chow Sang Sang Holdings International, which owns 14 per cent of the company. Guess what? Capital Group owns 12.31 per cent of Chow Sang Sang and they are also the controlling owner of Capital Research and Management Company, which owns just over 9 per cent of Tullow Oil! As the diagram above shows, the exact ownership of a firm can be highly complex and difficult to pin down.

CONCLUSION

The available theory and evidence are consistent with the view that shareholders control the firm, and that shareholder wealth maximization is the relevant goal of the corporation. Even so, there will undoubtedly be times when management goals are pursued at the expense of some or all shareholders, at least temporarily.

STAKEHOLDERS

Our discussion thus far implies that management and shareholders are the only parties with an interest in the firm's decisions. This is an oversimplification, of course. Employees, customers, suppliers and even the government all have a financial interest in the firm.

Taken together, these various groups are called **stakeholders**. In general, a stakeholder is someone, other than a shareholder or creditor, who potentially has a claim on the cash flows of the firm. Such groups will also attempt to exert control over the firm, perhaps to the detriment of the owners.

We can categorize a company's stakeholders into three main groups: *internal*, *connected* and *external*. An internal stakeholder will be an employee or ex-employee of the firm. A connected stakeholder will consist of shareholders, lenders, customers, suppliers and

> **stakeholder**
> someone, other than a shareholder or creditor, who potentially has a claim on the cash flows of the firm.

competitors. Finally, an external stakeholder would be the government, local communities, environmental pressure groups and regulatory bodies.

Each stakeholder group will have its own objectives, which may or may not be consistent with other stakeholder groups. For example, shareholders will want to maximize the value of their equity stake, whereas employees will want to maximize the value of their remuneration. The government will want to maximize tax revenues, while shareholders will want to minimize tax revenues.

> **CONCEPT QUESTIONS**
>
> **2.2a** What is an agency relationship?
> **2.2b** What are agency problems, and how do they come about? What are agency costs?
> **2.2c** What incentives do managers in large corporations have to maximize share value?

2.3 INTERNATIONAL CORPORATE GOVERNANCE

Variations in economic, social and religious culture can lead to differences in the way that companies are run. While corporate differences are to be expected across geographical regions, you may be surprised to learn that the corporate environment within Europe is very varied. Although monetary union has been enacted across much of the continent, the legal, institutional and governance structures in member countries are markedly different. In this section we shall discuss some differences in international corporate governance, and how they may impact upon the business decisions of corporations.

INVESTOR PROTECTION: THE LEGAL ENVIRONMENT

The legal environment in which a corporation does business can have a big impact on its decisions. In a common law system, the law evolves as a result of the judicial decisions of courts, whereas in a civil law system judges interpret the law; they cannot change it. With respect to commercial decisions, the UK and Ireland follow a common law system, whereas the rest of Europe follows civil law.

The third form of legal system is based on religious principles: canon law for Christianity, halakha for Judaism, and sharia for Islam. Under religious law, specific religious principles form the basis of legal decisions. This can have a considerable impact on business activity, especially when religion forbids specific activities. For example, Islam forbids the use of interest in any economic transaction, and so financial loans are not allowed.

Figure 2.4 presents a snapshot of countries that follow different legal systems. Many countries do not follow one system alone, and the exact legal environment can be a hybrid of two systems. For example, India's legal system is based on common law, but personal laws are driven by religious law depending on an individual's religion. Scotland has a different legal system from the rest of the UK, with most laws based on continental or Roman civil law. Commercial law is an exception, and it is similar to the rest of the UK in this regard.

Because the corporate environment must respond quickly to different economic events, common law systems are able to adapt faster to these changes. For example, if a company can identify a loophole in the law that allows it to legally expropriate wealth from shareholders, a common law system can quickly close this loophole through the courts. In a civil law system, any changes in regulation must be enacted through government statute, which can take a much longer time to process.

The inherent flexibility of common law legal environments ensures that shareholders and outside stakeholders are better protected than in civil law countries. This constrains the activities of corporate managers, and as a result, they are held more accountable to shareholders. In addition, because investor protection is better in common law environments, it would be expected that raising capital through the equity markets would be more popular in countries that follow this system.

The type of legal system is not the only factor that affects corporate investors. Adherence to the rule of law and efficiency of law enforcement can have a major impact on corporate decision-making and regulatory compliance. Clearly, a country can have very comprehensive laws, but if they are not enforced then their effect is meaningless. Even in Europe, law enforcement and corruption are exceptionally varied. Figure 2.5 presents the 2018 Corruption Perceptions Index as presented by Transparency International. The index is graded between 0 and 100, with a score of zero indicating that a country is exceptionally corrupt. As can be seen from the graph, Scandinavian countries have very little corruption, and this

FIGURE 2.4 Legal systems around the world

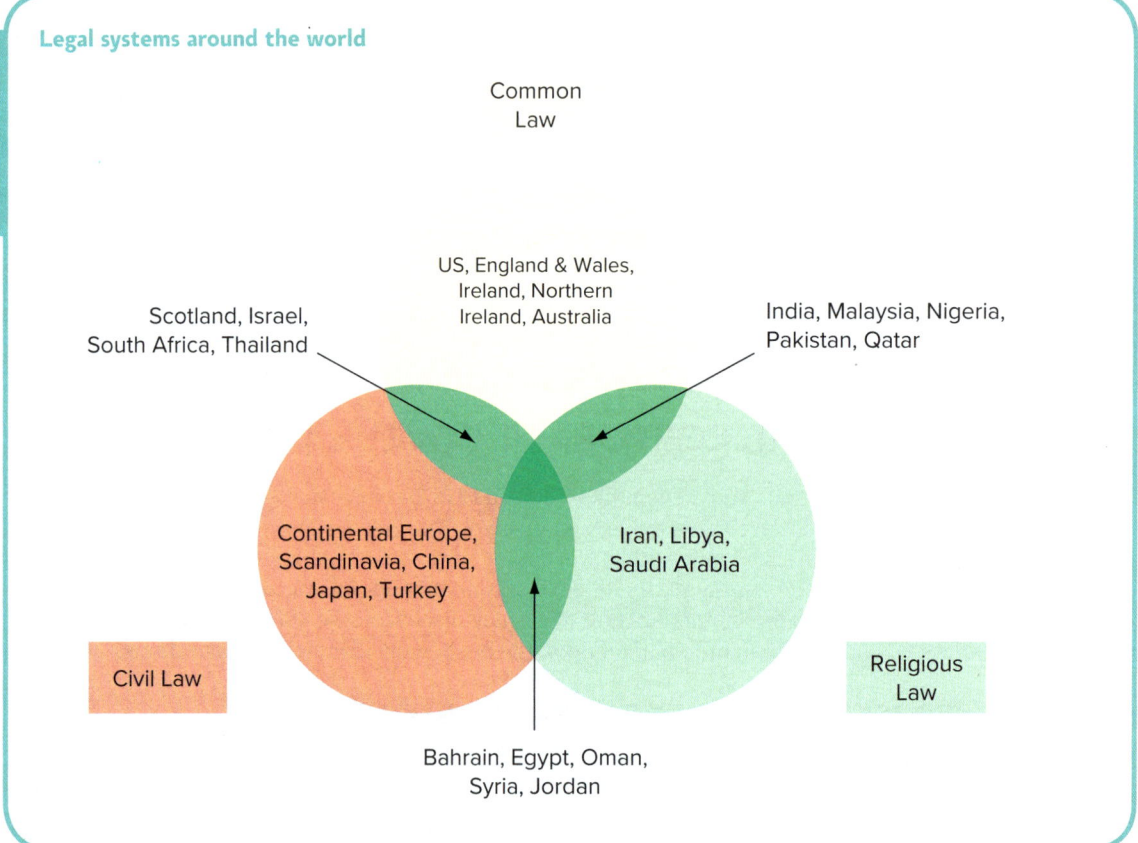

FIGURE 2.5 Transparency International Corruption Perceptions Index 2018

Source: Corruption Perceptions Index 2018.

tends to get worse as one goes towards the equator. Consistent with their lack of economic development, emerging markets tend to have more corruption than developed countries.

THE FINANCIAL SYSTEM: BANK-BASED AND MARKET-BASED COUNTRIES

In a bank-based financial system, banks play a major role in facilitating the flow of money between investors with surplus cash and organizations that require funding. In market-based systems, financial markets take on the role of the main financial intermediary. Corporations in countries with very well-developed financial markets find it easier to raise money by issuing debt and equity to the public than through bank borrowing. Countries with bank-based systems have very strong banks that actively monitor corporations and are often involved in long-term strategic decisions.

It has been argued that corporations in market-based countries have a shorter-term focus than in bank-based countries, because of the emphasis on share price and market performance. When banks are the major source of funding to a company, managers may have longer investment horizons and be less willing to take risks. On the other hand, market-based systems have been argued to be more efficient at funding companies than bank systems. There are many ways in which a country's financial system can be classified as bank or market-based. Table 2.2 shows, for a number of countries, the level of domestic deposits in banks divided by stock market size. A country with a high ratio would be regarded as a bank-based financial system.

TABLE 2.2

Bank versus market-based financial systems

Country	Deposit money banks' assets to GDP (%)	Stock market capitalization to GDP (%)	Deposit money banks' assets/stock market capitalization
South Africa	77.91	245.42	0.32
United States	60.20	143.31	0.42
Switzerland	177.55	219.31	0.81
Saudi Arabia	66.27	70.00	0.95
India	69.30	71.50	0.97
Belgium	81.08	80.37	1.01
United Kingdom	134.69	112.11	1.20
Oman	72.12	56.38	1.28
Netherlands	128.26	92.92	1.38
France	112.68	79.24	1.42
Sweden	133.60	92.81	1.44
Bahrain	101.27	66.67	1.52
Australia	136.01	88.36	1.54
Ireland	100.47	61.50	1.63
Finland	101.88	57.22	1.78
United Arab Emirates	102.65	54.09	1.90
Germany	96.60	47.12	2.05
Spain	154.51	67.26	2.30
Poland	68.15	29.30	2.33
China	153.41	64.14	2.39
Russian Federation	60.75	24.14	2.52
Norway	128.76	47.34	2.72
Denmark	184.59	61.18	3.02
Austria	104.09	23.42	4.44
Italy	130.17	28.02	4.65
Greece	128.45	22.59	5.69

Source: World Bank and authors' own calculations.

OWNERSHIP STRUCTURE

Another factor that can affect business decision-making and corporate objectives is the ownership structure of companies. This is the makeup and constitution of shareholdings in a firm. In the UK and US most large companies are widely held, which means that no single investor has a large ownership stake in a firm. In such environments, type I agency relationships dominate. The rest of the world is characterized by closely held firms, where governments, families and banks are the main shareholders in firms. Type II agency relationships are more important in closely held firms, and their corporate governance structure should reflect this.

Table 2.3 presents a breakdown of the ownership structure of all listed corporations in a number of selected companies across the world. It is very clear from the table that no two countries are the exact same. For example, the UK is characterized by a widely held ownership structure, whereas most of the large firms in Greece are run by families. Governments have a major role to play in many countries, with the Chinese, UAE and Omani governments being the most involved in firms.

TABLE 2.3

Ownership structure of companies in each country

Country	Widely held	Family (%)	State (%)	Other (%)	Country	Widely held	Family (%)	State (%)	Others (%)
Austria	32.3	19.8	8.3	39.6	Malaysia	51.3	16.1	5.9	26.7
Bahrain	58.5	12.2	19.5	9.8	Netherlands	66.1	10.5	2.3	21.1
Belgium	47.8	17.4	5.6	29.2	Norway	64.7	13.4	5	16.9
China	30	17.3	23.2	29.5	Omen	41.4	22	24.4	12.2
Denmark	75	7.1	0.6	17.3	Saudi Arabia	61.3	11.8	12.6	14.3
Finland	69.1	8.8	7.1	15	Singapore	57.9	19	5.9	17.2
France	43.0	29.2	2.9	24.9	South Africa	80.6	6.8	0.5	12.1
Germany	44.9	26.2	3.6	25.3	Spain	62.1	22	3.8	12.1
Greece	32.7	51.5	3.1	12.7	Sweden	66.1	13.4	1.2	19.3
Hong Kong	44.8	20.6	4.3	30.3	Switzerland	58.7	19.9	6.9	14.5
India	59.8	21.0	5.6	13.6	UAE	36.3	19.1	37.2	7.4
Italy	37.2	36.1	3.8	22.9	UK	83.3	10.1	0.9	5.7
Ireland	77	7.7	1.5	13.8	US	77.4	16.2	0.2	6.2

Note: The table presents the percentage of firms in a country that have a controlling shareholder with a greater than 20 per cent stake in the company. If no controlling shareholder exists, the firm is deemed to be widely held. Family firms also include individual shareholders.
Source: Adapted from Table 1 of Aminadav, G., & Papaioannou, E. (2020). Corporate control around the world. *Journal of Finance*, 75(3), 1191-1246.

Ownership structure has a massive impact on corporate objectives. Whereas all shareholders wish to maximize the value of their investment, how value is assessed differs according to the individual. For example, if a firm is widely held in a market-based economy, such as the UK, corporate objectives are likely to be focused on maximizing share price performance. Family firms have slightly different objectives because managers have to consider not only current shareholders but also the descendants of those shareholders. This would suggest that managers of family firms would have a longer-term perspective than other firms, which would influence the types of investment and funding they choose. Firms with a government as a major shareholder would have to consider political objectives, in addition to maximizing share value. A good example is the banking sector, which was bailed out by governments in 2008 and 2009 and still has governments as major shareholders in 2020. Although banks did not feel it appropriate to increase lending significantly under the economic conditions at the time, state shareholders insisted that lending be focused on first-time house buyers and small businesses.

CULTURE AND CORPORATE GOVERNANCE

Most of the discussion so far has related to Western governance environments where the principal-agent perspective is dominant. However, this is not fully accepted everywhere. For example, in the Middle East and parts of Asia and Africa, Islamic-based systems of governance are followed more closely. Furthermore, with governance scandals continuing to occur with regular frequency, Western commentators are questioning whether other approaches to governance may be more appropriate. One of the most important alternatives to principal-agent theory is the stewardship theory of corporate governance, which regards the manager as a steward of the firm's assets rather than an agent of the firm's shareholders.

Agency theory argues that managers are selfish agents who pursue their own objectives at the expense of all other stakeholders, including shareholders. As a result, contractual obligations between the firm and management must exist that bring managerial objectives in line with shareholders. One way to do this is to construct a remuneration package that incentivizes (but not too much!) managers to do their job well and seek maximization of firm value. Another strategy is to reduce the power of the manager so they will be constrained in their behaviour. One typical governance innovation is to split the role of chair and chief executive into two different jobs. Since the chief executive, who is responsible for the day-to-day running of the company, must report to the chair there is less scope for non-value maximizing activities to continue without getting queried.

When you think about it, to say a manager is selfish and only doing their own thing at the expense of everyone else is quite insulting! It also does not capture the vast majority of managers in business who are completely loyal to their firm and employees. Most companies in the world are run via families, founder-entrepreneurs, or long-term investors. In such a situation, managerial tenures can be very long and people are employed at the same company for many years. Basically, stewardship theory argues that managers are motivated to do the very best for a company because they view themselves as stewards of the firm. The best way to do this is to have exceptionally strong relationships with the shareholders of a firm. In addition, stewardship theory would suggest that the role of chair and chief executive should be combined so that the manager has enough power and authority to make decisions and take a long-term strategic perspective.

The stewardship theory concept is relevant in the Middle East and in those countries where long-term investors such as families are common, such as southern Europe and most of Asia and Africa. Both theories argue that managers must be helped to make the best decisions for the firm, which will also be the best decisions for shareholders. How this happens and how a firm is structured contributes to the decision-making process and influences the financial choices made by managers.

ETHICS AND CORPORATE GOVERNANCE

Many people confuse corporate governance with ethics and believe that if a company has strong corporate governance it will necessarily be more ethical. This is not necessarily true and many of the most significant corporate crises in recent times have been in companies with the highest level of observed corporate governance. Take the banking sector as an example. Although the industry is one of the most well-governed in the global economy, it still followed fairly unethical practices that led to the financial crisis and subsequent sovereign debt bailouts across the world. Another example is Carillion, the now-defunct multinational construction services firm. Arguably, Carillion had an absolutely top-quality governance structure, with non-executive directors, split chairman/chief executive position, a shareholder charter and corporate social responsibility policy, among other things. However, the UK government inquiry presented 'a story of recklessness, hubris and greed, its business model was a relentless dash for cash', which was anything but ethical.

The key to understanding corporate governance is that its objective is to facilitate the optimal allocation of resources in a firm. Resources do not only include physical assets like plant, property and equipment, but also human capital, such as employees. For the best financial decisions to be made, they must reflect both financial and social/ethical concerns. In sum, managers should optimize firm value conditional on an ethical framework of decision-making. Corporate governance can facilitate ethical decision-making but it is not a necessary requisite nor does it lead to ethical decision-making. This is something that goes deeper than rules and regulations and cannot be mandated through simple corporate governance structures.

Many firms now explicitly consider their business and strategic model within the framework of the UN Sustainable Development Goals and present these as part of their overall corporate governance framework. The goals span a range of socially optimal objectives and contribute in a small way to the environment and society. Figure 2.6 presents these in a graphical format.

FIGURE 2.6 UN Sustainable Development Goals

Source: United Nations.

2.4 BRINGING IT ALL TOGETHER

The basis of all good corporate finance decisions is a sound framework of corporate governance. This point can't be emphasized too much, because most of the problems that companies experience can usually be identified by failings in the way in which they are governed.

When covering subjects in later chapters, the underlying assumption is that corporate executives are acting in the interests of shareholders and that the firm is well-governed.

When a company does not have strong corporate governance, it may make decisions that do not maximize share value. For example, a firm may choose to invest in projects that maximize managers' own wealth and not that of shareholders. They may also make financing decisions that minimize the risk of the firm for the management but not necessarily for shareholders. This would lead them to make investment and financing decisions different from those that would be recommended in later chapters.

Transparency and timely information disclosure are major aspects of good governance. Without these, investors would find it extremely difficult to value a firm or assess the risk of its operations. Part Three of the textbook assumes that share prices efficiently incorporate information about a company. However, if the management of a firm does not see transparency and disclosure as important parts of their responsibilities, then share prices will be uninformative, and risk assessment would be meaningless.

Most countries have their own code of corporate governance that guides companies on how they should be governed. Largely, they are very similar, with only slight country-level differences. Table 2.4 lists the main corporate governance codes and their date of publication for different countries.

TABLE 2.4

Country codes of corporate governance

Country	Code
Australia	Corporate Governance Principles and Recommendations (2014)
Austria	Austrian Code of Corporate Governance (2015)
Bahrain	Corporate Governance Code Kingdom of Bahrain (2010)
Belgium	The 2009 Belgian Code on Corporate Governance (2009)
China	The Code of Corporate Governance for Listed Companies in China (2018)
Denmark	Recommendations for Corporate Governance (2017)
Dubai	Corporate Governance Code for Small and Medium Enterprises Dubai (2011)
EU	EFAMA Code for External Governance (2011)
	EVCA Corporate Governance Guidelines (2005)
Finland	Finnish Corporate Governance Code (2015)
France	AFEP-MEDEF Corporate Governance Code of Listed Corporations (2018)
Germany	German Corporate Governance Code (2017)
Greece	SEV Corporate Governance Code for Listed Companies (2013)
Hong Kong	Consultation Conclusions on Review of the Corporate Governance Code (2011)
India	Corporate Governance Voluntary Guidelines (2009)
Ireland	Follows the UK Corporate Governance Code (2018)
Netherlands	Dutch Corporate Governance Code (2016)
Norway	The Norwegian Code of Practice for Corporate Governance (2018)
OECD	OECD Principles of Corporate Governance (2015)
Oman	Code of Corporate Governance for Public Listed Companies (2016)
Pakistan	Code of Corporate Governance (2012)
Poland	Code of Best Practice for WSE Companies (2012)
Portugal	Corporate Governance Code (2016)
Saudi Arabia	Corporate Governance Regulations in the Kingdom of Saudi Arabia (2017)
Singapore	Code of Corporate Governance (2018)
South Africa	King Code of Corporate Governance for South Africa (2016)
Spain	Unified Good Governance Code (2006)
Sweden	Swedish Corporate Governance Code (2016)
Switzerland	Swiss Code of Best Practice for Corporate Governance (2014)
Thailand	The Principles of Good Corporate Governance for Listed Companies (2012)
UAE	Corporate Governance Code for Small and Medium Enterprises Dubai (2011)
	Ministerial Resolution No. (518) of 2009 Concerning Governance Rules and Corporate Discipline Standards (2009)
UK	The UK Corporate Governance Code (2018)
US	Corporate Governance Principles for US Listed Companies (2017)

SUMMARY AND CONCLUSIONS

All the material in this textbook makes the assumption that firms are run properly, efficiently and ethically. Unfortunately, in practice, this may not be the case. Corporate governance is concerned with the way in which a firm is managed. There are a number of basic principles that should be followed to minimize the danger of firms getting into difficulty because of the way they are managed. The budding financial manager must be aware of, and familiar with, the basic principles underlying the way in which his or her company should be run. Without this knowledge, he or she will not be in a position to make the best financial decisions for the company's shareholders.

In this chapter, we:

1. Considered the different types of business organization;
2. Introduced the concept of an 'agency problem' where (a) managers prioritize their welfare over that of the company's shareholders, and (b) large shareholder force managers to pursue their interests over that of minority shareholders; and
3. Provided an overview of the different business environments that exist across the world.

CHAPTER REVIEW AND SELF-TEST PROBLEMS

2.1 As the financial manager of an unlisted manufacturing company based in Amsterdam, you have been tasked with preparing your firm for potential listing on Euronext. The company is closely held with only five shareholders, each holding 20 per cent of the company's shares. The shareholders are all directors of the firm and they make up the board of directors. Because of the company's ownership structure, there has been no real consideration of corporate governance issues before.

The share listing will result in the total directors' cash ownership falling to 20 per cent of the total firm. This means that 80 per cent will be owned by external shareholders (mainly banks and financial institutions). However, the five directors have informed you that they do not wish to relinquish control of the firm. They have asked you to answer the following with respect to corporate governance issues:

(a) How can the board maintain control of the firm while having only 20 per cent of the shares?

(b) Should the company's board structure change? If so, what should be done and why?

(c) What processes should be put in place to ensure that all shareholders have some say in the company's strategy? How should the company deal with foreign shareholders?

(d) How should the company decide upon director remuneration? Are there any structures that should be put in place to ensure that the directors are fairly compensated for the work that they have done?

(e) There is a proposal that the company should instead possibly list in London or Shanghai and move headquarters to the listing location. Are there any institutional differences that the directors should be aware of before making their decision? Explain.

SOLUTIONS

2.1

(a) The board can maintain control by issuing shares without or with very few voting rights. This means that existing shareholders have the power to make decisions without being constrained by the new shareholders.

(b) It should change to meet the new governance needs and requirements. As the firm grows in size and attracts new investors, the need for accountability becomes greater. Corporate governance structures that establish an accountable and transparent culture in the firm will be required.

(c) The shareholders can control the corporation's direction, policies and activities by electing the board of directors. Also, cumulative voting and proxy voting procedures should be used.

(d) Incentive-based compensation should be used to ensure the board objectives are consistent with the shareholders.

(e) There are differences in the level of governance at the country level and this may affect the way in which the board is permitted to do its business.

QUESTIONS AND PROBLEMS

2.1 Partnerships Why are professional firms, such as accountants and lawyers, more likely to have a partnership form rather than a sole trader business or limited company structure?

2.2 Culture and Corporate Governance Explain the difference between the stewardship theory of corporate governance and agency theory.

2.3 Corporate Governance Principles In your opinion what is the most important issue in corporate governance? Explain your answer.

2.4 Corporate Governance Explain why the corporate governance of a sole trader should be different from that of a partnership, which in turn should be different from that of a limited corporation.

2.5 Ethics and Corporate Governance Do ethics have any role to play in a firm's corporate governance? Should this not be the responsibility of corporate regulation? Explain.

2.6 Sole Trader Why do you think that sole trader businesses are the most common types of business in the world?

2.7 Stakeholders Discuss what is meant by a stakeholder. In what ways are stakeholders represented in two-tier board structures? How does this differ from companies with a unitary board structure? Use real examples to illustrate your answer.

2.8 Agency Problems Who owns a corporation? Describe the process whereby the owners control the firm's management. What is the main reason why an agency relationship exists in the corporate form of organization? In this context, what kinds of problem can arise?

2.9 Board Committees Explain why you think publicly listed companies have board subcommittees like the remuneration committee, audit committee and risk management committee. Why could this responsibility not simply be left to the board of directors? Explain.

2.10 Corporate Governance Is it possible to improve one aspect of corporate governance in a firm but weaken another at the same time? Use an illustration to explain your answer.

2.11 Stakeholders What are the three main types of stakeholders in a company? Provide some examples of stakeholder types and how their respective objectives may conflict with other stakeholders.

2.12 Agency Problems Suppose you own equity in a company. The current share price is £25. Another company has just announced that it wants to buy your company and will pay £35 per share to acquire all the outstanding shares. Your company's management immediately begins fighting off this hostile bid. Is management acting in the shareholders' best interests? Why or why not?

2.13 Agency Problems and Corporate Ownership Corporate ownership varies around the world. Historically, individuals have owned the majority of shares in public corporations in the United States. In Germany and Japan, however, banks and other large financial institutions own most of the equity in public corporations. Do you think agency problems are likely to be more or less severe in Germany and Japan than in the United States? Why? In recent years, large financial institutions such as mutual funds and pension funds have been becoming the dominant owners of shares in the United Kingdom, and these institutions are becoming more active in corporate affairs. What are the implications of this trend for agency problems and corporate control?

2.14 Executive Compensation Why do you think chief executives in the UK are paid almost twice as much as their counterparts in Scandinavia?

2.15 Corporate Governance around the World In the Middle East, many companies have a Sharia Supervisory Board to which the board of directors reports. Evaluate the merits of such a governance structure and argue whether this approach to governance could be extended to other areas where the supervisory board guides on ethical, social or environmental matters.

2.16 Institutional Shareholders Regulators have developed a number of new policies with respect to institutional shareholder involvement in the running of firms. Review the reasons why regulators would prefer more or less involvement of institutions in the running of corporations. In addition, discuss the proposals that have been put forward by regulators in your own country, and whether these are likely to be effective.

2.17 Sustainable Development Goals Do you think that companies should pursue sustainable development goals to the detriment of profit maximization? Explain.

MINI CASE

GLYNDEBOURNE WINES LIMITED

Three years ago, husband and wife team, John and Beverly Glyndebourne formed Glyndebourne Wines. The company produced a full line of English wines, and its specialities included tonic wine, Crazy Dog wine, Temeke Wine and Tyson Wine. The two formed the company as an outside interest, and both continued to work at their existing jobs. John did all the wine-growing, and Beverly handled the marketing and distribution. With good product quality and a sound marketing plan, the company grew rapidly. Early this year, the company was featured in a widely distributed entrepreneurial magazine and just a few months ago the company was featured in *Gourmet Wines*, a leading speciality wine magazine. After the article appeared in *Gourmet Wines* sales exploded, and the company began receiving orders from all over the world.

Because of the increased sales, John left his other job, followed shortly by Beverly. The company hired additional workers to meet demand. Unfortunately, the fast growth experienced by the company led to cash flow and capacity problems. The company is currently producing as many wines as possible with the assets it owns, but demand for its wines is still growing. Further, the company has been approached by a national supermarket chain with a proposal to put four of its wines in all of the chain's stores, and a national restaurant chain has contacted the company about selling Glyndebourne Wines in its restaurants. The restaurant would sell the wines without a brand name.

John and Beverly have operated the company as a sole trader business with Beverly being the named owner of the firm and John as a paid employee. They have approached you to help manage and direct the company's growth. Specifically, they have asked you to answer the following questions.

QUESTIONS

1. Should they change the corporate form from sole trader, where Beverly is the only named owner, to a partnership with both John and Beverly as partners?
2. As an alternative, should they consider registering their firm as a private limited company with both John and Beverly holding 50 shares each?
3. In your opinion, what would be the optimal corporate form for Glyndebourne Wines?

ADDITIONAL READING

Corporate governance is a massive and very fertile area for research. The following papers are good papers to get an idea of the field.

1. Aminadav, G., & Papaioannou, E. (2020). Corporate control around the world. *Journal of Finance, 75*(3), 1191–1246.

2. Biermann, F., Kanie, N., & Kim, R. E. (2017). Global governance by goal-setting: The novel approach of the UN Sustainable Development Goals. *Current Opinion in Environmental Sustainability, 26*, 26–31.

3. De Haan, J., & Vlahu, R. (2016). Corporate governance of banks: A survey. *Journal of Economic Surveys, 30*(2), 228–277.

4. Edmans, A., & Holderness, C. G. (2017). Blockholders: A survey of theory and evidence. In B. Hermalin & M. Weisbach (eds), *The handbook of the economics of corporate governance* (Vol. 1, pp. 541–636). North-Holland.

5. Edmans, A., Gabaix, X., & Jenter, D. (2017). Executive compensation: A survey of theory and evidence. In B. Hermalin & M. Weisbach (eds), *The handbook of the economics of corporate governance* (Vol. 1, pp. 383–539). North-Holland.

6. McCahery, J. A., Sautner, Z., & Starks, L. T. (2016). Behind the scenes: The corporate governance preferences of institutional investors. *Journal of Finance, 71*(6), 2905–2932.

CHAPTER 3
FINANCIAL STATEMENT ANALYSIS

LEARNING OBJECTIVES
After studying this chapter, you should understand:
- **LO1** The three main financial statements that are produced by corporations: the statement of financial position, the income statement, and the statement of cash flows.
- **LO2** How to compute and, more importantly, interpret some common ratios.

KEY NOTATIONS
b	Retention ratio
NWC	Net working capital
P/E ratio	Price–earnings ratio
PPE	Property, plant and equipment
ROA	Return on assets
ROE	Return on equity

IF YOU are wondering how to assess the performance and value of a company, this chapter gives you some insights into how to build a preliminary picture. An analyst can draw on many information sources when undertaking a valuation assessment. She can take the most recent news stories and build an intuitive view of a firm's future prospects. Another information source is the firm's financial reports and the data presented therein. The analyst may also consider using market price information from stock exchanges (if available). Ideally, one would combine as much information as possible to provide the most complete picture possible of the company.

Underlying all corporate assessments is the concept of cash flow. Without a view of how much cash a firm generates, it is difficult to understand the future value that may be generated from a firm's operations. The title of this chapter is *Financial Statement Analysis* because we introduce the three main financial statements a firm produces and show you how to analyse these in a systematic way.

In this chapter we examine financial statements, taxes and cash flow. Our emphasis is not on preparing financial statements. Instead, we recognize that financial statements are frequently a key source of information for financial decisions, so our goal is to briefly examine such statements and point out some of their more relevant features. We also pay special attention to some of the practical details of cash flow.

As you read, pay particular attention to two important differences: (1) the difference between accounting value and market value; and (2) the difference between accounting income and cash flow. These distinctions will be important throughout the book.

3.1 THE ANNUAL REPORT

Every year, a company will release its annual report. In addition to information relating to the performance and activities of the firm over the previous year, the annual report presents three financial statements:

1. The statement of financial position, or balance sheet
2. The income statement
3. The statement of cash flows.

Financial statements have two main users: internal stakeholders and external stakeholders. Internal uses of financial statements are for forward planning and helping managers make financial decisions. External uses of financial statements are for legal requirements, such as reporting for tax and regulatory authorities. When financial reports are prepared for internal purposes, we call them management accounts. Management accounts do not necessarily follow a standard format. When financial reports are used for external purposes we call them financial accounts, and these tend to follow a standard format.

A key difference between management and financial accounts is that management accounts are forward-looking (helping to predict future performance) whereas financial accounts are backwards-looking (recording past performance).

We shall now discuss each statement in turn.

THE STATEMENT OF FINANCIAL POSITION

The **statement of financial position** or **balance sheet** is a snapshot of the firm. It is a convenient means of organizing and summarizing what a firm owns (its assets), what the firm owes (its liabilities), and the difference between the two (the firm's equity) at a given point in time. Figure. 3.1 illustrates how the statement of financial position is constructed. As shown, the left side lists the assets of the firm, and the right side lists the liabilities and equity.

> **statement of financial position (balance sheet)** financial statement showing a firm's accounting value on a particular date.

Assets: The Left Side

Assets are classified as either *current* or *non-current*. A non-current asset is one that has a relatively long life (greater than 12 months). Non-current assets can be either *tangible*, such as a truck or a computer, or *intangible*, such as a trademark or patent. A current asset has a life of less than 1 year. This means that the asset will convert to cash within 12 months. For example, inventory would normally be purchased and sold within a year and is thus classified as a current asset. Obviously, cash itself is a current asset. Trade receivables (money owed to the firm by its customers) are also current assets.

Liabilities and Owners' Equity: The Right Side

The firm's liabilities are the first thing listed on the right side of the statement of financial position. These are classified as either *current* or *non-current*. Current liabilities, like current assets, have a life of less than one year (meaning they must be paid within the year) and are usually listed before non-current liabilities. Trade payables (money the firm owes to its suppliers) are one example of a current liability.

A debt that is not due in the coming year is classified as a non-current liability. A loan the firm will pay off in 5 years is one such non-current liability. Firms borrow in the long term from a variety of sources. We shall tend to use the terms *bond* and *bondholders* generically to refer to long-term debt and long-term creditors, respectively.

Finally, by definition, the difference between the total value of the assets (current and non-current) and the total value of the liabilities (current and non-current) is the *shareholders' equity*, also called *ordinary*

FIGURE 3.1

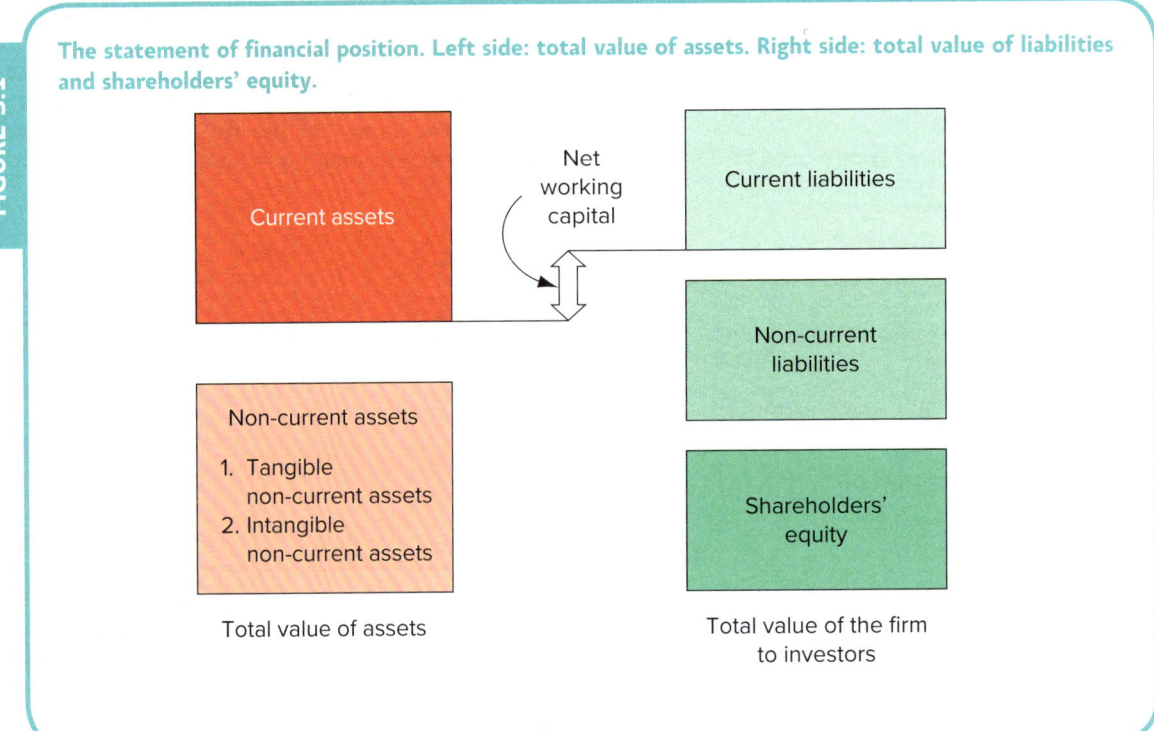

The statement of financial position. Left side: total value of assets. Right side: total value of liabilities and shareholders' equity.

equity or *owners' equity*. This feature of the statement of financial position is intended to reflect the fact that, if the firm were to sell all its assets and use the money to pay off its debts, then whatever residual value remained would belong to the shareholders. So the statement of financial position or balance sheet 'balances' because the value of the left side always equals the value of the right side. That is, the value of the firm's assets is equal to the sum of its liabilities and shareholders' equity:

$$\text{Assets} = \text{Liabilities} + \text{Shareholders' equity} \tag{3.1}$$

This is the *balance sheet identity*, or equation, and it always holds, because shareholders' equity is defined as the difference between assets and liabilities.

Net Working Capital

As shown in Figure 3.1, the difference between a firm's current assets and its current liabilities is called **net working capital**. Net working capital is positive when current assets exceed current liabilities. Based on the definitions of current assets and current liabilities, this means the cash that will become available over the next 12 months exceeds the cash that must be paid over the same period. For this reason, net working capital is usually positive in a healthy firm.

> **net working capital**
> current assets less current liabilities.

EXAMPLE 3.1

BUILDING THE STATEMENT OF FINANCIAL POSITION

Consider the statement of financial position below. The firm has current assets of DKK55.140 billion, non-current assets of DKK36.659 billion, current liabilities of DKK40.873 billion, and non-current liabilities of DKK3.957 billion. What does the statement of financial position or balance sheet look like? What is shareholders' equity? What is net working capital?

In this case, total assets are DKK55.140 + DKK36.659 = DKK91.799 billion and total liabilities are DKK40.873 + DKK3.957 = DKK44.830 billion, so shareholders' equity is the difference: DKK91.799 − DKK44.830 = DKK46.969 billion. The statement of financial position would look like this:

Assets (DKK billions)		Liabilities and shareholders' equity (DKK billions)	
Current assets	55.140	Current liabilities	40.873
Non-current assets	36.659	Non-current liabilities	3.957
		Shareholders' equity	46.969
Total assets	91.799	Total liabilities and shareholders' equity	91.799

Net working capital is the difference between current assets and current liabilities, or DKK55.140 − DKK40.873 = DKK14.267 billion.

Table 3.1 shows a real-life statement of financial position for the Italian high-tech firm, Leonardo SpA at 31 December 2018. The assets on the statement of financial position can be listed in order of the length of time it takes for them to convert to cash in the normal course of business. Similarly, the liabilities are listed in the order in which they would normally be paid. There are other ways in which the statements can be presented. For example, in the UK, non-current assets are sometimes called *fixed assets*, non-current liabilities are known as *long-term debt*, and the statement of financial position is presented as fixed assets + current assets − current liabilities = long-term debt + shareholders' equity.

TABLE 3.1

Leonardo SpA 2018 Statement of Financial Position

	€ millions		€ millions
Intangible assets	6,591	Share capital	2,495
Property, plant and equipment	2,166	Other reserves	2,015
Investment property	1,195	**Total equity**	**4,510**
Other non-current assets	1,904		
Non-current assets	**11,856**	Loans and borrowings (non-current)	3,423
		Other non-current liabilities	2,611
Inventories	5,449	**Non-current liabilities**	**6,034**
Contract assets	2,528		
Trade receivables	2,936	Contract liabilities	8,055
Income tax receivables	72	Trade payables	3,028
Loans and receivables	185	Loans and borrowings (current)	1,190
Other assets	444	Provisions for short-term risks and charges	1,125
Cash and cash equivalents	2,049	Other current liabilities	1,577
Current assets	**13,663**	**Current liabilities**	**14,975**
		Total liabilities	**21,009**
Total assets	**25,519**	**Total liabilities and equity**	**25,519**

Source: Yahoo! Finance. © 2020 Yahoo! All rights reserved.

Market Value versus Book Value

The values in the statement of financial position for the firm's assets are *book values* and generally are not what the assets are actually worth. Under **International Accounting Standards (IAS)** financial statements in Europe and many other countries can show assets in two ways. The most common presentation uses the *historical cost model*, in which assets are valued at what the firm paid for them, no matter how long ago they were purchased or how much they are worth today. Another approach uses the *revaluation model*, which presents an asset's value as what it is worth in the market today. This is known as the *fair value amount*.

> **International Accounting Standards (IAS)**
> the common set of standards and procedures by which audited financial statements are prepared in Europe and many other countries.

For current assets market value and book value might be somewhat similar because current assets are bought and converted into cash over a relatively short span of time. In other circumstances, the two values may differ quite a bit. Moreover, for non-current assets under the cost model, it would be purely a coincidence if the actual market value of an asset (what the asset could be sold for) were equal to its book value. For example, a railroad might own enormous tracts of land purchased a century or more ago. What the railroad paid for that land could be hundreds or thousands of times less than what the land is worth today. The statement of financial position would nonetheless show the historical cost if the cost model were used.

The statement of financial position is potentially useful to many different parties. A supplier might look at the size of trade payables to see how promptly the firm pays its bills. A potential creditor would examine the liquidity and degree of financial leverage. Managers within the firm can track things such as the amount of cash and the amount of inventory the firm keeps on hand. Uses such as these are discussed in more detail later in the chapter.

Managers and investors will frequently be interested in knowing the value of the firm. This information is not in the statement of financial position. The fact that assets may be listed at cost means that there is no necessary connection between the total assets shown and the value of the firm. Indeed, many of the most valuable assets a firm might have – good management, a good reputation, talented employees – don't appear in the statement of financial position at all.

Similarly, the shareholders' equity figure in the statement of financial position and the true value of the equity need not be related. For example, in 2020 the equity book value of the British insurer, Admiral Group was just over £918 million, whereas the market value was £6.46 billion. Similarly, Leonardo's book value of equity was approximately €4.51 billion, and its market value was €5.03 billion.

For financial managers, then, the accounting value of the equity is not an especially important concern; it is the market value that matters. Henceforth, whenever we speak of the value of an asset or the value of the firm, we shall normally mean its *market value*. So, for example, when we say the goal of the financial manager is to increase the value of the equity, we mean the market value of the equity.

EXAMPLE 3.2

MARKET VALUE VERSUS BOOK VALUE

Siouxsie plc has non-current assets with a book value of £700 and an appraised market value of about £1,000. Net working capital is £400 on the books, but approximately £600 would be realized if all the current accounts were liquidated. Siouxsie has £500 in long-term debt, both book value and market value. What is the book value of the equity? What is the market value?

We can construct two simplified statements of financial position, one in accounting (book value) terms and one in economic (market value) terms:

SIOUXSIE PLC
Statements of financial position
Market value versus book value

Assets	Book £	Market £	Liabilities and shareholders' equity	Book £	Market £
Net working capital	400	600	Non-current liabilities	500	500
Non-current assets	700	1,000	Shareholders' equity	600	1,100
	1,100	1,600		1,100	1,600

In this example shareholders' equity is actually worth almost twice as much as what is shown on the books. The distinction between book and market values is important precisely because book values can be so different from true economic value.

THE INCOME STATEMENT

The **income statement** or **statement of comprehensive income** measures performance over some period of time, usually a quarter, 6 months or a year. The income statement equation is:

$$\text{Revenues} - \text{Expenses} = \text{Income} \tag{3.2}$$

If you think of the statement of financial position as a snapshot, then you can think of the statement of comprehensive income as a video recording covering the period between before and after pictures. Table 3.2 shows a real-life income statement for Leonardo SpA.

The first thing reported in an income statement would usually be revenue and expenses from the firm's principal operations. Subsequent parts include, among other things, financing expenses such as interest paid. Taxes paid are reported separately.

income statement financial statement summarizing a firm's performance over a period of time.

TABLE 3.2

Leonardo SpA 2018 Statement of Comprehensive Income

	€ millions
Revenue	12,329
Cost of revenues	11,741
Profit before tax and financial expenses	588
Net financial expenses	14
Profit before taxes	574
Income taxes	64
Net income	510

Source: Yahoo! Finance. © 2020 Yahoo! All rights reserved.

The last item is *net income* (the so-called bottom line). Net income is often expressed on a per-share basis and called *earnings per share (EPS)*.

When looking at an income statement, the financial manager needs to keep two main things in mind: International Accounting Standards (IAS) and cash versus non-cash items.

EXAMPLE 3.3

CALCULATING EARNINGS PER SHARE

Leonardo had 574.34 million shares outstanding. Based on the income statement in Table 3.2, what was EPS? What were dividends per share?

From the income statement we see that Leonardo had a net income of €510 million for 2018. We can calculate earnings per share, or EPS, as follows:

$$\text{Earnings per share} = \text{Net Income}/\text{Total shares outstanding}$$
$$= €510.00/574.34 = €0.888 \text{ per share}$$

IAS and the Income Statement

An income statement prepared using International Accounting Standards will show revenue when it accrues. This is not necessarily when the cash comes in. The general rule (the *recognition* or *realization principle*) is to recognize revenue when the earnings process is virtually complete, and the value of an exchange of goods or services is known or can be reliably determined. In practice, this principle usually means that revenue is recognized at the time of sale, which need not be the same as the time of collection.

Expenses shown on the income statement are based on the *matching principle*. The basic idea here is to first determine revenues as described previously and then match those revenues with the costs associated with producing them. So, if we manufacture a product and then sell it on credit, the revenue is realized at the time of sale. The production and other costs associated with the sale of that product will likewise be recognized at that time. Once again, the actual cash outflows may have occurred at some different time.

As a result of the way revenues and expenses are realized, the figures shown on the income statement may not be at all representative of the actual cash inflows and outflows that occurred during a particular period.

> **non-cash items**
> expenses charged against revenues that do not directly affect cash flow, such as depreciation.

Non-Cash Items

A primary reason why accounting income differs from cash flow is that an income statement contains **non-cash items**. The most important of these is *depreciation*. Suppose a firm purchases an asset for €5,000 and pays in cash. Obviously, the firm has a €5,000 cash outflow at the time of purchase. However, instead of deducting the €5,000 as an expense, an accountant might depreciate the asset over its lifetime.

If the depreciation is straight-line and the asset is written down to zero over that period, then €5,000/5 = €1,000 will be deducted each year as an expense. The important thing to recognize is that this €1,000 deduction isn't cash – it's an accounting number. The actual cash outflow occurred when the asset was purchased.

The depreciation deduction is simply another application of the matching principle in accounting. The revenues associated with an asset would generally occur over some length of time. So the accountant seeks to match the expense of purchasing the asset with the benefits produced from owning it.

As we shall see, for the financial manager the actual timing of cash inflows and outflows is critical in coming up with a reasonable estimate of market value, so we need to learn how to separate the cash flows from the non-cash accounting entries. In reality, the difference between cash flow and accounting income can be quite high. For example, consider again Leonardo SpA. For its 2018 fiscal year, the company reported a net income of €510 million but only a positive cash flow of €150 million, a difference of about €360 million! (See Tables 3.2 and 3.3.)

TABLE 3.3

Leonardo SpA 2018 Statement of Cash Flows

	€ millions
Cash flows from operating activities	687
Cash flows from investing activities	−350
Cash flows from financing activities	−187
Net increase in cash and cash equivalents	**150**

A DIGRESSION: TAXES

Taxes can be one of the largest cash outflows a firm will experience. For example, for the year ending 2020, Tesco plc's profit before taxes was £1.315 billion. Its tax bill for this period was £380 million, which suggests an average tax rate of 28.89 per cent.

The size of a company's tax bill is determined by the tax code in each country it operates, and these are regularly changed by individual governments. In this section we examine corporate tax rates and how taxes are calculated. If the various rules of taxation seem a little bizarre or convoluted to you, keep in mind that the tax code is the result of political, not economic, forces. As a result, there is no reason why it has to make economic sense.

Corporate Tax Rates

An overview of corporate tax rates for a sample of countries that were in effect for 2016 is shown in Table 3.4. Corporate taxes are not normally a simple arithmetic deduction from profit before taxes. Almost all countries in the world allow firms to carry forward losses they've made in previous years to offset their tax bill in the future. In addition, there are a number of adjustments and modifications to the tax figure that affect what is actually paid.

TABLE 3.4

Corporate tax rates for large firms around the world

Country	Corporation tax (%)	Country	Corporation tax (%)
Australia	30	New Zealand	28
Austria	25	Norway	23
Bahrain	0	Oman	15
Belgium	29	Pakistan	35
Brazil	25	Poland	19
Canada	34	Portugal	21
China	25	Russia	20
Denmark	22	Singapore	17
Finland	20	South Africa	28
France	33.33	Spain	25
Germany	30	Sweden	22
Greece	29	Switzerland	18
Hong Kong	16.5	Tanzania	30
India	35	Thailand	20
Ireland	12.5	Turkey	20
Italy	24	United Arab Emirates	0
Japan	30.86	United Kingdom	19
Malaysia	24	United States	27
Netherlands	16/22.25		

Source: www.deloitte.com, Global Corporate Tax Rates 2020.

The tax rates presented in Table 3.4 are average tax rates for the largest companies. Many countries apply differential taxation, depending on how much a company earns in any given year.

Average versus Marginal Tax Rates

In making financial decisions, it is frequently important to distinguish between average and marginal tax rates. Your average tax rate is your tax bill divided by your taxable income – in other words, the percentage of your income that goes to pay taxes. Your marginal tax rate is the tax you would pay (in per cent) if you earned one more unit of currency. The percentage tax rates shown in Table 3.4 for the Netherlands are marginal rates. The first €200,000 earned by Dutch firms has a tax rate of 16 per cent. Any extra earnings are charged 22.25 per cent tax. Put another way, marginal tax rates apply to the part of income in the indicated range only, not all income.

The difference between average and marginal tax rates can best be illustrated with a simple example. Suppose our Dutch corporation has a taxable income of €400,000. What is the tax bill? Using Table 3.4, we can figure out the tax bill like this:

$$0.16 \times €200,000 = €32,000$$
$$0.2225 \times (€400,000 - 200,000) = €44,500$$
$$= €76,500$$

Our total tax is thus €76,500.

In our example, what is the average tax rate? We had a taxable income of €400,000 and a tax bill of €76,500, so the average tax rate is €76,500/400,000 = 19.125%. What is the marginal tax rate? If we made one more euro, the tax on that euro would be 22.25 cents, so our marginal rate is 22.25 per cent.

With a *flat-rate* tax, there is only one tax rate, so the rate is the same for all income levels. With such a tax, the marginal tax rate is always the same as the average tax rate. As it stands now, corporate taxation in the United Kingdom is based on a modified flat-rate tax.

Normally, the marginal tax rate will be relevant for financial decision-making. The reason is that any new cash flows will be taxed at that marginal rate. Because financial decisions usually involve new cash flows or changes in existing ones, this rate will tell us the marginal effect of a decision on our tax bill.

STATEMENT OF CASH FLOWS

At this point, we are ready to discuss perhaps one of the most important pieces of financial information that can be gleaned from financial statements: cash flow. By *cash flow* we simply mean the difference between the cash that came in and the cash that went out. For example, if you were the owner of a business, you might be very interested in how much cash you actually took out of your business in a given year. How to determine this amount is one of the things we discuss next.

No standard financial statement always presents this information in the way that we wish. We shall, therefore, discuss how to calculate cash flow for Leonardo SpA (Table 3.3), and point out how the result may differ from that of standard financial statement calculations. It is also important to note that the accounting standards used in Europe are different from those in the US, and this leads to differences in the way the cash flow statement is presented. Our focus is on International Accounting Standards, because these are followed by large European firms.

From the balance sheet identity, we know that the value of a firm's assets is equal to the value of its liabilities plus the value of its equity. Similarly, the cash flow from the firm's assets must equal the sum of the cash flow to creditors and the cash flow to shareholders (or owners):

$$\text{Cash flow from assets} = \text{Cash flow to creditors} + \text{Cash flow to shareholders} \quad (3.3)$$

This is the *cash flow identity*. It says that the cash flow from the firm's assets is equal to the cash flow paid to suppliers of capital to the firm. What it reflects is the fact that a firm generates cash through its various activities, and that cash is either used to pay creditors or paid out to the owners of the firm.

operating cash flow
cash generated from a firm's normal business activities.

Another way of presenting cash flow is to separate it according to the corporate activity to which it relates. Cash flows that arise because of the firm's core operations are known as **operating cash flow**. When a company buys or sells a warehouse, this is a long-term investment that will span many years, and a cash flow of this type relates to the firm's long-term investing activities. Finally, if a firm raises cash in the form of equity or debt, the cash flow would be part of its financing activities. Any cash flow that occurs can be identified as one of these three components:

$$\text{Total cash flow} = \frac{\text{Cash flow from}}{\text{operating activities}} + \frac{\text{Cash flow from}}{\text{investing activities}} + \frac{\text{Cash flow from}}{\text{financing activities}} \quad (3.4)$$

We discuss the various components that make up these cash flows next.

Cash Flow from Operating Activities

Operating cash flow refers to the cash flow that results from the firm's day-to-day activities of producing and selling. Expenses associated with the firm's financing of its assets or the purchase of buildings are not included, because they are not operating expenses.

To calculate operating cash flow (OCF), we want to calculate revenues minus costs plus changes in non-cash net working capital. We don't want to include depreciation, because it's not a cash outflow. We also don't want to include interest, because it's a financing expense. The only exception is when we are considering the accounts of a financial institution, such as a bank, where interest payments and receipts relate directly to operating income. Finally, we do want to include taxes, because they are (unfortunately) paid in cash.

International Accounting Standards require companies to present operating cash flows in one of two ways: the direct method, where actual cash outflows and inflows are presented; or the indirect method, which starts off with the company's profit or loss for the year and then extracts any non-cash items incurred (e.g. depreciation), cash flows arising from financing activities, and cash flows from investing activities. Both approaches will arrive at the same operating cash flow.

If we look at Leonardo SpA's statement of cash generated from core operations (Table 3.3), we see that Leonardo had a 2018 net cash flow of €687 million generated from its core operations. Operating cash flow is an important number because it tells us, on a very basic level, whether a firm's cash inflows from its business operations are sufficient to cover its everyday cash outflows. For this reason, negative operating cash flow is often a sign of trouble.

To complete our calculation of cash flow for Leonardo SpA, we need to consider how much was reinvested in the firm and how much was raised from outside financing. We consider spending on non-current assets first.

Cash Flow from Investing Activities

Cash flow from investing activities (net capital spending) is just money spent on non-current assets less money received from the sale of non-current assets. In Table 3.3 you can also see Leonardo SpA's net capital spending for financial year 2018.

During the year, Leonardo paid €577 million in buying other non-current assets such as property, plant and equipment (this is not shown in Table 3.3 but included in the company's full set of accounts). However, through a major restructuring of operations, the firm disposed of significant assets resulting in a lower net cash *outflow* of €350 million.

> **cash flow from investing activities** cash generated or expended from a firm's long-term investments.

Cash Flow from Financing Activities

The last major component of a firm's cash flow comes from any actions it has taken during the year to raise cash from investors. The company may also have paid back outstanding borrowings, or repurchased its own shares. **Cash flow from financing activities** can be substantial, and they constitute the third part of the cash flow statement.

During 2018, Leonardo SpA had a net *outflow* of €187 million from financing activities. Firms will have a positive cash flow if they raise capital via borrowing or issuing equity. Negative financing cash flow arises when a firm pays off its debt or buys back its equity. In Leonardo's case, the major restructuring also resulting in a change in the financing mix (Table 3.3).

> **cash flow from financing activities** cash generated or expended as a result of a firm's debt and equity choices.

Net Cash Flow

Given the figures we've come up with, we're ready to calculate cash flow for the firm. The total cash flow is found by adding the cash flow from operating activities to the cash flows from investing and financing

---

CONCEPT QUESTIONS

3.1a What is the balance sheet identity?
3.1b Explain the difference between accounting value and market value. Which is more important to the financial manager? Why?
3.1c What is the income statement equation?
3.1d Why is accounting income not the same as cash flow? Give two reasons.
3.1e What is the difference between a marginal and an average tax rate?
3.1f What is the cash flow identity? Explain what it says.
3.1g What are the components of operating cash flow?

activities. Leonardo had a net cash inflow of €150 million, once the effect of converting some foreign cash flows into euros had been factored into the analysis.

3.2 RATIO ANALYSIS

> **financial ratios**
> relationships determined from a firm's financial information and used for comparison purposes.

One of the main ways to understand how healthy a company is and how well it has performed is to carry out a ratio analysis and compare the **financial ratios** of the firm with those of its competitors. Such ratios are ways of comparing and investigating the relationships between different pieces of financial information.

Unfortunately, there is a problem in discussing financial ratios. Because a ratio is simply one number divided by another, and because there are so many accounting numbers out there, we could examine a huge number of possible ratios. Everybody has a favourite. We shall restrict ourselves to a representative sampling.

In this section we want only to introduce you to some commonly used financial ratios. These are not necessarily the ones we think are the best. In fact, some of them may strike you as illogical, or not as useful as some alternatives. If they do, don't be concerned. As a financial analyst, you can always decide how to compute your own ratios.

What you do need to worry about is the fact that different people and different sources seldom compute these ratios in exactly the same way, and this leads to much confusion. The specific definitions we use here may or may not be the same as ones you have seen or will see elsewhere. If you are ever using ratios as a tool for analysis, you should be careful to document how you calculate each one; and if you are comparing your numbers with numbers from another source, be sure you know how those numbers are computed.

We shall defer much of our discussion of how ratios are used, and some problems that come up with using them, until later in the chapter. For now, for each of the ratios we discuss, we consider several questions:

1. How is it computed?
2. What is it intended to measure, and why might we be interested?
3. What is the unit of measurement?
4. What might a high or low value tell us? How might such values be misleading?
5. How could this measure be improved?

Financial ratios are traditionally grouped into the following categories:

1. Short-term solvency, or liquidity, ratios
2. Long-term solvency, or financial leverage, ratios
3. Asset management, or turnover, ratios
4. Profitability ratios
5. Market value ratios.

We shall consider each of these in turn.

SHORT-TERM SOLVENCY, OR LIQUIDITY, MEASURES

As the name suggests, short-term solvency ratios as a group are intended to provide information about a firm's liquidity, and these ratios are sometimes called *liquidity measures*. The primary concern is the firm's ability to pay its bills over the short run without undue stress. Consequently, these ratios focus on current assets and current liabilities.

For obvious reasons, liquidity ratios are particularly interesting to short-term creditors. Because financial managers work constantly with banks and other short-term lenders, an understanding of these ratios is essential.

One advantage of looking at current assets and liabilities is that their book values and market values are likely to be similar. Often (though not always), these assets and liabilities just don't live long enough for the two to get seriously out of step. On the other hand, like any type of near-cash, current assets and liabilities can and do change fairly rapidly, so today's amounts may not be a reliable guide to the future. The most common liquidity ratios are as follows.

Current Ratio

One of the best known and most widely used ratios is the *current ratio*. As you might guess, the current ratio is defined as follows:

$$\text{Current ratio} = \frac{\text{Current assets}}{\text{Current liabilities}} \tag{3.5}$$

The Quick (or Acid-Test) Ratio

Inventory is often the least liquid current asset. It is also the one for which the book values are least reliable as measures of market value, because the quality of the inventory is not considered. Some of the inventory may later turn out to be damaged, obsolete or lost.

More to the point, relatively large inventories are often a sign of short-term trouble. The firm may have overestimated sales, and overbought or overproduced as a result. In this case, the firm may have a substantial portion of its liquidity tied up in slow-moving inventory.

To further evaluate liquidity, the *quick*, or *acid-test, ratio* is computed just like the current ratio, except that inventory is omitted:

$$\text{Quick ratio} = \frac{\text{Current assets} - \text{Inventory}}{\text{Current liabilities}} \tag{3.6}$$

Notice that using cash to buy inventory does not affect the current ratio, but it reduces the quick ratio. Again, the idea is that inventory is relatively illiquid compared with cash.

LONG-TERM SOLVENCY MEASURES

Long-term solvency ratios are intended to address the firm's long-term ability to meet its obligations, or, more generally, its financial leverage. These are sometimes called *financial leverage ratios* or just *leverage ratios*. We consider three commonly used measures and some variations.

Total Debt Ratio

The *total debt ratio* takes into account all debts of all maturities to all creditors. It can be defined in several ways, the easiest of which is this:

$$\text{Total debt ratio} = \frac{\text{Total assets} - \text{Total equity}}{\text{Total assets}} \tag{3.7}$$

We can define two useful variations on the total debt ratio – the *debt–equity ratio* and the *equity multiplier*:

$$\text{Debt–equity ratio} = \frac{\text{Total debt}}{\text{Total equity}} \tag{3.8}$$

$$\text{Equity multiplier} = \frac{\text{Total assets}}{\text{Total equity}} \tag{3.9}$$

The fact that the equity multiplier is 1 plus the debt–equity ratio is not a coincidence:

$$\begin{aligned}\text{Equity multiplier} &= \frac{\text{Total assets}}{\text{Total equity}} \\ &= \frac{\text{Total equity} + \text{Total debt}}{\text{Total equity ratio}} \\ &= 1 + \text{Debt–equity ratio}\end{aligned}$$

The thing to notice here is that, given any one of these three ratios, you can immediately calculate the other two; so they all say exactly the same thing.

Times Interest Earned

Another common measure of long-term solvency is the *times interest earned (TIE) ratio*. Once again, there are several possible (and common) definitions, but we'll stick with the most traditional:

$$\text{Times interest earned ratio} = \frac{\text{Operating profit}}{\text{Interest}} \tag{3.10}$$

Operating profit is also known as *earnings before interest and taxes (EBIT)*, and you will see this term used in many books. As the name *times interest earned ratio* suggests, this ratio measures how well a company has its interest obligations covered, and it is often called the *interest coverage ratio*.

Cash Coverage

A problem with the TIE ratio is that it is based on operating profit, which is not really a measure of cash available to pay interest. The reason is that depreciation and other non-cash expenses have been deducted out. Because interest is definitely a cash outflow (to creditors), one way to define the *cash coverage ratio* is this:

$$\text{Cash coverage ratio} = \frac{\text{Operating profit} + \text{Non-cash deductions}}{\text{Interest}} \tag{3.11}$$

The numerator here, operating profit plus non-cash deductions, is often abbreviated to EBITDA (earnings before interest, taxes, depreciation and amortization – say 'ebbit-dah'). It is a basic measure of the firm's ability to generate cash from operations, and it is frequently used as a measure of cash flow available to meet financial obligations.

A common variation on EBITDA is earnings before interest, taxes and depreciation (EBITD – say 'ebbit-dee'). In this variation, only depreciation is considered.

ASSET MANAGEMENT, OR TURNOVER MEASURES

We next turn our attention to the efficiency with which a company uses its assets. The measures in this section are sometimes called *asset utilization ratios*. The specific ratios we discuss can all be interpreted as measures of turnover. What they are intended to describe is how efficiently or intensively a firm uses its assets to generate sales. We first look at two important current assets: inventory and receivables.

Inventory Turnover and Days' Sales in Inventory

Inventory turnover can be calculated as follows:

$$\text{Inventory turnover} = \frac{\text{Cost of goods sold}}{\text{Inventory}} \tag{3.12}$$

As long as we are not running out of stock and thereby forgoing sales, the higher this ratio is, the more efficiently we are managing inventory.

If we know the inventory turnover, we can immediately figure out how long it took us to turn it over on average. The result is the average *days' sales in inventory*:

$$\text{Days' sales in inventory} = \frac{365 \text{ days}}{\text{Inventory turnover}} \tag{3.13}$$

In many of the ratios we discuss in this chapter, average figures could just as well be used. Again, it depends on whether we are worried about the past, in which case averages are appropriate, or the future, in which case ending figures might be better. Also, using ending figures is common in reporting industry averages; so, for comparison purposes, ending figures should be used in such cases.

Receivables Turnover and Days' Sales in Receivables

Our inventory measures give some indication of how fast we can sell our product. We now look at how fast we collect on those sales. The *receivables turnover* is defined much like inventory turnover:

$$\text{Receivables turnover} = \frac{\text{Sales}}{\text{Trade receivables}} \tag{3.14}$$

This ratio makes more sense if we convert it to days, so here is the *days' sales in receivables*:

$$\text{Days' sales in receivables} = \frac{365 \text{ days}}{\text{Receivables turnover}} \quad (3.15)$$

For obvious reasons, this ratio is frequently called the *average collection period (ACP)*.

Payables Turnover and Days' Payables in Receivables

A similar measure to Receivables Turnover is Payables Turnover. This gives an estimate of how long it takes to pay our supplier purchases.

$$\text{Payables turnover} = \frac{\text{Credit purchases}}{\text{Trade payables}} \quad (3.16)$$

This ratio makes more sense if we convert it to days, so here is the *days' purchases in receivables*:

$$\text{Days' purchases in payables} = \frac{365 \text{ days}}{\text{Payables turnover}} \quad (3.17)$$

For obvious reasons, this ratio is frequently called the *average payment period (APP)*.

Asset Turnover Ratios

Moving away from specific accounts such as inventory or receivables, we can consider several 'big picture' ratios. For example, *net working capital (NWC) turnover* is:

$$\text{NWC turnover} = \frac{\text{Sales}}{\text{NWC}} \quad (3.18)$$

This ratio measures how much 'work' we get out of our working capital. Once again, assuming we aren't missing out on sales, a high value is preferred. (Why?)

Similarly, *PPE turnover* is:

$$\text{PPE turnover} = \frac{\text{Sales}}{\text{Property, plant and equipment}} \quad (3.19)$$

REAL WORLD INSIGHTS

Understanding the linkages among financial statements, business forecasts and long-term financial planning can stretch experts, never mind beginners. All companies work with different types of information and it is from these that the business decisions of the firm are made. Financial statements like the income statement and balance sheet use data on past activities. Cash flow forecasts, on the other hand, use forward-looking predictions and estimates. The key to making correct finance decisions lies in an understanding of how accounting figures and cash flow forecasts are linked. You will also be faced with a number of different financial ratios that can sometimes seem contradictory. Cutting through the noise is sometimes very difficult and even experts can get confused.

For example, read the information below and decide whether or not the automobile parts manufacturer, Elringklinger GB, performed well in the last year.

Revenues increased to £20.4 million over the year but operating profit dropped to £1.802 million from £2.117 million. Gross profit rose to £4.6 million from £4.5 million but unfortunately, the profit margin percentage dropped to 23 per cent from 30 per cent. The number of employees jumped from 150 to 192, which increased overall salaries to £5.27 million from £4.08 million.

Difficult, isn't it? Clearly more analysis would be required before you could definitively come to a decision on Elringklinger GB's overall performance.

Our final asset management ratio, the *total asset turnover*, comes up quite a bit. We shall see it later in this chapter. As the name suggests, the total asset turnover is:

$$\text{Total asset turnover} = \frac{\text{Sales}}{\text{Total assets}} \quad (3.20)$$

PROFITABILITY MEASURES

The three measures we discuss in this section are probably the best known and most widely used of all financial ratios. In one form or another, they are intended to measure how efficiently a firm uses its assets and manages its operations. The focus in this group is on the bottom line, net income.

Profit Margin

Companies pay a great deal of attention to their *profit margins*:

$$\text{Profit margin} = \frac{\text{Net income}}{\text{Sales}} \quad (3.21)$$

All other things being equal, a relatively high profit margin is obviously desirable. This situation corresponds to low expense ratios relative to sales. However, we hasten to add that other things are often not equal.

For example, lowering our sales price will usually increase unit volume, but will normally cause profit margins to shrink. Total profit (or, more important, operating cash flow) may go up or down; so the fact that margins are smaller isn't necessarily bad.

Return on Assets

Return on assets (ROA) is a measure of profit per unit cash of assets. It can be defined in several ways, but the most common is this:

$$\text{Return on assets} = \frac{\text{Net income}}{\text{Total assets}} \quad (3.22)$$

Return on Equity

Return on equity (ROE) is a measure of how the shareholders fared during the year. Because benefiting shareholders is our goal, ROE is, in an accounting sense, the true bottom-line measure of performance. ROE is usually measured as follows:

$$\text{Return on equity} = \frac{\text{Net income}}{\text{Total equity}} \quad (3.23)$$

Return on Capital Employed

Return on capital employed (ROCE) or *return on investment (ROI)* is a similar measure to ROE except that gross profit (profit before interest and taxes) is used instead of the bottom line. The denominator (Total equity + non-current liabilities) measures the total long-term investment. ROCE shows the return you are getting from your assets before financing and taxation costs.

$$\text{Return on capital employed} = \frac{\text{Profit before interest and taxes}}{\text{Total equity + non-current liabilities}} \quad (3.24)$$

ROCE is also used when considering borrowing. If a company's ROCE is less than the cost of a loan, it may not be appropriate to borrow because the return on the investment is less than the return required to compensate lenders.

Because ROA, ROE and ROCE are such commonly cited numbers, it is important to remember they are accounting rates of return. For this reason, these measures should properly be called *return on book assets* and *return on book equity*. In fact, ROE is sometimes called *return on net worth*. Whatever it's called, it would be inappropriate to compare the result with, for example, an interest rate observed in the financial markets. We shall have more to say about accounting rates of return in later chapters.

MARKET VALUE MEASURES

Our final group of measures is based, in part, on information not necessarily contained in financial statements – the market price per share of equity. Obviously, these measures can be calculated directly only for publicly traded companies.

Price-Earnings Ratio

The first of our market value measures, the *price–earnings (P/E) ratio* (or multiple), is defined here:

$$\text{P/E ratio} = \frac{\text{Price per share}}{\text{Earnings per share}} \quad (3.25)$$

Earnings per share is simply net income divided by the number of shares.

Because the P/E ratio measures how much investors are willing to pay per unit of current earnings, higher P/Es are often taken to mean the firm has significant prospects for future growth. Of course, if a firm had no or almost no earnings, its P/E would probably be quite large: so, as always, care is needed in interpreting this ratio.

Sometimes analysts divide P/E ratios by expected future earnings growth rates (after multiplying the growth rate by 100). The result is the PEG ratio. The idea behind the PEG ratio is that whether a P/E ratio is high or low depends on expected future growth. High PEG ratios suggest that the P/E is too high relative to growth, and vice versa.

Price-Sales Ratio

In some cases, companies will have negative earnings for extended periods, so their P/E ratios are not very meaningful. A good example is a recent start-up. Such companies usually do have some revenues, so analysts will often look at the *price–sales ratio*:

$$\text{Price–sales ratio} = \frac{\text{Price per share}}{\text{Sales per share}} \quad (3.26)$$

As with P/E ratios, whether a particular price–sales ratio is high or low depends on the industry involved.

Market-to-Book Ratio

A second commonly quoted market value measure is the *market-to-book ratio*:

$$\text{Market-to-book ratio} = \frac{\text{Market value per share}}{\text{Book value per share}} \quad (3.27)$$

Notice that book value per share is total equity (not just ordinary shares) divided by the number of shares outstanding.

Because book value per share is an accounting number, it reflects historical costs. In a loose sense, the market-to-book ratio therefore compares the market value of the firm's investments with their cost. A value less than 1 could mean that the firm has not been successful overall in creating value for its shareholders.

Another ratio, called *Tobin's Q ratio*, is much like the market-to-book ratio. Tobin's Q is the market value of the firm's assets divided by their replacement cost:

$$\begin{aligned}\text{Tobin's Q} &= \frac{\text{Market value of firm's assets}}{\text{Replacement cost of firm's assets}} \\ &= \frac{\text{Market value of firm's debt and equity}}{\text{Replacement cost of firm's assets}}\end{aligned} \quad (3.28)$$

Notice that we used two equivalent numerators here: the market value of the firm's assets, and the market value of its debt and equity.

Conceptually, the Q ratio is superior to the market-to-book ratio, because it focuses on what the firm is worth today relative to what it would cost to replace it today. Firms with high Q ratios tend to be those with attractive investment opportunities or significant competitive advantages (or both). In contrast, the market-to-book ratio focuses on historical costs, which are less relevant.

As a practical matter, however, Q ratios are difficult to calculate with accuracy, because estimating the replacement cost of a firm's assets is not an easy task. Also, market values for a firm's debt are often unobservable. Book values can be used instead in such cases, but accuracy may suffer.

CONCLUSION

This completes our definitions of some common ratios. We could tell you about more of them, but these are enough for now. We'll go on to discuss some ways of using these ratios instead of just how to calculate them. Table 3.5 summarizes the ratios we've discussed.

TABLE 3.5

Common financial ratios

Short-term solvency or liquidity ratios

$$\text{Current ratio} = \frac{\text{Current assets}}{\text{Current liabilities}}$$

$$\text{Quick ratio} = \frac{\text{Current assets} - \text{Inventory}}{\text{Current liabilities}}$$

$$\text{Cash ratio} = \frac{\text{Cash}}{\text{Current liabilities}}$$

Net working capital to total assets

$$= \frac{\text{Net working capital}}{\text{Total assets}}$$

Asset management or turnover ratios

$$\text{Inventory turnover} = \frac{\text{Cost of goods sold}}{\text{Inventory}}$$

$$\text{Days' sales in inventory} = \frac{365 \text{ days}}{\text{Inventory turnover}}$$

$$\text{Receivables turnover} = \frac{\text{Sales}}{\text{Accounts receivables}}$$

$$\text{Days' sales in receivables} = \frac{365 \text{ days}}{\text{Receivables turnover}}$$

$$\text{Payables turnover} = \frac{\text{Credit purchases}}{\text{Trade payables}}$$

$$\text{Days' sales in receivables} = \frac{365 \text{ days}}{\text{Payables turnover}}$$

$$\text{NWC turnover} = \frac{\text{Sales}}{\text{NWC}}$$

$$\text{PPE turnover} = \frac{\text{Sales}}{\text{Property, plant and equipment}}$$

$$\text{Total asset turnover} = \frac{\text{Sales}}{\text{Total assets}}$$

Long-term solvency or financial leverage ratios

$$\text{Total debt ratio} = \frac{\text{Total assets} - \text{Total equity}}{\text{Total assets}}$$

$$\text{Debt-equity ratio} = \frac{\text{Total debt}}{\text{Total equity}}$$

$$\text{Equity multiplier} = \frac{\text{Total assets}}{\text{Total equity}}$$

$$\text{Long-term debt ratio} = \frac{\text{Long-term debt}}{\text{Long-term debt} + \text{Total equity}}$$

$$\text{Times interest earned ratio} = \frac{\text{Operating profit}}{\text{Interest}}$$

Cash coverage ratio

$$= \frac{\text{Operating profit} + \text{Non-cash deductions}}{\text{Interest}}$$

Profitability ratios

$$\text{Profit margin} = \frac{\text{Net income}}{\text{Sales}}$$

Return on capital employed (ROCE)

$$= \frac{\text{Profit before interest and taxes}}{\text{Total equity}}$$

$$\text{Return on assets (ROA)} = \frac{\text{Net income}}{\text{Total assets}}$$

$$\text{Return on equity (ROE)} = \frac{\text{Net income}}{\text{Total equity}}$$

$$\text{ROE} = \frac{\text{Net income}}{\text{Sales}} \times \frac{\text{Sales}}{\text{Assets}} \times \frac{\text{Assets}}{\text{Equity}}$$

Market value ratios

$$\text{Price-earnings ratio} = \frac{\text{Price per share}}{\text{Earnings per share}}$$

> **CONCEPT QUESTIONS**
>
> **3.2a** What are the five groups of ratios? Give two or three examples of each kind.
> **3.2b** Given the total debt ratio, what other two ratios can be computed? Explain how.
> **3.2c** Turnover ratios all have one of two figures as the numerator. What are these two figures? What do these ratios measure? How do you interpret the results?
> **3.2d** Profitability ratios all have the same figure in the numerator. What is it? What do these ratios measure? How do you interpret the results?

3.3 THE DU PONT IDENTITY

As we mentioned in discussing ROA and ROE, the difference between these two profitability measures is a reflection of the use of debt financing, or financial leverage. We illustrate the relationship between these measures in this section by investigating a famous way of decomposing ROE into its component parts.

A CLOSER LOOK AT ROE

To begin, let's recall the definition of ROE:

$$\text{Return on equity} = \frac{\text{Net income}}{\text{Total equity}}$$

If we were so inclined, we could multiply this ratio by Assets/Assets without changing anything:

$$\text{Return on equity} = \frac{\text{Net income}}{\text{Total equity}} = \frac{\text{Net income}}{\text{Total equity}} \times \frac{\text{Assets}}{\text{Assets}}$$

$$= \frac{\text{Net income}}{\text{Assets}} \times \frac{\text{Assets}}{\text{Total equity}}$$

Notice that we have expressed the ROE as the product of two other ratios – ROA and the equity multiplier:

$$\text{ROE} = \text{ROA} \times \text{Equity multiplier}$$
$$= \text{ROA} \times (1 + \text{Debt–equity ratio})$$

The difference between ROE and ROA can be substantial, particularly for certain businesses that have borrowed a lot of money. We can further decompose ROE by multiplying the top and bottom by total sales:

$$\text{ROE} = \frac{\text{Sales}}{\text{Sales}} \times \frac{\text{Net income}}{\text{Assets}} \times \frac{\text{Assets}}{\text{Total equity}}$$

If we rearrange things a bit, ROE looks like this:

$$\text{ROE} = \underbrace{\frac{\text{Net income}}{\text{Sales}} \times \frac{\text{Sales}}{\text{Assets}}}_{\text{Return on assets}} \times \frac{\text{Assets}}{\text{Total equity}}$$

$$= \text{Profit margin} \times \text{Total asset turnover} \times \text{Equity multiplier}$$

(3.29)

What we have now done is to partition ROA into its two component parts: profit margin and total asset turnover. The last expression of the preceding equation is called the **Du Pont identity**, after the Du Pont Corporation, which popularized its use.

The Du Pont identity tells us that ROE is affected by three things:

1. Operating efficiency (as measured by profit margin)
2. Asset use efficiency (as measured by total asset turnover)
3. Financial leverage (as measured by the equity multiplier).

Weakness in either operating or asset use efficiency (or both) will show up in a diminished return on assets, which will translate into a lower ROE.

> **Du Pont identity**
> popular expression breaking ROE into three parts: operating efficiency, asset use efficiency and financial leverage.

Considering the Du Pont identity, it appears that the ROE could be leveraged up by increasing the amount of debt in the firm. However, notice that increasing debt also increases interest expense, which reduces profit margins, which acts to reduce ROE. So ROE could go up or down. More important, the use of debt financing has a number of other effects, and as we discuss at some length in Part Six, the amount of leverage a firm uses is governed by its capital structure policy.

The decomposition of ROE we've discussed in this section is a convenient way of systematically approaching financial statement analysis. If ROE is unsatisfactory by some measure, then the Du Pont identity tells you where to start looking for the reasons.

> **REAL WORLD INSIGHTS**
>
> Consider AstraZeneca, the multinational pharmaceuticals firm, which has a return on equity of 9.90 per cent. What is driving this figure? The profit margin (Net income/Sales) is 4.7 per cent, asset turnover is 0.4432, and equity multiplier is 4.756.
> The Du Pont formula shows the following breakdown:
>
> %ROE = Profit margin × Asset turnover × Equity multiplier = 4.7 × 0.4432 × 4.756 = 9.90

> **CONCEPT QUESTIONS**
>
> **3.3a** Return on assets, or ROA, can be expressed as the product of two ratios. Which two?
> **3.3b** Return on equity, or ROE, can be expressed as the product of three ratios. Which three?

3.4 USING FINANCIAL STATEMENT INFORMATION

We now discuss in more detail some practical aspects of financial statement analysis. In particular, we shall look at reasons for analysing financial statements, how to get benchmark information, and some problems that come up in the process.

WHY EVALUATE FINANCIAL STATEMENTS?

As we have discussed, the primary reason for looking at accounting information is that we don't have, and can't reasonably expect to get, market value information. We stress that whenever we have market information, we shall use it instead of accounting data. Also, if there is a conflict between accounting and market data, market data should be given precedence.

Financial statement analysis is essentially an application of 'management by exception'. In many cases such analysis will boil down to comparing ratios for one business with average or representative ratios. Those ratios that seem to differ the most from the averages are tagged for further study.

Internal Uses

Financial statement information has a variety of uses within a firm. Among the most important of these is performance evaluation. For example, managers are frequently evaluated and compensated on the basis of accounting measures of performance such as profit margin and return on equity. Also, firms with multiple divisions frequently use financial statement information to compare the performance of those divisions.

Another important internal use we shall explore is planning for the future. As we shall see, historical financial statement information is useful for generating projections about the future, and for checking the realism of assumptions made in those projections.

External Uses

Financial statements are useful to parties outside the firm, including short-term and long-term creditors and potential investors. For example, we would find such information quite useful in deciding whether to grant credit to a new customer.

We would also use this information to evaluate suppliers, and suppliers would review our statements before deciding to extend credit to us. Large customers use this information to decide whether we are likely to be around in the future. Credit-rating agencies rely on financial statements in assessing a firm's overall creditworthiness. The common theme here is that financial statements are a prime source of information about a firm's financial health.

We would also find such information useful in evaluating our main competitors. We might be thinking of launching a new product. A prime concern would be whether the competition would jump in shortly thereafter. In this case we would be interested in learning about our competitors' financial strength to see whether they could afford the necessary development.

Finally, we might be thinking of acquiring another firm. Financial statement information would be essential in identifying potential targets and deciding what to offer.

CHOOSING A BENCHMARK

Given that we want to evaluate a division or a firm based on its financial statements, a basic problem immediately comes up. How do we choose a benchmark, or a standard of comparison? In this section we describe some ways of getting started.

Time Trend Analysis

One standard we could use is history. Suppose we find that the current ratio for a particular firm is 2.4, based on the most recent financial statement information. Looking back over the last 10 years, we might find that this ratio has declined fairly steadily over that period.

Based on this, we might wonder whether the liquidity position of the firm has deteriorated. It could be, of course, that the firm has made changes that allow it to use its current assets more efficiently, that the nature of the firm's business has changed, or that business practices have changed. If we investigate, we might find any of these possible explanations behind the decline. This is an example of what we mean by management by exception – a deteriorating time trend may not be bad, but it does merit investigation.

Peer Group Analysis

The second means of establishing a benchmark is to identify firms similar in the sense that they compete in the same markets, have similar assets and operate in similar ways. In other words, we need to identify a *peer group*. There are obvious problems with doing this, because no two companies are identical. Ultimately, the choice of which companies to use as a basis for comparison is subjective.

Also, we may be more concerned with a group of the top firms in an industry, not with the average firm. Such a group is called an *aspirant group*, because we aspire to be like its members. In this case, a financial statement analysis reveals how far we have to go.

PROBLEMS WITH FINANCIAL STATEMENT ANALYSIS

We close this section by discussing some additional problems that can arise from using financial statements. In one way or another, the basic problem with financial statement analysis is that there is no underlying theory to help us identify which quantities to look at or guide us in establishing benchmarks.

As we discuss in other chapters, there are many cases in which financial theory and economic logic provide guidance in making judgements about value and risk. Little such help exists with financial statements. This is why we can't say which ratios matter the most, or what a high or low value might be.

More generally, the kind of peer group analysis we have been describing works best when the firms are strictly in the same line of business, the industry is competitive, and there is only one way of operating. Another problem that is becoming increasingly common is that major competitors and natural peer group members in an industry may be scattered around the globe. The automobile industry is an obvious example. The problem here is that financial statements from outside Europe do not necessarily conform at all to International Accounting Standards. The existence of different standards and procedures makes it difficult to compare financial statements across national borders.

Several other general problems frequently crop up. First, different firms use different accounting procedures – for property, plant and equipment, for example. This makes it difficult to compare statements. Second, different firms end their fiscal years at different times. For firms in seasonal businesses (such as Tesco, with a large Christmas season), this can lead to difficulties in comparing statements of financial position, because of fluctuations in accounts during the year. Finally, for any particular firm, unusual or transient events – such as a one-time profit from an asset sale – may affect financial performance. In comparing firms, such events can give misleading signals.

> ### SUSTAINABILITY IN FINANCE
>
> The LEGO Group, based in Denmark, is one of the world's most reputable companies and a global leader in sustainability. The company has three key areas of focus in its sustainability strategy: Children, the Environment, and People. Under each category, LEGO has corporate objectives against which it wishes to be judged.
>
> For example, for children, LEGO strongly encourages its staff to engage in volunteering activities with young children. The company measures the number of employees who have chosen to help children and reports this number in its annual sustainability report. For the environment, Lego has committed to making its bricks only from sustainable sources. In 2020, this amounted to only 2 per cent of LEGO elements, but the objective is to have 100 per cent of their bricks made from sustainable sources by 2030. For people, the company has a zero injury target. In 2020, this was 0.9 injuries per million working hours. Have a look at LEGO Group's corporate website for many more triple bottom line objectives.
>
> The main criticism of the triple bottom line concept is that objectives and key performance ratios are subjective and it is difficult to identify quantitative measures that can be easily compared across peer companies. This is in contrast to financial information, which is quantitative and can be easily standardized.

> **CONCEPT QUESTIONS**
>
> **3.4a** What are some uses for financial statement analysis?
> **3.4b** Why do we say that financial statement analysis is management by exception?
> **3.4c** What are some problems that can come up with financial statement analysis?

SUMMARY AND CONCLUSIONS

This chapter has introduced some of the basics of financial statements. Financial statements are often the only basis on which to begin a financial analysis, and so it is important to understand them, how they are generated, and the weaknesses in using accounting information as compared with real cash flows.

In this chapter, We explored the following areas:

1. We defined and discussed a number of the most commonly reported and used financial ratios.
2. We categorized financial ratios into five distinct groups:
    - Short-term solvency, or liquidity, ratios
    - Long-term solvency ratios
    - Asset management, or turnover, measures
    - Profitability measures
    - Market value measures.
3. We discussed the famous Du Pont identity as a way of analysing financial performance.
4. Finally, we reviewed the problems that may arise with financial statement analysis.

One area that is linked and often discussed in the context of financial statement analysis and corporate finance is financial planning. We cover financial planning in some detail and introduce a number of ways in which to estimate the future growth rates of companies in the online appendix to this chapter.

CHAPTER REVIEW AND SELF-TEST PROBLEMS

3.1 Financial Ratios Consider the statement of financial position for John Stevens Group.

	£m		£m
Current assets		**Current liabilities**	
Cash	761.3	Accounts payable	855.5
Short-term investments	390.8	Accrued expenses	809.6
Trade receivables	347.1	Notes payable/short-term debt	188.1
Notes receivable: short term	19.9	Current portion of LT debt/capital leases	524.8
Receivables: other	131.6	Other current liabilities	1,370.4
Total inventory	24.2	**Total current liabilities**	**3,748.4**
Other current assets	404.8		
Total current assets	**2,079.7**	**Non-current liabilities**	
		Long-term debt	711.3
Non-current assets		Deferred income tax	97.8
Property/plant/equipment	897.6	Minority interest	12.7
Intangible assets	3,432.4	Other liabilities, total	451.7
Long-term investments	143.4	**Total non-current liabilities**	**1,273.5**
Note receivable: long term	126.4		
Other long-term assets	338.9	**Total liabilities**	**5,021.9**
Total non-current assets	**4,938.7**	Ordinary share capital	59.8
		Additional paid-in capital	8.9
		Retained earnings (accumulated deficit)	1,726.0
		Other equity, total	201.8
		Total equity	**1,996.5**
Total assets	**7,018.4**	**Total liabilities and shareholders' equity**	**7,018.4**

Based on the statement of financial position and income statement, calculate the following ratios:

Current ratio _____
Quick ratio _____
Cash ratio _____
Inventory turnover _____
Receivables turnover _____
Days' sales in inventory _____
Days' sales in receivables _____
Total debt ratio _____
Long-term debt ratio _____
Times interest earned ratio _____
Cash coverage ratio _____

3.2 ROE and the Du Pont Identity Calculate the ROE for John Stevens Group, and then break down your answer into its component parts using the Du Pont identity.

SOLUTIONS

3.1 We've calculated the following ratios based on the ending figures.

Current ratio	£2,079.70/£3,748.40	= 0.55 times
Quick ratio	£2,055.50/£3,748.40	= 0.55 times
Cash ratio	£761.30/£3,748.40	= 0.20 times
Inventory turnover	£6,282.50/£24.20	= 259.61 times
Receivables turnover	£8,167.10/£347.10	= 23.52 times
Days' sales in inventory	365/259.61	= 1.41 days
Days' sales in receivables	365/23.52	= 15.52 days
Total debt ratio	£5,021.90/£7,018.40	= 71.55%
Long-term debt ratio	£711.30/£2,707.80	= 26.27%
Times interest earned ratio	£109/£114	= 0.96 times
Cash coverage ratio	£236.60/£114	= 2.08 times

3.2 The return on equity is the ratio of net income to total equity. For John Stevens Group, this is £44.70/£1,996.60 = 2.2%, which is not outstanding.

Given the Du Pont identity, ROE can be written as follows:

$$\text{ROE} = \text{Profit margin} \times \text{Total asset turnover} \times \text{Equity multiplier}$$
$$= £44.70/£8,167.10/£8,167.10/£7,018.40/£1,996.50$$
$$= 0.55\% \times 1.16 \times 3.52$$
$$= 2.2\%$$

Notice that return on assets, ROA, is £44.70/£7,018.40 = 0.64%.

Level of difficulty: Basic | Intermediate | Challenge

QUESTIONS AND PROBLEMS

3.1 Building a Statement of Financial Position AEB Thompson plc financial statements showed current assets of £6 billion, non-current assets of £16 billion, current liabilities of £11 billion, and non-current liabilities of £6 billion. What is the value of the shareholders' equity for AEB Thompson? How much is net working capital?

3.2 Building an Income Statement Cavalry Cross had revenue of £38 million, total expenses of £30 million, tax of £4 million and zero depreciation. What is the net income for the firm? Cavalry Cross paid out £2 million in cash dividends. What is the addition to retained earnings?

3.3 Calculating Liquidity Ratios Havens Bags has current liabilities of £340,000, a quick ratio of 2, inventory turnover of 4 and a current ratio of 3. What is the cost of goods sold for the company?

3.4 Calculating Profitability Ratios Dylan AG had sales of €113 million, total assets of €167 million, and total debt of €69 million. If the profit margin is 20 per cent, what was net income? What was ROA? What was ROE?

3.5 Calculating Leverage Ratios GNR plc has a total debt ratio of 0.7. What is its debt–equity ratio? What is its equity multiplier?

3.6 Calculating Market Value Ratios Axel plc had additions to retained earnings for the year just ended of £430,000. The firm paid out £175,000 in cash dividends, and it has ending total equity of £5.3 million. If the company currently has 210,000 shares of equity outstanding, what are earnings per share? Dividends per share? Book value per share? If the equity currently sells for £63 per share, what is the market-to-book ratio? The price–earnings ratio? If the company had sales of £4.5 million, what is the price–sales ratio?

3.7 Book Values versus Market Values In preparing a balance sheet, why do you think International Accounting Standards allow both historical cost and fair value approaches?

3.8 Residual Claims Moneyback Limited is obligated to pay its creditors £7,300 during the year.

(a) What is the market value of the shareholders' equity if assets have a market value of £8,400?

(b) What if assets equal £6,700?

3.9 Net Income and OCF This year, Southern Coat Company had sales of £730,000. Cost of goods sold, administrative and selling expenses, and depreciation expenses were £580,000, £105,000 and £135,000 respectively. In addition, the company had an interest expense of £75,000 and a tax rate of 28 per cent. (Ignore any tax loss carry-back or carry-forward provisions.)

(a) What is Southern Coat Company's net income?

(b) What is its operating cash flow?

(c) Explain your results in (a) and (b).

3.10 Accounting Values versus Cash Flows In Problem 3.9, suppose Southern Coat Company paid out £25,000 in cash dividends. Is this possible? If spending on non-current assets and net working capital was zero, and if no new shares were issued during the year, what do you know about the firm's long-term debt?

3.11 Calculating Cash Flows Consider the following abbreviated financial statements for Parrothead Enterprises:

Parrothead Enterprises Partial Balance Sheets

Assets	Year $t-1$ £	Year t £	Liabilities and owners' equity	Year $t-1$ £	Year t £
Current assets	653	707	Current liabilities	261	293
Non-current assets	2,691	3,240	Non-current liabilities	1,422	1,512

Parrothead Enterprises Year t Income Statement

	£
Sales	8,280
Costs	3,861
Depreciation	738
Interest paid	211

(a) What is owners' equity for years $t-1$ and t?

(b) What is the change in net working capital for year t?

(c) In year *t*, Parrothead Enterprises had capital expenditure of £1,350. How much in non-current assets did Parrothead Enterprises sell? What is the cash flow from investing activities for the year? (The tax rate is 28 per cent.)

(d) During year *t*, Parrothead Enterprises raised £270 in new long-term debt. How much long-term debt must Parrothead Enterprises have paid off during the year? What is the cash flow from financing activities?

3.12 Profit Margin In response to complaints about high prices, a grocery chain runs the following advertising campaign: 'If you pay your child £3 to go and buy £50 worth of groceries, then your child makes twice as much on the trip as we do.' You've collected the following information from the grocery chain's financial statements:

	£m
Sales	750
Net income	22.5
Total assets	420
Total debt	280

(a) Evaluate the grocery chain's claim. What is the basis for the statement? Is this claim misleading? Why or why not?

(b) Use the financial accounts for Leonardo SpA that were provided in Section 3.1 to attempt Problems 3.13–3.16.

3.13 Calculating Financial Ratios Find the following financial ratios for Leonardo SpA.

Short-term solvency ratios:
(a) Current ratio   _____
(b) Quick ratio   _____
(c) Cash ratio   _____

Asset utilization ratios:
(d) Total asset turnover _____
(e) Inventory turnover   _____
(f) Receivables turnover _____

Long-term solvency ratios:
(g) Total debt ratio   _____
(h) Debt-equity ratio   _____
(i) Equity multiplier   _____
(j) Times interest earned ratio _____

Profitability ratios:
(k) Profit margin   _____
(l) Return on assets   _____
(m) Return on equity   _____

3.14 Du Pont Identity Construct the Du Pont identity for Leonardo SpA.

3.15 Market Value Ratios Leonardo SpA has 574.34 million ordinary shares outstanding, and the market price for a share of equity was €8.60. What is the price–earnings ratio? What is the market-to-book ratio? If the company's growth rate is 9 per cent, what is the PEG ratio?

3.16 Tobin's Q What is Tobin's Q for Leonardo SpA? What assumptions are you making about the book value of debt and the market value of debt? What about the book value of assets and the market value of assets? Are these assumptions realistic? Why or why not? Assume that the book value of debt is equal to the market value of debt and the assets can be replaced at the current value on the statement of financial position (balance sheet).

3.17 Earnings Management Companies often try to keep accounting earnings growing at a relatively steady pace, thereby avoiding large swings in earnings from period to period. They also try to meet earnings targets. To do so, they use a variety of tactics. The simplest way is to control the timing of accounting revenues and costs, which all firms can do to at least some extent. For example, if earnings are looking too low this year, then some accounting costs can be deferred until next year. This practice is called earnings management. It is common, and it raises a lot of questions. Why do firms do it? Why are firms even allowed to do it under International Accounting Standards? Is it ethical? What are the implications for cash flow and shareholder wealth?

3.18 Cash Flow What are some of the actions that a small company can take if it finds itself in a situation in which growth in sales outstrips production capacity and available financial resources? What other options (besides expansion of capacity) are available to a company when orders exceed capacity?

3.19 Non-Current Assets and Depreciation On the simplified statement of financial position, the non-current assets (NCA) account is equal to the gross property, plant and equipment (PPE) account (which records the acquisition cost of property, plant and equipment) minus the accumulated depreciation (AD) account (which records the total depreciation taken by the firm against its property, plant and equipment). Using the fact that NCA = PPE − AD, show that the expression for net capital spending, $NCA_{end} - NCA_{beg} + D$ (where D is the depreciation expense during the year), is equivalent to $PPE_{end} - PPE_{beg}$.

MINI CASE

FINANCIAL STATEMENT ANALYSIS AT FRIDAY QUANTUM SOLUTIONS (FQS)

Friday Quantum Solutions (FQS) develops and sells quantum technology solutions for the measurement of underwater sea-life diversity. It has only one product and, last year, FQS sold 10,000 units. This year, FQS reported sales of 16,000 units but net profit was lower than expected. You have been asked to prepare a report on the company's performance and financial position for the company's owners. Prior to the meeting, you have received the following information for the past two years:

	£000s This year	£000s Last year
Revenues	2,400	2,000
Cost of goods sold	1,440	900
Gross profit	960	1,100
Other expenses	600	400
Net profit before interest and tax	360	700
Interest expense for the year	170	100
Tax payable	57	180
Net profit after tax	133	420
Equity	3,410	3,230
Ratios		
Current ratio	4	3.7
Quick ratio	1.50	2.20
Debtor payment period	46	44
Creditor payment period	51	81
Debt/Assets	0.27	0.2
Times interest earned	2.1	7

QUESTION

1. Write a short report on FQS's performance and financial position. Your report should identify possible causes for the changes in profitability, liquidity and financial position. You should also recommend a turnaround strategy to improve the company's performance and financial position. It is generally accepted that the selling price per unit cannot be increased without a major loss of market share. In addition, reductions in the cost of materials and labour are not possible.

ADDITIONAL READING

The interested reader can find a whole range of readings to peruse in accounting journals such as *Journal of Accounting Research*, *The Accounting Review*, *Journal of Accounting and Economics*, *Journal of Business Finance and Accounting* and *Accounting and Business Research*. Important recent papers that relate to corporate finance are:

1. Faulkender, M., Flannery, M. J., Hankins, K. W., & Smith, J. M. (2012). Cash flows and leverage adjustments. *Journal of Financial Economics*, *103*(3), 632–646.

2. Konchitchki, Y., & Patatoukas, P. N. (2013). Taking the pulse of the real economy using financial statement analysis: Implications for macro forecasting and stock valuation. *The Accounting Review*, *89*(2), 669–694.

3. Lewellen, J. (2004). Predicting returns with financial ratios. *Journal of Financial Economics*, *74*(2), 209–235.

PART TWO

VALUATION OF FUTURE CASH FLOWS

4 Introduction to Valuation: The Time Value of Money   70

5 Discounted Cash Flow Valuation   91

6 Bond Valuation   126

7 Equity Valuation   159

CHAPTER 4
INTRODUCTION TO VALUATION: THE TIME VALUE OF MONEY

> **LEARNING OBJECTIVES**
>
> After studying this chapter, you should understand:
>
> **LO1** How to determine the future value of an investment made today.
> **LO2** How to determine the present value of cash to be received at a future date.
> **LO3** How to find the return on an investment.
> **LO4** How long it takes for an investment to reach a desired value.
>
> **KEY NOTATIONS**
>
> | | |
> |---|---|
> | **FV** | **Future value** |
> | **FVIF(r,t)** | **Future value interest factor for a sum of money invested at r per cent for t periods** |
> | **PV** | **Present value** |
> | **r** | **Interest rate or discount rate** |
> | **t** | **Number of periods** |

IN 2020, SYNGENTA FINANCE AG, a Swiss agribusiness operating in the crop protection and seeds business, sold a bond to investors that raised 200 million Swiss francs. Under the terms of the deal, Syngenta promised to repay the owner of one of these bonds SFr100,000 in 2 years and SFr125 in each of years 1 and 2. Investors paid Syngenta SFr100,000 for each of these bonds with the promise of receiving a total of SFr100,250 (SFr125 x 2 = SFr250 in interest and SFr100,000 original amount) over the subsequent 2 years. Is giving up SFr100,000 now in exchange for SFr100,250 over 2 years a good deal? On the plus side, you get back about SFr1.0025 for every SFr1 you put up. That probably sounds positive; but on the down side, you have to wait 2 years to get it. What you need to know is how to analyse this trade-off; this chapter gives you the tools you need.

One of the basic problems faced by the financial manager is how to determine the value today of cash flows expected in the future. For example, if a bond pays the owner €15,000 in one year, does this mean that it is worth €15,000 now? The answer is no, because if you had €15,000 today you could invest it or put the amount in a bank account allowing it to grow to more than €15,000. How much is the bond worth then? The answer depends on the time value of money, the subject of this chapter.

In the most general sense, the phrase *time value of money* refers to the fact that a euro (or pound) in the hand today is worth more than a euro promised at some time in the future. On a practical level, one reason for this is that you could earn interest while you waited; so a euro today would grow to more than a euro later. The trade-off between money now and money later thus depends on, among other things, the rate you can earn by investing. Our goal in this chapter is to evaluate explicitly this trade-off between euros (or any other currency) today and at some future time.

A thorough understanding of the material in this chapter is critical to understanding material in subsequent chapters, so you should study it with particular care. We shall present a number of examples in this chapter. In many problems your answer may differ from ours slightly. This can happen because of rounding, and is not a cause for concern.

4.1 FUTURE VALUE AND COMPOUNDING

The first thing we shall study is future value. **Future value (FV)** refers to the amount of money an investment will grow to over some period of time at some given interest rate. Put another way, future value is the cash value of an investment at some time in the future. We start out by considering the simplest case: a single-period investment.

> **Future value (FV)**
> the amount an investment is worth after one or more periods.

INVESTING FOR A SINGLE PERIOD

Suppose you invest £100 in a savings account that pays 10 per cent interest per year. How much will you have in one year? You will have £110. This £110 is equal to your original *principal* of £100 plus £10 in interest that you earn. We say that £110 is the future value of £100 invested for one year at 10 per cent, and we simply mean that £100 today is worth £110 in one year, given that 10 per cent is the interest rate.

In general, if you invest for one period at an interest rate of r, your investment will grow to $(1 + r)$ per pound invested. In our example, r is 10 per cent, so your investment grows to $1 + 0.10 = 1.1$ pounds per pound invested. You invested £100 in this case, so you ended up with £100 × 1.10 = £110.

REAL WORLD INSIGHTS

Would you invest in Uber, the innovative taxi company? Uber allows the user to order a taxi with the press of a button, using GPS to unite the customer with a free taxi. The technology has undermined existing licensing agreements with established taxi firms by taking the business online, thereby avoiding the need to pay licence fees.

In 2019, Uber announced a plan to raise $8.4 billion in the international capital markets. The total issue put a predicted value for the firm at $82.4 billion The $8.4 billion funding allowed the firm to expand aggressively in China and other countries throughout the world. However, is this worth the money?

Valuations of Uber were based on expected future growth across the globe. However, there is clearly uncertainty over these growth forecasts. Notwithstanding the worldwide effects of systemic crisis such as the Covid-19 pandemic, a backlash had been growing among taxi firms and governments against the firm. For example, London and some cities in Spain, France and some German cities banned the app, arguing the business model was uncompetitive because Uber did not need to pay local taxes or adhere to local regulations because of its online structure.

Focusing only on operational data, Uber lost $1.8 billion in the previous year, even though it reported revenues of $11.3 billion and a growth rate of 40 per cent. Even in the first three months of 2019, the company had lost more than $1 billion. The company operated in 700 cities around the world and had 91 million users every month.

Valuation of companies, like that of Uber, relies on forecasts of the future. Irrespective of the complexity of your models or techniques, if you get your forecasts and assumptions wrong, your valuations will be wrong as well. In Finance, the maxim is true: Rubbish in - Rubbish out. You would do well to remember this when using the methods outlined in this chapter.

Source: Uber website.

INVESTING FOR MORE THAN ONE PERIOD

> **compounding**
> the process of accumulating interest on an investment over time to earn more interest.

Going back to our £100 investment, what will you have after two years, assuming the interest rate doesn't change? If you leave the entire £110 in the bank, you will earn £110 × 0.10 = £11 in interest during the second year, so you will have a total of £110 + 11 = £121. This £121 is the future value of £100 in two years at 10 per cent. Another way of looking at it is that one year from now you are effectively investing £110 at 10 per cent for a year. This is a single-period problem, so you'll end up with £1.10 for every pound invested, or £110 × 1.1 = £121 total.

This £121 has four parts. The first part is the £100 original principal. The second part is the £10 in interest you earned in the first year, and the third part is another £10 you earn in the second year, for a total of £120. The last £1 you end up with (the fourth part) is interest you earn in the second year on the interest paid in the first year: £10 × 0.10 = £1.

> **interest on interest**
> interest earned on the reinvestment of previous interest payments.

This process of leaving your money and any accumulated interest in an investment for more than one period, and thereby *reinvesting* the interest, is called **compounding** Compounding the interest means earning **interest on interest**, so we call the result **compound interest**. With **simple interest** the interest is not reinvested, so interest is earned each period only on the original principal.

> **compound interest**
> interest earned on both the initial principal and the interest reinvested from prior periods.

We now take a closer look at how we calculated the £121 future value. We multiplied £110 by 1.1 to get £121. The £110, however, was £100 also multiplied by 1.1. In other words:

$$\begin{aligned} £121 &= £110 \times 1.1 \\ &= (£100 \times 1.1) \times 1.1 \\ &= £100 \times (1.1 \times 1.1) \\ &= £100 \times 1.1^2 \\ &= £100 \times 1.21 \end{aligned}$$

> **simple interest**
> interest earned only on the original principal amount invested.

At the risk of belabouring the obvious, let's ask: how much would our £100 grow to after three years? Once again, in two years we'll be investing £121 for one period at 10 per cent. We'll end up with £1.10 for every pound we invest, or £121 × 1.1 = £133.10 total. This £133.10 is thus:

$$\begin{aligned} £133.10 &= £121 \times 1.1 \\ &= (£110 \times 1.1) \times 1.1 \\ &= (£100 \times 1.1) \times 1.1 \times 1.1 \\ &= £100 \times (1.1 \times 1.1 \times 1.1) \\ &= £100 \times 1.1^3 \\ &= £100 \times 1.331 \end{aligned}$$

EXAMPLE 4.1

INTEREST ON INTEREST

Suppose you locate a two-year investment that pays 14 per cent per year. If you invest €325, how much will you have at the end of the two years? How much of this is simple interest? How much is compound interest?

At the end of the first year you will have €325 × (1 + 0.14) = €370.50. If you reinvest this entire amount and thereby compound the interest, you will have €370.50 × 1.14 = €422.37 at the end of the second year. The total interest you earn is thus €422.37 − 325 = €97.37. Your €325 original principal earns €325 × 0.14 = €45.50 in interest each year, for a two-year total of €91 in simple interest. The remaining €97.37 − 91 = €6.37 results from compounding. You can check this by noting that the interest earned in the first year is €45.50. The interest on interest earned in the second year thus amounts to €45.50 × 0.14 = €6.37, as we calculated.

You're probably noticing a pattern to these calculations, so we can now go ahead and state the general result. As our examples suggest, the future value of £1 invested for t periods at a rate of r per period is this:

$$\text{Future value} = £1 \times (1 + r)^t \qquad (4.1)$$

The expression $(1 + r)^t$ is sometimes called the *future value interest factor* (or just *future value factor*) for £1 invested at r per cent for t periods, and can be abbreviated as $\text{FVIF}(r, t)$.

In our example, what would your £100 be worth after five years? We can first compute the relevant future value factor as follows:

$$(1 + r)^t = (1 + 0.10)^5 = 1.1^5 = 1.6105$$

Your £100 will thus grow to:

$$£100 \times 1.6105 = £161.05$$

The growth of your £100 each year is illustrated in Table 4.1. As shown, the interest earned in each year is equal to the beginning amount multiplied by the interest rate of 10 per cent.

TABLE 4.1

Future value of £100 at 10 per cent

Year	Beginning amount (£)	Simple interest (£)	Compound interest (£)	Total interest earned (£)	Ending amount (£)
1	100.00	10	0.00	10.00	110.00
2	110.00	10	1.00	11.00	121.00
3	121.00	10	2.10	12.10	133.10
4	133.10	10	3.31	13.31	146.41
5	146.41	10	4.64	14.64	161.05
		Total £50 simple interest	Total £11.05 compound interest	Total £61.05 interest	

In Table 4.1, notice that the total interest you earn is £61.05. Over the five-year span of this investment the simple interest is £100 × 0.10 = £10 per year, so you accumulate £50 this way. The other £11.05 is from compounding.

Figure 4.1 illustrates the growth of the compound interest in Table 4.1. Notice how the simple interest is constant each year, but the amount of compound interest you earn gets bigger every year. The amount of the compound interest keeps increasing because more and more interest builds up and there is thus more to compound.

Future values depend critically on the assumed interest rate, particularly for long-lived investments. Figure 4.2 illustrates this relationship by plotting the growth of £1 for different rates and lengths of time. Notice that the future value of £1 after 10 years is about £6.20 at a 20 per cent rate, but it is only about £2.60 at 10 per cent. In this case, doubling the interest rate more than doubles the future value.

To solve future value problems, we need to come up with the relevant future value factors. There are several different ways of doing this. In our example, we could have multiplied 1.1 by itself five times. This would work just fine, but it would get to be very tedious for, say, a 30-year investment.

Fortunately, there are several easier ways to get future value factors. Most calculators have a key labelled 'y^x.' You can usually just enter 1.1, press this key, enter 5, and press the '=' key to get the answer. This is an easy way to calculate future value factors, because it's quick and accurate.

Alternatively, you can use a table that contains future value factors for some common interest rates and time periods. Table 4.2 contains some of these factors. Table A.1 in the appendix at the end of the book contains a much larger set. To use the table, find the column that corresponds to 10 per cent. Then look down the rows until you come to five periods. You should find the factor that we calculated, 1.6105.

FIGURE 4.1

Future value, simple interest and compound interest

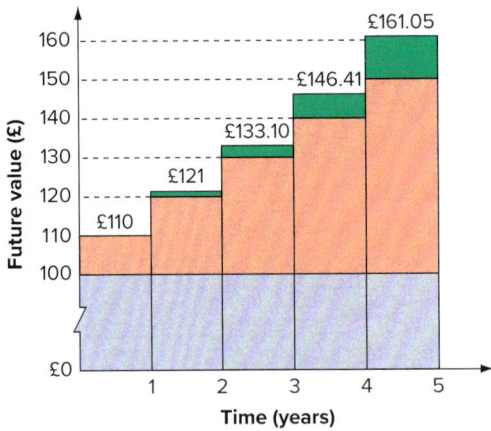

Growth of £100 original amount at 10% per year. The orange shaded area shows the simple interest. The green shaded area represents the portion of the total that results from compounding of interest.

FIGURE 4.2

Future value of £1 for different periods and rates

TABLE 4.2

Future value interest factors

Number of periods	Interest rate (%)			
	5	10	15	20
1	1.0500	1.1000	1.1500	1.2000
2	1.1025	1.2100	1.3225	1.4400
3	1.1576	1.3310	1.5209	1.7280
4	1.2155	1.4641	1.7490	2.0736
5	1.2763	1.6105	2.0114	2.4883

Tables such as these are not as common as they once were, because they pre-date inexpensive calculators or spreadsheets, and are available only for a relatively small number of rates. Interest rates are often quoted to three or four decimal places, so the tables needed to deal with these accurately would be quite large. As a result, the real world has moved away from using them. We shall emphasize the use of a calculator or spreadsheet in this chapter.

These tables still serve a useful purpose, though. To make sure you are doing the calculations correctly, pick a factor from the table and then calculate it yourself to see that you get the same answer. There are plenty of numbers to choose from.

EXAMPLE 4.2

COMPOUND INTEREST

You've located an investment that pays 12 per cent per year. That rate sounds good to you, so you invest €400. How much will you have in three years? How much will you have in seven years? At the end of seven years, how much interest will you have earned? How much of that interest results from compounding?

Based on our discussion, we can calculate the future value factor for 12 per cent and three years as follows:

$$(1 + r)^t = 1.12^3 = 1.4049$$

Your €400 thus grows to:

$$€400 \times 1.4049 = €561.97$$

After seven years you will have:

$$€400 \times 1.12^7 = €400 \times 2.2107 = €884.27$$

Thus you will more than double your money over seven years.

Because you invested €400, the interest in the €884.27 future value is €884.27 − 400 = €484.27. At 12 per cent your €400 investment earns €400 × 0.12 = €48 in simple interest every year. Over seven years the simple interest thus totals 7 × €48 = €336. The other €484.27 − 336 = €148.27 is from compounding.

The effect of compounding is not great over short time periods, but it really starts to add up as the horizon grows. To take an extreme case, suppose one of your more frugal ancestors had invested £5 for you at a 6 per cent interest rate 200 years ago. How much would you have today? The future value factor is a substantial $1.06^{200} = 115{,}125.90$ (you won't find this one in a table), so you would have £5 × 115,125.90 = £575,629.52 today. Notice that the simple interest is just £5 × 0.06 = £0.30 per year. After 200 years, this amounts to £60. The rest is from reinvesting. Such is the power of compound interest!

> **EXAMPLE 4.3**
>
> ### HOW MUCH FOR THAT ISLAND?
>
> To further illustrate the effect of compounding for long horizons, consider the case of Peter Minuit and the American Indians. In 1626 Minuit bought all of Manhattan Island for about $24 in goods and trinkets. This sounds cheap, but the Indians may have received the better end of the deal. To see why, suppose the Indians had sold the goods and invested the $24 at 10 per cent. How much would it be worth today?
>
> Assume about 390 years have passed since the transaction. At 10 per cent, $24 will grow by quite a bit over that time. How much? The future value factor is roughly:
>
> $$(1 + r)^t = 1.1^{390} \approx 13,904,238,598,204,900$$
>
> That is, 13.9 followed by 14 zeros. The future value is thus of the order of $24 × 13.9 = $334 *quadrillion* (give or take a few hundreds of trillions).
>
> Well, $334 quadrillion is a lot of money. How much? If you had it, you could buy the United States. All of it. Cash. With money left over to buy Canada, Mexico and the rest of the world, for that matter.
>
> This example is something of an exaggeration, of course. In 1626 it would not have been easy to locate an investment that would pay 10 per cent every year without fail for the next 390 years.

A NOTE ABOUT COMPOUND GROWTH

If you are considering depositing money in an interest-bearing account, then the interest rate on that account is just the rate at which your money grows, assuming you don't remove any of it. If that rate is 10 per cent, then each year you simply have 10 per cent more money than you had the year before. In this case the interest rate is just an example of a compound growth rate.

The way we calculated future values is actually quite general, and lets you answer some other types of question related to growth. For example, your company currently has 10,000 employees. You've estimated that the number of employees grows by 3 per cent per year. How many employees will there be in five years? Here, we start with 10,000 people instead of pounds or euros, and we don't think of the growth rate as an interest rate, but the calculation is exactly the same:

$$10,000 \times 1.03^5 = 10,000 \times 1.1593 = 11,593 \text{ employees}$$

There will be about 1,593 net new hires over the coming five years.

To give another example, according to Vodafone's 2015 annual report, its revenue was £42.2 billion. This was an increase of 10.1 per cent on the previous year's figures. Suppose sales are projected to increase at the same rate over the next seven years. What will Vodafone's sales be in the year 2022 if this is correct? Verify for yourself that the answer is about £82.8 billion – about twice as large.

> **EXAMPLE 4.4**
>
> ### DIVIDEND GROWTH
>
> Your company has just paid a cash dividend of €2.70 per share. You believe the dividend will increase by 4 per cent each year indefinitely. How big will the dividend be in eight years?
>
> Here we have a cash dividend growing because it is being increased by management; but once again the calculation is the same:
>
> $$\text{Future value} = €2.70 \times 1.04^8 = €2.70 \times 1.3686 = €3.6952$$
>
> The dividend will grow by nearly €1 over that period. Dividend growth is a subject we shall return to in a later chapter.

CONCEPT QUESTIONS

4.1a What do we mean by the future value of an investment?
4.1b What does it mean to compound interest? How does compound interest differ from simple interest?
4.1c In general, what is the future value of €1 invested at r per period for t periods?

4.2 PRESENT VALUE AND DISCOUNTING

When we discuss future value, we are thinking of questions such as: What will my €2,000 investment grow to if it earns a 6.5 per cent return every year for the next six years? The answer to this question is what we call the future value of €2,000 invested at 6.5 per cent for six years (verify that the answer is about €2,918).

Another type of question that comes up even more often is obviously related to future value. Suppose you need to have €10,000 in 10 years, and you can earn 6.5 per cent on your money. How much do you have to invest today to reach your goal? You can verify that the answer is €5,327.26. How do we know this? Read on.

THE SINGLE-PERIOD CASE

We've seen that the future value of £1 invested for one year at 10 per cent is £1.10. We now ask a slightly different question: how much do we have to invest today at 10 per cent to get £1 in one year? In other words, we know the future value here is £1, but what is the **present value (PV)**? The answer isn't too hard to figure out. Whatever we invest today will be 1.1 times bigger at the end of the year. Because we need £1 at the end of the year:

$$\text{Present value} \times 1.1 = £1$$

Or solving for the present value:

$$\text{Present value} = £1/1.1 = £0.909$$

In this case the present value is the answer to the following question: what amount, invested today, will grow to £1 in one year if the interest rate is 10 per cent? Present value is thus just the reverse of future value. Instead of compounding the money forward into the future, we **discount** it back to the present.

present value (PV)
the current value of future cash flows discounted at the appropriate discount rate.

discount
calculate the present value of some future amount.

EXAMPLE 4.5

SINGLE-PERIOD PV

Suppose you need €400 to buy textbooks next year. You can earn 7 per cent on your money. How much do you have to put up today?

We need to know the PV of €400 in one year at 7 per cent. Proceeding as in the previous example:

$$\text{Present value} \times 1.07 = €400$$

We can now solve for the present value:

$$\text{Present value} = €400 \times (1/1.07) = €373.83$$

Thus €373.83 is the present value. Again, this just means that investing this amount for one year at 7 per cent will give you a future value of €400.

From our examples, the present value of £1 to be received in one period is generally given as follows:

$$PV = £1 \times \left(\frac{1}{1+r}\right)$$

$$= \frac{£1}{1+r}$$

We next examine how to get the present value of an amount to be paid in two or more periods into the future.

PRESENT VALUES FOR MULTIPLE PERIODS

Suppose you need to have €1,000 in two years. If you can earn 7 per cent, how much do you have to invest to make sure you have the €1,000 when you need it? In other words, what is the present value of €1,000 in two years if the relevant rate is 7 per cent?

Based on your knowledge of future values, you know the amount invested must grow to €1,000 over the two years. In other words, it must be the case that:

$$€1,000 = PV \times 1.07 \times 1.07$$
$$= PV \times 1.07^2$$
$$= PV \times 1.1449$$

Given this, we can solve for the present value:

$$\text{Present value} = €1,000/1.1449 = €873.44$$

Therefore €873.44 is the amount you must invest to achieve your goal.

EXAMPLE 4.6

SAVING UP

You would like to buy a new car. You have £50,000 or so, but the car costs £68,500. If you can earn 9 per cent, how much do you have to invest today to buy the car in two years? Do you have enough? Assume the price will stay the same.

What we need to know is the present value of £68,500 to be paid in two years, assuming a 9 per cent rate. Based on our discussion, this is:

$$PV = £68,500/1.09^2 = £68,500/1.1881 = £57,655.08$$

You're still about £7,655 short, even if you're willing to wait two years.

As you have probably recognized by now, calculating present values is quite similar to calculating future values, and the general result looks much the same. The present value of £1 to be received t periods into the future at a discount rate of r is

$$PV = £1 \times \left[\frac{1}{(1+r)^t}\right]$$

$$= \frac{£1}{(1+r)^t} \qquad (4.2)$$

discount rate
the rate used to calculate the present value of future cash flows.

The quantity in brackets, $1/(1+r)^t$, goes by several different names. Because it's used to discount a future cash flow, it is often called a *discount factor*. With this name, it is not surprising that the rate used in the calculation is often called the **discount rate**. We shall tend to call it this in talking about present values. The quantity in brackets is also called the *present value interest factor* (or just *present value factor*) for £1 at r per cent for t periods, and is sometimes abbreviated as PVIF(r, t). Finally, calculating the present value of a future cash flow to determine its worth today is commonly called **discounted cash flow (DCF) valuation**.

> **discounted cash flow (DCF) valuation**
> calculating the present value of a future cash flow to determine its value today.

To illustrate, suppose you need €1,000 in three years. You can earn 15 per cent on your money. How much do you have to invest today? To find out, we have to determine the present value of €1,000 in three years at 15 per cent. We do this by discounting €1,000 back three periods at 15 per cent. With these numbers, the discount factor is:

$$1/(1 + 0.15)^3 = 1/1.5209 = 0.6575$$

The amount you must invest is thus:

$$€1,000 \times 0.6575 = €657.50$$

We say that €657.50 is the present or discounted value of €1,000 to be received in three years at 15 per cent.

There are tables for present value factors just as there are tables for future value factors, and you use them in the same way (if you use them at all). Table 4.3 contains a small set. A much larger set can be found in Table A.2 in the book's appendix.

TABLE 4.3

Present value interest factors

Number of periods	Interest rate (%)			
	5	10	15	20
1	0.9524	0.9091	0.8696	0.8333
2	0.9070	0.8264	0.7561	0.6944
3	0.8638	0.7513	0.6575	0.5787
4	0.8227	0.6830	0.5718	0.4823
5	0.7835	0.6209	0.4972	0.4019

In Table 4.3 the discount factor we just calculated (0.6575) can be found by looking down the column labelled '15%' until you come to the third row.

EXAMPLE 4.7

DECEPTIVE ADVERTISING?

Businesses sometimes advertise that you should 'Come try our product. If you do, we'll give you €100 just for coming by!' If you read the fine print, what you find out is that they will give you a savings certificate that will pay you €100 in 25 years or so. If the going interest rate on such certificates is 10 per cent per year, how much are they really giving you today?

What you're actually getting is the present value of €100 to be paid in 25 years. If the discount rate is 10 per cent per year, then the discount factor is:

$$1/1.1^{25} = 1/10.8347 = 0.0923$$

This tells you that a euro in 25 years is worth a little more than nine cents today, assuming a 10 per cent discount rate. Given this, the promotion is actually paying you about 0.0923 × €100 = €9.23. Maybe this is enough to draw customers, but it's not €100.

As the length of time until payment grows, present values decline. As Example 4.7 illustrates, present values tend to become small as the time horizon grows. If you look out far enough, they will always approach zero. Also, for a given length of time, the higher the discount rate is, the lower is the present value. Put another way, present values and discount rates are inversely related. Increasing the discount rate decreases the PV and vice versa.

The relationship between time, discount rates and present values is illustrated in Figure 4.3. Notice that by the time we get to 10 years, the present values are all substantially smaller than the future amounts.

FIGURE 4.3 Present value of £1 for different periods and rates

CONCEPT QUESTIONS

4.2a What do we mean by the present value of an investment?
4.2b The process of discounting a future amount back to the present is the opposite of doing what?
4.2c What do we mean by discounted cash flow, or DCF, valuation?
4.2d In general, what is the present value of £1 to be received in t periods, assuming a discount rate of r per period?

4.3 MORE ABOUT PRESENT AND FUTURE VALUES

If you look back at the expressions we came up with for present and future values, you will see a simple relationship between the two. We explore this relationship and some related issues in this section.

PRESENT VERSUS FUTURE VALUE

What we called the present value factor is just the reciprocal of (that is, 1 divided by) the future value factor:

$$\text{Future value factor} = (1+r)^t$$
$$\text{Present value factor} = 1/(1+r)^t$$

In fact, the easy way to calculate a present value factor on many calculators is to first calculate the future value factor and then press the '$1/x$' key to flip it over.

If we let FV_t stand for the future value after t periods, then the relationship between future value and present value can be written simply as one of the following:

$$PV \times (1+r)^t = FV_t$$
$$PV = \frac{FV_t}{(1+r)^t}$$
$$= FV_t \times \left[\frac{1}{(1+r)^t}\right] \tag{4.3}$$
$$= FV_t \times (1+r)^{-t}$$

This last result we shall call the *basic present value equation*. We shall use it throughout the text. A number of variations come up, but this simple equation underlies many of the most important ideas in corporate finance.

EXAMPLE 4.8

EVALUATING INVESTMENTS

To give you an idea of how we shall be using present and future values, consider the following simple investment. Your company proposes to buy an asset for £335. This investment is very safe. You would sell off the asset in three years for £400. You know you could invest the £335 elsewhere at 10 per cent with very little risk. What do you think of the proposed investment?

This is not a good investment. Why not? Because you can invest the £335 elsewhere at 10 per cent. If you do, after three years it will grow to:

$$£335 \times (1+r)^t = £335 \times 1.1^3$$
$$= £335 \times 1.331$$
$$= £445.89$$

Because the proposed investment pays out only £400, it is not as good as other alternatives we have. Another way of seeing the same thing is to notice that the present value of £400 in three years at 10 per cent is:

$$£400 \times \left[\frac{1}{(1+r)^t}\right] = £400/1.1^3$$
$$= £400/1.331$$
$$= £300.53$$

This tells us that we have to invest only about £300 to get £400 in three years, not £335. We shall return to this type of analysis later on.

DETERMINING THE DISCOUNT RATE

We frequently need to determine what discount rate is implicit in an investment. We can do this by looking at the basic present value equation:

$$PV = \frac{FV_t}{(1+r)^t}$$

There are only four parts to this equation: the present value (PV), the future value (FV_t), the discount rate (r), and the life of the investment (t). Given any three of these, we can always find the fourth.

> **EXAMPLE 4.9**
>
> ### FINDING R FOR A SINGLE-PERIOD INVESTMENT
>
> You are considering a one-year investment. If you put up €1,250 you will get back €1,350. What rate is this investment paying?
>
> First, in this single-period case, the answer is fairly obvious. You are getting a total of €100 in addition to your €1,250. The implicit rate on this investment is thus €100/1,250 = 8 per cent.
>
> More formally, from the basic present value equation, the present value (the amount you must put up today) is €1,250. The future value (what the present value grows to) is €1,350. The time involved is one period, so we have:
>
> $$€1{,}250 = €1{,}350/(1+r)^1$$
> $$1 + r = €1{,}350/1{,}250 = 1.80$$
> $$r = 8\%$$
>
> In this simple case, of course, there was no need to go through this calculation. But as we describe next, it gets a little harder with more than one period.

To illustrate what happens with multiple periods, let's say we are offered an investment that costs us £100 and will double our money in eight years. To compare this with other investments, we should like to know what discount rate is implicit in these numbers. This discount rate is called the *rate of return*, or sometimes just the *return*, on the investment. In this case we have a present value of £100, a future value of £200 (double our money), and an eight-year life. To calculate the return, we can write the basic present value equation as:

$$PV = \frac{FV_t}{(1+r)^t}$$

$$£100 = \frac{£200}{(1+r)^8}$$

It could also be written as:

$$(1+r)^8 = £200/100 = 2$$

We now need to solve for r. There are three ways we could do it:

1. Use a financial calculator or a spreadsheet.
2. Solve the equation for $1+r$ by taking the eighth root of both sides (i.e. $(1+r)^{(1/8)}$). Because this is the same thing as raising both sides to the power of 1/8 or 0.125, this is actually easy to do with the 'y^x' key on a calculator. Just enter 2, then press 'y^x', enter 0.125, and press the ' = ' key. The eighth root should be about 1.09, which implies that r is 9 per cent.
3. Use a future value table. The future value factor after eight years is equal to 2. If you look across the row corresponding to eight periods in Table A.1 (see Appendix A), you will see that a future value factor of 2 corresponds to the 9 per cent column, again implying that the return here is 9 per cent.

Actually, in this particular example there is a useful 'back of the envelope' means of solving for r: the Rule of 72. For reasonable rates of return, the time it takes to double your money is given approximately by 72/*r*%. In our example this means that 72/*r*% = 8 years, implying that *r* is 9 per cent, as we calculated. This rule is fairly accurate for discount rates in the range 5 to 20 per cent.

> **EXAMPLE 4.10**
>
> ### COMIC COLLECTIBLES AS INVESTMENTS
>
> In January 2017 *Amazing Fantasy* No. 15, the first Marvel comic in which Spider-Man appeared, was valued at $50,000 in mint condition. 'Experts' on such collectibles often argue that a mint condition *Amazing Fantasy* No. 15 would double in value to $100,000 by the end of 2026.
>
> So would the comic have been a good investment? By the Rule of 72, you already know the experts were predicting that the comic would double in value in 10 years; so the return predicted would be about 72/10 = 7.2 per cent per year, which is only so-so.

At one time at least, a rule of thumb in the rarefied world of fine art collecting was 'Your money back in 5 years, double your money in 10 years'. Given this, let's see how an investment stacked up. In 1998 the Alberto Giacometti bronze statue *Homme Qui Marche III* sold for €2,016,000. Five years later the statue was sold again, walking out of the door at a price of €2,740,000. How did the seller do?

The rule of thumb has us doubling our money in 10 years; so, from the Rule of 72, we have that 7.2 per cent per year was the norm. The statue was resold in almost exactly five years. The present value is €2,016,000, and the future value is €2,740,000. We need to solve for the unknown rate, *r*, as follows:

$$€2,016,000 = \frac{€2,740,000}{(1+r)^5}$$
$$(1+r)^5 = 1.3591$$
$$1+r = 1.3591^{1/5} = 1.0633$$

Solving for *r*, we find that the seller earned about 6.33 per cent per year – less than the 7.2 per cent rule of thumb. At least the seller made his money back.

> **EXAMPLE 4.11**
>
> ### SAVING FOR UNIVERSITY
>
> You estimate that you will need about £80,000 to send your child to university in eight years. You have about £35,000 now. If you can earn 20 per cent per year, will you make it? At what rate will you just reach your goal?
>
> If you can earn 20 per cent, the future value of your £35,000 in eight years will be:
>
> $$FV = £35,000 \times 1.20^8 = £35,000 \times 4.2998 = £150,493.59$$
>
> So you will make it easily. The minimum rate is the unknown *r* in the following:
>
> $$FV = £35,000 \times (1+r)^8 = £80,000$$
> $$(1+r)^8 = £80,000/35,000 = 2.2857$$
>
> Therefore the future value factor is 2.2857. Looking at the row in Table A.1 (see Appendix A) that corresponds to eight periods, we see that our future value factor is roughly halfway between the ones shown for 10 per cent (2.1436) and 12 per cent (2.4760), so you will just reach your goal if you earn approximately 11 per cent. To get the exact answer, we would solve for *r*:
>
> $$(1+r)^8 = £80,000/35,000 = 2.2857$$
> $$1+r = 2.2857^{(1/8)} = 2.2857^{0.125} = 1.1089$$
> $$r = 10.89\%$$

> **EXAMPLE 4.12**
>
> ### ONLY 18,262.5 DAYS TO RETIREMENT
>
> You would like to retire in 50 years as a millionaire. If you have €10,000 today, what rate of return do you need to earn to achieve your goal?
>
> The future value is €1,000,000. The present value is €10,000, and there are 50 years until payment. We need to calculate the unknown discount rate in the following:
>
> $$€10,000 = €1,000,000/(1 + r)^{50}$$
> $$(1 + r)^{50} = 100$$
>
> The future value factor is thus 100. You can verify that the implicit rate is about 9.65 per cent.

> **REAL WORLD INSIGHTS**
>
> In February 2020, Avagnought SA issued a thirty-year bond that pays €200,000 per bond when it expires in 2050. At the issue date, bonds of a similar structure, lifetime and risk gave a return to investors of 2.5 per cent. The value of the bond in the market is, therefore:
>
> $$Price = \frac{€200,000}{1.025^{30}} = €95,348.54$$

FINDING THE NUMBER OF PERIODS

Suppose we are interested in purchasing an asset that costs £50,000. We currently have £25,000. If we can earn 12 per cent on this £25,000, how long until we have the £50,000? Finding the answer involves solving for the last variable in the basic present value equation, the number of periods. You already know how to get an approximate answer to this particular problem. Notice that we need to double our money. From the Rule of 72, this will take about 72/12 = 6 years at 12 per cent.

To come up with the exact answer, we can again manipulate the basic present value equation. The present value is £25,000, and the future value is £50,000. With a 12 per cent discount rate, the basic equation takes one of the following forms:

$$£25,000 = £50,000/1.12^t$$
$$£50,000/25,000 = 1.12^t = 2$$

We thus have a future value factor of 2 for a 12 per cent rate. We now need to solve for t. If you look down the column in Table A.1 (see Appendix A) that corresponds to 12 per cent, you will see that a future value factor of 1.9738 occurs at six periods. It will thus take about six years, as we calculated.

To get the exact answer, we have to explicitly solve for t. This next part is only for mathematicians and uses the natural log function. An exact solution is achieved by taking the natural log of both sides of the equation to give:

$$t \ln(1.12) = \ln(2)$$
$$0.113t = 0.693$$
$$t = 0.693/0.113 = 6.116 \text{ years}$$

If you do this, you will see that the answer is 6.1163 years, so our approximation was quite close in this case.

EXAMPLE 4.13

WAITING FOR GODOT

You've been saving up to buy Godot Ltd. The total cost will be £10 million. You currently have about £2.3 million. If you can earn 5 per cent on your money, how long will you have to wait? At 16 per cent, how long must you wait?

At 5 per cent, you'll have to wait a long time. From the basic present value equation:

$$£2.3 \text{ million} = £10 \text{ million}/1.05^t$$
$$1.05^t = 4.35$$
$$t = 30 \text{ years}$$

At 16 per cent, things are a little better. Verify for yourself that it will take about 10 years.

SPREADSHEET STRATEGIES 4.1

Using a Spreadsheet for Time Value of Money Calculations

More and more, business people from many different areas (not just finance and accounting) rely on spreadsheets to do all the different types of calculation that come up in the real world. As a result, in this section we shall show you how to use a spreadsheet to handle the various time value of money problems we presented in this chapter. We shall use Microsoft Excel™, but the commands are similar for other types of software. We assume you are already familiar with basic spreadsheet operations.

As we have seen, you can solve for any one of the following four potential unknowns: future value, present value, the discount rate or the number of periods. With a spreadsheet, there is a separate formula for each. In Excel, these are as follows:

To find	Enter this formula
Future value	= FV (rate, nper, pmt, pv)
Present value	= PV (rate, nper, pmt, fv)
Discount rate	= RATE (nper, pmt, pv, fv)
Number of periods	= NPER (rate, pmt, pv, fv)

In these formulae, pv and fv are present and future value, nper is the number of periods, and rate is the discount, or interest, rate.

Two things are a little tricky here. First, the spreadsheet requires that the rate be entered as a decimal. Second, you have to put a negative sign on either the present value or the future value to solve for the rate or the number of periods. For the same reason, if you solve for a present value, the answer will have a negative sign unless you input a negative future value. The same is true when you compute a future value.

To illustrate how you might use these formulae, we shall go back to an example in the chapter. If you invest £25,000 at 12 per cent per year, how long until you have £50,000? You might set up a spreadsheet like this:

	A	B	C	D	E	F	G	H
1	Present Value (pv)	£25,000		Periods	6.116255			
2	Future Value (fv)	£50,000						
3	Rate (rate)	12%		Formula in cell E1 is =NPER (B3,0,-B1,B2)				
4								
5								

This example finishes our introduction to basic time value concepts. Table 4.4 summarizes present and future value calculations for future reference.

TABLE 4.4

Summary of time value calculations

Symbols

PV = Present value; what future cash flows are worth today
FV_t = Future value; what cash flows are worth in the future
R = Interest rate, rate of return, or discount rate per period - typically, but not always, one year
T = Number of periods - typically, but not always, the number of years
C = Cash amount

Future value of C invested at r per cent for t periods

$FV_t = C \times (1 + r)^t$
The term $(1 + r)^t$ is called the *future value factor*.

Present value of C to be received in t periods at r per cent per period

$PV = C/(1 + r)^t$
The term $1/(1 + r)^t$ is called the *present value factor*.

The basic present value equation giving the relationship between present and future value

$PV = FV_t/(1 + r)^t$

CONCEPT QUESTIONS

4.3a What is the basic present value equation?
4.3b What is the Rule of 72?

SUMMARY AND CONCLUSIONS

This chapter has introduced you to the basic principles of present value and discounted cash flow valuation. In it, we explained a number of things about the time value of money, including these:

1. For a given rate of return, we can determine the value at some point in the future of an investment made today by calculating the future value of that investment.
2. The property of compounding can lead to very large cash flows in the future.
3. We can determine the current worth of a future cash flow or series of cash flows for a given rate of return by calculating the present value of the cash flow(s) involved.
4. The relationship between present value (PV) and future value (FV) for a given rate r and time t is given by the basic present value equation:

$$PV = \frac{FV_t}{(1+r)^t}$$

5. Using the formula in (4), it is possible to find any one of the four components (PV, FV_t, r or t) given the other three.

The principles developed in this chapter will figure prominently in the chapters to come. The reason for this is that most investments, whether they involve real assets or financial assets, can be analysed using the discounted cash flow (DCF) approach. As a result, the DCF approach is broadly applicable and widely used in practice. Before going on, therefore, you might want to do some of the problems that follow.

CHAPTER REVIEW AND SELF-TEST PROBLEMS

4.1 Calculating Future Values Assume you deposit 10,000 Swedish kronor today in an account that pays 6 per cent interest. How much will you have in 5 years?

4.2 Calculating Present Values Suppose you have just celebrated your 19th birthday. A rich uncle has set up a trust fund for you that will pay you £150,000 when you turn 30. If the relevant discount rate is 9 per cent, how much is this fund worth today?

4.3 Calculating Rates of Return You've been offered an investment that will double your money in 10 years. What rate of return are you being offered? Check your answer using the Rule of 72.

4.4 Calculating the Number of Periods You've been offered an investment that will pay you 9 per cent per year. If you invest £15,000, how long until you have £30,000? How long until you have £45,000?

SOLUTIONS

4.1 We need to calculate the future value of SKr10,000 at 6 per cent for 5 years. The future value factor is:

$$1.06^5 = 1.3382$$

The future value is thus SKr10,000 × 1.3382 = SKr13,382.26.

4.2 We need the present value of £150,000 to be paid in 11 years at 9 per cent. The discount factor is:

$$1/1.09^{11} = 1/2.5804 = 0.3875$$

The present value is thus about £58,130.

4.3 Suppose you invest €1,000. You will have €2,000 in 10 years with this investment. So €1,000 is the amount you have today, or the present value, and €2,000 is the amount you will have in 10 years, or the future value. From the basic present value equation we have:

$$€2,000 = €1,000 \times (1 + r)^{10}$$
$$2 = (1 + r)^{10}$$

From here, we need to solve for r, the unknown rate. As shown in the chapter, there are several different ways to do this. We shall take the 10th root of 2 (by raising 2 to the power of 1/10):

$$2^{(1/10)} = 1 + r$$
$$1.0718 = 1 + r$$
$$r = 7.18\%$$

Using the Rule of 72, we have $72/t = r\%$, or $72/10 = 7.2\%$, so our answer looks good (remember that the Rule of 72 is only an approximation).

4.4 The basic equation is this:

$$£30,000 = £15,000 \times (1 + 0.09)^t$$
$$2 = (1 + 0.09)^t$$

If we solve for t, we find that $t = 8.04$ years. Using the Rule of 72, we get $72/9 = 8$ years, so once again our answer looks good. To get £45,000, verify for yourself that you will have to wait 12.75 years.

QUESTIONS AND PROBLEMS

4.1 Simple Interest versus Compound Interest First City Bank pays 8 per cent simple interest on its savings account balances, whereas Second City Bank pays 8 per cent interest compounded annually. If you made a £10,000 deposit in each bank, how much more money would you earn from your Second City Bank account at the end of 10 years?

4.2 Calculating Future Values Calculate the future value of a £100 cash flow for the following combinations of rates and times.

1. $r = 10\%$ and $t = 10$ years.
2. $r = 10\%$ and $t = 20$ years.
3. $r = 5\%$ and $t = 10$ years.
4. $r = 5\%$ and $t = 20$ years.

4.3 Calculating Present Values Calculate the present value of a £100 cash flow for the following combinations of rates and times.

1. $r = 10\%$ and $t = 10$ years.
2. $r = 10\%$ and $t = 20$ years.
3. $r = 5\%$ and $t = 10$ years.
4. $r = 5\%$ and $t = 20$ years.

4.4 Calculating Interest Rates Solve for the unknown interest rate in each of the following.

Present value	Years	Future value	Interest rate (%)
£240	4	£297	
£360	10	£1,080	
£39,000	11	£185,382	
£38,261	100	£531,618	

4.5 Calculating the Number of Periods Solve for the unknown number of years in each of the following.

Present value	Interest rate %	Future value	Years
NKr 460	10	NKr 1,284	
NKr 710	7	NKr 4,341	
NKr 8,400	15	NKr 364,518	
NKr 20,500	12	NKr 173,439	

4.6 Calculating Interest Rates Assume the total cost of a university education will be €290,000 when your child enters college in 18 years. You presently have €40,000 to invest. What annual rate of interest must you earn on your investment to cover the cost of your child's university education?

4.7 Calculating the Number of Periods At 6 per cent interest, how long does it take to double your money? To quadruple it?

4.8 Calculating Interest Rates In 2021, the average price per metre for owner-occupied flats in Copenhagen was about 23,000 Danish kroner. In 2002 the average price was around 6,000 Danish kroner. What was the annual increase in selling price?

4.9 Calculating the Number of Periods You're trying to save to buy a new €170,000 Ferrari. You have €40,000 today that can be invested at your bank. The bank pays 5 per cent annual interest on its accounts. How long will it be before you have enough to buy the car?

4.10 Calculating Present Values Imprudential plc has an unfunded pension liability of £800 million that must be paid in 20 years. To assess the value of the firm's equity, financial analysts want to discount this liability back to the present. If the relevant discount rate is 7 per cent, what is the present value of this liability?

4.11 Calculating Present Values You have just received notification that you have won the €1 million first prize in the Euro Lottery. However, the prize will be awarded on your 100th birthday (assuming you're around to collect), 70 years from now. What is the present value of your windfall if the appropriate discount rate is 12 per cent?

4.12 Calculating Future Values Your coin collection contains fifty 1952 silver dollars. If your grandparents purchased them for their face value when they were new, how much will your collection be worth when you retire in 2057, assuming they appreciate at a 4.5 per cent annual rate?

4.13 Calculating Interest Rates and Future Values In 1968 prize money for the Wimbledon Tennis Championships was first awarded. For the winner of the men's singles it was £2,000 and for the ladies' singles it was £750. In 2020 both winners received £2,350,000. What was the percentage increase per year in the winner's cheque for men and women over this period? If the winner's prize increases at the same rate, what will the men's and ladies' singles tournament winners receive in 2040?

4.14 Calculating Interest Rates In 2021 a gold Morgan dollar minted in 1895 sold for $28,786. For this to have been true, what rate of return did this coin return for the lucky numismatist? Assume interest is calculated annually.

4.15 Calculating Rates of Return On 8 February 2009 John Madejski, chairman of Reading Football Club, sold the Edgar Degas bronze sculpture *Petite Danseuse de Quatorze Ans* at auction for a world record price of £13.3 million. He bought the statue in 2004 for £5 million. What was his annual rate of return on this sculpture?

4.16 Calculating Rates of Return Consider a bond issued by Spanish Word Ltd in 2014 that, in return for receiving £24,099 from investors, it will pay back £100,000 in 30 years.

(a) Based on the £24,099 price, what rate was Spanish Word paying to borrow money?

(b) Suppose that in 2020 this security's price is £38,260. If an investor had purchased it for £24,099 in 2014 and sold it in 2020, what annual rate of return would she have earned?

(c) If an investor had purchased the security in the market in 2020, and held it until it matured, what annual rate of return would she have earned?

4.17 Calculating Present Values Suppose you are still committed to owning a €170,000 Ferrari (see Problem 4.9). If you believe your mutual fund can achieve a 12 per cent annual rate of return and you want to buy the car in 9 years' time, on the day you turn 30, how much must you invest today?

4.18 Calculating Future Values You have just made your first £4,000 contribution to your retirement account. Assuming you earn a 10 per cent rate of return and make no additional contributions, what will your account be worth when you retire in 45 years? What if you wait 10 years before contributing? (Does this suggest an investment strategy?)

4.19 Calculating Future Values You are scheduled to receive £30,000 in two years. When you receive it, you will invest it for 6 more years at 8.4 per cent per year. How much will you have in 8 years?

4.20 Calculating the Number of Periods You expect to receive €10,000 at graduation in 2 years. You plan on investing it at 10 per cent until you have €75,000. How long will you have to wait from now?

4.21 Balloon Payments On 1 September 2019, Susan Chao bought a motorcycle for £15,000. She paid £1,000 down and financed the balance with a 5-year loan at a stated annual interest rate of 9.6 per cent, compounded monthly. She started the monthly payments exactly 1 month after the purchase (i.e., 1 October 2019). Two years later, at the end of October 2021, Susan got a new job and decided to pay off the loan. If the bank charges her a 1 per cent prepayment penalty based on the loan balance, how much must she pay the bank on 1 November 2021?

4.22 Interest You receive a credit card application from Shady Banks plc offering an introductory rate of 2 per cent per year, compounded monthly for the first 6 months, increasing thereafter to 20 per cent per year compounded monthly. Assuming you transfer the £4,000 balance from your existing credit card and make no subsequent payments, how much interest will you owe at the end of the first year?

4.23 Future Values Your job pays you only once a year for all the work you did over the previous 12 months. Today, 31 December, you just received your salary of £100,000, and plan to spend all of it. However, you have also decided to join the company's employee pension scheme. Under the very generous scheme, your company contributes £2 for every £1 that you pay into the pension. You have decided that one year from today you will begin paying 2 per cent of your annual salary into the pension in which you are guaranteed to earn 8 per cent per year. How much money will you have on the date of your retirement 40 years from today?

4.24 Present Values A 3-year annuity of six £5,000 semi-annual payments will begin 10 years from now, with the first payment coming 10.5 years from now. If the discount rate is 10 per cent compounded monthly, what is the current value of the annuity?

MINI CASE

HREON SA

Hreon SA is an online technology company that provides services in outdated programming languages. As software upgrades, older languages such as VAX become obsolete. However, many organizations still have systems that use these languages and can't afford to purchase completely new systems. This emerging sector is entering the growth phase of development and so Hreon is considering an increase in its capability effectiveness.

Since the firm has little free cash around, it will need to borrow funds to support its investment. The problem facing Hreon is how much to borrow. The company has decided that an appropriate discount rate for its investment is 15 per cent, and it wishes to increase its cash flow one year from now by €250,000.

QUESTIONS

1. Assume that Hreon SA believes it will achieve an increase in cash flow of €250,000 in 10 years instead of one year from now. Why is €250,000 in year 10 worth less than €250,000 in year 1?
2. Hreon SA is assuming a discount rate of 15%. If they reassessed this and discovered that the discount rate should be 10%, what would this mean for the value of the investment?
3. Aside from the time value of money effect, do other factors influence how future cash flows are viewed?

ADDITIONAL READING

This chapter presents the time value of money concept. If you wish to delve much deeper into this area, you should read *Financial Markets and Corporate Strategy*, 2nd edition, McGraw-Hill, 2011, by David Hillier, Mark Grinblatt and Sheridan Titman.

CHAPTER 5
DISCOUNTED CASH FLOW VALUATION

LEARNING OBJECTIVES

After studying this chapter, you should understand:

LO1 How to determine the future and present value of investments with multiple cash flows.
LO2 How loan payments are calculated, and how to find the interest rate on a loan.
LO3 How loans are amortized or paid off.
LO4 How interest rates are quoted (and misquoted).

KEY NOTATIONS

APR	Annual percentage rate
C	Cash flow
EAR	Effective annual rate of return
g	Growth rate
m	Number of times interest is compounded a year
PVIFA	Present value interest factor for annuities
q	Quoted rate
r	Interest rate or discount rate
t	Number of periods

THERE ARE MANY WAYS TO VALUE A POTENTIAL INVESTMENT OR PROJECT, but almost all of the most common methods incorporate the time value of money. As a financial manager, you will identify the appropriate cash flows to include in your analysis (covered in detail in Part 3: Capital Budgeting) and discount these at an appropriate rate (identifying the correct discount rate is the subject of Part 5: Cost of Capital and Long-Term Financial Policy). In this chapter we show you some shortcuts and simplifications to make your job of discounting future cash flows easier.

In our previous chapter we covered the basics of discounted cash flow valuation. However, so far we have dealt only with single cash flows. In reality, most investments have multiple cash flows. For example, if Tesco is thinking of opening a new department store, there will be a large cash outlay in the beginning of the investment, and then cash inflows for many years. In this chapter, we begin to explore how to value such investments.

When you finish this chapter, you should have some very practical skills. For example, you will know how to calculate your own car payments or student loan payments. You will also be able to determine how long it will take to pay off a credit card if you make the minimum payment each month (a practice we do not recommend). We shall show you how to compare interest rates to determine which are the highest and which are the lowest, and we shall also show you how interest rates can be quoted in different – and at times deceptive – ways. Even financial securities, such as equities and bonds, can be valued using the techniques in this chapter.

5.1 FUTURE AND PRESENT VALUES OF MULTIPLE CASH FLOWS

Thus far we have restricted our attention to either the future value of a lump sum present amount or the present value of some single future cash flow. In this section, we begin to study ways to value multiple cash flows. We start with future value.

FUTURE VALUE WITH MULTIPLE CASH FLOWS

Suppose you deposit €100 today in an account paying 8 per cent. In one year you will deposit another €100. How much will you have in two years? This particular problem is relatively easy. At the end of the first year you will have €108 plus the second €100 you deposit, for a total of €208. You leave this €208 on deposit at 8 per cent for another year. At the end of this second year, it is worth:

$$€208 \times 1.08 = €224.64$$

Figure 5.1 is a *time line* that illustrates the process of calculating the future value of these two €100 deposits. Diagrams such as these are useful for solving complicated problems. Almost any time you are having trouble with a present or future value problem, drawing a time line will help you see what is happening.

In the first part of Figure 5.1 we show the cash flows on the time line. The most important thing is that we write them down where they actually occur. Here, the first cash flow occurs today, which we label as time 0. We, therefore, put €100 at time 0 on the time line. The second €100 cash flow occurs one year from today, so we write it down at the point labelled as time 1. In the second part of Figure 5.1 we calculate the future values, one period at a time, to come up with the final €224.64.

When we calculated the future value of the two €100 deposits, we simply calculated the balance as of the beginning of each year, and then rolled that amount forward to the next year. We could have done it another, quicker way. The first €100 is on deposit for two years at 8 per cent, so its future value is:

$$€100 \times 1.08^2 = €100 \times 1.1664 = €116.64$$

The second €100 is on deposit for one year at 8 per cent, and its future value is thus:

$$€100 \times 1.08 = €108$$

The total future value, as we previously calculated, is equal to the sum of these two future values:

$$€116.64 + 108 = €224.64$$

Based on this example, there are two ways to calculate future values for multiple cash flows: (1) compound the accumulated balance forward one year at a time, or (2) calculate the future value of each cash flow first and then add them up. Both give the same answer, so you can do it either way.

To illustrate the two different ways of calculating future values, consider the future value of €2,000 invested at the end of each of the next five years. The current balance is zero, and the rate is 10 per cent. We first draw a time line, as shown in Figure 5.2.

FIGURE 5.1

Drawing and using a time line

FIGURE 5.2

Time line for €2,000 per year for five years

On the time line, notice that nothing happens until the end of the first year when we make the first €2,000 investment. This first €2,000 earns interest for the next four (not five) years. Also, notice that the last €2,000 is invested at the end of the fifth year, so it earns no interest at all.

Figure 5.3 illustrates the calculations involved if we compound the investment one period at a time. As illustrated, the future value is €12,210.20.

FIGURE 5.3

Future value calculated by compounding forward one period at a time

Figure 5.4 goes through the same calculations, but the second technique is used. Naturally, the answer is the same.

FIGURE 5.4

Future value calculated by compounding each cash flow separately

---

EXAMPLE 5.1

SAVING UP ONCE AGAIN

If you deposit 100 Swedish kronor (SKr) in one year, SKr200 in two years, and SKr300 in three years, how much will you have in three years? How much of this is interest? How much will you have in five years if you don't add additional amounts? Assume a 7 per cent interest rate throughout.

We shall calculate the future value of each amount in three years. Notice that the SKr100 earns interest for two years, and the SKr200 earns interest for one year. The final SKr300 earns no interest. The future values are thus:

$$
\begin{aligned}
\text{SKr100} \times 1.07^2 &= \text{SKr114.49} \\
\text{SKr200} \times 1.07 &= 214.00 \\
+\text{SKr300} &= 300.00 \\
\text{Total future value} &= \text{SKr628.49}
\end{aligned}
$$

The total future value is thus SKr628.49. The total interest is:

$$\text{SKr628.49} - (100 + 200 + 300) = \text{SKr28.49}$$

How much will you have in five years? We know that you will have SKr628.49 in three years. If you leave that in for two more years, it will grow to:

$$\text{SKr628.49} \times 1.07^2 = \text{SKr628.49} \times 1.1449 = \text{SKr719.56}$$

Notice that we could have calculated the future value of each amount separately. Once again, be careful about the lengths of time. As we previously calculated, the first SKr100 earns interest for only four years, the second deposit earns three years' interest, and the last earns two years' interest:

$$
\begin{aligned}
\text{SKr100} \times 1.07^4 &= \text{SKr100} \times 1.3108 = \text{SKr131.08} \\
\text{SKr200} \times 1.07^3 &= \text{SKr200} \times 1.2250 = 245.01 \\
+\text{SKr300} \times 1.07^2 &= \text{SKr300} \times 1.1449 = 343.47 \\
\text{Total future value} &= \text{SKr719.56}
\end{aligned}
$$

PRESENT VALUE WITH MULTIPLE CASH FLOWS

We often need to determine the present value of a series of future cash flows. As with future values, there are two ways we can do it. We can either discount back one period at a time, or we can just calculate the present values individually and add them up.

Suppose you need €1,000 in one year and €2,000 more in two years. If you can earn 9 per cent on your money, how much do you have to put up today to exactly cover these amounts in the future? In other words, what is the present value of the two cash flows at 9 per cent?

The present value of €2,000 in two years at 9 per cent is:

$$€2,000/1.09^2 = €1,683.36$$

The present value of €1,000 in one year is:

$$€1,000/1.09 = €917.43$$

Therefore the total present value is:

$$€1,683.36 + 917.43 = €2,600.79$$

An alternative way of calculating present values for multiple future cash flows is to discount back to the present, one period at a time. To illustrate, suppose we had an investment that was going to pay £1,000 at the end of every year for the next five years. To find the present value, we could discount each £1,000 back to the present separately and then add them up. Figure 5.5 illustrates this approach for a 6 per cent discount rate; as shown, the answer is £4,212.37 (ignoring a small rounding error).

FIGURE 5.5 Present value calculated by discounting each cash flow separately

Alternatively, we could discount the last cash flow back one period and add it to the next-to last cash flow:

$$(£1,000/1.06) + 1,000 = £943.40 + 1,000 = £1,943.40$$

We could then discount this amount back one period and add it to the year 3 cash flow:

$$(£1,943.40/1.06) + 1,000 = £1,833.40 + 1,000 = £2,833.40$$

This process could be repeated as necessary. Figure 5.6 illustrates this approach and the remaining calculations.

FIGURE 5.6 Present value calculated by discounting back one period at a time

EXAMPLE 5.2

HOW MUCH IS IT WORTH?

You are offered an investment that will pay you £200 in one year, £400 the next year, £600 the next year, and £800 at the end of the fourth year. You can earn 12 per cent on similar investments. What is the most you should pay for this one?

We need to calculate the present value of these cash flows at 12 per cent. Taking them one at a time gives:

$$
\begin{aligned}
£200 \times 1/1.12^1 &= £200/1.1200 = &£178.57 \\
£400 \times 1/1.12^2 &= £400/1.2544 = &318.88 \\
£600 \times 1/1.12^3 &= £600/1.4049 = &427.07 \\
+£800 \times 1/1.12^4 &= £800/1.5735 = &\underline{508.41} \\
&\text{Total future value} = &\underline{£1{,}432.93}
\end{aligned}
$$

If you can earn 12 per cent on your money, then you can duplicate this investment's cash flows for £1,432.93, so this is the most you should be willing to pay.

EXAMPLE 5.3

HOW MUCH IS IT WORTH? PART 2

You are offered an investment that will make three €5,000 payments. The first payment will occur four years from today. The second will occur in five years, and the third will follow in six years. If you can earn 11 per cent, what is the most this investment is worth today? What is the future value of the cash flows?

We shall answer the questions in reverse order to illustrate a point. The future value of the cash flows in six years is:

$$(€5{,}000 \times 1.11^2) + (5{,}000 \times 1.11) + 5{,}000 = €6{,}160.50 + 5{,}550 + 5{,}000$$
$$= €16{,}710.50$$

The present value must be:

$$€16{,}710.50/1.11^6 = €8{,}934.12$$

Let's check this. Taking them one at a time, the PVs of the cash flows are:

$$
\begin{aligned}
€5{,}000 \times 1/1.11^6 &= €5{,}000/1.8704 = &€2{,}673.20 \\
€5{,}000 \times 1/1.11^5 &= €5{,}000/1.6851 = &2{,}967.26 \\
+€5{,}000 \times 1/1.11^4 &= €5{,}000/1.5181 = &\underline{3{,}293.65} \\
&\text{Total present value} = &\underline{€8{,}934.12}
\end{aligned}
$$

This is as we previously calculated (alert readers may see that the figures above only added up to €8,934.11 - this is because of rounding error). The point we want to make is that we can calculate present and future values in any order, and convert between them using whatever way seems most convenient. The answers will always be the same as long as we stick with the same discount rate, and are careful to keep track of the right number of periods.

> **SPREADSHEET STRATEGIES 5.1**
>
> **How to Calculate Present Values with Multiple Future Cash Flows Using a Spreadsheet**
>
> Just as we did in our previous chapter, we can set up a basic spreadsheet to calculate the present values of the individual cash flows as follows. Notice that we have simply calculated the present values one at a time and added them up:
>
> | | A | B | C | D | E |
> |---|---|---|---|---|---|
> | 1 | Rate | 0.12 | | | |
> | 2 | Year | 1 | 2 | 3 | 4 |
> | 3 | Cash Flow | £200 | £400.00 | £600.00 | £800.00 |
> | 4 | Present Value | £178.57 | £318.88 | £427.07 | £508.41 |
> | 5 | Formula Used | =PV(B1,B2,0,-B3) | =PV(B1,C2,0,-C3) | =PV(B1,D2,0,-D3) | =PV(B1,E2,0,-E3) |
> | 6 | | | | | |
> | 7 | Total PV | £1,432.93 | | | |
> | 8 | Formula Used | =SUM(B5:E5) | | | |
> | 9 | | | | | |

A NOTE ABOUT CASH FLOW TIMING

In present and future value problems, cash flow timing is critically important. In almost all such calculations, it is implicitly assumed that the cash flows occur at the *end* of each period. In fact, all the formulae we have discussed, all the numbers in a standard present value or future value table, and (very important) all the preset (or default) settings in a spreadsheet assume that cash flows occur at the end of each period. Unless you are explicitly told otherwise, you should always assume that this is what is meant.

As a quick illustration of this point, suppose you are told that a three-year investment has a first-year cash flow of £100, a second-year cash flow of £200, and a third-year cash flow of £300. You are asked to draw a time line. Without further information, you should always assume that the time line looks like this:

On our time line, notice how the first cash flow occurs at the end of the first period, the second at the end of the second period, and the third at the end of the third period.

We shall close this section by answering the question we posed at the beginning of the chapter concerning footballer Cristiano Ronaldo's contract. Recall that the contract called for £9.5 million in the first year, increasing by 25 per cent over the next five years. If 12 per cent is the appropriate interest rate, what kind of deal did the Real Madrid player have?

To answer, we can calculate the present value by discounting each year's salary back to the present as follows (notice we assume that all the payments are made at year-end):

$$
\begin{aligned}
&\text{Year 0 (2009): } £9{,}500{,}000 &&= £9{,}500{,}000.00 \\
&\text{Year 1 (2010): } £9{,}500{,}000 \times 1.25 \times 1/1.12^1 &&= £10{,}602{,}678.57 \\
&\text{Year 2 (2011): } £9{,}500{,}000 \times 1.25^2 \times 1/1.12^2 &&= £11{,}833{,}346.62 \\
&\text{Year 3 (2012): } £9{,}500{,}000 \times 1.25^3 \times 1/1.12^3 &&= £13{,}206{,}860.07 \\
&\text{Year 4 (2013): } £9{,}500{,}000 \times 1.25^4 \times 1/1.12^4 &&= £14{,}739{,}799.18 \\
&\text{Year 5 (2014): } £9{,}500{,}000 \times 1.25^5 \times 1/1.12^5 &&= £16{,}450{,}668.73
\end{aligned}
$$

Adding the individual cash flows together, you will see that Ronaldo's contract had a present value of about £76 million, or about 71 per cent of the stated £107 million value.

> **CONCEPT QUESTIONS**
>
> **5.1a** Describe how to calculate the future value of a series of cash flows.
> **5.1b** Describe how to calculate the present value of a series of cash flows.
> **5.1c** Unless we are explicitly told otherwise, what do we always assume about the timing of cash flows in present and future value problems?

5.2 VALUING LEVEL CASH FLOWS: ANNUITIES AND PERPETUITIES

We shall frequently encounter situations in which we have multiple cash flows that are all the same amount. For example, a common type of loan repayment plan calls for the borrower to repay the loan by making a series of equal payments over some length of time. Almost all consumer loans (such as car loans) and home mortgages feature equal payments, usually made each month.

annuity
a level stream of cash flows for a fixed period of time.

More generally, a series of constant or level cash flows that occur at the end of each period for some fixed number of periods is called an ordinary **annuity**; more correctly, the cash flows are said to be in *ordinary annuity form*. Annuities appear frequently in financial arrangements, and there are some useful shortcuts for determining their values. We consider these next.

PRESENT VALUE FOR ANNUITY CASH FLOWS

Suppose we are examining an asset that promises to pay £500 at the end of each of the next three years. The cash flows from this asset are in the form of a three-year, £500 annuity. If we wanted to earn 10 per cent on our money, how much would we offer for this annuity?

> **REAL WORLD INSIGHTS**
>
> How to value a company? Corporate valuation involves the same basic decision and details as valuing investments. One must estimate future cash flows and arrive at a risk assessment of the project.
>
> For example, to value a company like Adidas, one must forecast the future sales of all its athletic sports clothing and equipment lines, and estimate the total costs of manufacturing the company's products. The difference between revenues and costs each year is the net cash flow. Once you have estimated the annual Adidas cash flows, calculate their combined present value and you have a valuation!

From the previous section, we know that we can discount each of these £500 payments back to the present at 10 per cent to determine the total present value:

$$\begin{aligned} \text{Present value} &= (£500/1.1^1) + (500/1.1^2) + (500/1.1^3) \\ &= (£500/1.1) + (500/1.21) + (500/1.331) \\ &= £454.55 + 413.22 + 375.66 \\ &= £1{,}243.43 \end{aligned}$$

This approach works just fine. However, we shall often encounter situations in which the number of cash flows is quite large. For example, a typical home mortgage calls for monthly payments over 25 years, for a total of 300 payments. If we were trying to determine the present value of those payments, it would be useful to have a shortcut.

Because the cash flows of an annuity are all the same, we can come up with a handy variation on the basic present value equation (see the Appendix for a full derivation of the annuity present value factor). The present value of an annuity of £C (or any other currency) per period for t periods when the rate of return or interest rate is r is given by:

$$\text{Annuity present value} = C \times \left[\frac{1 - \text{Present value factor}}{r}\right]$$

$$= C \times \left\{\frac{1 - [1/(1+r)^t]}{r}\right\} \quad (5.1)$$

$$= C \times \left\{\frac{1}{r} - \frac{1}{r(1+r)^t}\right\}$$

The term in parentheses on the first line is sometimes called the *present value interest factor for annuities* and abbreviated PVIFA(r, t).

The expression for the annuity present value may look a little complicated, but it isn't difficult to use. Notice that the term in square brackets on the second line, $1/(1+r)^t$, is the same present value factor we've been calculating. In our example from the beginning of this section, the interest rate is 10 per cent, and there are three years involved. The usual present value factor is thus:

$$\text{Present value factor} = 1/1.1^3 = 1/1.331 = 0.751315$$

To calculate the annuity present value factor, we just plug this in:

$$\text{Annuity present value factor} = (1 - \text{Present value factor})/r$$
$$= (1 - 0.751315)/0.10$$
$$= 0.248685/0.10 = 2.48685$$

Just as we calculated before, the present value of our £500 annuity is then:

$$\text{Annuity present value} = £500 \times 2.48685 = £1,243.43$$

EXAMPLE 5.4

HOW MUCH CAN YOU AFFORD?

After carefully going over your budget, you have determined that you can afford to pay €632 per month towards a new sports car. You call up your local bank and find out that the going rate is 1 per cent per month for 48 months. How much can you borrow?

To determine how much you can borrow, we need to calculate the present value of €632 per month for 48 months at 1 per cent per month. The loan payments are in ordinary annuity form, so the annuity present value factor is:

$$\text{Annuity PV factor} = (1 - \text{Present value factor})/r$$
$$= [1 - (1/0.01^{48})]/0.01$$
$$= (1 - 0.6203)/0.01$$
$$= 37.9740$$

With this factor we can calculate the present value of the 48 payments of €632 each as:

$$\text{Present value} = €632 \times 37.9740 = €24,000$$

Therefore €24,000 is what you can afford to borrow and repay.

Annuity Tables

Just as there are tables for ordinary present value factors, there are tables for annuity factors as well. Table 5.1 contains a few such factors; Table A.3 in the appendix to the book contains a larger set. To find the annuity present value factor we calculated just before Example 5.4, look for the row corresponding to three periods and then find the column for 10 per cent. The number you see at that intersection should be 2.4869 (rounded to four decimal places), as we calculated. Once again, try calculating a few of these factors yourself and compare your answers with the ones in the table to make sure you know how to do it. If you are using a financial calculator, just enter £1 as the payment and calculate the present value; the result should be the annuity present value factor.

TABLE 5.1

Annuity present value interest factors

Number of periods	Interest rate (%)			
	5	10	15	20
1	0.9524	0.9091	0.8696	0.8333
2	1.8594	1.7355	1.6257	1.5278
3	2.7232	2.4869	2.2832	2.1065
4	3.5460	3.1699	2.8550	2.5887
5	4.3295	3.7908	3.3522	2.9906

SPREADSHEET STRATEGIES 5.2
Annuity Present Values

Using a spreadsheet to find annuity present values goes like this:

	A	B	C
1	Payment Amount per Period	£500	
2	Number of Payments	3	
3	Discount Rate	10%	
4			
5	Annuity Present Value	£1,243.43	
6			
7			

Formula used: = PV(B3,B2,−B1)

Finding the Payment

Suppose you wish to start up a new business that specializes in the latest of health food trends, frozen yak milk. To produce and market your product, the Yankee Doodle Dandy, you need to borrow €100,000. Because it strikes you as unlikely that this particular fad will be long-lived, you propose to pay off the loan quickly by making five equal annual payments. If the interest rate is 18 per cent, what will the payment be?

In this case, we know the present value is €100,000. The interest rate is 18 per cent, and there are five years. The payments are all equal, so we need to find the relevant annuity factor and solve for the unknown cash flow:

$$\text{Annuity present value} = €100{,}000$$
$$= C \times [(1 - \text{Present value factor})/r]$$
$$= C \times \{[1 - (1/1.18^5)]/0.18\}$$
$$= C \times [(1 - 0.4371)/0.18]$$
$$= C \times 3.1272$$
$$C = €100{,}000/3.1272 = €31{,}978$$

Therefore you'll make five payments of just under €32,000 each.

SPREADSHEET STRATEGIES 5.3

Annuity Payments

Using a spreadsheet to work the same problem goes like this:

	A	B	C
1	Annuity Present Value	100,000	
2	Number of Payments	5	
3	Discount Rate	18%	
4			
5	Annuity Payments	£31,977.78	
6			
7			

Formula used: = PV(B3,B2,−B1)

EXAMPLE 5.5

FINDING THE NUMBER OF PAYMENTS

You ran a little short on your spring break holiday, so you put €1,000 on your credit card. You can afford only the minimum payment of €20 per month. The interest rate on the credit card is 1.5 per cent per month. How long will you take to pay off the €1,000?

What we have here is an annuity of €20 per month at 1.5 per cent per month for some unknown length of time. The present value is €1,000 (the amount you owe today). We need to do a little algebra (or use a calculator):

$$€1{,}000 = €20 \times [(1 - \text{Present value factor})/0.015]$$
$$(€1{,}000/20) \times 0.015 = 1 - \text{Present value factor}$$
$$\text{Present value factor} = 0.25 = 1/(1 + r)^t$$
$$1.015^t = 1/0.25 = 4$$

At this point, the problem boils down to asking: how long does it take for your money to quadruple at 1.5 per cent per month? Based on our previous chapter, the answer is about 93 months:

$$1.015^{93} = 3.99 \approx 4$$

It will take you about 93/12 = 7.75 years to pay off the €1,000 at this rate.

Finding the Rate

The last question we might want to ask concerns the interest rate implicit in an annuity. For example, an insurance company offers to pay you £1,000 per year for 10 years if you will pay £6,710 up front. What rate is implicit in this 10-year annuity?

In this case, we know the present value (£6,710), we know the cash flows (£1,000 per year), and we know the life of the investment (10 years). What we don't know is the discount rate:

$$£6{,}710 = £1{,}000 \times [(1 - \text{Present value factor})/r]$$
$$£6{,}710/1{,}000 = 6.71$$
$$= \{1 - [1/(1+r)^{10}]\}/r$$

So the annuity factor for 10 periods is equal to 6.71, and we need to solve this equation for the unknown value of r. Unfortunately, this is mathematically impossible to do directly. The only way to do it is to use a table, or trial and error, to find a value for r.

If you look across the row corresponding to 10 periods in Table A.3 in the appendix you will see a factor of 6.7101 for 8 per cent, so we see right away that the insurance company is offering just about 8 per cent. Alternatively, we could just start trying different values until we got very close to the answer. Using this trial-and-error approach can be a little tedious, but fortunately, computers are good at that sort of thing.

To illustrate a situation in which finding the unknown rate can be useful, let us consider that a lottery offers you a choice of how to take your winnings. In a recent drawing, participants were offered the option of receiving a lump-sum payment of €250,000 or an annuity of €500,000 to be received in equal instalments over a 25-year period. Which option was better?

To answer, suppose you were to compare €250,000 today with an annuity of €500,000/25 = €20,000 per year for 25 years. At what rate do these have the same value? This is the same type of problem we've been looking at; we need to find the unknown rate r for a present value of €250,000, a €20,000 payment, and a 25-year period. If you grind through the calculations (or get a little computer assistance), you should find that the unknown rate is about 6.24 per cent. You should take the annuity option if that rate is attractive relative to other investments available to you. Notice that we have ignored taxes in this example, and taxes can significantly affect our conclusion. Be sure to consult your tax adviser any time you win the lottery.

FUTURE VALUE FOR ANNUITIES

Sometimes it's also handy to know a shortcut for calculating the future value of an annuity. As you might guess, there are future value factors for annuities as well as present value factors. In general, here is the future value factor for an annuity:

$$\text{Annuity FV factor} = \frac{\text{Future value factor} - 1}{r}$$
$$= \frac{(1+r)^t - 1}{r} \qquad (5.2)$$
$$= \frac{(1+r)^t}{r} - \frac{1}{r}$$

To see how we use annuity future value factors, suppose you plan to contribute £2,000 every year to a retirement account paying 8 per cent. If you retire in 30 years, how much will you have?

The number of years here, t, is 30, and the interest rate, r, is 8 per cent; so we can calculate the annuity future value factor as:

$$\text{Annuity FV factor} = (\text{Future value factor} - 1)/r$$
$$= (1.08^{30} - 1)/0.08$$
$$= (10.0627 - 1)/0.08$$
$$= 113.2832$$

The future value of this 30-year, £2,000 annuity is thus:

$$\text{Annuity future value} = £2{,}000 \times 113.28$$
$$= £226{,}566$$

A NOTE ABOUT ANNUITIES DUE

So far we have only discussed ordinary annuities. These are the most important, but there is a fairly common variation. Remember that with an ordinary annuity the cash flows occur at the end of each period. When you take out a loan with monthly payments, for example, the first loan payment normally occurs one month after you get the loan. However, when you lease an apartment, the first lease payment is usually due immediately. The second payment is due at the beginning of the second month, and so on. A lease is an example of an **annuity due**. An annuity due is an annuity for which the cash flows occur at the beginning of each period. Almost any type of arrangement in which we have to prepay the same amount each period is an annuity due.

> **annuity due**
> an annuity for which the cash flows occur at the beginning of the period.

Suppose an annuity due has five payments of £400 each, and the relevant discount rate is 10 per cent. The time line looks like this:

Notice how the cash flows here are the same as those for a *four*-year ordinary annuity, except that there is an extra £400 at time 0. For practice, check to see that the value of a four-year ordinary annuity at 10 per cent is £1,267.95. If we add on the extra £400, we get £1,667.95, which is the present value of this annuity due.

EXAMPLE 5.6

ANNUITY DUE VERSUS ORDINARY ANNUITY

You decide to buy a car and have a choice of two payment schemes. The first payment plan requires you to make 60 payments of £500 a month, with the first payment today. The second payment plan asks for 60 £500 monthly payments, but in this case the first payment is one month from now. If the monthly interest rate is 1 per cent, how much are you paying for the car under each payment plan?

Payment Plan 1 (Annuity Due):

$$PV = C + C\left[\frac{1}{r} - \frac{1}{r(1+r)^T}\right] = 500 + 500\left[\frac{1}{.01} - \frac{1}{.01(1.01^{59})}\right] = £22{,}702.29$$

Payment Plan 2 (Ordinary Annuity):

$$PV = C\left[\frac{1}{r} - \frac{1}{r(1+r)^T}\right] = 500\left[\frac{1}{.01} - \frac{1}{.01(1.01^{60})}\right] = £22{,}477.52$$

PERPETUITIES

We've seen that a series of level cash flows can be valued by treating those cash flows as an annuity. An important special case of an annuity arises when the level stream of cash flows continues for ever. Such an asset is called a **perpetuity**, because the cash flows are perpetual. Perpetuities are also called **consols**, particularly in the United Kingdom. See Example 5.7 for an important example of a perpetuity.

> **perpetuity**
> an annuity in which the cash flows continue for ever.

Because a perpetuity has an infinite number of cash flows, we obviously can't compute its value by discounting each one. Fortunately, valuing a perpetuity turns out to be the easiest possible case. The present value of a perpetuity (see the Appendix for a full derivation of the perpetuity shortcut formula) is simply:

> **consols**
> a type of perpetuity.

$$\text{PV for a perpetuity} = C/r \tag{5.3}$$

For example, an investment offers a perpetual cash flow of €500 every year. The return you require on such an investment is 8 per cent. What is the value of this investment? The value of this perpetuity is:

$$\text{Perpetuity PV} = C/r = €500/0.08 = €6{,}250$$

For future reference, Table 5.2 contains a summary of the annuity and perpetuity basic calculations we have described.

TABLE 5.2

Summary of annuity and perpetuity calculations

Symbols

PV = Present value, what future cash flows are worth today
FV_t = Future value, what cash flows are worth in the future
r = Interest rate, rate of return, or discount rate per period – typically, but not always, one year
t = Number of periods – typically, but not always, the number of years
C = Cash amount

Future value of C per period for t periods at r per cent per period

$FV_t = C \times \{[(1 + r)^t - 1]/r\}$
A series of identical cash flows is called an annuity and the term $[(1 + r)^t - 1]/r$ is called the *annuity future value factor*.

Present value of C per period for t periods at r per cent per period

$PV = C \times \{1 - [1/(1 + r)^t]\}/r$
The term $\{1 - [1/(1 + r)^t]\}/r$ is called the *annuity present value factor*.

Present value of a perpetuity of C per period

$PV = C/r$
A *perpetuity* has the same cash flow every year for ever.

EXAMPLE 5.7

PREFERENCE SHARES

Preference shares (or preferred stock) are an important example of a perpetuity. When a corporation sells preference shares, the buyer is promised a fixed cash dividend every period (usually every quarter or six months) forever. This dividend must be paid before any dividend can be paid to regular shareholders – hence the term *preference*.

Suppose Gesualdo SA wants to sell preference shares at €100 per share. A similar issue of preference shares already outstanding has a price of €40 per share and offers a dividend of €2 every six months. What dividend will Gesualdo have to offer if the preference shares are going to sell?

The issue that is already out has a present value of €40 and a cash flow of €2 every six months forever. Because this is a perpetuity:

$$\text{Present value} = €40 = €2 \times (1/r)$$
$$r = 5\%$$

To be competitive the new Gesualdo issue will also have to offer 5 per cent *per six months*; so if the present value is to be €100, the dividend must be such that:

$$\text{Present value} = €100 = C \times (1/0.05)$$
$$C = €5 \text{ (per six months)}$$

GROWING ANNUITIES AND PERPETUITIES

Annuities commonly have payments that grow over time. Suppose, for example, that we are looking at a lottery payout over a 20-year period. The first payment, made one year from now, will be €200,000. Every year thereafter the payment will grow by 5 per cent, so the payment in the second year will be €200,000 × 1.05 = €210,000. The payment in the third year will be €210,000 × 1.05 = €220,500, and so on. What's the present value if the appropriate discount rate is 11 per cent?

If we use the symbol g to represent the growth rate, we can calculate the value of a growing annuity using a modified version of our regular annuity formula:

$$\text{Growing annuity present value} = C \times \left[\frac{1 - \left(\frac{1+g}{1+r}\right)^t}{r - g} \right] \quad (5.4)$$

Plugging in the numbers from our lottery example (and letting $g = 0.05$), we get:

$$PV = €200{,}000 \times \left[\frac{1 - \left(\frac{1 + 0.05}{1 + 0.11}\right)^{20}}{0.11 - 0.05} \right]$$
$$= €200{,}000 \times 11.18169$$
$$= €2{,}236{,}337.6$$

There is also a formula for the present value of a growing perpetuity:

$$\text{Growing perpetuity present value} = C \times \left[\frac{1}{r - g} \right]$$
$$= \frac{C}{r - g} \quad (5.5)$$

In our lottery example, now suppose the payments continue for ever. In this case, the present value is:

$$PV = €200{,}000 \times \frac{1}{0.11 - 0.05}$$
$$= €200{,}000 \times 16.6667$$
$$= €3{,}333{,}333.33$$

The notion of a growing perpetuity may seem a little odd, because the payments get bigger every period for ever; but as we shall see in a later chapter, growing perpetuities play a key role in our analysis of share prices.

Before we go on, there is one important note about our formulae for growing annuities and perpetuities. In both cases, the cash flow in the formula, C, is the cash flow that is going to occur exactly one period from today.

CONCEPT QUESTIONS

5.2a In general, what is the present value of an annuity of C per period at a discount rate of r per period? The future value?

5.2b In general, what is the present value of a perpetuity?

5.3 COMPARING RATES: THE EFFECT OF COMPOUNDING

The next issue we need to discuss has to do with the way interest rates are quoted. This subject causes a fair amount of confusion, because rates are quoted in many different ways. Sometimes the way a rate is quoted is the result of tradition, and sometimes it's the result of legislation. Unfortunately, at times, rates are quoted in deliberately deceptive ways to mislead borrowers and investors. We shall discuss these topics in this section.

EFFECTIVE ANNUAL PERCENTAGE RATES AND COMPOUNDING

If a rate is quoted as 10 per cent compounded semi-annually, this means the investment actually pays 5 per cent every six months. A natural question then arises: is 5 per cent every six months the same thing as 10 per cent per year? It's easy to see that it is not. If you invest €1 at 10 per cent per year, you will have €1.10 at the end of the year. If you invest at 5 per cent every six months, then you'll have the future value of €1 at 5 per cent for two periods:

$$€1 \times 1.05^2 = €1.1025$$

> **nominal interest rate**
> the interest rate expressed in terms of the interest payment made each period. Also known as the stated or quoted interest rate.

This is €0.0025 more. The reason is simple: your account was credited with €1 × 0.05 = 5 cents in interest after six months. In the following six months, you earned 5 per cent on that five cents, for an extra 5 × 0.05 = 0.25 cents.

As our example illustrates, 10 per cent compounded semi-annually is actually equivalent to 10.25 per cent per year. Put another way, we would be indifferent between 10 per cent compounded semi-annually and 10.25 per cent compounded annually. Any time we have compounding during the year, we need to be concerned about what the rate really is.

> **effective annual percentage rate (EAR)**
> the interest rate expressed as if it were compounded once per year.

In our example, the 10 per cent is called a **nominal, stated or quoted interest rate**. Other names are used as well. The 10.25 per cent, which is actually the rate you will earn, is called the **effective annual percentage rate (EAR)**. To compare different investments or interest rates, we shall always need to convert to effective rates. Some general procedures for doing this are discussed next.

CALCULATING AND COMPARING EFFECTIVE ANNUAL RATES

To see why it is important to work only with effective rates, suppose you've shopped around and come up with the following three rates:

1. Bank A: 15 per cent compounded daily
2. Bank B: 15.5 per cent compounded quarterly
3. Bank C: 16 per cent compounded annually.

Which of these is the best if you are thinking of opening a savings account? Which of these is best if they represent loan rates?

To begin, Bank C is offering 16 per cent per year. Because there is no compounding during the year, this is the effective rate. Bank B is actually paying 0.155/4 = 0.03875 or 3.875 per cent per quarter. At this rate, an investment of £1 for four quarters would grow to:

$$£1 \times 1.03875^4 = £1.1642$$

The effective annual rate (EAR), therefore, is 16.42 per cent. For a saver, this is much better than the 16 per cent rate Bank C is offering; for a borrower, it's worse.

Bank A is compounding every day. This may seem a little extreme, but it is common to calculate interest daily. In this case, the daily interest rate is actually:

$$0.15/365 = 0.000411$$

This is 0.0411 per cent per day. At this rate, an investment of £1 for 365 periods would grow to:

$$£1 \times 1.000411^{365} = £1.1618$$

The EAR is 16.18 per cent. This is not as good as Bank B's 16.42 per cent for a saver, and not as good as Bank C's 16 per cent for a borrower.

This example illustrates two things. First, the highest quoted rate is not necessarily the best. Second, compounding during the year can lead to a significant difference between the quoted rate and the effective rate. Remember that the effective rate is what you actually get or what you pay.

If you look at our examples, you see that we computed the EARs in three steps. We first divided the quoted rate by the number of times that the interest is compounded. We then added 1 to the result and raised it to the power of the number of times the interest is compounded. Finally, we subtracted the 1. If we let m be the number of times the interest is compounded during the year, these steps can be summarized simply as:

$$\text{EAR} = [1 + (\text{Quoted rate}/m)]^m - 1 \tag{5.6}$$

For example, suppose you are offered 12 per cent compounded monthly. In this case, the interest is compounded 12 times a year; so m is 12. You can calculate the effective rate as:

$$\begin{aligned}\text{EAR} &= [1 + (\text{Quoted rate}/m)]^m - 1 \\ &= [1 + (0.12/12)]^{12} - 1 \\ &= 1.01^{12} - 1 \\ &= 1.126825 - 1 \\ &= 12.6825\%\end{aligned}$$

EXAMPLE 5.8

WHAT'S THE EAR?

A bank is offering 12 per cent compounded quarterly. If you put £100 in an account, how much will you have at the end of one year? What's the EAR? How much will you have at the end of two years?

The bank is effectively offering 12%/4 = 3% every quarter. If you invest £100 for four periods at 3 per cent per period, the future value is:

$$\begin{aligned}\text{Future value} &= £100 \times 1.03^4 \\ &= £100 \times 1.1255 \\ &= £112.55\end{aligned}$$

The EAR is 12.55 per cent: £100 × (1 + 0.1255) = £112.55.

We can determine what you would have at the end of two years in two different ways. One way is to recognize that two years is the same as eight quarters. At 3 per cent per quarter, after eight quarters, you would have:

$$£100 \times 1.03^8 = £100 \times 1.2668 = £126.68$$

Alternatively, we could determine the value after two years by using an EAR of 12.55 per cent; so after two years you would have:

$$£100 \times 1.1255^2 = £100 \times 1.2688 = £126.68$$

Thus the two calculations produce the same answer. This illustrates an important point. Whenever we do a present or future value calculation, the rate we use must be an actual or effective rate. In this case the actual rate is 3 per cent per quarter. The effective annual percentage rate is 12.55 per cent. It doesn't matter which one we use once we know the EAR.

EXAMPLE 5.9

QUOTING A RATE

Now that you know how to convert a quoted rate to an EAR, consider going the other way. As a lender, you know you want to actually earn 18 per cent on a particular loan. You want to quote a rate that features monthly compounding. What rate do you quote?

In this case we know the EAR is 18 per cent, and we know this is the result of monthly compounding. Let q stand for the quoted rate. We thus have:

$$\text{EAR} = \left[1 + (\text{Quoted Rate}/m)\right]^m - 1$$
$$0.18 = \left[1 + (q/12)\right]^{12} - 1$$
$$1.18 = \left[1 + (q/12)\right]^{12}$$

We need to solve this equation for the quoted rate. This calculation is the same as the ones we did to find an unknown interest rate in Chapter 4:

$$1.18^{(1/12)} = 1 + (q/12)$$
$$1.18^{0.083333} = 1 + (q/12)$$
$$1.0139 = 1 + (q/12)$$
$$q = 0.0139 \times 12$$
$$= 16.68\%$$

Therefore the rate you would quote is 16.68 per cent, compounded monthly.

THE ANNUAL PERCENTAGE RATE

Given the many different ways in which interest rates can be presented to the public, the European Union introduced a directive in 2010 that harmonized the way in which interest rates in any credit agreement for under €75,000 are presented. The UK extended the directive to all regulated loans, and the Netherlands also uses it for mortgage loans. This harmonized interest rate is the **annual percentage rate (APR)**, and it expresses the *total* cost of borrowing or investing as a percentage interest rate.

> **annual percentage rate (APR)**
> the harmonized interest rate that expresses the total cost of borrowing or investing as a percentage interest rate.

The reason for an APR is that a credit agreement may include not only interest payments, but also management fees, arrangement fees and other sundry costs that will affect the total charge for credit (TCC). In addition, knowledge of the interest rate is still not enough to guarantee full comparability of different loans or investments. As shown above, the compounding frequency and the date when interest is charged will influence the effective annual rate of interest.

Under the EU directive, all providers of credit must show the APR prominently in any document or advertising material that promotes a particular type of loan or investment. To calculate APR, we use the standard present value formula. The main difference is in the cash flows that are included in the calculation.

$$\text{PV} = C_o + \frac{C_1}{1 + APR} + \frac{C_2}{(1 + APR)^2} + \ldots + \frac{C_T}{(1 + APR)^T}$$
$$= C_o + \sum_{i=1}^{T} \frac{C_i}{(1 + APR)^i}$$

(5.7)

EXAMPLE 5.10

ANNUAL PERCENTAGE RATE

After much deliberation, Mary Moan decides to buy a new Mercedes-Benz car for her family. The sale price of the car is £30,000. Mary arranges financing through the Mercedes dealer, who quotes a simple annual interest rate of 12 per cent on the original borrowed amount over three years, payable in 36 monthly instalments. This means that the lender will charge 12 per cent interest on the original loan of £30,000 every year for three years. Each year, the interest charge will be £3,600 (12 per cent of £30,000), making a total interest payment of £10,800 over three years.

The regular monthly instalments that Mary must pay are:

$$\text{Monthly instalment} = (£30{,}000 + £10{,}800)/36 = £1{,}133.33$$

In addition to the interest payments, the Mercedes dealer charges a £250 administration fee, which must be paid when the financing agreement is made. We now solve for APR in Equation 5.7:

$$£30{,}000 = £250 + \frac{£1{,}133.33}{(1 + \text{APR})^{1/12}} + \frac{£1{,}133.33}{(1 + \text{APR})^{2/12}} + \cdots + \frac{£1{,}133.33}{(1 + \text{APR})^{36/12}}$$

This gives an annual percentage rate (APR) of 24.13 per cent! The lender must also state the total amount paid at the end of the loan, which in this case is £41,049.88, and the total charge for credit is £11,049.88 (£41,049.88 − £30,000).

The definition used by the European Union for APR is very different from the formula used in the United States, and this can cause considerable confusion when European students read finance textbooks aimed at an American market. In the US, the APR is simply the stated annual interest rate. Remember this if you ever plan to take out a loan overseas!

REAL WORLD INSIGHTS

What is a good interest rate for a loan? This all depends on whether you are an individual or a company, have a good history of making payments on time, or have missed payments on previous loans. It also matters if your company is very large or a start-up.

Let's start with individuals. If you borrow from a bank with an unsecured loan, interest rates will likely be around 10 per cent APR, but only if you have good credit. If your credit history has some missed payments or defaults, then expect a much higher rate (up to 40 per cent). There are some companies that lend till the end of a month (these are called pay-day loans because you are borrowing until you receive your next wages) and APRs can be as high as 2,000 per cent. Fortunately, governments are cracking down on these types of loans and it is hoped that such high interest rates will become illegal in time.

Companies have a different experience when borrowing because they have a much bigger asset value. For some exceptionally large companies, like BP, Vodafone, Apple, and Intel, interest rates can be almost the same as government borrowing rates. That is, they are almost risk free.

TAKING IT TO THE LIMIT: A NOTE ABOUT CONTINUOUS COMPOUNDING

If you made a deposit in a savings account, how often could your money be compounded during the year? If you think about it, there isn't really any upper limit. We've seen that daily compounding, for example, isn't a problem. There is no reason to stop here, however. We could compound every hour or minute or second. How high would the EAR get in this case? Table 5.3 illustrates the EARs that result as 10 per cent is compounded at shorter and shorter intervals. Notice that the EARs do keep getting larger, but the differences get very small.

As the numbers in Table 5.3 seem to suggest, there is an upper limit to the EAR. If we let q stand for the quoted rate, then, as the number of times the interest is compounded gets extremely large, the EAR approaches:

$$\text{EAR} = e^q - 1 \tag{5.8}$$

where e is the number 2.71828 (look for a key labelled 'e^x' on your calculator). For example, with our 10 per cent rate, the highest possible EAR is:

$$\begin{align}\text{EAR} &= e^q - 1 \\ &= 2.71828^{.10} - 1 \\ &= 1.1051709 - 1 \\ &= 10.51709\%\end{align}$$

In this case we say that the money is continuously, or instantaneously, compounded. Interest is being credited the instant it is earned, so the amount of interest grows continuously.

TABLE 5.3

Compounding frequency and effective annual rates

Compounding period	Number of times compounded	Effective annual rate (%)
Year	1	10.00000
Quarter	4	10.38129
Month	12	10.47131
Week	52	10.50648
Day	365	10.51558
Hour	8,760	10.51703
Minute	525,600	10.51709

CONCEPT QUESTIONS

5.3a If an interest rate is given as 12 per cent compounded daily, what do we call this rate?
5.3b What is an APR? What is an EAR? Are they the same thing?
5.3c In general, what is the relationship between a stated interest rate and an effective interest rate? Which is more relevant for financial decisions?
5.3d What does continuous compounding mean?

5.4 LOAN TYPES AND LOAN AMORTIZATION

Whenever a lender extends a loan, some provision will be made for repayment of the principal (the original loan amount). A loan might be repaid in equal instalments, for example, or it might be repaid in a single lump sum. Because the way that the principal and interest are paid is up to the parties involved, there are actually an unlimited number of possibilities.

In this section we describe a few forms of repayment that come up quite often, and more complicated forms can usually be built up from these. The three basic types of loan are pure discount loans, interest-only loans and amortized loans. Working with these loans is a very straightforward application of the present value principles that we have already developed.

PURE DISCOUNT LOANS

The *pure discount loan* is the simplest form of loan. With such a loan the borrower receives money today, and repays a single lump sum at some time in the future. A one-year, 10 per cent pure discount loan, for example, would require the borrower to repay £1.10 in one year for every pound borrowed today.

Because a pure discount loan is so simple, we already know how to value one. Suppose a borrower was able to repay £25,000 in five years. If we, acting as the lender, wanted a 12 per cent interest rate on the loan, how much would we be willing to lend? Put another way, what value would we assign today to that £25,000 to be repaid in five years? Based on our work in Chapter 4, we know the answer is just the present value of £25,000 at 12 per cent for five years:

$$\text{Present value} = £25,000/1.12^5$$
$$= £25,000/1.7623$$
$$= £14,186$$

Pure discount loans are common when the loan term is short – say a year or less. In recent years they have become increasingly common for much longer periods.

EXAMPLE 5.11

TREASURY BILLS

When a government borrows money on a short-term basis (a year or less), it does so by selling what are called *Treasury bills*, or *T-bills* for short. A T-bill is a promise by the government to repay a fixed amount at some time in the future - for example, 3 months or 12 months.

Treasury bills are pure discount loans. If a T-bill promises to repay £10,000 in 12 months, and the market interest rate is 7 per cent, how much will the bill sell for in the market?

Because the going rate is 7 per cent, the T-bill will sell for the present value of £10,000 to be repaid in one year at 7 per cent:

$$\text{Present value} = £10,000/1.07 = £9,345.79$$

INTEREST-ONLY LOANS

A second type of loan repayment plan calls for the borrower to pay interest each period, and to repay the entire principal (the original loan amount) at some point in the future. Loans with such a repayment plan are called *interest-only loans*. Notice that if there is just one period, a pure discount loan and an interest-only loan are the same thing.

For example, with a three-year, 10 per cent, interest-only loan of €1,000, the borrower would pay €1,000 × 0.10 = €100 in interest at the end of the first and second years. At the end of the third year the borrower would return the €1,000 along with another €100 in interest for that year. Similarly, a 50-year interest-only loan would call for the borrower to pay interest every year for the next 50 years, and then repay the principal. In the extreme, the borrower pays the interest every period for ever and never repays any principal. As we discussed earlier in the chapter, the result is a perpetuity.

Most corporate bonds have the general form of an interest-only loan. Because we shall be considering bonds in some detail in the next chapter, we shall defer further discussion of them for now.

AMORTIZED LOANS

With a pure discount or interest-only loan the principal is repaid all at once. An alternative is an *amortized loan*, with which the lender may require the borrower to repay parts of the loan amount over time. The process of providing for a loan to be paid off by making regular principal reductions is called *amortizing* the loan.

A simple way of amortizing a loan is to have the borrower pay the interest each period, plus some fixed amount. This approach is common with medium-term business loans. For example, suppose a business takes out a £5,000, five-year loan at 9 per cent. The loan agreement calls for the borrower to pay the interest on the loan balance each year, and to reduce the loan balance each year by £1,000. Because the loan amount declines by £1,000 each year, it is fully paid in five years.

In the case we are considering, notice that the total payment will decline each year. The reason is that the loan balance goes down, resulting in a lower interest charge each year, whereas the £1,000 principal reduction is constant. For example, the interest in the first year will be £5,000 × 0.09 = £450. The total payment will be £1,000 + 450 = £1,450. In the second year the loan balance is £4,000, so the interest is £4,000 × 0.09 = £360, and the total payment is £1,360. We can calculate the total payment in each of the remaining years by preparing a simple *amortization schedule* as follows:

Year	Beginning balance (£)	Total payment (£)	Interest paid (£)	Principal paid (£)	Ending balance (£)
1	5,000	1,450	450	1,000	4,000
2	4,000	1,360	360	1,000	3,000
3	3,000	1,270	270	1,000	2,000
4	2,000	1,180	180	1,000	1,000
5	1,000	1,090	90	1,000	0
Totals		£6,350	£1,350	£5,000	

Notice that in each year the interest paid is given by the beginning balance multiplied by the interest rate. Also notice that the beginning balance is given by the ending balance from the previous year.

Probably the most common way of amortizing a loan is to have the borrower make a single, fixed payment every period. Almost all consumer loans (such as car loans) and mortgages work this way. For example, suppose our five-year, 9 per cent, £5,000 loan was amortized this way. How would the amortization schedule look?

We first need to determine the payment. From our discussion earlier in the chapter we know that this loan's cash flows are in the form of an ordinary annuity. In this case, we can solve for the payment as follows:

$$£5,000 = C \times \{[1 - (1/1.09^5)]/0.09\}$$
$$= C \times [(1 - 0.6499)/0.09]$$

This gives us:

$$C = £5,000/3.8897$$
$$= £1,285.46$$

The borrower will therefore make five equal payments of £1,285.46. Will this pay off the loan? We shall check by filling in an amortization schedule.

In our previous example we knew the principal reduction each year. We then calculated the interest owed to get the total payment. In this example we know the total payment. We shall thus calculate the interest, and then subtract it from the total payment to calculate the principal portion in each payment.

In the first year the interest is £450, as we calculated before. Because the total payment is £1,285.46, the principal paid in the first year must be:

$$\text{Principal paid} = £1,285.46 - 450 = £835.46$$

The ending loan balance is thus:

$$\text{Ending balance} = £5,000 - 835.46 = £4,164.54$$

The interest in the second year is £4,164.54 × 0.09 = £374.81, and the loan balance declines by £1,285.46 − 374.81 = £910.65. We can summarize all of the relevant calculations in the following schedule:

Year	Beginning balance (£)	Total payment (£)	Interest paid (£)	Principal paid (£)	Ending balance (£)
1	5,000.00	1,285.46	450.00	835.46	4,164.54
2	4,164.54	1,285.46	374.81	910.65	3,253.88
3	3,253.88	1,285.46	292.85	992.61	2,261.27
4	2,261.27	1,285.46	203.51	1,081.95	1,179.32
5	1,179.32	1,285.46	106.14	1,179.32	0.00
Totals		6,427.30	1,427.31	5,000.00	

Because the loan balance declines to zero, the five equal payments do pay off the loan. Notice that the interest paid declines each period. This isn't surprising, because the loan balance is going down. Given that the total payment is fixed, the principal paid must be rising each period.

If you compare the two loan amortizations in this section, you will see that the total interest is greater for the equal total payment case: £1,427.31 versus £1,350. The reason for this is that the loan is repaid more slowly early on, so the interest is somewhat higher. This doesn't mean that one loan is better than the other; it simply means that one is effectively paid off faster than the other. For example, the principal reduction in the first year is £835.46 in the equal total payment case as compared to £1,000 in the first case.

EXAMPLE 5.12

PARTIAL AMORTIZATION, OR 'BITE THE BULLET'

A common arrangement in property lending might call for a 5-year loan with, say, a 15-year amortization. What this means is that the borrower makes a payment every month of a fixed amount based on a 15-year amortization. However, after 60 months the borrower makes a single, much larger payment called a 'balloon' or 'bullet' to pay off the loan. Because the monthly payments don't fully pay off the loan, the loan is said to be partially amortized.

Suppose we have a €100,000 commercial mortgage with a 1 per cent monthly effective interest rate and a 20-year (240-month) amortization. Further suppose the mortgage has a five-year balloon. What will the monthly payment be? How big will the balloon payment be?

The monthly payment can be calculated based on an ordinary annuity with a present value of €100,000. There are 240 payments, and the interest rate is 1 per cent per month. The payment is:

$$€100,000 = C \times \{[1 - (1/1.01^{240})]/0.01\}$$
$$= C \times 90.8194$$
$$C = €1,101.09$$

Now there is an easy way and a hard way to determine the balloon payment. The hard way is to actually amortize the loan for 60 months to see what the balance is at that time. The easy way is to recognize that, after 60 months, we have a 240 − 60 = 180-month loan. The payment is still €1,101.09 per month, and the interest rate is still 1 per cent per month. The loan balance is thus the present value of the remaining payments:

$$\text{Loan balance} = €1,101.09 \times \{[1 - (1/1.01^{180})]/0.01\}$$
$$= €1,101.09 \times 83.3217$$
$$= €91,744.69$$

The balloon payment is a substantial €91,744. Why is it so large? To get an idea, consider the first payment on the mortgage. The interest in the first month is €100,000 × 0.01 = €1,000. Your payment is €1,101.09, so the loan balance declines by only €101.09. Because the loan balance declines so slowly, the cumulative 'pay down' over five years is not great.

SPREADSHEET STRATEGIES 5.4

Loan Amortization Using a Spreadsheet

Loan amortization is a common spreadsheet application. To illustrate, we shall set up the problem that we examined earlier: a five-year, £5,000, 9 per cent loan with constant payments. Our spreadsheet looks like this:

	A	B
1	Loan Amount	£5,000
2	Interest Rate	9%
3	Loan Term	5
4	Loan Payment	£1,285.46
5		
6		

Loan payment formula: = PMT(B2,B3,−B1)

	A	B	C	D	E	F
6	Year	Beginning Balance	Total Payment	Interest Paid	Principal Paid	Ending Balance
7	1	£5,000	£1,285.46	£450	£835.46	£4,165
8	2	£4,165	£1,285.46	£374.809	£910.65	£3,254
9	3	£3,254	£1,285.46	£292.85	£992.61	£2,261
10	4	£2,261	£1,285.46	£203.515	£1,081.94	£1,179
11	5	£1,179	£1,285.46	£106.14	£1,179.32	£0
12	Totals		£6,427.30	£1427.31	£4,999.99	
13						
14						

Notice the slight rounding error in cell E12, which sometimes happens when one uses spreadsheets.

Year	Beginning balance (£)	Total payment (£)	Interest paid (£)	Principal paid (£)	Ending balance (£)
1	= B1	= B4	= B7*B2	= C7-D7	= B7-E7
2	= F7	= B4	= B8*B2	= C8-D8	= B8-E8
3	= F8	= B4	= B9*B2	= C9-D9	= B9-E9
4	= F9	= B4	= B10*B2	= C10-D10	= B10-E10
5	= F10	= B4	= B11*B2	= C11-D11	= B11-E11
Totals		= SUM(C7:C11)	= SUM(D7:D11)	= SUM(E7:E11)	

CONCEPT QUESTIONS

5.4a What is a pure discount loan? An interest-only loan?
5.4b What does it mean to amortize a loan?
5.4c What is a balloon payment? How do you determine its value?

> **REAL WORLD INSIGHTS**
>
> There are so many mortgages available to consumers that it is easy to get confused. Below is listed a couple of potential choices that are available to home-buyers:
>
> - Fixed Rate Mortgage: Provides you with an interest rate that will stay the same for the fixed term you choose. Example terms are 2, 3, 5 or even 10 years. At the end of the term, you can agree to a new fixed-rate for a set period or move to a tracker mortgage, where the interest rate is tied to a published benchmark rate, usually the bank's standard variable rate.
> - Offset Mortgage: Links your bank accounts to your mortgage in order to reduce the mortgage balance you're charged interest on. So, if your mortgage balance is £250,000 and you have £15,000 in your bank account, the monthly interest is based on (£250,000 − £15,000) = £235,000.

SUMMARY AND CONCLUSIONS

This chapter rounded out your understanding of fundamental concepts related to the time value of money and discounted cash flow valuation. Several important topics were covered:

1. There are two ways of calculating present and future values when there are multiple cash flows. Both approaches are straightforward extensions of our earlier analysis of single cash flows.
2. A series of constant cash flows that arrive or are paid at the end of each period is called an ordinary annuity, and we described some useful shortcuts for determining the present and future values of annuities.
3. Interest rates can be quoted in a variety of ways. For financial decisions, it is important that any rates being compared be first converted to effective rates. The relationship between a quoted rate and an effective annual rate (EAR) is given by:

$$\text{EAR} = \left[1 + (\text{Quoted Rate}/m)\right]^m - 1$$

   where m is the number of times during the year the money is compounded or, equivalently, the number of payments during the year.
4. Many loans are annuities. The process of providing for a loan to be paid off gradually is called amortizing the loan, and we discussed how amortization schedules are prepared and interpreted.
5. The annual percentage rate (APR) is used by countries in the European Union to provide a consistent way of presenting interest rates that have been applied to loans. The APR should include all fees and charges related to setting up a loan. The expression is:

$$\text{PV} = C_o + \frac{C_1}{1 + \text{APR}} + \frac{C_2}{(1 + \text{APR})^2} + \cdots + \frac{C_T}{(1 + \text{APR})^T}$$
$$= C_o + \sum_{i=1}^{T} \frac{C_i}{(1 + \text{APR})^i}$$

The principles developed in this chapter will figure prominently in the chapters to come. The reason for this is that most investments, whether they involve real assets or financial assets, can be analysed using the discounted cash flow (DCF) approach. As a result, the DCF approach is broadly applicable and widely used in practice. For example, the next two chapters show how to value bonds and shares using an extension of the techniques presented in this chapter. Before going on, therefore, you might want to do some of the problems that follow.

CHAPTER REVIEW AND SELF-TEST PROBLEMS

5.1 Present Values with Multiple Cash Flows A top footballer has been signed to a three-year, £10 million contract. The details provide for an immediate cash bonus of £2 million. The player is to receive £2 million in salary at the end of the first year, £3 million the next, and £3 million at the end of the last year. Assuming a 15 per cent discount rate, is this package worth £10 million? If not, how much is it worth?

5.2 Future Value with Multiple Cash Flows You plan to make a series of deposits in an individual retirement account. You will deposit £1,000 today, £2,000 in two years, and £2,000 in five years. If you withdraw £1,500 in three years and £1,000 in seven years, assuming no withdrawal penalties, how much will you have after eight years if the interest rate is 7 per cent? What is the present value of these cash flows?

5.3 Annuity Present Value You are looking into an investment that will pay you €12,000 per year for the next 10 years. If you require a 15 per cent return, what is the most you would pay for this investment?

5.4 It's the Principal that Matters Suppose you borrow £10,000. You are going to repay the loan by making equal annual payments for five years. The interest rate on the loan is 14 per cent per year. Prepare an amortization schedule for the loan. How much interest will you pay over the life of the loan?

5.5 Just a Little Bit Each Month You've recently finished your MBA. Naturally, you must purchase a new BMW immediately. The car costs about £21,000. The bank quotes a nominal annual interest rate of 15 per cent for a 72-month loan with a 10 per cent down payment. You plan on trading the car in for a new one in two years. What will your monthly payment be? What is the effective interest rate on the loan? What will the loan balance be when you trade the car in?

SOLUTIONS

5.1 Obviously, the package is not worth £10 million, because the payments are spread out over three years. The bonus is paid today, so it's worth £2 million. The present values for the three subsequent salary payments are:

$$(£2/1.15) + (3/1.15^2) + (3/1.15^3) = (2/1.15) + (3/1.32) + (3/1.52)$$
$$= £5.99 \text{ million}$$

The package is worth a total of £5.99 million.

5.2 We shall calculate the future values for each of the cash flows separately, and then add them up. Notice that we treat the withdrawals as negative cash flows:

$$\begin{array}{rcl}
£1,000 \times 1.07^8 = & £1,000 \times 1.7812 = & £1,718.19 \\
£2,000 \times 1.07^6 = & £2,000 \times 1.5007 = & £3,001.46 \\
-£1,500 \times 1.07^5 = & -£1,500 \times 1.4026 = & -£2,103.83 \\
£2,000 \times 1.07^3 = & £2,000 \times 1.2250 = & £2,450.09 \\
-£1,000 \times 1.07^1 = & -£1,000 \times 1.0700 = & \underline{-£1,070.00} \\
& \text{Total future value} & \underline{£3,995.91}
\end{array}$$

This value includes a small rounding error.

To calculate the present value, we could discount each cash flow back to the present, or we could discount back a single year at a time. However, because we already know that the future value in eight years is £3,995.91, the easy way to get the PV is just to discount this amount back eight years:

$$\text{Present value} = £3{,}995.91/1.07^8$$
$$= £3{,}995.91/1.7182$$
$$= £2{,}325.64$$

We again ignore a small rounding error. For practice, you can verify that this is what you get if you discount each cash flow back separately.

5.3 The most you would be willing to pay is the present value of €12,000 per year for 10 years at a 15 per cent discount rate. The cash flows here are in ordinary annuity form, so the relevant present value factor is:

$$\text{Annuity present value factor} = (1 - \text{Present value factor})/r$$
$$= [1 - (1/1.15^{10})]/0.15$$
$$= (1 - 0.2472)/0.15$$
$$= 5.0188$$

The present value of the 10 cash flows is thus:

$$\text{Present value} = €12{,}000 \times 5.0188$$
$$= €60{,}225$$

This is the most you would pay.

5.4 We first need to calculate the annual payment. With a present value of £10,000, an interest rate of 14 per cent, and a term of five years, the payment can be determined from:

$$£10{,}000 = \text{Payment} \times \{[1 - (1/1.14^5)]/0.14\}$$
$$= \text{Payment} \times 3.4331$$

Therefore the payment is £10,000/3.4331 = £2,912.84 (actually, it's £2,912.8355; this will create some small rounding errors in the following schedule). We can now prepare the amortization schedule as follows:

Year	Beginning balance (£)	Total payment (£)	Interest paid (£)	Principal paid (£)	Ending balance (£)
1	10,000.00	2,912.84	1,400.00	1,512.84	8,487.16
2	8,487.16	2,912.84	1,188.20	1,724.63	6,762.53
3	6,762.53	2,912.84	946.75	1,966.08	4,796.45
4	4,796.45	2,912.84	671.50	2,241.33	2,555.12
5	2,555.12	2,912.84	357.72	2,555.12	0.00
Totals		14,564.17	4,564.17	10,000.00	

5.5 The cash flows on the car loan are in annuity form, so we need to find only the payment. The interest rate is 15%/12 = 1.25% per month, and there are 72 months. The first thing we need is the annuity factor for 72 periods at 1.25 per cent per period:

$$\text{Annuity present value factor} = (1 - \text{Present value factor})/r$$
$$= [1 - (1/1.0125^{72})]/0.0125$$
$$= [1 - (1/2.4459)]/0.0125$$
$$= [1 - 0.4088]/0.0125$$
$$= 47.2925$$

The present value is the amount we finance. With a 10 per cent down payment, we shall be borrowing 90 per cent of £21,000, or £18,900. To find the payment, we need to solve for C:

$$£18,900 = C \times \text{Annuity present value factor}$$
$$= C \times 47.2925$$

Rearranging things a bit, we have:

$$C = £18,900 \times (1/47.2925)$$
$$= £18,900 \times 0.02115$$
$$= £399.64$$

Your payment is just under £400 per month.

The actual interest rate on this loan is 1.25 per cent per month. Based on our work in the chapter, we can calculate the effective annual rate as:

$$\text{EAR} = (1.0125)^{12} - 1 = 16.08\%$$

The effective rate is about one point higher than the quoted rate.

To determine the loan balance in two years, we could amortize the loan to see what the balance is at that time. This would be fairly tedious to do by hand. Using the information already determined in this problem, we can instead simply calculate the present value of the remaining payments. After two years, we have made 24 payments, so there are 72 − 24 = 48 payments left. What is the present value of 48 monthly payments of £399.64 at 1.25 per cent per month? The relevant annuity factor is:

$$\text{Annuity present value factor} = (1 - \text{Present value factor})/r$$
$$= [1 - (1/1.0125^{48})]/0.0125$$
$$= [1 - (1/1.8154)]/0.0125$$
$$= (1 - 0.5509)/0.0125$$
$$= 35.9315$$

The present value is thus:

$$\text{Present value} = £399.64 \times 35.9315 = £14,359.66$$

You will owe about £14,360 on the loan in two years.

QUESTIONS AND PROBLEMS

5.1 **Present Value and Multiple Cash Flows** Investment X offers to pay you £6,000 per year for nine years, whereas Investment Y offers to pay you £8,000 per year for six years. Which of these cash flow streams has the higher present value if the discount rate is 5 per cent? If the discount rate is 15 per cent?

5.2 **Future Value and Multiple Cash Flows** Herlige Narren AS has identified an investment project with the following cash flows. If the discount rate is 10 per cent, what is the future value of these cash flows at the end of year 5? What is the future value at a discount rate of 15 per cent? At 20 per cent? Assume all the cash flows have occurred at the beginning of the year.

Year	Cash flow (DKK)
1	950
2	1,190
3	1,540
4	1,905

5.3 **Calculating Annuity Present Value** An investment offers €4,000 per year for 10 years, with the first payment occurring one year from now. If the required return is 9 per cent, what is the value of the investment? What would the value be if the payments occurred for 20 years? For 50 years? For ever?

5.4 **Present Value** A 25-year fixed-rate mortgage has monthly payments of €717 per month and a mortgage interest rate of 6.14 per cent per year compounded monthly. If a buyer purchases a home with the cash proceeds of the mortgage loan plus an additional 20 per cent deposit, what is the purchase price of the home? Assume that the additional deposit amount is 20 per cent of the mortgage loan amount.

5.5 **Calculating Annuity Values** You want to have DKr450,000 in your savings account 10 years from now, and you're prepared to make equal annual deposits into the account at the end of the year. If the account pays 7 per cent interest, what must you deposit each year?

5.6 **Perpetuities** An investor purchasing a British consol is entitled to receive annual payments from the British government forever. What is the price of a consol that pays £4 annually if the next payment occurs one year from today? The market interest rate is 4 per cent.

5.7 **Calculating EAR** Find the EAR in each of the cases below.

Stated rate (APR)	Number of times compounded
4%	Quarterly
8%	Monthly
12%	Daily
16%	Infinite

5.8 **Continuous Compounding** A zero coupon bond that will pay €1,000 is selling today at €422.41. What is the continuously compounded annual interest rate on the bond?

5.9 **Calculating Future Values** If you invest €1,000 in a savings account that pays 4 per cent every year, how long would it take to triple your money?

5.10 **Calculating Present Values** An investment will pay you £58,000 in seven years. If the appropriate discount rate is 10 per cent compounded daily, what is the present value?

5.11 **Calculating EAR** Friendly's Quick Loans offers you 'three for four or I knock on your door'. This means you get £3 today and repay £4 when you get your wages in 1 week (or else). What's the effective annual return Friendly's earns on this lending business? If you were brave enough to ask, what quoted rate would Friendly's say you were paying?

5.12 **Calculating Annuity Future Values** You are planning to make monthly deposits of £400 into a retirement account that pays 7 per cent interest compounded monthly. If your first deposit will be made 1 month from now, how large will your retirement account be in 40 years?

5.13 **Calculating Annuity Present Values** Beginning three months from now, you want to be able to withdraw €1,200 each quarter from your bank account to cover university expenses over the next four years. If the account pays 2 per cent interest per quarter, how much do you need to have in your bank account today to meet your expense needs over the next 4 years? Assume the money is withdrawn at the beginning of the quarter.

5.14 **Discounted Cash Flow Analysis** If the appropriate discount rate for the following cash flows is 10 per cent per year, what is the present value of the cash flows? Assume cash flows are generated at the end of the year.

Year	Cash flow (£)
1	1,650
2	1,000
3	5,200
4	1,430

5.15 **Calculating Annuities** You are planning to save for retirement over the next 40 years. To do this, you will invest £1,000 a month in a share account and £1,000 a month in a bond account. The return of the share account is expected to be 6 per cent, and the bond account will pay 2 per cent. When you retire, you will combine your money into an account with a 5 per cent return. How much can you withdraw each month from your account, assuming a 25-year withdrawal period?

5.16 **Effective Annual Rate** You have been charged with putting together a redundancy package for a departing executive. The executive has asked for the following:

(a) The present value of the next two years' lost pay. The executive's current annual salary is £120,000 and a historical salary growth is 5 per cent per annum.

(b) £100,000 for reputation and non-disclosure contract.

(c) £20,000 non-competition agreement.

If the effective annual interest rate is 6 per cent, what is the size of the settlement? If you were the departing employee, would you like to see a higher or lower interest rate?

5.17 **Calculating Future Values** You have an investment that will pay you 2 per cent per month. How much will you have per euro invested in 1 year? 2 years?

5.18 **Calculating Rates of Return** Suppose an investment offers to triple your money in 12 months (don't believe it). Assume the rate is compounded quarterly. What rate of return per quarter are you being offered?

5.19 **Growing Perpetuity** Oasis Pods has been working on a new sustainable business that uses plastic waste to create standard office pods that can be placed in free spaces in a building. The new office pod technology has now been cleared for manufacture and development. Oasis Pods anticipates the first annual cash flow from the office pods to be €2,000,000, received 2 years from today. Subsequent annual cash flows will grow at 10 per cent in perpetuity. What is the present value of the new technology if the discount rate is 16 per cent?

5.20 **Present Value and Interest Rates** What is the relationship between the value of an annuity and the level of interest rates? Suppose you just bought a 20-year annuity of £19,000 per year at the current interest rate of 8 per cent per year. What happens to the value of your investment if interest rates suddenly drop to 3 per cent? What if interest rates suddenly rise to 13 per cent?

5.21 **Calculating Present Values** A 3-year annuity of six £5,000 semi-annual payments will begin 10 years from now, with the first payment coming 10.5 years from now. If the discount rate is 10 per cent compounded monthly, what is the value of the annuity 5 years from now, 3 years from now and its current value?

5.22 **Balloon Payments** You have just set up a new offsite catering business and purchased a warehouse facility to cook meals before sending out through food delivery apps. The cost of the warehouse is £1,000,000 and the seller requires a 20 per cent up-front payment. Although you can afford to pay the up-front payment, you will need to take out a mortgage loan to fund the remaining amount. A bank has offered you a 20-year mortgage with fixed payments. The APR of the mortgage loan is 4 per cent and you will be expected to make monthly payments (the first payment is due one month from now) over the life of the loan. To make the loan more attractive, the bank has given you the option of a 10-year balloon payment on the remaining balance of the load at that time. There are no other transaction costs or finance charges. How much will the balloon payment be in 10 years?

5.23 Interest You work for a jewellers and have sourced a good goldsmith who is able to sell you 100 ounces of gold for £100,000. You approach your two main customers. Mr Noel says he will buy the gold from you in 6 months for £104,000, whereas Ms Biggs tells you that she will be able to buy the gold from you in 2 years' time for £116,000. What is the annual percentage rate that Mr Noel and Ms Biggs are offering you?

5.24 Comparing Cash Flows You have your choice of two investment accounts. Investment A is a 20-year annuity that features end-of-month NKr12,000 payments and has an interest rate of 6 per cent compounded monthly. Investment B is an 8 per cent continuously compounded lump sum investment, also good for 15 years. How much money would you need to invest in B today for it to be worth as much as investment A 20 years from now?

5.25 Calculating APR A local finance company quotes a 12 per cent interest rate on one-year loans. So, if you borrow €20,000, the interest for the year will be €2,400. Because you must repay a total of €22,400 in one year, the finance company requires you to pay €22,400/12, or €1,867, per month over the next 12 months. Is this a 12 per cent loan? What rate would legally have to be quoted?

5.26 Annuities You have just turned 22 and you decide to play the stock market. Your fantastic corporate finance textbook leads you to believe that you can earn 10 per cent per annum from investing in equities. How much must you invest each year in order to become a millionaire in 40 years? You have decided that investing each year will be boring and so you just want to invest an amount today and leave it in an account for 40 years. How much should you invest today?

5.27 Annuities A couple will retire in 50 years; they plan to spend about £50,000 a year in retirement, which should last about 25 years. They believe that they can earn 4 per cent interest on retirement savings.

(a) If they make annual payments into a savings plan, how much will they need to save each year? Assume the first payment comes in one year.

(b) How would the answer to part (a) change if the couple also realizes that in 20 years, they will need to spend £30,000 on their child's college education?

5.28 Calculating Annuity Values You are serving on a jury. A plaintiff is suing the city for injuries sustained after a freak accident. In the trial, doctors testified that it will be 5 years before the plaintiff is able to return to work. The jury has already decided in favour of the plaintiff. You are the foreperson of the jury and propose that the jury give the plaintiff an award to cover the following:

(a) The present value of 2 years' back pay. The plaintiff's annual salary for the last 2 years would have been €25,000 and €28,000, respectively.

(b) The present value of 5 years' future salary. You assume the salary will be €28,000 per year.

(c) €100,000 for pain, suffering and humiliation.

(d) €20,000 for court costs.

Assume that the salary payments are equal amounts paid at the end of each month. If the interest rate you choose is a 4 per cent APR, what is the size of the settlement? If you were the plaintiff, would you like to see a higher or lower interest rate?

5.29 Discount Interest Rates This question illustrates what is known as *discount interest*. Imagine you are discussing a loan with a somewhat unscrupulous lender. You want to borrow £25,000 for one year. The interest rate is 15 per cent. You and the lender agree that the interest on the loan will be

0.15 × £25,000 = £3,750. So the lender deducts this interest amount from the loan up front and gives you £21,250. In this case, we say that the discount is £3,750. What is the correct interest rate to pay on the amount, assuming that all the other data in the question is correct?

5.30 Calculating EAR with Points You are looking at a one-year loan of €10,000. The interest rate is quoted as 8 per cent plus three points. A point on a loan is simply 1 per cent (one percentage point) of the loan amount. Quotes similar to this one are common with home mortgages. The interest rate quotation in this example requires the borrower to pay three points to the lender up front and repay the loan later with 8 per cent interest. What rate would you actually be paying here?

5.31 EAR versus APR Two banks in the area offer 30-year, £240,000 mortgages at 6.8 per cent quoted rate and charge a £2,300 loan application fee. However, the application fee charged by Insecurity Bank and Trust is refundable if the loan application is denied, whereas that charged by I.M. Greedy and Sons Mortgage Bank is not. The current disclosure law requires that any fees that will be refunded if the applicant is rejected be included in calculating the APR, but this is not required with non-refundable fees (presumably because refundable fees are part of the loan rather than a fee). What are the EARs on these two loans, assuming monthly mortgage payments?

5.32 Calculating Annuity Due You want to lease a set of golf clubs from Pings Ltd. The lease contract is in the form of 36 equal monthly payments at a 14 per cent stated annual interest rate, compounded monthly. Because the clubs cost £4,000 retail, Pings wants the PV of the lease payments to equal £4,000. Suppose that your first payment is due immediately. What will your monthly lease payments be?

5.33 Future Value and Multiple Cash Flows An insurance company is offering a new policy to its customers. Typically, the policy is bought by a parent or grandparent for a child at the child's birth. The details of the policy are as follows: The purchaser (say, the parent) makes the following six payments to the insurance company:

First birthday:	£ 900
Second birthday:	£ 900
Third birthday:	£1,000
Fourth birthday:	£1,000
Fifth birthday:	£1,100
Sixth birthday:	£1,100

After the child's sixth birthday, no more payments are made. When the child reaches age 65, he or she receives £500,000. If the relevant interest rate is 12 per cent for the first 6 years and 8 per cent for all subsequent years, is the policy worth buying?

5.34 Calculating Interest Rates A financial planning service offers a university savings programme. The plan calls for you to make six annual payments of £9,000 each, with the first payment occurring today, your child's 12th birthday. Beginning on your child's 18th birthday, the plan will provide £20,000 per year for four years. What return is this investment offering?

5.35 Unusual Perpetuities You have invested in a project that will pay you £1,000 every 2 years. If the interest rate is 8 per cent, how much is the project worth today?

5.36 Ordinary Annuities and Annuities Due As discussed in the text, an annuity due is identical to an ordinary annuity except that the periodic payments occur at the beginning of each period and not at the end of the period. Show that the relationship between the value of an ordinary annuity and the value of an otherwise equivalent annuity due is:

$$\text{Annuity due value} = \text{Ordinary annuity value} \times (1 + r)$$

Show this for both present and future values.

5.37 Calculating EAR A pawnbroker store is in the business of making personal loans to walk-up customers. The store makes only one-week loans at 7 per cent interest per week.

(a) What APR must the store report to its customers?

(b) The pawnbroker also makes one-month add-on interest loans at 7 per cent discount interest per week. Thus if you borrow €100 for one month (four weeks), the interest will be (€100 × 1.07⁴) − 100 = €31.08. Because this is discount interest, your net loan proceeds today will be €68.92. You must then repay the store €100 at the end of the month. To help you out, though, the store lets you pay off this €100 in instalments of €25 per week. What is the APR of this loan?

(c) Now suppose the store makes one-week loans at 7 per cent discount interest per week. What's the APR now?

5.38 Present Value of a Growing Perpetuity What is the equation for the present value of a growing perpetuity with a payment of C one period from today if the payments grow by C each period?

5.39 Rule of 72 Earlier, we discussed the Rule of 72, a useful approximation for many interest rates and periods for the time it takes a lump sum to double in value. For a 10 per cent interest rate, show that the 'Rule of 73' is slightly better. For what rate is the Rule of 72 exact? (*Hint:* Use the Solver function in Microsoft Excel.)

5.40 Rule of 69.3 A corollary to the Rule of 72 is the Rule of 69.3. The Rule of 69.3 is exactly correct except for rounding when interest rates are compounded continuously. Prove the Rule of 69.3 for continuously compounded interest.

MINI CASE

THE MBA DECISION

Ben Bates graduated from university six years ago with a finance undergraduate degree. Although he is satisfied with his current job, his goal is to become an investment banker. He feels that an MBA degree would allow him to achieve this goal. After examining schools, he has narrowed his choice to either Wilton University or Mount Perry University. Although internships are encouraged by both schools, to get class credit for the internship no salary can be paid. Other than internships, neither school will allow its students to work while enrolled in its MBA programme.

Ben currently works at the money management firm of Dewey and Louis. His annual salary at the firm is £75,000 per year, and his salary is expected to increase at 3 per cent per year until retirement. He is currently 28 years old and expects to work for 38 more years. His current job includes a fully paid health insurance plan, and his current average tax rate is 35 per cent. Ben has a savings account with enough money to cover the entire cost of his MBA programme.

The Ritter College of Business at Wilton University is one of the top MBA programmes in the country. The MBA degree requires two years of full-time enrolment at the university. The annual tuition fee is £30,000, payable at the beginning of each school year. Books and other supplies are estimated to cost £2,500 per year. Ben expects that after graduation from Wilton he will receive a job offer for about £98,000 per year, with a £15,000 signing bonus. The salary at this job will increase at 4 per cent per year. Because of the higher salary, his average income tax rate will increase to 40 per cent.

The Bradley School of Business at Mount Perry University began its MBA programme 16 years ago. The Bradley School is smaller and less well known than Ritter College. Bradley offers an accelerated one-year programme, with a tuition cost of £20,000 to be paid upon matriculation. Books and other supplies for the programme are expected to cost £3,500. Ben thinks that he will receive an offer of £90,000 per year upon graduation, with a £10,000 signing bonus. The salary at this job will increase at 3.5 per cent per year. His average tax rate at this level of income will be 35 per cent.

Both schools offer a health insurance plan that will cost £3,000 per year, payable at the beginning of the year. Ben also estimates that room and board expenses will cost £20,000 per year at both schools. The appropriate discount rate is 6.5 per cent.

QUESTIONS

1. How does Ben's age affect his decision to get an MBA?
2. What other, perhaps non-quantifiable, factors affect Ben's decision to get an MBA?

3. Assuming all salaries are paid at the end of each year, what is the best option for Ben from a strictly financial standpoint?
4. Ben believes that the appropriate analysis is to calculate the future value of each option. How would you evaluate this statement?
5. What initial salary would Ben need to receive to make him indifferent between attending Wilton University and staying in his current position?
6. Suppose, instead of being able to pay cash for his MBA, Ben must borrow the money. The current borrowing rate is 5.4 per cent. How would this affect his decision?

ADDITIONAL READING

Chapter 5 extends the material in Chapter 4 by delving deeper into the concepts of the time value of money. If you wish to go into the material in a much deeper way, you should read *Financial Markets and Corporate Strategy*, 2nd edition, McGraw-Hill, 2011, by David Hillier, Mark Grinblatt and Sheridan Titman.

APPENDIX: DERIVATIONS OF SELECTED FORMULAE

PRESENT VALUE OF A PERPETUITY

The present value of a constant cash flow, C, for an infinite number of periods is:

$$PV = \frac{C}{(1+r)} + \frac{C}{(1+r)^2} + \frac{C}{(1+r)^3} + \cdots$$

Multiply both sides of the equation by $1/(1+r)$ to get:

$$\frac{PV}{1+r} = \frac{C}{(1+r)^2} + \frac{C}{(1+r)^3} + \cdots$$

Subtract this equation from the first one:

$$PV - \frac{PV}{1+r} = \frac{C}{1+r}$$

This is equivalent to the following equation:

$$PV \times \frac{r}{1+r} = \frac{C}{1+r}$$

and this simplifies to:

$$PV = \frac{C}{r}$$

which is the perpetuity shortcut formula.

PRESENT VALUE OF AN ANNUITY

A standard annuity with payments of C per period from date *1* to date *T* has the following cash flows:

1	2	3	...	T	T+1	T+2	T+3	...
C	C	C	...	C	0	0	0	...

The standard annuity can be viewed as the difference between two perpetuities. The first perpetuity has cash flows that start at time 1 as shown below:

1	2	3	...	T	T+1	T+2	T+3	...
C	C	C	...	C	C	C	C	...

The second perpetuity begins at time $T+1$ and is represented by the following cash flow stream:

1	2	3	...	T	T+1	T+2	T+3	...
0	0	0	...	0	C	C	C	...

The first perpetuity has a present value of C/r and the second perpetuity has a time T value of C/r, which implies that the present value of the second perpetuity is:

$$PV = \frac{C/r}{(1+r)^T}$$

The difference in these two perpetuities has the same cash flows as the annuity. Therefore the present value of the annuity is the difference in the present values of the two perpetuities:

$$PV = \frac{C}{r} - \frac{C/r}{(1+r)^T} = \frac{C}{r}\left(1 - \frac{1}{(1+r)^T}\right) = C\left(\frac{1}{r} - \frac{1}{r(1+r)^T}\right)$$

This is the shortcut formula for the present value of an annuity.

CHAPTER 6
BOND VALUATION

> **LEARNING OBJECTIVES**
> After studying this chapter, you should understand:
> **LO1** Important bond features and types of bond.
> **LO2** Bond values and yields, and why they fluctuate.
> **LO3** Bond ratings, and what they mean.
> **LO4** The impact of inflation on interest rates.
> **LO5** The term structure of interest rates, and the determinants of bond yields.
>
> **KEY NOTATIONS**
> C Coupon
> **FV**   Face value of bond
> h Inflation rate
> **PV**   Present value
> r Interest rate or discount rate
> t Number of periods
> **YTM**   Yield to maturity

IN ITS MOST BASIC FORM, a bond is a fairly simple thing. You lend a company some money, say €1,000. The company pays you interest regularly, and it repays the original loan amount of €1,000 at some point in the future. Bonds can also have complex features.

An example is a *mortgage-backed security*, MBS, which, as the name suggests, is a bond that is backed by a pool of home mortgages. Bondholders receive payments derived from payments on the underlying mortgages, and these payments are divided up in various ways to create different classes of bond. In 2020, as a result of the Covid-19 pandemic, there was significant concern about widespread defaults on the underlying mortgages, which would have had a massive impact on these bonds. As a result, governments around the world bought these mortgage-backed securities from banks in government bail-outs as part of the rescue packages implemented.

Our goal in this chapter is to introduce you to bonds. We begin by showing how the techniques we developed in Chapters 4 and 5 can be applied to bond valuation. From there, we go on to discuss bond features, and how bonds are bought and sold. One important thing we learn is that bond values depend, in large part, on interest rates. We, therefore, close the chapter with an examination of interest rates and their behaviour.

6.1 BONDS AND BOND VALUATION

When a corporation or government wishes to borrow money from the public on a long-term basis, it usually does so by issuing or selling debt securities that are generically called *bonds*. In this section, we describe the various features of corporate bonds and some of the terminology associated with bonds. We then discuss the cash flows associated with a bond, and how bonds can be valued using our discounted cash flow procedure.

BOND FEATURES AND PRICES

As we mentioned in our previous chapter, a bond is normally an interest-only loan, meaning that the borrower will pay the interest every period, but none of the principal will be repaid until the end of the loan. For example, suppose Conegliano plc wants to borrow £1,000 for 30 years. The interest rate on similar debt issued by similar corporations is 12 per cent. Conegliano will thus pay 0.12 × £1,000 = £120 in interest every year for 30 years. At the end of 30 years, Conegliano will repay the £1,000. As this example suggests, a bond is a fairly simple financing arrangement. There is, however, a rich jargon associated with bonds, so we shall use this example to define some of the more important terms.

In our example, the £120 regular interest payments that Conegliano promises to make are called the bond's **coupons**. Because the coupon is constant and paid every year, the type of bond we are describing is sometimes called a *level coupon bond*. The amount that will be repaid at the end of the loan is called the bond's **face value**, or *par value*. As in our example, this par value is usually £1,000 for corporate bonds, and a bond that sells for its par value is called a *par value bond*. Government bonds frequently have much larger face, or par, values. Finally, the annual coupon divided by the face value is called the **coupon rate** on the bond: in this case, because £120/1,000 = 12%, the bond has a 12 per cent coupon rate.

The number of years until the face value is paid is called the bond's time to **maturity**. A corporate bond will frequently have a maturity of 30 years when it is originally issued, but this varies. Once the bond has been issued, the number of years to maturity declines as time passes. A bond with a maturity date is also called a **redeemable bond** and a bond with no maturity date is a perpetuity, and is sometimes called an **irredeemable bond** or consol bond.

BOND VALUES AND YIELDS

As time passes, interest rates change in the marketplace. The cash flows from a bond, however, stay the same. As a result, the value of the bond will fluctuate. When interest rates rise, the present value of the bond's remaining cash flows declines, and the bond is worth less. When interest rates fall, the bond is worth more.

To determine the value of a bond at a particular point in time, we need to know the number of periods remaining until maturity, the face value, the coupon, and the market interest rate for bonds with similar features. The interest rate required in the market on a bond is called the bond's **yield to maturity (YTM)**. This rate is sometimes called the bond's *yield* for short. Given all this information, we can calculate the present value of the cash flows as an estimate of the bond's current market value.

---

coupons the stated interest payment made on a bond.

face value the principal amount of a bond that is repaid at the end of the term. Also called *par value*.

coupon rate the annual coupon divided by the face value of a bond.

maturity the specified date on which the principal amount of a bond is paid.

redeemable bond a bond with a maturity date.

irredeemable bond a bond with no maturity date, also known as a consol.

yield to maturity (YTM) the rate required in the market on a bond.

For example, suppose Conegliano plc were to issue a bond with 10 years to maturity. The Conegliano bond has an annual coupon of £80. Similar bonds have a yield to maturity of 8 per cent. Based on our preceding discussion, the Conegliano bond will pay £80 per year for the next 10 years in coupon interest. In 10 years, Conegliano will pay £1,000 to the owner of the bond. The cash flows from the bond are shown in Figure 6.1. What would this bond sell for?

FIGURE 6.1

Cash flows for Conegliano plc bond

Cash flows

Year	0	1	2	3	4	5	6	7	8	9	10
Coupon		£80	£80	£80	£80	£80	£80	£80	£80	£80	£80
Face value											£1,000
		£80	£80	£80	£80	£80	£80	£80	£80	£80	£1,080

As shown, the Conegliano bond has an annual coupon of £80 and a face, or par, value of £1,000 paid at maturity in 10 years.

As illustrated in Figure 6.1, the Conegliano bond's cash flows have an annuity component (the coupons) and a lump sum (the face value paid at maturity). We thus estimate the market value of the bond by calculating the present value of these two components separately and adding the results together. First, at the going rate of 8 per cent, the present value of the £1,000 paid in 10 years is:

$$\text{Present value} = £1{,}000/1.08^{10} = £1{,}000/2.1589 = £463.19$$

Second, the bond offers £80 per year for 10 years; the present value of this annuity stream is:

$$\begin{aligned}\text{Annuity present value} &= £80 \times (1 - 1/1.08^{10})/0.08 \\ &= £80 \times (1 - 1/2.1589)/0.08 \\ &= £80 \times 6.7101 \\ &= £536.81\end{aligned}$$

We can now add the values for the two parts together to get the bond's value:

$$\text{Total bond value} = £463.19 + 536.81 = £1{,}000$$

This bond sells for exactly its face value. This is not a coincidence. The going interest rate in the market is 8 per cent. Considered as an interest-only loan, what interest rate does this bond have? With an £80 coupon, this bond pays exactly 8 per cent interest only when it sells for £1,000.

To illustrate what happens as interest rates change, suppose a year has gone by. The Conegliano bond now has 9 years to maturity. If the interest rate in the market has risen to 10 per cent, what will the bond be worth? To find out, we repeat the present value calculations with 9 years instead of 10, and a 10 per cent yield instead of an 8 per cent yield. First, the present value of the £1,000 paid in 9 years at 10 per cent is:

$$\text{Present value} = £1{,}000/1.10^9 = £1{,}000/2.3579 = £424.10$$

Second, the bond now offers £80 per year for 9 years; the present value of this annuity stream at 10 per cent is:

$$\begin{aligned}\text{Annuity present value} &= £80 \times (1 - 1/1.10^9)/0.10 \\ &= £80 \times (1 - 1/2.3579)/0.10 \\ &= £80 \times 5.7590 \\ &= £460.72\end{aligned}$$

We can now add the values for the two parts together to get the bond's value:

$$\text{Total bond value} = £424.10 + 460.72 = £884.82$$

Therefore the bond should sell for about £885. In the vernacular, we say that this bond, with its 8 per cent coupon, is priced to yield 10 per cent at £885.

The Conegliano plc bond now sells for less than its £1,000 face value. Why? The market interest rate is 10 per cent. Considered as an interest-only loan of £1,000, this bond pays only 8 per cent, its coupon rate. Because this bond pays less than the going rate, investors are willing to lend only something less than the £1,000 promised repayment. Because the bond sells for less than face value, it is said to be a *discount bond*.

The only way to get the interest rate up to 10 per cent is to lower the price to less than £1,000 so that the purchaser, in effect, has a built-in gain. For the Conegliano plc bond the price of £885 is £115 less than the face value, so an investor who purchased and kept the bond would get £80 per year and would have a £115 gain at maturity as well. This gain compensates the lender for the below-market coupon rate.

Another way to see why the bond is discounted by £115 is to note that the £80 coupon is £20 below the coupon on a newly issued par value bond, based on current market conditions. The bond would be worth £1,000 only if it had a coupon of £100 per year. In a sense, an investor who buys and keeps the bond gives up £20 per year for 9 years. At 10 per cent, this annuity stream is worth:

$$\text{Annuity present value} = £20 \times (1 - 1/1.10^9)/0.10$$
$$= £20 \times 5.7590$$
$$= £115.18$$

This is just the amount of the discount.

What would the Conegliano bond sell for if interest rates had dropped by 2 per cent instead of rising by 2 per cent? As you might guess, the bond would sell for more than £1,000. Such a bond is said to sell at a *premium*, and is called a *premium bond*.

This case is just the opposite of that of a discount bond. The Conegliano bond now has a coupon rate of 8 per cent when the market rate is only 6 per cent. Investors are willing to pay a premium to get this extra coupon amount. In this case, the relevant discount rate is 6 per cent, and there are 9 years remaining. The present value of the £1,000 face amount is:

$$\text{Present value} = £1,000/1.06^9 = £1,000/1.6895 = £591.89$$

The present value of the coupon stream is:

$$\text{Annuity present value} = £80 \times (1 - 1/1.06^9)/0.06$$
$$= £80 \times (1 - 1/1.6895)/0.06$$
$$= £80 \times 6.8017$$
$$= £544.14$$

We can now add the values for the two parts together to get the bond's value:

$$\text{Total bond value} = £591.89 + 544.14 = £1,136.03$$

Total bond value is therefore about £136 in excess of par value. Once again, we can verify this amount by noting that the coupon is now £20 too high, based on current market conditions. The present value of £20 per year for 9 years at 6 per cent is:

$$\text{Annuity present value} = £20 \times (1 - 1/1.06^9)/0.06$$
$$= £20 \times 6.8017$$
$$= £136.03$$

This is just as we calculated.

Based on our examples, we can now write the general expression for the value of a bond. If a bond has (1) a face value of F paid at maturity, (2) a coupon of C paid per period, (3) t periods to maturity, and (4) a yield of r per period, its value is:

$$\text{Bond value} = C \times \underbrace{\left[\frac{1 - 1/(1+r)^t}{r}\right]}_{\text{Present value of the coupons}} + \underbrace{\frac{F}{(1+r)^t}}_{\text{Present value of the face amount}} \quad (6.1)$$

> **EXAMPLE 6.1**
>
> ### SEMI-ANNUAL COUPONS
>
> Many bonds make coupon payments twice a year. So, if an ordinary bond has a coupon rate of 14 per cent and a face value of £100,000, then the owner will get a total of £14,000 per year, but this £14,000 will come in two payments of £7,000 each. Suppose we are examining such a bond. The yield to maturity is quoted at 16 per cent.
>
> Bond yields are presented in the same way as quoted rates, which is equal to the actual rate per period multiplied by the number of periods. In this case, with a 16 per cent quoted yield and semi-annual payments, the true yield is 8 per cent per 6 months. The bond matures in 7 years. What is the bond's price? What is the effective annual yield on this bond?
>
> Based on our discussion, we know the bond will sell at a discount, because it has a coupon rate of 7 per cent every 6 months when the market requires 8 per cent every 6 months. So, if our answer exceeds £100,000, we know we have made a mistake.
>
> To get the exact price, we first calculate the present value of the bond's face value of £100,000 paid in 7 years. This 7-year period has 14 periods of 6 months each. At 8 per cent per period, the value is:
>
> $$\text{Present value} = £100,000/1.08^{14} = £100,000/2.9372 = £34,046$$
>
> The coupons can be viewed as a 14-period annuity of £7,000 per period. At an 8 per cent discount rate, the present value of such an annuity is:
>
> $$\begin{aligned}\text{Annuity present value} &= £7,000 \times (1 - 1/1.08^{14})/0.08 \\ &= £7,000 \times (1 - 0.3405)/0.08 \\ &= £7,000 \times 8.2442 \\ &= £57,710\end{aligned}$$
>
> The total present value gives us what the bond should sell for:
>
> $$\text{Total present value} = £34,046 + 57,710 = £91,756$$
>
> To calculate the effective yield on this bond, note that 8 per cent every 6 months is equivalent to:
>
> $$\text{Effective annual rate} = (1 + 0.08)^2 - 1 = 16.64\%$$
>
> The effective yield, therefore, is 16.64 per cent.

As we have illustrated in this section, bond prices and interest rates always move in opposite directions. When interest rates rise, a bond's value, like any other present value, will decline. Similarly, when interest rates fall, bond values rise. Even if we are considering a bond that is riskless, in the sense that the borrower is certain to make all the payments, there is still risk in owning a bond. We discuss this next.

INTEREST RATE RISK

The risk that arises for bond owners from fluctuating interest rates is called *interest rate risk*. How much interest rate risk a bond has depends on how sensitive its price is to interest rate changes. This sensitivity depends directly on two things: the time to maturity and the coupon rate. As we shall see shortly, you should keep the following in mind when looking at a bond:

1. All other things being equal, the longer the time to maturity, the greater the interest rate risk.
2. All other things being equal, the lower the coupon rate, the greater the interest rate risk.

We illustrate the first of these two points in Figure 6.2. As shown, we compute and plot prices under different interest rate scenarios for 10 per cent coupon bonds with maturities of one year and 30 years. Notice how the slope of the line connecting the prices is much steeper for the 30-year maturity than it is for the one-year maturity. This steepness tells us that a relatively small change in interest rates will lead to a substantial change in the bond's value. In comparison, the one-year bond's price is relatively insensitive to interest rate changes.

FIGURE 6.2

Interest rate risk and time to maturity

Value of a bond with a 10 per cent coupon rate for different interest rates and maturities

Interest rate (%)	Time to maturity	
	1 year	30 years
5	€1,047.62	€1,768.62
10	1,000.00	1,000.00
15	966.52	671.70
20	916.67	502.11

Intuitively, we can see that longer-term bonds have greater interest rate sensitivity because a large portion of a bond's value comes from the €1,000 face amount. The present value of this amount isn't greatly affected by a small change in interest rates if the amount is to be received in one year. Even a small change in the interest rate, however, once it is compounded for 30 years, can have a significant effect on the present value. As a result, the present value of the face amount will be much more volatile with a longer-term bond.

The other thing to know about interest rate risk is that, like most things in finance and economics, it increases at a decreasing rate. In other words, if we compared a 10-year bond with a one-year bond, we would see that the 10-year bond has much greater interest rate risk. However, if you were to compare a 20-year bond with a 30-year bond, you would find that the 30-year bond had somewhat greater interest rate risk because it has a longer maturity, but the difference in the risk would be fairly small.

The reason why bonds with lower coupons have greater interest rate risk is essentially the same. As we discussed earlier, the value of a bond depends on the present value of its coupons and the present value of the face amount. If two bonds with different coupon rates have the same maturity, then the value of the one with the lower coupon is proportionately more dependent on the face amount to be received at maturity. As a result, all other things being equal, its value will fluctuate more as interest rates change. Put another way, the bond with the higher coupon has a larger cash flow early in its life, so its value is less sensitive to changes in the discount rate.

Bonds are rarely issued with maturities longer than 30 years. However, low interest rates in recent years have led to the issuance of much longer-term issues. In recent years, several European and Asian governments have issued 50-year bonds. These countries evidently want to lock in the historically low interest rates for a *long* time.

FINDING THE YIELD TO MATURITY: MORE TRIAL AND ERROR

Frequently, we will know a bond's price, coupon rate and maturity date, but not its yield to maturity. For example, suppose we are interested in a 6-year, 8 per cent coupon bond. A broker quotes a price of £955.14 for a bond with face value of £1,000. What is the yield on this bond?

We've seen that the price of a bond can be written as the sum of its annuity and lump sum components. Knowing that there is an £80 coupon for 6 years and a £1,000 face value, we can say that the price is:

$$£955.14 = £80 \times \left[\frac{1 - 1/(1+r)^6}{r}\right] + \frac{1,000}{(1+r)^6}$$

where r is the unknown discount rate, or yield to maturity. We have one equation here and one unknown, but we cannot solve it for r explicitly. The only way to find the answer is to use trial and error.

This problem is essentially identical to the one we examined in the last chapter when we tried to find the unknown interest rate on an annuity. However, finding the rate (or yield) on a bond is even more complicated, because of the £1,000 face amount.

We can speed up the trial-and-error process by using what we know about bond prices and yields. In this case, the bond has an £80 coupon and is selling at a discount. We thus know that the yield is greater than 8 per cent. If we compute the price at 10 per cent:

$$\begin{aligned}\text{Bond value} &= £80 \times (1 - 1/1.10^6)/0.10 + 1,000/1.10^6 \\ &= £80 \times 4.3553 + 1,000/1.7716 \\ &= £912.89\end{aligned}$$

At 10 per cent, the value we calculate is lower than the actual price, so 10 per cent is too high. The true yield must be somewhere between 8 and 10 per cent. At this point, it's 'plug and chug' to find the answer. You would probably want to try 9 per cent next. If you did, you would see that this is in fact the bond's yield to maturity.

A bond's yield to maturity should not be confused with its **current yield**, which is simply a bond's annual coupon divided by its price. In the previous example the bond's annual coupon was £80, and its price was £955.14. Given these numbers, we see that the current yield is £80/955.14 = 8.38 per cent, which is less than the yield to maturity of 9 per cent. The reason why the current yield is too low is that it considers only the coupon portion of your return; it doesn't consider the built-in gain from the price discount. For a premium bond the reverse is true, meaning that current yield would be higher because it ignores the built-in loss.

current yield
a bond's annual coupon divided by its price.

More information on interest rate theories is presented in the online appendix to this chapter.

EXAMPLE 6.2

CURRENT EVENTS

A bond has a quoted price of £108,042. It has a face value of £100,000, a semi-annual coupon of £3,000, and a maturity of five years. What is its current yield? What is its yield to maturity? Which is bigger? Why?

Notice that this bond makes semi-annual payments of £3,000, so the annual payment is £6,000. The current yield is thus £6,000/108,042 = 5.55 per cent. To calculate the yield to maturity, refer back to Example 6.1. In this case the bond pays £3,000 every 6 months, and has 10 six-month periods until maturity. So we need to find r as follows:

$$£108,042 = £3,000 \times \left[1 - 1/(1+r)^{10}\right]/r + 100,000/(1+r)^{10}$$

After some trial and error we find that r is equal to 2.1 per cent. But the tricky part is that this 2.1 per cent is the yield *per 6 months*. We have to double it to get the yield to maturity, so the yield to maturity is 4.2 per cent, which is less than the current yield. The reason is that the current yield ignores the built-in loss of the premium between now and maturity.

EXAMPLE 6.3

BOND YIELDS

You're looking at two bonds identical in every way except for their coupons and, of course, their prices. Both have 12 years to maturity. The first bond has a 10 per cent annual coupon rate and sells for £93,508. The second has a 12 per cent annual coupon rate. What do you think it would sell for?

Because the two bonds are similar, they will be priced to yield about the same rate. We first need to calculate the yield on the 10 per cent coupon bond. Proceeding as before, we know that the yield must be greater than 10 per cent, because the bond is selling at a discount. The bond has a fairly long maturity of 12 years. We've seen that long-term bond prices are relatively sensitive to interest rate changes, so the yield is probably close to 10 per cent. A little trial and error reveals that the yield is actually 11 per cent:

$$\text{Bond value} = £10{,}000 \times (1 - 1/1.11^{12})/0.11 + 100{,}000/1.11^{12}$$
$$= £10{,}000 \times 6.4924 + 100{,}000/3.4985$$
$$= £64{,}924 + 28{,}584$$
$$= £93{,}508$$

With an 11 per cent yield, the second bond will sell at a premium because of its £12,000 coupon. Its value is:

$$\text{Bond value} = £12{,}000 \times (1 - 1/1.11^{12})/0.11 + 100{,}000/1.11^{12}$$
$$= £12{,}000 \times 6.4924 + 100{,}000/3.4985$$
$$= £77{,}908 + 28{,}584$$
$$= £106{,}492$$

SPREADSHEET STRATEGIES 6.1

How to Calculate Bond Prices and Yields Using a Spreadsheet

Most spreadsheets have fairly elaborate routines available for calculating bond values and yields; many of these routines involve details we have not discussed. However, setting up a simple spreadsheet to calculate prices or yields is straightforward, as our next two spreadsheets show.

Suppose we have a bond with 22 years to maturity, a coupon rate of 8 per cent, and a yield to maturity of 9 per cent. If the bond makes semi-annual payments, what is its price today?

	A	B
1	Settlement Date	01/01/2021
2	Maturity Date	01/01/2043
3	Annual Coupon Rate	8%
4	Yield to Maturity	9%
5	Face Value (% of Par)	100
6	Coupons per Year	2
7		
8	Bond Price (% of Par)	90.49
9		

The formula for the bond price is given in the formula bar, and is '=PRICE(B1,B2,B3,B4,B5,B6)'. In our spreadsheet, notice that we had to enter two dates: a settlement date and a maturity date. The settlement date is just the date when you actually pay for the bond, and the maturity date is the day the bond actually matures. In most of our problems we don't explicitly have these dates, so we have to make them up. For example, because our bond has 22 years to maturity, we just picked 1/1/2021 (1 January 2021) as the settlement date and

1/1/2043 (1 January 2043) as the maturity date. Any two dates would do as long as they are exactly 22 years apart, but these are particularly easy to work with. Finally, notice that we had to enter the coupon rate and yield to maturity in annual terms and then explicitly provide the number of coupon payments per year.

Now suppose we have a bond with 22 years to maturity, a coupon rate of 8 per cent, and a price of €960.17. If the bond makes semi-annual payments, what is its yield to maturity?

	A	B
1	Settlement Date	01/01/2021
2	Maturity Date	01/01/2043
3	Annual Coupon Rate	8%
4	Bond Price (% of Par)	96.02
5	Face Value (% of Par)	100
6	Coupons per Year	2
7		
8	Yield to Maturity	8.40%

The formula for yield to maturity is '=YIELD(B1,B2,B3,B4,B5,B6)'.

CONCEPT QUESTIONS

6.1a What are the cash flows associated with a bond?
6.1b What is the general expression for the value of a bond?
6.1c Is it true that the only risk associated with owning a bond is that the issuer will not make all the payments? Explain.

6.2 MORE ABOUT BOND FEATURES

In this section, we continue our discussion of corporate debt by describing in some detail the basic terms and features that make up a typical long-term corporate bond. We discuss additional issues associated with long-term debt in subsequent sections.

Securities issued by corporations may be classified roughly as *equity securities* or *debt securities*. At the crudest level, a debt represents something that must be repaid; it is the result of borrowing money. When corporations borrow, they generally promise to make regularly scheduled interest payments and to repay the original amount borrowed (that is, the principal). The person or firm making the loan is called the *creditor* or *lender*. The corporation borrowing the money is called the *debtor* or *borrower*.

From a financial point of view, the main differences between debt and equity are the following.

1. Debt is not an ownership interest in the firm. Creditors generally do not have voting power.
2. The corporation's payment of interest on debt is considered a cost of doing business and is fully tax-deductible. Dividends paid to shareholders are *not* tax-deductible.
3. Unpaid debt is a liability of the firm. If it is not paid, the creditors can legally claim the assets of the firm. This action can result in liquidation or reorganization, two of the possible consequences of bankruptcy. Thus, one of the costs of issuing debt is the possibility of financial failure. This possibility does not arise when equity is issued.

IS IT DEBT OR EQUITY?

Sometimes it is not clear whether a particular security is debt or equity. For example, suppose a corporation issues a perpetual bond with interest payable solely from corporate income if and only if earned.

Whether this is really a debt is hard to say, and is primarily a legal and semantic issue. Courts and tax authorities would have the final say.

Corporations are adept at creating exotic, hybrid securities that have many features of equity but are treated as debt. Obviously, the distinction between debt and equity is important for tax purposes. So one reason why corporations try to create a debt security that is really equity is to obtain the tax benefits of debt and the bankruptcy benefits of equity.

As a general rule, equity represents an ownership interest, and it is a residual claim. This means that equity holders are paid after debt holders. As a result, the risks and benefits associated with owning debt and equity are different. To give just one example, note that the maximum reward for owning a debt security is ultimately fixed by the amount of the loan, whereas there is no upper limit to the potential reward from owning an equity interest.

REAL WORLD INSIGHTS

How do we value bonds and equities together? Are bond values related to equity values? How do we value bonds and equities during periods of massive disruption, like the Covid-19 pandemic?

If a company has both debt and equity, it would seem sensible to suggest that bond values and equity values are related. However, at the most basic level, you could argue the opposite. Bond cash flows (coupon payments) are normally predetermined and contractually set before the bond is issued, while equity cash flows (dividends) can vary over time depending on the company's fortunes. Theoretically then, there will be no correlation between bond and equity cash flows.

When it comes to risk, the issue is more complex. The risk of a bond is a function of how likely the coupon payments and principal will be repaid, whereas equity risk is dependent upon a number of factors, including the riskiness of business operations and how much the firm has borrowed (this topic is covered in more detail in Chapter 15).

A discounted cash flow valuation of bonds and equities in the same company is very likely to incorporate the interrelationship between bond and equity risk, as well as the cash flows of each security. There will also be periods when bonds are in more demand than equities, and vice versa because of global economic conditions, such as those caused by a global pandemic or technological disruption.

Take the bond (blue line) and equity (orange line) prices of Vodafone Group on the Deutsche Börse for the period January to September 2020. Notice how they moved together when the Covid-19 pandemic hit in March, affecting both bond and equity prices. Then prices diverged from about June 2020. Are these correlated? For the first six months of 2020, it would appear so. A different picture emerges after June, when there appears to be no relationship between bond and equity prices. The contrasting trends are driven by the risk and cash flow dynamics of bond and equities, and how these change over time.

Vodafone Group Bond (7%, 60-year bond, maturing in 2079) and Equity Prices between January and September 2020
Source: Deutsche Börse, 2020.

LONG-TERM DEBT: THE BASICS

Ultimately, all long-term debt securities are promises made by the issuing firm to pay principal when due and to make timely interest payments on the unpaid balance. Beyond this, a number of features distinguish these securities from one another. We discuss some of these features next.

The maturity of a long-term debt instrument is the length of time the debt remains outstanding with some unpaid balance. Debt securities can be *short term* (with maturities of one year or less) or *long term* (with maturities of more than one year).[1] Short-term debt is sometimes referred to as *unfunded debt*.[2]

Debt securities are typically called *notes*, *debentures* or *bonds*. Strictly speaking, a bond is a secured debt. However, in common usage, the word 'bond' refers to all kinds of secured and unsecured debt. We shall, therefore, continue to use the term generically to refer to long-term debt. Also, usually, the only difference between a note and a bond is the original maturity. Issues with an original maturity of 10 years or less are often called notes. Longer-term issues are called bonds.

The two major forms of long-term debt are *public issue* and *privately placed*. We concentrate on public-issue bonds. Most of what we say about them holds true for private-issue, long-term debt as well. The main difference between public-issue and privately placed debt is that the latter is placed directly with a lender and not offered to the public. Because this is a private transaction, the specific terms are up to the parties involved.

There are many other aspects of long-term debt, including such things as security, call features, sinking funds, ratings and protective covenants. Table 6.1 illustrates these features for a hypothetical bond. If some of these terms are unfamiliar, have no fear. We shall discuss them all presently.

Many of these features will be detailed in the bond indenture, so we discuss this first.

THE INDENTURE

indenture the written agreement between the corporation and the lender detailing the terms of the debt issue.

The **indenture** is the written agreement between the corporation (the borrower) and its creditors. It is sometimes referred to as the *deed of trust*.[3] Usually, a trustee (a bank, perhaps) is appointed by the corporation to represent the bondholders. The trust company must: (1) make sure the terms of the indenture are obeyed; (2) manage the sinking fund (described in the following pages); and (3) represent the bondholders in default – that is, if the company defaults on its payments to them.

TABLE 6.1

Features of a hypothetical bond issued on the London Stock Exchange

Term		Explanation
Amount of issue	£1 billion	The company issued £1 billion worth of bonds.
Date of issue	2021 and on a continuing basis	The bonds could be issued at any time over more than one date in separate tranches up to a cumulative amount of £1 billion.
Maturity	2030	The bonds mature in 2030. The term is thus 9 years.
Face value	£100,000	The denomination of the bonds is £100,000.
Annual coupon	6%	Each bondholder will receive £6,000 per bond per year (6% of face value).
Offer price	Variable	The issue price is determined by the issuing company prior to the offering of each tranche after taking into account certain factors including market conditions.
Security	None	The bonds are unsecured.
Sinking fund	None	The bonds have no sinking fund.
Call provision	None	The bonds do not have a call provision.

The bond indenture is a legal document. It can run to several hundred pages, and generally makes for tedious reading. It is an important document, however, because it generally includes the following provisions:

1. The basic terms of the bonds
2. The total quantity of bonds issued
3. A description of property used as security
4. The repayment arrangements
5. The call provisions
6. Details of the protective covenants

We discuss these features next.

Terms of a Bond

Corporate bonds usually have a face value (that is, a denomination) in multiples of 1,000 (for example, £1,000, £10,000 or £100,000). This *principal value* is stated on the bond certificate. So, if a corporation wanted to borrow £1 million, 1,000 bonds with a face value of £1,000 would have to be sold. The par value (that is, the initial accounting value) of a bond is almost always the same as the face value, and the terms are used interchangeably in practice.

Corporate bonds are usually in **registered form**. For example, the indenture might read as follows:

> Interest is payable semi-annually on 1 July and 1 January of each year to the person in whose name the bond is registered at the close of business on 15 June or 15 December respectively.

This means that the company has a registrar who will record the ownership of each bond, and record any changes in ownership. The company will pay the interest and principal by cheque, mailed directly to the address of the owner of record. A corporate bond may be registered and have attached 'coupons'. To obtain an interest payment the owner must separate a coupon from the bond certificate and send it to the company registrar (the paying agent).

Alternatively, the bond could be in **bearer form**. This means that the certificate is the basic evidence of ownership, and the corporation will 'pay the bearer'. Ownership is not otherwise recorded, and as with a registered bond with attached coupons, the holder of the bond certificate detaches the coupons and sends them to the company to receive payment.

There are two drawbacks to bearer bonds. First, they are difficult to recover if they are lost or stolen. Second, because the company does not know who owns its bonds, it cannot notify bondholders of important events. Bearer bonds are very common in Europe, and London is the financial centre of trading in these securities.

registered form the form of bond issue in which the registrar of the company records ownership of each bond; payment is made directly to the owner of record.

bearer form the form of bond issue in which the bond is issued without record of the owner's name; payment is made to whomever holds the bond.

Security

Debt securities are classified according to the collateral and mortgages used to protect the bondholder.

Collateral is a general term that frequently means securities (for example, bonds and equities) that are pledged as security for payment of debt. For example, collateral trust bonds often involve a pledge of equity shares held by the corporation. However, the term 'collateral' is commonly used to refer to any asset pledged on a debt.

Mortgage securities are secured by a mortgage on the real property of the borrower. The property involved is usually real estate – for example, land or buildings. The legal document that describes the mortgage is called a *mortgage trust indenture* or *trust deed*.

Sometimes mortgages are on specific property. More often, blanket mortgages are used. A *blanket mortgage* pledges all the real property owned by the company.[4]

Bonds frequently represent unsecured obligations of the company. An **unsecured bond** is a bond in which no specific pledge of property is made. The term **note** is

unsecured bond an unsecured debt security, usually with a maturity of 10 years or more.

note an unsecured debt security, usually with a maturity under 10 years.

generally used for such instruments if the maturity of the unsecured bond is less than 10 or so years when the bond is originally issued. Unsecured bondholders have a claim only on property not otherwise pledged – in other words, the property that remains after mortgages and collateral trusts are taken into account.

The terminology that we use here and elsewhere in this chapter is standard. However, across countries, these terms can have different meanings. For example, bonds ('gilts') issued by the British government are called treasury 'stock'. Also, in the United Kingdom, a debenture is a *secured* obligation, whereas in the US it is an *unsecured* obligation!

At present, public bonds issued in Europe by industrial and financial companies are typically unsecured.

Seniority

In general terms, *seniority* indicates preference in position over other lenders, and debts are sometimes labelled as *senior* or *junior* to indicate seniority. Some debt is *subordinated*, as in, for example, a subordinated unsecured bond.

In the event of default, holders of subordinated debt must give preference to other specified creditors. Usually, this means that the subordinated lenders will be paid off only after the specified creditors have been compensated. However, debt cannot be subordinated to equity.

> **sinking fund**
> an account managed by the bond trustee for early bond redemption.

Repayment

Bonds can be repaid at maturity, at which time the bondholder will receive the stated, or face, value of the bond; or they may be repaid in part or in entirety before maturity. Early repayment in some form is more typical and is often handled through a sinking fund.

A **sinking fund** is an account managed by the bond trustee for the purpose of repaying the bonds. The company makes annual payments to the trustee, who then uses the funds to retire a portion of the debt. The trustee does this either by buying up some of the bonds in the market or by calling in a fraction of the outstanding bonds. This second option is discussed in the next section.

> **call provision**
> an agreement giving the corporation the option to repurchase a bond at a specified price prior to maturity.

There are many different kinds of sinking fund arrangement, and the details would be spelled out in the indenture. For example:

1. Some sinking funds start about 10 years after the initial issuance.
2. Some sinking funds establish equal payments over the life of the bond.
3. Some high-quality bond issues establish payments to the sinking fund that are not sufficient to redeem the entire issue. As a consequence, there is the possibility of a large 'balloon payment' at maturity.

> **call premium**
> the amount by which the call price exceeds the par value of a bond.

The Call Provision

A **call provision** allows the company to repurchase or 'call' part or all of the bond issue at stated prices over a specific period. Corporate bonds are usually callable.

Generally, the call price is above the bond's stated value (that is, the par value). The difference between the call price and the stated value is the **call premium**. The amount of the call premium may become smaller over time. One arrangement is initially to set the call premium equal to the annual coupon payment, and then make it decline to zero as the call date moves closer to the time of maturity.

> **deferred call provision** a call provision prohibiting the company from redeeming a bond prior to a certain date.

Call provisions are often not operative during the first part of a bond's life. This makes the call provision less of a worry for bondholders in the bond's early years. For example, a company might be prohibited from calling its bonds for the first 10 years. This is a **deferred call provision**. During this period of prohibition, the bond is said to be **call protected**.

> **call-protected bond** a bond that, during a certain period, cannot be redeemed by the issuer.

In recent years a new type of call provision, a 'make-whole' call, has become widespread in the corporate bond market. With such a feature, bondholders receive approximately what the bonds are worth if they are called. Because bondholders don't suffer a loss in the event of a call, they are 'made whole'.

Protective Covenants

A **protective covenant** is that part of the indenture or loan agreement that limits certain actions a company might otherwise wish to take during the term of the loan. Protective covenants can be classified into two types: negative covenants and positive (or affirmative) covenants.

A *negative covenant* is a 'thou shalt not' type of covenant. It limits or prohibits actions the company might take. Here are some typical examples:

- The firm must limit the amount of dividends it pays according to some formula.
- The firm cannot pledge any assets to other lenders.
- The firm cannot merge with another firm.
- The firm cannot sell or lease any major assets without approval by the lender.
- The firm cannot issue additional long-term debt.

A *positive covenant* is a 'thou shalt' type of covenant. It specifies an action the company agrees to take, or a condition the company must abide by. Here are some examples:

- The company must maintain its working capital at or above some specified minimum level.
- The company must periodically furnish audited financial statements to the lender.
- The firm must maintain any collateral or security in good condition.

This is only a partial list of covenants; a particular indenture may feature many different ones.

> **protective covenant** a part of the indenture limiting certain actions that might be taken during the term of the loan, usually to protect the lender's interest.

REAL WORLD INSIGHTS

The bond discussed in Table 6.1 has both a negative covenant and a positive covenant.

The negative covenant (or pledge) requires that the company or its subsidiaries will not take out any further loans or provide financial guarantees without at the same time getting agreement from the existing lenders and providing security for the existing debt. For this to happen, there would need to be an extraordinary resolution of the bondholders.

The positive pledge is known as a Gearing Covenant. The issuing company agrees to keep the ratio of debt to equity below 100 per cent. That is, the value of debt is not allowed to exceed the value of equity on specified calculation dates during the life of the loan. The issuing company would be deemed to be in default if its debt to equity ratio was greater than 100 per cent only on these dates. It would not be in default if the debt to equity ratio was greater than 100 per cent on any other date.

CONCEPT QUESTIONS

6.2a What are the distinguishing features of debt compared with equity?
6.2b What is the indenture? What are protective covenants? Give some examples.
6.2c What is a sinking fund?

6.3 BOND RATINGS

Firms frequently pay to have their debt rated. The three leading bond-rating firms are Moody's, Standard & Poor's (S&P) and Fitch. The debt ratings are an assessment of the creditworthiness of the corporate issuer. The definitions of creditworthiness used by Moody's, S&P and Fitch are based on how likely the firm is to default, and on the protection that creditors have in the event of a default.

It is important to recognize that bond ratings are concerned *only* with the possibility of default. Earlier we discussed interest rate risk, which we defined as the risk of a change in the value of a bond resulting from a change in interest rates. Bond ratings do not address this issue. As a result, the price of a highly rated bond can still be quite volatile.

Bond ratings are constructed from information supplied by the corporation. The rating classes, and some information concerning them, are shown in Table 6.2.

TABLE 6.2

Bond rating

	Investment-quality bond ratings				Low-quality, speculative and/or 'junk' bond ratings					
	High grade		Medium grade		Low grade		Very low grade			
Moody's	Aaa	Aa	A	Baa	Ba	B	Caa	Ca	C	
Standard & Poor's	AAA	AA	A	BBB	BB	B	CCC	CC	C	D
Fitch	AAA	AA+	A	BBB	BB	B	CCC			D

Moody's	S&P	Fitch	
Aaa	AAA	AAA	Debt rated Aaa and AAA has the highest rating. Capacity to pay interest and principal is extremely strong.
Aa	AA	AA+	Debt rated Aa, AA and AA+ has a very strong capacity to pay interest and repay principal. Together with the highest rating, this group constitutes the high-grade bond class.
A	A	A	Debt rated A has a strong capacity to pay interest and repay principal, although it is somewhat more susceptible to the adverse effects of changes in circumstances and economic conditions than debt in high-rated categories.
Baa	BBB	BBB	Debt rated Baa and BBB is regarded as having an adequate capacity to pay interest and repay principal. Whereas it normally exhibits adequate protection parameters, adverse economic conditions or changing circumstances are more likely to lead to a weakened capacity to pay interest and repay principal for debt in this category than in higher-rated categories. These bonds are medium-grade obligations.
Ba; B Caa Ca C	BB; B CCC CC C	BB; B CCC	Debt rated in these categories is regarded, on balance, as predominantly speculative with respect to capacity to pay interest and repay principal in accordance with the terms of the obligation. BB and Ba indicate the lowest degree of speculation, and Ca, CC, and C the highest degree of speculation. Although such debt is likely to have some quality and protective characteristics, these are outweighed by large uncertainties or major risk exposures to adverse conditions. Issues rated C by Moody's are typically in default.
	D	D	Debt rated D is in default, and payment of interest and/or repayment of principal is in arrears.

Note: At times, Moody's, S&P and Fitch use adjustments (called notches) to these ratings. S&P uses plus and minus signs: A+ is the strongest A rating and A- the weakest. Moody's uses a 1, 2, or 3 designation, with 1 being the highest.

The highest rating a firm's debt can have is AAA or Aaa, and such debt is judged to be the best quality and to have the lowest degree of risk. A large part of corporate borrowing takes the form of low-grade, or 'junk', bonds. If these low-grade corporate bonds are rated at all, they are rated below investment grade by the major rating agencies. Investment-grade bonds are bonds rated at least BBB by S&P and Fitch, or Baa by Moody's.

A bond's credit rating can change as the issuer's financial strength improves or deteriorates. For example, in 2020, Standard & Poors downgraded many companies as a result of the economic fall-out of the global Covid-19 epidemic. Bonds that drop into junk territory are called *fallen angels*.

DETERMINANTS OF CREDIT RATINGS

Many factors can influence the credit rating that is awarded to a bond. Considering sovereign bonds (bonds issued by governments in local or foreign currency) first, the primary determinants are political risk, economic strength and growth prospects, government debt, and monetary and fiscal flexibility. Political risk relates to the stability of a country's government, transparency in government decisions, public security and corruption. Economic strength is fairly self-explanatory, but it also includes financial sector development, the efficiency of the public sector in a country, the income gap between rich and poor, and flexibility in workforce patterns. Monetary and fiscal flexibility means that the country's economy is less subject to economic cycles, plus central bank independence, timely, transparent and accountable government reporting, and a sustainable level of pension obligations.

Corporate bond ratings are driven by a number of other factors, but most notably the most important determinant is financial risk, and whether the company is able to meet its debt payments. Other firm-level factors relate to the company's debt burden, and whether it is growing or getting smaller. Planned and committed capital expenditures and forecast earnings performance can also impact upon a corporation's credit rating.

Macroeconomic factors can cause corporate credit ratings to change. For example, if inflation is expected to increase, the cost of borrowing will also increase, and this could affect a company's investment plans. More recently, global oil price demand has pushed the cost of manufacturing up, which has affected most firms. The strength of a country's currency is also important.

As you can see, many factors can influence the credit rating of a company's bond issue. Some factors are quantitative and easily measured, whereas others are very subjective and difficult to quantify. Credit ratings can be influenced by the economy, by an industry's prospects, by the issuing company's performance, and by the bond itself. With such complexity, it is understandable that companies and investors pay a lot of money to subscribe to credit rating agencies to access all of their services.

> **CONCEPT QUESTIONS**
>
> **6.3a** What does a bond rating say about the risk of fluctuations in a bond's value resulting from interest rate changes?
> **6.3b** What is a junk bond?

6.4 SOME DIFFERENT TYPES OF BOND

Thus far we have considered only 'plain vanilla' corporate bonds. In this section we briefly look at the characteristics of bonds issued by governments, and also at bonds with unusual features.

GOVERNMENT BONDS

The biggest borrowers in the world – by a wide margin – are governments. When a government wishes to borrow money for more than one year, it sells what are known as Treasury notes and bonds to the public (in fact, most governments do so every month). Treasury notes and bonds can have original maturities ranging from 2 to 100 years.

Most Treasury issues are just ordinary coupon bonds. Some older issues are callable, and a few have some unusual features. There are two important things to keep in mind, however. First, most government Treasury issues, unlike essentially all other bonds, have no default risk, because governments can always come up with the money to make the payments (i.e. print more money!). Countries in the European Monetary Union are an exception because the European Central Bank decides on money supply, which means that individual countries in the EMU can have default risk. Second, many Treasury issues are exempt from income taxes.

In some countries, state and local governments also borrow money by selling notes and bonds. Such issues are called *municipal* notes and bonds, or just 'munis'. Unlike Treasury issues, munis have varying degrees of default risk, and in fact, they are rated much like corporate issues. Also, they are almost always callable.

ZERO COUPON BONDS

zero coupon bond a bond that makes no coupon payments and is thus initially priced at a deep discount. Also called *pure discount bonds*.

A bond that pays no coupons at all must be offered at a price that is much lower than its stated value. Such bonds are called **zero coupon bonds**, *pure discount bonds*, or just *zeros*.[5]

Suppose Bocelli SpA issues a €1,000 face value, five-year zero coupon bond. The initial price is set at €508.35. Even though no interest payments are made on the bond, zero coupon bond calculations use semi-annual periods to be consistent with coupon bond calculations. Using semi-annual periods, it is straightforward to verify that, at this price, the bond yields 14 per cent to maturity. The total interest paid over the life of the bond is €1,000 − 508.35 = €491.65.

For tax purposes, the issuer of a zero coupon bond deducts interest every year, even though no interest is actually paid. Similarly, the owner must pay taxes on interest accrued every year, even though no interest is actually received. The way in which the yearly interest on a zero coupon bond is calculated is governed by the tax law existing in each country.

Some bonds are zero coupon bonds for only part of their lives. For example, General Motors has a 40-year debenture outstanding that matures on 15 March 2036. For the first 20 years of its life no coupon payments are made but after 20 years it will begin paying coupons semi-annually at a rate of 7.75 per cent per year.

FLOATING-RATE BONDS

The conventional bonds we have talked about in this chapter have fixed obligations because the coupon rates are set as fixed percentages of the par values. Similarly, the principal amounts are set equal to the par values. Under these circumstances, the coupon payments and principal are completely fixed.

With *floating-rate bonds (floaters)*, the coupon payments are adjustable. The adjustments are tied to an interest rate index such as the Treasury bill interest rate or the 30-year Treasury bond rate. The value of a floating-rate bond depends on exactly how the coupon payment adjustments are defined. In most cases, the coupon adjusts with a lag to some base rate. For example, suppose a coupon rate adjustment is made on 1 June. The adjustment might be based on the simple average of Treasury bond yields during the previous 3 months. In addition, the majority of floaters have the following features:

1. The holder has the right to redeem the note at par on the coupon payment date after some specified amount of time. This is called a *put provision* and is discussed in the following section.
2. The coupon rate has a floor and a ceiling, meaning that the coupon is subject to a minimum and a maximum. In this case, the coupon rate is said to be 'capped', and the upper and lower rates are sometimes called the *collar*.

A particularly interesting type of floating-rate bond is an *inflation-linked* bond. Such bonds have coupons that are adjusted according to the rate of inflation (the principal amount may be adjusted as well). The UK and French governments are the biggest European issuers of inflation-linked bonds, and they are called inflation-linked gilts (ILGs) in the UK and OATi and OAT€i in France. Other countries, including the US, Germany, Greece, Italy and Iceland, have issued similar securities.

OTHER TYPES OF BOND

Many bonds have unusual or exotic features. So-called *catastrophe*, or *cat, bonds* provide an interesting example. Catastrophe bonds are issued at a large discount to par value (are rated below investment grade) and lose all their value if there is a major specific catastrophe (such as a hurricane, flooding or earthquake) in a stated region.

Although the catastrophe bond market is relatively small, it is a fast-growing segment of the debt asset class. Given that we have now experienced the Covid-19 pandemic, cat bonds probably seem pretty risky. It might, therefore, be surprising to learn that, before Covid-19, very few cat bonds had not been paid in full.

Another possible bond feature is a *warrant*. A warrant gives the buyer of a bond the right to purchase shares of equity in the company at a fixed price. Such a right would be very valuable if the share price climbed substantially (a later chapter discusses this subject in greater depth). Because of the value of this feature, bonds with warrants are often issued at a very low coupon rate.

As these examples illustrate, bond features are really limited only by the imaginations of the parties involved. Unfortunately, there are far too many variations for us to cover in detail here. We, therefore, close this discussion by mentioning a few of the more common types.

Income bonds are similar to conventional bonds, except that coupon payments depend on company income. Specifically, coupons are paid to bondholders only if the firm's income is sufficient. This would appear to be an attractive feature, but income bonds are not very common.

A *convertible bond* can be swapped for a fixed number of shares of equity any time before maturity at the holder's option. Convertibles are relatively common, but the number has been decreasing in recent years.

A *put bond* allows the *holder* to force the issuer to buy back the bond at a stated price. For example, 3i Group plc, the private equity firm, has bonds outstanding that allow the holder to force 3i Group to buy the bonds back at 100 per cent of face value if certain relevant 'risk' events happen. One such event is a change in credit rating by Moody's or S&P from investment grade to lower than investment grade. The put feature is therefore just the reverse of the call provision.

A given bond may have many unusual features. Two of the most recent exotic bonds are *CoCo bonds*, which have a coupon payment, and *NoNo bonds*, which are zero-coupon bonds. CoCo and NoNo bonds are contingent convertible, puttable, callable, subordinated bonds. The contingent convertible clause is similar to the normal conversion feature, except that the contingent feature must be met. For example, a contingent feature may require that the company equity trade at 110 per cent of the conversion price for 20 out of the most recent 30 days. Because they are so complex, valuation of NoNo and CoCo bonds is exceptionally difficult.

REAL WORLD INSIGHTS

In 2017, the World Bank issued a new type of catastrophe bond that related solely to pandemics. These instruments were called Pandemic Emergency Financing Bonds and they paid out if the World Health Organization *did not* declare a global pandemic over the life of the bonds. If the WHO were to declare a pandemic, the bonds would default and the money raised would be used to fund efforts to deal with the pandemic in emerging markets.

The pandemic bonds were issued in two tranches. Class A bonds paid 6.9 per cent annually for the life of the bond, and Class B bonds paid 11.5 per cent annually. In total, $425 million was raised over both tranches.

Sadly, the coronavirus that ravaged the world in 2020 led to a default event, and many investors lost a lot of money. However, investors should have been content to know that people in Africa, Asia and South America benefited from the default and allowed the WHO to fund projects to alleviate victims' suffering.

CONCEPT QUESTIONS

6.4a Why might an income bond be attractive to a corporation with volatile cash flows? Can you think of a reason why income bonds are not more popular?

6.4b What do you think would be the effect of a put feature on a bond's coupon? How about a convertibility feature? Why?

6.5 BOND MARKETS

Bonds are bought and sold in enormous quantities every day. You may be surprised to learn that the trading volume in bonds on a typical day is many, many times larger than the trading volume in equities (by *trading volume* we simply mean the amount of money that changes hands). Here is a finance trivia question: where does most trading of financial securities take place? Most people would guess the stock exchanges. In fact, the largest securities market in the world in terms of trading volume is the government Treasury market.

HOW BONDS ARE BOUGHT AND SOLD

Most trading in bonds takes place over the counter, or OTC, which means there is no particular place where buying and selling occur. Instead, dealers around the world stand ready to buy and sell. The various dealers are connected electronically. The London Stock Exchange has an electronic trading system for bonds that allows private investors to buy bonds in denominations of £1,000. This retail market for individuals, which now has over 170 bonds, was an innovation for UK bonds since most British bonds have a face value of at least £50,000. In the Eurozone, the main bond markets are Deutsche Börse and Euronext, where many corporate bonds are traded through an electronic trading system.

One reason why the bond markets are so big is that the number of bond issues far exceeds the number of equity issues. There are two reasons for this. First, a corporation would typically have only one ordinary equity issue outstanding (there are exceptions to this, which we discuss in our next chapter). However, a single large corporation could easily have a dozen or more note and bond issues outstanding. Beyond this, government and local borrowing is simply enormous. For example, many large cities will have a wide variety of notes and bonds outstanding, representing money borrowed to pay for things such as roads, sewers and schools. When you think about how many large cities there are in the world, you begin to get the picture!

Although the total volume of trading in bonds far exceeds that in equities, only a small fraction of the total bond issues that exist actually trade on a given day. This fact, combined with the lack of transparency in the bond market, means that it can be difficult or impossible to get up-to-date prices on individual bonds, particularly for smaller corporate or municipal issues. Instead, a variety of sources of estimated prices exist and are commonly used.

BOND PRICE REPORTING

In recent years, transparency in the corporate bond market has improved dramatically. The advent of high-speed Internet connections has allowed real-time updates on bond prices and trading volumes directly from the stock exchange.

As shown in Table 6.3 for London Stock Exchange bonds, stock exchanges provide a daily snapshot of trading in the most active issues. The information shown is largely self-explanatory. Notice that the price of the GlaxoSmithKline 5.25 per cent coupon bond was trading at 123 per cent of its face value, which reflects the fall in yields experienced by bonds of this type.

If you go to the website and click on a particular bond, you will get a lot of information about the bond, including the credit rating, the call schedule, original-issue information and trade information.

As we mentioned before, the government Treasury market is the largest securities market in the world. As with bond markets in general, it is an OTC market, so there is limited transparency. However, unlike the situation with bond markets in general, trading in Treasury issues, particularly recently issued ones, is very heavy. Each day, representative prices for outstanding Treasury issues are reported.

TABLE 6.3

London Stock Exchange corporate bond quotations

Code	ISIN	Name	Currency	Price
A2D1	XS0975865949	A2D FUND. 22	GBP	98.75
A2D2	XS1103286305	A2D FUND.26	GBP	97.50
ALP2	XS1379593566	ALPHA PLUS24	GBP	61.00
4OLV	XS0089553282	ANGLIANWTR6.875	GBP	115.00
AE57	XS0138717441	AVIVA 6.125%36?	GBP	95.50
AA18	XS0134886067	BARCLAYS.5.75%	GBP	97.00
72NS	XS0097283096	BR.TEL.5T%BDS28	GBP	113.00
BRU1	XS0947705215	BRUNTWOOD 6%	GBP	98.50
BRU2	XS2104011304	BRUNTWOOD BD 6%	GBP	86.50
BUR4	XS1756325228	BURF CAP.F25	USD	71.75
BUR1	XS1088905093	BURFORD 22	GBP	78.50
BUR2	XS1391063424	BURFORD 24	GBP	68.00
BUR3	XS1614096425	BURFORD 26	GBP	66.38
93GR	XS0058209106	EAST.GP.8H%2025	GBP	126.00
52GO	XS0187202303	EAST.POWER5.75%	GBP	112.00
ENQ1	XS0880578728	ENQ 22 ?PIK TOG	GBP	30.30
ERO1	XS1112834608	EROS INT 21	GBP	47.38
92VF	XS0340495216	GE CAP.UK 33	GBP	108.25
AG99	XS0140516864	GLAXOSMSC 5.25%	GBP	123.00
72VH	XS0184639895	HAMMERSON 6%26	GBP	100.00

Source: London Stock Exchange. Prices as at 23 March 2020. All rights reserved.

A NOTE ABOUT BOND PRICE QUOTES

If you buy a bond between coupon payment dates, the price you pay is usually more than the price you are quoted. The reason is that standard convention in the bond market is to quote prices net of 'accrued interest', meaning that accrued interest is deducted to arrive at the quoted price. This quoted price is called the **clean price**. The price you actually pay, however, includes the accrued interest. This price is the **dirty price**, also known as the 'full' or 'invoice' price.

An example is the easiest way to understand these issues. Suppose you buy a bond with a 12 per cent annual coupon, payable semi-annually. You actually pay €1,080 for this bond, so €1,080 is the dirty, or invoice, price. Further, on the day you buy it, the next coupon is due in 4 months, so you are between coupon dates. Notice that the next coupon will be €60.

The accrued interest on a bond is calculated by taking the fraction of the coupon period that has passed, in this case 2 months out of 6, and multiplying this fraction by the next coupon, €60. So, the accrued interest in this example is 2/6 × €60 = €20. The bond's quoted price (that is, its clean price) would be €1,080 − €20 = €1,060.

> **clean price** the price of a bond net of accrued interest; this is the price that is typically quoted.
>
> **dirty price** the price of a bond including accrued interest, also known as the *full* or *invoice price*. This is the price the buyer actually pays.

CONCEPT QUESTIONS

6.5a What is meant by a bond's redemption yield and interest yield?
6.5b What is the difference between a bond's clean price and dirty price?

6.6 INFLATION AND INTEREST RATES

So far, we haven't considered the role of inflation in our various discussions of interest rates, yields and returns. Because this is an important consideration, we consider the impact of inflation next.

REAL VERSUS NOMINAL RATES

In examining interest rates, or any other financial market rates such as discount rates, bond yields, rates of return or required returns, it is often necessary to distinguish between **real rates** and **nominal rates**. Nominal rates are called 'nominal' because they have not been adjusted for inflation. Real rates are rates that have been adjusted for inflation.

To see the effect of inflation, suppose prices are currently rising by 5 per cent per year. In other words, the rate of inflation is 5 per cent. An investment is available that will be worth £115.50 in one year. It costs £100 today. Notice that with a present value of £100 and a future value in one year of £115.50, the investment has a 15.5 per cent rate of return. In calculating this 15.5 per cent return, we did not consider the effect of inflation, however, so this is the nominal return.

What is the impact of inflation here? To answer, suppose pizzas cost £5 apiece at the beginning of the year. With £100, we can buy 20 pizzas. Because the inflation rate is 5 per cent, pizzas will cost 5 per cent more, or £5.25, at the end of the year. If we take the investment, how many pizzas can we buy at the end of the year? Measured in pizzas, what is the rate of return on this investment?

Our £115.50 from the investment will buy us £115.50/5.25 = 22 pizzas. This is up from 20 pizzas, so our pizza rate of return is 10 per cent. What this illustrates is that even though the nominal return on our investment is 15.5 per cent, our buying power goes up by only 10 per cent, because of inflation. Put another way, we are really only 10 per cent richer. In this case we say that the real return is 10 per cent.

Alternatively, we can say that with 5 per cent inflation each of the £115.50 nominal pounds we get is worth 5 per cent less in real terms, so the real cash value of our investment in a year is:

$$£115.50/1.05 = £110$$

> **real rates** interest rates or rates of return that have been adjusted for inflation.
>
> **nominal rates** interest rates or rates of return that have not been adjusted for inflation.

What we have done is to *deflate* the £115.50 by 5 per cent. Because we give up £100 in current buying power to get the equivalent of £110, our real return is again 10 per cent. Because we have removed the effect of future inflation here, this £110 is said to be measured in current pounds.

The difference between nominal and real rates is important, and bears repeating:

The nominal rate on an investment is the percentage change in the amount of cash you have.

The real rate on an investment is the percentage change in how much you can buy with your cash – in other words, the percentage change in your buying power.

THE FISHER EFFECT

> **Fisher effect**
> the relationship between nominal returns, real returns and inflation.

Our discussion of real and nominal returns illustrates a relationship often called the **Fisher effect** (after the great economist Irving Fisher). Because investors are ultimately concerned with what they can buy with their money, they require compensation for inflation. Let R stand for the nominal rate and r stand for the real rate. The Fisher effect tells us that the relationship between nominal rates, real rates and inflation can be written as:

$$1 + R = (1 + r) \times (1 + h) \qquad (6.2)$$

where h is the inflation rate.

In the preceding example, the nominal rate was 15.50 per cent and the inflation rate was 5 per cent. What was the real rate? We can determine it by plugging in these numbers:

$$1 + 0.1550 = (1 + r) \times (1 + 0.05)$$
$$1 + r = 1.1550/1.05 = 1.10$$
$$r = 10\%$$

This real rate is the same as we found before. If we take another look at the Fisher effect, we can rearrange things a little as follows:

$$1 + R = (1 + r) \times (1 + h)$$
$$R = r + h + r \times h \qquad (6.3)$$

What this tells us is that the nominal rate has three components. First, there is the real rate on the investment, r. Next, there is the compensation for the decrease in the value of the money originally invested because of inflation, h. The third component represents compensation for the fact that the money earned on the investment is also worth less because of the inflation.

This third component is usually small, so it is often dropped. The nominal rate is then approximately equal to the real rate plus the inflation rate:

$$R \approx r + h \qquad (6.4)$$

EXAMPLE 6.4

THE FISHER EFFECT

If investors require a 1 per cent real rate of return, and the inflation rate is 5 per cent, what must be the approximate nominal rate? The exact nominal rate?

The nominal rate is approximately equal to the sum of the real rate and the inflation rate: 1% + 5% = 6%. From the Fisher effect, we have:

$$1 + R = (1 + r) \times (1 + h)$$
$$= 1.01 \times 1.05$$
$$= 1.0605$$

> Therefore the nominal rate will actually be higher at 6.05 per cent.
>
> When inflation and interest rates are low, the approximation above (6%) will give a good estimate of the actual nominal rate (6.05%), but this short-cut becomes significantly less accurate when inflation and interest rates are high.

It is important to note that financial rates, such as interest rates, discount rates and rates of return, are almost always quoted in nominal terms. To remind you of this, we shall henceforth use the symbol R instead of r in most of our discussions about such rates.

INFLATION AND PRESENT VALUES

One question that often comes up is the effect of inflation on present value calculations. The basic principle is simple: either discount nominal cash flows at a nominal rate, or discount real cash flows at a real rate. As long as you are consistent, you will get the same answer.

To illustrate, suppose you want to withdraw money each year for the next three years, and you want each withdrawal to have £25,000 worth of purchasing power as measured in current pounds. If the inflation rate is 4 per cent per year, then the withdrawals will simply have to increase by 4 per cent each year to compensate. The withdrawals each year will thus be:

$$C_1 = £25{,}000\,(1.04) = £26{,}000$$
$$C_2 = £25{,}000\,(1.04)^2 = £27{,}040$$
$$C_3 = £25{,}000\,(1.04)^3 = £28{,}121.60$$

What is the present value of these cash flows if the appropriate nominal discount rate is 10 per cent? This is a standard calculation, and the answer is:

$$PV = \frac{£26{,}000}{1.10} + \frac{£27{,}040}{1.10^2} + \frac{£28{,}121.60}{1.10^3}$$
$$= £67{,}111.65$$

Notice that we discounted the nominal cash flows at a nominal rate.

To calculate the present value using real cash flows, we need the real discount rate. Using the Fisher equation, the real discount rate is obtained from:

$$1 + R = (1 + r)(1 + h)$$
$$1 + 0.10 = (1 + r)(1 + 0.04)$$
$$r = 0.0577$$

By design, the real cash flows are an annuity of £25,000 per year. So the present value in real terms is:

$$PV = £25{,}000[1 - (1/1.0577^3)]/0.0577 = £67{,}111.65$$

Thus we get exactly the same answer (after allowing for a small rounding error in the real rate). Of course, you could also use the growing annuity equation we discussed in the previous chapter. The withdrawals are increasing at 4 per cent per year: so, using the growing annuity formula, the present value is:

$$PV = £26{,}000 \times \left[\frac{1 + \left(\frac{1 + 0.04}{1 + 0.10}\right)^3}{0.10 - 0.04}\right]$$
$$= £26{,}000(2.58122)$$
$$= £67{,}111.65$$

This is exactly the same present value we calculated before.

> **CONCEPT QUESTIONS**
>
> **6.6a** What is the difference between a nominal and a real return? Which is more important to a typical investor?
> **6.6b** What is the Fisher effect?

6.7 DETERMINANTS OF BOND YIELDS

We are now in a position to discuss the determinants of a bond's yield. As we shall see, the yield on any particular bond reflects a variety of factors, some common to all bonds and some specific to the issue under consideration.

THE TERM STRUCTURE OF INTEREST RATES

At any one time, short-term and long-term interest rates will generally be different. Sometimes short-term rates are higher, sometimes lower. Table 6.4 gives us a long-range perspective on this by showing UK government bond yields for securities of different maturities. As shown, in March 2020, long-term bond yields were around 0.6 per cent higher than short-term yields. This can vary over time and since 1992, the difference between short- and long-term rates has ranged from essentially zero to up to several percentage points, both positive and negative.

TABLE 6.4

UK Government bond yields, 23 March 2020

Maturity	Yield
1 Month	0.22%
3 Month	0.40%
6 Month	0.48%
1 Year	0.05%
2 Year	0.07%
3 Year	0.14%
4 Year	0.21%
5 Year	0.27%
7 Year	0.32%
8 Year	0.37%
9 Year	0.46%
10 Year	0.51%
15 Year	0.64%
20 Year	0.78%
30 Year	0.86%

Source: Data from FT.com.

term structure of interest rates the relationship between nominal interest rates on default-free, pure discount securities and time to maturity: that is, the pure time value of money.

The relationship between short- and long-term interest rates is known as the **term structure of interest rates**. To be a little more precise, the term structure of interest rates tells us what *nominal* interest rates are on *default-free, pure discount* bonds of all maturities. These rates are, in essence, 'pure' interest rates, because they involve no risk of default and a single, lump sum future payment. In other words, the term structure tells us the pure time value of money for different lengths of time.

When long-term rates are higher than short-term rates, we say that the term structure is upward sloping; when short-term rates are higher, we say it is downward sloping. The term structure can also be 'humped'. When this occurs, it is usually because rates increase at first, but then begin to decline as we look at longer and longer term rates.

The most common shape of the term structure, particularly in modern times, is upward sloping, but the degree of steepness has varied quite a bit.

What determines the shape of the term structure? There are three basic components. The first two are the ones we discussed in our previous section: the real rate of interest and the rate of inflation. The real rate of interest is the compensation that investors demand for forgoing the use of their money. You can think of it as the pure time value of money after adjusting for the effects of inflation.

The real rate of interest is the basic component underlying every interest rate, regardless of the time to maturity. When the real rate is high, all interest rates will tend to be higher, and vice versa. Thus the real rate doesn't really determine the shape of the term structure; instead, it mostly influences the overall level of interest rates.

In contrast, the prospect of future inflation strongly influences the shape of the term structure. Investors thinking about lending money for various lengths of time recognize that future inflation erodes the value of the cash that will be returned. As a result, investors demand compensation for this loss in the form of higher nominal rates. This extra compensation is called the **inflation premium**.

inflation premium
the portion of a nominal interest rate that represents compensation for expected future inflation.

If investors believe the rate of inflation will be higher in the future, then long-term nominal interest rates will tend to be higher than short-term rates. Thus an upward-sloping term structure may reflect anticipated increases in inflation. Similarly, a downward-sloping term structure probably reflects the belief that inflation will be falling in the future.

The third, and last, component of the term structure has to do with interest rate risk. As we discussed earlier in the chapter, longer-term bonds have much greater risk of loss resulting from changes in interest rates than do shorter-term bonds. Investors recognize this risk, and they demand extra compensation in the form of higher rates for bearing it. This extra compensation is called the **interest rate risk premium**. The longer is the term to maturity, the greater is the interest rate risk, so the interest rate risk premium increases with maturity. However, as we discussed earlier, interest rate risk increases at a decreasing rate, so the interest rate risk premium does as well.[6]

interest rate risk premium
the compensation investors demand for bearing interest rate risk.

Putting the pieces together, we see that the term structure reflects the combined effect of the real rate of interest, the inflation premium, and the interest rate risk premium. Figure 6.3 shows how these can interact to produce an upward-sloping term structure (in the top part of the figure) or a downward-sloping term structure (in the bottom part).

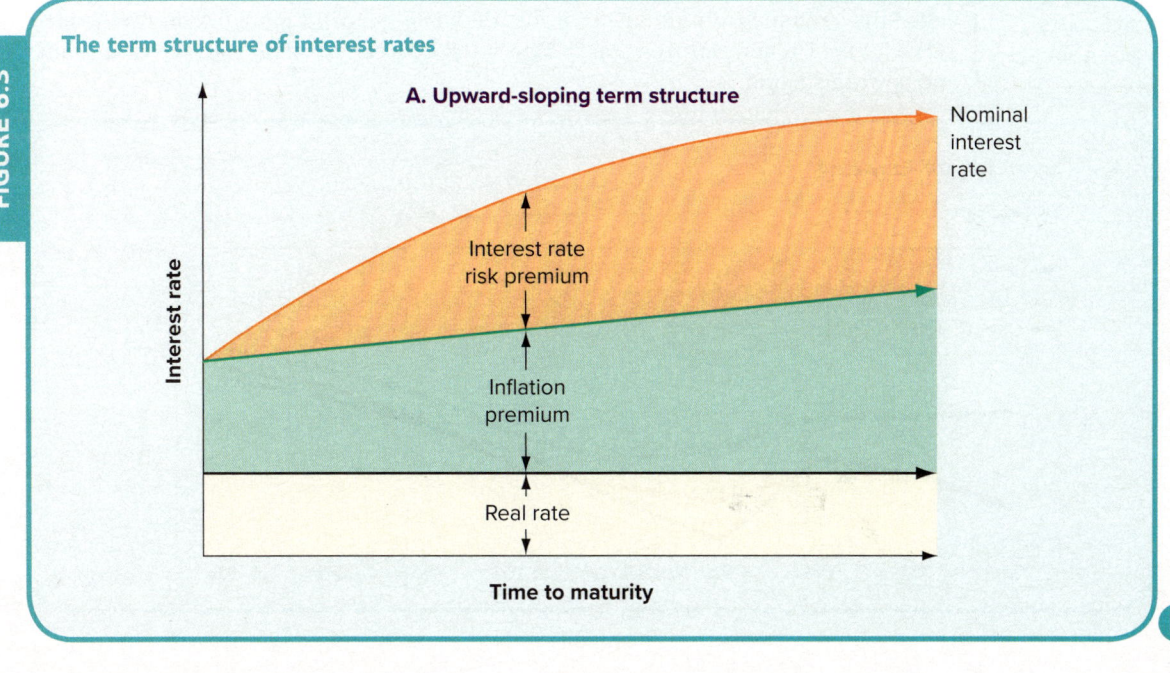

FIGURE 6.3 The term structure of interest rates

In the top part of Figure 6.3, notice how the rate of inflation is expected to rise gradually. At the same time, the interest rate risk premium increases at a decreasing rate, so the combined effect is to produce a pronounced upward-sloping term structure. In the bottom part of Figure 6.3, the rate of inflation is expected to fall in the future, and the expected decline is enough to offset the interest rate risk premium and produce a downward-sloping term structure. Notice that if the rate of inflation was expected to decline by only a small amount, we could still get an upward-sloping term structure because of the interest rate risk premium.

We assumed in drawing Figure 6.3 that the real rate would remain the same. Actually, expected future real rates could be larger or smaller than the current real rate. Also, for simplicity, we used straight lines to show expected future inflation rates as rising or declining, but they do not necessarily have to look like this. They could, for example, rise and then fall, leading to a humped yield curve.

BOND YIELDS AND THE YIELD CURVE: PUTTING IT ALL TOGETHER

Treasury yield curve a plot of the yields on Treasury notes and bonds relative to maturity.

Each day, in addition to the Treasury prices and yields shown in Table 6.4, the *Financial Times* provides a plot of Treasury yields relative to maturity. This plot is called the **Treasury yield curve** (or just the *yield curve*). Figure 6.4 shows the yield curve for the UK and Eurozone on 23 March 2020. As can be seen, both are very similar and upward sloping.

Source: http://markets.ft.com/data/bonds, 23 March 2020. © The Financial Times Ltd 2020.

As you probably now suspect, the shape of the yield curve reflects the term structure of interest rates. In fact, the Treasury yield curve and the term structure of interest rates are almost the same things. The only difference is that the term structure is based on pure discount bonds, whereas the yield curve is based on coupon bond yields. As a result, Treasury yields depend on the three components that underlie the term structure – the real rate, expected future inflation, and the interest rate risk premium.

Treasury notes and bonds have three important features that we need to remind you of: they are default-free (except for Eurozone countries), they are taxable, and they are highly liquid. This is not true of bonds in general, so we need to examine what additional factors come into play when we look at bonds issued by corporations or municipalities.

The first thing to consider is credit risk – that is, the possibility of default. Investors recognize that in most countries (except the Eurozone) issuers other than the Treasury may or may not make all the promised payments on a bond, so they demand a higher yield as compensation for this risk. This extra compensation is called the **default risk premium**. Earlier in the chapter, we saw how bonds were rated based on their credit risk. What you will find if you start looking at bonds of different ratings is that lower-rated bonds have higher yields.

An important thing to recognize about a bond's yield is that it is calculated assuming that all the promised payments will be made. As a result, it is really a promised yield, and it may or may not be what you will earn. In particular, if the issuer defaults, your actual yield will be lower – probably much lower. This fact is particularly important when it comes to junk bonds. Thanks to a clever bit of marketing, such bonds are now commonly called high-yield bonds, which has a much nicer ring to it; but now you recognize that these are really high *promised* yield bonds.

Next, recall that we discussed earlier how government bonds are free from most taxes and, as a result, have much lower yields than taxable bonds. Investors demand the extra yield on a taxable bond as compensation for the unfavourable tax treatment. This extra compensation is the **taxability premium**.

Finally, bonds have varying degrees of liquidity. As we discussed earlier, there is an enormous number of bond issues, most of which do not trade regularly. As a result, if you wanted to sell quickly, you would probably not get as good a price as you could otherwise. Investors prefer liquid assets to illiquid ones, so they demand a **liquidity premium** on top of all the other premiums we have discussed. As a result, all else being the same, less liquid bonds will have higher yields than more liquid bonds.

default risk premium
the portion of a nominal interest rate or bond yield that represents compensation for the possibility of default.

taxability premium
the portion of a nominal interest rate or bond yield that represents compensation for unfavourable tax status.

liquidity premium
the portion of a nominal interest rate or bond yield that represents compensation for lack of liquidity.

CONCLUSION

If we combine all of the things we have discussed regarding bond yields, we find that bond yields represent the combined effect of no fewer than six things. The first is the real rate of interest. On top of the real rate are five premiums representing compensation for:

1. Expected future inflation
2. Interest rate risk
3. Default risk
4. Taxability
5. Lack of liquidity

As a result, determining the appropriate yield on a bond requires careful analysis of each of these effects.

> **CONCEPT QUESTIONS**
>
> **6.7a** What is the term structure of interest rates? What determines its shape?
> **6.7b** What is the Treasury yield curve?
> **6.7c** What six components make up a bond's yield?

SUMMARY AND CONCLUSIONS

This chapter has explored bonds, bond yields and interest rates:

1. Determining bond prices and yields is an application of basic discounted cash flow principles.
2. Bond values move in the direction opposite to that of interest rates, leading to potential gains or losses for bond investors.
3. Bonds have a variety of features, spelled out in a document called the indenture.
4. Bonds are rated based on their default risk. Some bonds, such as Treasury bonds, have no risk of default, whereas so-called junk bonds have substantial default risk.
5. A wide variety of bonds exist, many of which contain exotic or unusual features.
6. Much bond trading is OTC, with little or no market transparency in many cases. As a result, bond price and volume information can be difficult to find for some types of bond.
7. Bond yields and interest rates reflect the effect of six different things: the real interest rate, and five premiums that investors demand as compensation for inflation, interest rate risk, default risk, taxability and lack of liquidity.

In closing, we note that bonds are a vital source of financing for governments and corporations of all types. Bond prices and yields are a rich subject, and our one chapter necessarily touches on only the most important concepts and ideas. There is a great deal more we could say, but instead we shall move on to equities in our next chapter.

CHAPTER REVIEW AND SELF-TEST PROBLEMS

6.1 Bond Values A Vodafone Group bond has a 7 per cent coupon rate and a £1,000 face value. Interest is paid semi-annually, and the bond has 60 years to maturity. If investors require a 6 per cent yield, what is the bond's value? What is the effective annual yield on the bond?

6.2 Bond Yields An Ekornes ASA bond carries an 8 per cent coupon, paid semi-annually. The par value is NKr1,000, and the bond matures in 6 years. If the bond currently sells for NKr911.37, what is its yield to maturity? What is the effective annual yield?

SOLUTIONS

6.1 Because the bond has a 7 per cent coupon yield and investors require a 6 per cent return, we know that the bond must sell at a premium. Notice that, because the bond pays interest semi-annually, the coupons amount to £70/2 = £35 every 6 months. The required yield is 6%/2 = 3% every 6 months. Finally, the bond matures in 60 years, so there are a total of 120 six-month periods.

The bond's value is thus equal to the present value of £35 every 6 months for the next 120 six-month periods plus the present value of the £1,000 face amount:

$$\text{Bond value} = £35 \times \left[\frac{1 - 1/1.03^{120}}{0.03}\right] + \frac{1{,}000}{1.03^{120}}$$
$$= £1{,}133.05579 + £28.80932$$
$$= £1{,}161.8651$$

Notice that we discounted the £1,000 back 120 periods at 3 per cent per period, rather than 60 years at 6 per cent. The reason is that the effective annual yield on the bond is $1.03^2 - 1 = 6.09\%$, not 6 per cent. We thus could have used 6.09 per cent per year for 60 years when we calculated the present value of the £1,000 face amount, and the answer would have been the same.

6.2 The present value of the bond's cash flows is its current price, NKr911.37. The coupon is NKr40 every 6 months for 12 periods. The face value is NKr1,000. So the bond's yield is the unknown discount rate in the following:

$$\text{NKr}911.37 = \text{NKr}40 \times \left[\frac{1 - 1/(1+r)^{12}}{r}\right] + \frac{1{,}000}{(1+r)^{12}}$$

The bond sells at a discount. Because the coupon rate is 8 per cent, the yield must be something in excess of that. If we were to solve this by trial and error, we might try 12 per cent (or 6 per cent per 6 months):

$$\text{Bond value} = \text{NKr}40 \times \left[\frac{1 - 1/1.06^{12}}{0.06}\right] + \frac{1{,}000}{1.06^{12}}$$
$$= \text{NKr}832.32$$

This is less than the actual value, so our discount rate is too high. We now know that the yield is somewhere between 8 and 12 per cent. With further trial and error (or a little computer assistance), the yield works out to be 10 per cent, or 5 per cent every 6 months. By convention, the bond's yield to maturity would be quoted as $2 \times 5\% = 10\%$. The effective yield is thus $1.05^2 - 1 = 10.25\%$.

QUESTIONS AND PROBLEMS

6.1 Interpreting Bond Yields Is the yield to maturity on a bond the same thing as the required return? Is YTM the same thing as the coupon rate? Suppose today a 10 per cent coupon bond sells at par. Two years from now, the required return on the same bond is 8 per cent. What is the coupon rate on the bond then? The YTM?

6.2 Interpreting Bond Yields Suppose you buy an 8 per cent coupon, 10-year bond today when it is first issued. If interest rates suddenly rise to 16 per cent, what happens to the value of your bond? Why?

6.3 Bond Prices Corvid plc has 5 per cent coupon bonds on the market that have 10 years left to maturity. The bonds make annual payments. If the YTM on these bonds is 7 per cent, what is the current bond price? The par value of the bond is £1,000.

6.4 Bond Yields Page plc has 10 per cent coupon bonds on the market, with nine years left to maturity. The bonds make annual payments. If the bond currently sells for £9,340 and the face value of the bonds is £10,000, what is its YTM?

6.5 Valuing Bonds Your company has just issued a five-year bond with face value of €1,000 and paying an annual coupon of 2 per cent. What is the price of the bond if the YTM is:

(a) 1 per cent.

(b) 2 per cent.

(c) 4 per cent.

Assume interest is calculated at the beginning of the period and paid annually.

6.6 Coupon Rates Steen Familie NV has bonds on the market making annual payments, with 10 years to maturity, and selling for €1,045. At this price, the bonds yield 5 per cent. The par value of the bond is €1,000. What must the coupon rate be on the bonds?

6.7 Bond Yields RCA Holdings plc has just issued an 24-month bond with a face value of €10,000, and an annual coupon rate of 8 per cent, paid every quarter. The issue price is €9,984.50. What is its quarterly YTM?

6.8 Bond Yields Ngata SA issued 10-year bonds five years ago at a coupon rate of 4 per cent. The bonds make semi-annual payments. If these bonds currently sell for 95 per cent of par value, what is the YTM?

6.9 Coupon Rates Stand AG has bonds on the market with 17.5 years to maturity, a YTM of 8 per cent, and a current price of €924. The bonds make semi-annual payments. The par value of the bond is €1,000. What must the coupon rate be on these bonds?

6.10 Calculating Real Rates of Return If Treasury bills are currently paying 7 per cent and the inflation rate is 3.8 per cent, what is the approximate real rate of interest? The exact real rate?

6.11 Inflation and Nominal Returns Suppose the real rate is 4 per cent and the inflation rate is 4.7 per cent. What rate would you expect to see on a Treasury bill?

6.12 Nominal and Real Returns An investment offers a 15 per cent total return over the coming year. You think the total real return on this investment will be only 9 per cent. What do you believe the inflation rate will be over the next year?

6.13 Total Returns The UK government issues a five-year bond which makes annual coupon payments of 2 per cent and offers a yield of 3 per cent annually compounded. Suppose that one year later the bond still yields 3 per cent. What return has the bondholder earned over the 12-month period? Now suppose that the bond yields 2 per cent at the end of the year. What return would the bondholder earn in this case? Assume the face value of the bond is €1,000 and that coupon payments are made at the beginning of the year.

6.14 Bond Price Movements Consider the bond in question 6.5(c). If yields remain unchanged, what do you expect the price of this bond will be one year from now? In two years? What's going on here? Illustrate your answers by graphing bond prices versus time to maturity. Assume the coupon payments are made at the beginning of the year and YTM is 4 per cent.

6.15 Bond Price Movements Bond X is a premium bond making annual payments. The bond pays an 8 per cent coupon, has a YTM of 6 per cent, and has 13 years to maturity. Bond Y is a discount bond making annual payments. This bond pays a 6 per cent coupon, has a YTM of 8 per cent, and also has 13 years to maturity. The par value of the bonds is £1,000. If interest rates remain unchanged, what do you expect the price of these bonds to be one year from now? In 3 years? In 8 years? In 12 years? In 13 years? What's going on here? Illustrate your answers by plotting bond prices against time to maturity.

6.16 Bond Returns You purchase a bond with an invoice price of £9,680. The bond has a coupon rate of 7.4 per cent, and there are four months to the next semi-annual coupon date. What is the clean price of the bond?

6.17 Interest Rate Risk Both Bond Tony and Bond Peter have 10 per cent coupons, make semi-annual payments, and are priced at par value. Bond Tony has 3 years to maturity, whereas Bond Peter has 20 years to maturity. If interest rates suddenly rise by 2 per cent, what is the percentage change in the price of Bond Tony? Of Bond Peter? If rates were to suddenly fall by 2 per cent instead, what would the percentage change in the price of Bond Tony be then? Of Bond Peter? Illustrate your answers by plotting bond prices against YTM. What does this problem tell you about the interest rate risk of longer-term bonds?

6.18 Interest Rate Risk Bond J is a 4 per cent coupon bond. Bond K is a 12 per cent coupon bond. Both bonds have nine years to maturity, make semi-annual payments, and have a YTM of 8 per cent. The par value of the bonds is £1,000. If interest rates suddenly rise by 2 per cent, what is the percentage price change of these bonds? What if rates suddenly fall by 2 per cent instead? What does this problem tell you about the interest rate risk of lower-coupon bonds?

6.19 Bond Yields Manish Quantum Sustainability plc has 6 per cent coupon bonds on the market with seven years to maturity. The bonds make semi-annual payments and currently sell for 102 per cent of par. What is the current yield on the bonds? The YTM? The effective annual yield?

6.20 Bond Yields Seether plc wants to issue new 20-year bonds for some much-needed expansion projects. The company currently has 8 per cent coupon bonds on the market that sell for £93,000 with a par value of £100,000, make semi-annual payments, and mature in 20 years. What coupon rate should the company set on its new bonds if it wants them to sell at par?

6.21 Finding the Bond Maturity Fluss AB has 8 per cent coupon bonds making annual payments with a YTM of 7.2 per cent. The current yield on these bonds is 7.55 per cent. How many years do these bonds have left until they mature?

6.22 Accrued Interest You purchase a bond with a coupon rate of 6.8 per cent and a clean price of £10,730, face value is £10,000. If the next semi-annual coupon payment is due in 2 months, what is the invoice price?

6.23 Using Bond Quotes Suppose the following bond quotes for Giorni d'Estate SpA appear in the financial page of today's newspaper. Assume the bond makes semi-annual payments, has a face value of €1,000 and the current date is 24 March 2021. What is the yield to maturity of the bond? What is the current yield?

Company	Coupon	Maturity	Last price	Last yield	Est. vol. (000s)
Giorni d'Estate	9.2	24 March 2032	1089.6	??	1,827

6.24 Bond Prices versus Yields

(a) What is the relationship between the price of a bond and its YTM?

(b) Explain why some bonds sell at a premium over par value while other bonds sell at a discount. What do you know about the relationship between the coupon rate and the YTM for premium bonds? What about for discount bonds? For bonds selling at par value?

(c) What is the relationship between the current yield and YTM for premium bonds? For discount bonds? For bonds selling at par value?

6.25 Interest on Zeros Tesla SA needs to raise funds to finance a plant expansion, and it has decided to issue 20-year zero coupon bonds to raise the money. The required return on the bonds will be 12 per cent. What will these bonds sell for at issuance? Assume semi-annual compounding. The par value is €1,000.

6.26 Zero Coupon Bonds Suppose your company needs to raise €20 million and you want to issue 10-year bonds for this purpose. Assume the required return on your bond issue will be 8 per cent, and you're evaluating two issue alternatives: an 8 per cent semi-annual coupon bond and a zero coupon bond. Your company's tax rate is 20 per cent. The par value of the bonds is €1,000.

(a) How many of the coupon bonds would you need to issue to raise the €20 million? How many of the zeros would you need to issue?

(b) In five years, what will your company's repayment be if you issue the coupon bonds? What if you issue the zeros?

(c) Based on your answers in (a) and (b), why would you ever want to issue the zeros? To answer, calculate the firm's after-tax cash outflows for the first year under the two different scenarios.

6.27 Finding the Maturity You've just found a 10 per cent coupon bond on the market that sells for par value. What is the yield to maturity on this bond?

6.28 Real Cash Flows When Marilyn Monroe died, ex-husband Joe DiMaggio vowed to place fresh flowers on her grave every Sunday as long as he lived. The week after she died in 1962, a bunch of fresh flowers that the former baseball player thought appropriate for the star cost about $5. Based on actuarial tables, 'Joltin' Joe' could expect to live for 30 years after the actress died. Assume that the EAR is 8.4 per cent. Also, assume that the price of the flowers will increase at 3.7 per cent per year, when expressed as an EAR. Assuming that each year has exactly 52 weeks, what is the present value of this commitment? Joe began purchasing flowers the week after Marilyn died.

6.29 Real Cash Flows You want to have €1.5 million in real euros in an account when you retire in 40 years. The nominal return on your investment is 11 per cent and the inflation rate is 3.8 per cent. What real amount must you deposit each year to achieve your goal?

6.30 Components of Bond Returns Bond P is a premium bond with a 10 per cent coupon. Bond D is a 7 per cent coupon bond currently selling at a discount. Both bonds make annual payments, have a YTM of 9 per cent, and have five years to maturity. The par value is £1,000. What is the current yield for bond P? For bond D? If interest rates remain unchanged, what is the expected capital gains yield over the next year for bond P? For bond D? Explain your answers and the interrelationships among the various types of yield.

6.31 Holding Period Yield The YTM on a bond is the interest rate you earn on your investment if interest rates don't change. If you actually sell the bond before it matures, your realized return is known as the *holding period yield* (HPY).

(a) Suppose that today you buy a 8 per cent annual coupon bond for €1,150. The bond has 10 years to maturity. What rate of return do you expect to earn on your investment?

(b) Two years from now, the YTM on your bond has declined by 1 per cent, and you decide to sell. What price will your bond sell for? What is the HPY on your investment? Compare this yield with the YTM when you first bought the bond. Why are they different?

6.32 Valuing Bonds Mallory plc has two different bonds currently outstanding. Bond M has a face value of £20,000 and matures in 20 years. The bond makes no payments for the first six years, then pays £1,200 every six months over the subsequent eight years, and finally pays £1,500 every six months over the last six years. Bond N also has a face value of £20,000 and a maturity of 20 years; it makes no coupon payments over the life of the bond. If the required return on both these bonds is 10 per cent compounded semi-annually, what is the current price of bond M? Of bond N?

6.33 Valuing the Call Feature Consider the prices in the following three Treasury issues as of 15 May:

Coupon	Maturity	Price	Change	YTM
6.500	16 May	106:10	−13	5.28
8.250	16 May	103:14	−3	5.24
12.000	16 May	134:25	−15	5.32

The bond in the middle is callable in February of next year. Assume £1,000 par value. What is the implied value of the call feature? (*Hint:* Is there a way to combine the two non-callable issues to create an issue that has the same coupon as the callable bond?)

6.34 Treasury Bonds Consider the following Treasury bond on 11 May:

| 9.125 | 15 May | 100:03 | ... | −2.15 |

Why would anyone buy this Treasury bond with a negative yield to maturity? How is this possible?

6.35 Real Cash Flows You are planning to save for retirement over the next 30 years. To save for retirement, you will invest £900 a month in an equity account in real pounds and £450 a month in a bond account in real pounds. The effective annual return of the equity account is expected to be 11 per cent, and the bond account will earn 7 per cent. When you retire, you will combine your money into an account with a 9 per cent effective return. The inflation rate over this period is expected to be 4 per cent. How much can you withdraw each month from your account in real terms, assuming a 25-year withdrawal period? What is the nominal pound amount of your last withdrawal?

MINI CASE

FINANCING EXPANSION PLANS WITH A BOND ISSUE

Peter Simon, the owner of West Coast Ventilators, has decided to expand his operations in relation to heightened demand for medical-grade oxygen ventilators. He asked his newly hired financial analyst, Cecilia Shaw, to enlist an underwriter to help raise £50 million in new five-year bonds to finance new manufacturing facilities and the technology required to produce ventilators at pace. Cecilia has entered into discussions with Arthur Brodie, an underwriter, about which bond features West Coast Ventilators should consider, and also what coupon rate the issue is likely to have. Although Cecilia is aware of bond features, she is uncertain of the costs and benefits of some features, so she isn't sure how each feature would affect the coupon rate of the bond issue.

QUESTIONS

1. In approaching potential lenders to finance the expansion of West Coast Ventilators, the lenders say that they would like to limit the actions that the firm can undertake over the duration of the loan. What is this type of agreement called?
2. Arthur has come to discuss the first covenants that the lenders wish to impose, which is a list of things the firm cannot do. What type of covenants are these?
3. Arthur has come back to discuss the second set of covenants that the lenders wish to impose, which is a list of things the firm must do. What type of covenants are these?
4. Arthur is also considering whether to issue coupon-bearing bonds or zero-coupon bonds. The yield to maturity on either bond issue will be 4 per cent. The coupon bond would have a 6 per cent coupon rate. The company's tax rate is 18 per cent. How many of the coupon bonds must West Coast Ventilators issue to raise the £50 million? How many of the zero-coupon bonds must it issue? Assume a £1,000 face value for the bonds.
5. In five years, what will be the principal repayment due if West Coast Ventilators issues the coupon bonds? What if it issues the zeros?
6. What are the company's considerations in issuing a coupon bond compared with a zero-coupon bond?

ADDITIONAL READING

The bond valuation methods used in this chapter can be extended easily to complex instruments that have a number of additional characteristics. If you wish to explore this area in more detail, you should read: *Financial Markets and Corporate Strategy*, 2nd edition, McGraw-Hill, 2011, by David Hillier, Mark Grinblatt and Sheridan Titman.

Endnotes

1. There is no universally agreed-upon distinction between short-term and long-term debt. In addition, people often refer to *intermediate-term debt*, which has a maturity of more than 1 year and less than 3 to 5, or even 10, years.
2. The word *funding* is part of the jargon of finance. It generally refers to the long term. Thus a firm planning to 'fund' its debt requirements may be replacing short-term debt with long-term debt.
3. The words *loan agreement* or *loan contract* are usually used for privately placed debt and term loans.
4. Real property includes land and things 'affixed thereto'. It does not include cash or inventories.
5. A bond issued with a very low coupon rate (as opposed to a zero coupon rate) is an *original-issue discount (OID) bond*.
6. In days of old, the interest rate risk premium was called a 'liquidity' premium. Today, the term *liquidity premium* has an altogether different meaning, which we explore in our next section. Also, the interest rate risk premium is sometimes called a *maturity risk premium*. Our terminology is consistent with the modern view of the term structure.

CHAPTER 7
EQUITY VALUATION

> ### LEARNING OBJECTIVES
> After studying this chapter, you should understand:
> **LO1** How share prices depend on future dividends and dividend growth.
> **LO2** The different ways corporate directors are elected to office.
> **LO3** How the equity markets work.
>
> ### KEY NOTATIONS
> D Dividend
> P Share price
> g Growth rate
> r The interest rate or discount rate
> t Number of periods

WHEN THE STOCK MARKET CLOSED ON 25 March 2020, the equity of Imperial Brands plc was selling for £13.31. On that same day, shares in Anglo American plc closed at £13.34, while shares in Royal Dutch Shell plc closed at £13.36. Because the share prices of these three companies were so similar, you might expect that they would be offering very similar dividends to their shareholders, but you would be wrong. Imperial Brand's annual dividend was £1.88 per share, Anglo American's was approximately £0.89 per share, and Royal Dutch Shell's was around £1.70 – opposite to perhaps what you would expect.

However, as we shall see in this chapter, dividends are one of the primary factors we look at when attempting to value equities. This chapter explores dividends, share prices, and the connection between the two.

In our previous chapter, we introduced you to bonds and bond valuation. In this chapter, we turn to the other primary source of financing for corporations: ordinary and preference shares. We first describe the cash flows associated with a share of equity and then go on to develop a famous result, the dividend growth or dividend discount model. The dividend growth model is just one of many ways we can value shares, but it gives us a lot of insight into the factors that drive equity valuations. From there, we move on to examine various important features of ordinary and preference shares, focusing on shareholder rights. We close the chapter with a discussion of how shares of equity are traded, and how share prices and other important information are reported in the financial press.

> **REAL WORLD INSIGHTS**
>
> Equity and bond valuation follow the same principles: identify the future cash flows of the security and estimate the risk of the investment. During the depths of the Covid-19 pandemic in March 2020, Apple's share price had dropped over 30 per cent within only 30 days. Yet, at the same time, the company had experienced record-breaking sales with revenues up to $267 billion.
>
> How is it possible to have such poor price performance on the one hand while delivering fantastic performance on the other? Analysts certainly take past performance into account, but their focus is on the future and what is likely to happen to sales in the next 8-10 quarters.
>
> The Covid-19 epidemic shook every country's economy to the core with complete lockdowns in many countries across the world. Apple shut every single one of its stores apart from in China, and the prospect of a long-term economic depression was real. Analysts considered not only Apple's future cash flows but other issues as well, such as future consumer spending, government tax increases and breaks in global supply chains. This revision in expectations led to the reassessment of the company's value.
>
> The Apple example gives us a powerful lesson in equity valuation: the past does not equal the future!
>
> *Source: FT.com.*

7.1 SHARE VALUATION

Share prices are more difficult to value in practice than a bond, for at least three reasons. First, with equity, not even the promised cash flows are known in advance. Second, the life of the investment is essentially forever because equity has no maturity. Third, there is no way to easily observe the rate of return that the market requires. Nonetheless, as we shall see, there are cases in which we can come up with the present value of the future cash flows for a share of equity, and thus determine its value.

CASH FLOWS

Imagine that you are considering buying a share of equity today. You plan to sell the equity in one year. You somehow know that it will be worth £70 at that time. You predict that the equity will also pay a £10 per share dividend at the end of the year. If you require a 25 per cent return on your investment, what is the most you would pay for the equity? In other words, what is the present value of the £10 dividend along with the £70 ending value at 25 per cent?

If you buy the equity today and sell it at the end of the year, you will have a total of £80 in cash. At 25 per cent:

$$\text{Present value} = \frac{£10 + 70}{1.25} = £64$$

Therefore £64 is the value you would assign to the equity today. It is important to note that the present value is an intrinsic value of the equity, and the observed share price may be quite different. Your assumptions and those of the market may be quite different, and this may lead to differences in your estimate.

More generally, let P_0 be the current share price, and assign P_1 to be the price in one period. If D_1 is the cash dividend paid at the end of the period, then:

$$P_0 = \frac{D_1 + P_1}{1 + R} \tag{7.1}$$

where R is the required return in the market on this investment.

Notice that we really haven't said much so far. If we wanted to determine the share price today (P_0), we would first have to come up with the value in one year (P_1). This is even harder to do, so we've only made the problem more complicated.

What is the price in one period, P_1? We don't know in general. Instead, suppose we somehow knew the price in two periods, P_2. Given a predicted dividend in two periods, D_2, the share price in one period would be:

$$P_1 = \frac{D_2 + P_2}{1 + R}$$

If we were to substitute this expression for P_1 into our expression for P_0, we would have:

$$P_0 = \frac{D_1 + P_1}{1 + R} = \frac{D_1 + (D_2 + P_2)/(1 + R)}{1 + R}$$
$$= \frac{D_1}{(1 + R)^1} + \frac{D_2}{(1 + R)^2} + \frac{P_2}{(1 + R)^2}$$

Now we need to get a price in two periods. We don't know this either, so we can procrastinate again and write:

$$P_2 = \frac{D_3 + P_3}{1 + R}$$

If we substitute this back in for P_2, we have:

$$P_0 = \frac{D_1}{(1 + R)^1} + \frac{D_2}{(1 + R)^2} + \frac{P_2}{(1 + R)^2}$$
$$= \frac{D_1}{(1 + R)^1} + \frac{D_2}{(1 + R)^2} + \frac{(D_3 + P_3)/(1 + R)}{(1 + R)^2}$$
$$= \frac{D_1}{(1 + R)^1} + \frac{D_2}{(1 + R)^2} + \frac{D_3}{(1 + R)^3} + \frac{P_3}{(1 + R)^3}$$

You should start to notice that we can push the problem of coming up with the share price off into the future forever. Note that no matter what the share price is, the present value is essentially zero if we push the sale of the equity far enough away.[1] We are eventually left with the result that the current price of the equity is the present value of the dividends beginning in one period and extending out forever:

$$P_0 = \frac{D_1}{(1 + R)^1} + \frac{D_2}{(1 + R)^2} + \frac{D_3}{(1 + R)^3} + \frac{D_4}{(1 + r)^4} + \frac{D_5}{(1 + R)^5} + \ldots$$

We have illustrated here that the share price today is equal to the present value of all of the future dividends. How many future dividends are there? In principle, there can be an infinite number, which means that we still can't compute a value for the equity, because we would have to forecast an infinite number of dividends and then discount them all. In the next section, we consider some special cases in which we can get around this problem.

> **EXAMPLE 7.1**
>
> ### GROWTH STOCKS
>
> Many companies do not pay dividends because they plough back all earnings into the firm. Are these companies' shares worth nothing? It depends. When we say that the value of the equity is equal to the present value of the future dividends, we don't rule out the possibility that some of those dividends are zero. They just can't *all* be zero.
>
> Imagine a company that has a provision in its articles and memorandum of association that prohibits the paying of dividends now or ever. The corporation never borrows any money, never pays out any cash to shareholders in any form whatsoever, and never sells any assets. Such a corporation couldn't really exist, because the tax authorities wouldn't like it, and the shareholders could always vote to amend the articles and memorandum if they wanted to. If it did exist, however, what would the equity be worth?
>
> The shares are worth absolutely nothing. Such a company is a financial 'black hole'. Money goes in, but nothing valuable ever comes out. Because nobody would ever get any return on this investment, the investment has no value. This example is a little absurd, but it illustrates that when we speak of companies that don't pay dividends, what we mean is that they are not *currently* paying dividends.

SOME SPECIAL CASES

In a few useful special circumstances, we can come up with a value for the equity. What we have to do is make some simplifying assumptions about the pattern of future dividends. The three cases we consider are the following:

1. The dividend has a zero growth rate.
2. The dividend grows at a constant rate.
3. The dividend grows at a constant rate after some length of time.

We consider each of these separately.

Zero Growth

The case of zero growth is one we've already seen. A share of equity in a company with a constant dividend is much like a preference share. For a zero-growth share of equity, this implies that:

$$D_1 = D_2 = D_3 = D = \text{constant}$$

So the value of the equity is:

$$P_0 = \frac{D}{(1+R)^1} + \frac{D}{(1+R)^2} + \frac{D}{(1+R)^3} + \frac{D}{(1+R)^4} + \frac{D}{(1+R)^5} + \ldots$$

Because the dividend is always the same, the share price can be viewed as an ordinary perpetuity with a cash flow equal to D every period. The per-share value is thus given by:

$$P_0 = D/R \qquad (7.2)$$

where R is the required return.

For example, suppose Paradise Prototyping has a policy of paying a €10 per share dividend every year. If this policy is to be continued indefinitely, what is the value of a share of equity if the required return is 20 per cent? The equity, in this case, amounts to an ordinary perpetuity, so it is worth €10/0.20 = €50 per share.

Constant Growth

Suppose we know that the dividend for some company always grows at a steady rate. Call this growth rate g. If we let D_0 be the dividend just paid, then the next dividend, D_1, is:

$$D_1 = D_0 \times (1+g)$$

The dividend in two periods is:

$$D_2 = D_1 \times (1+g)$$
$$= [D_0 \times (1+g)] \times (1+g)$$
$$= D_0 \times (1+g)^2$$

We could repeat this process to come up with the dividend at any point in the future. In general, from our discussion of compound growth in Chapter 4, we know that the dividend t periods into the future, D_t, is given by:

$$D_t = D_0 \times (1+g)^t$$

As we have previously seen, an asset with cash flows that grow at a constant rate forever is called a *growing perpetuity*.

The assumption of steady dividend growth might strike you as peculiar. Why would the dividend grow at a constant rate? The reason is that, for many companies, steady growth in dividends is an explicit goal. For example, in 2019, Procter & Gamble, the US-based maker of personal care and household products, increased its dividend by 4.00 per cent to $2.983 per share: this increase was notable because it was the 63rd in a row. The subject of dividend growth falls under the general heading of dividend policy, so we shall defer further discussion of it to a later chapter.

EXAMPLE 7.2

DIVIDEND GROWTH

Oasis plc has just paid a dividend of £3 per share. The dividend of this company grows at a steady rate of 8 per cent per year. Based on this information, what will the dividend be in 5 years?

Here we have a £3 current amount that grows at 8 per cent per year for 5 years. The future amount is thus:

$$£3 \times 1.08^5 = £3 \times 1.4693 = £4.41$$

The dividend will, therefore, increase by £1.41 over the coming 5 years.

If the dividend grows at a steady rate, then we have replaced the problem of forecasting an infinite number of future dividends with the issue of coming up with a single growth rate – a considerable simplification. In this case, if we take D_0 to be the dividend just paid, and g to be the constant growth rate, the value of a share of equity can be written as:

$$P_0 = \frac{D_1}{(1+R)^1} + \frac{D_2}{(1+R)^2} + \frac{D_3}{(1+R)^3} + \cdots$$
$$= \frac{D_0 \times (1+g)^1}{(1+R)^1} + \frac{D_0 \times (1+g)^2}{(1+R)^2} + \frac{D_0 \times (1+g)^3}{(1+R)^3} + \cdots$$

As long as the growth rate, g, is less than the discount rate, r, the present value of this series of cash flows can be written simply as:

$$P_0 = \frac{D_0 \times (1+g)}{R-g}$$
$$= \frac{D_1}{R-g}$$

(7.3)

This elegant result goes by a lot of different names. We shall call it the **dividend growth model**. It is also known as the *dividend discount model* and, by any name, it is very easy to use. To illustrate, suppose D_0 is £2.30, R is 13 per cent, and g is 5 per cent. The share price in this case is:

$$P_0 = D_0 \times (1+g)/(R-g)$$
$$= £2.30 \times 1.05/(0.13 - 0.05)$$
$$= £2.415/0.08$$
$$= £30.19$$

> **dividend growth model**
> a model that determines the current share price as its dividend next period divided by the discount rate less the dividend growth rate.

We can use the dividend growth model to get the share price at any point in time, not just today. In general, the share price as of time t is:

$$P_t = \frac{D_t \times (1+g)}{R-g} = \frac{D_{t+1}}{R-g} \tag{7.4}$$

In our example, suppose we are interested in the share price in 5 years, P_5. We first need the dividend at time 5, D_5. Because the dividend just paid is £2.30, and the growth rate is 5 per cent per year, D_5 is:

$$D_5 = £2.30 \times 1.05^5 = £2.30 \times 1.2763 = £2.935$$

From the dividend growth model, we get the share price in 5 years:

$$P_5 = \frac{D_5 \times (1+g)}{R-g}$$
$$= \frac{£2.935 \times 1.05}{0.13 - 0.05}$$
$$= \frac{£3.0822}{0.08}$$
$$= £38.53$$

Example 7.3 illustrates that the dividend growth model makes the implicit assumption that the share price will grow at the same constant rate as the dividend. This isn't too surprising. What it tells us is that if the cash flows on an investment grow at a constant rate through time, so does the value of that investment.

EXAMPLE 7.3

GORDON GROWTH LIMITED

The next dividend for Gordon Growth Limited will be £4 per share. Investors require a 16 per cent return on companies such as Gordon. Gordon's dividend increases by 6 per cent every year. Based on the dividend growth model, what is the value of Gordon's equity today? What is the value in 4 years?

The only tricky thing here is that the next dividend, D_1, is given as £4, so we won't multiply this by $(1 + g)$. With this in mind, the share price is given by:

$$P_0 = D_1/(R - g)$$
$$= £4/(0.16 - 0.06)$$
$$= £4/0.10$$
$$= £40$$

Because we already have the dividend in 1 year, we know that the dividend in 4 years is equal to $D_1 \times (1 + g)^3 = £4 \times 1.06^3 = £4.764$.

The price in 4 years is therefore

$$P_4 = D_4 \times (1 + g)/(R - g)$$
$$= £4.764 \times 1.06/(0.16 - 0/06)$$
$$= £5.50/0.10$$
$$= £50.50$$

Notice in this example that P_4 is equal to $P_0 \times (1 + g)^4$:

$$P_4 = £50.50$$
$$= £40 \times 1.06^4$$
$$= P_0 \times (1 + g)^4$$

To see why this is so, notice first that:

$$P_4 = D_5/(R - g)$$

However, D_5 is just equal to $D_1 \times (1 + g)^4$, so we can write P_4 as:

$$P_4 = D_1 \times (1 + g)^4/(R - g)$$
$$= [D_1/(R - g)] \times (1 + g)^4$$
$$= P_0 \times (1 + g)^4$$

You might wonder what would happen with the dividend growth model if the growth rate, g, were higher than the discount rate, R. It looks like we would get a negative share price because $R - g$ would be less than zero. This is not what would happen.

Instead, if the constant growth rate exceeds the discount rate, then the share price is infinitely large. Why? If the growth rate is bigger than the discount rate, the present value of the dividends keeps getting bigger. Virtually the same is true if the growth rate and the discount rate are equal. In both cases, the simplification that allows us to replace the infinite stream of dividends with the dividend growth model is 'illegal', so the answers we get from the dividend growth model are nonsense unless the growth rate is less than the discount rate.

Finally, the expression we came up with for the constant growth case will work for any growing perpetuity, not just dividends on ordinary equity. As we saw in Chapter 4, if C is the next cash flow on a growing perpetuity, then the present value of the cash flows is given by:

$$\text{Present value} = \frac{C_1}{(R - g)}$$
$$= \frac{C_0(1 + g)}{R - g}$$

Notice that this expression looks like the result for an ordinary perpetuity, except that we have $R - g$ on the bottom instead of just R.

Non-Constant Growth

The next case we consider is non-constant growth. The main reason for considering this case is to allow for 'supernormal' growth rates over some finite length of time. As we discussed earlier, the growth rate cannot exceed the required return indefinitely, but it certainly could do so for some number of years. To avoid the problem of having to forecast and discount an infinite number of dividends, we shall require that the dividends start growing at a constant rate at some time in the future.

For a simple example of non-constant growth, consider the case of a company that is currently not paying dividends. You predict that, in 5 years, the company will pay a dividend for the first time. The dividend will be €0.50 per share. You expect that this dividend will then grow at a rate of 10 per cent per year indefinitely. The required return on companies such as this one is 20 per cent. What is the share price today?

To see what the equity is worth today, we first find out what it will be worth once dividends are paid. We can then calculate the present value of that future price to get today's price. The first dividend will be paid in 5 years, and the dividend will grow steadily from then on. Using the dividend growth model, we can say that the price in 4 years will be:

$$P_4 = D_4 \times (1 + g)/(R - g)$$
$$= D_5/(R - g)$$
$$= €0.50/(0.20 - 0.10)$$
$$= €5$$

If the equity will be worth €5 in 4 years, then we can get the current value by discounting this price back 4 years at 20 per cent:

$$P_0 = €5/1.20^4$$
$$= €5/2.0736$$
$$= €2.41$$

The equity is, therefore, worth €2.41 today.

The problem of non-constant growth is only slightly more complicated if the dividends are not zero for the first several years. For example, suppose you have come up with the following dividend forecasts for the next 3 years:

Year	Expected dividend (€)
1	1.00
2	2.00
3	2.50

After the third year, the dividend will grow at a constant rate of 5 per cent per year. The required return is 10 per cent. What is the share price today?

In dealing with non-constant growth, a timeline can be helpful. Figure 7.1 illustrates one for this problem. The critical thing to notice is when constant growth starts. As we've shown, for this problem, constant growth begins at time 3, which means we can use our constant growth model to determine the share price at time 3, P_3. By far the most common mistake in this situation is to incorrectly identify the start of the constant growth phase and, as a result, calculate the future share price at the wrong time.

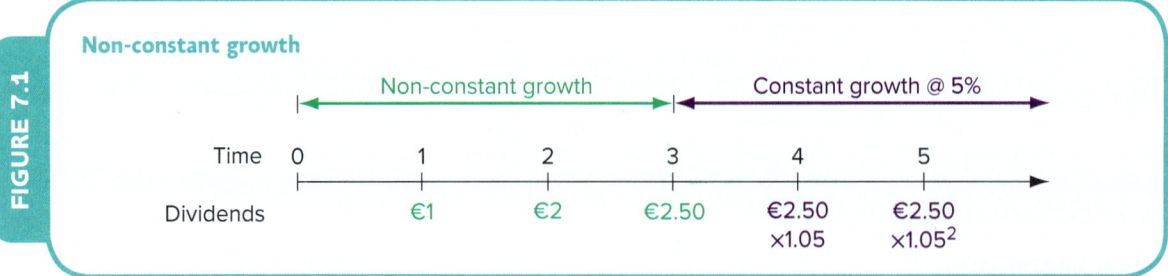

FIGURE 7.1

As always, the share price is the present value of all future dividends. To calculate this present value, we first have to compute the present value of the share price 3 years down the road, just as we did before. We then have to add in the present value of the dividends that will be paid between now and then. So the price in 3 years is:

$$P_3 = D_3 \times (1 + g)/(R - g)$$
$$= €2.50 \times 1.05/(0.10 - 0.05)$$
$$= €52.50$$

We can now calculate the total value of the equity as the present value of the first three dividends plus the present value of the price at time 3, P_3:

$$P_0 = \frac{D_1}{(1+R)^1} + \frac{D_2}{(1+R)^2} + \frac{D_3}{(1+R)^3} + \frac{P_3}{(1+R)^3}$$

$$= \frac{€1}{1.10} + \frac{2}{1.10^2} + \frac{2.50}{1.10^3} + \frac{52.50}{1.10^3}$$

$$= €0.91 + 1.65 + 1.88 + 39.44$$

$$= €43.88$$

The share price today is thus €43.88.

EXAMPLE 7.4

SUPERNORMAL GROWTH

Kettenreaktion AG has been growing at a phenomenal rate of 30 per cent per year because of its rapid expansion and explosive sales. You believe this growth rate will last for 3 more years, and will then drop to 10 per cent per year. If the growth rate then remains at 10 per cent indefinitely, what is the total value of the equity? Total dividends just paid were €5 million, and the required return is 20 per cent.

Kettenreaktion's situation is an example of supernormal growth. It is unlikely that a 30 per cent growth rate can be sustained for an extended time. To value the equity in this company, we first need to calculate the total dividends over the supernormal growth period:

Year	Total dividends (in millions)
1	€5.00 × 1.3 = €6.500
2	6.50 × 1.3 = 8.450
3	8.45 × 1.3 = 10.985

The price at time 3 can be calculated as:

$$P_3 = D_3 \times (1+g)/(R-g)$$

where g is the long-run growth rate. So we have:

$$P_3 = €10.985 \times 1.10/(0.20 - 0.10)$$
$$= €120.835$$

To determine the value today, we need the present value of this amount plus the present value of the total dividends:

$$P_0 = \frac{D_1}{(1+R)^1} + \frac{D_2}{(1+R)^2} + \frac{D_3}{(1+R)^3} + \frac{P_3}{(1+R)^3}$$

$$= \frac{€6.50}{1.20} + \frac{8.45}{1.20^2} + \frac{10.985}{1.20^3} + \frac{120.835}{1.20^3}$$

$$= €5.42 + 5.87 + 6.36 + 69.93$$

$$= €87.58$$

The total value of the equity today is thus €87.58 million. If there were, for example, 20 million shares, then the equity would be worth €87.58/20 = €4.38 per share.

Two-Stage Growth

The last case we consider is a particular case of non-constant growth: two-stage growth. Here, the idea is that the dividend will grow at a rate of g_1 for t years and then grow at a rate of g_2 thereafter forever. In this case, the value of the equity can be written as:

$$P_0 = \frac{D_1}{R - g_1} \times \left[1 - \left(\frac{1 + g_1}{1 + R}\right)^t\right] + \frac{P_t}{(1 + R)^t} \quad (7.5)$$

Notice that the first term in our expression is the present value of a growing annuity, which we discussed in Chapter 4. In this first stage, g_1 can be higher than R. The second part is the present value of the share price once the second stage begins at time t.

We can calculate P_t as follows:

$$P_t = \frac{D_{t+1}}{R - g_2} = \frac{D_0 \times (1 + g_1)^t \times (1 + g_2)}{R - g_2} \quad (7.6)$$

In this calculation we need the dividend at time $t + 1$, D_{t+1}, to get the share price at time t, P_t. Notice that, to get it, we grew the current dividend, D_0, at rate g_1 for t periods and then grew it one period at rate g_2. Also, in this second stage, g_2 must be less than R.

EXAMPLE 7.5

TWO-STAGE GROWTH

Alto Campo's dividend is expected to grow at 20 per cent for the next 5 years. After that, growth is expected to be 4 per cent forever. If the required return is 10 per cent, what is the value of the equity? The dividend just paid was €2.

There is a fair amount of computation here, but it is mostly just 'plug and chug' with a calculator. We can start by calculating the share price 5 years from now, P_5:

$$P_5 = \frac{D_6}{R - g_2} = \frac{D_0 \times (1 + g_1)^5 \times (1 + g_2)}{R - g_2}$$

$$= \frac{€2 \times (1 + 0.20)^5 \times (1 + 0.04)}{0.10 - 0.04}$$

$$= \frac{€5.18}{0.06}$$

$$= €86.26$$

We then plug into our two-stage growth formula to get the price today:

$$P_0 = \frac{D_1}{R - g_1} \times \left[1 - \left(\frac{1 + g_1}{1 + R}\right)^t\right] + \frac{P_t}{(1 + R)^t}$$

$$= \frac{€2 \times (1 + 0.20)}{0.10 - 0.20} \times \left[1 - \left(\frac{1 + 0.20}{1 + 0.10}\right)^5\right] + \frac{€86.26}{(1 + 0.10)^5}$$

$$= €66.64$$

Notice that we were given $D_0 = €2$ here, so we had to grow it by 20 per cent for one period to get D_1. Notice also that g_1 is bigger than R in this problem, but that fact does not cause a problem.

There are many reasons why dividend growth rates may change in the future. By far the most common cause is competition from other companies. Consider Apple, which has been incredibly successful over the past few years with its AirPods, iPhone, Watch, and iPad. Each product provided the company with robust growth. However, within 12 months of launch, competitors released similar products. As competition grows, sales growth will naturally decrease, having a direct effect on dividend growth rates.

Dividend payout policy may also change, and this will also have an impact on growth rates. In Chapter 3, we discussed sustainable growth rates. If a company increases its total dividend as a proportion of its overall earnings, growth will have to fall, because less money is retained to invest in value-maximizing projects. Holding everything else constant, if a company does increase its payout ratio, there will be a one-off increase in dividend (to reflect the bigger payout), followed by a lower growth rate in the future.

COMPONENTS OF THE REQUIRED RETURN

Thus far, we have taken the required return, or discount rate, R, as given. We shall have quite a bit to say about this subject in Chapters 11 and 13. For now, we want to examine the implications of the dividend growth model for this required return. Earlier, we calculated P_0 as:

$$P_0 = D_1/(R - g)$$

If we rearrange this to solve for R, we get:

$$R - g = D_1/P_0$$
$$R = D_1/P_0 + g \qquad (7.7)$$

This tells us that the total return, R, has two components. The first of these, D_1/P_0, is called the **dividend yield**. Because this is calculated as the expected cash dividend divided by the current price, it is conceptually similar to the current yield on a bond.

The second part of the total return is the growth rate, g. We know that the dividend growth rate is also the rate at which the share price grows (see Example 7.3 above). Thus, this growth rate can be interpreted as the **capital gains yield** – that is, the rate at which the value of the investment grows.[2]

To illustrate the components of the required return, suppose we observe an equity selling for €20 per share. The next dividend will be €1 per share. You think that the dividend will grow by 10 per cent per year more or less indefinitely. What return does this equity offer if this is correct?

The dividend growth model calculates total return as:

$$R = \text{Dividend yield} + \text{Capital gains yield}$$
$$= D_1/P_0 + g$$

> **dividend yield**
> an equity's expected cash dividend divided by its current price.

> **capital gains yield**
> the dividend growth rate, or the rate at which the value of an investment grows.

In this case, total return works out to be:

$$R = €1/20 + 10\%$$
$$= 5\% + 10\%$$
$$= 15\%$$

This equity, therefore, has an expected return of 15 per cent.

We can verify this answer by calculating the price in one year, P_1, using 15 per cent as the required return. Based on the dividend growth model, this price is:

$$P_1 = D_1 \times (1 + g)/(R - g)$$
$$= €1 \times 1.10/(0.15 - 0.10)$$
$$= €1.10/0.05$$
$$= €22$$

Notice that this €22 is €20 × 1.1, so the share price has grown by 10 per cent as it should. If you pay €20 for the equity today, you will get a €1 dividend at the end of the year, and you will have a €22 − 20 = €2 gain. Your dividend yield is thus €1/20 = 5%. Your capital gains yield is €2/20 = 10%, so your total return would be 5% + 10% = 15%.

To get a feel for actual numbers in this context, consider that, according to FT.com, Procter & Gamble's dividends were expected to grow by 3.57 per cent over the next few years, compared with a historical growth rate of 4 per cent. In 2019 the projected dividend for the coming year was given as $2.98, and the projected price was $127. The share price at that time was about $100 per share. What is the return investors require on P&G? Here, the dividend yield is 2.98 per cent and the capital gains yield is 27 per cent, giving a total required return of about 29.98 per cent on P&G shares.

Our discussion of equity valuation is summarized in Table 7.1.

TABLE 7.1

Summary of equity valuation

The general case

In general, the price today of a share of equity, P_0, is the present value of all of its future dividends, $D_1, D_2, D_3, \ldots$:

$$P_0 = \frac{D_1}{(1+R)^1} + \frac{D_2}{(1+R)^2} + \frac{D_3}{(1+R)^3} + \cdots$$

where R is the required return.

Constant growth case

If the dividend grows at a steady rate, g, then the price can be written as:

$$P_0 + \frac{D_1}{R-g}$$

This result is called the *dividend growth model*.

Non-constant growth

If the dividend grows steadily after t periods, then the price can be written as:

$$P_0 + \frac{D_1}{(1+R)^1} + \frac{D_2}{(1+R)^2} + \cdots + \frac{D_t}{(1+R)^t} + \frac{P_t}{(1+R)^t}$$

where:

$$P_t = \frac{D_t \times (1+g)}{(R-g)}$$

Two-stage growth

If the dividend grows at rate g_1 for t periods and then grows at rate g_2 thereafter, then the price can be written as:

$$P_0 = \frac{D_1}{R-g_1} \times \left[1 - \left(\frac{1+g_1}{1+R}\right)^t\right] + \frac{P_t}{(1+R)^t}$$

where:

$$P_t = \frac{D_{t+1}}{R-g_1} \times \frac{D_0 \times (1+g_1)^t \times (1+g_2)}{R-g_2}$$

The required return

The required return, R, can be written as the sum of two things:

$$R = D_1/P_0 + g$$

where D_1/P_0 is the *dividend yield* and g is the *capital gains yield* (which is the same thing as the growth rate in dividends for the steady growth case).

THE PRICE–EARNINGS RATIO

In Chapter 3, via our discussion on financial ratios, we introduced the price–earnings (P/E) ratio. Recall that the P/E ratio is the share price divided by earnings per share. P/E ratios are used by analysts to compare equity values across an industry, and they are used to complement other methods of equity valuation. The dividend growth model tells us that share value increases with growth rates, and so it implies that companies with high growth opportunities will have higher P/E ratios.

This explanation seems to hold fairly well in the real world. Electronic and other high-tech shares generally sell at very high P/E ratios (or multiples, as they are often called), because they are perceived to have high growth rates. In fact, some technology shares sell at high prices even though the companies have never earned a profit. Conversely, railroads, utilities and mining companies sell at lower multiples because of the prospects of lower growth. Table 7.2 contains summary data for different UK industries in March 2020.

Notice the variation across industries, and how the P/E ratios are related to growth opportunities. Care should be taken with blindly using data such as P/E ratios, because sometimes strange figures may appear. This data was collected in the depths of the Covid-19 pandemic, and share prices had collapsed across the world. As a result, the P/E ratios are very low for some industries, and this is known as the numerator effect. From looking at Table 7.2, you may also be surprised to learn that the average P/E ratio for a UK company over the past 40 years has been between 12 and 18. Sometimes, P/E ratios can be exceptionally high because average earnings in the past year within the sector are very low. This is known as the denominator effect.

TABLE 7.2

Summary equity data for selected UK industries, March 2020

Broad Sectors	P/E	Highest P/E Subsector	P/E	Lowest P/E Subsector	P/E
Oil & Gas	0.35	Integrated Oil & Gas	9.90	Oil: Crude Producers	−0.59
Basic Materials	13.68	Precious Metals & Mining	22.79	Industrial Materials	8.72
Industrials	7.93	Industrial Support Services	24.41	Electronic & Electrical Equipment	24.41
Consumer Discretion	9.96	Media	17.81	Leisure Goods	−1.15
Healthcare	36.35	Medical Equipment Services	228.59	Pharmaceutical & Biotech	5.59
Consumer Staples	15.67	Drug & Grocery Stores	35.59	Food Producers	−0.90
Telecommunications	12.47	Telecom. Equipment	6.45	Telecom. Services Providers	6.45
Utilities	122.85	Electricity	374.84	Gas, Water & Multinational Utilities	14.27
Financials	3.81	Life Insurance	19.34	Closed End Investments	1.63
Technology	18.17	Software & Computer Services	18.25	Technological Hardware and Equipment	17.48

Source: Data from Datastream 2020. All rights reserved.

> **CONCEPT QUESTIONS**
>
> **7.1a** What are the relevant cash flows for valuing a share of equity?
> **7.1b** Does the value of a share of equity depend on how long you expect to keep it?
> **7.1c** What is the value of a share of equity when the dividend grows at a constant rate?

7.2 SOME FEATURES OF ORDINARY AND PREFERENCE SHARES

In discussing ordinary equity features, we focus on shareholder rights and dividend payments. For preference shares, we explain what *preference* means, and we also debate whether preference shares are really debt or equity.

ORDINARY EQUITY FEATURES

ordinary equity
equity without priority for dividends or in bankruptcy.

The term **ordinary equity** means different things to different people, but it is usually applied to equity that has no special preference either in receiving dividends or in bankruptcy.

PREFERENCE SHARE FEATURES

preference shares
equity with dividend priority over ordinary shares, normally with a fixed dividend rate, sometimes without voting rights.

Preference shares differ from ordinary equity because they have preference over ordinary equity in the payment of dividends, and in the distribution of corporate assets in the event of a liquidation. *Preference* means only that the holders of the preference shares must receive a dividend (in the case of an ongoing firm) before holders of ordinary shares are entitled to anything.

A preference share is a form of equity, from a legal and tax standpoint. It is important to note, however, that holders of preference shares sometimes have no voting privileges.

Stated Value

Preference shares have a stated liquidating value, such as £100 or €100 per share. The cash dividend is described as a percentage of the stated value. For example, Unilever plc '4% preference shares' easily translates into a dividend yield of 4 per cent of stated value or £4 per share.

Cumulative and Non-Cumulative Dividends

A preference share dividend is *not* like interest on a bond. The board of directors may decide not to pay the dividends on preference shares, and their decision may have nothing to do with the current net income of the corporation.

Dividends payable on preference shares are either *cumulative* or *non-cumulative;* most are cumulative. If preferred dividends are cumulative and not paid in a particular year, they will be carried forward as an *arrearage*. Usually, both the accumulated (past) preferred dividends and the current preferred dividends must be paid before the ordinary shareholders can receive anything.

Unpaid preferred dividends are *not* debts of the firm. Directors elected by the ordinary shareholders can defer preferred dividends indefinitely. However, in such cases, ordinary shareholders must also forgo dividends. Furthermore, holders of preference shares are often granted voting and other rights if preferred dividends have not been paid for some time. Because preference shareholders receive no interest on the accumulated dividends, some have argued that firms have an incentive to delay paying preferred dividends, but, as we have seen, this may mean sharing control with preference shareholders.

Are Preference Shares Debt?

A good case can be made that preference shares are debt in disguise, a kind of equity bond. Preference shareholders receive a stated dividend only; and if the corporation is liquidated, preference shareholders get a stated value. Often, preference shares carry credit ratings much like those of bonds. Furthermore, preference shares are sometimes convertible into ordinary shares, and preference shares are usually callable.

Many preference share issues have obligatory sinking funds. The existence of such a sinking fund effectively creates a final maturity, because it means that the entire issue will ultimately be retired. For these reasons, preference shares seem to be a lot like debt. However, for tax purposes, preferred dividends are treated like ordinary share dividends.

International Accounting Standards (IAS 32: *Financial Instruments: Presentation*) recommend that the equity-like features of preference shares should be treated as equity in the company's financial accounts. Similarly, the bond-like features of a preference share should be treated as debt. So, if a preference share has a fixed dividend that has a mandatory redemption property at some future date, then it should be treated as a liability. If there is no redemption date, and the dividends are not mandatory, it should be treated as equity.

CONCEPT QUESTIONS

7.2a Why is a preference share called *preference*?
7.2b How can a preference share sometimes be treated as debt and at other times be treated as equity?
7.2c What is the difference between cumulative and non-cumulative dividends?

7.3 THE STOCK MARKETS

Back in Chapter 1, we briefly mentioned that shares of equity are bought and sold on various stock exchanges, the most important European exchanges being the London Stock Exchange, Euronext and Deutsche Börse. From our earlier discussion, recall that the stock market consists of a **primary market** and a **secondary market**. In the primary or new issue, market, shares of equity are first brought to the market and sold to investors. In the secondary market, existing shares are traded among investors.

In the primary market, companies sell securities to raise money. We shall discuss this process in detail in a later chapter. In this section, therefore, we focus mainly on secondary market activity. We conclude with a discussion of how share prices are quoted in the financial press.

> **primary market**
> the market in which new securities are originally sold to investors.

> **secondary market**
> the market in which previously issued securities are traded among investors.

DEALERS AND BROKERS

Because most securities transactions involve dealers and brokers, it is essential to understand what is meant by the terms *dealer* and *broker*. A **dealer** maintains an inventory and stands ready to buy and sell at any time. In contrast, a **broker** brings buyers and sellers together but does not maintain an inventory. Thus, when we speak of used car dealers and real estate brokers, we recognize that the used car dealer maintains an inventory, whereas the real estate broker does not.

In the securities markets, a dealer stands ready to buy securities from investors wishing to sell them and to sell securities to investors wanting to buy them. The price the dealer is willing to pay is called the *bid price*. The price at which the dealer will sell is called the *ask price* (sometimes called the asked, offered or offering price). The difference between the bid and ask prices is called the *spread*, and it is the primary source of dealer profits.

Dealers exist in all areas of the economy, not just the stock markets. For example, your local university bookshop is probably both a primary and a secondary market

> **dealer**
> an agent who buys and sells securities from inventory.

> **broker**
> an agent who arranges security transactions among investors.

textbook dealer. If you buy a new book, this is a primary market transaction. If you buy a used book, this is a secondary market transaction, and you pay the shop's ask price. If you sell the book back, you receive the shop's bid price (often half of the ask price). The bookshop's spread is the difference between the two prices.

In contrast, a securities broker arranges transactions between investors, matching investors wishing to buy securities with investors wanting to sell securities. The distinctive characteristic of security brokers is that they do not buy or sell securities for their own accounts. Facilitating trades by others is their business.

STOCK MARKET REPORTING

In recent years the reporting of share prices and related information has increasingly moved from traditional print media, such as the *Financial Times*, to various websites. Yahoo! Finance (finance.yahoo.com) and FT.com are good examples. We went to FT.com and requested a share price quote on Nokia Oyj, which is listed on the Helsinki Stock Exchange. A portion of what we found is shown in Table 7.3.

TABLE 7.3

Share price information for Nokia

Open	€2.82	Average volume	50.41m	Annual div (IAD)	€0
High	€2.83	Shares outstanding	5.65bn	Annual div yield (IAD)	0%
Low	€2.73	Free float	5.38bn	Div ex-date	Jul 29 2019
Bid	€2.76	P/E (TTM)	1,360.77	Div pay-date	Aug 08 2019
Offer	€2.76	Market cap	€16.08bn		
Previous close	€2.84	EPS (TTM)	€0.0021		

Source: FT.com.

Most of the information in Table 7.3 is self-explanatory. The last trade price is €2.76. The opening price is the first trade of the day. We see the bid and offer prices of €2.76.

Moving to the second column, Average volume is the average number of shares traded daily over the previous 10 days. Shares outstanding is the number of shares held by investors minus any shares held by the company. The Free float is the number of shares that can actually be traded in the company. P/E is the P/E ratio we discussed in Chapter 3. Market cap is the number of shares outstanding (from the most recent financial statements) multiplied by the current price per share. The earnings per share (EPS) used in the calculation is 'ttm', meaning 'trailing twelve months'.

In the third column, we have the annual dividend on the share and the dividend yield. Notice that the yield is zero because the dividend was zero.

CONCEPT QUESTIONS

7.3a What is the difference between a securities broker and a securities dealer?
7.3b Which is bigger, the bid price or the ask price? Why?

7.4 FIRM VALUATION

A look back at Chapter 3 shows that the assets of a firm are equal in value to the sum of a firm's liabilities and equity. Using the techniques in Chapters 6 and 7 to value bonds and equities, respectively, can assist you in the valuation process. However, firm valuation is a very imprecise science and the range of uncertainties the financial manager faces can make the task a very formidable one. In this section, we consider the most common approaches used in practice.

FREE CASH FLOW TO THE FIRM

In many countries, firms repurchase equity from shareholders as a substitute for paying dividends. This makes the dividend valuation models presented in this chapter more challenging to implement because we must not only value dividends but also the present value of future share repurchases. An alternative solution is to value the cash flows that accrue to the firm after removing the effect of financing. We do this through the statement of cash flows that is provided every year in the financial accounts (see **Chapter 3**). We can calculate free cash flow to the firm (FCFF) from either the statement of profit and loss or the statement of cash flows. Under International Accounting Standards, it is relatively straightforward to arrive at FCFF from the statement of cash flows, and this is what we will do in this section. The formula for FCFF (taking outflows as negative) is as follows:

$$\text{FCFF} = \text{Cash flow from operations} + \text{Cash flow from investing activities} \quad (7.8)$$

Under International Accounting Standards, firms will typically include interest expense under the heading *Cash Flow from Financing Activities*. However, firms have the option to include interest under *Cash Flow from Operations* if it is viewed to be part of a firm's operations. When this is the case, Equation 7.8 should be modified as follows:

$$\text{FCFF} = \text{Cash flow from operations} + \text{Cash flow from investing activities} \\ + \text{Net interest payment} \times (1 - \text{Tax rate}) \quad (7.9)$$

EXAMPLE 7.6

FREE CASH FLOW TO THE FIRM

Fresnillo plc is one of the world's largest mining firms, with particular strengths in silver and gold. It had the following statement of cash flows ($ millions) for 2017. What is the free cash flow to the firm?

Cash flow from operations	761
Cash flow from investing activities	−340
Cash flow from financing activities	−253

We calculate FCFF as follows:

$$\text{FCFF} = \$761 - \$340 = \$421 \text{ million}$$

Once we have calculated FCFF, it is a simple matter to discount the cash flows using the appropriate discount for the firm's operations. It is important to note that the discount rate used in the free cash flow valuation method will be different from the rate used for the dividend growth model. This is because the FCFF discount rate reflects the risk of the firm, whereas the discount rate used in the dividend growth model reflects the risk of the firm's equity. When a firm has no debt, the two discount rates will be the same.

EXAMPLE 7.7

FCFF VALUATION

In Example 7.6, we estimated that Fresnillo plc had an FCFF of $421 million. If the appropriate discount rate for Fresnillo is 12 per cent and the company's cash flows are expected to grow at 7 per cent every year, what was the value of Fresnillo?

To estimate the value of Fresnillo, we use the following valuation formula:

$$V_0 = \frac{FCFF_1}{r-g} = \frac{FCFF_0(1+g)}{r-g} = \frac{\$421(1.07)}{0.12 - 0.07}$$
$$= \$9{,}009.4 \text{ million}$$

If we compare the FCFF Fresnillo valuation to the actual market value, we are not far off in our estimate. In 2019, Fresnillo had a total equity market capitalization of $8.26 billion and total long-term debt of $1.02 billion, which is equal to a total firm value of $9.28 billion.

Although our calculation is not too far from the actual firm value, we still need to be careful about our assumptions regarding each of the formula's inputs.

VALUATION OF A FIRM'S CASH FLOWS

Suppose you are a business appraiser trying to determine the value of small companies. How can you determine what a firm is worth? One way to think about the question of how much a firm is worth is to calculate the present value of its future cash flows.

Consider the example of a firm that is expected to generate net cash flows (cash inflows minus cash outflows) of £5,000 in the first year and £2,000 for each of the next five years. The firm can be sold for £10,000 in seven years. The owners of the firm would like to be able to make 10 per cent on their investment in the firm.

We find the value of the firm by multiplying the net cash flows by the appropriate present value factor. The value of the firm is the sum of the present values of the individual net cash flows.

The present value of the net cash flows is next.

	The Present Value of the Firm		
End of Year	Net Cash Flow of the Firm (€)	Present Value Factor (10%)	Present Value of Net Cash Flows (€)
1	5,000	0.90909	4,545.45
2	2,000	0.82645	1,652.90
3	2,000	0.75131	1,502.62
4	2,000	0.68301	1,366.02
5	2,000	0.62092	1,241.84
6	2,000	0.56447	1,128.94
7	10,000	0.51316	5,131.58
		PV of firm	16,569.35

We can also use the simplifying formula for an annuity:

$$\frac{€5{,}000}{1.1} + \frac{(2{,}000 \times A^5_{0.10})}{1.1} + \frac{10{,}000}{(1.1)^7} = €16{,}569.35$$

Suppose you have the opportunity to acquire the firm for £12,000. Should you buy it? The answer is yes, because the NPV is positive:

$$NPV = PV - Cost$$
$$€4{,}569.35 = €16{,}569.35 - €12{,}000$$

The incremental value (NPV) of acquiring the firm is £4,569.35.

EXAMPLE 7.8

Poverty Alleviation International is a not-for-profit organization that is contemplating investing €1 million in an online platform that matches new start-up companies in Africa with wealthy investors from across the world who wish to donate or invest in these firms. It is expected that the platform will generate commission revenues of €200,000 per year for nine years and nothing after that. (The cash flows will occur at the end of each year, and there will be no cash flow after year 9.) Because the investment holds considerable risk, you have determined that the relevant discount rate for this investment is 15 per cent. The discount rate of 15 per cent is the rate of return the organization can earn on comparable projects. Should Poverty Alleviation International make the investment in the new platform?

We evaluate the decision as follows:

$$NPV = -€1,000,000 + \frac{€200,000}{1.15} + \frac{€200,000}{(1.15)^2} + \ldots + \frac{€200,000}{(1.15)^9}$$
$$= -€1,000,000 + €200,000 \times A^9_{0.15}$$
$$= -€1,000,000 + €954,316.78$$
$$= -€45,683.22$$

The present value of the online platform is only €954,316.78. The new platform is worth less than they cost. With the business plan as it currently stands, Poverty Alleviation International should not invest because the NPV is -€45,683.22. If Poverty Alleviation International requires a 15 per cent rate of return, the new platform is not a good investment. However, given the nature of the operation, it may seek donor funding from government organizations to offset the €45,683.22 reduction in value.

When valuing another firm, the financial manager will not typically have estimates of future cash flows to hand. As a result, other sources of information must be used. Chapter 3 illustrated the use of financial statements in assessing a firm's performance and growth rate. If the firm is listed on a stock exchange, past share price performance and volatility can also be used. Finally, comparative information on a firm's peers is necessary to calibrate your initial valuations.

MARKET MULTIPLES VALUATION

Many analysts use financial ratios like PE as a simple approach to valuing companies. The rationale is that if the financial markets are efficient, companies with similar characteristics will have similar values. Thus, two companies in the same industry with similar performance would be expected to have a similar PE ratio. There are a number of common valuation multiples in use, and the most used are presented in Table 7.4.

TABLE 7.4

Common valuation multiples

Price Multiples	Enterprise value (EV) Multiples	Other Ratios
Price/Earnings	EV/EBITDA	Dividend Yield
Price/Book Value of Equity	EV/Operating Profit	PEG (PE/Growth)
Price/Market Value of Equity		
Price/Cash Flow		
Price/Sales		

Note: Enterprise Value = Debt + Equity - Cash and Equivalents.

To value a firm using the multiples approach, you would first identify its peers in the industry. For each peer, calculate the valuation multiple and take an average of the multiple across the peers. This would become the benchmark valuation multiple for your target company, which allows you to value your firm. It is important to use forecasted figures in your valuations to reflect the future performance of the firm rather than the past.

> **REAL WORLD INSIGHTS**
>
> Eni SpA is an Italian gas firm and one of the largest in Europe. According to the Eni corporate website, its closest peers in terms of size (equity market capitalization) and industry are Equinor ($79 billion), ConocoPhillips ($70 billion) and Anadarko ($31 billion). Eni has an equity market capitalization of $64 billion.
>
> The PE ratios of Equinor, ConocoPhillips and Anadarko, are 11.1, 12.8 and 17.4, giving an average PE ratio of 13.8 for Eni's peers.
>
> Eni's net income was $6.845 billion in 2018, suggesting that its firm value should be ($6.845 billion x 13.8 =) $94.461 billion. Eni's equity market capitalization was $59.62 billion at the beginning of 2019, and its debt was $27.66 billion, giving a total estimated value of $87.28 billion.
>
> On first reading, it looks like Eni was undervalued and represented a good investment.

SUMMARY AND CONCLUSIONS

This chapter has covered the basics of equity and firm valuation:

1. The cash flows from owning a share of equity come in the form of future dividends. We saw that in certain special cases, it is possible to calculate the present value of all the future dividends and thus come up with a value for the equity.
2. In addition to ordinary shares, some corporations have issued preference shares. The name stems from the fact that preference shareholders must be paid first before ordinary shareholders can receive anything. Preference shares have a fixed dividend.
3. The three biggest stock markets in Europe are the London Stock Exchange, Euronext and Deutsche Börse. We discussed the organization and operation of these three markets, and we saw how share price information is reported in the financial press.
4. Approaches to firm valuation vary and span different levels of quantitative complexity.

This chapter completes Part Two of our book. By now, you should have a good grasp of what we mean by *present value*. You should also be familiar with how to calculate present values, loan payments, and so on. In Part Three, we cover capital budgeting decisions. As you will see, the techniques you learned in Chapters 4–7 form the basis for our approach to evaluating business investment decisions.

CHAPTER REVIEW AND SELF-TEST PROBLEMS

7.1 Dividend Growth and Share Valuation Gold and Silver plc has just paid a cash dividend of £4 per share. Investors require a 10 per cent return from investments such as this. If the dividend is expected to grow at a steady 5 per cent per year, what is the current value of the equity? What will the equity be worth in five years?

7.2 More Dividend Growth and Share Valuation In Self-Test Problem 7.1, what would the share sell for today if the dividend was expected to grow at 20 per cent per year for the next three years and then settle down to 5 per cent per year, indefinitely?

SOLUTIONS

7.1 The last dividend, D_0, was £4. The dividend is expected to grow steadily at 5 per cent. The required return is 10 per cent. Based on the dividend growth model, we can say that the current price is:

$$P_0 = D_1/(R - g) = D_0 \times (1 + g)/(R - g)$$
$$= £4 \times 1.05/(0.10 - 0.05)$$
$$= £4.20/0.05$$
$$= £84$$

We could calculate the price in five years by calculating the dividend in five years and then using the growth model again. Alternatively, we could recognize that the share price will increase by 5 per cent per year and calculate the future price directly. We'll do both. First, the dividend in five years will be:

$$D_5 = D_0 \times (1 + g)^5$$
$$= £4 \times 1.05^5$$
$$= £5.1051$$

The price in five years would therefore be:

$$P_5 = D_5 \times (1 + g)/(R - g)$$
$$= £5.1051 \times 1.05/0.05$$
$$= £5.3604/0.05$$
$$= £107.21$$

Once we understand the dividend model, however, it's easier to notice that:

$$P_5 = P_0 \times (1 + g)^5$$
$$= £84 \times 1.05^5$$
$$= £84 \times 1.2763$$
$$= £107.21$$

Notice that both approaches yield the same price in five years.

7.2 In this scenario, we have supernormal growth for the next three years. We'll need to calculate the dividends during the rapid growth period, and the share price in three years. The dividends are:

$$D_1 = £4.00 \times 1.20 = £4.800$$
$$D_2 = £4.80 \times 1.20 = £5.760$$
$$D_3 = £5.76 \times 1.20 = £6.912$$

After three years, the growth rate falls to 5 per cent indefinitely. The price at that time, P_3, is thus:

$$P_3 = D_3 \times (1 + g)/(R - g)$$
$$= £6.912 \times 1.05/(0.10 - 0.05)$$
$$= £7.2576/0.05$$
$$= £145.152$$

To complete the calculation of the share's present value, we have to determine the present value of the three dividends and the future price:

$$P_0 = \frac{D_1}{(1+R)^1} + \frac{D_2}{(1+R)^2} + \frac{D_3}{(1+R)^3} + \frac{P_3}{(1+R)^3}$$

$$= \frac{£4.80}{1.1} + \frac{5.76}{1.1^2} + \frac{6.912}{1.1^3} + \frac{145.152}{1.1^3}$$

$$= £4.36 + 4.76 + 5.19 + 109.05$$

$$= £123.37$$

Level of difficulty: Basic Intermediate Challenge

QUESTIONS AND PROBLEMS

7.1 Share Values Wild Horses plc has just announced that it will not pay a dividend because of atrocious trading conditions over the previous year. However, analysts expect the company to pay a dividend of £0.50 next year. If dividends are expected to grow at a constant rate of 10 per cent per year indefinitely, and investors require a 12 per cent return on the company, what is the current price? What will the price be in five years? In ten years?

7.2 Share Values A2A SpA is an Italian utility firm. Its most recent dividend was €0.013 per share. In the past year, the company has experienced financial difficulties and the share price has dropped by more than 20 per cent. However, long-term growth in dividends is anticipated to be 7 per cent forever. If A2A shares currently sell for €0.52, what is the required return?

7.3 Share Values The next dividend payment by Cannonball AG will be €3 per share. The dividends are anticipated to maintain a 5 per cent growth rate forever. The equity currently sells for €98 per share. What is the dividend yield? What is the expected capital gains yield?

7.4 Share Values XYZ plc will pay a dividend next year of 40p per share, and it is estimated that XYZ's dividend will increase by 4 per cent per year forever. Investors of XYZ require a rate of return of 10 per cent. What is the share price of XYZ plc?

7.5 Share Valuation Veggyburger is expected to maintain a constant 5 per cent growth rate in its dividends indefinitely. If the company has a dividend yield of 8 per cent, what is the required return on the company's shares?

7.6 Share Valuation Suppose you know that a company's equity currently sells for £64 per share, and the required return on the equity is 10 per cent. You also know that the total return on the equity is evenly divided between a capital gains yield and a dividend yield. If it is the company's policy to always maintain a constant growth rate in its dividends, what is the current dividend per share?

7.7 Share Valuation Vivendi SA pays a constant €1.40 dividend on its equity. The company will maintain this dividend for the next 11 years, and will then cease paying dividends for ever. If the required return on this equity is 10 per cent, what is the current share price?

7.8 Valuing Preference Shares Resnor plc has an issue of preference shares outstanding that pays a £3.40 dividend every year in perpetuity. If this issue currently sells for £69 per share, what is the required return?

7.9 Share Valuation and Required Return Red plc, Yellow plc and Blue plc each will pay a dividend of £2 next year. The growth rate in dividends for all three companies is 4 per cent. The required return for each company's shares is 8 per cent, 12 per cent and 16 per cent, respectively. What is the share price for each company? What do you conclude about the relationship between the required return and the share price?

7.10 Share Valuation Yoga Community plc, an international network of yoga studios, just paid a dividend of €2 on its equity. The growth rate in dividends is expected to be a constant 8 per cent per year indefinitely. Investors require a 20 per cent return on the equity for the first three years, a 10 per cent return for the next three years, and a 8 per cent return thereafter. What is the current share price?

7.11 Non-Constant Growth Dylan Bearings is a young start-up company. No dividends will be paid on the shares over the next nine years because the firm needs to plough back its earnings to fuel growth. The company will pay an £8 per share dividend in ten years and will increase the dividend by 6 per cent per year thereafter. If the required return is 13 per cent, what is the current share price?

7.12 Non-Constant Dividends Bread plc has an odd dividend policy. The company has just paid a dividend of £5 per share, and has announced that it will increase the dividend by £2 per share for each of the next five years, and then never pay another dividend. If you require an 18 per cent return on the company's equity, how much will you pay for a share today?

7.13 Non-Constant Dividends Far Side SpA is expected to pay the following dividends over the next four years: €12, €10, €6 and €3. Subsequently, the company pledges to maintain a constant 5 per cent growth rate in dividends forever. If the required return on the equity is 12 per cent, what is the current share price?

7.14 Supernormal Growth Marcel AG is growing quickly. Dividends are expected to grow at a 20 per cent rate for the next three years, with the growth rate falling off to a constant 5 per cent thereafter. If the required return is 16 per cent and the company just paid a €2 dividend, what is the current share price?

7.15 Growth Opportunities Yorkshire Humidifiers expects to earn £6 million per year in perpetuity if it does not undertake any new projects. The firm has an opportunity to invest £1 million today and £1.5 million in one year in real estate. The new investment will generate annual earnings of £1.5 million in perpetuity, beginning 2 years from today. The firm has 10 million shares outstanding, and the required rate of return on the equity is 16 per cent. Land investments are not depreciable. Ignore taxes.

(a) What is the share price if the firm does not undertake the new investment?

(b) What is the value of the investment?

(c) What is the share price if the firm undertakes the investment?

7.16 Supernormal Growth Eva AB is experiencing rapid growth. Dividends are expected to grow at 20 per cent per year during the next three years, 15 per cent over the following year, and then 10 per cent per year indefinitely. The required return on this equity is 13 per cent, and it currently sells for €56 per share. What is the projected dividend for the coming year?

7.17 Negative Growth Antiques R Us is a mature manufacturing firm. The company just paid a €12 dividend, but management expects to reduce the payout by 4 per cent per year indefinitely. If you require an 11 per cent return on this equity, what will you pay for a share today?

7.18 Finding the Dividend Teder plc shares currently sell for £64 per share. The market requires a 10 per cent return on the firm's equity. If the company maintains a constant 4.5 per cent growth rate in dividends, what was the most recent dividend per share paid on the equity?

7.19 Valuing Preference Shares Mark Bank just issued some new preference shares. The issue will pay a £5 annual dividend in perpetuity, beginning four years from now. If the market requires an 8 per cent return on this investment, how much do preference shares cost today?

7.20 Using Share Price Quotes You have found the following share price quote for HBooks plc, in the financial pages of today's newspaper. What was the closing price for this equity that appeared in *yesterday's* paper? If the company currently has 25 million shares of equity outstanding, what was the net income for the most recent year?

| 52-WEEK | | | | | | | NET |
HI	LO	EQUITY (DIV)	YLD %	P/E	VOL 100s	CLOSE	CHG
72.18	53.17	HBOOKS 1.48	2.1	19	17652	??	−0.23

7.21 Two-Stage Dividend Growth Model Thirsty Cactus SA has just paid a dividend of €2.50 per share. The dividends are expected to grow at 25 per cent for the next eight years, and then level off to an 8 per cent growth rate indefinitely. If the required return is 13 per cent, what is the share price today?

7.22 Two-Stage Dividend Growth Model Chartreuse County Choppers plc is experiencing rapid growth. The company expects dividends to grow at 20 per cent per year for the next 11 years before levelling off at 5 per cent into perpetuity. The required return on the company's equity is 14 per cent. If the dividend per share just paid was £1.74, what is the share price?

7.23 Capital Gains versus Income Consider four different equities, all of which have a required return of 15 per cent and a most recent dividend of £4.00 per share. Equities W, X and Y are expected to maintain constant growth rates in dividends for the foreseeable future of 10 per cent, 0 per cent, and −5 per cent per year, respectively. Equity Z is a growth stock that will increase its dividend by 20 per cent for the next two years and then maintain a constant 12 per cent growth rate thereafter. What is the dividend yield for each of these four equities? What is the expected capital gains yield? Discuss the relationship among the various returns that you find for each of these equities.

7.24 Share Valuation Most corporations pay semi-annual rather than annual dividends on their equity. Barring any unusual circumstances during the year, the board raises, lowers or maintains the current dividend once a year and then pays this dividend out in equal biannual instalments to its shareholders.

(a) Suppose a company currently pays a €3.00 annual dividend on its equity in a single annual instalment, and management plans on raising this dividend by 6 per cent per year indefinitely. If the required return on this equity is 14 per cent, what is the current share price?

(b) Now suppose that the company in (a) actually pays its annual dividend in equal six-monthly instalments; thus this company has just paid a €1.50 dividend per share, as it has in the previous six months. What is the current share price now? (*Hint:* Find the equivalent annual end-of-year dividend for each year. Assume the dividends grew by 6 per cent every six months.)

7.25 Non-Constant Growth Storico plc has just paid a dividend of £2.45 per share. The company will increase its dividend by 20 per cent next year, and will then reduce its dividend growth rate by 5 percentage points per year until it reaches the industry average of 5 per cent dividend growth, after which the company will keep a constant growth rate forever. If the required return on Storico shares is 11 per cent, what will a share of equity sell for today?

7.26 Non-Constant Growth This one is a little harder. Suppose the current share price for the firm in the previous problem is £63.82, and all the dividend information remains the same. What required return must investors be demanding on Storico equity? (*Hint:* Set up the valuation formula with all the relevant cash flows, and use trial and error to find the unknown rate of return.)

7.27 Constant Dividend Growth Model Assume an equity has dividends that grow at a constant rate forever. If you value the shares using the constant dividend growth model, how many years worth of dividends constitute one-half of the share's current price?

7.28 Two-Stage Dividend Growth Regarding the two-stage dividend growth model in the chapter, show that the price of a share of equity today can be written as follows:

$$P_0 = \frac{D_0 \times (1+g_1)}{R-g_1} \times \left[1 - \left(\frac{1+g_1}{1+R}\right)^t\right] + \left(\frac{1+g_1}{1+R}\right)^t \times \frac{D_0 \times (1+g_2)}{R-g_2}$$

Can you provide an intuitive interpretation of this expression?

7.29 Two-Stage Dividend Growth The chapter shows that in the two-stage dividend growth model, the growth rate in the first stage, g_1, can be greater than or less than the discount rate, R. Can they be exactly equal? (*Hint:* Yes, but what does the expression for the share value look like?)

MINI CASE

SHARE VALUATION AT ECORENEWABLE ENERGY

Ecorenewable Energy is a renewable wave energy firm, established in 2016 by two finance graduates. The company manufactures and installs wave energy converters through a point absorber buoy that floats on the surface of the water. Ecorenewable Energy has experienced rapid growth because of a proprietary technology that increases the energy efficiency of its systems. The company is owned equally by the two graduates, with each person holding 50,000 shares for a total of 100,000 shares in the company. In the event either wished to sell their shares, they first had to be offered to the other at a discounted price.

Both shareholders have decided they should value their holdings in the company for financial planning purposes. To accomplish this, they have gathered the following information about their main competitors:

Ecorenewable Energy plc Competitors					
	EPS (€)	DPS (€)	Share Price (€)	ROE (%)	R (%)
Surface Attenuator Systems	0.82	0.16	15.19	11	10
Wave Surge Oscillators plc	1.32	0.52	12.49	14	13
Water Column Oscillations SA	−0.47	0.54	48.60	14	12
Industry average	0.56	0.41	25.43	13	11.67

Water Column Oscillations SA's negative earnings per share (EPS) were the result of an accounting write-off last year. Without the write-off, EPS for the company would have been €2.34.

Last year, Ecorenewable Energy had an EPS of €4.32 and paid a total dividend of €108,000, shared equally between the two shareholders. The company had a return on equity of 25 per cent. This is more than the 20 per cent required return of the shareholders.

1. Assuming Ecorenewable Energy continues its current growth rate, what is the share price of the company's equity?

2. You have been hired to verify the share price valuation, and have been given information on Ecorenewable Energy and its three closest competitors. You believe that although Ecorenewable Energy has a technological advantage from the point absorber buoy, your research indicates that the firm's competitors are investigating a new technology that uses overtopping devices, which use wave velocity to power low-head turbines either on- or offshore. You expect Ecorenewable Energy's technological advantage will last for around five years, after which the company's growth rate will converge to the industry average growth rate. You also believe that the required return of 20 per cent is too high and that the industry average discount rate is more appropriate. With these assumptions, is your share price estimate higher or lower? What brings you to this conclusion?

3. What is the industry average price–earnings ratio? What is Ecorenewable Energy's price–earnings ratio? Comment on any differences and explain why they may exist.

4. Assume the company's growth rate declines to the industry average after five years. What percentage of the equity's value is attributable to growth opportunities?

5. Assume the company's growth rate slows to the industry average in five years. What future return on equity does this imply?
6. Both shareholders of Ecorenewable Energy wish to increase the value of the company equity but want to retain control of the company. They will not sell shares to outside investors and believe the company's debt is at a manageable level. They also do not wish to borrow more money. What steps can Ecorenewable Energy take to increase the share price? Are there any conditions under which this strategy would not increase the share price?

ADDITIONAL READING

A major challenge in equity valuation is measuring growth rates. The following paper investigates this issue:

1. Penman, S. (2011). Accounting for risk and return in valuation. *Journal of Applied Corporate Finance, 23*(2), 50–58.

The following papers are also of interest:

2. Bris, A., Koskine, Y., & Nilsson, M. (2009). The euro and corporate valuations. *Review of Financial Studies, 22*(8,) 3171–3209.

3. Penman, S. (2006). Handling valuation models. *Journal of Applied Corporate Finance, 18*(2), 48–55.

Endnotes

1. The only assumption we make about the share price is that it is a finite number, no matter how far away we push it. It can be extremely large, just not infinitely so. Because no one has ever observed an infinite share price, this assumption is plausible.
2. Here and elsewhere, we use the term *capital gains* a little loosely. For the record, a capital gain (or loss) is, strictly speaking, something defined by a country's tax authority. For our purposes, it would be more accurate (but less common) to use the term *price appreciation* instead of *capital gain*.

PART THREE
CAPITAL BUDGETING

8	Net Present Value and Other Investment Criteria	186
9	Making Capital Investment Decisions	223
10	Project Analysis and Evaluation	257

CHAPTER 8
NET PRESENT VALUE AND OTHER INVESTMENT CRITERIA

LEARNING OBJECTIVES
After studying this chapter, you should understand:

LO1 The reasons why the net present value criterion is the best way to evaluate proposed investments.
LO2 The payback rule, and some of its shortcomings.
LO3 The discounted payback rule, and some of its shortcomings.
LO4 Accounting rates of return, and some of the problems with them.
LO5 The internal rate of return criterion and its strengths and weaknesses.
LO6 The modified internal rate of return.
LO7 The profitability index, and its relation to net present value.

KEY NOTATIONS
AAR	Average accounting return
IRR	Internal rate of return
NPV	Net present value
PI	Profitability index
R	Discount rate

EVEN WHEN ECONOMIES ARE NOT PERFORMING WELL, companies must look to the future and scope out ways to enhance corporate value. This is especially the case for the telecommunications sector where technology never stands still. Over the past few years, the European telecommunications industry has had to expand its investment in 5G mobile telephone services. 5G is a significant improvement over 4G and opens up new revenue creation opportunities from premium streaming services to mobile customers.

Capital expenditure programmes in telecommunications are common because data requirements and Internet speeds evolve in a three- to five-year cycle. Investment in technology is expensive and constitutes a significant expenditure for firms that operate in telecommunications. Examples of substantial investments in telecommunications technology include AT&T ($130 billion between 2014 and 2020) and T-Mobile/Sprint ($40 billion between 2020 and 2022).

The AT&T and T-Mobile/Sprint investments are examples of a capital budgeting decision. Decisions such as these, with a price tag of billions, are major undertakings, and the risks and rewards must be carefully weighed. In this chapter, we discuss the necessary tools used in making such decisions.

In Chapter 1, we saw that increasing the value of equity in a company is the goal of financial management. Thus what we need to know is how to tell whether a particular investment will achieve that or not, and we will consider a variety of techniques for this purpose. More important, it shows how many of these techniques can be misleading, and it explains why the net present value approach is the right one.

In Chapter 1, we identified the three critical areas of concern to the financial manager. The first of these involved the question: what non-current assets should we buy? We called this the *capital budgeting decision*. In this chapter, we begin to deal with the issues that arise in answering this question.

The process of allocating or budgeting capital is usually more involved than just deciding whether to buy a particular non-current asset. We frequently face broader issues, such as whether we should launch a new product or enter a new market. Decisions such as these determine the nature of a firm's operations and products for years to come, primarily because non-current asset investments are generally long-lived and not easily reversed once they are made.

The most fundamental decision a business must make concerns its product line. What services shall we offer or what shall we sell? In what markets will we compete? What new products shall we introduce? The answer to any of these questions will require that the firm commit its scarce and valuable capital to certain types of asset. As a result, all these strategic issues fall under the general heading of capital budgeting. The process of capital budgeting could thus be given a more descriptive (not to mention impressive) name: *strategic asset allocation*.

For the reasons we have discussed, the capital budgeting question is probably the most important issue in corporate finance. How a firm chooses to finance its operations (the capital structure question) and how a firm manages its short-term operating activities (the working capital question) are indeed issues of concern, but the non-current assets define the business of the firm. Airlines, for example, are airlines because they operate aeroplanes, regardless of how they finance them.

Any firm possesses a vast number of possible investments. Each potential investment is an option available to the firm. Some options are valuable, and some are not. The essence of successful financial management, of course, is learning to identify which are which. With this in mind, our goal in this chapter is to introduce you to the techniques used to analyse potential business ventures to decide which are worth undertaking.

We present and compare different procedures used in practice. Our primary goal is to acquaint you with the advantages and disadvantages of the various approaches. As we shall see, the critical concept in this area is the idea of net present value, and we consider this next.

8.1 NET PRESENT VALUE

In Chapter 1, we argued that the goal of financial management is to create value for the shareholders. The financial manager must thus examine a potential investment in the light of its likely effect on the value of the firm's shares. In this section, we describe a widely used procedure for doing this: the net present value approach.

THE BASIC IDEA

An investment is worth undertaking if it creates value for its owners. In the most general sense, we create value by identifying an investment worth more in the marketplace than it costs us to acquire. How can something be worth more than it costs? It is a case of the whole being worth more than the cost of the parts.

For example, suppose you buy a run-down house for £25,000 and spend another £25,000 on painters, plumbers and so on to get it renovated. Your total investment is £50,000. When the work is completed, you place the house back on the market and find that it is worth £60,000. The market value (£60,000) exceeds the cost (£50,000) by £10,000. What you have done here is act as a manager and bring together some non-current assets (a house), some labour (plumbers, carpenters and others) and some materials (carpeting, paint and so on). The net result is that you have created £10,000 in value. Put another way, this £10,000 is the *value added* by management.

With our house example, it turned out *after the fact* that £10,000 in value had been created. Things thus worked out nicely. The real challenge, of course, would have been somehow to identify *ahead of time* whether investing the necessary £50,000 was a good idea in the first place. This is what capital budgeting is all about – namely, trying to determine whether a proposed investment or project will be worth more than it costs, once it is in place.

net present value (NPV) the difference between an investment's market value and its cost.

For reasons that will be obvious in a moment, the difference between an investment's market value and its cost is called the **net present value (NPV)** of the investment. In other words, the net present value is a measure of how much value is created or added today by undertaking an investment. Given our goal of creating value for the shareholders, we should view the capital budgeting process as a search for investments with positive NPVs.

With our run-down house, you can probably imagine how we would go about making the capital budgeting decision. We would first look at what comparable, renovated properties were selling for in the market. We would then get estimates of the cost of buying a particular property and bringing it to market. At this point, we would have an estimated total cost and an estimated market value. If the difference were positive, then this investment would be worth undertaking, because it would have a positive estimated NPV. There is a risk, of course, because there is no guarantee that our estimates will turn out to be correct.

As our example illustrates, investment decisions are greatly simplified when there is a market for assets similar to the investment we are considering. Capital budgeting becomes much more difficult when we cannot observe the market price for at least roughly comparable investments. The reason is that we then face the problem of estimating the value of an investment using only indirect market information. Unfortunately, this is precisely the situation the financial manager usually encounters. We examine this issue next.

ESTIMATING NET PRESENT VALUE

Imagine we are thinking of starting a business to produce and sell a new product – organic fertilizer, say. We can estimate the start-up costs with reasonable accuracy because we know what we shall need to buy to begin production. Would this be a good investment? Based on our discussion, you know that the answer depends on whether the value of the new business exceeds the cost of starting it. In other words, does this investment have a positive NPV?

This problem is much more complicated than our renovated house example because entire fertilizer companies are not routinely bought and sold in the marketplace, so it is practically impossible to observe the market value of a similar investment. As a result, we must somehow estimate this value by other means.

Based on our work in Chapters 4 and 5, you may be able to guess how we shall go about estimating the value of our fertilizer business. We shall first try to estimate the future cash flows we expect the new business to produce. We shall then apply our basic discounted cash flow procedure to calculate the present value of those cash flows. Once we have this estimate, we shall then estimate NPV as the difference between the present value of the future cash flows and the cost of the investment. As we mentioned in Chapter 5, this procedure is often called **discounted cash flow (DCF) valuation**.

discounted cash flow (DCF) valuation the process of valuing an investment by discounting its future cash flows.

To see how we might go about estimating NPV, suppose we believe the cash revenues from our fertilizer business will be £20,000 per year, assuming everything goes as expected. Cash costs (including taxes) will be £14,000 per year. We shall wind down the business in eight years. Plant, property and equipment will be worth £2,000 as salvage at that time. The project costs £30,000 to launch. We use a 15 per cent discount rate on new projects such as this one. Is this a good investment? If there are 1,000 shares of equity outstanding, what will be the effect on the share price of taking this investment?

From a purely mechanical perspective, we need to calculate the present value of the future cash flows at 15 per cent. The net cash inflow will be £20,000 cash income less £14,000 in costs per year for eight years. We illustrate these cash flows in Figure 8.1. As Figure 8.1 suggests, we effectively have an eight-year annuity of £20,000 − 14,000 = £6,000 per year, along with a single lump-sum inflow of £2,000 in eight years. Calculating the present value of the future cash flows thus comes down to the same type of problem we considered in Chapter 5. The total present value is:

$$\text{Present value} = £6,000 \times \left[1 - \left(1/1.15^8\right)\right]/0.15 + \left(2,000/1.15^8\right)$$
$$= (£6,000 \times 4.4873) + (2,000/3.0590)$$
$$= £26,924 + 654$$
$$= £27,578$$

FIGURE 8.1

Project cash flows (£000)

Time (years)	0	1	2	3	4	5	6	7	8
Initial cost	−£30								
Inflows		£20	£20	£20	£20	£20	£20	£20	£20
Outflows		−14	−14	−14	−14	−14	−14	−14	−14
Net inflow		£ 6	£ 6	£ 6	£ 6	£ 6	£ 6	£ 6	£ 6
Salvage									2
Net cash flow	−£30	£ 6	£ 6	£ 6	£ 6	£ 6	£ 6	£ 6	£ 8

When we compare this with the £30,000 estimated cost, we see that the NPV is:

$$\text{NPV} = -£30{,}000 + 27{,}578 = -£2{,}422$$

Therefore this is *not* a good investment. Based on our estimates, taking it would *decrease* the total value of the equity by £2,422. With 1,000 shares outstanding, our best estimate of the impact of taking this project is a loss of value of £2,422/1,000 = £2.42 per share.

Our fertilizer example illustrates how NPV estimates can be used to determine whether an investment is desirable. From our example, notice that if the NPV is negative, the effect on share value will be unfavourable. If the NPV were positive, the effect would be favourable. As a consequence, all we need to know about a particular proposal to make an accept–reject decision is whether the NPV is positive or negative.

Given that the goal of financial management is to increase share value, our discussion in this section leads us to the *net present value rule*:

An investment should be accepted if the net present value is positive and rejected if it is negative.

In the unlikely event that the NPV turned out to be exactly zero, we would be indifferent between making the investment and not taking it.

Two comments about our example are in order. First and foremost, it is not the rather mechanical process of discounting the cash flows that is important. Once we have the cash flows and the appropriate discount rate, the required calculations are relatively straightforward. The task of coming up with the cash flows and the discount rate is much more challenging. We shall have much more to say about this in the next few chapters. For the remainder of this chapter, we take it as a given that we have estimates of the cash revenues and costs and, where needed, an appropriate discount rate.

The second thing to keep in mind about our example is that the −£2,422 NPV is an estimate. Like any estimate, it can be high or low. The only way to find out the actual NPV would be to place the investment up for sale and see what we could get for it. We generally won't be doing this, so we must have reliable estimates of NPV. Once again, we shall say more about this later. For the rest of this chapter, we shall assume that the NPV estimates are accurate.

EXAMPLE 8.1

USING THE NPV RULE

Suppose we are asked to decide whether a new consumer product should be launched. Based on projected sales and costs, we expect that the cash flows over the five-year life of the project will be £2,000 in the first two years, £4,000 in the next two, and £5,000 in the last year. It will cost about £10,000 to begin production. We use a 10 per cent discount rate to evaluate new products. What should we do here?

Given the cash flows and discount rate, we can calculate the total value of the product by discounting the cash flows back to the present:

$$\text{Present value} = (£2{,}000/1.1) + (2{,}000/1.1^2) + (4{,}000/1.1^3)$$
$$+ (4{,}000/1.1^4) + (5{,}000/1.1^5)$$
$$= £1{,}818 + 1{,}653 + 3{,}005 + 2{,}732 + 3{,}105$$
$$= £12{,}313$$

The present value of the expected cash flows is £12,313, but the cost of getting those cash flows is only £10,000, so the NPV is £12,313 − 10,000 = £2,313. This is positive; so, based on the net present value rule, we should take on the project.

As we have seen in this section, estimating NPV is one way of assessing the value of a proposed investment. It is certainly not the only way value is considered, and we now turn to some alternatives. As we shall see, when compared with NPV, each of the alternative approaches we shall examine is flawed in some way; so NPV is the preferred approach in principle, if not always in practice.

SPREADSHEET STRATEGIES 8.1
Calculating NPVs with a Spreadsheet

Spreadsheets are commonly used to calculate NPVs. Examining the use of spreadsheets in this context also allows us to issue an important warning. Let's redo Example 8.1:

	A	B	C	D	E	F	G	H
1	Year	0	1	2	3	4	5	
2	Cash Flow	-£10,000	£2,000	£2,000	£4,000	£4,000	£5,000	
3								
4	Discount Rate	10%						
5								
6	NPV =	£2,102.72	WRONG!!! Incorrect formula is =NPV(B4,B2:G2)					
7	NPV =	"2,312.99	CORRECT!!! Formula is =NPV(B4,C2:G2)+B2					
8								
9								

In our spreadsheet example, notice that we have provided two answers. By comparing the answers with that found in Example 8.1, we see that the first answer is wrong, even though we used the spreadsheet's NPV formula. What happened is that the 'NPV' function in our spreadsheet is actually a PV function; unfortunately, one of the original spreadsheet programs many years ago got the definition wrong, and subsequent spreadsheets have copied it! Our second answer shows how to use the formula correctly.

The example here illustrates the danger of blindly using calculators or computers without understanding what is going on; we shudder to think of how many capital budgeting decisions in the real world are based on incorrect use of this particular function. We shall see another example of something that can go wrong with a spreadsheet later in the chapter.

CONCEPT QUESTIONS

8.1a What is the net present value rule?
8.1b If we say an investment has an NPV of €1,000, what exactly do we mean?

SUSTAINABILITY IN FINANCE

One of Europe's largest investment projects is the Trans-Adriatic Pipeline (TAP). The pipeline is connected to the Trans-Anatolian Pipeline (TANAP) on the Greek-Turkey border and spans 870 km across Greece and Albania before ending in southern Italy. Once complete, the pipeline will allow the transport and distribution of natural gas from Azerbaijan throughout Europe.

Natural gas is an improvement on other energy types for a number of reasons. First, natural gas is up to 50 per cent cleaner than other fossil fuels and compared to coal-fired power plants, natural gas produces less than 1 per cent as much sulphur oxide and a third of nitrogen oxides. Natural gas is an important component of Europe's carbon reduction strategy and the Trans-Adriatic Pipeline is a key component of Europe's strategy to reduce overall greenhouse gas emissions.

A construction project of TAP's size is extremely rare and involves years of planning. Upon announcement of the project by EGL Group, a full feasibility study that lasted seven years had to be undertaken. During this time, applications to build the pipeline in Greece, Albania and Italy were prepared, submitted, and accepted by the respective country authorities.

Once the regulatory compliance issues were resolved, negotiations were then held with a wide variety of companies to become partners in an international consortium to build and manage the pipeline. As of 2016, the investment stage of the project had been implemented.

TAP is expected to provide a very cost-effective transportation route stretching from the Caspian Sea into Europe, and during the next few years, cash inflows will be generated to pay off the initial investment and create value for the shareholders of the consortium.

When the initial plans for TAP were announced in 2003, the oil and gas sector was completely different. Energy was four times as expensive as it was in 2021 and nobody knows what will happen over the next few years. Will the pipeline maximize shareholder value? Only time will tell.

8.2 THE PAYBACK RULE

It is common in practice to talk of the payback on a proposed investment. Loosely, the *payback* is the length of time it takes to recover our initial investment. Because this idea is widely understood and used, we shall examine it in some detail.

DEFINING THE RULE

We can illustrate how to calculate a payback with an example. Figure 8.2 shows the cash flows from a proposed investment. How many years do we have to wait until the accumulated cash flows from this investment equal or exceed the cost of the investment? As Figure 8.2 indicates, the initial investment is £50,000. After the first year, the firm has recovered £30,000, leaving £20,000. The cash flow in the second year is exactly £20,000, so this investment 'pays for itself' in precisely two years. Put another way, the **payback period** is two years. If we require a payback of, say, three years or less, then this investment is acceptable. This illustrates the *payback period rule*:

payback period the amount of time required for an investment to generate cash flows sufficient to recover its initial cost.

> Based on the payback rule, an investment is acceptable if its calculated payback period is less than some pre-specified number of years.

FIGURE 8.2

Net project cash flows

In our example, the payback works out to be exactly two years. This won't usually happen, of course. When the numbers don't work out exactly, it is customary to work with fractional years. For example, suppose the initial investment is £60,000, and the cash flows are £20,000 in the first year and £90,000 in the second. The cash flows over the first two years are £110,000, so the project pays back some time in the second year. After the first year, the project has paid back £20,000, leaving £40,000 to be recovered. To figure out the fractional year, note that this £40,000 is £40,000/90,000 = 4/9 of the second year's cash flow. Assuming that the £90,000 cash flow is received uniformly throughout the year, the payback would be 1 4/9 years.

> **EXAMPLE 8.2**
>
> **CALCULATING PAYBACK**
>
> Here are the projected cash flows from a proposed investment:
>
> | Year | Cash flow (€) |
> |------|---------------|
> | 1 | 100 |
> | 2 | 200 |
> | 3 | 500 |
>
> This project costs €500. What is the payback period for this investment?
>
> The initial cost is €500. After the first two years, the cash flows total €300. After the third year, the total cash flow is €800, so the project pays back some time between the end of year 2 and the end of year 3. Because the accumulated cash flows for the first two years are €300, we need to recover €200 in the third year. The third-year cash flow is €500, so we shall have to wait €200/500 = 0.4 years to do this. The payback period is thus 2.4 years, or about two years and five months.

Now that we know how to calculate the payback period on an investment, using the payback period rule for making decisions is straightforward. A particular cut-off time is selected – say, two years – and all investment projects that have payback periods of two years or less are accepted, whereas any that pay off in more than two years are rejected.

Table 8.1 illustrates cash flows for five different projects. The figures shown as the year 0 cash flows are the costs of the investments. We examine these to indicate some peculiarities that can, in principle, arise with payback periods.

TABLE 8.1

Expected cash flows for projects A–E

Year	A (€)	B (€)	C (€)	D (€)	E (€)
0	−100	−200	−200	−200	−50
1	30	40	40	100	100
2	40	20	20	100	−50,000,000
3	50	10	10	−200	
4	60		130	200	

The payback for the first project, A, is easily calculated. The sum of the cash flows for the first two years is €70, leaving us with €100 − 70 = €30 to go. Because the cash flow in the third year is €50, the payback occurs sometime in that year. When we compare the €30 we need with the €50 that will be coming in, we get €30/50 = 0.6: so payback will occur 60 per cent of the way into the year. The payback period is thus 2.6 years.

Project B's payback is also easy to calculate: it *never* pays back because the cash flows never total up to the original investment. Project C has a payback of exactly four years because it supplies the €130 that B is missing in year 4. Project D is a little strange. Because of the negative cash flow in year 3, you can easily verify that it has two different payback periods, two years and four years. Which of these is correct? Both of them; the way the payback period is calculated doesn't guarantee a single answer. Finally, project E is unrealistic, but it does pay back in six months, thereby illustrating the point that a rapid payback does not guarantee a good investment.

ANALYSING THE RULE

When compared with the NPV rule, the payback period rule has some rather severe shortcomings. First, we calculate the payback period by adding up the future cash flows. There is no discounting involved, so the time value of money is completely ignored. The payback rule also fails to consider risk differences because payback would be calculated the same way for both very risky and very safe projects.

Perhaps the biggest problem with the payback period rule is coming up with the right cut-off period: we don't really have an objective basis for choosing a particular number. Put another way, there is no economic rationale for looking at payback in the first place, so we have no guide for how to pick the cut-off. As a result, we end up using a number that is arbitrarily chosen.

Suppose we have somehow decided on an appropriate payback period of two years or less. As we have seen, the payback period rule ignores the time value of money for the first two years. More seriously, cash flows after the second year are ignored entirely. To see this, consider the two investments, Long and Short, in Table 8.2. Both projects cost €250. Based on our discussion, the payback on Long is $2 + (€50/100) = 2.5$ years, and the payback on Short is $1 + (€150/200) = 1.75$ years. With a cut-off of two years, Short is acceptable and Long is not.

TABLE 8.2

Investment projected cash flows

Year	Long (€)	Short (€)
0	−250	−250
1	100	100
2	100	200
3	100	0
4	100	0

Is the payback period rule guiding us to the right decisions? Maybe not. Suppose we require a 15 per cent return on this type of investment. We can calculate the NPV for these two investments as:

$$\text{NPV(Short)} = -€250 + (100/1.15) + (200/1.15^2) = -11.81$$

$$\text{NPV(Long)} = -€250 + (100 \times \{[1 - (1/1.15^4)]/0.15\}) = €35.50$$

Now we have a problem. The NPV of the shorter-term investment is negative, meaning that taking it diminishes the value of the shareholders' equity. The opposite is true for the longer-term investment – it increases share value.

Our example illustrates two primary shortcomings of the payback period rule. First, by ignoring time value, we may make investments (like Short) that are worth less than they cost. Second, by ignoring cash flows beyond the cut-off, we may be led to reject profitable long-term investments (like Long). More generally, using a payback period rule will tend to bias us towards shorter-term investments.

REDEEMING QUALITIES OF THE RULE

Despite its shortcomings, the payback period rule is often used by large and sophisticated companies when they are making relatively minor decisions. There are several reasons for this. The primary reason is that many investment decisions do not warrant detailed analysis, because the cost of the analysis would exceed the possible loss from a mistake. As a practical matter, an investment that pays back rapidly and has benefits extending beyond the cut-off period probably has a positive NPV.

Small investment decisions are made by the hundreds every day in large organizations and at all levels. As a result, it would not be uncommon for a corporation to require, for example, a two-year payback on all investments of a minimal amount (say, less than £10,000). Larger investments would be subjected to greater scrutiny. The requirement of a two-year payback is not perfect, for reasons we have seen, but it does exercise some control over expenditures, and thus limits possible losses.

In addition to its simplicity, the payback rule has two other positive features. First, because it is biased towards short-term projects, it is biased towards liquidity. In other words, a payback rule tends to favour investments that free up cash for other uses quickly, which could be necessary for a small business; it would be less so for a large corporation. Second, cash flows expected to occur later in a project's life are probably more uncertain. Arguably, a payback period rule adjusts for the extra riskiness of later cash flows, but it does so in a rather draconian fashion – by ignoring them altogether.

We should note here that some of the apparent simplicity of the payback rule is an illusion. The reason is that we must still come up with the cash flows first, and, as we discussed earlier, this is not at all easy to do. Thus it would probably be more accurate to say that the *concept* of a payback period is both intuitive and easy to understand.

SUMMARY OF THE RULE

To summarize, the payback period is a kind of 'break-even' measure. Because time value is ignored, you can think of the payback period as the length of time it takes to break even in an accounting sense, but not in an economic sense. The biggest drawback to the payback period rule is that it doesn't ask the right question. The relevant issue is the impact an investment will have on the value of the equity, not how long it takes to recover the initial investment.

Nevertheless, because it is so simple, companies often use it as a screen for dealing with the myriad minor investment decisions they have to make. There is certainly nothing wrong with this practice. As with any simple rule of thumb, there will be some errors in using it; but it wouldn't have survived all this time if it weren't useful. Now that you understand the rule, you can be on the alert for circumstances under which it might lead to problems. To help you remember, Table 8.3 lists the pros and cons of the payback period rule.

TABLE 8.3

Advantages and disadvantages of the payback period rule

Advantages	Disadvantages
1. Easy to understand.	1. Ignores the time value of money.
2. Adjusts for uncertainty of later cash flows.	2. Requires an arbitrary cut-off point.
3. Biased towards liquidity.	3. Ignores cash flows beyond the cut-off date.
	4. Biased against long-term projects, such as research and development, and new projects.

CONCEPT QUESTIONS

8.2a In words, what is the payback period? The payback period rule?
8.2b Why do we say that the payback period is, in a sense, an accounting break-even measure?

8.3 THE DISCOUNTED PAYBACK

discounted payback period
the length of time required for an investment's discounted cash flows to equal its initial cost.

We saw that one shortcoming of the payback period rule was that it ignored time value. A variation of the payback period, the discounted payback period, fixes this particular problem. The **discounted payback period** is the length of time until the sum of the discounted cash flows is equal to the initial investment. The *discounted payback rule* would be:

Based on the discounted payback rule, an investment is acceptable if its discounted payback is less than some pre-specified number of years.

To see how we might calculate the discounted payback period, suppose we require a 12.5 per cent return on new investments. We have an investment that costs €300 and has cash flows of €100 per year for five years. To get the discounted payback, we have to discount each cash flow at 12.5 per cent and then start adding them. We do this in Table 8.4. In Table 8.4, we have both the discounted and the undiscounted cash flows. Looking at the accumulated cash flows, we see that the regular payback is exactly three years. The discounted cash flows total €300 only after four years, however, so the discounted payback is four years, as shown.[1]

TABLE 8.4

Ordinary and discounted payback

Year	Cash flow (€)		Accumulated cash flow (€)	
	Undiscounted	Discounted	Undiscounted	Discounted
1	100	89	100	89
2	100	79	200	168
3	100	70	300	238
4	100	62	400	300
5	100	55	500	355

How do we interpret the discounted payback? Recall that the ordinary payback is the time it takes to break even in an accounting sense. Because it includes the time value of money, the discounted payback is the time it takes to break even in an economic or financial sense. Loosely speaking, in our example, we get our money back, along with interest we could have earned elsewhere, in four years.

Figure 8.3 illustrates this idea by comparing the *future* value at 12.5 per cent of the €300 investment with the *future* value of the €100 annual cash flows at 12.5 per cent. Notice that the two lines cross at

FIGURE 8.3

Year	Future value at 12.5% (€)	
	€100 Annuity (projected cash flow)	€300 Lump sum (projected investment)
0	0	300
1	100	338
2	213	390
3	339	427
4	481	481
5	642	541

precisely four years, which tells us that the value of the project's cash flows catches up and then passes the original investment in four years.

Table 8.4 and Figure 8.3 illustrate another interesting feature of the discounted payback period. If a project ever pays back on a discounted basis, then it must have a positive NPV.[2] This is true because, by definition, the NPV is zero when the sum of the discounted cash flows equals the initial investment. For example, the present value of all the cash flows in Table 8.4 is €355. The cost of the project was €300, so the NPV is €55. This €55 is the value of the cash flow that occurs *after* the discounted payback (see the last line in Table 8.4). In general, if we use a discounted payback rule, we won't accidentally take any projects with a negative estimated NPV.

Based on our example, the discounted payback would seem to have much to recommend it. You may be surprised to find that it is rarely used in practice. Why? Probably because it isn't any simpler to use than NPV. To calculate a discounted payback, you have to discount cash flows, add them up, and compare them with the cost, just as you do with NPV. So, unlike an ordinary payback, the discounted payback is not especially simple to calculate.

A discounted payback period rule has a couple of other significant drawbacks. The biggest one is that the cut-off still has to be arbitrarily set, and cash flows beyond that point are ignored.[3] As a result, a project with a positive NPV may be found unacceptable because the cut-off is too short. Also, just because one project has a shorter discounted payback than another does not mean it has a larger NPV.

The discounted payback is a compromise between a regular payback and NPV that lacks the simplicity of the first and the conceptual rigour of the second. Nonetheless, if we need to assess the time it will take to recover the investment required by a project, then the discounted payback is better than the ordinary payback because it considers time value. In other words, the discounted payback recognizes that we could have invested the money elsewhere and earned a return on it. The ordinary payback does not take this into account. We now summarize the advantages and disadvantages of the discounted payback rule in Table 8.5.

TABLE 8.5

Advantages and disadvantages of the discounted payback period rule

Advantages	Disadvantages
1. Includes time value of money.	1. May reject positive NPV investments.
2. Easy to understand.	2. Requires an arbitrary cut-off point.
3. Does not accept negative estimated NPV investments.	3. Ignores cash flows beyond the cut-off date.
4. Biased towards liquidity.	4. Biased against long-term projects, such as research and development, and new projects.

EXAMPLE 8.3

CALCULATING DISCOUNTED PAYBACK

Consider an investment that costs £400 and pays £100 per year forever. We use a 20 per cent discount rate on this type of investment. What is the ordinary payback? What is the discounted payback? What is the NPV?

The NPV and ordinary payback are easy to calculate in this case, because the investment is a perpetuity. The present value of the cash flow is £100/0.2 = £500, so the NPV is £500 − 400 = £100. The ordinary payback is thus four years.

To get the discounted payback, we need to find the number of years such that a £100 annuity has a present value of £400 at 20 per cent. In other words, the present value annuity factor is £400/100 = 4, and the interest rate is 20 per cent per period; so what's the number of periods? If we solve for the number of periods, we find that the answer is a little less than nine years, so this is the discounted payback.

> **CONCEPT QUESTIONS**
>
> **8.3a** In words, what is the discounted payback period? Why do we say it is, in a sense, a financial or economic break-even measure?
>
> **8.3b** What advantage(s) does the discounted payback have over the ordinary payback?

8.4 THE AVERAGE ACCOUNTING RETURN

Another attractive, but flawed, approach to making capital budgeting decisions involves the **average accounting return (AAR)**. There are many different definitions of the AAR. However, in one form or another, the AAR is always defined as:

$$\frac{\text{Some measure of average accounting profit}}{\text{Some measure of average accounting value}}$$

The specific definition we shall use is:

$$\frac{\text{Average net income}}{\text{Average book value}}$$

> **average accounting return (AAR)** an investment's average net income divided by its average book value.

To see how we might calculate this number, suppose we are deciding whether to open a store in a new shopping centre. The required investment in improvements is £500,000. The store would have a five-year life, because everything reverts to the centre owners after that time. We shall assume that the required investment would be 100 per cent depreciated (straight-line) over five years,[4] so the depreciation would be £500,000/5 = £100,000 per year. The tax rate is 25 per cent. Table 8.6 contains the projected revenues and expenses. Net income in each year, based on these figures, is also shown.

TABLE 8.6

Projected yearly revenue and costs for average accounting return

	Year 1	Year 2	Year 3	Year 4	Year 5
Revenue (£)	433,333	450,000	266,667	200,000	133,333
Expenses (£)	200,000	150,000	100,000	100,000	100,000
Earnings before depreciation (£)	233,333	300,000	166,667	100,000	33,333
Depreciation (£)	100,000	100,000	100,000	100,000	100,000
Earnings before taxes (£)	133,333	200,000	66,667	0	−66,667
Taxes (25%) (£)	33,333	50,000	16,667	0	−66,667
Net income (£)	100,000	150,000	50,000	0	−50,000

$$\text{Average net income} = \frac{£100,000 + 150,000 + 50,000 + 0 - 50,000}{5} = £50,000$$

$$\text{Average book value} = \frac{£500,000 + 0}{2} = £250,000$$

To calculate the average book value for this investment, we note that we started out with a book value of £500,000 (the initial cost) and ended up at £0. The average book value during the life of the investment is thus (£500,000 + 0)/2 = £250,000. As long as we use straight-line depreciation, the average investment will always be one-half of the initial investment.[5]

Looking at Table 8.6, we see that net income is £100,000 in the first year, £150,000 in the second year, £50,000 in the third year, £0 in Year 4, and −£50,000 in Year 5. The average net income, then, is:

$$[£100,000 + 150,000 + 50,000 + 0 + (-50,000)]/5 = £50,000$$

The average accounting return is:

$$\text{AAR} = \frac{\text{Average net income}}{\text{Average book value}} = \frac{£50{,}000}{£250{,}000} = 20\%$$

If the firm has a target AAR of less than 20 per cent, then this investment is acceptable; otherwise it is not. The *average accounting return rule* is thus:

> Based on the average accounting return rule, a project is acceptable if its average accounting return exceeds a target average accounting return.

As we shall now see, the use of this rule has a number of problems.

You should recognize the chief drawback of the AAR immediately. Above all else, the AAR is not a rate of return in any meaningful economic sense. Instead, it is the ratio of two accounting numbers, and it is not comparable to the returns offered, for example, in financial markets.[6]

One of the reasons why the AAR is not a true rate of return is that it ignores time value. When we average figures that occur at different times, we are treating the near future and the more distant future in the same way. There was no discounting involved when we computed the average net income, for example.

The second problem with the AAR is similar to the problem we had with the payback period rule concerning the lack of an objective cut-off period. Because a calculated AAR is really not comparable to a market return, the target AAR must somehow be specified. There is no generally agreed-upon way to do this. One way of doing it is to calculate the AAR for the firm as a whole and use this as a benchmark, but there are lots of other ways as well.

The third, and perhaps worst, flaw in the AAR is that it doesn't even look at the right things. Instead of cash flow and market value, it uses net income and book value. These are both poor substitutes. As a result, an AAR doesn't tell us what the effect on share price will be of taking an investment, so it doesn't tell us what we really want to know.

Does the AAR have any redeeming features? About the only one is that it almost always can be computed. The reason is that accounting information will almost always be available, both for the project under consideration and for the firm as a whole. We hasten to add that once the accounting information is available, we can always convert it to cash flows, so even this is not a particularly important fact. The AAR is summarized in Table 8.7.

TABLE 8.7

Advantages and disadvantages of the average accounting return

Advantages	Disadvantages
1. Easy to calculate.	1. Not a true rate of return; time value of money is ignored.
2. Needed information will usually be available.	2. Uses an arbitrary benchmark cut-off rate.
	3. Based on accounting (book) values, not cash flows and market values.

CONCEPT QUESTIONS

8.4a What is an average accounting rate of return (AAR)?
8.4b What are the weaknesses of the AAR rule?

8.5 THE INTERNAL RATE OF RETURN

internal rate of return (IRR) the discount rate that makes the NPV of an investment zero.

We now come to the most important alternative to NPV, the **internal rate of return**, universally known as the IRR. As we shall see, the IRR is closely related to NPV. With the IRR, we try to find a single rate of return that summarizes the merits of a project. Furthermore, we want this rate to be an 'internal' rate in the sense that it depends only on the cash flows of a particular investment, not on rates offered elsewhere.

To illustrate the idea behind the IRR, consider a project that costs €100 today and pays €110 in one year. Suppose you were asked, 'What is the return on this investment?' What would you say? It seems both natural and obvious to say that the return is 10 per cent, because for every euro we put in, we get €1.10 back. In fact, as we shall see in a moment, 10 per cent is the internal rate of return, or IRR, on this investment.

Is this project with its 10 per cent IRR a good investment? Once again, it would seem apparent that this is a good investment only if our required return is less than 10 per cent. This intuition is also correct, and illustrates the *IRR rule:*

> Based on the IRR rule, an investment is acceptable if the IRR exceeds the required return. It should be rejected otherwise.

Imagine that we want to calculate the NPV for our simple investment. At a discount rate of R, the NPV is:

$$\text{NPV} = -€100 + [110/(1 + R)]$$

Now, suppose we don't know the discount rate. This presents a problem, but we can still ask how high the discount rate would have to be before this project was deemed unacceptable. We know that we are indifferent between taking and not taking this investment when its NPV is just equal to zero. In other words, this investment is *economically* a break-even proposition when the NPV is zero, because value is neither created nor destroyed. To find the break-even discount rate we set NPV equal to zero and solve for R:

$$\text{NPV} = 0 = -€100 + [110/(1 + R)]$$
$$€100 = €110/(1 + R)$$
$$1 + R = €110/100 = 1.1$$
$$R = 10\%$$

This 10 per cent is what we have already called the return on this investment. What we have now illustrated is that the IRR on an investment (or just 'return' for short) is the discount rate that makes the NPV equal to zero. This is an important observation, so it bears repeating:

> The IRR on an investment is the required return that results in a zero NPV when it is used as the discount rate.

The fact that the IRR is simply the discount rate that makes the NPV equal to zero is important, because it tells us how to calculate the returns on more complicated investments. As we have seen, finding the IRR turns out to be relatively easy for a single-period investment. However, suppose you were now looking at an investment with the cash flows shown in Figure 8.4. As illustrated, this investment costs €100 and has a cash flow of €60 per year for two years, so it's only slightly more complicated than our single-period example. However, if you were asked for the return on this investment, what would you say? There doesn't seem to be any obvious answer (at least not to us). However, based on what we now know, we can set the NPV equal to zero and solve for the discount rate:

$$\text{NPV} = 0 = -€100 + \left[60/(1 + \text{IRR})\right] + \left[60/(1 + \text{IRR})^2\right]$$

FIGURE 8.4 **Project cash flows**

Unfortunately, the only way to find the IRR in general is by trial and error, either by hand or by calculator. This is precisely the same problem that came up in Chapter 4 when we found the unknown rate for an annuity and in Chapter 6 when we found the yield to maturity on a bond. In fact, we now see that in both of those cases we were finding an IRR.

In this particular case the cash flows form a two-period, €60 annuity. To find the unknown rate, we can try some different rates until we get the answer. If we were to start with a 0 per cent rate, the NPV would obviously be €120 − 100 = €20. At a 10 per cent discount rate, we would have:

$$\text{NPV} = -€100 + (60/1.1) + (60/1.1^2) = €4.13$$

Now, we're getting close. We can summarize these and some other possibilities as shown in Table 8.8. From our calculations the NPV appears to be zero with a discount rate between 10 per cent and 15 per cent, so the IRR is somewhere in that range. With a little more effort we can find that the IRR is about 13.1 per cent.[7] So, if our required return were less than 13.1 per cent, we would take this investment. If our required return exceeded 13.1 per cent, we would reject it.

TABLE 8.8

NPV at different discount rates

Discount rate (%)	NPV (€)
0	20.00
5	11.56
10	4.13
15	−2.46
20	−8.33

net present value profile a graphical representation of the relationship between an investment's NPVs and various discount rates.

By now you have probably noticed that the IRR rule and the NPV rule appear to be quite similar. In fact, the IRR is sometimes simply called the *discounted cash flow return*, or *DCF return*. The easiest way to illustrate the relationship between NPV and IRR is to plot the numbers we calculated for Table 8.8. We put the different NPVs on the vertical axis, or *y*-axis, and the discount rates on the horizontal axis, or *x*-axis. If we had a very large number of points the resulting picture would be a smooth curve called a **net present value profile**. Figure 8.5 illustrates the NPV profile for this project. Beginning with a 0 per cent discount rate, we have €20 plotted directly on the *y*-axis. As the discount rate increases, the NPV declines smoothly. Where will the curve cut through the *x*-axis? This will occur where the NPV is just equal to zero, so it will happen right at the IRR of 13.1 per cent.

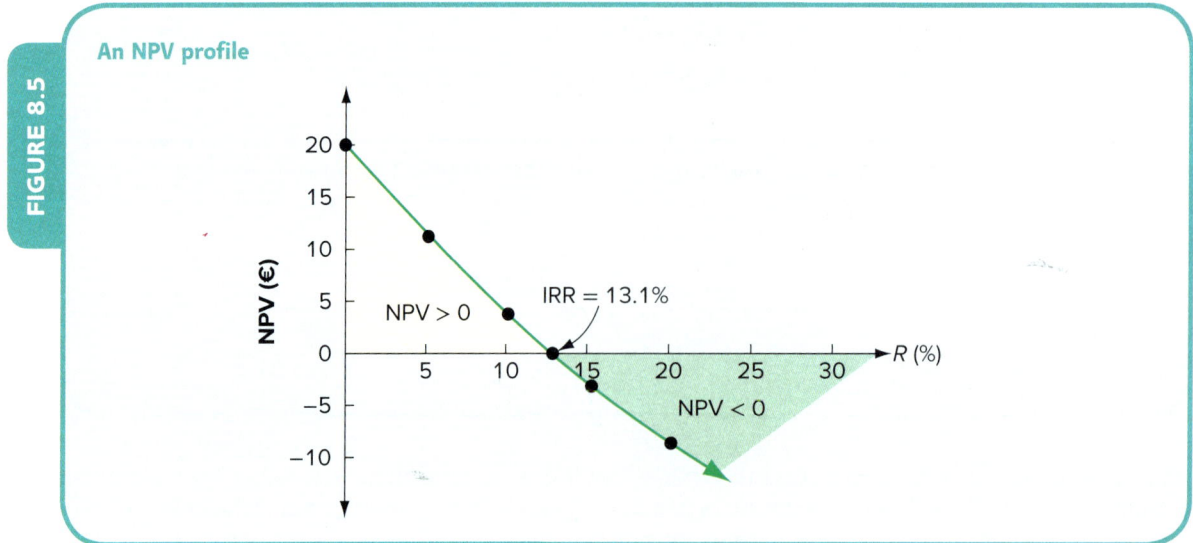

FIGURE 8.5 An NPV profile

In our example the NPV rule and the IRR rule lead to identical accept–reject decisions. We shall accept an investment using the IRR rule if the required return is less than 13.1 per cent. As Figure 8.5 illustrates, however, the NPV is positive at any discount rate less than 13.1 per cent, so we would accept the investment using the NPV rule as well. The two rules give equivalent results in this case.

EXAMPLE 8.4

CALCULATING THE IRR

A project has a total up-front cost of €435.44. The cash flows are €100 in the first year, €200 in the second year, and €300 in the third year. What's the IRR? If we require an 18 per cent return, should we take this investment?

We'll describe the NPV profile and find the IRR by calculating some NPVs at different discount rates. You should check our answers for practice. Beginning with 0 per cent, we have:

Discount rate (%)	NPV (€)
0	164.56
5	100.36
10	46.15
15	0.00
20	−39.61

The NPV is zero at 15 per cent, so 15 per cent is the IRR. If we require an 18 per cent return, then we should not take the investment. The reason is that the NPV is negative at 18 per cent (verify that it is −€24.47). The IRR rule tells us the same thing in this case. We shouldn't take this investment, because its 15 per cent return is below our required 18 per cent return.

At this point you may be wondering whether the IRR and NPV rules always lead to identical decisions. The answer is yes, as long as two very important conditions are met. First, the project's cash flows must be *conventional*, meaning that the first cash flow (the initial investment) is negative and all the rest are positive. Second, the project must be *independent*, meaning that the decision to accept or reject this project does not affect the decision to accept or reject any other. The first of these conditions is typically met, but the second often is not. In any case, when one or both of these conditions are not met, problems can arise. We discuss some of these next.

SPREADSHEET STRATEGIES 8.2

Calculating IRRs with a Spreadsheet

Because IRRs are so tedious to calculate by hand, spreadsheets are generally used and, as the following example illustrates, using a spreadsheet is easy.

Suppose we have a four-year project that costs £500. The cash flows over the four-year life will be £100, £200, £300 and £400, respectively. What is the IRR?

The spreadsheet could be laid out as follows:

	A	B	C	D	E	F
1	Year	0	1	2	3	4
2	Cash Flow	-500	100	200	300	400
3						
4	IRR =	IRR=(B2:F2)				
5						

The formula in cell B4 gives an IRR of 27.27 per cent.

PROBLEMS WITH THE IRR

The problems with the IRR come about when the cash flows are not conventional, or when we are trying to compare two or more investments to see which is best. In the first case, surprisingly, the simple question 'What's the return?' can become difficult to answer. In the second case, the IRR can be a misleading guide.

Non-Conventional Cash Flows

Suppose we have a strip-mining project that requires a €60 investment. Our cash flow in the first year will be €155. In the second year, the mine will be depleted, but we shall have to spend €100 to restore the terrain. As Figure 8.6 illustrates, both the first and third cash flows are negative.

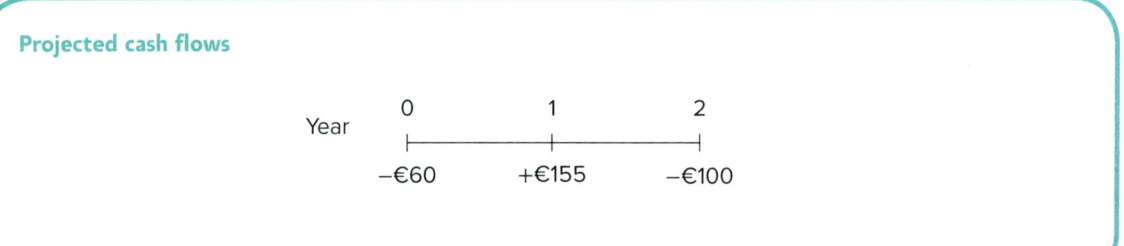

FIGURE 8.6 Projected cash flows

To find the IRR on this project, we can calculate the NPV at various rates:

Discount rate (%)	NPV (€)
0	−5.00
10	−1.74
20	−0.28
30	0.06
40	−0.31

The NPV appears to be behaving peculiarly here. First, as the discount rate increases from 0 per cent to 30 per cent, the NPV starts negative and becomes positive. This seems counterintuitive, because the NPV is rising as the discount rate rises. It then starts getting smaller and becomes negative again. What's the IRR? To find out, we draw the NPV profile, as shown in Figure 8.7.

In Figure 8.7, notice that the NPV is zero when the discount rate is 25 per cent, so this is the IRR. Or is it? The NPV is also zero at 33⅓ per cent. Which of these is correct? The answer is both or neither; more precisely, there is no unambiguously correct answer. This is the **multiple rates of return** problem. Many financial computer packages (including a best-seller for personal computers) aren't aware of this problem and report the first IRR that is found. Others state only the smallest positive IRR, even though this answer is no better than any other.

> **multiple rates of return** the possibility that more than one discount rate will make the NPV of an investment zero.

In our current example, the IRR rule breaks down completely. Suppose our required return is 10 per cent. Should we take this investment? Both IRRs are greater than 10 per cent, so, by the IRR rule, perhaps we should. However, as Figure 8.7 shows, the NPV is negative at any discount rate less than 25 per cent, so this is not a good investment. When should we take it? Looking at Figure 8.7 one last time, we see that the NPV is positive only if our required return is between 25 per cent and 33⅓ per cent.

Non-conventional cash flows can occur in a variety of ways. For example, ore mining firms open and close operations depending on the price of the ore that is being extracted. This results in negative cash flows during the periods in which the mine is closed, and positive cash flows when it is open. Sometimes the cost of maintaining a disused mine is significantly better than running a loss-making mining operation.

The moral of the story is that when the cash flows aren't conventional, strange things can start to happen to the IRR. This is not anything to get upset about, however, because the NPV rule, as always,

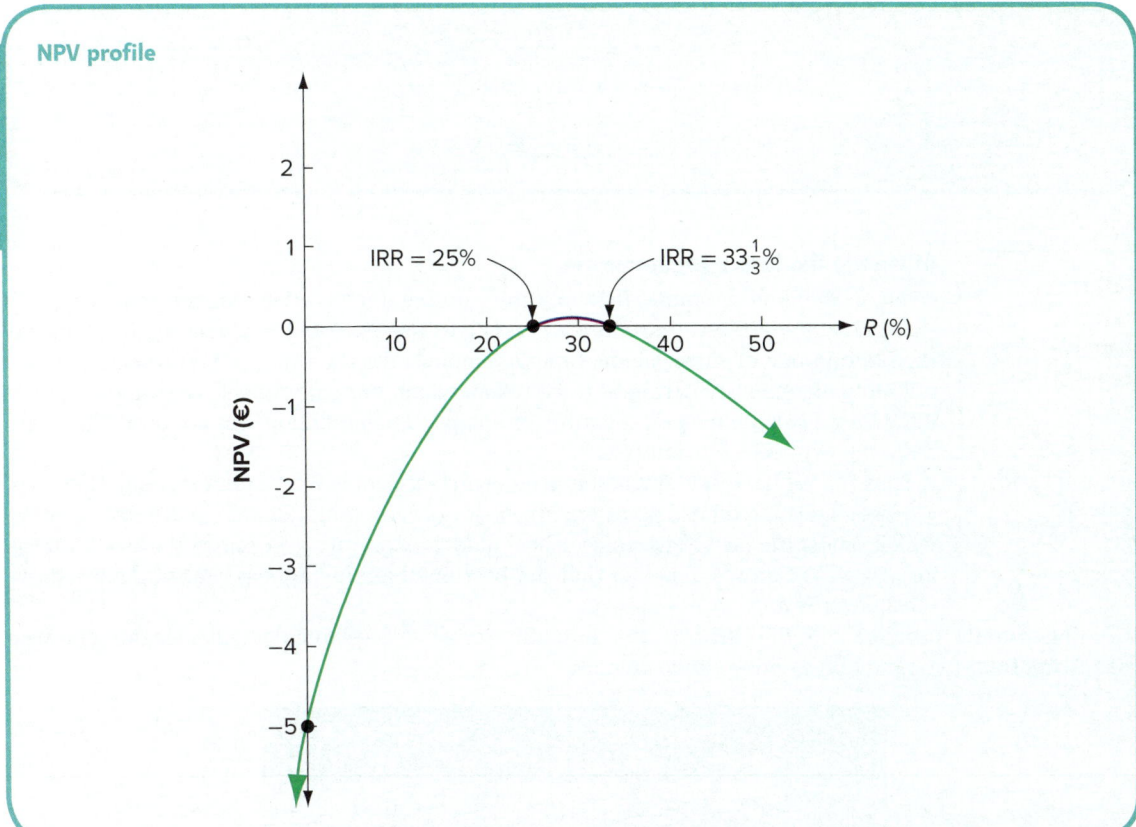

FIGURE 8.7 NPV profile

works just fine. This illustrates the fact that, oddly enough, the obvious question – What's the rate of return? – may not always have a good answer.

EXAMPLE 8.5

WHAT'S THE IRR?

You are looking at an investment that requires you to invest €51 today. You'll get €100 in one year, but you must pay out €50 in two years. What is the IRR of this investment?

You're on the alert now for the non-conventional cash flow problem, so you probably wouldn't be surprised to see more than one IRR. However, if you start looking for an IRR by trial and error, it will take you a long time. The reason is that there is no IRR. The NPV is negative at every discount rate, so we shouldn't take this investment under any circumstances. What's the return on this investment? Your guess is as good as ours.

EXAMPLE 8.6

'I THINK, THEREFORE I KNOW HOW MANY IRRS THERE CAN BE'

We've seen that it's possible to get more than one IRR. If you wanted to make sure that you had found all the possible IRRs, how could you do it? The answer comes from the great mathematician, philosopher and financial analyst Descartes (of 'I think, Therefore I am' fame). Descartes' Rule of Sign says that the maximum number of IRRs that there can be is equal to the number of times that the cash flows change sign from positive to negative and/or negative to positive.[8]

> In our example with the 25 per cent and 33⅓ per cent IRRs, could there be yet another IRR? The cash flows flip from negative to positive, then back to negative, for a total of two sign changes. Therefore, according to Descartes' rule, the maximum number of IRRs is two, and we don't need to look for any more. Note that the actual number of IRRs can be less than the maximum (see Example 8.5).

Mutually Exclusive Investments

mutually exclusive investment decisions a situation in which taking one investment prevents the taking of another.

Even if there is a single IRR, another problem can arise concerning **mutually exclusive investment decisions**. If two investments, X and Y, are mutually exclusive, then taking one of them means that we cannot take the other. Two projects that are not mutually exclusive are said to be independent. For example, if we own one corner lot, then we can build a petrol station or an apartment building, but not both. These are mutually exclusive alternatives.

Thus far, we have asked whether a given investment is worth undertaking. However, a related question comes up often: given two or more mutually exclusive investments, which one is the best? The answer is simple enough: the best one is the one with the largest NPV. Can we also say that the best one has the highest return? As we show, the answer is no.

To illustrate the problem with the IRR rule and mutually exclusive investments, consider the following cash flows from two mutually exclusive investments:

Year	Investment A (€)	Investment B (€)
0	−100	−100
1	50	20
2	40	40
3	40	50
4	30	60

The IRR for A is 24 per cent, and the IRR for B is 21 per cent. Because these investments are mutually exclusive, we can take only one of them. Simple intuition suggests that investment A is better because of its higher return. Unfortunately, simple intuition is not always correct.

To see why investment A is not necessarily the better of the two investments, we've calculated the NPV of these investments for different required returns:

Discount rate (%)	NPV (A) (€)	NPV (B) (€)
0	60.00	70.00
5	43.13	47.88
10	29.06	29.79
15	17.18	14.82
20	7.06	2.31
25	−1.63	−8.22

The IRR for A (24 per cent) is larger than the IRR for B (21 per cent). However, if you compare the NPVs, you'll see that which investment has the higher NPV depends on our required return. B has greater total cash flow, but it pays back more slowly than A. As a result, it has a higher NPV at lower discount rates.

In our example, the NPV and IRR rankings conflict for some discount rates. If our required return is 10 per cent, for instance, then B has the higher NPV and is thus the better of the two, even though A has a higher return. If our required return is 15 per cent, then there is no ranking conflict: A is better.

The conflict between the IRR and NPV for mutually exclusive investments can be illustrated by plotting the investments' NPV profiles as we have done in Figure 8.8. In Figure 8.8 notice that the NPV profiles cross at about 11 per cent. Notice also that at any discount rate less than 11 per cent the NPV for B is higher. In this range, taking B benefits us more than taking A, even though A's IRR is higher. At any rate greater than 11 per cent, investment A has the greater NPV.

FIGURE 8.8 NPV profiles for mutually exclusive investments

This example illustrates that when we have mutually exclusive projects, we shouldn't rank them based on their returns. More generally, whenever we are comparing investments to determine which is best, looking at IRRs can be misleading. Instead, we need to look at the relative NPVs to avoid the possibility of choosing incorrectly. Remember, we're ultimately interested in creating value for the shareholders, so the option with the higher NPV is preferred, regardless of the relative returns.

If this seems counterintuitive, think of it this way. Suppose you have two investments. One has a 10 per cent return and makes you €100 richer immediately. The other has a 20 per cent return and makes you €50 richer immediately. Which one do you like better? We would rather have €100 than €50, regardless of the returns, so we like the first one better.

EXAMPLE 8.7

CALCULATING THE CROSSOVER RATE

In Figure 8.8, the NPV profiles cross at about 11 per cent. How can we determine just what this crossover point is? The *crossover rate*, by definition, is the discount rate that makes the NPVs of two projects equal. To illustrate, suppose we have the following two mutually exclusive investments:

Year	Investment A (€)	Investment B (€)
0	−400	−500
1	250	320
2	280	340

What is the crossover rate?

To find the crossover, first consider moving out of investment A and into investment B. If you make the move, you'll have to invest an extra €100 (= €500 − 400). For this €100 investment, you'll get an additional €70 (= €320 − 250) in the first year and an extra €60 (= €340 − 280) in the second year. Is this a good move? In other words, is it worth investing the extra €100?

Based on our discussion, the NPV of the switch, NPV(B − A), is

$$\text{NPV}(B - A) = -€100 + \left[70/(1+R)\right] + \left[60/(1+R)^2\right]$$

We can calculate the return on this investment by setting the NPV equal to zero and solving for the IRR:

$$\text{NPV}(B - A) = 0$$
$$= -€100 + \left[70/(1+R)\right] + \left[60/(1+R)^2\right]$$

If you go through this calculation, you will find the IRR is exactly 20 per cent. What this tells us is that, at a 20 per cent discount rate, we are indifferent between the two investments, because the NPV of the difference in their cash flows is zero. As a consequence, the two investments have the same value, so this 20 per cent is the crossover rate. Check to see that the NPV at 20 per cent is €2.78 for both investments.

In general, you can find the crossover rate by taking the difference in the cash flows and calculating the IRR using the difference. It doesn't make any difference which one you subtract from which. To see this, find the IRR for (A − B); you'll see it's the same number. Also, for practice, you might want to find the exact crossover in Figure 8.8. (*Hint:* It's 11.0704 per cent.)

Investing or Financing?

Consider the following two independent investments:

Year	Investment A (€)	Investment B (€)
0	−100	+100
1	130	−130

The company initially pays out cash with investment A and initially receives cash for investment B. Most projects are more like investment A, but projects like investment B also occur. For example, consider a corporation conducting a seminar where the participants pay in advance. Because large expenses are frequently incurred at the seminar date, cash inflows precede cash outflows.

For these two projects, suppose the required return for each investment project is 12 per cent. According to the IRR decision rule, which, if either, project should we accept? If you calculate the IRRs, you will find that they are 30 per cent for both projects.

According to the IRR decision rule, we should accept both projects. However, if we calculate the NPV of B at 12 per cent, we get:

$$€100 - \frac{€130}{1.12} = -€16.07$$

In this case, the NPV and IRR decision rules disagree. To see what's going on, Figure 8.9 shows the NPV profile for each project. As you can see, the NPV profile for B is upward sloping. Thus the project should be accepted if the required return is *greater* than 30 per cent.

When a project has cash flows like investment B's, the IRR is a rate that you are paying, not receiving. For this reason, we say that the project has *financing-type* cash flows, whereas investment A has *investing-type* cash flows. You should take a project with financing-type cash flows only if it is an inexpensive source of financing, meaning that its IRR is *lower* than your required return.

FIGURE 8.9 NPV profile for investing and financing investments

REDEEMING QUALITIES OF THE IRR

Despite its flaws, the IRR is very popular in practice – more so even than the NPV. It probably survives because it fills a need that the NPV does not. In analysing investments, people in general, and financial analysts in particular, seem to prefer talking about rates of return rather than cash values.

In a similar vein, the IRR also appears to provide a simple way of communicating information about a proposal. One manager might say to another, 'Remodelling the clerical wing has a 20 per cent return.' This may somehow seem more straightforward than saying, 'At a 10 per cent discount rate, the net present value is £4,000.'

Finally, under certain circumstances, the IRR may have a practical advantage over the NPV. We can't estimate the NPV unless we know the appropriate discount rate, but we can still calculate the IRR. Suppose we didn't know the required return on an investment, but we found, for example, that it had a 40 per cent return. We would probably be inclined to take it because it would be unlikely that the required return would be that high. We summarize the advantages and disadvantages of IRR in Table 8.9.

TABLE 8.9

Advantages and disadvantages of the internal rate of return

Advantages	Disadvantages
1. Closely related to NPV, often leading to identical decisions.	1. May result in multiple answers, or not deal with non-conventional cash flows.
2. Easy to understand and communicate.	2. May lead to incorrect decisions in comparisons of mutually exclusive investments.

THE MODIFIED INTERNAL RATE OF RETURN (MIRR)

We sometimes use a modified version of IRR to address the problems that crop up with the standard IRR. As we shall see, there are several different ways of calculating a modified IRR, or MIRR, but the basic idea is to modify the cash flows first and then calculate an IRR using the modified cash flows.

To illustrate, let's go back to the cash flows in Figure 8.6: −€60, +€155 and −€100. As we saw, there are two IRRs, 25 per cent and 33⅓ per cent. We next illustrate three different MIRRs, all of which have the property that only one answer will result, thereby eliminating the multiple IRR problem.

Method 1: The Discounting Approach

With the discounting approach, the idea is to discount all negative cash flows back to the present at the required return and add them to the initial cost, and then calculate the IRR. Because only the first modified cash flow is negative, there will be only one IRR. The discount rate used might be the required return, or it might be some other externally supplied rate. We shall use the project's required return.

If the required return on the project is 20 per cent, then the modified cash flows look like this:

$$\text{Time 0:} -€60 + \frac{-€100}{1.20^2} = -€129.44$$

Time 1: +€155

Time 2: +€0

If you calculate the MIRR now, you should get 19.74 per cent.

Method 2: The Reinvestment Approach

With the reinvestment approach, we compound *all* cash flows (positive and negative) except the first out to the end of the project's life, and then calculate the IRR. In a sense, we are 'reinvesting' the cash flows, and not taking them out of the project until the very end. The rate we use could be the required return on the project, or it could be a separately specified 'reinvestment rate'. We shall use the project's required return. When we do, here are the modified cash flows:

Time 0: −€60
Time 1: +0
Time 2: −€100 + (€155 × 1.2) = €86

The MIRR on this set of cash flows is 19.72 per cent, or a little lower than we got using the discounting approach.

Method 3: The Combination Approach

As the name suggests, the combination approach blends our first two methods. Negative cash flows are discounted back to the present, and positive cash flows are compounded to the end of the project. In practice, different discount or compounding rates might be used, but we shall again stick with the project's required return.

With the combination approach, the modified cash flows are as follows:

$$\text{Time 0:} -€60 + \frac{-€100}{1.20^2} = -€129.44$$

Time 1: +0
Time 2: €155 × 1.2 = €186

See if you disagree that the MIRR is 19.87 per cent, the highest of the three.

MIRR or IRR: Which Is Better?

MIRRs are controversial. At one extreme are those who claim that MIRRs are always superior to IRRs. For example, by design, they don't suffer from the multiple rates of return problem.

At the other end, detractors say that MIRR should stand for 'meaningless internal rate of return'. As our example makes clear, one problem with MIRRs is that there are different ways of calculating them, and there is no apparent reason to say that one of our three methods is better than any other. The differences are small with our simple cash flows, but they could be much larger for a more complex project. Moreover, it's not clear how to interpret an MIRR. It may look like a rate of return, but it's a rate of return on a modified set of cash flows, not the project's actual cash flows.

We're not going to take sides. However, notice that calculating an MIRR requires discounting, compounding, or both, which leads to two apparent observations. First, if we have the appropriate discount rate, why not calculate the NPV and be done with it? Second, because an MIRR depends on an externally supplied discount (or compounding) rate, the answer you get is not truly an 'internal' rate of return, which by definition depends only on the project's cash flows.

We shall take a stand on one issue that frequently comes up in this context. The value of a project does not depend on how a firm uses the cash flows generated by it. A firm might use a project's cash flows to fund other projects, to pay dividends, or to buy an executive jet. It doesn't matter: how the cash flows are spent in the future does not affect their value today. As a result, there is generally no need to consider reinvestment of interim cash flows.

> **CONCEPT QUESTIONS**
>
> **8.5a** Under what circumstances will the IRR and NPV rules lead to the same accept-reject decisions? When might they conflict?
>
> **8.5b** Is it generally true that an advantage of the IRR rule over the NPV rule is that we don't need to know the required return to use the IRR rule?

8.6 THE PROFITABILITY INDEX

Another tool used to evaluate projects is called the **profitability index (PI)** or benefit–cost ratio. This index is defined as the present value of the future cash flows divided by the initial investment. So, if a project costs €200 and the present value of its future cash flows is €220, the profitability index value would be €220/200 = 1.1. Notice that the NPV for this investment is €20, so it is a desirable investment.

More generally, if a project has a positive NPV, then the present value of the future cash flows must be bigger than the initial investment. The profitability index would thus be bigger than 1 for a positive-NPV investment and less than 1 for a negative-NPV investment.

How do we interpret the profitability index? In our example, the PI was 1.1. This tells us that, per euro invested, €1.10 in value or €0.10 in NPV results. The profitability index thus measures the value created per cash unit invested. For this reason, it is often proposed as a measure of performance for government or other not-for-profit investments. Also, when capital is scarce, it may make sense to allocate it to projects with the highest PIs. We shall return to this issue in a later chapter.

profitability index (PI) the present value of an investment's future cash flows divided by its initial cost. Also called the *benefit–cost ratio.*

The PI is similar to the NPV. However, consider an investment that costs €5 and has a €10 present value, and an investment that costs €100 with a €150 present value. The first of these investments has an NPV of €5 and a PI of 2. The second has an NPV of €50 and a PI of 1.5. If these are mutually exclusive investments, then the second one is preferred even though it has a lower PI. This ranking problem is similar to the IRR ranking problem we saw in the previous section. In all, there seems to be little reason to rely on the PI instead of the NPV. We summarize our discussion of the PI in Table 8.10.

TABLE 8.10

Advantages and disadvantages of the profitability index

Advantages	Disadvantages
1. Closely related to NPV, generally leading to identical decisions. 2. Easy to understand and communicate. 3. May be useful when available investment funds are limited.	1. May lead to incorrect decisions in comparisons of mutually exclusive investments.

> **CONCEPT QUESTIONS**
>
> **8.6a** What does the profitability index measure?
>
> **8.6b** How would you state the profitability index rule?

8.7 THE PRACTICE OF CAPITAL BUDGETING

Given that NPV seems to be telling us directly what we want to know, you might be wondering why there are so many other procedures, and why alternative procedures are commonly used. Recall that we are trying to make an investment decision, and that we are frequently operating under considerable uncertainty about the future. We can only *estimate* the NPV of an investment in this case. The resulting estimate can be very 'soft', meaning that the true NPV might be quite different.

Because the true NPV is unknown, the astute financial manager seeks clues to help in assessing whether the estimated NPV is reliable. For this reason, firms would typically use multiple criteria for evaluating a proposal. For example, suppose we have an investment with a positive estimated NPV. Based on our experience with other projects, this one appears to have a short payback and a very high AAR. In this case, the different indicators seem to agree that it's 'all systems go'. Put another way, the payback and the AAR are consistent with the conclusion that the NPV is positive.

On the other hand, suppose we had a positive estimated NPV, a long payback and a low AAR. This could still be a good investment, but it looks as though we need to be much more careful in making the decision, because we are getting conflicting signals. If the estimated NPV is based on projections in which we have little confidence, then further analysis is probably in order. We shall consider how to evaluate NPV estimates in more detail in the next two chapters.

EXAMPLE 8.8

BRINGING IT ALL TOGETHER: EVALUATING A PROJECT USING SEVERAL CAPITAL BUDGETING APPRAISAL TECHNIQUES

Sandy Grey Ltd is in the process of deciding whether or not to revise the line of mobile phones that it manufactures and sells. Its sole market is large corporations, and it has not as yet focused on the retail sector. The company has estimated that the revision will cost £220,000. Cash flows from increased sales will be £80,000 in the first year. These cash flows will increase by 5 per cent per year. The company estimates that the new line will be obsolete five years from now. Assume the initial cost is paid now, and all revenues are received at the end of each year. If the company requires a 10 per cent return for such an investment, should it undertake the revision? Use three investment evaluation techniques to arrive at your answer.

We shall look at NPV, IRR and PI. However, it is easy to consider the payback period or discounted payback period.

If the cash flows increase by 5 per cent per year, they will be as follows:

Year	0	1	2	3	4	5
Cash flow (£)	−220,000	80,000	84,000	88,200	92,610	97,240.5

The NPV of the investment is:

$$NPV = -£220,000 + \frac{£80,000}{(1+0.10)} + \frac{£84,000}{(1+0.10)^2} + \frac{£88,200}{(1+0.10)^3} + \frac{£92,610}{(1+0.10)^4} + \frac{£97,240.5}{(1+0.10)^5}$$

$$= £112,047$$

The IRR of the investment is:

$$NPV = 0$$
$$= -£220,000 + \frac{£80,000}{(1+IRR)} + \frac{£84,000}{(1+IRR)^2} + \frac{£88,200}{(1+IRR)^3} + \frac{£92,610}{(1+IRR)^4} + \frac{£97,240.5}{(1+IRR)^5}$$

Using trial and error, the IRR is:

$$IRR = 27.69\%$$

The profitability index of the investment is:

$$PI = \left[\frac{£80{,}000}{(1+R)} + \frac{£84{,}000}{(1+R)^2} + \frac{£88{,}200}{(1+R)^3} + \frac{£92{,}610}{(1+R)^4} + \frac{£97{,}240.5}{(1+R)^5}\right] / £220{,}000$$

$$= 1.509$$

With all methods the project looks viable, and should be undertaken.

So far this chapter has asked 'Which capital budgeting methods should companies be using?' An equally important question is this: which methods are companies *actually* using? Table 8.11 helps to answer this question. The figures in the table are the percentage of firms from the country sample that said they 'Always Used' or 'Almost Always Used' a method. As can be seen from the table, there is quite a substantial variation in the frequency with which different techniques are utilized. Most companies use the IRR and NPV methods, which is not surprising given the theoretical advantages of these approaches. The most interesting point is that, for a number of countries, the payback period is very popular.

TABLE 8.11

Percentage of firms in selected countries that use capital budgeting techniques

Country	NPV	IRR	Payback Period	Average Accounting Return
Poland	76%	48%	87%	63%
Finland	62%	43%	51%	3%
France	70%	44%	51%	16%
Germany	78%	42%	50%	32%
Netherlands	89%	56%	65%	35%
Sweden	84%	30%	54%	24%
UK	80%	53%	69%	38%
USA	95%	76%	57%	20%
Australia	96%	64%	59%	19%
China	84%	89%	84%	9%
Malaysia	91%	69%	71%	37%
Singapore	86%	71%	71%	47%
India	50%	52%	38%	0%
South Africa	99%	79%	54%	14%

Source: Adapted from Table 10, Andor, G., S.K. Mohanty and T. Toth (2015). Capital budgeting practices: A survey of Central and Eastern European firms. Emerging Markets Review, 23, 148–172.

An astute reader will ask why, if NPV is so good, do all firms not use this method? The issue is that NPV's strength is also its weakness. That is, because NPV uses all cash flow information, analysts must actually forecast these cash flows. Forecast may be good or bad and long-term forecasts are more likely to be less accurate than short-term forecasts. If a company operates in an industry or geography with long-term uncertainty, NPV may give very inaccurate estimates of present value. Another problem with NPV is that you must also estimate the discount rate of the project. This is always estimated and so a further source of error is introduced.

The use of quantitative techniques in capital budgeting varies with the industry. As one would imagine, firms that are better able to estimate cash flows are more likely to use NPV. For example, estimation of cash flow in certain aspects of the oil business is entirely feasible. Because of this, energy-related firms were among the first to use NPV analysis. Conversely, the cash flows in the motion picture business are very hard to project. The gross revenues of great hits like *Titanic*, *Black Panther* and *Avengers: Endgame* were far,

far higher than anyone imagined. The substantial failures like *King Arthur: Legend of the Sword* and *Mortal Engines* were unexpected as well. Because of this, NPV analysis is frowned upon in the movie business.

Another insight from Table 8.11 is that companies use a combination of investment appraisal methods to make capital expenditure decisions. This is without a doubt the most sensible strategy, and combinations of the techniques introduced in this chapter can be the basis for hybrid decision rules for investment appraisal. For example, consider an energy firm that is capital rationed and experiences large winding-down costs for projects (such as dismantling oil rigs and clean-up costs at the end of an oil field's life). An appropriate combination would be NPV and payback period. NPV tells the financial manager whether the project will add value and includes all cash flows, while the payback period will say how long it takes to get the initial investment back. A decision rule that requires both a payback period less than four years and a positive NPV would be a typical decision rule. As can be seen, combining investment appraisal methods can open up a whole set of innovative decision rules to make financial decisions.

For future reference, the various criteria we have discussed are summarized in Table 8.12.

TABLE 8.12

Summary of investment criteria

Discounted cash flow criteria

A. *Net present value (NPV):* The NPV of an investment is the difference between its market value and its cost. The NPV rule is to take a project if its NPV is positive. NPV is frequently estimated by calculating the present value of the future cash flows (to estimate market value) and then subtracting the cost. NPV has no serious flaws; it is the preferred decision criterion.

B. *Internal rate of return (IRR):* The IRR is the discount rate that makes the estimated NPV of an investment equal to zero; it is sometimes called the *discounted cash flow (DCF) return*. The IRR rule is to take a project when its IRR exceeds the required return. IRR is closely related to NPV, and it leads to exactly the same decisions as NPV for conventional, independent projects. When project cash flows are not conventional there may be no IRR, or there may be more than one. More seriously, the IRR cannot be used to rank mutually exclusive projects; the project with the highest IRR is not necessarily the preferred investment.

C. *Modified internal rate of return (MIRR):* The MIRR is a modification to the IRR. A project's cash flows are modified by: (1) discounting the negative cash flows back to the present; (2) compounding cash flows to the end of the project's life; or (3) combining (1) and (2). An IRR is then computed on the modified cash flows. MIRRs are guaranteed to avoid the multiple rate of return problem, but it is unclear how to interpret them; and they are not truly 'internal', because they depend on externally supplied discounting or compounding rates.

D. *Profitability index (PI):* The PI, also called the *benefit–cost ratio*, is the ratio of present value to cost. The PI rule is to take an investment if the index exceeds 1. The PI measures the present value of an investment per unit of currency invested. It is quite similar to NPV, but, like IRR, it cannot be used to rank mutually exclusive projects. However, it is sometimes used to rank projects when a firm has more positive NPV investments than it can currently finance.

Payback criteria

A. *Payback period:* The payback period is the length of time until the sum of an investment's cash flows equals its cost. The payback period rule is to take a project if its payback is less than some cut-off. The payback period is a flawed criterion, primarily because it ignores risk, the time value of money, and cash flows beyond the cut-off point.

B. *Discounted payback period:* The discounted payback period is the length of time until the sum of an investment's discounted cash flows equals its cost. The discounted payback period rule is to take an investment if the discounted payback is less than some cut-off. The discounted payback rule is flawed, primarily because it ignores cash flows after the cut-off.

Accounting criterion

A. *Average accounting return (AAR):* The AAR is a measure of accounting profit relative to book value. It is *not* related to the IRR, but it is similar to the accounting return on assets (ROA) measure in Chapter 3. The AAR rule is to take an investment if its AAR exceeds a benchmark AAR. The AAR is seriously flawed for a variety of reasons, and it has little to recommend it.

> **CONCEPT QUESTIONS**
>
> **8.7a** What are the most commonly used capital budgeting procedures?
> **8.7b** If NPV is conceptually the best procedure for capital budgeting, why do you think multiple measures are used in practice?

SUMMARY AND CONCLUSIONS

This chapter has covered the different criteria used to evaluate potential investments. The seven criteria, in the order we discussed them, are these:

1. Net present value (NPV)
2. Payback period
3. Discounted payback period
4. Average accounting return (AAR)
5. Internal rate of return (IRR)
6. Modified internal rate of return (MIRR)
7. Profitability index (PI)

We illustrated how to calculate each of these and discussed the interpretation of the results. We also described the advantages and disadvantages of each of them. Ultimately a good capital budgeting criterion must tell us two things. First, is a particular project a good investment? Second, if we have more than one good project, but we can take only one of them, which one should we take? The main point of this chapter is that only the NPV criterion can always provide the correct answer to both questions.

For this reason, NPV is one of the two or three most important concepts in finance, and we shall refer to it many times in the chapters ahead. When we do, keep two things in mind: (1) NPV is always just the difference between the market value of an asset or project and its cost; and (2) the financial manager acts in the shareholders' best interests by identifying and taking positive-NPV projects.

Finally, we cannot usually observe NPVs in the market; instead, we must estimate them. Because there is always the possibility of a poor estimate, financial managers use multiple criteria for examining projects. The other criteria provide additional information about whether a project truly has a positive NPV.

CHAPTER REVIEW AND SELF-TEST PROBLEMS

8.1 Investment Criteria This problem will give you some practice calculating NPVs and paybacks. A proposed overseas expansion has the following cash flows:

Year	Cash flow (£)
0	−200
1	50
2	60
3	70
4	200

Calculate the payback, the discounted payback, and the NPV at a required return of 10 per cent.

8.2 Mutually Exclusive Investments Consider the following two mutually exclusive investments. Calculate the IRR for each and the crossover rate. Under what circumstances will the IRR and NPV criteria rank the two projects differently?

Year	Investment A (€)	Investment B (€)
0	−75	−75
1	20	60
2	40	50
3	70	15

8.3 Average Accounting Return You are looking at a three-year project with a projected net income of €2,000 in year 1, €4,000 in year 2, and €6,000 in year 3. The cost is €12,000, which will be depreciated straight-line to zero over the three-year life of the project. What is the average accounting return (AAR)?

SOLUTIONS

8.1 In the following table, we have listed the cash flow, cumulative cash flow, discounted cash flow (at 10 per cent), and cumulative discounted cash flow for the proposed project.

Year	Cash flow (£)	Cumulative cash flow (£)	Present value cash flow (£)	Cumulative present value cash flow (£)
0	−200	−200	−200	−200
1	50	−150	45.45	−154.55
2	60	−90	49.59	−104.96
3	70	−20	52.59	−52.37
4	200	180	136.60	84.24

Recall that the initial investment was £200. When we compare this with accumulated undiscounted cash flows, we see that payback occurs between years 3 and 4. The cash flows for the first three years are £180 total, so, going into the fourth year, we are short by £20. The total cash flow in year 4 is £200, so the payback is 3 + (£20/200) = 3.10 years. Looking at the accumulated discounted cash flows, we see that the discounted payback occurs between years 3 and 4. The sum of the discounted cash flows is £284.23, so the NPV is £84.23. Notice that this is the present value of the cash flows that occur after the discounted payback.

8.2 To calculate the IRR, we might try some guesses, as in the following table:

Discount rate (%)	NPV(A) (€)	NPV(B) (€)
0	55.00	50.00
10	28.83	32.14
20	9.95	18.40
30	−4.09	7.57
40	−14.80	−1.17

Several things are immediately apparent from our guesses. First, the IRR on A must be between 20 per cent and 30 per cent (why?). With some more effort, we find that it is 26.79 per cent. For B, the IRR must be a little less than 40 per cent (again, why?); it works out to be 38.54 per cent. Also, notice that at rates between 0 per cent and 10 per cent, the NPVs are very close, indicating that the crossover is in that vicinity.

To find the crossover exactly, we can compute the IRR on the difference in the cash flows. If we take the cash flows from A minus the cash flows from B, the resulting cash flows are:

Year	A − B (€)
0	0
1	−40
2	−10
3	55

These cash flows look a little odd, but the sign changes only once, so we can find an IRR. With some trial and error, you'll see that the NPV is zero at a discount rate of 5.42 per cent, so this is the crossover rate. The IRR for B is higher. However, as we've seen, A has the larger NPV for any discount rate less than 5.42 per cent, so the NPV and IRR rankings will conflict in that range. Remember, if there's a conflict, we shall go with the higher NPV. Our decision rule is thus simple: take A if the required return is less than 5.42 per cent, take B if the required return is between 5.42 per cent and 38.54 per cent (the IRR on B), and take neither if the required return is more than 38.54 per cent.

8.3 Here we need to calculate the ratio of average net income to average book value to get the AAR. Average net income is:

$$\text{Average net income} = (€2{,}000 + 4{,}000 + 6{,}000)/3 + €4{,}000$$

Average book value is:

$$\text{Average book value} = €12{,}000/2 = €6{,}000$$

So the average accounting return is:

$$\text{AAR} = €4{,}000/6{,}000 = 66.67\%$$

This is an impressive return. Remember, however, that it isn't a rate of return like an interest rate or an IRR, so the size doesn't tell us a lot. In particular, our money is probably not going to grow at a rate of 66.67 per cent per year, we're sorry to say.

QUESTIONS AND PROBLEMS

8.1 Calculating Payback What is the payback period for this project?

Year	Cash flow (€)
0	−55,000
1	45,000
2	25,000
3	15,000

8.2 Payback Your company has identified a project that will cost £15 million to initiate, have start-up costs of £2 million in year 1 and provide a net cash flow of £5 million per year for six years. If your company had a payback benchmark of three years, would you accept the project? What would be the reasons for the company to have such a low benchmark payback period?

8.3 Calculating Payback An investment project provides cash inflows of £765 per year for eight years. What is the project payback period if the initial cost is £2,400? What if the initial cost is £3,600? What if it is £6,500?

8.4 Calculating Payback Dream plc has the following mutually exclusive projects. Suppose Shire's payback period cut-off is two years. Which of these two projects should be chosen?

Year	Cash flow (A) (€)	Cash flow (B) (€)
0	−14,000	−6,000
1	4,000	4,500
2	5,500	2,200
3	10,000	200

8.5 Calculating Discounted Payback An investment project has annual cash inflows of £20,000, £35,400, £48,000 and £54,000 and a discount rate of 14 per cent. What is the discounted payback period for these cash flows if the initial cost is £100,000? What if the initial cost is £120,000? What if it is £170,000?

8.6 Calculating Discounted Payback An investment project costs €30,000, and has annual cash flows of €8,300 for six years. What is the discounted payback period if the discount rate is zero per cent? What if the discount rate is 7 per cent? If it is 20 per cent?

8.7 Calculating AAR You're trying to determine whether to expand your business by building a new manufacturing plant. The plant has an installation cost of £15 million, which will be depreciated straight-line to zero over its four-year life. If the plant has projected net income of £1,938,200, £2,201,600, £1,876,000 and £1,329,500 over these four years, what is the project's average accounting return (AAR)?

8.8 Calculating IRR A firm evaluates all of its projects by applying the IRR rule. If the required return is 20 per cent, should the firm accept the following project?

Year	Cash flow (€)
0	−30,000
1	15,000
2	17,000
3	14,000

8.9 Calculating NPV For the cash flows in the previous problem, suppose the firm uses the NPV decision rule. At a required return of 12 per cent, should the firm accept this project? What if the required return was 40 per cent?

8.10 Calculating NPV and IRR A project that provides annual cash flows of €28,500 for nine years costs €138,000 today. Is this a good project if the required return is 8 per cent? What if it's 20 per cent? At what discount rate would you be indifferent between accepting the project and rejecting it?

8.11 Calculating IRR What is the IRR of the following set of cash flows?

Year	Cash flow (£)
0	−£19,500
1	9,800
2	10,300
3	8,600

8.12 Calculating NPV For the cash flows in the previous problem, what is the NPV at a discount rate of zero per cent? What if the discount rate is 8 per cent? If it is 12 per cent? If it is 20 per cent?

8.13 Project Evaluation Software games company, Avalanche Entertainment, is considering expanding its highly successful online game franchise to the board game or trading card environment. The company has decided that it will invest in one project but not both. Consider the following cash flows of the two mutually exclusive projects. Assume the discount rate for Avalanche Entertainment is 10 per cent.

Year	Trading Cards (€)	Board Game (€)
0	−200	−2,000
1	300	−2,200
2	300	900
3	100	500

(a) Based on the payback period, which project should be taken?
(b) Based on the NPV, which project should be taken?
(c) Based on the IRR, which project should be taken?
(d) Calculate the incremental IRR; which project should be taken?

8.14 NPV versus IRR Consider the following cash flows on two mutually exclusive projects for Tomatina Recreation SA. Both projects require an annual return of 15 per cent.

Year	Deepwater Fishing (€)	New Submarine Ride (€)
0	−600,000	−1,800,000
1	270,000	1,000,000
2	350,000	700,000
3	300,000	900,000

(a) Calculate the IRR for both projects. Which project should you choose?
(b) Compute the NPV for both projects. Which project should you choose?

8.15 NPV versus IRR Consider the following two mutually exclusive projects:

Year	Cash flow (X) (DKr)	Cash flow (Y) (DKr)
0	−15,000	−15,000
1	8,150	7,700
2	5,050	5,150
3	6,800	7,250

Sketch the NPV profiles for X and Y over a range of discount rates from zero to 25 per cent. What is the crossover rate for these two projects?

8.16 Problems with IRR Sustainable Drainage Systems plc is trying to evaluate the introduction of a new generation of drainage systems with the following cash flows:

Year	Cash flow (£)
0	−45,000,000
1	78,000,000
2	−14,000,000

(a) The company requires a 12 per cent return on its investments. Using the NPV decision rule, should it accept this project? Why?

(b) Compute the IRR for this project. How many IRRs are there? Using the IRR decision rule, should the company accept the project? What's going on here?

8.17 Calculating Profitability Index What is the profitability index for the following set of cash flows? Should the project be accepted or rejected if the discount rate is 14 per cent?

Year	Cash flow (€)
0	−14,000
1	7,300
2	6,900
3	5,700

8.18 Calculating Profitability Index Suppose the following two independent investment opportunities are available to Greenplain Ltd. The appropriate discount rate is 10 per cent.

Year	Project Alpha (€)	Project Beta (€)
0	−600	−3,000
1	400	400
2	800	2,500
3	700	3,200

(a) Compute the profitability index for each of the two projects.

(b) Which project(s) should Greenplain accept based on the profitability index rule?

8.19 Comparing Investment Criteria Consider the following cash flows of two mutually exclusive projects for Tadcaster Rubber Company. Assume the discount rate for Tadcaster Rubber Company is 10 per cent.

Year	Dry Prepreg (€)	Solvent Prepreg (€)
0	−800,000	−600,000
1	500,000	400,000
2	300,000	600,000
3	900,000	200,000

(a) Calculate the payback period. Which project should be taken?

(b) Calculate the NPV. Which project should be taken?

(c) Calculate the IRR. Which project should be taken?

(d) Calculate the incremental IRR. Is incremental IRR analysis necessary? Please conduct the analysis.

8.20 NPV and Discount Rates An investment has an installed cost of €700,000. The cash flows over the four-year life of the investment are projected to be €250,000, €300,000, €225,000 and €175,000. If the discount rate is zero, what is the NPV? If the discount rate is infinite, what is the NPV? At what discount rate is the NPV just equal to zero? Sketch the NPV profile for this investment, based on these three points.

8.21 MIRR Slow Ride plc is evaluating a project with the following cash flows:

Year	Cash flow (£)
0	−25,000
1	9,000
2	11,000
3	12,000
4	5,000
5	−5,000

The company uses a 12 per cent interest rate on all of its projects. Calculate the MIRR of the project using all three methods.

8.22 MIRR Suppose the company in the previous problem uses an 11 per cent discount rate and an 8 per cent reinvestment rate on all of its projects. Calculate the MIRR of the project using all three methods using these interest rates.

8.23 NPV and the Profitability Index If we define the NPV index as the ratio of NPV to cost, what is the relationship between this index and the profitability index?

8.24 Cash Flow Intuition A project has an initial cost of I, has a required return of R, and pays C annually for N years.

(a) Find C in terms of I and N such that the project has a payback period just equal to its life.

(b) Find C in terms of I, N and R such that this is a profitable project according to the NPV decision rule.

(c) Find C in terms of I, N and R such that the project has a benefit–cost ratio of 3.

8.25 Payback and NPV An investment under consideration has a payback of seven years and a cost of €724,000. If the required return is 12 per cent, what is the worst-case NPV? The best-case NPV? Explain. Assume the cash flows are conventional.

8.26 Multiple IRRs This problem is useful for testing the ability of financial calculators and computer software. Consider the following cash flows. How many different IRRs are there? (*Hint:* Search between 20 per cent and 70 per cent.) When should we take this project?

Year	Cash flow (£)
0	−1,512
1	8,586
2	−18,210
3	17,100
4	−6,000

8.27 NPV Valuation Yuvhadit Ltd wants to set up a private cemetery business. According to the CFO, Barry M. Deep, business is 'looking up'. As a result, the cemetery project will provide a net cash inflow of €100,000 for the firm during the first year, and the cash flows are projected to grow at a rate of 5 per cent per year forever. The project requires an initial investment of €1,000,000.

(a) If Yuvhadit requires a 10 per cent return on such undertakings, should the cemetery business be started?

(b) The company is somewhat unsure about the assumption of a 5 per cent growth rate in its cash flows. At what constant growth rate would the company just break even if it still required a 10 per cent return on investment?

8.28 **Problems with IRR** A project has the following cash flows:

Year	Cash flow (£)
0	58,000
1	−34,000
2	−45,000

What is the IRR for this project? If the required return is 12 per cent, should the firm accept the project? What is the NPV of this project? What is the NPV of the project if the required return is 0 per cent? 24 per cent? What is going on here? Sketch the NPV profile to help you with your answer.

8.29 **Problems with IRR** Kilmaheedin Ltd has a project with the following cash flows:

Year	Cash flow (£)
0	30,000
1	−36,000
2	20,000

What is the IRR of the project? What is happening here?

8.30 **NPV and IRR** Gulliver International Limited is evaluating a project in Lilliput. The project will create the following cash flows:

Year	Cash flow (LP)
0	−750,000
1	205,000
2	265,000
3	346,000
4	220,000

All cash flows will occur in Lilliput and are expressed in Lilliputian pounds (LP). In an attempt to improve its economy, the Lilliputian government has declared that all cash flows created by a foreign company are 'blocked', and must be reinvested with the government for one year. The reinvestment rate for these funds is 4 per cent. If Gulliver uses an 11 per cent required return on this project, what are the NPV and IRR of the project? Is the IRR you calculated the MIRR of the project? Why or why not?

MINI CASE

DAVIES GOLD MINING

Dick Davies, the owner of Davies Gold Mining, is evaluating a new gold mine in Tanzania. Barry Koch, the company's geologist, has just finished his analysis of the mine site. He has estimated that the mine would be productive for eight years, after which the gold would be completely mined. Barry has taken an estimate of the gold deposits to Andy Marshall, the company's financial officer. Andy has been asked by Dick to perform an analysis of the new mine and present his recommendation on whether the company should open the new mine.

Andy has used the estimates provided by Barry to determine the revenues that could be expected from the mine. He has also projected the expense of opening the mine, and the annual operating expenses. If the company opens the mine, it will cost £500 million today, and it will have a cash outflow of £80 million nine years from today in costs associated with closing the mine and reclaiming the area surrounding it. The expected cash flows each year from the mine are shown in the following table. Davies Gold Mining has a 12 per cent required return on all of its gold mines.

Year	Cash flow (£)
0	−500,000,000
1	60,000,000
2	90,000,000
3	170,000,000
4	230,000,000
5	205,000,000
6	140,000,000
7	110,000,000
8	70,000,000
9	−80,000,000

1. Andy is asked by Dick to rank the different valuation methods by how appropriate they are for analysing the project. Rank the different methods used.
2. In discussing the payback period rule Dick asks Andy to highlight its strengths and weaknesses, what are they?
3. In analysing the mine, Andy advises Dick that this mine is riskier than other mines in the Davies Gold Mining portfolio and so the discount rate should increase. What impact will this have on the cash flows of the project?

ADDITIONAL READING

The techniques presented in this chapter are used in all industries to assess the value of potential investments. The papers below give the reader some insight into their strengths and weaknesses:

1. Chiang, Y.H., Cheng, E.W.L., & Lam, P.T.I. (2010). Employing the net present value – Consistent IRR methods for PFI contracts. *Journal of Construction Engineering and Management, 136*(7), 811–814.

2. Johnson, N.H., & Solomon, B.D. (2010). A net-present value analysis for a wind turbine purchase at a small US college. *Energies, 3*(5), 943–959.

Endnotes

1. In this case the discounted payback is an even number of years. This won't ordinarily happen, of course. However, calculating a fractional year for the discounted payback period is more involved than it is for the ordinary payback, and it is not commonly done.
2. This argument assumes that the cash flows, other than the first, are all positive. If they are not, then these statements are not necessarily correct. Also, there may be more than one discounted payback.
3. If the cut-off were forever, then the discounted payback rule would be the same as the NPV rule. It would also be the same as the profitability index rule considered in a later section.
4. Straight-line depreciation is not the normal way to depreciate assets in Europe, where the reducing-balance method is more common. To estimate reducing-balance depreciation you would subtract a certain percentage from the residual value of the asset. For example, assume that the asset is worth

£500,000 and you are applying 20 per cent reducing-balance depreciation. The depreciation for this year would be 20 per cent of £500,000, which is equal to £100,000. Next year, the residual value is £500,000 − £100,000 = £400,000, and depreciation next year would be 20 per cent of this amount, £400,000, which is £80,000, and so on.

5. We could, of course, calculate the average of the six book values directly. In thousands, we would have (£500 + 400 + 300 + 200 + 100 + 0)/6 = £250.

6. The AAR is closely related to the return on assets (ROA) discussed in Chapter 3. In practice, the AAR is sometimes computed by first calculating the ROA for each year and then averaging the results. This produces a number that is similar, but not identical, to the one we computed.

7. With a lot more effort (or a personal computer), we can find that the IRR is approximately (to nine decimal places) 13.066238629 per cent – not that anybody would ever want this many decimal places!

8. To be more precise, the number of IRRs that are larger than −100 per cent is equal to the number of sign changes, or it differs from the number of sign changes by an even number. Thus, for example, if there are five sign changes, there are five IRRs, three IRRs, or one IRR. If there are two sign changes, there are either two IRRs or no IRRs.

CHAPTER 9
MAKING CAPITAL INVESTMENT DECISIONS

LEARNING OBJECTIVES
After studying this chapter, you should understand:
- **LO1** How to determine the relevant cash flows for a proposed project.
- **LO2** How to determine whether a project is acceptable.
- **LO3** How to set a bid price for a project.
- **LO4** How to evaluate the equivalent annual cost of a project.

KEY NOTATIONS
AAR	Average accounting return
EAC	Equivalent annual cost
EBIT	Earnings before interest and taxes
NPV	Net present value
OCF	Operating cash flow

MAKING CAPITAL INVESTMENT DECISIONS is not just about investing in one specific project. In an environment where cash is scarce, an investment decision in one area may lead to spending cuts in another. Technological change can also have a massive impact on corporate investment plans, and a very salient example of this is the lighting sector. Traditionally, the market leaders in lighting (predominantly lightbulbs) have been Philips and General Electric. However, with European Union legislation that effectively banned the sale of inefficient lightbulbs and a rash of new start-ups selling internet-connected lightbulbs, the sector has been forced to consider further investment in advanced technologies. Philips, for example, was forced to restructure its operations with asset sales and redundancies, as well as new investment. With the company scaling back on traditional lighting technology, it has invested heavily in internet-enabled lighting. A hybrid contraction and investment policy are common in industries that have experienced a disruptive change in technology.

As you no doubt recognize from your study of the previous chapter, the decision of Philips to invest in internet-enabled lightbulbs represents a capital budgeting decision. However, other decisions made by the firm are inextricably linked to the investments. In this chapter, we further investigate such decisions, how they are made, and how to look at them objectively.

This chapter follows up on the previous one by delving more deeply into capital budgeting. We have two primary goals. First, recall that in the last chapter we saw that cash flow estimates are the critical input into a net present value analysis, but we didn't say much about where these cash flows come from, so we shall now examine this question in some detail. Our second goal is to learn how to assess NPV estimates and, in particular, how to evaluate the sensitivity of NPV estimates to assumptions made about the uncertain future.

So far we've covered various parts of the capital budgeting decision. Our task in this chapter is to start bringing these pieces together. In particular, we'll show you how to 'spread the numbers' for a proposed investment or project and, based on those numbers, make an initial assessment about whether the project should be undertaken.

In the discussion that follows, we focus on the process of setting up a discounted cash flow analysis. From the previous chapter, we know that the projected future cash flows are the critical element in such an evaluation. Accordingly, we emphasize working with financial and accounting information to come up with these figures.

In evaluating a proposed investment, we pay special attention to deciding what information is relevant to the decision at hand, and what information is not. As we shall see, it is easy to overlook important pieces of the capital budgeting puzzle.

We shall wait until the next chapter to describe in detail how to go about evaluating the results of our discounted cash flow analysis. Also, where needed, we shall assume that we know the relevant required return or discount rate. We continue to defer in-depth discussion of this subject to Part Five.

9.1 PROJECT CASH FLOWS: A FIRST LOOK

The effect of taking a project is to change the firm's overall cash flows today and in the future. To evaluate a proposed investment we must consider these changes in the firm's cash flows, and then decide whether they add value to the firm. The first (and most important) step, therefore, is to decide which cash flows are relevant.

RELEVANT CASH FLOWS

incremental cash flows
the difference between a firm's future cash flows with a project and those without the project.

What is a relevant cash flow for a project? The general principle is simple enough: a relevant cash flow for a project is a change in the firm's overall future cash flow that comes about as a *direct* consequence of the decision to take that project. Because the relevant cash flows are defined in terms of changes in, or increments to, the firm's existing cash flow, they are called the **incremental cash flows** associated with the project.

The concept of incremental cash flow is central to our analysis, so we shall state a general definition, and refer back to it as needed:

> The incremental cash flows for project evaluation consist of any changes in the firm's future cash flows that are a direct consequence of taking the project.

This definition of incremental cash flows has an obvious and important corollary: any cash flow that exists regardless of *whether or not* a project is undertaken is *not* relevant.

THE STAND-ALONE PRINCIPLE

stand-alone principle
the assumption that evaluation of a project may be based on the project's incremental cash flows.

In practice, it would be cumbersome to actually calculate the future total cash flows to the firm with and without a project, especially for a large firm. Fortunately, it is not really necessary to do so. Once we have identified the effect of undertaking the proposed project on the firm's cash flows, we need to focus only on the project's resulting incremental cash flows. This is called the **stand-alone principle**.

What the stand-alone principle says is that, once we have determined the incremental cash flows from undertaking a project, we can view that project as a kind of 'mini-firm' with its own future revenues and costs, its own assets and, of course, its own cash flows. We shall then be interested primarily in comparing the cash flows from this mini-firm with the cost of acquiring it. An important consequence of this approach is that we shall be evaluating the proposed project purely on its own merits, in isolation from any other activities or projects.

> **CONCEPT QUESTIONS**
>
> **9.1a** What are the relevant incremental cash flows for project evaluation?
> **9.1b** What is the stand-alone principle?

9.2 INCREMENTAL CASH FLOWS

We are concerned here only with cash flows that are incremental, and which result from a project. Looking back at our general definition, we might think it would be easy enough to decide whether a cash flow is incremental. Even so, in a few situations, it is easy to make mistakes. In this section, we describe some common pitfalls and how to avoid them.

SUNK COSTS

A **sunk cost**, by definition, is a cost we have already paid, or have already incurred the liability to pay. Such a cost cannot be changed by the decision today to accept or reject a project. Put another way, the firm will have to pay this cost no matter what. Based on our general definition of incremental cash flow, such a cost is not relevant to the decision at hand. So we shall always be careful to exclude sunk costs from our analysis.

That a sunk cost is not relevant seems obvious given our discussion. Nonetheless, it is easy to fall prey to the fallacy that a sunk cost should be associated with a project. For example, suppose General Milk plc hires a financial consultant to help evaluate whether a line of organic milk should be launched. When the consultant turns in the report, General Milk objects to the analysis, because the consultant did not include the hefty consulting fee as a cost of the organic milk project.

Who is correct? By now, we know that the consulting fee is a sunk cost: it must be paid whether or not the chocolate milk line is actually launched (this is an attractive feature of the consulting business).

> **sunk cost** a cost that has already been incurred and cannot be removed, and which therefore should not be considered in an investment decision.

OPPORTUNITY COSTS

When we think of costs, we usually think of out-of-pocket expenses – namely those that require us to spend some amount of cash. An **opportunity cost** is slightly different; it requires us to give up a benefit. A common situation arises in which a firm already owns some of the assets a proposed project will be using. For example, we might be thinking of converting an old rustic cotton mill we bought years ago for €100,000 into up-market apartments.

If we undertake this project, there will be no direct cash outflow associated with buying the old mill, because we already own it. For purposes of evaluating the apartment project, should we then treat the mill as 'free'? The answer is no. The mill is a valuable resource used by the project. If we didn't use it here, we could do something else with it. Like what? The obvious answer is that, at a minimum, we could sell it. Using the mill for the apartment complex thus has an opportunity cost: we give up the valuable opportunity to do something else with the mill.

There is another issue here. Once we agree that the use of the mill has an opportunity cost, how much should we charge the apartment project for this use? Given that we paid €100,000, it might seem that we should charge this amount to the apartment project. Is this correct? The answer is no, and the reason is based on our discussion concerning sunk costs.

The fact that we paid €100,000 some years ago is irrelevant. That cost is sunk. At a minimum, the opportunity cost that we charge the project is what the mill would sell for today (net of any selling costs) because this is the amount we give up by using the mill instead of selling it.[1]

> **opportunity cost** the most valuable alternative that is given up if a particular investment is undertaken.

REAL WORLD INSIGHTS

How does one assess the value created by a large infrastructure project? In the UK, the HS2 high-speed rail link between the north and south of England has generated countless newspaper headlines arguing for and against the worth of this investment. The same applies to the extra runway at Heathrow Airport and its impact on the regional economy.

Fortunately, the approach to investment appraisal is the same for substantial strategic investments as it is for small discrete projects. The only difference is that the consequences of large infrastructure investment are much more significant in scope.

Considering HS2, which has a construction budget of £106 billion, planners argue that value will be created in the north of England with an increase of nearly £5 billion in annual output by 2037. Almost 30,000 construction jobs are expected to be created, and once the line is in full operation, 100,000 additional jobs are anticipated from its beneficial effects. According to KPMG, UK productivity will rise by £15 billion per annum as a result of HS2. Other practical consequences of the investment have been proposed, including its effect on the environment.

Some readers will think that the figures given above are just forecasts and may not be accurate at all. This is a criticism of any capital budgeting analysis. If you are undertaking a similar assignment, make sure you justify every single forecast and assumption and be ready to defend each one of them if challenged.

Source: KPMG.

SIDE EFFECTS

Remember that the incremental cash flows for a project include all the resulting changes in the *firm's* future cash flows. It would not be unusual for a project to have side, or spillover, effects, both good and bad. For example, in 2021, the time between the theatrical release of a movie and home streaming had shrunk to as low as two weeks in some cases, compared to 200 days in 2001. This shortened release time was blamed for at least part of the decline in average movie theatre box office receipts. Of course, retailers, such as Disney+, Netflix, Apple and Amazon, cheered the move, because it increased their sales. A negative impact on the cash flows of an existing product from the introduction of a new product is called **erosion**.[2] In this case, the cash flows from the new line should be adjusted downwards to reflect lost profits on other lines.

> **erosion** the cash flows of a new project that come at the expense of a firm's existing projects.

In accounting for erosion, it is important to recognize that any sales lost as a result of launching a new product might be lost anyway because of future competition. Erosion is relevant only when the sales would not otherwise be lost.

Side effects show up in a lot of different ways. For example, one of Walt Disney Company's concerns, when it built Euro Disney (now known as Disneyland Paris), was that the new park would drain visitors from the Florida park, a popular vacation destination for Europeans.

There are beneficial spillover effects, of course. For example, you might think that Hewlett-Packard would have been concerned when the price of a printer that sold for £500–£600 in 1994 declined to £35 by 2021. HP realized that the big money is in the consumables that printer owners buy to keep their printers going, such as inkjet cartridges, laser toner cartridges and special paper. The profit margins for these products are substantial.

NET WORKING CAPITAL

Normally a project will require that the firm invest in net working capital in addition to long-term assets. For example, a project will generally need some amount of cash on hand to pay any expenses that arise. In addition, a project will need an initial investment in inventories and trade receivables (to cover credit sales). Some of the financing for this will be in the form of amounts owed to suppliers (trade payables), but the firm will have to supply the balance. This balance represents the investment in net working capital.

It is easy to overlook an important feature of net working capital in capital budgeting. As a project winds down, inventories are sold, receivables are collected, bills are paid, and cash balances can be drawn down. These activities free up the net working capital originally invested. So the firm's investment in project net working capital closely resembles a loan. The firm supplies working capital at the beginning, and recovers it towards the end.

Students often get confused with net working capital's effect on cash flows. Assume you spend €100,000 on inventory this year. This represents a cash outflow of €100,000 in year 0. In year 1 (365 days from now), you increase the level of raw materials to €200,000, which means that you need to invest a further €100,000 in net working capital. Although net working capital is €200,000, your cash outflow in year 1 is only €100,000 because you already had €100,000 of raw materials in stock from year 0.

At the end of the project, say year 4, you've finished producing new goods for sale and you are left with €200,000 net working capital. To close off the project, you would look to sell the inventory to other bodies or use it in other projects within the firm. This would result in a cash inflow of €200,000 in year 4, even as the level of net working capital has fallen to zero.

The cash flows and net working capital are given below for each year.

	0	1	2	3	4
Net Working Capital	100	200	200	200	0
Cash Flow	−100	−100	0	0	200

Typically, corporate worksheets treat net working capital as a whole. The individual components of working capital (receivables, inventory and the like) do not generally appear in the worksheets. However, the reader should remember that the working capital numbers in the worksheets are not pulled out of thin air. Instead, they result from a meticulous forecast of the components, just as we illustrated for year 1.

FINANCING COSTS

In analysing a proposed investment, we shall *not* include interest paid or any other financing costs such as dividends or principal repaid, because we are interested in the cash flow generated by the assets of the project. As we mentioned in Chapter 3, interest paid, for example, is a component of cash flow to creditors, not cash flow from assets.

More generally, our goal in project evaluation is to compare the cash flow from a project with the cost of acquiring that project in order to estimate NPV. The particular mixture of debt and equity a firm actually chooses to use in financing a project is a managerial variable and determines primarily how project cash flows are divided between owners and creditors. This is not to say that financing arrangements are unimportant; they are just something to be analysed separately. We shall cover this in later chapters.

For example, assume you are considering an investment in a new company-wide security system. You've estimated the future cash flow savings that will result from the investment (cash inflows) and you know the cost of the initial investment (cash outflow). The discount rate you use reflects the risk of the project. To fund the initial investment you can choose to give up some ownership of your company in return for the cash, or you can borrow the money needed in return for contractual future payments.

Both options give you the money needed to fund the project. However, your financing decision has nothing to do with the viability or risk of the project itself and therefore should be ignored in the core investment appraisal.

OTHER ISSUES

There are some other things to consider. First, we are interested only in measuring cash flow. Moreover, we are interested in measuring it when it occurs, not when it accrues in an accounting sense. Second, we are always interested in *after-tax* cash flow, because taxes are definitely a cash outflow. Whenever we write *incremental cash flows*, we mean after-tax incremental cash flows. Remember, however, that after-tax cash flow and accounting profit, or net income, are entirely different things.

> **CONCEPT QUESTIONS**
>
> **9.2a** What is a sunk cost? An opportunity cost?
> **9.2b** Explain the concept of erosion and why it is relevant.
> **9.2c** Explain why interest paid is not a relevant cash flow for project evaluation.

9.3 PRO FORMA FINANCIAL STATEMENTS AND PROJECT CASH FLOWS

The first thing we need when we begin evaluating a proposed investment is a set of pro forma or projected financial statements. Given these, we can develop the projected cash flows from the project. Once we have the cash flows, we can estimate the value of the project using the techniques we described in the previous chapter.

GETTING STARTED: PRO FORMA FINANCIAL STATEMENTS

pro forma financial statements
financial statements projecting future years' operations.

Pro forma financial statements are a convenient and easily understood means of summarizing much of the relevant information for a project. To prepare these statements, we shall need estimates of quantities such as unit sales, the selling price per unit, the variable cost per unit, and total fixed costs. We shall also need to know the total investment required, including any investment in net working capital.

To illustrate, suppose we think we can sell 50,000 cans of shark attractant per year at a price of £4 per can. It costs us about £2.50 per can to make the attractant, and a new product such as this one typically has only a three-year life (perhaps because the customer base dwindles rapidly). We require a 20 per cent return on new products.

Fixed costs for the project, including such things as rent on the production facility, will run to £12,000 per year.[3] Further, we shall need to invest a total of £90,000 in manufacturing equipment. For simplicity, we shall assume that this £90,000 will be 100 per cent depreciated straight-line over the three-year life of the project.[4] Furthermore, the cost of removing the equipment will roughly equal its actual value in three years, so it will be essentially worthless on a market value basis as well. Finally, the project will require an initial £20,000 investment in net working capital, and the tax rate is 34 per cent.

In Table 9.1, we organize these initial projections by first preparing the pro forma income statement. Once again, notice that we have *not* deducted any interest expense. This will always be so. As we described earlier, interest paid is a financing expense, not a component of operating cash flow.

We can also prepare a series of abbreviated statements of financial position that show the capital requirements for the project, as we've done in Table 9.2. Here we have a net working capital of £20,000 each year. Non-current assets are £90,000 at the start of the project's life (year 0), and they decline by the £30,000 in depreciation each year, ending up at zero. Notice that the total investment given here for future years is the total book, or accounting, value, not market value.

TABLE 9.1

Projected income statement, shark attractant project

Sales (50,000 units at £4/unit)	200,000
Variable costs (£2.50/unit)	125,000
Gross profit (£)	75,000
Fixed costs (£)	12,000
Depreciation (£90,000/3)	30,000
Profit before taxes (£)	33,000
Taxes (34%) (£)	11,220
Net income (£)	21,780

TABLE 9.2

Projected capital requirements, shark attractant project

	Year 0	Year 1	Year 2	Year 3
Net working capital (£)	20,000	20,000	20,000	20,000
Net non-current assets (£)	90,000	60,000	30,000	0
Total investment (£)	110,000	80,000	50,000	20,000

	Year				
	1	2	3	4	5
Initial value (€)	500,000	410,000	336,200	275,684	226,061
Depreciation (18%) (€)	90,000	73,800	60,516	49,623	226,061
Written-down value (€)	410,000	336,200	275,684	226,061	0

Note how the depreciation amounts fall over time. This is because the amount depreciated is less each year. In addition, given that the asset is worthless at the end of five years, the final-year depreciation is simply the starting year 5 value.

Currently, each country in the European Union has its own tax system, and this is seen as one of the major obstacles for the full integration of European economies. However, in 2016, the European Commission launched the Common Consolidated Corporate Tax Base (CCCTB) for all countries. Although it will take several years for it to be enacted, the CCCTB is a step in the right direction. The main recommendations of the working group are that all countries will work on a common tax basis so that European companies can efficiently operate in all countries within the EU. At the time of writing, a decision on how the UK remains involved (if at all), is still to be made.

Book Value versus Market Value

In calculating depreciation under current tax law, the economic life and future market value of the asset are not an issue. As a result, the book value of an asset can differ substantially from its actual market value. Take, for example, a Toyota Landcruiser that is worth £48,000 new. With 18 per cent reducing-balance depreciation, the book value after the first year is £48,000 less the first year's depreciation of £8,640, or £39,360. The remaining book values are summarized in Table 9.5. After five years, the book value of the car is £17,796.

TABLE 9.5

Toyota Landcruiser book values

	Year				
	1	2	3	4	5
Initial value (£)	48,000	39,360	32,275	26,466	21,702
Depreciation (18%) (£)	8,640	7,085	5,810	4,764	3,906
Written-down value (£)	39,360	32,275	26,466	21,702	17,796

Suppose we wanted to sell the car after five years. Based on historic averages, it would be worth, say, 50 per cent of the purchase price, or 0.50 × £48,000 = £24,000. If we sold it for this, then we would have to pay taxes at the ordinary income tax rate on the difference between the sale price of £24,000 and the book value of £17,796. For a corporation in the 23 per cent bracket, the tax liability would be 0.23 × £6,204 = £1,427.

The reason why taxes must be paid in this case is that the difference between market value and book value is 'excess' depreciation, and it must be 'recaptured' when the asset is sold. What this means is that, as it turns out, we over-depreciated the asset by £24,000 – £17,796 = £6,204. Because we deducted £6,204 too much in depreciation, we paid £1,427 too little in taxes, and we have to make up the difference.

Notice that this is *not* a tax on a capital gain. As a general (albeit rough) rule, a capital gain occurs only if the market price exceeds the original cost. However, what is and what is not a capital gain is ultimately up to the taxation authorities, and the specific rules can be complex. We shall ignore capital gains taxes for the most part.

Finally, if the book value exceeds the market value, then the difference is treated as a loss for tax purposes. For example, if we sell the car after five years for £10,000, then the book value exceeds the market value by £7,796. In this case, a tax saving of 0.23 × £7,796 = £1,793 occurs.

EXAMPLE 9.2

REDUCING-BALANCE DEPRECIATION

Staple Supply Ltd has just purchased a new computerized information system with an installed cost of €160,000. What are the yearly depreciation allowances if 20 per cent reducing-balance depreciation is used? Based on historical experience, we think that the system will be worth only €10,000 when Staple gets rid of it in four years. What are the tax consequences of the sale if the tax rate is 34 per cent? What is the total after-tax cash flow from the sale?

The yearly depreciation allowances are presented below:

	Year			
	1	2	3	4
Initial value (€)	160,000	128,000	102,400	81,920
Depreciation (20%) (€)	32,000	25,600	20,480	16,384
Written-down value (€)	128,000	102,400	81,920	65,536

Notice that we have also computed the book value of the system as at the end of each year. The book value at the end of year 4 is €65,536. If Staple sells the system for €10,000 at that time, it will have a loss of €55,536 (the difference) for tax purposes. This loss, of course, is like depreciation because it isn't a cash expense.

What really happens? Two things. First, Staple gets €10,000 from the buyer. Second, it saves 0.34 × €55,536 = €18,882 in taxes. So the total after-tax cash flow from the sale is a €28,882 cash inflow.

AN EXAMPLE: MAJESTIC MULCH AND COMPOST LTD (MMC)

At this point, we want to go through a somewhat more involved capital budgeting analysis. Keep in mind as you read that the basic approach here is exactly the same as that in the shark attractant example used earlier. We have just added some real-world detail (and a lot more numbers).

MMC is investigating the feasibility of a new line of power mulching tools aimed at the growing number of home composters. Based on exploratory conversations with buyers for large garden shops, MMC projects unit sales as follows:

Year	Unit sales
1	3,000
2	5,000
3	6,000
4	6,500
5	6,000
6	5,000
7	4,000
8	3,000

The new power mulcher will sell for £120 per unit to start. When the competition catches up after three years, however, MMC anticipates that the price will drop to £110.

The power mulcher project will require £20,000 in net working capital at the start. Subsequently, the total net working capital at the end of each year will be about 15 per cent of sales for that year. The variable cost per unit is £60, and total fixed costs are £25,000 per year.

It will cost about £800,000 to buy the equipment necessary to begin production. This investment is primarily in industrial equipment, which should be depreciated using the 18 per cent reducing-balance method. The equipment will actually be worth about 20 per cent of its cost in eight years, or 0.20 × £800,000 = £160,000. The relevant tax rate is 23 per cent, and the required return is 15 per cent. Based on this information, should MMC proceed?

Operating Cash Flows

There is a lot of information here that we need to organize. The first thing we can do is calculate projected sales. Sales in the first year are projected at 3,000 units at £120 apiece, or £360,000 total. The remaining figures are shown in Table 9.6.

TABLE 9.6

Projected revenues, power mulcher project

Year	Unit price (£)	Unit sales	Revenues (£)
1	120	3,000	360,000
2	120	5,000	600,000
3	120	6,000	720,000
4	110	6,500	715,000
5	110	6,000	660,000
6	110	5,000	550,000
7	110	4,000	440,000
8	110	3,000	330,000

Next, we compute the depreciation on the £800,000 investment in Table 9.7. With this information, we can prepare the pro forma income statements, as shown in Table 9.8. From here, computing the operating cash flows is straightforward. The results are illustrated in the first part of Table 9.10.

TABLE 9.7

Annual depreciation, power mulcher project

Year	Initial value	Depreciation (£)	Residual value (£)
1	800,000	144,000	656,000
2	656,000	118,080	537,920
3	537,920	96,826	441,094
4	441,094	79,397	361,697
5	361,697	65,106	296,592
6	296,592	53,387	243,205
7	243,205	43,777	199,428
8	199,428	39,428	160,000

TABLE 9.8

Projected income statements, power mulcher project

	Year							
	1	2	3	4	5	6	7	8
Unit price (£)	120	120	120	110	110	110	110	110
Unit sales	3,000	5,000	6,000	6,500	6,000	5,000	4,000	3,000
Revenues (£)	360,000	600,000	720,000	715,000	660,000	550,000	440,000	330,000
Variable costs (£)	180,000	300,000	360,000	390,000	360,000	300,000	240,000	180,000
Fixed costs (£)	25,000	25,000	25,000	25,000	25,000	25,000	25,000	25,000
Depreciation (£)	144,000	118,080	96,826	79,397	65,106	53,387	43,777	39,428
Profit before taxes (£)	11,000	156,920	238,174	220,603	209,894	171,613	131,223	85,572
Taxes (23%) (£)	2,530	36,092	54,780	50,739	48,276	39,471	30,181	19,681
Net income (£)	8,470	120,828	183,394	169,864	161,619	132,142	101,042	65,890

Change in NWC

Now that we have the operating cash flows, we need to determine the changes in NWC. By assumption, net working capital requirements change as sales change. In each year, MMC will generally either add to or recover some of its project net working capital. Recalling that NWC starts out at £20,000 and then rises to 15 per cent of sales, we can calculate the amount of NWC for each year, as shown in Table 9.9.

TABLE 9.9

Changes in net working capital, power mulcher project

Year	Revenues (£)	Net working capital (£)	Cash flow (£)
0		20,000	−20,000
1	360,000	54,000	−34,000
2	600,000	90,000	−36,000
3	720,000	108,000	−18,000
4	715,000	107,250	750
5	660,000	99,000	8,250
6	550,000	82,500	16,500
7	440,000	66,000	16,500
8	330,000	49,500	16,500

As illustrated, during the first year net working capital grows from £20,000 to $0.15 \times £360,000 = £54,000$. The increase in net working capital for the year is thus £54,000 − 20,000 = £34,000. The remaining figures are calculated in the same way.

Remember that an increase in net working capital is a cash outflow, so we use a negative sign in this table to indicate an additional investment that the firm makes in net working capital. A positive sign represents net working capital returning to the firm. Thus, for example, £16,500 in NWC flows back to the firm in year 6. Over the project's life, net working capital builds to a peak of £108,000, and declines from there as sales begin to drop off.

We show the result for changes in net working capital in the second part of Table 9.10. Notice that at the end of the project's life, there is £49,500 in net working capital still to be recovered. Therefore, in the last year, the project returns £16,500 of NWC during the year and then returns the remaining £49,500 at the end of the year for a total of £66,000.

Capital Spending

Finally, we have to account for the long-term capital invested in the project. In this case, MMC invests £800,000 at year 0. By assumption, this equipment will be worth £160,000 at the end of the project. In Table 9.7, this figure is given as the ending value, and the depreciation has been calculated accordingly. This means that the book and market values of the equipment are the same, resulting in no tax effects from the disposal. These figures are shown in the third part of Table 9.10.

Total Cash Flow and Value

We now have all the cash flow pieces, and we put them together in Table 9.11. In addition to the total project cash flows, we have calculated the cumulative cash flows and the discounted cash flows. At this point, it's essentially plug-and-chug to calculate the net present value, internal rate of return and payback.

If we sum the discounted cash flows and the initial investment, the net present value (at 15 per cent) works out to be £124,925. This is positive, so, based on these preliminary projections, the power mulcher project is acceptable. The internal, or DCF, rate of return is greater than 15 per cent because the NPV is positive. It works out to be 19.1 per cent, again indicating that the project is acceptable.

Looking at the cumulative cash flows, we can see that the project has paid back after 4 years because the table shows that the cumulative cash flow is just above zero at that time. As indicated, the fractional year works out to be £236,402/£250,011 = 0.95, so the payback is 3.95 years. We can't say whether or not this is good because we don't have a benchmark for MMC. This is the usual problem with payback periods.

More About Project Cash Flow   237

TABLE 9.10

Projected cash flows, power mulcher project

					Year				
	0	1	2	3	4	5	6	7	8
I. Operating cash flow									
Net income (£)		8,470	120,828	183,394	169,864	161,619	132,142	101,042	65,890
Depreciation (£)		144,000	118,080	96,826	79,397	65,106	53,387	43,777	39,428
Operating cash flow (£)		152,470	238,908	280,220	249,261	226,724	185,529	144,819	105,318
II. Net working capital									
Initial NWC (£)	−20,000								
Change in NWC (£)		−34,000	−36,000	−18,000	750	8,250	16,500	16,500	16,500
NWC recovery (£)									49,500
Total change in NWC (£)	−20,000	−34,000	−36,000	−18,000	750	8,250	16,500	16,500	66,000
III. Capital spending									
Initial outlay (£)	−800,000								
After-tax salvage (£)									160,000

TABLE 9.11

Projected total cash flows, power mulcher project

					Year				
	0	1	2	3	4	5	6	7	8
Operating cash flow (£)		152,470	238,908	280,220	249,261	226,724	185,529	144,819	105,318
Change in NWC (£)	−20,000	−34,000	−36,000	−18,000	750	8,250	16,500	16,500	66,000
Capital spending (£)	−800,000								160,000
Net cash flow (£)	−820,000	118,470	202,908	262,220	250,011	234,974	202,029	161,319	331,319
Cumulative cash flow (£)	−820,000	−701,530	−498,622	−236,402	13,610	248,584	450,613	611,931	943,250
DCF @ 15% (£)	−820,000	103,017	153,428	172,414	142,945	116,824	87,343	60,646	108,309
NPV @ 15% (£)	124,925								
Internal rate of return (%)	19.1								
Payback (years)	3.95								

Conclusion

This completes our preliminary DCF analysis. Where do we go from here? If we have a great deal of confidence in our projections, there is no further analysis to be done. MMC should begin production and marketing immediately. It is unlikely that this will be the case. It is important to remember that the result of our analysis is an estimate of NPV, and we shall usually have less than complete confidence in our projections. This means we have more work to do. In particular, we shall almost surely want to spend some time evaluating the quality of our estimates. We shall take up this subject in the next chapter. For now, we look at some alternative definitions of operating cash flow, and we illustrate some different cases that arise in capital budgeting.

> **CONCEPT QUESTIONS**
>
> **9.4a** Why is it important to consider changes in net working capital in developing cash flow? What is the effect of doing so?
>
> **9.4b** How is depreciation calculated for non-current assets under current tax law? What effects do expected salvage value and estimated economic life have on the calculated depreciation deduction?

9.5 ALTERNATIVE DEFINITIONS OF OPERATING CASH FLOW

The analysis we went through in the previous section is quite general, and can be adapted to just about any capital investment problem. In the next section we illustrate some particularly useful variations. Before we do so, we need to discuss the fact that there are different definitions of project operating cash flow that are commonly used, both in practice and in finance texts.

As we shall see, the different approaches to operating cash flow that exist all measure the same thing. If they are used correctly, they all produce the same answer, and one is not necessarily any better or more useful than another. Unfortunately, the fact that alternative definitions are used does sometimes lead to confusion. For this reason, we examine several of these variations next, to see how they are related.

In the discussion that follows, keep in mind that when we speak of cash flow, we literally mean cash in less cash out. This is all we are concerned with. Different definitions of operating cash flow simply amount to different ways of manipulating basic information about sales, costs, depreciation and taxes to get at cash flow.

For a particular project and year under consideration, suppose we have the following estimates:

$$\text{Sales} = €1{,}500$$
$$\text{Costs} = €700$$
$$\text{Depreciation} = €600$$

With these estimates, notice that earnings before interest and taxes (EBIT) is:

$$\begin{aligned}\text{EBIT} &= \text{Sales} - \text{Costs} - \text{Depreciation}\\ &= €1{,}500 - 700 - 600\\ &= €200\end{aligned}$$

Once again, we assume that no interest is paid, so the tax bill is:

$$\begin{aligned}\text{Taxes} &= \text{EBIT} \times T\\ &= €200 \times 0.34 = €68\end{aligned}$$

where T, the corporate tax rate, is 34 per cent.

When we put all of this together, we see that project operating cash flow, OCF, is:

$$\begin{aligned}\text{OCF} &= \text{EBIT} + \text{Depreciation} - \text{Taxes}\\ &= €200 + 600 - 68 = €732\end{aligned}$$

There are some other ways to determine OCF that could be (and are) used. We consider these next.

THE BOTTOM-UP APPROACH

Because we are ignoring any financing expenses, such as interest, in our calculations of project OCF, we can write project net income as:

$$\begin{aligned} \text{Project net income} &= \text{EBIT} - \text{Taxes} \\ &= €200 - 68 \\ &= €132 \end{aligned}$$

If we simply add the depreciation to both sides, we arrive at a slightly different and very common expression for OCF:

$$\begin{aligned} \text{OCF} &= \text{Net income} + \text{Depreciation} \\ &= €132 + 600 \\ &= €732 \end{aligned} \quad (9.1)$$

This is the *bottom-up* approach. Here, we start with the accountant's bottom line (net income) and add back any non-cash deductions such as depreciation. It is crucial to remember that this definition of operating cash flow as net income plus depreciation is correct only if there is no interest expense subtracted in the calculation of net income.

For the shark attractant project, net income was £21,780 and depreciation was £30,000, so the bottom-up calculation is:

$$\text{OCF} = £21{,}780 + 30{,}000 = £51{,}780$$

THE TOP-DOWN APPROACH

Perhaps the most obvious way to calculate OCF is:

$$\begin{aligned} \text{OCF} &= \text{Sales} - \text{Costs} - \text{Taxes} \\ &= €1{,}500 - 700 - 68 = €732 \end{aligned} \quad (9.2)$$

This is the *top-down* approach, the second variation on the basic OCF definition. Here, we start at the top of the income statement with sales and work our way down to net cash flow by subtracting costs, taxes and other expenses. Along the way, we simply leave out any strictly non-cash items such as depreciation.

For the shark attractant project, the operating cash flow can be readily calculated using the top-down approach. With sales of £200,000, total costs (fixed plus variable) of £137,000, and a tax bill of £11,220, the OCF is:

$$\text{OCF} = £200{,}000 - 137{,}000 - 11{,}220 = £51{,}780$$

This is just as we had before.

THE TAX SHIELD APPROACH

The third variation on our basic definition of OCF is the *tax shield* approach. This approach will be useful for some problems we consider in the next section. The tax shield definition of OCF is:

$$\text{OCF} = (\text{Sales} - \text{Costs}) \times (1 - T) + \text{Depreciation} \times T \quad (9.3)$$

where T is again the corporate tax rate. Assuming that $T = 34\%$, the OCF works out to be:

$$\begin{aligned} \text{OCF} &= (€1{,}500 - 700) \times 0.66 + 600 \times 0.34 \\ &= €528 + 204 \\ &= €732 \end{aligned}$$

This is just as we had before.

This approach views OCF as having two components. The first part is what the project's cash flow would be if there were no depreciation expense. In this case, this would-have-been cash flow is €528.

> **depreciation tax shield**
>
> the tax saving that results from the depreciation deduction, calculated as depreciation multiplied by the corporate tax rate.

The second part of OCF in this approach is the depreciation deduction multiplied by the tax rate. This is called the **depreciation tax shield**. We know that depreciation is a non-cash expense. The only cash flow effect of deducting depreciation is to reduce our taxes, a benefit to us. At a 34 per cent corporate tax rate, every euro in depreciation expense saves us 34 cents in taxes. So, in our example, the €600 depreciation deduction saves us €600 × 0.34 = €204 in taxes.

For the shark attractant project we considered earlier in the chapter, the depreciation tax shield would be £30,000 × 0.34 = £10,200. The after-tax value for sales less costs would be (£200,000 − 137,000) × (1 − 0.34) = £41,580. Adding these together yields the value of OCF:

$$OCF = £41,580 + 10,200 = £51,780$$

This calculation verifies that the tax shield approach is completely equivalent to the approach we used before.

CONCLUSION

Now that we've seen that all of these approaches are the same, you're probably wondering why everybody doesn't just agree on one of them. One reason, as we shall see in the next section, is that different approaches are useful in different circumstances. The best one to use is whichever happens to be the most convenient for the problem at hand.

> **CONCEPT QUESTIONS**
>
> **9.5a** What are the top-down and bottom-up definitions of operating cash flow?
> **9.5b** What is meant by the term *depreciation tax shield*?

9.6 SOME SPECIAL CASES OF DISCOUNTED CASH FLOW ANALYSIS

To finish our chapter, we look at three common cases involving discounted cash flow analysis. The first case involves investments that are aimed primarily at improving efficiency and thereby cutting costs. The second case we consider comes up when a firm is involved in submitting competitive bids. The third and final case arises in choosing between equipment options with different economic lives.

We could consider many other special cases, but these three are particularly important because problems similar to these are so common. Also, they illustrate some diverse applications of cash flow analysis and DCF valuation.

EVALUATING COST-CUTTING PROPOSALS

One decision we frequently face is whether to upgrade existing facilities to make them more cost-effective. The issue is whether the cost savings are large enough to justify the necessary capital expenditure.

For example, suppose we are considering automating some part of an existing production process. The necessary equipment costs €80,000 to buy and install. The automation will save €22,000 per year (before taxes) by reducing labour and material costs. For simplicity, assume that the equipment has a five-year life and is depreciated to zero on a straight-line basis over that period. It will actually be worth €20,000 in five years. Should we automate? The tax rate is 34 per cent, and the discount rate is 10 per cent.

As always, the first step in making such a decision is to identify the relevant incremental cash flows. First, determining the relevant capital spending is easy enough. The initial cost is €80,000. The after-tax salvage value is €20,000 × (1 − 0.34) = €13,200, because the book value will be zero in five years. Second, there are no working capital consequences here, so we don't need to worry about changes in net working capital.

Operating cash flows are the third component to consider. Buying new equipment affects our operating cash flows in two ways. First, we save €22,000 before taxes every year. In other words, the firm's operating income increases by €22,000, so this is the relevant incremental project operating income.

Second (and it's easy to overlook this), we have an additional depreciation deduction. In this case, the depreciation is €80,000/5 = €16,000 per year.

Because the project has an operating income of €22,000 (the annual pre-tax cost saving) and a depreciation deduction of €16,000, taking the project will increase the firm's EBIT by €22,000 – 16,000 = €6,000, so this is the project's EBIT.

Finally, because EBIT is rising for the firm, taxes will increase. This increase in taxes will be €6,000 × 0.34 = €2,040. With this information, we can compute the operating cash flow in the usual way:

	€
EBIT	6,000
+ Depreciation	16,000
− Taxes	2,040
Operating cash flow	19,960

So our after-tax operating cash flow is €19,960.

It might be somewhat more enlightening to calculate operating cash flow using a different approach. What is actually going on here is very simple. First, the cost savings increase our pre-tax income by €22,000. We have to pay taxes on this amount, so our tax bill increases by 0.34 × €22,000 = €7,480. In other words, the €22,000 pre-tax saving amounts to €22,000 × (1 − 0.34) = €14,520 after taxes.

Second, the extra €16,000 in depreciation isn't really a cash outflow, but it does reduce our taxes by €16,000 × 0.34 = €5,440. The sum of these two components is €14,520 + 5,440 = €19,960, just as we had before. Notice that the €5,440 is the depreciation tax shield we discussed earlier, and we have effectively used the tax shield approach here.

We can now finish our analysis. Based on our discussion, here are the relevant cash flows:

	Year					
	0	1	2	3	4	5
Operating cash flow (€)		19,960	19,960	19,960	19,960	19,960
Capital spending (€)	−80,000					13,200
Total cash flow (€)	−80,000	19,960	19,960	19,960	19,960	33,160

At 10 per cent, it's straightforward to verify that the NPV here is €3,860, so we should go ahead and automate.

EXAMPLE 9.3

TO BUY OR NOT TO BUY?

We are considering the purchase of a €200,000 computer-based inventory management system. It will be depreciated 20 per cent reducing-balance over its four-year life. It will be worth €30,000 at the end of that time. The system will save us €60,000 before taxes in inventory-related costs. The relevant tax rate is 39 per cent. Because the new set-up is more efficient than our existing one, we shall be able to carry less total inventory and thus free up €45,000 in net working capital. What is the NPV at 16 per cent? What is the DCF return (the IRR) on this investment?

We can first calculate the operating cash flow. The depreciation schedule is given below:

Year	Initial value (€)	Depreciation (€)	Residual value (€)
1	200,000	40,000	160,000
2	160,000	32,000	128,000
3	128,000	25,600	102,400
4	102,400	72,400	30,000

Operating cash flow now follows:

	Year			
	1	2	3	4
Cash savings (€)	60,000	60,000	60,000	60,000
Depreciation (€)	40,000	32,000	25,600	72,400
Profit before taxes (€)	20,000	28,000	34,400	−12,400
Taxes (39%) (€)	7,800	10,920	13,416	−4,836
Net income (€)	12,200	17,080	20,984	−7,564
Plus depreciation (€)	40,000	32,000	25,600	72,400
Operating cash flow (€)	52,200	49,080	46,584	64,836

Finally, and this is the somewhat tricky part, the initial investment in net working capital is a €45,000 *inflow* because the system frees up working capital. Furthermore, we shall have to put this back in at the end of the project's life. What this really means is simple: while the system is in operation, we have €45,000 to use elsewhere.

To finish our analysis, we can compute the total cash flows:

	Year				
	0	1	2	3	4
Operating cash flow (€)		52,200	49,080	46,584	64,836
Change in NWC (€)	45,000				−45,000
Capital spending (€)	−200,000				30,000
Net cash flow (€)	−155,000	52,200	49,080	46,584	49,836

At 16 per cent the NPV is −€16,157, so the investment is not attractive. After some trial and error, we find that the NPV is zero when the discount rate is 10.62 per cent, so the IRR on this investment is about 10.6 per cent.

REAL WORLD INSIGHTS

Although much of finance relates to investment decisions to generate revenues, in every industry, managers will also consider the opposite of investment, which is cost-cutting. This happens when sectors go into a downturn, and investment opportunities become scarce. Reducing costs can be just as effective in improving corporate profits as revenue generation, and managers should focus both on managing the top line (revenues) and the bottom line (profits).

For example, in 2020, most industrial sectors faced a bleak environment because of the economic disaster from the Covid-19 pandemic. Many companies had to implement a suite of cost-cutting measures to manage the catastrophic decline in demand. If you were a manager in an airline, you would need to compare a range of different turnaround strategies and assess the value impact of each option. For example, easyJet ground all of their flights to reduce operating costs, it streamlined its operations and postponed a £4.5 billion aeroplane order from Airbus. If a company can reduce cash costs by at least the forecasted fall in cash revenues, the value generated can remain unaffected.

Source: Reuters, FT.com.

SETTING THE BID PRICE

Early on, we used a discounted cash flow analysis to evaluate a proposed new product. A somewhat different (and common) scenario arises when we must submit a competitive bid to win a job. Under such circumstances, the winner is whoever submits the lowest bid.

There is an old joke concerning this process: the low bidder is whoever makes the biggest mistake. This is called the *winner's curse*. In other words, if you win, there is a good chance you underbid. In this section, we look at how to go about setting the bid price to avoid the winner's curse. The procedure we describe is useful whenever we have to set a price on a product or service.

As with any other capital budgeting project, we must be careful to account for all relevant cash flows. For example, industry analysts estimated that the materials in Sony PlayStation 5 cost more than the retail price of each unit. Why would a manufacturer sell at a price well below break-even? This is because the revenues coming from associated products, such as games, online monthly payments, and accessories make the project value-creative.

To illustrate how to go about setting a bid price, imagine we are in the business of buying stripped-down truck platforms and then modifying them to customer specifications for resale. A local distributor has requested bids for five specially modified trucks each year for the next four years, for a total of 20 trucks in all.

We need to decide what price per truck to bid. The goal of our analysis is to determine the lowest price we can profitably charge. This maximizes our chances of being awarded the contract while guarding against the winner's curse.

Suppose we can buy the truck platforms for €10,000 each. The facilities we need can be leased for €24,000 per year. The labour and material cost to do the modification works out to be about €4,000 per truck. Total cost per year will thus be €24,000 + 5 × (10,000 + 4,000) = €94,000.

We shall need to invest €60,000 in new equipment. For simplicity, this equipment will be depreciated straight-line to a zero salvage value over the four years. It will be worth about €5,000 at the end of that time. We shall also need to invest €40,000 in raw materials inventory and other working capital items. The relevant tax rate is 39 per cent. What price per truck should we bid if we require a 20 per cent return on our investment?

We start by looking at capital spending and net working capital investment. We have to spend €60,000 today for new equipment. The after-tax salvage value is €5,000 × (1 − 0.39) = €3,050. Furthermore, we have to invest €40,000 today in working capital. We shall get this back in four years.

We can't determine the operating cash flow just yet, because we don't know the sales price. Thus, if we draw a timeline, here is what we have so far:

	Year				
	0	1	2	3	4
Operating cash flow (€)		+OCF	+OCF	+OCF	+OCF
Change in NWC (€)	−40,000				40,000
Capital spending (€)	−60,000				3,050
Net cash flow (€)	−100,000	+OCF	+OCF	+OCF	+OCF + 43,050

With this in mind, note that the key observation is the following: the lowest possible price we can profitably charge will result in a zero NPV at 20 per cent. At that price, we earn exactly 20 per cent on our investment.

Given this observation, we first need to determine what the operating cash flow must be for the NPV to equal zero. To do this, we calculate the present value of the €43,050 non-operating cash flow from the last year, and subtract it from the €100,000 initial investment:

$$€100,000 - 43,050/1.20^4 = €100,000 - 20,761$$
$$= €79,239$$

Once we have done this, our timeline is as follows:

	Year				
	0	1	2	3	4
Total cash flow (€)	−79,239	+OCF	+OCF	+OCF	+OCF

As the timeline suggests, the operating cash flow is now an unknown ordinary annuity amount. The four-year annuity factor for 20 per cent is 2.58873, so we have:

$$\text{NPV} = 0 = -€79{,}239 + \text{OCF} \times 2.58873$$

This implies that:

$$\text{OCF} = €79{,}239/2.58873 = €30{,}609$$

So the operating cash flow needs to be €30,609 each year.

We're not quite finished. The final problem is to find out what sales price results in an operating cash flow of €30,609. The easiest way to do this is to recall that operating cash flow can be written as net income plus depreciation (the bottom-up definition). The depreciation here is €60,000/4 = €15,000. Given this, we can determine what net income must be:

$$\text{Operating cash flow} = \text{Net income} + \text{Depreciation}$$
$$€30{,}609 = \text{Net income} + €15{,}000$$
$$\text{Net income} = €15{,}609$$

From here, we work our way back up the income statement. If net income is €15,609, then our income statement is as follows:

Sales	?
Costs (€)	94,000
Depreciation (€)	15,000
Taxes (39%) (€)	?
Net income (€)	15,609

We can solve for sales by noting that:

$$\text{Net income} = (\text{Sales} - \text{Costs} - \text{Depreciation}) \times (1 - T)$$
$$€15{,}609 = (\text{Sales} - €94{,}000 - €15{,}000) \times (1 - 0.39)$$
$$\text{Sales} = €15{,}609/0.61 + 94{,}000 + 15{,}000$$
$$= €134{,}589$$

Sales per year must be €134,589. Because the contract calls for five trucks per year, the sales price has to be €134,589/5 = €26,918. If we round this up a bit, it looks as though we need to bid about €27,000 per truck. At this price, were we to get the contract, our return would be just over 20 per cent.

EVALUATING EQUIPMENT OPTIONS WITH DIFFERENT LIVES

The final problem we consider involves choosing among different possible systems, equipment set-ups or procedures. Our goal is to choose the most cost effective. The approach we consider here is necessary only when two special circumstances exist. First, the possibilities under evaluation have different economic lives. Second, and just as important, we shall need whatever we buy more or less indefinitely. As a result, when it wears out, we shall buy another one.

We can illustrate this problem with a simple example. Imagine we are in the business of manufacturing stamped metal subassemblies. Whenever a stamping mechanism wears out, we have to replace it with a new one to stay in business. We are considering which of two stamping mechanisms to buy.

Machine A costs €100 to buy and €10 per year to operate. It wears out, and must be replaced every 2 years. Machine B costs €140 to buy and €8 per year to operate. It lasts for 3 years, and must then be replaced. Ignoring taxes, which one should we choose if we use a 10 per cent discount rate?

In comparing the two machines, we notice that the first is cheaper to buy, but it costs more to operate, and it wears out more quickly. How can we evaluate these trade-offs? We can start by computing the present value of the costs for each:

$$\text{Machine A: PV} = -€100 + -10/1.1 + -10/1.1^2 = -€117.36$$
$$\text{Machine B: PV} = -€140 + -8/1.1 + -8/1.1^2 + -8/1.1^3 = -€159.89$$

Notice that *all* the numbers here are costs, so they all have negative signs. If we stopped here, it might appear that A is more attractive, because the PV of the costs is less. However, all we have really discovered so far is that A effectively provides 2 years' worth of stamping service for €117.36, whereas B effectively provides 3 years' worth for €159.89. These costs are not directly comparable, because of the difference in service periods.

We need to somehow work out a cost per year for these two alternatives. To do this, we ask: what amount, paid each year over the life of the machine, has the same PV of costs? This amount is called the **equivalent annual cost (EAC)**.

> **equivalent annual cost (EAC)** the present value of a project's costs, calculated on an annual basis.

Calculating the EAC involves finding an unknown payment amount. For example, for machine A we need to find a two-year ordinary annuity with a PV of −€117.36 at 10 per cent. Going back to Chapter 5, we know that the two-year annuity factor is:

$$\text{Annuity factor} = (1 - 1/1.10^2)/0.10 = 1.7355$$

For machine A, then, we have:

$$\text{PV of costs} = -€117.36 = \text{EAC} \times 1.7355$$
$$\text{EAC} = -€117.36/1.7355$$
$$= -€67.62$$

For machine B the life is 3 years, so we first need the three-year annuity factor:

$$\text{Annuity factor} = (1 - 1/1.10^3)/0.10 = 2.4869$$

We calculate the EAC for B just as we did for A:

$$\text{PV of costs} = -€159.89 = \text{EAC} \times 2.4869$$
$$\text{EAC} = -€159.89/2.4869$$
$$= -€64.29$$

Based on this analysis, we should purchase B, because it effectively costs €64.29 per year compared with €67.62 for A. In other words, all things considered, B is cheaper. In this case, the longer life and lower operating cost are more than enough to offset the higher initial purchase price.

EXAMPLE 9.4

EQUIVALENT ANNUAL COSTS

This extended example illustrates what happens to the EAC when we consider taxes. You are evaluating two different pollution control options. A filtration system will cost €1.1 million to install and €60,000 annually, before taxes, to operate. It will have to be completely replaced every five years. A precipitation system will cost €1.9 million to install but only €10,000 per year to operate. The precipitation equipment has an effective operating life of eight years. To simplify matters, straight-line depreciation is used throughout, and neither system has any salvage value. Which option should we select if we use a 12 per cent discount rate? The tax rate is 34 per cent.

We need to consider the EACs for the two systems, because they have different service lives and will be replaced as they wear out. The relevant information can be summarized as follows:

	Filtration system	Precipitation system
After-tax operating cost (€)	−39,600	−6,600
Depreciation tax shield (€)	74,800	80,750
Operating cash flow (€)	35,200	74,150
Economic life (years)	5	8
Annuity factor (12%) (€)	3.6048	4.9676
Present value of operating cash flow (€)	126,888	368,350
Capital spending (€)	−1,100,000	−1,900,000
Total PV of costs (€)	−973,112	−1,531,650

Notice that the operating cash flow is actually positive in both cases because of the large depreciation tax shields. This can occur whenever the operating cost is small relative to the purchase price.

To decide which system to purchase, we compute the EACs for both using the appropriate annuity factors:
Filtration system:

$$-€973,112 = EAC \times 3.6048$$
$$EAC = -€269,951$$

Precipitation system:

$$-€1,531,650 = EAC \times 4.9676$$
$$EAC = -€308,328$$

The filtration system is the cheaper of the two, so we select it. In this case the longer life and smaller operating cost of the precipitation system are not sufficient to offset its higher initial cost.

CONCEPT QUESTIONS

9.6a In setting a bid price, we used a zero NPV as our benchmark. Explain why this is appropriate.
9.6b Under what circumstances do we have to worry about unequal economic lives? How do you interpret the EAC?

SUMMARY AND CONCLUSIONS

This chapter has described how to put together a discounted cash flow analysis. In it, we covered:

1. The identification of relevant project cash flows. We discussed project cash flows and described how to handle some issues that often come up, including sunk costs, opportunity costs, financing costs, net working capital and erosion.
2. Preparing and using pro forma, or projected, financial statements. We showed how information from such financial statements is useful in coming up with projected cash flows, and we also looked at some alternative definitions of operating cash flow.
3. The role of net working capital and depreciation in determining project cash flows. We saw that including the change in net working capital was important in cash flow analysis because it adjusted for the discrepancy between accounting revenues and costs and cash revenues and costs. We also went over the calculation of depreciation expense under current tax law.
4. Some special cases encountered in using discounted cash flow analysis. Here we looked at three special issues: evaluating cost-cutting investments, how to go about setting a bid price, and the unequal lives problem.

The discounted cash flow analysis we've covered here is a standard tool in the business world. It is a very powerful tool, so care should be taken in its use. The most important thing is to identify the cash flows in a way that makes economic sense. This chapter gives you a good start in learning to do this.

CHAPTER REVIEW AND SELF-TEST PROBLEMS

9.1 Capital Budgeting for Project X Based on the following information for project X, should we undertake the venture? To answer, first prepare a pro forma income statement for each year. Next, calculate the operating cash flow. Finish the problem by determining total cash flow and then calculating NPV assuming a 28 per cent required return. Use a 34 per cent tax rate throughout. For help, look back at our shark attractant and power mulcher examples. Project X involves a new type of graphite composite in-line skate wheel. We think we can sell 6,000 units per year at a price of €1,000 each. Variable costs will be about €400 per unit, and the product should have a four-year life. Fixed costs for the project will be €450,000 per year. Further, we shall need to invest a total of €1,250,000 in manufacturing equipment. This equipment is depreciated using 20 per cent reducing-balance for tax purposes. In four years the equipment will be worth about half of what we paid for it. We shall have to invest €1,150,000 in net working capital at the start. After that, the net working capital requirements will be 25 per cent of sales.

9.2 Calculating Operating Cash Flow Kilimanjaro Tents Ltd have projected a sales volume of R1,650 for the second year of a proposed expansion project. Costs normally run at 60 per cent of sales, or about R990 in this case. The depreciation expense will be R100, and the tax rate is 35 per cent. What is the operating cash flow? Calculate your answer using all the approaches (including the top-down, bottom-up and tax shield approaches) described in the chapter.

9.3 Are we Spending Money to Save Money? For help on this one, refer back to the computerized inventory management system in Example 9.3. Here, we're contemplating a new automatic surveillance system to replace our current contract security system. It will cost SKr450,000 to get the new system. The cost will be depreciated straight-line to zero over the system's four-year expected life. The system is expected to be worth SKr250,000 at the end of four years after removal costs. We think the new system will save us SKr125,000, before taxes, per year in contract security costs. The tax rate is 34 per cent. What are the NPV and IRR for buying the new system? The required return is 17 per cent.

SOLUTIONS

9.1 To develop the pro forma income statements, we need to calculate the depreciation for each of the four years. The asset is worth €625,000 in the fourth year, so the depreciation schedule is as follows:

Year	Initial value (€)	Depreciation (€)	Residual value (€)
1	1,250,000	250,000	1,000,000
2	1,000,000	200,000	800,000
3	800,000	160,000	640,000
4	640,000	15,000	625,000

The projected income statements, therefore, are as follows:

	Year			
	1	2	3	4
Sales (€)	6,000,000	6,000,000	6,000,000	6,000,000
Variable costs (€)	2,400,000	2,400,000	2,400,000	2,400,000
Fixed costs (€)	450,000	450,000	450,000	450,000
Depreciation (€)	250,000	200,000	160,000	15,000
Profit before taxes (€)	2,900,000	2,950,000	2,990,000	3,135,000
Taxes (34%) (€)	986,000	1,003,000	1,016,600	1,065,900
Net income (€)	1,914,000	1,947,000	1,973,400	2,069,100

Based on this information, here are the operating cash flows:

	Year			
	1	2	3	4
Net income (€)	1,914,000	1,947,000	1,973,400	2,069,100
Plus depreciation (€)	250,000	200,000	160,000	15,000
Operating cash flow (€)	2,164,000	2,147,000	2,133,400	2,084,100

We now have to worry about the non-operating cash flows. Net working capital starts out at €1,150,000 and then rises to 25 per cent of sales, or €1,500,000. This is a €350,000 change in net working capital.

Finally, we have to invest €1,250,000 to get started, and in four years the estimated market value is €625,000 (half of the cost). When we combine all this information, the projected cash flows for project X are as follows:

	Year				
	0	1	2	3	4
Operating cash flow (€)		2,164,000	2,147,000	2,133,400	2,084,100
Change in NWC (€)	−1,150,000	−350,000			1,500,000
Capital spending (€)	−1,250,000				625,000
Net cash flow (€)	−2,400,000	1,814,000	2,147,000	2,133,400	4,209,100

With these cash flows, the NPV at 28 per cent is:

$$\text{NPV} = -€2,400,000 + 1,814,000/1.28 + 2,147,000/1.28^2$$
$$+ 2,133,400/1.28^3 + 4,209,100/1.28^4$$
$$= €2,912,909$$

So this project appears quite profitable.

9.2 First, we can calculate the project's EBIT, its tax bill, and its net income:

$$\text{EBIT} = \text{Sales} - \text{Costs} - \text{Depreciation}$$
$$= R1,650 - 990 - 100 = R560$$
$$\text{Taxes} = R560 \times 0.35 = R196$$
$$\text{Net income} = R560 - 196 = R364$$

With these numbers, operating cash flow is:

$$\text{OCF} = \text{EBIT} + \text{Depreciation} - \text{Taxes}$$
$$= R560 + 100 - 196$$
$$= R464$$

Using the other OCF definitions, we have:

$$\text{Bottom-up OCF} = \text{Netincome} + \text{Depreciation}$$
$$= R364 + 100$$
$$= R464$$
$$\text{Top-down OCF} = \text{Sales} - \text{Costs} - \text{Taxes}$$
$$= R1,650 - 990 - 196$$
$$= R464$$
$$\text{Tax shield OCF} = (\text{Sales} - \text{Costs}) \times (1 - 0.35) + \text{Depreciation} \times 0.35$$
$$= (R1,650 - 990) \times 0.65 + 100 \times 0.35$$
$$= R464$$

As expected, all these definitions produce exactly the same answer.

9.3 The SKr125,000 pre-tax saving amounts to (1 − 0.34) × SKr125,000 = SKr82,500 after taxes. The annual depreciation of SKr450,000/4 = SKr112,500 generates a tax shield of 0.34 × SKr112,500 = SKr38,250 each year. Putting these together, we calculate that the operating cash flow is SKr82,500 + 38,250 = SKr120,750. Because the book value is zero in four years, the after-tax salvage value is (1 − 0.34) × SKr250,000 = SKr165,000. There are no working capital consequences, so here are the cash flows:

	Year				
	0	1	2	3	4
Operating cash flow (SKr)		120,750	120,750	120,750	120,750
Capital spending (SKr)	−450,000				165,000
Net cash flow (SKr)	−450,000	120,750	120,750	120,750	285,750

You can verify that the NPV at 17 per cent is −SKr30,702, and the return on the new surveillance system is only about 13.96 per cent. The project does not appear to be profitable.

Level of difficulty: Basic | Intermediate | Challenge

QUESTIONS AND PROBLEMS

9.1 Relevant Cash Flows Parker & Stone NV is looking at setting up a new manufacturing plant in Rotterdam to produce garden tools. The company bought some land six years ago for €6 million in anticipation of using it as a warehouse and distribution site, but the company has since decided to rent these facilities from a competitor instead. If the land were sold today, the company would net €6.4 million. The company wants to build its new manufacturing plant on this land; the plant will cost €14.2 million to build, and the site requires €890,000 worth of grading before it is suitable for construction. What is the proper cash flow amount to use as the initial investment in non-current assets when evaluating this project? Why?

9.2 Relevant Cash Flows Gabon Education plc currently sells 50,000 solar powered mobile smartbooks for use in sub-Saharan schools every year at £500 each, and 120,000 solar powered phones per year at £200 each. The company wants to introduce a new combined solar powered laptop to fill out its product line; it hopes to sell 30,000 of these laptops per year at £300 each. An independent consultant has determined that if Gabon Education introduces the new laptops, it should boost the sales of its existing phones by 5,000 units per year, and reduce the sales of its mobile smartbooks by 2,000 units per year. What is the amount to use as the annual sales figure when evaluating this project? Why?

9.3 Calculating Projected Net Income A proposed new investment has projected sales of £800,000. Variable costs are 50 per cent of sales, and fixed costs are £150,000; depreciation is £50,000. Prepare a pro forma income statement assuming a tax rate of 18 per cent. What is the projected net income?

9.4 Calculating OCF Consider the following income statement:

Sales (£)	1,824,500
Costs (£)	838,900
Depreciation (£)	226,500
Profit before taxes (£)	?
Taxes (28%) (£)	?
Net income (£)	?

Fill in the missing numbers and then calculate the OCF. What is the depreciation tax shield?

9.5 OCF from Several Approaches A proposed new project has projected sales of NKr108,000, costs of NKr51,000, and depreciation of NKr6,800. The tax rate is 35 per cent. Calculate operating cash flow using the four different approaches described in the chapter, and verify that the answer is the same in each case.

9.6 Calculating Depreciation A piece of newly purchased industrial equipment costs €1,080,000, and is depreciated using 20 per cent reducing-balance. Calculate the annual depreciation allowances and end-of-the-year book values for this equipment.

9.7 Calculating Salvage Value Consider an asset that costs €1,000,000 and is depreciated using 20 per cent reducing-balance. The asset is to be used in a five-year project; at the end of the project, the asset can be sold for €200,000. If the relevant tax rate is 18 per cent, what is the after-tax cash flow from the sale of this asset?

9.8 Calculating Salvage Value An asset used in a four-year project is depreciated at 20 per cent reducing-balance for tax purposes. The asset has an acquisition cost of £9,300,000 and will be sold for £3,100,000 at the end of the project. If the tax rate is 28 per cent, what is the after-tax salvage value of the asset?

9.9 Calculating Project NPV AXA is considering a new Insurtech investment in Paris. Financial projections for the investment are tabulated here. The French corporate tax rate is 28 per cent and the investment is depreciated using 20 per cent reducing balances. Assume all sales revenue is received in cash, all operating costs and income taxes are paid in cash, and all cash flows occur at the end of the year. All net working capital is recovered at the end of the project and the investment is sold at its residual value after depreciation.

	Year 0 (€)	Year 1 (€)	Year 2 (€)	Year 3 (€)	Year 4 (€)
Investment	325,000	-	-	-	
Sales Revenue	-	105,000	105,000	105,000	105,000
Operating costs	-	20,000	20,000	20,000	20,000
Net working capital spending	10,000	2,000	3,000	4,000	?

(a) Compute the incremental net income of the investment for each year.

(b) Compute the incremental cash flows of the investment for each year.

(c) Suppose the appropriate discount rate is 8 per cent. What is the NPV of the project?

9.10 Calculating Project Cash Flow from Assets In the previous problem, suppose the project requires an initial investment in net working capital of €20,000 and the investment will have a market value of €100,000 at the end of the project. Assume the discounting rate to be 8 per cent. What is the projects net cash flow? Year 1? Year 2? Year 3? What is the new NPV?

9.11 NPV and Reducing Balance Depreciation In the previous problem, suppose the investment is depreciated using the reducing balance method at 25 per cent per annum. All the other facts are the same. What is the project's year 1 net income now? Year 2? Year 3? What is the new NPV?

9.12 Calculating Project NPV You have been appointed by a retail store as its new financial manager. The firm has opened a new store in the south of France that is specifically targeted at holiday makers. The firm has decided that it will install a rotisserie which allows customers to directly pick cooked chickens to eat. The cost of the rotisserie is €37,000. Because the food is made on the premises, the store must pay a one-off insurance fee of €8,000 to avoid any liability from food poisoning. The chief executive has asked you to deal with the transaction. Should you include the insurance fee as capital investment or is it an expense? The tax rate is 25 per cent and the relevant discount rate is 10 per cent. If the insurance is treated as a capital investment cost, what is the present value of tax savings using a depreciation method of 20 per cent reducing balance? Assume that the rotisserie will be scrapped for nothing in five years. Which is better for the store: treating the insurance cost as a capital investment or as an expense?

9.13 Project Evaluation Dog Up! Franks is looking at a new sausage system with an installed cost of €390,000. This cost will be depreciated straight-line to zero over the projects five-year life, at the end of which the sausage system can be scrapped for €60,000. The sausage system will save the firm €120,000 per year in pre-tax operating costs, and the system requires an initial investment in net working capital of €28,000. If the tax rate is 34 per cent and the discount rate is 10 per cent, what is the NPV of this project?

9.14 Bid Price Blue Operations plc needs someone to supply it with 150,000 cartons of machine screws per year to support its manufacturing needs over the next five years, and you've decided to bid on the contract. It will cost you £780,000 to install the equipment necessary to start production; you'll depreciate this cost using 18 per cent reducing balances over the project's life. You estimate that in five years this equipment can be salvaged for £50,000. Your fixed production costs will be £240,000 per year, and your variable production costs should be £8.50 per carton. You also need an initial investment in net working capital of £75,000. If your tax rate is 23 per cent and you require a 16 per cent return on your investment, what bid price should you submit?

9.15 Project Evaluation Your firm is contemplating the purchase of a new £925,000 computer-based order entry system. The system will be depreciated using the 20 per cent reducing-balance method over its five-year life. It will be worth £90,000 at the end of that time. You will save £360,000 before taxes per year in order-processing costs, and you will be able to reduce working capital by £125,000 (this is a onetime reduction). If the tax rate is 18 per cent, what is the IRR for this project?

9.16 Calculating EAC A five-year project has an initial fixed non-current asset investment of £270,000, an initial NWC investment of £25,000, and an annual OCF of –£42,000. The non-current asset is depreciated 20 per cent reducing-balance over the life of the project, and has no salvage value. If the required return is 11 per cent, what is this projects equivalent annual cost, or EAC?

9.17 Calculating EAC Machine A costs £10,000 and costs £3,000 per year to maintain. It is expected to last three years. Machine B costs £8,000 and costs £5,000 per year to maintain. It is expected to last two years. Assume the discount rate is 20 per cent, which system should the firm choose?

9.18 Calculating a Bid Price Renton Superstores needs a company to supply it with 185,000 pallets per year of mozzarella cheese to support forecasted demand over the next five years, and, as a family-owned enterprise in Italy, you've decided to bid for the contract. It will cost you €2,000,000 to install the equipment necessary to start production; you'll depreciate this cost straight-line to zero over the project's life. You estimate that, in five years, this equipment can be salvaged for €350,000. Your fixed production costs will be €305,000 per year, and your variable production costs should be €9.25 per pallet. You also need an initial investment in net working capital of €75,000. If your tax rate is 23 per cent and you require a 12 per cent return on your investment, what bid price should you submit?

9.19 Cost-Cutting Proposals Geary Machine Shop is considering a four-year project to improve its production efficiency. Buying a new machine press for £560,000 is estimated to result in £210,000 in annual pre-tax cost savings. The press is depreciated using the 20 per cent reducing-balance method, and it will have a salvage value at the end of the project of £80,000. The press also requires an initial investment in spare parts inventory of £20,000, along with an additional £3,000 in inventory for each succeeding year of the project. If the shops tax rate is 28 per cent and its discount rate is 9 per cent, should the company buy and install the machine press?

9.20 Comparing Mutually Exclusive Projects Hagar Industrial Systems Company (HISC) is trying to decide between two different conveyor belt systems. System A costs 430,000 Norwegian kroner (NKr), has a four-year life, and requires NKr120,000 in pre-tax annual operating costs. System B costs NKr540,000, has a six-year life, and requires NKr80,000 in pre-tax annual operating costs. Both systems are to be depreciated using the reducing-balance method of 50 per cent per annum, and will have zero salvage value at the end of their life. Whichever system is chosen, it will not be replaced when it wears out. If the tax rate is 28 per cent and the discount rate is 20 per cent, which system should the firm choose?

9.21 Comparing Mutually Exclusive Projects Suppose in the previous problem that HISC always needs a conveyor belt system; when one wears out, it must be replaced. Which project should the firm choose now?

9.22 Calculating a Bid Price Consider a project to supply 100 million postage stamps per year to the Royal Mail for the next five years. You have an idle parcel of land available that cost £2,400,000 five years ago; if the land were sold today, it would net you £2,700,000 after tax. In five years the land can be sold for £3,200,000 after tax. You will need to install £4.1 million in new manufacturing plant and equipment to actually produce the stamps: this plant and equipment will be depreciated straight-line to zero over the project's five-year life. The equipment can be sold for £540,000 at the end of the project. You will also need £600,000 in initial net working capital for the project, and an additional investment of £50,000 in every year thereafter. Your production costs are 0.5 pence per stamp, and you have fixed costs of £950,000 per year. If your tax rate is 34 per cent and your required return on this project is 12 per cent, what bid price should you submit on the contract?

9.23 Interpreting a Bid Price In the previous problem, suppose you could keep working capital investments down to only £25,000 per year. How would this new information affect your calculated bid price?

9.24 Comparing Mutually Exclusive Projects Vandalay Industries is considering the purchase of a new machine for the production of latex. Machine A costs £2,900,000 and will last for six years. Variable costs are 35 per cent of sales, and fixed costs are £170,000 per year. Machine B costs £5,100,000 and will last for nine years. Variable costs for this machine are 30 per cent of sales, and fixed costs are £130,000 per year. The sales for each machine will be £10 million per year. The required return is 10 per cent, and the tax rate is 35 per cent. Both machines will be depreciated on a straight-line basis. If the company plans to replace the machine when it wears out on a perpetual basis, which machine should you choose?

9.25 Equivalent Annual Cost Compact fluorescent lamps (CFLs) have become more popular in recent years, but do they make financial sense? Suppose a typical 60 watt incandescent light bulb costs £0.50 and lasts 1,000 hours. A 15 watt CFL, which provides the same light, costs £3.50 and lasts for 12,000 hours. A kilowatt-hour of electricity costs £0.101, which is about the national average. A kilowatt-hour is 1,000 watts for 1 hour. If you require a 10 per cent return and use a light fixture for 500 hours per year, what is the equivalent annual cost of each light bulb?

9.26 Break-Even Cost The previous problem suggests that using CFLs instead of incandescent bulbs is a no-brainer. However, electricity costs actually vary quite a bit, depending on location and user type (you can get information on your rates from your local power company). An industrial user in the Scottish Highlands might pay £0.04 per kilowatt-hour, whereas a residential user in Essex might pay £0.25. What's the break-even cost per kilowatt-hour in Problem 9.25?

9.27 Break-Even Replacement The previous two problems suggest that using CFLs is a good idea from a purely financial perspective unless you live in an area where power is relatively inexpensive, but there is another wrinkle. Suppose you have a residence with a lot of incandescent bulbs that are used on average for 500 hours a year. The average bulb will be about halfway through its life, so it will have 500 hours remaining (and you can't tell which bulbs are older or newer). At what cost per kilowatt-hour does it make sense to replace your incandescent bulbs today?

9.28 Issues in Capital Budgeting The debate regarding CFLs versus incandescent bulbs (see Problems 9.25–9.27) has even more wrinkles. In no particular order:

- Incandescent bulbs generate a lot more heat than CFLs.
- CFL prices will probably decline relative to incandescent bulbs.
- CFLs unavoidably contain small amounts of mercury, a significant environmental hazard, and special precautions must be taken in disposing of burned-out units (and also in cleaning up a broken lamp). Currently, there is no agreed-upon way to recycle a CFL. Incandescent bulbs pose no disposal/breakage hazards.
- Depending on a lights location (or the number of lights), there can be a non-trivial cost to change bulbs (i.e., labour cost in a business).

- Coal-fired power generation accounts for a substantial portion of the mercury emissions in Europe, though the emissions will drop sharply in the relatively near future.
- Power generation accounts for a substantial portion of CO_2 emissions in Europe.
- CFLs are more energy and material intensive to manufacture. On-site mercury contamination and worker safety are issues.
- If you install a CFL in a permanent lighting fixture in a building, you will probably move long before the CFL burns out.
- Another lighting technology based on light-emitting diodes (LEDs) exists, and is improving. LEDs are currently much more expensive than CFLs, but costs are coming down. LEDs last much longer than CFLs, and use even less power. Also, LEDs don't contain mercury.

Qualitatively, how do these issues affect your position in the CFL versus incandescent light bulb debate? Australia recently proposed banning the sale of incandescent bulbs altogether, as have several European countries. Does your analysis suggest such a move is wise? Are there other regulations, short of an outright ban, that make sense to you?

9.29 Replacement Decisions Your small remodelling business has two hydrogen-battery/petrol hybrid eco-vehicles. One is a small passenger car used for jobsite visits and for other general business purposes. The other is a heavy truck used to haul equipment. The car gets 50 miles per litre. The truck gets 20 miles per litre. You want to improve petrol mileage to save money, and you have enough money to upgrade one vehicle. The upgrade cost will be the same for both vehicles. An upgraded car will get 80 miles per litre; an upgraded truck will get 25 miles per litre. The cost of petrol is £1.09 per litre. Assuming an upgrade is a good idea in the first place, which one should you upgrade? Both vehicles are driven 12,000 miles per year.

9.30 Calculating Project NPV With the growing popularity of casual surf print clothing, two recent MBA graduates decided to broaden this casual surf concept to encompass a surf lifestyle for the home. With limited capital, they decided to focus on surf print table and floor lamps to accent people's homes. They projected unit sales of these lamps to be 5,000 in the first year, with growth of 15 per cent each year for the next five years. Production of these lamps will require £28,000 in net working capital to start. Total fixed costs are £75,000 per year, variable production costs are £20 per unit, and the units are priced at £45 each. The equipment needed to begin production will cost £60,000. The equipment will be depreciated using the reducing-balance (20 per cent) method and is not expected to have a salvage value. The effective tax rate is 28 per cent, and the required rate of return is 25 per cent. What is the NPV of this project?

9.31 Project Evaluation Aguilera Acoustics (AA) projects unit sales for a new seven-octave voice emulation implant as follows:

Year	Unit sales
1	85,000
2	98,000
3	106,000
4	114,000
5	93,000

Production of the implants will require €1,500,000 in net working capital to start, and additional net working capital investments each year equal to 15 per cent of the projected sales for the following year. Total fixed costs are €900,000 per year, variable production costs are €240 per unit, and the units are priced at €325 each. The equipment needed to begin production has an installed cost of €21,000,000. Because the implants are intended for professional singers, this equipment is considered industrial machinery, and is thus depreciated by the reducing-balance method at 20 per cent per annum. In five years this equipment can be sold for about 20 per cent of its acquisition cost. AA is in the 35 per cent marginal tax bracket, and has a required return on all its projects of 18 per cent. Based on these preliminary project estimates, what is the NPV of the project? What is the IRR?

9.32 Calculating Required Savings A proposed cost-saving device has an installed cost of £360,000. The device will be used in a five-year project and be depreciated using the reducing balance method at 20 per cent per annum. The required initial net working capital investment is £20,000, the marginal tax rate is 24 per cent, and the project discount rate is 12 per cent. The device has an estimated year 5 salvage value of £60,000. What level of pre-tax cost savings do we require for this project to be profitable?

9.33 Calculating a Bid Price Another utilization of cash flow analysis is setting the bid price on a project. To calculate the bid price, we set the project NPV equal to zero and find the required price. Thus the bid price represents a financial break-even level for the project. Guthrie Enterprises needs someone to supply it with 150,000 cartons of machine screws per year to support its manufacturing needs over the next five years, and you have decided to bid on the contract. It will cost you €780,000 to install the equipment necessary to start production; you will depreciate this cost using 20 per cent reducing balances over the project's life. You estimate that in five years this equipment can be salvaged for €50,000. Your fixed production costs will be €240,000 per year, and your variable production costs should be €8.50 per carton. You also need an initial investment in net working capital of €75,000. If your tax rate is 35 per cent and you require a 16 per cent return on your investment, what bid price should you submit?

9.34 Calculating a Bid Price Your company has been approached to bid on a contract to sell 10,000 voice recognition (VR) computer keyboards a year for four years. Because of technological improvements, beyond that time they will be outdated, and no sales will be possible. The equipment necessary for the production will cost £2.4 million and will be depreciated on a reducing-balance (20 per cent) method. Production will require an investment in net working capital of £75,000 to be returned at the end of the project, and the equipment can be sold for £200,000 at the end of production. Fixed costs are £500,000 per year, and variable costs are £165 per unit. In addition to the contract, you feel your company can sell 3,000, 6,000, 8,000 and 5,000 additional units to companies in other countries over the next four years, respectively, at a price of £275. This price is fixed. The tax rate is 28 per cent, and the required return is 13 per cent. Additionally, the managing director of the company will undertake the project only if it has an NPV of £100,000. What bid price should you set for the contract?

9.35 Replacement Decisions Suppose we are thinking about replacing an old computer with a new one. The old one cost us €650,000; the new one will cost €780,000. The new machine will be depreciated straight-line to zero over its five-year life. It will probably be worth about €150,000 after five years.

The old computer is being depreciated straight-line at a rate of €130,000 per year. It will be completely written off in three years. If we don't replace it now, we shall have to replace it in two years. We can sell it now for €210,000; in two years, it will probably be worth €60,000. The new machine will save us €145,000 per year in operating costs. The tax rate is 38 per cent, and the discount rate is 12 per cent.

(a) Suppose we recognize that, if we don't replace the computer now, we shall be replacing it in two years. Should we replace now or should we wait? (*Hint:* What we effectively have here is a decision either to invest in the old computer (by not selling it) or to invest in the new one. Notice that the two investments have unequal lives.)

(b) Suppose we consider only whether we should replace the old computer now without worrying about what is going to happen in two years. What are the relevant cash flows? Should we replace it or not? (*Hint:* Consider the net change in the firm's after-tax cash flows if we do the replacement.)

MINI CASE

CONCHBIT, PART 1

Conch Republic Electronics is a midsized electronics manufacturer located in Emilia-Romagna, Italy. The company president is Morena Moscardini, who inherited the company. When it was founded, over 70 years ago, the company originally repaired radios and other household appliances. Over the years the company expanded into manufacturing, and is now a reputable manufacturer of various electronic items. Jay McCanless, a recent MBA graduate, has been hired by the company's finance department.

One of the major revenue-producing items manufactured by Conch Republic is a wearable fitness device (Conchbit). Conch Republic currently has one fitness device on the market, and sales have been excellent. The Conchbit is a unique item in that it comes in a variety of designs and has real time feedback on blood oxygen levels. However, as with any electronic item, technology changes rapidly, and the current model has limited features in comparison with newer models. Conch Republic spent €750,000 to develop a prototype for a new Conchbit that has all the features of the existing model but adds new features such as real-time blood glucose monitoring. The company has spent a further €200,000 for a marketing study to determine the expected sales figures for the new Conchbit.

Conch Republic can manufacture the new Conchbit for €155 each in variable costs. Fixed costs for the operation are estimated to be €4.7 million per year. The estimated sales volumes are 74,000, 95,000, 125,000, 105,000 and 80,000 per year for the next five years, respectively. The unit price of the new Conchbit will be €360. The necessary equipment can be purchased for €21.5 million, and will be depreciated using the 20 per cent reducing-balance method. It is believed the value of the equipment in five years will be €4.1 million.

As previously stated, Conch Republic currently manufactures a health wearable model. Production of the existing model is expected to be terminated in two years. If Conch Republic does not introduce the new Conchbit, sales will be 80,000 units and 60,000 units for the next two years, respectively. The price of the existing model is €290 per unit, with variable costs of €120 each and fixed costs of €1,800,000 per year. If Conch Republic does introduce the new Conchbit, sales of the existing model will fall by 15,000 units per year, and the price of the existing units will have to be lowered to €255 each. Net working capital for the models will be 20 per cent of sales, and will occur with the timing of the cash flows for the year: for example, there is no initial outlay for NWC, but changes in NWC will first occur in year 1 with the first year's sales. Conch Republic has a 35 per cent corporate tax rate and a 12 per cent required return.

Morena has asked Jay to prepare a report that answers the following questions.

QUESTIONS

1. Explain why the €750,000 on developing the prototype and the €200,000 on testing the market have been ignored in the calculations. Why should they have been ignored?
2. What is the impact of introducing the new Conchbit on the existing sales of the current Conchbit called?
3. In assessing the cash flows that occur from introducing the new Conchbit, what is the valuation principle that is being applied?

ADDITIONAL READING

A very interesting paper that links stock market efficiency and capital budgeting is Durnev, Morck and Yeung (2004). This has implications for capital budgeting when carried out in emerging and developed markets. Although the research uses US data, the authors do present a nice figure of stock market synchronicity (Figure 1) for many countries and link this to market efficiency and capital budgeting.

1. Durnev, A., Morck, R., & Yeung, B. (2004). Value-enhancing capital budgeting and firm-specific stock return variation. *Journal of Finance, 59*(1), 65–105.

Some other interesting papers on capital budgeting methods include:

2. Brunzell, T., Liljeblom, E., & Vaikekoski, M. (2013). Determinants of capital budgeting methods and hurdle rates in Nordic firms. *Accounting & Finance, 53*(1), 85–110.
3. Holmén, M., & Pramborg, B. (2009). Capital budgeting and political risk: Empirical evidence. *Journal of International Financial Management & Accounting, 20*(2), 105–134.

Endnotes

1. If the asset in question is unique, then the opportunity cost might be higher, because there might be other valuable projects we could undertake that would use it. However, if the asset in question is of a type that is routinely bought and sold (a used car, perhaps), then the opportunity cost is always the going price in the market, because that is the cost of buying another similar asset.
2. More colourfully, erosion is sometimes called *piracy* or *cannibalism*.
3. By *fixed cost* we mean a cash outflow that will occur regardless of the level of sales. This should not be confused with some sort of accounting period charge.
4. We shall also assume that a full year's depreciation can be taken in the first year.
5. In reality, the firm would probably recover something less than 100 per cent of this amount because of bad debts, inventory loss, and so on. If we wanted to, we could just assume that, for example, only 90 per cent was recovered, and proceed from there.
6. We're guilty of a minor inconsistency here. When we calculated the NPV and the IRR, we assumed that all the cash flows occurred at end of year. When we calculated the payback, we assumed that the cash flows occurred uniformly throughout the year.
7. Notice that the average total book value is not the initial total of £110,000 divided by 2. The reason is that the £20,000 in working capital doesn't 'depreciate'.
8. If there were other accounts, we might have to make some further adjustments. For example, a net increase in inventory would be a cash outflow.

CHAPTER 10
PROJECT ANALYSIS AND EVALUATION

LEARNING OBJECTIVES
After studying this chapter, you should understand:

- **LO1** How to perform and interpret a sensitivity analysis for a proposed investment.
- **LO2** How to perform and interpret a scenario analysis for a proposed investment.
- **LO3** How to determine and interpret cash, accounting and financial break-even points.
- **LO4** How the degree of operating leverage can affect the cash flows of a project.
- **LO5** How capital rationing affects the ability of a company to accept projects.

KEY NOTATIONS

D	Depreciation
DCF	Discounted cash flow
DOL	Degree of operating leverage
FC	Total fixed cost
NPV	Net present value
P	Price per unit
Q	Total quantity of output
S	Total sales = $P \times Q$
T	Tax rate
TC	Total cost
v	Variable cost per unit
VC	Total variable cost

FOR SEVERAL YEARS NOW, companies have been making strategic investment decisions in an uncertain and harsh economic environment. The United Kingdom, in particular, has experienced an unprecedented upheaval with the fallout from the Brexit vote affecting every British firm. Then, when companies felt there was going to be a period of stability after Brexit, the Covid-19 pandemic swept the world, and almost every company faced its strategic crisis. Social distancing became a new factor that affected all companies, irrespective of where they operate, and business models were reassessed under new business protocols.

Strategic decisions that reflect future uncertainty, such as those relating to a post-pandemic Covid-19 world, must be analysed in a way that incorporates all potential future events. Standard net present value valuation does not adequately capture alternative scenarios, and so a modification of the methods must be developed. This chapter explores how firms can assess strategic investments in uncertain environments and what they can do to mitigate the risk of their decisions.

In our previous chapter, we discussed how to identify and organize the relevant cash flows for capital investment decisions. Our primary interest there was in coming up with a preliminary estimate of the net present value for a proposed project. In this chapter, we focus on assessing the reliability of such an estimate, and on some additional considerations in project analysis.

We begin by discussing the need for an evaluation of cash flow and NPV estimates. We go on to develop some useful tools for such an assessment. We also examine additional complications and concerns that can arise in project evaluation.

10.1 EVALUATING NPV ESTIMATES

As we discussed in Chapter 9, an investment has a positive net present value if its market value exceeds its cost. Such an investment is desirable because it creates value for its owner. The primary problem in identifying such opportunities is that usually, we can't actually observe the relevant market value; instead, we estimate it. Having done so, it is only natural to wonder whether our estimates are at least close to the true values. We consider this question next.

THE BASIC PROBLEM

Suppose we are working on a preliminary discounted cash flow analysis along the lines we described in the previous chapter. We carefully identify the relevant cash flows, avoiding such things as sunk costs, and we remember to consider working capital requirements. We add back any depreciation, we account for possible erosion, and we pay attention to opportunity costs. Finally, we double-check our calculations; when all is said and done, the bottom line is that the estimated NPV is positive.

Now what? Do we stop here and move on to the next proposal? Probably not. The fact that the estimated NPV is positive is definitely a good sign; but, more than anything, this tells us that we need to take a closer look.

If you think about it, there are two circumstances under which a DCF analysis could lead us to conclude that a project has a positive NPV. The first possibility is that the project really does have a positive NPV. That's good news. The bad news is the second possibility: a project may appear to have a positive NPV because our estimate is inaccurate.

Notice that we could also err in the opposite way. If we conclude that a project has a negative NPV when the true NPV is positive, we lose a valuable opportunity.

PROJECTED VERSUS ACTUAL CASH FLOWS

There is a somewhat subtle point we need to make here. When we say something like 'The projected cash flow in year 4 is €700', what exactly do we mean? Does this mean that we think the cash flow will actually be €700? Not really. It could happen, of course, but we would be surprised to see it turn out exactly that way. The reason is that the €700 projection is based only on what we know today. Almost anything could happen between now and then to change that cash flow.

Loosely speaking, we really mean that if we took all the possible cash flows that could occur in four years and averaged them, the result would be €700. So we don't really expect a projected cash flow to be exactly right in any one case. What we *do* expect is that, if we evaluate a large number of projects, our projections will be right – on average.

FORECASTING RISK

> **forecasting risk** the possibility that errors in projected cash flows will lead to incorrect decisions. Also, *estimation risk.*

The key inputs into a DCF analysis are projected future cash flows. If the projections are seriously in error, then we have a classic GIGO (garbage in, garbage out) system. In such a case, no matter how carefully we arrange the numbers and manipulate them, the resulting answer can still be grossly misleading. This is the danger in using a relatively sophisticated technique like DCF. It is sometimes easy to get caught up in number crunching and forget the underlying nuts-and-bolts economic reality.

The possibility that we shall make a bad decision because of errors in the projected cash flows is called **forecasting risk** (or *estimation risk*). Because of forecasting risk, there is the danger that we shall think a project has a positive NPV when really it does not. How is this possible? It happens if we are overly optimistic about the future, and, as a result, our projected cash flows don't realistically reflect the possible future cash flows.

So far, we have not explicitly considered what to do about the possibility of errors in our forecasts, so one of our goals in this chapter is to develop some tools that are useful in identifying areas where potential errors exist, and where they might be especially damaging. In one form or another, we shall be trying to assess the economic 'reasonableness' of our estimates. We shall also be wondering how much damage will be done by errors in those estimates.

SOURCES OF VALUE

The first line of defence against forecasting risk is simply to ask, 'What is it about this investment that leads to a positive NPV?' We should be able to point to something specific as the source of value. For example, if the proposal under consideration involved a new product, then we might ask questions such as the following: Are we certain that our new product is significantly better than that of the competition? Can we truly manufacture at a lower cost, or distribute more effectively, or identify undeveloped market niches, or gain control of a market?

A key factor to keep in mind is the degree of competition in the market. A basic principle of economics is that positive-NPV investments will be rare in a highly competitive environment. Therefore proposals that appear to show significant value in the face of stiff competition are particularly troublesome, and the likely reaction of the competition to any innovations must be closely examined. Anyone thinking of entering highly profitable markets would do well to reflect on what the supply (and profit margin) situation will look like in just a few years from existing and potentially new competitors.

The point to remember is that positive-NPV investments are probably not all that common, and the number of positive-NPV projects is almost certainly limited for any given firm. If we can't articulate some sound economic basis for thinking – ahead of time – that we have found something special, then the conclusion that our project has a positive NPV should be viewed with some suspicion.

> **CONCEPT QUESTIONS**
>
> **10.1a** What is forecasting risk? Why is it a concern for the financial manager?
> **10.1b** What are some potential sources of value in a new project?

10.2 SCENARIO AND OTHER WHAT-IF ANALYSES

Our basic approach to evaluating cash flow and NPV estimates involves asking what-if questions. Accordingly, we discuss some organized ways of going about a what-if analysis. Our goal in performing such an analysis is to assess the degree of forecasting risk and to identify the most critical components of the success or failure of an investment.

GETTING STARTED

We are investigating a new project. Naturally, the first thing we do is estimate NPV, based on our projected cash flows. We shall call this initial set of projections the *base case*. Now, however, we recognize the possibility of error in these cash flow projections. After completing the base case, we thus wish to investigate the impact on our estimates of different assumptions about the future.

One way to organize this investigation is to put upper and lower bounds on the various components of the project. For example, suppose we forecast sales at 100 units per year. We know this estimate may be high or low, but we are relatively sure it is not off by more than 10 units in either direction. We thus pick a lower bound of 90 and an upper bound of 110. We then go on to assign such bounds to any other cash flow components of which we are unsure.

When we pick these upper and lower bounds, we are not ruling out the possibility that the actual values could be outside this range. What we are saying, again loosely speaking, is that it is unlikely that the actual average (as opposed to our estimated average) of the possible values is outside this range.

An example is useful to illustrate the idea here. The project under consideration costs €200,000, has a five-year life and has no salvage value. For simplicity, depreciation is straight-line to zero. The required return is 12 per cent, and the tax rate is 34 per cent. In addition, we have compiled the following information:

	Base case	Lower bound	Upper bound
Unit sales	6,000	5,500	6,500
Price per unit (€)	80	75	85
Variable costs per unit (€)	60	58	62
Fixed costs per year (€)	50,000	45,000	55,000

With this information, we can calculate the base-case NPV by first calculating net income:

Sales (€)	480,000
Variable costs (€)	360,000
Fixed costs (€)	50,000
Depreciation (€)	40,000
Profit before taxes (€)	30,000
Taxes (34%) (€)	10,200
Net income	19,800

Operating cash flow is thus €19,800 + 40,000 = €59,800 per year. At 12 per cent, the five-year annuity factor is 3.6048, so the base-case NPV is:

$$\text{Base-case NPV} = -€200,000 + 59,800 \times 3.6048$$
$$= €15,567$$

Thus the project looks good so far.

SCENARIO ANALYSIS

scenario analysis the determination of what happens to NPV estimates when we ask what-if questions.

The basic form of what-if analysis is called **scenario analysis**. What we do is investigate the changes in our NPV estimates that result from asking questions such as: what if unit sales realistically should be projected at 5,500 units instead of 6,000?

Once we start looking at alternative scenarios, we might find that most of the plausible ones result in positive NPVs. In this case, we have some confidence in proceeding with the project. If a substantial percentage of the scenarios look bad, the degree of forecasting risk is high, and further investigation is in order.

We can consider several possible scenarios. An excellent place to start is with the worst-case scenario, which will tell us the minimum NPV of the project. If this turns out to be positive, we shall be in good shape. While we are at it, we shall go ahead and determine the other extreme, the best case. This puts an upper bound on our NPV.

To get the worst case, we assign the least favourable value to each item. This means *low* values for items such as units sold and price per unit, and *high* values for costs. We do the reverse for the best case. For our project, these values would be the following:

	Worst case	Best case
Unit sales	5,500	6,500
Price per unit (€)	75	85
Variable costs per unit (€)	62	58
Fixed costs per year (€)	55,000	45,000

With this information, we can calculate the net income and cash flows under each scenario (check these for yourself):

Scenario	Net income (€)	Cash flow (€)	Net present value (€)	IRR (%)
Base case	19,800	59,800	15,567	15.1
Worst case*	−15,510	24,490	−111,719	−14.4
Best case	59,730	99,730	159,504	40.9

*We assume a tax credit is created in our worst-case scenario.

What we learn is that, under the worst scenario, the cash flow is still positive at €24,490. That's good news. The bad news is that the return is −14.4 per cent in this case, and the NPV is −€111,719. Because the project costs €200,000, we stand to lose a little more than half of the original investment under the worst possible scenario. The best case offers an attractive 41 per cent return.

The terms *best case* and *worst case* are commonly used, and we shall stick with them, but they are somewhat misleading. The absolutely best thing that could happen would be something absurdly unlikely, such as launching a new diet soft drink and subsequently learning that our (patented) formulation also happens to cure the common cold. Similarly, the true worst case would involve some incredibly remote possibility of total disaster. We're not claiming that these things don't happen; once in a while they do. Some products, such as iPhones, succeed beyond the wildest expectations; and some, such as asbestos, turn out to be absolute catastrophes. Our point is that, in assessing the reasonableness of an NPV estimate, we need to stick to cases that are reasonably likely to occur.

Instead of *best* and *worst*, then, it is probably more accurate to use the words *optimistic* and *pessimistic*. In broad terms, if we were thinking about a reasonable range for, say, unit sales, then what we call the best case would correspond to something near the upper end of that range. The worst case would simply correspond to the lower end.

Depending on the project, the best- and worst-case estimates can vary greatly. For example, Roche Carolina, a subsidiary of the Roche Group, a Swiss global health care company, announced plans for converting its site to a solar heating and cooling system. The initial cost was estimated at €350,000, including a government grant. The range used for this initial cost was ±15 per cent. The annual savings were calculated as €29,000, with a range of ±30 per cent. In the end, the NPV was estimated at €125,000, with a range of €42,000 to €208,000, and the IRR was 18 per cent, with a range of 11 per cent to 25 per cent.

As we have mentioned, there is an unlimited number of different scenarios that we could examine. At a minimum, we might want to investigate two intermediate cases by going halfway between the base amounts and the extreme amounts. This would give us five scenarios in all, including the base case.

Beyond this point, it is hard to know when to stop. As we generate more and more possibilities, we run the risk of experiencing 'paralysis of analysis'. The difficulty is that, no matter how many scenarios we run, all we can learn are possibilities – some good and some bad. Beyond that, we don't get any guidance as to what to do. Scenario analysis is thus useful in telling us what could happen, and in helping us gauge the potential for disaster, but it does not tell us whether to adopt a project.

Unfortunately, in practice, even the worst-case scenarios may not be low enough. Two recent examples show what we mean. The Eurotunnel under the English Channel connects Britain to France and covers 38 km. It took 8,000 workers eight years to remove 7.5 million cubic metres of rock. When the tunnel was finally built, it cost £11.9 billion (€13.1 billion), or slightly more than twice the original estimate of £5.9 billion (€6.5 billion). And things got worse. Forecasts called for 16.8 million passengers in the first year, but only 4 million actually used it. Revenue estimates were £1.92 billion (€2.12 billion), but actual revenue was only about one-third of that. The major problems faced by the Eurotunnel included increased competition from ferry services, which dropped their prices, and the rise of low-cost airlines. In 2006 things got so bad that the company operating the Eurotunnel was forced into negotiations with creditors to chop its £7.4 billion (€8.2 billion) debt in half to avoid bankruptcy. The debt reduction appeared to help. In 2007 the Eurotunnel reported its first profit, of £0.9 million (€1 million). Of course, this profit paled in comparison with the £185 million (€204 million) in losses accumulated since the Chunnel first opened in 1994.

Another example is Volkswagen, which had long been regarded as a very reliable and trustworthy carmaker. In 2015, the US Environmental Protection Agency accused Volkswagen of installing a 'defeat device' to reduce the recorded carbon emissions when the cars were tested. Unfortunately, more than 10 million vehicles were fitted with the device, leading to a total recall of all affected vehicles and catastrophic damage to its reputation.

> **REAL WORLD INSIGHTS**
>
> Possibly the highest growth market to emerge over the coming few years is the internet of things, where everyday objects are connected and controlled through the internet. Virtually every single household item will benefit from having remote access, from defrosting food, to cooking at a specific temperature, to switching on and off lights, to closing and opening curtains, and setting the heating to the desired temperature, to even feeding a pet.
>
> Valuing these projects, however, can be extremely difficult because the central assumptions underlying future cash flow estimations are so nebulous. For example, what is the potential market size of driverless cars? How much of the market would you expect to capture if you created a workable model? What price would you set for the car?
>
> For this, and other disruptive technologies, an analyst should consider worst- and best-case scenarios at the very minimum. It may be that the best approach is to consider the break-even sales figure and develop plans to surpass that in the early years.
>
> These questions now face big technology firms, such as Alphabet and Apple. They have whole divisions focused on 'Moonshot' ventures and are relying on a small subset of these projects to deliver the future growth expected by investors.

SENSITIVITY ANALYSIS

sensitivity analysis
investigation of what happens to NPV when only one variable is changed.

Sensitivity analysis is a variation on scenario analysis that is useful in pinpointing the areas where forecasting risk is especially severe. The basic idea with a sensitivity analysis is to freeze all of the variables except one, and then see how sensitive our estimate of NPV is to changes in that one variable. If our NPV estimate turns out to be very sensitive to relatively small changes in the projected value of some component of project cash flow, then the forecasting risk associated with that variable is high.

To illustrate how sensitivity analysis works, we go back to our base case for every item except unit sales. We can then calculate cash flow and NPV using the largest and smallest unit sales figures:

Scenario	Unit sales	Cash flow (€)	Net present value (€)	IRR (%)
Base case	6,000	59,800	15,567	15.1
Worst case	5,500	53,200	−8,226	10.3
Best case	6,500	66,400	39,357	19.7

For comparison, we now freeze everything except fixed costs and repeat the analysis:

Scenario	Fixed costs (€)	Cash flow (€)	Net present value (€)	IRR (%)
Base case	50,000	59,800	15,567	15.1
Worst case	55,000	56,500	3,670	12.7
Best case	45,000	63,100	27,461	17.4

What we see here is that, given our ranges, the estimated NPV of this project is more sensitive to changes in projected unit sales than it is to changes in projected fixed costs. In fact, under the worst case for fixed costs, the NPV is still positive.

The results of our sensitivity analysis for unit sales can be illustrated graphically as in Figure 10.1. Here we place NPV on the vertical axis and unit sales on the horizontal axis. When we plot the combinations of unit sales versus NPV, we see that all possible combinations fall on a straight line. The steeper the resulting line, the greater the sensitivity of the estimated NPV to changes in the projected value of the variable being investigated.

FIGURE 10.1 Sensitivity analysis for unit sales

As we have illustrated, sensitivity analysis is useful in pinpointing which variables deserve the most attention. If we find that our estimated NPV is especially sensitive to changes in a variable that is difficult to forecast (such as unit sales), then the degree of forecasting risk is high. We might decide that further market research would be a good idea in this case.

Because sensitivity analysis is a form of scenario analysis, it suffers from the same drawbacks. Sensitivity analysis is useful for pointing out where forecasting errors will do the most damage, but it does not tell us what to do about possible errors.

CASE STUDY: EASYJET PLC

In this section, we shall consider the challenges you face when valuing a full company instead of a single project. Recall the balance sheet Equation (3.1) from Chapter 3, where the value of a firm's assets equals the value of its debt plus equity. We've already shown how to value debt and equity, and this is good enough when a company is large, and its securities are frequently traded on a stock exchange. However, in many cases, you may prefer to work with the other side of the balance sheet equation and value a company's assets directly.

Valuing a firm's assets is similar to valuing a project. You estimate the future cash flows coming from all the operations of the company, and discount those cash flows at the appropriate discount rate. If the firm has several distinct operations in different industries or geographical locations, you may wish to use different discount rates for each stream of cash flows.

In this case study, we shall arrive at a valuation for easyJet plc, which is a budget airline firm with all of its operations in Europe. You can visit its website, corporate.easyjet.com, for more information on the company's history and operations. Our approach will be necessarily simplistic to focus on the fundamentals of valuation. However, although we may seem to be making lots of assumptions, the basic process is the same as provided by many commercial valuation services.

In August 2020, easyJet was listed on the UK London Stock Exchange, and its share price was £6.43. It had 216.66 million shares outstanding, making its market capitalization of equity equal to £6.43 × 397.36 million = £2.55 billion. The company had £1.92 billion of debt, and so, according to the share price, the value of the company was (£2.55 + £1.92 billion) = £4.47 billion.

Firm valuation requires an identification of the significant risk factors for the company. For our purposes, we will simplify matters and consider only three major risk factors: the macroeconomic environment, external competition and the fuel price. All three affect each division differently, and this must be reflected in our valuation.

Macroeconomic Environment

The macroeconomic conditions facing easyJet will have a direct impact on ticket revenues and impact the fixed costs the company bears as a percentage of net income. The value of the aircraft owned by easyJet is affected by the number of miles each plane completes. In a weak economy or one with travel restrictions, this will be lower. Servicing revenue will change by a smaller percentage than ticketing because aviation support requirements are less sensitive to macroeconomic changes than ticket revenues (planes must be serviced regularly irrespective of their mileage).

	Recession (%)	Status quo (%)	Strong economic recovery (%)
Probability	30	40	30
Cash Flow impact (£m)	−69	0	+28

External Competition

A major risk factor facing any company is market share. All firms focus on this statistic, and easyJet is no different from others in this regard. Based on information in the 2019 annual report and the company's response to the Covid-19 pandemic, we can envisage the following scenarios and impacts.

	Loss of market share (%)	Maintain market share (%)	Increase market share (%)
Probability	20	50	30
Cash Flow impact (£m)	−55	0	+55

Fuel Price

The price of jet fuel is one of the primary factors in airline profitability. However, companies have several options to reduce the impact of fuel price volatility. The main approach is for a firm to enter into hedging contracts (Chapter 20) or pass on any increase via ticket prices. This means that an airline can effectively minimize the risk it faces from oil price uncertainty. easyJet has an active risk management policy and engages in many hedge positions, so we will assume that fuel price volatility has a negligible effect on easyJet market value and will not consider its impact.

A valuation must consider every possible risk factor facing a company. For publicly listed companies, the first place to look is the annual report. For private companies, identifying key risks is more difficult but not impossible. One could look at the risk factors of public listed companies in the same industry sector, or even contact the company in person for their view.

Assume that in 2020, the company had a cash flow of £260 million (this is a simplification of the actual cash flow for easyJet), which is expected to grow at 6 per cent per annum. Assume that the applicable discount rate for easyJet is 12 per cent. Assume also that the firm will last forever and so the cash flows are a perpetuity.

Now that we have our different assumptions, we are in a position to value easyJet plc.

Taking the expected scenario first, analysts believe that net operating cash flows will be £275.6 (£260 × 1.06) million next year and that it will continue to grow by 6 per cent per annum indefinitely.

$$V_{easyJet} = \frac{NCF}{r-g} = \frac{£275.6 \text{ m}}{0.12 - 0.06} = £4.59 \text{ bn}$$

The value of easyJet of £4.59 billion compares with the market value of £4.47 billion presented early in this section.

The next stage in our valuation should be the sensitivity analysis. We first present the impact of market conditions and market share on easyJet's overall cash flow in £ millions in the table below.

	Lose market share	Maintain market share	Increase market share
Recession	151.6	206.6	261.6
Status quo	220.6	275.6	330.6
Recovery	248.6	303.6	358.6

We now present the expected share price in each situation. From the table, we see that the value of easyJet (in £ millions) is sensitive to changes in the macroeconomy and market share.

	Lose market share	Maintain market share	Increase market share
Recession	2,527	3,443	4,360
Status quo	3,677	4,593	5,510
Recovery	4,143	5,060	5,977

We can also carry out a scenario analysis for easyJet by looking at the best- and worst-case scenarios. These are the times when the worst- (or best-) case estimates for all the inputs coincide. When the worst-case scenario occurs, the value of easyJet will be £2,527 million, significantly less than the current value. Similarly, under the best-case scenario, easyJet will be worth £5,977 million.

So what should the value of easyJet be? It all depends on the likelihood of each scenario or outcome in the future. We may require further analysis. For example, we have not considered the impact of fuel prices, and which hedging strategy will be most effective. In addition, we could have investigated our assumptions in more detail and, for example, examined market share and macroeconomic changes for every year in the future.

SIMULATION ANALYSIS

Scenario analysis and sensitivity analysis are widely used. With scenario analysis, we let all the different variables change, but allow them to take on only a few values. With sensitivity analysis, we let only one variable change, but we let it take on many values. If we combine the two approaches, the result is a crude form of **simulation analysis**.

simulation analysis a combination of scenario and sensitivity analysis.

If we want to let all the items vary at the same time, we have to consider a huge number of scenarios, and computer assistance is almost certainly needed. In the simplest case, we start with unit sales and assume that any value in a specific range is equally likely. We start by randomly picking one value (or by instructing a computer to do so). We then randomly select a price, a variable cost and so on.

Once we have values for all the relevant components, we calculate an NPV. We repeat this sequence as many times as we desire, probably several thousand times. The result is many NPV estimates that we summarize by calculating the average value and some measure of how spread out the different possibilities are. For example, it would be of some interest to know what percentage of the possible scenarios result in negative estimated NPVs.

Because simulation analysis (or simulation) is an extended form of scenario analysis, it has the same problems. Once we have the results, no simple decision rule tells us what to do. Also, we have described a relatively simple form of simulation. To really do it right, we would have to consider the interrelationships between the different cash flow components. Furthermore, we assumed that the possible values were equally likely to occur. It is probably more realistic to assume that values near the base case are more likely than extreme values, but coming up with the probabilities is difficult.

For these reasons, the use of simulation is somewhat limited in practice. However, recent advances in computer software and hardware (and user sophistication) lead us to believe it may become more common in the future, particularly for large-scale projects.

> **CONCEPT QUESTIONS**
>
> **10.2a** What are scenario, sensitivity and simulation analysis?
> **10.2b** What are the drawbacks to the various types of what-if analysis?

10.3 BREAK-EVEN ANALYSIS

It will frequently turn out that the crucial variable for a project is sales volume. If we are thinking of creating a new product or entering a new market, for example, the hardest thing to forecast accurately is how much we can sell. For this reason, sales volume is usually analysed more closely than other variables.

Break-even analysis is a popular and commonly used tool for analysing the relationship between sales volume and profitability. There are a variety of different break-even measures, and we have already seen several types. For example, we discussed (in Chapter 8) how the payback period can be interpreted as the length of time until a project breaks even, ignoring time value.

All break-even measures have a similar goal. Loosely speaking, we shall always be asking, 'How bad do sales have to get before we actually begin to lose money?' Implicitly, we shall also be asking, 'Is it likely that things will get that bad?' To get started on this subject, we first discuss fixed and variable costs.

FIXED AND VARIABLE COSTS

In discussing break-even, the difference between fixed and variable costs becomes significant. As a result, we need to be a little more explicit about the difference than we have been so far.

Variable Costs

> **variable costs** costs that change when the quantity of output changes.

By definition, **variable costs** change as the quantity of output changes, and they are zero when production is zero. For example, direct labour costs and raw material costs are usually considered variable. This makes sense because if we shut down operations tomorrow, there will be no future costs for labour or raw materials.

We shall assume that variable costs are a constant amount per unit of output, which means that the total variable cost is equal to the cost per unit multiplied by the number of units. In other words, the relationship between total variable cost (VC), cost per unit of output (v) and the total quantity of output (Q) can be written simply as:

Total variable cost = Total quantity of output × Cost per unit of output

$$VC = Q \times v$$

For example, suppose variable costs (v) are €2 per unit. If total output (Q) is 1,000 units, what will total variable costs (VC) be?

$$\begin{aligned} VC &= Q \times v \\ &= 1{,}000 \times €2 \\ &= €2{,}000 \end{aligned}$$

Similarly, if Q is 5,000 units, then VC will be $5{,}000 \times €2 = €10{,}000$.

Figure 10.2 illustrates the relationship between output level and variable costs in this case. In Figure 10.2, notice that increasing output by one unit results in variable costs rising by €2, so 'the rise over the run' (the slope of the line) is given by €2/1 = €2.

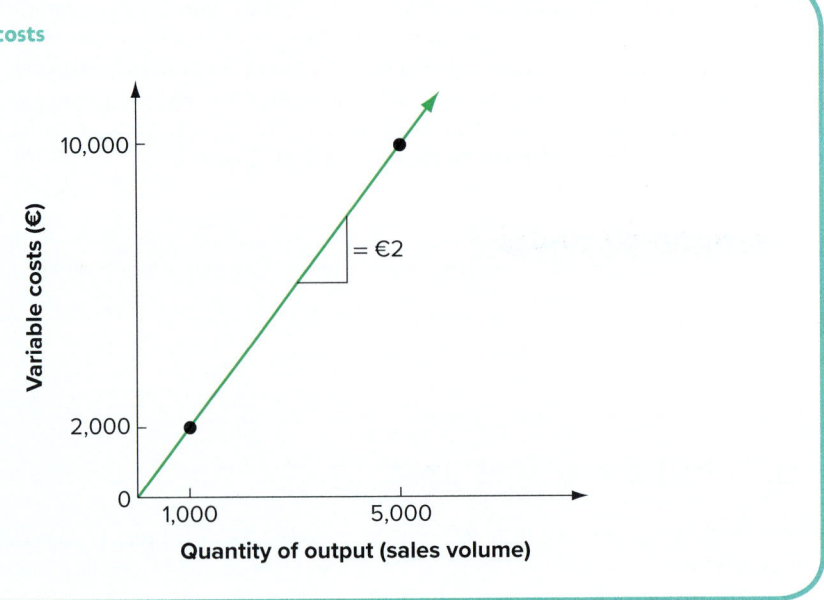

FIGURE 10.2 Output level and variable costs

> **EXAMPLE 10.1**
>
> ### VARIABLE COSTS
>
> Blume plc is a manufacturer of pencils. It has received an order for 5,000 pencils, and the company has to decide whether to accept the order. From recent experience, the company knows that each pencil requires £0.05 in raw materials and £0.50 in direct labour costs. These variable costs are expected to continue to apply in the future. What will Blume's total variable costs be if it accepts the order?
>
> In this case, the cost per unit is £0.50 in labour plus £0.05 in materials, for a total of £0.55 per unit. At 5,000 units of output, we have
>
> $$\begin{aligned} VC &= Q \times v \\ &= 5{,}000 \times £0.55 \\ &= £2{,}750 \end{aligned}$$
>
> Therefore total variable costs will be £2,750.

Fixed Costs

Fixed costs, by definition, do not change during a specified period. So, unlike variable costs, they do not depend on the amount of goods or services produced during a period (at least within some range of production). For example, the lease payment on a production facility and the company chairman's salary are fixed costs, at least over some period.

fixed costs costs that do not change when the quantity of output changes during a particular time period.

Naturally, fixed costs are not fixed forever. They are fixed only during some particular time, say a quarter or a year. Beyond that time, leases can be terminated and executives 'retired'. More to the point, any fixed cost can be modified or eliminated given enough time; so, in the long run, all costs are variable.

Notice that when a cost is fixed, that cost is effectively a sunk cost, because we are going to have to pay it no matter what.

Total Costs

Total costs (TC) for a given level of output are the sum of variable costs (VC) and fixed costs (FC):

$$\begin{aligned} TC &= VC + FC \\ &= v \times Q + FC \end{aligned}$$

So, for example, if we have variable costs of €3 per unit and fixed costs of €8,000 per year, our total cost is:

$$TC = €3 \times Q + €8{,}000$$

If we produce 6,000 units, our total production cost will be €3 × 6,000 + €8,000 = €26,000. At other production levels, we have the following:

Quantity produced	Total variable costs (€)	Fixed costs (€)	Total costs (€)
0	0	8,000	8,000
1,000	3,000	8,000	11,000
5,000	15,000	8,000	23,000
10,000	30,000	8,000	38,000

By plotting these points in Figure 10.3, we see that the relationship between quantity produced and total costs is given by a straight line. In Figure 10.3, notice that total costs equal fixed costs when sales are zero. Beyond that point, every one-unit increase in production leads to a €3 increase in total costs, so the slope of the line is 3. In other words, the **marginal, or incremental, cost** of producing one more unit is €3.

marginal or incremental cost the change in costs that occurs when there is a small change in output.

EXAMPLE 10.2

AVERAGE COST VERSUS MARGINAL COST

Suppose Blume plc has a variable cost per pencil of £0.55. The lease payment on the production facility is £5,000 per month. If Blume produces 100,000 pencils per year, what are the total costs of production? What is the average cost per pencil?

The fixed costs are £5,000 per month, or £60,000 per year. The variable cost is £0.55 per pencil. So the total cost for the year, assuming that Blume produces 100,000 pencils, is:

$$\text{Total cost} = v \times Q + FC$$
$$= £0.55 \times 100,000 + £60,000$$
$$= £115,000$$

The average cost per pencil is £115,000/100,000 = £1.15.

Now suppose that Blume has received a special, one-off order for 5,000 pencils. Blume has sufficient capacity to manufacture the 5,000 pencils on top of the 100,000 already produced so that no additional fixed costs will be incurred. Also, there will be no effect on existing orders. If Blume can get £0.75 per pencil for this order, should the order be accepted?

marginal or incremental revenue the change in revenue that occurs when there is a small change in output.

What this boils down to is a simple proposition. It costs £0.55 to make another pencil. Anything Blume can get for this pencil more than the £0.55 incremental cost contributes in a positive way towards covering fixed costs. The £0.75 **marginal, or incremental, revenue** exceeds the £0.55 marginal cost, so Blume should take the order.

The fixed cost of £60,000 is not relevant to this decision, because it is effectively sunk, at least for the current period. In the same way, the fact that the average cost is £1.15 is irrelevant, because this average reflects the fixed cost. As long as producing the extra 5,000 pencils truly does not cost anything beyond the £0.55 per pencil, then Blume should accept anything over £0.55.

FIGURE 10.3 Output level and total costs

ACCOUNTING BREAK-EVEN

The most widely used measure of break-even is **accounting break-even**. The accounting break-even point is simply the sales level that results in a zero project net income.

> **accounting break-even** the sales level that results in zero project net income.

To determine a project's accounting break-even, we start with some common sense. Suppose we retail USB flash drives for £5 apiece. We can buy drives from a wholesale supplier for £3 apiece. We have accounting expenses of £600 in fixed costs and £300 in depreciation. How many drives do we have to sell to break even – that is, for net income to be zero?

For every drive we sell, we pick up £5 − 3 = £2 towards covering our other expenses (this £2 difference between the selling price and the variable cost is often called the *contribution margin per unit*). We have to cover a total of £600 + 300 = £900 in accounting expenses, so we need to sell £900/2 = 450 drives. We can check this by noting that at a sales level of 450 units our revenues are £5 × 450 = £2,250 and our variable costs are £3 × 450 = £1,350. Thus here is the income statement:

Sales (£)	2,250
Variable costs (£)	1,350
Fixed costs (£)	600
Depreciation (£)	300
Profit before taxes (£)	0
Taxes (28%) (£)	0
Net income (£)	0

Remember, because we are discussing a proposed new project, we do not consider any interest expense in calculating net income or cash flow from the project. Also, notice that we include depreciation in calculating expenses here, even though depreciation is not a cash outflow. That is why we call it an *accounting* break-even. Finally, notice that when net income is zero, so are pre-tax income and, of course, taxes. In accounting terms, our revenues are equal to our costs, so there is no profit to tax.

Figure 10.4 presents another way to see what is happening. This figure looks a lot like Figure 10.3, except that we add a line for revenues. As indicated, total revenues are zero when output is zero. Beyond that, each unit sold brings in another £5, so the slope of the revenue line is 5.

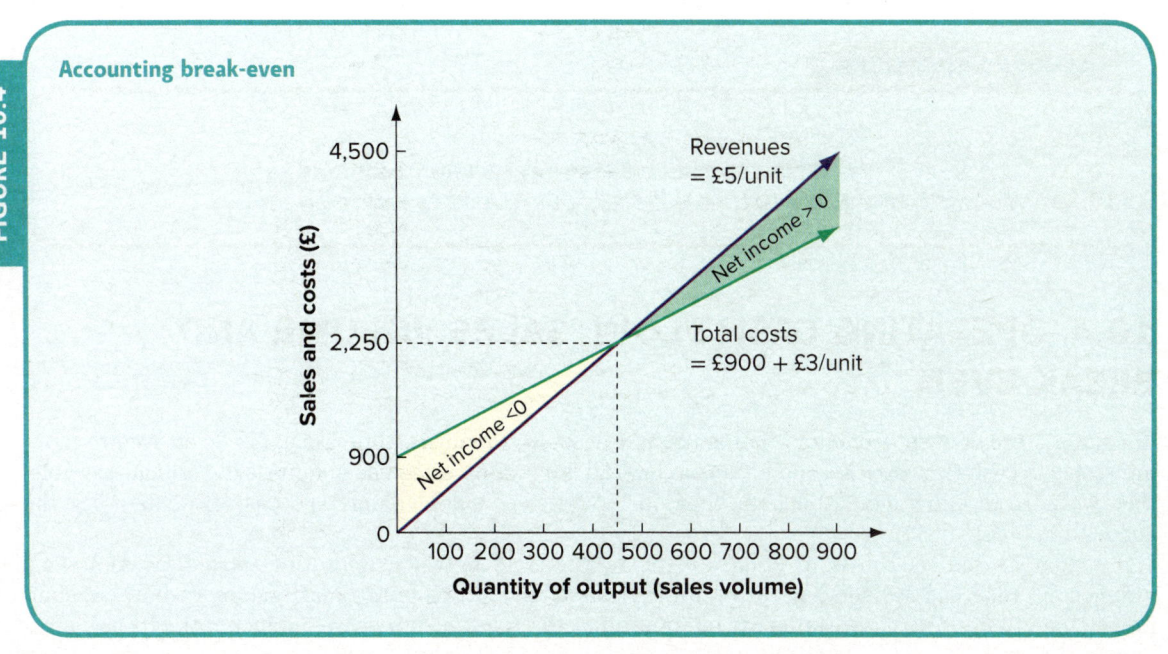

FIGURE 10.4 Accounting break-even

From our preceding discussion, we know that we break even when revenues are equal to total costs. The line for revenues and the line for total costs cross exactly where output is at 450 units. As illustrated, at any level of output below 450, our accounting profit is negative, and at any level above 450, we have a positive net income.

USES FOR THE ACCOUNTING BREAK-EVEN

Why would anyone be interested in knowing the accounting break-even point? To illustrate how it can be useful, suppose we are a small ice cream manufacturer with a strictly local distribution. We are thinking about expanding into new markets. Based on the estimated cash flows, we find that the expansion has a positive NPV.

Going back to our discussion of forecasting risk, we know that it is likely that what will make or break our expansion is sales volume. The reason is that in this case at least, we probably have a reasonably good idea of what we can charge for the ice cream. Further, we know relevant production and distribution costs reasonably well because we are already in the business. What we do not know with any real precision is how much ice cream we can sell.

Given the costs and selling price, however, we can immediately calculate the break-even point. Once we have done so, we might find that we need to get 30 per cent of the market to break even. If we think that this is unlikely to occur, because, for example, we have only 10 per cent of our current market, then we know our forecast is questionable, and there is a real possibility that the actual NPV is negative. On the other hand, we might find that we already have firm commitments from buyers for about the break-even amount, so we are almost sure we can sell more. In this case, the forecasting risk is much lower, and we have greater confidence in our estimates.

There are several other reasons why knowing the accounting break-even can be useful. First, as we shall discuss in more detail later, accounting break-even and payback period are similar measures. Like payback period, accounting break-even is relatively easy to calculate and explain.

Second, managers are often concerned with the contribution a project will make to the firm's total accounting earnings. A project that does not break even in an accounting sense reduces total earnings.

Third, a project that just breaks even on an accounting basis loses money in a financial or opportunity cost sense. This is true because we could have earned more by investing elsewhere. Such a project does not lose money in an out-of-pocket sense. As described in the following pages, we get back exactly what we put in. For non-economic reasons, opportunity losses may be easier to live with than out-of-pocket losses.

> **CONCEPT QUESTIONS**
>
> **10.3a** How are fixed costs similar to sunk costs?
> **10.3b** What is net income at the accounting break-even point? What about taxes?
> **10.3c** Why might a financial manager be interested in the accounting break-even point?

10.4 OPERATING CASH FLOW, SALES VOLUME AND BREAK-EVEN

Accounting break-even is one tool that is useful for project analysis. Ultimately, however, we are more interested in cash flow than in accounting income. So, for example, if sales volume is the critical variable, then we need to know more about the relationship between sales volume and cash flow than just the accounting break-even.

Our goal in this section is to illustrate the relationship between operating cash flow and sales volume. We also discuss some other break-even measures. To simplify matters somewhat, we shall ignore the effect of taxes. We start off by looking at the relationship between accounting break-even and cash flow.

ACCOUNTING BREAK-EVEN AND CASH FLOW

Now that we know how to find the accounting break-even, it is natural to wonder what happens with cash flow. To illustrate, suppose Wettway Yachts Ltd is considering whether to launch its new Margo-class yacht. The selling price will be £40,000 per boat. The variable costs will be about half that, or £20,000 per boat, and fixed costs will be £500,000 per year.

The Base Case

The total investment needed to undertake the project is £3,500,000. For simplicity, this amount will be depreciated straight-line to zero over the five-year life of the equipment.[1] The salvage value is zero, and there are no working capital consequences. Wettway has a 20 per cent required return on new projects.

Based on market surveys and historical experience, Wettway projects total sales for the five years at 425 boats, or about 85 boats per year. Ignoring taxes, should this project be launched?

To begin, ignoring taxes, the operating cash flow at 85 boats per year is:

$$\begin{aligned} \text{Operating cash flow} &= \text{EBIT} + \text{Depreciation} - \text{Taxes} \\ &= (S - VC - FC - D) + D - 0 \\ &= 85 \times (£40{,}000 - 20{,}000) - 500{,}000 \\ &= £1{,}200{,}000 \text{ per year} \end{aligned}$$

At 20 per cent, the five-year annuity factor is 2.9906, so the NPV is:

$$\begin{aligned} \text{NPV} &= -£3{,}500{,}000 + 1{,}200{,}000 \times 2.9906 \\ &= -£3{,}500{,}000 + 3{,}588{,}720 \\ &= £88{,}720 \end{aligned}$$

In the absence of additional information, the project should be launched.

Calculating the Break-Even Level

Looking a little closer at this project, you might ask a series of questions. For example, how many new boats does Wettway need to sell for the project to break even on an accounting basis? If Wettway does break even, what will be the annual cash flow from the project? What will be the return on the investment in this case?

Before fixed costs and depreciation are considered, Wettway generates £40,000 − 20,000 = £20,000 per boat (this is revenue less variable cost). Depreciation is £3,500,000/5 = £700,000 per year. Fixed costs and depreciation together total £1.2 million, so Wettway needs to sell $(FC + D)/(P - v)$ = £1.2 million/20,000 = 60 boats per year to break even on an accounting basis. This is 25 boats fewer than projected sales: so, assuming that Wettway is confident its projection is accurate to within, say, 15 boats, it appears unlikely that the new investment will fail to at least break even on an accounting basis.

To calculate Wettway's cash flow in this case, we note that if 60 boats are sold, net income will be exactly zero. Recalling from the previous chapter that operating cash flow for a project can be written as net income plus depreciation (the bottom-up definition), we can see that the operating cash flow is equal to the depreciation, or £700,000 in this case. The internal rate of return is exactly zero (why?).

Payback and Break-Even

As our example illustrates, whenever a project breaks even on an accounting basis, the cash flow for that period will equal the depreciation. This result makes perfect accounting sense. For example, suppose we invest £100,000 in a five-year project. The depreciation is straight-line to a zero salvage, or £20,000 per year. If the project exactly breaks even in every period, then the cash flow will be £20,000 per period.

The sum of the cash flows for the life of this project is 5 × £20,000 = £100,000, the original investment. What this shows is that a project's payback period is precisely equal to its life if the project breaks even in every period. Similarly, a project that does better than break even has a payback that is shorter than the life of the project and has a positive rate of return.

The bad news is that a project that just breaks even on an accounting basis has a negative NPV and a zero return. For our yacht project, the fact that Wettway will almost surely break even on an accounting basis is partially comforting, because it means that the firm's 'downside' risk (its potential loss) is limited. However, we still don't know whether the project is truly profitable. More work is needed.

SALES VOLUME AND OPERATING CASH FLOW

At this point, we can generalize our example and introduce some other break-even measures. From our discussion in the previous section, we know that ignoring taxes, a project's operating cash flow, OCF, can be written simply as EBIT plus depreciation:

$$\begin{aligned} \text{OCF} &= [(P - v) \times Q - \text{FC} - D] + D \\ &= (P - v) \times Q - \text{FC} \end{aligned} \quad (10.1)$$

For the Wettway yacht project, the general relationship (in thousands of pounds) between operating cash flow and sales volume is thus:

$$\begin{aligned} \text{OCF} &= (P - v) \times Q - FC \\ &= (£40 - 20) \times Q - 500 \\ &= -£500 + 20 \times Q \end{aligned}$$

What this tells us is that the relationship between operating cash flow and sales volume is given by a straight line with a slope of £20 and a y-intercept of −£500. If we calculate some different values, we get:

Quantity sold	Operating cash flow (£)
0	−500
15	−200
30	100
50	500
75	1,000

These points are plotted in Figure 10.5, where we have indicated three different break-even points. We discuss these next.

FIGURE 10.5

CASH FLOW, ACCOUNTING AND FINANCIAL BREAK-EVEN POINTS

We know from the preceding discussion that the relationship between operating cash flow and sales volume (ignoring taxes) is:

$$\text{OCF} = (P - v) \times Q - \text{FC}$$

If we rearrange this and solve for Q, we get:

$$Q = \frac{FC + OCF}{P - v} \qquad (10.2)$$

This tells us what sales volume (Q) is necessary to achieve any given OCF, so this result is more general than the accounting break-even. We use it to find the various break-even points in Figure 10.5.

Accounting Break-Even Revisited

Looking at Figure 10.5, suppose operating cash flow is equal to depreciation (D). Recall that this situation corresponds to our break-even point on an accounting basis. To find the sales volume, we substitute the £700 depreciation amount for OCF in our general expression:

$$\begin{aligned} Q &= (FC + OCF)/(P - v) \\ &= (£500 + 700)/20 \\ &= 60 \end{aligned}$$

This is the same quantity we had before.

Cash Break-Even

We have seen that a project that breaks even on an accounting basis has a net income of zero, but it still has a positive cash flow. At some sales level below the accounting break-even, the operating cash flow goes negative. This is a particularly unpleasant occurrence. If it happens, we have to supply additional cash to the project to keep it afloat.

To calculate the **cash break-even** (the point where operating cash flow is equal to zero), we put in a zero for OCF:

> **cash break-even** the sales level that results in a zero operating cash flow.

$$\begin{aligned} Q &= (FC + 0)/(P - v) \\ &= £500/20 \\ &= 25 \end{aligned}$$

Wettway must therefore sell 25 boats to cover the £500 in fixed costs. As we show in Figure 10.5, this point occurs exactly where the operating cash flow line crosses the horizontal axis.

Notice that a project that just breaks even on a cash flow basis can cover its own fixed operating costs, but that is all. It never pays back anything, so the original investment is a complete loss (the IRR is −100 per cent).

Financial Break-Even

The last case we consider is that of **financial break-even**, the sales level that results in a zero NPV. To the financial manager, this is the most interesting case. What we do is first determine what the operating cash flow has to be for the NPV to be zero. We then use this amount to determine the sales volume.

> **financial break-even** the sales level that results in a zero NPV.

To illustrate, recall that Wettway requires a 20 per cent return on its £3,500 (in thousands) investment. How many yachts does Wettway have to sell to break even once we account for the 20 per cent per year opportunity cost?

The yacht project has a five-year life. The project has a zero NPV when the present value of the operating cash flows equals the £3,500 investment. Because the cash flow is the same each year, we can solve for the unknown amount by viewing it as an ordinary annuity. The five-year annuity factor at 20 per cent is 2.9906, and the OCF can be determined as follows:

$$\begin{aligned} £3,500 &= OCF \times 2.9906 \\ OCF &= £3,500/2.9906 \\ &= £1,170 \end{aligned}$$

Wettway thus needs an operating cash flow of £1,170 each year to break even. We can now plug this OCF into the equation for sales volume:

$$\begin{aligned} Q &= (£500 + 1,170)/20 \\ &= 83.5 \end{aligned}$$

So, Wettway needs to sell about 84 boats per year. This is not good news.

As indicated in Figure 10.5, the financial break-even is substantially higher than the accounting break-even. This will often be the case. Moreover, what we have discovered is that the yacht project has a substantial degree of forecasting risk. We project sales of 85 boats per year, but it takes 84 to earn the required return.

Conclusion

Overall, it seems unlikely that the Wettway yacht project would fail to break even on an accounting basis. However, there appears to be a good chance that the true NPV is negative. This illustrates the danger in looking at just the accounting break-even.

What should Wettway do? Is the new project all wet? The decision at this point is essentially a managerial issue – a judgement call. The crucial questions are these:

1. How much confidence do we have in our projections?
2. How important is the project for the future of the company?
3. How badly will the company be hurt if sales turn out to be low? What options are available to the company in this case?

We shall consider questions such as these in a later section. For future reference, our discussion of the different break-even measures is summarized in Table 10.1.

TABLE 10.1

Summary of break-even measures

The general break-even expression

Ignoring taxes, the relation between operating cash flow (OCF) and quantity of output or sales volume (Q) is:

$$Q = \frac{FC + OCF}{P - v}$$

where:
- FC = Total fixed costs
- P = Price per unit
- v = Variable cost per unit

As shown next, this relation can be used to determine the accounting, cash, and financial break-even points.

The accounting break-even point

Accounting break-even occurs when net income is zero. Operating cash flow is equal to depreciation when net income is zero, so the accounting break-even point is:

$$Q = \frac{FC + D}{P - v}$$

A project that always just breaks even on an accounting basis has a payback exactly equal to its life, a negative NPV, and an IRR of zero.

The cash break-even point

Cash break-even occurs when operating cash flow is zero. The cash break-even point is thus:

$$Q = \frac{FC}{P - v}$$

A project that always just breaks even on a cash basis never pays back, has an NPV that is negative and equal to the initial outlay, and has an IRR of −100 per cent.

The financial break-even point

Financial break-even occurs when the NPV of the project is zero. The financial break-even point is thus:

$$Q = \frac{FC + OCF^*}{P - v}$$

where OCF^* is the level of OCF that results in a zero NPV. A project that breaks even on a financial basis has a discounted payback equal to its life, a zero NPV, and an IRR just equal to the required return.

> **CONCEPT QUESTIONS**
>
> **10.4a** If a project breaks even on an accounting basis, what is its operating cash flow?
> **10.4b** If a project breaks even on a cash basis, what is its operating cash flow?
> **10.4c** If a project breaks even on a financial basis, what do you know about its *discounted* payback?

10.5 OPERATING LEVERAGE

We have discussed how to calculate and interpret various measures of break-even for a proposed project. What we have not explicitly discussed is what determines these points, and how they might be changed. We now turn to this subject.

THE BASIC IDEA

Operating leverage is the degree to which a project or firm is committed to fixed production costs. A firm with low operating leverage will have low fixed costs compared with a firm with high operating leverage. Generally speaking, projects with a relatively heavy investment in plant and equipment will have a relatively high degree of operating leverage. Such projects are said to be *capital intensive*.

> **operating leverage** the degree to which a firm or project relies on fixed costs.

Whenever we are thinking about a new venture, there will normally be alternative ways of producing and delivering the product. For example, Wettway can purchase the necessary equipment and build all the components for its yachts in-house. Alternatively, some of the work could be farmed out to other firms. The first option involves a greater investment in plant and equipment, greater fixed costs and depreciation, and, as a result, a higher degree of operating leverage.

IMPLICATIONS OF OPERATING LEVERAGE

Regardless of how it is measured, operating leverage has important implications for project evaluation. Fixed costs act as a lever in the sense that a small percentage change in operating revenue can be magnified into a large percentage change in operating cash flow and NPV. This explains why we call it operating 'leverage'.

The higher the degree of operating leverage, the greater is the potential danger from forecasting risk. The reason is that relatively small errors in forecasting sales volume can get magnified, or 'levered up', into large errors in cash flow projections.

From a managerial perspective, one way of coping with highly uncertain projects is to keep the degree of operating leverage as low as possible. This will generally have the effect of maintaining the break-even point (however measured) at its minimum level. We shall illustrate this point shortly, but first, we need to discuss how to measure operating leverage.

MEASURING OPERATING LEVERAGE

One way of measuring operating leverage is to ask: if quantity sold rises by 5 per cent, what will be the percentage change in operating cash flow? In other words, the **degree of operating leverage (DOL)** is defined such that:

> **degree of operating leverage (DOL)** the percentage change in operating cash flow relative to the percentage change in quantity sold.

$$\text{Percentage change in OCF} = \text{DOL} \times \text{Percentage change in } Q$$

Based on the relationship between OCF and Q, DOL can be written as[2]:

$$\text{DOL} = 1 + \text{FC/OCF} \qquad (10.3)$$

The ratio FC/OCF simply measures fixed costs as a percentage of total operating cash flow. Notice that zero fixed costs would result in a DOL of 1, implying that percentage changes in quantity sold would show up one for one in operating cash flow. In other words, no magnification, or leverage, effect would exist.

To illustrate this measure of operating leverage, we go back to the Wettway yacht project. Fixed costs were £500 and $(P - v)$ was £20, so OCF was:

$$\text{OCF} = -£500 + 20 \times Q$$

Suppose Q is currently 50 boats. At this level of output, OCF is $-£500 + 1,000 = £500$.

If Q rises by 1 unit to 51, then the percentage change in Q is $(51 - 50)/50 = 0.02$, or 2 per cent. OCF rises to £520, a change of $P - v = £20$. The percentage change in OCF is $(£520 - 500)/500 = 0.04$, or 4 per cent. So a 2 per cent increase in the number of boats sold leads to a 4 per cent increase in operating cash flow. The degree of operating leverage must be exactly 2.00. We can check this by noting that:

$$\begin{aligned} \text{DOL} &= 1 + \text{FC}/\text{OCF} \\ &= 1 + £500/500 \\ &= 2 \end{aligned}$$

This verifies our previous calculations.

Our formulation of DOL depends on the current output level, Q. However, it can handle changes from the current level of any size, not just one unit. For example, suppose Q rises from 50 to 75, a 50 per cent increase. With DOL equal to 2, operating cash flow should increase by 100 per cent, or exactly double. Does it? The answer is yes, because, at a Q of 75, OCF is:

$$\text{OCF} = -£500 + 20 \times 75 = £1,000$$

Notice that operating leverage declines as output (Q) rises. For example, at an output level of 75, we have:

$$\text{DOL} = 1 + £500/1,000 = 1.50$$

The reason why DOL declines is that fixed costs, considered as a percentage of operating cash flow, get smaller and smaller, so the leverage effect diminishes.

EXAMPLE 10.3

OPERATING LEVERAGE

VisorX Ltd currently sells eco-friendly workplace sanitization consumables. Each sanitization consumable is sold for £3.50 per application with a variable cost of £2 per application. Marketing and packaging operations have fixed costs of £400,000 per year. Depreciation is £50,000 per year. What is the accounting break-even? Ignoring taxes, what will be the increase in operating cash flow if the quantity sold rises to 10 per cent above the break-even point?

The accounting break-even is £450,000/1.50 = 300,000 applications. As we know, the operating cash flow is equal to the £50,000 depreciation at this level of production, so the degree of operating leverage is:

$$\begin{aligned} \text{DOL} &= 1 + \text{FC}/\text{OCF} \\ &= 1 + £400,000/50,000 \\ &= 9 \end{aligned}$$

Given this, a 10 per cent increase in the number of sanitization applications sold will increase operating cash flow by a substantial 90 per cent.

To check this answer, we note that if sales rise by 10 per cent, then the quantity sold will rise to 300,000 × 1.1 = 330,000. Ignoring taxes, the operating cash flow will be 330,000 × £1.50 − 400,000 = £95,000. Compared with the £50,000 cash flow we had, this is exactly 90 per cent more: £95,000/50,000 = 1.90.

OPERATING LEVERAGE AND BREAK-EVEN

We illustrate why operating leverage is an important consideration by examining the Wettway yacht project under an alternative scenario. At a Q of 85 boats, the degree of operating leverage for the yacht project under the original scenario is:

$$DOL = 1 + FC/OCF$$
$$= 1 + £500/1,200$$
$$= 1.42$$

Also, recall that the NPV at a sales level of 85 boats was £88,720 and that the accounting break-even was 60 boats.

An option available to Wettway is to subcontract production of the boat hull assemblies. If the company does this, the necessary investment falls to £3,200,000 and the fixed operating costs fall to £180,000. However, variable costs will rise to £25,000 per boat, because subcontracting is more expensive than producing in-house. Ignoring taxes, evaluate this option.

For practice, see if you don't agree with the following:

NPV at 20% (85 units) = £74,720
Accounting break-even = 55 boats
Degree of operating leverage = 1.16

What has happened? This option results in a slightly lower estimated NPV, and the accounting break-even point falls to 55 boats from 60 boats.

Given that this alternative has the lower NPV, is there any reason to consider it further? Perhaps there is. The degree of operating leverage is substantially lower in the second case. If Wettway is worried about the possibility of an overly optimistic projection, then it might prefer to subcontract.

There is another reason why Wettway might consider the second arrangement. If sales turned out to be better than expected, the company would always have the option of starting to produce in-house at a later date. As a practical matter, it is much easier to increase operating leverage (by purchasing equipment) than to decrease it (by selling off equipment). As we discuss in a later chapter, one of the drawbacks of discounted cash flow analysis is that it is difficult to explicitly include options of this sort in the analysis, even though they may be quite important.

> **CONCEPT QUESTIONS**
>
> **10.5a** What is operating leverage?
> **10.5b** How is operating leverage measured?
> **10.5c** What are the implications of operating leverage for the financial manager?

10.6 CAPITAL RATIONING

Capital rationing is said to exist when we have profitable (positive-NPV) investments available, but we can't get the funds needed to undertake them. For example, as division managers for a large corporation, we might identify €5 million in excellent projects, but find that, for whatever reason, we can spend only €2 million. Now what? Unfortunately, for reasons we shall discuss, there may be no truly satisfactory answer.

SOFT RATIONING

The situation we have just described is called **soft rationing**. This occurs when, for example, different units in a business are allocated some fixed amount of money each year for capital spending. Such an allocation is primarily a means of controlling and keeping track of overall expenditure. The important thing to note about soft rationing is that the corporation as a whole isn't short of capital; more can be raised if management so desires.

If we face soft rationing, the first thing to do is to try to get a larger allocation. Failing that, one common suggestion is to generate as large an NPV as possible within the existing budget. This amounts to choosing projects with the largest benefit–cost ratio (profitability index).

> **capital rationing** the situation that exists if a firm has positive-NPV projects but cannot find the necessary financing.

> **soft rationing** the situation that occurs when units in a business are allocated a certain amount of financing for capital budgeting.

Strictly speaking, this is the correct thing to do only if the soft rationing is a one-time event – that is if it won't exist next year. If soft rationing is a chronic problem, then something is amiss. The reason goes back to Chapter 1. Ongoing soft rationing means we are continually bypassing positive-NPV investments, and this contradicts our goal of the firm. If we are not trying to maximize value, then the question of which projects to take becomes ambiguous, because we no longer have an objective goal in the first place.

HARD RATIONING

> **hard rationing** the situation that occurs when a business cannot raise financing for a project under any circumstances.

With **hard rationing**, a business cannot raise capital for a project under any circumstances. For healthy corporations, this situation probably does not occur very often. This is fortunate because, with hard rationing, our DCF analysis breaks down, and the best course of action is ambiguous.

The reason why DCF analysis breaks down has to do with the required return. Suppose we say our required return is 20 per cent. Implicitly, we are saying we shall take a project with a return that exceeds this. However, if we face hard rationing, then we are not going to take a new project, no matter what the return on that project is, so the whole concept of a required return is ambiguous. About the only interpretation we can give this situation is that the required return is so large that no project has a positive NPV in the first place.

Hard rationing can occur when a company experiences financial distress, meaning that bankruptcy is a possibility. Also, a firm may not be able to raise capital without violating a pre-existing contractual agreement. We discuss these situations in greater detail in a later chapter.

SUSTAINABILITY IN FINANCE

With the oil price tumbling to levels not seen in years (it was negative in April 2020!), most European oil firms have had no choice but to pull back on planned investments. Revenue forecasts have been reined back, and concomitant planned expenditures have been halted, with redundancy programmes now standard in the sector.

Oil extraction costs vary from site to site and depend upon the difficulty in getting the commodity out of the ground. Whereas the average cost of oil extraction in Saudi Arabia is less than $20 a barrel, in Norway and the North Sea, it is more than double that amount. As a result, very few European oil projects are viable with sub-$30 barrel prices, and there is little appetite for expenditure on these types of investments.

What can oil companies do in such a harsh environment? In response to low revenue projections, many oil firms are exploring alternative and very agile operating models that return profitability even with depressed oil prices. Some oil companies have started to explore alternative renewable energy sources, like water, solar and wind power. Over time, these firms will expand, and capital will return to the sector for investment. As with any severe downturn, the most efficient and well-run companies will survive and form the foundation for future economic growth. Unfortunately, there will be many companies that find it too difficult to adapt, and their future is much less certain.

Source: Reuters, FT.com.

CONCEPT QUESTIONS

10.6a What is capital rationing? What types are there?
10.6b What problems does capital rationing create for discounted cash flow analysis?

SUMMARY AND CONCLUSIONS

In this chapter, we looked at some ways of evaluating the results of a discounted cash flow analysis; we also touched on some of the problems that can come up in practice:

1. Net present value estimates depend on projected future cash flows. If there are errors in those projections, then our estimated NPVs can be misleading. We called this possibility *forecasting risk*.
2. Scenario and sensitivity analysis are useful tools for identifying which variables are critical to the success of a project, and where forecasting problems can do the most damage.
3. Break-even analysis in its various forms is a particularly common type of scenario analysis that is useful for identifying critical levels of sales.
4. Operating leverage is a key determinant of break-even levels. It reflects the degree to which a project or a firm is committed to fixed costs. The degree of operating leverage tells us the sensitivity of operating cash flow to changes in sales volume.
5. Projects usually have future managerial options associated with them. These options may be important, but standard discounted cash flow analysis tends to ignore them.
6. Capital rationing occurs when profitable projects cannot be funded. Standard discounted cash flow analysis is troublesome in this case because NPV is not necessarily the appropriate criterion.

The most important thing to carry away from reading this chapter is that estimated NPVs or returns should not be taken at face value. They depend critically on projected cash flows. If there is room for significant disagreement about those projected cash flows, the results from the analysis have to be taken with a pinch of salt.

Despite the problems we have discussed, discounted cash flow analysis is still *the* way of attacking problems because it forces us to ask the right questions. What we have learned in this chapter is that knowing the questions to ask does not guarantee we shall get all the answers.

CHAPTER REVIEW AND SELF-TEST PROBLEMS

Use the following base-case information to work the self-test problems:

A project under consideration costs €750,000, has a five-year life and has no salvage value. Depreciation is straight-line to zero. The required return is 17 per cent, and the tax rate is 34 per cent. Sales are projected at 500 units per year. Price per unit is €2,500, variable cost per unit is €1,500, and fixed costs are €200,000 per year.

10.1 Scenario Analysis Suppose you think that the unit sales, price, variable cost and fixed cost projections given here are accurate to within 5 per cent. What are the upper and lower bounds for these projections? What is the base-case NPV? What are the best- and worst-case scenario NPVs?

10.2 Break-Even Analysis Given the base-case projections in the previous problem, what are the cash, accounting and financial break-even sales levels for this project? Ignore taxes in answering.

SOLUTIONS

10.1 We can summarize the relevant information as follows:

	Base case	Lower bound	Upper bound
Unit sales	500	475	525
Price per unit (€)	2,500	2,375	2,625
Variable cost per unit (€)	1,500	1,425	1,575
Fixed cost per year (€)	200,000	190,000	210,000

Depreciation is €150,000 per year; knowing this, we can calculate the cash flows under each scenario. Remember that we assign high costs and low prices and volume for the worst case, and just the opposite for the best case:

Scenario	Unit sales	Unit price (€)	Unit variable cost (€)	Fixed costs (€)	Cash flow (€)
Base case	500	2,500	1,500	200,000	249,000
Best case	525	2,625	1,425	190,000	341,400
Worst case	475	2,375	1,575	210,000	163,200

At 17 per cent the five-year annuity factor is 3.19935, so the NPVs are:

$$\begin{aligned}
\text{Base-case NPV} &= -€750,000 + 3.19935 \times €249,000 \\
&= €46,638 \\
\text{Best-case NPV} &= -€750,000 + 3.19935 \times €341,400 \\
&= €342,258 \\
\text{Worst-case NPV} &= -€750,000 + 3.19935 \times €163,200 \\
&= -€227,866
\end{aligned}$$

10.2 In this case we have €200,000 in cash fixed costs to cover. Each unit contributes €2,500 − 1,500 = €1,000 towards covering fixed costs. The cash break-even is thus €200,000/€1,000 = 200 units. We have another €150,000 in depreciation, so the accounting break-even is (€200,000 + 150,000)/€1,000 = 350 units.

To get the financial break-even, we need to find the OCF such that the project has a zero NPV. As we have seen, the five-year annuity factor is 3.19935 and the project costs €750,000, so the OCF must be such that:

$$€750,000 = \text{OCF} \times 3.19935$$

So, for the project to break even on a financial basis, the project's cash flow must be €750,000/3.19935, or €234,423 per year. If we add this to the €200,000 in cash fixed costs, we get a total of €434,423 that we have to cover. At €1,000 per unit, we need to sell €434,423/€1,000 = 435 units.

QUESTIONS AND PROBLEMS

10.1 Calculating Costs and Break-Even Rolling Stone (RS) quarries quartz. The variable materials cost is €2.50 per unit, and the variable labour cost is €4.90 per unit.

(a) What is the variable cost per unit?

(b) Suppose RS incurs fixed costs of €500,000 during a year in which total production is 300,000 units. What are the total costs for the year?

(c) If the selling price is €25 per unit, does RS break even on a cash basis? If depreciation is €200,000 per year, what is the accounting break-even point?

10.2 Computing Average Cost Makaveli SpA can manufacture mountain climbing shoes for €24.86 per pair in variable raw material costs and €14.08 per pair in variable labour expense. The shoes sell for €135 per pair. Last year, production was 120,000 pairs. Fixed costs were €1,550,000. What were total production costs? What is the marginal cost per pair? What is the average cost? If the company is considering a one-time order for an extra 5,000 pairs, what is the minimum acceptable total revenue from the order? Explain.

10.3 Scenario Analysis You have been given the following figures to assess the viability of a new portable hospital scanner. It is expected you will capture 10 per cent of the total market of 1.1 million units. The market price will be €400,000 and the unit variable cost is 90 per cent of the market price. Fixed costs of running and manufacture amount to €2 billion per annum.

(a) What is the net income of the project?

(b) You have been approached by management, who disagree on the figures that were originally used in the analysis. They want you to consider the following scenarios proposed by different Directors in the company. Carry out a sensitivity analysis of the project. What are the main uncertainties in the project?

	Director A	Director B	Director C
Market size	0.8 million	1 million	1.2 million
Market share (%)	4	10	16
Unit price (€)	300,000	375,000	400,000
Variable cost (%)	116	80	70
Fixed cost (€)	5 billion	3 billion	1 billion

10.4 Sensitivity Analysis For the company in the previous problem, suppose management is most concerned about the impact of its price estimate on the project's profitability. How could you address this concern? Describe how you would calculate your answer. What values would you use for the other forecast variables?

10.5 Sensitivity Analysis and Break-Even A retail clothing firm is evaluating the development of a new range of all-weather coats. These coats contain an internal solar battery to provide heating whenever the garment is worn. The solar battery cost £3.2 million to make and the expectation is that the project will last for five years. At the end of the project, the machinery to make the battery will be worthless because of new technological developments. Assume that depreciation is 20 per cent reducing-balance method. Sales are projected at 250,000 units per year. Price per battery is £10, variable cost per unit is £2.50, and fixed costs are £900,000 per year. The tax rate is 23 per cent, and we require a 13 per cent return on this project.

(a) Calculate the accounting break-even point.

(b) Calculate the base-case cash flow and NPV. What is the sensitivity of NPV to changes in the sales figure? Explain what your answer tells you about a 50,000-unit decrease in projected sales.

(c) What is the sensitivity of OCF to changes in the variable cost figure? Explain what your answer tells you about a £2 decrease in estimated variable costs.

10.6 Scenario Analysis A retail clothing firm is evaluating the development of a new range of all-weather coats. These coats contain an internal solar battery to provide heating whenever the garment is worn. The solar battery cost £3.2 million to make and the expectation is that the project will last for five years. At the end of the project, the machinery to make the battery will be worthless because of new technological developments. Assume that depreciation is 20 per cent reducing-balance method. Sales are projected at 250,000 units per year. Price per battery is £10, variable cost per unit is £1.50, and fixed costs are £900,000 per year. The tax rate is 23 per cent, and we require a 13 per cent return on this project. Suppose the projections given for price, quantity, variable costs and fixed costs are all accurate to within ±10 per cent. Calculate the best-case and worst-case NPV figures.

10.7 Calculating Break-Even L.J.'s Toys just purchased a £200,000 machine to produce toy cars. The machine will be fully depreciated using 20 per cent reducing balances over its five-year economic life. Each toy sells for £25. The variable cost per toy is £5, and the firm incurs fixed costs of £350,000 each year. The corporate tax rate for the company is 25 per cent. The appropriate discount rate is 12 per cent.

What is the financial break-even point for the project?

10.8 Calculating Break-Even You are considering investing in a company that cultivates truffles for sale to local restaurants. Use the following information:

Sales price per truffle	£100.00
Variable cost per truffle	£72.00
Fixed costs per year	£340,000
Depreciation per year	£20,000
Tax rate	35%

The discount rate for the company is 15 per cent, the initial investment in truffle-detecting equipment is £140,000, and the project's economic life is seven years. Assume, for simplicity, that the equipment is depreciated on a straight-line basis over the project's life.

(a) What is the accounting break-even level for the project?

(b) What is the financial break-even level for the project?

10.9 Calculating Break-Even You are considering investing in a company that cultivates abalone for sale to local restaurants. The discount rate for the company is 15 per cent, the initial investment in equipment is £140,000, and the project's economic life is seven years. Assume, for simplicity, that the equipment is depreciated on a straight-line basis over the project's life.

(a) What is the accounting break-even level for the project?

(b) What is the financial break-even level for the project?

Use the following information:

Sales price per abalone	£2.00
Variable cost per abalone	£0.72
Fixed costs per year	£340,000
Depreciation per year	£20,000
Tax rate	18%

10.10 Using Break-Even Analysis Consider a project with the following data: accounting break-even quantity = 15,500 units; cash break-even quantity = 13,200 units; life = 5 years; fixed costs = £140,000; variable costs = £24 per unit; required return = 16 per cent. Ignoring the effect of taxes, find the financial break-even quantity.

10.11 Calculating Operating Leverage At an output level of 100,000 units, you calculate that the degree of operating leverage is 3.40. If output falls to 80,000 units, what will the percentage change in operating cash flow be? Will the new level of operating leverage be higher or lower? Explain.

10.12 Leverage In the previous problem, suppose fixed costs are £130,000. What is the operating cash flow at 58,000 units? The degree of operating leverage?

10.13 Operating Cash Flow and Leverage Bellstar manufacturing is planning a restructuring of operations. The company has fixed costs of £320,000 per year. The operating cash flow at 20,000 units is £400,000. Ignoring the effect of taxes, what is the degree of operating leverage? If units sold rise from 20,000 to 25,000 as a result of the restructuring, what will be the increase in operating cash flow? What is the new degree of operating leverage?

10.14 Cash Flow and Leverage At an output level of 10,000 units, you have calculated that the degree of operating leverage is 2.1. The operating cash flow is £43,000 in this case. Ignoring the effect of taxes, what are fixed costs? What will the operating cash flow be if output rises to 11,000 units? If output falls to 9,000 units?

10.15 Leverage In the previous problem, what will be the new degree of operating leverage in each case?

10.16 Break-Even Intuition Consider a project with a required return of R per cent that costs £I and will last for N years. The project uses straight-line depreciation to zero over the N-year life; there is no salvage value or net working capital requirements.

(a) At the accounting break-even level of output, what is the IRR of this project? The payback period? The NPV?

(b) At the cash break-even level of output, what is the IRR of this project? The payback period? The NPV?

(c) At the financial break-even level of output, what is the IRR of this project? The payback period? The NPV?

10.17 Sensitivity Analysis Consider a project to supply Italy with 40,000 tons of machine screws annually for automobile production. You will need an initial €1,500,000 investment in threading equipment to get the project started; the project will last for five years. The accounting department estimates that annual fixed costs will be €600,000 and that variable costs should be €210 per ton; accounting will depreciate the initial fixed asset investment using 20 per cent reducing-balance method over the five-year project life. It also estimates a salvage value of €800,000 after dismantling costs. The marketing department estimates that the automakers will let the contract at a selling price of €230 per ton. The engineering department estimates you will need an initial net working capital investment of €450,000. You require a 13 per cent return and face a marginal tax rate of 32 per cent on this project.

(a) Suppose you are confident about your own projections, but you are a little unsure about Italy's actual machine screw requirement. What is the sensitivity of the project OCF to changes in the quantity supplied?

(b) What about the sensitivity of NPV to changes in quantity supplied?

(c) Given the sensitivity number you calculated, is there some minimum level of output below which you would not want to operate? Why?

10.18 Operating Leverage In the previous problem, what is the degree of operating leverage at the given level of output? What is the degree of operating leverage at the accounting break-even level of output?

10.19 Project Analysis You are considering a new product launch. The project will cost £1,700,000, have a four-year life, and have no salvage value; depreciation is 20 per cent reducing-balance. Sales are projected at 190 units per year; price per unit will be £18,000, variable cost per unit will be £11,200, and fixed costs will be £410,000 per year. The required return on the project is 12 per cent, and the relevant tax rate is 28 per cent.

  (a) Based on your experience, you think the unit sales, variable cost and fixed cost projections given here are probably accurate to within ±10 per cent. What are the upper and lower bounds for these projections? What is the base-case NPV? What are the best-case and worst-case scenarios?

  (b) Evaluate the sensitivity of your base-case NPV to changes in fixed costs.

  (c) What is the cash break-even level of output for this project (ignoring taxes)?

  (d) What is the accounting break-even level of output for this project? What is the degree of operating leverage at the accounting break-even point? How do you interpret this number?

10.20 Project Analysis McGilla Golf has decided to sell a new line of golf clubs. The clubs will sell for £700 per set and have a variable cost of £320 per set. The company has spent £150,000 for a marketing study that determined the company will sell 55,000 sets per year for seven years. The marketing study also determined that the company will lose sales of 13,000 sets of its high-priced clubs. The high-priced clubs sell at £1,100 and have variable costs of £600. The company will also increase sales of its cheap clubs by 10,000 sets. The cheap clubs sell for £400 and have variable costs of £180 per set. The fixed costs each year will be £7,500,000. The company has also spent £1,000,000 on research and development for the new clubs. The plant and equipment required will cost £18,200,000 and will be depreciated on a 20 per cent reducing-balance basis. At the end of the seven years, the salvage value of the plant and equipment will be equal to the written down or residual value. The new clubs will also require an increase in net working capital of £950,000 that will be returned at the end of the project. The tax rate is 28 per cent, and the cost of capital is 14 per cent. Calculate the payback period, the NPV and the IRR for base case.

10.21 Scenario Analysis In the previous problem, you feel that the values are accurate to within only ±10 per cent. What are the best-case and worst-case NPVs? (*Hint:* The price and variable costs for the two existing sets of clubs are known with certainty; only the sales gained or lost are uncertain.)

10.22 Sensitivity Analysis McGilla Golf would like to know the sensitivity of NPV to changes in the price of the new clubs and the quantity of new clubs sold. What is the sensitivity of the NPV to each of these variables?

10.23 Break-Even Analysis Hybrid cars are touted as a green alternative; however, the financial aspects of hybrid ownership are not as clear. Consider the Toyota Prius Hatchback, which had a list price of £18,390 (including tax consequences) compared with an equivalent Toyota Corolla with a list price of £15,855. Additionally, the annual ownership costs (other than fuel) for the Prius are expected to be £300 more than the Corolla. The EPA mileage estimate was 40 km/l for the Prius and 32 km/l for the Corolla.

  (a) Assume that fuel costs are £1.03 per litre, and you plan to keep either car for six years. How many kilometres per year would you need to drive to make the decision to buy the Prius worthwhile, ignoring the time value of money?

  (b) If you drive 15,000 miles per year and keep either car for six years, what price per litre would make the decision to buy the Prius worthwhile, ignoring the time value of money?

  (c) Rework parts (a) and (b) assuming the appropriate interest rate is 10 per cent and all cash flows occur at the end of the year.

  (d) What assumption did the analysis in the previous parts make about the resale value of each car?

10.24 Break-Even Analysis In an effort to capture the large jet market, Airbus invested €10.2 billion developing its A380, which is capable of carrying 800 passengers. The plane has a list price of €206 million. In discussing the plane, Airbus stated that the company would break even when 249 A380s were sold.

(a) Assuming the break-even sales figure given is the cash flow break-even, what is the cash flow per plane?

(b) Airbus promised its shareholders a 20 per cent rate of return on the investment. If sales of the plane continue in perpetuity, how many planes must the company sell per year to deliver on this promise?

(c) Suppose instead that the sales of the A380 last for only 10 years. How many planes must Airbus sell per year to deliver the same rate of return?

10.25 Break-Even and Taxes This problem concerns the effect of taxes on the various break-even measures.

(a) Show that, assuming straight-line depreciation, when we consider taxes, the general relationship between operating cash flow, OCF, and sales volume, Q, can be written as:

$$Q = \frac{FC + (OCF - T \times D/(1 - T)}{P - v}$$

(b) Use the expression in part (a) to find the cash, accounting and financial break-even points for the Wettway yacht example in the chapter. Assume a 38 per cent tax rate.

(c) In part (b), the accounting break-even should be the same as before. Why? Verify this algebraically.

10.26 Operating Leverage and Taxes Show that if we consider the effect of taxes, the degree of operating leverage can be written as:

$$DOL = 1 + \frac{FC \times (1 - T) - T \times D}{OCF}$$

Assume straight-line depreciation. Notice that this reduces to our previous result if $T = 0$. Can you interpret this in words?

10.27 Scenario Analysis Refer to the information in Problem 10.17 when answering this question.

(a) What is the estimated OCF for this project? The NPV? Should you pursue this project?

(b) Suppose you believe that the accounting department's initial cost and salvage value projections are accurate only to within ±15 per cent; the marketing department's price estimate is accurate only to within ±10 per cent; and the engineering department's net working capital estimate is accurate only to within ±5 per cent. What is your worst-case scenario for this project? Your best-case scenario? Do you still want to pursue the project?

10.28 Sensitivity Analysis In Problem 10.27, suppose you are confident about your own projections, but you're a little unsure about Italy's actual machine screw requirement. What is the sensitivity of the project OCF to changes in the quantity supplied? What about the sensitivity of NPV to changes in quantity supplied? Given the sensitivity number you calculated, is there some minimum level of output below which you wouldn't want to operate? Why?

10.29 Break-Even Analysis The Wheatchopper Company is considering the purchase of a new harvester. Wheatchopper has hired you to determine the break-even purchase price in terms of present value of the harvester. This break-even purchase price is the price at which the projects NPV is zero.

Base your analysis on the following facts:

- The new harvester is not expected to affect revenues, but pre-tax operating expenses will be reduced by €10,000 per year for 10 years.

- The old harvester is now 5 years old, with 10 years of its scheduled life remaining. It was originally purchased for €45,000 and has been depreciated using the 20 per cent reducing-balance method.
- The old harvester can be sold for €20,000 today.
- The new harvester will be depreciated by the 20 per cent reducing balance method over its 10-year life.
- The corporate tax rate is 34 per cent.
- The firm's required rate of return is 15 per cent.
- The initial investment, the proceeds from selling the old harvester, and any resulting tax effects occur immediately.
- All other cash flows occur at year-end.
- The market value of each harvester at the end of its economic life is equal to its residual or written down value.

10.30 Operating Leverage Use the results of Problem 10.26 to find the degree of operating leverage for the company in Problem 10.27 at the base-case output level of 35,000 units. How does this number compare with the sensitivity figure you found in Problem 10.28? Verify that either approach will give you the same OCF figure at any new quantity level.

MINI CASE

WHITE MOUNTAIN THYME WHISKY LTD

Heinrich Schutz, the chief executive of White Mountain Thyme Whisky Ltd, was evaluating the possibility of new fixed-life distillery facilities. These were primarily to initiate production of Scottish White Whisky, a departure from the single malts they had previously focused on. The distillery extension would have an additional benefit in that it would allow the firm to draw water from a nearby water source rather than buying it in the open market from other whisky distillers.

The proposed distillery extension will utilize a new renewable technology that allows for a more streamlined production process. This will increase the efficiency of the malting process and reduce the firm's reliance on a nearby distillery, White Heather Whisky, to undertake the task for them. In fact, the new technology will allow Wild Mountain Thyme to compete directly with White Heather in the market for white whisky.

If the project is to go ahead, construction will begin this year with an investment of £20 million. When the distillery begins operations next year, the existing operating costs of White Mountain Thyme Whisky will fall significantly because of technology upgrades and it is expected these will be £5 million every year of the project.

Schutz plans to sell the white whisky in Europe at the earliest possible opportunity. Next year, the white whisky revenues of Wild Mountain Thyme are expected to be £10 million, growing by 10 per cent every year. Production costs (before accounting adjustments) are 10 per cent of revenues, and administrative and selling costs are 50 per cent of revenues.

The upgrade in production capacity will result in an increase of working capital, corresponding to 15 per cent of revenue every year. This means that working capital requirements change whenever revenues change.

After five years of production, the distillery will come to the end of its natural working life. At that time all the working capital would be recovered. The company can also expect to sell some of the components of the initial investment in the market at the end of the project for £2 million (before taxes).

The marginal corporate tax rate is 23 per cent, and depreciation is calculated at 20 per cent reducing balance over the life of the project. The company's cost of capital is 12 per cent.

QUESTIONS

1. In discussing your project appraisal and sensitivity analysis, Heinrich Schutz asks why you have undertaken a sensitivity analysis. Why is it important to undertake sensitivity analysis in project appraisal?
2. As well as undertaking sensitivity analysis we could also undertake a scenario analysis at the same time, what would this result in?
3. To help Heinrich Schutz you have to explain estimation risk. What causes estimation risk?

ADDITIONAL READING

Apart from textbooks, there is not much research literature on project evaluation and capital budgeting. An interesting paper that considers the effect of CEO turnover on capital budgeting activity is:

1. Hornstein, A. S. (2013). Corporate capital budgeting and CEO turnover. *Journal of Corporate Finance*, *20*, 41–58.

Endnotes

1. We use straight-line depreciation to provide the intuition underlying break-even analysis. In practice, one would use the reducing-balance method. Given that the depreciation amount would be different each year, one would need to use a spreadsheet to find the break-even level. However, the intuition underlying the discussion remains the same.
2. To see this, note that if Q goes up by one unit, OCF will go up by $(P - v)$. In this case, the percentage change in Q is $1/Q$, and the percentage change in OCF is $(P - v)/\text{OCF}$. Given this, we have:

$$\text{Percentage change in OCF} = \text{DOL} \times \text{Percentage change in } Q$$
$$(P - v)/\text{OCF} = \text{DOL} \times 1/Q$$
$$\text{DOL} = (P - v) \times Q/\text{OCF}$$

Also, based on our definitions of OCF:

$$\text{OCF} + \text{FC} = (P - v) \times Q$$

Thus DOL can be written as:

$$\text{DOL} = (\text{OCF} + \text{FC})/\text{OCF}$$
$$= 1 + \text{FC}/\text{OCF}$$

PART FOUR

RISK AND RETURN

11 Some Lessons from Recent Capital Market History   289

12 Return, Risk and the Security Market Line   317

CHAPTER 11
SOME LESSONS FROM RECENT CAPITAL MARKET HISTORY

LEARNING OBJECTIVES
After studying this chapter, you should understand:

LO1 How to calculate the return on an investment.
LO2 The historical returns on various important types of investment.
LO3 The historical risks on various important types of investment.
LO4 The implications of market efficiency.

KEY NOTATIONS
D	Dividend
P	Share price
R	Return
$\overline{R}$	Average return
$SD(R)$ or σ	Standard deviation of returns
T	Number of historical returns
$Var(R)$ or σ^2	Variance of returns

RECENT YEARS have seen significant movements in financial markets, both up and down. Take the FTSE 100 as an example. Representing the fortunes of the 100 largest companies in the UK, it had an index value of 7,604 at the beginning of 2020. However, when the impact of Covid-19 spread throughout the world in March, the FTSE 100 fell nearly 30 per cent to 4,993 and its lowest level since the global financial crisis 12 years before. One month later, the index had jumped over 20 per cent to 5,893. Clearly, the Covid-19 pandemic was unprecedented in living memory and the FTSE 100 index volatility was extremely unusual. However, the stock market does regularly see large market movement for individual stocks. In 2020, like any other year, there were tremendous potential profits to be made, but there was also the risk of losing money – lots of it. So what should you, as a stock market investor, expect when you invest your own money? In this chapter, we study market history to find out.

Thus far, we haven't had much to say about what determines the required return on an investment. In one sense, the answer is simple: the required return depends on the risk of the investment. The greater the risk, the greater is the required return.

Having said this, we are left with a somewhat more difficult problem. How can we measure the amount of risk present in an investment? Put another way, what does it mean to say that one investment is riskier than another? Obviously, we need to define what we mean by *risk* if we are going to answer these questions. This is our task in the next two chapters.

From the last several chapters, we know that one of the responsibilities of the financial manager is to assess the value of proposed real asset investments. In doing this, it is important that we first look at what financial investments have to offer. At a minimum, the return we require from a proposed non-financial investment must be greater than what we can get by buying financial assets of similar risk.

Our goal in this chapter is to provide a perspective on what capital market history can tell us about risk and return. The most important thing to get out of this chapter is a feel for the numbers. What is a high return? What is a low one? More generally, what returns should we expect from financial assets, and what are the risks of such investments? This perspective is essential for understanding how to analyse and value risky investment projects.

We start our discussion of risk and return by describing the experience of investors in the world's financial markets. The introduction to this chapter showed the extent of volatility in the UK equity markets in 2020, which experienced the greatest daily movements since the 2008 global financial crisis. Every stock market experienced the same volatility, so what lessons, if any, can financial managers learn from such volatility? We shall explore market history to find out.

Two central lessons emerge from our study of market history. First, there is a reward for bearing risk. Second, the greater the potential reward is, the greater is the risk. To illustrate these facts about market returns, we devote much of this chapter to reporting the statistics and numbers that make up modern European capital market history. In the next chapter, these facts provide the foundation for our study of how financial markets put a price on risk.

11.1 RETURNS

We wish to discuss historical returns on different types of financial asset. The first thing we need to do, then, is briefly discuss how to calculate the return from investing.

CASH RETURNS

If you buy an asset of any sort, your gain (or loss) from that investment is called the *return on your investment*. This return will usually have two components. First, you may receive some cash directly while you own the investment. This is called the *income component* of your return. Second, the value of the asset you purchase will often change. In this case, you have a capital gain or capital loss on your investment.[1]

To illustrate, suppose Video Concept has several thousand shares of equity outstanding. You purchased some of these shares at the beginning of the year. It is now year-end, and you want to determine how well you have done on your investment.

First, over the year, a company may pay cash dividends to its shareholders. As a shareholder in Video Concept, you are a part owner of the company. If the company is profitable, it may choose to distribute some of its profits to shareholders (we discuss the details of dividend policy in a later chapter). So, as the owner of some equity, you will receive some cash. This cash is the income component from owning the shares.

In addition to the dividend, the other part of your return is the capital gain or capital loss on the equity. This part arises from changes in the value of your investment. For example, consider the cash flows illustrated in Figure 11.1. At the beginning of the year the equity was selling for £37 per share. If you had bought 100 shares, you would have had a total outlay of £3,700. Suppose that, over the year, the equity paid a dividend of £1.85 per share. By the end of the year, then, you would have received income of:

$$\text{Dividend} = £1.85 \times 100 = £185$$

FIGURE 11.1 Cash returns

Also, the value of the equity has risen to £40.33 per share by the end of the year. Your 100 shares are now worth £4,033, so you have a capital gain of:

$$\text{Capital gain} = (£40.33 - 37) \times 100 = £333$$

On the other hand, if the price had dropped to, say, £34.78, you would have a capital loss of:

$$\text{Capital loss} = (£34.78 - 37) \times 100 = -£222$$

Notice that a capital loss is the same thing as a negative capital gain.

The total cash return on your investment is the sum of the dividend and the capital gain:

$$\text{Total cash return} = \text{Dividend income} + \text{Capital gain (or loss)} \quad (11.1)$$

In our first example, the total cash return is thus given by:

$$\text{Total cash return} = £185 + 333 = £518$$

Notice that if you sold the equity at the end of the year, the total amount of cash you would have would equal your initial investment plus the total return. In the preceding example, then:

$$\begin{aligned}\text{Total cash if equity is sold} &= \text{Initial investment} + \text{Total return} \\ &= £3{,}700 + 518 \\ &= £4{,}218\end{aligned} \quad (11.2)$$

As a check, notice that this is the same as the proceeds from the sale of the equity plus the dividends:

$$\begin{aligned}\text{Proceeds from equity sale} + \text{Dividends} &= £40.33 \times 100 + 185 \\ &= £40.33 + 185 \\ &= £4{,}218\end{aligned}$$

Suppose you hold on to your Video Concept shares and don't sell them at the end of the year. Should you still consider the capital gain as part of your return? Isn't this only a 'paper' gain and not really a cash flow if you don't sell the equity?

The answer to the first question is a strong yes, and the answer to the second is an equally strong no. The capital gain is every bit as much a part of your return as the dividend, and you should certainly count it as part of your return. That you actually decide to keep the shares and not sell (you don't 'realize' the gain) is irrelevant, because you could have converted it to cash if you had wanted to. Whether you choose to do so or not is up to you.

After all, if you insisted on converting your gain to cash, you could always sell the shares at year-end and immediately reinvest by buying the shares back. There is no net difference between doing this and just not selling (assuming, of course, that there are no tax consequences from selling the shares). Again, the point is that whether you actually cash out and buy beer (or whatever) or reinvest by not selling doesn't affect the return you earn.

PERCENTAGE RETURNS

It is usually more convenient to summarize information about returns in percentage terms, rather than cash terms, because that way your return doesn't depend on how much you actually invest. The question we want to answer is this: how much do we get for each unit of cash we invest?

To answer this question, let P_t be the share price at the beginning of the year and let D_{t+1} be the dividend paid during the year. Consider the cash flows in Figure 11.2. These are the same as those in Figure 11.1, except that we have now expressed everything on a per-share basis.

FIGURE 11.2

In our example, the price at the beginning of the year was £37 per share and the dividend paid during the year on each share was £1.85. As we discussed in Chapter 7, expressing the dividend as a percentage of the beginning share price results in the dividend yield:

$$\text{Dividend yield} = D_{t+1}/P_t$$
$$= £1.85/37 = 0.05 = 5\%$$

This says that for each pound we invest, we get 5 pence in dividends.

The second component of our percentage return is the capital gains yield. Recall (from Chapter 7) that this is calculated as the change in the price during the year (the capital gain) divided by the beginning price:

$$\begin{aligned}\text{Capital gains yield} &= (P_{t+1} - P_t)/P_t \\ &= (£40.33 - 37)/37 \\ &= £3.33/37 \\ &= 9\%\end{aligned}$$

So, per pound invested, we get 9 pence in capital gains.

Putting it together, per pound invested, we get 5 pence in dividends and 9 pence in capital gains; so we get a total of 14 pence. Our percentage return is 14 pence on the pound, or 14 per cent.

To check this, notice that we invested £3,700 and ended up with £4,218. By what percentage did our £3,700 increase? As we saw, we picked up £4,218 − 3,700 = £518. This is a £518/3,700 = 14% increase.

EXAMPLE 11.1

CALCULATING RETURNS

Suppose you bought some equity at the beginning of the year for €25 per share. At the end of the year, the share price is €35. During the year, you got a €2 dividend per share. This is the situation illustrated in Figure 11.3. What is the dividend yield? The capital gains yield? The percentage return? If your total investment was €1,000, how much do you have at the end of the year?

FIGURE 11.3 Cash flow: an investment example

Your €2 dividend per share works out to a dividend yield of:

$$\text{Dividend yield} = D_{t+1}/P_t$$
$$= €2/25 = 0.08 = 8\%$$

The per-share capital gain is €10, so the capital gains yield is:

$$\text{Capital gains yield} = (P_{t-1} - P_t)/P_t$$
$$= (€35 - 25)/25$$
$$= €10/25$$
$$= 40\%$$

The total percentage return is thus 48 per cent.

If you had invested €1,000, you would have €1,480 at the end of the year, representing a 48 per cent increase. To check this, note that your €1,000 would have bought you €1,000/25 = 40 shares. Your 40 shares would then have paid you a total of 40 × €2 = €80 in cash dividends. Your €10 per share gain would give you a total capital gain of €10 × 40 = €400. Add these together, and you get the €480 increase.

To give extreme examples, equity in the sports retailer, JD Sports plc began 2019 at £3.639 per share. The company paid £0.0144 dividends during 2019, and the share price at the end of the year was £8.374. What was the return on JD Sports for the year? For practice, see if you agree that the answer is 130.51 per cent. Of course, negative returns occur as well. For example, at the start of 2019 educational publisher Pearson plc had a share price of £9.63. Dividends of £0.19 were paid during the year and the equity ended 2019 at £6.55 per share. Do you agree that the loss was 30 per cent for the year?

CONCEPT QUESTIONS

11.1a What are the two parts of total return?
11.1b Why are unrealized capital gains or losses included in the calculation of returns?
11.1c What is the difference between a cash return and a percentage return? Why are percentage returns more convenient?

11.2 THE HISTORICAL RECORD

In this section we shall discuss the historical rates of return on a number of different securities in different countries across Europe. The countries we look at are Belgium, China, Denmark, France, Germany, India, the Netherlands, Sweden and the UK. The large company share portfolios are based on indices representing the largest companies in each country. These are, respectively, the Bel-20 Index (Belgium), SSE Composite (China), OMX Copenhagen 20 (Denmark), CAC 40 (France), DAX30 (Germany), S&P BSE Sensex (India), Amsterdam SE All Shares (Netherlands), OMX Stockholm 30 (Sweden), and the FTSE 100 (UK). We have also included the FTSE 250 Midcap Index, which represents smaller companies on the London Stock Exchange.

None of the returns are adjusted for taxes, transaction costs or inflation. Figure 11.4 shows the relative performance of different stock markets over the period 2010–2020. Clearly, a much longer period could have been considered, since European stock exchanges have been open for years and, in some cases, hundreds of years. The year 2020 shows the systemic impact of Covid-19 on economic activity and market values. Note that, although countries are geographically dispersed, the financial markets all followed the same general trajectory, with variation around a similar trend line. This illustrates the integrated nature of economies driven by globalization.

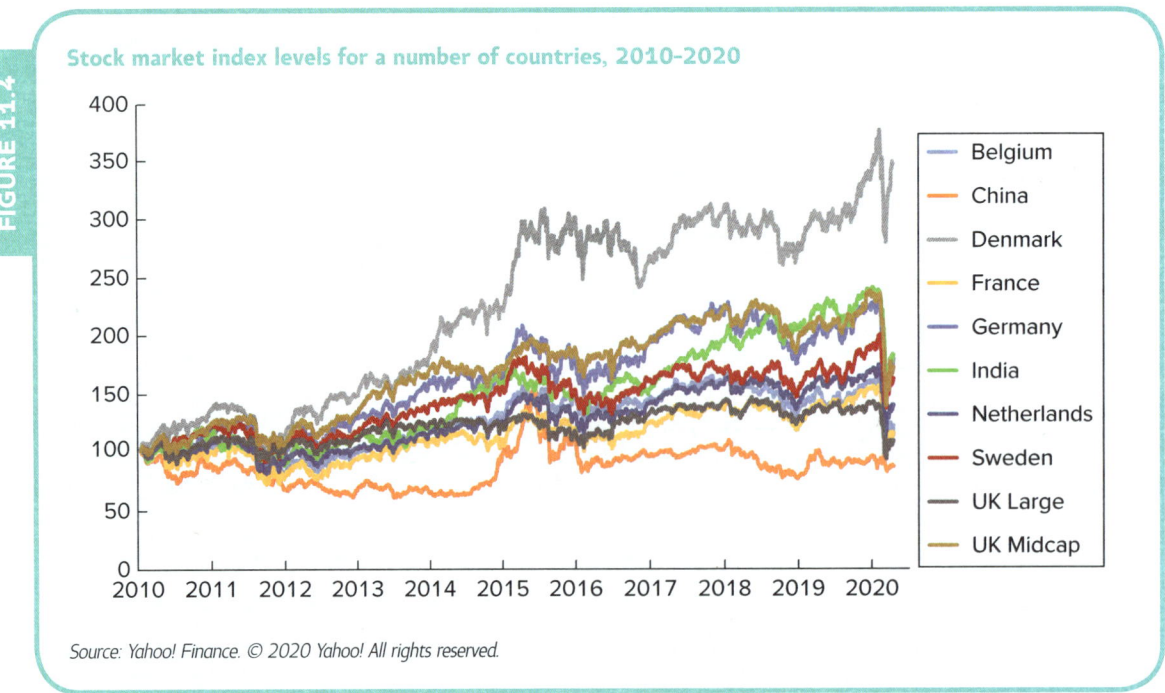

FIGURE 11.4 Stock market index levels for a number of countries, 2010-2020

Source: Yahoo! Finance. © 2020 Yahoo! All rights reserved.

Table 11.1 presents the index values for each stock market for every year between 2010 and 2020. The numbers in Table 11.1 show that an investor must be careful when reading information on company or stock market performance. For example, if one were to look at the return for China between 2005 and 2015, and compare this with the return for the same country in, say, 2008, conflicting messages would be given. Over the full 10 years, the Chinese stock market has more than doubled, whereas in 2008, it halved in value! Which is the correct performance measure? Unfortunately, both are correct from different perspectives.

TABLE 11.1

Year-by-year stock market index levels for different countries, 2010–2020

Date	Belgium	China	Denmark	France	Germany	India	Netherlands	Sweden	UK Large	UK Midcap
01/01/2010	100	100	100	100	100	100	100	100	100	100
03/01/2011	104.7866	85.68684	137.1855	99.09891	117.3281	117.7284	108.7594	123.6551	108.9982	124.1962
02/01/2012	84.18152	67.11394	118.2393	81.86051	101.9822	88.8525	95.12705	105.013	102.9448	108.5529
01/01/2013	98.57423	69.24113	147.364	92.4991	127.7798	112.1158	101.5277	116.0772	108.9588	132.9657
01/01/2014	116.4117	64.56784	182.8091	109.1359	160.3403	121.0461	116.6859	140.0569	124.6857	171.221
01/01/2015	130.8024	98.7043	221.1055	108.5465	164.5936	157.5027	124.3858	153.8845	121.3049	172.8337
01/01/2016	147.3272	107.9961	301.2177	117.8016	180.3296	149.7921	130.5811	152.0216	115.3235	187.2787
02/01/2017	144.537	94.70578	267.2963	124.0338	194.6868	152.2802	140.9585	160.4285	131.9599	194.2353
01/01/2018	158.3791	100.9164	304.2027	134.9623	216.8324	193.605	156.4486	165.6937	142.0273	222.698
01/01/2019	129.1449	76.09992	264.8014	120.1802	177.2402	207.5864	138.2351	148.0204	124.2985	188.0548
01/01/2020	157.5011	93.07265	337.34	151.8689	222.3947	236.51	166.3538	186.1735	139.3425	235.1314
27/04/2020	120.8957	85.91305	347.2096	114.4533	178.9361	181.7545	138.7302	161.7608	108.0163	171.4076

Source: Yahoo! Finance. © 2020 Yahoo! All rights reserved.

Figure 11.4 gives the growth of an investment in various stock markets between 2010 and 2020. In other words, it shows what the worth of the investment would have been if the money that was initially invested had been left in the stock market, and if each year the dividends from the previous year had been reinvested in more shares. If R_t is the return in year t (expressed in decimals), the value you would have at the end of year T is the product of 1 plus the return in each of the years:

$$(1 + R_1) \times (1 + R_2) \times \ldots \times (1 + R_t) \times \ldots \times (1 + R_T)$$

For example, in Table 11.2 the index values in Table 11.1 are presented as annual percentage returns.

TABLE 11.2

Annual returns for different countries, 2010–2020

Date	Belgium	China	Denmark	France	Germany	India	Netherlands	Sweden	UK Large	UK Midcap
2010	4.79%	−4.31%	37.19%	−0.90%	17.33%	17.73%	8.76%	23.66%	9.00%	24.20%
2011	−19.66%	−21.68%	−13.81%	−17.40%	−13.08%	−24.53%	−12.53%	−15.08%	−5.55%	−12.60%
2012	17.10%	3.17%	24.63%	13.00%	25.30%	26.18%	6.73%	10.54%	5.84%	22.49%
2013	18.10%	−6.75%	24.05%	17.99%	25.48%	7.97%	14.93%	20.66%	14.43%	28.77%
2014	12.36%	52.87%	20.95%	−0.54%	2.65%	30.12%	6.60%	9.87%	−2.71%	0.94%
2015	12.63%	9.41%	36.23%	8.53%	9.56%	−4.90%	4.98%	−1.21%	−4.93%	8.36%
2016	−1.89%	−12.31%	−11.26%	5.29%	7.96%	1.66%	7.95%	5.53%	14.43%	3.71%
2017	9.58%	6.56%	13.81%	8.81%	11.37%	27.14%	10.99%	3.28%	7.63%	14.65%
2018	−8.46%	−24.59%	−12.95%	−10.95%	−18.26%	7.22%	−11.64%	−10.67%	−12.48%	−15.56%
2019	21.96%	22.30%	27.39%	26.37%	25.48%	13.93%	20.34%	25.78%	12.10%	25.03%
Jan–Apr 2020	−23.24%	−7.69%	2.93%	−24.64%	−19.54%	−23.15%	−16.61%	−13.11%	−22.48%	−27.10%

Source: Yahoo! Finance. © 2013 Yahoo! All rights reserved. Note: returns are for period January–December of stated year.

The next thing to consider is the difference in performance between large and small companies (shown here for the UK). Notice how, in almost every year, small companies had larger returns (whether positive or negative) than large companies. We shall discuss why later in the chapter.

> **CONCEPT QUESTIONS**
>
> **11.2a** With 20/20 hindsight, what would you say was the best investment for the period from 2010 through 2020?
> **11.2b** Why doesn't everyone just buy small equities as investments?
> **11.2c** About how many times did large-company equities return more than 20 per cent? How many times did they return less than −20 per cent?
> **11.2d** What was the longest 'winning streak' (years without a negative return) for large-company equities?

11.3 AVERAGE RETURNS: THE FIRST LESSON

As you've probably begun to notice, the history of capital market returns is too complicated to be of much use in its undigested form. We need to begin summarizing all these numbers. Accordingly, we discuss how to go about condensing the detailed data. We start out by calculating average returns.

CALCULATING AVERAGE RETURNS

The obvious way to calculate the average returns on the different indices in Table 11.2 is simply to add up the yearly returns and divide by 10. The result is the historical average of the individual values.

For example, if you add up the returns for the UK large company equities for the 10 years (excluding the first four months of 2020), you will get about 37.75. The average annual return is thus 37.75/10 = 3.78%. You interpret this 3.78 per cent just like any other average. If you were to pick a year at random from the 10-year history, and you had to guess what the return in that year was, the best guess would be 3.78 per cent.

AVERAGE RETURNS: THE HISTORICAL RECORD

Table 11.3 shows the average returns (excluding the first four months of 2020) for the indices we have discussed. As shown, in a typical year, UK small company equities increased in value by 10.0 per cent. Notice also how much larger the small company returns are than the large company returns.

TABLE 11.3

Average annual returns, 2011-2020

Investment	Average return (%)
UK large companies	3.78
UK small companies	10.00
Belgian companies	5.65
Chinese companies	1.47
Danish companies	14.62
French companies	5.02
German companies	9.38
Indian companies	10.25
Dutch companies	5.71
Swedish companies	7.24

Source: Yahoo! Finance. © 2020 Yahoo! All rights reserved.

RISK PREMIUMS

Now that we have computed the average return on the stock market, it seems sensible to compare it with the returns on other securities. The most obvious comparison is with the low-variability returns in the government bond market. These are free of most of the volatility we see in the stock market.

Governments borrow money by issuing bonds, which the investing public holds. As we discussed in an earlier chapter, these bonds come in many forms, and the ones we will look at here are called *Treasury bills*, or *T-bills*. Once a week the government sells some bills at an auction. A typical bill is a pure discount bond that will mature in a year or less. Because governments can raise taxes to pay for the debt they incur – a trick that many of us would like to be able to perform – this debt is virtually free of the risk of default. Thus we will call this the *risk-free return* over a short time (one year or less).

An interesting comparison, then, is between the virtually risk-free return on T-bills and the very risky return on equity. This difference between risky returns and risk-free returns is often called the *excess return on the risky asset*. It is called *excess* because it is the additional return resulting from the riskiness of equities and is interpreted as an equity **risk premium**.

risk premium the excess return required from an investment in a risky asset over that required from a risk-free investment.

Table 11.4 shows the risk premium of equities in a number of countries in April 2020. The equity risk premium relates to two securities: long-term government bonds and short-term treasury bills. The table also presents the country risk premium, which is the difference between the individual country equity risk premium and a mature economy equity risk premium.

TABLE 11.4

Equity and Country Risk Premiums, April 2020

Country	Equity Risk Premium	Country Risk Premium	Country	Equity Risk Premium	Country Risk Premium
Abu Dhabi	6.29%	0.91%	Norway	5.96%	0.00%
Austria	6.74%	0.73%	Oman	9.02%	3.06%
Bahrain	16.8%	7.64%	Poland	7.14%	1.18%
Belgium	6.80%	0.84%	Portugal	9.02%	3.06%
China	6.94%	0.98%	Russia	9.43%	3.47%
Denmark	5.96%	0.00%	Saudi Arabia	6.94%	0.98%
Finland	6.51%	0.55%	Singapore	5.96%	0.00%
France	6.65%	0.69%	South Africa	9.02%	3.06%
Germany	5.96%	0.00%	Spain	8.18%	2.22%
Greece	14.99%	9.03%	Sweden	5.96%	0.00%
India	8.60%	2.64%	Switzerland	5.96%	0.00%
Ireland	7.14%	1.18%	Turkey	10.96%	5.00%
Italy	9.02%	3.06%	United Arab Emirates	6.65%	0.69%
Malaysia	7.63%	1.67%	United Kingdom	6.65%	0.69%
Netherlands	5.96%	0.00%	United States	5.96%	0.00%

Source: Aswath Damodaran website, http://pages.stern.nyu.edu/~adamodar/New_Home_Page/datafile/ctryprem.html.

Clearly, the 10-year period between 2011 and 2020 has been exceptional in the history of stock markets. A much longer period to assess average returns and risk premiums would be better, because then short-term volatility would likely even out. Figure 11.5 presents the risk premium for a number of countries between 1900 and 2010. Notice that in every country, equities gave a higher return than both bills and bonds over the full time period.

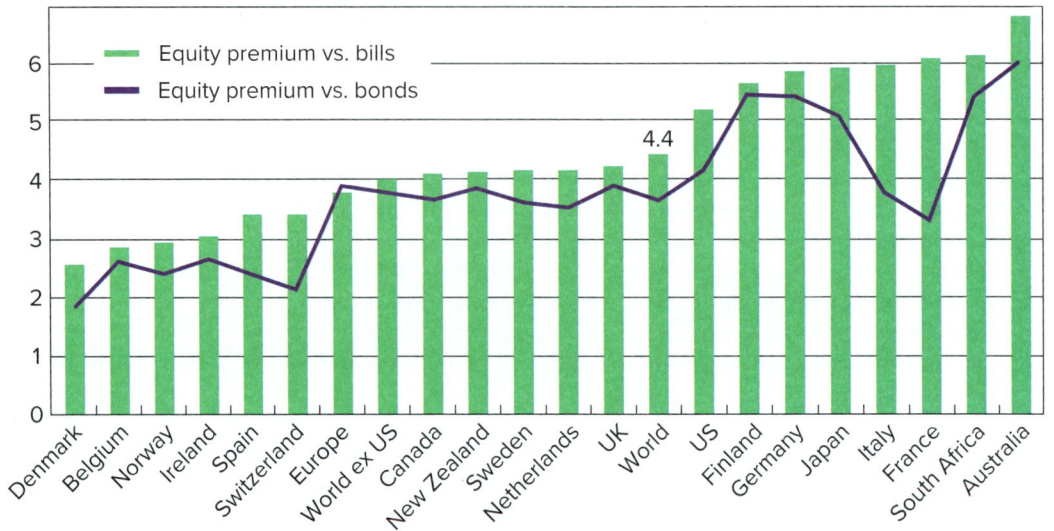

FIGURE 11.5 Worldwide annualized equity risk premium (%) relative to bonds and bills, 1900–2010

Note: Premiums for Germany are based on 109 years, excluding hyperinflationary 1922-23.

Source: E. Dimson, P. Marsh and M. Staunton (2002) *Triumph of the Optimists* (Princeton, NJ: Princeton University Press) and subsequent research. E. Dimson, P. Marsh and M. Staunton (2011) 'Equity Premia around the World', in *Rethinking the Equity Risk Premium* (December), CFA Institute. Copyright 2011, CFA Institute Research Foundation. Reproduced and republished from Rethinking the Equity Risk Premium with permission from the CFA Institute Research Foundation. All rights reserved.

THE FIRST LESSON

Looking at Table 11.3, there appears a lot of uncertainty from investing in European equities. However, over the long term there is much less volatility in returns. For UK securities over a significantly longer period (Figure 11.5), we see that the average risk premium earned by a typical UK large-company equity is about 4 per cent. This is a fairly significant reward. The fact that it exists historically is an important observation, and it is the basis for our first lesson: over the long term, risky assets, on average, earn a risk premium. Put another way, there is a reward for bearing risk.

Why is this so? Why, for example, is the risk premium for small-company equities so much larger than the risk premium for large-company equities? More generally, what determines the relative sizes of the risk premiums for the different assets? The answers to these questions are at the heart of modern finance, and the next chapter is devoted to them. For now, we can find part of the answer by looking at the historical variability of the returns on these different investments. So, to get started, we now turn our attention to measuring variability in returns.

REAL WORLD INSIGHTS

Is it possible to manipulate prices in large stock markets? Although it may appear highly unlikely, if individuals have access to a large enough amount of money they can make prices change temporarily – and take advantage of that change. Alternatively, senior executives can release unnecessarily optimistic or pessimistic news to make the market react accordingly. Clearly, all these activities are illegal and will lead to criminal convictions if the perpetrators are caught, but it does happen.

One activity, known as 'spoofing', involves the submission of a very large number of orders and bids to a market in order to change prices. Before these orders or bids are executed, however, they are cancelled or altered. This may sound innocuous but many automated trading strategies are based on the analysis of an order book, and if done skilfully, market prices can change significantly.

A case on spoofing went through the courts in 2020 regarding two ex-Deutsche Bank traders. It was alleged they spoofed precious metals prices by sending orders, which changed quoted prices, and later cancelled them before it was possible for a transaction to take place. According to court documents, one of the traders wrote in an email after the alleged spoofing activity, 'Got that up 2 bucks … that does show you how easy it is to manipulate sometimes.'

While the traders did not deny the activity (it would be difficult to do so given all orders are recorded), their defence was that an order does not convey intent or promise to trade, but is like a poker bluff that 'ups the ante' without revealing cards.

We'll leave it to you to decide if that is a valid argument.

CONCEPT QUESTIONS

11.3a What do we mean by excess *return* and *risk premium*?
11.3b What was the real (as opposed to nominal) risk premium on the US large company portfolio?
11.3c What was the nominal risk premium on US corporate bonds? The real risk premium?
11.3d What is the first lesson from capital market history?

11.4 THE VARIABILITY OF RETURNS: THE SECOND LESSON

We have already seen that the year-to-year returns on equities tend to be more volatile than the returns on, say, long-term government bonds. We now discuss measuring this variability of equity returns so that we can begin examining the subject of risk.

RETURN VARIABILITY

What we need to do is to measure the spread in returns. From Section 11.3, we know that the return on UK small company equities in a typical year was 10 per cent. We now want to know how much the actual return deviates from this average in a typical year. In other words, we need a measure of how volatile the return is. The **variance**, and its square root, the **standard deviation** are the most commonly used measures of volatility. We describe how to calculate them next.

variance
the average squared difference between the actual return and the average return.

standard deviation
the positive square root of the variance.

THE HISTORICAL VARIANCE AND STANDARD DEVIATION

The variance essentially measures the average squared difference between the actual returns and the average return. The bigger this number is, the more the actual returns tend to differ from the average return. Also, the larger the variance or standard deviation is, the more spread out the returns will be.

The way we calculate the variance and standard deviation will depend on the specific situation. In this chapter we are looking at historical returns, so the procedure we describe here is the correct one for calculating the *historical* variance and standard deviation. If we were examining projected future returns, then the procedure would be different. We describe this procedure in the next chapter.

To illustrate how we calculate the historical variance, suppose a particular investment has had returns of 10 per cent, 12 per cent, 3 per cent and −9 per cent over the last 4 years. The average return is $(0.10 + 0.12 + 0.03 − 0.09)/4 = 4\%$. Notice that the return is never actually equal to 4 per cent. Instead, the first return deviates from the average by $0.10 − 0.04 = 0.06$, the second return deviates from the average by $0.12 − 0.04 = 0.08$, and so on. To compute the variance, we square each of these deviations, add them up, and divide the result by the number of returns less 1, or 3 in this case. Most of this information is summarized in the following table:

	(1) Actual return	(2) Average return	(3) Deviation (1)−(2)	(4) Squared deviation
	0.10	0.04	0.06	0.0036
	0.12	0.04	0.08	0.0064
	0.03	0.04	−0.01	0.0001
	−0.09	0.04	−0.13	0.0169
Totals	0.16		0.00	0.0270

In the first column, we write the four actual returns. In the third column, we calculate the difference between the actual returns and the average by subtracting 4 per cent. Finally, in the fourth column, we square the numbers in the third column to get the squared deviations from the average.

The variance can now be calculated by dividing 0.0270, the sum of the squared deviations, by the number of returns less 1. Let Var(R), or σ^2 (read this as 'sigma squared'), stand for the variance of the return:

$$\text{Var}(R) = \sigma^2 = \frac{0.027}{(4-1)} = 0.009$$

The standard deviation is the square root of the variance. So if SD(R), or σ, stands for the standard deviation of return:

$$\text{SD}(R) = \sigma = \sqrt{0.009} = 0.09487$$

The square root of the variance is used because the variance is measured in 'squared' percentages and thus is hard to interpret. The standard deviation is an ordinary percentage, so the answer here could be written as 9.487 per cent.

In the preceding table, notice that the sum of the deviations is equal to zero. This will always be the case, and it provides a good way to check your work. In general, if we have T historical returns, where T is some number, we can write the historical variance as:

$$\text{Var}(R) = \frac{1}{T-1}\left[(R_1 - \overline{R})^2 + \ldots + (R_T - \overline{R})^2\right] \quad (11.3)$$

This formula tells us to do what we just did: take each of the T individual returns ($R_1, R_2, \ldots$) and subtract the average return, $\overline{R}$; square the results, and add them all up; and finally, divide this total by the number of returns less 1, (T− 1). The standard deviation is always the square root of Var(R). Standard deviations are a widely used measure of volatility.

EXAMPLE 11.2

CALCULATING THE VARIANCE AND STANDARD DEVIATION

Suppose Supertech and Hyperdrive have experienced the following returns in the last 4 years:

Year	Supertech return	Hyperdrive return
2010	−0.20	0.05
2011	0.50	0.09
2012	0.30	−0.12
2013	0.10	0.20

What are the average returns? The variances? The standard deviations? Which investment was more volatile?

To calculate the average returns, we add up the returns and divide by 4. The results are:

Supertech average return $\overline{R} = 0.70/4 = 0.175$
Hyperdrive average return $\overline{R} = 0.22/4 = 0.055$

To calculate the variance for Supertech, we can summarize the relevant calculations as follows:

Year	(1) Actual return	(2) Average return	(3) Deviation (1) − (2)	(4) Squared deviation
2010	−0.20	0.175	−0.375	0.140625
2011	0.50	0.175	0.325	0.105625
2012	0.30	0.175	0.125	0.015625
2013	0.10	0.175	−0.075	0.005625
Totals	0.70		0.000	0.267500

Because there are 4 years of returns, we calculate the variance by dividing 0.2675 by (4 − 1) = 3:

	Supertech	Hyperdrive
Variance (σ^2)	0.2675/3 = 0.0892	0.0529/3 = 0.0176
Standard deviation (σ)	$\sqrt{0.0892} = 0.2987$	$\sqrt{0.0176} = 0.1327$

For practice, verify that you get the same answer as we do for Hyperdrive. Notice that the standard deviation for Supertech, 29.87 per cent, is a little more than twice Hyperdrive's 13.27 per cent: Supertech is thus the more volatile investment.

THE HISTORICAL RECORD

Figure 11.6 summarizes UK capital market history in more detail. It plots a histogram of the yearly stock market return of the UK largest companies between 1926 and 2019. The height of the graph gives the number of sample observations in the range on the horizontal axis. Notice the higher frequency of large positive returns than large negative returns.

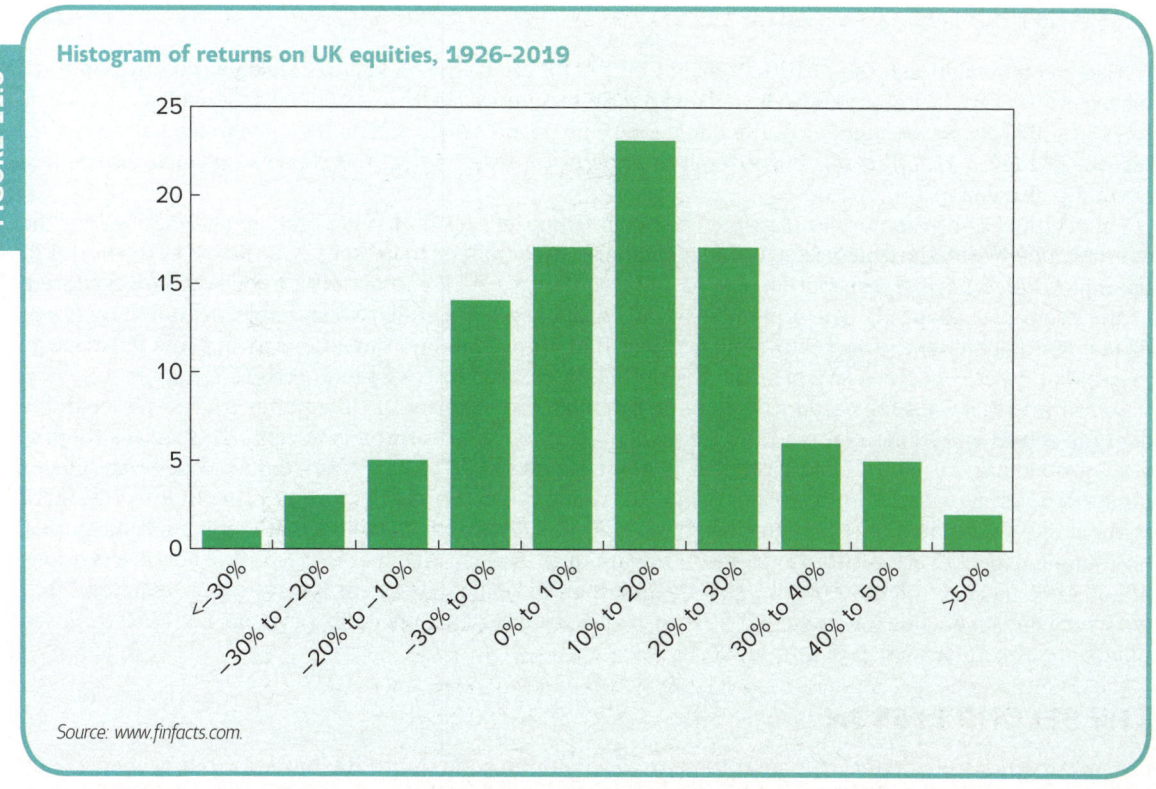

FIGURE 11.6

Histogram of returns on UK equities, 1926–2019

Source: www.finfacts.com.

NORMAL DISTRIBUTION

normal distribution
a symmetric, bell-shaped frequency distribution that is completely defined by its mean and standard deviation.

For many different random events in nature, a particular frequency distribution, the **normal distribution** (or *bell curve*), is useful for describing the probability of ending up in a given range.

Figure 11.7 illustrates a normal distribution, and its distinctive bell shape. As you can see, this distribution has a much cleaner appearance than the actual return distributions illustrated in Figure 11.6. Even so, like the normal distribution, the actual distributions do appear to be at least roughly mound-shaped and symmetric. When this is true, the normal distribution is often a very good approximation.

FIGURE 11.7 The normal distribution

Also, keep in mind that the distributions in Figure 11.6 are based on just over 200 yearly observations, whereas Figure 11.7 is, in principle, based on an infinite number. So if we had been able to observe returns for, say, 1,000 years, we might have filled in a lot of the irregularities and ended up with a much smoother picture in Figure 11.6. For our purposes it is enough to observe that the returns are at least roughly normally distributed.

The usefulness of the normal distribution stems from the fact that it is completely described by the average and the standard deviation. If you have these two numbers, then there is nothing else to know. For example, with a normal distribution, the probability that we shall end up within one standard deviation of the average is about 2/3. The probability that we shall end up within two standard deviations is about 95 per cent. Finally, the probability of being more than three standard deviations away from the average is less than 1 per cent. These ranges, and the probabilities, are illustrated in Figure 11.7.

To see why this is useful, assume the standard deviation of returns on UK equities is 17.82 per cent, the average return is 3.73 per cent and the frequency distribution of returns is normal. This means there is a 2/3 probability the return in a given year is in the range −14.09 to 21.55 per cent (3.73 per cent plus or minus one standard deviation, 17.82 per cent). The range is illustrated in Figure 11.7. In other words, there is about one chance in three the return will be *outside* this range, which means that if you buy UK equities, you should expect to be outside this range in 1 year out of every 3. This reinforces our earlier observations about stock market volatility. Taking this further, there is only a 5 per cent chance (approximately) that we would end up outside the range −31.91 to 39.37 per cent (3.73 per cent plus or minus 2 × 17.82%). These points are also illustrated in Figure 11.7.

THE SECOND LESSON

Our observations concerning the year-to-year variability in returns are the basis for our second lesson from capital market history. On average, bearing risk is handsomely rewarded; but in a given year there is a significant chance of a dramatic change in value. Thus our second lesson is this: the greater the potential reward, the greater is the risk.

USING CAPITAL MARKET HISTORY

Based on the discussion in this section, you should begin to have an idea of the risks and rewards from investing. For example, in 2020 one-year UK Treasury bills were paying roughly 0 (zero) per cent. Suppose we had an investment that we thought had about the same risk as a portfolio of small UK company equities. At a minimum, what return would this investment have to offer for us to be interested?

> **REAL WORLD INSIGHTS**
>
> What drives market movements? Investors and analysts across the world scour the financial press for anything that may provide insights on how prices will evolve in the future. A scan of the newspapers presents the reader with various reports predicting where the markets may go. Take, for example, the news on a single day in 2020 (15 September): US stock markets climbed 0.9 per cent for S&P 500 and the Nasdaq was up 1.2 per cent. Tech stocks had a particularly good day with Tesla, Netflix and Apple up 5, 3 and 1 per cent respectively. At the same time, Carnival, a cruise operator experienced a share price collapse of 7 per cent.
>
> Less than 24 hours earlier, China's currency hit its highest level in over year on the back of strong retail sales in the country. A manufacturing survey by the Federal Reserve Bank of New York showed manufacturing activity above forecasts in the US. In Europe, big retailers also did well with H&M and Ocado doing better than expected. In Germany, investor sentiment was the highest it had been in over 20 years. The UK was the only country to give negative news, with unemployment hitting a high of 4.1 per cent.
>
> Does any of this information inform us about the value of stock prices? History will show this day as just one in a time series of events that led to either lower or higher prices. Although the information on this day is important, it is simply one more daily observation in a distribution of daily observations, with no more importance in the long term than any other day.

From Table 11.3 we see that the average return earned by small UK company equities was 10 per cent per annum, and so a reasonable estimate of the risk premium was roughly 10 per cent (10 − 0) over the 10-year period 2010 to 2020. This may strike you as being high, but if we were thinking of starting a new business, then the risks of doing so might resemble those of investing in small-company equities.

We shall discuss the relationship between risk and required return in more detail in the next chapter. For now, you should notice that a projected internal rate of return, or IRR, on a risky investment in the 10 to 20 per cent range isn't particularly outstanding. It depends on how much risk there is. This, too, is an important lesson from capital market history.

> **CONCEPT QUESTIONS**
>
> **11.4a** In words, how do we calculate a variance? A standard deviation?
> **11.4b** With a normal distribution, what is the probability of ending up more than one standard deviation below the average?
> **11.4c** Assuming that long-term corporate bonds have an approximately normal distribution, what is the approximate probability of earning 14.6 per cent or more in a given year? With T-bills, roughly what is this probability?
> **11.4d** What is the second lesson from capital market history?

11.5 MORE ABOUT AVERAGE RETURNS

Thus far in this chapter we have looked closely at simple average returns. But there is another way of computing an average return. The fact that average returns are calculated in two different ways leads to some confusion, so our goal in this section is to explain the two approaches, and also the circumstances under which each is appropriate.

ARITHMETIC VERSUS GEOMETRIC AVERAGES

Let's start with a simple example. Suppose you buy a particular equity for £100. Unfortunately, the first year you own it, it falls to £50. The second year you own it, it rises back to £100, leaving you where you started (no dividends were paid).

What was your average return on this investment? Common sense seems to say that your average return must be exactly zero, because you started with £100 and ended with £100. But if we calculate the returns year by year, we see that you lost 50 per cent the first year (you lost half of your money). The second year, you made 100 per cent (you doubled your money). Your average return over the 2 years was thus (−50% + 100%)/2 = 25%!

> **geometric average return**
> the average compound return earned per year over a multi-year period.
>
> **arithmetic average return**
> the return earned in an average year over a multi-year period.

So which is correct, 0 per cent or 25 per cent? Both are correct: they just answer different questions. The 0 per cent is called the **geometric average return**. The 25 per cent is called the **arithmetic average return**. The geometric average return answers the question 'What was your average compound return per year over a particular period?' The arithmetic average return answers the question 'What was your return in an average year over a particular period?'

Notice that in previous sections the average returns we calculated were all arithmetic averages, so we already know how to calculate them. What we need to do now is: (1) learn how to calculate geometric averages; and (2) learn the circumstances under which one average is more meaningful than the other.

CALCULATING GEOMETRIC AVERAGE RETURNS

First, to illustrate how we calculate a geometric average return, suppose a particular investment had annual returns of 10 per cent, 12 per cent, 3 per cent, and −9 per cent over the last 4 years. The geometric average return over this 4-year period is calculated as $(1.10 \times 1.12 \times 1.03 \times 0.91)^{1/4} - 1 = 3.66\%$. In contrast, the average arithmetic return we have been calculating is $(0.10 + 0.12 + 0.03 - 0.09)/4 = 4.0\%$.

In general, if we have T years of returns, the geometric average return over these T years is calculated using this formula:

$$\text{Geometric average return} = [(1 + R_1) \times (1 + R_2) \times \ldots \times (1 + R_T)]^{1/T} - 1 \quad (11.4)$$

This formula tells us that four steps are required:

1. Take each of the T annual returns $R_1, R_2, \ldots, R_T$ and add 1 to each (after converting them to decimals!).
2. Multiply all the numbers from step 1 together.
3. Take the result from step 2 and raise it to the power $1/T$.
4. Finally, subtract 1 from the result of step 3. The result is the geometric average return.

EXAMPLE 11.3

CALCULATING THE GEOMETRIC AVERAGE RETURN

Calculate the geometric average return for Danish equities for the first 5 years in Table 11.2, 2010–2014.
First, convert percentages to decimal returns, add 1, and then calculate their product:

Danish returns (%)	Product
27.19	1.3719
−13.81	× 0.8619
24.63	× 1.2463
24.05	× 1.2405
20.95	× 1.2095
	2.2111

> Notice that the number 2.2111 is what our investment is worth after 5 years if we started with a 1 kroner investment. The geometric average return is then calculated as follows:
>
> $$\text{Geometric average return} = 2.2111^{1/5} - 1 = 0.1720, \text{ or } 17.20\%$$
>
> Thus the geometric average return is about 17.20 per cent in this example. Here is a tip: if you are using a financial calculator, you can put '1' in as the present value, '2.2111' as the future value, and '5' as the number of periods. Then solve for the unknown rate. You should get the same answer that we did.

Table 11.5 shows the arithmetic average risk premiums and standard deviations for a number of different countries, along with the geometric average risk premiums and other information.

TABLE 11.5

Worldwide risk premiums relative to bonds, 1900–2010

Country	Geometric Mean (%)	Arithmetic Mean (%)	Standard Dev. (%)	Min. Return (%)	Year	Max. Return (%)	Year
Australia	5.9	7.8	19.8	−52.9	2008	66.3	1980
Belgium	2.6	4.9	21.4	−60.3	2008	84.4	1940
Canada	3.7	5.3	18.2	−40.7	2008	48.6	1950
Denmark	2.0	3.4	17.2	−54.3	2008	74.9	1972
Finland	5.6	9.2	30.3	−56.3	2008	173.1	1999
France	3.2	5.6	22.9	−50.3	2008	84.3	1946
Germany	5.4	8.8	28.4	−50.8	2008	116.6	1949
Ireland	2.9	4.9	19.8	−66.6	2008	83.2	1972
Italy	3.7	7.2	29.6	−49.4	2008	152.2	1946
Japan	5.0	9.1	32.8	−45.2	2008	193.0	1948
The Netherlands	3.5	2.1	22.2	−55.6	2008	107.6	1940
New Zealand	3.8	1.7	18.1	−59.7	1987	72.7	1983
Norway	2.5	5.5	28.0	−57.8	2008	192.1	1979
South Africa	5.5	1.9	19.6	−34.3	2008	70.9	1979
Spain	2.3	4.3	20.8	−42.7	2008	69.1	1986
Sweden	3.8	6.1	22.3	−48.1	2008	87.5	1905
Switzerland	2.1	3.6	17.6	−40.6	2008	52.2	1985
UK	3.9	1.6	17.0	−38.4	2008	80.8	1975
US	4.4	1.9	20.5	−50.1	2008	57.2	1933
Europe	3.9	5.2	16.6	−47.6	2008	67.9	1923
World ex-US	3.8	1.5	15.5	−47.1	2008	51.7	1923
World	3.8	5.0	15.5	−47.9	2008	38.3	1954

Note: Premiums for Germany are based on 109 years, excluding hyperinflationary 1922-23.

Source: E. Dimson, P. Marsh and M. Staunton (2002) *Triumph of the Optimists* (Princeton, NJ: Princeton University Press) and subsequent research. E. Dimson, P. Marsh and M. Staunton (2011) 'Equity Premia around the World', in *Rethinking the Equity Risk Premium (December)*, CFA Institute. Copyright 2011, CFA Institute Research Foundation. Reproduced and republished from Rethinking the Equity Risk Premium with permission from the CFA Institute Research Foundation. All rights reserved.

ARITHMETIC AVERAGE RETURN OR GEOMETRIC AVERAGE RETURN?

When we look at historical returns, the difference between the geometric and arithmetic average returns isn't too hard to understand. To put it slightly differently, the geometric average tells you what you actually earned per year on average, compounded annually. The arithmetic average tells you what you earned in a typical year. You should use whichever one answers the question you want answered.

> **EXAMPLE 11.4**
>
> **MORE GEOMETRIC AVERAGES**
>
> Take a look back at Table 11.1. There we showed that the UK Midcap index grew from 100 to 171.4 over 10 years. The 10-year return is given below:
>
> $$\text{10 year return} = (171.4/100) - 1 = 71.4\%$$
>
> The geometric average annual return is thus:
>
> $$\text{Geometric average return} = 1.714^{1/10} - 1 = 0.0554, \text{ or } 5.54\%$$
>
> For practice, check some of the other countries in Table 11.1 the same way.

A somewhat trickier question concerns which average return to use when forecasting future wealth levels, and there's a lot of confusion on this point among analysts and financial planners. First, let's get one thing straight: if you *know* the true arithmetic average return, then this is what you should use in your forecast. For example, if you know the arithmetic return is 10 per cent, then your best guess of the value of a €1,000 investment in 10 years is the future value of €1,000 at 10 per cent for 10 years, or €2,593.74.

The problem we face, however, is that we usually have only *estimates* of the arithmetic and geometric returns, and estimates have errors. In this case the arithmetic average return is probably too high for longer periods, and the geometric average is probably too low for shorter periods. So you should regard long-run projected wealth levels calculated using arithmetic averages as optimistic. Short-run projected wealth levels calculated using geometric averages are probably pessimistic. The key thing here is to be aware of the strengths and weaknesses of each average estimate and act accordingly in your decision-making.

> **CONCEPT QUESTIONS**
>
> **11.5a** If you want to forecast what the stock market is going to do over the next year, should you use an arithmetic or geometric average?
> **11.5b** If you want to forecast what the stock market is going to do over the next century, should you use an arithmetic or geometric average?

11.6 CAPITAL MARKET EFFICIENCY

efficient capital market
a market in which security prices reflect available information.

Capital market history suggests that the market values of equities and bonds can fluctuate widely from year to year. Why does this occur? At least part of the answer is that prices change because new information arrives, and investors reassess asset values based on that information.

The behaviour of market prices has been extensively studied. A question that has received particular attention is whether prices adjust quickly and correctly when new information arrives. A market is said to be 'efficient' if this is the case. To be more precise, in an **efficient capital market** current market prices fully reflect available information. By this we simply mean that, based on available information, there is no reason to believe that the current price is too low or too high.

The concept of market efficiency is a rich one, and much has been written about it. A full discussion of the subject goes beyond the scope of our study of corporate finance. However, because the concept figures so prominently in studies of market history, we briefly describe the key points here.

PRICE BEHAVIOUR IN AN EFFICIENT MARKET

To illustrate how prices behave in an efficient market, suppose F-Stop Camera Corporation (FCC) has, through years of secret research and development, developed a camera with an autofocusing system whose speed will double that of the autofocusing systems now available. FCC's capital budgeting analysis suggests that launching the new camera will be a highly profitable move; in other words, the NPV appears to be positive and substantial. The key assumption thus far is that FCC has not released any information about the new system, so the fact of its existence is 'inside' information only.

Now consider a share of equity in FCC. In an efficient market, its price reflects what is known about FCC's current operations and profitability, and it reflects market opinion about FCC's potential for future growth and profits. The value of the new autofocusing system is not reflected, however, because the market is unaware of the system's existence.

If the market agrees with FCC's assessment of the value of the new project, FCC's share price will rise when the decision to launch is made public. For example, assume the announcement is made in a press release on Wednesday morning. In an efficient market, the price of shares in FCC will adjust quickly to this new information. Investors should not be able to buy the equity on Wednesday afternoon and make a profit on Thursday. This would imply that it took the stock market a full day to realize the implication of the FCC press release. If the market is efficient, the FCC share price on Wednesday afternoon will already reflect the information contained in the Wednesday morning press release.

Figure 11.8 presents three possible share price adjustments for FCC. In Figure 11.8 day 0 represents the announcement day. As illustrated, before the announcement FCC sells for £140 per share. The NPV per share of the new system is, say, £40, so the new price will be £180 once the value of the new project is fully reflected.

The solid line in Figure 11.8 represents the path taken by the share price in an efficient market. In this case the price adjusts immediately to the new information, and no further changes in the share price take place. The broken line in Figure 11.8 depicts a delayed reaction. Here it takes the market 8 days or so to fully absorb the information. Finally, the dotted line illustrates an overreaction and subsequent adjustment to the correct price.

The broken line and the dotted line in Figure 11.8 illustrate paths that the share price might take in an inefficient market. If, for example, share prices don't adjust immediately to new information (the broken line), then buying shares immediately following the release of new information and then selling them several days later would be a positive-NPV activity because the price is too low for several days after the announcement.

THE EFFICIENT MARKETS HYPOTHESIS

The **efficient markets hypothesis (EMH)** asserts that well-organized capital markets, such as the London Stock Exchange or Euronext, are efficient markets, at least as a practical matter. In other words, an advocate of the EMH might argue that although inefficiencies may exist, they are relatively small and not common.

efficient markets hypothesis (EMH) the hypothesis that actual capital markets are efficient.

If a market is efficient, then there is a very important implication for market participants: all investments in that market are zero-NPV investments. The reason is not complicated. If prices are neither too low nor too high, then the difference between the market value of an investment and its cost is zero: hence the NPV is zero. As a result, in an efficient market, investors get exactly what they pay for when they buy securities, and firms receive exactly what their equities and bonds are worth when they sell them.

What makes a market efficient is competition among investors. Many individuals spend their entire lives trying to find mispriced equities. For any given equity, they study what has happened in the past to the share price and the equity's dividends. They learn, to the extent possible, what a company's earnings have been, how much the company owes to creditors, what taxes it pays, what businesses it is in, what new investments are planned, how sensitive it is to changes in the economy, and so on.

FIGURE 11.8 Share price reaction to new information in efficient and inefficient markets

Efficient market reaction: The price instantaneously adjusts to and fully reflects new information; there is no tendency for subsequent increases and decreases to occur.
Delayed reaction: The price partially adjusts to the new information; 8 days elapse before the price completely reflects the new information.
Over-reaction: The price over-adjusts to the new information; it overshoots the new price and subsequently corrects.

Not only is there a great deal to know about any particular company, but there is also a powerful incentive for knowing it – namely, the profit motive. If you know more about some company than other investors in the marketplace, you can profit from that knowledge by investing in the company's shares if you have good news and by selling them if you have bad news.

The logical consequence of all this information-gathering and analysis is that mispriced equities will become fewer and fewer. In other words, because of competition among investors, the market will become increasingly efficient. A kind of equilibrium comes into being, with which there is just enough mispricing around for those who are best at identifying it to make a living at it. For most other investors the activity of information-gathering and analysis will not pay.[2]

SOME COMMON MISCONCEPTIONS ABOUT THE EMH

No other idea in finance has attracted as much attention as that of efficient markets, and not all of the attention has been flattering. Rather than rehash the arguments here, we shall be content to observe that some markets are more efficient than others. For example, financial markets on the whole are probably much more efficient than real asset markets.

Having said this, however, we can also say that much of the criticism of the EMH is misguided, because it is based on a misunderstanding of what the hypothesis says and what it doesn't say. For example, when the notion of market efficiency was first publicized and debated in the popular financial press, it was often characterized by words to the effect that 'throwing darts at the financial page will produce a portfolio that can be expected to do as well as any managed by professional security analysts'.[3]

Confusion over statements of this sort has often led to a failure to understand the implications of market efficiency. For example, sometimes it is wrongly argued that market efficiency means that it doesn't matter how you invest your money, because the efficiency of the market will protect you from making a mistake. However, a random dart thrower might wind up with all of the darts sticking into one or two high-risk equities that deal in genetic engineering. Would you really want all of your money in two such companies?

A contest run by the *Wall Street Journal* provides a good example of the controversy surrounding market efficiency. Each month the *Journal* asked four professional money managers to pick one equity each. At the same time it threw four darts at the equities page to select a comparison group. In the 147 contests from over a 13-year period, the pros won 90 times.

The fact that the pros are ahead of the darts by 90 to 57 suggests that markets are not efficient. Or does it? One problem is that the darts naturally tend to select equities of average risk. The pros, however, are playing to win, and naturally select riskier equities, or so it is argued. If this is true, then on average we *expect* the pros to win. Furthermore, the pros' picks are announced to the public at the start. This publicity may boost the prices of the shares involved somewhat, leading to a partially self-fulfilling prophecy. Unfortunately, the *Journal* discontinued the contest in 2002, so this test of market efficiency is no longer continuing.

More than anything else, what efficiency implies is that the price a firm will obtain when it sells a share of its equity is a 'fair' price in the sense that it reflects the value of that equity, given the information available about the firm. Shareholders do not have to worry that they are paying too much for an equity with a low dividend or some other sort of characteristic, because the market has already incorporated that characteristic into the price. We sometimes say that the information has been 'priced out'.

The concept of efficient markets can be explained further by replying to a frequent objection. It is sometimes argued that the market cannot be efficient, because share prices fluctuate from day to day. If the prices are right, the argument goes, then why do they change so much and so often? From our discussion of the market we can see that these price movements are in no way inconsistent with efficiency. Investors are bombarded with information every day. The fact that prices fluctuate is, at least in part, a reflection of that information flow. In fact, the absence of price movements in a world that changes as rapidly as ours would suggest inefficiency.

THE FORMS OF MARKET EFFICIENCY

It is common to distinguish between three forms of market efficiency. Depending on the degree of efficiency, we say that markets are either *weak-form efficient, semi-strong-form efficient,* or *strong-form efficient*. The difference between these forms relates to what information is reflected in prices.

We start with the extreme case. If the market is strong-form efficient, then *all* information of *every* kind is reflected in share prices. In such a market there is no such thing as inside information. Therefore, in our FCC example, we apparently were assuming that the market was not strong-form efficient.

Casual observation, particularly in recent years, suggests that inside information does exist, and it can be valuable to possess. Whether it is lawful or ethical to use that information is another issue. In any event, we conclude that private information about a particular equity may exist that is not currently reflected in the share price. For example, prior knowledge of a takeover attempt could be very valuable.

The second form of efficiency, semi-strong-form efficiency, is the most controversial. If a market is semi-strong-form efficient, then all *public* information is reflected in the share price. The reason why this form is controversial is that it implies that a security analyst who tries to identify mispriced equities using, for example, financial statement information is wasting time, because that information is already reflected in the current price.

The third form of efficiency, weak-form efficiency, suggests that, at a minimum, the current share price reflects the equity's own past prices. In other words, studying past prices in an attempt to identify mispriced securities is futile if the market is weak-form efficient. Although this form of efficiency might seem rather mild, it implies that searching for patterns in historical prices that will be useful in identifying mispriced equities will not work (this practice is quite common).

What does capital market history say about market efficiency? Here again there is great controversy. At the risk of going out on a limb, we can say that the evidence seems to tell us three things. First, prices appear to respond rapidly to new information, and the response is at least not grossly different from what we would expect in an efficient market. Second, the future of market prices, particularly in the short run, is difficult to predict based on publicly available information. Third, if mispriced equities exist, then there is no obvious means of identifying them. Put another way, simple-minded schemes based on public information will probably not be successful.

Many people do not believe that markets are efficient at all. The recent stock market bubbles at the beginning of the century and, more recently, in the mid-2000s have led to a new interest in what is known as *behavioural finance*. This is covered in more detail in Chapter 19.

CONCEPT QUESTIONS

11.6a What is an efficient market?
11.6b What are the forms of market efficiency?

SUMMARY AND CONCLUSIONS

This chapter has explored the subject of capital market history. Such history is useful, because it tells us what to expect in the way of returns from risky assets. We summed up our study of market history with two key lessons:

1. Risky assets, on average, earn a risk premium. There is a reward for bearing risk.
2. The greater the potential reward from a risky investment, the greater is the risk.

These lessons have significant implications for the financial manager. We shall consider these implications in the chapters ahead.

We also discussed the concept of market efficiency. In an efficient market, prices adjust quickly and correctly to new information. Consequently, asset prices in efficient markets are rarely too high or too low. How efficient capital markets (such as the London Stock Exchange or Euronext) are is a matter of debate; but, at a minimum, they are probably much more efficient than most real asset markets.

CHAPTER REVIEW AND SELF-TEST PROBLEMS

11.1 Recent Return History Use Table 11.2 to calculate the average return over the years 2010–2019 for all the indices presented in the table.

11.2 More Recent Return History Calculate the standard deviation for each index using information from the previous problem. Which of the investments was the most volatile over this period?

SOLUTIONS

11.1 We calculate the averages as follows:

Date	Belgium	China	Denmark	France	Germany	India	Netherlands	Sweden	UK Large	UK Midcap
2010	4.79%	−14.31%	37.19%	−0.90%	17.33%	17.73%	8.76%	23.66%	9.00%	24.20%
2011	−19.66%	−21.68%	−13.81%	−17.40%	−13.08%	−24.53%	−12.53%	−15.08%	−5.55%	−12.60%
2012	17.10%	3.17%	24.63%	13.00%	25.30%	26.18%	6.73%	10.54%	5.84%	22.49%
2013	18.10%	−6.75%	24.05%	17.99%	25.48%	7.97%	14.93%	20.66%	14.43%	28.77%
2014	12.36%	52.87%	20.95%	−0.54%	2.65%	30.12%	6.60%	9.87%	−2.71%	0.94%
2015	12.63%	9.41%	36.23%	8.53%	9.56%	−4.90%	4.98%	−1.21%	−4.93%	8.36%
2016	−1.89%	−12.31%	−11.26%	5.29%	7.96%	1.66%	7.95%	5.53%	14.43%	3.71%
2017	9.58%	6.56%	13.81%	8.81%	11.37%	27.14%	10.99%	3.28%	7.63%	14.65%
2018	−18.46%	−24.59%	−12.95%	−10.95%	−18.26%	7.22%	−11.64%	−10.67%	−12.48%	−15.56%
2019	21.96%	22.30%	27.39%	26.37%	25.48%	13.93%	20.34%	25.78%	12.10%	25.03%
Average	5.65%	1.47%	14.62%	5.02%	9.38%	10.25%	5.71%	7.24%	3.78%	10.00%

11.2 We first need to calculate the deviations from the average returns. Using the averages from Problem 11.1 above, we get the following values:

	Belgium	China	Denmark	France	Germany	India	Netherlands	Sweden	UK Large	UK Midcap
Average	5.65%	1.47%	14.62%	5.02%	9.38%	10.25%	5.71%	7.24%	3.78%	10.00%
Variance	0.021564	0.054323	0.040086	0.017086	0.023939	0.028114	0.010862	0.019106	0.009022	0.024949
Standard Deviation	14.68%	23.31%	20.02%	13.07%	15.47%	16.77%	10.42%	13.82%	9.50%	15.80%

Notice that most of the equity indices had roughly the same level of volatility.

QUESTIONS AND PROBLEMS

11.1 Calculating Yields At the beginning of the year, the price of Anheuser-Busch was €19.67; a dividend of €0.28 per share was paid during the year; and the ending share price was €36.40. What is the dividend yield? What is the capital gains yield?

11.2 Return Calculations At the beginning of the year the price of Deutsche Lufthansa was €17.54; it paid a dividend of €0.80 per share during the year, and had an ending share price of €8.29. Compute the percentage total return. What is the dividend yield? What is the capital gains yield?

11.3 Calculating Returns Suppose you bought an 8 per cent coupon bond one year ago for €980. The bond sells for €1,074 today.

(a) Assuming a €1,000 face value, what was your total euro return on this investment over the past year?

(b) What was your total nominal rate of return on this investment over the past year?

(c) If the inflation rate last year was 1 per cent, what was your total real rate of return on this investment?

11.4 Nominal versus Real Returns Assume inflation rates have been as follows, 2020: 0.2 per cent; 2019: 0.8 per cent; 2018: 1.2 per cent; 2017: 1.1 per cent; and in 2016: 1.6 per cent.

Year	Hardy Group (%)	Gainsbourg (%)
2020	−60.7	−3.6
2019	24.1	37.5
2018	33.6	105.5
2017	−62.3	−61.8
2016	−21.8	−33.2

Calculate the average real return of Hardy Group and Gainsbourg.

11.5 Bond Returns

(a) What is the historical real return on long-term US government bonds? Nominal return is 2.8 per cent, inflation rate is 1.1 per cent.

(b) What is the historical real return on long-term US corporate bonds? Nominal return is 3.2 per cent, inflation rate is 1.1 per cent.

11.6 Calculating Returns and Variability Using the returns from Problem 11.4, calculate the average returns, the variances and the standard deviations for Hardy Group and Gainsbourg.

11.7 Risk Premiums Refer to the table below.

Date	Belgium	China	Denmark	France	Germany	India	Netherlands	Sweden
2010	4.79%	−14.31%	37.19%	−0.90%	17.33%	−17.73%	8.76%	23.66%
2011	−19.66%	−21.68%	−13.81%	−17.40%	−13.08%	−24.53%	−12.53%	−15.08%
2012	17.10%	3.17%	24.63%	13.00%	25.30%	26.18%	6.73%	10.54%
2013	18.10%	−6.75%	24.05%	17.99%	25.48%	7.97%	14.93%	20.66%
2014	12.36%	52.87%	20.95%	−0.54%	2.65%	30.12%	6.60%	9.87%
2015	12.63%	9.41%	36.23%	8.53%	9.56%	−4.90%	4.98%	−1.21%
2016	−1.89%	−12.31%	−11.26%	5.29%	7.96%	1.66%	7.95%	5.53%
2017	9.58%	6.56%	13.81%	8.81%	11.37%	27.14%	10.99%	3.28%
2018	−18.46%	−24.59%	−12.95%	−10.95%	−18.26%	7.22%	−11.64%	−10.67%
2019	21.96%	22.30%	27.39%	26.37%	25.48%	13.93%	20.34%	25.78%

(a) Calculate the arithmetic average returns for all the indices in the table over the period 2015–2019.

(b) Calculate the standard deviation of the returns for all the indices over the period 2015–2019.

11.8 Calculating Returns and Variability You have observed the following prices for British Autos, the luxury car maker for a number of years. Jan 2012: €26.87; Jan 2013: €35.19; Jan 2014: €32.17; Jan 2015: €37.23; Jan 2016: €46.84; Jan 2017: €36.80; Jan 2018: €18.61; Jan 2019: €30.96; Jan 2020: €56.08; Jan 2021: €65.39. The company paid the following dividends: 2012: €0.52; 2013: €0.58; 2014: €0.62; 2015: €0.64; 2016: €0.70; 2017: Nil; 2018: €0.30; 2019: €0.30; 2020: Nil.

(a) What was the arithmetic average return on British Auto's shares over this period?

(b) What was the variance of British Auto's returns over this period?

(c) What was the standard deviation of British Auto's returns over this period?

11.9 Calculating Real Returns and Risk Premiums In Problem 11.8, suppose the average inflation rate over this period was 1.2 per cent and the average T-bill rate over the period was 1.4 per cent.

(a) What was the average real return on British Auto's shares?

(b) What was the average nominal risk premium on British Auto's shares?

(c) What was the average real risk-free rate over this time period?

11.10 Calculating Real Rates You have observed the following returns on Crash-n-Burn Computer's equity over the past 5 years: 7 per cent, –12 per cent, 11 per cent, 38 per cent, and 14 per cent. Suppose the average inflation rate over this period was 3.5 per cent and the average T-bill rate over the period was 4.2 per cent.

(a) What was the average real risk-free rate over this time period?

(b) What was the average real risk premium?

11.11 Calculating Investment Returns You bought one of Bergen Manufacturing's 8 per cent coupon bonds one year ago for NKr1,028.50. These bonds make annual payments and mature 6 years from now. Suppose you decide to sell your bonds today, when the required return on the bonds is 7 per cent. If the inflation rate was 4.8 per cent over the past year, what would be your total real return on the investment?

11.12 Calculating Returns and Variability You find a certain equity that had returns of 7 per cent, –12 per cent, 18 per cent and 19 per cent for 4 of the last 5 years. If the average return of the equity over this period was 10.5 per cent, what was the equity's return for the missing year? What is the standard deviation of the equity's return?

11.13 Arithmetic and Geometric Returns An equity has had returns of 10 per cent, 15 per cent, 20 per cent, –12 per cent, 2 per cent, and –5 per cent over the last 6 years. What are its arithmetic and geometric returns?

11.14 Arithmetic and Geometric Returns An equity has had the following year-end prices and dividends:

Year	Price (£)	Dividend (£)
1	43.12	–
2	49.07	0.55
3	51.19	0.60
4	47.24	0.63
5	56.09	0.72
6	67.21	0.81

What are the arithmetic and geometric returns?

11.15 Using Return Distributions Suppose the returns on your company are normally distributed. The historical average share price return for your firm is 5.8 per cent with a standard deviation of 9.3 per cent. What is the approximate probability that your return will be less than –3.5 per cent in a given year? What range of returns would you expect to see 95 per cent of the time? What range would you expect to see 99 per cent of the time?

11.16 Using Return Distributions Refer to Table 11.6. Assuming that the returns from holding Danish equities are normally distributed, what is the approximate probability that your money will double in value in a single year? What about triple in value?

11.17 Distributions Assume that the returns from holding Dutch equities in Table 11.6 are normally distributed. What is the probability that the return is less than –100 per cent (think)? What are the implications for the distribution of returns?

TABLE 11.6

Average annual returns, 2011–2020

Investment	Average return (%)	Standard Deviation (%)
UK large companies	3.78	9.50
UK small companies	10.00	15.80
Belgian companies	5.65	14.68
Chinese companies	1.47	23.31
Danish companies	14.62	20.02
French companies	5.02	13.07
German companies	9.38	15.47
Indian companies	10.25	16.77
Dutch companies	5.71	10.42
Swedish companies	7.24	13.82

Source: Yahoo! Finance. © 2020 Yahoo! All rights reserved.

11.18 Using Probability Distributions Refer to Table 11.6. Suppose the returns on large company UK equities are normally distributed. Based on the historical record, determine the probability that in any given year you will lose money by investing in large company UK equities.

11.19 Using Probability Distributions Refer to Table 11.6. Suppose the returns on German equities are normally distributed. Based on the historical record, answer the following questions.

(a) What is the probability that, in any given year, the return on German equities will be greater than 10 per cent? Less than 0 per cent?

(b) In 2018 the return on German equities was –18.26 per cent. How likely is it that such a low return will recur at some point in the future? In 2019, German equities had a return of 25.48 per cent. How likely is it that such a high return on German equities will recur at some point in the future?

11.20 Returns Go to the Yahoo! Finance website and look up Nestlé. Click on the *Historical Prices* link. Find its closing price yesterday and its closing price exactly one year earlier. From the historical prices in Yahoo! Finance you will see the total dividend paid out in the last year. What has been the annual return on Nestlé? What was the dividend yield? The capital gains yield?

11.21 Returns and Industries Choose three companies from your country, download the historical share prices for the previous year. Find the annual return, dividend yield and capital gains yield. Do you see any relationship between dividend yield and industry? Can you explain it?

MINI CASE

HOLDON SUSTAINABLE INVESTMENT FUND

You have been appointed to manage a new sustainable investment fund and must choose an appropriate asset class mix to ensure you maximize return within the ethical constraints of the investment strategy. The Holdon Sustainable Investment Fund has to follow a set ethical and sustainable investment approach to investments:

1. The fund has a long-term sustainable investment horizon and rejects investments that maximize short-term profits at the expense of longer-term sustainable value creation.
2. The fund will only invest in business with the highest internal standards, that encompass environmental, social and governance (ESG) expectations.
3. Investment criteria: Sustainable themes as measured by the UN Sustainable Development Goals, best-in-class ESG standards.

The Holdon fund will invest in other funds that represent various asset classes. The return on the Holden fund is the weighted average of the return of the individual portfolios minus any expenses. The largest expense is typically the management fee paid to the fund manager. The management fee is compensation for the manager, who makes all the investment decisions for the fund.

Your investment universe consists of the following:

- **Private Ethical Businesses** A distinctive feature of the Holdon fund is that it can invest directly in private businesses that expect to go public in the next 3 to 5 years. These are inherently long-term investments and there is no publicly traded share price for the firm.
- **ESG Index Fund** This mutual fund tracks the largest 100 firms that have the highest ESG standards. Equities in the fund are weighted proportionately by their market values. Because an index fund purchases assets based on publicly available pre-set criteria, the fund manager is not required to research stocks or make investment decisions. The result is that fund expenses are usually low. The ESG Index Fund charges expenses of 0.15 per cent of assets per year.
- **Sustainable Start-Up Fund** This fund invests primarily in small-capitalization companies with prominent ESG objectives. The returns of the fund are therefore more volatile. This fund charges 1.70 per cent in expenses.
- **Renewables Equity Fund** This fund invests primarily in large-capitalization companies involved in renewable energy. The fund has outperformed the market in 4 of the last 5 years. The fund charges 1.50 per cent in expenses.
- **ESG Bond Fund** This fund invests in long-term corporate bonds issued by European firms. The fund is restricted to investments in bonds in firms with the highest ESG standards. This fund charges 1.40 per cent in expenses.
- **Money Market Fund** This fund invests in short-term, high-credit quality debt instruments, which include Treasury bills. The return on the money market fund is therefore only slightly higher than the return on Treasury bills. Because of the credit quality and short-term nature of the investments, there is only a very slight risk of negative return. The fund charges 0.60 per cent in expenses.

QUESTIONS

1. What advantages do the mutual funds offer compared with private business investments?
2. Assume you decide you should invest at least 30 per cent of the Holdon fund's assets in the Renewables Equity Fund. What are the advantages and disadvantages of choosing the Renewables Equity Fund compared with the ESG Index Fund?
3. The returns on the Sustainable Start-Up Fund are the most volatile of all the ESG funds available to Holdon. Why would you ever want to invest in this fund? When you examine the expenses of the ESG funds, you will notice that this fund also has the highest expenses. Does this affect your decision to invest in this fund?
4. A measure of risk-adjusted performance that is often used is the Sharpe ratio. The Sharpe ratio is calculated as the risk premium of an asset divided by its standard deviation. The standard deviation

and return of the funds over the past 5 years are listed here. Calculate the Sharpe ratio for each of these funds. Assume that the expected return and standard deviation of private ethical businesses will be 18 per cent and 70 per cent, respectively. Calculate the Sharpe ratio for Private Ethical Businesses. How appropriate is the Sharpe ratio for these firms? When would you use the Sharpe ratio?

	10-year annual return(%)	Standard deviation(%)
ESG Index Fund	11.48	15.82
Sustainable Start-Up Fund	16.68	19.64
Renewables Equity Fund	11.85	15.41
ESG Bond Fund	9.67	10.83

5. What portfolio allocation would you choose for Holdon Sustainable Investment Fund? Why? Explain your thinking carefully.

ADDITIONAL READING

The number of research papers about the financial markets would fill a whole book and more. As a result, we've had to be exceptionally selective in picking those papers that are most appropriate to the understanding and study of corporate finance.

1. Bartram, S.M., Griffin, J.M., Lim, T.H., & Ng, D.T. (2015). How important are foreign ownership linkages for international stock returns? *Review of Financial Studies, 28*(11), 3036–3072.
2. Bekaert, G., Hodrick, R.J., & Zhang, X. (2009). International stock return comovements. *Journal of Finance, 64*(6), 2591–2626.
3. Braione, M., & Scholtes, N.K. (2016). Forecasting value-at-risk under different distributional assumptions. *Econometrics, 4*(1), 3.
4. Diaz, E.M., Molero, J.C., & de Gracia, F.P. (2016). Oil price volatility and stock returns in the G7 economies. *Energy Economics, 54*, 417–430.
5. Gay, R.D. (2016). Effect of macroeconomic variables on stock market returns for four emerging economies: Brazil, Russia, India, and China. *International Business & Economics Research Journal* (online), *15*(3), 119.
6. Lundblad, C. (2007). The risk return tradeoff in the long run: 1836–2003. *Journal of Financial Economics, 85*(1), 123–150.
7. Marimoutoi, V., Raggad, B., & Tabelsi, A. (2009). Extreme value theory and value at risk: Application to oil market. *Energy Economics, 31*(4), 519–530.
8. Yuan, Y. (2015). Market-wide attention, trading, and stock returns. *Journal of Financial Economics, 116*(3), 548–564.

Endnotes

1. As we mentioned in an earlier chapter, strictly speaking, what is and what is not a capital gain (or loss) is determined by a country's tax authority. We thus use the terms loosely.
2. The idea behind the EMH can be illustrated by the following short story. A student was walking down the hall with her finance professor when they both saw a €500 note on the ground. As the student bent down to pick it up, the professor shook his head slowly and, with a look of disappointment on his face, said patiently to the student, 'Don't bother. If it were really there, someone else would have picked it up already.' The moral of the story reflects the logic of the efficient markets hypothesis: if you think you have found a pattern in share prices or a simple device for picking winners, you probably have not.
3. Malkiel, B.G. (2003). *A random walk down Wall Street* (revised and updated edn). Norton.

CHAPTER 12
RETURN, RISK AND THE SECURITY MARKET LINE

LEARNING OBJECTIVES
After studying this chapter, you should understand:

LO1 How to calculate expected returns.
LO2 The impact of diversification.
LO3 The systematic risk principle.
LO4 The security market line and the risk–return trade-off.

KEY NOTATIONS

CAPM	Capital asset pricing model
E(R)	Expected return
R_f	Risk-free rate of return
R_p	Portfolio return
β	Beta or systematic risk
β_p	Portfolio beta
σ	Standard deviation of returns
σ^2	Variance of returns

SOMETIMES THE FINANCIAL MARKETS ARE A MYSTERY TO THE AVERAGE PERSON IN THE STREET. It is a regular occurrence to see bad news come out regarding the economy but share prices going up on the same day. Similarly, it may seem that a company has announced positive information about its operations only for the share price to drop significantly. Share price volatility can be significant during periods of market stress and investors may find it difficult to separate random noise from the underlying price signal. This was particularly severe in 2020 as the world's financial markets faced the effects of Covid-19 and its long-term ramifications on country economies, international supply chains and global trade.

So when are prices driven by information, and do the random changes in prices reflect news or just noise? In the midst of all this uncertainty, how can investors create efficient financial portfolios? The answer is fundamental to understanding risk and return, and the good news is that this chapter explores it in some detail.

In our last chapter, we learned some important lessons from capital market history. Most importantly, we learned that there is a reward, on average, for bearing risk. We called this reward a *risk premium*. The second lesson is that this risk premium is larger for riskier investments. This chapter explores the economic and managerial implications of this basic idea.

Thus far we have concentrated mainly on the return behaviour of a few large portfolios. We need to expand our consideration to include individual assets. Specifically, we have two tasks to accomplish. First, we have to define risk and discuss how to measure it. We then must quantify the relationship between an asset's risk and its required return.

When we examine the risks associated with individual assets, we find there are two types of risk: systematic and unsystematic. This distinction is crucial, because as we shall see, systematic risk affects almost all assets in the economy, at least to some degree, whereas unsystematic risk affects at most a small number of assets. We then develop the principle of diversification, which shows that highly diversified portfolios will tend to have almost no unsystematic risk.

The principle of diversification has an important implication: to a diversified investor, only systematic risk matters. It follows that in deciding whether to buy a particular individual asset, a diversified investor will be concerned only with that asset's systematic risk. This is a key observation, and it allows us to say a great deal about the risks and returns on individual assets. In particular, it is the basis for a famous relationship between risk and return called the *security market line*, or SML. To develop the SML we introduce the equally famous *beta* coefficient, one of the centrepieces of modern finance. Beta and the SML are key concepts because they supply us with at least part of the answer to the question of how to determine the required return on an investment.

12.1 EXPECTED RETURNS AND VARIANCES

In our previous chapter, we discussed how to calculate average returns and variances using historical data. We now begin to discuss how to analyse returns and variances when the information we have concerns possible future returns and their probabilities.

EXPECTED RETURN

We start with a straightforward case. Consider a single period of time – say a year, and we have two equities, L and U, which have the following characteristics. Equity L is expected to have a return of 25 per cent in the coming year. Equity U is expected to have a return of 20 per cent for the same period.

In a situation like this, if all investors agreed on the expected returns, why would anyone want to hold Equity U? After all, why invest in one equity when the expectation is that another will do better? Clearly, the answer must depend on the risk of the two investments. The return on Equity L, although it is *expected* to be 25 per cent, could turn out to be higher or lower.

For example, suppose the economy booms. In this case, we think Equity L will have a 70 per cent return. If the economy enters a recession, we believe the return will be −20 per cent. In this case, we say that there are two *states of the economy*, which means that these are the only two possible situations. This set-up is oversimplified, of course, but it allows us to illustrate some critical ideas without a lot of computation.

Suppose we think a boom and a recession are equally likely to happen, for a 50–50 chance of each. Table 12.1 illustrates the basic information we have described, and some additional information about Equity U. Notice that Equity U earns 30 per cent if there is a recession, and 10 per cent if there is a boom.

TABLE 12.1

States of the economy and equity returns

		Rate of return if state occurs (%)	
State of economy	Probability of state of economy	Equity L	Equity U
Recession	0.50	−20	30
Boom	0.50	70	10
	1.00		

If you buy one of these equities, say Equity U, what you earn in any particular year depends on what the economy does during that year. However, suppose the probabilities stay the same through time. If you hold Equity U for several years, you'll earn 30 per cent about half the time and 10 per cent the other half. In this case, we say that your **expected return** on Equity U, $E(R_U)$, is 20 per cent:

expected return
the return on a risky asset expected in the future.

$$E(R_U) = 0.50 \times 30\% + 0.50 \times 10\% = 20\%$$

In other words, you should expect to earn 20 per cent from this equity, on average.

For Equity L, the probabilities are the same, but the possible returns are different. Here, we lose 20 per cent half the time, and we gain 70 per cent the other half. The expected return on L, $E(R_L)$, is thus 25 per cent:

$$E(R_L) = 0.50 \times -20\% + 0.50 \times 70\% = 25\%$$

Table 12.2 illustrates these calculations.

TABLE 12.2

Calculation of expected return

		Equity L		Equity U	
(1) State of economy	(2) Probability of state of economy	(3) Rate of return if state occurs	(4) Product (2) × (3)	(5) Rate of return if state occurs	(6) Product (2) × (5)
Boom	0.50	−0.20	−0.10	0.30	0.15
Recession	0.50	0.70	0.35	0.10	0.05
	1.00		$E(R_L) = 0.25 = 25\%$		$E(R_U) = 0.20 = 20\%$

In our previous chapter, we defined the risk premium as the difference between the return on a risky investment and that on a risk-free investment, and we calculated the historical risk premiums on some different investments. Using our projected returns, we can calculate the *projected*, or *expected*, *risk premium* as the difference between the expected return on a risky investment and the certain return on a risk-free investment.

For example, suppose risk-free investments are currently offering 8 per cent. We shall say that the risk-free rate, which we label as R_f, is 8 per cent. Given this, what is the projected risk premium on Equity U? On Equity L? Because the expected return on Equity U, $E(R_U)$, is 20 per cent, the projected risk premium is:

$$\begin{aligned}\text{Risk premium} &= \text{Expected return} - \text{Risk-free rate} \\ &= E(R_U) - R_f \\ &= 20\% - 8\% \\ &= 12\%\end{aligned} \quad (12.1)$$

Similarly, the risk premium on Equity L is 25% − 8% = 17%.

In general, the expected return on a security or other asset is equal to the sum of the possible returns multiplied by their probabilities. So, if we had 100 possible returns, we would multiply each one by its probability and add up the results. The result would be the expected return. The risk premium would then be the difference between this expected return and the risk-free rate.

EXAMPLE 12.1

UNEQUAL PROBABILITIES

Look again at Tables 12.1 and 12.2. Suppose you think a boom will occur only 20 per cent of the time instead of 50 per cent. What are the expected returns on Equities U and L in this case? If the risk-free rate is 10 per cent, what are the risk premiums?

The first thing to notice is that a recession must occur 80 per cent of the time (1 − 0.20 = 0.80) because there are only two possibilities. With this in mind, we see that Equity U has a 30 per cent return in 80 per cent of the years and a 10 per cent return in 20 per cent of the years. To calculate the expected return, we again multiply the possibilities by the probabilities and add up the results:

$$E(R_U) = 0.80 \times 30\% + 0.20 \times 10\% = 26\%$$

Table 12.3 summarizes the calculations for both equities. Notice that the expected return on L is −2 per cent.

TABLE 12.3

Calculation of expected return

		Equity L		Equity U	
(1) State of economy	(2) Probability of state of economy	(3) Rate of return if state occurs	(4) Product (2) × (3)	(5) Rate of return if state occurs	(6) Product (2) × (5)
Recession	0.80	−0.20	−0.16	0.30	0.24
Boom	0.20	0.70	0.14	0.10	0.02
		$E(R_L) = -2\%$		$E(R_U) = 26\%$	

The risk premium for Equity U is 26% − 10% = 16% in this case. The risk premium for Equity L is negative: −2% − 10% = −12%. This is a little odd; but, for reasons we discuss later, it is not impossible.

CALCULATING THE VARIANCE

To calculate the variances of the returns on our two equities, we first determine the squared deviations from the expected return. We then multiply each possible squared deviation by its probability. We add these up, and the result is the variance. The standard deviation, as always, is the square root of the variance.

To illustrate, let us return to the Equity U we originally discussed, which has an expected return of $E(R_U) = 20\%$. In a given year it will actually return either 30 per cent or 10 per cent. The possible deviations are thus 30% − 20% = 10% and 10% − 20% = −10%. In this case, the variance is:

$$\text{Variance} = \sigma^2 = 0.50 \times (10\%)^2 + 0.50 \times (-10\%)^2 = 0.01$$

The standard deviation is the square root of this:

$$\text{Standard deviation} = \sigma \sqrt{0.01} = 0.10 = 10\%$$

Table 12.4 summarizes these calculations for both equities. Notice that Equity L has a much larger variance.

When we put the expected return and variability information for our two equities together, we have the following:

	Equity L	Equity U
Expected return, E(R) (%)	25	20
Variance, σ^2	0.2025	0.0100
Standard deviation, $\sigma(\%)$	45	10

Equity L has a higher expected return, but U has less risk. You could get a 70 per cent return on your investment in L, but you could also lose 20 per cent. Notice that an investment in U will always pay at least 10 per cent.

TABLE 12.4

Calculation of variance

(1) State of economy	(2) Probability of state of economy	(3) Return deviation from expected return	(4) Squared return deviation from expected return	(5) Product (2) × (4)
Equity L				
Recession	0.50	−0.20 − 0.25 = −0.45	−0.45² = 0.2025	0.10125
Boom	0.50	0.70 − 0.25 = 0.45	0.45² = 0.2025	0.10125
				$\sigma_L^2 = 0.20250$
Equity U				
Recession	0.50	0.30 − 0.20 = 0.10	0.10² = 0.01	0.005
Boom	0.50	−0.10 − 0.20 = −0.45	−0.10² = 0.01	0.005
				$\sigma_U^2 = 0.010$

Which of these two equities should you buy? We can't really say; it depends on your personal preferences. We can be reasonably sure that some investors would prefer L to U, and some would prefer U to L.

You've probably noticed that the way we have calculated expected returns and variances here is somewhat different from the way we did it in the last chapter. The reason is that in Chapter 11 we were examining actual historical returns, so we estimated the average return and the variance based on some actual events. Here, we have projected *future* returns and their associated probabilities, so this is the information with which we must work.

EXAMPLE 12.2

MORE UNEQUAL PROBABILITIES

Going back to Example 12.1, what are the variances on the two equities once we have unequal probabilities? The standard deviations?

We can summarize the needed calculations as follows:

(1) State of economy	(2) Probability of state of economy	(3) Return deviation from expected return	(4) Squared return deviation from expected return	(5) Product (2) × (4)
Equity L				
Recession	0.80	−0.20 − (−0.02) = −0.18	0.0324	0.02592
Boom	0.20	0.70 − (−0.02) = 0.72	0.5184	0.10368
				$\sigma_L^2 = 0.12960$
Equity U				
Recession	0.80	0.30 − 0.26 = 0.04	0.0016	0.00128
Boom	0.20	0.10 − 0.26 = −0.16	0.0256	0.00512
				$\sigma_U^2 = 0.00640$

Based on these calculations, the standard deviation for L is $\sigma_L = \sqrt{0.1296} = 0.36 = 36\%$. The standard deviation for U is much smaller: $\sigma_U = \sqrt{0.0064} = 0.08 = 8\%$.

CONCEPT QUESTIONS

12.1a How do we calculate the expected return on a security?
12.1b In words, how do we calculate the variance of the expected return?

12.2 PORTFOLIOS

portfolio
a group of assets such as equities and bonds held by an investor.

Thus far, in this chapter, we have concentrated on individual assets considered separately. However, most investors actually hold a **portfolio** of assets. All we mean by this is that investors tend to own more than just a single equity, bond or other asset. Given that this is so, portfolio return and portfolio risk are of obvious relevance. Accordingly, we now discuss portfolio expected returns and variances.

PORTFOLIO WEIGHTS

portfolio weight
the percentage of a portfolio's total value that is in a particular asset.

There are many equivalent ways of describing a portfolio. The most convenient approach is to list the percentage of the total portfolio's value that is invested in each portfolio asset. We call these percentages the **portfolio weights**.

For example, if we have €50 in one asset and €150 in another, our total portfolio is worth €200. The percentage of our portfolio in the first asset is €50/€200 = 0.25. The percentage of our portfolio in the second asset is €150/€200, or 0.75. Our portfolio weights are thus 0.25 and 0.75. Notice that the weights have to add up to 1.00 because all of our money is invested somewhere.[1]

PORTFOLIO EXPECTED RETURNS

Let's go back to Equities L and U. You put half your money in each. The portfolio weights are obviously 0.50 and 0.50. What is the pattern of returns on this portfolio? The expected return?

To answer these questions, suppose the economy enters a recession. In this case, half your money (the half in L) loses 20 per cent. The other half (the half in U) gains 30 per cent. Your portfolio return, R_P, in a recession is thus:

$$R_P = 0.50 \times -20\% + 0.50 \times 30\% = 5\%$$

Table 12.5 summarizes the remaining calculations. Notice that when a boom occurs, your portfolio will return 40 per cent:

$$R_P = 0.50 \times 70\% + 0.50 \times 10\% = 40\%$$

As indicated in Table 12.5, the expected return on your portfolio, $E(R_P)$, is 22.5 per cent.

TABLE 12.5

Expected return on an equally weighted portfolio of Equity L and Equity U

(1) State of economy	(2) Probability of state of economy	(3) Portfolio return if state occurs	(4) Product (2) ×(3)
Recession	0.50	0.50 × −20% + 0.50 × 30% = 5%	0.025
Boom	0.50	0.50 × 70% + 0.50 × 10% = 40%	0.200
			$E(R_P)$ = 22.5%

We can save ourselves some work by calculating the expected return more directly. Given these portfolio weights, we could have reasoned that we expect half of our money to earn 25 per cent (the half in L) and half of our money to earn 20 per cent (the half in U). Our portfolio expected return is thus:

$$E(R_P) = 0.50 \times E(R_L) + 0.50 \times E(R_U)$$
$$= 0.50 \times 25\% + 0.50 \times 20\%$$
$$= 22.5\%$$

This is the same portfolio expected return we calculated previously.

This method of calculating the expected return on a portfolio works no matter how many assets there are in the portfolio. Suppose we had n assets in our portfolio, where n is any number. If we let x_i stand for the percentage of our money in Asset i, then the expected return would be:

$$E(R_P) = x_1 \times E(R_1) + x_2 \times E(R_2) + \ldots + x_n \times E(R_n) \tag{12.2}$$

This says that the expected return on a portfolio is a straightforward combination of the expected returns on the assets in that portfolio. This seems somewhat obvious; but, as we shall examine next, the obvious approach is not always the right one.

EXAMPLE 12.3

PORTFOLIO EXPECTED RETURN

Suppose we have the following projections for three equities:

State of economy	Probability of state of economy	Returns if state occurs (%)		
		Equity A	Equity B	Equity C
Boom	0.40	10	15	20
Bust	0.60	8	4	0

We want to calculate portfolio expected returns in two cases. First, what would be the expected return on a portfolio with equal amounts invested in each of the three equities? Second, what would be the expected return if half of the portfolio were in A, with the remainder equally divided between B and C?

Based on what we've learned from our earlier discussions, we can determine that the expected returns on the individual equities are (check these for practice):

$$E(R_A) = 8.8\%$$
$$E(R_B) = 8.4\%$$
$$E(R_C) = 8.0\%$$

If a portfolio has equal investments in each asset, the portfolio weights are all the same. Such a portfolio is said to be *equally weighted*. Because there are three equities, in this case, the weights are all equal to ⅓. The portfolio expected return is thus:

$$E(R_P) = (1/3) \times 8.8\% + (1/3) \times 8.4\% + (1/3) \times 8\% = 8.4\%$$

In the second case, verify that the portfolio expected return is 8.5 per cent.

PORTFOLIO VARIANCE

From our earlier discussion, the expected return on a portfolio that contains equal investments in Equities U and L is 22.5 per cent. What is the standard deviation of return on this portfolio? Simple intuition might suggest that because half of the money has a standard deviation of 45 per cent and the other half has a standard deviation of 10 per cent, the portfolio's standard deviation might be calculated as:

$$\sigma_P = 0.50 \times 45\% + 0.50 \times 10\% = 27.5\%$$

Unfortunately, this approach is completely incorrect!

TABLE 12.6

Variance on an equally weighted portfolio of Equity L and Equity U

(1) State of economy	(2) Probability of state of economy	(3) Portfolio return if state occurs (%)	(4) Squared deviation from expected return	(5) Product (2) × (4)
Recession	0.50	5	$(0.05 - 0.225)^2 = 0.030625$	0.0153125
Boom	0.50	40	$(0.40 - 0.225)^2 = 0.030625$	0.0153125
				$\sigma_P^2 = 0.030625$

$$\sigma_P = \sqrt{0.030625} = 17.5\%$$

Let's see what the standard deviation really is. Table 12.6 summarizes the relevant calculations. As we see, the portfolio's variance is about 0.031, and its standard deviation is less than we thought – it's only 17.5 per cent. What is illustrated here is that the variance on a portfolio is not generally a simple combination of the variances of the assets in the portfolio.

We can illustrate this point a little more dramatically by considering a slightly different set of portfolio weights. Suppose we put 2/11 (about 18 per cent) in L and the other 9/11 (about 82 per cent) in U. If a recession occurs, this portfolio will have a return of:

$$R_P = (2/11) \times -20\% + (9/11) \times 30\% = 20.91\%$$

If a boom occurs, this portfolio will have a return of:

$$R_P = (2/11) \times 70\% + (9/11) \times 10\% = 20.91\%$$

Notice that the return is the same, no matter what happens. No further calculations are needed: this portfolio has a zero variance. Apparently, combining assets into portfolios can substantially alter the risks faced by the investor. This is a crucial observation, and we shall begin to explore its implications in the next section.

EXAMPLE 12.4

PORTFOLIO VARIANCE AND STANDARD DEVIATION

In Example 12.3, what are the standard deviations on the two portfolios? To answer, we first have to calculate the portfolio returns in the two states. We shall work with the second portfolio, which has 50 per cent in Equity A and 25 per cent in each of Equities B and C. The relevant calculations can be summarized as follows:

State of economy	Probability of state of economy	Rate of return if state occurs (%)			
		Equity A	Equity B	Equity C	Portfolio
Boom	0.40	10	15	20	13.75
Bust	0.60	8	4	0	5.00

The portfolio return when the economy booms is calculated as:

$$E(R_P) = 0.50 \times 10\% + 0.25 + 15\% + 0.25 \times 20\% = 13.75\%$$

The return when the economy goes bust is calculated the same way. The expected return on the portfolio is 8.5 per cent. The variance is thus:

$$\sigma_P^2 = 0.40 \times (0.1375 - 0.085)^2 + 0.60 \times (0.05 - 0.085)^2$$
$$= 0.0018375$$

The standard deviation is thus about 4.3 per cent. For our equally weighted portfolio, check to see that the standard deviation is about 5.4 per cent.

> **CONCEPT QUESTIONS**
>
> **12.2a** What is a portfolio weight?
> **12.2b** How do we calculate the expected return on a portfolio?
> **12.2c** Is there a simple relationship between the standard deviation on a portfolio and the standard deviations of the assets in the portfolio?

12.3 ANNOUNCEMENTS, SURPRISES AND EXPECTED RETURNS

Now that we know how to construct portfolios and evaluate their returns, we begin to describe more carefully the risks and returns associated with individual securities. Thus far, we have measured volatility by looking at the difference between the actual return on an asset or portfolio, R, and the expected return, $E(R)$. We now look at why those deviations exist.

EXPECTED AND UNEXPECTED RETURNS

To begin, for concreteness, we consider the return on the equity of a company called Flyers. What will determine this equity's return in, say, the coming year?

The return on any equity traded in a financial market is composed of two parts. First, the normal, or expected, return from the equity is the part of the return that shareholders in the market predict or expect. This return depends on the information shareholders have that bears on the equity, and it is based on the market's understanding today of the important factors that will influence the share price in the coming year.

The second part of the return on the equity is the uncertain, or risky, part. This is the portion that comes from unexpected information revealed within the year. A list of all possible sources of such information would be endless, but here are a few examples:

- News about Flyers research
- Government figures released on gross domestic product (GDP)
- The results from the latest arms control talks
- The news that Flyers' sales figures are higher than expected
- A sudden, unexpected drop in interest rates

Based on this discussion, one way to express the return on Flyers' equity in the coming year would be:

$$\text{Total return} = \text{Expected return} + \text{Unexpected return}$$
$$R = E(R) + U \tag{12.3}$$

where R stands for the actual total return in the year, $E(R)$ stands for the expected part of the return, and U stands for the unexpected part of the return. What this says is that the actual return, R, differs from the expected return, $E(R)$, because of surprises that occur during the year. In any given year, the unexpected return will be positive or negative; but, through time, the average value of U will be zero. This means that, on average, the actual return equals the expected return.

ANNOUNCEMENTS AND NEWS

We must be careful when we talk about the effect of news events on share price returns. For example, suppose Flyers' business is such that the company prospers when GDP grows at a relatively high rate, and suffers when GDP is stagnant. In this case, in deciding what return to expect this year from owning equity in Flyers, shareholders either implicitly or explicitly must think about what GDP is likely to be for the year.

When the government announces GDP figures for the year, what will happen to the value of Flyers' equity? The answer depends on what figure is released. More to the point, however, the impact depends on how much of that figure is *new* information.

At the beginning of the year, market participants will have some idea or forecast of what the yearly GDP will be. To the extent that shareholders have predicted GDP, that prediction will already be factored into the expected part of the return on the equity, $E(R)$. On the other hand, if the announced GDP is a surprise, the effect will be part of U, the unanticipated portion of the return. As an example, suppose shareholders in the market had forecast that the GDP increase this year would be 0.5 per cent. If the actual announcement this year is precisely 0.5 per cent, the same as the forecast, then the shareholders don't learn anything, and the information isn't news. There will be no impact on the share price as a result. This is like receiving confirmation of something you suspected all along; it doesn't reveal anything new.

A common way of saying that an announcement isn't news is to say that the market has already 'discounted' the information in the announcement. The use of the word *discount* here is different from the use of the term in computing present values, but the spirit is the same. When we discount cash in the future, we say it is worth less to us because of the time value of money. When we discount an announcement or a news item, we say that it has less of an impact on the price, because the market already knew much of it.

Going back to Flyers, suppose the government announces that the actual GDP increase during the year has been 1.5 per cent. Now shareholders have learned something – namely, that the increase is one percentage point higher than they had forecast. This difference between the actual result and the forecast, one percentage point in this example, is sometimes called the *innovation* or the *surprise*.

This distinction explains why what seems to be good news can be bad news (and vice versa). We regularly see examples where companies like Netflix and Apple report subscriber growth but the share price falls on the announcement. Company performance is mapped to expectations, and if these are not met, then the share price will fall. The opposite applies when companies exceed expectations. News may seem initially bad, but if the market was expecting worse, then prices will increase.

A key idea to keep in mind about news and price changes is that information about the future is what matters. When companies publish their annual accounts, the figures presented are, in a genuine sense, yesterday's news because they report what has happened in the previous year. Looking to the future, investors scrutinise annual reports to identify whether future growth is likely to be higher, lower, or as expected.

To summarize, an announcement can be broken into two parts: the anticipated, or expected, part and the surprise, or innovation:

$$\text{Announcement} = \text{Expected part} + \text{Surprise} \qquad (12.4)$$

The expected part of any announcement is the part of the information that the market uses to form the expectation, $E(R)$, of the return on the equity. The surprise is the news that influences the unanticipated return on the equity, U.

Our discussion of market efficiency in the previous chapter bears on this discussion. We are assuming that relevant information known today is already reflected in the expected return. This is identical to saying that the current price reflects relevant, publicly available information. We are thus implicitly assuming that markets are at least reasonably efficient in the semi-strong form.

Henceforth, when we speak of news, we shall mean the surprise part of an announcement and not the portion that the market has expected and therefore already discounted.

> **CONCEPT QUESTIONS**
>
> **12.3a** What are the two basic parts of a return?
> **12.3b** Under what conditions will a company's announcement have no effect on share prices?

12.4 RISK: SYSTEMATIC AND UNSYSTEMATIC

The unanticipated part of the return, that portion resulting from surprises, is the true risk of any investment. After all, if we always receive exactly what we expect, then the investment is perfectly predictable and, by definition, risk-free. In other words, the risk of owning an asset comes from surprises – unanticipated events.

There are significant differences, though, among various sources of risk. Look back at our previous list of news stories. Some of these stories are specifically directed at Flyers, and some are more general. Which of the news items are of specific importance to Flyers?

Announcements about interest rates or GDP are important for nearly all companies, whereas news about Flyers' chairman, its research, or its sales is of specific interest to Flyers. We shall distinguish between these two types of event because, as we shall see, they have different implications.

SYSTEMATIC AND UNSYSTEMATIC RISK

The first type of surprise – the one that affects many assets – we shall label **systematic risk**. A systematic risk is one that influences a large number of assets, each to a greater or lesser extent. Because systematic risks have market-wide effects, they are sometimes called *market risks*.

The second type of surprise we shall call **unsystematic risk**. An unsystematic risk is one that affects a single asset or a small group of assets. Because these risks are unique to individual companies or assets, they are sometimes called *unique* or *asset-specific risks*. We shall use these terms interchangeably.

As we have seen, uncertainties about general economic conditions (such as GDP, interest rates or inflation) are examples of systematic risks. These conditions affect nearly all companies to some degree. An unanticipated increase, or surprise, in inflation, for example, affects wages, the costs of raw materials, the value of assets that companies own, and the prices at which companies sell their products. Forces such as these, to which all companies are susceptible, are the essence of systematic risk.

In contrast, the announcement of an oil strike by a company will primarily affect that company and, perhaps, a few others (such as main competitors and suppliers). It is unlikely to have much of an effect on the world oil market, however, or on the affairs of companies not in the oil business, so this is an unsystematic event.

> **systematic risk**
> a risk that influences a large number of assets. Also, *market risk*.
>
> **unsystematic risk**
> a risk that affects at most a small number of assets. Also, *unique* or *asset-specific risk*.

SYSTEMATIC AND UNSYSTEMATIC COMPONENTS OF RETURN

The distinction between a systematic risk and an unsystematic risk is never really as exact as we make it out to be. Even the most narrow and peculiar bit of news about a company ripples through the economy. This is true because every enterprise, no matter how tiny, is a part of the economy. It's like the tale of a kingdom that was lost because one horse lost a shoe. This is mostly hairsplitting, however. Some risks are clearly much more general than others. We'll see some evidence on this point in just a moment.

The distinction between the types of risk allows us to break down the surprise portion, U, of the return on Flyers' equity into two parts. Earlier, we had the actual return broken down into its expected and surprise components:

$$R = E(R) + U$$

We now recognize that the total surprise component for Flyers, U, has a systematic and an unsystematic component, so:

$$R = E(R) + \text{Systematic portion} + \text{Unsystematic portion}$$

Because it is traditional, we shall use the Greek letter epsilon, ε, to stand for the unsystematic portion. Because systematic risks are often called market risks, we shall use the letter m to stand for the systematic part of the surprise. With these symbols, we can rewrite the formula for the total return:

$$\begin{aligned} R &= E(R) + U \\ &= E(R) + m + e \end{aligned}$$

The important thing about the way we have broken down the total surprise, U, is that the unsystematic portion, ε, is more or less unique to Flyers. For this reason, it is unrelated to the unsystematic portion of return on most other assets. To see why this is important, we need to return to the subject of portfolio risk.

> **CONCEPT QUESTIONS**
>
> **12.4a** What are the two basic types of risk?
> **12.4b** What is the distinction between the two types of risk?

12.5 DIVERSIFICATION AND PORTFOLIO RISK

We've seen earlier that portfolio risks can, in principle, be quite different from the risks of the assets that make up the portfolio. We now look more closely at the riskiness of an individual asset versus the risk of a portfolio of many different assets. We shall once again examine some market history to get an idea of what happens with actual investments in European capital markets.

THE EFFECT OF DIVERSIFICATION: ANOTHER LESSON FROM MARKET HISTORY

In our previous chapter, we saw that the standard deviation of the annual return on a portfolio of large European equities has historically been between 20 and 30 per cent per year. Does this mean that the standard deviation of the annual return on a typical European equity is between 20 and 30 per cent? As you might suspect by now, the answer is *no*. This is a significant observation.

To illustrate the relationship between portfolio size and portfolio risk, Table 12.7 presents typical average annual standard deviations for equally weighted portfolios that contain different numbers of randomly selected securities.

TABLE 12.7

Standard deviations of annual portfolio returns

(1) Number of equities in portfolio	(2) Average standard deviation of annual portfolio returns (%)	(3) Ratio of portfolio standard deviation to standard deviation of a single equity
1	49.24	1.00
2	37.36	0.76
4	29.69	0.60
6	26.64	0.54
8	24.98	0.51
10	23.93	0.49
20	21.68	0.44
30	20.87	0.42
40	20.46	0.42
50	20.20	0.41
100	19.69	0.40
200	19.42	0.39
300	19.34	0.39
400	19.29	0.39
500	19.27	0.39
1,000	19.21	0.39

Source: Table 1 in M. Statman (1987). How many stocks make a diversified portfolio? Journal of Financial and Quantitative Analysis, 22(3), 353-364. Derived from E.J. Elton and M.J. Gruber (1977). Risk reduction and portfolio size: An analytic solution. Journal of Business, 50, October, 415-437.

In column 2 of Table 12.7, we see that the standard deviation for a 'portfolio' of one security is about 49 per cent. What this means is that if you randomly selected a single equity and put all your money into it, your standard deviation of return would typically be a substantial 49 per cent per year. If you were to randomly select two equities and invest half your money in each, your standard deviation would be about 37 per cent on average, and so on.

The important thing to notice in Table 12.7 is that the standard deviation declines as the number of securities is increased. By the time we have 100 randomly chosen equities, the portfolio's standard deviation has declined by about 60 per cent, from 49 per cent to about 20 per cent. With 500 securities the standard deviation is 19.27 per cent, similar to the 20 per cent we saw in our previous chapter for the large UK company portfolio.

REAL WORLD INSIGHTS

Many investors ask the question, what is the best asset class (e.g. emerging market equities, UK small companies, US government bonds, commodities, etc.) in which to invest to avoid significant losses but also give decent returns? This is more difficult to answer than you would expect because individual asset class financial performance has varied dramatically over the past 20 years.

As one would expect, the asset class that avoided any losses was cash. However, it is also the worst performer because cash generates almost no returns. More risky asset classes have provided bumper years (e.g. small company equities in 2016 and emerging markets in 2017 and large company equities in 2019), and have performed very poorly in other years (2018 for emerging markets and small companies). Even commodities such as gold, oil and industrial metals have had excellent years (2010) and awful years (2014 and 2015).

Since it is tough to predict ahead of time how well an asset class will perform in any particular year, a diversified strategy of investing in several asset classes works very well over the long term.

THE PRINCIPLE OF DIVERSIFICATION

Figure 12.1 illustrates the point we've been discussing. What we have plotted is the standard deviation of return versus the number of equities in the portfolio. Notice in Figure 12.1 that the benefit in terms of

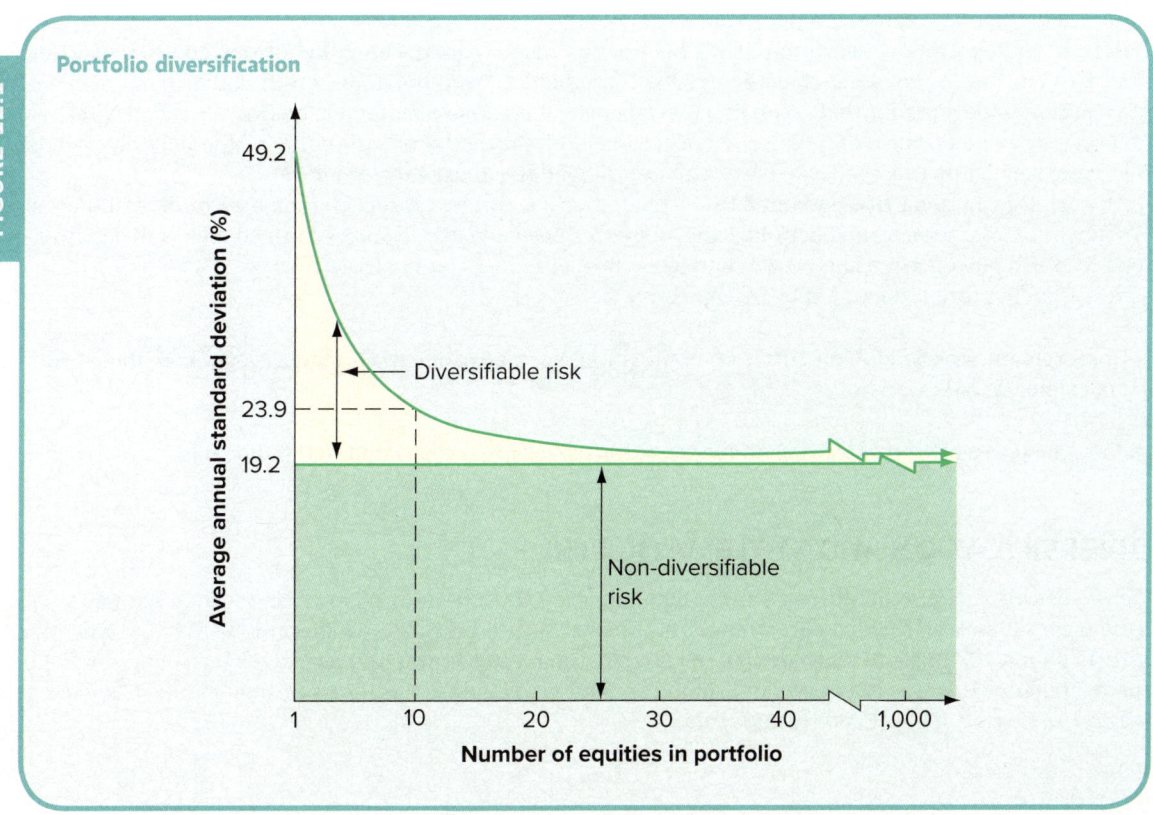

FIGURE 12.1 Portfolio diversification

risk reduction from adding securities drops off as we add more and more. By the time we have 10 securities, most of the effect is already realized; and by the time we get to 30 or so, there is little remaining benefit.

> **principle of diversification**
> spreading an investment across a number of assets will eliminate some, but not all, of the risk.

Figure 12.1 illustrates two key points. First, some of the riskiness associated with individual assets can be eliminated by forming portfolios. The process of spreading an investment across assets (and thereby creating a portfolio) is called *diversification*. The **principle of diversification** tells us that spreading an investment across many assets will eliminate some of the risk. The orange shaded area in Figure 12.1, labelled 'Diversifiable risk', is the part that can be eliminated by diversification.

The second point is equally important. There is a minimum level of risk that cannot be eliminated simply by diversifying. This minimum level is labelled 'Non-diversifiable risk' in Figure 12.1. Taken together, these two points are another vital lesson from capital market history: diversification reduces risk, but only up to a point. Put another way, some risk is diversifiable, and some is not.

To give a recent example of the impact of diversification, the FTSE 100, which is a widely followed stock market index of 100 large, well-known British companies, stayed about level on 17 July 2020. Big individual gainers for the day were BT Group (up 3.51 per cent), Flutter Entertainment (up 3.24%) and Imperial Brands (up 2.47 per cent). However, losers included International Consolidated Airlines (down 6.91 per cent), Rolls-Royce (down 5.55 per cent) and Halma (down 5.37 per cent) Again, the lesson is clear: diversification reduces exposure to extreme outcomes, both good and bad.

DIVERSIFICATION AND UNSYSTEMATIC RISK

From our discussion of portfolio risk, we know that some of the risk associated with individual assets can be diversified away, and some cannot. We are left with an obvious question: why is this so? It turns out that the answer hinges on the distinction we made earlier between systematic and unsystematic risk.

By definition, an unsystematic risk is one that is particular to a single asset or, at most, a small group. For example, if the asset under consideration is equity in a single company, the discovery of positive-NPV projects such as successful new products and innovative cost savings will tend to increase the value of the equity. Unanticipated lawsuits, industrial accidents, strikes and similar events will tend to decrease future cash flows and thereby reduce share values.

Here is an important observation: if we held only a single equity, the value of our investment would fluctuate because of company-specific events. If we hold a large portfolio, on the other hand, some of the equities in the portfolio will go up in value because of positive company-specific events and some will go down in value because of adverse events. The net effect on the overall value of the portfolio will be relatively small, however, because these effects will tend to cancel each other out.

Now we see why some of the variability associated with individual assets is eliminated by diversification. When we combine assets into portfolios, the unique, or unsystematic, events – both positive and negative – tend to 'wash out' once we have more than just a few assets.

This is an important point that bears repeating:

> Unsystematic risk is eliminated by diversification, so a portfolio with many assets has almost no unsystematic risk.

In fact, the terms *diversifiable risk* and *unsystematic risk* are often used interchangeably.

DIVERSIFICATION AND SYSTEMATIC RISK

We've seen that unsystematic risk can be eliminated by diversifying. What about systematic risk? Can it also be eliminated by diversification? The answer is no, because, by definition, a systematic risk affects almost all assets to some degree. As a result, no matter how many assets we put into a portfolio, the systematic risk doesn't go away. Thus, for obvious reasons, the terms *systematic risk* and *non-diversifiable risk* are used interchangeably.

Because we have introduced so many different terms, it is useful to summarize our discussion before moving on. What we have seen is that the total risk of an investment, as measured by the standard deviation of its return, can be written as:

$$\text{Total risk} = \text{Systematic risk} + \text{Unsystematic risk} \quad (12.5)$$

Systematic risk is also called *non-diversifiable risk* or *market risk*. Unsystematic risk is also called *diversifiable risk*, *unique risk* or *asset-specific risk*. For a well-diversified portfolio, the unsystematic risk is negligible. For such a portfolio, essentially all of the risk is systematic.

> **CONCEPT QUESTIONS**
>
> **12.5a** What happens to the standard deviation of return for a portfolio if we increase the number of securities in the portfolio?
> **12.5b** What is the principle of diversification?
> **12.5c** Why is some risk diversifiable? Why is some risk not diversifiable?
> **12.5d** Why can't systematic risk be diversified away?

12.6 SYSTEMATIC RISK AND BETA

The question that we now begin to address is this: what determines the size of the risk premium on a risky asset? Put another way, why do some assets have a larger risk premium than other assets? The answer to these questions, as we discuss next, is also based on the distinction between systematic and unsystematic risk.

THE SYSTEMATIC RISK PRINCIPLE

Thus far, we've seen that the total risk associated with an asset can be decomposed into two components: systematic and unsystematic risk. We have also seen that unsystematic risk can virtually be eliminated by diversification. The systematic risk present in an asset, on the other hand, cannot be eliminated by diversification.

Based on our study of capital market history, we know that there is a reward, on average, for bearing risk. However, we now need to be more precise about what we mean by risk. The **systematic risk principle** states that the reward for bearing risk depends only on the systematic risk of an investment. The underlying rationale for this principle is straightforward: because unsystematic risk can be eliminated at virtually no cost (by diversifying), there is no reward for bearing it. Put another way, the market does not reward risks that are taken unnecessarily.

The systematic risk principle has a remarkable and significant implication:

> The expected return on an asset depends only on that asset's systematic risk.

There is an obvious corollary to this principle: no matter how much total risk an asset has, only the systematic portion is relevant in determining the expected return (and the risk premium) on that asset.

systematic risk principle
the expected return on a risky asset depends only on that asset's systematic risk.

beta coefficient
the amount of systematic risk present in a particular risky asset relative to that in an average risky asset.

MEASURING SYSTEMATIC RISK

Because systematic risk is the crucial determinant of an asset's expected return, we need some way of measuring the level of systematic risk for different investments. The specific measure we shall use is called the **beta coefficient**, for which we shall use the Greek letter β. A beta coefficient, or beta for short, tells us how much systematic risk a particular asset has relative to an average asset. By definition, an average asset has a beta of 1.0 relative to itself. An asset with a beta of 0.50, therefore, has half as much systematic risk as an average asset; an asset with a beta of 2.0 has twice as much.

Table 12.8 contains the estimated beta coefficients for the equities of some well-known companies. The range of betas in Table 12.8 is typical for equities of large European corporations. Betas outside this range occur, but they are less common.

TABLE 12.8

Beta coefficients for selected companies

Equity	Beta
Adidas	0.68
L'Oréal	0.54
SAP	0.94
Siemens	1.20
Daimler	1.55
Telefonica	1.06
Renault	1.70
Volkswagen	1.54

Source: The Financial Times Limited (2020). All rights reserved.

The important thing to remember is that the expected return, and thus the risk premium, of an asset depends only on its systematic risk. Because assets with larger betas have greater systematic risks, they will have greater expected returns. Thus, from Table 12.8, an investor who buys equity in L'Oréal, with a beta of 0.54, should expect to earn less, on average, than an investor who buys equity in Renault, with a beta of about 1.70.

One cautionary note is in order: not all betas are created equal. Different providers use somewhat different methods for estimating betas, and significant differences sometimes occur. As a result, it is a good idea to look at several sources.

EXAMPLE 12.5

TOTAL RISK VERSUS BETA

Consider the following information about two securities. Which has a greater total risk? Which has greater systematic risk? Greater unsystematic risk? Which asset will have a higher risk premium?

	Standard deviation (%)	Beta
Security A	40	0.50
Security B	20	1.50

From our discussion in this section, Security A has greater total risk, but it has substantially less systematic risk. Because total risk is the sum of systematic and unsystematic risk, Security A must have greater unsystematic risk. Finally, from the systematic risk principle, Security B will have a higher risk premium and a greater expected return, even though it has less total risk.

PORTFOLIO BETAS

Earlier, we saw that the riskiness of a portfolio has no simple relationship to the risks of the assets in the portfolio. A portfolio beta, however, can be calculated, just like a portfolio expected return. For example, looking again at Table 12.8, suppose you put half of your money in L'Oréal and half in Siemens. What would the beta of this combination be? Because L'Oréal has a beta of 0.54 and Siemens has a beta of 1.20 the portfolio's beta, β_P, would be:

$$\begin{aligned}\beta_P &= 0.50 \times \beta_{\text{L'Oréal}} + 0.50 \times \beta_{\text{Siemens}} \\ &= 0.50 \times 0.54 + 0.50 \times 1.20 \\ &= 0.87\end{aligned}$$

In general, if we had many assets in a portfolio, we would multiply each asset's beta by its portfolio weight and then add the results to get the portfolio's beta.

EXAMPLE 12.6

PORTFOLIO BETAS

Suppose we had the following investments:

Security	Amount invested (€)	Expected return (%)	Beta
Equity A	1,000	8	0.80
Equity B	2,000	12	0.95
Equity C	3,000	15	1.10
Equity D	4,000	18	1.40

What is the expected return on this portfolio? What is the beta of this portfolio? Does this portfolio have more or less systematic risk than an average asset?

To answer, we first have to calculate the portfolio weights. Notice that the total amount invested is €10,000. Of this, €1,000/10,000 = 10% is invested in Equity A. Similarly, 20 per cent is invested in Equity B, 30 per cent is invested in Equity C, and 40 per cent is invested in Equity D. The expected return, $E(R_P)$, is thus:

$$\begin{aligned}E(R_P) &= 0.10 \times E(R_A) + 0.20 \times E(R_B) + 0.30 \times E(R_C) + 0.40 \times E(R_D) \\ &= 0.10 \times 8\% + 0.20 \times 12\% + 0.30 \times 15\% + 0.40 \times 18\% \\ &= 14.9\%\end{aligned}$$

Similarly, the portfolio beta, β_P, is:

$$\begin{aligned}\beta_P &= 0.10 \times \beta_A + 0.20 \times \beta_B + 0.30 \times \beta_C + 0.40 \times \beta_D \\ &= 0.10 \times 0.80 + 0.20 \times 0.95 + 0.30 \times 1.10 + 0.40 \times 1.40 \\ &= 1.16\end{aligned}$$

This portfolio thus has an expected return of 14.9 per cent and a beta of 1.16. Because the beta is larger than 1, this portfolio has greater systematic risk than an average asset.

CONCEPT QUESTIONS

12.6a What is the systematic risk principle?
12.6b What does a beta coefficient measure?
12.6c True or false: the expected return on a risky asset depends on that asset's total risk. Explain.
12.6d How do you calculate a portfolio beta?

12.7 THE SECURITY MARKET LINE

We're now in a position to see how risk is rewarded in the marketplace. To begin, suppose that Asset A has an expected return of $E(R_A) = 20\%$ and a beta of $\beta_A = 1.6$. Furthermore, suppose that the risk-free rate is $R_f = 8\%$. Notice that a risk-free asset, by definition, has no systematic risk (or unsystematic risk), so a risk-free asset has a beta of zero.

BETA AND THE RISK PREMIUM

Consider a portfolio made up of Asset A and a risk-free asset. We can calculate some different possible portfolio expected returns and betas by varying the percentages invested in these two assets. For example, if 25 per cent of the portfolio is invested in Asset A, then the expected return is:

$$E(R_P) = 0.25 \times E(R_A) + (1 - 0.25) \times R_f$$
$$= 0.25 \times 20\% + 0.75 \times 8\%$$
$$= 11\%$$

Similarly, the beta on the portfolio, β_P, would be:

$$\beta_P = 0.25 \times \beta_A + (1 - 0.25) \times 0$$
$$= 0.25 \times 1.6$$
$$= 0.40$$

Notice that because the weights have to add up to 1, the percentage invested in the risk-free asset is equal to 1 minus the percentage invested in Asset A.

One thing that you might wonder about is whether it is possible for the percentage invested in Asset A to exceed 100 per cent. The answer is yes. This can happen if the investor borrows at the risk-free rate. For example, suppose an investor has €100 and borrows an additional €50 at 8 per cent, the risk-free rate. The total investment in Asset A would be €150, or 150 per cent of the investor's wealth. The expected return, in this case, would be:

$$E(R_P) = 1.50 \times E(R_A) + (1 - 1.50) \times R_f$$
$$= 1.50 \times 20\% - 0.50 \times 8\%$$
$$= 26\%$$

The beta on the portfolio would be:

$$\beta_P = 1.50 \times \beta + (1 - 1.50) \times 0$$
$$= 1.50 \times 1.6$$
$$= 2.4$$

We can calculate some other possibilities, as follows:

Percentage of portfolio in Asset A (%)	Portfolio expected return (%)	Portfolio beta
0	8	0.0
25	11	0.4
50	14	0.8
75	17	1.2
100	20	1.6
125	23	2.0
150	26	2.4

In Figure 12.2, these portfolio expected returns are plotted against the portfolio betas. Notice that all the combinations fall on a straight line.

The Reward-to-Risk Ratio

What is the slope of the straight line in Figure 12.2(a)? As always, the slope of a straight line is equal to 'the rise over the run'. In this case, as we move out of the risk-free asset into Asset A, the beta increases from zero to 1.6 (a 'run' of 1.6). At the same time, the expected return goes from 8 per cent to 20 per cent, a 'rise' of 12 per cent. The slope of the line is thus 12% / 1.6 = 7.5%.

FIGURE 12.2

(a) Portfolio expected returns and betas for Asset A; (b) Portfolio expected returns and betas for Asset B; (c) Portfolio expected returns and betas for both assets

Notice that the slope of our line is just the risk premium on Asset A, $E(R_A) - R_f$, divided by Asset A's beta, β_A:

$$\text{Slope} = \frac{E(R_A) - R_f}{\beta_A}$$
$$= \frac{20\% - 8\%}{1.6}$$
$$= 7.5\%$$

This tells us that Asset A offers a *reward-to-risk* ratio of 7.5 per cent.[2] In other words, Asset A has a risk premium of 7.50 per cent per 'unit' of systematic risk.

The Basic Argument

Now suppose we consider a second asset, Asset B. This asset has a beta of 1.2 and an expected return of 16 per cent. Which investment is better, Asset A or Asset B? You might think that once again, we really cannot say – some investors might prefer A; some investors might prefer B. Actually, however, we *can* say A is better, because, as we shall demonstrate, B offers inadequate compensation for its level of systematic risk, at least relative to A.

To begin, we calculate different combinations of expected returns and betas for portfolios of Asset B and a risk-free asset, just as we did for Asset A. For example, if we put 25 per cent in Asset B and the remaining 75 per cent in the risk-free asset, the portfolio's expected return will be:

$$\begin{aligned} E(R_P) &= 0.25 \times E(R_B) + (1 - 0.25) \times R_f \\ &= 0.25 \times 16\% + 0.75 \times 8\% \\ &= 10\% \end{aligned}$$

Similarly, the beta on the portfolio, β_P, would be:

$$\begin{aligned} \beta_P &= 0.25 \times \beta_B + (1 - 0.25) \times 0 \\ &= 0.25 \times 1.2 \\ &= 0.30 \end{aligned}$$

Some other possibilities are as follows:

Percentage of portfolio in Asset B (%)	Portfolio expected return (%)	Portfolio beta
0	8	0.0
25	10	0.3
50	12	0.6
75	14	0.9
100	16	1.2
125	18	1.5
150	20	1.8

When we plot these combinations of portfolio expected returns and portfolio betas in Figure 12.2(b) we get a straight line, just as we did for Asset A.

The key thing to notice is that when we compare the results for Assets A and B, as in Figure 12.2(c), the line describing the combinations of expected returns and betas for Asset A is higher than the one for Asset B. This tells us that for any given level of systematic risk (as measured by β), some combination of Asset A and the risk-free asset always offers a larger return. This is why we were able to state that Asset A is a better investment than Asset B.

Another way of seeing that A offers a superior return for its level of risk is to note that the slope of our line for Asset B is:

$$\begin{aligned} \text{Slope} &= \frac{E(R_B) - R_f}{\beta_B} \\ &= \frac{16\% - 8\%}{1.2} \\ &= 6.67\% \end{aligned}$$

Thus Asset B has a reward-to-risk ratio of 6.67 per cent, which is less than the 7.5 per cent offered by Asset A.

The Fundamental Result

The situation we have described for Assets A and B could not persist in a well-organized, active market because investors would be attracted to Asset A and away from Asset B. As a result, Asset A's price would rise and Asset B's price would fall. Because prices and returns move in opposite directions, A's expected return would decline, and B's would rise.

This buying and selling would continue until the two assets plotted on the same line, which means they would offer the same reward for bearing risk. In other words, in an active, competitive market, we must have the situation that:

$$\frac{E(R_A) - R_f}{\beta_A} = \frac{E(R_B) - R_f}{\beta_B}$$

This is the fundamental relationship between risk and return.

Our basic argument can be extended to more than just two assets. In fact, no matter how many assets we had, we would always reach the same conclusion:

The reward-to-risk ratio must be the same for all the assets in the market.

This result is really not so surprising. What it says is that, for example, if one asset has twice as much systematic risk as another asset, its risk premium will be twice as large.

Because all of the assets in the market must have the same reward-to-risk ratio, they all must plot on the same line. This argument is illustrated in Figure 12.3. As shown, Assets A and B plot directly on the line and thus have the same reward-to-risk ratio. If an asset plotted above the line, such as C in Figure 12.3, its price would rise, and its expected return would fall until it plotted exactly on the line. Similarly, if an asset plotted below the line, such as D in Figure 12.3, its expected return would rise until it too plotted directly on the line.

The arguments we have presented apply to active, competitive, well-functioning markets. The financial markets, including the LSE, Euronext and Deutsche Börse, best meet these criteria. Other markets, such as real asset markets, may or may not. For this reason, these concepts are most useful in examining financial markets. We shall thus focus on such markets here. However, as discussed in a later section, the information about risk and return gleaned from financial markets is crucial in evaluating the investments that a corporation makes in real assets.

FIGURE 12.3

Expected returns and systematic risk

The fundamental relationship between beta and expected return is that all assets must have the same reward-to-risk ratio, $[E(R_i) - R_f]/\beta_i$. This means that they would all plot on the same straight line. Assets A and B are examples of this behaviour. Asset C's expected return is too high; asset D's is too low.

EXAMPLE 12.7

BUY LOW, SELL HIGH

An asset is said to be *overvalued* if its price is too high, given its expected return and risk. Suppose you observe the following situation:

Security	Beta	Expected return (%)
SWMS plc	1.3	14
Insec plc	0.8	10

The risk-free rate is currently 6 per cent. Is one of the two securities overvalued relative to the other?
To answer, we compute the reward-to-risk ratio for both. For SWMS, this ratio is (14% − 6%) / 1.3 = 6.15%. For Insec, this ratio is 5 per cent. What we conclude is that Insec offers an insufficient expected return for its level of risk, at least relative to SWMS. Because its expected return is too low, its price is too high. In other words, Insec is overvalued relative to SWMS, and we would expect to see its price fall relative to SWMS's. Notice that we could also say SWMS is undervalued relative to Insec.

THE SECURITY MARKET LINE

security market line (SML)
a positively sloped straight line displaying the relationship between expected return and beta.

The line that results when we plot expected returns and beta coefficients is obviously of some importance, so it's time we gave it a name. This line, which we use to describe the relationship between systematic risk and expected return in financial markets, is usually called the **security market line (SML)**. After NPV, the SML is arguably the most important concept in modern finance.

Market Portfolios

It will be very useful to know the equation of the SML. There are many different ways we could write it, but one way is particularly common. Suppose we consider a portfolio made up of all of the assets in the market. Such a portfolio is called a *market portfolio*, and we shall express the expected return on this market portfolio as $E(R_M)$.

Because all the assets in the market must plot on the SML, so must a market portfolio made up of those assets. To determine where it plots on the SML, we need to know the beta of the market portfolio, β_M. Because this portfolio is representative of all of the assets in the market, it must have average systematic risk. In other words, it has a beta of 1. We could therefore express the slope of the SML as:

$$\text{SML slope} = \frac{E(R_M) - R_f}{\beta_M}$$
$$= \frac{E(R_M) - R_f}{1}$$
$$= E(R_M) - R_f$$

The term $E(R_M) - R_f$ is often called the **market risk premium** because it is the risk premium on a market portfolio.

market risk premium
the slope of the SML - the difference between the expected return on a market portfolio and the risk-free rate.

The Capital Asset Pricing Model

To finish up, if we let $E(R_i)$ and β_i stand for the expected return and beta, respectively, on any asset in the market, then we know that asset must plot on the SML. As a result, we know that its reward-to-risk ratio is the same as the overall market's:

$$\frac{E(R_i) - R_f}{\beta_i} = E(R_M) - R_f$$

If we rearrange this, then we can write the equation for the SML as:

$$E(R_i) = R_f + [E(R_M) - R_f] \times \beta_i \qquad (12.6)$$

This result is the famous **capital asset pricing model (CAPM)**.

The CAPM shows that the expected return for a particular asset depends on three things:

capital asset pricing model (CAPM)
the equation of the SML showing the relationship between expected return and beta.

1. *The pure time value of money:* As measured by the risk-free rate, R_f, this is the reward for merely waiting for your money, without taking any risk.
2. *The reward for bearing systematic risk:* As measured by the market risk premium, $E(R_M) - R_f$, this component is the reward the market offers for bearing an average amount of systematic risk in addition to waiting.
3. *The amount of systematic risk:* As measured by β_i, this is the amount of systematic risk present in a particular asset or portfolio, relative to that in an average asset.

By the way, the CAPM works for portfolios of assets just as it does for individual assets. In an earlier section, we saw how to calculate a portfolio's β. To find the expected return on a portfolio, we use this β in the CAPM equation.

Figure 12.4 summarizes our discussion of the SML and the CAPM. As before, we plot expected return against beta. Now we recognize that, based on the CAPM, the slope of the SML is equal to the market risk premium, $E(R_M) - R_f$.

FIGURE 12.4

The security market line (SML)

The slope of the security market line is equal to the market risk premium – that is, the reward for bearing an average amount of systematic risk. The equation describing the SML can be written:

$$E(R_i) = R_f + [E(R_M) - R_f] \times \beta_i$$

which is the capital asset pricing model (CAPM).

This concludes our presentation of concepts related to the risk-return trade-off. For future reference, Table 12.9 summarizes the various concepts in the order in which we discussed them.

TABLE 12.9

Summary of risk and return

Total risk

The *total risk* of an investment is measured by the variance or, more commonly, the standard deviation of its return.

Total return

The *total return* on an investment has two components: the expected return and the unexpected return. The unexpected return comes about because of unanticipated events – the risk from investing stems from the possibility of an unanticipated event.

Systematic and unsystematic risks

Systematic risks (also called *market risks*) are unanticipated events that affect almost all assets to some degree because the effects are economy-wide. *Unsystematic risks* are unforeseen events that affect single assets or small groups of assets. Unsystematic risks are also called *unique or asset-specific risks*.

The effect of diversification
Some, but not all, of the risk associated with a risky investment can be eliminated by diversification. The reason is that unsystematic risks, which are unique to individual assets, tend to wash out in a large portfolio, but systematic risks, which affect all of the assets in a portfolio to some extent, do not.

The systematic risk principle and beta
Because unsystematic risk can be freely eliminated by diversification, the *systematic risk principle* states that the reward for bearing risk depends only on the level of systematic risk. The systematic risk of a particular asset is given by its beta.

The reward-to-risk ratio and the security market line
The *reward-to-risk ratio* for asset i is the ratio of its risk premium, $E(R) - R_f$, to its beta, β_i:

$$\frac{E(R_i) - R_f}{\beta_i}$$

In a well-functioning market, this ratio is the same for every asset. As a result, when asset expected returns are plotted against asset betas, all assets plot on the same straight line, called the *security market line* (SML).

The capital asset pricing model
From the SML, the expected return on asset i can be written:

$$E(R_i) = R_f + [E(R_M) - R_f] \times \beta_i$$

This is the *capital asset pricing model* (CAPM). The expected return on a risky asset thus has three components. The first is the pure time value of money (R_f), the second is the market risk premium $[E(R_M) - R_f]$, and the third is the beta for that asset, (β_i).

EXAMPLE 12.8

RISK AND RETURN

Suppose the risk-free rate is 4 per cent, the market risk premium is 8.6 per cent, and a particular equity has a beta of 1.3. Based on the CAPM, what is the expected return on this equity? What would the expected return be if the beta were to double?

With a beta of 1.3, the risk premium for the equity is 1.3 × 8.6%, or 11.18 per cent. The risk-free rate is 4 per cent, so the expected return is 15.18 per cent. If the beta were to double to 2.6, the risk premium would double to 22.36 per cent, so the expected return would be 26.36 per cent.

REAL WORLD INSIGHTS

Never before have so many intelligent people spent so much time painstakingly unpicking the devilishly complex world of finance. Visit any business school, and you will find legions of relatively well-paid, dedicated academics scrutinizing reams of financial data. For years, finance academics longed for a rational subject that they could study rigorously, measure and hypothesize upon. They longed to copy the rigour of the physical sciences and to treat data objectively. They just needed the means to do it.

The answer came in the 1960s in the guise of the Capital Asset Pricing Model. The CAPM is used by investors to value shares by modelling the relationship between expected risk and expected return. It assumes rationality underpins the financial markets and has been the unchallenged core of academic finance ever since it was

> adopted. Mainstream academics take data from the real world of finance then devote their time to reconciling it with these core principles. It results in an endless stream of puzzles that keep the academic finance industry busy. Unfortunately, this misses the point of the CAPM. The model is a reasonable basis for understanding the markets, but that is all it can ever be - a basis upon which to build.
>
> Source: Excerpts from 'Academics must address the problems of the financial markets' by Kevin Keasey and Iain Clacher, FT.com, 18 June 2012.

CRITICISMS OF THE CAPM

Although the CAPM represents one of the most critical advances in financial economics, it is not immune to criticism. Nobody who works in finance will ever say that they believe the CAPM fully explains the returns on securities, investments or financial portfolios. All the CAPM does, as with any other theoretical model, is give insights into the truth. It is argued that, because it is practically impossible to construct a portfolio that contains every single security (i.e. the true market portfolio), any test of the CAPM that uses a market proxy (e.g. FTSE 100, DAX, CAC 40, etc.) will be testing that specific portfolio and not the true market portfolio. This means that the CAPM is empirically untestable because the underlying market portfolio is unobservable. This is known as Roll's (1977)[a] critique and any tests of the CAPM that use market proxies will be affected by this criticism.

EMPIRICAL TESTS OF THE CAPM

The first empirical tests of the CAPM occurred more than 30 years ago and were quite supportive of the model. Using data from the 1930s to the 1960s on US stock markets, researchers showed that the average return on a portfolio of stocks was positively related to the beta of the portfolio, a finding consistent with the CAPM. The model was not seriously called into question until the 1990s with two papers by researchers, Fama and French (1992[b], 1993[c]), which made two related points. First, the relationship between average return and beta was virtually non-existent from 1963 to 1990. Second, the average return on a security was found to be negatively related to a firm's price–earnings (PE) ratio and market-to-book (MB) ratios. Other research has highlighted past share price performance as being positive related to future returns (Carhart's 1997[d] momentum factor).

Fama and French (2015[e], 2016[f], 2017[g]) extended their earlier analysis and presented further evidence against beta. Specifically, average returns were positively related to operating efficiency and eliminated the explanatory power of beta in average European stock returns. These contentions, if confirmed by other research, would be quite damaging to the CAPM. After all, the CAPM states that the expected returns on equities should be related only to beta, and not to other factors such as PE, MB, momentum or market volatility.

Although a lot of time has been spent debating the relevance of beta, CAPM is still widely used. Financial websites, such as Yahoo! Finance, Bloomberg, and FT.com, frequently provide estimates of the beta of listed firms. Investors use beta to understand the risk of companies, and corporate managers use CAPM to understand their cost of capital, a topic we cover in considerable detail later.

---

[a]Roll, R. (1977). A critique of the asset pricing theory's tests Part I: On past and potential testability of the theory. *Journal of Financial Economics*, *4*(2), 129–176.

[b]Fama, E.F., & French, K.R. (1992). The cross-section of expected stock returns. *Journal of Finance*, 47, 427–465.

[c]Fama, E.F., & French, K.R. (1993). Common risk factors in the returns on stocks and bonds. *Journal of Financial Economics*, 33, 3–56.

[d]Carhart, M.M. (1997). On persistence in mutual fund performance. *Journal of Finance*, *52*(1), 57–82.

[e]Fama, E.F., & French, K.R. (2015). A five-factor asset pricing model. *Journal of Financial Economics*, *116*(1), 1–22.

[f]Fama, E.F., & French, K.R. (2016). Dissecting anomalies with a five-factor model. *Review of Financial Studies*, *29*(1), 69–103.

[g]Fama, E.F., & French, K.R. (2017). International tests of a five-factor asset pricing model. *Journal of Financial Economics*, *123*(3), 441–463.

> **CONCEPT QUESTIONS**
>
> **12.7a** What is the fundamental relationship between risk and return in well-functioning markets?
> **12.7b** What is the security market line? Why must all assets plot directly on it in a well-functioning market?
> **12.7c** What is the capital asset pricing model (CAPM)? What does it tell us about the required return on a risky investment?

12.8 THE SML AND THE COST OF CAPITAL: A PREVIEW

Our goal in studying risk and return is twofold. First, risk is an extremely important consideration in almost all business decisions, so we want to discuss just what risk is and how it is rewarded in the market. Our second purpose is to learn what determines the appropriate discount rate for future cash flows. We briefly discuss this second subject now; we shall discuss it in more detail in a subsequent chapter.

THE BASIC IDEA

The security market line tells us the reward for bearing risk in financial markets. At an absolute minimum, any new investment our firm undertakes must offer an expected return that is no worse than what the financial markets offer for the same risk. The reason for this is simply that our shareholders can always invest for themselves in the financial markets.

The only way we benefit our shareholders is by finding investments with expected returns that are superior to what the financial markets offer for the same risk. Such an investment will have a positive NPV. So, if we ask 'What is the appropriate discount rate?', the answer is that we should use the expected return offered in financial markets on investments with the same systematic risk.

In other words, to determine whether an investment has a positive NPV, we essentially compare the expected return on that new investment with what the financial market offers on an investment with the same beta. This is why the SML is so important: it tells us the 'going rate' for bearing risk in the economy.

THE COST OF CAPITAL

cost of capital
the minimum required return on a new investment.

The appropriate discount rate on a new project is the minimum expected rate of return an investment must offer to be attractive. This minimum required return is often called the **cost of capital** associated with the investment. It is called this because the required return is what the firm must earn on its capital investment in a project to break even. It can thus be interpreted as the opportunity cost associated with the firm's capital investment.

Notice that when we say an investment is attractive if its expected return exceeds what is offered in financial markets for investments of the same risk, we are effectively using the internal rate of return (IRR) criterion that we developed and discussed in Chapter 8. The only difference is that we now have a much better idea of what determines the required return on an investment. This understanding will be critical when we discuss cost of capital and capital structure in Part Five of our book.

> **CONCEPT QUESTIONS**
>
> **12.8a** If an investment has a positive NPV, would it plot above or below the SML? Why?
> **12.8b** What is meant by the term *cost of capital*?

SUMMARY AND CONCLUSIONS

This chapter has covered the essentials of risk. Along the way, we have introduced many definitions and concepts. The most important of these is the security market line, or SML. The SML is important because it tells us the reward offered in financial markets for bearing risk. Once we know this, we have a benchmark against which we can compare the returns expected from real asset investments to determine whether they are desirable.

Because we have covered quite a bit of ground, it is useful to summarize the basic economic logic underlying the SML as follows:

1. Based on capital market history, there is a reward for bearing risk. This reward is the risk premium on an asset.
2. The total risk associated with an asset has two parts: systematic risk and unsystematic risk. Unsystematic risk can be freely eliminated by diversification (this is the principle of diversification), so only systematic risk is rewarded. As a result, the risk premium on an asset is determined by its systematic risk. This is the systematic risk principle.
3. An asset's systematic risk, relative to the average, can be measured by its beta coefficient, β_i. The risk premium on an asset is then given by its beta coefficient multiplied by the market risk premium, $[E(R_M) - R_f] \times \beta_i$.
4. The expected return on an asset, $E(R_i)$, is equal to the risk-free rate, R_f, plus the risk premium:

$$E(R_i) = R_f + [E(R_M) - R_f] \times \beta_i$$

This is the equation of the SML, and it is often called the capital asset pricing model (CAPM).

This chapter completes our discussion of risk and return. Now that we have a better understanding of what determines a firm's cost of capital for an investment, the next several chapters will examine more closely how firms raise the long-term capital needed for investment.

CHAPTER REVIEW AND SELF-TEST PROBLEMS

12.1 Expected Return and Standard Deviation This problem will give you some practice calculating measures of prospective portfolio performance. There are two assets and three states of the economy:

State of economy	Probability of state of economy	Rate of return if state occurs	
		Equity A	Equity B
Recession	0.20	−0.15	0.20
Normal	0.50	0.20	0.30
Boom	0.30	0.60	0.40

What are the expected returns and standard deviations for these two equities?

12.2 Portfolio Risk and Return Using the information in the previous problem, suppose you have £20,000 total. If you put £15,000 in Equity A and the remainder in Equity B, what will be the expected return and standard deviation of your portfolio?

12.3 Risk and return Suppose you observe the following situation:

Security	Beta	Expected return (%)
Cooley NV	1.8	22.00
Moyer NV	1.6	20.44

If the risk-free rate is 7 per cent, are these securities correctly priced? What would the risk-free rate have to be if they are correctly priced?

12.4 CAPM Suppose the risk-free rate is 8 per cent. The expected return on the market is 16 per cent. If a particular equity has a beta of 0.7, what is its expected return based on the CAPM? If another equity has an expected return of 24 per cent, what must its beta be?

SOLUTIONS

12.1 The expected returns are just the possible returns multiplied by the associated probabilities:

$$E(R_A) = (0.20 \times -0.15) + (0.50 \times 0.20) + (0.30 \times 0.60) = 25\%$$
$$E(R_B) = (0.20 \times 0.20) + (0.50 \times 0.30) + (0.30 \times 0.40) = 31\%$$

The variances are given by the sums of the squared deviations from the expected returns multiplied by their probabilities:

$$\begin{aligned}\sigma_A^2 &= 0.20 \times (-0.15 - 0.25)^2 + 0.50 \times (0.20 - 0.25)^2 + 0.30 \times (0.60 - 0.25)^2 \\ &= (0.20 \times -0.40)^2 + (0.50 \times -0.05^2) + (0.30 \times 0.35^2) \\ &= (0.20 \times 0.16) + (0.50 \times 0.0025) + (0.30 \times 0.1225) \\ &= 0.0700\end{aligned}$$

$$\begin{aligned}\sigma_B^2 &= 0.20 \times (0.20 - 0.31)^2 + 0.50 \times (0.30 - 0.31)^2 + 0.30 \times (0.40 - 0.31)^2 \\ &= (0.20 \times 0.11^2) + (0.50 \times 0.01^2) + (0.30 \times 0.09^2) \\ &= (0.20 \times 0.0121) + (0.50 \times 0.001) + (0.30 \times 0.0081) \\ &= 0.0049\end{aligned}$$

The standard deviations are thus:

$$\sigma_A = \sqrt{0.0700} = 26.46\%$$
$$\sigma_B = \sqrt{0.0049} = 7\%$$

12.2 The portfolio weights are £15,000/20,000 = 0.75 and £5,000/20,000 = 0.25. The expected return is thus:

$$\begin{aligned}E(R_P) &= 0.75 \times E(R_A) + 0.25 \times E(R_B) \\ &= (0.75 \times 25\%) + (0.25 \times 31\%) \\ &= 26.5\%\end{aligned}$$

Alternatively, we could calculate the portfolio's return in each of the states:

State of economy	Probability of state of economy	Portfolio return if state occurs
Recession	0.20	(0.75 × −0.15) + (0.25 × 0.20) = −0.0625
Normal	0.50	(0.75 × 0.20) + (0.25 × 0.30) = 0.2250
Boom	0.30	(0.75 × 0.60) + (0.25 × 0.40) = 0.5500

The portfolio's expected return is:

$$E(R_P) = (0.25 \times -0.0625) + (0.50 \times 0.2250) + (0.30 \times 0.5500) = 26.5\%$$

This is the same as we had before.

The portfolio's variance is:

$$\sigma_P^2 = 0.20 \times (-0.0625 - 0.265)^2 + 0.50 \times (0.225 - 0.265)^2$$
$$+ 0.30 \times (0.55 - 0.265)^2$$
$$= 0.0466$$

So the standard deviation is $\sqrt{0.0466} = 21.59\%$

12.3 If we compute the reward-to-risk ratios, we get $(22\% - 7\%)/1.8 = 8.33\%$ for Cooley versus 8.4% for Moyer. Relative to that of Cooley, Moyer's expected return is too high, so its price is too low.

If they are correctly priced, then they must offer the same reward-to-risk ratio. The risk-free rate would have to be such that:

$$(22\% - R_f)/1.8 = (20.44\% - R_f)/1.6$$

With a little algebra, we find that the risk-free rate must be 8 per cent:

$$22\% - R_f = (20.44\% - R_f)(1.8/1.6)$$
$$22\% - 20.44\% \times 1.125 = R_f - R_f \times 1.125$$
$$R_f = 8\%$$

12.4 Because the expected return on the market is 16 per cent, the market risk premium is $16\% - 8\% = 8\%$. The first equity has a beta of 0.7, so its expected return is $8\% + 0.7 \times 8\% = 13.6\%$.

For the second equity, notice that the risk premium is $24\% - 8\% = 16\%$. Because this is twice as large as the market risk premium, the beta must be exactly equal to 2. We can verify this using the CAPM:

$$E(R_i) = R_f + [E(R_M) - R_f]\beta_i$$
$$24\% = 8\% + (16\% - 8\%) \times \beta_i$$
$$\beta_i = 16\%/8\%$$
$$= 2.0$$

QUESTIONS AND PROBLEMS

12.1 **Determining Portfolio Weights** What are the portfolio weights for a portfolio that has 200 shares of Equity A that sell for £4.50 per share and 100 shares of Equity B that sell for £2.70 per share?

12.2 **Portfolio Expected Return** You own a portfolio that has €2,950 invested in Equity A and €3,700 invested in Equity B. If the expected returns on these equities are 11 per cent and 15 per cent, respectively, what is the expected return on the portfolio?

12.3 **Portfolio Expected Return** You own a portfolio that is 60 per cent invested in Equity X, 25 per cent in Equity Y, and 15 per cent in Equity Z. The expected returns on these three equities are 9 per cent, 17 per cent and 13 per cent, respectively. What is the expected return on the portfolio?

12.4 **Portfolio Expected Return** You have £10,000 to invest in an equity portfolio. Your choices are Equity X with an expected return of 14 per cent and Equity Y with an expected return of 11 per cent. If your goal is to create a portfolio with an expected return of 12 per cent, how much money will you invest in Equity X? In Equity Y?

12.5 **Calculating Expected Return** Based on the following information, calculate the expected return:

State of economy	Probability of state of economy	Portfolio return if state occurs
Recession	0.25	−0.08
Boom	0.75	0.21

12.6 **Calculating Expected Return** Based on the following information, calculate the expected return:

State of economy	Probability of state of economy	Portfolio return if state occurs
Recession	0.15	−0.08
Normal	0.60	0.10
Boom	0.25	0.28

12.7 **Calculating Returns and Standard Deviations** Based on the following information, calculate the expected return and standard deviation for the two equities:

		Rate of return if state occurs	
State of economy	Probability of state of economy	Equity A	Equity B
Recession	0.25	0.05	−0.17
Normal	0.55	0.08	0.12
Boom	0.20	0.13	0.29

12.8 **Calculating Expected Returns** A portfolio is invested 25 per cent in Equity G, 55 per cent in Equity J and 20 per cent in Equity K. The expected returns on these equities are 8 per cent, 15 per cent and 24 per cent, respectively. What is the portfolio's expected return? How do you interpret your answer?

12.9 **Returns and Variances** Consider the following information:

		Rate of return if state occurs		
State of economy	Probability of state of economy	Equity A	Equity B	Equity C
Boom	0.35	0.07	0.15	0.33
Bust	0.65	0.13	0.03	−0.06

(a) What is the expected return on an equally weighted portfolio of these three equities?

(b) What is the variance of a portfolio invested 20 per cent each in A and B and 60 per cent in C?

12.10 Returns and Standard Deviations Consider the following information:

State of economy	Probability of state of economy	Rate of return if state occurs		
		Equity A	Equity B	Equity C
Boom	0.05	0.30	0.45	0.33
Good	0.45	0.12	0.10	0.15
Poor	0.35	0.01	−0.15	−0.05
Bust	0.15	−0.06	−0.30	−0.09

(a) Your portfolio is invested 30 per cent each in A and C, and 40 per cent in B. What is the expected return of the portfolio?

(b) What is the variance of this portfolio? The standard deviation?

12.11 Calculating Portfolio Betas Your equity portfolio has 25 per cent in L'Oréal, 20 per cent in Carrefour, 15 per cent in Unicredit, and 40 per cent in LVMH Moët Hennesey Louis Vuitton. The betas for these four equities are 0.65, 0.89, 1.93 and 1.04, respectively. What is the portfolio beta?

12.12 Calculating Portfolio Betas You own a portfolio equally invested in a risk-free asset and two mining stocks, Vedanta Resources and Glencore plc. The beta of Vedanta is 2.63 and the total portfolio is equally as risky as the market. What is the beta of Glencore?

12.13 Using CAPM L'Oréal has a beta of 0.65, the expected return on the CAC 40 Index is 8 per cent, and the risk-free rate is 1.5 per cent. What is the expected return of L'Oréal?

12.14 Using CAPM The German chemicals firm, Lanxess AG, has an expected return of 13 per cent, the risk-free rate is 1.5 per cent, and the market risk premium is 8.5 per cent. What is the beta of Lanxess?

12.15 Using CAPM An equity has an expected return of 7.5 per cent, its beta is 0.67, and the risk-free rate is 1 per cent. What must the expected return on the market be?

12.16 Using CAPM The beta of Banco de Sabadell SA is 1.48 and the company has an expected return of 11 per cent over the next year. What is the risk-free rate if the expected return on the market is 8 per cent. What must the risk-free rate be?

12.17 Using the SML Asset W has an expected return of 15.2 per cent and a beta of 1.25. If the risk-free rate is 5.3 per cent, complete the following table for portfolios of Asset W and a risk-free asset. Illustrate the relationship between portfolio expected return and portfolio beta by plotting the expected returns against the betas. What is the slope of the line that results?

Percentage of portfolio in Asset W	Portfolio expected return	Portfolio beta
0		
25		
50		
75		
100		
125		
150		

12.18 Using CAPM An equity has a beta of 1.1 and an expected return of 9 per cent. A risk-free asset currently earns 0.8 per cent.

(a) What is the expected return on a portfolio that is equally invested in the two assets?

(b) If a portfolio of the two assets has a beta of 0.8, what are the portfolio weights?

(c) If a portfolio of the two assets has an expected return of 11 per cent, what is its beta?

(d) If a portfolio of the two assets has a beta of 2.2, what are the portfolio weights? How do you interpret the weights for the two assets in this case? Explain.

12.19 Reward-to-Risk Ratios Equity Y has a beta of 1.4 and an expected return of 10.5 per cent. Equity Z has a beta of 0.80 and an expected return of 6 per cent. If the risk-free rate is 0.5 per cent and the market risk premium is 8 per cent, are these equities correctly priced? Explain.

12.20 Reward-to-Risk Ratios In the previous problem, what would the risk-free rate have to be for the two equities to be correctly priced?

12.21 Portfolio Returns Using information from the previous chapter on capital market history, determine the return on a portfolio that is equally invested in large UK company equities and small UK company equities. What is the return on a portfolio that is equally invested in German and French equities?

12.22 CAPM Using the CAPM, show that the ratio of the risk premiums on two assets is equal to the ratio of their betas.

12.23 Portfolio Returns and Deviations Consider the following information about three equities:

State of economy	Probability of state of economy	Rate of return if state occurs		
		Equity A	Equity B	Equity C
Boom	0.25	0.24	0.36	0.55
Good	0.50	0.17	0.13	0.09
Bust	0.25	0.00	−0.28	−0.45

(a) If your portfolio is invested 40 per cent each in A and B and 20 per cent in C, what is the portfolio expected return? The variance? The standard deviation?

(b) If the expected T-bill rate is 3.80 per cent, what is the expected risk premium on the portfolio?

(c) If the expected inflation rate is 3.50 per cent, what are the approximate and exact expected real returns on the portfolio? What are the approximate and exact expected real risk premiums on the portfolio?

12.24 Analysing a Portfolio You want to create a portfolio equally as risky as the market, and you have £1,000,000 to invest. Given this information, fill in the rest of the following table:

Asset	Investment (£)	Beta
Equity A	210,000	0.85
Equity B	320,000	1.20
Equity C	?	1.35
Risk-free asset	?	?

12.25 Analysing a Portfolio You have £24,000 to invest in a portfolio containing X, Y and a risk-free asset. You must invest all of your money. Your goal is to create a portfolio that has an expected return of 8.5 per cent and that has only 70 per cent of the risk of the overall market. If X has an expected return of 12 per cent and a beta of 1.5, Y has an expected return of 9 per cent and a beta of 1.2, and the risk-free rate is 3 per cent. How much money will you invest in X? How do you interpret your answer?

12.26 Systematic versus Unsystematic Risk Consider the following information about Equities I and II:

State of economy	Probability of state of economy	Rate of return if state occurs	
		Equity I	Equity II
Recession	0.20	0.09	−0.30
Normal	0.60	0.42	0.12
Irrational exuberance	0.20	0.26	0.44

The market risk premium is 10 per cent, and the risk-free rate is 1 per cent. Compute the β_i and standard deviation of security I. Compute the β_i and standard deviation of security II. Which equity is 'riskier'? Explain.

12.27 SML Suppose you observe the following situation:

Security	Beta	Expected return
Renewable Energy Corp	1.3	0.23
STATOIL	0.6	0.13

Assume these securities are correctly priced. Based on the CAPM, what is the expected return on the market? What is the risk-free rate?

12.28 SML Suppose you observe the following situation:

State of economy	Probability of state of economy	Rate of return if state occurs	
		Equity A	Equity B
Bust	0.25	−0.10	−0.30
Normal	0.50	0.10	0.05
Boom	0.25	0.20	0.40

(a) Calculate the expected return on each equity.

(b) Assuming the capital asset pricing model holds, and equity B's beta is greater than equity A's beta by 0.25, what is the expected market risk premium?

MINI CASE

THE BETA FOR ØRSTED A/S

As an analyst in Holdon Sustainable Investment Fund, you have been looking at potential investments in the renewable energy sector. Widely recognized as one of the most sustainable firms in the world, Ørsted A/S, the Danish power supplier is a potential target for your Renewables fund.

As with any investment, you are concerned about the risk of an investment in Ørsted A/S, as well as its potential return. Holdon currently uses a commercial data vendor for information about its positions. Because of this, you are unsure exactly how the numbers provided are calculated. The data provider considers its methods proprietary, and it will not disclose how equity betas and other information are calculated. Not knowing exactly how these numbers are being computed, you believe it may be more appropriate and less expensive to calculate the necessary statistics in-house. To explore this question, you have decided to undertake the following assignment:

QUESTIONS

1. Go to Yahoo! Finance and download the ending monthly equity prices for Ørsted A/S (code: ORSTED. CO) for the last 60 months. Use the adjusted closing price, which adjusts for dividend payments and stock splits. Next, find a website to download the monthly value of the OMX Copenhagen 20 index over the same period. For the historical risk-free rate, download the historical three-month Danish Treasury bill secondary market rate. What are the monthly returns, average monthly returns and standard deviations for Ørsted A/S equity, the three-month Treasury bill, and the OMX Copenhagen 20 for this period?

2. Beta is often estimated by linear regression. A model often used is called the *market model*, which is:

$$R_t - R_{ft} = \alpha_i + \beta_i[R_{Mt} - R_{ft}] + \varepsilon_t$$

In this regression R_t is the return on the equity and R_{ft} is the risk-free rate for the same period. R_{Mt} is the return on a stock market index such as the FTSE 100 index. α_i is the regression intercept, and β_i is the slope (and the equity's estimated beta). ε_t represents the residuals for the regression. What do you think is the motivation for this particular regression? The intercept, α_i, is often called *Jensen's alpha*.

What does it measure? If an asset has a positive Jensen's alpha, where would it plot with respect to the SML? What is the financial interpretation of the residuals in the regression?

3. Use the market model to estimate the beta for Ørsted A/S using the last 36 months of returns (the regression procedure in Microsoft Excel is one easy way to do this). Plot the monthly returns on Ørsted A/S against the index, and also show the fitted line.

4. When the beta of an equity is calculated using monthly returns, there is a debate over the number of months that should be used in the calculation. Rework the previous questions using the last 60 months of returns. How does this answer compare with what you calculated previously? What are some arguments for and against using shorter versus longer periods? Also, you've used monthly data, which are a common choice. You could have used daily, weekly, quarterly or even annual data. What do you think are the issues here?

5. Compare your beta for Ørsted A/S with the beta you find on Yahoo! Finance. How similar are they? Why might they be different?

ADDITIONAL READING

Capital asset pricing theory is probably the most tested theory in modern investment finance. Given this, it is important that the interested reader is directed to the most relevant recent research in the area. A number of papers listed below directly test the power of the CAPM or market model beta under a variety of environments and with a number of other control variables. While it is easy to say that the range of CAPM anomalies suggests that the model is inferior to other, more complex models, it is still the most commonly used way to estimate the cost of equity (discount rate) of a listed firm. Most of the papers listed below study the US markets. Those papers that consider other countries are highlighted in bold. The list does not follow any real theme, as is the case in other chapters. Moreover, the listing is a very small representation of recent research in the area. Those who wish to specialize should view the references as the tip of the iceberg and use them to build up their own reading list.

Good starting points for exploring the research on cross-sectional returns are:

1. Linnainmaa, J.T., & Roberts, M.R. (2018). The history of the cross-section of stock returns. *Review of Financial Studies, 31*(7), 2606–2649.

2. McLean, R.D., & Pontiff, J. (2016). Does academic research destroy stock return predictability? *Journal of Finance, 71*(1), 5–32.

Other more specialized papers follow:

1. Burlacu, R., Fontaine, P., Jimenez-Garcès, S., & Seasholes, M.S. (2012). Risk and the cross section of stock returns. *Journal of Financial Economics, 105*(3), 511–522.

2. Dimson, E., Marsh, P., & Staunton, M. (2017). Factor-based investing: The long-term evidence. *Journal of Portfolio Management, 43*(5), 15.

3. Fama, E.F., & French, K.R. (2012). Size, value, and momentum in international stock returns. *Journal of Financial Economics, 105*(3), 457–472.

4. Fama, E.F., & French, K.R. (2018). Choosing factors. *Journal of Financial Economics,* 128(2), 234–252.

5. Gârleanu, N., Kogan, L., & Panageas, S. (2012). Displacement risk and asset returns. *Journal of Financial Economics, 105*(3), 491–510.

6. Harvey, C.R., Liu, Y., & Zhu, H. (2016). … And the cross-section of expected returns. *Review of Financial Studies, 29*(1), 5–68.

7. Hou, K., Xue, C. & Zhang, L. (2015). Digesting anomalies: An investment approach. *Review of Financial Studies, 28*(3), 650–705.

8. Koijen, R.S., Lustig, H., & Van Nieuwerburgh, S. (2017). The cross-section and time series of stock and bond returns. *Journal of Monetary Economics, 88,* 50–69.

9. Novy-Marx, R. (2013). The other side of value: The gross profitability premium. *Journal of Financial Economics, 108*(1), 1–28.

10. Roll, R. (1977). A critique of the asset pricing theory's tests Part I: On past and potential testability of the theory. *Journal of Financial Economics, 4*(2), 129–176.

11. Trigeorgis, L., & Lambertides, N. (2014). The role of growth options in explaining stock returns. *Journal of Financial and Quantitative Analysis, 49*(3), 749–771.

Endnotes

1. Some of it could be in cash, of course, but we would then just consider the cash to be one of the portfolio assets.
2. This ratio is sometimes called the *Treynor index,* after one of its originators.

PART FIVE

COST OF CAPITAL AND LONG-TERM FINANCIAL POLICY

13 Cost of Capital — 353

14 Raising Capital — 383

15 Financial Leverage and Capital Structure Policy — 414

16 Dividends and Payout Policy — 452

CHAPTER 13
COST OF CAPITAL

LEARNING OBJECTIVES
After studying this chapter, you should understand:
- **LO1** How to determine a firm's cost of equity.
- **LO2** How to determine a firm's cost of debt.
- **LO3** How to determine a firm's overall cost of capital.
- **LO4** How to correctly include flotation costs in capital budgeting projects.
- **LO5** Some of the pitfalls associated with a firm's overall cost of capital, and what to do about them.

KEY NOTATIONS
D	Dividend
D	Market value of debt
E	Market value of equity
f_A	Weighted average flotation cost
f_D	Debt flotation cost
f_E	Equity flotation cost
g	Growth rate
NPV	Net present value
P	Share price
PV	Present value
R	Discount rate
R_D	Return on debt
R_E	Return on equity
R_f	Risk-free rate of return
R_M	Market return
SML	Security market line
T_C	Corporate tax rate
V	Market value of firm
WACC	Weighted average cost of capital
β	Beta or systematic risk

WITH NEARLY 120,000 EMPLOYEES ON FIVE CONTINENTS, Germany-based BASF is a major international company. The company operates in a variety of industries, including agriculture, oil and gas, chemicals, and plastics. In an attempt to increase value, BASF follows a comprehensive plan that includes all functions within the company and challenges and encourages employees to act in an entrepreneurial manner. BASF expects to earn its weighted average cost of capital, also known as WACC, plus a premium. So, what exactly is WACC?

The WACC is the minimum return a company needs to earn to satisfy all of its investors, including shareholders, bondholders and preference shareholders. For example, BASF pegs WACC for its general business at just over 7 per cent and uses 8.49 per cent for its overseas exploration and production unit. In this chapter, we learn how to compute a firm's cost of capital, and find out what it means to the firm and its investors. We shall also learn when to use the firm's cost of capital and, perhaps more importantly, when not to use it.

Suppose you have just become the chief executive of a large company, and the first decision you face is whether to go ahead with a plan to renovate the company's warehouse distribution system. The plan will cost the company €50 million, and it is expected to save €12 million per year after taxes over the next 6 years.

This is a familiar problem in capital budgeting. To address it, you would determine the relevant cash flows, discount them and, if the net present value was positive, take on the project; if the NPV was negative, you would scrap it. So far, so good; but what should you use as the discount rate?

From our discussion of risk and return, you know that the correct discount rate depends on the riskiness of the project to renovate the warehouse distribution system. In particular, the new project will have a positive NPV only if its return exceeds what the financial markets offer on investments of similar risk. We called this minimum required return the *cost of capital* associated with the project.

Thus, to make the right decision as chief executive, you must examine what the capital markets have to offer, and use this information to arrive at an estimate of the project's cost of capital. Our primary purpose in this chapter is to describe how to go about doing this. There are a variety of approaches to this task, and some conceptual and practical issues arise.

One of the most important concepts we develop is that of the *weighted average cost of capital* (WACC). This is the cost of capital for the firm as a whole, and it can be interpreted as the required return on the overall firm. In discussing the WACC, we shall recognize the fact that a firm will normally raise capital in a variety of forms, and that these different forms of capital may have different costs associated with them.

We also recognize in this chapter that taxes are an important consideration in determining the required return on an investment: we are always interested in valuing the after-tax cash flows from a project. We shall, therefore, discuss how to incorporate taxes explicitly into our estimates of the cost of capital.

13.1 THE COST OF CAPITAL: SOME PRELIMINARIES

In Chapter 12 we developed the security market line, or SML, and used it to explore the relationship between the expected return on a security and its systematic risk. We concentrated on how the risky returns from buying securities looked from the viewpoint of, for example, a shareholder in the firm. This helped us understand more about the alternatives available to an investor in the capital markets.

In this chapter, we turn things around a bit and look more closely at the other side of the problem, which is how these returns and securities look from the viewpoint of the companies that issue them. The important fact to note is that the return an investor in a security receives is the cost of that security to the company that issued it.

REQUIRED RETURN VERSUS COST OF CAPITAL

When we say that the required return on an investment is, say, 10 per cent, we usually mean that the investment will have a positive NPV only if its return exceeds 10 per cent. Another way of interpreting the required return is to observe that the firm must earn 10 per cent on the investment just to compensate its investors for the use of the capital needed to finance the project. This is why we could also say that 10 per cent is the cost of capital associated with the investment.

To illustrate the point further, imagine that we are evaluating a risk-free project. In this case, how to determine the required return is obvious: we look at the capital markets and observe the current rate offered by risk-free investments, and we use this rate to discount the project's cash flows. Thus the cost of capital for a risk-free investment is the risk-free rate.

If a project is risky, then, assuming that all the other information is unchanged, the required return is obviously higher. In other words, the cost of capital for this project, if it is risky, is greater than the risk-free rate, and the appropriate discount rate would exceed the risk-free rate.

We shall henceforth use the terms *required return, appropriate discount rate* and *cost of capital* more or less interchangeably, because, as the discussion in this section suggests, they all mean essentially the same thing. The key fact to grasp is that the cost of capital associated with an investment depends on the risk of that investment. This is one of the most important lessons in corporate finance, so it bears repeating:

The cost of capital depends primarily on the use of the funds, not the source.

It is a common error to forget this crucial point and fall into the trap of thinking that the cost of capital for an investment depends primarily on how and where the capital is raised.

FINANCIAL POLICY AND COST OF CAPITAL

We know that the particular mixture of debt and equity a firm chooses to employ – its capital structure – is a managerial decision. In this chapter, we shall take the firm's financial policy as given. In particular, we assume that the firm has a fixed debt–equity ratio it seeks to maintain. This ratio reflects the firm's *target* capital structure. How a firm might choose that ratio is the subject of a later chapter.

From the preceding discussion, we know that a firm's overall cost of capital will reflect the required return on the firm's assets as a whole. Given that a firm uses both debt and equity capital, this overall cost of capital will be a mixture of the returns needed to compensate its creditors and those needed to compensate its shareholders. In other words, a firm's cost of capital will reflect both its cost of debt capital and its cost of equity capital. We discuss these costs separately in the sections that follow.

> **CONCEPT QUESTIONS**
>
> **13.1a** What is the primary determinant of the cost of capital for an investment?
> **13.1b** What is the relationship between the required return on an investment and the cost of capital associated with that investment?

13.2 THE COST OF EQUITY

We begin with the most difficult question on the subject of cost of capital: what is the firm's overall **cost of equity**? The reason why this is a difficult question is that there is no way of directly observing the return that the firm's equity investors require on their investment. Instead, we must somehow estimate it. This section discusses two approaches to determining the cost of equity: the dividend growth model approach and the security market line (SML) approach.

cost of equity
the return that equity investors require on their investment in the firm.

THE DIVIDEND GROWTH MODEL APPROACH

The easiest way to estimate the cost of equity capital is to use the dividend growth model we developed in Chapter 7. Recall that, under the assumption that the firm's dividend will grow at a constant rate g, the share price, P_0, can be written as:

$$P_0 = \frac{D_0 \times (1+g)}{R_E - g} = \frac{D_1}{R_E - g}$$

where D_0 is the dividend just paid and D_1 is the next period's projected dividend. Notice that we have used the symbol R_E (the E stands for equity) for the required return on the equity.

As we discussed in Chapter 7, we can rearrange this to solve for R_E as follows:

$$R_E = D_1/P_0 + g \tag{13.1}$$

Because R_E is the return that the shareholders require on the equity, it can be interpreted as the firm's cost of equity capital.

Implementing the Approach

To estimate R_E using the dividend growth model approach, we obviously need three pieces of information: P_0, D_0 and g.[1] Of these, for a publicly traded, dividend-paying company, the first two can be observed directly, so they are easily obtained. Only the third component, the expected growth rate for dividends, must be estimated.

To illustrate how we estimate R_E, suppose Great Country Public Service, a large public utility, paid a dividend of €4 per share last year. The equity currently sells for €60 per share. You estimate that the dividend will grow steadily at a rate of 6 per cent per year into the indefinite future. What is the cost of equity capital for Great Country?

Using the dividend growth model, we can calculate that the expected dividend for the coming year, D_1, is:

$$D_1 = D_0 \times (1 + g)$$
$$= €4 \times 1.06$$
$$= €4.24$$

Given this, the cost of equity, R_E, is:

$$R_E = D_1/P_0 + g$$
$$= €4.24/60 + 0.06$$
$$= 13.07\%$$

The cost of equity is thus 13.07 per cent.

Estimating g

To use the dividend growth model, we must come up with an estimate for g, the growth rate. There are essentially two ways of doing this: (1) use historical growth rates; or (2) use analysts' forecasts of future growth rates. Analysts' forecasts are available from a variety of sources, such as Yahoo! Finance. Naturally, different sources will have different estimates, so one approach might be to obtain multiple estimates and then average them.

Alternatively, we might observe dividends for the previous, say, 5 years, calculate the year-to-year growth rates and average them. For example, suppose we observe the following for some company:

Year	Dividend (£)
2010	1.10
2011	1.20
2012	1.35
2013	1.40
2014	1.55

We can calculate the percentage change in the dividend for each year as follows:

Year	Dividend (£)	Absolute change (£)	Percentage change (%)
2010	1.10	–	–
2011	1.20	0.10	9.09
2012	1.35	0.15	12.50
2013	1.40	0.05	3.70
2014	1.55	0.15	10.71

Notice that we calculated the change in the dividend on a year-to-year basis, and then expressed the change as a percentage. Thus in 2011, for example, the dividend rose from £1.10 to £1.20, an increase of £0.10. This represents a £0.10/1.10 = 9.09% increase.

If we average the four growth rates the result is (9.09 + 12.50 + 3.70 + 10.71)/4 = 9%, so we could use this as an estimate for the expected growth rate, g. Notice that this 9 per cent growth rate we have calculated is a simple, or arithmetic, average. Going back to Chapter 11, we could also calculate a geometric growth rate. Here, the dividend grows from £1.10 to £1.55 over a four-year period. What's the compound, or geometric, growth rate? See if you don't agree that it's 8.95 per cent; you can view this as a simple time value of money problem, where £1.10 is the present value and £1.55 is the future value.

As usual, the geometric average (8.95 per cent) is lower than the arithmetic average (9 per cent), but the difference here is not likely to be of any practical significance. In general, if the dividend has grown at a relatively steady rate, as we assume when we use this approach, then it can't make much difference which way we calculate the average dividend growth rate.

Advantages and Disadvantages of the Approach

The primary advantage of the dividend growth model approach is its simplicity. It is both easy to understand and easy to use. There are a number of associated practical problems and disadvantages.

First and foremost, the dividend growth model is obviously applicable only to companies that pay dividends. This means that the approach is useless in many cases. Furthermore, even for companies that do pay dividends, the key underlying assumption is that the dividend grows at a constant rate. As our previous example illustrates, this will never be *exactly* the case. More generally, the model is really applicable only to cases in which reasonably steady growth is likely to occur.

A second problem is that the estimated cost of equity is very sensitive to the estimated growth rate. For a given share price, an upward revision of g by just one percentage point, for example, increases the estimated cost of equity by at least a full percentage point. Because D_1 will probably be revised upwards as well, the increase will actually be somewhat larger than that.

Finally, this approach really does not explicitly consider risk. Unlike the SML approach (which we consider next), there is no direct adjustment for the riskiness of the investment. For example, there is no allowance for the degree of certainty or uncertainty surrounding the estimated growth rate for dividends. As a result, it is difficult to say whether or not the estimated return is commensurate with the level of risk.[2]

THE SML APPROACH

In Chapter 12 we discussed the security market line, or SML. Our primary conclusion was that the required or expected return on a risky investment depends on three things:

1. The risk-free rate, R_f.
2. The market risk premium, $E(R_M) - R_f$.
3. The systematic risk of the asset relative to average, which we called its beta coefficient, β.

Using the SML, we can write the expected return on the company's equity, $E(R_E)$, as:

$$E(R_E) = R_f + \beta_E \times [E(R_M) - R_f]$$

where β_E is the estimated beta. To make the SML approach consistent with the dividend growth model, we shall drop the Es denoting expectations and henceforth write the required return from the SML, R_E, as:

$$R_E = R_f + \beta_E \times (R_M - R_f) \tag{13.2}$$

Implementing the Approach

To use the SML approach, we need a risk-free rate, R_f, an estimate of the market risk premium, $R_M - R_f$, and an estimate of the relevant beta, β_E. In Chapter 11, we saw that one estimate of the market risk premium (based on large UK equities) is about 4 per cent (see Figure 11.5). Assume that Treasury bills are paying about 2.2 per cent, so we shall use this as our risk-free rate for the UK. Beta coefficients for publicly traded companies are widely available.[3]

To illustrate, according to FT.com, ITV plc had an estimated beta of 1.90 in 2016. We could thus estimate ITV's cost of equity as:

$$\begin{aligned} R_E &= R_f + \beta_{ITV} \times (R_M - R_f) \\ &= 2.2\% + 1.90 \times 4\% \\ &= 9.80\% \end{aligned}$$

Thus, using the SML approach, we calculate that ITV's cost of equity is about 9.80 per cent.

Advantages and Disadvantages of the Approach

The SML approach has two primary advantages. First, it explicitly adjusts for risk. Second, it applies to companies other than just those with steady dividend growth. Thus it may be useful in a wider variety of circumstances.

There are drawbacks, of course. The SML approach requires that two things be estimated: the market risk premium and the beta coefficient. To the extent that our estimates are poor, the resulting cost of equity will be inaccurate. For example, our estimate of the UK market risk premium, 4 per cent, is based on a large number of years of returns on particular equity portfolios and markets. Using different time periods or different equities and markets could result in very different estimates.

Finally, as with the dividend growth model, we essentially rely on the past to predict the future when we use the SML approach. Economic conditions can change quickly, so, as always, the past may not be a good guide to the future. In the best of all worlds, both approaches (the dividend growth model and the SML) are applicable, and the two result in similar answers. If this happens, we might have some confidence in our estimates. We might also wish to compare the results with those for other similar companies as a reality check.

EXAMPLE 13.1

THE COST OF EQUITY

Suppose equity in Alpha Air Freight has a beta of 1.2. The market risk premium is 7 per cent, and the risk-free rate is 6 per cent. Alpha's last dividend was €2 per share, and the dividend is expected to grow at 8 per cent indefinitely. The equity currently sells for €30. What is Alpha's cost of equity capital?

We can start by using the SML. Doing this, we find that the expected return on the equity of Alpha Air Freight is:

$$R_E = R_f + \beta_E \times (R_M - R_f)$$
$$= 6\% + 1.2 \times 7\%$$
$$= 14.4\%$$

This suggests that 14.4 per cent is Alpha's cost of equity. We next use the dividend growth model. The projected dividend is $D_0 \times (1 + g) = €2 \times 1.08 = €2.16$, so the expected return using this approach is:

$$R_E = D_1/P_0 + g$$
$$= €2.16/30 + 0.08$$
$$= 15.2\%$$

Our two estimates are reasonably close, so we might average them to find that Alpha's cost of equity is approximately 14.8 per cent.

HOW DO CORPORATIONS ESTIMATE COST OF CAPITAL IN PRACTICE?

The material in this chapter is quite complex, and the reader may be left wondering what firms actually do when they calculate the cost of capital in practice. Results of the most recent survey undertaken of executives in France, the Netherlands and the UK on methods they used to estimate the cost of capital is presented in Table 13.1.

There are notable differences across countries, but the most commonly used method is CAPM and beta. Historical returns on share prices are also commonly used, and in the Netherlands a surprisingly large number of companies use a cost of capital estimate that is set by investors. Notice that regulators play an important role in the UK and France.

CONCEPT QUESTIONS

13.2a What do we mean when we say that a corporation's cost of equity capital is 16 per cent?
13.2b What are two approaches to estimating the cost of equity capital?

TABLE 13.1

Of firms that estimate cost of capital, the percentage that use specific methods

	US	UK	The Netherlands	France
Capital asset pricing model	73.49	47.06	55.56	45.16
Historical returns	39.41	31.25	30.77	27.27
Multifactor models[4]	34.29	27.27	15.38	30.30
Backed out from dividend growth model (i.e. $P = Div/r$)	15.74	10.00	10.71	10.34
Determined by investors	13.93	18.75	44.83	34.38
Determined by regulators	7.04	16.13	3.70	16.13

Source: Data from Table 2 from D. Brounen, A. de Jong and K. Koedijk (2004). Corporate finance in Europe: Confronting theory with practice. Financial Management, 33(4), 71-101.

13.3 THE COSTS OF DEBT AND PREFERENCE SHARES

In addition to ordinary equity, firms use debt and, to a lesser extent, preference shares to finance their investments. As we discuss next, determining the costs of capital associated with these sources of financing is much easier than determining the cost of equity.

THE COST OF DEBT

The **cost of debt** is the return the firm's creditors demand on new borrowing. In principle, we could determine the beta for the firm's debt and then use the SML to estimate the required return on debt, just as we estimated the required return on equity. This isn't really necessary, however.

> **cost of debt**
> the return that lenders require on the firm's debt.

Unlike a firm's cost of equity, its cost of debt can normally be observed either directly or indirectly: the cost of debt is simply the interest rate the firm must pay on new borrowing, and we can observe interest rates in the financial markets. For example, if the firm already has bonds outstanding, then the yield to maturity on those bonds is the market-required rate on the firm's debt.

Alternatively, if we know that the firm's bonds are rated, say, AA, then we can simply find the interest rate on newly issued AA-rated bonds. Either way, there is no need to estimate a beta for the debt, because we can directly observe the rate we want to know.

There is one thing to be careful about, though. The coupon rate on the firm's outstanding debt is irrelevant here. That rate just tells us roughly what the firm's cost of debt was back when the bonds were issued, not what the cost of debt is today.[5] This is why we have to look at the yield on the debt in today's marketplace. For consistency with our other notation, we shall use the symbol R_D for the cost of debt.

If bond prices are available, we can rearrange the present value formulae presented in Chapter 6 and solve for the cost of debt.

EXAMPLE 13.2

THE COST OF REDEEMABLE AND IRREDEEMABLE DEBT

Recall that redeemable debt is a bond that has a fixed life and irredeemable debt is in the form of a consol bond with no expiry date. Suppose General Tools issued a 30-year, 7 per cent bond 8 years ago. The bond is currently selling for 96 per cent of its face value of £50,000, or £48,000. What is General Tools' cost of redeemable debt?

Going back to Chapter 6, we need to calculate the yield to maturity on this bond. Because the bond is selling at a discount, the yield is apparently greater than 7 per cent, but not much greater, because the discount is fairly small. You can check to see that the yield to maturity is about 7.37 per cent, assuming annual coupons. General Tool's cost of debt, R_D, is thus 7.37 per cent.

Now assume General Tools also has a console bond that pays 7 per cent and is also selling for 96 per cent of its face value. The cost of irredeemable debt for General Tools would then be:

$$\text{Price} = £48{,}000 = \frac{0.07 \times £50{,}000}{r_D} \Rightarrow r_D = \frac{£3{,}500}{£48{,}000} = 0.0729 = 7.29\%$$

Floating Rate Bonds With floating rate bonds, the coupon rate varies with an underlying benchmark, such as SONIA (Sterling Overnight Index Average) for sterling-denominated loans, SOFR (Secured Overnight Financing Rate) for dollar-denominated loans, or EONIA (Euro Overnight Index Average) for euro-denominated loans). To estimate the cost of floating rate debt, one must accurately forecast the coupons in each period over the remaining life of the bond. This will entail forecasting future economic conditions, which is difficult. A simplifying heuristic is to calculate the cost of debt of a fixed rate bond with a similar maturity for a firm of similar risk and profile. This will provide a rough estimate of the cost of debt.

Bank Loans A bank loan is a private contract between a bank and borrower and, consequently, there will be no observed price of the loan, as one would see with a bond. The cost of the bank loan is therefore the interest rate on the loan.

THE COST OF PREFERENCE SHARES

Determining the *cost of preference shares* is quite straightforward. As we discussed in Chapters 5 and 7, preference shares have a fixed dividend paid every period forever, so a single preference share is essentially a perpetuity. The cost of preference shares, R_P, is thus:

$$R_P = D/P_0 \tag{13.3}$$

where D is the fixed dividend and P_0 is the current preference share price. Notice that the cost of preference shares is simply equal to the dividend yield on the preference share. Alternatively, because preference shares are rated in much the same way as bonds, the cost of preference shares can be estimated by observing the required returns on other, similarly rated preference shares.

EXAMPLE 13.3

EDINBURGH POWER'S COST OF PREFERENCE SHARES

Edinburgh Power has two issues of ordinary preference shares with a £25 par value. One issue pays £1.30 annually per share and sells for £21.05 per share. The other pays £1.46 per share annually and sells for £24.35 per share. What is Edinburgh Power's cost of preference shares?

Using the first issue, we calculate that the cost of preference shares is:

$$R_P = D/P_0$$
$$= £1.30/21.05$$
$$= 6.2\%$$

Using the second issue, we calculate that the cost is:

$$R_P = D/P_0$$
$$= £1.46/24.35$$
$$= 6\%$$

So Edinburgh Power's cost of preference shares appears to be about 6.1 per cent.

> **CONCEPT QUESTIONS**
>
> **13.3a** Why is the coupon rate a bad estimate of a firm's cost of debt?
> **13.3b** How can the cost of debt be calculated?
> **13.3c** How can the cost of preference shares be calculated?

13.4 THE WEIGHTED AVERAGE COST OF CAPITAL

Now that we have the costs associated with the main sources of capital the firm employs, we need to worry about the specific mix. As we mentioned earlier, we shall take this mix, which is the firm's capital structure, as given for now. Also, we shall focus mostly on debt and ordinary equity in this discussion.

In Chapter 3 we mentioned that financial analysts frequently focus on a firm's total capitalization, which is the sum of its long-term debt and equity. This is particularly true in determining cost of capital; short-term liabilities are often ignored in the process. We shall not explicitly distinguish between total value and total capitalization in the following discussion; the general approach is applicable with either.

SUSTAINABILITY IN FINANCE

The weighted cost of capital for renewable energy significantly varies across the European Union, amounting to 3.5 per cent in Germany and 12 per cent in Greece. These are the findings of the 'DiaCore project', funded by the Executive Agency for Small and Medium Enterprises (EASME). The research was led by Ecofys, Fraunhofer ISI, eclareon, EPU-NTUA, TU Wien and LEI. The project team is the first to estimate the costs of capital for onshore wind energy projects across the 27 EU Member States.

The European Union set itself a binding target of 'at least' 20 per cent renewable energy in final energy consumption by 2020, and to meet this target, annual investments of €60-70 billion were needed. Renewable energy technologies are capital-intensive, hence the cost of capital plays an important role in investment decisions and costs of target achievement.

The cost of capital is determined by the cost of debt and the cost of equity. The cost of equity for onshore wind projects ranges between 6 per cent (in Germany) and more than 15 per cent in Estonia, Greece, Latvia, Lithuania, Romania and Slovenia. The cost of debt varies between 1.8 per cent in Germany and 12.6 per cent in Greece. This results in weighted average cost of capital (WACC) ranging from 3.5 to 12 per cent.

Note: The UK is no longer a member of the European Union.

> 'There is a growing gap among EU Member States on the financing of renewable energy projects. From the very start of a project, project developers in the EU do not face the same financing conditions. Why does the cost of capital vary so much? Because of the risks for investors: if an investment is risky, the cost of capital increases', explains Ecofys Principal Consultant David deJager.
>
> Based on interviews with more than 110 banks and project developers in the EU, the consortium found that next to country risk, the main risk for investors in renewable energy is policy-induced risk. Unstable policies, such as sudden retroactive regulatory changes, automatically increase the cost of reaching renewable energy targets. Fortunately, by the middle of 2020 almost all EU countries were on track to hit their targets.
>
> Source: © DiaCore, Ecofys et al.: WACC across the EU-28 (interview results onshore wind). In: The impact of risks in renewable energy investments and the role of smart policies, February 2016. URL: http://diacore.eu/images/files2/WP3-Final%20Report/diacore-2016-impact-of-risk-in-res-investments.pdf.

THE CAPITAL STRUCTURE WEIGHTS

We shall use the symbol E (for equity) to stand for the *market* value of the firm's equity. We calculate this by taking the number of shares outstanding and multiplying it by the share price. Similarly, we shall use the symbol D (for debt) to stand for the *market* value of the firm's debt. For long-term debt we calculate this by multiplying the market price of a single bond by the number of bonds outstanding.

If there are multiple bond issues (as there normally would be), we repeat this calculation of D for each, and then add up the results. If there is debt that is not publicly traded (because it is held by a life insurance company, for example), we must observe the yield on similar publicly traded debt and then estimate the market value of the privately held debt, using this yield as the discount rate. For short-term debt the book (accounting) values and market values should be somewhat similar, so we might use the book values as estimates of the market values.

Finally, we shall use the symbol V (for value) to stand for the combined market value of the debt and equity:

$$V = E + D \qquad (13.4)$$

If we divide both sides by V, we can calculate the percentages of the total capital represented by the debt and equity:

$$100\% = E/V + D/V \qquad (13.5)$$

These percentages can be interpreted just like portfolio weights, and they are often called the *capital structure weights*.

For example, if the total market value of a company's equity and debt were calculated as £200 million and £50 million, respectively, then the combined value would be £250 million. Of this total, E/V = £200 million/250 million = 80%, so 80 per cent of the firm's financing would be equity and the remaining 20 per cent would be debt.

We emphasize here that the correct way to proceed is to use the *market* values of debt and equity. Under certain circumstances, such as when calculating figures for a privately owned company, it may not be possible to get reliable estimates of these quantities. In this case, we might go ahead and use the accounting values for debt and equity. Although this would probably be better than nothing, we would have to take the answer with a pinch of salt.

TAXES AND THE WEIGHTED AVERAGE COST OF CAPITAL

There is one final issue we need to discuss. Recall that we are always concerned with after-tax cash flows. If we are determining the discount rate appropriate to those cash flows, then the discount rate also needs to be expressed on an after-tax basis.

As we have discussed previously in various places in this book (and as we shall discuss later), the interest paid by a corporation is deductible for tax purposes. Payments to shareholders, such as dividends, are not. What this means, effectively, is that the government pays some of the interest. Thus, in determining an after-tax discount rate, we need to distinguish between the pre-tax and the after-tax cost of debt.

To illustrate, suppose a firm borrows €1 million at 9 per cent interest. The corporate tax rate is 34 per cent. What is the after-tax interest rate on this loan? The total interest bill will be €90,000 per year. This amount is tax-deductible, however, so the €90,000 interest reduces the firm's tax bill by 0.34 × €90,000 = €30,600. The after-tax interest bill is thus €90,000 − 30,600 = €59,400. The after-tax interest rate is thus €59,400/1 million = 5.94%.

Notice that, in general, the after-tax interest rate is simply equal to the pre-tax rate multiplied by 1 minus the tax rate. If we use the symbol T_C to stand for the corporate tax rate, then the after-tax rate can be written as $R_D \times (1 - T_C)$. For example, using the numbers from the preceding paragraph, we find that the after-tax interest rate is 9% × (1 − 0.34) = 5.94%.

Bringing together the various topics we have discussed in this chapter, we now have the capital structure weights along with the cost of equity and the after-tax cost of debt. To calculate the firm's overall cost of capital we multiply the capital structure weights by the associated costs and add them up. The total is the **weighted average cost of capital (WACC)**:

> **weighted average cost of capital (WACC)**
> the weighted average of the cost of equity and the after-tax cost of debt.

$$\text{WACC} = (E/V) \times R_E + (D/V) \times R_D \times (1 - T_C) \quad (13.6)$$

This WACC has a straightforward interpretation. It is the overall return the firm must earn on its existing assets to maintain the value of its equity. It is also the required return on any investments by the firm that have essentially the same risks as existing operations. So, if we were evaluating the cash flows from a proposed expansion of our existing operations, this is the discount rate we would use.

If a firm uses preference shares in its capital structure, then our expression for the WACC needs a simple extension. If we define P/V as the percentage of the firm's financing that comes from preference shares, then the WACC is simply:

$$\text{WACC} = (E/V) \times R_E + (P/V) \times R_P + (D/V) \times R_D \times (1 - T_C) \quad (13.7)$$

where R_P is the cost of preference shares.

EXAMPLE 13.4

CALCULATING THE WACC

Travis SpA has 1.4 million shares of equity outstanding. The equity currently sells for €20 per share. The firm's debt is publicly traded, and was recently quoted at 93 per cent of face value. It has a total face value of €5 million, and it is currently priced to yield 11 per cent. The risk-free rate is 8 per cent, and the market risk premium is 7 per cent. You've estimated that Travis has a beta of 0.74. If the corporate tax rate is 34 per cent, what is the WACC of Travis SpA?

We can first determine the cost of equity and the cost of debt. Using the SML, we find that the cost of equity is 8% + 0.74 × 7% = 13.18%. The total value of the equity is 1.4 million × €20 = €28 million. The pre-tax cost of debt is the current yield to maturity on the outstanding debt, 11 per cent. The debt sells for 93 per cent of its face value, so its current market value is 0.93 × €5 million = €4.65 million. The total market value of the equity and debt together is €28 million + 4.65 million = €32.65 million.

From here, we can calculate the WACC easily enough. The percentage of equity used by Travis to finance its operations is €28 million/€32.65 million = 85.76%. Because the weights have to add up to 1, the percentage of debt is 1 − 0.8576 = 14.24%. The WACC is thus:

$$\begin{aligned}\text{WACC} &= (E/V) \times R_E + (D/V) \times R_D \times (1 - T_C) \\ &= 0.8576 \times 13.18\% + 0.1424 \times 11\% \times (1 - 0.34) \\ &= 12.34\%\end{aligned}$$

Travis thus has an overall weighted average cost of capital of 12.34 per cent.

CALCULATING THE WACC FOR RWE AG

In this section, we illustrate how to calculate the WACC for the German energy supplier, RWE AG. Our goal is to take you through, on a step-by-step basis, the process of finding and using the information needed using online sources. As you will see, there is a fair amount of detail involved, but the necessary information is, for the most part, readily available.

RWE's Cost of Equity

Our first stop is the main screen for RWE available at Yahoo! Finance. In 2020, here's what it looked like:

TABLE 13.2

OVERALL	
Beta:	1.49
Market Cap. (Mil.):	19,750
Shares Outstanding (Mil.):	615.07
Dividend:	0.80
Yield (%):	2.44

©Yahoo! Finance.

As you can see, the total value of equity is €19.75 billion (the share price is 19.750/0.61507 = €31.11). To estimate RWE's cost of equity, we shall assume a market risk premium of 5.96 per cent (see Figure 11.5 for Germany). RWE's beta on Reuters is 1.49, which is higher than the beta of the average equity. According to the bond section of FT.com, German government bonds were paying about −0.54 per cent. Using the CAPM to estimate the cost of equity, we find:

$$R_E = -0.0054 + 1.49(0.0596) = 0.0834 \text{ or } 8.34\%$$

To calculate the growth rate for RWE, we check the Analysis link in the RWE page at Yahoo! Finance. The average 5-year growth rate is listed as 5.86 per cent. For now, we shall use this growth rate in the dividend discount model to estimate the cost of equity. The estimated cost of equity using the dividend discount model is:

$$R_E = \frac{Div_1}{P_0} + g = \frac{€0.80}{€32.11} + 0.0586 = 0.0835 \text{ or } 8.35\%$$

Notice that the estimates for the cost of equity are very similar. This is often the case, but it does not always happen. Remember that each method of estimating the cost of equity relies on different assumptions, so different estimates of the cost of equity should not surprise us. If the estimates are different, there are two simple solutions. First, we could ignore one of the estimates. We would look at each estimate to see whether one of them seemed too high or too low to be reasonable. Second, we could average the two estimates. Averaging the two estimates for RWE's cost of equity gives us a cost of equity of 8.345 per cent. This seems like a reasonable number, so we shall use it in calculating the cost of capital in this example.

RWE's Cost of Debt

We found out about RWE's outstanding bonds by going to its annual report and looking at its financial information. It has a number of relatively long-term bond issues plus private loans that account for essentially all of its long-term debt. Fortunately, RWE states explicitly in its annual report that the company cost of debt was 5 per cent and its effective tax rate was 25 per cent.

RWE's WACC

We now have the various pieces necessary to calculate RWE's WACC. First, we need to calculate the capital structure weights. If we use market value weights, RWE's equity is worth €19.75 billion (from Yahoo! Finance) and its debt is worth €46.74 billion (from the annual report). The capital structure weights are therefore €19.75 billion/66.49 billion = 0.30 and €46.324 billion/53.473 billion = 0.70, so the debt percentage is much higher. With these weights, RWE's WACC is:

$$\text{WACC} = 0.30 \times 8.345\% + 0.70 \times 5\% \times (1 - 0.25) = 5.13\%$$

Thus, using market value weights, we get about 5.13 per cent for RWE's WACC.

SOLVING THE WAREHOUSE PROBLEM AND SIMILAR CAPITAL BUDGETING PROBLEMS

Now we can use the WACC to solve the warehouse problem we posed at the beginning of the chapter. However, before we rush to discount the cash flows at the WACC to estimate NPV, we need to make sure we are doing the right thing.

Going back to first principles, we need to find an alternative in the financial markets that is comparable to the warehouse renovation. To be comparable, an alternative must be of the same level of risk as the warehouse project. Projects that have the same risk are said to be in the same risk class.

The WACC for a firm reflects the risk and the target capital structure of the firm's existing assets as a whole. As a result, strictly speaking, the firm's WACC is the appropriate discount rate only if the proposed investment is a replica of the firm's existing operating activities.

In broader terms, whether or not we can use the firm's WACC to value the warehouse project depends on whether the warehouse project is in the same risk class as the firm. We shall assume that this project is an integral part of the overall business of the firm. In such cases, it is natural to think that the cost savings will be as risky as the general cash flows of the firm, and the project will thus be in the same risk class as the overall firm. More generally, projects like the warehouse renovation that are intimately related to the firm's existing operations are often viewed as being in the same risk class as the overall firm.

We can now see what the chief executive should do. Suppose the firm has a target debt–equity ratio of 1/3. From Chapter 3 we know that a debt–equity ratio of $D/E = 1/3$ implies that E/V is 0.75 and D/V is 0.25. The cost of debt is 10 per cent, and the cost of equity is 20 per cent. Assuming a 34 per cent tax rate, the WACC will be:

$$\begin{aligned}\text{WACC} &= (E/V) \times R_E + (D/V) \times R_D \times (1 - T_C) \\ &= 0.75 \times 20\% + 0.25 \times 10\% \times (1 - 0.34) \\ &= 16.65\%\end{aligned}$$

Recall that the warehouse project had a cost of €50 million and expected after-tax cash flows (the cost savings) of €12 million per year for 6 years. The NPV (in millions) is thus:

$$\text{NPV} = -€50 + \frac{12}{(1 + \text{WACC})^1} + \cdots + \frac{12}{(1 + \text{WACC})^6}$$

Because the cash flows are in the form of an ordinary annuity, we can calculate this NPV using 16.65 per cent (the WACC) as the discount rate as follows:

$$\begin{aligned}\text{NPV} &= -€50 + 12 \times \frac{1 - [1/(1 + 0.1665)^6]}{0.1665} \\ &= -€50 + 12 \times 3.6222 \\ &= -€6.53\end{aligned}$$

Should the firm take on the warehouse renovation? The project has a negative NPV using the firm's WACC. This means that the financial markets offer superior projects in the same risk class (namely, the firm itself). The answer is clear: the project should be rejected. For future reference, our discussion of the WACC is summarized in Table 13.3.

TABLE 13.3

Summary of capital cost calculations

The cost of equity, R_E

A. Dividend growth model approach (from Chapter 7):

$$R_E = D_1/P_0 + g$$

where D_1 is the expected dividend in one period, g is the dividend growth rate, and P_0 is the current share price.

B. SML approach (from Chapter 12):

$$R_E = R_f + \beta_E \times (R_M - R_f)$$

where R_E is the risk-free rate, R_M is the expected return on the overall market, and β_E is the systematic risk of the equity.

The cost of debt, R_D

A. For a firm with publicly held debt, the cost of debt can be measured as the yield to maturity on the outstanding debt. The coupon rate is irrelevant. Yield to maturity is covered in Chapter 6. Alternatively, a simple estimate of the risk-free rate plus the credit spread can provide a very broad benchmark figure.

B. If the firm has no publicly traded debt, then the cost of debt can be measured as the yield to maturity on similarly rated bonds (bond ratings are discussed in Chapter 6).

The weighted average cost of capital, WACC

A. The firm's WACC is the overall required return on the firm as a whole. It is the appropriate discount rate to use for cash flows similar in risk to those of the overall firm.

B. The WACC is calculated as:

$$\text{WACC} = (E/V) \times R_E + (D/V) \times R_D \times (1 - T_C)$$

where T_C is the corporate tax rate, E is the *market* value of the firm's equity, D is the *market* value of the firm's debt, and $V = E + D$. Note that E/V is the percentage of the firm's financing (in market value terms) that is equity, and D/V is the percentage that is debt.

EXAMPLE 13.5

USING THE WACC

A firm is considering a project that will result in initial after-tax cash savings of £5 million at the end of the first year. These savings will grow at a rate of 5 per cent per year. The firm has a debt–equity ratio of 0.5, a cost of equity of 29.2 per cent, and a cost of debt of 10 per cent. The cost-saving proposal is closely related to the firm's core business, so it is viewed as having the same risk as the overall firm. Should the firm take on the project?

Assuming a 28 per cent tax rate, the firm should take on this project if it costs less than £29.64 million. To see this, note that the PV is:

$$PV = \frac{£5 \text{ million}}{\text{WACC} - 0.05}$$

This is an example of a growing perpetuity, as discussed in Chapter 7. The WACC is:

$$\begin{aligned}\text{WACC} &= (E/V) \times R_E + (D/V) \times R_D \times (1 - T_C) \\ &= 2/3 \times 29.2\% + 1/3 \times 10\% \times (1 - 0.28) \\ &= 21.87\%\end{aligned}$$

The PV is thus:

$$PV = \frac{£5 \text{ million}}{0.217 - 0.05} = £29.64 \text{ million}$$

The NPV will be positive only if the cost is less than £29.64 million.

PERFORMANCE EVALUATION: ANOTHER USE OF THE WACC

Performance evaluation is another use of the WACC. Probably the best-known approach in this area is the economic value added (EVA) method developed by Stern Stewart and Co. Similar approaches include market value added (MVA) and shareholder value added (SVA).

Although the details differ, the basic idea behind EVA and similar strategies is straightforward. Suppose we have €100 million in capital (debt and equity) tied up in our firm, and our overall WACC is 12 per cent. If we multiply these together, we get €12 million. Referring back to Chapter 3, if our cash flow from assets is less than this, we are, on an overall basis, destroying value; if cash flow from assets exceeds €12 million, we are creating value.

In practice, evaluation strategies such as these suffer to a certain extent from problems with implementation. For example, it appears that many companies make extensive use of book values for debt and equity in computing cost of capital. Even so, by focusing on value creation, WACC-based evaluation procedures force employees and management to pay attention to the real bottom line: increasing the share price.

CONCEPT QUESTIONS

13.4a How is the WACC calculated?
13.4b Why do we multiply the cost of debt by $(1 - T_C)$ when we compute the WACC?
13.4c Under what conditions is it correct to use the WACC to determine NPV?

13.5 DIVISIONAL AND PROJECT COSTS OF CAPITAL

As we have seen, using the WACC as the discount rate for future cash flows is appropriate only when the proposed investment is similar to the firm's existing activities. This is not as restrictive as it sounds. If we are in the pizza business, for example, and we are thinking of opening a new location, then the WACC is the discount rate to use. The same is true of a retailer thinking of a new store, a manufacturer thinking of expanding production, or a consumer products company thinking of expanding its markets.

Nonetheless, despite the usefulness of the WACC as a benchmark, there will clearly be situations in which the cash flows under consideration have risks distinctly different from those of the overall firm. We consider how to cope with this problem next.

THE SML AND THE WACC

When we are evaluating investments with risks that are substantially different from those of the overall firm, use of the WACC will potentially lead to poor decisions. Figure 13.1 illustrates why.

In Figure 13.1 we have plotted an SML corresponding to a risk-free rate of 7 per cent and a market risk premium of 8 per cent. To keep things simple, we consider an all-equity company with a beta of 1. As we have indicated, the WACC and the cost of equity are exactly equal to 15 per cent for this company, because there is no debt.

Suppose our firm uses its WACC to evaluate all investments. This means that any investment with a return of greater than 15 per cent will be accepted, and any investment with a return of less than 15 per cent will be rejected. We know from our study of risk and return, however, that a desirable investment is one that plots above the SML. As Figure 13.1 illustrates, using the WACC for all types of project can result in the firm incorrectly accepting relatively risky projects and incorrectly rejecting relatively safe ones.

For example, consider point A. This project has a beta of $\beta_A = 0.60$, as compared with the firm's beta of 1.0. It has an expected return of 14 per cent. Is this a desirable investment? The answer is yes because its required return is only:

$$\begin{aligned}\text{Required return} &= R_f + \beta_A \times (R_M - R_f) \\ &= 7\% + 0.60 \times 8\% \\ &= 11.8\%\end{aligned}$$

However, if we use the WACC as a cut-off, then this project will be rejected, because its return is less than 15 per cent. This example illustrates that a firm that uses its WACC as a cut-off will tend to reject profitable projects with risks less than those of the overall firm.

FIGURE 13.1 The security market line (SML) and the weighted average cost of capital (WACC)

If a firm uses its WACC to make accept–reject decisions for all types of project, it will have a tendency towards incorrectly accepting risky projects and incorrectly rejecting less risky projects.

At the other extreme, consider point B. This project has a beta of $\beta_B = 1.2$. It offers a 16 per cent return, which exceeds the firm's cost of capital. This is not a good investment, however, because, given its level of systematic risk, its return is inadequate. Nonetheless, if we use the WACC to evaluate it, it will appear to be attractive. So the second error that will arise if we use the WACC as a cut-off is that we shall tend to make unprofitable investments with risks greater than those of the overall firm. As a consequence, through time, a firm that uses its WACC to evaluate all projects will have a tendency both to accept unprofitable investments and to become increasingly risky.

DIVISIONAL COST OF CAPITAL

The same type of problem with the WACC can arise in a corporation with more than one line of business. Imagine, for example, a corporation that has two divisions: a regulated telephone company and an electronics manufacturing operation. The first of these (the phone operation) has relatively low risk; the second has a relatively high risk.

In this case, the firm's overall cost of capital is really a mixture of two different costs of capital, one for each division. If the two divisions were competing for resources, and the firm used a single WACC as a cut-off, which division would tend to be awarded greater funds for investment?

The answer is that the riskier division would tend to have greater returns (ignoring the greater risk), so it would tend to be the 'winner'. The less glamorous operation might have great profit potential that would end up being ignored. Large corporations in Europe are aware of this problem, and many work to develop separate divisional costs of capital.

THE PURE PLAY APPROACH

We've seen that using the firm's WACC inappropriately can lead to problems. How can we come up with the appropriate discount rates in such circumstances? Because we cannot observe the returns on these investments, there generally is no direct way of coming up with a beta, for example. Instead, what we must do is examine other investments outside the firm that are in the same risk class as the one we are considering, and use the market-required return on these investments as the discount rate. In other words, we shall try to determine what the cost of capital is for such investments by trying to locate some similar investments in the marketplace.

For example, going back to our telephone division, suppose we wanted to come up with a discount rate to use for that division. What we could do is identify several other phone companies that have publicly traded securities. We might find that a typical phone company has a beta of 0.80, AA-rated debt, and a capital structure that is about 50 per cent debt and 50 per cent equity. Using this information, we could develop a WACC for a typical phone company and use this as our discount rate.

Alternatively, if we were thinking of entering a new line of business, we would try to develop the appropriate cost of capital by looking at the market-required returns on companies already in that business. In the language of financial markets, a company that focuses on a single line of business is called a *pure play*. For example, if you wanted to bet on the price of crude oil by purchasing equities, you would try to identify companies that dealt exclusively with this product, because they would be the most affected by changes in the price of crude oil. Such companies would be called 'pure plays on the price of crude oil'.

What we try to do here is to find companies that focus as exclusively as possible on the type of project in which we are interested. Our approach, therefore, is called the **pure play approach** to estimating the required return on an investment. To illustrate, suppose McDonald's decides to enter the personal computer and network server business with a line of machines called McPuters. The risks involved are quite different from those in the fast-food business. As a result, McDonald's would need to look at companies already in the personal computer business to compute a cost of capital for the new division. An obvious pure play candidate would be Dell, which is predominantly in this line of business. Apple, on the other hand, would not be as good a choice because its primary focus is elsewhere, and it has many different product lines.

pure play approach the use of a WACC that is unique to a particular project, based on companies in similar lines of business.

In Chapter 3 we discussed the subject of identifying similar companies for comparison purposes. The same problems we described there come up here. The most obvious one is that we may not be able to find any suitable companies. In this case, how to determine a discount rate objectively becomes a difficult question. Even so, the important thing is to be aware of the issue, so that we at least reduce the possibility of the kinds of mistake that can arise when the WACC is used as a cut-off on all investments.

THE SUBJECTIVE APPROACH

Because of the difficulties that exist in establishing discount rates objectively for individual projects, firms often adopt an approach that involves making subjective adjustments to the overall WACC. To illustrate, suppose a firm has an overall WACC of 14 per cent. It places all proposed projects into four categories, as follows:

Category	Examples	Adjustment factor (%)	Discount rate (%)
High risk	New products	+6	20
Moderate risk	Cost savings, expansion of existing lines	+0	14
Low risk	Replacement of existing equipment	−4	10
Mandatory	Pollution control equipment	n/a	n/a

n/a = Not applicable.

The effect of this crude partitioning is to assume that all projects either fall into one of three risk classes or else are mandatory. In the last case, the cost of capital is irrelevant, because the project must be taken. With the subjective approach, the firm's WACC may change through time as economic conditions change. As this happens, the discount rates for the different types of projects will also change.

Within each risk class, some projects will presumably have more risk than others, and the danger of making incorrect decisions still exists. Figure 13.2 illustrates this point. Comparing Figures 13.1 and 13.2, we see that similar problems exist, but the magnitude of the potential error is less with the subjective approach. For example, the project labelled A would be accepted if the WACC were used, but it is rejected once it is classified as a high-risk investment. What this illustrates is that some risk adjustment, even if it is subjective, is probably better than no risk adjustment.

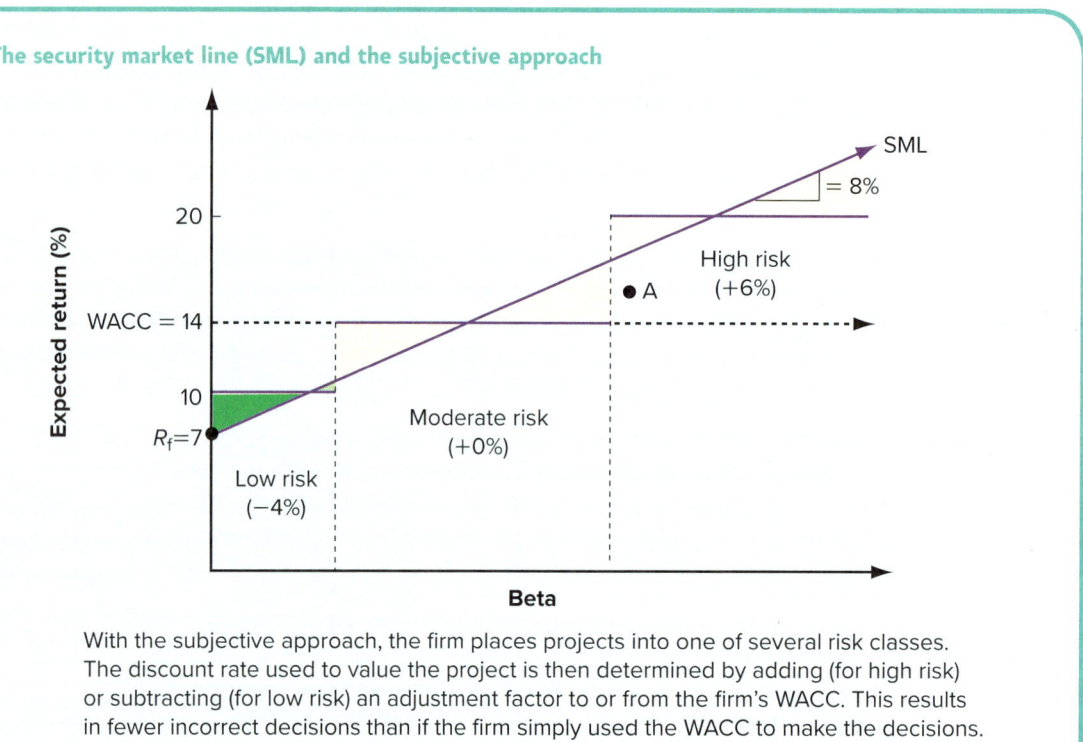

FIGURE 13.2

The security market line (SML) and the subjective approach

With the subjective approach, the firm places projects into one of several risk classes. The discount rate used to value the project is then determined by adding (for high risk) or subtracting (for low risk) an adjustment factor to or from the firm's WACC. This results in fewer incorrect decisions than if the firm simply used the WACC to make the decisions.

It would be better, in principle, to determine the required return objectively for each project separately. However, as a practical matter, it may not be possible to go much beyond subjective adjustments, because either the necessary information is unavailable or the cost and effort required are simply not worthwhile.

REAL WORLD INSIGHTS

The weighted average cost of capital (WACC) can be used as a good rule of thumb to assess the attractiveness of an investment in a company. Compare WACC to a company's return on invested capital (ROIC) to ascertain if a company is likely to earn higher returns than it costs to raise capital. Take, for example, the Oil and Gas sector in 2020 - a period of very low oil prices and returns for oil companies. Table 13.4 lists the WACCs and ROICs for a selection of companies in the industry.

TABLE 13.4

Weighted average cost of capital (WACC) and return on invested capital (ROIC) for a selection of firms in the oil and gas sector, 2020

Company	WACC	ROIC
Exxon Mobil Corp	8.12%	2.06%
Royal Dutch Shell	3.70%	2.77%
BP	4.20%	9.17%
Repsol	3.69%	1.71%
Total SE	3.82%	3.68%
Chevron	7.32%	−0.17%

Source: Gurufocus.com.

Whereas the companies' WACCs are similar, their ROICs vary substantially. Only BP was able to generate returns above what it would cost them to raise in the market. For all other companies, it would cost too much to raise new financing given the returns they earned from their business in 2020.

Obviously, the oil industry is affected by the oil price and if this increases, the sector will again become attractive to investors.

CONCEPT QUESTIONS

13.5a What are the likely consequences if a firm uses its WACC to evaluate all proposed investments?

13.5b What is the pure play approach to determining the appropriate discount rate? When might it be used?

ONLINE SUPPLEMENT – FLOTATION COSTS AND THE WEIGHTED AVERAGE COST OF CAPITAL

In Chapter 13, we did not include issue, or flotation, costs in our discussion of the weighted average cost of capital. If a company accepts a new project, it may be required to issue, or float, new bonds and shares. This means that the firm will incur some costs, which we call *flotation costs*. The nature and magnitude of flotation costs are discussed in some detail in Chapter 14.

Sometimes it is suggested that the firm's WACC should be adjusted upwards to reflect flotation costs. This is really not the best approach, because, once again, the required return on an investment depends on the risk of the investment, not on the source of the funds. This is not to say that flotation costs should be ignored. Because these costs arise as a consequence of the decision to undertake a project, they are relevant cash flows. We therefore briefly discuss how to include them in project analysis.

THE BASIC APPROACH

We start with a simple case. Spatt Ltd, an all-equity firm, has a cost of equity of 20 per cent. Because this firm is 100 per cent equity, its WACC and its cost of equity are the same. Spatt is contemplating a large-scale, €100 million expansion of its existing operations. The expansion would be funded by selling new equity.

Based on conversations with its investment banker, Spatt believes its flotation costs will run to 10 per cent of the amount issued. This means that Spatt's proceeds from the equity sale will be only 90 per cent of the amount sold. When flotation costs are considered, what is the cost of the expansion?

As we discuss in more detail in Chapter 14, Spatt needs to sell enough equity to raise €100 million *after* covering the flotation costs. In other words:

$$€100 \text{ million} = (1 - 0.10) \times \text{Amount raised}$$
$$\text{Amount raised} = €100 \text{ million}/0.90 = €111.11 \text{ million}$$

Spatt's flotation costs are thus €11.11 million, and the true cost of the expansion is €111.11 million once we include flotation costs.

Things are only slightly more complicated if the firm uses both debt and equity. For example, suppose Spatt's target capital structure is 60 per cent equity, 40 per cent debt. The flotation costs associated with equity are still 10 per cent, but the flotation costs for debt are less – say 5 per cent.

Earlier, when we had different capital costs for debt and equity, we calculated a weighted average cost of capital using the target capital structure weights. Here we shall do much the same thing. We can calculate a weighted average flotation cost, f_A, by multiplying the equity flotation cost, f_E, by the percentage of equity (E/V) and the debt flotation cost, f_D, by the percentage of debt (D/V), and then adding the two together:

$$\begin{aligned} f_A &= (E/V) \times f_E + (D/V) \times f_D \\ &= 60\% \times 0.10 + 40\% \times 0.05 \\ &= 8\% \end{aligned} \quad (13.8)$$

The weighted average flotation cost is thus 8 per cent. What this tells us is that for every euro in outside financing needed for new projects, the firm must actually raise €1/(1 − 0.08) = €1.087. In our example, the project cost is €100 million when we ignore flotation costs. If we include them, then the true cost is €100 million/(1 − f_A) = €100 million/0.92 = €108.7 million.

In taking issue costs into account, the firm must be careful not to use the wrong weights. The firm should use the target weights, even if it can finance the entire cost of the project with either debt or equity. The fact that a firm can finance a specific project with debt or equity is not directly relevant. If a firm has a target debt–equity ratio of 1, for example, but chooses to finance a particular project with all debt, it will have to raise additional equity later on to maintain its target debt–equity ratio. To take this into account, the firm should always use the target weights in calculating the flotation cost.

EXAMPLE 13.6

CALCULATING THE WEIGHTED AVERAGE FLOTATION COST

Wendy plc has a target capital structure that is 80 per cent equity, 20 per cent debt. The flotation costs for equity issues are 20 per cent of the amount raised; the flotation costs for debt issues are 6 per cent. If Wendy needs £65 million for a new manufacturing facility, what is the true cost once flotation costs are considered?

We first calculate the weighted average flotation cost, f_A:

$$\begin{aligned} f_A &= (E/V) \times f_E + (D/V) \times f_D \\ &= 80\% \times 0.20 + 20\% \times 0.06 \\ &= 17.2\% \end{aligned}$$

The weighted average flotation cost is thus 17.2 per cent. The project cost is £65 million when we ignore flotation costs. If we include them, then the true cost is £65 million/(1 − f_A) = £65 million/0.828 = £78.5 million, again illustrating that flotation costs can be a considerable expense.

FLOTATION COSTS AND NPV

To illustrate how flotation costs can be included in an NPV analysis, suppose Tripleday Printing SA is currently at its target debt–equity ratio of 100 per cent. It is considering building a new €500,000 printing plant in Lyon. This new plant is expected to generate after-tax cash flows of €73,150 per year forever. The tax rate is 34 per cent. There are two financing options:

1. A €500,000 new issue of equity. The issuance costs of the new equity would be about 10 per cent of the amount raised. The required return on the company's new equity is 20 per cent.
2. A €500,000 issue of 30-year bonds. The issuance costs of the new debt would be 2 per cent of the proceeds. The company can raise new debt at 10 per cent.

What is the NPV of the new printing plant?

To begin, because printing is the company's main line of business, we shall use the company's weighted average cost of capital to value the new printing plant:

$$\begin{aligned} \text{WACC} &= (E/V) \times R_E + (D/V) \times R_D \times (1 - T_C) \\ &= 0.50 \times 20\% + 0.50 \times 10\% \times (1 - 0.34) \\ &= 13.3\% \end{aligned}$$

Because the cash flows are €73,150 per year forever, the PV of the cash flows at 13.3 per cent per year is:

$$\text{PV} = \frac{€73,150}{0.133} = €550,000$$

If we ignore flotation costs, the NPV is:

$$\text{NPV} = €550,000 - 500,000 = €50,000$$

With no flotation costs, the project generates an NPV that is greater than zero, so it should be accepted.

What about financing arrangements and issue costs? Because new financing must be raised, the flotation costs are relevant. From the information given, we know that the flotation costs are 2 per cent for debt and 10 per cent for equity. Because Tripleday uses equal amounts of debt and equity, the weighted average flotation cost, f_A, is:

$$\begin{aligned} f_A &= (E/V) \times f_E + (D/V) \times f_D \\ &= 0.50 \times 10\% + 0.50 \times 2\% \\ &= 6\% \end{aligned}$$

Remember, the fact that Tripleday can finance the project with all debt or all equity is irrelevant. Because Tripleday needs €500,000 to fund the new plant, the true cost, once we include flotation costs, is €500,000/$(1 - f_A) = €500,000/0.94 = €531,915$. Because the PV of the cash flows is €550,000, the plant has an NPV of €550,000 − 531,915 = €18,085, so it is still a good investment. However, its value is less than we initially might have thought.

INTERNAL EQUITY AND FLOTATION COSTS

Our discussion of flotation costs to this point implicitly assumes that firms always have to raise the capital needed for new investments. In reality, most firms rarely sell equity at all. Instead, their internally generated cash flow is sufficient to cover the equity portion of their capital spending. Only the debt portion must be raised externally.

The use of internal equity doesn't change our approach. However, we now assign a value of zero to the flotation cost of equity, because there is no such cost. In our Tripleday example, the weighted average flotation cost would therefore be:

$$\begin{aligned} f_A &= (E/V) \times f_E + (D/V) \times f_D \\ &= 0.50 \times 0\% + 0.50 \times 2\% \\ &= 1\% \end{aligned}$$

Notice that whether equity is generated internally or externally makes a big difference, because external equity has a relatively high flotation cost.

> **CONCEPT QUESTIONS**
>
> **13.6a** What are flotation costs?
> **13.6b** How are flotation costs included in an NPV analysis?

SUMMARY AND CONCLUSIONS

This chapter has discussed cost of capital. The most important concept is the weighted average cost of capital, or WACC, which we interpreted as the required rate of return on the overall firm. It is also the discount rate appropriate for cash flows that are similar in risk to those of the overall firm. We described how the WACC can be calculated, and we illustrated how it can be used in certain types of analysis.

We also pointed out situations in which it is inappropriate to use the WACC as the discount rate. To handle such cases we described some alternative approaches to developing discount rates, such as the pure play approach. We also discussed how the flotation costs associated with raising new capital can be included in an NPV analysis.

To finish, the chapter material can be summarized as follows:

1. The cost of capital depends primarily on the use of the funds and the risk of the investment, not the source.
2. The cost of equity can be estimated by the dividend growth model and/or the security market line.
3. The cost of debt can be measured at discrete times as the interest rate on new loans. Apart from those days when new debt is issued, the cost of debt will not normally be equal to the interest rate because of the risk of debt changes over time.
4. A firm's overall cost of capital is measured by WACC, the weighted average cost of capital. Remember to use market values and not book values when calculating WACC.

CHAPTER REVIEW AND SELF-TEST PROBLEMS

13.1 Calculating the Cost of Equity Suppose equity in Watta plc has a beta of 0.80. The market risk premium is 6 per cent, and the risk-free rate is 6 per cent. Watta's last dividend was £1.20 per share, and the dividend is expected to grow at 8 per cent indefinitely. The equity currently sells for £45 per share. What is Watta's cost of equity capital?

13.2 Calculating the WACC In addition to the information given in the previous problem, suppose Watta has a target debt–equity ratio of 50 per cent. Its cost of debt is 9 per cent before taxes. If the tax rate is 28 per cent, what is the WACC?

13.3 Flotation Costs Suppose in the previous problem Watta is seeking £30 million for a new project. The necessary funds will have to be raised externally. Watta's flotation costs for selling debt and equity are 2 per cent and 16 per cent, respectively. If flotation costs are considered, what is the true cost of the new project?

SOLUTIONS

13.1 We start off with the SML approach. Based on the information given, the expected return on Watta's equity is:

$$\begin{aligned} R_E &= R_f + \beta_E \times (R_M - R_f) \\ &= 6\% + 0.80 \times 6\% \\ &= 10.80\% \end{aligned}$$

We now use the dividend growth model. The projected dividend is $D_0 \times (1 + g) = £1.20 \times 1.08 = £1.296$, so the expected return using this approach is:

$$\begin{aligned} R_E &= D_1/P_0 + g \\ &= £1.296/45 + 0.08 \\ &= 10.88\% \end{aligned}$$

Because these two estimates, 10.80 per cent and 10.88 per cent, are fairly close, we shall average them. Watta's cost of equity is approximately 10.84 per cent.

13.2 Because the target debt–equity ratio is 0.50, Watta uses £0.50 in debt for every £1 in equity. In other words, Watta's target capital structure is 1/3 debt and 2/3 equity. The WACC is thus:

$$\begin{aligned} \text{WACC} &= (E/V) \times R_\text{E} + (D/V) \times R_\text{D} \times (1 - T_\text{C}) \\ &= 2/3 \times 10.84\% + 1/3 \times 9\% \times (1 - 0.28) \\ &= 9.387\% \end{aligned}$$

13.3 Because Watta uses both debt and equity to finance its operations, we first need the weighted average flotation cost. As in the previous problem, the percentage of equity financing is 2/3, so the weighted average cost is:

$$\begin{aligned} f_\text{A} &= (E/V) \times f_\text{E} + (D/V) \times f_\text{D} \\ &= 2/3 \times 16\% + 1/3 \times 2\% \\ &= 11.33\% \end{aligned}$$

If Watta needs £30 million after flotation costs, then the true cost of the project is £30 million/$(1 - f_\text{A})$ = £30 million/0.8867 = £33.83 million.

QUESTIONS AND PROBLEMS

13.1 **Calculating Cost of Equity** Down and Out NV has just issued a dividend of €2.40 per share on its equity. The company is expected to maintain a constant 5.5 per cent growth rate in its dividends indefinitely. If the equity sells for €52 a share, what is the company's cost of equity?

13.2 **Calculating Cost of Equity** Dybvig plc's equity has a beta of 1.3. If the risk-free rate is 4.5 per cent and the expected return on the market is 12 per cent, what is Dybvig's cost of equity capital?

13.3 **Cost of Capital** As financial manager of Cosco Pacific Limited, you have been tasked with determining your firm's cost of equity capital. The shares currently sell for HK$10.40, and the dividend per share will probably be about HK$0.05736. Your assistant argues: 'It will cost us HK$0.05736 per share to use the shareholders' money this year, so the cost of equity is only equal to 0.55 per cent' (HK$0.05736/HK$10.40). What is wrong with this conclusion?

13.4 **Calculating Cost of Equity** Equity in Landsväg AG has a beta of 0.85. The market risk premium is 8 per cent, and T-bills are currently yielding 5 per cent. The company's most recent dividend was SKr1.60 per share, and dividends are expected to grow at a 6 per cent annual rate indefinitely. If the equity sells for SKr37 per share, what is your best estimate of the company's cost of equity?

13.5 **Cost of Capital** You are the financial manager of a multinational construction firm with operations in a number of countries in Europe, the Gulf and in South Africa. Is it appropriate for the firm to use different costs of capital for its operations in different countries? If the overall firm WACC were used as the hurdle rate for all countries, would the riskier countries tend to get most of the investment projects? Why? If you were to try to estimate the appropriate cost of capital for the firm's operations in different countries, what problems might you encounter? What are two techniques you could use to develop a rough estimate for each country's cost of capital?

13.6 **Estimating the DCF Growth Rate** Suppose Found Ltd issued a dividend of £1.43 per share on its equity. The company paid dividends of £1.05, £1.12, £1.19 and £1.30 per share in the last four years. If the equity currently sells for £45, what is your best estimate of the company's cost of equity capital using the arithmetic average growth rate in dividends? What if you use the geometric average growth rate?

13.7 **Calculating Cost of Preference Shares** Holdup Bank has an issue of preference shares with a €6 stated dividend that just sold for €96 per share. What is the bank's cost of preference shares?

13.8 **Calculating Cost of Debt** Blue Suede plc is trying to determine its cost of debt. The firm has a debt issue outstanding with 10 years to maturity that is quoted at 104 per cent of face value. The issue makes pays a coupon of 6 per cent annually. What is Blue Suede's pre-tax cost of debt? If the tax rate is 18 per cent, what is the after-tax cost of debt? Assume the face value of the debt is €1,000.

13.9 **Calculating Cost of Debt** Shanken NV issued a 30-year, 10 per cent semi-annual bond 7 years ago. The bond currently sells for 108 per cent of its face value. The company's tax rate is 35 per cent. Assume the face value of the debt is €1,000.

(a) What is the pre-tax cost of debt?

(b) What is the after-tax cost of debt?

(c) Which is more relevant, the pre-tax or the after-tax cost of debt? Why?

13.10 **Calculating Cost of Debt** For the firm in Problem 13.9, suppose the book value of the debt issue is €20 million. In addition, the company has a second debt issue on the market, a zero-coupon bond with 7 years left to maturity; the book value of this issue is €80 million, and the bonds sell for 58 per cent of par. Assume the face value of the debt is €1,000. What is the company's total book value of debt? The total market value? What is your best estimate of the after-tax cost of debt now?

13.11 Calculating WACC Crosstown is a transport firm with a target capital structure of 70 per cent equity and 30 per cent debt. Its cost of equity is 15 per cent and the cost of debt is 4 per cent. The relevant tax rate is 18 per cent. What is Crosstown's WACC?

13.12 Taxes and WACC Miller Manufacturing has a target debt–equity ratio of 0.60. Its cost of equity is 18 per cent, and its cost of debt is 10 per cent. If the tax rate is 35 per cent, what is Miller's WACC?

13.13 Beta The returns of Siracha plc have a standard deviation of 40 per cent per annum and have a correlation with the FTSE 100 of 0.65. The standard deviation of the FTSE 100 is 20 per cent. What is Siracha's beta?

13.14 Book Value versus Market Value Garden Electronics has 25 million shares of equity outstanding. The current share price is £16, and the book value per share is £12. Garden Electronics has issued two bonds in the past. The first bond was issued 20 years ago, has a face value of £50 million, has a 6 per cent coupon, and sells for 101 per cent of par. The second bond was issued five years ago, has a face value of £30 million, a 4 per cent coupon, and sells for 105 per cent of par. The first issue matures in 10 years, the second in 5 years.

(a) What are Garden Electronics' capital structure weights on a book value basis?

(b) What are Garden Electronics' capital structure weights on a market value basis?

(c) Which are more relevant, the book or market value weights? Why?

13.15 Calculating the WACC In Problem 13.14, suppose the company's equity has a beta of 1.2. The risk-free rate is 1 per cent, and the market premium is 9 per cent. Assume that the overall cost of debt is the weighted average cost of two outstanding debt issues. Both bonds make annual payments. The tax rate is 18 per cent. What is the company's WACC? Assume the face value of the debt is £1,000.

13.16 WACC Kose SA has a target debt–equity ratio of 0.80. Its WACC is 10.5 per cent, and the tax rate is 35 per cent.

(a) If Kose's cost of equity is 15 per cent, what is its pre-tax cost of debt?

(b) If instead you know that the after-tax cost of debt is 6.4 per cent, what is the cost of equity?

13.17 Finding the WACC Bottled Water is a listed European company which has a corporate finance structure as shown below. What is the company's WACC?

Debt:	50,000 bonds with a quoted price of 119.80, providing an 8% coupon rate. The bonds have 25 years to maturity. There are also 150,000 zero-coupon bonds outstanding, with a quoted price of 13.85 and 30 years until maturity.
Preferred stock:	120,000 shares of 6.5% preferred with a current price of €112 and a par value of €100.
Common stock:	2 million shares of common stock. The current share price is €65, and the beta of the stock is 1.1.
Market:	The corporate tax rate is 40%, the market risk premium is 5%, and the risk-free rate is 4%.

13.18 Finding the WACC Titan Mining Corporation has 9 million shares of equity outstanding and 1,200,000 8.5 per cent semi-annual bonds outstanding, par value £100 each. The equity currently sells for £34 per share and has a beta of 1.20, and the bonds have 15 years to maturity and sell for 93 per cent of par. The market risk premium is 10 per cent, T-bills are yielding 5 per cent, and Titan Mining's tax rate is 28 per cent.

(a) What is the firm's market value capital structure?

(b) If Titan Mining is evaluating a new investment project that has the same risk as the firm's typical project, what rate should the firm use to discount the projects cash flows?

13.19 SML and WACC An all-equity firm is considering the following projects:

Project	Beta	Expected return (%)
W	0.80	6
X	0.70	5
Y	1.15	9
Z	1.30	13

The T-bill rate is 1 per cent, and the expected return on the market is 9 per cent.

(a) Which projects have a higher expected return than the firm's 10 per cent cost of capital?

(b) Which projects should be accepted?

(c) Which projects would be incorrectly accepted or rejected if the firm's overall cost of capital were used as a hurdle rate?

13.20 Calculating Flotation Costs Suppose your company needs £20 million to build a new assembly line. Your target debt–equity ratio is 0.75. The flotation cost for new equity is 8 per cent, but the flotation cost for debt is only 5 per cent. Your boss has decided to fund the project by borrowing money, because the flotation costs are lower and the required funds are relatively small.

(a) What do you think about the rationale behind borrowing the entire amount?

(b) What is your company's weighted average flotation cost, assuming all equity is raised externally?

(c) What is the true cost of building the new assembly line after taking flotation costs into account? Does it matter in this case that the entire amount is being raised from debt?

13.21 Calculating Flotation Costs Southern Alliance needs to raise €45 million to start a new project, and will raise the money by selling new bonds. The company will generate no internal equity for the foreseeable future. The company has a target capital structure of 65 per cent equity, 5 per cent preference shares, and 30 per cent debt. Flotation costs for issuing new equity are 9 per cent, for new preference shares, 6 per cent, and for new debt, 3 per cent. What is the true initial cost figure Southern should use when evaluating its project?

13.22 Flotation Costs Purple Haze recently issued new securities to finance a new TV show. The project cost €15 million, and the company paid €850,000 in flotation costs. In addition, the equity issued had a flotation cost of 7 per cent of the amount raised, whereas the debt issued had a flotation cost of 3 per cent of the amount raised. If Purple Haze issued new securities in the same proportion as its target capital structure, what is the company's target debt–equity ratio?

13.23 Calculating the Cost of Debt HTR Renewable Energy Ltd has issued four separate bonds in the past 10 years. Each bond makes semi-annual payments and they are listed in the following table. If the corporate tax rate is 18 per cent, what is the after-tax cost of HTR Renewable Energy's debt? Assume the face value of the debt is £1,000.

Bond	Coupon rate (%)	Price quote (% of face value)	Maturity (years)	Face value (£)
1	7.00	103.00	5	40,000,000
2	8.50	108.00	8	35,000,000
3	8.20	97.00	15½	55,000,000
4	9.80	111.00	25	50,000,000

13.24 Calculating the Cost of Equity Floyd Industries equity has a beta of 1.50. The company has just paid a dividend of £0.80, and dividends are expected to grow at 5 per cent. The expected return of the market is 12 per cent, and Treasury bills are yielding 5.5 per cent. The most recent share price for Floyd is £61.

(a) Calculate the cost of equity using the DCF method.

(b) Calculate the cost of equity using the SML method.

(c) Why do you think your estimates in (a) and (b) are so different?

13.25 Flotation Costs and NPV Photochronograph Creative (PC) manufactures time series photographic equipment. It is currently at its target debt–equity ratio of 0.70. It is considering building a new £45 million manufacturing facility. This new plant is expected to generate after-tax cash flows of £6.2 million in perpetuity. The company raises all equity from outside financing. There are three financing options:

(a) *A new issue of equity.* The flotation costs of the new equity would be 8 per cent of the amount raised. The required return on the company's new equity is 14 per cent.

(b) *A new issue of 20-year bonds.* The flotation costs of the new bonds would be 4 per cent of the proceeds. If the company issues these new bonds at an annual coupon rate of 8 per cent, they will sell at par.

(c) *Increased use of accounts payable financing.* Because this financing is part of the company's ongoing daily business, it has no flotation costs, and the company assigns it a cost that is the same as the overall firm WACC. Management has a target ratio of accounts payable to long-term debt of 0.20. (Assume there is no difference between the pre-tax and after-tax accounts payable cost.) What is the NPV of the new plant? Assume that PC has a 28 per cent tax rate.

13.26 Flotation Costs Fratelli Tutti has a debt–equity ratio of 0.80 and is considering an expansion of operations into a new country. The total capital expenditure for the new investment is expected to be €24 million. When the company issues new equity, it incurs a flotation cost of 6 per cent, while the costs of issuing new debt are only 4 per cent. If Fratelli Tutti raises all its required funding from external equity, what is the initial cost of the new operations? Assume a combination of funding sources is used: 40 per cent of the required investment comes from external equity and 60 per cent of its funds comes from retained earnings. What will the cost be now? Finally, what is the initial cost, if the investment was funded completely from retained earnings?

13.27 Project Evaluation This is a comprehensive project evaluation problem bringing together much of what you have learned in this and previous chapters. Suppose you have been hired as a financial consultant to Defence Electronics International (DEI), a large, publicly traded firm that is the market share leader in radar detection systems (RDSs). The company is looking at setting up a manufacturing plant overseas to produce a new line of RDSs. This will be a five-year project. The company bought some land three years ago for £4 million in anticipation of using it as a toxic dump site for waste chemicals, but it built a piping system to discard the chemicals safely instead. The land was appraised last week at £5.1 million. In five years the after-tax value of the land will be £6 million, but the company expects to keep the land for a future project. The company wants to build its new manufacturing plant on this land; the plant and equipment will cost £35 million to build. The following market data on DEI's securities are current:

Debt: 2,400,000 7.5 per cent coupon bonds outstanding, 20 years to maturity, selling for 94 per cent of par; the bonds have a £100 par value each and make semi-annual payments.
Equity: 9,000,000 shares outstanding, selling for £71 per share; the beta is 1.2.
Preference shares: 400,000 of 5.5 per cent preference shares outstanding, selling for £81 per share.
Market: 8 per cent expected market risk premium; 5 per cent risk-free rate.

DEI uses G.M. Wharton as its lead underwriter. Wharton charges DEI spreads of 8 per cent on new equity issues, 6 per cent on new preference share issues, and 4 per cent on new debt issues. Wharton has included all direct and indirect issuance costs (along with its profit) in setting these spreads. Wharton has recommended to DEI that it raise the funds needed to build the plant by issuing new shares of equity. DEI's tax rate is 28 per cent. The project requires £1,300,000 in initial net working capital investment to get operational. Assume Wharton raises all equity for new projects externally. Assume that the face value of a preference share is £100.

(a) Calculate the project's initial time 0 cash flow, taking into account all side effects.

(b) The new RDS project is somewhat riskier than a typical project for DEI, primarily because the plant is being located overseas. Management has told you to use an adjustment factor of +2 per cent to account for this increased riskiness. Calculate the appropriate discount rate to use when evaluating DEI's project.

(c) The manufacturing plant has an eight-year tax life, and DEI uses 20 per cent reducing-balance depreciation. At the end of the project (that is, the end of year 5), the plant and equipment can be scrapped for £6 million. What is the after-tax salvage value of this plant and equipment?

(d) The company will incur £7,000,000 in annual fixed costs. The plan is to manufacture 18,000 RDSs per year and sell them at £10,900 per machine; the variable production costs are £9,400 per RDS. What is the annual operating cash flow (OCF) from this project?

(e) DEI's financial controller is interested primarily in the impact of DEI's investments on the bottom line of reported accounting statements. What will you tell her is the accounting break-even quantity of RDSs sold for this project?

(f) Finally, DEI's chief executive wants you to throw all your calculations, assumptions and everything else into the report for the chief financial officer; all he wants to know is what the RDS project's internal rate of return (IRR) and net present value (NPV) are. What will you report?

MINI CASE

THE COST OF CAPITAL FOR PAVEGEN

Pavegen (www.pavegen.com) is a UK technology firm that manufactures paving tiles to convert footsteps into kinetic energy via electromagnetic generators. The company's products have been installed in 36 countries in a range of locations where footfall is high, such as shopping centres and train stations. Because it is a private company, calculating the cost of capital for Pavegen is a difficult task and, although it is a very poor comparator, you have decided the closest firm to Pavegen is Powerhouse Energy (www.powerhouseenergy.net). You plan to use this company as a representative firm to estimate the cost of Pavegen's cost of capital. The following steps will allow you to calculate this estimate.

QUESTIONS

1. All publicly traded UK corporations are required to submit financial reports to Companies House detailing their financial operations over the previous six months or year, respectively. These corporate filings are always available on the company's website. Go to the Powerhouse Energy website, follow the *'Investors'* link, and download the most recent set of financial accounts. Look in the balance sheet to find the book value of debt and the book value of equity.

2. To estimate the cost of equity for Powerhouse Energy, go to any of the standard financial websites (Yahoo! finance, FT.com, Reuters, etc.) and find the company's most recent share price, the market value of equity, beta, and number of shares outstanding. Now go to www.ft.com, follow the *'Markets Data'* link and then the *'Bonds and Rates'* link. What is the yield on 10-year UK Treasury bonds?

3. We now need to estimate the historical market risk premium. Go to Yahoo! Finance, and download the monthly historical prices for the FTSE 100 index for the last five years. Calculate the monthly returns,

take the average, and multiply this by 12 to get the annualized historical return on the FTSE 100. What is the historical market risk premium for the UK? Using the historical market risk premium, what is Powerhouse Energy's cost of equity using the CAPM?

4. Find the beta of five other UK renewable energy firms and calculate the average beta. Using the industry average beta, what is the cost of equity? Does it matter if you use the beta for Powerhouse Energy or the beta for the industry in this case?

5. You now need to calculate Powerhouse Energy's cost of debt. There are several ways to do this, all of which are broad approximations. One approach is to divide the tax paid by Powerhouse Energy in the previous year by the average total long term debt over the past two years. This gives a very rough estimate of the company's cost of debt.

6. You now have all the necessary information to calculate the weighted average cost of capital for Powerhouse Energy. Calculate WACC using book value weights and market value weights, assuming Powerhouse Energy has an 18 per cent effective tax rate. Which cost of capital number is more relevant?

7. You used Powerhouse Energy as a representative company to estimate the cost of capital for Pavegen. What are some of the potential problems with this approach? What improvements might you suggest?

ADDITIONAL READING

The following papers consider the cost of capital for both debt and equity, and how it is affected by different factors, such as default risk, growth opportunities, and information quality. Brav (2009) considers the much wider issue of financing choices for private and public firms and should also be read as additional reading for Chapters 14, 19 and 20.

1. Brav, O. (2009). Access to capital, capital structure, and the funding of the firm. *Journal of Finance, 64*(1), 263–308.

2. Chen, K.C.W., Chen, Z., & Wei, K.C.J. (2009). Legal protection of investors, corporate governance, and the cost of equity capital. *Journal of Corporate Finance, 15*(3), 273–289.

3. Driessen, J. (2005). Is default event risk priced in corporate bonds? *Review of Financial Studies, 18*(1), 165–195.

4. Easley, D., & O'Hara, M. (2004). Information and the cost of capital. *Journal of Finance, 59*(4), 1553–1583.

5. Hail, L., & Leuz, C. (2009). Cost of capital effects and changes in growth expectations around US cross-listings. *Journal of Financial Economics, 93*(3), 428–454.

6. Hirst, I., Danbolt, J., & Jones, E. (2008). Required rates of return for corporate investment appraisal in the presence of growth opportunities. *European Financial Management, 14*(5), 989–1006.

7. Kisgen, D.J., & Strahan, P.E. (2010). Do regulations based on credit ratings affect a firm's cost of capital? *Review of Financial Studies, 23*(12), 4324–4347.

8. Sabal, J. (2004). The discount rate in emerging markets: A guide. *Journal of Applied Corporate Finance, 16*(2 and 3), 155–166.

9. Zou, H., & Adams, M.B. (2008). Debt capacity, cost of debt, and corporate insurance. *Journal of Financial and Quantitative Analysis, 43*(2), 433–466.

Endnotes

1. Notice that if we have D_0 and g, we can simply calculate D_1 by multiplying D_0 by $(1+g)$.
2. There is an implicit adjustment for risk, because the current share price is used. All other things being equal, the higher the risk, the lower is the share price. Further, the lower the share price, the greater is the cost of equity, again assuming all the other information is the same.
3. We can also estimate beta coefficients directly by using historical data. For a discussion of how to do this, see Chapters 10, 11 and 13 in D. Hillier, S.A. Ross, R.W. Westerfield and J.J. Jaffe (2009). *Corporate finance: European edition*, 1st edn. McGraw-Hill.
4. For a discussion of multifactor models, see D. Hillier, S.A. Ross, R.W. Westerfield and J.J. Jaffe (2009). *Corporate finance: European edition*, 1st edn. McGraw-Hill.
5. The firm's cost of debt based on its historic borrowing is sometimes called the *embedded debt cost*.

CHAPTER 14
RAISING CAPITAL

> **LEARNING OBJECTIVES**
> After studying this chapter, you should understand:
> **LO1** The venture capital market, and its role in the financing of new, high-risk ventures.
> **LO2** How securities are sold to the public, and the role of investment banks in the process.
> **LO3** Initial public offerings, and some of the costs of going public.
> **LO4** How rights are issued to existing shareholders, and how to value those rights.
>
> **KEY NOTATIONS**
> EPS   Earnings per share
> IPO   Initial public offering
> SEO   Seasoned equity offering

WHEN A FIRM WISHES TO RAISE CAPITAL for new investment, it has two basic choices. It can either issue new equity or borrow funds privately from financial institutions, or through the public issue of debt. Every day you will read about companies raising capital in the financial markets, and in recent years there have been a number of very high public issues. These include Saudi Aramco, Uber, Slack, Peloton, and Trainline, all of which have met with varying levels of success.

In this chapter, we examine the process by which companies sell equity to the public, the costs of doing so, and the role of intermediaries in the process. We pay particular attention to what is probably the most important stage in a company's financial life cycle – the initial public offering. Such offerings are the process by which companies convert from being privately owned to being publicly owned. For many people, starting a company, growing it, and taking it public is the ultimate entrepreneurial dream.

All firms must, at different times, obtain capital. To do so, a firm must either borrow the money (debt financing), or sell a portion of the firm (equity financing), or both. How a firm raises capital depends a great deal on the size of the firm, its life-cycle stage, and its growth prospects.

In this chapter, we examine some of the ways in which firms actually raise capital. We begin by looking at companies in the early stages of their lives, and the importance of venture capital for such firms. We then look at the process of going public, and the role of investment banks. Along the way, we discuss many of the issues associated with selling securities to the public and their implications for all types of firm. We close the chapter with a discussion of sources of debt capital.

14.1 THE FINANCING LIFE CYCLE OF A FIRM: EARLY-STAGE FINANCING AND VENTURE CAPITAL

One day, you and a friend have a great idea for a new computer software product that helps users communicate using the next-generation meganet. Filled with entrepreneurial zeal, you christen the product Megacomm and set about bringing it to market.

Working at nights and weekends, you are able to create a prototype of your product. It doesn't actually work, but at least you can show it around to illustrate your idea. To develop the product you need to hire programmers, buy computers, rent office space, and so on. Unfortunately, because you are both university students, your combined assets are not sufficient to fund a *pizza* party, much less a start-up company. You need what is often referred to as OPM – other people's money.

> **venture capital (VC)**
> financing for new, often high-risk, ventures.

Your first thought might be to approach a bank for a loan. You would probably discover, however, that banks are generally not interested in making loans to start-up companies with no assets (other than an idea) run by fledgling entrepreneurs with no track record. Instead, your search for capital would probably lead you to the private equity and **venture capital (VC)** market.

THE PRIVATE EQUITY FIRM

A large amount of private equity investment is undertaken by professional private equity managers representing large institutional investors such as mutual funds and pension funds. Private equity has been important for both traditional start-up companies and established public firms. The private equity market can be divided into venture equity and non-venture equity markets. A large part of the non-venture market is made up of firms in financial distress. Firms in financial distress are not likely to be able to issue public equity, and typically cannot use traditional forms of debt such as bank loans or public debt. For these firms, the best alternative is to find a private equity market firm.

According to Invest Europe, the world's largest association of private capital providers, France and the US were the leading centres for private equity fundraising in the world. The majority of private equity firms are based in the US and UK, with branches in geographical regions. Table 14.1 presents the world's largest private equity fundraising firms by total deal size between 2015 and 2020. Note the dominance of US private equity firms in the list.

TABLE 14.1

Largest private equity fundraisers

Private equity fund manager	Location
Blackstone	US
The Carlyle Group	US
KKR	US
TPG	US
Warburg Pincus	US
NB Private Equity Partners	US

TABLE 14.1

Private equity fund manager	Location
CVC Capital Partners	Luxembourg
EQT	Sweden
Advent International	US
Vista Equity Partners	US
Leonard Green and Partners	US
Cinven	UK

Source: privateequityinternational.com.

SUPPLIERS OF VENTURE CAPITAL

Venture capital is a significant part of the private equity market. There are at least four types of organization that supply venture capital. First, a few old-line, wealthy families have traditionally provided start-up capital to promising businesses. For example, over the years, the Rockefeller family has made the initial capital contribution to a number of successful businesses. Such families have been involved in venture capital for at least a century.

Second, a number of private partnerships and corporations have been formed to provide investment funds. The organizer behind the partnership might raise capital from institutional investors, such as insurance companies and pension funds. Alternatively, a group of individuals might provide the funds to be ultimately invested with budding entrepreneurs.

Venture capital is a sub-activity of all private equity financing. The most common form of private equity financing in recent years is through buy-outs. Examples of private equity buy-out activity include EMI, Boots and Chrysler. Figure 14.1 provides a breakdown of European private equity funding in 2020 across

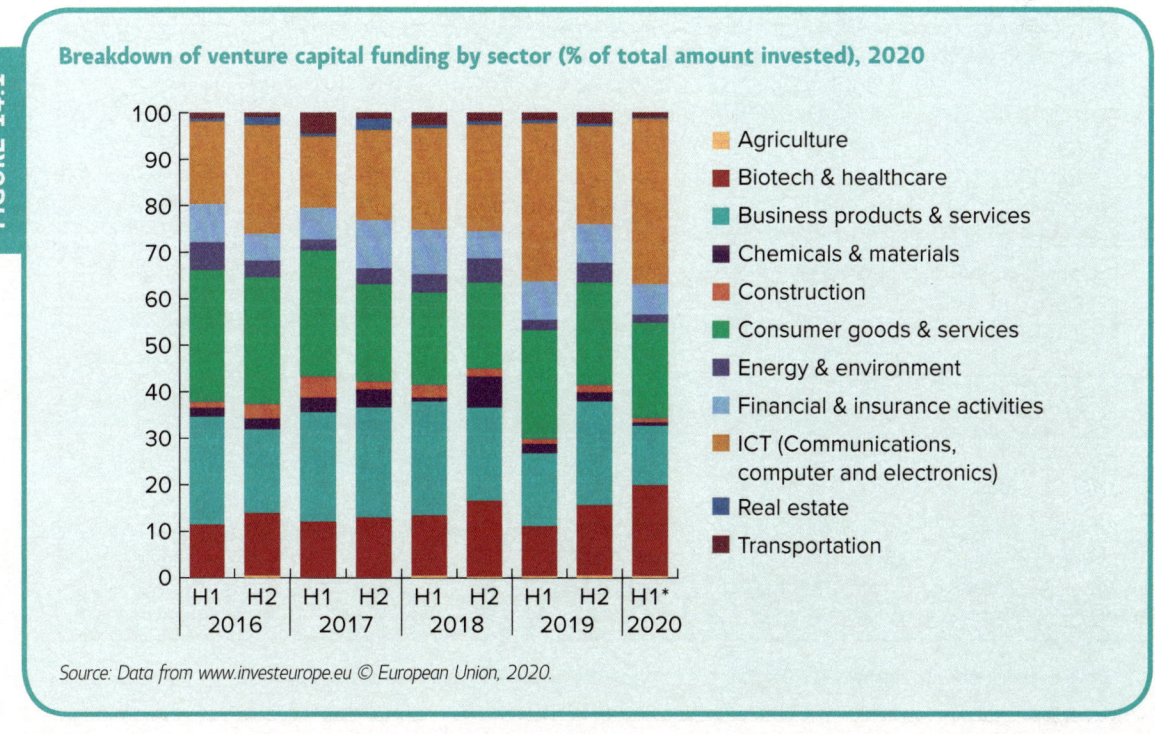

FIGURE 14.1 Breakdown of venture capital funding by sector (% of total amount invested), 2020

Source: Data from www.investeurope.eu © European Union, 2020.

industrial sectors. Although there is annual variation in where investment lands, the majority of venture capital investments were in Biotech, Healthcare and ICT.

Stories used to abound about how easily an individual could obtain venture capital. Though that may have been the case in an earlier era, it is certainly not the case today. Venture capital firms employ various screening procedures to prevent inappropriate funding. For example, because of the large demand for funds, many venture capitalists have at least one employee whose full-time job consists of reading business plans. Only the very best plans can expect to attract funds.

Third, large industrial or financial corporations have established venture capital subsidiaries. Manufacturers Hanover Venture Capital Corp., Citicorp Venture Capital and Chemical Venture Capital Corporation of Chemical Bank are examples of this type. However, private equity subsidiaries appear to make up only a small portion of the venture capital market.

Fourth, there are also participants in an informal venture capital market. Rather than belonging to any venture capital firm, these investors (often referred to as *business angels*) act as individuals when providing financing. They should not, by any means, be viewed as isolated, and there is a rich network of angels, continually relying on each other for advice. The venture capital community has unfortunately chosen to refer to business angels as 'dumb dentists'. Although a number indeed may be dentists, their intelligence should not be called into question. The typical angel has income over $100,000, net worth over $1,000,000, and substantial business experience and knowledge. As we might expect, the informal venture capitalist is able to tolerate high risks. Table 14.2 presents data held by the European Business Angel Network on its business angel membership. The UK, Germany and Spain are the largest countries for business angels, and this reflects the overall size of each country's economy. However, business angels are in every country and form an important, if small, component of the European financing sector. Though this informal market may seem small and unimportant, it is perhaps the largest of all sources of venture capital in Europe.

TABLE 14.2

International business angel networks

Country	Number of business angel networks	Number of business angels	Number of investments	Total investment (€m)
UK	74	9,000	848	109.4
Germany	40	2,000	198	86.6
Spain	48	3,742	221	58.7
Russia	24	250	140	49.0
France	64	5,000	455	37.0
Finland	6	670	435	36.0
Sweden	12	820	78	25.5
Denmark	1	250	191	23.1
Netherlands	19	1,200	72	22.3
Italy	9	450	55	21.2
Switzerland	10	710	133	20.1
Austria	4	385	23	18.5
Belgium	2	450	68	18
Poland	5	500	34	16.8
Portugal	20	344	65	16.5
Ireland	12	780	44	12.5
Greece	4	52	19	2.7
Norway	6	350	31	6.48

Source: European Business Angel Network, EBAN Statistics Compendium, European Early Stage Market Statistics (2018).

STAGES OF FINANCING

There are six stages in private equity financing:

1. *Seed money:* A small amount of financing needed to prove a concept or develop a product. Marketing is not included in this stage.
2. *Start-up:* Financing for firms that started within the past year. Funds are likely to pay for marketing and product development expenditures.
3. *Later stage capital:* Additional money to begin sales and manufacturing after a firm has spent its start-up funds.
4. *Growth capital:* Funds earmarked for a firm to enable it to reach its potential and achieve successful growth.
5. *Replacement capital:* Financing for a company to buy out other investors in the firm.
6. *Buyout financing:* Money provided for managers and outside investors to acquire a fully functioning firm.

Figure 14.2 presents a breakdown of where private equity funding was made in Europe in the first six months of 2020. The vast majority of investment was in buyouts to take a firm off the stock exchange, followed by venture and growth capital.

FIGURE 14.2 Breakdown of European private equity investments into European companies by investment stage, 2020

Source: Data from www.investeurope.eu.

The penultimate stage in venture capital finance is the initial public offering. Venture capitalists are important participants in initial public offerings. Venture capitalists rarely sell all of their shares at the time of the initial public offering. Instead they usually sell out in subsequent public offerings. However, there is considerable evidence that venture capitalists can successfully time IPOs by taking firms public when the market values are at the highest.

SOME VENTURE CAPITAL REALITIES

Although there is a large venture capital market, the truth is that access to venture capital is really very limited. Venture capital companies receive huge numbers of unsolicited proposals, the vast majority of which end up in the bin, unread. Venture capitalists rely heavily on informal networks of lawyers, accountants, bankers and other venture capitalists to help identify potential investments. As a result, personal contacts are important in gaining access to the venture capital market; it is very much an 'introduction' market.

Another simple fact about venture capital is that it is incredibly expensive. In a typical deal the venture capitalist will demand (and get) 40 per cent or more of the equity in the company. Venture capitalists frequently hold voting preference shares, giving them various priorities in the event that the company is sold or liquidated. The venture capitalist will typically demand (and get) several seats on the company's board of directors, and may even appoint one or more members of senior management.

> ### SUSTAINABILITY IN FINANCE
>
> Bill Gates has predicted researchers will 'discover a clean energy breakthrough that will save our planet and power our world' within the next 15 years. In their annual open letter, Bill and Melinda Gates provide an update on their plans to stimulate innovation in technologies for tackling climate change, energy poverty and gender inequality.
>
> In Bill's section of the letter, which is addressed to teenagers, the Microsoft founder and billionaire philanthropist argues it should be a development priority to deliver clean energy to the 1.3 billion people who do not have access to power.
>
> 'New green technologies are allowing the world to produce more carbon-free energy from solar and wind power,' he writes. 'Maybe you live near a wind farm or have seen solar panels near your school. It's great that these are getting cheaper and more people are using them. We should use more of them where it makes sense, like in places where it's especially sunny or windy. And by installing special new power lines we could make even more use of solar and wind power.'
>
> Gates argues that a combination of private sector research and development, such as his recently launched Energy Breakthrough Coalition, government action, and individual endeavour can combine to deliver a new generation of clean energy technologies.
>
> He also revealed the Breakthrough Energy Coalition is working on new investment approaches that would provide more 'patient capital' than that offered by traditional venture capital funds, allowing for greater investment in long term R&D efforts.
>
> *Excerpts from: 'Bill Gates: World will deliver "clean energy breakthrough" within 15 years', BusinessGreen.com.*

CONCLUSION

If a start-up succeeds, the big pay-off frequently comes when the company is sold to another company or goes public. Either way, investment bankers are often involved in the process. We discuss the process of selling securities to the public in the next several sections, paying particular attention to the process of going public.

> **CONCEPT QUESTIONS**
>
> **14.1a** What is venture capital?
> **14.1b** Why is venture capital often provided in stages?

14.2 SELLING SECURITIES TO THE PUBLIC: THE BASIC PROCEDURE

When considering the steps involved in a public issue of securities, it is important to remember that each country has its own specific regulations and traditions, although the European Union has a comprehensive directive that covers all member countries. Table 14.3 illustrates the general process for European public issues

TABLE 14.3

The process of raising capital

Steps in public offering	Time	Activities
Preparatory period	6 months before	Advisors appointed; listing eligibility established, due diligence starts, prospectus prepared
First draft prospectus	3 months before	Advisors submit first draft of prospectus to regulator
Listing announcement	2 months before	Company announces intention to list, draft prospectus published
Blackout period	1 month before	Research by connected brokers is published; no more connected research permitted after this period
Pathfinder prospectus	14 days before	Pathfinder prospectus issued with indicative issue price range, underwriters appointed and begin selling, pre-underwriting conferences held by company directors
Pricing date	3 days before	Issue price set and shares are allocated to subscribers, final prospectus published, price stabilization begins
Issue date	Day 0	Shares start trading

CONCEPT QUESTIONS

14.2a What are the basic procedures in selling a new issue?
14.2b What is a prospectus?

14.3 ALTERNATIVE ISSUE METHODS

When a company issues a security, it can have a public or a private issue. In a public issue, the firm must register the issue with the stock exchange on which it plans to list. However, if the issue is to be sold to a small number of investors, the sale may be carried out privately.

For equity sales, there are two kinds of public issue: a **general cash offer** and a **rights issue** (or *rights offering*). With a cash offer, securities are offered to the general public. With a rights issue, securities are initially offered only to existing owners. Rights issues are very common in Europe.

The first public equity issue that is made by a company is referred to as an **initial public offering**, an *IPO*, or an *unseasoned new issue*. This issue occurs when a company decides to go public. Obviously, all initial public offerings are cash offers. If the firm's existing shareholders wanted to buy the shares, the firm wouldn't have to sell them publicly in the first place.

A **seasoned equity offering (SEO)** is a new issue for a company with securities that have been previously issued.[1] A seasoned equity offering can be made by using a cash offer or a rights offer.

These methods of issuing new securities are shown in Table 14.4. They are discussed in Sections 14.4–14.8.

---

general cash offer
an issue of securities offered for sale to the general public on a cash basis.

rights issue
a public issue of securities in which securities are first offered to existing shareholders. Also called a *rights offering*.

initial public offering (IPO)
a company's first equity issue made available to the public. Also called an *unseasoned new issue* or an *IPO*.

seasoned equity offering (SEO)
a new equity issue of securities by a company that has previously issued securities to the public.

TABLE 14.4

The methods of issuing new securities

Method	Type	Definition
Public traditional negotiated cash offer	Firm commitment cash offer	The company negotiates an agreement with an investment firm or bank to underwrite and distribute the new shares. A specified number of shares are bought by underwriters and sold at a higher price.
	Best efforts cash offer	The company has an investment firm or bank sell as many of the new shares as possible at the agreed-upon price. There is no guarantee concerning how much cash will be raised.
	Dutch auction cash offer	The company has an investment firm or bank auction shares to determine the highest offer price obtainable for a given number of shares to be sold.
Privileged subscription	Direct rights issue	The company offers the new equity directly to its existing shareholders.
	Standby rights issue	Like the direct rights issue, this contains a privileged subscription arrangement with existing shareholders. The net proceeds are guaranteed by the underwriters.
Non-traditional cash offer	Shelf cash offer	Qualifying companies can authorize all shares they expect to sell over a two-year period and sell them when needed.
	Competitive firm cash offer	The company can elect to award the underwriting contract through a public auction instead of negotiation.
Private	Direct placement	Securities are sold directly to the purchaser, who, at least until recently, generally could not resell securities for at least two years.

CONCEPT QUESTIONS

14.3a What is the difference between a rights offer and a cash offer?
14.3b Why is an initial public offering necessarily a cash offer?

14.4 UNDERWRITERS

If the public issue of securities is a cash offer, **underwriters** are usually involved. Underwriting is an important line of business for large investment firms (such as Morgan Stanley) and banks (such as Credit Suisse). Underwriters perform services such as the following for corporate issuers:

> **underwriters**
> investment firms that act as intermediaries between a company selling securities and the investing public.

- Formulating the method used to issue the securities
- Pricing the new securities
- Selling the new securities

Typically, the underwriter buys the securities for less than the offering price, and accepts the risk of not being able to sell them. Because underwriting involves risk, underwriters usually combine to form an underwriting group called a **syndicate** to share the risk and to help sell the issue.

In a syndicate, one or more managers arrange, or co-manage, the offering. The lead manager typically has the responsibility of dealing with the issuer and pricing the securities. The other underwriters in the syndicate serve primarily to distribute the issue and produce research reports later on. In recent years it has become fairly common for a syndicate to consist of only a small number of co-managers.

The difference between the underwriter's buying price and the offering price is called the **gross spread**, or underwriting discount. It is the basic compensation received by the underwriter. Sometimes, on smaller deals, the underwriter will get non-cash compensation in the form of warrants and shares in addition to the spread.[2]

CHOOSING AN UNDERWRITER

A firm can offer its securities to the highest bidding underwriter on a *competitive offer* basis, or it can negotiate directly with an underwriter. Except for a few large firms, companies usually do new issues of debt and equity on a *negotiated offer* basis.

There is evidence that competitive underwriting is cheaper to use than negotiated underwriting. The underlying reasons for the dominance of negotiated underwriting in Europe are the subject of ongoing debate.

TYPES OF UNDERWRITING

Three basic types of underwriting are involved in a cash offer: firm commitment, best efforts, and Dutch auction.

Firm Commitment Underwriting

In **firm commitment underwriting** the issuer sells the entire issue to the underwriters, who then attempt to resell it. This is the most prevalent type of underwriting in Europe. For a new issue of seasoned equity, the underwriters can look at the market price to determine what the issue should sell for, and more than 95 per cent of all such new issues are firm commitments.

If the underwriter cannot sell all of the issue at the agreed-upon offering price, it may have to lower the price on the unsold shares. Nonetheless, with firm commitment underwriting the issuer receives the agreed-upon amount, and all the risk associated with selling the issue is transferred to the underwriter.

Because the offering price usually isn't set until the underwriters have investigated how receptive the market is to the issue, this risk is usually minimal. Also, because the offering price usually is not set until just before selling commences, the issuer doesn't know precisely what its net proceeds will be until that time.

Best Efforts Underwriting

In **best efforts underwriting** the underwriter is legally bound to use 'best efforts' to sell the securities at the agreed-upon offering price. Beyond this, the underwriter does not guarantee any particular amount of money to the issuer. This form of underwriting has become uncommon in recent years.

Dutch Auction Underwriting

With **Dutch auction underwriting** the underwriter does not set a fixed price for the shares to be sold. Instead, the underwriter conducts an auction in which investors bid for shares. The offer price is determined based on the submitted bids. A Dutch auction is also known by the more descriptive name *uniform price auction*. This approach to selling securities to the public is relatively new in the IPO market and has not been widely used there, but it is very common in the bond markets. For example, it is the sole procedure used by governments to sell enormous quantities of notes, bonds and bills to the public.

---

syndicate
a group of underwriters formed to share the risk and to help sell an issue.

gross spread
compensation to the underwriter, determined by the difference between the underwriter's buying price and the offering price.

firm commitment underwriting
the type of underwriting in which the underwriter buys the entire issue, assuming full financial responsibility for any unsold shares.

best efforts underwriting
the type of underwriting in which the underwriter sells as much of the issue as possible, but can return any unsold shares to the issuer without financial responsibility.

dutch auction underwriting
the type of underwriting in which the offer price is set based on competitive bidding by investors. Also known as a *uniform price auction*.

The best way to understand a Dutch or uniform price auction is to consider a simple example. Suppose Rial plc wants to sell 400 shares to the public. The company receives five bids as follows:

Bidder	Quantity (shares)	Price (£)
A	100	16
B	100	14
C	200	12
D	100	12
E	200	10

Thus bidder A is willing to buy 100 shares at £16 each, bidder B is willing to buy 100 shares at £14, and so on. Rial plc examines the bids to determine the highest price that will result in all 400 shares being sold. So, for example, at £14, A and B would buy only 200 shares, so that price is too high. Working our way down, all 400 shares won't be sold until we hit a price of £12, so £12 will be the offer price in the IPO. Bidders A–D will receive shares; bidder E will not.

There are two additional important points to observe in our example. First, all the winning bidders will pay £12 – even bidders A and B, who actually bid a higher price. The fact that all successful bidders pay the same price is the reason for the name 'uniform price auction'. The idea in such an auction is to encourage bidders to bid aggressively, by providing some protection against bidding a price that is too high.

Second, notice that at the £12 offer price there are actually bids for 500 shares, which exceeds the 400 shares Rial wants to sell. Thus there has to be some sort of allocation. How this is done varies, but in the IPO market, the approach has been to simply compute the ratio of shares offered to shares bid at the offer price or better, which in our example is 400/500 = 0.8, and allocate bidders that percentage of their bids. In other words, bidders A–D would each receive 80 per cent of the shares they bid at a price of £12 per share.

THE AFTERMARKET

The period after a new issue is initially sold to the public is referred to as the *aftermarket*. During this time the members of the underwriting syndicate generally do not sell securities for less than the offering price.

green shoe provision
a contract provision giving the underwriter the option to purchase additional shares from the issuer at the offering price. Also called the *overallotment option*.

In most countries, the principal underwriter is permitted to buy shares if the market price falls below the offering price. The purpose of this would be to support the market and stabilize the price against temporary downward pressure. If the issue remains unsold after a time (for example, 30 days), members can leave the group and sell their shares at whatever price the market will allow.

THE GREEN SHOE PROVISION

Many underwriting contracts contain a **Green Shoe provision** (sometimes called the *overallotment option*), which gives the members of the underwriting group the option to purchase additional shares from the issuer at the offering price.[3] Essentially all IPOs and SEOs include this provision, but ordinary debt offerings generally do not. The stated reason for the Green Shoe option is to cover excess demand and oversubscriptions. Green Shoe options usually last for 30 days and involve 15 per cent of the newly issued shares.

In practice, usually underwriters initially go ahead and sell 115 per cent of the shares offered. If the demand for the issue is strong after the offering, the underwriters exercise the Green Shoe option to get the extra 15 per cent from the company. If demand for the issue is weak, the underwriters buy the needed shares in the open market, thereby helping to support the price of the issue in the aftermarket.

lock-up agreement
the part of the underwriting contract that specifies how long insiders must wait after an IPO before they can sell equity.

LOCK-UP AGREEMENTS

Although they are not required by law, almost all underwriting contracts contain so-called **lock-up agreements**. Such agreements specify how long insiders must wait after an IPO before they can sell some or all of their equity. Lock-up periods have become fairly standardized in recent years at 180 days. Thus, following an

IPO, insiders can't cash out until 6 months have gone by, which ensures that they maintain a significant economic interest in the company going public.

Lock-up periods are also important because it is not unusual for the number of locked-up shares to exceed the number of shares held by the public, sometimes by a substantial multiple. On the day the lock-up period expires, there is the possibility that a large number of shares will hit the market on the same day and thereby depress values. The evidence suggests that, on average, venture-capital-backed companies are particularly likely to experience a loss in value on the lock-up expiration day.

THE QUIET PERIOD

Once a firm begins to seriously contemplate an IPO, stock exchange authorities normally require that a firm and its managing underwriters observe a 'quiet period'. This means that all communications with the public must be limited to ordinary announcements and other purely factual matters. The logic is that all relevant information should be contained in the prospectus, and an important result of this requirement is that the underwriter's analysts are prohibited from making recommendations to investors. As soon as the quiet period ends, however, the managing underwriters typically publish research reports, usually accompanied by a favourable 'buy' recommendation.

> **CONCEPT QUESTIONS**
>
> **14.4a** What do underwriters do?
> **14.4b** What is the Green Shoe provision?

14.5 IPOS AND UNDERPRICING

Determining the correct offering price is the most difficult thing an underwriter must do for an initial public offering. The issuing firm faces a potential cost if the offering price is set too high or too low. If the issue is priced too high, it may be unsuccessful and have to be withdrawn. If the issue is priced below the true market value, the issuer's existing shareholders will experience an opportunity loss when the issuer sells shares for less than they are worth.

Underpricing is common. It obviously helps new shareholders earn a higher return on the shares they buy. However, the existing shareholders of the issuing firm are not helped by underpricing. To them, it is an indirect cost of issuing new securities. For example, consider a hypothetical IPO. The new issue opens at €44 and rises to a first-day high of €69, before closing at €56.50, a gain of about 28 per cent. Based on these numbers, the IPO is underpriced by about €12.50 per share, which means the company missed out on significant capital that could be used in its operations.

IPO UNDERPRICING

Unseasoned new equity issues are generally offered below their true market price. Table 14.5 shows the issue date average return on new IPOs for a variety of countries.

TABLE 14.5

Equal weighted average initial IPO returns for 47 countries

Country	Sample size	Time period	Average initial return (%)	Country	Sample size	Time period	Average initial return (%)
Australia	2,069	1976-2018	19.8	Netherlands	212	1982-2017	13.3
Austria	106	1971-2018	6.2	New Zealand	269	1979-2018	15.9

TABLE 14.5

Country	Sample size	Time period	Average initial return (%)	Country	Sample size	Time period	Average initial return (%)
Belgium	114	1984-2017	11.0	Nigeria	125	1989-2017	12.8
Bulgaria	9	2004-2007	36.5	Norway	266	1984-2018	6.7
Canada	758	1971-2017	6.4	Pakistan	80	2000-2013	22.1
China	3,798	1990-2019	157.7	Philippines	173	1987-2018	17.3
Cyprus	73	1999-2012	20.3	Poland	350	1991-2019	11.7
Denmark	173	1984-2017	7.4	Portugal	33	1992-2017	11.5
Egypt	74	1990-2017	9.4	Russia	64	1999-2013	3.3
Finland	209	1971-2018	14.2	Saudi Arabia	80	2003-2011	239.8
France	834	1983-2017	9.7	Singapore	687	1973-2017	25.8
Germany	779	1978-2014	23.0	South Africa	342	1980-2018	17.2
Greece	373	1976-2013	50.8	Spain	199	1986-2018	9.2
Hong Kong	2,042	1980-2017	44.5	Sri Lanka	134	1987-2018	28.9
India	3,145	1990-2017	85.2	Sweden	405	1980-2015	25.9
Indonesia	531	1990-2017	26.4	Switzerland	164	1983-2018	25.2
Iran	279	1991-2004	22.4	Taiwan	1,915	1980-2019	37.2
Ireland	38	1999-2013	21.6	Thailand	697	1987-2018	40.0
Israel	348	1990-2006	13.8	Turkey	404	1990-2014	9.6
Italy	413	1985-2018	13.1	United Arab Emirates	24	2003-2010	270.1
Korea	1,758	1980-2018	55.2	United Kingdom	5,185	1959-2016	15.8
Malaysia	562	1980-2018	51.0	United States	13,244	1960-2019	16.9

Source: Professor Jay R. Ritter's website, University of Florida, https://site.warrington.ufl.edu/ritter/files/Int.pdf.

There are some incredibly high initial returns experienced by IPO firms. IPOs in China, India, Saudi Arabia and UAE have experienced underpricing of greater than 80 per cent, which dwarfs the nearest countries. Even with their highly developed capital markets, German and UK firms experienced IPO returns of 23 and 15.8 per cent, respectively.

WHY DOES UNDERPRICING EXIST?

Based on the evidence we've examined, an obvious question is why underpricing continues to exist. As we discuss, there are various explanations but, to date, there is a lack of complete agreement among researchers as to which is correct.

We present some pieces of the underpricing puzzle by stressing two important caveats to our preceding discussion. First, the average figures we have examined tend to obscure the fact that much of the apparent underpricing is attributable to the smaller, more highly speculative issues between 1980 and 2000, but less so since then. This point is illustrated in Table 14.6, which shows the extent of underpricing for US IPOs over the period from 1980 through to 2019. Here, the firms are grouped based on their total sales in the 12 months prior to the IPO.

Other factors explaining underpricing include positive media attention before the IPO date, local bias, recent market return, recent IPO activity, top-tier underwriters, VC-backed IPOs, an integer offer price, the IPO has a strong order flow, the underwriter has made a firm commitment to sell the issue, and

TABLE 14.6

Average first-day returns, categorized by sales, for IPOs, 1980–2019

	1980–1989		1990–1998		1999–2000		2001–2019	
	Return (%)	N	Return (%)	N	Return (%)	N	Return (%)	N
0 ≤ sales < $10m	10.3	420	17.2	741	68.9	331	10.6	429
$10m ≤ sales < $20m	8.7	243	18.7	393	81.4	138	13.1	85
$20m ≤ sales < $50m	7.8	500	18.8	791	75.0	155	16.8	228
$50m ≤ sales < $100m	6.3	356	12.9	589	61.8	87	21.3	293
$100m ≤ sales < $200m	5.1	234	11.8	454	35.8	56	19.9	259
$200m ≤ sales	3.4	290	8.7	645	25.0	91	12.3	686
All	7.3	2,043	14.8	3,613	64.5	858	14.8	2,090

Notes: Sales, measured in millions, are for the last 12 months prior to going public. All sales have been converted into dollars of 2003 purchasing power, using the Consumer Price Index. There are 8,608 IPOs, after excluding IPOs with an offer price of less than $5.00 per share, units, REITs, ADRs, closed-end funds, banks and S&Ls, firms not listed on CRSP, and 18 firms with missing sales. Sales are from Thomson Financial's SDC, Dealogic, EDGAR, and the Graeme Howard-Todd Huxster collection of pre-EDGAR prospectuses. The average first-day return is 18.0 per cent.

Source: Professor Jay Ritter's website, University of Florida, Table 2, https://site.warrington.ufl.edu/ritter/files/IPOs2019_Sales.pdf.

the IPO is high-tech. Table 14.7 presents an overview of the international evidence on the determinants of IPO underpricing across countries. A '+' entry means there is a positive relationship between the characteristic and IPO underpricing; A '−' entry means there is a negative relationship and '0' means there is no relationship. So, as an example, in all countries, recent market performance is strongly associated with greater levels of underpricing.

TABLE 14.7

Determinants of underpricing by country

Country	Offer size	Recent market return	Recent IPO activity	Stock market turnover	Top-tier underwriter	VC-backed IPO	Firm commitment	High-tech firm
United States	−	+	+	−	+	+	−	+
China	−	+	−	−	−	−	−	−
United Kingdom	−	+	+	+	−	−	−	+
France	0	+	+		0	−	0	+
Singapore	−	+	0	+	0	−	0	0
Germany	0	+	+	0	0	−	−	+
Malaysia	−	+	+	0	0	0	0	+
India	−	+	0	0	−	0	−	0

Source: Adapted from Table 4.2 of Boulton, T., Smart, S., & Zutter, C. (2018). Determinants of variation in IPO underpricing. The Oxford handbook of IPOs, 81.Oxford University Press.

The second caveat is that relatively few IPO buyers will actually get the initial high average returns observed in IPOs, and many will lose money. Although it is true that, on average, IPOs have positive initial returns, a significant fraction of them have price drops. Furthermore, when the issue price is too low, the issue is often 'oversubscribed'. This means investors will not be able to buy all the shares they want, and the underwriters will allocate the shares *pro rata* among investors.

The average investor will find it difficult to get shares in a 'successful' offering (one in which the price increases), because there will not be enough shares to go around. On the other hand, an investor blindly submitting orders for IPOs tends to get more shares in issues that go down in price.

To illustrate, consider this tale of two investors. Smith knows very accurately what Bonanza Ltd is worth when its shares are offered. They are confident that the shares are underpriced. Jones knows only that prices usually rise one month after an IPO. Armed with this information, Jones decides to buy 1,000 shares of every IPO. Does he actually earn an abnormally high return on the initial offering?

The answer is no, and at least one reason is Smith. Knowing about Bonanza Ltd, Smith invests all their money in its IPO. When the issue is oversubscribed, the underwriters have to somehow allocate the shares between Smith and Jones. The net result is that when an issue is underpriced, Jones doesn't get to buy as much of it as he wanted.

Smith also knows that the Blue Sky Ltd IPO is overpriced. In this case, they avoid its IPO altogether, and Jones ends up with a full 1,000 shares. To summarize this tale, Jones gets fewer shares when more knowledgeable investors swarm to buy an underpriced issue, and gets all he wants when the smart money avoids the issue.

This is an example of a 'winner's curse', and it is thought to be another reason why IPOs have such a large average return. When the average investor 'wins' and gets the entire allocation, it may be because those who knew better avoided the issue. The only way underwriters can counteract the winner's curse and attract the average investor is to underprice new issues (on average) so that the average investor still makes a profit.

Another reason for underpricing is that it is a kind of insurance for the underwriters. Conceivably, an underwriter could be sued successfully by angry customers if it consistently overpriced securities. Underpricing guarantees that, at least on average, customers will come out ahead.

A final reason for underpricing is that, before the offer price is established, underwriters talk to big institutional investors to gauge the level of interest in the equity, and to gather opinions about a suitable price. Underpricing is a way that the bank can reward these investors for truthfully revealing what they think the equity is worth and the number of shares they would like to buy.

> **CONCEPT QUESTIONS**
>
> **14.5a** Why is underpricing a cost to the issuing firm?
> **14.5b** Suppose a stockbroker calls you up out of the blue and offers to sell you 'all the shares you want' of a new issue. Do you think the issue will be more or less underpriced than average?

14.6 NEW EQUITY SALES AND THE VALUE OF THE FIRM

We now turn to a consideration of seasoned offerings, which, as we discussed earlier, are offerings by firms that already have outstanding securities. It seems reasonable to believe that new long-term financing is arranged by firms after positive net present value projects are put together. As a consequence, when the announcement of external financing is made, the firm's market value should go up. Interestingly, this is not what happens. Share prices tend to decline following the announcement of a new equity issue, although they tend to not change much following a debt announcement. A number of researchers have studied this issue. Plausible reasons for this strange result include the following:

1. *Managerial information:* If management has superior information about the market value of the firm, it may know when the firm is overvalued. If it does, it will attempt to issue new shares of equity when the market value exceeds the correct value. This will benefit existing shareholders. However, the potential new shareholders are not stupid, and they will anticipate this superior information and discount it in lower market prices at the new-issue date.

2. *Debt usage:* A company issuing new equity may reveal that the company has too much debt or too little liquidity. One version of this argument says that the equity issue is a bad signal to the market. After all, if the new projects are favourable ones, why should the firm let new shareholders in on them? It could just issue debt and let the existing shareholders have all the gain.
3. *Issue costs:* As we discuss next, there are substantial costs associated with selling securities.

The drop in the value of existing shares following the announcement of a new issue is an example of an indirect cost of selling securities. This drop might typically be of the order of 3 per cent for an industrial corporation (and somewhat smaller for a public utility); so, for a large company, it can represent a substantial amount of money. We label this drop the *abnormal return* in our discussion of the costs of new issues that follows.

> **CONCEPT QUESTIONS**
>
> **14.6a** What are some possible reasons why the share price drops on the announcement of a new equity issue?
>
> **14.6b** Explain why we might expect a firm with a positive-NPV investment to finance it with debt instead of equity.

14.7 THE COSTS OF ISSUING SECURITIES

Issuing securities to the public isn't free, and the costs of different methods are important determinants of which is used. These costs associated with *floating* a new issue are generically called *flotation costs*. In this section we take a closer look at the flotation costs associated with equity sales to the public.

THE COSTS OF SELLING STOCK TO THE PUBLIC

The costs of selling equity are classified in the following list, and fall into six categories:

1. *Gross spread:* The gross spread consists of direct fees paid by the issuer to the underwriting syndicate – the difference between the price the issuer receives and the offer price.
2. *Other direct expenses:* These are direct costs, incurred by the issuer, that are not part of the compensation to underwriters. These costs include filing fees, legal fees and taxes – all reported on the prospectus.
3. *Indirect expenses:* These costs are not reported on the prospectus, and include the costs of management time spent working on the new issue.
4. *Abnormal returns:* In a seasoned issue of equity, the price of the existing shares drops on average by 3 per cent on the announcement of the issue. This drop is called the abnormal return.
5. *Underpricing:* For initial public offerings, losses arise from selling the equity below the true value.
6. *Green Shoe option:* The Green Shoe option gives the underwriters the right to buy additional shares at the offer price to cover overallotments.

Research on issues costs provides a number of insights. First, with the possible exception of straight debt offerings (about which we shall have more to say later), there are substantial economies of scale. The underwriter spreads are smaller on larger issues, and other direct costs fall sharply as a percentage of the amount raised – a reflection of the mostly fixed nature of such costs. Second, the costs associated with selling debt are substantially less than the costs of selling equity. Third, IPOs have higher expenses than SEOs, but the difference is not as great as might originally be guessed. Finally, straight bonds are cheaper to float than convertible bonds.

Finally, with regard to debt offerings, there is a general pattern in issue costs. Recall from Chapter 6 that bonds carry different credit ratings. Higher-rated bonds are said to be investment grade, whereas lower-rated bonds are non-investment grade. Research has shown that there are substantial economies of scale with debt offerings as well, and that investment-grade issues have much lower direct costs, particularly for straight bonds.

> **CONCEPT QUESTIONS**
>
> **14.7a** What are the different costs associated with security offerings?
> **14.7b** What lessons do we learn from studying issue costs?

14.8 RIGHTS

When new shares of equity are sold to the general public, the proportional ownership of existing shareholders is likely to be reduced. However, if a pre-emptive right is contained in the firm's articles of incorporation, the firm must first offer any new issue of equity to existing shareholders. If the articles of incorporation do not include a pre-emptive right, the firm has a choice of offering the issue of equity directly to existing shareholders or to the public.

An issue of equity offered to existing shareholders is called a *rights issue, rights offering* or a *privileged subscription*. In a rights issue each shareholder is issued rights to buy a specified number of new shares from the firm at a specified price within a specified time, after which the rights are said to *expire*. The terms of the rights offering are evidenced by certificates known as *share warrants* or *rights*. Such rights are often traded on securities exchanges or over the counter.

Rights issues have some interesting advantages relative to cash offers. For example, they appear to be cheaper for the issuing firm than cash offers. In fact, a firm can undertake a rights issue without using an underwriter, whereas, as a practical matter, an underwriter is almost a necessity in a cash offer. In Europe, rights issues are more common than cash offers, but fairly rare in the United States. Why this is true is a bit of a mystery, and the source of much debate; but to our knowledge no definitive answer exists.

THE MECHANICS OF A RIGHTS ISSUE

The various considerations confronting a financial manager in a rights issue are illustrated by the situation of Babcock International in April 2014 to partially fund the £1.6 billion acquisition of French helicopter firm, Avincis. Babcock's share price was £13.66 on the day of the announcement and the rights issue allowed existing shareholders to buy new Babcock shares for £7.90 each.

The process of issuing rights differs from the process of issuing shares of equity for cash. Existing shareholders are notified that they have been given one right for each share of equity they own. Exercise occurs when a shareholder sends payment to the firm's subscription agent (usually a bank) and turns in the required number of rights. Babcock's shareholders had three choices: (1) subscribe for the full number of entitled shares; (2) order all the rights sold; or (3) do nothing and let the rights expire.

Babcock executives had to answer the following questions:

1. What price should the existing shareholders be allowed to pay for a share of new equity?
2. How many rights will be required to purchase one share of equity?
3. What effect will the rights offering have on the existing share price of the company?

Subscription Price

In a rights issue the subscription price is the price that existing shareholders are allowed to pay for a share of equity. A rational shareholder will subscribe to the rights offering only if the subscription price is below the market price of the equity on the offer's expiration date. For example, if the share price at expiration is £5 and the subscription price is £7.90, no rational shareholder will subscribe. Why pay £7.90

for something worth £5? Babcock International chose a price of £7.90, which was well below the existing market price of £13.66. As long as the market price did not fall below the subscription price of £7.90 before expiration, the rights offering would succeed.

Number of Rights Needed to Purchase a Share

Babcock International wanted to raise just over £1.1 billion in new equity. With a subscription price of £7.90, it needed to issue 139,259,204 new shares. This can be determined by dividing the total amount to be raised by the subscription price:

$$\text{Number of new shares} = \frac{\text{Funds to be raised}}{\text{Subscription price}}$$
$$= \frac{£1{,}100{,}147{,}712}{£7.90}$$
$$= 139{,}259{,}204 \text{ shares}$$

To determine how many rights must be exercised to get one share of equity, we can divide the number of existing shares by the number of new shares:

$$\frac{\text{Number of rights needed}}{\text{to buy a share of equity}} = \frac{\text{'Old' shares}}{\text{'New' shares}}$$
$$= \frac{362{,}073{,}930}{139{,}259{,}204}$$
$$= 2.6 \text{ rights}$$

Clearly, it is impossible to own exactly 2.6 shares, and so in a rights issue one must construct terms so that the number of rights and shares are integers. In Babcock's case the correct terms were 13 'old' shares for 5 'new' shares (13/5 = 2.6). In market parlance this would be called a '5 for 13 rights issue of 139,259,204 shares at £7.90 per share'. Thus each shareholder had to give up 13 rights plus £7.90 to receive 5 shares of new equity. If all the shareholders do this, Babcock International will raise the required £1.1 billion.

It should be clear that the subscription price, the number of new shares, and the number of rights needed to buy a new share of equity are interrelated. If Babcock International lowered the subscription price, it would have had to issue more new shares to raise £1.1 billion in new equity. Several alternatives appear here:

Subscription price (£)	Number of new shares	Number of rights needed to buy a share of equity
9.00	122,238,635	2.962
7.90	139,259,204	2.600
5.00	220,029,542	1.646

The Effect of a Rights Offer on the Share Price

Rights clearly have value. In Babcock's case, the right to be able to buy a share of equity worth £13.66 for £7.90 was valuable.

Suppose a Babcock shareholder owns 13 shares of equity just before the rights offering. This situation is depicted in Table 14.8. Initially the Babcock share price was £13.66 per share, so the shareholder's total holding is worth 13 × £13.66 = £177.58. The shareholder who has 13 shares will receive 13 rights. The Babcock International rights issue gave shareholders with 13 rights the opportunity to purchase 5 additional shares for £7.90. The holding of the shareholder who exercises these rights and buys the new shares would increase to 13 + 5 = 18 shares. The value of the new holding would be £177.57 + £39.50 = £217.08 (the £177.58 initial value plus the £39.50 paid to the company). Because the shareholder now holds 18 shares, the price per share would drop to £217.08/18 = £12.06 (rounded to two decimal places).

The difference between the old share price of £13.66 and the new share price of £12.06 reflects the fact that the old shares carried rights to subscribe to the new issue. The difference must be equal to the value of one right – that is, £13.66 − £12.06 = £1.60.

TABLE 14.8

The value to the individual shareholder of Babcock International's rights

	The shareholder
Initial position	
Number of shares	13
Share price	£13.66
Value of holding	£177.58
Terms of offer	
Subscription price	£7.90
Number of old shares for new shares	13 for 5
After offer	
Number of shares	18
Value of holding	£217.08
Share price	£12.06
Value of a right	
Old price − New price	£13.66 − £12.06 = £1.60
$\dfrac{\text{New price} - \text{Subscription price}}{\text{Number of rights for a share}}$	(£12.06 − £7.90)/2.6 = £1.60

Table 14.9 shows what happens to Babcock International. If all shareholders exercise their rights, the number of shares will increase to 501,333,134 and the value of the firm will increase to £6,046,077,601. After the rights offering the value of each share will drop to £12.06 (= £6,046,077,601/501,333,134).

An investor holding no shares of Babcock International who wants to subscribe to the new issue can do so by buying rights. An outside investor buying 13 rights will pay £1.60 × 13 = £20.80 (to account for previous rounding). If the investor exercises the rights at a subscription cost of £7.90 to purchase five new shares, the total cost will be £20.80 + £39.50 = £60.30. In return for this expenditure the investor will receive five shares of the new equity (worth £12.06 per share), totalling £60.30.

Of course, outside investors can also buy Babcock International shares directly at £12.06 per share. In an efficient stock market it will make no difference whether new equity is obtained via rights or via direct purchase.

Effects on Shareholders

Shareholders can exercise their rights or sell them. In either case the shareholder will neither win nor lose by the rights offering. The hypothetical holder of 13 Babcock International shares has a portfolio worth £177.58. On the one hand, if the shareholder exercises the rights, he or she ends up with five shares worth a total of £60.30. In other words, by spending £60.30 the investor increases the value of the holding by £60.30, which means that he or she is neither better nor worse off.

TABLE 14.9

The Babcock International rights offering

Initial position	
Number of 'old' shares	362,073,930
Share price (£)	£13.66
Value of equity (£)	£4,945,929,889

Terms of offer	
Subscription price (£)	7.90
Number of 'new' shares	139,259,204
After offer	
Number of shares	501,333,134
Share price	£12.06
Value of firm	£6,046,077,601
Value of one right	£13.66 − £12.06 = £1.60
	or (£12.06 − £7.90)/2.6 = £1.60

On the other hand, a shareholder who sells the 13 rights for £1.60 each obtains £1.60 × 13 = £20.80 in cash. Because the 13 shares are each worth £12.06, the holdings are valued at:

$$\begin{aligned} \text{Shares} &= 13 \times £12.06 = £156.78 \\ \text{Sold rights} &= 13 \times £1.60 = £20.80 \\ \text{Total} &= £177.58 \end{aligned}$$

The new £156.78 market value plus £20.80 in cash is exactly the same as the original holding of £177.58. Thus shareholders can neither lose nor gain from exercising or selling rights.

It is obvious that the new market price of the firm's equity will be lower after the rights offering than it was before the rights issue. The lower the subscription price, the greater the price decline of a rights issue. However, our analysis shows that the shareholders have suffered no loss because of the rights issue.

REAL WORLD INSIGHTS

In 2020, the software firm Aveva Group announced a £2.8 billion rights issue to part-fund a $5 billion acquisition of its rival, OSIsoft. Under the terms of the issue, Aveva's shareholders could buy seven new shares for every nine shares held. The subscription price for the new shares was £22.55, representing a discount of 32.2 per cent on the company's existing shares. The number of new shares issued was 125.7 million.

Upon announcement of the rights issue, Aveva's share price immediately fell by 2.1 per cent to £41.18.

THE UNDERWRITING ARRANGEMENTS

Rights issues are typically arranged using **standby underwriting**. In standby underwriting the issuer makes a rights issue, and the underwriter makes a firm commitment to 'take up' (that is, purchase) the unsubscribed portion of the issue. The underwriter usually gets a **standby fee** and additional amounts based on the securities taken up.

Standby underwriting protects the firm against undersubscription, which can occur if investors throw away rights, or if bad news causes the market price of the equity to fall below the subscription price.

In practice, only a small percentage (fewer than 10 per cent) of shareholders fail to exercise valuable rights. This failure can probably be attributed to ignorance or holidays. Furthermore, shareholders are usually given an **oversubscription privilege**, which enables them to purchase unsubscribed shares at the subscription price. The oversubscription privilege makes it unlikely that the corporate issuer would have to turn to its underwriter for help.

standby underwriting
the type of underwriting in which the underwriter agrees to purchase the unsubscribed portion of the issue.

standby fee
an amount paid to an underwriter participating in a standby underwriting agreement.

oversubscription privilege
a privilege that allows shareholders to purchase unsubscribed shares in a rights offering at the subscription price.

> **CONCEPT QUESTIONS**
>
> **14.8a** How does a rights issue work?
> **14.8b** What questions must financial managers answer in a rights issue?
> **14.8c** How is the value of a right determined?
> **14.8d** When does a rights issue affect the value of a company's shares?
> **14.8e** Does a rights issue cause share prices to decrease? How are existing shareholders affected by a rights offering?

14.9 DILUTION

A subject that comes up quite a bit in discussions involving the selling of securities is **dilution**. Dilution refers to a loss in existing shareholders' value. There are several kinds:

1. Dilution of proportionate ownership
2. Dilution of market value
3. Dilution of book value and earnings per share

dilution
loss in existing shareholders' value in terms of ownership, market value, book value or EPS.

The differences between these three types can be a little confusing, and there are some common misconceptions about dilution, so we discuss it in this section.

DILUTION OF PROPORTIONATE OWNERSHIP

The first type of dilution can arise whenever a firm sells shares to the general public. For example, Ellis Smith owns 5,000 shares of Merit Shoes. Merit Shoes currently has 50,000 shares of equity outstanding; each share gets one vote. Ellis thus controls 10 per cent (= 5,000/50,000) of the votes, and gets 10 per cent of the dividends.

If Merit Shoes issues 50,000 new shares of equity to the public via a general cash offer, Ellis's ownership in Merit Shoes may be diluted. If Ellis does not participate in the new issue, their ownership will drop to 5 per cent (= 5,000/100,000). Notice that the value of Ellis's shares is unaffected; they just own a smaller percentage of the firm.

Because a rights issue would ensure that Ellis Smith has an opportunity to maintain their proportionate 10 per cent share, dilution of the ownership of existing shareholders can be avoided by using a rights issue.

DILUTION OF VALUE: BOOK VERSUS MARKET VALUES

We now examine the dilution of value by looking at some accounting numbers. We do this to illustrate a fallacy concerning dilution; we do not mean to suggest that accounting value dilution is more important than market value dilution. As we illustrate, quite the reverse is true.

Suppose North Country Manufacturing (NCM) wants to build a new electricity-generating plant to meet future anticipated demands. As shown in Table 14.10, NCM currently has 1 million shares outstanding and no debt. Each share is selling for €5, and the company has a €5 million market value. NCM's book value is €10 million total, or €10 per share.

TABLE 14.10

New issues and dilution: the case of North Country Manufacturing

	Initial	After taking on new project	
		With dilution	With no dilution
Number of shares	1,000,000	1,400,000	1,400,000
Book value (€)	10,000,000	12,000,000	12,000,000
Book value per share, B (€)	10	8.57	8.57

	Initial	After taking on new project	
		With dilution	With no dilution
Market value (€)	5,000,000	6,000,000	8,000,000
Market price, P (€)	5	4.29	5.71
Net income (€)	1,000,000	1,200,000	1,600,000
Return on equity, ROE	0.10	0.10	0.13
Earnings per share, EPS (€)	1	0.86	1.14
EPS/P	0.20	0.20	0.20
P/EPS	5	5	5
P/B	0.5	0.5	0.67
Project cost	€2,000,000	NPV = −€1,000,000	NPV = €1,000,000

NCM has experienced a variety of difficulties in the past, including cost overruns, regulatory delays in building a nuclear-powered electricity-generating plant, and below-normal profits. These difficulties are reflected in the fact that NCM's market-to-book ratio is €5/10 = 0.50 (successful firms rarely have market prices below book values).

Net income for NCM is currently €1 million. With 1 million shares, earnings per share are €1, and the return on equity is €1/10 = 10%.[4] NCM thus sells for five times earnings (the price–earnings ratio is 5). NCM has 200 shareholders, each of whom holds 5,000 shares. The new plant will cost €2 million, so NCM will have to issue 400,000 new shares (€5 × 400,000 = €2 million). There will thus be 1.4 million shares outstanding after the issue.

The ROE on the new plant is expected to be the same as for the company as a whole. In other words, net income is expected to go up by 0.10 × €2 million = €200,000. Total net income will thus be €1.2 million. The following will result if the plant is built:

1. With 1.4 million shares outstanding, EPS will be €1.2/1.4 = €0.857, down from €1.
2. The proportionate ownership of each old shareholder will drop from 0.50 per cent to 5,000/1.4 million = 0.36 per cent.
3. If the equity continues to sell for five times earnings, then the value will drop to 5 × €0.857 = €4.29, representing a loss of €0.71 per share.
4. The total book value will be the old €10 million plus the new €2 million, for a total of €12 million. Book value per share will fall to €12 million/1.4 million = €8.57.

If we take this example at face value, then dilution of proportionate ownership, accounting dilution and market value dilution all occur. NCM's shareholders appear to suffer significant losses.

A Misconception

Our example appears to show that selling equity when the market-to-book ratio is less than 1 is detrimental to shareholders. Some managers claim that the resulting dilution occurs because EPS will go down whenever shares are issued when the market value is less than the book value.

When the market-to-book ratio is less than 1, increasing the number of shares does cause EPS to go down. Such a decline in EPS is accounting dilution, and accounting dilution will always occur under these circumstances.

Is it also true that market value dilution will necessarily occur? The answer is *no*. There is nothing incorrect about our example, but why the market price has decreased is not obvious. We discuss this next.

The Correct Arguments

In this example the market price falls from €5 per share to €4.29. This is true dilution, but why does it occur? The answer has to do with the new project. NCM is going to spend €2 million on the new plant. However, as shown in Table 14.10, the total market value of the company is going to rise from €5 million to €6 million, an increase of only €1 million. This simply means that the NPV of the new project is −€1 million. With 1.4 million shares, the loss per share is €1/1.4 = €0.71, as we calculated before.

So true dilution takes place for the shareholders of NCM because the NPV of the project is negative, not because the market-to-book ratio is less than 1. This negative NPV causes the market price to drop, and the accounting dilution has nothing to do with it.

Suppose the new project has a positive NPV of €1 million. The total market value rises by €2 million + 1 million = €3 million. As shown in Table 14.10 (third column), the share price rises to €5.71. Notice that accounting dilution still takes place because the book value per share still falls, but there is no economic consequence of that fact. The market value of the equity rises.

The €0.71 increase in share value comes about because of the €1 million NPV, which amounts to an increase in value of about €0.71 per share. Also, as shown, if the ratio of price to EPS remains at 5, then EPS must rise to €5.71/5 = €1.14. Total earnings (net income) rises to €1.14 per share × 1.4 million shares = €1.6 million. Finally, ROE will rise to €1.6 million/12 million = 13.33%.

> **CONCEPT QUESTIONS**
>
> **14.9a** What are the different kinds of dilution?
> **14.9b** Is dilution important?

14.10 ISSUING LONG-TERM DEBT

term loans
direct business loans of typically 1 to 5 years.

private placements
loans (usually long-term) provided directly by a limited number of investors.

The general procedures followed in a public issue of bonds are the same as those for equities: the issue must be registered with the stock exchange authorities, there must be a prospectus, and so on. The registration statement for a public issue of bonds, however, is different from the one for equities. For bonds, the registration statement must indicate an indenture.

Another important difference is that more than 50 per cent of all debt is issued privately. There are two basic forms of direct private long-term financing: term loans and private placement.

Term loans are direct business loans. These loans have maturities of between 1 year and 5 years. Most term loans are repayable during the life of the loan. The lenders include commercial banks, insurance companies and other lenders that specialize in corporate finance. **Private placements** are similar to term loans except that the maturity is longer.

The important differences between direct private long-term financing and public issues of debt are these:

- A direct long-term loan avoids the cost of stock exchange registration.
- Direct placement is likely to have more restrictive covenants.
- It is easier to renegotiate a term loan or a private placement in the event of a default. It is harder to renegotiate a public issue, because hundreds of holders are usually involved.
- Life insurance companies and pension funds dominate the private placement segment of the bond market. Banks are significant participants in the term loan market.
- The costs of distributing bonds are lower in the private market.

The interest rates on term loans and private placements are usually higher than those on an equivalent public issue. This difference reflects the trade-off between a higher interest rate and more flexible arrangements in the event of financial distress, as well as the lower costs associated with private placements.

An additional, and very important, consideration is that the flotation costs associated with selling debt are much less than the comparable costs associated with selling equity.

> **CONCEPT QUESTIONS**
>
> **14.10a** What is the difference between private and public bond issues?
> **14.10b** A private placement is likely to have a higher interest rate than a public issue. Why?

14.11 BANK LOANS

Bank loans form a major part of debt financing across the world. Although the amount of credit available from banks has declined somewhat from pre-financial crisis levels, it still dominates other forms of funding in many countries. Figure 14.3 presents a time series of bank loan data versus other financing types for the Eurozone area over the recent period. As can be seen, bank loans have declined significantly since 2008 and, in some years, more bank loans were paid back than new ones created.

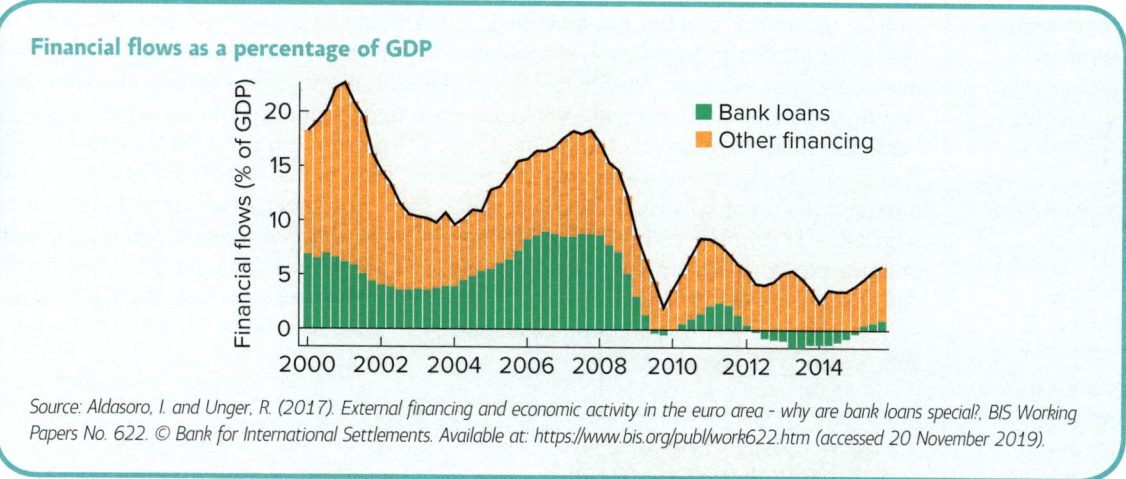

FIGURE 14.3 Financial flows as a percentage of GDP

Source: Aldasoro, I. and Unger, R. (2017). External financing and economic activity in the euro area - why are bank loans special?, BIS Working Papers No. 622. © Bank for International Settlements. Available at: https://www.bis.org/publ/work622.htm (accessed 20 November 2019).

Figure 14.4 presents data on the popularity of bank loans by country, clearly illustrating the importance of bank debt to Italian firms. Although bank debt is the most common form of external financing, the pattern is quite varied across countries and reflects different financing cultures as well as liquidity in domestic financial markets.

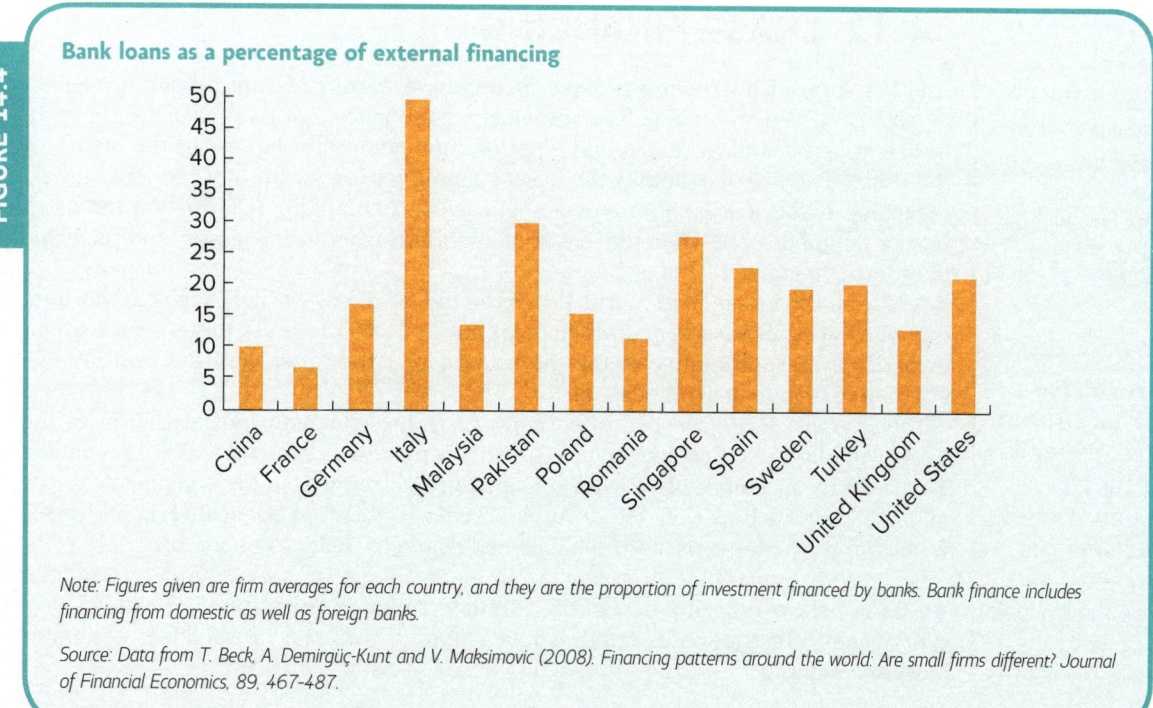

FIGURE 14.4 Bank loans as a percentage of external financing

Note: Figures given are firm averages for each country, and they are the proportion of investment financed by banks. Bank finance includes financing from domestic as well as foreign banks.

Source: Data from T. Beck, A. Demirgüç-Kunt and V. Maksimovic (2008). Financing patterns around the world: Are small firms different? Journal of Financial Economics, 89, 467-487.

TYPES OF BANK LOAN

Bank loans come in two types: lines of credit and loan commitments. A **line of credit** is an arrangement between a bank and a firm, typically for a short-term loan, whereby the bank authorizes the maximum loan amount, but not the interest rate, when setting up the line of credit. Lines of credit do not in a practical sense commit the bank to lend money because the bank is free to quote any interest rate it wishes at the time the borrowing firm requests funds. If the interest rate is too high, the firm will decline the available line of credit.

A **loan commitment** on the other hand, is an arrangement that requires a bank to lend up to a maximum pre-specified loan amount at a pre-specified interest rate. The commitment is in place and available at the firm's request as long as the firm meets the requirements established when the commitment was drawn up. There are two types of loan commitment. A **revolver** is a loan commitment in which funds flow back and forth between the bank and the firm without any predetermined schedule. Funds are drawn from the revolver whenever the company needs them, up to the maximum amount specified. Revolvers may also be subject to an annual clean-up in which the firm must retire all borrowings. A **non-revolving loan commitment** is one in which the firm cannot pay down the loan and then subsequently increases the amount of borrowing. Research has shown that firms with high levels of cash flow are able to obtain lines of credit but less liquid firms tend to rely on cash for their short-term capital requirements.[5]

> **line of credit**
> an arrangement between a bank and a firm, typically for a short-term loan, whereby the bank authorizes the maximum loan amount, but not the interest rate, when setting up the line of credit.

> **loan commitment**
> an arrangement that requires a bank to lend up to a maximum pre-specified loan amount at a prespecified interest rate.

> **revolver**
> a loan commitment in which funds flow back and forth between the bank and the firm without any predetermined schedule.

> **non-revolving loan commitment**
> a loan commitment where the firm cannot pay down the loan and then subsequently increase the amount of borrowing.

> **CONCEPT QUESTIONS**
>
> **14.11a** What is the difference between a line of credit and a loan commitment?
> **14.11b** What are the different types of loan commitment and why are they used?

14.12 LEASE FINANCING

Another form of borrowing is lease financing. A *lease* is a contractual agreement between a lessee and lessor. The agreement establishes that the lessee has the right to use an asset and in return make periodic payments to the lessor, the owner of the asset. The lessor is either the asset's manufacturer or an independent leasing company. If the lessor is an independent leasing company, it must buy the asset from a manufacturer. Then the lessor delivers the asset to the lessee, and the lease goes into effect.

As far as the lessee is concerned, it is the use of the asset that is most important, not who owns the asset, and a lease contract allows the asset to be used without ownership. The alternative is for the user to buy the asset, and this will involve alternative financing arrangements.

The example in Figure 14.5 often happens in the computer industry. Firm U, the lessee, might be a hospital, a law firm, or any other firm that uses computers. The lessor is an independent leasing company that purchased the equipment from a manufacturer such as Dell, HP or Apple. Leases of this type are called direct leases. In the figure, the lessor issued both debt and equity to finance the purchase.

Of course, a manufacturer like Apple could lease its *own* computers, though we do not show this situation in the example. Leases of this type are called sales-type leasing. In this case, Apple would compete with the independent computer leasing company.

FIGURE 14.5 Buying versus leasing

OPERATING LEASES

Years ago, a lease where the lessee received an operator along with the equipment was called an operating lease. Though the operating lease defies an exact definition today, this form of leasing has several salient characteristics:

1. Operating leases are usually not fully amortized. This means that the payments required under the terms of the lease are not enough to recover the full cost of the asset for the lessor. This occurs because the term or life of the operating lease is usually less than the economic life of the asset. Thus, the lessor must expect to recover the costs of the asset by renewing the lease or by selling the asset for its residual value.
2. Operating leases usually require the lessor to maintain and insure the leased assets.
3. Perhaps the most interesting feature of an operating lease is the cancellation option. This option gives the lessee the right to cancel the lease contract before the expiration date. If the option to cancel is exercised, the lessee must return the equipment to the lessor. The value of a cancellation clause depends on whether future technological or economic conditions are likely to make the value of the asset to the lessee less than the value of the future lease payments under the lease.

To leasing practitioners, these characteristics constitute an operating lease. However, accountants use the term in a slightly different way, as we will see shortly.

FINANCIAL LEASES

Financial leases are the exact opposite of operating leases, as seen from their characteristics:

1. Financial leases do not provide for maintenance or service by the lessor.
2. Financial leases are fully amortized.
3. The lessee usually has a right to renew the lease on expiration.
4. Generally, financial leases cannot be cancelled. In other words, the lessee must make all payments or face the risk of bankruptcy.

Because of these characteristics, particularly (2), this lease provides an alternative method of financing to purchase. Hence, its name is a sensible one. Two particular types of financial lease are the sale and leaseback arrangement, and the leveraged lease.

Sale and Leaseback

A sale and leaseback occurs when a company sells an asset it owns to another firm and immediately leases it back. In a sale and leaseback two things happen:

1. The lessee receives cash from the sale of the asset.
2. The lessee makes periodic lease payments, thereby retaining use of the asset.

For example, in 2019, the British rail operator, Transport for London, had a £1 billion sale and leaseback initiative to raise capital to purchase new trains for the London underground network. The contract will last until 2039 and Transport for London will pay a group of lessors, called the 345 Rail Leasing Consortium, lease payments over this period in return for the £1 billion.

Leveraged Leases

A leveraged lease is a three-sided arrangement among the lessee, the lessor and the lenders:

1. The lessee uses the assets and makes periodic lease payments.
2. The lessor purchases the assets, delivers them to the lessee and collects the lease payments. However, the lessor puts up no more than 40 to 50 per cent of the purchase price.
3. The lenders supply the remaining financing and receive interest payments from the lessor. Thus, the arrangement on the right side of Figure 14.5 would be a leveraged lease if creditors supplied the bulk of the financing.

Lenders in a leveraged lease typically use a non-recourse loan, which means the lessor is not obligated to the lender in a default. However, the lender is protected in two ways:

1. The lender has a first claim on the asset.
2. In the event of loan default, the lease payments are made directly to the lender.

The lessor puts up only part of the funds but gets the lease payments and all the tax benefits of ownership. These lease payments are used to pay the debt service of the non-recourse loan. The lessee benefits because, in a competitive market, the lease payment is lowered when the lessor saves taxes.

ACCOUNTING FOR LEASES

Twenty years ago, a firm could arrange to use an asset through a lease and not disclose the asset or the lease contract on the balance sheet. Lessees reported leasing activity in the footnotes of their financial statements, which led leasing to be known as off-balance-sheet financing. Things have changed significantly in recent years and leasing now has an accounting standard all to itself: IFRS 16 *Leases*.

Leases have different characteristics and this affects how they should be recorded in a firm's financial statements. An issue relates to the effective ownership of an asset, the risks and rewards of ownership, and to whom this should be attributed. Specifically, a lease is considered a finance lease if the lessee bears the majority of risks and reward of the asset, whereas it is viewed as an operating lease if the lessor bears the risk.

The IFRS accounting treatment of leases (applicable to most European and South African companies, IFRS 16) underwent a substantial evolution in 2019 and there were a number of major changes to the way leases impact the balance sheet of lessees (lessors were largely unimpacted by the changes). Older textbooks will treat leases differently and the reader must be very careful when drawing on these sources.

For the lessee, operating and finance leases are treated in the same way (this was not the situation in previous accounting standards), with the leased asset appearing on the statement of financial position and depreciated as a normal owned asset. The value to be recorded in the statement of financial position must be the fair/realizable value of the asset or, if lower, the present value of the lease payments. This means that, to all intents and purposes, assets funded by a lease are regarded in the same way as normal assets in a company. To offset the addition of a new asset in the statement of financial position, a financial liability of equivalent value is also recorded. Each of these items (the leased asset and financial liability) must be treated separately in the financial statements.

Short-term leases of less than 12 months, or low-value assets (such as tablets, laptops and mobile phones) are treated differently. Short-term and low-value leases treat the lease payments as simple expenses in the income statement, without the need to add the lease to the statement of financial position.

SUMMARY AND CONCLUSIONS

This chapter has looked at how corporate securities are issued. The following are the main points:

1. The costs of issuing securities can be quite large. They are much lower (as a percentage) for larger issues.
2. The direct and indirect costs of going public can be substantial. However, once a firm is public, it can raise additional capital with much greater ease.
3. Rights issues are cheaper than general cash offers.
4. The private equity market consists of taking public firms private, and the venture capital industry. In recent years the private equity market has been dominated by buy-outs.

CHAPTER REVIEW AND SELF-TEST PROBLEMS

14.1 Flotation Costs L5 plc is considering an equity issue to finance a new space station. A total of €15 million in new equity is needed. If the direct costs are estimated at 7 per cent of the amount raised, how large does the issue need to be? What is the euro amount of the flotation cost?

14.2 Rights Issues Hadron SA currently has 3 million shares outstanding. The equity sells for €40 per share. To raise €20 million for a new particle accelerator, the firm is considering a rights offering at €25 per share. What is the value of a right in this case? The ex-rights price?

SOLUTIONS

14.1 The firm needs to net €15 million after paying the 7 per cent flotation costs. So the amount raised is given by:

$$\text{Amount raised} \times (1 - 0.07) = €15 \text{ million}$$
$$\text{Amount raised} = €15 \text{ million}/0.93 = €16.129 \text{ million}$$

The total flotation cost is thus €1.129 million.

14.2 To raise €20 million at €25 per share, €20 million/25 = 800,000 shares will have to be sold. Before the offering, the firm is worth 3 million × €40 = €120 million. The issue will raise €20 million, and there will be 3.8 million shares outstanding. The value of an ex-rights share will therefore be €140 million/3.8 million = €36.84. The value of a right is thus €40 − 36.84 = €3.16.

QUESTIONS AND PROBLEMS

14.1 **Long-Term Financing** There are a number of different long-term sources of financing. Review the main financing sources and discuss some reasons why some forms of financing are used more often than others.

14.2 **Rights Issues** In 2020, Aveva Group plc had a £2.8 billion rights offering. Under the terms of the issue, Aveva shareholders could buy seven new shares for every nine shares held. The subscription price was £22.55, which was a discount of 32.2 per cent on the company's existing shares. The number of new shares issued was 125.7 million.

(a) What was the share price prior to announcement of the rights issue?

(b) How many shares were outstanding prior to the rights issue?

(c) What is the ex-rights price?

(d) What is the value of a right?

(e) Ignoring regulations, why might a company have a rights offering rather than a general cash offer?

14.3 **Venture Capital** What is the difference between venture capital financing and other forms of external financing? What factors influence a firm's choices of venture capital financing versus other forms of equity financing?

14.4 **Rights Issues** Faff plc has announced a rights issue to raise £50 million for a new journal, the *Journal of Financial Excess*. This journal will review potential articles after the author pays a non-refundable reviewing fee of £5,000 per page. The equity currently sells for £40 per share, and there are 5.2 million shares outstanding.

(a) What is the maximum possible subscription price? What is the minimum?

(b) If the subscription price is set at £35 per share, how many shares must be sold? How many rights will it take to buy one share?

(c) What is the ex-rights price? What is the value of a right?

(d) Show how a shareholder with 1,000 shares before the offering and no desire (or money) to buy additional shares is not harmed by the rights offer.

14.5 **Rights** Glasauge AB concluded that additional equity financing will be needed to expand operations and that the needed funds will be best obtained through a rights issue. It has correctly determined that as a result of the rights issue, the share price will fall from €3.38 to €3.00 (€3.38 is the rights-on price; €3.00 is the ex-rights price, also known as the when-issued price). The company is seeking €2 million in additional funds with a per-share subscription price equal to €2. How many shares are there currently, before the offering? (Assume that the increment to the market value of the equity equals the gross proceeds from the offering.)

14.6 **IPO Underpricing** Carlyle plc and Mullan plc have both announced IPOs at £40 per share. One of these is undervalued by £11, and the other is overvalued by £6, but you have no way of knowing which is which. You plan on buying 1,000 shares of each issue. If an issue is underpriced, it will be rationed, and only half your order will be filled. If you *could* get 1,000 shares in Carlyle and 1,000 shares in Mullan, what would your profit be? What profit do you actually expect? What principle have you illustrated?

14.7 Calculating Flotation Costs Educated Horses plc needs to raise £60 million to finance its expansion into new markets. The company will sell new shares of equity via a general cash offering to raise the needed funds. If the offer price is £21 per share and the company's underwriters charge a 9 per cent spread, how many shares need to be sold?

14.8 Calculating Flotation Costs In the previous problem, if the stock exchange filing fee and associated administrative expenses of the offering are £900,000, the offer price is £21 per share and the company's underwriters charge a 9 per cent spread, how many shares need to be sold?

14.9 Calculating Flotation Costs Groene Heuvels NV has just gone public. Under a firm commitment agreement, Groene Heuvels received €19.75 for each of the 5 million shares sold. The initial offering price was €21 per share, and the equity rose to €26 per share in the first few minutes of trading. Groene Heuvels paid €800,000 in direct legal and other costs and €250,000 in indirect costs. What was the flotation cost as a percentage of funds raised?

14.10 Price Dilution Raggio SpA has 100,000 shares of equity outstanding. Each share is worth €90, so the company's market value of equity is €9,000,000. Suppose the firm issues 20,000 new shares at the following prices: €90, €85 and €70. What will the effect be of each of these alternative offering prices on the existing price per share?

14.11 Dilution SustainGenius is planning to expand its operations into a new country. The company currently has 100 million shares outstanding, and no debt. The equity sells for €7 per share, but the book value per share is €5. Net income for SustainGenius is currently €35 million. The new facility will cost €10 million, and it will increase net income by €100,000.

(a) Assuming a constant price–earnings ratio, what will the effect be of issuing new equity to finance the investment? To answer, calculate the new book value per share, the new total earnings, the new EPS, the new share price, and the new market-to-book ratio. What is going on here?

(b) What would the new net income for SustainGenius have to be for the share price to remain unchanged?

14.12 Dilution Elvis Heavy Metal Mining (EHMM) plc wants to diversify its operations. Some recent financial information for the company is shown here:

EHMM is considering an investment that has the same P/E ratio as the firm. The cost of the investment is £1,100,000, and it will be financed with a new equity issue. The return on the investment will equal EHMM's current ROE. What will happen to the book value per share, the market value per share, and the EPS? What is the NPV of this investment? Does dilution take place?

14.13 Dilution In the previous problem, what would the ROE on the investment have to be if we wanted the price after the offering to be £98 per share? (Assume the P/E ratio remains constant.) What is the NPV of this investment? Does any dilution take place?

14.14 Rights Charlesray plc requires €50 million in funding to develop its operations in a new sector. It is unable to raise debt and so has decided that a rights issue is the appropriate funding vehicle. Charlesray is aiming for an ex-rights price of €10, when the current price is €15. There are 10 million shares outstanding. What is the subscription price?

14.15 Value of a Right Show that the value of a right just prior to expiration can be written as:

$$\text{Value of a right} = P_{RO} - P_X = (P_{RO} - P_S)/(N + 1)$$

where P_{RO}, P_S and P_X stand for the rights-on price, the subscription price and the ex-rights price, respectively, and N is the number of rights needed to buy one new share at the subscription price.

14.16 Selling Rights Wuttke plc wants to raise £3.65 million via a rights issue. The company currently has 490,000 ordinary shares outstanding that sell for £30 per share. Its underwriter has set a subscription price of £22 per share, and will charge Wuttke a 6 per cent spread. If you currently own 6,000 shares of equity in the company and decide not to participate in the rights issue, how much money can you get by selling your rights?

14.17 Valuing a Right Mitsi Inventory Systems has announced a rights offer. The company has announced that it will take four rights to buy a new share in the offering at a subscription price of €40. At the close of business the day before the ex-rights day the company's shares sell for €80 per share. The next morning you notice that the equity sells for €72 per share and the rights sell for €6 each. Are the equity and/or the rights correctly priced on the ex-rights day? Describe a transaction in which you could use these prices to create an immediate profit.

14.18 Equity Finance In a public share issue, the probability of receiving an allocation of an underpriced security is less than or equal to the probability of receiving an allocation of an overpriced issue. Discuss this statement in the context of initial public offerings.

MINI CASE

FINANCING EXPANSION WITH A BOND ISSUE

The year 2021 saw the roll-out of Covid-19 vaccine production in response to successful trials for a number of vaccines, most notably those developed by Pfizer and BioNTech, which used mRNA technology and required to be kept at −70°C. The German super-cold container firm, va-Q-tec, experienced a massive jump in demand for its rental containers to transport the vaccines across the world. The sharp increase in orders meant the company's growth could no longer be funded by internal sources, so the management of va-Q-tec decided the time was right to make a 25 million Swiss franc bond issue.

The following case captures a hypothetical decision-making scenario facing va-Q-tec executives.

To ensure the bond issue was successful, va-Q-tec hired an underwriter to manage the capital raising. Bond issues of this type attract a typical underwriter fee of 7 per cent on monies raised. The issuing firm would also expect to pay about SFr1,200,000 in legal fees and expenses, SFr12,000 in registration fees, and SFr15,000 in other filing fees. Additionally, to be listed on the Deutsche Börse, the company must pay SFr100,000. The company should also expect to pay SFr75,000 for other expenses associated with the IPO.

Finally, va-Q-tec must provide 3 years' worth of audited financial statements, and the cost of the audit is currently unknown. The company currently provides audited financial statements as part of its bond indenture, and the company pays SFr300,000 per year for the outside auditor.

QUESTIONS

1. After some negotiation, va-Q-tec has negotiated that the issue will be underwritten on a firm commitment basis. Why would va-Q-tec prefer a firm commitment contract to best efforts?
2. From a potential investor's perspective, which type of underwriter contract (firm commitment or best efforts) would attract the most demand and why?
3. The bond issue will be for SFr80 million. Ignoring underpricing, how much will the issue cost the company as a percentage of the funds received?

ADDITIONAL READING

The literature in this section investigates the factors that determine long-term financing decisions. References [3] and [4] are particularly relevant given their international focus.

1. Chang, X., Dasgupta, S., & Hilary, G. (2006). Analyst coverage and financing decisions. *Journal of Finance, 61*(6), 3009–3048.
2. Dittmar, A.K., & Dittmar, R.F. (2008). The timing of financing decisions: An examination of the correlation in financing waves. *Journal of Financial Economics, 90*(1), 59–83.

3. Martinsson, G. (2010). Equity financing and innovation: Is Europe different from the United States? *Journal of Banking and Finance, 34*(6), 1215–1224.

4. Megginson, W.L., Nash, R.C., Netter, J.M., & Poulsen, A.B. (2004). The choice of private versus public capital markets: Evidence from privatizations. *Journal of Finance, 59*(6), 2835–2870.

Endnotes

1. The terms *follow-on offering* and *secondary offering* are also commonly used.
2. Warrants are options to buy shares at a fixed price for some fixed period.
3. The term *Green Shoe provision* sounds quite exotic, but the origin is relatively mundane. The term comes from the name of the Green Shoe Manufacturing Company, which in 1963 was the first issuer that granted such an option.
4. Return on equity, or ROE, is equal to earnings per share divided by book value per share, or, equivalently, net income divided by common equity. We discuss this and other financial ratios in some detail in Chapter 3.
5. Sufi, A. (2009). Bank lines of credit in corporate finance: An empirical analysis. *Review of Financial Studies, 22*, 1057–1088.

CHAPTER 15
FINANCIAL LEVERAGE AND CAPITAL STRUCTURE POLICY

LEARNING OBJECTIVES
After studying this chapter, you should understand:
- **LO1** The effect of financial leverage.
- **LO2** The impact of taxes and bankruptcy on capital structure choice.
- **LO3** The essentials of the bankruptcy process.

KEY NOTATIONS
D	Market value of debt
E	Market value of equity
EBIT	Earnings before interest and taxes
EPS	Earnings per share
R_A	Return on assets
R_D	Return on debt
R_E	Return on equity
ROE	Return on equity
T_C	Corporate tax rate
V_L	Market value of a levered firm
V_U	Market value of an unlevered firm
WACC	Weighted average cost of capital

IN THE WAKE of the closure of stadia for outdoor sporting events as a result of the Covid-19 pandemic, the viability of European football business models and their level of indebtedness has come under scrutiny. European clubs, and in particular English clubs, have seen unparalleled injections of cash from worldwide television deals. This additional spending power has led to massive transfer fees, which in turn requires more funding to sustain high footballer salaries. Some clubs, including Liverpool and Manchester United, were bought by wealthy individuals backed by significant debt. As with all debt, the loans taken out by football clubs will expire and need to be renewed. Several questions arise: Is the level of debt in European soccer too high? Will we see a fallout in the soccer sector in the same way as the banking sector? How should a company choose a capital structure for itself, and what are the important factors driving this? To answer these questions, this chapter covers the basic ideas underlying optimal debt policies, and how firms establish them.

Thus far we have taken the firm's capital structure as given. Debt–equity ratios don't just drop on firms from the sky, of course, so now it's time to wonder where they come from. Going back to Chapter 1, recall that we refer to decisions about a firm's debt–equity ratio as *capital structure decisions*.[1]

For the most part, a firm can choose any capital structure it wants. If management so desired, a firm could issue some bonds and use the proceeds to buy back some equity, thereby increasing the debt–equity ratio. Alternatively, it could issue equity and use the money to pay off some debt, thereby reducing the debt–equity ratio. Activities such as these, which alter the firm's existing capital structure, are called capital *restructurings*. In general, such restructurings take place whenever the firm substitutes one capital structure for another while leaving the firm's assets unchanged.

Because the assets of a firm are not directly affected by a capital restructuring, we can examine the firm's capital structure decision separately from its other activities. This means that a firm can consider capital restructuring decisions in isolation from its investment decisions. In this chapter, then, we shall ignore investment decisions and focus on the long-term financing, or capital structure, question.

What we shall see in this chapter is that capital structure decisions can have important implications for the value of the firm and its cost of capital. We shall also find those important elements of the capital structure decision are easy to identify, but precise measures of these elements are generally not obtainable. As a result, we are able to give only an incomplete answer to the question of what the best capital structure might be for a particular firm at a particular time.

15.1 THE CAPITAL STRUCTURE QUESTION

How should a firm go about choosing its debt–equity ratio? Here, as always, we assume that the guiding principle is to choose the course of action that maximizes the value of a share of equity. As we discuss next, however, when it comes to capital structure decisions, this is essentially the same thing as maximizing the value of the whole firm, and, for convenience, we shall tend to frame our discussion in terms of firm value.

FIRM VALUE AND EQUITY VALUE: AN EXAMPLE

The following example illustrates that the capital structure that maximizes the value of the firm is the one that financial managers should choose for the shareholders, so there is no conflict in our goals. To begin, suppose the market value of J.J. Sprint plc is £1,000. The company currently has no debt, and J.J. Sprint's 100 shares sell for £10 each. Further suppose that J.J. Sprint restructures itself by borrowing £500 and then paying out the proceeds to shareholders as an extra dividend of £500/100 = £5 per share.

This restructuring will change the capital structure of the firm, with no direct effect on the firm's assets. The immediate effect will be to increase debt and decrease equity. However, what will be the final impact of the restructuring? Table 15.1 illustrates three possible outcomes in addition to the original no-debt case. Notice that in Scenario II the value of the firm is unchanged at £1,000. In Scenario I firm value rises to £1,250; it falls by £250, to £750, in Scenario III. We haven't yet said what might lead to these changes. For now, we just take them as possible outcomes to illustrate a point.

TABLE 15.1

Possible firm values: no debt versus debt plus dividend

	No debt	Debt plus dividend		
		I	II	III
Debt (£)	0	500	500	500
Equity (£)	1,000	750	500	250
Firm value (£)	1,000	1,250	1,000	750

Because our goal is to benefit the shareholders, we next examine, in Table 15.2, the net pay-offs to the shareholders in these scenarios. We see that, if the value of the firm stays the same, shareholders will experience a capital loss exactly offsetting the extra dividend. This is Scenario II. In Scenario I, the value of the firm increases to £1,250, and the shareholders come out ahead by £250. In other words, the restructuring has an NPV of £250 in this scenario. The NPV in Scenario III is −£250.

TABLE 15.2

Possible pay-offs to shareholders: debt plus dividend

	Debt plus dividend		
	I	II	III
Equity value reduction (£)	−250	−500	−750
Dividends (£)	500	500	500
Net effect (£)	+250	0	−250

The key observation to make here is that the change in the value of the firm is the same as the net effect on the shareholders. Financial managers can therefore try to find the capital structure that maximizes the value of the firm. Put another way, the NPV rule applies to capital structure decisions, and the change in the value of the overall firm is the NPV of a restructuring. Thus J.J. Sprint should borrow £500 if it expects Scenario I. The crucial question in determining a firm's capital structure is, of course, which scenario is likely to occur.

CAPITAL STRUCTURE AND THE COST OF CAPITAL

In Chapter 13 we discussed the concept of the firm's weighted average cost of capital, or WACC. You may recall that the WACC tells us that the firm's overall cost of capital is a weighted average of the costs of the various components of the firm's capital structure. When we described the WACC, we took the firm's capital structure as given. Thus one important issue that we shall want to explore in this chapter is what happens to the cost of capital when we vary the amount of debt financing or the debt–equity ratio.

A primary reason for studying the WACC is that the value of the firm is maximized when the WACC is minimized. To see this, recall that the WACC is the appropriate discount rate for the firm's overall cash flows. Because values and discount rates move in opposite directions, minimizing the WACC will maximize the value of the firm's cash flows.

Thus, we shall want to choose the firm's capital structure so that the WACC is minimized. For this reason, we shall say that one capital structure is better than another if it results in a lower weighted average cost of capital. Further, we say that a particular debt–equity ratio represents the *optimal capital structure* if it results in the lowest possible WACC. This optimal capital structure is sometimes called the firm's *target* capital structure as well.

> #### CONCEPT QUESTIONS
>
> **15.1a** Why should financial managers choose the capital structure that maximizes the value of the firm?
> **15.1b** What is the relationship between the WACC and the value of the firm?
> **15.1c** What is an optimal capital structure?

15.2 THE EFFECT OF FINANCIAL LEVERAGE

The previous section described why the capital structure that produces the highest firm value (or the lowest cost of capital) is the one most beneficial to shareholders. In this section, we examine the impact of financial leverage on the pay-offs to shareholders. As you may recall, *financial leverage* refers to the extent to which a firm relies on debt. The more debt financing a firm uses in its capital structure, the more financial leverage it employs.

As we describe, financial leverage can dramatically alter the pay-offs to shareholders in the firm. Remarkably, however, financial leverage may not affect the overall cost of capital. If this is true, then a firm's capital structure is irrelevant, because changes in capital structure won't affect the value of the firm. We shall return to this issue a little later.

THE BASICS OF FINANCIAL LEVERAGE

We start by illustrating how financial leverage works. For now, we ignore the impact of taxes. Also, for ease of presentation, we describe the impact of leverage in terms of its effects on earnings per share, EPS, and return on equity, ROE. These are of course accounting numbers, and as such are not our primary concern. Using cash flows instead of these accounting numbers would lead to precisely the same conclusions, but a little more work would be needed. We discuss the impact on market values in a subsequent section.

Financial Leverage, EPS and ROE: An Example

Autoveloce SpA currently has no debt in its capital structure. The firm is considering a restructuring that would involve issuing debt and using the proceeds to buy back some of the outstanding equity. Table 15.3 presents both the current and proposed capital structures. As shown, the firm's assets have a market value of €8 million, and there are 400,000 shares outstanding. Because Autoveloce is an all-equity firm, the price per share is €20.

TABLE 15.3

Current and proposed capital structures for Autoveloce SpA

	Current	Proposed
Assets (€)	8,000,000	8,000,000
Debt (€)	0	4,000,000
Equity (€)	8,000,000	4,000,000
Debt–equity ratio	0	1
Share price (€)	20	20
Shares outstanding	400,000	200,000
Interest rate (%)	10	10

The proposed debt issue would raise €4 million; the interest rate would be 10 per cent. Because the equity sells for €20 per share, the €4 million in new debt would be used to purchase €4 million/20 = 200,000 shares, leaving 200,000. After the restructuring, Autoveloce would have a capital structure that was 50 per cent debt, so the debt–equity ratio would be 1. Notice that, for now, we assume that the equity price will remain at €20.

To investigate the impact of the proposed restructuring, Table 15.4 compares the firm's current capital structure with the proposed capital structure under three scenarios. The scenarios reflect different assumptions about the firm's EBIT. Under the expected scenario, the EBIT is €1 million. In the recession scenario, EBIT falls to €500,000. In the expansion scenario, it rises to €1.5 million.

TABLE 15.4

Capital structure scenarios for Autoveloce SpA

	Current capital structure: no debt		
	Recession	Expected	Expansion
EBIT (€)	500,000	1,000,000	1,500,000
Interest (€)	0	0	0
Net income (€)	500,000	1,000,000	1,500,000
ROE (%)	6.25	12.50	18.75
EPS (€)	1.25	2.50	3.75

	Proposed capital structure: Debt = €4 million		
EBIT (€)	500,000	1,000,000	1,500,000
Interest (€)	400,000	400,000	400,000
Net income (€)	100,000	600,000	1,100,000
ROE (%)	2.50	15.00	27.50
EPS (€)	0.50	3.00	5.50

To illustrate some of the calculations behind the figures in Table 15.4, consider the expansion case. EBIT is €1.5 million. With no debt (the current capital structure) and no taxes, net income is also €1.5 million. In this case, there are 400,000 shares worth €8 million total. EPS is therefore €1.5 million/400,000 = €3.75. Also, because accounting return on equity, ROE, is net income divided by total equity, ROE is €1.5 million/8 million = 18.75%.[2]

With €4 million in debt (the proposed capital structure), things are somewhat different. Because the interest rate is 10 per cent, the interest bill is €400,000. With EBIT of €1.5 million, interest of €400,000, and no taxes, net income is €1.1 million. Now there are only 200,000 shares worth €4 million total. EPS is, therefore, €1.1 million/200,000 = €5.50, versus the €3.75 that we calculated in the previous scenario. Furthermore, ROE is €1.1 million/4 million = 27.5%. This is well above the 18.75 per cent we calculated for the current capital structure.

EPS versus EBIT

The impact of leverage is evident when the effect of the restructuring on EPS and ROE is examined. In particular, the variability in both EPS and ROE is much larger under the proposed capital structure. This illustrates how financial leverage acts to magnify gains and losses to shareholders.

In Figure 15.1 we take a closer look at the effect of the proposed restructuring. This figure plots earnings per share, EPS, against earnings before interest and taxes, EBIT, for the current and proposed capital structures. The first line, labelled 'No debt', represents the case of no leverage. This line begins at the origin, indicating that EPS would be zero if EBIT were zero. From there, every €400,000 increase in EBIT increases EPS by €1 (because there are 400,000 shares outstanding).

The second line represents the proposed capital structure. Here, EPS is negative if EBIT is zero. This follows because €400,000 of interest must be paid, regardless of the firm's profits. Because there are 200,000 shares in this case, the EPS is −€2 as shown. Similarly, if EBIT were €400,000, EPS would be exactly zero.

The important thing to notice in Figure 15.1 is that the slope of the line in this second case is steeper. In fact, for every €400,000 increase in EBIT, EPS rises by €2, so the line is twice as steep. This tells us that EPS is twice as sensitive to changes in EBIT because of the financial leverage employed.

Another observation to make in Figure 15.1 is that the lines intersect. At that point, EPS is exactly the same for both capital structures. To find this point, note that EPS is equal to EBIT/400,000 in the no-debt case. In the with-debt case, EPS is (EBIT − €400,000)/200,000. If we set these equal to each other, EBIT is given by:

$$\text{EBIT}/400{,}000 = (\text{EBIT} - €400{,}000)/200{,}000$$
$$\text{EBIT} = 2 \times (\text{EBIT} - €400{,}000)$$
$$= €800{,}000$$

When EBIT is €800,000, EPS is €2 under either capital structure. This is labelled as the break-even point in Figure 15.1; we could also call it the indifference point. If EBIT is above this level, leverage is beneficial; if it is below this point, it is not.

There is another, more intuitive, way of seeing why the break-even point is €800,000. Notice that, if the firm has no debt and its EBIT is €800,000, its net income is also €800,000. In this case, the ROE is 10 per cent. This is precisely the same as the interest rate on the debt, so the firm earns a return that is just sufficient to pay the interest.

FIGURE 15.1

Financial leverage: EPS and EBIT for Autoveloce SpA

EXAMPLE 15.1

BREAK-EVEN EBIT

MPD plc has decided in favour of a capital restructuring. Currently, MPD uses no debt financing. Following the restructuring, however, debt will be £1 million. The interest rate on the debt will be 9 per cent. MPD currently has 200,000 shares outstanding, and the share price is £20. If the restructuring is expected to increase EPS, what is the minimum level for EBIT that MPD's management must be expecting? Ignore taxes in answering.

To answer, we calculate the break-even EBIT. At any EBIT above this, the increased financial leverage will increase EPS, so this will tell us the minimum level for EBIT. Under the old capital structure EPS is simply EBIT/200,000. Under the new capital structure, the interest expense will be £1 million × 0.09 = £90,000. Furthermore, with the £1 million proceeds, MPD will repurchase £1 million/20 = 50,000 shares of equity, leaving 150,000 outstanding. EPS will thus be (EBIT − £90,000)/150,000.

Now that we know how to calculate EPS under both scenarios, we set them equal to each other and solve for the break-even EBIT:

$$\text{EBIT}/200{,}000 = (\text{EBIT} - £90{,}000)/150{,}000$$
$$\text{EBIT} = 4/3 \times (\text{EBIT} - £90{,}000)$$
$$= £360{,}000$$

Verify that, in either case, EPS is £1.80 when EBIT is £360,000. Management at MPD is apparently of the opinion that EPS will exceed £1.80.

CORPORATE BORROWING AND HOMEMADE LEVERAGE

Based on Tables 15.3 and 15.4 and Figure 15.1, Autoveloce draws the following conclusions:

1. The effect of financial leverage depends on the company's EBIT. When EBIT is relatively high, leverage is beneficial.
2. Under the expected scenario, leverage increases the returns to shareholders, as measured by both ROE and EPS.
3. Shareholders are exposed to more risk under the proposed capital structure because the EPS and ROE are much more sensitive to changes in EBIT in this case.
4. Because of the impact that financial leverage has on both the expected return to shareholders and the riskiness of the equity, capital structure is an important consideration.

The first three of these conclusions are clearly correct. Does the last conclusion necessarily follow? Surprisingly, the answer is no. As we discuss next, the reason is that shareholders can adjust the amount of financial leverage by borrowing and lending on their own. This use of personal borrowing to alter the degree of financial leverage is called **homemade leverage**.

We shall now illustrate that it actually makes no difference whether or not Autoveloce adopts the proposed capital structure because any shareholder who prefers the proposed capital structure can simply create it using homemade leverage. To begin, the first part of Table 15.5 shows what will happen to an investor who buys €2,000 worth of Autoveloce equity if the proposed capital structure is adopted. This investor purchases 100 shares of equity. From Table 15.4 we know that EPS will be €0.50, €3 or €5.50, so the total earnings for 100 shares will be either €50, €300 or €550 under the proposed capital structure.

> **homemade leverage**
> the use of personal borrowing to change the overall amount of financial leverage to which the individual is exposed.

TABLE 15.5

Proposed capital structure versus original capital structure with homemade leverage

	Proposed capital structure		
	Recession	Expected	Expansion
EPS (€)	0.50	3.00	5.50
Earnings for 100 shares (€)	50.00	300.00	550.00
Net cost = 100 shares × €20 = €2,000			
Original capital structure and homemade leverage			
EPS (€)	1.25	2.50	3.75
Earnings for 200 shares (€)	250.00	500.00	750.00
Less: Interest on €2,000 at 10% (€)	200.00	200.00	200.00
Net earnings (€)	50.00	300.00	550.00
Net cost = 200 shares × €20 − Amount borrowed = €4,000 − 2,000 = €2,000			

Now, suppose that Autoveloce does not adopt the proposed capital structure. In this case, EPS will be €1.25, €2.50 or €3.75. The second part of Table 15.5 demonstrates how a shareholder who prefers the pay-offs under the proposed structure can create them using personal borrowing. To do this, the shareholder borrows €2,000 at 10 per cent on her or his own. Our investor uses this amount, along with the original €2,000, to buy 200 shares of equity. As shown, the net pay-offs are exactly the same as those for the proposed capital structure.

How did we know to borrow €2,000 to create the right pay-offs? We are trying to replicate Autoveloce's proposed capital structure at a personal level. The proposed capital structure results in a debt–equity ratio of 1. To replicate this structure at the personal level, the shareholder must borrow enough to create this same debt–equity ratio. Because the shareholder has €2,000 in equity invested, the borrowing of another €2,000 will create a personal debt–equity ratio of 1.

This example demonstrates that investors can always increase financial leverage themselves to create a different pattern of pay-offs. It thus makes no difference whether Autoveloce chooses the proposed capital structure.

> **EXAMPLE 15.2**
>
> ### UNLEVERING THE EQUITY
>
> In our Autoveloce example, suppose management adopts the proposed capital structure. Further, suppose that an investor who owned 100 shares preferred the original capital structure. Show how this investor could 'delever' the equity to recreate the original pay-offs.
>
> To create leverage, investors borrow on their own. To undo leverage, investors must lend money. In the case of Autoveloce, the corporation borrowed an amount equal to half its value. The investor can delever the equity by simply lending money in the same proportion. In this case, the investor sells 50 shares for €1,000 total and then lends the €1,000 at 10 per cent. The pay-offs are calculated in the following table:
>
> | | Recession | Expected | Expansion |
> |---|---|---|---|
> | EPS (proposed structure) (€) | 0.50 | 3.00 | 5.50 |
> | Earnings for 50 shares (€) | 25.00 | 150.00 | 275.00 |
> | Plus: Interest on €1,000 (€) | 100.00 | 100.00 | 100.00 |
> | Total pay-off (€) | 125.00 | 250.00 | 375.00 |
>
> These are precisely the pay-offs the investor would have experienced under the original capital structure.

> **CONCEPT QUESTIONS**
>
> **15.2a** What is the impact of financial leverage on shareholders?
> **15.2b** What is homemade leverage?
> **15.2c** Why is Autoveloce's capital structure irrelevant?

15.3 CAPITAL STRUCTURE AND THE COST OF EQUITY CAPITAL

> **M&M Proposition I**
> the proposition that the value of the firm is independent of the firm's capital structure.

We have seen that there is nothing special about corporate borrowing because investors can borrow or lend on their own. As a result, whichever capital structure Autoveloce chooses, the equity price will be the same. Autoveloce's capital structure is thus irrelevant, at least in the simple world we have examined.

Our Autoveloce example is based on a famous argument advanced by two Nobel laureates, Franco Modigliani and Merton Miller, whom we shall henceforth call M&M. What we illustrated for the Autoveloce Corporation is a special case of **M&M Proposition I**. M&M Proposition I states that it is completely irrelevant how a firm chooses to arrange its finances.

M&M PROPOSITION I: THE PIE MODEL

One way to illustrate M&M Proposition I is to imagine two firms that are identical on the left side of the balance sheet. Their assets and operations are exactly the same. The right sides are different because the two firms finance their operations differently. In this case, we can view the capital structure question in terms of a 'pie' model. Why we choose this name is apparent from Figure 15.2. Figure 15.2 gives two possible ways of cutting up the pie between the equity slice, E, and the debt slice, D: 40%–60% and 60%–40%. However, the size of the pie in Figure 15.2 is the same for both firms, because the value of the assets is the same. This is precisely what M&M Proposition I states: The size of the pie doesn't depend on how it is sliced.

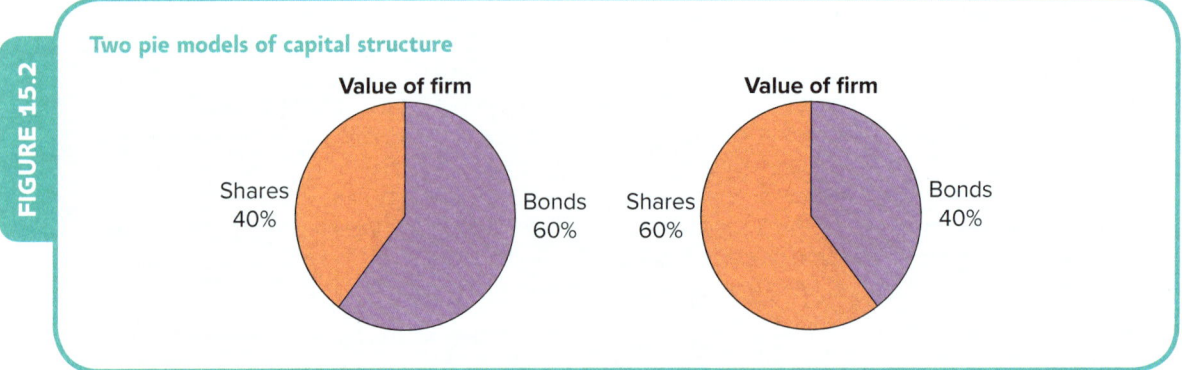

FIGURE 15.2 Two pie models of capital structure

THE COST OF EQUITY AND FINANCIAL LEVERAGE: M&M PROPOSITION II

Although changing the capital structure of the firm does not change the firm's *total* value, it does cause important changes in the firm's debt and equity. We now examine what happens to a firm financed with debt and equity when the debt–equity ratio is changed. To simplify our analysis, we shall continue to ignore taxes.

Based on our discussion in Chapter 13, if we ignore taxes, the weighted average cost of capital, WACC, is:

$$\text{WACC} = (E/V) \times R_E + (D/V) \times R_D$$

where $V = E + D$. We also saw that one way of interpreting the WACC is as the required return on the firm's overall assets. To remind us of this, we shall use the symbol R_A to stand for the WACC, and write:

$$R_A = (E/V) \times R_E + (D/V) \times R_D$$

If we rearrange this to solve for the cost of equity capital, we see that:

$$R_E = R_A + (R_A - R_D) \times (D/E) \qquad (15.1)$$

This is the famous **M&M Proposition II**, which tells us that the cost of equity depends on three things: the required rate of return on the firm's assets, R_A; the firm's cost of debt, R_D; and the firm's debt–equity ratio, D/E.

Figure 15.3 summarizes our discussion thus far by plotting the cost of equity capital, R_E, against the debt–equity ratio. As shown, M&M Proposition II indicates that the cost of equity, R_E, is given by a straight line with a slope of $(R_A - R_D)$. The y-intercept corresponds to a firm with a debt–equity ratio of zero, so $R_A = R_E$ in that case. Figure 15.3 shows that as the firm raises its debt–equity ratio, the increase in leverage raises the risk of the equity and therefore the required return or cost of equity (R_E).

Notice in Figure 15.3 that the WACC doesn't depend on the debt–equity ratio; it's the same no matter what the debt–equity ratio is. This is another way of stating M&M Proposition I: the firm's overall cost of capital is unaffected by its capital structure.

As illustrated, the fact that the cost of debt is lower than the cost of equity is exactly offset by the increase in the cost of equity from borrowing. In other words, the change in the capital structure weights (E/V and D/V) is exactly offset by the change in the cost of equity (R_E), so the WACC stays the same.

M&M Proposition II the proposition that a firm's cost of equity capital is a positive linear function of the firm's capital structure.

FIGURE 15.3

The cost of equity and the WACC: M&M Propositions I and II with no taxes

$R_E = R_A + (R_A - R_D) \times (D/E)$ by M&M Proposition II

$R_A = \text{WACC} = \left(\dfrac{E}{V}\right) \times R_E + \left(\dfrac{D}{V}\right) \times R_D$

Where $V = D + E$

EXAMPLE 15.3

THE COST OF EQUITY CAPITAL

Ricard NV has a weighted average cost of capital (ignoring taxes) of 12 per cent. It can borrow at 8 per cent. Assuming that Ricard has a target capital structure of 80 per cent equity and 20 per cent debt, what is its cost of equity? What is the cost of equity if the target capital structure is 50 per cent equity? Calculate the WACC using your answers to verify that it is the same.

According to M&M Proposition II, the cost of equity, R_E, is:

$$R_E = R_A + (R_A - R_D)(D/E)$$

In the first case, the debt–equity ratio is 0.2/0.8 = 0.25, so the cost of the equity is:

$$R_E = 12\% + (12\% - 8\%) \times 0.25$$
$$= 13\%$$

In the second case, verify that the debt–equity ratio is 1.0, so the cost of equity is 16 per cent.

We can now calculate the WACC assuming that the percentage of equity financing is 80 per cent, the cost of equity is 13 per cent, and the tax rate is zero:

$$\text{WACC} = (E/V) \times R_E + (D/V) \times R_D$$
$$= 0.50 \times 16\% + 0.50 \times 8\%$$
$$= 12\%$$

In the second case, the percentage of equity financing is 50 per cent and the cost of equity is 16 per cent. The WACC is:

$$\text{WACC} = (E/V) \times R_E + (D/V) \times R_D$$
$$= 0.80 \times 13\% + 0.20 \times 8\%$$
$$= 12\%$$

As we have calculated, the WACC is 12 per cent in both cases.

BUSINESS AND FINANCIAL RISK

business risk
the equity risk that comes from the nature of the firm's operating activities.

M&M Proposition II shows that the firm's cost of equity can be broken down into two components. The first component, R_A, is the required return on the firm's assets overall, and it depends on the nature of the firm's operating activities. The risk inherent in a firm's operations is called the **business risk** of the firm's equity. Referring back to Chapter 12, note that this business risk depends on the systematic risk of the firm's assets. The greater a firm's business risk, the greater R_A will be, and, all other things being the same, the greater will be the firm's cost of equity.

REAL WORLD INSIGHTS

MERTON H. MILLER ON CAPITAL STRUCTURE: M&M 30 YEARS LATER

'How difficult it is to summarize briefly the contribution of these papers was brought home to me very clearly after Franco Modigliani was awarded the Nobel Prize in Economics, in part – but, of course, only in part – for his work in finance. The television camera crews from our local stations in Chicago immediately descended upon me. "We understand," they said, "that you worked with Modigliani some years back in developing these M&M theorems, and we wonder if you could explain them briefly to our television viewers." "How briefly?" I asked. "Oh, take 10 seconds," was the reply.

Ten seconds to explain the work of a lifetime! Ten seconds to describe two carefully reasoned articles, each running to more than 30 printed pages and each with 60 or so long footnotes! When they saw the look of dismay on my face, they said, "You don't have to go into details. Just give us the main points in simple, commonsense terms."

The main point of the cost-of-capital article was, in principle at least, simple enough to make. It said that in an economist's ideal world, the total market value of all the securities issued by a firm would be governed by the earning power and risk of its underlying real assets and would be independent of how the mix of securities issued to finance it was divided between debt instruments and equity capital. Some corporate treasurers might well think that they could enhance total value by increasing the proportion of debt instruments because yields on debt instruments, given their lower risk, are, by and large, substantially below those on equity capital. But, under the ideal conditions assumed, the added risk to the shareholders from issuing more debt will raise required yields on the equity by just enough to offset the seeming gain from use of low-cost debt.

Such a summary would not only have been too long, but it relied on shorthand terms and concepts that are rich in connotations to economists, but hardly so to the general public. I thought, instead, of an analogy that we ourselves had invoked in the original paper. "Think of the firm," I said, "as a gigantic tub of whole milk. The farmer can sell the whole milk as is. Or he can separate out the cream and sell it at a considerably higher price than the whole milk would bring. (Selling cream is the analogue of a firm selling low-yield and hence high-priced debt securities.) But, of course, what the farmer would have left would be skim milk, with low butterfat content, and that would sell for much less than whole milk. Skim milk corresponds to the levered equity. The M&M proposition says that if there were no costs of separation (and, of course, no government dairy support programmes), the cream plus the skim milk would bring the same price as the whole milk."

The television people conferred among themselves for a while. They informed me that it was still too long, too complicated, and too academic. "Have you anything simpler?" they asked. I thought of another way in which the M&M proposition is presented that stresses the role of securities as devices for "partitioning" a firm's pay-offs among the group of its capital suppliers. "Think of the firm," I said, "as a gigantic pizza, divided into quarters. If, now, you cut each quarter in half into eighths, the M&M proposition says that you will have more pieces, but not more pizza."

Once again whispered conversation. This time, they shut the lights off. They folded up their equipment. They thanked me for my co-operation. They said they would get back to me. But I knew that I had somehow lost my chance to start a new career as a packager of economic wisdom for TV viewers in convenient 10-second sound bites. Some have the talent for it; and some just don't.'

The late Merton H. Miller was famous for his groundbreaking work with Franco Modigliani on corporate capital structure, cost of capital, and dividend policy. He received the Nobel Prize in Economics for his contributions shortly after this essay was prepared.

Reproduced with permission from GSB Chicago, University of Chicago (Autumn 1986).

The second component in the cost of equity, $(R_A - R_D) \times (D/E)$, is determined by the firm's financial structure. For an all-equity firm, this component is zero. As the firm begins to rely on debt financing, the required return on equity rises. This occurs because debt financing increases the risks borne by the shareholders. This extra risk that arises from the use of debt financing is called the **financial risk** of the firm's equity.

The total systematic risk of the firm's equity thus has two parts: business risk and financial risk. The first part (the business risk) depends on the firm's assets and operations and is not affected by capital structure. Given the firm's business risk (and its cost of debt), the second part (the financial risk) is completely determined by financial policy. As we have illustrated, the firm's cost of equity rises when the firm increases its use of financial leverage, because the financial risk of the equity increases while the business risk remains the same.

> **financial risk**
> the equity risk that comes from the financial policy (the capital structure) of the firm.

CONCEPT QUESTIONS

15.3a What does M&M Proposition I state?
15.3b What are the three determinants of a firm's cost of equity?
15.3c The total systematic risk of a firm's equity has two parts. What are they?

15.4 M&M PROPOSITIONS I AND II WITH CORPORATE TAXES

Debt has two distinguishing features that we have not taken into proper account. First, as we have mentioned in a number of places, interest paid on debt is tax-deductible. This is good for the firm, and it may be an added benefit of debt financing. Second, failure to meet debt obligations can result in bankruptcy. This is not good for the firm, and it may be an added cost of debt financing. Because we haven't explicitly considered either of these two features of debt, we realize that we may get a different answer about capital structure once we do. Accordingly, we consider taxes in this section and bankruptcy in the next.

We can start by considering what happens to M&M Propositions I and II when we consider the effect of corporate taxes. To do this, we shall examine two firms: Firm U (unlevered) and Firm L (levered). These two firms are identical on the left side of the balance sheet, so their assets and operations are the same.

We assume that EBIT is expected to be €1,000 every year forever for both firms. The difference between the firms is that Firm L has issued €1,000 worth of perpetual bonds on which it pays 8 per cent interest each year. The interest bill is thus 0.08 × €1,000 = €80 every year forever. Also, we assume that the corporate tax rate is 30 per cent.

For our two firms, U and L, we can now calculate the following:

	Firm U	Firm L
EBIT (€)	1,000	1,000
Interest (€)	0	80
Taxable income (€)	1,000	920
Taxes (30%) (€)	300	276
Net income	700	644

THE INTEREST TAX SHIELD

To simplify things, we shall assume that depreciation is zero. We shall also assume that capital spending is zero, and that there are no changes in NWC. In this case, cash flow from assets is simply equal to EBIT − Taxes. For Firms U and L we thus have:

Cash flow from assets	Firm U	Firm L
EBIT (€)	1,000	1,000
− Taxes (€)	300	276
Total (€)	700	724

We immediately see that capital structure is now having some effect, because the cash flows from U and L are not the same, even though the two firms have identical assets.

To see what's going on, we can compute the cash flow to shareholders and bondholders:

Cash flow (€)	Firm U	Firm L
To shareholders	700	644
To bondholders	0	80
Total	700	724

interest tax shield
the tax saving attained by a firm from interest expense.

What we are seeing is that the total cash flow to L is €24 more. This occurs because L's tax bill (which is a cash outflow) is €24 less. The fact that interest is deductible for tax purposes has generated a tax-saving equal to the interest payment (€80) multiplied by the corporate tax rate (30 per cent): €80 × 0.30 = €24. We call this tax-saving the **interest tax shield**.

TAXES AND M&M PROPOSITION I

Because the debt is perpetual, the same €24 shield will be generated every year forever. The after-tax cash flow to L will thus be the same €700 that U earns plus the €24 tax shield. Because L's cash flow is always €24 greater, Firm L is worth more than Firm U, the difference being the value of this €24 perpetuity.

Because the tax shield is generated by paying interest, it has the same risk as the debt, and 8 per cent (the cost of debt) is, therefore, the appropriate discount rate. The value of the tax shield is thus:

$$\begin{aligned} PV &= \frac{€24}{0.08} \\ &= \frac{0.30 \times €1{,}000 \times 0.08}{0.08} \\ &= 0.30 \times €1{,}000 \\ &= €300 \end{aligned}$$

As our example illustrates, the present value of the interest tax shield can be written as:

$$\text{Present value of the interest tax shield} = \frac{T_C \times D \times R_D}{R_D} \qquad (15.2)$$
$$= T_C \times D$$

We have now come up with another famous result, M&M Proposition I with corporate taxes. We have seen that the value of Firm L, V_L, exceeds the value of Firm U, V_U, by the present value of the interest tax shield, $T_C \times D$. M&M Proposition I with taxes, therefore, states that:

$$V_L = V_U + T_C \times D \qquad (15.3)$$

The effect of borrowing, in this case, is illustrated in Figure 15.4. We have plotted the value of the levered firm, V_L, against the amount of debt, D. M&M Proposition I with corporate taxes implies that the relationship is given by a straight line with a slope of T_C and a y-intercept of V_U.

FIGURE 15.4 M&M Proposition I with taxes

The value of the firm increases as total debt increases, because of the interest tax shield. This is the basis of M&M Proposition I with taxes.

In Figure 15.4 we have also drawn a horizontal line representing V_U. As indicated, the distance between the two lines is $T_C \times D$, the present value of the tax shield.

Suppose that the cost of capital for Firm U is 10 per cent. We shall call this the **unlevered cost of capital**, and we shall use the symbol R_U to represent it. We can think of R_U as the cost of capital a firm would have if it had no debt. Firm U's cash flow is €700 every year forever, and, because U has no debt, the appropriate discount rate is $R_U = 10\%$. The value of the unlevered firm, V_U, is simply:

> **unlevered cost of capital**
> the cost of capital for a firm that has no debt.

$$V_U = \frac{\text{EBIT} \times (1 - T_C)}{R_U}$$
$$= \frac{€700}{0.10}$$
$$= €7{,}000$$

The value of the levered firm, V_L, is:

$$V_L = V_U + T_C \times D$$
$$= €7{,}000 + 0.30 \times 1{,}000$$
$$= €7{,}300$$

As Figure 15.4 indicates, the value of the firm goes up by €0.30 for every €1 in debt. In other words, the NPV *per euro* of debt is €0.30. It is difficult to imagine why any corporation would not borrow to the absolute maximum under these circumstances.

The result of our analysis in this section is the realization that, once we include taxes, capital structure definitely matters. However, we immediately reach the illogical conclusion that the optimal capital structure is 100 per cent debt.

TAXES, THE WACC AND PROPOSITION II

We can also conclude that the best capital structure is 100 per cent debt by examining the weighted average cost of capital. From Chapter 13 we know that once we consider the effect of taxes, the WACC is:

$$\text{WACC} = (E/V) \times R_E + (D/V) \times R_D \times (1 - T_C)$$

To calculate this WACC we need to know the cost of equity. M&M Proposition II with corporate taxes states that the cost of equity is:

$$R_E = R_U + (R_U - R_D) \times (D/E) \times (1 - T_C) \qquad (15.4)$$

To illustrate, recall that we saw a moment ago that Firm L is worth €7,300 in total. Because the debt is worth €1,000, the equity must be worth €7,300 − 1,000 = €6,300. For Firm L, the cost of equity is thus:

$$R_E = 0.10 + (0.10 - 0.08) \times (€1{,}000/6{,}300) \times (1 - 0.30)$$
$$= 10.22\%$$

The weighted average cost of capital is:

$$\text{WACC} = (€6{,}300/7{,}300) \times 10.22\% + (1{,}000/7{,}300) \times 8\% \times (1 - 0.30)$$
$$= 9.6\%$$

Without debt, the WACC is over 10 per cent; with debt, it is 9.6 per cent. Therefore the firm is better off with debt.

CONCLUSION

Figure 15.5 summarizes our discussion concerning the relationship between the cost of equity, the after-tax cost of debt, and the weighted average cost of capital. For reference, we have included R_U, the unlevered cost of capital. In Figure 15.5 we have the debt–equity ratio on the horizontal axis. Notice how the WACC declines as the debt–equity ratio grows. This illustrates again that the more debt the firm uses, the lower is its WACC. Table 15.6 summarizes the key results of our analysis of the M&M propositions for future reference.

FIGURE 15.5 The cost of equity and the WACC: M&M Proposition II with taxes

M&M Proposition I with taxes implies that a firm's WACC decreases as the firm relies more heavily on debt financing:

$$\text{WACC} = \left(\frac{E}{V}\right) \times R_E + \left(\frac{D}{V}\right) \times R_D \times (1 - T_C)$$

M&M Proposition II with taxes implies that a firm's cost of equity, R_E, rises as the firm relies more heavily on debt financing:

$$R_E = R_U + (R_U - R_D) \times (D/E) \times (1 - T_C)$$

TABLE 15.6

Modigliani and Miller summary

The no-tax case

A Proposition I: The value of the firm levered (V_L) is equal to the value of the firm unlevered (V_U):

$$V_L = V_U$$

Implications of Proposition I:
1. A firm's capital structure is irrelevant.
2. A firm's weighted average cost of capital (WACC) is the same, no matter what mixture of debt and equity is used to finance the firm.

B Proposition II: The cost of equity, R_E, is:

$$R_E = R_A + (R_A - R_D) \times (D/E)$$

where R_A is the WACC, R_D is the cost of debt, and D/E is the debt–equity ratio.
Implications of Proposition II:
1. The cost of equity rises as the firm increases its use of debt financing.
2. The risk of equity depends on two things: the riskiness of the firm's operations *(business risk)*, and the degree of financial leverage *(financial risk)*. Business risk determines R_A; financial risk is determined by D/E.

The tax case

A Proposition I with taxes: The value of the firm levered (V_L) is equal to the value of the firm unlevered (V_U) plus the present value of the interest tax shield:

$$V_L = V_U + T_C \times D$$

where T_C is the corporate tax rate and D is the amount of debt.
Implications of Proposition I:
1. Debt financing is highly advantageous, and in the extreme, a firm's optimal capital structure is 100 per cent debt.
2. A firm's weighted average cost of capital (WACC) decreases as the firm relies more heavily on debt financing.

B Proposition II with taxes: The cost of equity, R_E, is:

$$R_E = R_U + (R_U - R_D) \times (D/E) \times (1 - T_C)$$

where R_U is the *unlevered cost of capital* - that is, the cost of capital for the firm if it has no debt. Unlike the case with Proposition I, the general implications of Proposition II are the same whether there are taxes or not.

THE COST OF EQUITY AND THE VALUE OF THE FIRM

This is a comprehensive example that illustrates most of the points we have discussed thus far. You are given the following information for Fermat SA:

$$\text{EBIT} = €151.52$$
$$T_C = 0.34$$
$$D = €500$$
$$R_U = 0.20$$

The cost of debt capital is 10 per cent. What is the value of Fermat's equity? What is the cost of equity capital for Fermat? What is the WACC?

This one's easier than it looks. Remember that all the cash flows are perpetuities. The value of the firm if it has no debt, V_U, is:

$$V_U = \frac{\text{EBIT} - \text{Taxes}}{R_U}$$
$$= \frac{\text{EBIT} \times (1 - T_C)}{R_U}$$
$$= \frac{€100}{0.20}$$
$$= €500$$

From M&M Proposition I with taxes we know that the value of the firm with debt is:

$$V_L = V_U + T_C \times D$$
$$= €500 + 0.34 \times 500$$
$$= €670$$

Because the firm is worth €670 total, and the debt is worth €500, the equity is worth €170:

$$E = V_L - D$$
$$= €670 - 500$$
$$= €170$$

Based on M&M Proposition II with taxes, the cost of equity is:

$$R_E = R_U + (R_U - R_D) \times (D/E) \times (1 - T_C)$$
$$= 0.20(0.20 - 0.10)(€500/170)(1 - 0.34)$$
$$= 39.4\%$$

Finally, the WACC is:

$$\text{WACC} = (€170/670) \times 39.4\% (500/670) \times 10\% \times (1 - 0.34)$$
$$= 14.92\%$$

Notice that this is substantially lower than the cost of capital for the firm with no debt ($R_U = 20\%$), so debt financing is highly advantageous.

> **CONCEPT QUESTIONS**
>
> **15.4a** What is the relationship between the value of an unlevered firm and the value of a levered firm once we consider the effect of corporate taxes?
>
> **15.4b** If we consider only the effect of taxes, what is the optimal capital structure?

15.5 BANKRUPTCY COSTS

One limiting factor affecting the amount of debt a firm might use comes in the form of *bankruptcy costs*. As the debt–equity ratio rises, so too does the probability that the firm will be unable to pay its bondholders what was promised to them. When this happens, ownership of the firm's assets is ultimately transferred from the shareholders to the bondholders.

In principle, a firm becomes bankrupt when the value of its assets equals the value of its debt. When this occurs, the value of equity is zero, and the shareholders turn over control of the firm to the bondholders. When this takes place, the bondholders hold assets whose value is exactly equal to what is owed on the debt. In a perfect world, there are no costs associated with this transfer of ownership, and the bondholders don't lose anything.

This idealized view of bankruptcy is not, of course, what happens in the real world. Ironically, it is expensive to go bankrupt. As we discuss, the costs associated with bankruptcy may eventually offset the tax-related gains from leverage.

DIRECT BANKRUPTCY COSTS

When the value of a firm's assets equals the value of its debt, then the firm is economically bankrupt in the sense that the equity has no value. However, the formal turning over of the assets to the bondholders is a *legal* process, not an economic one. There are legal and administrative costs to bankruptcy, and it has been remarked that bankruptcies are to lawyers what blood is to sharks.

Bankruptcy costs can be absolutely massive with large multinational firms. For example, as of 2020, the direct costs of Enron's bankruptcy (in 2001) included thousands of jobs, more than $60 billion in market value, $2 billion in pension plans, $7.3 billion in compensation, and at least $30 billion of claims still in courts.

Because of the expenses associated with bankruptcy, bondholders won't get all that they are owed. Some fraction of the firm's assets will 'disappear' in the legal process of going bankrupt. These are the legal and administrative expenses associated with the bankruptcy proceeding. We call these costs **direct bankruptcy costs**.

These direct bankruptcy costs are a disincentive to debt financing. If a firm goes bankrupt, then, suddenly, a piece of the firm disappears. This amounts to a bankruptcy 'tax'. So a firm faces a trade-off: borrowing saves a firm money on its corporate taxes, but the more a firm borrows, the more likely it is that the firm will become bankrupt and have to pay the bankruptcy tax.

> **direct bankruptcy costs**
> the costs that are directly associated with bankruptcy, such as legal and administrative expenses.

> **REAL WORLD INSIGHTS**
>
> The largest-ever bankruptcy concerned Lehman Brothers, which at the time was one of the biggest banks in the world. This bankruptcy followed large write-downs on subprime mortgage assets and a general collapse in interbank credit in September 2008. Estimates vary on the total cost of the bank's collapse but a conservative estimate is around $2 billion, and it is very likely to be much higher. According to Lehman Brothers' official documentation, the total fees that were paid to administrators, lawyers and other parties amounted to $1.05 billion within just two years of the bankruptcy. Given its enormous size, the bankruptcy affected nearly every country in Europe and the cost of winding up Lehman's European subsidiaries was almost as high at $900 million. These are just the direct costs. The total (direct and indirect) costs of the bankruptcy will have been astronomical once the company's demise is considered more broadly in terms of impacting the local community and the wider financial sector.

INDIRECT BANKRUPTCY COSTS

Because it is expensive to go bankrupt, a firm will spend resources to avoid doing so. When a firm is having significant problems in meeting its debt obligations, we say that it is experiencing financial distress. Some financially distressed firms ultimately file for bankruptcy, but most do not, because they are able to recover or otherwise survive.

The costs of avoiding a bankruptcy filing incurred by a financially distressed firm are called **indirect bankruptcy costs**. We use the term **financial distress costs** to refer generically to the direct and indirect costs associated with going bankrupt or avoiding a bankruptcy filing.

The problems that come up in financial distress are particularly severe, and the financial distress costs are thus larger when the shareholders and the bondholders are different groups. Until the firm is legally bankrupt, the shareholders control it. They, of course, will take actions in their own economic interests. Because the shareholders can be wiped out in a legal bankruptcy, they have a very strong incentive to avoid a bankruptcy filing.

The bondholders, on the other hand, are concerned primarily with protecting the value of the firm's assets and will try to take control away from shareholders.

> **indirect bankruptcy costs**
> the costs of avoiding a bankruptcy filing incurred by a financially distressed firm.

> **financial distress costs**
> the direct and indirect costs associated with going bankrupt or experiencing financial distress.

They have a strong incentive to seek bankruptcy to protect their interests and keep shareholders from further dissipating the assets of the firm. The net effect of all this fighting is that a long, drawn-out and potentially quite expensive legal battle gets started.

Meanwhile, as the wheels of justice turn in their ponderous way, the assets of the firm lose value because management is busy trying to avoid bankruptcy instead of running the business. Normal operations are disrupted, and sales are lost. Valuable employees leave, potentially fruitful programmes are dropped to preserve cash, and otherwise profitable investments are not taken.

These are all indirect bankruptcy costs, or costs of financial distress. Whether or not the firm ultimately goes bankrupt, the net effect is a loss of value because the firm chose to use debt in its capital structure. It is this possibility of loss that limits the amount of debt that a firm will choose to use.

> **REAL WORLD INSIGHTS**
>
> Financial distress can hit any company, whether it is well run or mismanaged. Think of a fishing boat sailing from Norway to Italy. The boat's crew may be efficient and have the ability to sail the boat adeptly in all weathers, but if the boat is engulfed in a major storm, the crew may not be able to adapt quickly enough to the rapidly deteriorating environment.
>
> Managing a corporation is similar to piloting a boat because a company can also be hit by major external events. Like a boat's captain, a company's leadership team must adapt quickly to extraneous shocks and even change the way they approach their business if the impact of the shock is strong enough.
>
> Take Carillion, one of the world's largest construction and services management firms, that went into bankruptcy in 2018. Issues with the company's debt borrowing had been raised three years before and by the end of November 2017, Carillion was having difficulty paying interest on debt amounting to nearly £1 billion. Despite intensive discussions with the UK Financial Conduct Authority about a potential rescue deal, the firm collapsed in January 2018 with less than £30 million in the bank.
>
> Even though debt brings benefits to a company through its tax shield, it can also kill it if interest payments can't be made. Carillion, like many other financially distressed firms, tried to go into administration to give them protection from creditors and to provide time to turn its operations around.
>
> Ultimately, the direct and indirect costs ran into billions and the effects of the bankruptcy are still being borne by investors today.

AGENCY COSTS

When a firm has debt, conflicts of interest arise between shareholders and bondholders. Because of this, shareholders are tempted to pursue selfish strategies. These conflicts of interest, which are magnified when financial distress is incurred, impose agency costs on the firm. We describe three kinds of selfish strategy that shareholders use to hurt the bondholders and help themselves. These strategies are costly because they will lower the market value of the whole firm.

Selfish Investment Strategy 1: Incentive to Take Large Risks

Firms near bankruptcy often take great chances because they believe that they are playing with someone else's money. To see this, imagine a levered firm considering two mutually exclusive projects, a low-risk one and a high-risk one. There are two equally likely outcomes, recession and boom. The firm is in such dire straits that, should a recession hit, it will come near to bankruptcy with one project and actually fall into bankruptcy with the other. To save themselves and their jobs managers will take the high-risk project, because, irrespective of a recession or boom, the firm will become bankrupt with the low-risk investment. With the high-risk project, there is a strong probability the firm will fail and a very small chance that the firm will survive. Clearly, managers will choose the high-risk project, even though it may not actually have a positive NPV.

Thus, financial economists argue that shareholders expropriate value from the bondholders by selecting high-risk projects.

Selfish Investment Strategy 2: Incentive towards Underinvestment

Shareholders of a firm with a significant probability of bankruptcy often find that new investment helps the bondholders at the shareholders' expense. The simplest case might be a property owner facing imminent bankruptcy. If he took €100,000 out of his own pocket to refurbish the building, he could increase the building's value by, say, €150,000. Although this investment has a positive net present value, he will turn it down if the increase in value cannot prevent bankruptcy. 'Why,' he asks, 'should I use my own funds to improve the value of a building that the bank will soon repossess?'

The discussion of selfish strategy 2 is quite similar to the discussion of selfish strategy 1. In both cases, an investment strategy for the levered firm is different from the one for the unlevered firm. Thus leverage results in distorted investment policy. Whereas the unlevered corporation always chooses projects with positive net present value, the levered firm may deviate from this policy.

Selfish Investment Strategy 3: Milking the Property
Another strategy is to pay out extra dividends or other distributions in times of financial distress, leaving less in the firm for the bondholders. This is known as *milking the property*, a phrase taken from real estate. Strategies 2 and 3 are very similar. In Strategy 2 the firm chooses not to raise new equity. Strategy 3 goes one step further because equity is actually withdrawn through the dividend.

Summary of Selfish Strategies
The distortions just discussed occur only when there is a probability of bankruptcy or financial distress. Thus these distortions should not affect, say, Vodafone, because bankruptcy is not a realistic possibility for a diversified, blue-chip firm such as this. In other words, Vodafone's debt will be virtually risk-free, regardless of the projects it accepts. The same argument could be made for nationalized banks, such as the Royal Bank of Scotland, that are protected by the government. By contrast, small firms in risky industries, such as computers, are more likely to experience financial distress and, in turn, to be affected by such distortions.

Who pays for the cost of selfish investment strategies? We argue that it is ultimately the shareholders. Rational bondholders know that when financial distress is imminent, they cannot expect help from shareholders. Rather, shareholders are likely to choose investment strategies that reduce the value of the bonds. Bondholders protect themselves accordingly by raising the interest rate that they require on the bonds. Because the shareholders must pay these high rates, they ultimately bear the costs of selfish strategies. For firms that face these distortions, debt will be difficult and costly to obtain. These firms will have low leverage ratios.

> **CONCEPT QUESTIONS**
>
> **15.5a** What are direct bankruptcy costs?
> **15.5b** What are indirect bankruptcy costs?
> **15.5c** Explain what is meant by agency costs.

15.6 OPTIMAL CAPITAL STRUCTURE

Our previous two sections have established the basis for determining an optimal capital structure. A firm will borrow because the interest tax shield is valuable. At relatively low debt levels the probability of bankruptcy and financial distress is low, and the benefit from debt outweighs the cost. At very high debt levels the possibility of financial distress is a chronic, ongoing problem for the firm, so the benefit from debt financing may be more than offset by the financial distress costs. Based on our discussion, it would appear that an optimal capital structure exists somewhere in between these extremes.

static theory of capital structure
the theory that a firm borrows up to the point where the tax benefit from an extra pound or euro in debt is exactly equal to the cost that comes from the increased probability of financial distress.

THE STATIC THEORY OF CAPITAL STRUCTURE

The theory of capital structure that we have outlined is called the **static theory of capital structure**. It says that firms borrow up to the point where the tax benefit from an extra pound or euro in debt is exactly equal to the cost that comes from the increased probability of financial distress. We call this the static theory because it assumes that the firm is fixed in terms of its assets and operations, and it considers only possible changes in the debt–equity ratio.

The static theory is illustrated in Figure 15.6, which plots the value of the firm, V_L, against the amount of debt, D. In Figure 15.6 we have drawn lines corresponding to three different stories. The first represents M&M Proposition I with no taxes. This is the horizontal line extending from V_U, and it indicates that the value of the firm is unaffected by its capital structure. The second case, M&M Proposition I with corporate taxes, is represented by the upward-sloping straight line. These two cases are exactly the same as the ones we previously illustrated in Figure 15.4.

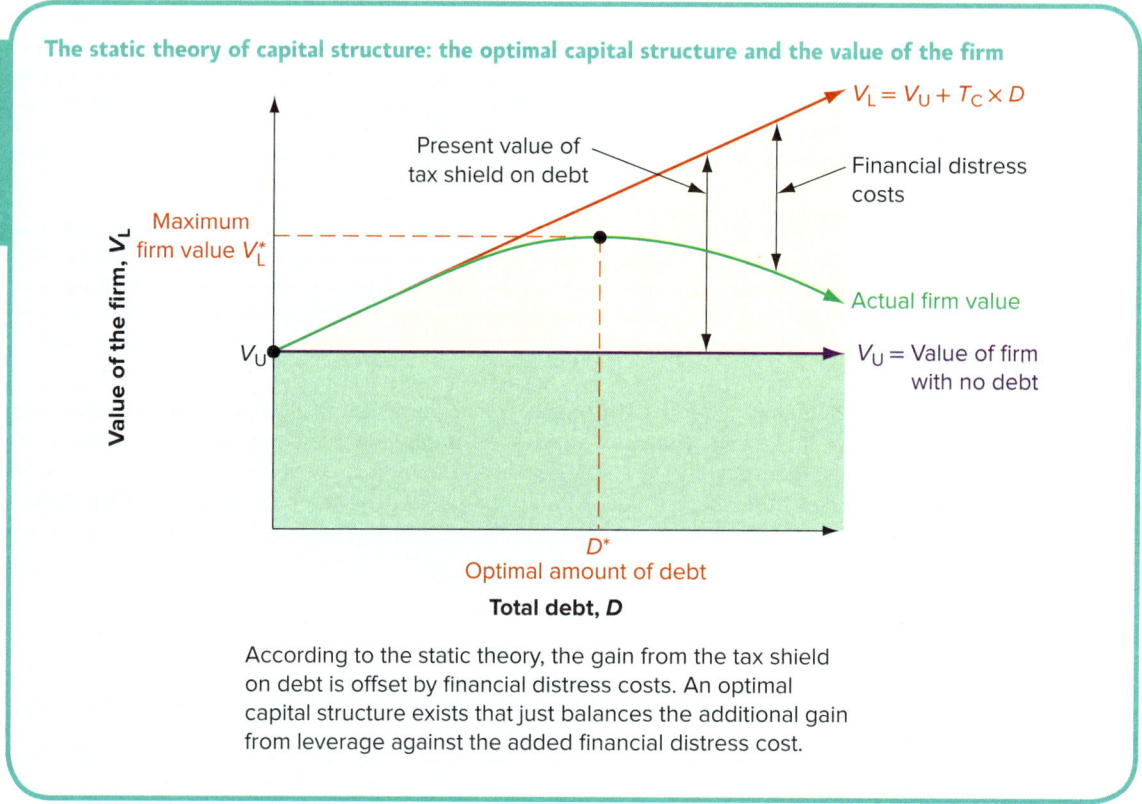

FIGURE 15.6

The static theory of capital structure: the optimal capital structure and the value of the firm

According to the static theory, the gain from the tax shield on debt is offset by financial distress costs. An optimal capital structure exists that just balances the additional gain from leverage against the added financial distress cost.

The third case in Figure 15.6 illustrates our current discussion: the value of the firm rises to a maximum and then declines beyond that point. This is the picture that we get from our static theory. The maximum value of the firm, V^*_L is reached at D^*, so this point represents the optimal amount of borrowing. Put another way, the firm's optimal capital structure is composed of D^*/V^*_L in debt and $1 - D^*/V^*_L$ in equity.

The final thing to notice in Figure 15.6 is that the difference between the value of the firm in our static theory and the M&M value of the firm with taxes is the loss in value from the possibility of financial distress. Also, the difference between the static theory value of the firm and the M&M value with no taxes is the gain from leverage, net of distress costs.

OPTIMAL CAPITAL STRUCTURE AND THE COST OF CAPITAL

As we discussed earlier, the capital structure that maximizes the value of the firm is also the one that minimizes the cost of capital. Figure 15.7 illustrates the static theory of capital structure in terms of the weighted average cost of capital and the costs of debt and equity. Notice in Figure 15.7 that we have plotted the various capital costs against the debt–equity ratio, D/E.

Figure 15.7 is much the same as Figure 15.5 except that we have added a new line for the WACC. This line, which corresponds to the static theory, declines at first. This occurs because the after-tax cost of debt is cheaper than equity, so, at least initially, the overall cost of capital declines.

FIGURE 15.7

The static theory of capital structure: the optimal capital structure and the cost of capital

According to the static theory the WACC falls initially, because of the tax advantage of debt. Beyond the point D^*/E^* it begins to rise, because of financial distress costs.

At some point, the cost of debt begins to rise, and the fact that debt is cheaper than equity is more than offset by the financial distress costs. From this point, further increases in debt actually increase the WACC. As illustrated, the minimum WACC* occurs at point D^*/E^*, just as we described before.

OPTIMAL CAPITAL STRUCTURE: A RECAP

With the help of Figure 15.8, we can review our discussion of capital structure and cost of capital. As we have noted, there are essentially three cases. We shall use the simplest of the three cases as a starting point, and then build up to the static theory of capital structure. Along the way, we shall pay particular attention to the connection between capital structure, firm value and cost of capital.

Figure 15.8 presents the original M&M no-tax, no-bankruptcy argument as Case I. This is the most basic case. In the top part of the figure we have plotted the value of the firm, V_L, against total debt, D. When there are no taxes, bankruptcy costs or other real-world imperfections, we know that the total value of the firm is not affected by its debt policy, so V_L is simply constant. The bottom part of Figure 15.8 tells the same story in terms of the cost of capital. Here the weighted average cost of capital, WACC, is plotted against the debt–equity ratio, D/E. As with total firm value, the overall cost of capital is not affected by debt policy in this basic case, so the WACC is constant.

Next, we consider what happens to the original M&M argument once taxes are introduced. As Case II illustrates, we now see that the firm's value critically depends on its debt policy. The more the firm borrows, the more it is worth. From our earlier discussion, we know this happens because interest payments are tax-deductible, and the gain in firm value is just equal to the present value of the interest tax shield.

In the bottom part of Figure 15.8 notice how the WACC declines as the firm uses more and more debt financing. As the firm increases its financial leverage, the cost of equity does increase; but this increase is more than offset by the tax break associated with debt financing. As a result, the firm's overall cost of capital declines.

FIGURE 15.8 The capital structure question

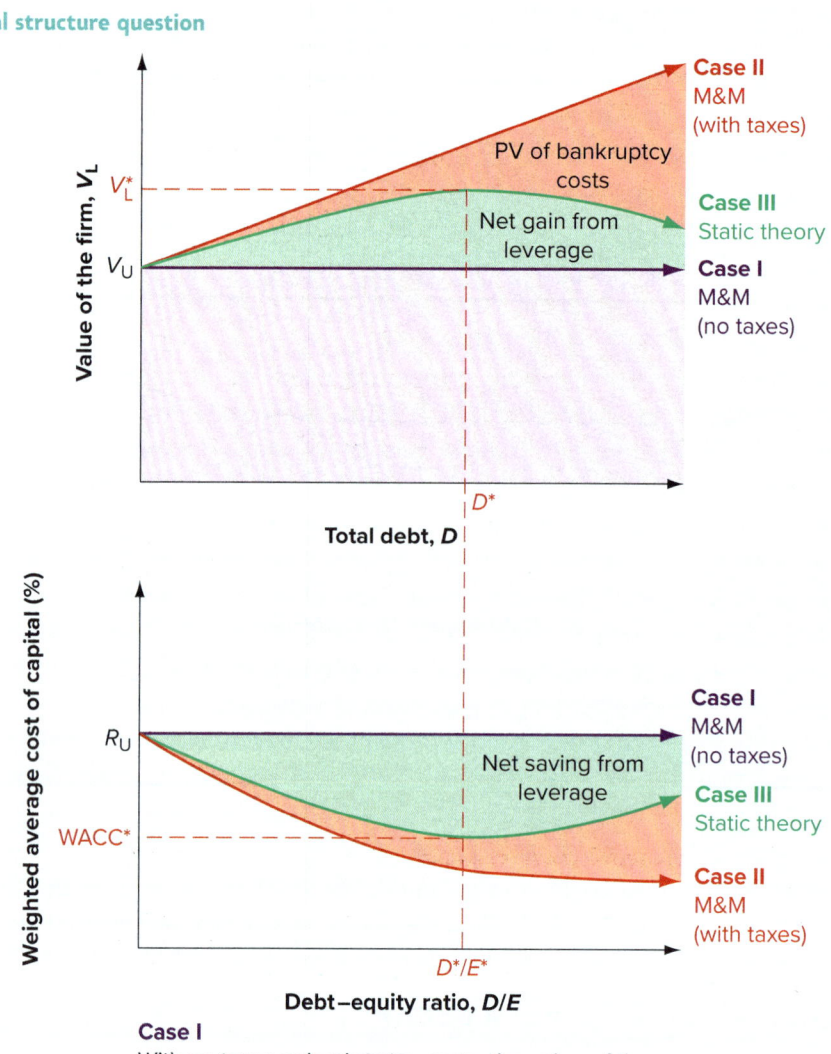

Case I
With no taxes or bankruptcy costs, the value of the firm and its weighted average cost of capital are not affected by capital structures.

Case II
With corporate taxes and no bankruptcy costs, the value of the firm increases and the weighted average costs of capital decreases as the amount of debt goes up.

Case III
With corporate taxes and bankruptcy costs, the value of the firm, V_L, reaches a maximum at D^*, the point representing the optimal amount of borrowing. At the same time the weighted average cost of capital, WACC, is minimized at D^*/E^*.

To finish our story, we include the impact of bankruptcy or financial distress costs to get Case III. As shown in the top part of Figure 15.8, the value of the firm will not be as large as we previously indicated. The reason is that the firm's value is reduced by the present value of the potential future bankruptcy costs. These costs grow as the firm borrows more and more, and they eventually overwhelm the tax advantage of debt financing. The optimal capital structure occurs at D^*, the point at which the tax saving from an additional pound or euro in debt financing is exactly balanced by the increased bankruptcy costs associated with the additional borrowing. This is the essence of the static theory of capital structure.

The bottom part of Figure 15.8 presents the optimal capital structure in terms of the cost of capital. Corresponding to D^*, the optimal debt level, is the optimal debt–equity ratio, D^*/E^*. At this level of debt financing the lowest possible weighted average cost of capital, WACC*, occurs.

CAPITAL STRUCTURE: SOME MANAGERIAL RECOMMENDATIONS

The static model that we have described is not capable of identifying a precise optimal capital structure, but it does point out two of the more relevant factors: taxes and financial distress. We can draw some limited conclusions concerning these.

Taxes

First, the tax benefit from leverage is obviously important only to firms that are in a tax-paying position. Firms with substantial accumulated losses will get little value from the interest tax shield. Furthermore, firms that have substantial tax shields from other sources, such as depreciation, will get less benefit from leverage.

Also, not all firms have the same tax rate. The higher the tax rate, the greater the incentive to borrow.

Financial Distress

Firms with a greater risk of experiencing financial distress will borrow less than firms with a lower risk of financial distress. For example, all other things being equal, the greater the volatility in EBIT, the less a firm should borrow.

In addition, financial distress is more costly for some firms than for others. The costs of financial distress depend primarily on the firm's assets. In particular, financial distress costs will be determined by how easily ownership of those assets can be transferred.

For example, a firm with mostly tangible assets that can be sold without great loss in value will have an incentive to borrow more. For firms that rely heavily on intangibles, such as employee talent or growth opportunities, debt will be less attractive, because these assets effectively cannot be sold.

> **CONCEPT QUESTIONS**
>
> **15.6a** Can you describe the trade-off that defines the static theory of capital structure?
> **15.6b** What are the important factors in making capital structure decisions?

15.7 THE PIE AGAIN

Although it is comforting to know that the firm might have an optimal capital structure when we take account of such real-world matters as taxes and financial distress costs, it is disquieting to see the elegant original M&M intuition (that is, the no-tax version) fall apart in the face of these matters.

Critics of the M&M theory often say that it fails to hold as soon as we add in real-world issues and that the M&M theory is really just that: a theory that doesn't have much to say about the real world that we live in. In fact, they would argue that it is the M&M theory that is irrelevant, not capital structure. As we discuss next, however, taking that view blinds critics to the real value of the M&M theory.

THE EXTENDED PIE MODEL

To illustrate the value of the original M&M intuition, we briefly consider an expanded version of the pie model that we introduced earlier. In the extended pie model taxes just represent another claim on the cash flows of the firm. Because taxes are reduced as leverage is increased, the value of the government's claim (G) on the firm's cash flows decreases with leverage.

Bankruptcy costs are also a claim on the cash flows. They come into play as the firm comes close to bankruptcy and has to alter its behaviour to attempt to stave off the event itself, and they become large when bankruptcy actually takes place. Thus the value of this claim (B) on the cash flows rises with the debt–equity ratio.

The extended pie theory simply holds that all these claims can be paid from only one source: the cash flows (CF) of the firm. Algebraically, we must have:

CF = Payments to shareholders + Payments to creditors
   + Payments to the government
   + Payments to bankruptcy courts and lawyers
   + Payments to any and all other claimants to the cash flows of the firm

The extended pie model is illustrated in Figure 15.9. Notice that we have added a few slices for the additional groups. Notice also the change in the relative sizes of the slices as the firm's use of debt financing is increased.

FIGURE 15.9

The extended pie model

Lower financial leverage — Bondholder claim, Shareholder claim, Bankruptcy claim, Tax claim

Higher financial leverage — Bondholder claim, Shareholder claim, Bankruptcy claim, Tax claim

In the extended pie model the value of all the claims against the firm's cash flows is not affected by capital structure, but the *relative* values of claims change as the amount of debt financing is increased.

With the list we have developed, we have not even begun to exhaust the potential claims on the firm's cash flows. To give an unusual example, we might say that everyone reading this book has an economic claim on the cash flows of Mercedes-Benz. After all, if you are injured in an accident, you might sue Mercedes-Benz, and, win or lose, Mercedes-Benz will expend some of its cash flow in dealing with the matter. For Mercedes-Benz or any other company, there should thus be a slice of the pie representing potential lawsuits. This is the essence of the M&M intuition and theory: the value of the firm depends on the total cash flow of the firm. The firm's capital structure just cuts that cash flow up into slices without altering the total. What we recognize now is that the shareholders and the bondholders may not be the only ones who can claim a slice.

MARKETED CLAIMS VERSUS NON-MARKETED CLAIMS

With our extended pie model, there is an important distinction between claims such as those of shareholders and bondholders, on the one hand, and those of the government and potential litigants in lawsuits on the other. The first set of claims is *marketed claims,* and the second set is *non-marketed claims.* A key difference is that the marketed claims can be bought and sold in financial markets, but the non-marketed claims cannot.

When we speak of the value of the firm, we are generally referring to just the value of the marketed claims, V_M, and not the value of the non-marketed claims, V_N. If we write V_T for the total value of *all* the claims against a corporation's cash flows, then:

$$V_T = E + D + G + B + \ldots$$
$$= V_M + V_N$$

The essence of our extended pie model is that this total value, V_T, of all the claims to the firm's cash flows is unaltered by capital structure. However, the value of the marketed claims, V_M, may be affected by changes in the capital structure.

Based on the pie theory, any increase in V_M must imply an identical decrease in V_N. The optimal capital structure is thus the one that maximizes the value of the marketed claims or, equivalently, minimizes the value of non-marketed claims such as taxes and bankruptcy costs.

CONCEPT QUESTIONS

15.7a What are some of the claims on a firm's cash flows?
15.7b What is the difference between a marketed claim and a non-marketed claim?
15.7c What does the extended pie model say about the value of all the claims on a firm's cash flows?

15.8 SIGNALLING

The previous section pointed out that the corporate leverage decision involves a trade-off between a tax subsidy and financial distress costs. This idea was graphed in Figure 15.8, where the marginal tax subsidy of debt exceeds the distress costs of debt for low levels of debt. The reverse holds for high levels of debt. The firm's capital structure is optimized where the marginal subsidy to debt equals the marginal cost.

Let's explore this idea a little more. What is the relationship between a company's profitability and its debt level? A firm with low anticipated profits will probably take on a low level of debt. A small interest deduction is all that is needed to offset all of this firm's pre-tax profits. And too much debt would raise the firm's expected distress costs. A more successful firm would probably take on more debt. This firm could use the extra interest to reduce the taxes from its greater earnings. Being more financially secure, this firm would find its extra debt increases the risk of bankruptcy only slightly. In other words, rational firms raise debt levels (and the concomitant interest payments) when profits are expected to increase.

How do investors react to an increase in debt? Rational investors are likely to infer a higher firm value from a higher debt level. Thus these investors are likely to bid up a firm's share price after the firm has, say, issued debt in order to buy back equity. We say that investors view debt as a signal of firm value.

Now we get to the incentives of managers to fool the public. Consider a firm whose level of debt is optimal. That is, the marginal tax benefit of debt exactly equals the marginal distress costs of debt. However, imagine that the firm's manager desires to increase the firm's current share price, perhaps because he knows that many of his shareholders want to sell their equity soon. This manager might want to increase the level of debt just to make investors think that the firm is more valuable than it really is. If the strategy works, investors will push up the price of the shares.

This implies that firms can fool investors by taking on some additional leverage. Now let's ask the big question. Are there benefits to extra debt but no costs, implying that all firms will take on as much debt as possible? The answer, fortunately, is that there are costs as well. Imagine that a firm has issued extra debt just to fool the public. At some point, the market will learn that the company is not that valuable after all. At this time the share price should actually fall below what it would have been had the debt never been increased. Why? Because the firm's debt level is now above the optimal level. That is, the marginal tax benefit of debt is below the marginal cost of debt. Thus, if the current shareholders plan to sell, say, half of their shares now and retain the other half, an increase in debt will help them on immediate sales but probably hurt them on later ones.

Now here is the important point: we said that in a world where managers do not attempt to fool investors, valuable firms issue more debt than less valuable ones. It turns out that even when managers attempt to fool investors, the more valuable firms will still want to issue more debt than the less valuable firms. That is, while all firms will increase debt levels somewhat to fool investors, the costs of extra debt prevent the less valuable firms from issuing more debt than the more valuable firms issue. Thus investors can still treat the debt level as a signal of firm value. In other words, investors can still view an announcement of debt as a positive sign for the firm.

The foregoing is a simplified example of debt signalling, and you might argue that it is too simplified. For example, perhaps the shareholders of some firms want to sell most of their equity immediately, whereas the shareholders of other firms want to sell only a little of theirs now. It is impossible to tell here whether the firms with the most debt are the most valuable, or merely the ones with the most impatient shareholders. Because other objections can be brought up as well, signalling theory is best validated by empirical evidence. Fortunately, empirical evidence tends to support the theory.

CONCEPT QUESTIONS

15.8a What is meant by signalling?
15.8b Why would managers wish to fool investors if, by doing so, they run the risk of getting discovered?

15.9 THE PECKING-ORDER THEORY

The static theory we have developed in this chapter has dominated thinking about capital structure for a long time, but it has some shortcomings. Perhaps the most obvious is that many large, financially sophisticated, and highly profitable firms use little debt. This is the opposite of what we would expect. Under the static theory, these are the firms that should use the *most* debt, because there is little risk of bankruptcy and the value of the tax shield is substantial. Why do they use so little debt? The pecking-order theory, which we consider next, may be part of the answer.

INTERNAL FINANCING AND THE PECKING ORDER

The pecking-order theory is an alternative to the static theory. A key element in the pecking-order theory is that firms prefer to use internal financing whenever possible. A simple reason is that selling securities to raise cash can be expensive, so it makes sense to avoid doing so if possible. If a firm is very profitable, it might never need external financing: so it would end up with little or no debt. For example, in 2020, Alphabet Inc's (the trading name for the Google group of companies) balance sheet showed assets of $275 billion, of which $120 billion was classified as either cash or marketable securities. In fact, Alphabet held so much of its assets in the form of securities that, at one point, it was in danger of being regulated as a mutual fund!

There is a more subtle reason why companies may prefer internal financing. Suppose you are the manager of a firm, and you need to raise external capital to fund a new venture. As an insider, you are privy to a lot of information that isn't known to the public. Based on your knowledge, the firm's future prospects are considerably brighter than outside investors realize. As a result, you think your equity is currently undervalued. Should you issue debt or equity to finance the new venture?

If you think about it, you definitely don't want to issue equity in this case. The reason is that your equity is undervalued, and you don't want to sell it too cheaply. So you issue debt instead.

Would you ever want to issue equity? Suppose you thought your firm's equity was overvalued. It makes sense to raise money at inflated prices, but a problem crops up. If you try to sell equity, investors will realize that the shares are probably overvalued, and your equity price will take a hit. In other words, if you try to raise money by selling equity, you run the risk of signalling to investors that the price is too high. In fact, in the real world, companies rarely sell new equity, and the market reacts negatively to such sales when they occur.

So we have a pecking order. Companies will use internal financing first. Then they will issue debt if necessary. Equity will be sold pretty much as a last resort.

IMPLICATIONS OF THE PECKING ORDER

The pecking-order theory has several significant implications, a couple of which are at odds with our static trade-off theory:

1. *No target capital structure:* Under the pecking-order theory there is no target or optimal debt–equity ratio. Instead, a firm's capital structure is determined by its need for external financing, which dictates the amount of debt the firm will have.
2. *Profitable firms use less debt:* Because profitable firms have greater internal cash flow, they will need less external financing, and will therefore have less debt. As we mentioned earlier, this is a pattern that we seem to observe, at least for some companies.
3. *Companies will want financial slack:* To avoid selling new equity, companies will want to stockpile internally generated cash. Such a cash reserve is known as *financial slack*. It gives management the ability to finance projects as they appear and to move quickly if necessary.

Which theory, static trade-off or pecking order, is correct? Financial researchers have not reached a definitive conclusion on this issue, but we can make a few observations. The trade-off theory speaks more to long-run financial goals or strategies. The issues of tax shields and financial distress costs are plainly important in that context. The pecking-order theory is concerned more with the shorter-run, tactical issue of raising external funds to finance investments. So both theories are useful ways of understanding corporate use of debt. For example, it is probably the case that firms have long-run, target capital structures, but it is also probably true that they will deviate from those long-run targets as needed to avoid issuing new equity.

> **CONCEPT QUESTIONS**
>
> **15.9a** Under the pecking-order theory, what is the order in which firms will obtain financing?
> **15.9b** Why might firms prefer not to issue new equity?
> **15.9c** What are some differences in implications of the static and pecking-order theories?

15.10 OBSERVED CAPITAL STRUCTURES

No two firms have identical capital structures. Nonetheless, we see some regular elements when we start looking at actual capital structures. We discuss a few of these next.

The most striking thing we observe about European capital structures is that they are so varied across countries. Most corporations use much less debt financing than equity financing. To illustrate, Figure 15.10 shows the debt-to-equity ratios of firms in different countries in recent years.

There are also significant inter-industry differences in debt ratios that persist over time. As can be seen in Table 15.7, debt–asset ratios tend to be quite low in high-growth industries, such as the healthcare and technology industries, with ample future investment opportunities. This is true even when the need for external financing is great. Industries with large investments in tangible assets, such as real estate, tend to have high leverage. Consistent with Figure 15.10, there are also differences in average industry capital structures across countries.

Table 15.7 makes it clear that corporations have not, in general, issued debt up to the point where tax shelters have been completely used up, and we conclude that there must be limits to the amount of debt corporations can use.

FIGURE 15.10

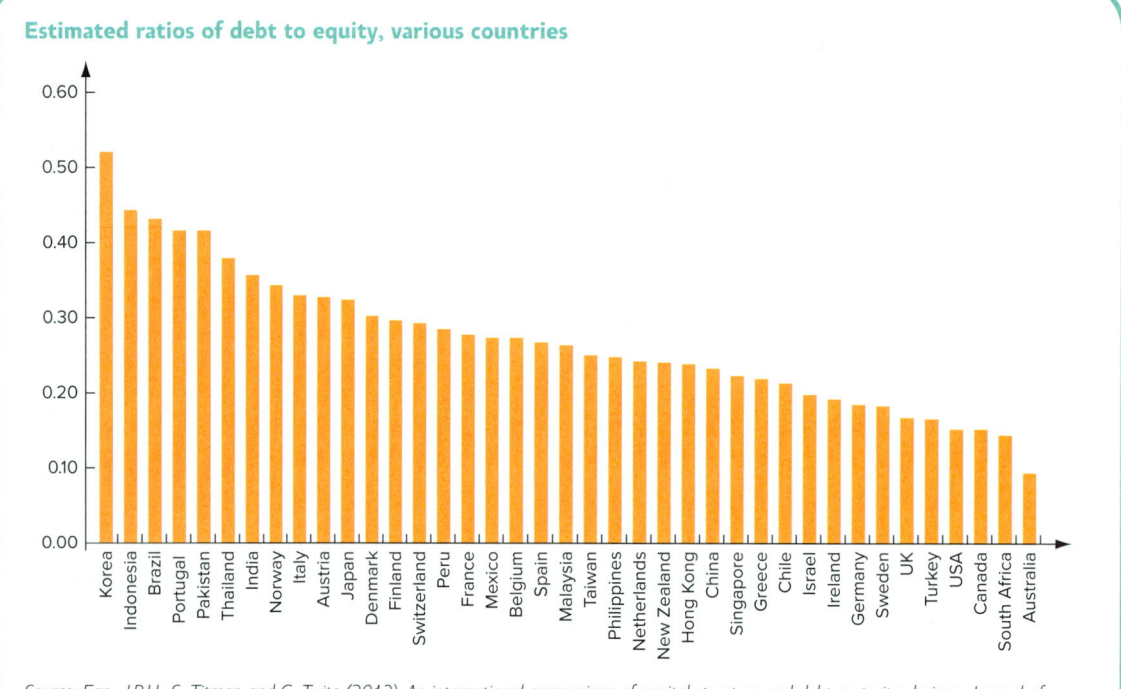

Estimated ratios of debt to equity, various countries

Source: Fan, J.P.H., S. Titman and G. Twite (2012). An international comparison of capital structure and debt maturity choices. *Journal of Financial and Quantitative Analysis*, 47(1), 23-56.

TABLE 15.7

European industry debt ratios

Debt Ratio	From 0 to 10% (%)	From 10 to 50% (%)	From 50 to 70% (%)	From 70 to 100% (%)	More than 100% (%)	Number of Companies
Basic Materials	39.27	24.77	12.99	10.57	12.39	331
Consumer Goods	24.42	31.16	12	14.53	17.89	475
Consumer Services	31.34	25.35	8.27	8.98	26.06	568
Financials	41.99	19.52	5.43	5.62	27.44	1086
Health Care	47.92	28.82	5.21	6.6	11.46	288
Industrials	24.28	32.13	11.56	10.39	21.63	943
Oil & Gas	45.59	25.49	9.31	5.88	13.73	204
Technology	47.22	32.74	8.91	2.9	8.24	449
Telecommunications	35.94	21.88	3.13	15.63	23.44	64
Utilities	15.84	14.85	7.92	11.88	49.5	101
n/a	25	25	0	0	50	4
Total	1592	1201	399	380	941	4513

Note: Debt ratio is defined as (1 - Shareholder funds) / Total assets. All firms are from the European Union. Countries included in the sample are Austria, Belgium, Croatia, Denmark, Finland, France, Germany, Greece, Hungary, Ireland, Italy, Lithuania, Luxembourg, Malta, Netherlands, Poland, Portugal, Spain, Sweden, UK.

Source: Datastream.

Because different industries have different operating characteristics in terms of, for example, EBIT volatility and asset types, there does appear to be some connection between these characteristics and capital structure. Our story involving tax savings, financial distress costs and potential pecking orders undoubtedly supplies part of the reason, but to date, there is no fully satisfactory theory that explains these regularities in capital structures.

Research has shown (Brounen, de Jong and Koedjik, 2006*) that the majority of European firms across countries have a target debt–equity ratio, though the strictness of the targets varies across companies. A notable exception to this is in France, where most firms do not pursue a target debt ratio. Even in the UK, nearly half of all firms do not consider a target debt ratio to be important.

> **CONCEPT QUESTIONS**
>
> **15.10a** Do European corporations rely heavily on debt financing?
> **15.10b** What regularities do we observe in capital structures?

15.11 A QUICK LOOK AT THE BANKRUPTCY PROCESS

As we have discussed, one consequence of using debt is the possibility of financial distress, which can be defined in several ways:

1. *Business failure:* This term is usually used to refer to a situation in which a business has terminated with a loss to creditors; but even an all-equity firm can fail.
2. *Legal bankruptcy:* Firms or creditors bring petitions to a court for bankruptcy. **Bankruptcy** is a legal proceeding for liquidating or reorganizing a business.
3. *Technical insolvency:* Technical insolvency occurs when a firm is unable to meet its financial obligations.
4. *Accounting insolvency:* Firms with negative net worth are insolvent on the books. This happens when the total book liabilities exceed the book value of the total assets.

> **bankruptcy**
> a legal proceeding for liquidating or reorganizing a business.

We now very briefly discuss some of the terms and more relevant issues associated with bankruptcy and financial distress.

LIQUIDATION AND REORGANIZATION

Firms that cannot or choose not to make contractually required payments to creditors have two basic options: liquidation or reorganization. **Liquidation** means termination of the firm as a going concern, and it involves selling off the assets of the firm. The proceeds, net of selling costs, are distributed to creditors in order of established priority. **Reorganization** is the option of keeping the firm a going concern; it often involves issuing new securities to replace old securities. Liquidation or reorganization is the result of a bankruptcy proceeding. Which occurs depends on whether the firm is worth more 'dead or alive'.

> **liquidation**
> termination of the firm as a going concern.

> **reorganization**
> financial restructuring of a failing firm to attempt to continue operations as a going concern.

BANKRUPTCY LAW

Bankruptcy law across the world is converging to a similar process. However, there are important country-level differences. The European Union introduced its bankruptcy regulation in 2002, 'Regulation on Insolvency Proceedings', which has been adopted by all EU countries, with the exception of Denmark. This was updated in 2015 to

---

*Brounen, D., De Jong, A., & Koedijk, K. (2006). Capital structure policies in Europe: Survey evidence. *Journal of Banking & Finance*, 30(5), 1409–1442.

accommodate new thinking on financial distress and recovery. As European bankruptcy law is very similar, the regulations facing British bankruptcy will be discussed in detail, followed by an overview of the salient differences in other countries.

Financially distressed firms in the UK can be voluntarily or compulsorily dissolved or liquidated. Liquidation means that the firm's assets are sold to allow payment of the outstanding liabilities of the firm. However, this is the very last and least desirable option, and it will be considered only when all other strategies have been exhausted. An alternative is to appoint an administrator, who will attempt to restructure the firm's outstanding claims, introduce a viable business model, or look for a potential buyer. It is important to note that when a firm is in administration, it will continue business until a solution (which may be liquidation) is found.

Liquidation

For a firm to be liquidated or made insolvent, a creditor, the directors or shareholders must petition a court for a winding-up order. If a judge decides that there is a case for liquidation, an official receiver will be appointed who liquidates the assets of the firm and distributes the proceeds to all creditors. Normally, creditors will not be paid all that they are due, because of direct bankruptcy costs from legal and administration fees.

Priority of Claims

Once a corporation is determined to be bankrupt, liquidation takes place. The distribution of the proceeds of the liquidation occurs according to the following general priority:

1. Administration expenses associated with liquidating the bankrupt's assets
2. Unsecured claims arising after the filing of an involuntary bankruptcy petition
3. Wages, salaries and commissions
4. Contributions to employee benefit plans arising within a set period before the filing date
5. Consumer claims
6. Tax claims
7. Secured and unsecured creditors' claims
8. Preference shareholder claims
9. Ordinary shareholder claims

absolute priority rule (APR)
the order of creditor claims distribution in the event of a liquidation.

The priority rule in liquidation is known as the **absolute priority rule (APR)**.

One qualification to this list concerns secured creditors. Liens on property are outside APR ordering. However, if the secured property is liquidated, and provides cash insufficient to cover the amount owed them, the secured creditors join with unsecured creditors in dividing the remaining liquidating value. In contrast, if the secured property is liquidated for proceeds greater than the secured claim, the net proceeds are used to pay unsecured creditors and others.

Administration

When a company enters administration, the administrator will attempt to restructure the company's liabilities, look for a buyer, or break up the company into viable parts. Possible strategies also include exchanging debt for equity, which allows the financially distressed firm to dispense with paying interest on the debt and at the same time gives the creditor a stake in the company should it recover.

The legal agreement that details how the firm's liabilities are to be restructured is known as a *company voluntary agreement* (CVA). If creditors reject the CVA, or the company does not submit a CVA to the court, the judge can give the corporation an extension during which it must come up with an acceptable plan or ask the creditors to come up with their own reorganization plan. In most cases, at least one extension is granted. Under UK bankruptcy law a CVA will be accepted if at least 75 per cent of the company's claim holders, including shareholders, vote in favour of it. Once accepted, the agreement is legally binding.

In Scotland, bankruptcy law is slightly more complex. In addition to administration and insolvency procedures, firms may also go into receivership. This is also a characteristic of bankruptcy law in England and Wales for firms that have outstanding securities issued before 2003. The differences between administration and receivership are important. When in administration, the financially distressed firm is legally protected from its creditors while a CVA is prepared. An insolvency practitioner, such as an accounting firm, is normally appointed to run the business while the agreement is being drawn up. A firm will go into receivership if its creditors do not believe that the company can recover and repay its liabilities. A receiver, again normally an accounting firm, will thus be appointed to sell the assets of the firm so that the creditors can be paid.

Bankruptcy in Other Countries

Bankruptcy procedures in most countries follow the same model as that in the United Kingdom. In the United States, financially distressed firms may file for Chapter 11 bankruptcy (equivalent to administration) or for Chapter 7 bankruptcy (equivalent to liquidation). All other aspects of the system are practically the same.

Countries in the European Union follow the 2015 amended version of 'Regulation on Insolvency Proceedings'. Some country-level differences do exist, however. France has two types of bankruptcy proceedings and these were updated in 2015. The first stage involves out-of-court hearings. These are voluntary and designed to facilitate a resolution of the financial distress by working out a solution that suits the company and its major creditors. If the hearings cannot resolve the situation, a petition will be made to a commercial court to restructure the company's liabilities, organize a sale of assets or liquidate the firm.

South Africa follows a similar system to other countries, there is no administration process. Thus, creditors, shareholders or the company itself will go directly to the South African High Court to request that the firm be placed in liquidation. The process is then worked through the system, and restructuring or winding-up may be an outcome of this process.

> **CONCEPT QUESTIONS**
>
> **15.11a** What is the APR?
> **15.11b** What is the difference between liquidation and reorganization?

SUMMARY AND CONCLUSIONS

In this chapter, we considered the second key question of corporate finance: capital structure (can you remember the other two questions?) and the ideal mixture of debt and equity for a firm. We discussed a number of concepts:

1. The optimal capital structure maximizes the value of a firm and minimizes its overall cost of capital.
2. If we ignore taxes, financial distress costs and any other imperfections, we find that there is no optimal capital structure and the mixture of debt and equity is simply irrelevant.
3. If we consider the effect of corporate taxes, capital structure matters a great deal. Interest paid is tax deductible and generates a valuable tax shield. Unfortunately, we also find that the optimal capital structure is 100 per cent debt, which is not something we observe in healthy firms.
4. The costs associated with bankruptcy or, more generally, financial distress reduce the attractiveness of debt financing. We concluded that an optimal capital structure exists when the net tax saving from an additional pound or euro in interest just equals the increase in expected financial distress costs. This is the essence of the static theory of capital structure.
5. The pecking-order theory of capital structure suggests that firms will use internal financing as much as possible, followed by debt financing if needed. Equity will not be issued if possible. As a result, a firm's capital structure just reflects its historical needs for external financing, so there is no optimal capital structure.
6. When we examine actual capital structures, we find two regularities. First, firms in Europe typically do not use great amounts of debt, but they pay substantial taxes. This suggests that there is a limit to the use of debt financing to generate tax shields. Second, firms in similar industries tend to have similar capital structures, suggesting that the nature of their assets and operations is an important determinant of capital structure.

CHAPTER REVIEW AND SELF-TEST PROBLEMS

15.1 EBIT and EPS Suppose Blackhead plc has decided in favour of a capital restructuring that involves increasing its existing £80 million in debt to £125 million. The interest rate on the debt is 9 per cent, and is not expected to change. The firm currently has 10 million shares outstanding, and the share price is £45. If the restructuring is expected to increase the ROE, what is the minimum level for EBIT that Blackhead's management must be expecting? Ignore taxes in your answer.

15.2 M&M Proposition II (No Taxes) Habitat has a WACC of 16 per cent. Its cost of debt is 13 per cent. If Habitat's debt–equity ratio is 2, what is its cost of equity capital? Ignore taxes in your answer.

15.3 M&M Proposition I (with Corporate Taxes) Gypco expects an EBIT of €10,000 every year for ever. Gypco can borrow at 7 per cent. Suppose Gypco currently has no debt, and its cost of equity is 17 per cent. If the corporate tax rate is 35 per cent, what is the value of the firm? What will the value be if Gypco borrows €15,000 and uses the proceeds to repurchase equity?

SOLUTIONS

15.1 To answer, we can calculate the break-even EBIT. At any EBIT above this the increased financial leverage will increase EPS. Under the old capital structure the interest bill is £80 million × 0.09 = £7,200,000. There are 10 million shares of equity: so, ignoring taxes, EPS is (EBIT − £7.2 million)/10 million.

Under the new capital structure the interest expense will be £125 million × 0.09 = £11.25 million. Furthermore, the debt rises by £45 million. This amount is sufficient to repurchase £45 million/£45 = 1 million shares of equity, leaving 9 million outstanding. EPS is thus (EBIT − £11.25 million)/9 million. Now that we know how to calculate EPS under both scenarios, we set the two calculations equal to each other and solve for the break-even EBIT:

$$(\text{EBIT} - £7.2 \text{ million})/10 \text{ million} = (\text{EBIT} - £11.25 \text{ million})/9 \text{ million}$$
$$\text{EBIT} - £7.2 \text{ million} = 1.11 \times (\text{EBIT} - £11.25 \text{ million})$$
$$\text{EBIT} = £47,700,000$$

Verify that, in either case, EPS is £4.05 when EBIT is £47.7 million.

15.2 According to M&M Proposition II (no taxes), the cost of equity is:

$$R_E = R_A + (R_A - R_D) \times (D/E)$$
$$= 16\% + (16\% - 13\%) \times 2$$
$$= 22\%$$

15.3 With no debt, Gypco's WACC is 17 per cent. This is also the unlevered cost of capital. The after-tax cash flow is €10,000 × (1 − 0.35) = €6,500, so the value is just V_U = €6,500/0.17 = €38,235. After the debt issue, Gypco will be worth the original €38,235 plus the present value of the tax shield. According to M&M Proposition I with taxes, the present value of the tax shield is $T_C \times D$, or 0.35 × €15,000 = €5,250: so the firm is worth €38,235 + 5,250 = €43,485.

QUESTIONS AND PROBLEMS

15.1 EBIT and Leverage Drum Surfing SpA has no debt outstanding, and a total market value of €600,000. Earnings before interest and taxes, EBIT, are projected to be €150,000 if economic conditions are normal. If there is a strong expansion in the economy, then EBIT will be 20 per cent higher. If there is a recession, then EBIT will be 50 per cent lower. Drum Surfing is considering a €300,000 debt issue with a 5 per cent interest rate. The proceeds will be used to repurchase shares of equity. There are currently 200,000 shares outstanding. Ignore taxes for this problem.

  (a) Calculate earnings per share, EPS, under each of the three economic scenarios before any debt is issued. Also, calculate the percentage changes in EPS when the economy expands or enters a recession.

  (b) Repeat part (a) assuming that Drum Surfing goes through with recapitalization. What do you observe?

15.2 EBIT, Taxes and Leverage Repeat parts (a) and (b) in Problem 15.1 assuming Drum Surfing has a tax rate of 20 per cent.

15.3 M&M and Equity Value Jour de Pluie SA is comparing two different capital structures, an all-equity plan (Plan I) and a levered plan (Plan II). Under Plan I, Jour de Pluie would have 100,000 shares of equity outstanding. Under Plan II, there would be 50,000 shares of equity outstanding and €1 million in debt outstanding. The interest rate on the debt is 10 per cent and there are no taxes. Use M&M Proposition I to find the share price under each of the two proposed plans. What is the value of the firm?

15.4 Break-Even EBIT and Leverage Dovey Prosthetics SA is comparing two different capital structures. Plan I would result in 2,000 shares of equity and €50,000 in debt. Plan II would result in 1,000 shares of equity and €75,000 in debt. The interest rate on the debt is 10 per cent.

  (a) Ignoring taxes, compare both of these plans with an all-equity plan assuming that EBIT will be €100,000. The all-equity plan would result in 4,000 shares of equity outstanding. Which of the three plans has the highest EPS? The lowest?

  (b) In part (a) what are the break-even levels of EBIT for each plan as compared with that for an all-equity plan? Is one higher than the other? Why?

  (c) Ignoring taxes, when will EPS be identical for Plans I and II?

  (d) Repeat parts (a), (b) and (c) assuming that the corporate tax rate is 20 per cent. Are the break-even levels of EBIT different from before? Why or why not?

15.5 Leverage and Share Value Ignoring taxes in Problem 15.4, what is the share price under Plan I? Plan II? What principle is illustrated by your answers?

15.6 M&M Nina plc uses no debt. The weighted average cost of capital is 13 per cent. If the current market value of the equity is £35 million, and there are no taxes, what is EBIT?

15.7 M&M and Taxes In the previous problem, suppose the corporate tax rate is 28 per cent. What is EBIT in this case? What is the WACC? Explain.

15.8 ROE and Leverage Dickdale & Co has no debt outstanding and a total market value of €6.5 billion. Earnings before interest and taxes, EBIT, are projected to be €1 billion if economic conditions are normal. If there is a strong expansion in the economy, then EBIT will be 20 per cent higher. If there is a recession, then EBIT will be 20 per cent lower. Dickdale is considering a €1 billion debt issue with a 5 per cent interest rate. The proceeds will be used to repurchase shares of equity. There are currently 1 billion shares outstanding. Ignore taxes for this problem. Suppose that Dickdale has a book value of €6.5 billion.

(a) Calculate the return on equity, ROE, under each of the three economic scenarios before any debt is issued. Also, calculate the percentage changes in ROE for economic expansion and recession, assuming no taxes.

(b) Repeat part (a) assuming the firm goes through with the proposed recapitalization.

(c) Repeat parts (a) and (b) of this problem assuming the firm has a tax rate of 20 per cent.

15.9 Break-Even EBIT Hammerson plc is comparing two different capital structures: an all-equity plan (Plan I) and a levered plan (Plan II). Under Plan I, Hammerson would have 712 million shares of equity outstanding. Under Plan II, there would be 475 million shares of equity outstanding and £1 billion in debt outstanding. The interest rate on the debt is 5 per cent and there are no taxes.

(a) If EBIT is £459 million, what is the EPS?

(b) If EBIT is £80 million, what is the EPS?

(c) What is the break-even EBIT?

15.10 Homemade Leverage Star plc, a prominent consumer products firm, is debating whether or not to convert its all-equity capital structure to one that is 40 per cent debt. Currently, there are 2,000 shares outstanding, and the share price is £70. EBIT is expected to remain at £16,000 per year forever. The interest rate on new debt is 8 per cent, and there are no taxes. Assume that the firm has a dividend payout rate of 100 per cent.

(a) Ms Brown, a shareholder of the firm, owns 100 shares of equity. What is her cash flow under the current capital structure?

(b) What will Ms Brown's cash flow be under the proposed capital structure of the firm? Assume that she keeps all 100 of her shares.

(c) Suppose Star does convert, but Ms Brown prefers the current all-equity capital structure. Show how she could unlever her shares to recreate the original capital structure.

(d) Using your answer to part (c), explain why Star's choice of capital structure is irrelevant.

15.11 Homemade Leverage and WACC Verpfändung AG and Zeit AG are identical firms in all respects except for their capital structure. Verpfändung is all-equity financed, with €500,000 in equity shares. Zeit AG uses both shares and perpetual debt; its equity is worth €250,000, and the interest rate on its debt is 10 per cent. Both firms expect EBIT to be €100,000. Assume that both firms maintain a dividend payout rate of 100 per cent and that the book value exactly resembles the market value for both debt and equity. Ignore taxes.

(a) Robert owns €25,000 worth of Zeit AG's shares. What rate of return is he expecting if the payout ratio is 50 per cent?

(b) What is the cost of equity for Verpfändung? What is it for Zeit?

(c) What is the WACC for Verpfändung? For Zeit? What principle have you illustrated?

15.12 Calculating WACC Renewable Tripping has a debt–equity ratio of 1. Its WACC is 5 per cent, and its cost of debt is 2 per cent. The corporate tax rate is 18 per cent.

(a) What is Renewable Tripping's cost of equity capital?

(b) What is Renewable Tripping's unlevered cost of equity capital?

(c) What would the cost of equity be if the debt–equity ratio were 2? What if it were zero?

15.13 Calculating WACC Shadow plc has no debt, but can borrow at 8 per cent. The firm's WACC is currently 12 per cent, and the tax rate is 28 per cent.

(a) What is Shadow's cost of equity?

(b) If the firm converts to 25 per cent debt, what will its cost of equity be?

(c) If the firm converts to 50 per cent debt, what will its cost of equity be?

(d) What is Shadow's WACC in part (b)? In part (c)?

15.14 M&M and Taxes Bruce & Co. expects its EBIT to be £100,000 every year forever. The firm can borrow at 10 per cent. Bruce currently has no debt, and its cost of equity is 20 per cent. The tax rate is 21 per cent. What is the value of the firm? What will the value be if Bruce borrows £80,000 and uses the proceeds to repurchase shares?

15.15 M&M and Taxes For the company in Problem 15.14, what is the cost of equity after recapitalization? What is the WACC? What are the implications for the firm's capital structure decision?

15.16 M&M Tool Manufacturing has an expected EBIT of £35,000 in perpetuity and a tax rate of 28 per cent. The firm has £70,000 in outstanding debt at an interest rate of 9 per cent, and its unlevered cost of capital is 14 per cent. What is the value of the firm according to M&M Proposition I with taxes? Should Tool change its debt–equity ratio if the goal is to maximize the value of the firm? Explain.

15.17 Firm Value Old School Corporation expects an EBIT of £9,000 every year forever. Old School currently has no debt, and its cost of equity is 17 per cent. The firm can borrow at 10 per cent. If the corporate tax rate is 28 per cent, what is the value of the firm? What will the value be if Old School converts to 50 per cent debt? To 100 per cent debt?

15.18 Homemade Leverage The Veblen Company and the Knight Company are identical in every respect except that Veblen is not levered. The market value of Knight Company's 6 per cent bonds is SKr1 million. Financial information for the two firms appears here. All earnings streams are perpetuities. Neither firm pays taxes. Both firms distribute all earnings available to ordinary shareholders immediately.

	Veblen	Knight
Projected operating income (SKr)	300,000	300,000
Year-end interest on debt (SKr)	–	60,000
Market value of stock (SKr)	2,400,000	1,714,000
Market value of debt (SKr)	–	1,000,000

(a) An investor who can borrow at 6 per cent per year wishes to purchase 5 per cent of Knight's equity. Can they increase their kronor return by purchasing 5 per cent of Veblen's equity if they borrow so that the initial net costs of the two strategies are the same?

(b) Given the two investment strategies in (a), which will investors choose? When will this process cease?

15.19 Weighted Average Cost of Capital In a world of corporate taxes only, show that the WACC can be written as $WACC = R_U \times [1 - T_c(D/V)]$.

15.20 Cost of Equity and Leverage Assuming a world of corporate taxes only, show that the cost of equity, R_E, is as given in the chapter by M&M Proposition II with corporate taxes.

15.21 Business and Financial Risk Assume a firm's debt is risk-free so that the cost of debt equals the risk-free rate, R_f. Define β_A as the firm's *asset* beta – that is, the systematic risk of the firm's assets. Define β_E to be the beta of the firm's equity. Use the capital asset pricing model (CAPM) along with M&M Proposition II to show that $\beta_E = \beta_A \times (1 + D/E)$, where D/E is the debt–equity ratio. Assume the tax rate is zero.

15.22 Shareholder Risk Suppose a firm's business operations are such that they mirror movements in the economy as a whole very closely: that is, the firm's asset beta is 1.0. Use the result of Problem 15.21 to find the equity beta for this firm for debt–equity ratios of 0, 1, 5 and 20. What does this tell you about the relationship between capital structure and shareholder risk? How is the shareholders' required return on equity affected? Explain.

MINI CASE

SUSTAINABLE LAKES' RECAPITALIZATION

Sustainable Lakes was founded 10 years ago to ensure recyclable safe water systems are in place in countries lacking clean water infrastructure. The company has only recently started making a profit after 9 years of loss-making activity. The company's management are dedicated professionals and Sustainable Lakes' shareholders have supported the company since inception as it developed its operations. In the past, the management of Sustainable Lakes has found it difficult to raise debt financing because of the nature of its business and, as a result, the company is entirely equity-financed, with 15 million shares outstanding. The shares currently trade at £32.50 per share.

The majority of Sustainable Lakes' operations are in sub-Saharan Africa and the company has just been awarded a large contract in Tanzania to provide clean water in the Morogoro region. The Sustainable Lakes' business model is to enter into a long-term contract with a region or country's authorities, invest upfront in recycling facilities and provide sustainable water recycling services in the longer term. Set-up costs are estimated to be £100 million and the new contract is expected to increase pre-tax earnings by £25 million in perpetuity.

You have been put in charge of the project and have determined that Sustainable Lakes' current cost of capital is 12.5 per cent. You believe the company would be more valuable if it was able to borrow and have debt in its capital structure. A possible option is to issue debt to finance the project entirely. Based on some conversations with investment banks, you think Sustainable Lakes can issue bonds at par value with an 8 per cent coupon rate. You also believe that a capital structure in the range of 70 per cent equity/30 per cent debt would be optimal. If the company goes beyond 30 per cent debt, its bonds would carry a lower rating and a much higher coupon, because the possibility of financial distress and the associated costs would rise sharply. Sustainable Lakes has a 28 per cent corporate tax rate.

QUESTIONS

1. If Sustainable Lakes wishes to maximize its total market value, would you recommend that it issue debt or equity to finance the land purchase? Explain.
2. Construct Sustainable Lake's market value balance sheet before it announces the contract.
3. Suppose Sustainable Lakes decides to issue equity to finance the purchase.
   (a) What is the net present value of the project?
   (b) Construct Sustainable Lakes' market value balance sheet after it announces that the firm will finance the contract using equity. What would be the new price per share of the firm's equity? How many shares will Sustainable Lakes need to issue to finance the purchase?
   (c) Construct Sustainable Lakes' market value balance sheet after the equity issue but before the initial investment has been made. How many shares of equity does Sustainable Lakes have outstanding? What is the price per share of the firm's equity?
   (d) Construct Sustainable Lakes' market value balance sheet after the initial investment has been made.
4. Suppose Sustainable Lakes decides to issue debt to finance the contract.
   (a) What will the market value of Sustainable Lakes be if the initial investment is financed with debt?
   (b) Construct Sustainable Lakes' market value balance sheet after both the debt issue and the initial investment. What is the price per share of the firm's equity?
5. Which method of financing maximizes the per-share price of Sustainable Lakes' equity?

ADDITIONAL READING

If you wish to delve deeper into the theory of capital structure and how it affects corporate strategy, you should read:

1. Hillier, D., Grinblatt, M., & Titman, S. (2012). *Financial markets and corporate strategy: European edition*, 2nd edn. McGraw-Hill.

An excellent paper that looks at the determinants of capital structure in a number of different countries is:

2. Antoniou, A., Guney, Y., & Paudyal, K. (2008). The determinants of capital structure: Capital market-oriented versus bank-oriented institutions. *Journal of Financial and Quantitative Analysis, 43,*(1), 59–92.

Another paper of interest is:

3. De Jong, A., Kabir, R., & Nguyen, T.T. (2008). Capital structure around the world: The roles of firm- and country-specific determinants. *Journal of Banking and Finance, 32*(9), 1954–1969.

Endnotes

1. It is conventional to refer to decisions regarding debt and equity as *capital structure decisions*. However, the term *financial structure decisions* would be more accurate, and we use the terms interchangeably.
2. ROE is discussed in some detail in Chapter 3.

CHAPTER 16
DIVIDENDS AND PAYOUT POLICY

LEARNING OBJECTIVES
After studying this chapter, you should understand:
LO1 Dividend types, and how dividends are paid.
LO2 The issues surrounding dividend policy decisions.
LO3 The difference between cash and stock dividends.
LO4 Why share repurchases are an alternative to dividends.

KEY NOTATIONS
D   Dividend
P   Share price
r   Interest rate or discount rate

THE COVID-19 PANDEMIC disrupted the business models of most industry sectors and almost destroyed standard operating principles in others. Airlines, tourism, restaurants, and outdoor entertainment suffered most because of the physical distancing and lockdown measures imposed in almost all countries. With revenues plummeting and cash liquidity of paramount importance, many firms reduced or removed their dividend payments in 2020. However, at the same time, other companies maintained or even increased their dividends. This chapter explores the whole concept of dividends and asks the question: Are dividends and dividend policy important to shareholders? We also explore several other issues concerning dividends and their implications for corporate decision-making.

Dividend policy is an important subject in corporate finance, and dividends are a major cash outlay for many corporations. For example, before the Covid-19 pandemic in 2020, British companies paid over £110 billion in dividends in 2019, up 10.8 per cent on the previous year. At first glance, it may seem obvious that a firm would always want to give as much as possible back to its shareholders by paying dividends. It might seem equally obvious, however, that a firm could always invest the money for its shareholders instead of paying it out. The heart of the dividend policy question is just this: should the firm pay out money to its shareholders, or should it take that money and invest it for its shareholders?

In this chapter, we shall cover a variety of topics related to dividends and corporate payout policies. We first discuss the various types of cash dividend and how they are paid. We ask whether dividend policy matters, and we consider arguments in favour of both high- and low-dividend payouts. Next, we examine share repurchases, which have become an important alternative to cash dividends. We then bring together several decades of research on dividends and corporate payouts to describe the key trade-offs involved in establishing a payout policy. We conclude the chapter by discussing stock splits and stock dividends.

16.1 CASH DIVIDENDS AND DIVIDEND PAYMENT

A **dividend** usually refers to cash paid out of earnings. If payment is made from sources other than current or accumulated retained earnings, the term **distribution**, rather than *dividend*, is used. However, it is acceptable to refer to a distribution from earnings as a dividend, and a distribution from capital as a liquidating dividend. More generally, any direct payment by the corporation to the shareholders may be considered a dividend or a part of dividend policy.

Dividends come in several different forms. The basic types of cash dividend are these:

1. Regular cash dividends
2. Extra dividends
3. Special dividends
4. Liquidating dividends

Later in the chapter, we discuss dividends paid in equity instead of cash. We also consider another alternative to cash dividends: share repurchases.

> **dividend**
> a payment made out of a firm's earnings to its owners, in the form of either cash or stock.

> **distribution**
> a payment made by a firm to its owners from sources other than current or accumulated retained earnings.

CASH DIVIDENDS

The most common type of dividend is a cash dividend. Commonly, public companies pay **regular cash dividends** two or four times a year. As the name suggests, these are cash payments made directly to shareholders, and they are made in the regular course of business. In other words, management sees nothing unusual about the dividend, and no reason why it won't be continued.

Sometimes firms will pay a regular cash dividend and an *extra cash dividend*. By calling part of the payment 'extra', management is indicating that the 'extra' part may or may not be repeated in the future. A *special dividend* is similar, but the name usually indicates that this dividend is viewed as a truly unusual or one-time event, and won't be repeated. Finally, the payment of a *liquidating dividend* usually means that some or all of the business has been liquidated – that is, sold off.

However it is labelled, a cash dividend payment reduces corporate cash and retained earnings, except in the case of a liquidating dividend (which may reduce paid-in capital).

> **regular cash dividend**
> a cash payment made by a firm to its owners in the normal course of business, usually paid four times a year.

STANDARD METHOD OF CASH DIVIDEND PAYMENT

The decision to pay a dividend rests in the hands of the board of directors of the corporation. When a dividend has been declared, it becomes a debt of the firm, and cannot easily be rescinded. Sometime after it has been declared, a dividend is distributed to all shareholders as of some specific date.

declaration date
the date on which the board of directors passes a resolution to pay a dividend.

ex-dividend date
the date two business days before the date of record, establishing those individuals entitled to a dividend.

date of record
the date by which a holder must be on record to be designated to receive a dividend.

date of payment
the date on which the dividend is paid.

Commonly, the amount of the cash dividend is expressed in terms of cash per share (*dividends per share*). As we have seen in other chapters, it is also expressed as a percentage of the market price (the *dividend yield*), or as a percentage of net income or earnings per share (the *dividend payout*).

DIVIDEND PAYMENT: A CHRONOLOGY

We illustrate the mechanics of a cash dividend payment in Figure 16.1 and the following description:

1. **Declaration date**: On 15 January the board of directors passes a resolution to pay a dividend of £1 per share on 16 February to all holders of record as of 30 January.
2. **Ex-dividend date**: To make sure that dividend payments go to the right people, brokerage firms and stock exchanges establish an ex-dividend date. This date is normally 2 business days before the date of record (discussed next). If you buy the equity before this date, you are entitled to the dividend. If you buy on this date or after, the previous owner will get the dividend.

   In Figure 16.1, Wednesday 28 January is the ex-dividend date. Before this date, the equity is said to trade 'with dividend' or 'cum dividend'. Afterwards, the equity trades 'ex-dividend'.

   The ex-dividend date convention removes any ambiguity about who is entitled to the dividend. Because the dividend is valuable, the share price will be affected when the equity goes 'ex'. We examine this effect in a moment.
3. **Date of record**: Based on its records, the corporation prepares a list on 30 January of all individuals believed to be shareholders. These are the *holders of record*, and 30 January is the date of record (or record date). The word *believed* is important here. If you buy the equity just before this date, the corporation's records may not reflect that fact, because of mailing or other delays. Without some modification, some of the dividend payments will go to the wrong people. This is the reason for the ex-dividend day convention.
4. **Date of payment**: The dividend is paid on 16 February.

FIGURE 16.1

Example of procedure for dividend payment

1 *Declaration date*: The board of directors declares a payment of dividends.
2 *Record date*: The declared dividends are distributable to shareholders of record on a specific date.
3 *Ex-dividend date*: A share of equity becomes ex-dividend on the date the seller is entitled to keep the dividend; under stock exchange rules, shares are traded ex-dividend on and after the second business day before the record date.
4 *Payment date*: The dividend cheques are mailed to shareholders of record.

MORE ABOUT THE EX-DIVIDEND DATE

The ex-dividend date is important, and a common source of confusion. We examine what happens to the equity when it goes ex, meaning that the ex-dividend date arrives. To illustrate, suppose we have an equity that sells for £10 per share. The board of directors declares a dividend of £1 per share, and the record date is set to be Tuesday 12 June. Based on our previous discussion, we know that the ex-date will be 2 business (not calendar) days earlier, on Friday 8 June.

If you buy the equity on Thursday 7 June, just as the market closes, you'll get the £1 dividend, because the equity is trading cum dividend. If you wait and buy it just as the market opens on Friday, you won't get the £1 dividend. What happens to the value of the equity overnight?

If you think about it, you will see that the equity is worth about £1 less on Friday morning, so its price will drop by this amount between the close of business on Thursday and the Friday opening. In general, we expect that the share price will go down by about the dividend amount when the equity goes ex-dividend. The keyword here is *about*. Because dividends are taxed, the actual price drop might be closer to some measure of the after-tax value of the dividend. Determining this value is complicated because of the different tax rates and tax rules that apply for different buyers.

The series of events described here is illustrated in Figure 16.2.

FIGURE 16.2

Price behaviour around the ex-dividend date for a £1 cash dividend

The share price will fall by the amount of the dividend on ex-dividend date (Time 0). If the dividend is £1 per share, the price will be £10 − 1 = £9 on the ex-dividend date:

Before ex-dividend date (Time −1), dividend = £0	Price = £10
On ex-dividend date (Time 0), dividend = £1	Price = £9

EXAMPLE 16.1

'EX' MARKS THE DAY

The board of directors of Divided Airlines has declared a dividend of €2.50 per share payable on Tuesday 30 May, to shareholders of record as of Tuesday 9 May. You buy 100 shares of Divided on Tuesday 2 May for €150 per share. What is the ex-date? Describe the events that will occur with regard to the cash dividend and the share price.

The ex-date is 2 business days before the date of record, Tuesday 9 May: so the equity will go ex on Friday 5 May. You buy the shares on Tuesday 2 May, so you purchase the equity cum dividend. In other words, you will get €2.50 × 100 = €250 in dividends. You will be paid on Tuesday 30 May. Just before the equity does go ex on Friday, its value will drop overnight by about €2.50 per share.

> **CONCEPT QUESTIONS**
>
> **16.1a** What are the different types of cash dividend?
> **16.1b** What are the mechanics of the cash dividend payment?
> **16.1c** How should the share price change when it goes ex-dividend?

16.2 DOES DIVIDEND POLICY MATTER?

To decide whether or not dividend policy matters, we first have to define what we mean by dividend *policy*. All other things being the same, of course, dividends matter. Dividends are paid in cash, and cash is something that everybody likes. The question we shall be discussing here is whether the firm should pay out cash now, or invest the cash and pay it out later. Dividend policy, therefore, is the time pattern of dividend payout. In particular, should the firm pay out a large percentage of its earnings now or a small (or even zero) percentage? This is the dividend policy question.

AN ILLUSTRATION OF THE IRRELEVANCE OF DIVIDEND POLICY

A powerful argument can be made that dividend policy does not matter. We illustrate this by considering the simple case of Bristol plc. Bristol is an all-equity firm that has existed for 10 years. The current financial managers plan to dissolve the firm in 2 years. The total cash flows the firm will generate, including the proceeds from liquidation, will be £10,000 in each of the next 2 years.

Current Policy: Dividends Set Equal to Cash Flow

At present, dividends at each date are set equal to the cash flow of £10,000. There are 100 shares outstanding, so the dividend per share is £100. In Chapter 7, we showed that the value of the equity is equal to the present value of future dividends. Assuming a 10 per cent required return, the share price today, P_0, is:

$$P_0 = \frac{D_1}{(1+R)^1} + \frac{D_2}{(1+R)^2}$$
$$= \frac{£100}{1.10} + \frac{100}{1.10^2}$$
$$= £173.55$$

The firm as a whole is thus worth $100 \times £173.55 = £17,355$.

Several members of the board of Bristol have expressed dissatisfaction with the current dividend policy, and have asked you to analyse an alternative policy.

Alternative Policy: Initial Dividend Greater than Cash Flow

Another possible policy is for the firm to pay a dividend of £110 per share on the first date (Date 1), which is, of course, a total dividend of £11,000. Because the cash flow is only £10,000, an extra £1,000 must somehow be raised. One way to do this is to issue £1,000 worth of bonds or equity at Date 1. Assume that equity is issued. The new shareholders will desire enough cash flow at Date 2 that they earn the required 10 per cent return on their Date 1 investment.[1]

What is the value of the firm with this new dividend policy? The new shareholders invest £1,000. They require a 10 per cent return, so they will demand $£1,000 \times 1.10 = £1,100$ of the Date 2 cash flow, leaving only £8,900 to the old shareholders. The dividends to the old shareholders will be as follows:

	Date 1	Date 2
Aggregate dividends to old shareholders (£)	11,000	8,900
Dividends per share (£)	110	89

The present value of the dividends per share is therefore:

$$P_0 = \frac{£110}{1.10} + \frac{89}{1.10^2} = £173.55$$

This is the same value we had before.

The value of the equity is not affected by this switch in dividend policy, even though we have to sell some new equity to finance the new dividend. In fact, no matter what pattern of dividend payout the firm chooses, the value of the equity will always be the same in this example. In other words, for Bristol plc, dividend policy makes no difference. The reason is simple: any increase in a dividend at some point in time is exactly offset by a decrease somewhere else, so the net effect, once we account for time value, is zero.

> **REAL WORLD INSIGHTS**
>
> Although dividend policy may be irrelevant, companies and investors definitely value the importance of dividends in practice. When pressed on why the pharmaceutical firm, GlaxoSmithKline (GSK), continues to invest in low margin high volume products like toothpaste and over-the-counter painkillers, the firm clearly puts the reason as ensuring the maintenance of dividend levels for investors.
>
> GSK (with a dividend yield of over 5.9 per cent) has historically high levels of dividends compared to its sector peers, such as Johnson & Johnson (2.6 per cent) and Pfizer (3.6 per cent). GSK's strategy of focusing on products like Sensodyne and Panadol has allowed the company to generate significant levels of cash, which is passed on directly to investors in the form of dividends. To GSK executives, avoiding troublesome issues like patents and heavy R&D expense has meant the firm can generate steady and predictable dividend growth in the future.

HOMEMADE DIVIDENDS

There is an alternative and perhaps more intuitively appealing explanation of why dividend policy doesn't matter in our example. Suppose individual investor X prefers dividends per share of £100 at both Dates 1 and 2. Would they be disappointed if informed that the firm's management was adopting the alternative dividend policy (dividends of £110 and £89 on the two dates, respectively)? Not necessarily: they could easily reinvest the £10 of unneeded funds received on Date 1 by buying more Bristol plc shares. At 10 per cent, this investment would grow to £11 by Date 2. Thus X would receive their desired net cash flow of £110 − 10 = £100 at Date 1 and £89 + 11 = £100 at Date 2.

Conversely, imagine that investor Z, preferring £110 of cash flow at Date 1 and £89 of cash flow at Date 2, finds that management will pay dividends of £100 at both Dates 1 and 2. This investor can sell £10 worth of equity to boost their total cash at Date 1 to £110. Because this investment returns 10 per cent, Investor Z gives up £11 at Date 2 (£10 × 1.1), leaving them with £100 − 11 = £89.

Our two investors can transform the corporation's dividend policy into a different policy by buying or selling on their own. The result is that investors can create a **homemade dividend policy**. This means that dissatisfied shareholders can alter the firm's dividend policy to suit themselves. As a result, there is no particular advantage to any single dividend policy the firm might choose.

Many corporations actually assist their shareholders in creating homemade dividend policies by offering *automatic dividend reinvestment plans* (ADRs or DRIPs). As the name suggests, with such a plan, shareholders have the option of automatically reinvesting some or all of their cash dividend in shares of equity. In some cases, they actually receive a discount on the shares, which makes such a plan very attractive.

> **homemade dividend policy** the tailored dividend policy created by individual investors who undo corporate dividend policy by reinvesting dividends or selling shares of equity.

A TEST

Our discussion to this point can be summarized by considering the following true-false test questions:

1. Dividends are irrelevant: true or false?
2. Dividend policy is irrelevant: true or false?

The first statement is surely false, and the reason follows from common sense. Clearly, investors prefer higher dividends to lower dividends at any single date if the dividend level is held constant at every other date. To be more precise regarding the first question, if the dividend per share at a given date is raised while the dividend per share at every other date is held constant, the share price will rise. The reason is that the present value of future dividends must go up if this occurs. This action can be accomplished by management decisions that improve productivity, increase tax savings, strengthen product marketing or otherwise improve cash flow.

The second statement is true, at least in the simple case we have been examining. Dividend policy by itself cannot raise the dividend at one date while keeping it the same at all other dates. Rather, dividend policy merely establishes the trade-off between dividends at one date and dividends on another date. Once we allow for time value, the present value of the dividend stream is unchanged. Thus, in this simple world, dividend policy does not matter, because managers choosing either to raise or to lower the current dividend do not affect the current value of their firm. However, we have ignored several real-world factors that might lead us to change our minds; we pursue some of these in subsequent sections.

> **CONCEPT QUESTIONS**
>
> **16.2a** How can an investor create a homemade dividend?
> **16.2b** Are dividends irrelevant?

16.3 REAL-WORLD FACTORS FAVOURING A LOW-DIVIDEND PAYOUT

The example we used to illustrate the irrelevance of dividend policy ignored taxes and flotation costs. In this section, we shall see that these factors might lead us to prefer a low-dividend payout.

TAXES

Tax laws are complex, and they affect dividend policy in several ways. The key tax feature has to do with the taxation of dividend income and capital gains. For individual shareholders, *effective* tax rates on dividend income are normally higher than the tax rates on capital gains. However, this is not always the case, and in many countries, the opposite is true. Historically, dividends received have been taxed as ordinary income. Capital gains have been taxed at somewhat lower rates, and the tax on a capital gain is deferred until the equity is sold. This second aspect of capital gains taxation makes the effective tax rate much lower because the present value of the tax is less.[2]

FLOTATION COSTS

In our example showing that dividend policy doesn't matter, we saw that the firm could sell some new equity if necessary, to pay a dividend. As we mentioned in Chapter 13, selling new equity can be very expensive. If we include flotation costs in our argument, then we shall find that the share price decreases if we sell new equity.

More generally, imagine two firms identical in every way except that one pays out a greater percentage of its cash flow in the form of dividends. Because the other firm ploughs back more, its equity grows faster. If these two firms are to remain identical, then the one with the higher payout will have to periodically sell some equity to catch up. Because this is expensive, a firm might be inclined to have a low payout.

DIVIDEND RESTRICTIONS

In some cases, a corporation may face restrictions on its ability to pay dividends. For example, as we discussed in Chapter 6, a common feature of a bond indenture is a covenant prohibiting dividend payments above some level. Also, a corporation may be prohibited by law from paying dividends if the dividend amount exceeds the firm's retained earnings.

> **CONCEPT QUESTIONS**
>
> **16.3a** What are the tax benefits of low dividends?
> **16.3b** Why do flotation costs favour a low payout?

16.4 REAL-WORLD FACTORS FAVOURING A HIGH-DIVIDEND PAYOUT

In this section, we consider reasons why a firm might pay its shareholders higher dividends, even if it means the firm must issue more shares of equity to finance the dividend payments.

Commonly held views are that firms should generally have high-dividend payouts because:

1. 'The discounted value of near dividends is higher than the present worth of distant dividends.'
2. Between 'two companies with the same general earning power and same general position in an industry, the one paying the larger dividend will almost always sell at a higher price'.[3]

Two additional factors favouring a high-dividend payout have also been mentioned frequently by proponents of this view: the desire for current income, and the resolution of uncertainty.

A DESIRE FOR CURRENT INCOME

It has been argued that many individuals desire current income. The classic example is the group of retired people and others living on a fixed income (the proverbial widows and orphans). It is argued that this group is willing to pay a premium to get a higher dividend yield. If this is true, then it lends support to the claim that dividends are important to investors.

It is easy to see, however, that this argument is not relevant in our simple case. An individual preferring high current cash flow but holding low-dividend securities can easily sell off shares to provide the necessary funds. Similarly, an individual desiring a low current cash flow but holding high-dividend securities can simply reinvest the dividend. This is just our homemade dividend argument again. Thus, in a world of no transaction costs, a policy of high current dividends would be of no value to the shareholder.

The current income argument may have relevance in the real world. Here the sale of low-dividend equities would involve brokerage fees and other transaction costs. These direct cash expenses could be avoided by an investment in high-dividend securities. Also, the expenditure of the shareholder's own time in selling securities, and the natural (though not necessarily rational) fear of consuming out of principal, might further lead many investors to buy high-dividend securities.

Even so, to put this argument in perspective, remember that financial intermediaries such as mutual funds can (and do) perform these 'repackaging' transactions for individuals at marginal cost. Such intermediaries could buy low-dividend equities and, through a controlled policy of realizing gains, they could pay their investors at a higher rate.

TAX AND OTHER BENEFITS FROM HIGH DIVIDENDS

Earlier, we saw that dividends were regularly taxed unfavourably for individual investors, and this is a powerful argument for a low payout. However, many other investors do not receive unfavourable tax treatment from holding high-dividend yield relative to low-dividend yield securities.

Tax-Exempt Investors

We have pointed out both the tax advantages and the tax disadvantages of a low-dividend payout. Of course, this discussion is irrelevant to those in zero-tax brackets. This group includes (in most countries) some of the largest investors in the economy, such as pension funds, endowment funds and trust funds.

Institutions such as university endowment funds and trust funds are frequently prohibited from spending any of the principal. Such institutions might therefore prefer to hold high-dividend yield equities so they have some ability to spend. Like widows and orphans, this group thus prefers current income. However, unlike widows and orphans, this group is huge in terms of the amount of equity owned.

CONCLUSION

Overall, individual investors (for whatever reason) may have a desire for current income, and may thus be willing to pay the dividend tax. Also, large investors, such as tax-free institutions may have a strong preference for high-dividend payouts.

> **CONCEPT QUESTIONS**
>
> **16.4a** Why might some individual investors favour a high-dividend payout?
> **16.4b** Why might some non-individual investors prefer a high-dividend payout?

16.5 A RESOLUTION OF REAL-WORLD FACTORS?

In previous sections, we presented some factors that favour a low-dividend policy and others that favour a high-dividend policy. Here, we discuss two important concepts related to dividends and dividend policy: the information content of dividends, and the clientele effect. The first topic illustrates both the importance of dividends in general and the importance of distinguishing between dividends and dividend policy. The second topic suggests that, despite the many real-world considerations we have discussed, the dividend payout ratio may not be as important as we originally imagined.

INFORMATION CONTENT OF DIVIDENDS

To begin, we quickly review some of our earlier discussion. Previously, we examined three different positions on dividends:

1. Based on the homemade dividend argument, dividend policy is irrelevant.
2. Because of tax effects for individual investors and new issue costs, a low-dividend policy is best.
3. Because of the desire for current income and related factors, a high-dividend policy is best.

If you wanted to decide which of these positions is the right one, an obvious way to get started would be to look at what happens to share prices when companies announce dividend changes. You would find with some consistency that share prices rise when the current dividend is unexpectedly increased (except for our opening example!), and they generally fall when the dividend is unexpectedly decreased. What does this imply about any of the three positions just stated?

At first glance, the behaviour we describe seems consistent with the third position and inconsistent with the other two. In fact, many writers have argued this. If share prices rise in response to dividend increases and fall in response to dividend decreases, then isn't the market saying that it approves of higher dividends?

Other authors have pointed out that this observation doesn't really tell us much about dividend policy. Everyone agrees that dividends are important, all other things being equal. Companies cut dividends only with great reluctance. Thus a dividend cut is often a signal that the firm is in trouble.

More to the point, a dividend cut is usually not a voluntary, planned change in dividend policy. Instead, it usually signals that management does not think that the current dividend policy can be maintained. As a result, expectations of future dividends should generally be revised downwards. The present value of expected future dividends falls, and so does the share price.

In this case, the share price declines following a dividend cut because future dividends are generally expected to be lower, not because the firm has changed the percentage of its earnings it will pay out in the form of dividends.

In a similar vein, an unexpected increase in the dividend signals good news. Management will raise the dividend only when future earnings, cash flow and general prospects are expected to rise to such an extent that the dividend will not have to be cut later. A dividend increase is management's signal to the market that the firm is expected to do well. The share price reacts favourably because expectations of future dividends are revised upwards, not because the firm has increased its payout.

In both of these cases, the share price reacts to the dividend change. The reaction can be attributed to changes in the expected amount of future dividends, not necessarily a change in dividend payout policy. This reaction is called the **information content effect** of the dividend. The fact that dividend changes convey information about the firm to the market makes it difficult to interpret the effect of the dividend policy of the firm.

> **information content effect** the market's reaction to a change in corporate dividend payout.

A BEHAVIOURAL FINANCE RATIONALE FOR HIGH DIVIDENDS

Suppose it turned out that the transaction costs in selling no-dividend securities could not account for the preference of investors for dividends. Would there still be a reason for high dividends? Behavioural finance may provide an answer to our question.

Every investor has different degrees of *self-control*, a concept that is quite important in psychology but receives virtually no emphasis in finance. Although we cannot review all that psychology has to say about self-control, let us focus on one example – losing weight. Suppose Kiran Harland, a university student, just got back from the Christmas break a few pounds heavier than he would like. Kiran wishes to lose weight by doing HIIT (high intensity interval training) classes. Each day, Kiran would balance the costs and benefits of doing HIIT classes. Perhaps he would choose to exercise on most days because losing weight is important to him. However, when he is too busy with exams, he might rationally choose not to exercise because he cannot afford the time. So, he may rationally choose to avoid doing HIIT classes on days when other social commitments become too time-consuming.

Unfortunately, Kiran must make a proactive choice to exercise every day, and there may be too many days when his other priorities get the better of him. He may tell himself that he does not have the time to exercise on a particular day, simply because he is starting to find the classes boring, not because he really does not have the time. Before long, he is avoiding HIIT classes on most days!

Is there an alternative? One way would be to set rigid rules. Perhaps Kiran may decide to do HIIT classes every day *no matter what*. This is not necessarily the best approach for everyone, but there is no question that many of us (perhaps most of us) live by a set of rules.

What does this have to do with dividends? Investors must also deal with self-control. Suppose a retiree wants to consume £20,000 a year from savings, in addition to their pension. On one hand, they could buy shares with a dividend yield high enough to generate £20,000 in dividends. On the other hand, they could place savings in non-dividend paying shares, selling off £20,000 each year for consumption. Though these two approaches seem financially equivalent, the second one may allow for too much leeway. If lack of self-control gets the better of the retiree, they might sell off too much, leaving little for later years. Better, perhaps, to short-circuit this possibility by investing in dividend-paying equities with a firm personal rule of *never* 'dipping into principal'. Although behaviourists do not claim this approach is for everyone, they argue that enough people think this way to explain why firms pay dividends – even though, as we said earlier, dividends are tax-disadvantaged.

Does behavioural finance argue for increased share repurchases as well as increased dividends? The answer is no, because investors will sell the shares that firms repurchase. As we have said, selling shares involves too much leeway. Investors might sell too many shares, leaving little for later years. Thus, the behaviourist argument may explain why companies pay dividends in a world with personal taxes.

THE CLIENTELE EFFECT

In our earlier discussion, we saw that some groups (wealthy individuals, for example) have an incentive to pursue low-payout (or zero-payout) equities. Other groups (charities, for example) have an incentive to pursue high-payout equities. Companies with high payouts will thus attract one group, and low-payout companies will attract another.

These different groups are called *clienteles*, and what we have described is a **clientele effect**. The clientele effect argument states that different groups of investors desire different levels of dividend. When a firm chooses a particular dividend policy, the only effect is to attract a particular clientele. If a firm changes its dividend policy, then it just attracts a different clientele.

> **clientele effect** the observable fact that equities attract particular groups based on dividend yield and the resulting tax effects.

What we are left with is a simple supply and demand argument. Suppose 40 per cent of all investors prefer high dividends, but only 20 per cent of the firms pay high dividends. Here the high-dividend firms will be in short supply: thus their share prices will rise. Consequently, low-dividend firms will find it advantageous to switch policies until 40 per cent of all firms have high payouts. At this point, the *dividend market* is in equilibrium. Further changes in dividend policy are meaningless because all clienteles are satisfied. The dividend policy for any individual firm is now irrelevant.

To see if you understand the clientele effect, consider the following statement. Despite the theoretical argument that dividend policy is irrelevant, or that firms should not pay dividends, many investors like high dividends: because of this fact, a firm can boost its share price by having a higher dividend payout ratio. True or false?

The answer is 'false' if clienteles exist. As long as enough high-dividend firms satisfy the dividend-loving investors, a firm won't be able to boost its share price by paying high dividends. An unsatisfied clientele must exist for this to happen, and there is no evidence that this is the case.

> **CONCEPT QUESTIONS**
>
> **16.5a** How does the market react to unexpected dividend changes? What does this tell us about dividends? About dividend policy?
>
> **16.5b** What is a dividend clientele? All things considered, would you expect a risky firm with significant but highly uncertain growth prospects to have a low- or high-dividend payout?

THE CATERING THEORY OF DIVIDENDS

It is not unreasonable to expect there will be times when companies are temporarily mispriced in the stock market or that there will be changes in the demand for dividend-paying equities. This may be because of the clientele effect, which predicts that if the proportion of dividend-paying companies in a market increases or decreases, the demand for dividend-paying shares will shift to a new equilibrium, temporarily creating a premium or discount on shares of companies that pay dividends.

Instead of focusing on investor decisions, the Catering Theory of Dividends predicts that managers will rationally respond to time variation in investor demand for dividends by modifying their company's dividend policy. In effect, the theory makes less of a statement about market efficiency or behavioural finance than it does about the logical business decisions by corporate management. Research (Ferris, Sen and Yui, 2006) has shown that UK dividend policy is somewhat consistent with this theory.

Does this mean that dividend increases lead to a positive price reaction? Not necessarily. If the time-varying demand for dividend-paying shares is low, an announcement by a company that it is increasing its dividend is not likely to be met with a positive reaction. In this situation, a dividend omission may elicit a more positive market response.

16.6 SHARE REPURCHASES: AN ALTERNATIVE TO CASH DIVIDENDS

Thus far in our chapter, we have considered cash dividends. However, cash dividends are not the only way corporations distribute cash. Instead, a company can **repurchase** its own equity. Repurchases (or *buybacks*) have become an increasingly popular tool, and the amount spent on repurchases has become huge.

share repurchase
the purchase, by a corporation, of its own shares of equity; also known as a *buyback*.

Across Europe, share repurchases were historically not common. For example, in 2002, less than 1 per cent of all British firms repurchased shares. Share repurchases have taken on increased importance in recent years. Consider the situation in Europe, where share repurchase activity has exploded to now comprise more than half the value of all cash dividends in the European Union. Between 1992 and 2000, share repurchases were only 32 per cent of capital expenditure, growing to over 85 per cent in 2020. In comparison, dividends were around 55 per cent of capital expenditures in 2020.

Share repurchases are typically accomplished in one of three ways. First, companies may purchase their own equity, just as anyone would buy shares of a particular equity.

In these *open market purchases*, the firm does not reveal itself as the buyer. Thus the seller does not know whether the shares were sold back to the firm, or just another investor.

Second, the firm could institute a *tender offer*. Here the firm announces to all of its shareholders that it is willing to buy a fixed number of shares at a specific price. For example, suppose Kunst en Ambacht NV (K&A) has one million shares of equity outstanding, with a share price of €50 per share. The firm makes a tender offer to buy back 300,000 shares at €60 per share. K&A chooses a price above €50 to induce shareholders to sell – that is, tender – their shares. In fact, if the tender price is set high enough, shareholders may very well want to sell more than the 300,000 shares. In the extreme case where all outstanding shares are tendered, K&A will buy back 3 out of every 10 shares that a shareholder has.

Finally, firms may repurchase shares from specific individual shareholders. This procedure has been called a *targeted repurchase*. For example, suppose International Biotechnology AB purchased approximately 10 per cent of the outstanding equity of Prime Robotics Ltd (P-R Ltd) in April at around SKr38 per share. At that time, International Biotechnology announced to the Stockholm Stock Exchange that it might eventually try to take control of P-R Ltd. In May, P-R Ltd repurchased the International Biotechnology holdings in P-R Ltd at SKr48 per share, well above the market price at that time. This offer was not extended to other shareholders.

CASH DIVIDENDS VERSUS REPURCHASE

Imagine an all-equity company with excess cash of £300,000. The firm pays no dividends, and its net income for the year just ended is £49,000. The market value balance sheet at the end of the year is represented here:

Market value balance sheet (before paying out excess cash)			
	£		£
Excess cash	300,000	Debt	0
Other assets	700,000	Equity	1,000,000
Total	1,000,000	Total	1,000,000

There are 100,000 shares outstanding. The total market value of the equity is £1 million, so the share price is £10. Earnings per share (EPS) are £49,000/100,000 = £0.49, and the price-earnings ratio (P/E) is £10/0.49 = 20.4.

One option the company is considering is a £300,000/100,000 = £3 per share extra cash dividend. Alternatively, the company is thinking of using the money to repurchase £300,000/10 = 30,000 shares of equity.

If commissions, taxes and other imperfections are ignored in our example, the shareholders shouldn't care which option is chosen. Does this seem surprising? It shouldn't, really. What is happening here is that the firm is paying out £300,000 in cash. The new balance sheet is represented here:

Market value balance sheet (after paying out excess cash)			
	£		£
Excess cash	0	Debt	0
Other assets	700,000	Equity	700,000
Total	700,000	Total	700,000

If the cash is paid out as a dividend, there are still 100,000 shares outstanding, so each is worth £7.

The fact that the per-share value fell from £10 to £7 is not a cause for concern. Consider a shareholder who owns 100 shares. At £10 per share before the dividend, the total value is £1,000.

After the £3 dividend, this same shareholder has 100 shares worth £7 each, for a total of £700, plus 100 × £3 = £300 in cash, for a combined total of £1,000. This illustrates what we saw early on: a cash dividend doesn't affect a shareholder's wealth if there are no imperfections. In this case, the share price fell by £3 when the equity went ex-dividend.

Also, because total earnings and the number of shares outstanding haven't changed, EPS is still 49 pence. The price-earnings ratio, however, falls to £7/0.49 = 14.3. Why we are looking at accounting earnings and P/E ratios will be apparent in just a moment.

Alternatively, if the company repurchases 30,000 shares, there are 70,000 left outstanding. The balance sheet looks the same:

Market value balance sheet (after share repurchase)			
	£		£
Excess cash	0	Debt	0
Other assets	700,000	Equity	700,000
Total	700,000	Total	700,000

The company is worth £700,000 again, so each remaining share is worth £700,000/70,000 = £10. Our shareholder with 100 shares is obviously unaffected. For example, if they were so inclined, they could sell 30 shares and end up with £300 in cash and £700 in equity, just as they would have if the firm pays the cash dividend. This is another example of a homemade dividend.

In this second case, EPS goes up because total earnings remain the same while the number of shares goes down. The new EPS is £49,000/70,000 = £0.70. However, the important thing to notice is that the P/E ratio is £10/0.70 = 14.3, just as it was following the dividend.

This example illustrates the important point that, if there are no imperfections, a cash dividend and a share repurchase are essentially the same things. This is just another illustration of dividend policy irrelevance when there are no taxes or other imperfections.

REAL-WORLD CONSIDERATIONS IN A REPURCHASE

The example we have just described shows that a repurchase and a cash dividend are the same things in a world without taxes and transaction costs. In the real world, there are some accounting differences between a share repurchase and a cash dividend, but the most important difference is in the tax treatment.

Under current tax laws, a repurchase has a significant tax advantage over a cash dividend. A dividend is taxed, and a shareholder has no choice about whether or not to receive the dividend. In a repurchase, a shareholder pays taxes only if: (1) the shareholder actually chooses to sell; and (2) the shareholder has a capital gain on the sale.

For example, suppose a dividend of £1 per share is taxed at ordinary rates. Investors in the 28 per cent tax bracket who own 100 shares of the security pay £100 × 0.28 = £28 in taxes. Selling shareholders would pay far lower taxes if £100 worth of equity were repurchased. This is because taxes are paid only on the profit from a sale. Thus the gain on a sale would be only £40 if shares sold at £100 were originally purchased at £60. The capital gains tax would be 0.28 × £40 = £11.20.

> ### REAL WORLD INSIGHTS
>
> During recessions and world crises like the recent Covid-19 pandemic, share repurchase activity tends to fall. Many reasons have been given: when unemployment levels are high, there are real political pressures for large companies to focus on investment in value-maximizing (and personnel-heavy) projects. Share repurchases are regarded in the financial press as vehicles to maximize earnings per share and minimize tax expenditure. With stronger shareholder activism in recent years, managers have understandably shied away from any activity that will cause them to come under the scrutiny of a diligent media.
>
> Perceptions change, though. Low refinancing rates and a slowly stabilizing economy may allow companies to create new value by shifting their capital structure away from equity and into debt, which will increase the tax shield benefit from having more debt in the balance sheet. Also, when share prices are deflated, and corporate operating performance is improving, debt-funded share repurchases make a lot of sense to managers, who see this activity as a sustainable way to create value through a combination of low-cost debt (compared to equity) and an improved tax shield.
>
> This is what Warren Buffett, one of the world's most successful and famous investors, did in 2020 to his company, Berkshire Hathaway. During the pandemic, when share prices were deflated, Buffet spent significant sums of money repurchasing shares to take advantage of the low share price at the time.

SHARE REPURCHASES AND EARNINGS PER SHARE

You may read in the popular financial press that a share repurchase is beneficial because it causes earnings per share to increase. As we have seen, this will happen. The reason is simply that a share repurchase reduces the number of outstanding shares, but it has no effect on total earnings. As a result, EPS rises.

Although equity value isn't affected by share repurchase-induced EPS improvements, the academic evidence suggests managers prioritize them over cash dividends in certain situations. Research undertaken by Almeida, Fos and Kronlund (2016) showed that companies are likely to have share repurchases when they are in danger of not meeting EPS forecasts. Managers may also prioritize share repurchases over cash dividends if their personal remuneration is linked to changes in EPS. This is more of an issue in the USA than in Europe, where top executive compensation packages are more likely to be tied to earnings per share.

> **CONCEPT QUESTIONS**
>
> **16.6a** Why might a share repurchase make more sense than an extra cash dividend?
> **16.6b** What is the effect of a share repurchase on a firm's EPS? On its P/E?

16.7 WHAT WE KNOW AND DO NOT KNOW ABOUT DIVIDEND AND PAYOUT POLICIES

Although companies have paid dividends for centuries, and dividend policy has a well-established theoretical development, there are still areas where there are either anomalies to academic wisdom or corporate behaviour unexplained by existing theories. In this section, we explore a few of these areas.

DIVIDENDS AND DIVIDEND PAYERS

As we have discussed, there are several good reasons to favour a dividend policy of low (or no) payout. Nonetheless, in Europe, aggregate dividends paid by companies are quite large. However, even before the Covid-19 pandemic, the total real dividends (share repurchases and cash dividends) of European firms were falling. In addition, the percentage of European companies that pay dividends has also declined.

One important reason why the percentage of dividend-paying firms has declined is that the population of firms has changed. There has been a huge increase in the number of newly listed firms over the last 25 or so years. Newly listed firms tend to be younger and less profitable. Such firms need their internally generated cash to fund growth, and typically do not pay dividends.

Another factor at work is that firms appear to be more likely to begin making payouts using share repurchases, which are flexible, rather than committing themselves to make cash distributions. Such a policy seems quite sensible, given our previous discussions. However, after controlling for the changing mix of firms and the increase in share repurchasing activity, there still appears to be a decreased propensity to pay dividends among certain types of older, better-established firms, although further research is needed on this question.

CORPORATIONS SMOOTH DIVIDENDS

As we previously observed, dividend cuts are frequently viewed as negative news by market participants, and companies cut dividends only when there is no other acceptable alternative. For the same reason, companies are also reluctant to increase dividends unless they are sure the new dividend level can be sustained.

In practice, what we observe is that dividend-paying companies tend to raise dividends only after earnings have risen. Companies don't increase or cut dividends in response to temporary earnings fluctuations. In other words: (1) dividend growth lags earnings growth, and (2) dividend growth will tend to be much smoother than earnings growth.

PUTTING IT ALL TOGETHER

Much of what we have discussed in this chapter (and much of what we know about dividends from decades of research) can be pulled together and summarized in the following five observations:[4]

1. Aggregate dividend and share repurchases are massive.
2. Dividends are heavily concentrated among a relatively small number of large, mature firms.
3. Managers are very reluctant to cut dividends, normally doing so only because of firm-specific problems.
4. Managers smooth dividends, raising them slowly and incrementally as earnings grow.
5. Share prices react to unanticipated changes in dividends.

The challenge now is to fit these five pieces into a reasonably coherent picture. Concerning payouts in general, meaning the combination of share repurchases and cash dividends, a simple life cycle theory fits points 1 and 2. The key ideas are straightforward. First, relatively young and less profitable firms generally should not make cash distributions. They need the cash to fund investments (and flotation costs discourage the raising of outside cash).

However, as a firm matures, it begins to generate free cash flow (which, you will recall, is internally generated cash flow beyond that needed to fund profitable investment activities). Significant free cash flow can lead to agency problems if it is not distributed. Managers may become tempted to pursue empire building or otherwise spend the excess cash in ways not in the shareholders' best interests. Thus firms come under pressure to make distributions rather than hoard cash. And, consistent with what we observe, we expect large firms with a history of profitability to make large distributions.

Thus the life-cycle theory says that firms trade off the agency costs of excess cash retention against the potential future costs of external equity financing. A firm should begin making distributions when it generates sufficient internal cash flow to fund its investment needs now and into the foreseeable future.

The more complex issue concerns the type of distribution: cash dividends versus repurchase. The tax argument in favour of repurchases is a clear and strong one. Further, repurchases are a much more flexible option (and managers greatly value financial flexibility), so the question is: why would firms ever choose a cash dividend?

If we are to answer this question, we have to ask a different question. What can a cash dividend accomplish that a share repurchase cannot? One answer is that when a firm commits to pay a cash dividend now and into the future, it sends a two-part signal to the markets. As we have already discussed, one signal is that the firm anticipates being profitable, with the ability to make the payments on an ongoing basis. Note that a firm cannot benefit by trying to fool the market in this regard, because the firm would ultimately be punished when it couldn't make the dividend payment (or couldn't make it without relying on external financing). Thus a cash dividend may let a firm distinguish itself from less profitable rivals.

A second, and more subtle, signal takes us back to the agency problem of free cash flow. By committing itself to pay cash dividends now and in the future, the firm signals that it won't be hoarding cash (or at least not as much cash), thereby reducing agency costs and enhancing shareholder wealth.

This two-part signalling story is consistent with points 3–5 above, but an obvious objection remains. Why don't firms commit themselves to a policy of setting aside whatever money would be used to pay dividends, and use it instead to buy back shares? After all, either way, a firm is committing itself to pay out cash to shareholders.

A fixed repurchase strategy suffers from two drawbacks. The first is verifiability. A firm could announce an open market repurchase and then not do it. By suitably fudging its books, it would be some time before the deception was discovered. Thus it would be necessary for shareholders to develop a monitoring mechanism, meaning some way for shareholders to know for sure that the repurchase was in fact done. Such a mechanism wouldn't be difficult to build (it could be a simple trustee relationship, such as we observe in the bond markets), but it currently does not exist. Of course, a tender offer repurchase needs little or no verification, but such offers have expenses associated with them. The beauty of a cash dividend is that it needs no monitoring. A firm is forced to make dividend payments two or four times a year, year in and year out.

A second objection to a fixed repurchase strategy is more controversial. Suppose managers, as insiders, are better able than shareholders to judge whether their share price is too high or too low. (Note that this idea does not conflict with semi-strong market efficiency if inside information is the reason.) In this case, a fixed repurchase commitment forces management to buy back shares even in circumstances when the equity is overvalued. In other words, it forces management into making negative-NPV investments.

More research on the cash dividend versus share repurchase question is needed, but the historical trend seems to be favouring continued growth in repurchases relative to dividends. Table 16.1 provides a summary of the pros and cons of paying dividends.

TABLE 16.1

The pros and cons of paying dividends

Pros	Cons
1 Cash dividends can underscore good results and provide support for the share price.	1 Dividends are taxed to recipients.
2 Dividends may attract institutional investors who prefer some return in the form of dividends. A mix of institutional and individual investors may allow a firm to raise capital at a lower cost because of the ability of the firm to reach a wider market.	2 Dividends can reduce internal sources of financing. Dividends may force the firm to forgo positive-NPV projects or rely on costly external equity financing.
3 Share prices usually increase with the announcement of a new or increased dividend.	3 Once dividends are established, dividend cuts are hard to make without adversely affecting a firm's share price.
4 Dividends absorb excess cash flow and may reduce the agency costs that arise from conflicts between management and shareholders.	

SOME SURVEY EVIDENCE ON DIVIDENDS

A recent study surveyed a large number of financial executives regarding dividend policy. One of the questions asked was, 'Do these statements describe factors that affect your company's dividend decisions?' Table 16.2 shows some of the results.

As shown in Table 16.2, financial managers are very disinclined to cut dividends. Moreover, they are very conscious of their previous dividends and desire to maintain a relatively steady dividend. In contrast, the cost of external capital and the desire to attract 'prudent man' investors (those with fiduciary duties) are less important.

Table 16.3 is drawn from the same survey, but here the responses are to the question, 'How important are the following factors to your company's dividend decision?' Not surprisingly, given the responses in Table 16.2 and our earlier discussion, the highest priority is maintaining a consistent dividend policy. The next several items are also consistent with our previous analysis. Financial managers are very concerned about earnings stability and future earnings levels in making dividend decisions, and they consider the availability of good investment opportunities. Survey respondents also believed that attracting both institutional and individual (retail) investors was relatively important.

In contrast to our discussion of taxes and flotation costs in the earlier part of this chapter, the financial managers in this survey did not think that personal taxes paid on dividends by shareholders were that important. And even fewer thought that equity flotation costs were relevant.

TABLE 16.2

Survey responses on dividend decisions

Policy statements	The proportion of respondents who agree or strongly agree (%)
1 We try to avoid reducing dividends per share.	93.8
2 We try to maintain a smooth dividend from year to year.	89.6
3 We consider the level of dividends per share that we have paid in recent quarters.	88.2
4 We are reluctant to make dividend changes that might have to be reversed in the future.	77.9
5 We consider the change or growth in dividends per share.	66.7
6 We consider the cost of raising external capital to be smaller than the cost of cutting dividends.	42.8
7 We pay dividends to attract investors subject to 'prudent man' investment restrictions.	41.7

Survey respondents were asked the question, 'Do these statements describe factors that affect your company's dividend decisions?'

Source: Adapted from Table 4 of A. Brav, J.R. Graham, C.R. Harvey and R. Michaely (2005). Payout policy in the 21st century. Journal of Financial Economics, 77(3), 483-527.

TABLE 16.3

Survey responses on dividend decisions

Policy statements	The proportion of respondents who think this is important or very important (%)
1 Maintaining consistency with our historic dividend policy.	84.1
2 Stability of future earnings.	71.9
3 A sustainable change in earnings.	67.1
4 Attracting institutional investors to purchase our stock.	52.5
5 The availability of good investment opportunities for our firm to pursue.	47.6
6 Attracting retail investors to purchase our stock.	44.5
7 Personal taxes our shareholders pay when receiving dividends.	21.1
8 Flotation costs of issuing new equity.	9.3

Survey respondents were asked the question, 'How important are the following factors to your company's dividend decision?'

Source: Adapted from Table 5 of A. Brav, J.R. Graham, C.R. Harvey and R. Michaely (2005). Payout policy in the 21st century. Journal of Financial Economics, 77(3), 483-527.

16.8 STOCK DIVIDENDS AND STOCK SPLITS

Another type of dividend is paid out in shares of equity. This type of dividend is called a share or **stock dividend**. A stock dividend is not a true dividend because it is not paid in cash. The effect of a stock dividend is to increase the number of shares that each owner holds. Because more shares are outstanding, each share is worth less.

A stock dividend is commonly expressed as a percentage: for example, a 20 per cent stock dividend means that a shareholder receives one new share for every five currently owned (a 20 per cent increase). Because every shareholder receives 20 per cent more shares, the total number of shares outstanding rises by 20 per cent. As we shall see in a moment, the result is that each share of equity is worth about 20 per cent less.

A **stock split** is essentially the same thing as a stock dividend, except that it is expressed as a ratio instead of a percentage. When a split is declared, each share is split up to create additional shares. For example, in a three-for-one stock split, each old share is split into three new shares.

> **stock dividend**
> a payment made by a firm to its owners in the form of equity, diluting the value of each share outstanding.

SOME DETAILS ABOUT STOCK SPLITS AND STOCK DIVIDENDS

Stock splits and stock dividends have essentially the same impacts on the corporation and the shareholder: they increase the number of shares outstanding and reduce the value per share. Unlike US accounting standards, IFRS makes no distinction between a cash dividend and a stock dividend. IFRS considers a stock dividend as being a cash dividend to shareholders with a simultaneous purchase of shares by the same shareholders.

> **stock split**
> an increase in a firm's shares outstanding without any change in owners' equity.

By convention, stock dividends of less than 20 to 25 per cent are called *small stock dividends*. The accounting procedure for such a dividend is discussed next. A stock dividend greater than this value of 20 to 25 per cent is called a *large stock dividend*. Large stock dividends are not uncommon, and except for some relatively minor accounting differences, a stock dividend has the same effect as a stock split.

VALUE OF STOCK SPLITS AND STOCK DIVIDENDS

The laws of logic tell us that stock splits and stock dividends can: (1) leave the value of the firm unaffected; (2) increase its value; or (3) decrease its value. Unfortunately, the issues are complex enough that we cannot easily determine which of the three relationships holds.

The Benchmark Case

A strong case can be made that stock dividends and splits do not change either the wealth of any shareholder or the wealth of the firm as a whole. Consider an all-equity firm with a total market value of €660,000 and 10,000 shares. With a 10 per cent stock dividend, the number of shares increases to 11,000, so it seems that each would be worth €660,000/11,000 = €60.

For example, a shareholder who had 100 shares worth €66 each before the dividend would have 1,110 shares worth €60 each afterwards. The total value of the equity is €6,600 either way; so the stock dividend doesn't really have any economic effect.

Now consider a two-for-one split. After the stock split, 20,000 shares are outstanding, so each should be worth €660,000/20,000 = €33. In other words, the number of shares double and the price halves. From these calculations, it appears that stock dividends and splits are just paper transactions.

Although these results are relatively obvious, reasons are often given to suggest that there may be some benefits to these actions. The typical financial manager is aware of many real-world complexities: for that reason, the stock split or stock dividend decision is not treated lightly in practice.

Popular Trading Range

Proponents of stock dividends and stock splits frequently argue that a security has a proper **trading range**. When the security is priced above this level, many investors do not have the funds to buy the common trading unit of 100 shares, called a *round lot*. Although securities can be purchased in *odd-lot* form (fewer than 100 shares), the commissions are greater. Thus firms will split the equity to keep the price in this trading range.

> **trading range**
> the price range between the highest and lowest prices at which an equity is traded.

Although this argument is a popular one, its validity is questionable, for several reasons. Mutual funds, pension funds and other institutions have steadily increased their trading activity since World War II, and now handle a sizeable percentage of total trading volume (of the order of 80 per cent of stock exchange trading volume, for example). Because these institutions buy and sell in huge amounts, the individual share price is of little concern.

Furthermore, we sometimes observe share prices that are quite large that do not appear to cause problems. To take an extreme case, consider the Swiss chocolatier Lindt. In 2016 Lindt shares were selling for around 70,000 Swiss francs each, or about €64,000. This is fairly expensive, but also consider Berkshire-Hathaway, the company run by legendary investor Warren Buffet. In 2016 each share in the company sold for about $213,000!

Finally, there is evidence that stock splits may actually decrease the liquidity of the company's shares. Following a two-for-one split, the number of shares traded should more than double if the split increases liquidity. This doesn't appear to happen, and the reverse is sometimes observed.

REVERSE SPLITS

> **reverse split**
> a stock split in which a firm's number of shares outstanding is reduced.

A less frequently encountered financial manoeuvre is the **reverse split**. For example, in 2020, Eyepoint Pharmaceuticals underwent a one-for-ten reverse stock split. In a one-for-ten reverse split, each investor exchanges ten old shares for one new share. The par value is multiplied by ten in the process. As with stock splits and stock dividends, a case can be made that a reverse split has no real effect.

Given real-world imperfections, three related reasons are cited for reverse splits. First, transaction costs to shareholders may be less after the reverse split. Second, the liquidity and marketability of a company's equity might be improved when its price is raised to the popular trading range. Third, equities selling at prices below a certain level are not considered respectable, meaning that investors underestimate these firms' earnings, cash flow, growth and stability. Some financial analysts argue that a reverse split can achieve instant respectability. As was the case with stock splits, none of these reasons is particularly compelling, especially not the third one.

There are two other reasons for reverse splits. First, stock exchanges have minimum share price requirements. A reverse split may bring the share price up to such a minimum. Second, companies sometimes perform reverse splits and, at the same time, buy out any shareholders who end up with less than a certain number of shares.

> **CONCEPT QUESTIONS**
>
> **16.8a** What is the effect of a stock split on shareholder wealth?
> **16.8b** How does the accounting treatment of a stock split differ from that used with a stock dividend?

SUMMARY AND CONCLUSIONS

In this chapter, we first discussed the types of dividend and how they are paid. We then defined dividend policy and examined whether or not dividend policy matters. Next, we illustrated how a firm might establish a dividend policy, and described an important alternative to cash dividends, a share repurchase.
In covering these subjects, we saw these points:

1. Dividend policy is irrelevant when there are no taxes or other imperfections because shareholders can effectively undo the firm's dividend strategy. Shareholders who receive dividends greater than desired can reinvest the excess. Conversely, shareholders who receive dividends smaller than desired can sell off extra shares of equity.
2. Individual shareholder income taxes and new issue flotation costs are real-world considerations that favour a low-dividend payout. With taxes and new issue costs, the firm should pay out dividends only after all positive-NPV projects have been fully financed.
3. There are groups in the economy that may favour a high payout. These include many large institutions, such as pension plans. Recognizing that some groups prefer a high payout, and some prefer a low payout, the clientele-effect argument supports the idea that dividend policy responds to the needs of shareholders. For example, if 40 per cent of the shareholders prefer low dividends and 60 per cent of the shareholders prefer high dividends, approximately 40 per cent of companies will have a

low-dividend payout, and 60 per cent will have a high payout. This sharply reduces the impact of any individual firm's dividend policy on its market price.
4. A share repurchase acts much like a cash dividend but has a significant tax advantage. Stock repurchases are, therefore, an important part of overall dividend policy.
5. We discussed recent research and thinking on dividend policy. We saw that dividends are heavily concentrated in a relatively small number of larger, older firms and that the use of share repurchases continues to grow. We described a simple life cycle theory of distributions, in which firms trade off the agency costs of excess cash retention against the future costs of external equity financing. The implication is that younger firms with significant growth opportunities will not distribute cash, but older, profitable firms with significant free cash flow will do so.

To close our discussion of dividends, we emphasize one last time the difference between dividends and dividend policy. Dividends are important because the value of a share of equity is ultimately determined by the dividends that will be paid. What is less clear is whether the time pattern of dividends (more now versus more later) matters. This is the dividend policy question, and it is not easy to give a definitive answer to it.

CHAPTER REVIEW AND SELF-TEST QUESTIONS

16.1 Thesepe plc has declared a £2 per-share dividend and sells for £8.40 per share. Assuming that the tax rate on capital gains and dividends is zero, what do you think the ex-dividend price will be? Explain.

16.2 Eurasion Natural Resources Corporation currently has 2.4 million shares outstanding that sell for £5.16 per share. Assuming no market imperfections or tax effects exist, what will the share price be after:

   (a) a three-for-two stock split?

   (b) an 8 per cent stock dividend?

   (c) a 20 per cent stock dividend?

   (d) a two-for-three reverse stock split?

   Determine the new number of shares outstanding in parts (a) through (d).

SOLUTIONS

16.1 The ex-dividend price will be (£8.40 − £2 =) £6.40.

16.2 To find the new share price, we multiply the current share price by the ratio of old shares to new shares, so:

   (a) £5.16(2/3) = £3.44

   (b) £5.16(1/1.08) = £4.78

   (c) £5.16(1/1.20) = £4.30

   (d) £5.16(3/2) = £7.74

   To find the new shares outstanding, we multiply the current shares outstanding times the ratio of new shares to old shares, so:

   (a) 2.4(3/2) = 3.6 million

   (b) 2.4(1.08) = 2.592 million

   (c) 2.4(1.20) = 2.88 million

   (d) 2.4(2/3) = 1.6 million

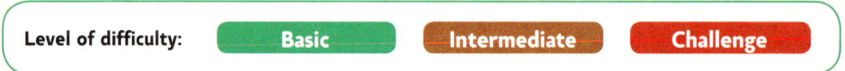

QUESTIONS AND PROBLEMS

16.1 **Dividends and Taxes** Thesepe plc has declared a £2 per share dividend and sells for £8.40 per share. Assuming the tax rate on capital gains and dividends is zero, what do you think the ex-dividend price will be? Explain.

16.2 **Stock Dividends** The shareholder equity accounts for Ochsphil are shown here:

	£
Ordinary shares (£1 par value)	20,000
Capital surplus	180,000
Retained earnings	500,000
Total owners' equity	700,000

(a) If Ochsphil shares currently sell for £10 per share, and a 10 per cent stock dividend is declared, how many new shares will be distributed? Show how the equity accounts would change.

(b) Ochsphil shares currently sell for £10 per share, and a 5 per cent stock dividend is declared. How many new shares will be distributed? Show how the equity accounts would change.

16.3 **Stock Splits** For the company in Problem 16.2, show how the equity accounts will change if:

(a) Ochsphil declares a four-for-one stock split. How many shares are outstanding now? What is the new par value per share?

(b) Ochsphil declares a one-for-five reverse stock split. How many shares are outstanding now? What is the new par value per share?

16.4 **Dividend Policy** Bodyswerve plc has experienced significant performance gains over previous years and there is no reason to expect any different in the future. The firm has engaged with a potential investor to purchase its shares in the open market. However, the investor has argued that a Bodyswerve investment is not good value for money because the firm has never paid a dividend and their preference is to choose equities that only pay dividends.

(a) Does the investor's argument make sense? Explain.

(b) What argument should be used to convince the investor that Bodyswerve equity is the investment for them?

(c) What counter-arguments could be made?

16.5 **Stock Splits and Stock Dividends** Sustainable Development Corporation currently has 6.2 million shares outstanding that sell for £25 per share. Assume no market imperfections or tax effects exist. Determine the new share price and the new number of shares outstanding in parts (a) through (d).

(a) A three-for-two stock split?

(b) A 10 per cent stock dividend?

(c) A 25 per cent stock dividend?

(d) A two-for-five reverse stock split?

16.6 Dividends versus Capital Gains It is clear in many countries that investors prefer dividend-paying stocks to those that pay no dividends. How do you explain this if dividend policy is irrelevant? Explain.

16.7 Regular Dividends The balance sheet for Allianz SE is shown here in market value terms. There are 412.29 million shares outstanding. The company has declared an annual dividend of €0.96 per share. The equity goes ex-dividend tomorrow. Ignoring any tax effects, what are the shares selling for today? What will they sell for tomorrow? What will the market value balance sheet look like after the dividends are paid?

Market value balance sheet			
	€ m		€ m
Cash	351	Equity	40,427
Non-current assets	121,274	Liabilities	81,198
Total	121,625	Total	121,625

16.8 Share Repurchase For the company in Problem 16.7, assume Allianz SE has announced it is going to repurchase €10 billion worth of equity.

(a) What effect will this transaction have on the equity of the firm?

(b) How many shares will be outstanding?

(c) What will the price per share be after the repurchase?

(d) Ignoring tax effects, show how the share repurchase is effectively the same as a cash dividend.

16.9 Stock Dividends The market value balance sheet for KL Air is shown here. KL Air has declared a 20 per cent stock dividend. The stock goes ex-dividend tomorrow (the chronology for a stock dividend is similar to that for a cash dividend). There are 15,000 shares of equity outstanding. What will the ex-dividend price be?

Market value balance sheet			
	R		R
Cash	1,290,000	Debt	1,682,500
Non-current assets	5,440,000	Equity	5,047,500
Total	6,730,000	Total	6,730,000

16.10 Stock Dividends The company with the equity accounts shown here has declared a 12 per cent stock dividend when the market value of its equity is €20 per share. What effects on the equity accounts will the distribution of the stock dividend have?

	€
Ordinary shares (£1 par value)	350,000
Capital surplus	1,650,000
Retained earnings	3,000,000
Total owners' equity	5,000,000

16.11 Stock Splits In the previous problem, suppose the company instead decides on a five-for-one stock split. The firm's 70 pence per share cash dividend on the new (post-split) shares represents an increase of 10 per cent over last year's dividend on the pre-split equity. What effect does this have on the equity accounts? What was last year's dividend per share?

16.12 Homemade Dividends You own 2,000 shares of equity in Avondale Property plc. You will receive a £0.25 per share dividend in 1 year. In 2 years, Avondale will pay a liquidating dividend of £0.75 per share. The required return on Avondale shares is 18 per cent. What is the current share price of your equity (ignoring taxes)? If you would rather have equal dividends in each of the next 2 years, show how you can accomplish this by creating homemade dividends.

16.13 Homemade Dividends In the previous problem, suppose you want £400 total in dividends the first year. What will your homemade dividend be in 2 years?

16.14 Share Repurchase Wilemere NV is evaluating an extra dividend versus a share repurchase. In either case €100,000 would be spent. Current earnings are €0.95 per share, and the equity currently sells for €40 per share. There are 4,000 shares outstanding. Ignore taxes and other imperfections in answering parts (a) and (b).

(a) Evaluate the two alternatives in terms of the effect on the price per share of the equity and shareholder wealth.

(b) What will be the effect on Wilemere's EPS and P/E ratio under the two different scenarios?

(c) In the real world, which of these actions would you recommend? Why?

16.15 Expected Return, Dividends and Taxes Gecko Company and Gordon Company are two firms whose business risk is the same but which have different dividend policies. Gecko pays no dividend, whereas Gordon has an expected dividend yield of 6 per cent. Suppose the capital gains tax rate is zero, whereas the dividend tax rate is 12.5 per cent. Gecko has an expected earnings growth rate of 15 per cent annually, and its share price is expected to grow at this same rate. If the after-tax expected returns on the two equities are equal (because they are in the same risk class), what is the pre-tax required return on Gordon's shares?

16.16 Dividends and Taxes In the absence of market imperfections and tax effects, we would expect the share price to decline by the amount of the dividend payment when the equity goes ex dividend. Once we consider the role of taxes, however, this is not necessarily true. One model has been proposed that incorporates tax effects into determining the ex-dividend price (Elton and Gruber, 1970):

$$(P_0 - P_X)/D = (1 - t_P)/(1 - t_G)$$

where P_0 is the price just before the share goes ex, P_X is the ex-dividend share price, D is the amount of the dividend per share, t_P is the relevant marginal personal tax rate on dividends, and t_G is the effective marginal tax rate on capital gains.

(a) If $t_P = t_G = 0$, how much will the share price fall when the equity goes ex?

(b) If $t_P = 36.1$ per cent and $t_G = 0$, how much will the share price fall?

(c) If $t_P = 36.1$ per cent and $t_G = 28$ per cent, how much will the share price fall?

(d) What does this problem tell you about real-world tax considerations and the dividend policy of the firm?

16.17 Residual Dividend Policy Worthington AG has declared an annual dividend of 1.50 Swiss Francs (SFr) per share. For the year just ended, earnings were SFr14 per share. What is Worthington's payout ratio? Suppose Worthington has 12 million shares outstanding. Borrowing for the coming year is planned at SFr25 million. What are planned investment outlays assuming a residual dividend policy? Determine the D/E ratio.

16.18 Dividends versus Reinvestment National Business Machine plc (NBM) has £2 million of extra cash after taxes have been paid. NBM has two choices to make use of this cash. One alternative is to invest the cash in financial assets. The resulting investment income will be paid out as a special dividend at the end of 3 years. In this case, the firm can invest in either Treasury bills yielding 7 per cent or an 11 per cent preferred stock. Another alternative is to pay out the cash now as dividends. This would allow the shareholders to invest on their own in Treasury bills with the same yield, or in preferred stock. The corporate tax rate is 28 per cent. Assume the investor has a 40 per cent personal income tax rate, which is applied to interest income and preferred stock dividends.

The personal dividend tax rate is 12.5 per cent on cash dividends. Should the cash be paid today or in 3 years? Which of the two options generates the highest after-tax income for the shareholders?

16.19 Dividends versus Reinvestment After completing its capital spending for the year, Carlson Manufacturing has £1,000 extra cash. Carlson's managers must choose between investing the cash in Treasury bonds that yield 8 per cent or paying the cash out to investors who would invest in the bonds themselves.

(a) If the corporate tax rate is 28 per cent, what personal tax rate would make the investors equally willing to receive the dividend or to let Carlson invest the money?

(b) Is the answer to (a) reasonable? Why or why not?

MINI CASE

HOMEWARE SUSTAINABLES

Homeware Sustainables (HS) is an online furniture and homeware firm based in Marseilles founded 15 years ago by entrepreneurs Georges Thiébald and Louis-Lucien Klotz. HS manufactures low-cost but high-quality sustainably sourced furniture products for distribution around Europe.

The sustainability ethos permeates all parts of the business, from its sales approaches to the maintenance of the supply chain. All raw materials are sourced from sustainable suppliers. For example, the wood used in all the company's products comes only from lumber mills following sustainable replanting practices. Homeware Sustainables pursues a triple bottom line business model and targets net-zero carbon emissions every year.

In addition to Georges and Louis-Lucien, Katherine Pancol, who provided capital for the company, is the third primary owner. Each owns 25 per cent of the 1 million shares outstanding. Several other individuals, including current employees, own the remaining company shares.

Recently, the company has designed a new solar panel for sale to homeowners. The company believes the solar panel's design is both more efficient and less expensive to manufacture than existing models, and expects to capture significant market share from the product. After investigating the possibility of manufacturing the solar panels, HS determined that the costs involved in building a new manufacturing plant would be prohibitive. The owners also decided that they were unwilling to bring in another large outside owner. Instead, HS sold the design to an outside firm. The sale of the solar panel design was completed for an after-tax payment of €30 million.

QUESTIONS

1. Georges believes the company should use the extra cash to pay a special one-time dividend. How will this proposal affect the share price? How will it affect the value of the company?
2. Louis-Lucent believes that the company should use the extra cash to pay off debt and upgrade its existing manufacturing capability. How would Louis-Lucent's proposals affect the company?
3. Katherine is in favour of a share repurchase. She argues that a repurchase will increase the company's P/E ratio, return on assets, and return on equity. Are her arguments correct? How will a share repurchase affect the value of the company?
4. Another option discussed by Georges, Louis-Lucent and Katherine would be to begin a regular dividend payment to shareholders. How would you evaluate this proposal?
5. One way to value a share of equity is the dividend growth, or growing perpetuity, model. Consider the following. The dividend payout ratio is 1 minus b, where b is the 'retention' or 'ploughback' ratio. So the dividend next year will be the earnings next year, E_1, times 1 minus the retention ratio. The most commonly used equation to calculate the sustainable growth rate is the return on equity times the retention ratio. Substituting these relationships into the dividend growth model, we get the following equation to calculate the price of a share of equity today:

$$P_0 = \frac{E_1(1-b)}{R_s - \text{ROE} \times b}$$

What are the implications of this result regarding whether the company should pay a dividend or upgrade and expand its manufacturing capability? Explain.

6. Does the question of whether the company should pay a dividend depend on whether the company is organized as a corporation or as a partnership?

ADDITIONAL READING

Dividend policy, the reasons why firms issue dividends, the factors affecting dividend policy, and their importance to investors are issues that have been bothering academics since Modigliani and Miller published their original dividend irrelevance theorem. The papers that are referenced below consider dividends in detail.

Theoretical Developments

1. Allen, F., Bernardo, A.E., & Welch, I. (2000). A theory of dividends based on tax clienteles. *Journal of Finance, 55*(6), 2499–2536.

2. Almeida, H., Fos, V., & Kronlund, M. (2016). The real effects of share repurchases. *Journal of Financial Economics, 119*(1), 168–185.

3. DeAngelo, H., & DeAngelo, L. (2006). The irrelevance of the MM dividend irrelevance theorem. *Journal of Financial Economics, 80*(2), 299–315.

4. Ohlson, J.A., Ostaszewski, A.J., & Gao, Z. (2011). Dividend policy irrelevancy and the construct of earnings. Working Paper.

Dividend Policy, Share Repurchases and Stock Splits

5. Andres, C., Betzer, A., Goergen, M., & Renneboog, L. (2009). Dividend policy of German firms: A panel data analysis of partial adjustment models. *Journal of Empirical Finance, 16*(2), 175–187.

6. Berkman, H., & Koch, P.D. (2017). Drips and the dividend pay date effect. *Journal of Financial and Quantitative Analysis, 52*(4), 1765–1795

7. Brav, A., Graham, J.R., Harvey, C.R., & Michaely, R. (2005). Payout policy in the 21st century. *Journal of Financial Economics, 77*(3), 483–527.

8. Bremberger, F., Cambini, C., Gugler, K., & Rondi, L. (2016). Dividend policy in regulated network industries: Evidence from the EU. *Economic Inquiry, 54*(1), 408–432.

9. Chen, J., Leung, W.S., & Goergen, M. (2017). The impact of board gender composition on dividend payouts. *Journal of Corporate Finance, 43*, 86–105.

10. Ferris, S., Sen, N., & Yui, H. (2006). God save the Queen and her dividends: Corporate payouts in the United Kingdom. *Journal of Business, 79*(3), 1149–1173.

11. Ferris, S.P., Jayaraman, N., & Sabherwal, S. (2009). Catering effects in corporate dividend policy: The international evidence. *Journal of Banking and Finance, 33*(9), 1730–1738.

12. Floyd, E., Li. N., & Skinner, D.J. (2015). Payout policy through the financial crisis: The growth of repurchases and the resilience of dividends. *Journal of Financial Economics, 118*(2), 299–316.

13. Graham, J.R., & Kumar, A. (2006). Do dividend clienteles exist? Evidence on dividend preferences of retail investors. *Journal of Finance, 61*(3), 1305–1336.

14. Grennan, J. (2019). Dividend payments as a response to peer influence. *Journal of Financial Economics, 131*(3), 549–570.

15. Grinstein, Y., & Michaely, R. (2005). Institutional holdings and payout policy. *Journal of Finance, 60*(3), 1389–1426.

16. He, W., Ng, L., Zaiats, N., & Zhang, B. (2017). Dividend policy and earnings management across countries. *Journal of Corporate Finance, 42*, 267–286.

17. Jacob, M., & Michaely, R. (2017). Taxation and dividend policy: The muting effect of agency issues and shareholder conflicts. *Review of Financial Studies, 30*(9), 3176–3222.

18. Kinkki, S. (2008). Minority protection and dividend policy in Finland. *European Financial Management, 14*(3), 470–502.

19. Kunz, R.M., & Rosa-Majhensek, S. (2008). Stock splits in Switzerland: To signal or not to signal. *Financial Management, 37*(2), 193–226.

20. La Porta, L., Lopez-de-Silanes, F., Shliefer, A., & Vishney, R. (2000). Agency problems and dividend policy around the world. *Journal of Finance, 55*(1), 1–33.

21. Li, W., & Lie, E. (2006). Dividend changes and catering incentives. *Journal of Financial Economics, 80*(2), 293–308.

22. Renneboog, L., & Trojanowski, G. (2011). Patterns in payout policy and payout channel choice. *Journal of Banking and Finance, 35*(6), 1477–1490.

Endnotes

1. The same results would occur after an issue of bonds, although the arguments would be less easily presented.
2. In fact, capital gains taxes can sometimes be avoided altogether. Although we do not recommend this particular tax avoidance strategy, the capital gains tax may be avoided by dying. Your heirs are not considered to have a capital gain, so the tax liability dies when you do. In this instance, you can take it with you.
3. Graham, B., Dodd, D. & Cottle, S. (1962). *Security analysis*. McGraw-Hill.
4. This list is distilled in part from a longer list in DeAngelo, H., & DeAngelo, L. (2007). Payout policy pedagogy: What matters and why. *European Financial Management, 13*(1), 11–27.

PART SIX

TOPICS IN CORPORATE FINANCE

17	Short-Term Financial Planning and Management	479
18	International Corporate Finance	520
19	Behavioural Finance	552
20	Financial Risk Management	000
21	Options and Corporate Finance	000
22	Mergers and Acquisitions	000

CHAPTER 17
SHORT-TERM FINANCIAL PLANNING AND MANAGEMENT

LEARNING OBJECTIVES
After studying this chapter, you should understand:
- **LO1** The importance of float, and how it affects the cash balances.
- **LO2** How firms manage their cash, and some of the collection, concentration and disbursement techniques used.
- **LO3** The advantages and disadvantages of holding cash, and some of the ways to invest idle cash.
- **LO4** How firms manage their receivables, and the basic components of a firm's credit policies.
- **LO5** How to analyse the decision by a firm to grant credit.
- **LO6** The types of inventory and inventory management system used by firms.
- **LO7** How to determine the costs of carrying inventory and the optimal inventory level.

KEY NOTATIONS

ACP	Average collection period
C	Cash balance
C^*	Optimal or target cash balance
CC	Carrying costs per unit
EAR	Effective annual rate of return
EOQ	Economic order quantity
F	The fixed cost of making a securities trade to replenish cash
L	Lower cash balance limit
NPV	Net present value
P	Price per unit
PV	Present value
Q	Quantity sold per period or quantity of inventory ordered per period
R	The opportunity cost of holding cash
r	Monthly required return
T	The total amount of new cash needed for transaction purposes over the relevant planning period
T (Sec. 17.2)	Total sales per period
U^*	Upper cash balance limit
v	Variable cost per unit
π	Percentage of bad debts
σ^2	Variance of the net cash flow per period

CONVENTIONAL WISDOM states the main reason a company will go out of business is because of a poor product or business plan. In fact, a key factor in predicting financial distress is poor cash and inventory management. Another reason for business failure is attempting to grow too fast. A lot of start-ups fail because they have not implemented a sustainable growth plan, invested too heavily in anticipation of new business, and quickly run out of cash because they needed to honour their increased fixed costs. With the pandemic recovery underway, most firms have had to readjust their business models to optimize cash, credit and inventory management. Remember, even if a firm is growing and has excellent performance, if it runs out of cash it cannot survive.

This chapter is about how firms manage cash and other short-term financial assets. The basic objective in short-term financial management is to keep the investment in cash and other short-term assets as low as possible while still keeping the firm operating efficiently and effectively. This goal usually reduces to the dictum 'Collect early and pay late'. Accordingly, we discuss ways of accelerating collections and managing disbursements.

In addition, firms must invest temporarily idle cash in short-term marketable securities. As we discuss in various places, these securities can be bought and sold in the financial markets. As a group, they have minimal default risk, and most are highly marketable. There are different types of these so-called money market securities, and we discuss a few of the most important ones.

17.1 REASONS FOR HOLDING CASH

John Maynard Keynes, in his classic work *The General Theory of Employment, Interest and Money*, identified three motives for liquidity: the speculative motive, the precautionary motive, and the transaction motive. We discuss these next.

THE SPECULATIVE AND PRECAUTIONARY MOTIVES

speculative motive
the need to hold cash to take advantage of additional investment opportunities, such as bargain purchases.

The **speculative motive** is the need to hold cash in order to be able to take advantage of, for example, bargain purchases that might arise, attractive interest rates and (in the case of international firms) favourable exchange rate fluctuations.

For most firms, reserve borrowing ability and marketable securities can be used to satisfy speculative motives. Thus there might be a speculative motive for maintaining liquidity, but not necessarily for holding cash *per se*. Think of it this way: if you have a credit card with a very large credit limit, then you can probably take advantage of any unusual bargains that come along without carrying any cash.

precautionary motive
the need to hold cash as a safety margin to act as a financial reserve.

This is also true, to a lesser extent, for precautionary motives. The **precautionary motive** is the need for a safety supply to act as a financial reserve. Once again, there probably is a precautionary motive for maintaining liquidity. However, given that the value of money market instruments is relatively certain, and that instruments such as T-bills are extremely liquid, there is no real need to hold substantial amounts of cash for precautionary purposes.

THE TRANSACTION MOTIVE

transaction motive
the need to hold cash to satisfy normal disbursement and collection activities associated with a firm's ongoing operations.

Cash is needed to satisfy the **transaction motive**: the need to have cash on hand to pay bills. Transaction-related needs come from the normal disbursement and collection activities of the firm. The disbursement of cash includes the payment of wages and salaries, trade debts, taxes and dividends.

Cash is collected from product sales, the selling of assets and new financing. The cash inflows (collections) and outflows (disbursements) are not perfectly synchronized, and some level of cash holdings is necessary to serve as a buffer.

As electronic funds transfers and other high-speed 'paperless' payment mechanisms continue to develop, even the transaction demand for cash may all but disappear. Even if it does, however, there will still be a demand for liquidity and a need to manage it efficiently.

COMPENSATING BALANCES

Compensating balances are another reason to hold cash. Cash balances are kept at banks to compensate for banking services the firm receives. A minimum compensating balance requirement may impose a lower limit on the level of cash a firm holds.

COSTS OF HOLDING CASH

When a firm holds cash in excess of some necessary minimum, it incurs an opportunity cost. The opportunity cost of excess cash (held in currency or bank deposits) is the interest income that could be earned in the next best use, such as investment in marketable securities.

Given the opportunity cost of holding cash, why would a firm hold cash in excess of its compensating balance requirements? The answer is that a cash balance must be maintained to provide the liquidity necessary for transaction needs – paying bills. If the firm maintains too small a cash balance, it may run out of cash. If this happens, the firm may have to raise cash on a short-term basis. This could involve, for example, selling marketable securities or borrowing.

Activities such as selling marketable securities and borrowing involve various costs. As we've discussed, holding cash has an opportunity cost. To determine the appropriate cash balance, the firm must weigh the benefits of holding cash against these costs. We discuss this subject in more detail in the sections that follow.

CASH MANAGEMENT VERSUS LIQUIDITY MANAGEMENT

Before we move on, we should note that it is important to distinguish between true cash management and a more general subject, liquidity management. The distinction is a source of confusion, because the word *cash* is used in practice in two different ways. First of all, it has its literal meaning: actual cash on hand. However, financial managers frequently use the word to describe a firm's holdings of cash along with its marketable securities, and marketable securities are sometimes called *cash equivalents* or *near-cash*.

The distinction between liquidity management and cash management is straightforward. Liquidity management concerns the optimal quantity of liquid assets a firm should have on hand, and it is one particular aspect of the current asset management policies we discuss in this chapter. Cash management is much more closely related to optimizing mechanisms for collecting and disbursing cash.

> **CONCEPT QUESTIONS**
>
> **17.1a** What is the transaction motive, and how does it lead firms to hold cash?
> **17.1b** What is the cost to the firm of holding excess cash?

17.2 MANAGING SHORT-TERM CAPITAL

In large companies, the responsibility for managing short-term capital will reside in the *Treasury Department*. A treasury department normally consists of a small group of specialists focused on one or more of the following:

1. **Liquidity Management.** All firms must manage their cash flow and optimize its efficiency through maintaining cash balances through the cycle of short-term deficit and surplus positions.
2. **Credit Management.** The treasury department will be responsible for designing the firm's optimal trade credit policy and the use of credit instruments for short-term financing needs.
3. **Inventory Management.** If inventory and raw materials are a significant component of current assets, the treasury department will be concerned with its impact on liquidity and may be responsible for ensuring optimal inventory control systems are in place.

4. **Risk Management.** Treasury departments are most commonly recognized for their involvement in managing the firm's risk. This is covered in more detail in Chapter 20.
5. **Advisory.** Many treasury departments provide financial advisory services to corporate management because of the number of accountants and financially literate staff in the treasury team.

TEMPORARY CASH SURPLUSES

Firms have temporary cash surpluses for various reasons. Two of the most important are the financing of seasonal or cyclical activities of the firm and the financing of planned or possible expenditures.

Seasonal or Cyclical Activities

Some firms have a predictable cash flow pattern. They have surplus cash flows during part of the year and deficit cash flows for the rest of the year. For example, companies that sell Christmas trees, gazebos, barbecues, and garden furniture will have a seasonal cash flow pattern influenced by the weather. Restaurants and department stores are heavily reliant on the holiday season. Firms like these may buy marketable securities when surplus cash flows occur, and sell marketable securities when deficits occur. Of course, bank loans are another short-term financing device. The use of bank loans and marketable securities to meet temporary financing needs is illustrated in Figure 17.1. In this case, the firm is following a compromise working capital policy.

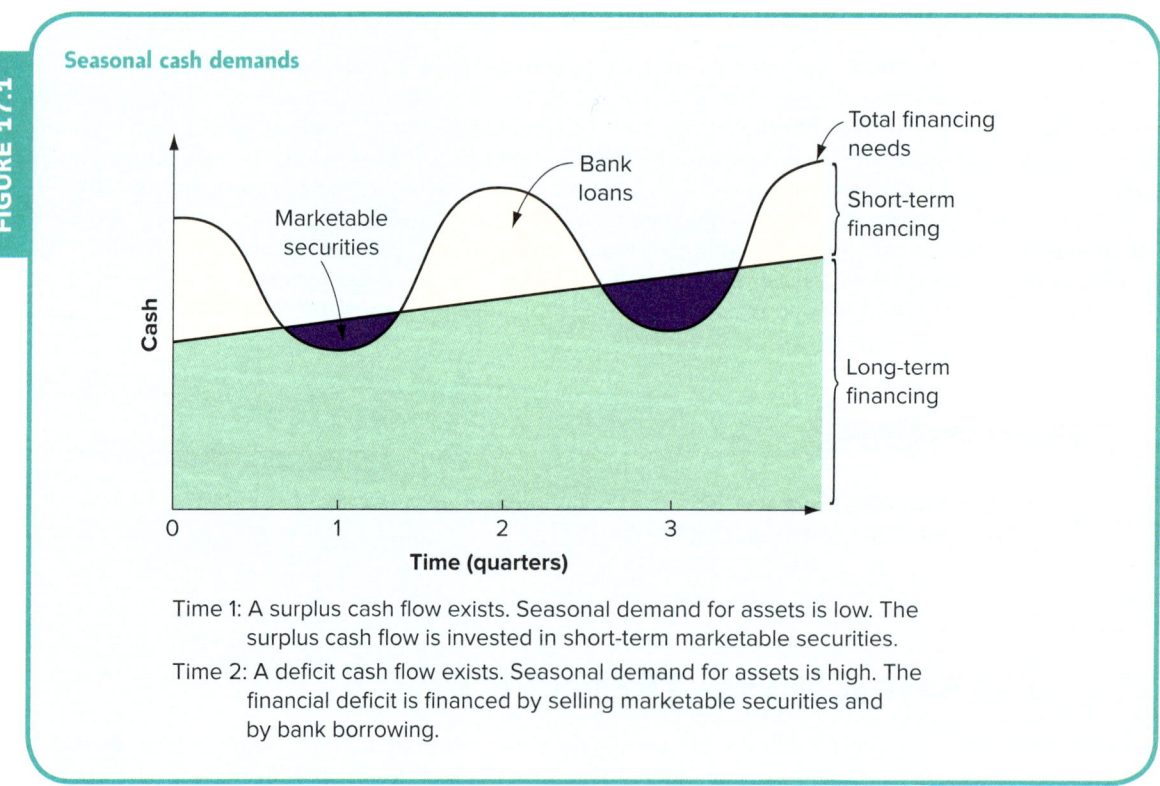

FIGURE 17.1

Time 1: A surplus cash flow exists. Seasonal demand for assets is low. The surplus cash flow is invested in short-term marketable securities.

Time 2: A deficit cash flow exists. Seasonal demand for assets is high. The financial deficit is financed by selling marketable securities and by bank borrowing.

Planned or Possible Expenditures

Firms frequently accumulate temporary investments in marketable securities to provide the cash for a plant construction programme, dividend payment or other large expenditure. Thus firms may issue bonds and shares before the cash is needed, investing the proceeds in short-term marketable securities and then selling the securities to finance the expenditures. Also, firms may face the possibility of having to make a large cash outlay. An obvious example would involve the possibility of losing a large lawsuit. Firms may build up cash surpluses against such a contingency.

> **CONCEPT QUESTIONS**
>
> **17.2a** What are some reasons why firms find themselves with idle cash?

SOURCES OF SHORT-TERM FINANCE

Liquidity management requires the firm to dynamically manage liquidity so that the short-term fluctuations of cash and inventory are smoothed over time. The one thing a treasury department hates is volatility because this creates the risk of a liquidity crunch and the possibility it will not be able to pay its creditors or purchase inventory for its production processes.

When a firm has temporary surplus cash balances, it will want to invest this in very short-term money market instruments. When it has a temporary deficit cash balance it will want to draw on short-term financing to offset the liquidity shortage. The four main sources of short-term finance are:

1. Bank overdrafts
2. Short-term loans
3. Trade credit
4. Short-term leases

We will cover bank overdrafts, short-term loans and leases in this section, and trade credit in Sections 17.5 to 17.10.

BANK OVERDRAFTS

Bank overdrafts allow a firm to temporarily borrow from a bank through its current account. Once the overdraft has been set up, it can be used to smooth out short-term volatility in the firm's cash flow. Every firm will aim to have an overdraft facility because it provides flexibility in cash management at a relatively low cost.

A commitment fee will normally be required when a firm initially sets up the overdraft and there will also be an annual fee for the service. An overdraft limit will be agreed and when a firm utilizes the overdraft, it will be charged interest on a daily basis for the amount overdrawn. Sometimes collateral will be required against the overdraft limit but this is unusual and only occurs when there is a material risk in the borrowing firm's operations.

SHORT-TERM LOANS

Short-term loans will be for a set period and the normal lender is the bank. Unlike a bank overdraft, the funds are released immediately and contracted payments are required over the life of the loan.

Short-term loans and bank overdrafts are sometimes compared because they both provide funding for short periods. Bank overdrafts are attractive when a firm wishes to smooth cash flow volatility arising from day-to-day trading, whereas a short-term loan will normally be used to purchase an asset.

Most firms have an overdraft facility as well as short-term loans, which provides the maximum flexibility in cash flow management. The overdraft is available to manage the day-to-day fluctuations in cash flow and short-term loans are used to finance property or equipment.

SHORT-TERM LEASES

A *lease* is a contractual agreement between a lessee and lessor. The agreement establishes that the lessee has the right to use an asset and in return must make periodic payments to the lessor, the owner of the asset. The lessor is either the asset's manufacturer or an independent leasing company. If the lessor is an independent leasing company, it must buy the asset from a manufacturer. Then the lessor delivers the asset to the lessee, and the lease goes into effect.

TABLE 17.1

Bank overdrafts versus short-term loans

Bank overdraft	Short-term loan
Commitment fee and annual fee	No set-up fee
An overdraft is a credit facility that is available to a firm when required. Interest is due only when a firm's current account balance is in deficit. This is known as the bank account being overdrawn.	The cash from the loan is transferred immediately upon the contract being signed. Interest is charged from the moment the loan is set up.
Firms will pay off overdraft when able.	Loan repayments are set for the life of the loan. Interest rates are lower for short-term loans than for bank overdrafts.
There is always a risk the lender will reduce or remove the overdraft facility.	The borrowing firm received the money immediately and so has certainty in the money being available during the lifetime of the loan.

As far as the lessee is concerned, it is the use of the asset that is most important, not who owns the asset, and a lease contract allows the asset to be used without ownership. The alternative is for the user to buy the asset, and this will involve alternative financing arrangements.

There are two types of leases: operating leases and financial leases.

OPERATING LEASES

Years ago, a lease where the lessee received an operator along with the equipment was called an operating lease. Though the operating lease defies an exact definition today, this form of leasing has several salient characteristics:

1. Operating leases are usually not fully amortized. This means that the payments required under the terms of the lease do not cover the full cost of the asset for the lessor. This is because the term or life of the operating lease is usually less than the economic life of the asset. Thus, the lessor must expect to recover the costs of the asset by renewing the lease or by selling the asset for its residual value.
2. Operating leases usually require the lessor to maintain and insure the leased assets.
3. Perhaps the most interesting feature of an operating lease is the cancellation option. This option gives the lessee the right to cancel the lease contract before the expiration date. If the option to cancel is exercised, the lessee must return the equipment to the lessor. The value of a cancellation clause depends on whether future technological or economic conditions are likely to make the value of the asset to the lessee less than the value of the future lease payments under the lease.

FINANCIAL LEASES

Financial leases are the exact opposite of operating leases, as seen from their characteristics:

1. Financial leases do not provide for maintenance or service by the lessor.
2. Financial leases are fully amortized.
3. The lessee usually has a right to renew the lease on expiration.
4. Generally, financial leases cannot be cancelled. In other words, the lessee must make all payments or face the risk of bankruptcy.

Because of these characteristics, particularly (2), this lease provides an alternative method of financing to purchase. Hence, its name is a sensible one. Operating leases will normally be for short periods and used as an alternative to purchasing an item.

> **CONCEPT QUESTIONS**
>
> **17.2b** What are the options available to firms that require short-term finance?
> **17.2c** In what ways are bank overdrafts different from short-term loans?
> **17.2d** What are the two types of leases? Which one is better for short-term financing? Why?

17.3 INVESTING IDLE CASH

If a firm has a temporary cash surplus, it can invest in short-term securities. As we have mentioned at various times, the market for short-term financial assets is called the *money market*. The maturity of short-term financial assets that trade in the money market is one year or less.

Most large firms manage their own short-term financial assets, carrying out transactions through banks and dealers. Some large firms and many small firms use money market mutual funds. These are funds that invest in short-term financial assets for a management fee. The management fee is compensation for the professional expertise and diversification provided by the fund manager.

Among the many money market mutual funds, some specialize in corporate customers. In addition, banks offer arrangements in which the bank takes all excess available funds at the close of each business day and invests them for the firm.

Money market instruments can be divided into three broad categories:

1. Interest bearing instruments
2. Discount instruments
3. Derivatives

INTEREST-BEARING INSTRUMENTS

Interest-bearing instruments are simply very short-term loans. The main interest-bearing instruments are:

1. Money market deposits (loans between banks)
2. Certificates of deposit (loans from companies to banks)
3. Repurchase agreements (loans between companies and/or banks)

Money Market Deposits

The term of a money market deposit ranges from overnight to up to 12 months. Money market deposits are either *fixed* (interest rate and term are decided at the beginning of the contract) or *call* (interest rate is determined by a benchmark rate and term can be shortened if prior notice is given).

Typical benchmark rates are SONIA (Sterling Overnight Index Average), LIBOR (London Interbank Offer Rate, to be phased out in 2021), and €STR (euro short-term rate). These are collectively known as SOFR (Secured Overnight Financing Rates).

Certificates of Deposit (CD)

A certificate of deposit is a very short-term loan from a company with excess cash to a bank. The certificate of deposit has a specified interest rate and term. Negotiable certificates of deposit can be sold before the instrument's expiry date whereas a non-negotiable certificate of deposit cannot be traded and must be held to maturity.

Certificates of deposit are just like money market deposits except that the former is a loan by a company to a bank instead of between banks.

Repurchase Agreements (Repo)

The third type of interest-bearing instrument is the repurchase agreement, or repo as it is commonly known. With a repo, a firm will sell a security to another firm and simultaneously agrees to buy it back in the future at a higher price. The difference between the sale price and the subsequent purchase price is equivalent to interest.

Typical securities are government treasury bills or other low-risk short-term securities.

> **EXAMPLE 17.1**
>
> ### CALCULATING THE REPURCHASE PRICE OF A REPO
>
> Your firm requires £100 million over the next 30 days to manage a potential cash shortage from supply chain investments. Your treasury department has decided the appropriate instrument is a repo and sold £100 million of 30-day UK treasury bills to a multinational bank. The repo rate is 1.9 per cent per annum. How much is due in 30 days?
>
> Assuming a 365 day year, the interest payment will be:
>
> Interest = £100 million × 30/365 × 0.019 = £157,808
>
> The amount due in 30 days is £100 million + £157,808 interest = £100,157,808

DISCOUNT INSTRUMENTS

Discount instruments are zero-coupon debt securities with a very short life of less than 12 months. The main discount instruments are:

1. Treasury bills
2. Commercial paper
3. Banker's acceptances

Treasury Bills

Treasury bills are short-term government debt securities. The typical maturity ranges from 1 month to 12 months.

Commercial Paper

Commercial paper is the corporate equivalent of treasury bills. They are short-term debt securities of up to 12 months, with the most common maturity being either 1 or 3 months. Only the largest companies can issue commercial paper and the instruments are almost always unsecured.

Banker's Acceptances

A banker's acceptance is an instrument used by importers and exporters in countries where they do not have a strong corporate presence. A company must first set up a banker's acceptance facility with a bank and will issue discount instruments against the facility. The banker's acceptance will have a maturity and will sell at a discount. The distinctive characteristic of a banker's acceptance is that the bank guarantees the payment and so credit risk is lower than it otherwise may be. The borrowing firm will pay the bank any moneys owed. Banker's acceptances are short-term instruments with less than 12 months to maturity.

DERIVATIVE INSTRUMENTS

The three most common short-term derivative instruments are forwards, futures and options.

1. **Forwards.** A bespoke agreement between two firms to exchange an asset (such as cash or foreign exchange) for a set price at a specified date in the future.
2. **Futures.** A standardized exchange-traded forward contract. The asset characteristics, asset quantity, price and contract maturity are standardized. Futures contracts can be traded on an exchange.
3. **Options.** contract that gives the holder the right but not the obligation to buy or sell an asset for a set price at or before a specified date in the future. Option contracts may be bespoke or exchange traded.

Derivate securities are discussed in much greater depth in Chapter 21.

17.4 DETERMINING THE TARGET CASH BALANCE

The **target cash balance** involves a trade-off between the opportunity costs of holding too much cash (the carrying costs) and the costs of holding too little (the shortage costs, also called **adjustment costs**). The nature of these costs depends on the firm's working capital policy.

If the firm has a flexible working capital policy, it will probably maintain a marketable securities portfolio. In this case the adjustment, or shortage, costs will be the trading costs associated with buying and selling securities. If the firm has a restrictive working capital policy, it will probably borrow in the short term to meet cash shortages. The costs in this case will be the interest and other expenses associated with arranging a loan.

In our discussion that follows, we shall assume the firm has a flexible policy. Its cash management, then, consists of moving money in and out of marketable securities. This is a traditional approach to the subject, and it is a nice way of illustrating the costs and benefits of holding cash. Keep in mind, however, that the distinction between cash and money market investments is becoming increasingly blurred.

target cash balance
a firm's desired cash level as determined by the trade-off between carrying costs and shortage costs.

adjustment costs
the costs associated with holding too little cash. Also, *shortage costs*.

THE BASIC IDEA

Figure 17.2 presents the cash management problem for our flexible firm. If a firm tries to keep its cash holdings too low, it will find itself running out of cash more often than is desirable, and thus selling marketable securities (and perhaps later buying marketable securities to replace those sold) more frequently than would be the case if the cash balance were higher. Thus trading costs will be high when the cash balance is small. These costs will fall as the cash balance becomes larger.

In contrast, the opportunity costs of holding cash are low if the firm holds little cash. These costs increase as the cash holdings rise, because the firm is giving up more interest that could have been earned.

FIGURE 17.2

Trading costs are increased when the firm must sell securities to establish a cash balance. Opportunity costs are increased when there is a cash balance because there is no return on cash.

In Figure 17.2 the sum of the costs is given by the total cost curve. As shown, the minimum total cost occurs where the two individual cost curves cross at point C^*. At this point the opportunity costs and the trading costs are equal. This point represents the target cash balance, and it is the point the firm should try to find.

THE BAT MODEL

The Baumol–Allais–Tobin (BAT) model is a classic means of analysing our cash management problem. We shall show how this model can be used to actually establish the target cash balance. It is a straightforward model useful for illustrating the factors in cash management and, more generally, current asset management.

To develop the BAT model, suppose Golden Socks plc starts off at week 0 with a cash balance of $C =$ £1.2 million. Each week, outflows exceed inflows by £600,000. As a result, the cash balance will drop to zero at the end of week 2. The average cash balance will be the beginning balance (£1.2 million) plus the ending balance (£0) divided by 2, or (£1.2 million + 0)/2 = £600,000, over the two-week period. At the end of week 2, Golden Socks replenishes its cash by depositing another £1.2 million.

As we have described, the simple cash management strategy for Golden Socks boils down to depositing £1.2 million every 2 weeks. This policy is shown in Figure 17.3. Notice how the cash balance declines by £600,000 per week. Because the company brings the account up to £1.2 million, the balance hits zero every 2 weeks.

Implicitly, we assume that the net cash outflow is the same every day and is known with certainty. These two assumptions make the model easy to handle. We shall indicate in the next section what happens when they do not hold.

If C were set higher, at £2.4 million, say, cash would last 4 weeks before the firm would have to sell marketable securities; but the firm's average cash balance would increase to £1.2 million (from £600,000). If C were set at £600,000, cash would run out in one week, and the firm would have to replenish cash more frequently; but the average cash balance would fall from £600,000 to £300,000.

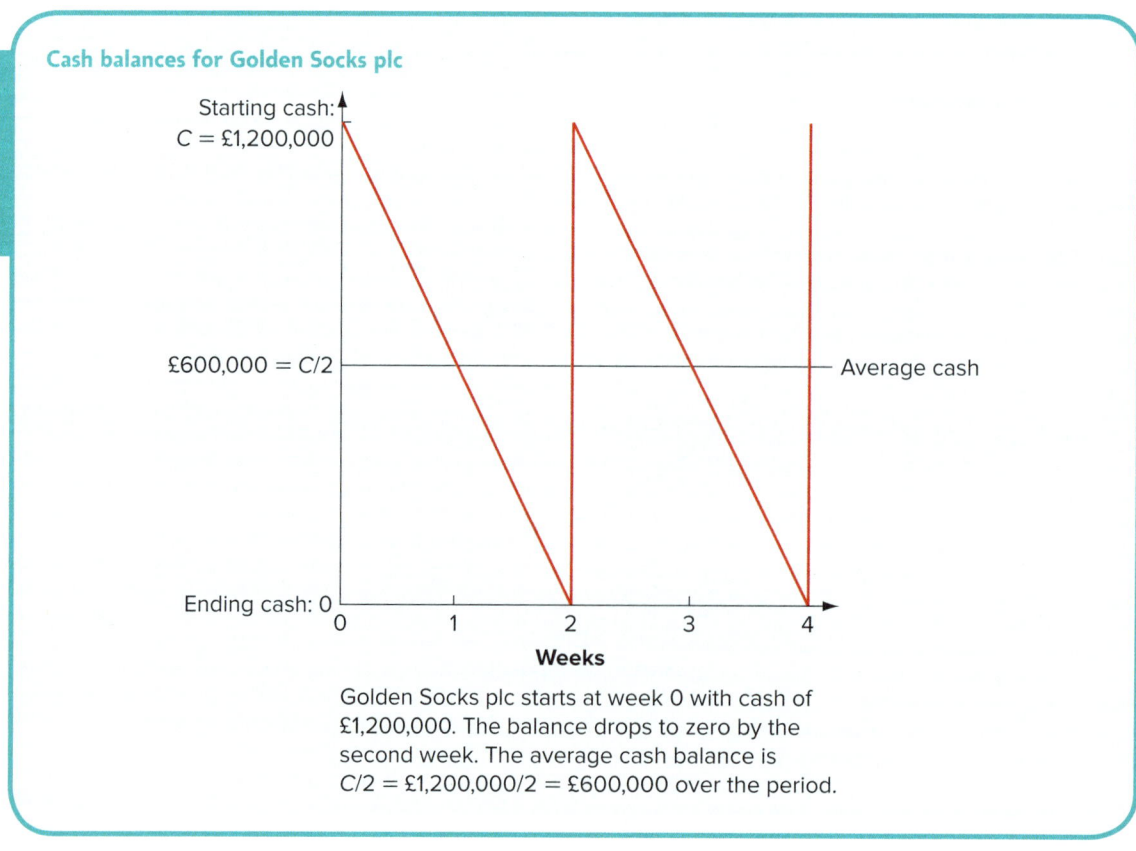

FIGURE 17.3

Cash balances for Golden Socks plc

Golden Socks plc starts at week 0 with cash of £1,200,000. The balance drops to zero by the second week. The average cash balance is $C/2$ = £1,200,000/2 = £600,000 over the period.

Because transaction costs (for example, the brokerage costs of selling marketable securities) must be incurred whenever cash is replenished, establishing large initial balances will lower the trading costs connected with cash management. However, the larger the average cash balance, the greater is the opportunity cost (the return that could have been earned on marketable securities).

To determine the optimal strategy, Golden Socks needs to know the following three things:

F = The fixed cost of making a securities trade to replenish cash.
T = The total amount of new cash needed for transaction purposes over the relevant planning period – say, one year.
R = The opportunity cost of holding cash. This is the interest rate on marketable securities.

With this information, Golden Socks can determine the total costs of any particular cash balance policy. It can then determine the optimal cash balance policy.

The Opportunity Costs

To determine the opportunity costs of holding cash, we have to find out how much interest is forgone. Golden Socks has, on average, $C/2$ in cash. This amount could be earning interest at rate R. So the total opportunity costs of cash balances are equal to the average cash balance multiplied by the interest rate:

$$\text{Opportunity costs} = (C/2) \times R \tag{17.1}$$

For example, the opportunity costs of various alternatives are given here, assuming that the interest rate is 10 per cent:

Initial cash balance, C (£)	Average cash balance, $C/2$ (£)	Opportunity cost, $(C/2) \times R$ (£) ($R = 0.10$)
4,800,000	2,400,000	240,000
2,400,000	1,200,000	120,000
1,200,000	600,000	60,000
600,000	300,000	30,000
300,000	150,000	15,000

In our original case, in which the initial cash balance is £1.2 million, the average balance is £600,000. The interest Golden Socks could have earned on this (at 10 per cent) is £60,000, so this is what the firm gives up with this strategy. Notice that the opportunity costs increase as the initial (and average) cash balance rises.

The Trading Costs

To determine the total trading costs for the year, we need to know how many times Golden Socks will have to sell marketable securities during the year. First, the total amount of cash disbursed during the year is £600,000 per week, so T = £600,000 × 52 weeks = £31.2 million. If the initial cash balance is set at C = £1.2 million, Golden Socks will sell £1.2 million in marketable securities: T/C = £31.2 million/ £1.2 million = 26 times per year. It costs F pounds each time, so trading costs are given by:

$$\frac{£31.2 \text{ million}}{£1.2 \text{ million}} \times F = 26 \times F$$

In general, the total trading costs will be given by:

$$\text{Trading costs} = (T/C) \times F \tag{17.2}$$

In this example, if F were £1,000 (an unrealistically large amount), the trading costs would be £26,000.

We can calculate the trading costs associated with some different strategies as follows:

Total amount of disbursements during relevant period, T (£)	Initial cash balance, C (£)	Trading costs, (T/C) × F (£) (F = £1,000)
31,200,000	4,800,000	6,500
31,200,000	2,400,000	13,000
31,200,000	1,200,000	26,000
31,200,000	600,000	52,000
31,200,000	300,000	104,000

The Total Cost

Now that we have the opportunity costs and the trading costs, we can calculate the total cost by adding them together:

$$\text{Total cost} = \text{Opportunity costs} + \text{Trading costs}$$
$$= (C/2) \times R + (T/C) \times F \tag{17.3}$$

Using the numbers generated earlier, we have the following:

Cash balance (£)	Opportunity costs (£)	+	Trading costs (£)	=	Total cost (£)
4,800,000	240,000		6,500		246,500
2,400,000	120,000		13,000		133,000
1,200,000	60,000		26,000		86,000
600,000	30,000		52,000		82,000
300,000	15,000		104,000		119,000

Notice how the total cost starts out at almost £250,000 and declines to about £82,000 before starting to rise again.

The Solution

We can see from the preceding schedule that a £600,000 cash balance results in the lowest total cost of the possibilities presented: £82,000. But what about £700,000 or £500,000, or other possibilities? It appears that the optimal balance is somewhere between £300,000 and £1.2 million. With this in mind, we could easily proceed by trial and error to find the optimal balance. It is not difficult to find it directly, however, so we do this next.

Take a look back at Figure 17.2. As the figure is drawn, the optimal size of the cash balance, C^*, occurs right where the two lines cross. At this point the opportunity costs and the trading costs are exactly equal. So, at C^*, we must have that:

$$\text{Opportunity costs} = \text{Trading costs}$$
$$(C^*/2) \times R = (T/C^*) \times F$$

With a little algebra, we can write:

$$C^{*2} = (2T \times F)/R$$

To solve for C^*, we take the square root of both sides to get:

$$C^* = \sqrt{(2T \times F)/R} \tag{17.4}$$

This is the optimal initial cash balance.

For Golden Socks we have $T = £31.2$ million, $F = £1,000$, and $R = 10\%$. We can now find the optimal cash balance:

$$C^* = \sqrt{(2 \times £31,200,000 \times 1,000)/0.10}$$
$$= \sqrt{£624 \text{ billion}}$$
$$= £789,937$$

We can verify this answer by calculating the various costs at this balance, as well as a little above and a little below:

Cash balance (£)	Opportunity costs (£)	+	Trading costs (£)	=	Total cost (£)
850,000	42,500		36,706		79,206
800,000	40,000		39,000		79,000
789,937	39,497		39,497		78,994
750,000	37,500		41,600		79,100
700,000	35,000		44,571		79,571

The total cost at the optimal cash level is £78,994, and it does appear to increase as we move in either direction.

EXAMPLE 17.2

THE BAT MODEL

Vulcan SA has cash outflows of €100 per day, 7 days a week. The interest rate is 5 per cent, and the fixed cost of replenishing cash balances is €10 per transaction. What is the optimal initial cash balance? What is the total cost?

The total cash needed for the year is 365 days × €100 = €36,500. From the BAT model, we have that the optimal initial balance is:

$$C^* = \sqrt{(2T \times F)/R}$$
$$= \sqrt{(2 \times €36,500 \times 10)/0.05}$$
$$= \sqrt{€14.6 \text{ million}}$$
$$= €3,821$$

The average cash balance is €3,821/2 = €1,911, so the opportunity cost is €1,911 × 0.05 = €96. Because Vulcan needs €100 per day, the €3,821 balance will last €3,821/100 = 38.21 days. The firm needs to resupply the account 365/38.21 = 9.6 times per year, so the trading (order) cost is €96. The total cost is €192.

Conclusion

The BAT model is possibly the simplest and most stripped-down sensible model for determining the optimal cash position. Its chief weakness is that it assumes steady, certain cash outflows. We next discuss a more involved model designed to deal with this limitation.

THE MILLER-ORR MODEL: A MORE GENERAL APPROACH

We now describe a cash management system designed to deal with cash inflows and outflows that fluctuate randomly from day to day. With this model we again concentrate on the cash balance. But in contrast to the situation with the BAT model, we assume that this balance fluctuates up and down randomly, and that the average change is zero.

The Basic Idea

Figure 17.4 shows how the system works. It operates in terms of an upper limit (U^*) and a lower limit (L) to the amount of cash, as well as a target cash balance (C^*). The firm allows its cash balance to wander around between the lower and upper limits. As long as the cash balance is somewhere between U^* and L, nothing happens.

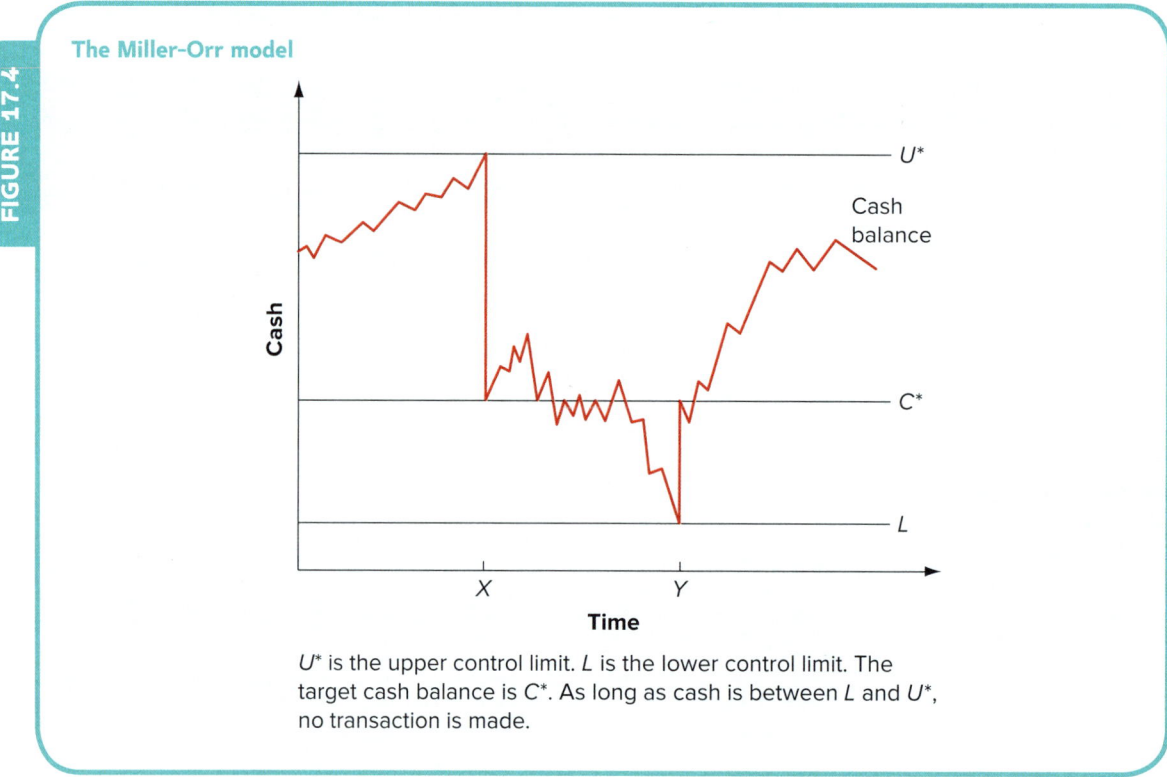

FIGURE 17.4 The Miller-Orr model

U^* is the upper control limit. L is the lower control limit. The target cash balance is C^*. As long as cash is between L and U^*, no transaction is made.

When the cash balance reaches the upper limit (U^*), as it does at point X, the firm moves $U^* - C^*$ cash out of the account and into marketable securities. This action moves the cash balance down to C^*. In the same way, if the cash balance falls to the lower limit (L), as it does at point Y, the firm will sell $C^* - L$ worth of securities and deposit the cash in the account. This action takes the cash balance up to C^*.

Using the Model

To get started, management sets the lower limit (L). This limit essentially defines a safety stock, so where it is set depends on how much risk of a cash shortfall the firm is willing to tolerate. Alternatively, the minimum might just equal a required compensating balance.

As with the BAT model, the optimal cash balance depends on trading costs and opportunity costs. Once again, the cost per transaction of buying and selling marketable securities, F, is assumed to be fixed. Also, the opportunity cost of holding cash is R, the interest rate per period on marketable securities.

The only extra piece of information needed is σ^2, the variance of the net cash flow per period. For our purposes the period can be anything – a day or a week, for example – as long as the interest rate and the variance are based on the same length of time.

Given L, which is set by the firm, Miller and Orr show that the cash balance target, C^*, and the upper limit, U^*, that minimize the total costs of holding cash are:

$$C^* = L + \left(3/4 \times F \times \sigma^2 / R\right)^{1/3} \tag{17.5}$$

$$U^* = 3 \times C^* - 2 \times L \tag{17.6}$$

Also, the average cash balance in the Miller–Orr model is:

$$\text{Average cash balance} = (4 \times C^* - L)/3 \tag{17.7}$$

The derivation of these expressions is relatively complex, so we shall not present it here. Fortunately, as we illustrate next, the results are not difficult to use.

For example, suppose $F = €10$, the interest rate is 1 per cent per month, and the standard deviation of the monthly net cash flows is €200. The variance of the monthly net cash flows is:

$$\sigma^2 = €200^2 = €40,000$$

We assume a minimum cash balance of $L = €100$. We can calculate the cash balance target, C^*, as follows:

$$\begin{align}C^* &= L + (3/4 \times F \times \sigma^2/R)^{1/3} \\ &= €100 + (3/4 \times 10 \times 40,000/0.01)^{1/3} \\ &= €100 + 30,000,000^{1/3} \\ &= €100 + 311 = €411\end{align}$$

The upper limit, U^*, is thus:

$$\begin{align}U^* &= 3 \times C^* - 2 \times L \\ &= 3 \times €411 - 2 \times 100 \\ &= €1,033\end{align}$$

Finally, the average cash balance will be:

$$\begin{align}\text{Average cash balance} &= (4 \times C^* - L)/3 \\ &= (4 \times €411 - 100)/3 \\ &= €515\end{align}$$

IMPLICATIONS OF THE BAT AND MILLER–ORR MODELS

Our two cash management models differ in complexity, but they have some similar implications. In both cases, all other things being equal, we see that:

1. The greater the interest rate, the lower is the target cash balance.
2. The greater the order cost, the higher is the target balance.

These implications are both fairly obvious. The advantage of the Miller–Orr model is that it improves our understanding of the problem of cash management by considering the effect of uncertainty, as measured by the variation in net cash inflows.

The Miller–Orr model shows that the greater the uncertainty is (the higher σ^2 is), the greater is the difference between the target balance and the minimum balance. Similarly, the greater the uncertainty is, the higher is the upper limit and the higher is the average cash balance. These statements all make intuitive sense. For example, the greater the variability is, the greater is the chance that the balance will drop below the minimum. We thus keep a higher balance to guard against this happening.

OTHER FACTORS INFLUENCING THE TARGET CASH BALANCE

Before moving on, we briefly discuss two additional considerations that affect the target cash balance.

First, in our discussion of cash management, we assume cash is invested in marketable securities such as Treasury bills. The firm obtains cash by selling these securities. Another alternative is to borrow cash. Borrowing introduces additional considerations to cash management:

1. Borrowing is likely to be more expensive than selling marketable securities, because the interest rate is likely to be higher.
2. The need to borrow will depend on management's desire to hold low cash balances. A firm is more likely to have to borrow to cover an unexpected cash outflow with greater cash flow variability and lower investment in marketable securities.

Second, for large firms, the trading costs of buying and selling securities are small when compared with the opportunity costs of holding cash. For example, suppose a firm has £1 million in cash that won't be needed for 24 hours. Should the firm invest the money or leave it sitting?

Suppose the firm can invest the money at an annualized rate of 7.57 per cent per year. The daily rate in this case is about two basis points (0.02 per cent or 0.0002). The daily return earned on £1 million is thus 0.0002 × £1 million = £200. In many cases, the order cost will be much less than this; so a large firm will buy and sell securities very often before it will leave substantial amounts of cash idle.

> **CONCEPT QUESTIONS**
>
> **17.4a** What is a target cash balance?
> **17.4b** What is the basic trade-off in the BAT model?
> **17.4c** Describe how the Miller-Orr model works.

17.5 CREDIT AND RECEIVABLES

When a firm sells goods and services, it can demand cash on or before the delivery date, or it can extend credit to customers and allow some delay in payment. The next few sections provide an idea of what is involved in the firm's decision to grant credit to its customers. Granting credit is making an investment in a customer – an investment tied to the sale of a product or service.

Why do firms grant credit? Not all do, but the practice is extremely common. The obvious reason is that offering credit is a way of stimulating sales. The costs associated with granting credit are not trivial. First, there is the chance that the customer will not pay. Second, the firm has to bear the costs of carrying the receivables. The credit policy decision thus involves a trade-off between the benefits of increased sales and the costs of granting credit.

From an accounting perspective, when credit is granted, a trade receivable is created. Such receivables include credit to other firms, called *trade credit*, and credit granted to consumers, called *consumer credit*. About one-sixth of all the assets of industrial firms are in the form of trade receivables, so receivables obviously represent a major investment of financial resources by businesses.

> **REAL WORLD INSIGHTS**
>
> Bank overdrafts and trade credit (where a business allows its customers to obtain goods and pay an agreed number of days later) are the most flexible and popular ways for SMEs to access short-term funding and manage cash flow. Traditional industries (such as building and construction) in particular often rely on this to buy vital equipment and materials in advance of their jobs.
>
> Trade credit is important for all firms, and especially for small companies with low cash flow. Clearly, trade credit helps smaller firms purchase raw materials without the accompanying cash outlay. It also generates opportunities for companies that supply small businesses who would otherwise struggle to find resources for upfront inventory or working capital requirements.
>
> A new form of short-term capital management includes barter exchanges, where firms present services or goods instead of cash in transactions. These are listed on public exchanges and are an innovative way to conserve cash. An example of a barter transaction is a marketing firm providing advertising services to a restaurant, who supplies the firm with a number of meals to be used by the marketing firm's clients.

COMPONENTS OF CREDIT POLICY

If a firm decides to grant credit to its customers, then it must establish procedures for extending credit and collecting. In particular, the firm will have to deal with the following components of credit policy:

1. **Terms of sale**: The terms of sale establish how the firm proposes to sell its goods and services. A basic decision is whether the firm will require cash or will extend credit. If the firm does grant credit to a

customer, the terms of sale will specify (perhaps implicitly) the credit period, the cash discount and discount period, and the type of credit instrument.

2. **Credit analysis**: In granting credit, a firm determines how much effort to expend trying to distinguish between customers who will pay and customers who will not pay. Firms use a number of devices and procedures to determine the probability that customers will not pay: put together, these are called credit analysis.

3. **Collection policy**: After credit has been granted, the firm has the potential problem of collecting the cash, for which it must establish a collection policy.

In the next several sections, we shall discuss these components of credit policy, which collectively make up the decision to grant credit.

> **terms of sale**
> the conditions under which a firm sells its goods and services for cash or credit.

> **credit analysis**
> the process of determining the probability that customers will not pay.

THE INVESTMENT IN RECEIVABLES

The investment in trade receivables for any firm depends on the amount of credit sales and the average collection period. For example, if a firm's average collection period, ACP, is 30 days, then at any given time there will be 30 days' worth of sales outstanding. If credit sales run £1,000 per day, the firm's trade receivables will then be equal to 30 days × £1,000 per day = £30,000, on average.

As our example illustrates, a firm's receivables generally will be equal to its average daily sales multiplied by its average collection period:

$$\text{Trade receivables} = \text{Average daily sales} \times \text{ACP} \qquad (17.8)$$

Thus a firm's investment in trade receivables depends on factors that influence credit sales and collections.

We have seen the average collection period in various places, including Chapter 3. Recall that we use the terms *days' sales in receivables, receivables period* and *average collection period* interchangeably to refer to the length of time it takes for the firm to collect on a sale.

> **collection policy**
> the procedures followed by a firm in collecting trade receivables.

CONCEPT QUESTIONS

17.5a What are the basic components of credit policy?
17.5b What are the basic components of the terms of sale if a firm chooses to sell on credit?

17.6 TERMS OF THE SALE

As we described previously, the terms of a sale are made up of three distinct elements:

1. The period for which credit is granted (the credit period)
2. The cash discount and the discount period
3. The type of credit instrument

Within a given industry, the terms of sale are usually fairly standard, but these terms vary quite a bit across industries. In many cases the terms of sale are remarkably archaic, and literally date to previous centuries. Organized systems of trade credit that resemble current practice can be easily traced to the great fairs of medieval Europe, and they almost surely existed long before then.

THE BASIC FORM

The easiest way to understand the terms of sale is to consider an example. Terms such as '2/10, net 60' are common. This means that customers have 60 days from the invoice date (discussed a bit later) to pay the full amount; however, if payment is made within 10 days, a 2 per cent cash discount can be taken.

Consider a buyer who places an order for €1,000, and assume that the terms of the sale are 2/10, net 60. The buyer has the option of paying €1,000 × (1 − 0.02) = €980 in 10 days, or paying the full €1,000 in 60 days. If the terms are stated as just net 30, then the customer has 30 days from the invoice date to pay the entire €1,000, and no discount is offered for early payment.

In general, credit terms are interpreted in the following way:

[take this discount off the invoice price] / [if you pay in this many days], [else pay the full invoice amount in this many days]

Thus '5/10, net 45' means take a 5 per cent discount from the full price if you pay within 10 days, or else pay the full amount in 45 days.

THE CREDIT PERIOD

> **credit period**
> the length of time for which credit is granted.

The **credit period** is the basic length of time for which credit is granted. The credit period varies widely from industry to industry, but it is almost always between 30 and 120 days. If a cash discount is offered, then the credit period has two components: the net credit period and the cash discount period.

The net credit period is the length of time the customer has to pay. The cash discount period is the time during which the discount is available. With 2/10, net 30, for example, the net credit period is 30 days and the cash discount period is 10 days.

> **invoice**
> a bill for goods or services provided by the seller to the purchaser.

The Invoice Date

The invoice date is the beginning of the credit period. An **invoice** is a written account of services provided or merchandise shipped to the buyer. For individual items, by convention, the invoice date is usually the shipping date or the billing date, *not* the date on which the buyer receives the goods or the bill.

Many other arrangements exist. For example, the terms of sale might be ROG, for *receipt of goods*. In this case the credit period starts when the customer receives the order. This might be used when the customer is in a remote location.

With EOM dating, all sales made during a particular month are assumed to be made at the end of that month. This is useful when a buyer makes purchases throughout the month, but the seller bills only once a month.

For example, terms of '2/10th, EOM' tell the buyer to take a 2 per cent discount if payment is made by the 10th of the month; otherwise the full amount is due. Confusingly, the end of the month is sometimes taken to be the 25th day of the month. MOM, for middle of month, is another variation.

Seasonal dating is sometimes used to encourage sales of seasonal products during the off-season. A product sold primarily in the summer (suntan oil?) can be shipped in January with credit terms of '2/10, net 30'. However, the invoice might be dated 1 May so that the credit period actually begins at that time. This practice encourages buyers to order early.

Length of the Credit Period

Several factors influence the length of the credit period. Two important ones are the *buyer's* inventory period and operating cycle. All else equal, the shorter these are, the shorter the credit period will be.

The operating cycle has two components: the inventory period and the receivables period. The buyer's inventory period is the time it takes the buyer to acquire inventory (from us), process it and sell it. The buyer's receivables period is the time it then takes the buyer to collect on the sale. Note that the credit period we offer is effectively the buyer's payables period.

By extending credit, we finance a portion of our buyer's operating cycle and thereby shorten that buyer's cash cycle. If our credit period exceeds the buyer's inventory period, then we are financing not only the buyer's inventory purchases, but also part of the buyer's receivables.

Furthermore, if our credit period exceeds our buyer's operating cycle, then we are effectively providing financing for aspects of our customer's business beyond the immediate purchase and sale of our merchandise. The reason is that the buyer effectively has a loan from us even after the merchandise is resold, and the buyer can use that credit for other purposes. For this reason, the length of the buyer's operating cycle is often cited as an appropriate upper limit to the credit period.

There are a number of other factors that influence the credit period. Many of these also influence our customer's operating cycles; so, once again, these are related subjects. Among the most important are these:

1. *Perishability and collateral value:* Perishable items have relatively rapid turnover and relatively low collateral value. Credit periods are thus shorter for such goods. For example, a food wholesaler selling fresh fruit and produce might use net 7 days. Alternatively, jewellery might be sold for 5/30, net 4 months.
2. *Consumer demand:* Products that are well established generally have more rapid turnover. Newer or slow-moving products will often have longer credit periods associated with them to entice buyers. Also, as we have seen, sellers may choose to extend much longer credit periods for off-season sales (when customer demand is low).
3. *Cost, profitability and standardization:* Relatively inexpensive goods tend to have shorter credit periods. The same is true for relatively standardized goods and raw materials. These all tend to have lower mark-ups and higher turnover rates, both of which lead to shorter credit periods. However, there are exceptions. Car dealers, for example, generally pay for the vehicles as they are received.
4. *Credit risk:* The greater the credit risk of the buyer, the shorter the credit period is likely to be (if credit is granted at all).
5. *Size of the account:* If an account is small, the credit period may be shorter because small accounts cost more to manage, and the customers are less important.
6. *Competition:* When the seller is in a highly competitive market, longer credit periods may be offered as a way of attracting customers.
7. *Customer type:* A single seller might offer different credit terms to different buyers. A food wholesaler, for example, might supply groceries, bakeries and restaurants. Each group would probably have different credit terms. More generally, sellers often have both wholesale and retail customers, and they frequently quote different terms to the two types.

CASH DISCOUNTS

As we have seen, **cash discounts** are often part of the terms of sale. One reason why discounts are offered is to speed up the collection of receivables. This will have the effect of reducing the amount of credit being offered, and the firm must trade this off against the cost of the discount.

cash discount
a discount given to induce prompt payment. Also, *sales discount*.

Notice that when a cash discount is offered, the credit is essentially free during the discount period. The buyer pays for the credit only after the discount expires. With 2/10, net 30, a rational buyer either pays in 10 days to make the greatest possible use of the free credit or pays in 30 days to get the longest possible use of the money in exchange for giving up the discount. By giving up the discount, the buyer effectively gets $30 - 10 = 20$ days' credit.

Another reason for cash discounts is that they are a way of charging higher prices to customers that have had credit extended to them. In this sense, cash discounts are a convenient way of charging for the credit granted to customers.

Cost of the Credit

In our examples it might seem that the discounts are rather small. With 2/10, net 30, for example, early payment gets the buyer only a 2 per cent discount. Does this provide a significant incentive for early payment? The answer is yes, because the implicit interest rate is extremely high.

To see why the discount is important, we shall calculate the cost to the buyer of not paying early. To do this, we shall find the interest rate that the buyer is effectively paying for the trade credit. Suppose the order is for £1,000. The buyer can pay £980 in 10 days or wait another 20 days and pay £1,000. It's obvious that the buyer is effectively borrowing £980 for 20 days and that the buyer pays £20 in interest on the 'loan'. What's the interest rate?

This interest is ordinary discount interest, which we discussed in Chapter 5. With £20 in interest on £980 borrowed, the rate is £20/980 = 2.0408%. This is relatively low, but remember that this is the rate per 20-day period. There are 365/20 = 18.25 such periods in a year: so, by not taking the discount, the buyer is paying an effective annual rate (EAR) of:

$$\text{EAR} = 1.020408^{18.25} - 1 = 44.6\%$$

From the buyer's point of view this is an expensive source of financing!

Given that the interest rate is so high here, it is unlikely that the seller benefits from early payment. Ignoring the possibility of default by the buyer, the decision of a customer to forgo the discount almost surely works to the seller's advantage.

Trade Discounts

In some circumstances the discount is not really an incentive for early payment but is instead a *trade discount*, a discount routinely given to some type of buyer. For example, with our 2/10th, EOM terms, the buyer takes a 2 per cent discount if the invoice is paid by the 10th, but the bill is considered due on the 10th, and overdue after that. Thus the credit period and the discount period are effectively the same, and there is no reward for paying before the due date.

The Cash Discount and the ACP

To the extent that a cash discount encourages customers to pay early, it will shorten the receivables period and, all other things being equal, reduce the firm's investment in receivables.

For example, suppose a firm currently has terms of net 30 and an average collection period (ACP) of 30 days. If it offers terms of 2/10, net 30, then perhaps 50 per cent of its customers (in terms of volume of purchases) will pay in 10 days. The remaining customers will still take an average of 30 days to pay. What will the new ACP be? If the firm's annual sales are £15 million (before discounts), what will happen to the investment in receivables?

If half of the customers take 10 days to pay and half take 30, then the new average collection period will be:

$$\text{New ACP} = 0.50 \times 10 \text{ days} + 0.50 \times 30 \text{ days} = 20 \text{ days}$$

The ACP thus falls from 30 days to 20 days. Average daily sales are £15 million/365 = £41,096 per day. Receivables will thus fall by £41,096 × 10 = £410,960.

CREDIT INSTRUMENTS

credit instrument
the evidence of indebtedness.

The **credit instrument** is the basic evidence of indebtedness. Most trade credit is offered on *open account*. This means that the only formal instrument of credit is the invoice, which is sent with the shipment of goods and which the customer signs as evidence that the goods have been received. Afterwards, the firm and its customers record the exchange on their books of account.

At times, the firm may require that the customer sign a *promissory note*. This is a basic IOU, and might be used when the order is large, when there is no cash discount involved, or when the firm anticipates a problem in collections. Promissory notes are not common, but they can eliminate possible controversies later about the existence of debt.

One problem with promissory notes is that they are signed after delivery of the goods. One way to obtain a credit commitment from a customer before the goods are delivered is to arrange a *commercial draft*. Typically, the firm draws up a commercial draft calling for the customer to pay a specific amount by a specified date. The draft is then sent to the customer's bank with the shipping invoices.

If immediate payment is required on the draft, it is called a *sight draft*. If immediate payment is not required, then the draft is a *time draft*. When the draft is presented and the buyer 'accepts' it, meaning that the buyer promises to pay it in the future, then it is called a *trade acceptance* and is sent back to the selling firm. The seller can then keep the acceptance or sell it to someone else. If a bank accepts the draft, meaning that the bank is guaranteeing payment, then the draft becomes a *banker's acceptance*. This arrangement is common in international trade, and banker's acceptances are actively traded in the money market.

A firm can also use a conditional sales contract as a credit instrument. With such an arrangement the firm retains legal ownership of the goods until the customer has completed payment. Conditional sales contracts are usually paid in instalments, and have an interest cost built into them.

CONCEPT QUESTIONS

17.6a What considerations enter the determination of the terms of sale?
17.6b Explain what terms of '3/45, net 90' mean. What is the effective interest rate?

17.7 ANALYSING CREDIT POLICY

In this section we take a closer look at the factors that influence the decision to grant credit. Granting credit makes sense only if the NPV from doing so is positive. We thus need to look at the NPV of the decision to grant credit.

CREDIT POLICY EFFECTS

In evaluating credit policy, there are five basic factors to consider:

1. *Revenue effects:* If the firm grants credit, then there will be a delay in revenue collections as some customers take advantage of the credit offered and pay later. However, the firm may be able to charge a higher price if it grants credit, and it may be able to increase the quantity sold. Total revenues may thus increase.
2. *Cost effects:* Although the firm may experience delayed revenues if it grants credit, it will still incur the costs of sales immediately. Whether the firm sells for cash or credit, it will still have to acquire or produce the merchandise (and pay for it).
3. *The cost of debt:* When the firm grants credit, it must arrange to finance the resulting receivables. As a result, the firm's cost of short-term borrowing is a factor in the decision to grant credit.
4. *The probability of non-payment:* If the firm grants credit, some percentage of the credit buyers will not pay. This can't happen, of course, if the firm sells for cash.
5. *The cash discount:* When the firm offers a cash discount as part of its credit terms, some customers will choose to pay early to take advantage of the discount.

EVALUATING A PROPOSED CREDIT POLICY

To illustrate how credit policy can be analysed, we shall start with a relatively simple case. Locust Software has been in existence for 2 years, and it is one of several successful firms that develop computer programs. Currently, Locust sells for cash only.

Locust is evaluating a request from some major customers to change its current policy to net 1 month (30 days). To analyse this proposal, we define the following:

P Price per unit
v Variable cost per unit
Q Current quantity sold per month
Q' Quantity sold under new policy
r Monthly required return

For now, we ignore discounts and the possibility of default. Also, we ignore taxes, because they don't affect our conclusions.

NPV of Switching Policies

To illustrate the NPV of switching credit policies, suppose we have the following for Locust:

$$P = €49$$
$$v = €20$$
$$Q = 100$$
$$Q' = 110$$

If the required return, r, is 2 per cent per month, should Locust make the switch?

Currently, Locust has monthly sales of $P \times Q = €4,900$. Variable costs each month are $v \times Q = €2,000$, so the monthly cash flow from this activity is:

$$\begin{aligned} \text{Cash flow with old policy} &= (P - v)Q \\ &= (€49 - 20) \times 100 \\ &= €2,900 \end{aligned} \quad (17.9)$$

This is not the total cash flow for Locust, of course, but it is all that we need to look at, because fixed costs and other components of cash flow are the same whether or not the switch is made.

If Locust does switch to net 30 days on sales, then the quantity sold will rise to $Q' = 110$. Monthly revenues will increase to $P \times Q'$, and costs will be $v \times Q'$. The monthly cash flow under the new policy will thus be:

$$\begin{aligned} \text{Cash flow with new policy} &= (P - v)Q' \\ &= (€49 - 20) \times 110 \\ &= €290 \end{aligned} \quad (17.10)$$

Going back to Chapter 9, we know that the relevant incremental cash flow is the difference between the new and old cash flows:

$$\begin{aligned} \text{Incremental cash inflow} &= (P - v)(Q' - Q) \\ &= (€49 - 20) \times (110 - 100) \\ &= €290 \end{aligned}$$

This says that the benefit each month of changing policies is equal to the gross profit per unit sold, $P - v = €29$, multiplied by the increase in sales, $Q' - Q = 10$. The present value of the future incremental cash flows is thus:

$$\text{PV} = [(P - v)(Q' - Q)]/r \quad (17.11)$$

For Locust, this present value works out to be:

$$\text{PV} = (€29 \times 10)/0.02 = €14,500$$

Notice that we have treated the monthly cash flow as a perpetuity, because the same benefit will be realized each month for ever.

Now that we know the benefit of switching, what's the cost? There are two components to consider. First, because the quantity sold will rise from Q to Q', Locust will have to produce $Q' - Q$ more units at a cost of $v(Q' - Q) = €20 \times (110 - 100) = €200$. Second, the sales that would have been collected this month under the current policy ($P \times Q = €4,900$) will not be collected. Under the new policy, the sales made this month won't be collected until 30 days later. The cost of the switch is the sum of these two components:

$$\text{Cost of switching} = PQ + v(Q' - Q) \quad (17.12)$$

For Locust this cost would be $€4,900 + 200 = €5,100$.

Putting it all together, we see that the NPV of the switch is:

$$\text{NPV of switching} = -[PQ + v(Q' - Q)] + [(P - v)(Q' - Q)]/r \quad (17.13)$$

For Locust, the cost of switching is €5,100. As we saw earlier, the benefit is €290 per month, for ever. At 2 per cent per month, the NPV is:

$$\begin{aligned} \text{NPV} &= -€5,100 + 290/0.02 \\ &= -€5,100 + 14,500 \\ &= €9,400 \end{aligned}$$

Therefore the switch is very profitable.

> **EXAMPLE 17.3**
>
> **WE'D RATHER FIGHT THAN SWITCH**
>
> Suppose a company is considering a switch from all cash to net 30, but the quantity sold is not expected to change. What is the NPV of the switch? Explain.
>
> In this case, $Q' - Q$ is zero, so the NPV is just $-PQ$. What this says is that the effect of the switch is simply to postpone one month's collections for ever, with no benefit from doing so.

A Break-Even Application

Based on our discussion thus far, the key variable for Locust is $Q' - Q$, the increase in unit sales. The projected increase of 10 units is only an estimate, so there is some forecasting risk. Under the circumstances, it's natural to wonder what increase in unit sales is necessary to break even.

Earlier, the NPV of the switch was defined as:

$$\text{NPV} = -[PQ + v(Q' - Q)] + [(P - v)(Q' - Q)]/r$$

We can calculate the break-even point explicitly by setting the NPV equal to zero and solving for $(Q' - Q)$:

$$\text{NPV} = 0 = -[PQ + v(Q' - Q)] + \frac{(P - v)(Q' - Q)}{r}$$
$$Q' - Q = \frac{PQ}{(P - v)/(r - v)} \quad (17.14)$$

For Locust, the break-even sales increase is thus:

$$Q' - Q = €4{,}900/(29/0.02 - 20)$$
$$= 3.43 \text{ units}$$

This tells us that the switch is a good idea as long as Locust is confident that it can sell at least 3.43 more units per month.

> **CONCEPT QUESTIONS**
>
> **17.7a** What are the important effects to consider in a decision to offer credit?
> **17.7b** Explain how to estimate the NPV of a credit policy switch.

17.8 OPTIMAL CREDIT POLICY

So far, we've discussed how to compute net present values for a switch in credit policy. We have not discussed the optimal amount of credit, or the optimal credit policy. In principle, the optimal amount of credit is determined by the point at which the incremental cash flows from increased sales are exactly equal to the incremental costs of carrying the increase in investment in trade receivables.

THE TOTAL CREDIT COST CURVE

The trade-off between granting credit and not granting credit isn't hard to identify, but it is difficult to quantify precisely. As a result, we can only describe an optimal credit policy.

To begin, the carrying costs associated with granting credit come in three forms:

1. The required return on receivables
2. The losses from bad debts
3. The costs of managing credit and credit collections

We have already discussed the first and second of these. The third cost, the cost of managing credit, consists of the expenses associated with running the credit department. Firms that don't grant credit have no such department, and no such expense. These three costs will all increase as credit policy is relaxed.

If a firm has a very restrictive credit policy, then all the associated costs will be low. In this case the firm will have a 'shortage' of credit, so there will be an opportunity cost. This opportunity cost is the extra potential profit from credit sales that are lost because credit is refused. This forgone benefit comes from two sources: the increase in quantity sold, Q' minus Q, and (potentially) a higher price. The opportunity costs go down as credit policy is relaxed.

> **credit cost curve**
> a graphical representation of the sum of the carrying costs and the opportunity costs of a credit policy.

The sum of the carrying costs and the opportunity costs of a particular credit policy is called the total **credit cost curve**. We have drawn such a curve in Figure 17.5. As Figure 17.5 illustrates, there is a point where the total credit cost is minimized. This point corresponds to the optimal amount of credit or, equivalently, the optimal investment in receivables.

If the firm extends more credit than this minimum, the additional net cash flow from new customers will not cover the carrying costs of the investment in receivables. If the level of receivables is below this amount, then the firm is forgoing valuable profit opportunities.

In general, the costs and benefits from extending credit will depend on the characteristics of particular firms and industries. All other things being equal, for example, it is likely that firms with (1) excess capacity, (2) low variable operating

FIGURE 17.5

The costs of granting credit

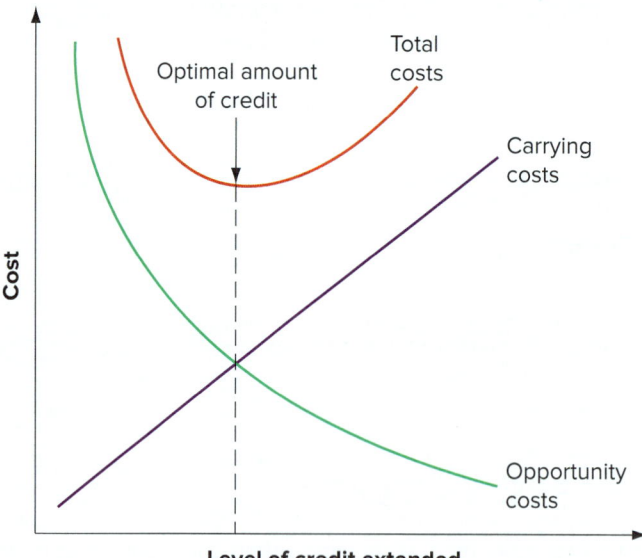

Carrying costs are the costs that must be incurred when credit is granted. They are positively related to the amount of credit extended.

Opportunity costs are the lost sales from refusing credit. These costs drop when credit is granted.

costs, and (3) repeat customers will extend credit more liberally than other firms. See if you can explain why each of these characteristics contributes to a more liberal credit policy.

> **CONCEPT QUESTIONS**
>
> **17.8a** What are the carrying costs of granting credit?
> **17.8b** What are the opportunity costs of not granting credit?

17.9 CREDIT ANALYSIS

Thus far we have focused on establishing credit terms. Once a firm decides to grant credit to its customers, it must then establish guidelines for determining who will and who will not be allowed to buy on credit. *Credit analysis* refers to the process of deciding whether or not to extend credit to a particular customer. It usually involves two steps: gathering relevant information, and determining creditworthiness.

WHEN SHOULD CREDIT BE GRANTED?

Imagine that a firm is trying to decide whether or not to grant credit to a customer. This decision can get complicated. For example, note that the answer depends on what will happen if credit is refused. Will the customer simply pay cash? Or will the customer not make the purchase at all? To avoid being bogged down by this and other difficulties, we shall use some special cases to illustrate the key points.

A One-Time Sale

We start by considering the simplest case. A new customer wishes to buy one unit on credit at a price of P per unit. If credit is refused, the customer will not make the purchase.

Furthermore, we assume that, if credit is granted, then, in one month, the customer will either pay up or default. The probability of the second of these events is π. In this case the probability (π) can be interpreted as the percentage of *new* customers who will not pay. Our business does not have repeat customers, so this is strictly a one-time sale. Finally, the required return on receivables is r per month, and the variable cost is v per unit.

The analysis here is straightforward. If the firm refuses credit, then the incremental cash flow is zero. If it grants credit, then it spends v (the variable cost) this month, and expects to collect $(1 - \pi)P$ next month. The NPV of granting credit is:

$$\text{NPV} = -v + (1 - \pi)P/(1 + r) \tag{17.15}$$

For example, for Locust Software, this NPV is:

$$\text{NPV} = -€20 + (1 - \pi) \times 49/1.02$$

With, say, a 20 per cent rate of default, this works out to be:

$$\text{NPV} = -€20 + 0.80 \times 49/1.02 = €18.43$$

Therefore credit should be granted. Notice that we have divided by $(1 + r)$ here, instead of by r, because we now assume that this is a one-time transaction.

Our example illustrates an important point. In granting credit to a new customer, a firm risks its variable cost (v) but it stands to gain the full price (P). For a new customer, then, credit may be granted even if the default probability is high. For example, the break-even probability, in this case, can be determined by setting the NPV equal to zero and solving for π:

$$\text{NPV} = 0 = -€20 + (1 - \pi) \times 49/1.02$$
$$1 - \pi = €20/49 \times 1.02$$
$$\pi = 58.4\%$$

Locust should extend credit as long as there is a 1 − 0.584 = 41.6% chance or better of collecting. This explains why firms with higher mark-ups tend to have looser credit terms.

This percentage (58.4%) is the maximum acceptable default probability for a *new* customer. If a returning, cash-paying customer wanted to switch to a credit basis, the analysis would be different, and the maximum acceptable default probability would be much lower.

The important difference is that, if we extend credit to a returning customer, we risk the total sales price (P), because this is what we collect if we don't extend credit. If we extend credit to a new customer, we risk only our variable cost.

Repeat Business

A second, very important factor to keep in mind is the possibility of repeat business. We can illustrate this by extending our one-time sale example. We make one important assumption: a new customer who does not default the first time around will remain a customer for ever and never default.

If the firm grants credit, it spends v this month. Next month, it gets nothing if the customer defaults, or it gets P if the customer pays. If the customer pays, then the customer will buy another unit on credit and the firm will spend v again. The net cash inflow for the month is thus $P - v$. In every subsequent month, this same $P - v$ will occur as the customer pays for the previous month's order and places a new one.

It follows from our discussion that, in one month, the firm will receive €0 with probability π. With probability $(1 - \pi)$, however, the firm will have a permanent new customer. The value of a new customer is equal to the present value of $(P - v)$ every month for ever:

$$PV = (P - v)/r$$

The NPV of extending credit is therefore:

$$NPV = -v + (1 - \pi)(P - v)/r \qquad (17.16)$$

For Locust, this is:

$$NPV = -€20 + (1 - \pi) \times (49 - 20)/0.02$$
$$= -€20 + (1 - \pi) \times 1{,}450$$

Even if the probability of default is 90 per cent, the NPV is:

$$NPV = -€20 + 0.10 \times 1{,}450 = €125$$

Locust should extend credit unless default is a virtual certainty. The reason is that it costs only €20 to find out who is a good customer and who is not. A good customer is worth €1,450, however, so Locust can afford quite a few defaults.

Our repeat business example probably exaggerates the acceptable default probability, but it does illustrate that it will often turn out that the best way to do credit analysis is simply to extend credit to almost anyone. It also points out that the possibility of repeat business is a crucial consideration. In such cases the important thing is to control the amount of credit initially offered to any one customer, so that the possible loss is limited. The amount can be increased with time. Most often, the best predictor of whether or not someone will pay in the future is whether or not they have paid in the past.

> **CONCEPT QUESTIONS**
>
> **17.9a** What is credit analysis?
> **17.9b** Should credit always be given?

17.10 COLLECTION POLICY

Collection policy is the final element in credit policy. Collection policy involves monitoring receivables to spot trouble, and obtaining payment on past-due accounts.

MONITORING RECEIVABLES

To keep track of payments by customers, most firms will monitor outstanding accounts. First of all, a firm will normally keep track of its average collection period (ACP) through time. If a firm is in a seasonal business, the ACP will fluctuate during the year; but unexpected increases in the ACP are a cause for concern. Either customers in general are taking longer to pay, or some percentage of trade receivables are seriously overdue.

> **ageing schedule**
> a compilation of trade receivables by the age of each account.

The **ageing schedule** is a second basic tool for monitoring receivables. To prepare one, the credit department classifies accounts by age. Suppose a firm has £100,000 in receivables. Some of these accounts are only a few days old, but others have been outstanding for quite some time. The following is an example of an ageing schedule:

Age of account (days)	Amount (£)	Percentage of total value of trade receivables (%)
0-10	50,000	50
11-60	25,000	25
61-80	20,000	20
Over 80	5,000	5
	100,000	100

If this firm has a credit period of 60 days, then 25 per cent of its accounts are late. Whether or not this is serious depends on the nature of the firm's collections and customers. It is often the case that accounts beyond a certain age are almost never collected. Monitoring the age of accounts is very important in such cases.

Firms with seasonal sales will find the percentages on the ageing schedule changing during the year. For example, if sales in the current month are very high, then total receivables will also increase sharply. This means that the older accounts, as a percentage of total receivables, become smaller and might appear less important. Some firms have refined the ageing schedule so that they have an idea of how it should change with peaks and valleys in their sales.

COLLECTION EFFORT

A firm usually goes through the following sequence of procedures for customers whose payments are overdue:

1. It sends out a delinquency letter informing the customer of the past-due status of the account.
2. It makes a telephone call to the customer.
3. It employs a collection agency.
4. It takes legal action against the customer.

At times, a firm may refuse to grant additional credit to customers until arrears are cleared up. This may antagonize a normally good customer, which points to a potential conflict between the collections department and the sales department.

In probably the worst case, the customer files for bankruptcy. When this happens, the credit-granting firm is just another unsecured creditor. The firm can simply wait, or it can sell its receivable.

> **CONCEPT QUESTIONS**
>
> **17.10a** What tools can a manager use to monitor receivables?
> **17.10b** What is an ageing schedule?

17.11 INVENTORY MANAGEMENT

Like receivables, inventories represent a significant investment for many firms. For a typical manufacturing operation, inventories will often exceed 15 per cent of assets. For a retailer, inventories could represent more than 25 per cent of assets. From our discussion earlier, we know that a firm's operating cycle is made up of its inventory period and its receivables period. This is one reason for considering credit and inventory policy in the same chapter. Beyond this, both credit policy and inventory policy are used to drive sales, and the two must be co-ordinated to ensure that the process of acquiring inventory, selling it, and collecting on the sale proceeds smoothly. For example, changes in credit policy designed to stimulate sales must be accompanied by planning for adequate inventory.

THE FINANCIAL MANAGER AND INVENTORY POLICY

Despite the size of a typical firm's investment in inventories, the financial manager of a firm will not normally have primary control over inventory management. Instead, other functional areas such as purchasing, production and marketing will usually share decision-making authority regarding inventory. Inventory management has become an increasingly important speciality in its own right, and financial management will often only have input into the decision. For this reason we shall just survey some basics of inventory and inventory policy.

INVENTORY TYPES

For a manufacturer, inventory is normally classified into one of three categories. The first category is *raw material*. This is whatever the firm uses as a starting point in its production process. Raw materials might be something as basic as iron ore for a steel manufacturer, or something as sophisticated as touch sensitive screens for a smartphone manufacturer.

The second type of inventory is *work in progress*, which is just what the name suggests – unfinished product. How big this portion of inventory is depends in large part on the length of the production process. For an airframe manufacturer, for example, work in progress can be substantial. The third and final type of inventory is *finished goods* – that is, products ready to ship or sell.

INVENTORY COSTS

Two basic types of costs are associated with current assets in general, and with inventory in particular. The first of these is *carrying costs*. Here, carrying costs represent all of the direct and opportunity costs of keeping inventory on hand. These include:

- Storage and tracking costs
- Insurance and taxes
- Losses due to obsolescence, deterioration or theft
- The opportunity cost of capital on the invested amount

The sum of these costs can be substantial, ranging roughly from 20 to 40 per cent of inventory value per year.

The other type of costs associated with inventory is *shortage costs*. Shortage costs are costs associated with having inadequate inventory on hand. The two components of shortage costs are restocking costs and costs related to safety reserves. Depending on the firm's business, restocking or order costs are either the costs of placing an order with suppliers or the costs of setting up a production run. The costs related to safety reserves are opportunity losses such as lost sales and loss of customer goodwill that result from having inadequate inventory.

A basic trade-off exists in inventory management, because carrying costs increase with inventory levels, whereas shortage or restocking costs decline with inventory levels. The basic goal of inventory management is thus to minimize the sum of these two costs. We consider ways to reach this goal in the next section.

> **CONCEPT QUESTIONS**
>
> **17.11a** What are the different types of inventory?
> **17.11b** What is the basic goal of inventory management?

17.12 INVENTORY MANAGEMENT TECHNIQUES

As we described earlier, the goal of inventory management is usually framed as cost minimization. Three techniques are discussed in this section, ranging from the relatively simple to the very complex.

THE ABC APPROACH

The ABC approach is a simple approach to inventory management, in which the basic idea is to divide inventory into three (or more) groups. The underlying rationale is that a small portion of inventory in terms of quantity might represent a large portion in terms of inventory value. For example, this situation would exist for a manufacturer that uses some relatively expensive, high-tech components and some relatively inexpensive basic materials in producing its products.

Figure 17.6 illustrates an ABC comparison of items in terms of the percentage of inventory value represented by each group versus the percentage of items represented. As Figure 17.6 shows, the A Group constitutes only 10 per cent of inventory by item count, but it represents over half of the value of inventory. The A Group items are thus monitored closely, and inventory levels are kept relatively low. At the other end, basic inventory items, such as nuts and bolts, also exist; but because these are crucial and inexpensive, large quantities are ordered and kept on hand. These would be C Group items. The B Group is made up of in-between items.

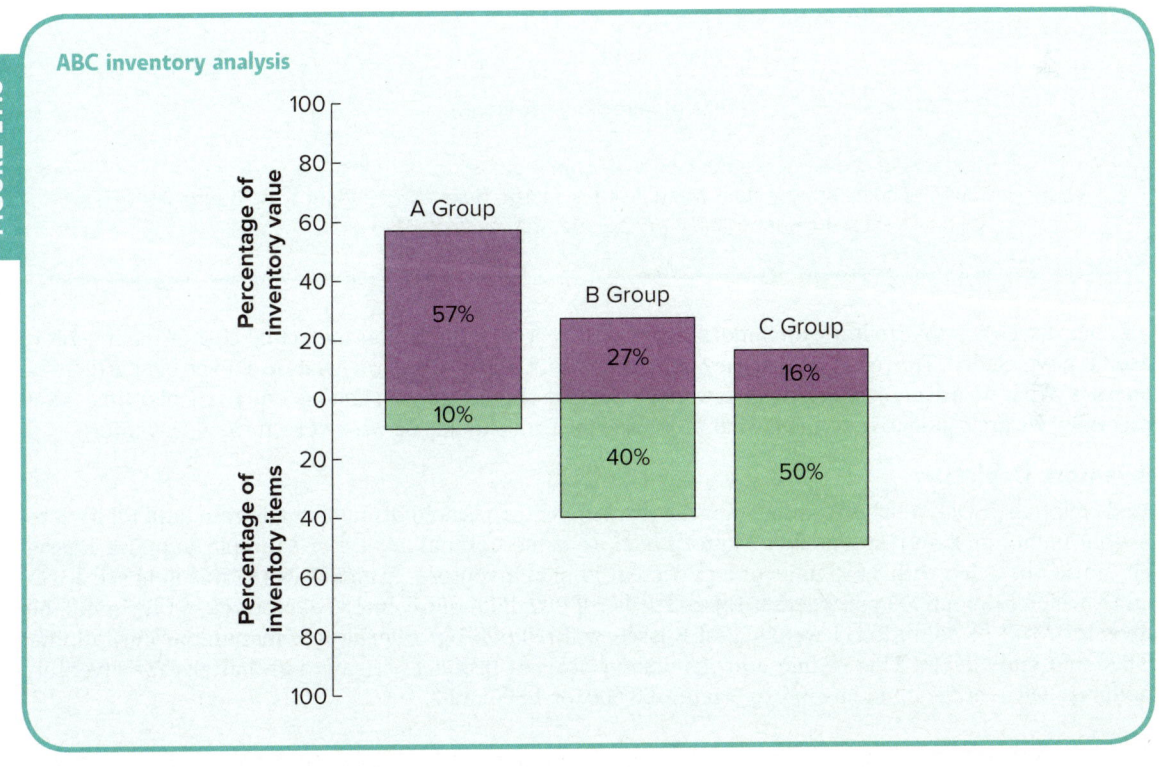

FIGURE 17.6 ABC inventory analysis

THE ECONOMIC ORDER QUANTITY MODEL

The economic order quantity (EOQ) model is the best-known approach for explicitly establishing an optimal inventory level. The basic idea is illustrated in Figure 17.7, which plots the various costs associated with holding inventory (on the vertical axis) against inventory levels (on the horizontal axis). As shown, inventory-carrying costs rise and restocking costs decrease as inventory levels increase. From our general discussion earlier in this chapter, and our discussion of the total credit cost curve, the general shape of the total inventory cost curve is familiar. With the EOQ model, we shall attempt to specifically locate the minimum total cost point, Q^*.

FIGURE 17.7 Costs of holding inventory

Restocking costs are greatest when the firm holds a small quantity of inventory.
Carrying costs are greatest when there is a large quantity of inventory on hand.
Total costs are the sum of the carrying and restocking costs.

In our discussion that follows, an important point to keep in mind is that the actual cost of the inventory itself is not included. The reason is that the *total* amount of inventory the firm needs in a given year is dictated by sales. What we are analysing here is how much the firm should have on hand at any particular time. More precisely, we are trying to determine what order size the firm should use when it restocks its inventory.

Inventory Depletion

To develop the EOQ, we shall assume that the firm's inventory is sold off at a steady rate until it hits zero. At that point, the firm restocks its inventory back to some optimal level. For example, suppose Eyssell plc starts out today with 3,600 units of a particular item in inventory. Annual sales of this item are 46,800 units, which is about 900 per week. If Eyssell sells off 900 units of inventory each week, all the available inventory will be sold after 4 weeks, and Eyssell will restock by ordering (or manufacturing) another 3,600 and start again. This selling and restocking process produces a sawtooth pattern for inventory holdings. On average, then, inventory is half of 3,600, or 1,800 units.

The Carrying Costs

As Figure 17.7 illustrates, carrying costs are normally assumed to be directly proportional to inventory levels. Suppose we let Q be the quantity of inventory that Eyssell orders each time (3,600 units): we shall call this the *restocking quantity*. Average inventory would then just be $Q/2$, or 1,800 units. If we let CC be the carrying cost per unit per year, Eyssell's total carrying costs will be:

$$\text{Total carrying costs} = \text{Average inventory} \times \text{Carrying costs per unit}$$
$$= (Q/2) \times \text{CC} \quad (17.17)$$

In Eyssell's case, if carrying costs were £0.75 per unit per year, total carrying costs would be the average inventory of 1,800 multiplied by £0.75, or £1,350 per year.

The Shortage Costs

For now, we shall focus only on the restocking costs. In essence, we shall assume that the firm never actually runs short of inventory, so that costs relating to safety reserves are not important. We shall return to this issue later.

Restocking costs are normally assumed to be fixed. In other words, every time we place an order, fixed costs are associated with that order (remember that the cost of the inventory itself is not considered here). Suppose we let T be the firm's total unit sales per year. If the firm orders Q units each time, then it will need to place a total of T/Q orders. For Eyssell, annual sales are 46,800, and the order size is 3,600. Eyssell thus places a total of $46,800/3,600 = 13$ orders per year. If the fixed cost per order is F, the total restocking cost for the year would be:

$$\text{Total restocking cost} = \text{Fixed cost per order} \times \text{Number of orders}$$
$$= F \times (T/Q) \qquad (17.18)$$

For Eyssell, order costs might be £50 per order, so the total restocking cost for 13 orders would be £50 × 13 = £650 per year.

The Total Costs

The total costs associated with holding inventory are the sum of the carrying costs and the restocking costs:

$$\text{Total costs} = \text{Carrying costs} \times \text{Restocking costs}$$
$$= (Q/2) \times \text{CC} + F \times (T/Q) \qquad (17.19)$$

Our goal is to find the value of Q, the restocking quantity, that minimizes this cost. To see how we might go about this, we can calculate total costs for some different values of Q. For Eyssell plc we had carrying costs (CC) of £0.75 per unit per year, fixed costs (F) of £50 per order, and total unit sales (T) of 46,800 units. With these numbers, here are some possible total costs (check some of these for practice):

Restocking quantity, Q	Carrying costs, $Q/2 \times \text{CC}$ (£)	+	Restocking costs, $F \times T/Q$ (£)	=	Total costs (£)
500	187.50		4,680.00		4,867.50
1,000	375.00		2,340.00		2,715.00
1,500	562.50		1,560.00		2,122.50
2,000	750.00		1,170.00		1,920.00
2,500	937.50		936.00		1,873.50
3,000	1,125.00		780.00		1,905.00
3,500	1,312.50		668.60		1,981.10

Inspecting the numbers, we see that total costs start out at almost £5,000 and decline to just under £1,900. The cost-minimizing quantity is about 2,500.

To find the cost-minimizing quantity, we can look back at Figure 17.7. What we notice is that the minimum point occurs exactly where the two lines cross. At this point, carrying costs and restocking costs are the same. For the particular types of costs we have assumed here, this will always be true; so we can find the minimum point just by setting these costs equal to each other and solving for Q^*:

$$\text{Carrying costs} = \text{Restocking costs}$$
$$(Q^*/2) \times \text{CC} = F \times (T/Q^*) \qquad (17.20)$$

With a little algebra, we get:

$$Q^{*2} = \frac{2T \times F}{\text{CC}} \qquad (17.21)$$

To solve for Q^*, we take the square root of both sides to find:

$$Q^* = \sqrt{\frac{2T \times F}{CC}} \qquad (17.22)$$

This reorder quantity, which minimizes the total inventory cost, is called the **economic order quantity (EOQ)**. For Eyssell plc, the EOQ is:

$$\begin{aligned} Q^* &= \sqrt{\frac{2T \times F}{CC}} \\ &= \sqrt{\frac{(2 \times 46{,}800) \times £50}{0.75}} \\ &= \sqrt{6{,}240{,}000} \\ &= 2{,}498 \text{ units} \end{aligned}$$

> **economic order quantity (EOQ)**
> the restocking quantity that minimizes the total inventory costs.

Thus, for Eyssell, the economic order quantity is 2,498 units. At this level, verify that the restocking costs and carrying costs are both £936.75.

EXAMPLE 17.4

CARRYING COSTS

Thiewes Shoes begins each period with 100 pairs of hiking boots in stock. This stock is depleted each period and reordered. If the carrying cost per pair of boots per year is £3, what are the total carrying costs for the hiking boots?

Inventories always start at 100 items and end up at zero, so average inventory is 50 items. At an annual cost of £3 per item, total carrying costs are £150.

EXAMPLE 17.5

RESTOCKING COSTS

In Example 17.4, suppose Thiewes sells a total of 600 pairs of boots in a year. How many times per year does Thiewes restock? Suppose the restocking cost is £20 per order. What are total restocking costs?

Thiewes orders 100 items each time. Total sales are 600 items per year, so Thiewes restocks six times per year, or about every two months. The restocking costs would be 6 orders × £20 per order = £120.

EXAMPLE 17.6

THE EOQ

Based on our previous two examples, what size orders should Thiewes place to minimize costs? How often will Thiewes restock? What are the total carrying and restocking costs? The total costs?

We know that the total number of pairs of boots ordered for the year (T) is 600. The restocking cost (F) is £20 per order, and the carrying cost (CC) is £3. We can calculate the EOQ for Thiewes as follows:

$$\begin{aligned} EOQ &= \sqrt{\frac{2T \times C}{CC}} \\ &= \sqrt{\frac{(2 \times 600) \times £20}{3}} \\ &= \sqrt{8{,}000} \\ &= 89.44 \text{ units} \end{aligned}$$

Because Thiewes sells 600 pairs per year, it will restock 600/89.44 = 6.71 times. The total restocking costs will be £20 × 6.71 = £134.16. Average inventory will be 89.44/2 = 44.72. The carrying costs will be £3 × 44.72 = £134.16, the same as the restocking costs. The total costs are thus £268.33.

EXTENSIONS TO THE EOQ MODEL

Thus far we have assumed that a company will let its inventory run down to zero and then reorder. In reality, a company will wish to reorder before its inventory goes to zero, for two reasons. First, by always having at least some inventory on hand, the firm minimizes the risk of a stock-out and the resulting losses of sales and customers. Second, when a firm does reorder, there will be some time lag before the inventory arrives. Thus, to finish our discussion of the EOQ, we consider two extensions: safety stocks and reordering points.

Safety Stocks

A *safety stock* is the minimum level of inventory that a firm keeps on hand. Inventories are reordered whenever the level of inventory falls to the safety stock level. The top of Figure 17.8 illustrates how a safety stock can be incorporated into an EOQ model. Notice that adding a safety stock simply means that the firm does not run its inventory all the way down to zero. Other than this, the situation here is identical to that described in our earlier discussion of the EOQ.

Reorder Points

To allow for delivery time, a firm will place orders before inventories reach a critical level. The *reorder points* are the times at which the firm will actually place its inventory orders. These points are illustrated in the middle of Figure 17.8. As shown, the reorder points simply occur some fixed number of days (or weeks or months) before inventories are projected to reach zero.

One of the reasons why a firm will keep a safety stock is to allow for uncertain delivery times. We can therefore combine our reorder point and safety stock discussions in the bottom part of Figure 17.8. The result is a generalized EOQ model in which the firm orders in advance of anticipated needs, and also keeps a safety stock of inventory.

MANAGING DERIVED-DEMAND INVENTORIES

The third type of inventory management technique is used to manage derived-demand inventories. As we described earlier, demand for some inventory types is derived from or dependent on other inventory needs. A good example is given by the car manufacturing industry, in which the demand for finished products depends on consumer demand, marketing programmes, and other factors related to projected unit sales. The demand for inventory items such as tyres, batteries, headlights and other components is then completely determined by the number of vehicles planned. **Materials requirements planning (MRP)** and just-in-time inventory management are two methods for managing demand-dependent inventories.

Materials Requirements Planning

Production and inventory specialists have developed computer-based systems for ordering and/or scheduling production of demand-dependent types of inventory. These systems fall under the general heading of materials requirements planning. The basic idea behind MRP is that, once finished goods inventory levels are set, it is possible to determine what levels of work-in-progress inventories must exist to meet the need for finished goods. From there, it is possible to calculate the quantity of raw materials that must be on hand. This ability to schedule backwards from finished goods inventories stems from the dependent nature of work-in-progress and raw materials inventories. MRP is particularly important for complicated products for which a variety of components are needed to create the finished product.

Just-in-Time Inventory

Just-in-time (JIT) inventory is a modern approach to managing dependent inventories. The goal of JIT is to minimize such inventories, thereby maximizing

> **materials requirements planning (MRP)**
> a set of procedures used to determine inventory levels for demand-dependent inventory types such as work in progress and raw materials.

> **just-in-time (JIT) inventory**
> a system for managing demand-dependent inventories that minimizes inventory holdings.

FIGURE 17.8

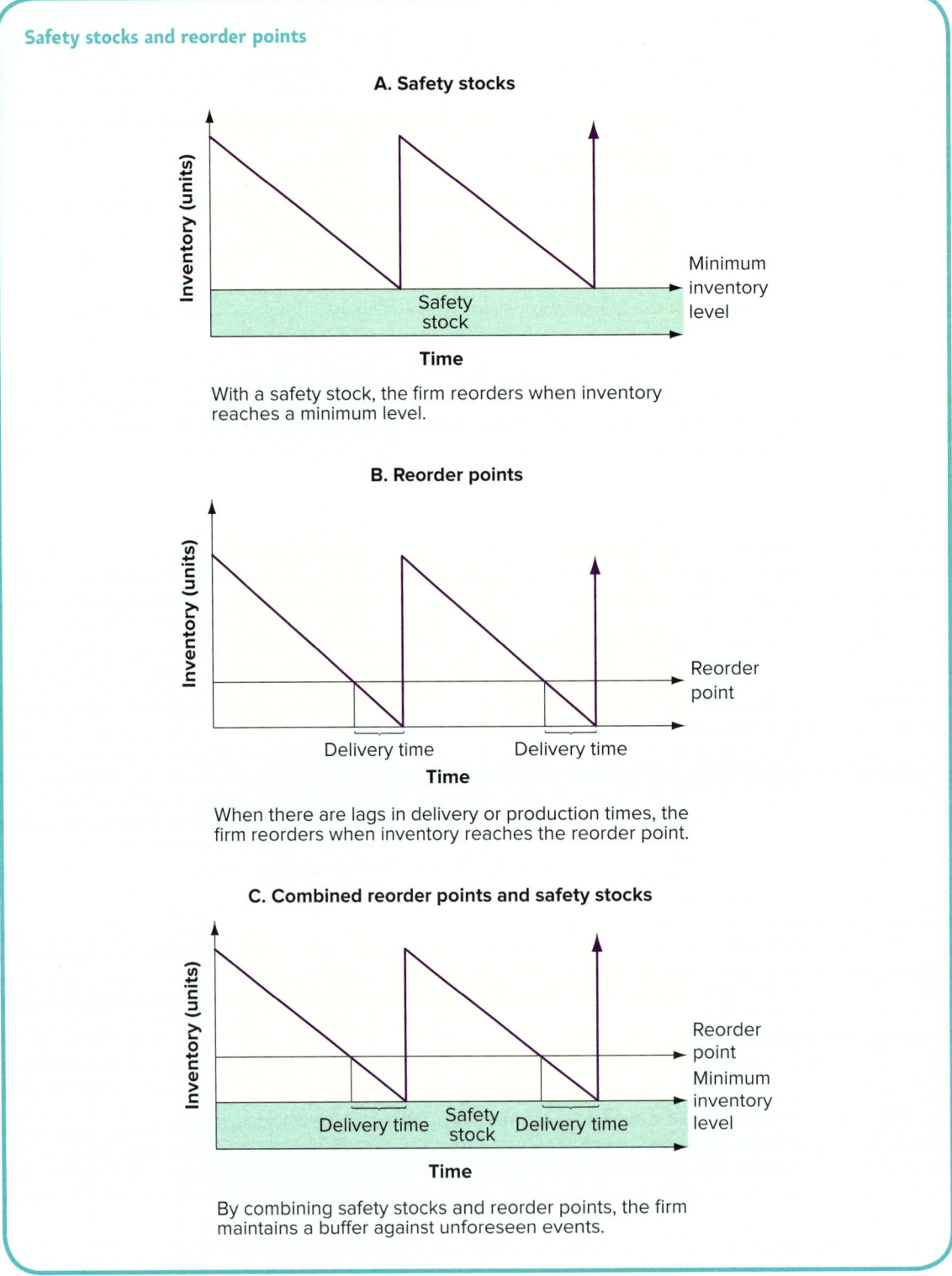

Safety stocks and reorder points

A. Safety stocks

With a safety stock, the firm reorders when inventory reaches a minimum level.

B. Reorder points

When there are lags in delivery or production times, the firm reorders when inventory reaches the reorder point.

C. Combined reorder points and safety stocks

By combining safety stocks and reorder points, the firm maintains a buffer against unforeseen events.

turnover. The approach began in Japan, and it is a fundamental part of Japanese manufacturing philosophy. As the name suggests, the basic goal of JIT is to have only enough inventory on hand to meet immediate production needs.

The result of the JIT system is that inventories are reordered and restocked frequently. Making such a system work and avoiding shortages requires a high degree of co-operation among suppliers. Japanese manufacturers often have a relatively small, tightly integrated group of suppliers, with whom they work closely to achieve the needed co-ordination. These suppliers are a part of a large manufacturer's (such as Toyota's) industrial group, or *keiretsu*. Each large manufacturer tends to have its own *keiretsu*. It also helps to have suppliers located nearby, a situation that is common in Japan.

The *kanban* is an integral part of a JIT inventory system, and JIT systems are sometimes called *kanban systems*. The literal meaning of *kanban* is 'card' or 'sign'; but, broadly speaking, a kanban is a signal to a supplier to send more inventory. For example, a kanban can literally be a card attached to a bin of parts. When a worker pulls that bin, the card is detached and routed back to the supplier, who then supplies a replacement bin.

A JIT inventory system is an important part of a larger production planning process. A full discussion of it would necessarily shift our focus away from finance to production and operations management, so we shall leave it here.

REAL WORLD INSIGHTS

During economic downturns, only the most innovative companies can survive. In this book, we've looked at different ways companies can create value through investment and financing. Inventory control is no different and can be a major source of value generation if done well.

The European oil and gas sector is an industry that has seen its fair share of external market shocks, principally through what seems a permanent reduction in prices due to new technology. As revenues dwindle, the only way to increase profit margins and share value is by managing costs.

Inventory control is an area in which oil and gas companies are particularly exposed because of high fixed costs in maintaining drilling rigs, be they offshore or in inhospitable environments. An original solution to minimize costs has been developed in recent years. Instead of purchasing new raw materials from suppliers when stocks got low, a group of oil and gas firms agreed to trade their inventories of over 200,000 items between each other using a bespoke trading platform specially designed for this initiative.

By creating a market platform for standardized items already in existence, inventory costs fell by between 15 and 20 per cent per annum, which is equivalent to a significant annual cash injection to each firm.

CONCEPT QUESTIONS

17.12a What does the EOQ model determine for the firm?
17.12b Which cost component of the EOQ model does JIT inventory minimize?

SUMMARY AND CONCLUSIONS

This chapter has covered the basics of short-term financial planning. With respect to cash management:

1. A firm holds cash to conduct transactions, and to compensate banks for the various services they render.
2. The difference between a firm's available balance and its book balance is the firm's net float. The float reflects the fact that some cheques have not cleared, and are thus uncollected. The financial manager must always work with collected cash balances, and not with the company's book balance. To do otherwise is to use the bank's cash without the bank's knowing it, which raises ethical and legal questions.
3. The firm can make use of a variety of procedures to manage the collection and disbursement of cash in such a way as to speed up the collection of cash and slow down the payments.

4. Because of seasonal and cyclical activities, to help finance planned expenditures, or as a contingency reserve, firms temporarily hold a cash surplus. The money market offers a variety of possible vehicles for 'parking' this idle cash.

With respect to credit and working capital:

1. We discussed the terms of sale, credit analysis and collection policy. Under the general subject of terms of sale, the credit period, the cash discount and discount period, and the credit instrument were described.
2. We developed the cash flows from the decision to grant credit, and showed how the credit decision can be analysed in an NPV setting. The NPV of granting credit depends on five factors: revenue effects, cost effects, the cost of debt, the probability of non-payment, and the cash discount.
3. The optimal amount of credit the firm should offer depends on the competitive conditions under which the firm operates. These conditions will determine the carrying costs associated with granting credit, and the opportunity costs of the lost sales resulting from refusing to offer credit. The optimal credit policy minimizes the sum of these two costs.
4. We looked at the decision to grant credit to a particular customer. We saw that two considerations are very important: the cost relative to the selling price, and the possibility of repeat business.
5. Collection policy determines the method of monitoring the age of trade receivables and dealing with past-due accounts. We described how an ageing schedule can be prepared, and the procedures a firm might use to collect on past-due accounts.
6. We described the different inventory types, and how they differ in terms of liquidity and demand.
7. The two basic inventory costs are carrying costs and restocking costs; we discussed how inventory management involves a trade-off between these two costs.
8. We described the ABC approach and the EOQ model approach to inventory management. We also briefly touched on materials requirements planning (MRP) and just-in-time (JIT) inventory management.

CHAPTER REVIEW AND SELF-TEST PROBLEMS

17.1 The BAT Model Given the following information, calculate the target cash balance using the BAT model:

Annual interest rate	12%
Fixed order cost	€100
Total cash needed	€240,000

What are the opportunity cost of holding cash, the trading cost and the total cost? What would these be if €15,000 were held instead? If €25,000 were held?

17.2 Credit Policy Cold Fusion plc (manufacturer of the Mr Fusion home power plant) is considering a new credit policy. The current policy is cash only. The new policy would involve extending credit for one period. Based on the following information, determine if a switch is advisable. The interest rate is 2.0 per cent per period:

	Current policy	New policy
Price per unit (£)	175	175
Cost per unit (£)	130	130
Sales per period (units)	1,000	1,100

17.3 Credit Where Credit Is Due You are trying to decide whether or not to extend credit to a particular customer. Your variable cost is €15 per unit; the selling price is €22. This customer wants to buy 1,000 units today and pay in 30 days. You think there is a 15 per cent chance of default. The required return is 3 per cent per 30 days. Should you extend credit? Assume that this is a one-time sale, and that the customer will not buy if credit is not extended.

17.4 The EOQ Annondale Manufacturing starts each period with 10,000 'Long John' golf clubs in stock. This stock is depleted each month and reordered. If the carrying cost per golf club is £1, and the fixed order cost is £5, is Annondale following an economically advisable strategy?

SOLUTIONS

17.1 From the BAT model, we know that the target cash balance is:

$$C^* = \sqrt{(2T \times F)/R}$$
$$= \sqrt{(2 \times €240,000 \times 100)/0.12}$$
$$= \sqrt{€400,000,000}$$
$$= €20,000$$

The average cash balance will be $C^*/2 = €20,000/2 = €10,000$. The opportunity cost of holding €10,000 when the going rate is 12 per cent is €10,000 × 0.12 = €1,200. There will be €240,000/20,000 = 12 orders during the year, so the order cost, or trading cost, is also 12 × €100 = €1,200. The total cost is thus €2,400. If €15,000 is held, the average balance is €7,500. Verify that the opportunity, trading and total costs in this case are €900, €1,600 and €2,500, respectively. If €25,000 is held, these numbers are €1,500, €960 and €2,460, respectively.

17.2 If the switch is made, an extra 100 units per period will be sold at a gross profit of £175 − 130 = £45 each. The total benefit is thus £45 × 100 = £4,500 per period. At 2.0 per cent per period for ever, the PV is £4,500/0.02 = £225,000. The cost of the switch is equal to this period's revenue of £175 × 1,000 units = £175,000 plus the cost of producing the extra 100 units: 100 × £130 = £13,000. The total cost is thus £188,000, and the NPV is £225,000 − 188,000 = £37,000. The switch should be made.

17.3 If the customer pays in 30 days, then you will collect €22 × 1,000 = €22,000. There's only an 85 per cent chance of collecting this; so you expect to get €22,000 × 0.85 = €18,700 in 30 days. The present value of this is €18,700/1.03 = €18,155.34. Your cost is €15 × 1,000 = €15,000; so the NPV is €18,155.34 − 15,000 = €3,155.34. Credit should be extended.

17.4 We can answer by first calculating Annondale's carrying and restocking costs. The average inventory is 5,000 clubs and, because the carrying costs are £1 per club, total carrying costs are £5,000. Annondale restocks every month at a fixed order cost of £5, so the total restocking costs are £60. What we see is that carrying costs are large relative to reorder costs, so Annondale is carrying too much inventory.

To determine the optimal inventory policy, we can use the EOQ model. Because Annondale orders 10,000 golf clubs 12 times per year, total needs (T) are 120,000 golf clubs. The fixed order cost is £5, and the carrying cost per unit (CC) is £1. The EOQ is therefore:

$$EOQ = \sqrt{\frac{2T \times F}{CC}}$$
$$= \sqrt{\frac{(2 \times 120,000) \times £5}{1}}$$
$$= \sqrt{1,200,000}$$
$$= 1,095.45 \text{ units}$$

We can check this by noting that the average inventory is about 550 clubs, so the carrying cost is £550. Annondale will have to reorder 120,000/1,095.45 = 109.54 ≈ 110 times. The fixed order cost is £5, so the total restocking cost is also £550.

Level of difficulty: Basic | Intermediate | Challenge

QUESTIONS AND PROBLEMS

17.1 **Net Working Capital** What is short-term financial planning? Why is short-term financial planning crucial to a company? Provide an example of a company that has either undergone an insolvency event or is in financial distress due to poor short-term financial planning.

17.2 **Cash** Review the different ways in which cash can increase or decrease in a firm. Use the accounting equation to support your answer. What are some of the characteristics of a firm with a long operating cycle? Similarly, what are some of the characteristics of a firm with a long cash cycle?

17.3 **Short-Term Financing Needs** Which type of company is likely to have large short-term financing needs? Provide an example using a company from your country.

17.4 **Short-Term Financial Policy** Your friend has recently started up a new ice-cream shop business but is worried about the seasonality of cash flows the business will face. This is because the demand for ice cream will most likely be higher in summer than in other seasons, particularly winter. He asks you for help on how he should manage this risk. What would your advice be?

17.5 **Cash Discounts** You place an order for 200 units of inventory at a unit price of £95. The supplier offers terms of 2/10, net 30.

(a) How long do you have to pay before the account is overdue? If you take the full period, how much should you remit?

(b) What is the discount being offered? How quickly must you pay to get the discount? If you take the discount, how much should you remit?

(c) If you do not take the discount, how much interest are you paying implicitly? How many days' credit are you receiving?

17.6 **ACP and Trade Receivables** Dalglish plc sells earnings forecasts for British securities. Its credit terms are 2/10, net 30. Based on experience, 65 per cent of all customers will take the discount.

(a) What is the average collection period for Dalglish?

(b) If Dalglish sells 1,200 forecasts every month at a price of £2,200 each, what is its average balance sheet amount in accounts receivable?

17.7 **Terms of Sale** A firm offers terms of 2/9, net 40. What effective annual interest rate does the firm earn when a customer does not take the discount?

(a) All other things remaining the same, if the discount is changed to 3 per cent, what will be the effective annual interest rate?

(b) All other things remaining the same, if the credit period is increased to 60 days, what will be the effective annual interest rate?

(c) All other things remaining the same, if the discount period is increased to 15 days, what will be the effective annual interest rate?

17.8 **Size of Trade Receivables** Baker Ginger Ltd sells on credit terms of net 25. Its accounts are, on average, 9 days past due. If annual credit sales are £8 million, what is the company's balance sheet amount in accounts receivable?

17.9 **Evaluating Credit Policy** Silicon Wafers plc (SW), is debating whether to extend credit to a particular customer. SW's products, primarily used in the manufacture of semiconductors, currently sell for

£1,850 per unit. The variable cost is £1,200 per unit. The order under consideration is for 12 units today; payment is promised in 30 days. Assume that this is a one-time sale and the customer will not buy if credit is not extended.

(a) If there is a 20 per cent chance of default, calculate the net present value. Should SW fill the above order?

(b) What is the break-even probability in part (a)?

17.10 EOQ Redan Manufacturing uses 2,500 switch assemblies per week and then reorders another 2,500. If the relevant carrying cost per switch assembly is €9, and the fixed order cost is €1,700, is Redan's inventory policy optimal? Why or why not?

17.11 EOQ Derivation Prove that when carrying costs and restocking costs are as described in the chapter, the EOQ must occur at the point where the carrying costs and restocking costs are equal.

17.12 Credit Policy Evaluation Harrington plc is considering a change in its cash-only policy. The new terms would be net one period. Based on the following information, determine whether Harrington should proceed or not. The required return is 2.5 per cent per period.

	Current policy	New policy
Price per unit (£)	91	94
Cost per unit (£)	47	47
Unit sales per month	3,850	3,940

17.13 Credit Policy Evaluation. Consider the information in the following table about two alternative credit strategies. The higher cost per unit reflects the expense associated with credit orders, and the higher price per unit reflects the existence of a cash discount. The credit period will be 90 days, and the cost of debt is 0.75 per cent per month. Based on this information

(a) Calculate the cash discount and the default probability. Should credit be granted?

(b) What does the credit price per unit have to be to break even?

	Refuse credit	Grant credit
Price per unit (£)	51	55
Cost per unit (£)	29	31
Quantity sold per quarter	3,300	3,500
Probability of payment	1.0	0.9

17.14 Safety Stocks and Order Points Saché SA expects to sell 700 of its designer suits every week. The store is open 7 days a week, and expects to sell the same number of suits every day. The company has an EOQ of 500 suits and a safety stock of 100 suits. Once an order is placed, it takes 3 days for Saché to get the suits in. How many orders does the company place per year? Assume that it is Monday morning before the store opens, and a shipment of suits has just arrived. When will Saché place its next order?

17.15 Cash Budgeting The sales budget for your company in the coming year is based on a 20 per cent quarterly growth rate with the first-quarter sales projection at £100 million. In addition to this basic trend, the seasonal adjustments for the four quarters are 0, −£10, −£5, and £15 million, respectively. Generally, 50 per cent of the sales can be collected within the quarter and 45 per cent in the following quarter; the rest of sales are bad debt. The bad debts are written off in the second quarter after the sales are made. The beginning accounts payable balance is £81 million. Assuming all sales are on credit, compute the cash collections from sales for each quarter.

17.16 Calculating the Cash Budget Wildcat SA has estimated sales (in millions) for the next four quarters as follows:

	Q1	Q2	Q3	Q4
Sales	€230	€195	€270	€290

Sales for the first quarter of the year after this one are projected at €250 million. Accounts receivable at the beginning of the year were €79 million. Wildcat has a 45-day collection period. Wildcat's purchases from suppliers in a quarter are equal to 45 per cent of the next quarter's forecast sales, and suppliers are normally paid in 36 days. Wages, taxes and other expenses run at about 30 per cent of sales. Interest and dividends are €15 million per quarter. Wildcat plans a major capital outlay in the second quarter of €90 million. Finally, the company started the year with a €73 million cash balance and wishes to maintain a €30 million minimum balance.

(a) Complete a cash budget for Wildcat by filling in the following:

WILDCAT SA Cash budget (in millions)				
	Q1	Q2	Q3	Q4
Beginning cash balance	€73			
Net cash inflow				
Ending cash balance				
Minimum cash balance	−30			
Cumulative surplus (deficit)				

(b) Assume that Wildcat can borrow any needed funds on a short-term basis at a rate of 3 per cent per quarter, and can invest any excess funds in short-term marketable securities at a rate of 2 per cent per quarter. Prepare a short-term financial plan by filling in the following schedule. What is the net cash cost (total interest paid minus total investment income earned) for the year?

WILDCAT SA Short-term financial plan (in millions)				
	Q1	Q2	Q3	Q4
Beginning cash balance	€30			
Net cash inflow				
New short-term investments				
Income from short-term investments				
Short-term investments sold				
New short-term borrowing				
Interest on short-term borrowing				
Short-term borrowing repaid			_____	
Ending cash balance				
Minimum cash balance	−30		_____	
Cumulative surplus (deficit)				
Beginning short-term investments				
Ending short-term investments				
Beginning short-term debt				
Ending short-term debt				

17.17 Cash Management Policy Rework Problem 17.16 assuming the following:

(a) Wildcat maintains a minimum cash balance of €45 million.

(b) Wildcat maintains a minimum cash balance of €15 million.

(c) Based on your answers in (a) and (b), do you think the firm can boost its profit by changing its cash management policy? Should other factors be considered as well? Explain.

MINI CASE

CREDIT POLICY AT SCHWARZWALD AG

Dagmar Bamberger, the president of Schwarzwald AG, has been exploring ways of improving the company's financial performance. Schwarzwald manufactures and sells office equipment to retailers. The company's growth has been relatively slow in recent years, but with an expansion in the economy it appears that sales may increase more quickly in the future. Dagmar has asked Johann Rüstow, the company's treasurer, to examine Schwarzwald's credit policy to see whether a different credit policy could help increase profitability.

The company currently has a policy of net 30. As with any credit sales, default rates are always of concern. Because of Schwarzwald's screening and collection process, the default rate on credit is currently only 1.5 per cent. Johann has examined the company's credit policy in relation to other vendors, and he has determined that three options are available.

The first option is to relax the company's decision on when to grant credit. The second option is to increase the credit period to net 45, and the third option is a combination of the relaxed credit policy and the extension of the credit period to net 45. On the positive side, each of the three policies under consideration would increase sales. The three policies have the drawbacks that default rates would increase, the administrative costs of managing the firm's receivables would increase, and the receivables period would increase. The credit policy change would affect all four of these variables to different degrees. Johann has prepared the following table outlining the effect on each of these variables:

	Annual sales (€ millions)	Default rate (% of sales)	Administrative costs (% of sales)	Receivables period (days)
Current policy	120	1.5	2.1	38
Option 1	140	2.4	3.1	41
Option 2	137	1.7	2.3	51
Option 3	150	2.1	2.9	49

Schwarzwald's variable costs of production are 45 per cent of sales, and the relevant interest rate is a 6 per cent effective annual rate.

QUESTIONS

1. Which credit policy should the company use?
2. Also, notice that in option 3 the default rate and administrative costs are below those in option 2. Is this plausible? Why or why not?

ADDITIONAL READING

The literature on cash holdings has exploded in recent years and the papers below give a flavour of the work in this area.

1. Bigelli, M., & Sánchez-Vidal, J. (2012). Cash holdings in private firms. *Journal of Banking and Finance*, 36(1), 26–35.
2. Chen, Y., Dou, P. Y., Rhee, S. G., Truong, C., & Veeraraghavan, M. (2015). National culture and corporate cash holdings around the world. *Journal of Banking & Finance*, 50, 1–18.
3. Duchin, R. (2010). Cash holdings and corporate diversification. *Journal of Finance*, 65(3), 955–992.
4. Lins, K. V., Servaes, H., & Tufano, P. (2010). What drives corporate liquidity? An international survey of cash holdings and lines of credit. *Journal of Financial Economics*, 98(1), 160–176.
5. Palazzo, B. (2012). Cash holdings, risk and expected returns. *Journal of Financial Economics*, 104(1), 162–185.

CHAPTER 18
INTERNATIONAL CORPORATE FINANCE

LEARNING OBJECTIVES

After studying this chapter, you should understand:

- **LO1** How exchange rates are quoted, what they mean, and the difference between spot and forward exchange rates.
- **LO2** Purchasing power parity, interest rate parity, unbiased forward rates, uncovered interest rate parity and the international Fisher effect, and their implications for exchange rate changes.
- **LO3** The different types of exchange rate risk, and ways in which firms manage exchange rate risk.
- **LO4** The impact of political risk on international business investing.

KEY NOTATIONS

F	Forward exchange rate
FC	Foreign country
h	Inflation rate
HC	Home country
IFE	International Fisher effect
IRP	Interest rate parity
NPV	Net present value
P	Price
PPP	Purchasing power parity
R	Risk-free rate
S	Exchange rate
UFR	Unbiased forward rate
UIP	Uncovered interest parity

RELATIVELY FEW COMPANIES operate fully in a single country. Even if your firm's sales solely focus on the domestic market, you will likely have competitors or suppliers with operations overseas. In most industries, raw materials and components are sourced and imported from abroad, and many services and products are sold to other countries.

Firms, such as dropshippers, use the international supply chain to source goods to sell. When a dropshipper receives orders, it routes them to an international exporter to complete the transaction. In this way, the dropshipper avoids the need for inventory and can concentrate wholly on generating sales.

If your company has international sales, an international supply chain or even international competitors, currency fluctuations will impact costs, revenues and profitability. For example, if the euro strengthens against the British pound, British exports become more competitive in Europe. Similarly, raw materials from Europe will become more expensive, and British corporations will look elsewhere for cheaper inputs. One of the reasons why European

Monetary Union was adopted was that many countries in the Eurozone traded heavily with each other. With a single currency, the risk of fluctuations is eradicated. For companies outside the Eurozone who have Eurozone customers or suppliers, currency fluctuations (and hence currency risk) may even become worse.

The UK's exit from the European Union has meant that international corporate finance has become significantly more important to British and European firms. The EU is the UK's largest trading partner, with nearly 50 per cent of the UK's total trade involving the European Union. Likewise, the UK is the EU's third-largest trading partner, behind the United States and China in that order. To cap it off, increasing global tensions involving the world's global trading powers will undoubtedly increase international trade volatility. This chapter explores the roles of currencies and exchange rates, along with several other key topics in international corporate finance.

Corporations with significant foreign operations are called *international corporations* or *multinationals*. Such corporations must consider many financial factors that do not directly affect purely domestic firms. These include foreign exchange rates, differing interest rates from country to country, complex accounting methods for foreign operations, foreign tax rates and foreign government intervention.

The basic principles of corporate finance still apply to international corporations. Like domestic companies, these firms seek to invest in projects that create more value for the shareholders than they cost and to arrange financing that raises cash at the lowest possible cost. In other words, the net present value principle holds for both foreign and domestic operations, although it is usually more complicated to apply the NPV rule to foreign investments.

One of the most significant complications of international finance is foreign exchange. The foreign exchange markets provide important information and opportunities for an international corporation to undertake capital budgeting and financing decisions. As we shall discuss, international exchange rates, interest rates and inflation rates are closely related. We shall spend much of this chapter exploring the connection between these financial variables.

18.1 TERMINOLOGY

A common buzzword for the student of business finance is *globalization*. The first step in learning about the globalization of financial markets is to conquer a new vocabulary. As with any speciality, international finance is rich in jargon. Accordingly, we get started on the subject with a highly eclectic vocabulary exercise.

The terms that follow are presented alphabetically, and they are not all of equal importance. We choose these particular ones either because they frequently appear in the financial press, or because they illustrate the colourful nature of the language of international finance.

1. An **American depositary receipt (ADR)** is a security issued in the United States representing shares of foreign equity, allowing that equity to be traded in the United States. Foreign companies use ADRs issued in US dollars, to expand the pool of potential US investors. ADRs are available in two forms for a large and growing number of foreign companies: company-sponsored, which are listed on an exchange; and unsponsored, which usually are held by the bank that makes a market in the ADR. Both forms are available to individual investors, but only company-sponsored issues are quoted daily in newspapers. A *global depositary receipt* (GDR) is an equivalent security denominated in sterling or euros and traded in financial centres such as London or Frankfurt.
2. The **cross-rate** is the implicit exchange rate between two currencies when both are quoted in some third currency.
3. A **eurobond** (or external bond) is a bond issued in multiple countries but denominated in a single currency, usually the issuer's home currency. Such bonds have become an important way to raise capital for many international companies

> **American depositary receipt (ADR)**
> a security issued in the United States representing shares of a foreign equity, and allowing that equity to be traded in the United States.

> **cross-rate**
> the implicit exchange rate between two currencies quoted in some third currency.

> **eurobond**
> international bond issued in multiple countries but denominated in a single currency (usually the issuer's currency).

Eurocurrency
money deposited in a financial centre outside the country whose currency is involved.

and governments. Eurobonds are issued outside the restrictions that apply to domestic offerings and are syndicated and traded mostly from London. Trading takes place anywhere there is a buyer and a seller. Notice that eurobonds are not related in a special way to the euro currency, as the term has evolved before the euro even existed. A eurobond should also not be confused with a Eurobond (spot the capital 'E'), which is a bond issued by the European Union.

4. **Eurocurrency** is money deposited in a financial centre outside the country whose currency is involved. For instance, eurodollars – the most widely used eurocurrency – are US dollars deposited in banks outside the United States. Eurosterling, euroeuro and euroyen are British, European and Japanese equivalents.

foreign bonds
international bonds issued in a single country, usually denominated in that country's currency.

5. Unlike eurobonds, **foreign bonds** are issued in a single country and are usually denominated in that country's currency. Often, the country in which these bonds are issued will draw distinctions between them and bonds issued by domestic issuers, including different tax laws, restrictions on the amount issued, and tougher disclosure rules.

Foreign bonds often are nicknamed for the country where they are issued: Yankee bonds (United States), Panda bonds (China), Samurai bonds (Japan), Matilda bonds (Australia), Rembrandt bonds (the Netherlands), and Bulldog bonds (Britain). Partly because of tougher regulations and disclosure requirements, the foreign bond market hasn't grown in past years with the vigour of the eurobond market.

gilts
british and Irish government securities.

6. **Gilts**, technically, are British and Irish government securities, although the term also includes issues of local British authorities and some overseas public sector offerings.

Secured Overnight Financing Rate (SOFR)
a benchmark interest rate for dollar-denominated loans.

7. The **Secured Overnight Financing Rate (SOFR)** is the rate that most international banks charge one another for overnight dollar loans. SOFR is the successor to LIBOR (London Interbank Offer Rate) and is a cornerstone in the pricing of money market issues and other short-term debt issued by both government and corporate borrowers. Interest rates are frequently quoted as some spread over SOFR, and they then float with the SOFR rate. In the UK, the reference rate is SONIA (Sterling Overnight Index Average), and in the Eurozone, it is €STR (euro short-term rate).

swaps
agreements to exchange two securities or currencies.

8. There are two basic kinds of **swaps**: interest rate swaps and currency swaps. An interest rate swap occurs when two parties exchange a floating-rate payment for a fixed-rate payment or vice versa. Currency swaps are agreements to deliver one currency in exchange for another. Both types of swap are often used in the same transaction when debt denominated in different currencies is swapped.

> **CONCEPT QUESTIONS**
>
> **18.1a** What are the differences between a eurobond and a foreign bond?
> **18.1b** What are eurodollars?

18.2 FOREIGN EXCHANGE MARKETS AND EXCHANGE RATES

foreign exchange market
the market in which one country's currency is traded for another's.

The **foreign exchange market** is undoubtedly the world's largest financial market. It is the market where one country's currency is traded for another's. Most of the trading takes place in a few currencies: the US dollar ($), British pound sterling (£), Japanese yen (¥) and euro (€). Table 18.1 lists some of the more common currencies and their symbols.

The foreign exchange market is an over-the-counter market, so there is no single location where traders get together. Instead, market participants are located in the major banks around the world. They communicate using computer terminals, telephones and other telecommunications devices. For example, one communications network for foreign transactions is maintained by the Society for Worldwide Interbank Financial Telecommunication (SWIFT), a Belgian not-for-profit co-operative. Using data transmission lines, a bank in New York can send messages to a bank in London via SWIFT regional processing centres.

TABLE 18.1

International currency symbol

Country	Currency	Symbol
Australia	Dollar	A$
Canada	Dollar	C$
China	Yuan (renminbi)	¥
Denmark	Krone	DKr
Eurozone	Euro	€
India	Rupee	Rs
Iran	Rial	IR
Japan	Yen	¥
Kuwait	Dinar	KD
Mexico	Peso	Ps
Norway	Krone	NKr
Saudi Arabia	Riyal	SR
Singapore	Dollar	S$
South Africa	Rand	R
Sweden	Krona	SKr
Switzerland	Franc	SFr
United Kingdom	Pound	£
United States	Dollar	$

The many different types of participant in the foreign exchange market include the following:

1. Importers who pay for goods using foreign currencies
2. Exporters who receive foreign currency and may want to convert it to the domestic currency
3. Portfolio managers who buy or sell foreign equities and bonds
4. Foreign exchange brokers who match buy and sell orders
5. Traders who 'make a market' in foreign currencies
6. Speculators who try to profit from changes in exchange rates

EXCHANGE RATES

An **exchange rate** is simply the price of one country's currency expressed in another country's currency. Exchange rates are constantly changing.

> **exchange rate**
> the price of one country's currency expressed in terms of another country's currency.

Exchange Rate Quotations

Table 18.2 reproduces exchange rate quotations from January 2021. The three main columns give the number of foreign currency units it takes to buy one pound, euro and dollar, respectively. Because this is the price of the currency in dollars, euros or pounds, it is called an indirect quote. For example, the Bahraini dinar is quoted at 0.5116 against the British pound, which means that you can buy one British pound with 0.5116 Bahraini dinars.

Bid and Offer Rates

The foreign exchange market is dominated by large currency dealers, such as banks, and the profit made by these dealers is the difference between the price paid for a currency and the price at which the currency is sold. So, if the euro is quoted at €1.1079/£, a currency dealer wishing to buy euros with sterling will look to pay lower (such as €1.1080/£). A currency dealer wishing to sell euros for sterling will quote a higher rate (for example, €1.078/£). If the dealer was able to trade at these quotes, a round trip transaction of a buy and then a sale would result in a net profit of €0.0002/£ against the quote of €1.1079/£. The price at which a dealer wishes to buy currency is known as the *bid rate* and the corresponding sale price is known as the *offer or ask rate*. The difference between the bid and offer (ask) rates is called the **bid-ask spread**.

> **bid-ask spread**
> the difference between bid and offer (ask) rates.

Cross-Rates and Triangle Arbitrage

There are 180 currencies in the world and to quote each currency with respect to all other currencies would require a massive 180 × 180 table. To simplify, all exchange rates can be quoted with respect to the dollar, euro, yen or sterling. Using the exchange rates with respect to any one of the major currencies, it is straightforward to find a cross rate between any two currencies.

TABLE 18.2

Exchange rate quotations

Currencies	GBP £	EUR €	USD $
Bahrain	0.5116	0.4620	0.3768
China	8.8652	8.0000	6.5274
Denmark	8.2372	7.4349	6.0643
Eurozone	1.1079	1.0000	0.8156
India	100.0000	90.0901	73.5294
Malaysia	5.4765	4.9407	4.0306
Norway	11.4811	10.3627	8.4531
Oman	0.5225	0.4716	0.3845
Saudi Arabia	5.0916	4.5956	3.7467
Singapore	1.8005	1.6247	1.3247
South Africa	20.7469	18.7266	15.2672
Sweden	11.1607	10.0705	8.2169
Switzerland	1.2006	1.0835	0.8836
UAE	4.9875	4.5005	3.6697
United Kingdom	1.0000	0.9024	0.7359
United States	1.3587	1.2264	1.0000

Source: Bloomberg real-time feed, 7 January 2021.

EXAMPLE 18.1

A YEN FOR EUROS

Suppose you have €1,000. If the exchange rate in terms of rand per euro is 18.7266, how many South African rand can you get? Alternatively, if a Porsche costs €100,000, how many pounds will you need to buy it, if the exchange rate is £0.9024/€?

The exchange rate in terms of rand per euro is 18.7266. Your €1,000 will thus get you:

$$€1,000 \times 18.7255 \text{ rand per } €1 = 18,725.5 \text{ rand}$$

Because the exchange rate in terms of pounds per euro is 0.9024, you will need:

$$€100,000 \times £0.9024 \text{ per } € = £90,240$$

Earlier, we defined the cross-rate as the exchange rate for a foreign currency expressed in terms of another foreign currency. For example, suppose we observe the following for the Russian rouble and the Bahraini dinar:

$$\text{Russian rouble per } €1 = 45.8022$$
$$\text{Bahraini dinar per } €1 = 0.4831$$

Suppose the cross-rate is quoted as:

$$\text{Dinars per rouble} = 0.01$$

What do you think?

The cross-rate here is inconsistent with the exchange rates. To see this, suppose you have €100. If you convert this to Russian roubles, you will receive:

$$€100 \times 45.8022 \text{ roubles per } €1 = 4{,}580.22 \text{ roubles}$$

If you then convert the roubles to dinar at the cross-rate, you will have:

$$4{,}580.22 \text{ roubles} \times 0.01 \text{ per rouble} = 45.8022 \text{ dinar}$$

However, if you convert your euros to dinar without going through Russian roubles, you will have:

$$€100 \times 0.4831 \text{ dinars per } €1 = 48.31 \text{ dinar}$$

We see that the dinar has two prices, 0.4831 dinars per €1 and 0.4580 dinars per €1, with the price we pay depending on how we get the dinar.

To make money, we want to buy low and sell high. The important thing to note is that dinar are cheaper if you buy them with euros because you get 0.4831 dinars instead of just 0.4580 dinars. You should proceed as follows:

1. Buy 48.31 dinars for €100.
2. Use the 48.31 dinars to buy Russian roubles at the cross-rate. Because it takes 0.01 dinar to buy a Russian rouble, you will receive 48.31 dinar/0.01 roubles = 4,831 roubles.
3. Use the 4,831 roubles to buy euros. Because the exchange rate is 45.8022 roubles per euro, you receive 4,831 roubles/45.8022 = €105.48, for a round-trip profit of €5.48.
4. Repeat steps 1–3.

This particular activity is called *triangle arbitrage* because the arbitrage involves moving through three different exchange rates:

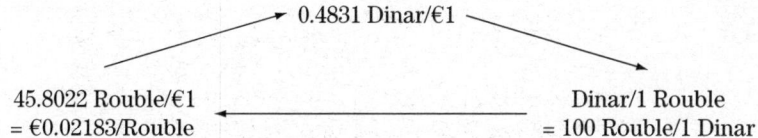

To prevent such opportunities, it is not difficult to see that because a euro will buy you either 45.8022 Russian roubles or 0.4831 Bahraini dinars, the cross-rate must be:

$$(0.4831 \text{ dinar}/€1)/(45.8022 \text{ rouble}/€1) = 0.010548 \text{ dinar/rouble}$$

That is, the cross-rate must be 0.010548 Bahraini dinars per 1 Russian rouble. If it were anything else, there would be a triangle arbitrage opportunity.

EXAMPLE 18.2

SHEDDING SOME POUNDS

Assume the exchange rates for the British pound against the euro and dollar are:

$$€/£ = 1.1079$$
$$\$/£ = 1.3587$$

The US dollar/euro exchange rate is quoted as \$1.2264/€. Show that the exchange rates are consistent. Taking the two British pound exchange rates, we find that the cross-rate is:

$$\$/€ = (\$/£)/(€/£) = 1.3587/1.1079 = 1.2264$$

The exchange rates are consistent.

Types of Transaction

spot trade
an agreement to trade currencies based on the exchange rate today for settlement within 2 business days.

spot exchange rate
the exchange rate on a spot trade.

forward trade
an agreement to exchange currency at some time in the future.

There are two basic types of trade in the foreign exchange market: spot trades and forward trades. A **spot trade** is an agreement to exchange currency 'on the spot', which actually means that the transaction will be completed or settled within two business days. The exchange rate on a spot trade is called the **spot exchange rate**. Implicitly, all the exchange rates and transactions we have discussed so far have referred to the spot market.

A **forward trade** is an agreement to exchange currency at some time in the future. The exchange rate that will be used is agreed upon today and is called the **forward exchange rate**. A forward trade will normally be settled at some point in the next 12 months.

For example, assume the spot €/£ exchange rate is €1.1079/£. The one-year forward exchange rate is €1.1010/£. This means that you can buy a pound today for €1.1079, or you can agree to take delivery of a pound in one year and pay €1.1010 at that time.

Notice that the British pound is less expensive in the forward market (€1.1010 versus €1.1079). Because the British pound is less expensive in the future than it is today, it is said to be selling at a *discount* relative to the euro. For the same reason, the euro is selling at a *premium* relative to the British pound.

Why does the forward market exist? One answer is that it allows businesses and individuals to lock in a future exchange rate today, thereby eliminating any risk from unfavourable shifts in the exchange rate.

EXAMPLE 18.3

LOOKING FORWARD

Suppose you are a British business and expect to receive one million euros in three months, and you agree to a forward trade to exchange your euros for pounds. Based on a spot rate of £0.8662/€ and three-month forward rate of £0.8665/€, how many pounds will you get in three months? Is the euro selling at a discount or a premium relative to the pound?

The spot exchange rate and the three-month forward rate in terms of pounds per euros are £0.8662 = €1 and £0.8665 = €1, respectively. If you expect €1 million in three months, then you will get €1 million × 0.8665 per pound = £866,500. Because it is less expensive to buy a pound in the forward market than in the spot market (£0.8665 versus £0.8662), the pound is said to be selling at a discount relative to the euro.

As we mentioned earlier, it is standard practice worldwide (with a few exceptions) to quote exchange rates in terms of the dollar, euro or pound. This means that rates are quoted as the amount of currency per dollar, euro or pound. For the remainder of this chapter, we shall stick with this form. Things can get extremely confusing if you forget this. Thus, when we say things like 'the exchange rate is expected to rise', it is important to remember that we are talking about the exchange rate quoted as units of foreign currency per dollar, euro or pound.

> **forward exchange rate**
> the agreed-upon exchange rate to be used in a forward trade.

CONCEPT QUESTIONS

18.2a What is triangle arbitrage?
18.2b What do we mean by the 90-day forward exchange rate?
18.2c If we say that the exchange rate is €1.1/£, what do we mean?

18.3 PURCHASING POWER PARITY

Now that we have discussed what exchange rate quotations mean, we can address an obvious question: what determines the spot exchange rate level? Also, because we know that exchange rates change through time, we can ask the related question: what determines the rate of change in exchange rates? At least part of the answer in both cases goes by the name of **purchasing power parity (PPP)**: the idea that the exchange rate adjusts to keep purchasing power constant among currencies. As we discuss next, there are two forms of PPP, *absolute* and *relative*.

> **purchasing power parity (PPP)**
> the idea that the exchange rate adjusts to keep purchasing power constant among currencies.

ABSOLUTE PURCHASING POWER PARITY

The basic idea behind *absolute purchasing power parity* is that a commodity costs the same, regardless of what currency is used to purchase it or where it is selling. This is a straightforward concept. If a beer costs 50 kroner in Oslo, and the exchange rate is NKr10 per pound, then a beer costs NKr50/10 = £5 in London. In other words, absolute PPP says that £1 or €1 will buy you the same number of beers anywhere in the world.

More formally, let S_0 be the spot exchange rate between the euro and the dollar today (time 0), and we are quoting exchange rates as the amount of foreign currency per euro. Let P_{US} and P_{euro} be the current US and euro prices, respectively, on a particular commodity, say, apples. Absolute PPP says that:

$$P_{US} = S_0 \times P_{euro}$$

This tells us that the US price for something is equal to the euro price for that same something multiplied by the exchange rate.

The rationale behind PPP is similar to that behind triangle arbitrage. If PPP did not hold, arbitrage would be possible (in principle) if apples were moved from one country to another. For example, suppose apples are selling in Madrid for €2 per bushel, whereas in New York the price is $3 per bushel. Absolute PPP implies that:

$$P_{US} = S_0 \times P_{euro}$$
$$\$3 = S_0 \times €2$$
$$S_0 = \$3/€2 = \$1.50/€$$

That is, the implied spot exchange rate is $1.50 per euro. Equivalently, a dollar is worth €1/$1.5 = €0.667/$.

Suppose instead that the actual exchange rate is $1.2815/€. Starting with €2, a trader could buy a bushel of apples in Madrid, ship it to New York, and sell it there for $3. Our trader could then convert the $3 into euros at the prevailing exchange rate, $S_0 = \$1.2815/€$, yielding a total of $3/€1.2815 = €2.34. The round-trip gain would be 34 cents.

Because of this profit potential, forces are set in motion to change the exchange rate and/or the price of apples. In our example, apples would begin moving from Madrid to New York. The reduced supply of apples in Madrid would raise the price of apples there, and the increased supply in the US would lower the price of apples in New York.

In addition to moving apples around, apple traders would be busily converting dollars back into euros to buy more apples. This activity would increase the supply of dollars and simultaneously increase the demand for euros. We would expect the value of a dollar to fall. This means that the euro would be getting more valuable, so it would take more dollars to buy one euro. Because the exchange rate is quoted as dollars per euro, we would expect the exchange rate to rise from $1.2815/€.

For absolute PPP to hold absolutely, several things must be true:

1. The transactions costs of trading apples – shipping, insurance, spoilage, and so on – must be zero.
2. There must be no barriers to trading apples – no tariffs, taxes, or other political barriers.
3. Finally, an apple in New York must be identical to an apple in Madrid. It won't do for you to send red apples to Madrid if the Spanish eat only green apples.

Given that the transactions costs are not zero, and that the other conditions are rarely exactly met, it is not surprising that absolute PPP is really applicable only to traded goods, and then only to very uniform ones.

For this reason, absolute PPP does not imply that a Mercedes costs the same as a Ford, or that a nuclear power plant in France costs the same as one in New York. In the case of cars, they are not identical. In the case of nuclear power plants, even if they were identical, they are expensive and would be very difficult to ship. On the other hand, we would be surprised to see a significant violation of absolute PPP for gold.

Examples of violations of absolute purchasing power parity are not too hard to find. One of the more famous violations of absolute PPP is the Big Mac Index constructed by *The Economist*. To construct the index, prices for a Big Mac in different countries are gathered from McDonald's using dollars, euros and sterling as the base currency. Table 18.3 presents the under- and over-valuation of currencies using the July 2020 Big Mac index from www.economist.com. (We shall leave it to you to find the most recent index.)

TABLE 18.3

The Economist **Big Mac index**

Country	Local price	US price	$ Over/under valuation (%)	€ Over/under valuation (%)	£ Over/under valuation (%)
United Arab Emirates	14.75	4.02	−29.67	−16.09	−6.11
Bahrain	1.40	3.71	−34.97	−22.42	−13.19
Switzerland	6.50	6.91	20.94	44.29	61.45
China	21.70	3.10	−45.74	−35.26	−27.56
Denmark	30	4.58	−19.78	−4.29	7.09
Eurozone	4.21	4.79	−16.18	0.00	11.90
India	190	2.53	−55.75	−47.21	−40.93
Malaysia	9.99	2.34	−58.98	−51.07	−45.25
Norway	52	5.55	−2.82	15.94	29.73
Oman	1.10	2.86	−49.96	−40.30	−33.20
Russia	135	1.91	−66.51	−60.04	−55.29
Saudi Arabia	14	3.73	−34.64	−22.02	−12.74
Singapore	5.90	4.25	−25.54	−11.16	−0.59
South Africa	31	1.86	−67.44	−61.15	−56.63
Sweden	52.60	5.76	0.80	20.26	34.57
United Kingdom	3.39	4.28	−25.09	−10.63	0.00
United States	5.71	5.71	0.00	19.30	33.49

Source: www.economist.com, July 2020.

As you can see from the index, absolute PPP does not seem to hold, at least for the Big Mac. In fact, in very few countries surveyed by *The Economist* is the exchange rate within 10 per cent of that predicted by absolute PPP. The largest disparity is in South Africa, where a Big Mac costs the equivalent of $1.86. The most overvalued currency is the Swiss franc, where a Big Mac's cost is $6.91!

RELATIVE PURCHASING POWER PARITY

As a practical matter, a relative version of purchasing power parity has evolved. *Relative purchasing power parity* does not tell us what determines the absolute level of the exchange rate. Instead, it tells what determines the *change* in the exchange rate over time.

The Basic Idea

Suppose the British pound–US dollar exchange rate is currently $S_0 = \$1.30$. Further, suppose that the inflation rate in the United States is predicted to be 10 per cent over the coming year, and (for the moment) the inflation rate in the United Kingdom is predicted to be zero. What do you think the exchange rate will be in a year?

If you think about it, you see that a pound currently costs $1.30 in the United States. With 10 per cent inflation, we expect prices in the United States to generally rise by 10 per cent. So we expect that the price of a pound will go up by 10 per cent, and the exchange rate should rise to $\$1.30 \times 1.1 = \$1.43$.

If the United Kingdom's inflation rate is not zero, we need to worry about the relative inflation rates in the two countries. For example, suppose the UK inflation rate is predicted to be 4 per cent. Relative to prices in the United Kingdom, prices in the United States are rising at a rate of 10 per cent − 4 per cent = 6 per cent per year. So we expect the value of the pound to rise by 6 per cent, and the predicted exchange rate is $\$1.30 \times 1.06 = \$1.378$.

The Result

In general, relative PPP says that the change in the exchange rate is determined by the difference in the two countries' inflation rates. To be more specific, we shall use the following notation:

S_0 Current (time 0) spot exchange rate (foreign currency per dollar)
$E(S_t)$ Expected exchange rate in
h_{HC} Inflation rate in the home currency
h_{FC} Foreign country inflation rate

Based on our preceding discussion, relative PPP says that the expected percentage change in the exchange rate over the next year, $[E(S_1) - S_0]/S_0$, is:

$$\frac{E(S_1) - S_0}{S_0} = h_{FC} - h_{HC} \tag{18.1}$$

In words, relative PPP says that the expected percentage change in the exchange rate is equal to the difference in inflation rates. If we rearrange this slightly, we get:

$$E(S_1) = S_0 \times [1 + (h_{FC} - h_{HC})] \tag{18.2}$$

This result makes a certain amount of sense, but care must be used in quoting the exchange rate.

In our example involving the United Kingdom and the United States, relative PPP tells us that the exchange rate will rise by $h_{FC} - h_{HC} = 10\% - 4\% = 6\%$ per year. Assuming the difference in inflation rates doesn't change, the expected exchange rate in two years, $E(S_2)$, will therefore be:

$$\begin{aligned} E(S_2) &= E(S_1) \times (1 + 0.06) \\ &= 1.378 \times 1.06 \\ &= 1.461 \end{aligned}$$

Notice that we could have written this as:

$$\begin{aligned} E(S_2) &= 1.378 \times 1.06 \\ &= 1.30 \times (1.06 \times 1.06) \\ &= 1.30 \times 1.06^2 \end{aligned}$$

In general, relative PPP says that the expected exchange rate at some time in the future, $E(S_t)$, is:

$$E(S_t) = S_0 \times [1 + (h_{FC} - h_{HC})]^t$$

As we shall see, this is a very useful relationship.

Because we don't really expect absolute PPP to hold for most goods, we shall focus on relative PPP in our following discussion. Henceforth, when we refer to PPP without further qualification, we mean relative PPP.

> **EXAMPLE 18.4**
>
> ### IT'S ALL RELATIVE
>
> Assume the Turkish lira-euro exchange rate is 2.3600 lira per euro. The inflation rate in Turkey over the next three years will be, say, 10 per cent per year, whereas the Eurozone inflation rate will be 2 per cent. Based on relative PPP, what will the exchange rate be in three years?
>
> Because the Eurozone inflation rate is lower, we expect that a euro will become more valuable. The exchange rate change will be 10 per cent − 2 per cent = 8 per cent per year. Over three years the exchange rate will rise to:
>
> $$\begin{aligned} E(S_3) &= S_0 \times [1 + (h_{FC} - h_{HC})]^3 \\ &= 2.3600 \times [1 + (0.08)]^3 \\ &= 2.9729 \end{aligned}$$

Currency Appreciation and Depreciation

We frequently hear things like 'the euro strengthened (or weakened) in financial markets today' or 'the euro is expected to appreciate (or depreciate) relative to the pound'. When we say that the euro strengthens or appreciates, we mean that the value of a euro rises, so it takes more foreign currency to buy a euro.

What happens to the exchange rates as currencies fluctuate in value depends on how exchange rates are quoted. Because we are quoting them as units of foreign currency per home currency, the exchange rate moves in the same direction as the value of the home currency: it rises as the home currency strengthens, and it falls as the home currency weakens.

Relative PPP tells us that the exchange rate will rise if the home currency inflation rate is lower than the foreign country's. This happens because the foreign currency depreciates in value and therefore weakens relative to the home currency.

> **CONCEPT QUESTIONS**
>
> **18.3a** What does absolute PPP say? Why might it not hold for many types of goods?
> **18.3b** According to relative PPP, what determines the change in exchange rates?

18.4 INTEREST RATE PARITY, UNBIASED FORWARD RATES AND THE INTERNATIONAL FISHER EFFECT

We now need to address the relationship between spot exchange rates, forward exchange rates and interest rates. To get started, we use some additional notation:

F_t Forward exchange rate for settlement at time
R_{HC} Home country nominal risk-free interest rate
R_{FC} Foreign country nominal risk-free interest rate

As before, we shall use S_0 to stand for the spot exchange rate. You can take the home country's nominal risk-free rate, R_{HC}, to be the home country's T-bill rate.

COVERED INTEREST ARBITRAGE

We observe the following information about the British pound and the US dollar:

$$S_0 = \$1.5193$$
$$F_1 = \$1.5167$$
$$R_{HC} = 2.13\%$$
$$R_{FC} = 0.27\%$$

where R_{FC} is the nominal risk-free rate in the United States. The period is 1 year, so F_1 is the 360-day forward rate.

Do you see an arbitrage opportunity here? Suppose you have £10,000 to invest, and you want a riskless investment. One option you have is to invest the £10,000 in a riskless UK investment such as a 360-day T-bill. If you do this, then in one period your £1 will be worth:

$$\text{£ value in 1 period} = £1 \times (1 + R_{HC})$$
$$= £10,213$$

Alternatively, you can invest in the US risk-free investment. To do this, you need to convert your £10,000 to US dollars and simultaneously execute a forward trade to convert dollars back to pounds in 1 year. The necessary steps would be as follows:

1. Convert your £10,000 to £10,000 × S_0 = $15,193.
2. At the same time, enter into a forward agreement to convert US dollars back to pounds in 1 year. Because the forward rate is $1.5167, you will get £1 for every $1.5167 that you have in 1 year.
3. Invest your $15,193 in the United States at R_{FC}. In 1 year, you will have:

$$\$ \text{ value in 1 year} = \$15,193 \times (1 + R_{FC})$$
$$= \$15,193 \times 1.0027$$
$$= \$15,234$$

4. Convert your $15,234 back to pounds at the agreed-upon rate of $1.5167 = £1. You end up with:

$$\text{£ value in 1 year} = \$15,234/1.5167$$
$$= £10,044$$

Notice that the value in 1 year resulting from this strategy can be written as:

$$\text{£ value in 1 year} = £10,000 \times S_0 \times (1 + R_{FC})/F_1$$
$$= £10,000 \times 1,5193 \times 1.0027/1.5167$$
$$= £10,044$$

The return on this investment is apparently 0.44 per cent. This is lower than the 2.13 per cent we get from investing in the United Kingdom. Because both investments are risk-free, there is an arbitrage opportunity.

To exploit the difference in interest rates, you need to borrow, say, $10 million at the lower US rate and invest it at the higher UK rate. What is the round-trip profit from doing this? To find out, we can work through the steps outlined previously:

1. Convert the $10 million at $1.5193/£ to get £6,581,979.
2. Agree to exchange dollars for pounds in 1 year at $1.5167 to the pound.
3. Invest the £6,581,979 for 1 year at R_{UK} = 2.13 per cent. You end up with £6,722,175.

4. Convert the £6,722,175 back to dollars to fulfil the forward contract. You receive £6,722,175 × $1.5167/£ = $10,195,522.
5. Repay the loan with interest. You owe $10 million plus 0.27 per cent interest, for a total of $10,027,000. You have $10,195,522, so your round-trip profit is a risk-free $168,522.

The activity that we have illustrated here goes by the name of *covered interest arbitrage*. The term *covered* refers to the fact that we are covered in the event of a change in the exchange rate because we lock in the forward exchange rate today.

INTEREST RATE PARITY

If we assume that significant covered interest arbitrage opportunities do not exist, then there must be some relationship between spot exchange rates, forward exchange rates and relative interest rates. To see what this relationship is, note that, in general, Strategy 1 from the preceding discussion, investing in a riskless home country investment, gives us $1 + R_{HC}$ for every unit of cash in home currency we invest. Strategy 2, investing in a foreign risk-free investment, gives us $S_0 \times (1 + R_{FC})/F_1$ for every unit of cash in home currency we invest. Because these have to be equal to prevent arbitrage, it must be the case that:

$$1 + R_{HC} = S_0 \times \frac{1 + R_{FC}}{F_1}$$

Rearranging this a bit gets us the famous **interest rate parity (IRP)** condition:

$$\frac{F_1}{S_0} = \frac{1 + R_{FC}}{1 + R_{HC}} \tag{18.3}$$

> **interest rate parity (IRP)**
> the condition stating that the interest rate differential between two countries is equal to the percentage difference between the forward exchange rate and the spot exchange rate.

There is a handy approximation for IRP that clearly illustrates what is going on, and it is not difficult to remember. If we define the percentage forward premium or discount as $(F_1 - S_0)/S_0$, then IRP says that this percentage premium or discount is *approximately* equal to the difference in interest rates:

$$(F_1 - S_0)/S_0 = R_{FC} - R_{HC} \tag{18.4}$$

Very loosely, what IRP says is that any difference in interest rates between two countries for some period is just offset by the change in the relative value of the currencies, thereby eliminating any arbitrage possibilities. Notice that we could also write:

$$F_1 = S_0 \times [1 + (R_{FC} - R_{HC})] \tag{18.5}$$

In general, if we have t periods instead of just one, the IRP approximation is written as:

$$F_t = S_0 \times [1 + (R_{FC} - R_{HC})]^t \tag{18.6}$$

EXAMPLE 18.5

PARITY CHECK

Suppose the exchange rate for the South African rand, S_0, is currently R13.0745 = €1. If the interest rate in the Eurozone is $R_{Euro} = 2.12$ per cent and the interest rate in South Africa is $R_{SA} = 10.95$ per cent, what must the forward rate be to prevent covered interest arbitrage?

From IRP, we have:

$$\begin{aligned}
F_1 &= S_0 \times [1 + (R_{SA} - R_{Euro})] \\
&= R13.0745 \times [1 + (0.1095 - 0.0212)] \\
&= R13.0745 \times 1.0883 \\
&= R14.2290
\end{aligned}$$

Notice that the rand will sell at a discount relative to the euro. (Why?)

FORWARD RATES AND FUTURE SPOT RATES

In addition to PPP and IRP, we need to discuss one more basic relationship. What is the connection between the forward rate and the expected future spot rate? The **unbiased forward rates (UFR)** condition says that the forward rate, F_1, is equal to the *expected* future spot rate, $E(S_1)$:

$$F_1 = E(S_1)$$

With t periods, UFR would be written as:

$$F_t = E(S_t)$$

> **unbiased forward rates (UFR)**
> the condition stating that the current forward rate is an unbiased predictor of the future spot exchange rate.

Loosely, the UFR condition says that, on average, the forward exchange rate is equal to the future spot exchange rate.

If we ignore risk, then the UFR condition should hold. Suppose the forward rate for the South African rand is consistently lower than the future spot rate by, say, 10 rand. This means that anyone who wanted to convert euros to rand in the future would consistently get more rand by not agreeing to a forward exchange. The forward rate would have to rise to get anyone interested in a forward exchange.

Similarly, if the forward rate were consistently higher than the future spot rate, anyone who wanted to convert rand to euros would get more euros per rand by not agreeing to a forward trade. The forward exchange rate would have to fall to attract such traders.

> **uncovered interest parity (UIP)**
> the condition stating that the expected percentage change in the exchange rate is equal to the difference in interest rates.

For these reasons, the forward and actual future spot rates should be equal to each other on average. What the future spot rate will actually be is uncertain, of course. The UFR condition may not hold if traders are willing to pay a premium to avoid this uncertainty. If the condition does hold, then the 180-day forward rate that we see today should be an unbiased predictor of what the exchange rate will actually be in 180 days.

PUTTING IT ALL TOGETHER

We have developed three relationships, PPP, IRP and UFR, that describe the interaction between key financial variables such as interest rates, exchange rates and inflation rates. We now explore the implications of these relationships as a group.

Uncovered Interest Parity

To start, it is useful to collect our international financial market relationships in one place:

$$\text{PPP:} \quad E(S_1) = S_0 \times [1 + (h_{FC} - h_{HC})]$$
$$\text{IPR:} \quad F_1 = S_0 \times [1 + (R_{FC} - R_{HC})]$$
$$\text{UFR:} \quad F_1 = E(S_1)$$

We begin by combining UFR and IRP. Because we know that $F_1 = E(S_1)$ from the UFR condition, we can substitute $E(S_1)$ for F_1 in IRP. The result is:

$$\text{UIP:} \quad E(S_1) = S_0 \times [1 + (R_{FC} - R_{HC})] \quad (18.7)$$

This important relationship is called **uncovered interest parity (UIP)**, and it will play a key role in our international capital budgeting discussion that follows. With t periods, UIP becomes:

$$E(S_t) = S_0 \times [1 + (R_{FC} - R_{HC})]^t \quad (18.8)$$

The International Fisher Effect

Next, we compare PPP and UIP. Both have $E(S_1)$ on the left-hand side, so their right-hand sides must be equal. We thus have:

$$S_0 \times [1 + (h_{FC} - h_{HC})] = S_0 \times [1 + (R_{FC} - R_{HC})]$$
$$h_{FC} - h_{HC} = R_{FC} - R_{HC}$$

international Fisher effect (IFE)
the theory that real interest rates are equal across countries.

This tells us that the difference in returns between the home country and a foreign country is just equal to the difference in inflation rates. Rearranging this slightly gives us the **international Fisher effect (IFE)**:

$$\text{IFE: } R_{HC} - h_{HC} = R_{FC} - h_{FC} \tag{18.9}$$

The IFE says that *real* rates are equal across countries.[1]

The conclusion that real returns are equal across countries is really basic economics. If real returns were higher in, say, Britain than in the Eurozone, money would flow out of Eurozone financial markets and into British markets. Asset prices in Britain would rise, and their returns would fall. At the same time, asset prices in Europe would fall, and their returns would rise. This process acts to equalize real returns.

Having said all this, we need to note a couple of things. First of all, we really haven't explicitly dealt with risk in our discussion. We might reach a different conclusion about real returns once we do, particularly if people in different countries have different tastes and attitudes towards risk. Second, there are many barriers to the movement of money and capital around the world. Real returns might differ in two separate countries for long periods of time if money can't move freely between them.

Despite these problems, we expect that capital markets will become increasingly internationalized. As this occurs, any differences in real rates that do exist will probably diminish. The laws of economics have very little respect for national boundaries.

> **CONCEPT QUESTIONS**
>
> **18.4a** What is covered interest arbitrage?
> **18.4b** What is the international Fisher effect?

18.5 INTERNATIONAL CAPITAL BUDGETING

Kihlstrom Equipment, a US-based international company, is evaluating an overseas investment. Kihlstrom's exports of drill bits have increased to such a degree that it is considering building a French distribution centre. The project will cost €2 million to launch. The cash flows are expected to be €0.9 million a year for the next three years.

The current spot exchange rate for euros is €0.5. Recall that this is euros per dollar, so a euro is worth $1/0.5 = $2. The risk-free rate in the United States is 5 per cent, and the risk-free rate in the Eurozone is 7 per cent. Note that the exchange rate and the two interest rates are observed in financial markets, not estimated.[2] Kihlstrom's required return on dollar investments of this sort is 10 per cent.

Should Kihlstrom take this investment? As always, the answer depends on the NPV; but how do we calculate the net present value of this project in US dollars? There are two basic methods:

1. *The home currency approach:* Convert all the euro cash flows into dollars, and then discount at 10 per cent to find the NPV in dollars. Notice that we have to come up with the future exchange rates to convert the future projected euro cash flows into dollars.
2. *The foreign currency approach:* Determine the required return on euro investments, and then discount the euro cash flows to find the NPV in euros. Then convert this euro NPV to a dollar NPV. This approach requires us to convert the 10 per cent dollar required return to the equivalent euro required return.

The difference between these two approaches is primarily a matter of when we convert from euros to dollars. In the first case, we convert before estimating the NPV. In the second case, we convert after estimating the NPV.

It might appear that the second approach is superior because we have to come up with only one number, the euro discount rate. Furthermore, because the first approach requires us to forecast future exchange rates, it probably seems that there is greater room for error with this approach. As we illustrate next, however, based on our previous results, the two approaches are really the same.

METHOD 1: THE HOME CURRENCY APPROACH

To convert the projected future cash flows into dollars, we shall invoke the uncovered interest parity, or UIP, relation to come up with the projected exchange rates. Based on our earlier discussion, the expected exchange rate at time t, $E(S_t)$, is:

$$E(S_t) = S_0 \times [1 + (R_\euro - R_{US})]^t$$

where $R_\euro$ stands for the nominal risk-free rate in the Eurozone. Since $R_\euro$ is 7 per cent, R_{US} is 5 per cent, and the current exchange rate (S_0) is €0.5:

$$E(S_t) = 0.5 \times [1 + (0.07 - 0.05)]^t$$
$$= 0.5 \times 1.02^t$$

The projected exchange rates for the drill bit project are thus:

Year	Expected exchange rate
1	€0.5 × 1.02¹ = €0.5100
2	€0.5 × 1.02² = €0.5202
3	€0.5 × 1.02³ = €0.5306

Using these exchange rates, along with the current exchange rate, we can convert all of the euro cash flows to dollars (note that all of the cash flows in this example are in millions):

Year	(1) Cash flow in € millions	(2) Expected exchange rate (€/$)	(3) Cash flow in $ millions (1)/(2)
0	−2.0	0.5000	−4.00
1	0.9	0.5100	1.76
2	0.9	0.5202	1.73
3	0.9	0.5306	1.70

To finish off, we calculate the NPV in the usual way:

$$NPV_\$ = -\$4 + \$1.76/1.10 + \$1.73/1.10^2 + \$1.70/1.10^3$$
$$= \$0.3 \text{ million}$$

So the project appears to be profitable.

METHOD 2: THE FOREIGN CURRENCY APPROACH

Kihlstrom requires a nominal return of 10 per cent on the dollar-denominated cash flows. We need to convert this to a rate suitable for euro-denominated cash flows. Based on the international Fisher effect, we know that the difference in the nominal rates is:

$$R_\euro - R_{US} = h_\euro - h_{US}$$
$$= 7\% - 5\%$$
$$= 2\%$$

The appropriate discount rate for estimating the euro cash flows from the drill bit project is approximately equal to 10 per cent plus an extra 2 per cent to compensate for the greater euro inflation rate.

If we calculate the NPV of the euro cash flows at this rate, we get:

$$NPV_\euro = -\euro 2 + \euro 0.9/1.12 + \euro 0.9/1.12^2 + \euro 0.9/1.12^3$$
$$= \euro 0.16 \text{ million}$$

The NPV of this project is €0.16 million. Taking this project makes us €0.16 million richer today. What is this in dollars? Because the exchange rate today is €0.5, the dollar NPV of the project is:

$$\begin{aligned} NPV_\$ &= NPV_\euro / S_0 \\ &= \euro\ 0.16/0.5 \\ &= \$0.3 \text{ million} \end{aligned}$$

This is the same dollar NPV that we previously calculated.

The important thing to recognize from our example is that the two capital budgeting procedures are actually the same, and will always give the same answer.[3] In this second approach, the fact that we are implicitly forecasting exchange rates is hidden. Even so, the foreign currency approach is computationally a little easier.

UNREMITTED CASH FLOWS

The previous example assumed that all after-tax cash flows from the foreign investment could be remitted to (paid out to) the parent firm. Actually, substantial differences can exist between the cash flows generated by a foreign project and the amount that can actually be remitted, or 'repatriated', to the parent firm.

A foreign subsidiary can remit funds to a parent in many forms, including the following:

- Dividends
- Management fees for central services
- Royalties on the use of trade names and patents

In whichever way cash flows are repatriated, international firms must pay special attention to remittances, because there may be current and future controls on remittances. Many governments are sensitive to the charge of being exploited by foreign national firms. In such cases, governments are tempted to limit the ability of international firms to remit cash flows. Funds that cannot currently be remitted are sometimes said to be *blocked*.

> **CONCEPT QUESTIONS**
>
> **18.5a** What financial complications arise in international capital budgeting? Describe two procedures for estimating NPV in the case of an international project.
> **18.5b** What are blocked funds?

18.6 EXCHANGE RATE RISK

exchange rate risk
the risk related to having international operations in a world where relative currency values vary.

Exchange rate risk is the natural consequence of international operations in a world where relative currency values move up and down. Managing exchange rate risk is an important part of international finance. As we discuss next, there are three different types of exchange rate risk, or exposure: short-run exposure, long-run exposure and translation exposure.

SHORT-RUN EXPOSURE

The day-to-day fluctuations in exchange rates create short-run risks for international firms. Most such firms have contractual agreements to buy and sell goods in the near future at set prices. When different currencies are involved, such transactions have an extra element of risk.

Imagine that you are importing imitation pasta from Italy and reselling it in the United Kingdom under the Impasta brand name. Your largest customer has ordered 10,000 cases of Impasta. You place the order with your supplier today, but you won't pay until the goods arrive in 60 days. Your selling price is £6 per case. Your cost is €8.40 per case, and the exchange rate is currently €1.50, so it takes €1.50 to buy £1.

At the current exchange rate, your cost in pounds of filling the order is €8.40/0.5 = £5.60 per case, so your pre-tax profit on the order is 10,000 × (£6 − 5.60) = £4,000. However, the exchange rate in 60 days will probably be different, so your profit will depend on what the future exchange rate turns out to be.

For example, if the rate goes to €1.60, your cost is €8.40/1.6 = £5.25 per case. Your profit goes to £7,500. If the exchange rate goes to, say, €1.40, your cost is €8.40/1.4 = £6, and your profit is zero.

The short-run exposure in our example can be reduced or eliminated in several ways. The most obvious way is by entering into a forward exchange agreement to lock in an exchange rate. For example, suppose the 60-day forward rate is €1.58. What will be your profit if you hedge? What profit should you expect if you don't?

If you hedge, you lock in an exchange rate of €1.58. Your cost in pounds will thus be €8.40/1.58 = £5.32 per case, so your profit will be 10,000 × (£6 − 5.32) = £6,800. If you don't hedge, then, assuming that the forward rate is an unbiased predictor (in other words, assuming the UFR condition holds), you should expect that the exchange rate will actually be €1.58 in 60 days. You should expect to make £6,800.

Alternatively, if this strategy is not feasible, you could borrow the pounds today, convert them into euros, and invest the euros for 60 days to earn some interest. Based on IRP, this amounts to entering into a forward contract.

LONG-RUN EXPOSURE

In the long run, a foreign operation's value can fluctuate because of unanticipated changes in relative economic conditions. For example, imagine that we own a labour-intensive assembly operation located in another country to take advantage of lower wages. Through time, unexpected changes in economic conditions can raise the foreign wage levels to the point where the cost advantage is eliminated, or even becomes negative.

Hedging long-run exposure is more difficult than hedging short-term risks. For one thing, organized forward markets don't exist for such long-term needs. Instead, firms' primary option is to try to match up foreign currency inflows and outflows. The same thing goes for matching foreign-currency-denominated assets and liabilities. For example, a firm that sells in a foreign country might concentrate its raw material purchases and labour expense in that country. In that way, the home currency values of its revenues and costs will move up and down together. Probably the best examples of this type of hedging are the so-called *transplant auto manufacturers* such as BMW, Honda, Mercedes and Toyota, who now build in the United States a substantial portion of the cars they sell there, thereby obtaining some degree of immunization against exchange rate movements.

For example, BMW produces 160,000 cars in the United States and exports about 100,000 of them. The costs of manufacturing cars are paid mostly in dollars; when BMW exports cars to Europe, it receives euros. When the dollar weakens, these vehicles become more profitable for BMW. At the same time, BMW exports about 217,000 cars to the United States each year. The costs of manufacturing these imported cars are mostly in euros, so they become less profitable when the dollar weakens. Taken together, these gains and losses tend to offset each other and provide BMW with a natural hedge.

Similarly, a firm can reduce its long-run exchange rate risk by borrowing in the foreign country because changes in the value of foreign borrowing will partially offset fluctuations in the foreign subsidiary's asset value.

TRANSLATION EXPOSURE

When a British company calculates its accounting net income and EPS for some period, it must 'translate' everything into pounds. This can create some problems for the accountants when there are significant foreign operations. In particular, two issues arise:

1. What is the appropriate exchange rate to use for translating each balance sheet account?
2. How should balance sheet accounting gains and losses from foreign currency translation be handled?

To illustrate the accounting problem, suppose we started a small foreign subsidiary in Lilliputia a year ago. The local currency is the gulliver, abbreviated GL. At the beginning of the year, the exchange rate was GL2 = €1, and the balance sheet in gullivers looked like this:

	GL		GL
Assets	1,000	Liabilities	500
		Equity	500

At 2 gullivers to the euro, the beginning balance sheet in euros was as follows:

	€		€
Assets	500	Liabilities	250
		Equity	250

Lilliputia is a quiet place, and nothing at all actually happened during the year. As a result, net income was zero (before consideration of exchange rate changes). However, the exchange rate changed to 4 gullivers = €1 because the Lilliputian inflation rate is much higher than the Eurozone inflation rate.

Because nothing happened, the accounting ending balance sheet in gullivers is the same as the beginning one. However, if we convert it to euros at the new exchange rate, we get:

Notice that the equity value has gone down by €125, even though net income was exactly zero. Even though absolutely nothing really happened, there is a €125 accounting loss. How to handle this €125 loss has been a controversial accounting question.

One obvious and consistent way to handle this loss is to report the loss on the parent's income statement. During periods of volatile exchange rates, this kind of treatment can dramatically impact an international company's reported EPS. This is a purely accounting phenomenon; but, even so, such fluctuations are disliked by some financial managers.

The current approach to handling translation gains and losses is based on rules set out in the International Accounting Standards Board (IASB) International Accounting Standard No. 21 (IAS 21). For the most part, IAS 21 requires that all assets and liabilities be translated from the subsidiary's currency into the parent's currency using the exchange rate that currently prevails. Income and expenses are treated differently, and these are translated at the exchange rate that prevails at the time of the transaction, or at the average rate for the period when this is a reasonable approximation. In contrast to US accounting rules, the impact of translation gains and losses is explicitly recognized in net income. In the US, the translation gain or loss is not recognized until the underlying assets and liabilities are sold or otherwise liquidated.

MANAGING EXCHANGE RATE RISK

For a large multinational firm, the management of exchange rate risk is complicated because there can be many different currencies involved in many different subsidiaries. A change in some exchange rate will probably benefit some subsidiaries and hurt others. The net effect on the overall firm depends on its net exposure.

For example, suppose a firm has two divisions. Division A buys goods in Italy for euros and sells them in Britain for pounds. Division B buys goods in Britain for pounds and sells them in Italy for euros. If these two divisions are of roughly equal size in terms of their inflows and outflows, the firm at the aggregate level obviously has little exchange rate risk.

In our example, the firm's net position in pounds (the amount coming in less the amount going out) is small, so the exchange rate risk is small. However, if one division, acting on its own, were to start hedging its exchange rate risk, the overall firm's exchange rate risk would go up. The moral of the story is that multinational firms have to be conscious of their overall positions in a foreign currency. For this reason, management of exchange rate risk is probably best handled on a centralized basis.

Firms use various approaches to manage exchange risk and there is no one method that dominates others. The main approaches are: (a) home currency invoicing, (b) receipt and payment matching, and (c) cash payment and receipt management.

Home Currency Invoicing

The simplest approach to managing foreign exchange risk is to invoice customers in your home currency and agree to pay suppliers in your home currency. Although this approach appears optimal, it means the counterparty absorbs all risk associated with future exchange rate movements, which is clearly suboptimal to them.

An alternative is to denominate invoices in the foreign currency (home currency of the counterparty) and agree on an exchange rate at which the transaction will take place. This is known as a currency forward contract and will be discussed in more detail in Chapter 20.

Receipt and Payment Matching

Another way to minimize foreign exchange risk is to schedule foreign currency payments and receipts so that they take place at roughly the same time. Any exposure to currency volatility will be netted out, with only the difference between receipts and payments exposed to exchange rate risk.

Cash Payment and Receipt Management

There is a fundamental rule in business: *collect cash due as soon as possible and negotiate the longest possible credit terms with suppliers.* Companies can manage foreign exchange risk by flipping the previous statement on its head by offering counterparties something of value in reward for mitigating exchange rate risk. There are two strategies:

1. Lead payments. Offer to pay for foreign currency-denominated goods upfront to remove exchange rate risk.
2. Lag receipts. Offer to delay receipt of foreign currency payments until such times as exchange rates move in a favourable direction.

A prudent financial manager will utilize all three of the methods discussed above to minimize exchange rate risk.

> **CONCEPT QUESTIONS**
>
> **18.6a** What are the different types of exchange rate risk?
> **18.6b** How can a firm hedge short-run exchange rate risk? Long-run exchange rate risk?

> **REAL WORLD INSIGHTS**
>
> At any one time, the world faces several major risks to global and political stability. This undoubtedly affects corporate growth prospects, and an adept financial manager must be cognizant of the possibilities of major risk events. Normally, companies rank risk events in terms of probability of occurrence and degree of impact. Risks can also be categorized into different areas, such as economic, technological and political. Some of the most important risks (in no particular order) facing European companies between 2021 and 2024 are listed below. These may change over time, and new risks can and will emerge.
>
> 1. Climate change (major weather events such as flooding and drought)
> 2. Social and political upheaval because of conflict-induced immigration
> 3. High levels of unemployment
> 4. Wars between national states
> 5. An economic slowdown in Europe, the United States or China
> 6. The economic fall-out from low energy prices
> 7. Automation and artificial intelligence
> 8. Another global pandemic

18.7 POLITICAL RISK

One final element of risk in international investing is **political risk**. Political risk refers to changes in value that arise as a consequence of political actions. This is not a problem faced exclusively by international firms. For example, changes in British tax laws and regulations may benefit some British firms and hurt others, so political risk exists nationally and internationally.

political risk risk related to changes in value that arise because of political actions.

Some countries do have more political risk than others, however. When firms operate in these riskier countries, the extra political risk may lead the firms to require higher returns on overseas investments to compensate for the possibility that funds may be blocked, critical operations interrupted, or contracts abrogated. In the most extreme case, the possibility of outright confiscation may be a concern in countries with relatively unstable political environments.

Political risk also depends on the nature of the business. Some businesses are less likely to be confiscated because they are not particularly valuable in a different owner's hands. An assembly operation supplying subcomponents that only the parent company uses would not be an attractive 'takeover' target, for example. Similarly, a manufacturing operation that requires the use of specialized components from the parent is of little value without the parent company's co-operation.

Natural resource developments, such as copper mining or oil drilling, are just the opposite. Once the operation is in place, much of the value is in the commodity. The political risk for such investments is much higher for this reason. Also, the issue of exploitation is more pronounced with such investments, again increasing the political risk.

Corruption is a huge issue in many countries, where kickbacks or 'business facilitation fees' are the norm. Government officials, petty bureaucrats and cumbersome administrative regulations can significantly restrict the efficiency of international operations.

Many organizations present rankings of political risk in countries, which should be considered before any foreign direct investment occurs. Transparency International's 'perceptions of corruption' ranking is an example of such an assessment and is presented in Table 18.4.

> **REAL WORLD INSIGHTS**
>
> The Transparency International Corruption Perceptions Index is graded between 0 and 100 (see Table 18.4), with a lower score indicating a country in which the public sector is perceived to be exceptionally corrupt. Scandinavian countries are perceived to have very little public-sector corruption, but this tends to worsen as

TABLE 18.4

Transparency International Corruption Perceptions Index 2019

Country	CPI score 2019	Country	CPI score 2019
Denmark	87	Italy	53
Finland	86	Malaysia	53
Singapore	85	Saudi Arabia	53
Sweden	85	Oman	52
Switzerland	85	Greece	48
Norway	84	Jordan	48
Netherlands	82	South Africa	44
Germany	80	Bahrain	42
Luxembourg	80	China	41
Iceland	78	India	41
Austria	77	Brazil	35
United Kingdom	77	Russia	28
Belgium	75	Iran	26
Ireland	74	Nigeria	26
United Arab Emirates	71	Iraq	20
France	69	Syria	13
United States	69	South Sudan	12
Spain	62	Somalia	9

Note: Transparency International's Corruption Perceptions Index measures the perceived level of public-sector corruption in countries and territories worldwide on a scale of 0 (highly corrupt) to 100 (very clean). Source: © Transparency International. All Rights Reserved. For more information, visit www.transparency.org.

one goes further south-east through Europe. Consistent with their economic development, emerging markets tend to have more public-sector corruption than developed countries. Notably, China and India's public sector is perceived to be exceptionally corrupt, even with these countries' incredible growth over the past 20 years.

Political risk can be hedged in several ways, particularly when confiscation or nationalization is a concern. The use of local financing, perhaps from the foreign country's government in question, reduces the possible loss because the company can refuse to pay the debt in the event of unfavourable political activities. Based on our discussion in this section, structuring the operation so that it requires significant parent company involvement to function is another way to reduce political risk.

CONCEPT QUESTIONS

18.7a What is political risk?
18.7b What are some ways of hedging political risk?

18.8 ISLAMIC CORPORATE FINANCE

In recent years, many countries have developed financial instruments and business practices reflecting Islam's religious values. This is known as Islamic financing, with the main characteristic that interest of any kind is not allowed to be charged on financial securities. The United Kingdom is at the forefront of Islamic financing in Western Europe, followed by Switzerland, France, and Luxembourg. In the Middle East, Bahrain is the Islamic financing centre, and Malaysia is the main country in South East Asia. Islamic financing need not be confined only to Muslims and in Malaysia, for example, nearly a quarter of all users of Islamic products are non-Muslims.

Not having interest-bearing securities presents challenges to firms wishing to raise financing for investment projects. In response, banks have created innovative instruments and financing methods consistent with Islamic or Shariah principles and have debt-like characteristics. The most common of these involve elements of profit-sharing, known as *mudharabah,* joint ventures (*musharakah*), leasing (*ijarah*), and compensation for facilitating the financing activity (*murabahah*). Islamic securities that can be traded on exchanges are known as *sukuk*.

TYPES OF ISLAMIC FINANCING METHODS

Advanced Payment Sale

A *bai salam* is a contract where two parties trade today in return for a good to be delivered at some specified date in the future. The transfer of cash must be made today, and the quality and quantity of the good must be specified at the time of the trade. One of the requirements of *bai salam* is that there can be no uncertainty in the quality or quantity of a good or commodity. Therefore, raw agricultural produce is not allowed to be traded in this way because flooding or an earthquake may result in loss of quality or quantity.

EXAMPLE 18.6

BAI SALAM
Shukran plc is undertaking a new warehouse expansion and has commissioned a company, Temsaah Ltd, to build it on an existing warehouse site. The warehouse with full facilities will take one year to build, and the price of the new warehouse will be £3,000,000 in one year. In a *bai salam* sale, Shukran may pay £2.7 million today for the warehouse (fully specified at the time of the contract) to be ready for use exactly one year from the trade date.

Stated Cost Plus Profit

Murabahah is one of the most common forms of Islamic financing contracts. In this transaction, the seller of a commodity expressly states the cost that has been incurred in producing, manufacturing or buying a commodity or asset. A pre-agreed mark-up or profit margin is then applied to the cost to find the trade price. Clearly, a *murabahah* contract requires the seller to be honest about the base cost of the commodity. *Murabahah* is used for the financing of asset purchases and property investments. So that there is no doubt that it was the underlying asset that has been traded (to avoid accusations of interest payments in another form), the seller of the commodity or asset must be the owner before selling it. As in other Islamic financing contracts, a seller may consult the debt markets to ascertain competitive mark-up rates.

In a *murabahah* sale, the purchaser may pay the stated amount in fixed instalments. When only one payment in the future is made, this is known as a *bai' bithaman ajil* contract.

EXAMPLE 18.7

MURABAHAH

Shukran plc is undertaking a new warehouse expansion and has commissioned a company, Temsaah Ltd, to build it on an existing warehouse site. Temsaah needs cash equalling the construction costs of £2.7 million today to finance the building of the warehouse. Unfortunately, Shukran does not have the funds in place. The CEO of Shukran goes to Bahrain Bank and enters into a *murabahah* transaction.

Bahrain Bank agrees to pay £2.7 million today to Temsaah and notifies Shukran's CEO of the cost. Given market conditions, with comparable loans currently at 10 per cent, the Bahrain Bank manager agrees with the CEO of Shukran to charge a mark-up of £270,000 on the building to be paid in one year. This mark-up of 10 per cent makes the murabahah contract competitive with Western financing deals.

In this transaction, Bahrain Bank owns the warehouse until the date of the trade. In one year, Bahrain Bank sells the warehouse for £2,970,000 (£2,700,000 cost plus £270,000 mark-up), and the transfer of title deeds to Shukran takes place on that date. As you will have noticed, this transaction is actually a *bai' bithaman ajil* contract, a subtype of *murabahah* financing.

Goodwill Loan

Perhaps unique to the global financial markets, a *qard hassan* is a loan without any interest. The lender will provide the borrower with funds and, at some point in the future, these will be paid back to the bank. At their own discretion, the borrower may repay an extra amount to compensate the lender for supplying the funds. A *qard hassan* is normally very small, say £2,000, and pays for school education, medical fees or some other social improving purpose.

Hire Purchase

Hire purchase agreements originally came from the United Kingdom and are most commonly used in the automobile industry. In a Western hire purchase agreement, the buyer of an asset puts down an initial deposit on an asset's price and agrees to hire or rent it for a set period. When the sum of the rental payments reaches a certain amount, the buyer may purchase the asset outright for a pre-agreed price and take ownership.

With a little modification, hire purchase agreements are ideal instruments for Islamic financing. In an *ijarah thumma al bai'* contract, the buyer agrees to initially lease or rent the asset for a certain period. When this period has expired, the buyer may purchase the asset for a specific price agreed at the beginning of the contract.

Joint Venture

A *musharakah* is a contract between two parties to invest in a joint venture and share any profit or losses that may arise from the investment. Companies that require partial funding for an investment can go to an Islamic bank and enter into a *musharakah* agreement and raise the required funds.

> **EXAMPLE 18.8**
>
> ### IJARAH THUMMA AL BAI'
>
> Shufaa Al Beity wishes to purchase a car whose sale price is €25,000. Unfortunately, she is a student and cannot afford to part with that amount of money today. She decides to enter into an *ijarah thumma al bai'* contract to buy the car over 5 years in monthly instalments. How much would she pay?
>
> To determine a set of monthly payments that is competitive with other Western lenders, an Islamic bank would study the range of Western loans on offer today. Assume that most banks are giving personal loans with an APR of 10 per cent. This is the effective interest rate on car loans for €25,000 over 5 years and equates to a rate of 0.7974 per cent per month (work it out yourself!). Using the standard annuity formula, the monthly payment on a loan of €25,000 paid over 60 monthly instalments at a rate of 0.7974 per cent per month is:
>
> $$C = \frac{€25,000}{A^{60}_{0.007974}} = \frac{€25,000}{47.5385} = €525.89$$
>
> The total payments that Shufaa will need to make if she takes out a Western loan are 60 × €525.89 = €31,553.37. For an Islamic bank to be competitive with its Western counterpart, the total amount paid in an *ijarah thumma al bai'* must be equal to or less than €31,553.37.
>
> Shufaa can only afford a monthly payment of €500, so she enters into an *ijarah thumma al bai'* contract where the Islamic bank buys the car from the car dealer for €25,000. It then leases the car to Shufaa for a monthly payment of €500 a month for 60 months. At the end of the term of the *ijarah thumma al bai'*, she will have paid a total of €30,000. To be competitive with Western loans, the final payment must be less than or equal to €31,553.37 − €30,000 = €1,553.37.

This type of financing is an important alternative to standard bank loans and illustrates the co-operative nature of the Islamic approach to doing business. In each transaction, the supplier and demander of funds directly bear the underlying investment's cash flow risk.

Leasing
Leasing or *ijarah* is a form of financing that is available to companies. With a lease, the lessee pays rent for an asset for a period of time from the lessor. In this type of contract, the payments are for the use of the asset. Lease financing is covered in more detail later in the text.

Profit-Sharing
In a *mudharabah* contract, a company uses a bank or lender's funds to invest in a project. The two parties share the profits of the business according to predetermined ratios. In this transaction, the lender bears the financial risk of the investment but gains from the entrepreneur's specialized skills. Both parties benefit financially from the joint investment through the contribution of different skills or assets.

Safekeeping
Like Western banks, Islamic banks require deposits to fund their activities. A company or individual may lodge funds at an Islamic bank and draw those funds from the bank. In some situations, the bank may give the depositor a *hibah*, a small sum of money to compensate the depositor for leaving the funds with the Islamic bank. This is known as *wadiah*. Although this could be seen as an interest payment in any other name, because the *hibah* payment is not contractual, it is not viewed as such under Shariah law.

Sale and Buyback
With a *bai' al-inah* agreement, a company buys an asset from a seller and agrees to pay for it at some point in the future. The seller immediately repurchases the asset at a discount.

> **EXAMPLE 18.9**
>
> **BAI' AL-INAH**
>
> Shukran plc needs £2,700,000 to undertake another new warehouse expansion. They approach an Islamic bank, which agrees to participate in a *bai' al-inah* agreement. In this transaction, the bank sells a building today to Shukran for £3,000,000 to be paid in one year. Immediately, the bank repurchases the building for £2,700,000 today. In this transaction, Shukran now has £2,700,000 but must pay £3,000,000 to the bank in one year. This is very similar to a one-year loan, but the crucial thing is that a real asset and not money drives the payments. This is acceptable under Islamic law.

Islamic Bonds

Having read so far, you may think it would be impossible for any bond to be acceptable to Islamic law. This is because any interest payment or attempt to make money from money is forbidden. With the massive increase in the oil price over the last few years, many Islamic investment funds and banks have been seeking ways to diversify their investment portfolios in ways consistent with their religious beliefs. One such instrument is a *sukuk*, otherwise known as an Islamic bond.

A *sukuk* is not a simple certificate like a bond that promises set periodic payments over the period of the bond. It is more akin to a financing company that is involved in profit sharing (*musharakah*), stated cost plus profit (*murabahah*) or sale and leasebacks (*ijarah*). Taking an *ijarah sukuk* as an example, a company wishes to raise funds just now in return for a set periodic payment in the future. To be compliant with Islamic law, the financing instrument cannot have any interest or make money from money. An *ijarah sukuk* is structured as follows:

1. The company that wishes to raise funds creates a subsidiary specifically for the *ijarah sukuk*. This is generally known as a special purpose vehicle (SPV) or special investment vehicle (SIV).
2. The company sells its own assets (for example, a manufacturing plant, technical machinery, or property) to the SPV with a value equal to the amount of financing required.
3. The SPV issues securities or *sukuk* to the market. The *sukuk* pays periodic payments (fixed or floating depending on the underlying asset) from the cash flows generated by the assets. The money raised by the *sukuk* issue is used to pay for the assets in step 2.
4. The company immediately leases the assets back from the SPV making periodic payments (fixed or floating depending on the asset) to the SPV. The payments are passed on to the *sukuk* holders.
5. At the end of the financing period, the company repurchases the assets from the SPV and the SPV passes these on to the holders of the *sukuk*.

The cash flows from the *sukuk* to different parties are presented in the table below. Notice how the cash flows from the *sukuk* are the same as that of a bond, except that money is being generated from the underlying asset and not money in itself.

Step	Company	SPV	Sukuk holders
1. Create SPV			
2. Company sells assets	+ Asset value	− Asset value	
3. SPV issues securities to market		+ Asset value	− Asset value
4. Company leases asset from SPV	− Periodic payment − Periodic payment	+ Periodic payment	+ Periodic payment
5. Company repurchases assets from SPV. SPV pays back *sukuk* holders	− Asset value	+ Asset value − Asset value	+ Asset value

> **REAL WORLD INSIGHTS**
>
> In 2021, the First Abu Dhabi Bank (FAB) issued a five-year $500 million *sukuk* with payments set to provide a yield of 1.411 per cent. This was the first *sukuk* issue in 2021 denominated in dollars, and it attracted orders of $1.5 billion, amounting to three times the available bonds on offer. The buyers consisted of high quality international and domestic institutions, with 53 per cent of orders going to international investors. Islamic investors made up 76 per cent of the buyers and came from across the world.

18.9 BREXIT AND INTERNATIONAL CORPORATE FINANCE

On 31 December 2020, the UK left the European Union. The ramifications of the trade deal between the UK and EU will take many years to become apparent and there will undoubtedly be refinements in laws contained in the 1,246-page trade deal. A full analysis of the intricacies of the deal is far beyond the scope of this book and so we will only discuss the central implications of the deal on UK and EU businesses.

TRADE IN GOODS

Within the European Union, there is free movement and trade of goods. This means there are no quotas, tariffs or bureaucracy when goods move from one part of the bloc to another. Under the UK–EU trade deal, there will continue to be no tariffs and quotas for goods, but there will be necessary customs paperwork to be completed. This friction adds costs to every import and export transaction, and these need to be borne, directly and indirectly, by companies and consumers.

TRADE IN SERVICES

At the beginning of 2021, services were not included in the trade deal and so there is no free movement in economic activities involving consultancies, financial services, or any form of service provision. It is important to note there is nothing to stop the UK and EU refining the trade deal over the coming months and it is to be expected this will happen in some sectors, most notably the digital and finance industries.

FREE MOVEMENT

Another big change in the trade deal is the removal of free movement of workers between the UK and EU. Europeans and British citizens now require a visa to work in each other's countries.

IMPACT ON CORPORATE FINANCE

While there are undoubtedly more frictions than before, the trading environment for EU–UK trade is still very good and the two trading blocs will continue to be very important partners. Just like any other new regulation, businesses will adapt to changes in their environment and optimize operations to maximize revenues across the whole region.

SUMMARY AND CONCLUSIONS

The international firm has a more complicated life than the purely domestic firm. Management must understand the connection between interest rates, foreign currency exchange rates and inflation, and it must become aware of many different financial market regulations and tax systems. This chapter is intended to be a concise introduction to some of the financial issues that come up in international investing. Our coverage has been necessarily brief. The main topics we discussed are the following:

1. **Some basic vocabulary:** We briefly defined some exotic terms such as LIBOR and Eurocurrency.
2. **The basic mechanics of exchange rate quotations:** We discussed the spot and forward markets, and how exchange rates are interpreted.
3. **The fundamental relationships between international financial variables:**
   (a) Absolute and relative purchasing power parity, PPP.
   (b) Interest rate parity, IRP.
   (c) Unbiased forward rates, UFR.

   Absolute purchasing power parity states that £1 or €1 should have the same purchasing power in each country. This means that an orange costs the same whether you buy it in London or in Madrid.

   Relative purchasing power parity means that the expected percentage change in exchange rates between the currencies of two countries is equal to the difference in their inflation rates.

   Interest rate parity implies that the percentage difference between the forward exchange rate and the spot exchange rate is equal to the interest rate differential. We showed how covered interest arbitrage forces this relationship to hold.

   The unbiased forward rates condition indicates that the current forward rate is a good predictor of the future spot exchange rate.

4. **International capital budgeting:** We showed that the basic foreign exchange relationships imply two other conditions:
   (a) Uncovered interest parity.
   (b) The international Fisher effect.

   By invoking these two conditions, we learned how to estimate NPVs in foreign currencies and how to convert foreign currencies into home currencies to estimate NPV in the usual way.

5. **Exchange rate and political risk:** We described the various types of exchange rate risk, and discussed some commonly used approaches to managing the effect of fluctuating exchange rates on the cash flows and value of the international firm. We also discussed political risk, and some ways of managing exposure to it.

CHAPTER REVIEW AND SELF-TEST PROBLEMS

18.1 Relative Purchasing Power Parity The inflation rate in the United Kingdom is projected at 3 per cent per year for the next several years. The Swiss inflation rate is projected to be 5 per cent during that time. The exchange rate is currently SFr 1.66. Based on relative PPP, what is the expected exchange rate in 2 years?

18.2 Covered Interest Arbitrage The spot and 360-day forward rates on the Turkish lira to the euro are L2.1/€ and L1.9/€, respectively. Assume that the risk-free interest rate in Europe is 6 per cent, and the risk-free rate in Turkey is 4 per cent. Is there an arbitrage opportunity here? How would you exploit it?

SOLUTIONS

18.1 Based on relative PPP, the expected exchange rate in 2 years, $E(S_2)$, is:

$$E(S_2) = S_0 \times [1 + (h_{FC} - h_{HC})]^2$$

where h_{FC} is the Swiss inflation rate. The current exchange rate is SFr1.66, so the expected exchange rate is

$$E(S_2) = \text{SFr}1.66 \times [1 + (0.05 - 0.03)]^2$$
$$= \text{SFr}1.66 \times 1.02^2$$
$$= \text{SFr}1.73$$

18.2 Based on interest rate parity, the forward rate should be (approximately):

$$F_1 = S_0 \times [1 + (R_{\text{FC}} - R_{\text{HC}})]$$
$$= 2.1 \times [1 + (0.04 - 0.06)]$$
$$= 2.06$$

Because the forward rate is actually L1.9/€, there is an arbitrage opportunity. To exploit the arbitrage opportunity, you first note that euros are selling for L1.9 each in the forward market. Based on IRP, this is too cheap, because they should be selling for L2.06. So you want to arrange to buy euros with Turkish lira in the forward market. To do this, you can:

(a) *Today:* Borrow, say, €1 million for 360 days. Convert it to L2.1 million in the spot market, and buy a forward contract at L1.9 to convert it back to euros in 360 days. Invest the L2.1 million at 4 per cent.

(b) *In 1 year:* Your investment has grown to L2.1 million × 1.04 = L2.184 million. Convert this to euros at the rate of L1.9/€. You will have L2.184 million/1.9 = €1,149,474. Pay off your loan with 6 per cent interest at a cost of €1 million × 1.06 = €1,060,000 and pocket the difference of €89,474.

QUESTIONS AND PROBLEMS

18.1 **Using Exchange Rates** Take a look back at Table 18.2 to answer the following questions:

  (a) If you have 100 Omani rials, how many British pounds can you get? How many euros can you get?

  (b) How much is £1 worth in terms of euro?

  (c) If you have £10 million, how many euros do you have?

  (d) Which is worth more, a Singaporean dollar or Malaysian ringgit?

  (e) Which is worth more, a UAE dirham or a Saudi Arabian ryal?

  (f) How many Bahraini dinars can you get for a Chinese yuan? What do you call this rate?

  (g) Per unit, what is the most valuable currency of those listed? The least valuable?

18.2 **Using the Cross-Rate** Use the information in Table 18.2 to answer the following questions:

  (a) Which would you rather have, €100 or £100? Why?

  (b) Which would you rather have, 100 Swedish krona or 100 Swiss francs? Why?

  (c) What is the cross-rate for South African rand in terms of the Norwegian krone? For Norwegian krone in terms of South African rand?

18.3 **Forward Exchange Rates** If the $/€ spot rate is $1.14/€ and the three-month forward rate is $1.15/€? Is the dollar selling at a premium or a discount? Explain.

18.4 **Using Spot and Forward Exchange Rates** Suppose the spot exchange rate for the South African rand is R15/£ and the six-month forward rate is R16/£.

(a) Which is worth more, the British pound or the South African rand?

(b) Assuming absolute PPP holds, what is the cost in the United Kingdom of a Castle beer if the price in South Africa is R20? Why might the beer actually sell at a different price in the United Kingdom?

(c) Is the British pound selling at a premium or a discount relative to the South African rand?

(d) Which currency is expected to appreciate?

(e) Which country do you think has higher interest rates – the United Kingdom or South Africa? Explain.

18.5 **Cross-Rates and Arbitrage** Use Table 18.2 to answer the following questions:

(a) What is the cross-rate in terms of Singaporean dollar per Indian rupee?

(b) Suppose the cross-rate is 50 Indian rupee = 1 Singapore dollar. Is there an arbitrage opportunity here? If there is, explain how to take advantage of the mispricing.

18.6 **Interest Rate Parity** The £/€ exchange rate is £0.7635/€, and the one-year forward rate is £0.76/€. Suppose interest rate parity holds, and the current one-year risk-free rate in the Eurozone is 0.8 per cent. What must the one-year risk-free rate be in the UK?

18.7 **Interest Rates and Arbitrage** Your Dutch company wishes to invest €50 million in either the Netherlands or UK for the next 4 months. The annual interest rate in both countries is 0.1 per cent per month. The spot exchange rate is €1.10/£, and the 4-month forward rate is €1.15/€. Ignoring transaction costs, in which country would the treasurer want to invest the company's funds? Why?

18.8 **Inflation and Exchange Rates** Suppose the current exchange rate for the Polish zloty is Z5/£. The expected exchange rate in 3 years is Z5.2/£. What is the difference in the annual inflation rates for the United Kingdom and Poland over this period? Assume that the anticipated rate is constant for both countries. What relationship are you relying on when answering?

18.9 **Exchange Rate Risk** Suppose your company, which is based in Nantes, imports computer motherboards from Singapore. The exchange rate is S$1.9361/€1. You have just placed an order for 30,000 motherboards at a cost to you of 168.5 Singapore dollars each. You will pay for the shipment when it arrives in 90 days. You can sell the motherboards for €100 each. Calculate your profit if the exchange rate goes up or down by 10 per cent over the next 90 days. What is the break-even exchange rate? What percentage rise or fall does this represent in terms of the Singapore dollar versus the euro?

18.10 **Exchange Rates and Arbitrage** The spot rate of foreign exchange between the United States and the United Kingdom is $1.3587/£. If the United States' interest rate is 2 per cent and it is 1 per cent in the United Kingdom. What would you expect the one-year forward rate to be if no immediate arbitrage opportunities existed?

18.11 **The International Fisher Effect** You observe that the United Kingdom's inflation rate is 3.5 per cent per year and that T-bills currently yield 3.9 per cent annually. What do you estimate the inflation rate to be in

(a) Australia, if short-term Australian government securities yield 5 per cent per year?

(b) Canada, if short-term Canadian government securities yield 7 per cent per year?

(c) Taiwan, if short-term Taiwanese government securities yield 10 per cent per year?

18.12 **Spot versus Forward Rates** Suppose the spot and three-month forward rates for the Indian rupee are R68.81/€ and R61.8/€, respectively.

(a) Is the rupee expected to get stronger or weaker?

(b) What would be your estimate regarding the effective annual inflation rate differential between the Eurozone and India?

18.13 Expected Spot Rates Suppose the spot exchange rate for the Tanzanian shilling is TSh2500/£. The United Kingdom's inflation rate is 3.5 per cent, and it is 8.6 per cent in Tanzania. What do you predict the exchange rate will be in 1 year? In 2 years? In 5 years? What relationship are you using?

18.14 Capital Budgeting The Dutch firm ABS Equipment has an investment opportunity in the United Kingdom. The project costs £12 million, and is expected to produce cash flows of £2.7 million in year 1, £3.5 million in year 2, and £3.3 million in year 3. The current spot exchange rate is €1.12/£, and the current risk-free rate in the Eurozone is 2.12 per cent, compared with that in the United Kingdom of 2.13 per cent. The appropriate discount rate for the project is estimated to be 13 per cent, the Eurozone cost of capital for the company. In addition, the subsidiary can be sold at the end of 3 years for an estimated £7.4 million. What is the NPV of the project?

18.15 Capital Budgeting As a German company, you must evaluate a proposed expansion of an existing subsidiary in Switzerland. The cost of the expansion would be SFr27.0 million. The cash flows from the project would be SFr7.5 million per year for the next 5 years. The euro required return is 13 per cent per year, and the current exchange rate is SFr1.48/€. The going rate on EURIBOR is 8 per cent per year. It is 7 per cent per year on Swiss francs.

(a) What do you project will happen to exchange rates over the next 4 years?

(b) Based on your answer in (a), convert the projected franc flows into euro cash flows and calculate the NPV.

(c) What is the required return on franc cash flows? Based on your answer, calculate the NPV in francs and then convert to euros.

18.16 Translation Exposure Akbulut International has operations in Istanbul. This company's balance sheet shows assets of 23 million Turkish lira, debt to the amount of 9 million lira, and equity of 14 million lira.

(a) If the current exchange rate is 9 lira per euro, what does the balance sheet look like in euros?

(b) Assume that 1 year from now, the balance sheet in lira is the same as at the beginning of the year. If the exchange rate is 10 lira per euro, what does the balance sheet look like in euros now?

18.17 Translation Exposure In the previous problem, assume the equity increases by 1.25 million lira due to retained earnings. If the exchange rate at the end of the year is 10 lira per euro, what does the balance sheet look like?

18.18 Using the Exact International Fisher Effect From our discussion of the Fisher effect in Chapter 6, we know that the actual relationship between a nominal rate R, a real rate r and an inflation rate h can be written as:

$$1 + r = (1 + R)/(1 + h)$$

This is the *domestic* Fisher effect.

(a) What is the non-approximate form of the international Fisher effect?

(b) Based on your answer in (a), what is the exact form for UIP? (*Hint:* Recall the exact form of IRP, and use UFR.)

(c) What is the exact form for relative PPP? (*Hint:* Combine your previous two answers.)

(d) Recalculate the NPV for the Kihlstrom drill bit project (discussed in Section 18.5) using the exact forms for UIP and the international Fisher effect. Verify that you get precisely the same answer either way.

18.19 Capital Budgeting Stolt-Neilsen Ltd is a Norwegian maritime transportation company with operations all over the world. Piracy is becoming an increasingly worrying problem for firms like Stolt-Neilsen, and they continually seek ways to counter this threat. The company is considering a microthreat weapons system that will provide countermeasures capability against small hostile naval craft. The system costs £35 million to install in its whole fleet, but it is expected to save £12 million per annum for the next 4 years in lower insurance premiums, retained custom and new orders. The current spot exchange rate is Nkr9/£, and the current risk-free rate in Norway is 4 per cent, compared with that in the United Kingdom of 2 per cent. The appropriate discount rate for the investment is estimated to be 20 per cent, the Norwegian cost of capital for the company. At the end of 4 years, it is expected that enough pirate groups will have access to technology that makes the system obsolete. As a result, there is no resale value. What is the NPV of the project?

MINI CASE

WEST COAST ELECTRONICS GOES CARBON NEUTRAL

West Coast Electronics is a high-end music system manufacturer and has been in discussions with a climate change entrepreneurial firm, Kestävyys, to open a carbon-neutral manufacturing site in Finland. Kestävyys believes that by embracing sustainability in Finland, West Coast Electronics will increase Scandinavian sales by approximately €5 million per month. All sales will be made in euros, and Kestävyys will act as a distributor of all products in Scandinavia. The commission fee for all Scandinavian sales will be 5 per cent of the sales price, which will be paid in euros. It will take a few weeks to set up operations and so it is expected that sales will start in one month. Kestävyys will pay West Coast Electronics for every sale it makes 90 days after it is filled. This payment schedule will continue for the length of the contract between the West Coast Electronics and Kestävyys.

West Coast Electronics is confident it can handle the extra volume with its existing facilities but is unsure about any potential financial risks of constructing a new carbon-neutral operation in Finland. In discussion with Kestävyys, West Coast Electronics found that at the current exchange rate of €1.12/£, the company would spend 70 per cent of the sales income on production costs. This number does not reflect the sales commission to be paid to Kestävyys.

You have been asked by West Coast Electronics to prepare an analysis of the proposed international sales. Specifically:

QUESTIONS

1. What are the pros and cons of the carbon-neutral Finnish sales plan? What additional risks will the company face?
2. What will happen to the company's profits if the British pound strengthens? What if the British pound weakens?
3. Ignoring taxes, what are West Coast Electronics' projected gains or losses from this proposed arrangement at the current exchange rate of €1.12/£? What will happen to profits if the exchange rate changes to €1.20/£? At what exchange rate will the company break even?
4. How can the company hedge its exchange rate risk? What are the implications for this approach?
5. Taking all factors into account, should the company pursue the carbon-neutral Finnish project further? Why or why not?

ADDITIONAL READING

Very few papers exist that examine international capital budgeting in any detail. However, there are a few:

1. Bekaert, G., Harvey, C.R., Lundblad, C.T., & Siegel, S. (2013). The European Union, the euro, and equity market integration. *Journal of Financial Economics, 109*(3), 583–603.
2. Colacito, R., Riddiough, S. J., & Sarno, L. (2020). Business cycles and currency returns. *Journal of Financial Economics, 137*(3), 659–678.

3. Greene, W.H., Hornstein, A.S., & White, L.J. (2009). Multinationals do it better: Evidence on the efficiency of corporations' capital budgeting. *Journal of Empirical Finance, 16*(5), 703–720.

4. Holmén, M., & Pramborg, B. (2009). Capital budgeting and political risk: Empirical evidence. *Journal of International Financial Management and Accounting, 20*(2), 105–134.

Endnotes

1. Notice that our result here is in terms of the approximate real rate, $R - h$ (see Chapter 6), because we used approximations for PPP and IRP. For the exact result see Problem 18.18 at the end of the chapter.
2. For example, the interest rates might be the short-term eurodollar and euro deposit rates offered by large money centre banks.
3. Actually, there will be a slight difference because we are using the approximate relationships. If we calculate the required return as $1.10 \times (1 + 0.02) - 1 = 12.2\%$, then we get exactly the same NPV. See Problem 18.18 for more detail.

CHAPTER 19
BEHAVIOURAL FINANCE

> **LEARNING OBJECTIVES**
>
> After studying this chapter, you should understand:
>
> **LO1** How behaviours such as overconfidence, over-optimism and confirmation bias can affect decision-making.
> **LO2** How framing effects can result in inconsistent and/or incorrect decisions.
> **LO3** How the use of heuristics can lead to suboptimal financial decisions.
> **LO4** The shortcomings of and limitations to market efficiency from the behavioural finance view.

THE CRYPTOCURRENCY, bitcoin, regularly appears in financial news reports with sensationalist reports of it being (a) a replacement for gold as a hedge asset and (b) a market fad with very little real value. In the 12-month period, January 2020 to January 2021, the bitcoin price increased by 500 per cent from $8,000 to $40,000. However, the increase wasn't consistent, and in a single day (10-11 January 2021), bitcoin's value fell by 25 per cent from $41,134 to $30,970.

Opinions on the real value of bitcoin and its future importance are starkly contrasting. When the bitcoin price is rising, the view on financial markets tends to be that it is heralding a future where economic value will be maintained on decentralized technological platforms based on financial blockchain technology. When the price falls, it is seen as a highly speculative investment that must be regulated by central banks. Bitcoin's volatility does appear to be too high for it to be anything but a speculative asset, and the increase in price over 2020 has been described by many as a major bubble. The argument is that bitcoin prices were inflated to economically ridiculous levels by market participants betting against the value of the dollar. Eventually, the bubble will burst, and bitcoin's value will fall to more realistic levels.

In this chapter, we introduce the subject of behavioural finance, which deals with questions such as how bubbles can come to exist. Some of the issues we discuss are quite controversial and unsettled. We shall describe competing ideas, present some evidence on both sides, and examine behavioural finance implications for corporate managers.

Be honest: do you think of yourself as a better than average driver? If you do, you are not alone. About 80 per cent of the people who are asked this question will say yes. Evidently, we tend to overestimate our abilities behind the wheel. Is the same true when it comes to making financial management decisions?

It will probably not surprise you when we say that human beings sometimes make errors in judgement. How these errors, and other aspects of human behaviour, affect financial managers falls under the general heading of *behavioural finance*. Our goal is to acquaint you with some common types of mistake and their financial implications in this chapter. As you will see, researchers have identified a wide variety of potentially damaging behaviours. By learning to recognize situations in which mistakes are common, you will become a better decision-maker, both in the context of financial management and elsewhere.

19.1 INTRODUCTION TO BEHAVIOURAL FINANCE

Sooner or later, you are going to make a financial decision that winds up costing you (and possibly your employer and/or shareholders) a lot of money. Why is this going to happen? You already know the answer. Sometimes you make sound decisions, but you get unlucky in the sense that something happens that you could not have reasonably anticipated. At other times (however painful it is to admit) you make a bad decision, one that could (and should) have been avoided. The beginning of business wisdom is to recognize the circumstances that lead to poor decisions and thereby cut down on the damage done by financial blunders.

As we have previously noted, the research area known as **behavioural finance** attempts to understand and explain how reasoning errors influence financial decisions. Much of the research done in the behavioural finance area stems from work in cognitive psychology, which is how people, including financial managers, think, reason and make decisions. Errors in reasoning are often called *cognitive errors*. In the next several subsections we shall review three main categories of such errors: (1) biases; (2) framing effects; and (3) heuristics.

> **behavioural finance**
> the area of finance dealing with the implications of reasoning errors on financial decisions.

19.2 BIASES

If your decisions exhibit systematic biases, then you will make systematic errors in judgement. The type of error depends on the type of bias. In this section, we discuss five particularly relevant biases: (1) overconfidence; (2) over-optimism; (3) confirmation bias; (4) self-attribution bias; and (5) the planning fallacy.

OVERCONFIDENCE

Serious errors in judgement occur in the business world as a result of **overconfidence**. We are all overconfident about our abilities in at least some areas (recall our question about driving ability at the beginning of the chapter). Here is another example that we see a lot: ask yourself what grade you will receive in this course (despite the arbitrary and capricious nature of the professor). In our experience, almost everyone will either say 'A' or, at worst, 'B'. Sadly, when this happens, we are always confident (but not overconfident) that at least some of our students will be disappointed.

> **overconfidence**
> the belief that your abilities are better than they really are.

In general, you are overconfident when you overestimate your ability to make the correct choice or decision. For example, most business decisions require judgements about the unknown future. The belief that you can forecast the future with precision is a common form of overconfidence.

Another good example of overconfidence comes from studies of equity investors. Researchers have examined large numbers of actual brokerage accounts to see how investors fare when they choose equities. Overconfidence by investors would cause them to overestimate their ability to pick the best equities, leading to excessive trading. The evidence supports this view. First, investors hurt themselves by trading. The accounts with the most trading significantly underperform the accounts with the least trading, primarily because of the costs associated with trades.

A second finding is equally interesting. Accounts registered to men underperform those registered to women. The reason is that men trade more on average. This extra trading is consistent with evidence from psychology that men have greater degrees of overconfidence than women.

OVER-OPTIMISM

over-optimism
taking an overly optimistic view of potential outcomes.

Over-optimism leads to overestimating the likelihood of a good outcome and underestimating the likelihood of a bad outcome. Over-optimism and overconfidence are related, but they are not the same thing. An overconfident individual could (overconfidently) forecast a bad outcome, for example.

Optimism is usually thought of as a good thing. Optimistic people have 'upbeat personalities' and 'sunny dispositions'. However, excessive optimism leads to bad decisions. In a capital budgeting context, overly optimistic analysts will consistently overestimate cash flows and underestimate the probability of failure. Doing so leads to upward-biased estimates of project NPVs, a common occurrence in the business world.

CONFIRMATION BIAS

confirmation bias
searching for (and giving more weight to) information and opinion that confirms what you believe, rather than information and opinion to the contrary.

When you are evaluating a decision, you collect information and opinions. A common bias in this regard is focusing more on information that agrees with your opinion and downplays or ignores information that doesn't support your position. This phenomenon is known as **confirmation bias**, and people who suffer from it tend to spend too much time trying to prove themselves right rather than searching for information that might prove them wrong.

Here is a classic example from psychology. Below are four cards. Notice that the cards are labelled *a*, *b*, 2 and 3. You are asked to evaluate the following statement: 'Any card with a vowel on one side has an even number on the other.' You are asked which of the four cards has to be turned over to decide whether the statement is true or false. It costs €100 to turn over a card, so you want to be as economical as possible. What do you do?

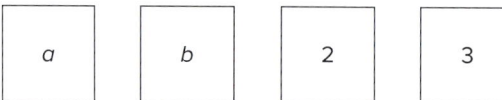

You would probably begin by turning over the card with an *a* on it, which is correct. If we find an odd number, then we are done, because the statement is not correct.

Suppose we find an even number. What next? Most people will turn over the card with a 2. Is that the right choice? If we find a vowel, we confirm the statement, but we don't learn anything if we find a consonant. In other words, this card can't prove that the statement is wrong; it can only confirm it, so selecting this card is an example of confirmation bias.

Continuing, there is no point in turning over the card labelled '*b*' because the statement doesn't say anything about consonants, which leaves us with the last card. Do we have to turn it over? The answer is 'yes' because it might have a vowel on the other side, which would disprove the statement, but most people will choose the 2 card over the 3 card.

Confirmation bias can lead managers to ignore negative information about potential investments and focus only on that information which proves they are correct in their opinions. This can lead to poor decisions that reduce firm value.

SELF-ATTRIBUTION BIAS

Self-attribution bias relates to the feeling that when things go to plan, it is because of your decisions and ability to perform. However, when bad outcomes occur, you blame others or external events for the failure. In other words, you get all the credit when the company performs well but never take the blame when business doesn't go as expected. Self-attribution bias is a close relation to confirmation bias in that you selectively perceive past events or information as supporting your own ability. In contrast, confirmation bias selectivity identifies information that supports your decision and ignores everything else.

In his book, *Fooled by Randomness*, the author Nassim Taleb recounts successful financial markets traders who irrationally believed their performance to be a result of superior trading ability, only to lose it all when market movements went against their positions. Although their strategy was effectively lucky until they lost money, it did not stop traders from trumpeting their models and decisions to other investors and traders. Taleb argues that, when you see a successful trader, you observe only one potential outcome in a distribution of random hypothetical outcomes relating to a particular strategy. What is more important is the unobserved potential outcomes that could have happened but didn't. To clarify, out of 10,000 traders who follow a particular strategy, 50 traders are successful and 9,950 are failures. Who do you hear bragging about the strategy? Clearly, successful traders! What you don't see is that their strategy is high risk with a strong chance of failure. Just because one person is successful in following a strategy, doesn't mean it is a good one.

Self-attribution bias can lead managers to adhere to a poor business strategy because they believe that the reason it is not working is because of events outside their control. In addition, they may put any success in a company down to their decisions, leading to a further behavioural bias: overconfidence.

THE PLANNING FALLACY

Some of the most common problems with new investments are cost and time overruns. How many times have you read that a major infrastructure project is over budget and/or taking a lot longer to complete than originally expected? The planning fallacy predicts that this is expected because managers have a natural tendency to underestimate the costs, risks and time of undertaking new projects.

A more complex interpretation of the planning fallacy is that managers only consider a single forecast point (say, NPV) when they decide to undertake new investments and ignore the overall distribution of potential outcomes that may occur. This is an analogous point to that made by Nassim Taleb about self-attribution bias.

Although the outcomes can be catastrophic, it is fairly straightforward to mitigate the risk of underestimating the effort (time, risk or money) in a new venture. Reference class forecasting uses large datasets of previous similar projects to allow a manager to statistically estimate the likelihood of budget or time overruns. In addition, senior managers can ensure that the proposers of new projects have considered in detail the assumptions underlying each cost and income variable.

CONCEPT QUESTIONS

19.2a What is meant by overconfidence and over-optimism? How are they likely to be costly?
19.2b Explain how self-attribution bias is similar but subtly different from confirmation bias.
19.2c What are the most effective ways for companies to overcome the planning fallacy?

19.3 FRAMING EFFECTS

You are susceptible to framing effects if your decisions depend on how a problem or question is framed. Consider the following example. A disaster has occurred, 600 people are at risk, and you are in charge. You must choose between the two following rescue operations:

Scenario 1

Option A: Exactly 200 people will be saved.
Option B: There is a 1/3 chance that all 600 people will be saved and a 2/3 chance that no people will be saved.

Which would you choose? There is no necessarily right answer, but most people will choose option A. Now suppose your choices are as follows:

Scenario 2

Option C: Exactly 400 people will die.
Option D: There is a 1/3 chance that nobody will die and a 2/3 chance that all 600 will die.

Now, which do you pick? Again, there is no right answer, but most people will choose option D. Although most people will choose options A and D in our hypothetical scenarios, you probably see that doing so

> **frame dependence**
> the tendency of individuals to make different (and potentially inconsistent) decisions, depending on how a question or problem is framed.

is inconsistent, because options A and C are identical, as are options B and D. Why do people make inconsistent choices? It's because the options are framed differently. The first scenario is positive because it emphasizes the number that will be saved. The second is negative, because it focuses on losses, and people react differently to positive and negative framing, which is a form of **frame dependence**.

LOSS AVERSION

Here is another example that illustrates a particular type of frame dependence:

Scenario 1

Suppose we give you £1,000. You have the following choices:

Option A: You can receive another £500 for sure.

Option B: You can flip a fair coin. If the coin flip comes up heads, you get another £1,000, but you get nothing if it comes up tails.

Scenario 2

Suppose we give you £2,000. You have the following choices:

Option C: You can lose £500 for sure.

Option D: You can flip a fair coin. If the coin flip comes up heads, you lose £1,000, but you lose nothing if it comes up tails.

What were your answers? Did you choose option A in the first scenario and option D in the second? If that's what you did, you are guilty of focusing just on gains and losses, and not paying attention to what really matters, namely the impact on your wealth. However, you are not alone. About 85 per cent of the people presented with the first scenario choose option A and about 70 per cent of the people presented with the second scenario choose option D.

If you look closely at the two scenarios, you will see that they are actually identical. You end up with £1,500 for sure if you pick option A or C, or else you end up with a 50–50 chance of either £1,000 or £2,000 if you pick option B or D. So you should pick the same option in both scenarios. Which option you prefer is up to you, but the point is that you should never pick option A in our first scenario and option D in our second one.

This example illustrates an important aspect of financial decision-making. Focusing on gains and losses instead of overall wealth is an example of narrow framing, leading to a phenomenon known as *loss aversion*. In fact, most people avoid option C in scenario 2 in our example because it is expressed as a sure loss of £500. In general, researchers have found that individuals are reluctant to realize losses and will, for example, gamble at unfavourable odds to avoid doing so.

Loss aversion is also known as the *break-even effect*. It frequently shows up as individuals and companies hang on to bad investments and projects (and perhaps even invest more), hoping that something will happen that will allow them to break even and thereby escape without a loss. For example, we discussed the irrelevance of sunk costs in the context of capital budgeting, and the idea of a sunk cost seems clear. Nonetheless, we constantly see companies (and individuals) throw good money after bad rather than recognize a loss in the face of sunk costs.

How destructive is the break-even effect? Perhaps the most famous case occurred in 1995 when 28-year-old Nicholas Leeson caused his employer's collapse, the 233-year-old Barings Bank. At the end of 1992, Mr Leeson had lost about £2 million, which he hid in a secret account. By the end of 1993, his losses were about £23 million, and they mushroomed to £208 million at the end of 1994.

Instead of admitting to these losses, Mr Leeson gambled more of the bank's money in an attempt to 'double up and catch up'. On 23 February 1995 Mr Leeson's losses were about £827 million, and his trading irregularities were uncovered. Although he attempted to flee from prosecution, he was caught, arrested, tried, convicted and imprisoned. Also, his wife divorced him.

Do you suffer from the break-even effect? Perhaps so. Consider the following scenario. You have just lost €78 somehow. You can just live with the loss, or you can make a bet. If you make a bet, there is an 80 per cent chance that your loss will grow to €100 (from €78) and a 20 per cent chance that your loss will be nothing. Do you take the loss or take the bet? We bet you choose the bet. If you do, you suffer from the break-even effect, because the bet is a bad one. Instead of a sure loss of €78, your expected loss from the bet is $0.80 \times €100 + 0.20 \times €0 = €80$.

In corporate finance, loss aversion can be quite damaging. We have already mentioned the pursuit of sunk costs. We also might see managers bypassing positive-NPV projects because they have the possibility of large losses (perhaps with low probability). Another phenomenon that we see is *debt avoidance*. As we discuss in our coverage of capital structure, debt financing generates valuable tax shields for profitable companies. Even so, there are hundreds of profitable companies listed on major stock exchanges that completely (or almost completely) avoid debt financing. Because debt financing increases the likelihood of losses, and even bankruptcy, this potentially costly behaviour could be due to loss aversion.

HOUSE MONEY

Casinos know all about a concept called *playing with house money*. They have found that gamblers are far more likely to take big risks with money they have won from the casino (i.e., house money). Also, casinos have found that gamblers are not as upset about losing house money as they are about losing the money they brought with them to gamble.

It may seem natural for you to feel that some money is precious, because you earned it through hard work, sweat and sacrifice, whereas other money is less precious because it came to you as a windfall. But these feelings are plainly irrational, because any cash you have buys the same amount of goods and services, no matter how you obtained that cash.

Let's consider another common situation to illustrate several of the ideas we have explored thus far. Consider the following two investments:

Investment 1: You bought 100 shares in Tayz plc for £35 per share. The shares immediately fell to £20 each.

Investment 2: At the same time, you bought 100 shares in Streets plc for £5 per share. The shares immediately jumped to £20 each.

How would you feel about your investments? You would probably feel pretty good about your Streets investment and be unhappy with your Tayz investment. Here are some other things that might occur:

1. You might tell yourself that your Streets investment was a great idea on your part; you're a stock-picking genius. The drop in value on the Tayz shares wasn't your fault – it was just bad luck. This is a form of confirmation bias. It also illustrates self-attribution bias, which is taking credit for good outcomes that occur for reasons beyond your control, while attributing bad outcomes to bad luck or misfortune.
2. You might be unhappy that your big winner was essentially nullified by your loser, but notice in our example that your overall wealth did not change. Suppose instead that shares in both companies didn't change in price at all so that your overall wealth was unchanged. Would you feel the same way?
3. You might be inclined to sell your Streets shares to 'realize' the gain, but hold on to your Tayz shares in hopes of avoiding the loss (which is, of course, loss aversion). The tendency to sell winners and hold losers is known as the *disposition effect*. Plainly, the rational thing to do is to decide whether the equities are attractive investments at their new prices, and react accordingly.

Suppose you decide to keep both equities a little longer. Once you do, both decline to £15. You might now feel very differently about the decline, depending on which equity you looked at. With Tayz, the decline makes a bad situation even worse. Now you are down £20 per share on your investment. On the other hand, with Streets, you only 'give back' some of your 'paper profit'. You are still way ahead. This kind of thinking is playing with house money; whether you lose from your original investment or from your investment gains is irrelevant.

Our Tayz and Streets example illustrates what can happen when you become emotionally invested in decisions such as equity purchases. When you add a new equity to your portfolio, it is human nature to associate the equity with its purchase price. As the share price changes through time, you will have unrealized gains or losses when you compare the current price with the purchase price. You will mentally account for these gains and losses, and how you feel about the investment depends on whether you are ahead or behind. This behaviour is known as *mental accounting*.

When you engage in mental accounting, you unknowingly have a personal relationship with each of your investments. As a result, it becomes harder to sell one of them. It is as if you have to 'break up' with this investment, or 'fire' it from your portfolio. As with personal relationships, these investment relationships can be complicated and, believe it or not, make selling shares or dropping projects difficult at times. What can you do about mental accounting? Legendary investor Warren Buffet offers the following advice: 'The investment doesn't know you own it. You have feelings about it, but it has no feelings about you. The investment doesn't know what you paid. People shouldn't get emotionally involved with their investments.'

Loss aversion, mental accounting and the house money effect are important examples of how narrow framing leads to poor decisions. Other related types of judgement error have been documented. Here are a few examples:

1. **Myopic loss aversion:** This behaviour tends to focus on avoiding short-term losses, even at the expense of long-term gains. For example, you might fail to invest in equities for long-term retirement purposes because you have a fear of loss in the near term. Another example is that managers may avoid investing in long-term projects with little positive cash flow for several years because they fear the impact the investment has on the firm's short-term earnings. Projects with shorter payback periods may be preferred in this case.

2. **Regret aversion:** This aversion is the tendency to avoid making a decision because you fear that, in hindsight, the decision would have been less than optimal. Regret aversion relates to myopic loss aversion.

3. **Endowment effect:** This effect is the tendency to consider something that you own to be worth more than it would be if you did not own it. Because of the endowment effect, people sometimes demand more money to give up something than they would be willing to pay to acquire it. The endowment effect can sometimes explain why acquiring firms find it so difficult to persuade shareholders of a target firm that the value of the target is less than the shareholders believe.

4. **Money illusion:** If you suffer from a money illusion, you are confused between real buying power and nominal buying power (i.e., you do not account for the effects of inflation).

> **CONCEPT QUESTIONS**
>
> **19.3a** What is frame dependence? How is it likely to be costly?
> **19.3b** What is loss aversion? How is it likely to be costly?
> **19.3c** What is the house money effect? Why is it irrational?

19.4 HEURISTICS

heuristics
shortcuts or rules of thumb used to make decisions.

Financial managers (and managers in general) often rely on rules of thumb, or **heuristics**, in making decisions. For example, a manager might decide that any project with a payback period of less than 2 years is acceptable, and therefore not bother with additional analysis. As a practical matter, this mental shortcut might be fine for most circumstances, but we know that it will lead to the acceptance of a negative-NPV project sooner or later.

THE AFFECT HEURISTIC

affect heuristic
the reliance on instinct instead of analysis in making decisions.

We frequently hear business and political leaders talk about following their gut instinct. In essence, such people are making decisions based on whether the chosen outcome or path feels 'right' emotionally. Psychologists use the term *affect* (as in *affection*) to refer to emotional feelings, and the reliance on gut instinct is called the **affect heuristic**.

Reliance on instinct is closely related to reliance on intuition and/or experience. Both intuition and experience are important, and, used properly, help decision-makers identify potential risks and rewards. However, instinct, intuition and experience should be viewed as complements to formal analysis, not substitutes. Over-reliance on emotions in making decisions will almost surely lead (at least on occasion) to costly outcomes that could have been avoided with careful, structured thinking. An obvious example would be making capital budgeting decisions based on instinct rather than on market research and discounted cash flow analysis.

THE REPRESENTATIVENESS HEURISTIC

People often assume that a particular person, object or outcome is broadly representative of a larger class. For example, suppose an employer hired a graduate of your high-quality educational institution and, in fact, is quite pleased with that person. The employer might be inclined to look to your institution again for future employees because the students are so good. Of course, in doing so, the employer assumes that the recent hire is representative of all the students, which is an example of the **representativeness heuristic**. A little more generally, the representativeness heuristic relies on stereotypes, analogies or limited samples to form opinions about an entire class.

representativeness heuristic the reliance on limited samples or stereotypes to make decisions.

REPRESENTATIVENESS AND RANDOMNESS

Another implication of the representativeness heuristic has to do with perceiving patterns or causes where none exist. For example, soccer fans generally believe that success breeds success. Suppose we look at the recent performance of two football players named Wayne and Cristiano. Both of these players have a 50 per cent goal-to-shoot ratio. But Wayne has just scored two goals in a row, whereas Cristiano has just missed two in a row. Researchers have found that if they ask 100 football fans which player has the better chance of scoring the next goal, 91 of them will say Wayne. Further, 84 of these fans believe that it is important for teammates to pass the ball to Wayne after he has scored two or three goals in a row.

But, and the sports fans among you will have a hard time with this, researchers have found that this (known as the *hot hands effect* from basketball) is an illusion. That is, players really do not deviate much from their long-run scoring averages – although fans, players, commentators and coaches think they do.

Cognitive psychologists actually studied the shooting percentage of one professional basketball team for a season. Here is what they found:

Shooting percentages and the history of previous attempts	
Shooting percentage on next shot (%)	History of previous attempts
46	Has made 3 in a row
50	Has made 2 in a row
51	Has made 1 in a row
52	First shot of the game
54	Has missed 1 in a row
53	Has missed 2 in a row
56	Has missed 3 in a row

Detailed analysis of scoring data failed to show that players score or miss shots more or less frequently than what would be expected by chance. That is, statistically speaking, all the scoring percentages listed here are the same.

Footballers indeed score in streaks. But these streaks are within the bounds of long-run goal-scoring percentages. So it is an illusion that players are either 'hot' or 'cold'. If you are a believer in the hot hand (or hot foot), however, you are likely to reject these facts, because you 'know better' from watching your favourite teams over the years. If you do, you are being fooled by randomness.

The *clustering illusion* is our human belief that random events that occur in clusters are not really random. For example, it strikes most people as very unusual if heads comes up four times in a row during a series of coin flips. However, if a fair coin is flipped 20 times, there is about a 50 per cent chance of getting four heads in a row. Ask yourself, if you flip four heads in a row, do you think you have a 'hot hand' at coin flipping?

> **REAL WORLD INSIGHTS**
>
> It's not often that a company will admit it has acted irrationally but to its credit, Tesla Motors, the electronic automobile company led by its CEO and founder, Elon Musk, did just that. When asked by investors and analysts why they had not met target sales figures, the company put it down to excessive pride and over-confidence.
>
> In a press release to investors, it admitted to '. . . hubris in adding far too much new technology to the Model X in version 1.0'.
>
> With its extremely innovative technological design, the Model X requires over 8,000 distinct components for manufacture. Having so many different and technologically advanced parts meant that even with a supply shortage of only six components, the car production was halted.
>
> With hindsight, the company may have been better off avoiding the boutique suppliers of parts that give the company such trendy reputation and focused on more standard component types that can be purchased from many suppliers.
>
> When business meets art, only one can win if you want to make money in the long run.
>
> Source: Tesla Motors Inc press release, 'Tesla Delivers 14,820 Vehicles in Q1 2016; On Track for Full-Year Delivery Guidance', 4 April 2016.

THE GAMBLER'S FALLACY

People commit the *gambler's fallacy* when they assume that a departure from what occurs on average, or in the long run, will be corrected in the short run. Interestingly, some people suffer from both the hot-hand illusion (which predicts continuation in the short run) and the gambler's fallacy (which predicts reversal in the short run)! The idea is that because an event has not happened recently, it has become overdue and is more likely to occur. People sometimes refer (wrongly) to the law of averages in such cases.

Roulette is a random gambling game where gamblers can make various bets on the spin of the wheel. There are 37 numbers on a roulette table: 1 green one, 18 red ones and 18 black ones. One possible bet is whether the spin will result in a red number or a black number. Suppose a red number has appeared five times in a row. Gamblers will often become (over) confident that the next spin will be black, when the true chance remains at about 50 per cent (of course, it is exactly 18 in 37).

The misconception arises from the human intuition that the overall odds of the wheel must be reflected in a small number of spins. Gamblers often become convinced that the wheel is 'due' to hit a black number after a series of red numbers. Gamblers do know that the odds of a black number appearing are always unchanged: 18 in 37. But gamblers cannot help but feel that after a long series of red numbers, a black one must appear to restore the balance between red and black numbers over time.

Of course, there are many other related errors and biases due to heuristics. Here is a partial list:

1. **Law of small numbers:** If you believe in the law of small numbers, you believe that a small sample of outcomes always resembles the long-run distribution of outcomes. If your investment guru has been right five out of seven times recently, you might believe that his long-run average of being correct is also five out of seven. The law of small numbers is related to recency bias (see our next item) and the gambler's fallacy.
2. **Recency bias:** Humans tend to give recent events more importance than less recent events. For example, during the great bull market that occurred from 2003 to 2007, many investors thought the market would continue its big gains for a long time – forgetting that bear markets also occur (which happened from 2007 to 2008). Recency bias is related to the law of small numbers.
3. **Anchoring and adjustment:** People have an anchoring bias when they cannot account for new information in the correct way. That is, they become 'anchored' to a previous price or other value. If you have an anchoring bias, you will tend to be overly conservative in the face of fresh news.
4. **Ambiguity aversion:** This bias results when people shy away from the unknown. For example, consider the following choice. You get £1,000 for sure, or you can draw a ball out of a big bin containing 100 balls. If the ball is blue, you win £2,000. If it is red, you win nothing. When people are told that there are 50 blue balls and 50 red balls in the bin, about 40 per cent choose to draw a ball. When they are told nothing about how many balls in the bin are blue, most choose to take the £1,000 – ignoring the possibility that the odds might really be in their favour. That is, there could be more than 50 blue balls in the bin.

5. **False consensus:** This is the tendency to assume that other people think the same thing you are thinking (with no real evidence). False consensus relates to overconfidence and confirmation bias.
6. **Availability bias:** You suffer from availability bias when you put too much weight on easily available information and place too little weight on information that is hard to obtain. Your financial decisions will suffer if you consider only information that is easy to obtain.

> **CONCEPT QUESTIONS**
>
> **19.4a** What is the affect heuristic? How is it likely to be costly?
> **19.4b** What is the representativeness heuristic? How is it likely to be costly?
> **19.4c** What is the gambler's fallacy?

19.5 BEHAVIOURAL FINANCE AND MARKET EFFICIENCY

Our discussion thus far has focused on how cognitive errors by individuals can lead to poor business decisions. It seems both clear and non-controversial that such errors are both real and financially important. We now venture into a much less clear area – the implications of behavioural finance for share prices.

In Chapter 11, we introduced the notion of market efficiency. The key idea is that, in an efficient market, prices fully reflect available information. Put differently, prices are correct in the sense that an equity purchase or sale is a zero-NPV investment. In a well-organized, liquid market such as the LSE or Euronext, the argument is that competition among profit-motivated, economically rational traders ensures that prices can never drift far from their zero-NPV level.

In this chapter, we have already seen a few examples of how cognitive errors, such as overconfidence, can lead to damaging decisions in the context of share ownership. If many traders behave in ways that are economically irrational, then is there still reason to think that markets are efficient?

First off, it is important to realize that the efficient markets hypothesis does not require every investor to be rational. Instead, all that is required for a market to be efficient is at least some smart and well-financed investors. These investors are prepared to buy and sell to take advantage of any mispricing in the marketplace. This activity is what keeps markets efficient. It is sometimes said that market efficiency doesn't require that *everyone* be rational, just that *some* be.

FOUNDATIONS OF MARKET EFFICIENCY

Is it possible for a market to be efficient while investors are irrational and display behavioural biases? To answer this question, one must consider the fundamental axioms of market efficiency and whether these are affected by investor behaviour.

According to Shleifer (2000), there are three conditions for which only one is needed for market efficiency. These are: (1) investor rationality, (2) independent deviations of investors from rationality, and (3) arbitrage. A discussion of these conditions follows.

Investor Rationality

Imagine that all investors are rational. When new information is released in the marketplace, all investors will adjust their estimates of share prices in a rational way. For example, consider the highly innovative firm, Tesla Motors, that produces high-tech electric cars. In 2016, it announced the release of its first mass-market car, the Model-X. Within days, the company had received over 275,000 pre-orders suggesting increased annual revenues of $10 billion. If investors are rational, they will immediately raise the company's valuation to reflect the new information and the share price would rise immediately because rational investors would see no reason to wait before trading at the new price.

Of course, we all know times when family members, friends, and yes, even we seem to behave less than perfectly rationally. Thus, perhaps it is too much to ask that all investors behave rationally, but the market will still be efficient if the following scenario holds.

Independent Deviations from Rationality

Going back to the Tesla Motors example, many analysts in the media questioned the company's ability to actually produce 275,000 models. In the first quarter of 2016, Tesla had only produced 15,000 models – far short of demand. In addition, they had experienced significant component shortages that led to manufacturing delays. Clearly, the questions raised on the value that could be achieved with the Model-X were valid, given the information available in the market at the time. If it is difficult to identify the market share, sale price and unit cost of new products, it will be challenging to estimate NPV.

Now imagine that with so many questions going unanswered, many investors do not think clearly. Some investors might get caught up in the romance of the new Model-X, hoping for and ultimately believing in sales projections well above what is rational. They would overpay for new shares. And if they needed to sell shares (perhaps to finance current consumption), they would do so only at a high price. If these individuals dominate the market, the share price would likely rise beyond what market efficiency would predict.

However, due to emotional resistance, investors could just as easily react to new information in a pessimistic manner. After all, we have discussed the planning fallacy in a previous section of this chapter and the tendency for managers to underestimate production costs and the time to take new products to market. If investors believe Tesla Motors won't be capable of manufacturing 275,000 Model-X motors, the share price would likely rise less than market efficiency would predict.

Now suppose that about as many individuals were irrationally optimistic as were irrationally pessimistic. Prices would likely rise in a manner consistent with market efficiency, even though most investors would be classified as less than fully rational. Thus market efficiency does not require rational individuals – only countervailing irrationalities.

However, this assumption of offsetting irrationalities at all times may be unrealistic. Perhaps at certain times, most investors are swept away by excessive optimism and at other times are caught in the throes of extreme pessimism. But even here there is an assumption that will produce efficiency.

Arbitrage

Imagine a world with two types of individuals: irrational amateurs and rational professionals. The amateurs get caught up in their emotions, at times believing irrationally that an equity is undervalued and at other times believing the opposite. If the passions of the different amateurs do not cancel each other out, these amateurs, by themselves, would tend to carry shares either above or below their efficient prices.

Now let us bring in the professionals. Suppose professionals go about their business methodically and rationally. They study companies thoroughly, evaluate the evidence objectively, estimate share prices, and act accordingly. If an equity is underpriced, they will buy it. If it is overpriced, they will sell it. And their confidence would likely be greater than that of the amateurs. Whereas an amateur might risk only a small sum, these professionals might risk large ones, knowing as they do that the security is mispriced. Furthermore, they would be willing to rearrange their entire portfolio in search of a profit. Arbitrage is the word that comes to mind here because arbitrage generates profit from the simultaneous purchase and sale of different, but substitute, securities. If the arbitrage of professionals dominates the speculation of amateurs, markets would still be efficient.

LIMITS TO ARBITRAGE

> **limits to arbitrage**
> the notion that the price of an asset may not equal its correct value because of barriers to arbitrage.

Investors who buy and sell to exploit mispricings are engaging in a form of *arbitrage* and are known as *arbitrageurs* (or just *arbs* for short). Sometimes, however, a problem arises in this context. The term **limits to arbitrage** refers to the notion that, under certain circumstances, it may not be possible for rational, well-capitalized traders to correct a mispricing, at least not quickly. The reason is that strategies designed to eliminate mispricings are often risky, costly or somehow restricted.

Three important such problems are:

1. **Firm-specific risk:** This issue is the most obvious risk facing a would-be arbitrageur. Suppose that you believe that the observed price of BMW equity is too low, so you purchase many, many shares. Then there is some unanticipated negative news that drives the share price of BMW even lower. Of course, you could try to hedge some of the firm-specific risk, but any hedge you create is likely to be either imperfect and/or costly.

2. **Noise trader risk:** A **noise trader** is someone whose trades are not based on information or financially meaningful analysis. Noise traders could, in principle, act together to worsen mispricing in the short run. Noise trader risk is important because the worsening of a mispricing could force the arbitrageur to liquidate early and sustain steep losses. As Keynes once famously observed, 'Markets can remain irrational longer than you can remain solvent'.

    Noise trader risk is also called **sentiment-based risk**, meaning the risk that an asset's price is being influenced by sentiment (or irrational belief) rather than fact-based financial analysis. If sentiment-based risk exists, it is another source of risk beyond the systematic and unsystematic risks discussed in an earlier chapter.

3. **Implementation costs:** All trades cost money. In some cases, the cost of correcting a mispricing may exceed the potential gains. For example, suppose you believe a small, thinly traded equity is significantly undervalued. You want to buy a large quantity. The problem is that as soon as you try to place a huge order, the price would jump because the equity isn't heavily traded.

> **noise trader**
> a trader whose trades are not based on information or meaningful financial analysis.
>
> **sentiment-based risk**
> a source of risk to investors above and beyond firm-specific risk and overall market risk.

When these or other risks and costs are present, mispricing may persist because arbitrage is too risky or too costly. Collectively, these risks and costs create barriers or limits to arbitrage. How important these limits are is difficult to say, but we do know that mispricings occur, at least on occasion. To illustrate, we next consider two well-known examples.

The 3Com/Palm Mispricing

On 2 March 2000, 3Com, a profitable provider of computer networking products and services, sold 5 per cent of its Palm subsidiary to the public via an initial public offering (IPO). 3Com planned to distribute the remaining Palm shares to 3Com shareholders at a later date. Under the plan, if you owned one share of 3Com, you would receive 1.5 shares of Palm. So, after 3Com sold part of Palm via the IPO, investors could buy Palm shares directly, or indirectly by purchasing shares of 3Com.

What makes this case interesting is what happened in the days that followed the Palm IPO. If you owned one 3Com share, you would be entitled, eventually, to 1.5 shares of Palm. Therefore each 3Com share should be worth *at least* 1.5 times the value of each Palm share. We say *at least* because the other parts of 3Com were profitable. As a result, each 3Com share should have been worth much more than 1.5 times the value of one Palm share. But, as you might guess, things did not work out this way.

The day before the Palm IPO, shares in 3Com sold for $104.13. After the first day of trading, Palm closed at $95.06 per share. Multiplying $95.06 by 1.5 results in $142.59, which is the minimum value one would expect to pay for 3Com. But the day Palm closed at $95.06, 3Com shares closed at $81.81, more than $60 lower than the price implied by Palm. It gets stranger.

A 3Com price of $81.81 when Palm sells for $95.06 implies that the market values the rest of 3Com's businesses (per share) at: $81.81 − 142.59 = −$60.78. Given the number of 3Com shares outstanding at the time, this means the market placed a *negative value* of about −$22 billion on the rest of 3Com's businesses. Of course, a share price cannot be negative. This means, then, that the price of Palm relative to 3Com was much too high, and investors should have bought and sold such that the negative value was instantly eliminated.

What happened? As you can see in Figure 19.1, the market valued 3Com and Palm shares so that the non-Palm part of 3Com had a negative value for about 2 months, from 2 March 2000 until 8 May 2000. Even then, it took approval by the US tax authorities for 3Com to proceed with the planned distribution of Palm shares before the non-Palm part of 3Com once again had a positive value.

The Royal Dutch/Shell Price Ratio

Another fairly well-known example of apparent mispricing involves two large oil companies. In 1907 Royal Dutch of the Netherlands and Shell of the UK agreed to merge their business enterprises and split operating profits on a 60–40 basis. So, whenever the share prices of Royal Dutch and Shell are not in a 60–40 ratio, there is a potential opportunity to make an arbitrage profit.

Figure 19.2 contains a plot of the daily deviations from the 60–40 ratio of the Royal Dutch price to the Shell price. If the prices of Royal Dutch and Shell are in a 60–40 ratio, there is a zero percentage deviation. If the price of Royal Dutch is too high compared with the Shell price, there is a positive deviation. If the price of Royal Dutch is too low compared with the price of Shell, there is a negative deviation. As you can

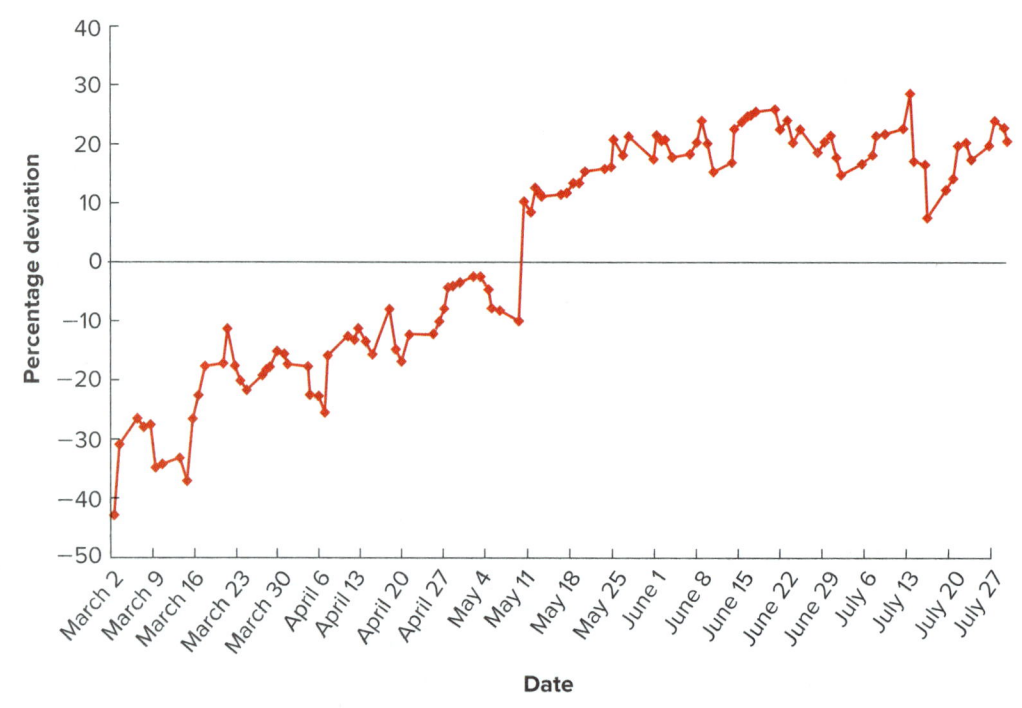

FIGURE 19.1 The percentage difference between 1 share of 3Com and 1.5 shares of Palm, 2 March 2000 to 27 July 2000

FIGURE 19.2 Royal Dutch and Shell 60–40 price ratio deviations, 1962 to 2005

Source: ft.com. © The Financial Times Ltd 2016. Used under licence from the Financial Times. All rights reserved.

see in Figure 19.2, there have been large and persistent deviations from the 60–40 ratio. In fact, the ratio is seldom at 60–40 for most of the time from 1962 until mid-2005 (when the companies merged).

BUBBLES AND CRASHES

A **bubble** occurs when market prices soar far in excess of what normal and rational analysis would suggest. Investment bubbles eventually pop because they are not based on fundamental values. When a bubble does pop, investors find themselves holding assets with plummeting values.

A **crash** is a significant and sudden drop in market-wide values. Crashes are generally associated with a bubble. Typically, a bubble lasts much longer than a crash. A bubble can form over weeks, months or even years. Crashes, on the other hand, are sudden, generally lasting less than a week. However, the disastrous financial aftermath of a crash can last for years.

> **bubble**
> a situation where observed prices soar far higher than fundamentals and rational analysis would suggest.
>
> **crash**
> a situation where market prices collapse significantly and suddenly.

The Bitcoin Bubble?

Bitcoin is a currency like a euro or a dollar, except it is digital and based on a financial technology called blockchain. Bitcoins are known as a cryptocurrency because all information on the bitcoin is recorded by an encrypted algorithm (a blockchain) near impossible to hack by outside organizations. Because bitcoins are digital currencies based on a mathematical code, they have been criticized for having no intrinsic value. They are not based on a real asset like gold, so there is no real 'value' tied to the currency. For people who have had no experience of games like Fortnite or World of Warcraft, it isn't easy to understand this concept of value. However, for those familiar with in-app purchases and virtual world economies, the idea that a digital asset has value is not too strange.

At the beginning of 2021, during a winter dominated by the Covid-19 pandemic and political unrest in the United States, many investors began to believe that bitcoin represented a store of value that bypassed the US dollar and gold. As a result of increasing demand, the bitcoin price grew quickly over a period of months. However, regulators in Europe and across the world raised serious concerns about the asset and called for it to be regulated much more than it is currently. In addition, central bankers argued that the price increase was a bubble and had no basis in economic reality.

Figure 19.3 presents the bitcoin price in 2020 and early 2021. At the time of writing, bitcoin volatility was exceptionally high, but its value still appeared to be trajecting upward. When you read this, you should check the bitcoin price and decide if the price levels in early 2021 were a bubble or represented real value. This is the real problem with considering bubbles. You only know you were in one once it has burst!

FIGURE 19.3 Bitcoin price January 2020–January 2021

Source: Coindesk data, 14 January 2021.

The Global Credit Crunch

One of the worst financial crises in modern history was the Global Credit Crunch of 2007/2008. Analysts will be dissecting the events for many decades, but almost all agree the cause of the crisis was a combination of investor irrationality and an almost blind view of the riskiness of bank strategies in the years before the crash.

Although the crisis originated in the United States through the mass provision of risky subprime mortgages to people ill-placed to afford them over the longer term, Europe gleefully took full advantage of the cheap credit available at the time. Faced with increasing competition from other countries, many banks maximized their loan portfolio sizes through significantly increased lending levels to risky borrowers. What made this strategy particularly risky was that the long-term loans were funded by short-term borrowing in the money markets.

Several behavioural biases were at work here. First, everyone was overly optimistic about the cheap credit continuing. Even with inflation growing fast, and bad debt levels increasing, market participants ignored the warning signs. Confirmation bias was also exhibited by bankers and shareholders, who argued that the bank funding and lending strategy was obviously a good one because it had such strong performance in the recent past.

The global financial crisis of 2008 is the most dramatic example of a bubble and crash. However, there are many more examples of bubbles, and some of these are presented in Table 19.1.

TABLE 19.1

Bubbles in history

Period	Name	Description
1633-1637	Tulpenmanie	The price of one tulip bulb in The Netherlands rose to 10 times the annual income of a skilled worker, and cost the equivalent of 12 acres (5 hectares) of land. When the bubble burst, the bulb price fell to 0.001 per cent of its previous high.
1720	The South Sea Bubble	Share valuations in European companies that traded in South America grew 1,000 per cent and collapsed to pre-bubble levels within one year. A very famous example of the silliness was the successful public equity issue of a company whose business model was to 'carry out an undertaking of great advantage'. We still don't know today what that undertaking was.
1920-1929	The Roaring Twenties	Very similar to the bubbles of this century in that new technologies and economic prosperity drove stock market valuations to extreme highs. The crash led to the great depression of the 1930s.
1997	The South-East Asian Bubble	Significant foreign capital inflows in search of lucrative gains led to the South East Asian economies becoming overheated. When the bubble burst, the economies went with it.
1995-2007	The Celtic Tiger	The Irish economy grew sharply over this period until the global credit crisis in 2007. The economy subsequently contracted by more than 10 per cent in a year and made the country one of the riskiest in the Eurozone.
2006-present	The Property Bubble	Property prices are at historically extreme levels, with most individuals being unable to comfortably afford mortgages. It is argued that property bubbles currently exist in China, France, Greece, India, Ireland, Italy, the Netherlands, Norway, Spain, the United Kingdom and the United States. The bubble hasn't burst yet . .

> **REAL WORLD INSIGHTS**
>
> **Hersh Shefrin on Behavioural Finance**
>
> 'Most of the chief financial officers (CFOs) I know admit that there is a gap between what they learned about corporate finance in business schools and what they put into practice as executives. A major reason for this gap is the material you are studying in this chapter. It really is true that financial managers do not practise textbook corporate finance. In the 1990s I became convinced that this was the case after I joined the organization Financial Executives International (FEI), which gave me an opportunity to meet many CFOs on a regular basis and discuss with them how they practise corporate finance. In doing so, I gained a great deal of information that led me to conclude that behavioural finance was highly applicable to corporate life.
>
> 'Behavioural corporate finance is important for at least three reasons. First, being human, financial managers are susceptible to the behavioural phenomena you are reading about in this chapter. Textbook corporate finance offers many valuable concepts, tools and techniques. My point is not that the material in traditional corporate finance textbooks lacks value, but that psychological obstacles often stand in the way of this material being implemented correctly. Second, the people with whom financial managers interact are also susceptible to mistakes. Expecting other people to be immune to mistakes is itself an error that can lead managers to make bad decisions. Third, investors' mistakes can sometimes lead prices to be inefficient. In this respect, managers can make one of two different mistakes. They might believe that prices are efficient when they are actually inefficient. Or they might believe that prices are inefficient when they are actually efficient. Managers need to know how to think about the vulnerability to both types of errors and how to deal with each.'
>
> 'The material in this chapter is a wonderful start to learning about behavioural finance. However, for this material to really make a difference, you need to integrate the material with what you are learning about traditional topics such as capital budgeting, capital structure, valuation, payout policy, market efficiency, corporate governance, and mergers and acquisition. You need to study behavioural cases about real people making real decisions and see how psychology impacts those decisions. You need to learn from their mistakes in an effort to make better decisions yourself. This is how behavioural corporate finance will generate value for you.'
>
> *Source: Hersh Shefrin holds the Mario Belotti Chair in the Department of Finance at Santa Clara University's Leavey School of Business. Professor Shefrin is a pioneer of behavioural finance.*

SUMMARY AND CONCLUSIONS

This chapter has examined some of the implications of research in cognitive psychology and behavioural finance. We learned the following:

1. By studying behavioural finance, you can see the potential damage from errors due to biases, frame dependence and heuristics.
2. Biases can lead to bad decisions because they lead to unnecessarily poor estimates of future outcomes. Over-optimism, for example, leads to overly favourable estimates and opinions.
3. Frame dependence leads to narrow framing, which is focusing on the smaller picture instead of the bigger one.
4. The use of heuristics as shortcuts ignores potentially valuable insights that more detailed analysis would reveal.
5. Market inefficiencies can be difficult for arbitrageurs to exploit because of firm-specific risk, noise trader (or sentiment-based) risk, and implementation costs. We called these difficulties limits (or barriers) to arbitrage.
6. Markets appear to be susceptible to bubbles and crashes, suggesting significant inefficiency at specific points in time.

CHAPTER REVIEW AND SELF-TEST PROBLEMS

19.1 In 2015, Volkswagen's share price fell dramatically when the US Environmental Protection Agency announced that many of their cars had 'defeat devices' that led to a mismeasurement of carbon emissions. However, within two months of the scandal, Volkswagen's share price had recovered much of its losses. Is this consistent with a behavioural finance interpretation? If so, what behavioural characteristic is represented here?

19.2 Is the share price reaction to the Volkswagen scandal explained by the efficient markets hypothesis? If so, explain why.

SOLUTIONS

19.1 If the share price fall and subsequent reversal resulted from investor sentiment or investor over-reaction, then it is definitely possible to explain Volkswagen's price movements as being caused by a psychological irrationality of the market.

19.2 The efficient markets hypothesis could also explain the share price movements of Volkswagen around the emissions scandal. At the time of the announcement (18 September 2015), there was considerable uncertainty of the scandal's extent, how many models were affected, and the legal costs involved with any litigation that could arise. By combining these factors' potential impacts, one could conclude that Volkswagen's operations would be severely curtailed. The price reversal can be explained by the resolution of uncertainty over time and the more accurate information relating to the emissions scandal's effects on Volkswagen's market value.

QUESTIONS AND PROBLEMS

19.1 **Efficient Market Hypothesis** The efficient market hypothesis implies that all mutual funds should obtain the same expected risk-adjusted returns. Therefore we can simply pick mutual funds at random. Is this statement true or false? Explain.

19.2 **Behavioural Finance and Efficient Markets** Proponents of behavioural finance use three concepts to argue that markets are not efficient. What are these arguments?

19.3 **Frame Dependence** In the chapter we presented an example where you had lost €78 and were given the opportunity to make a wager in which your loss would increase to €100 for 80 per cent of the time and decrease to €0 for 20 per cent of the time. Using the stand-alone principle from capital budgeting, explain how your decision to accept or reject the proposal could have been affected by frame dependence. In other words, reframe the question in a way in which most people are likely to analyse the proposal correctly.

19.4 **Empirical Challenges to Market Efficiency** Discuss some of the anomalies to market efficiency that have been detected in academic research. Taken together, do these anomalies provide concrete evidence that the market is inefficient? Why or why not? Explain.

19.5 **Efficient Market Theory versus Behavioural Finance** Compare and contrast both theories. In your opinion, which is the most reflective of market behaviour? Explain.

19.6 Implications for Corporate Finance What do efficient market theory and behavioural finance imply for corporate decision-making? Provide three examples of how each theory may affect managerial behaviour.

19.7 Technical Trading 'Every day I check the price patterns from the day before to identify the shares I wish to trade that day.' What do the efficient markets hypothesis and behavioural finance hypothesis say about this statement? Which explanation do you believe as being most valid?

19.8 Bitcoin and Bubbles Many investors earned significantly positive returns during 2020 from investing in Bitcoin. How can you explain this using the efficient markets hypothesis and behavioural finance theory?

19.9 Technical Analysis What would a technical analyst say about market efficiency? What would a technical analyst say about behavioural finance?

19.10 Corporate Insider Trading Across the world, corporate insiders appear to consistently earn positive abnormal returns when they buy the equity of their own company. Although it could be argued that executives are exploiting private information in their trades, is it possible to interpret their performance using behavioural finance theories? Explain why or why not.

19.11 Behavioural Finance Do you think cryptocurrencies are more or less efficient than established currencies, such as sterling or the euro? Do you think they will be more or less sensitive to general market sentiment? Explain.

19.12 Behavioural Finance versus Market Efficiency Some people argue that the efficient market hypothesis cannot explain the Bitcoin price increases in 2020. What alternative hypothesis could be proposed?

19.13 Efficient Markets When President Donald Trump tweeted that he was planning to impose 10 per cent tariffs on $300 billion of Chinese imports, the S&P 500 fell by 3 per cent and the Chinese yuan weakened against the dollar. What do the efficient market theory and behavioural finance say about the effect of Donald Trump's tweets? Is this evidence that investors believe in efficient markets, behavioural finance or both? Explain.

19.14 Initial Public Offerings Research has shown that managers of newly listed firms rein in their capital expenditure plans if the market share price performance is not particularly strong around the IPO date. This is regularly put down to 'poor market sentiment'. Is this evidence that corporate managers believe in efficient markets, behavioural finance or both? Explain.

19.15 Investor Sentiment Some people believe that following the European Commission's Economic Sentiment Indicator (see chart below) allows you to predict future market movements. What is the Economic Sentiment Indicator intended to capture? How might it be useful in technical analysis? Look at the stock market indices of any European country. Do you think it is a good indicator? Explain.

MINI CASE

SUPERCOLD SKIS

SuperCold Skis is an alpine sports manufacturing firm based in Northern Europe. Three years ago, in an attempt to exploit growth opportunities in Scandinavia, the company raised £10 million on the London Stock Exchange. The recent history of the company has not been good, however, and the expected revenue growth has not materialized. Moreover, the company's new shareholders (mostly small-scale skiing enthusiasts) are putting pressure on the management to change direction. Specifically, they want more say in the strategic direction of the company and have asked for a seat on the board of directors.

The company has hired you as an external consultant to manage the firm's engagement with the media and its unhappy shareholders. The directors believe that behavioural finance can help the firm maximize its value and have asked you to come up with an effective communications strategy.

QUESTIONS

1. Use a method learned in this chapter as the basis of a communications strategy to investors. Explain what your strategy is, the behavioural concept it is founded on, and the expected outcome of the strategy.
2. Assume that you are an activist investor wishing to purchase the firm at a cheap price. What behavioural strategy would you use to pressurize the management into giving you a seat on the board of directors?
3. If the market is efficient, how effective would the strategies in questions 1 and 2 be? Explain your reasoning.

ADDITIONAL READING

In recent years, behavioural finance has captured the minds of researchers and managers and led to a sizeable body of work using it to explore behaviours and anomalies in finance. Subrahmanyam (2008) provides a very readable review of this research.

1. Subrahmanyam, A. (2008). Behavioural finance: A review and synthesis. *European Financial Management*, 14(1), 12–29.

A good book on understanding randomness in financial markets is the following:

2. Taleb, N. (2005). *Fooled by randomness: The Hidden Role of Chance in Life and in the Markets* (Vol. 1). Penguin Random House.

CHAPTER 20
FINANCIAL RISK MANAGEMENT

LEARNING OBJECTIVES
After studying this chapter, you should understand:
- **LO1** The exposures to risk in a company's business and how a company could choose to hedge these risks.
- **LO2** The similarities and differences between futures and forward contracts, and how these contracts are used to hedge risk.
- **LO3** The basics of swap contracts, and how they are used to hedge interest rates.
- **LO4** The pay-offs of option contracts, and how they are used to hedge risk.

ANYONE STUDYING CORPORATE FINANCE must be familiar with the principles of financial risk management. Many students think that only financial institutions use derivatives such as futures and swaps. However, every company that does business overseas, sources raw materials from other countries, borrows or lends money, or buys commodities today for delivery in the future will use risk management techniques to manage risk and optimize its business.

When the UK left the European Union, the Covid-19 pandemic had caused a widespread lockdown with restrictions on social distancing and business operations in many industrial sectors. The whole region entered a period of uncertainty and firms had to predict future economic conditions, raw material prices, supply chain dynamics, and future exchange rates. Car exporters, for example, were faced with some of the worst trading conditions in living memory and had to chart a route through a number of potential future scenarios, all requiring some form of risk mitigation.

In this environment, financial risk management becomes fundamental to lessening the risk of doing business. There are a variety of methods firms can adopt, and in this chapter we review the main approaches and financial risk management instruments in use today.

Prices for all types of goods and services have become increasingly volatile in recent years. This is a cause for concern because sudden and unexpected shifts in prices create expensive disruptions in operating activities, even for well-run firms. As a result, firms shield themselves from price volatility through the use of innovative financial arrangements.

The purpose of this chapter is to introduce you to some of the basics of financial risk management. The activities we discuss are on the frontier of modern, real-world financial management. By describing one of the rapidly developing areas in corporate finance, we hope to leave you with a sense of how the art and practice of corporate finance evolves in response to changes in the financial environment.[1]

20.1 HEDGING AND PRICE VOLATILITY

hedging
reducing a firm's exposure to price or rate fluctuations. Also, *immunization*.

derivative security
a financial asset that represents a claim to another financial asset.

In broad terms, reducing a firm's exposure to price or rate fluctuations is called **hedging**. The term *immunization* is sometimes used as well. As we shall discuss, there are many different types of hedging and risk management techniques. Frequently, when a firm desires to hedge a particular risk, there will be no direct way of doing so. In such cases, the financial manager's job is to innovate by using available financial instruments to create new ones. This process has come to be called *financial engineering*.

Corporate risk management often involves the buying and selling of **derivative securities**. A derivative security is a financial asset that represents a claim to another financial asset. For example, an equity option gives the owner the right to buy or sell equities, a financial asset: so equity options are derivative securities.

In a world where prices were very stable and changed only slowly, there would be very little demand for financial risk management. Given the economic turmoil in the last five years, financial risk management has become central to every business's operations.

There are three specific areas of particular importance in which volatility has increased dramatically in recent years: interest rates, exchange rates and commodity prices.

INTEREST RATE VOLATILITY

We know that debt is a vital source of financing for corporations, and interest rates are a key component of a firm's cost of capital. Since the Brexit vote in 2016, interest rates have been fairly volatile in Europe. Figure 20.1 illustrates this volatility by plotting the monthly percentage changes in 10-year UK Treasury bond yields between 2010 and 2021. European interest rates have the same level of volatility. In today's financial world, firms must manage their exposure to movements in interest rates because of the uncertainty surrounding government bond yields in the UK, Eurozone and beyond.

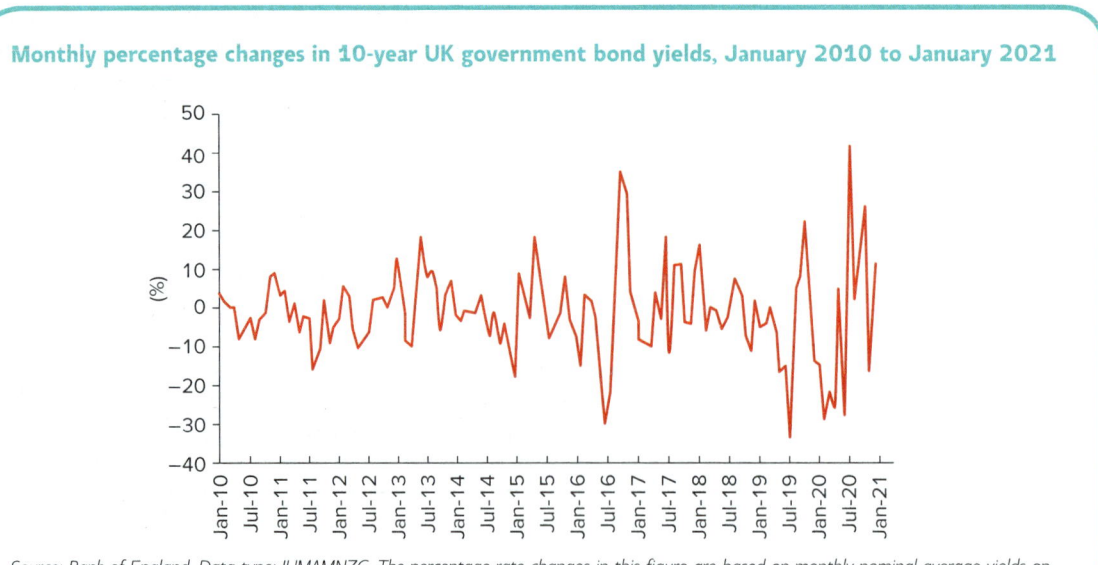

FIGURE 20.1 Monthly percentage changes in 10-year UK government bond yields, January 2010 to January 2021

Source: Bank of England. Data type: IUMAMNZC. The percentage rate changes in this figure are based on monthly nominal average yields on 10-year zero discount UK government bonds.

EXCHANGE RATE VOLATILITY

As discussed in Chapter 18, international operations are of fundamental importance to European businesses. The UK's vote to leave the European Union created substantial volatility in £/€ exchange rates and this impacted importers and exporters alike. However, most currencies have become more volatile in recent years and this has increased the risk of business for many companies in a wide range of industrial sectors.

Like interest rates, foreign exchange volatility can impact the revenues and costs of a business. To avoid exposure to adverse exchange rate movements, financial managers will seek to minimize the probability of large shifts in foreign exchange by investing in currency hedge instruments.

COMMODITY PRICE VOLATILITY

Commodity prices (the prices for basic goods and materials) are the third major area in which volatility has risen. Oil is one of the most important commodities and, as Figure 20.2 shows (and recent experience confirms), oil prices can change dramatically from one month to the next. The behaviour of oil prices is not unique; many other key commodities have experienced increased volatility over the past decade.

FIGURE 20.2 Monthly percentage change in Europe Brent spot oil price ($/barrel), 2010–2021

Source: US Energy Information Administration.

CONCEPT QUESTIONS

20.1a What is hedging?
20.1b Why do firms place greater emphasis on hedging now than they did in the past?

20.2 MANAGING FINANCIAL RISK

We've seen that price and interest rate volatility have been very high in recent years. Whether or not this is a cause for concern for a particular firm depends on the nature of the firm's operations, and of its financing. For example, an all-equity firm would not be concerned about interest rate fluctuations as a highly leveraged one. Similarly, a firm with little or no international activity would not be overly concerned about exchange rate fluctuations.

To manage financial risk effectively, financial managers will identify the types of price fluctuation that have the most significant impact on the firm's value. Sometimes these will be obvious, but sometimes they will not be. For example, consider a timber company. If interest rates increase, then its borrowing costs will clearly rise. Beyond this, however, the demand for housing typically declines as interest rates rise. As housing demand falls, so too does the need for timber. An increase in interest rates leads to increased financing costs and, at the same time, decreased revenues.[2]

THE RISK PROFILE

risk profile
a plot showing how the value of the firm is affected by changes in prices or rates.

The primary tool for identifying and measuring a firm's exposure to financial risk is the **risk profile**. The risk profile is a plot showing the relationship between changes in the price of some good, service or rate and changes in the firm's value. Constructing a risk profile is conceptually very similar to performing a sensitivity analysis (described in Chapter 10).

To illustrate, consider an agricultural products company that has a large-scale wheat-farming operation. Because wheat prices can be very volatile, we might wish to investigate the firm's exposure to wheat price fluctuations – that is, its risk profile with regard to wheat prices. To do this, we plot changes in the value of the firm (ΔV) against unexpected changes in wheat prices (ΔP_{wheat}). Figure 20.3 shows the result. The risk profile in Figure 20.3 tells us two things. First, because the line slopes up, increases in wheat prices will increase the firm's value. Because wheat is an output, this comes as no surprise. Second, because the line has a fairly steep slope, this firm has significant exposure to wheat price fluctuations, and it may wish to take steps to reduce that exposure.

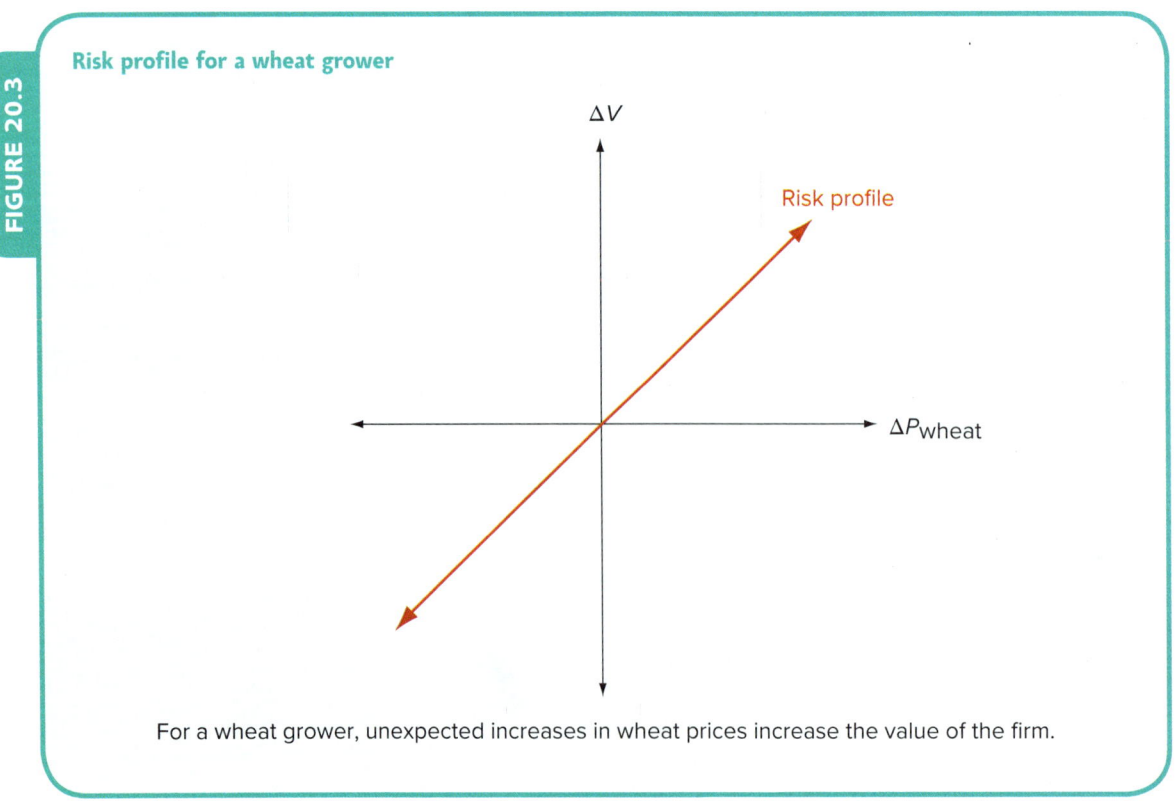

FIGURE 20.3 Risk profile for a wheat grower

For a wheat grower, unexpected increases in wheat prices increase the value of the firm.

REDUCING RISK EXPOSURE

Fluctuations in the price of any particular good or service can have very different effects on different types of firm. Going back to wheat prices, we now consider the case of a food-processing operation. The food processor buys large quantities of wheat and has a risk profile like the one illustrated in Figure 20.4. As with the agricultural products firm, this firm's value is sensitive to wheat prices; but because wheat is an input, increases in wheat prices lead to decreases in firm value.

FIGURE 20.4

Risk profile for a wheat buyer

For a wheat buyer, unexpected increases in wheat prices decrease the value of the firm.

Both the agricultural products firm and the food processor are exposed to wheat price fluctuations, but such fluctuations have opposite effects for the two firms. If these two firms get together, then much of the risk can be eliminated. The grower and the processor can agree that the grower will deliver a certain quantity of wheat at set dates in the future, and the processor will pay a set price. Once the agreement is signed, both firms will have locked in the price of wheat for as long as the contract is in effect, and both of their risk profiles with regard to wheat prices will be completely flat during that time.

We should note that, in reality, a firm that hedges financial risk usually won't be able to create a completely flat risk profile. For example, our wheat grower doesn't actually know what the crop's size will be ahead of time. If the crop is larger than expected, then some portion of the crop will be unhedged. If the crop is small, then the grower will have to buy more to fulfil the contract and will thereby be exposed to the risk of price changes. Either way, there is some exposure to wheat price fluctuations; but hedging sharply reduces that exposure.

There are other reasons why perfect hedging is usually impossible, but this is not really a problem. With most financial risk management, the goal is to reduce risk to more bearable levels and flatten out the risk profile, not necessarily eliminate it.

In thinking about financial risk, there is an important distinction to be made. Price fluctuations have two components. Short-run, essentially temporary changes are the first component. The second component has to do with more long-run, essentially permanent changes. As we discuss next, these two types of change have very different implications for the firm.

HEDGING SHORT-RUN EXPOSURE

Short-run, temporary changes in prices result from unforeseen events or shocks. Some examples are sudden increases in orange juice prices because of a late-season freeze, increases in oil prices because of political turmoil, and increases in coffee prices because of a serious drought. Price fluctuations of this sort are often called *transitory* changes.

Short-run price changes can drive a business into financial distress even though, in the long run, the company is fundamentally sound. When a firm finds itself with sudden cost increases, it cannot immediately pass this on to customers. A negative cash flow position is created, and the firm may be unable to meet its financial obligations.

For example, wheat crops might be much larger than expected in a particular year because of excellent growing conditions. At harvest time, wheat prices will be unexpectedly low. By that time, a wheat farmer will have already incurred most of the costs of production. If prices drop too low, revenues from the crop will be insufficient to cover the costs, and financial distress may result.

> **transactions exposure**
> short-run financial risk arising from the need to buy or sell at uncertain prices or rates in the near future.

Short-run financial risk is often called **transactions exposure**. This name stems from the fact that short-term financial exposure typically arises because a firm must make transactions in the near future at uncertain prices or rates. For example, with our wheat farmer, the crop must be sold at the end of the harvest, but the wheat price is uncertain. Alternatively, a firm may have a bond issue maturing next year that it will have to replace, but the new interest rate the firm will pay is unknown.

As we shall see, short-run financial risk can be managed in a variety of ways. The opportunities for short-term hedging have grown tremendously in recent years, and firms worldwide are increasingly hedging away transitory price changes.

CASH FLOW HEDGING: A CAUTIONARY NOTE

One thing to notice is that in our discussion thus far, we have talked conceptually about hedging the value of the firm. However, in our example concerning wheat prices, what is really hedged is the firm's near-term cash flow. In fact, at the risk of ignoring some subtleties, we shall say that hedging short-term financial exposure, hedging transactions exposure and hedging near-term cash flows amount to much the same thing.

It will usually be the case that directly hedging the value of the firm is not really feasible; instead, the firm will try to reduce the uncertainty of its near-term cash flows. If the firm is thereby able to avoid expensive disruptions, cash flow hedging will act to hedge the value of the firm, but the linkage is indirect. In such cases, care must be taken to ensure that the cash flow hedging does have the desired effect.

For example, imagine a vertically integrated firm with an oil-producing division and a petrol-retailing division. Both divisions are affected by fluctuations in oil prices. However, it may well be that the firm as a whole has minimal transactions exposure because any transitory shifts in oil prices simply benefit one division and cost the other. The firm's overall risk profile with regard to oil prices is essentially flat. Put another way, the firm's net exposure is small. However, if one division, acting on its own, were to begin hedging its cash flows, then the firm as a whole would suddenly be exposed to financial risk. Cash flow hedging should therefore not be done in isolation. Instead, a firm needs to worry about its net exposure and hedging activities should probably be done on a centralized, or at least co-operative, basis.

HEDGING LONG-TERM EXPOSURE

> **economic exposure**
> long-term financial risk arising from permanent changes in prices or other economic fundamentals.

Price fluctuations can also be longer-run, more permanent changes. These result from fundamental shifts in the underlying economics of a business. If improvements in agricultural technology come about, for example, then wheat prices will permanently decline (in the absence of agricultural price subsidies!). If a firm cannot adapt to new technology, it will not be economically viable over the long term.

A firm's exposure to long-run financial risks is often called its **economic exposure**. Because long-term exposure is rooted in fundamental economic forces, it is much more difficult, if not impossible, to hedge on a permanent basis. For example, is it possible that a wheat farmer and a food processor could permanently eliminate exposure to wheat price fluctuations by agreeing on a fixed price forever?

The answer is no; in fact, the effect of such an agreement might even be the opposite of the one desired. The reason is that if over the long run, wheat prices were to change on a permanent basis, one party to this agreement would ultimately be unable to honour it. Either the buyer would be paying too much, or the seller would be receiving too little. In either case, the loser would become uncompetitive and fail. Something of the sort happened in the 1970s when public utilities and other energy consumers entered into long-run contracts with natural gas producers. Natural gas prices plummeted in later years, and a great deal of turmoil followed.

CONCLUSION

In the long run, either a business is economically viable, or it will fail. No amount of hedging can change this simple fact. Nonetheless, by hedging over the near term, a firm gives itself time to adjust its operations and adapt to new conditions without expensive disruptions. So, drawing our discussion in this section together, we can say that, by managing financial risks, the firm can accomplish two important things. The first is that the firm insulates itself from otherwise troublesome transitory price fluctuations. The second is that the firm gives itself a little breathing space to adapt to fundamental changes in market conditions.

> **CONCEPT QUESTIONS**
>
> **20.2a** What is a risk profile? Describe the risk profiles with regard to oil prices for an oil producer and a petrol retailer.
>
> **20.2b** What can a firm accomplish by hedging financial risk?

20.3 HEDGING WITH FORWARD CONTRACTS

Forward contracts are among the oldest and most basic tools for managing financial risk. Our goal in this section is to describe forward contracts and discuss how they hedge financial risk.

FORWARD CONTRACTS: THE BASICS

A **forward contract** is a legally binding agreement between two parties calling for the sale of an asset or product in the future at a price agreed on today. The terms of the contract call for one party to deliver the goods to the other on a specific date in the future called the *settlement date*. The other party pays the previously agreed *forward price* and takes the goods. Looking back, note that the agreement we discussed between the wheat grower and the food processor was, in fact, a forward contract.

Forward contracts can be bought and sold. The *buyer* of a forward contract has an obligation to take delivery and pay for the goods; the *seller* has an obligation to make delivery and accept payment. The buyer of a forward contract benefits if prices increase, because the buyer will have locked in a lower price. Similarly, the seller wins if prices fall, because a higher selling price has been locked in. Note that one party to a forward contract can win only at the other's expense, so a forward contract is a zero-sum game.

forward contract
a legally binding agreement between two parties calling for the sale of an asset or product in the future at a price agreed on today.

THE PAY-OFF PROFILE

The **pay-off profile** is the key to understanding how forward contracts (and other contracts we discuss later) are used to hedge financial risks. In general, a pay-off profile is a plot showing the gains and losses on a contract that result from unexpected price changes. For example, suppose we were examining a forward contract on oil. Based on our discussion, the buyer of the forward contract is obligated to accept delivery of a specified quantity of oil at a future date and pay a set price. Part A of Figure 20.5 shows the forward contract's resulting pay-off profile from the buyer's perspective.

pay-off profile
a plot showing the gains and losses that will occur on a contract as the result of unexpected price changes.

What Figure 20.5 shows is that, as oil prices increase, the buyer of the forward contract benefits by having locked in a lower-than-market price. If oil prices decrease, the buyer loses because that buyer ends up paying a higher-than-market price. For the seller of the forward contract, things are simply reversed. The pay-off profile of the seller is illustrated in Part B of Figure 20.5.

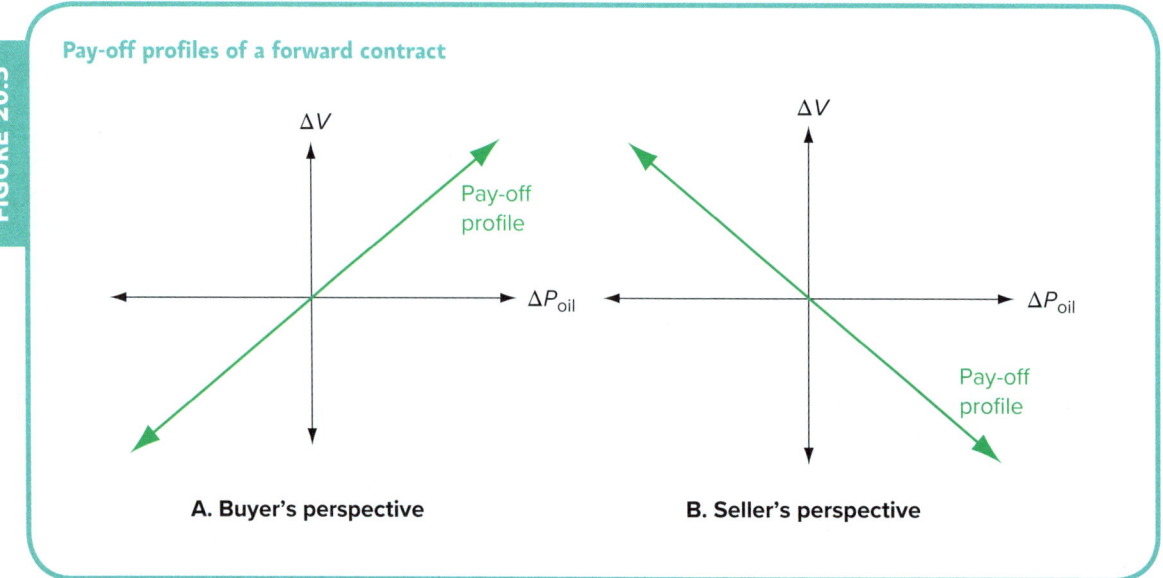

FIGURE 20.5 Pay-off profiles of a forward contract

A. Buyer's perspective

B. Seller's perspective

HEDGING WITH FORWARDS

To illustrate how forward contracts can be used to hedge, we consider the case of a public utility that uses oil to generate power. The prices our utility can charge are regulated and cannot be changed rapidly. As a result, sudden increases in oil prices are a source of financial risk. The utility's risk profile is illustrated in Figure 20.6.

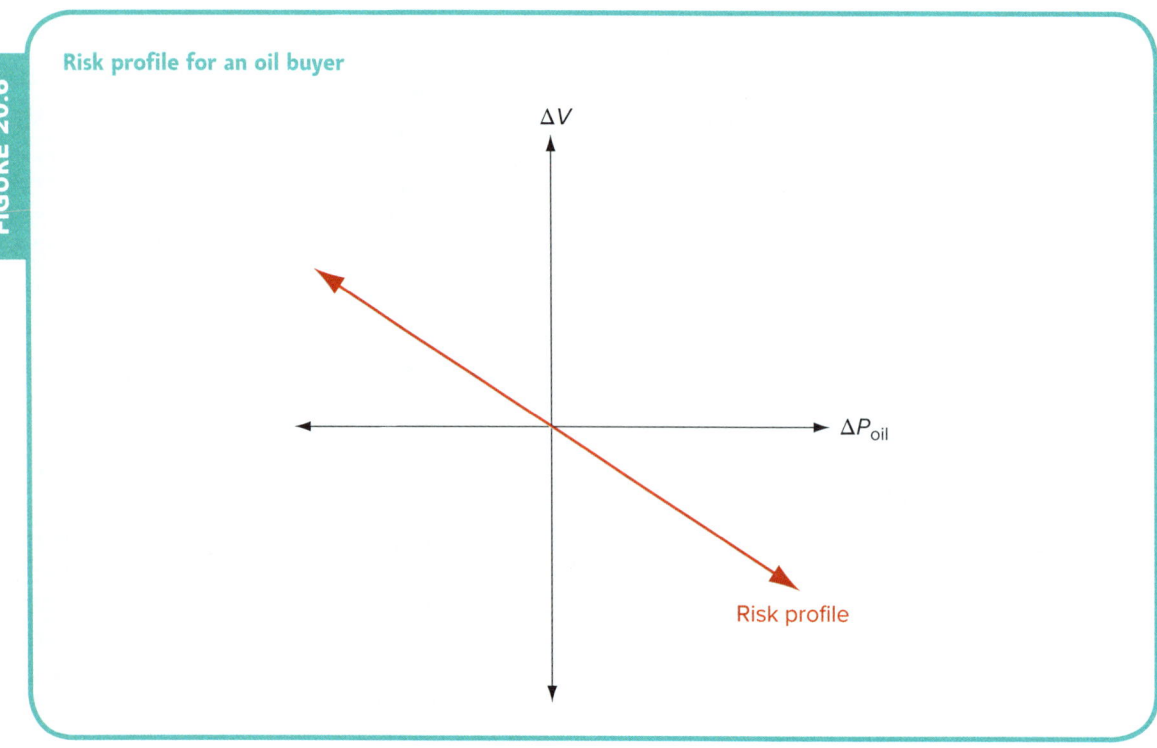

FIGURE 20.6 Risk profile for an oil buyer

If we compare the risk profile in Figure 20.6 with the buyer's pay-off profile on a forward contract shown in Figure 20.5, we see what the utility needs to do. The pay-off profile for the buyer of a forward contract on oil is exactly the opposite of the utility's risk profile with respect to oil. If the utility buys a forward contract, its exposure to unexpected changes in oil prices will be eliminated. This result is shown in Figure 20.7.

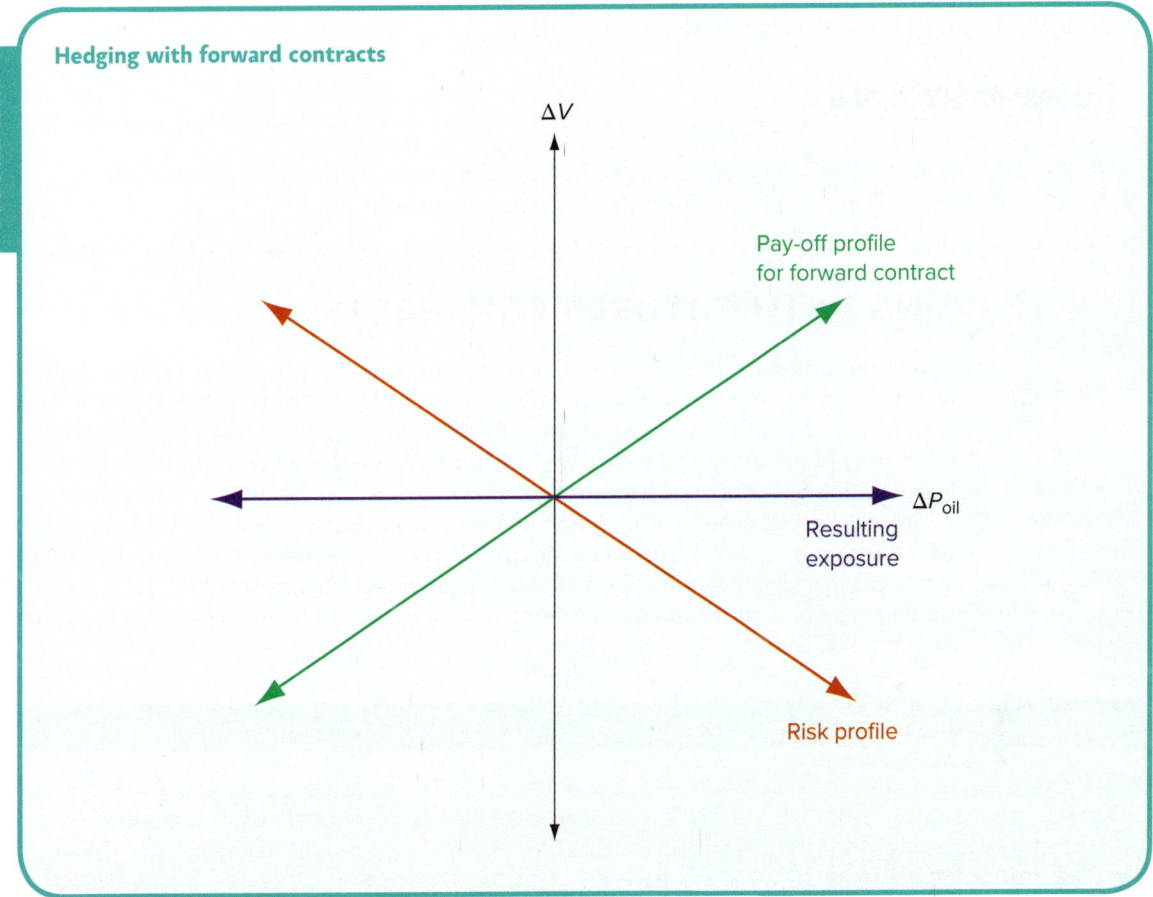

FIGURE 20.7 Hedging with forward contracts

Our public utility example illustrates the fundamental approach to managing financial risk. We first identify the firm's exposure to financial risk using a risk profile. We then try to find a financial arrangement, such as a forward contract, that has an offsetting pay-off profile.

A Caveat

Figure 20.7 shows that the utility's net exposure to oil price fluctuations is zero. If oil prices rise, the gains on the forward contract will offset the damage from increased costs. However, if oil prices decline, the benefit from lower costs will be offset by losses on the forward contract.

This illustrates an important thing to remember about hedging with forward contracts. Price fluctuations can be good or bad, depending on which way they go. If we hedge with forward contracts, we eliminate the risk associated with an adverse price change. However, we also eliminate the potential gain from a favourable move. You might wonder whether we couldn't somehow hedge against unfavourable moves. We can, and we describe how in a subsequent section.

Credit Risk

Another important thing to remember is that, with a forward contract, no money changes hands when the contract is initiated. The contract is simply an agreement to transact in the future, so there is no up-front cost to the contract. However, because a forward contract is a financial obligation, there is credit risk.

When the settlement date arrives, the party on the losing end of the contract has a significant incentive to default on the agreement. As discussed in the next section, a variation on the forward contract exists that greatly diminishes this risk.

Forward Contracts in Practice

Where are forward contracts commonly used to hedge? Because exchange rate fluctuations can have disastrous consequences for firms with significant import or export operations, forward contracts are routinely used by such firms to hedge exchange rate risk.

> **CONCEPT QUESTIONS**
>
> **20.3a** What is a forward contract? Describe the pay-off profiles for the buyer and the seller of a forward contract.
> **20.3b** Explain how a firm can alter its risk profile using forward contracts.

20.4 HEDGING WITH FUTURES CONTRACTS

futures contract
a forward contract with the feature that gains and losses are realized each day rather than only on the settlement date.

A **futures contract** is the same as a forward contract, with one exception. With a forward contract, the buyer and seller realize gains or losses only on the settlement date. With a futures contract, gains and losses are realized daily. If we buy a futures contract on oil, then if oil prices rise today, we have a profit and the seller of the contract has a loss. The seller pays up, and we start again tomorrow with neither party owing the other.

The daily resettlement feature found in futures contracts is called *marking to market*. As we mentioned earlier, there is a significant risk of default with forward contracts. With daily marking to market, this risk is greatly reduced. This is probably why organized trading is much more common in futures contracts than in forward contracts (outside international trade).

> **REAL WORLD INSIGHTS**
>
> Technically, any commodity, good or service can have a futures contract written on it. As long as there are standardized characteristics that are quantifiable and measurable, a futures contract can hedge price uncertainty. However, exchanges also have contracts on instruments where there is no real hedging requirement.
>
> Take, for example, bitcoin and ethereum, which are both cryptocurrencies. While it can be difficult for traditional investors to invest directly in crypto assets, investing in crypto futures contracts is straightforward.
>
> It is difficult to see how futures contracts in cryptocurrencies can hedge underlying risk unless payment for goods or services was required in either bitcoin or ethereum. More likely, the contracts are used to speculate on future growth in the value of each currency and for investors to capture price movements associated with bitcoin and ethereum.

TRADING IN FUTURES

Futures contracts are routinely bought and sold for a remarkable variety of items. The types of contract available are traditionally divided into two groups: commodity futures and financial futures. With a financial future, the underlying goods are financial assets such as equities, bonds or currencies. With a commodity future, the underlying goods can be just about anything other than a financial asset.

There are commodity futures contracts on various agricultural products, such as corn, orange juice and, yes, pork bellies. There is even a contract on fertilizer. There are commodity contracts on precious metals such as gold and silver, and there are contracts on basic goods such as copper and timber. There are contracts on various petroleum products such as crude oil, heating oil and gasoline. Wherever there is price volatility, there may be a demand for a futures contract, and new futures contracts are introduced on a fairly regular basis.

FUTURES EXCHANGES

There are many futures exchanges around the world, and more are being established. The big three exchanges are the National Stock Exchange of India, the Chicago Mercantile Exchange, and B3 (Brazil). While trading on these exchanges spans whole geographic regions, there are many other exchanges, such as the Intercontinental Exchange (ICE), Eurex, CBOE Holdings, OMX (Nordic and Baltic markets), IDEM (Italy), MEFF (Spain) and LME (London).

Figure 20.8 gives a partial *Financial Times* listing for selected futures contracts. Taking a look at the NYSE LIFFE cocoa contracts, note that the contracts are for delivery of 10 tonnes of cocoa, and are quoted in pounds per tonne. The price of cocoa for delivery in the future is expected to fall over 2021. For example, the price of a May 2021 cocoa futures contract is £1,662, falling to £1,633 for a September contract, before rising to £1,644 for a December 2021 contract.

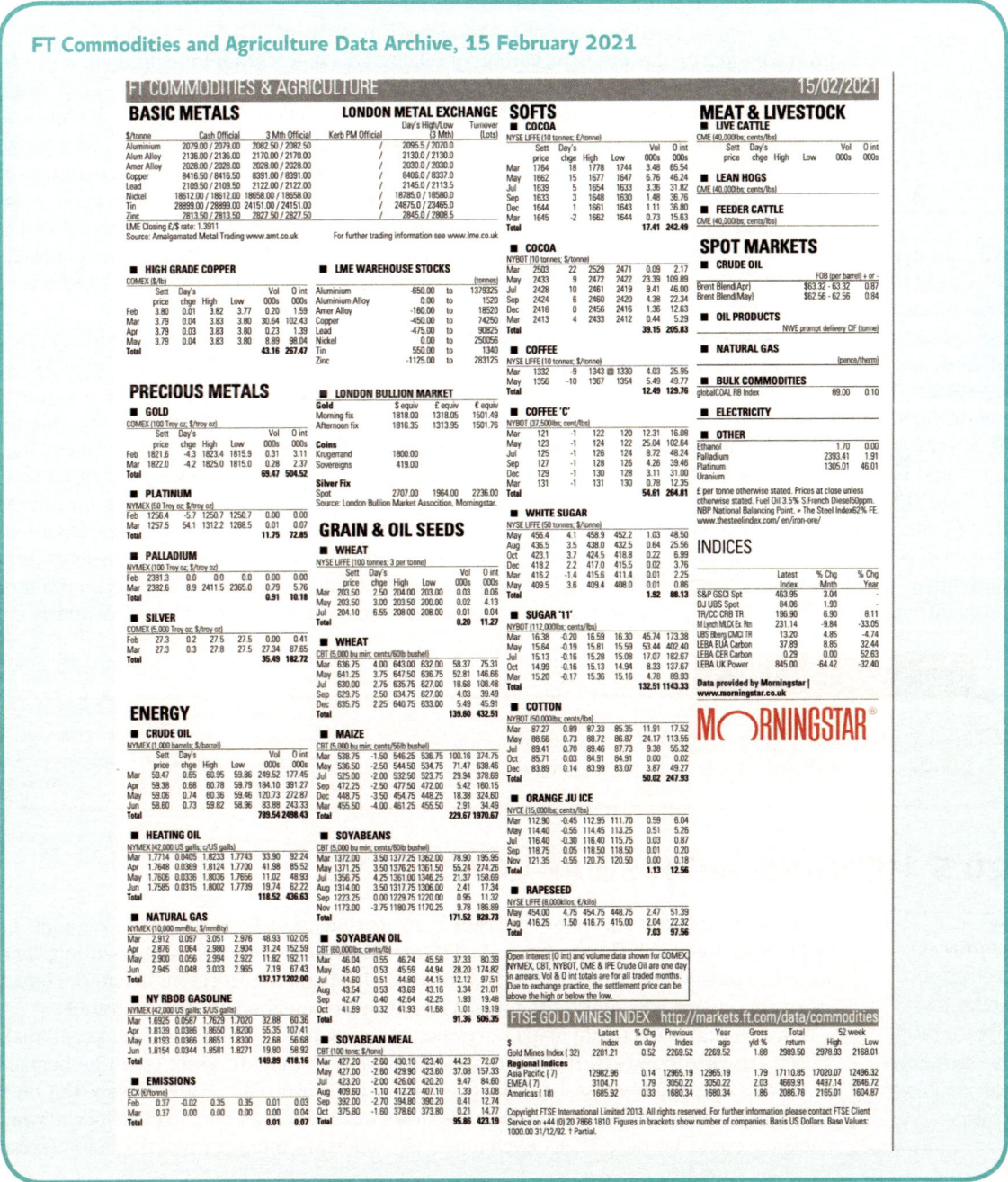

FIGURE 20.8 FT Commodities and Agriculture Data Archive, 15 February 2021

For the LIFFE cocoa contract with a May maturity, the first number in the row is the settlement price (£1,662) and is essentially the closing price for the day. For purposes of marking to market, this is the figure used. The change, listed next, is the movement in the settlement price since the previous trading session (+£15). The highest price (£1,677) and the lowest price (£1,647) over the contract's life are shown next. Finally, there were 6,760 contracts traded, and open interest (46,240) – the number of contracts outstanding at the end of the day – is shown.

HEDGING WITH FUTURES

Hedging with futures contracts is conceptually identical to hedging with forward contracts, and the pay-off profile on a futures contract is drawn just like the profile for a forward contract. The only difference in hedging with futures is that the firm will have to maintain an account with a broker so that gains and losses can be credited or debited each day as a part of the marking-to-market process.

> **cross-hedging**
> hedging an asset with contracts written on a closely related, but not identical, asset.

Even though there are many futures contracts, it is unlikely that a particular firm will be able to find the precise hedging instrument it needs. For example, we might produce a particular grade or variety of oil, but find no contract for exactly that grade. However, all oil prices tend to move together, so we could hedge our output using futures contracts on other grades of oil. Using a contract on a related, but not identical, asset as a means of hedging is called **cross-hedging**.

When a firm *does* cross-hedge, it does not actually want to buy or sell the underlying asset. This presents no problem because the firm can reverse its futures position at some point before maturity. This means that if the firm sells a futures contract to hedge something, it will buy the same contract at a later date, thereby eliminating its futures position. In fact, futures contracts are rarely held to maturity by anyone (despite horror stories of individuals waking up to find mountains of soya beans in their front yards); as a result, actual physical delivery very rarely takes place.

A related issue has to do with contract maturity. A firm might wish to hedge over a relatively long period of time, but the available contracts might have shorter maturities. A firm could therefore decide to roll over short-term contracts, but this entails some risks. For example, Metallgesellschaft AG, a German firm, nearly went bankrupt in 1993 after losing more than $1 billion in the oil markets, mainly through derivatives. The trouble began in 1992 when MG Corp., a US subsidiary, began marketing gasoline, heating oil and diesel fuel. It entered into contracts to supply products for fixed prices for up to 10 years. Thus, if the price of oil rose, the firm stood to lose money. MG protected itself by, among other things, buying short-term oil futures that fluctuated with near-term energy prices. Under these contracts, if the price of oil rose, the derivatives gained in value. Unfortunately for MG, oil prices dropped, and the firm incurred huge losses on its short-term derivatives positions without an immediate, offsetting benefit on its long-term contracts. Thus its primary problem was that it was hedging a long-term contract with short-term contracts – a less than ideal approach.

> **CONCEPT QUESTIONS**
>
> **20.4a** What is a futures contract? How does it differ from a forward contract?
> **20.4b** What is cross-hedging? Why is it important?

20.5 HEDGING WITH SWAP CONTRACTS

> **swap contract**
> an agreement by two parties to exchange, or swap, specified cash flows at specified intervals in the future.

As the name suggests, a **swap contract** is an agreement by two parties to exchange, or swap, specified cash flows at specified intervals. Swaps are a recent innovation; they were first introduced to the public in 1981 when IBM and the World Bank entered into a swap agreement. The market for swaps has grown tremendously since that time.

A swap contract is really just a portfolio, or series, of forward contracts. Recall that, with a forward contract, one party promises to exchange an asset (such as bushels of wheat) for another asset (cash) on a specific future date. With a swap, the only difference is that there are multiple exchanges instead of just one. In principle, a swap contract could be tailored to exchange just about anything. In practice, most swap contracts fall into one of three basic categories: currency swaps, interest rate swaps and commodity swaps. Other types will surely develop, but we shall concentrate on just these three.

CURRENCY SWAPS

With a *currency swap*, two parties agree to exchange a specific amount of one currency for a specific amount of another at specific dates in the future. For example, suppose a US firm has a German subsidiary and wishes to obtain debt financing to expand the subsidiary's operations. Because most of the subsidiary's cash flows are in euros, the company would like the subsidiary to borrow and make payments in euros, thereby hedging against changes in the euro-dollar exchange rate. Unfortunately, the company has good access to US debt markets but not to German debt markets.

At the same time, a German firm would like to obtain US dollar financing. It can borrow cheaply in euros, but not in dollars. Both firms face a similar problem. They can borrow at favourable rates – but not in the desired currency. A currency swap is a solution. These two firms agree to exchange dollars for euros at a fixed rate at specific future dates (the payment dates on the loans). Thus, each firm obtains the best possible rate and then arranges to eliminate exposure to exchange rate changes by agreeing to swap currencies – a neat solution.

INTEREST RATE SWAPS

Imagine a firm that wishes to obtain a fixed-rate loan, but can get a good deal on only a floating-rate loan – that is, a loan for which the payments are adjusted periodically to reflect changes in interest rates. Another firm can obtain a fixed-rate loan, but wishes to obtain the lowest possible interest rate: it is, therefore, willing to take a floating-rate loan. (Rates on floating-rate loans are generally lower than rates on fixed-rate loans. Why?) Both firms could accomplish their objectives by agreeing to exchange loan payments: in other words, the two firms would make each other's loan payments. This is an example of an *interest rate swap*; what is really being exchanged is a floating interest rate for a fixed one.

Interest rate swaps and currency swaps are often combined. One firm obtains floating-rate financing in a particular currency and swaps it for fixed-rate financing in another currency. Also, note that payments on floating-rate loans are always based on some index, such as the one-year Treasury rate. An interest rate swap might involve exchanging one floating-rate loan for another as a way of changing the underlying index.

COMMODITY SWAPS

As the name suggests, a *commodity swap* is an agreement to exchange a fixed quantity of a commodity at fixed times in the future. For example, airlines hedge fuel costs using jet fuel swaps. Commodity swaps are the newest type of swap, and the market for them is small relative to that for other types. However, the growth potential is enormous.

Swap contracts for oil have been engineered. For example, say that an oil user needs 20,000 barrels every quarter. The oil user could enter into a swap contract with an oil producer to supply the needed oil. What price would they agree on? As we mentioned previously, they can't fix a price forever. Instead, they could agree that the price would be equal to the *average* daily oil price from the previous 90 days. As a result of their using an average price, the impact of the relatively large daily price fluctuations in the oil market would be reduced, and both firms would benefit from a reduction in transactions exposure.

THE SWAP DEALER

Unlike futures contracts, swap contracts are not traded on organized exchanges. The main reason is that they are not sufficiently standardized. Instead, the *swap dealer* plays a key role in the swaps market. In the absence of a swap dealer, a firm that wished to enter into a swap would have to track down another firm that wanted the opposite end of the deal. This search would probably be expensive and time-consuming.

Instead, a firm wishing to enter into a swap agreement contacts a swap dealer, and the swap dealer takes the other side of the agreement. The swap dealer will then try to find an offsetting transaction with some other party or parties (perhaps another firm or another dealer). Failing this, a swap dealer will hedge its exposure using futures contracts.

Banks are the dominant swap dealers in Europe. As a large swap dealer, a bank would be involved in a variety of contracts. It would be swapping fixed-rate loans for floating-rate loans with some parties, and doing just the opposite with other participants. The total collection of contracts in which a dealer is involved is called the swap *book*. The dealer will try to keep a balanced book to limit its net exposure. A balanced book is often called a *matched* book.

INTEREST RATE SWAPS: AN EXAMPLE

To get a better understanding of swap contracts and the swap dealer's role, we consider a floating-for-fixed interest rate swap. Suppose Company A can borrow at a floating rate equal to EURIBOR plus 1 per cent, or at a fixed rate of 10 per cent. Company B can borrow at a floating rate of EURIBOR plus 2 per cent, or at a fixed rate of 9.5 per cent. Company A desires a fixed-rate loan, whereas Company B desires a floating-rate loan. Clearly, a swap is in order.

Company A contacts a swap dealer, and a deal is struck. Company A borrows the money at a rate of EURIBOR plus 1 per cent. The swap dealer agrees to cover the loan payments; in exchange, the company agrees to make fixed-rate payments to the swap dealer at a rate of, say, 9.75 per cent. Notice that the swap dealer is making floating-rate payments and receiving fixed-rate payments. The company is making fixed-rate payments, so it has swapped a floating payment for a fixed one.

Company B also contacts a swap dealer. The deal here calls for Company B to borrow the money at a fixed rate of 9.5 per cent. The swap dealer agrees to cover the fixed loan payments, and the company agrees to make floating-rate payments to the swap dealer at a rate of EURIBOR plus, say, 1.5 per cent. In this second arrangement, the swap dealer is making fixed-rate payments and receiving floating-rate payments.

What's the net effect of these machinations? First, Company A gets a fixed-rate loan at a rate of 9.75 per cent, which is cheaper than the 10 per cent rate it can obtain on its own. Second, Company B gets a floating-rate loan at EURIBOR plus 1.5 instead of EURIBOR plus 2. The swap benefits both companies.

The swap dealer also wins. When all the dust settles, the swap dealer receives (from Company A) fixed-rate payments at a rate of 9.75 per cent and makes fixed-rate payments (for Company B) at a rate of 9.5 per cent. At the same time, it makes floating-rate payments (for Company A) at a rate of EURIBOR plus 1 per cent and receives floating-rate payments at a rate of EURIBOR plus 1.5 per cent (from Company B). Notice that the swap dealer's book is perfectly balanced in terms of risk, and it has no exposure to interest rate volatility.

Figure 20.9 illustrates the transactions in our interest rate swap. Note that the essence of the swap transactions is that one company swaps a fixed payment for a floating payment, while the other exchanges a floating payment for a fixed one. The swap dealer acts as an intermediary and profits from the spread between the rates it charges and the rates it receives.

FIGURE 20.9 Illustration of an interest rate swap

Company A borrows at EURIBOR plus 1% and swaps for a 9.75% fixed rate.
Company B borrows at 9.5% fixed and swaps for a EURIBOR plus 1.5% floating rate.

> **CONCEPT QUESTIONS**
>
> **20.5a** What is a swap contract? Describe three types.
> **20.5b** Describe the role of the swap dealer.
> **20.5c** Explain the cash flows in Figure 20.9.

20.6 HEDGING WITH OPTION CONTRACTS

The contracts we have discussed thus far – forwards, futures and swaps – are conceptually similar. In each case, two parties agree to transact on a future date or dates. The key is that both parties are obligated to complete the transaction.

In contrast, an **option contract** is an agreement that gives the owner the right, but not the obligation, to buy or sell (depending on the option type) some asset at a specified price for a specified time. Options are covered in detail in Chapter 21. Here we shall only quickly discuss some options basics, and then focus on using options to hedge volatility in commodity prices, interest rates and exchange rates. In doing so, we shall sidestep a wealth of detail concerning option terminology, option trading strategies and option valuation.

option contract
an agreement that gives the owner the right, but not the obligation, to buy or sell a specific asset at a specific price for a set period of time.

OPTION TERMINOLOGY

Options come in two flavours: puts and calls. The owner of a **call option** has the right, but not the obligation, to *buy* an underlying asset at a fixed price, called the *strike price* or *exercise price*, for a specified time. The owner of a **put option** has the right, but not the obligation, to sell an underlying asset at a fixed price for a specified time.

The act of buying or selling the underlying asset using the option contract is called *exercising* the option. Some options ('American' options) can be exercised at any time up to and including the *expiration date* (the last day); other options ('European' options) can be exercised only on the expiration date. Most options are American.

Because the buyer of a call option has the right to buy the underlying asset by paying the strike price, the seller of a call option is obligated to deliver the asset and accept the strike price if the option is exercised. Similarly, the put option buyer has the right to sell the underlying asset and receive the strike price. In this case, the seller of the put option must accept the asset and pay the strike price.

call option
an option that gives the owner the right, but not the obligation, to buy an asset at a fixed price during a particular period.

put option
an option that gives the owner the right, but not the obligation, to sell an asset. The opposite of a call option.

OPTIONS VERSUS FORWARDS

There are two key differences between an options contract and a forward contract. The first is obvious. With a forward contract, both parties are obligated to transact; one party delivers the asset, and the other party pays for it. With an option, the transaction occurs only if the owner of the option chooses to exercise it.

The second difference between an option and a forward contract is that no money changes hands when a forward contract is created, but the buyer of an option contract gains a valuable right and must pay the seller for that right. The price of the option is frequently called the *option premium*.

OPTION PAY-OFF PROFILES

Figure 20.10 shows the general pay-off profile for a call option from the owner's viewpoint. The horizontal axis shows the difference between the asset's value and the strike price on the option (ΔP). As illustrated, if the price of the underlying asset rises above the strike price, then the option's owner will exercise the option and enjoy a profit (ΔV). If the asset's value falls below the strike price, the owner of the option will not exercise it. Notice that this pay-off profile does not consider the premium that the buyer paid for the option.

FIGURE 20.10

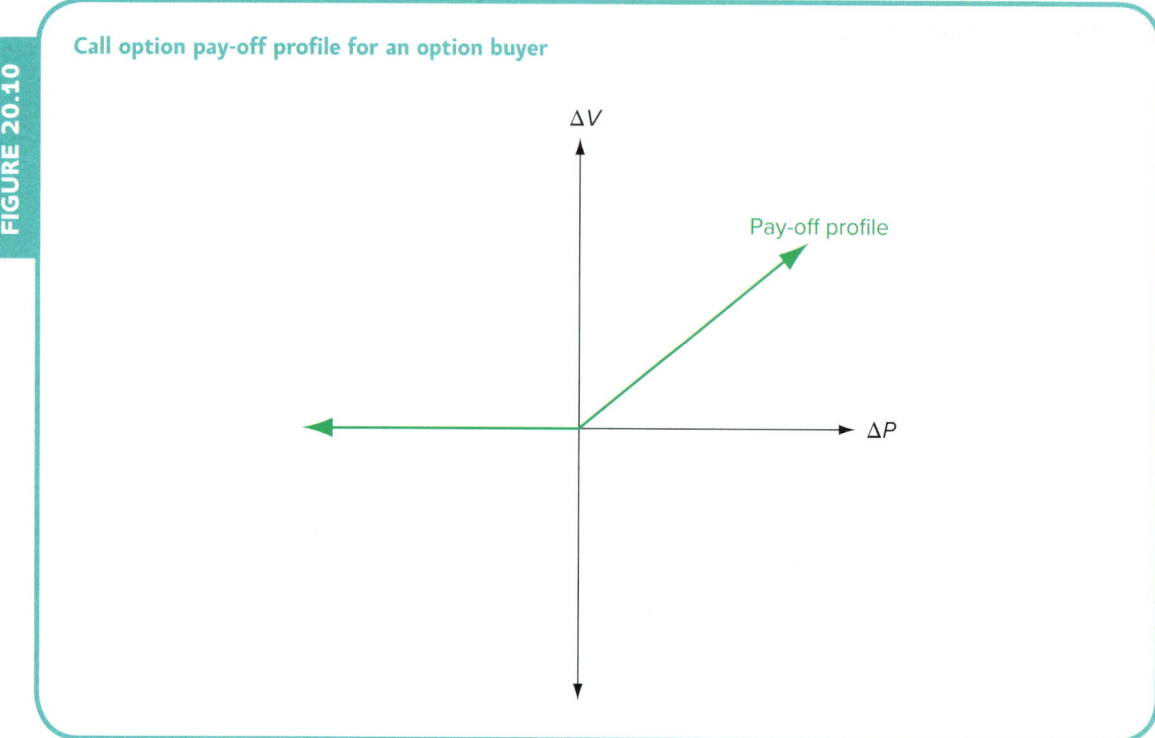

Call option pay-off profile for an option buyer

The pay-off profile that results from buying a call is repeated in Part A of Figure 20.11. Part B shows the pay-off profile on a call option from the seller's side. A call option is a zero-sum game, so the seller's pay-off profile is exactly the opposite of the buyer's.

Part C of Figure 20.11 shows the pay-off profile for the buyer of a put option. In this case, if the asset's value falls below the strike price, then the buyer profits because the seller of the put must pay the strike price. Part D shows that the seller of the put option loses out when the price falls below the strike price.

FIGURE 20.11

Option pay-off profiles

OPTION HEDGING

Suppose a firm has a risk profile that looks like the one in Part A of Figure 20.12. If the firm wishes to hedge against adverse price movements using options, what should it do? Examining the different pay-off profiles in Figure 20.11, we see that the one with the desired shape is C, buying a put. If the firm buys a put, its net exposure is as illustrated in Part B of Figure 20.12.

FIGURE 20.12

Hedging with options

A. The unhedged risk profile

B. The hedged risk profile
The hedged profile is created by purchasing a put option, thereby eliminating the downside risk.

In this case, by buying a put option, the firm has eliminated the downside risk, which is the risk of an adverse price movement. However, the firm has retained the upside potential. In other words, the put option acts as a kind of insurance policy. Remember that this desirable insurance is not free: the firm pays for it when it buys the put option.

HEDGING COMMODITY PRICE RISK WITH OPTIONS

We saw earlier that futures contracts are available for a variety of basic commodities. In addition, an increasing number of options are available on these same commodities. In fact, the options that are typically traded on commodities are actually options on futures contracts: for this reason, they are called *futures options*.

These work as follows. When a futures call option on, for example, wheat is exercised, the owner of the option receives two things. The first is a futures contract on wheat at the current futures price. This contract can be immediately closed at no cost. The second thing the owner of the option receives is the difference between the strike price on the option and the current futures price. The difference is simply paid in cash.

HEDGING EXCHANGE RATE RISK WITH OPTIONS

Futures options are available on foreign currencies as well as on commodities. These work in exactly the same way as commodities futures options. In addition, there are other traded options for which the underlying asset is just currency rather than a futures contract on a currency. Firms with significant exposure to exchange rate risk frequently purchase put options to protect against adverse exchange rate changes.

SUSTAINABILITY IN FINANCE

As investors focus more on sustainable investment, and specifically companies with strong environmental, social and governance objectives, it is not surprising that derivatives contracts have sprung up to take advantage of this heightened interest. What is surprising is the enormous success of these instruments.

For example, the derivatives exchange, Eurex, launched a range of sustainable derivatives offerings in 2019 to cover sustainable investments in five regions: the US, emerging markets, developed markets, Canada and Japan. These instruments have become exceptionally popular with traders who are more sophisticated in their asset class risk preferences, and wish to differentiate between types of companies (such as sustainable firms) within broad asset classes.

The ESG derivatives, as they are known, reached daily record trading volumes in early 2021, with 104,000 contracts traded on one day in February alone. Within two years of launching the ESG derivatives, more than 2 million ESG contracts were traded on the Eurex exchange.

HEDGING INTEREST RATE RISK WITH OPTIONS

The use of options to hedge against interest rate risk is a widespread practice, and there are a variety of options available to serve this purpose. Some are futures options like the ones we have been discussing, and these trade on organized exchanges. Beyond this, there is a thriving over-the-counter market in interest rate options. We shall describe some of these options in this section.

A Preliminary Note

Some interest rate options are actually options on interest-bearing assets such as bonds (or on futures contracts for bonds). Most of the options that are traded on exchanges fall into this category. As we shall discuss in a moment, some others are actually options on interest rates. The distinction is important if we are thinking about using one type or the other to hedge. To illustrate, suppose we want to protect ourselves against an increase in interest rates using options: what should we do?

We need to buy an option that increases in value as interest rates go up. One thing we can do is buy a *put* option on a bond. Why a put? Remember that when interest rates go up, bond values go down; so one way to hedge against interest rate increases is to buy put options on bonds. The other way to hedge is to buy a *call* option on interest rates. We discuss this alternative in more detail in the next section.

We actually saw interest rate options in Chapter 6 when we discussed the call feature on a bond. Remember that the call provision gives the issuer the right to buy back the bond at a set price, known as the *call price*. What happens is that if interest rates fall, the bond's price will rise. If it rises above the call price, the issuer will exercise the option and acquire the bond at a bargain price. Thus, the call provision can be viewed as either a call option on a bond or a put option on interest rates.

Interest Rate Caps

An interest rate cap is a call option on an interest rate. Suppose a firm has a floating-rate loan. It is concerned that interest rates will rise sharply, and the firm will experience financial distress because of the increased loan payment. To guard against this, the firm can purchase an interest rate cap from a bank (there are banks that specialize in such products). What will happen is that if the loan payment ever rises above an agreed-upon limit (the 'ceiling'), the bank will pay the difference between the actual payment and the ceiling to the firm in cash.

A *floor* is a put option on an interest rate. If a firm buys a cap and sells a floor, the result is a *collar*. By selling the put and buying the call, the firm protects itself against increases in interest rates beyond the ceiling by the cap. However, if interest rates drop below the floor, the put will be exercised against the firm. The result is that the rate the firm pays will not drop below the floor rate. In other words, the rate the firm pays will always be between the floor and the ceiling.

Other Interest Rate Options

We shall close our chapter by briefly mentioning two relatively new types of interest rate option. Suppose a firm has a floating-rate loan. The firm is comfortable with its floating-rate loan, but it would like to have the right to convert it to a fixed-rate loan in the future.

What can the firm do? It wants the right, but not the obligation, to swap its floating-rate loan for a fixed-rate loan. In other words, the firm needs to buy an option on a swap. Swap options exist, and they have the charming name *swaptions*.

We've seen that there are options on futures contracts and options on swap contracts, but what about options on options? Such options are called *compound* options. As we have just discussed, a cap is a call option on interest rates. Suppose a firm thinks that, depending on interest rates, it might like to buy a cap in the future. As you can probably guess, in this case, what the firm might want to do today is buy an option on a cap. Inevitably, it seems, an option on a cap is called a *caption*, and there is a large market for these instruments.

FINANCIAL RISK MANAGEMENT IN PRACTICE

Because the true extent of derivatives does not usually appear in financial statements, it is much more difficult to observe the use of derivatives by firms compared to, say, bank debt. Much of our knowledge of corporate derivative use comes from academic surveys. Most surveys report that the use of derivatives appears to vary widely among large publicly traded firms. Large firms are far more likely to use derivatives than are small firms. Table 20.1 shows the percentage of firms worldwide that use derivatives, where it can be seen that foreign currency and interest rate derivatives are most popular.

TABLE 20.1

Derivative usage around the world (% of all firms)

	Number of firms	% of firms using derivatives	Hedging intensity	FX General	FX Forward	FX Swap	FX Option	Interest Rate General	Interest Rate Forward	Interest Rate Swap	Interest Rate Option	Commodity Price General	Commodity Price Futures	Commodity Price Swaps	Commodity Price Options
Austria	41	56.1	1.3	56.1	43.9	17.1	22	22	0	17.1	7.3	7.3	2.4	4.9	2.4
Belgium	60	50	0.8	36.7	26.7	8.3	6.7	23.3	0	21.7	3.3	3.3	0	1.7	0
China	32	12.5	0.2	6.3	6.3	3.1	0	3.1	0	3.1	0	3.1	3.1	0	0
Denmark	80	87.5	1.5	80	72.5	12.5	18.8	26.3	1.3	21.3	6.3	5	1.3	2.5	1.3
Finland	100	64	1.7	58	45	18	27	37	9	29	17	8	3	1	3
France	159	66	1.6	52.8	37.1	22.6	25.8	44.7	1.9	38.4	15.1	3.8	1.3	1.3	0.6
Germany	395	47.1	1	39	27.3	10.6	12.4	24.1	1.8	17.7	9.4	4.8	1.8	0.5	0.5
Greece	19	21.1	0.5	21.1	10.5	5.3	5.3	10.5	0	10.5	0	5.3	5.3	0	0
India	40	70	0.9	62.5	60	7.5	0	12.5	0	12.5	0	5	2.5	0	0
Ireland	47	85.1	1.9	70.2	61.7	27.7	8.5	53.2	4.3	46.8	8.5	14.9	2.1	6.4	4.3
Italy	93	61.3	1	38.7	29	16.1	3.2	33.3	3.2	23.7	3.2	2.2	1.1	2.2	0
Malaysia	289	20.1	0.2	16.3	12.5	1.4	0.7	4.2	0	3.8	1	1	0.7	0	0
Netherlands	131	56.5	1.2	48.1	38.9	18.3	12.2	33.6	1.5	27.5	9.2	4.6	0.8	0.8	0.8
Norway	85	67.1	1.4	56.5	48.2	17.6	17.6	29.4	2.4	24.7	5.9	8.2	2.4	0	3.5
Poland	11	45.5	1.1	36.4	18.2	18.2	27.3	18.2	9.1	9.1	9.1	9.1	0	0	0
Singapore	219	55.3	0.8	50.7	42.5	5.9	3.7	11.4	0.5	9.6	1.8	2.3	0	1.8	0
South Africa	55	89.1	1.7	89.1	87.3	9.1	14.5	38.2	0	32.7	5.5	14.5	5.5	0	1.8
Spain	29	62.1	1.5	37.9	27.6	10.3	10.3	37.9	3.4	34.5	13.8	20.7	6.9	6.9	6.9
Sweden	135	63.7	0.9	45.2	35.6	7.4	8.1	13.3	2.2	9.6	2.2	4.4	0.7	0.7	1.5
Switzerland	119	77.3	1.6	68.1	61.3	14.3	23.5	42.9	3.4	35.3	7.6	5.9	0.8	0.8	0.8
United Kingdom	860	64.4	1.3	55	49.4	17.1	7.8	36.5	0.6	32.1	10.8	3.7	1.5	1.4	0.7
United States	2,076	65.1	1.2	37.8	30.9	6.4	7.5	40.4	0.7	36	6.8	16.1	6	5.2	3.3
Europe	2,421	61.5	1.3	51.1	42.3	15.3	12.5	32.3	1.8	26.9	9.2	5	1.6	1.4	1
All firms	6,896	60.5	1.2	45.5	37.9	11.2	9.8	33.1	1.1	29.1	7.4	9.8	3	2.9	2.3

Note: Hedging intensity is the number of instruments used by an average firm.

Source: Adapted from Bartram (2019), Table A-2.

The prevailing view is that derivatives can help reduce the variability of corporate cash flows, which in turn reduces the various costs associated with financial distress. Therefore it is somewhat puzzling that large firms use derivatives more often than small firms – because large firms tend to have less cash flow variability than small firms. Also, some surveys report that firms occasionally use derivatives when they want to speculate about future prices and not just to hedge risks. However, most of the evidence is consistent with the theory that derivatives are most frequently used by firms where financial distress costs are high, and access to the capital markets is constrained.

> **CONCEPT QUESTIONS**
>
> **20.6a** Suppose that the unhedged risk profile in Figure 20.12 sloped down instead of up. What options-based hedging strategy would be suitable in this case?
> **20.6b** What is a futures option?
> **20.6c** What is a caption? Who might want to buy one?

SUMMARY AND CONCLUSIONS

This chapter has introduced some of the basic principles of financial risk management.

1. The motivation for risk management stems from the fact that a firm will frequently have an undesirable exposure to some type of risk.
2. We describe a firm's exposure to a particular risk with a risk profile.
3. The goal of financial risk management is to alter the firm's risk profile through buying and selling derivative assets such as futures contracts, swap contracts and options contracts.
4. By finding instruments with appropriate pay-off profiles, a firm can reduce or even eliminate its exposure to many types of risk.
5. Hedging cannot change the fundamental economic reality of a business. What it can do is allow a firm to avoid expensive and troublesome disruptions that might otherwise result from short-run, temporary price fluctuations.
6. Hedging gives a firm time to react and adapt to changing market conditions.

Many other option types are available in addition to those we have discussed, and more are created every day. One very important aspect of financial risk management that we have not discussed is that options, forwards, futures and swaps can be combined in a wide variety of ways to create new instruments. These basic contract types are really just the building blocks used by financial engineers to create new and innovative products for corporate risk management.

CHAPTER REVIEW AND SELF-TEST QUESTIONS

20.1 Futures Contracts Suppose Golden Grain Farms (GGF) expects to harvest 50,000 bushels of wheat in September. GGF is concerned about the possibility of price fluctuations between now and September. The futures price for September wheat is £2 per bushel, and the relevant contract calls for 5,000 bushels. What action should GGF take to lock in the £2 price? Suppose the price of wheat actually turns out to be £3. Evaluate GGF's gains and losses. Do the same for a price of £1. Ignore marking to market.

20.2 Options Contracts In the previous question, suppose that September futures put options with a strike price of £2 per bushel cost £0.15 per bushel. Assuming that GGF hedges using put options, evaluate its gains and losses for wheat prices of £1, £2 and £3.

SOLUTIONS

20.1 GGF wants to deliver wheat and receive a fixed price, so it needs to sell futures contracts. Each contract calls for delivery of 5,000 bushels, so GGF needs to sell 10 contracts. No money changes hands today. If wheat prices actually turn out to be £3, then GGF will receive £150,000 for its crop; but it will have a loss of £50,000 on its futures position when it closes that position, because the contracts require it to sell 50,000 bushels of wheat at £2, when the going price is £3. It thus nets £100,000 overall. If wheat prices turn out to be £1 per bushel, then the crop will be worth only £50,000. However, GGF will have a profit of £50,000 on its futures position, so GGF again nets £100,000.

20.2 If GGF wants to insure against a price decline only, it can buy 10 put contracts. Each contract is for 5,000 bushels, so the cost per contract is 5,000 × £0.15 = £750. For 10 contracts, the cost will be £7,500. If wheat prices turn out to be £3, then GGF will not exercise the put options (why not?). Its crop is worth £150,000, but the £7,500 cost of the options has already been incurred, so it nets £142,500. If wheat prices fall to £1, the crop is worth £50,000. GGF will exercise its puts (why?) and thereby force the seller of the puts to pay £2 per bushel. GGF receives a total of £100,000. If we subtract the cost of the puts, we see that GGF's net is £92,500. In fact, verify that its net at any price of £2 or lower is £92,500.

QUESTIONS AND PROBLEMS

20.1 **Swaps** Giving Back Food Banks (GBFB) is an international marketing firm that runs promotions to raise money that is then reinvested in food banks in Eastern Europe. It has announced that it has entered into an interest rate swap, which converts the company's €100 million, 4.9 per cent interest rate bonds for a variable-rate payment, which is the six-month EURIBOR plus 1.26 per cent. Why would GBFB use a swap agreement? In other words, why doesn't GBFB just go ahead and issue floating-rate bonds, because the net effect of issuing fixed-rate bonds and then doing a swap is to create a variable-rate bond?

20.2 **Futures Quotes** Suppose you purchased a June Live Cattle futures contract on 4 March at $1.00 per lb. What would your profit or loss have been if Live Cattle prices turn out to be $1.20 per lb at expiration?

20.3 **Futures Quotes** Suppose you sell five April high grade copper futures contracts on 4 March at $350 each. What will your per contract profit or loss be if copper prices turn out to be $400 at expiration? What if copper prices are $300 at expiration?

20.4 **Trading with Futures: Marking to Market** You are long 10 gold futures contracts, established at an initial settle price of €1,000 per ounce, where each contract represents 100 ounces. Over the subsequent 4 trading days, gold settles at €1,003, €1,009, €1,012 and €1,004, respectively. Compute the cash flows at the end of each trading day. Compute your total profit or loss at the end of the trading period.

20.5 **Put and Call Pay-offs** Suppose a financial manager buys call options on 1,000 troy ounces of 22 carat gold with the same exercise price of $1,800 per 100 troy ounces. They simultaneously sell a put option on 1,000 troy ounces of 22 carat gold with the same exercise price of $1,800 per 100 troy ounces. Consider their gains and losses if gold prices are $1,600, $1,700, $1,800, $1,900 and $2,000. What do you notice about the pay-off profile?

20.6 Hedging with Futures Suppose today is 16 April, and your firm produces chocolate and needs 75,000 tonnes of cocoa in July for an upcoming promotion. You would like to lock in your costs today because you are concerned that cocoa prices might go up between now and July. The closing price for July futures is £1,468 per tonne of cocoa. Each contract is for the delivery of 10 tonnes of cocoa. How could you use cocoa futures contracts to hedge your risk exposure? Suppose cocoa prices are £1,500 per contract in July. What is the profit or loss on your futures position? Explain how your futures position has eliminated your exposure to price risk in the cocoa market.

20.7 Hedging with Futures Suppose today is 17 February, your firm produces chocolate and needs 10,000 tonnes of cocoa in July for an upcoming promotion. The July cocoa futures price is £1,639 per tonne. You would like to lock in your costs today, because you are concerned that cocoa prices might go up between now and July.

(a) How could you use cocoa futures contracts to hedge your risk exposure? What price would you effectively be locking in, based on the closing price of the day?

(b) Suppose cocoa prices are £1,700 per tonne in July. What is the profit or loss on your futures position? Explain how your futures position has eliminated your exposure to price risk in the cocoa market.

20.8 Interest Rate Swaps ABC Company and XYZ Company need to raise funds to pay for capital improvements at their manufacturing plants. ABC Company is a well-established firm with an excellent credit rating in the debt market; it can borrow funds either at 11 per cent fixed rate or at EURIBOR +1 per cent floating rate. XYZ Company is a fledgling start-up firm without a strong credit history. It can borrow funds either at 10 per cent fixed rate or at EURIBOR +3 per cent floating rate.

(a) Is there an opportunity here for ABC and XYZ to benefit by means of an interest rate swap?

(b) Suppose you've just been hired at a bank that acts as a dealer in the swaps market, and your boss has shown you the borrowing rate information for your clients ABC and XYZ. Describe how you could bring these two companies together in an interest rate swap that would make both firms better off while netting your bank a 2.0 per cent profit.

20.9 Financial Engineering Suppose there were call options and forward contracts available on wind energy, but no put options. Show how a financial engineer could create a put option using the available contracts. What does your answer tell you about the general relationship between puts, calls and forwards?

20.10 Hedging You are the finance director of a British company, which is expecting a payment of €200 million at the end of September and wishes to hedge against currency risk. However, the nearest maturity date for a euro futures contract is on 13 December and it is now 29 January. The face value of one euro futures contract is €100,000. The spot rate today is £0.9/€ and the futures rate is £0.85/€.

(a) Estimate the number of futures contracts required.

(b) Assume that at the end of September, the spot rate turns out to be £0.95/€ and a futures contract taken out at the end of September to expire on 13 December is quoted at £0.92/€. Estimate the total gain or loss earned by your company.

(c) Estimate the effective exchange rate received by your company.

20.11 Swaps Consider two firms, Yakwanza plc and Yamwisho plc. Yakwanza plc has a better credit rating and can borrow cheaper than Yamwisho plc in both fixed- and floating-rate markets. Specifically, Yakwanza plc pays 4 per cent fixed and €STR plus 1 per cent floating. Yamwisho plc pays 6 per cent fixed and €STR plus 2 per cent floating. If Yakwanza plc prefers to borrow floating and Yamwisho plc prefers to borrow fixed, determine the spread differential that they will split if they do a swap with each other.

20.12 Swaps Construct a swap in which both Yakwanza plc and Yamwisho plc (see Problem 20.11) can exploit a comparative advantage belonging to one of the firms. Your answer should include a swap diagram and a description of the cash flows transferred as a result of the swap.

MINI CASE

MCAFEE MORTGAGES LTD

Jennifer McAfee recently received her university Master's degree, and has decided to enter the mortgage brokerage business. Rather than work for someone else, she has decided to open her own shop. Her cousin Finn has approached her about a mortgage for a house he is building. The house will be completed in 3 months, and he will need the mortgage at that time. Finn wants a 25-year, fixed-rate mortgage for the amount of £500,000 with monthly payments.

Jennifer has agreed to lend Finn the money in 3 months at the current market rate of 8 per cent. Because Jennifer is just starting out, she does not have £500,000 available for the loan, so she approaches Ian MacDuff, the president of IM Insurance, about purchasing the mortgage from her in 3 months. Ian has agreed to purchase the mortgage in 3 months, but he is unwilling to set a price on the mortgage. Instead, he has agreed in writing to purchase the mortgage at the market rate in 3 months. There are Treasury bond futures contracts available for delivery in 3 months. A Treasury bond contract is for £100,000 in face value of Treasury bonds.

QUESTIONS

1. What is the monthly mortgage payment on Finn's mortgage?
2. What is the most significant risk Jennifer faces in this deal?
3. How can Jennifer hedge this risk?
4. Suppose that in the next 3 months the market rate of interest rises to 9 per cent.
   (a) How much will Ian be willing to pay for the mortgage?
   (b) What will happen to the value of Treasury bond futures contracts? Will the long or short position increase in value?
5. Suppose that in the next 3 months the market rate of interest falls to 7 per cent.
   (a) How much will Ian be willing to pay for the mortgage?
   (b) What will happen to the value of T-bond futures contracts? Will the long or short position increase in value?
6. Are there any possible risks Jennifer faces in using Treasury bond futures contracts to hedge her interest rate risk?

ADDITIONAL READING

The following papers look at corporate hedging activities and the way in which firms use financial derivatives to manage risk.

1. Aretz, K., & Bartram, S.M. (2010). Corporate hedging and shareholder value. *Journal of Financial Research, 33*(4), 317–371.
2. Bartram, S.M., Brown, G.W., & Fehle, F.R. (2009). International evidence on financial derivatives usage. *Financial Management, 38*(1), 185–206.
3. Bartram, S.M. (2019). Corporate hedging and speculation with derivatives. *Journal of Corporate Finance, 57*, 9–34.
4. Campello, M., Lin, C., Ma, Y., & Zou, H. (2011). The real and financial implications of corporate hedging. *Journal of Finance, 66*(5), 1615–1647.
5. Guay, W., & Kothari, S.P. (2003). How much do firms hedge with derivatives? *Journal of Financial Economics, 70*(3), 423–461.
6. Lel, U. (2012). Currency hedging and corporate governance: A cross-country analysis. *Journal of Corporate Finance, 18*(2), 221–237.

Endnotes

1. Financial risk management is a complex topic. If you wish to explore this topic further, a good place to start is D. Hillier, S. Ross, R. Westerfield, J. Jaffe and B. Jordan (2020) *Corporate Finance*, 4th edn. McGraw Hill.
2. For further discussion on this topic, I again direct you to Hillier et al., *Corporate Finance*, 4th edn.

CHAPTER 21
OPTIONS AND CORPORATE FINANCE

LEARNING OBJECTIVES
After studying this chapter, you should understand:

LO1 The basics of call and put options and how to calculate their pay-offs and profits.
LO2 The factors that affect option values and how to price call and put options using no-arbitrage conditions.
LO3 The relationship between stock prices, call prices and put prices using put-call parity.
LO4 The famous Black–Scholes option pricing model and its uses.
LO5 The basics of employee stock options and their benefits and disadvantages.
LO6 How to value a firm's equity as an option on the firm's assets.
LO7 How option valuation can be used to evaluate capital budgeting projects, including timing options, the option to expand, the option to abandon, and the option to contract.

KEY NOTATIONS

C	Call price
$N(d)$	Probability that a standardized, normally distributed, random variable will be less than or equal to d
P	Put price
$PV(E)$	Present value of exercise price
R_f	Risk-free rate of return
S	Equity or share price
t	Time (in years) to the expiration date
σ^2	Variance (per year) of the continuous share price return

MANY COMPANIES have now stopped issuing employee share options and moved to restricted stock units (RSUs). An RSU is a share of equity that can't be sold or exchanged until it is vested. The vesting period can vary but is usually between 3 and 5 years. When an RSU vests, the employee receives a full share of the equity. The biggest advantage of RSUs for employees is that they receive the equity no matter the share price. With employee share options, on the other hand, the employee may receive nothing.

Employee share options are just one kind of option. This chapter introduces you to options and explains their features and what determines their value. The chapter also shows you that options show up in many places in corporate finance. In fact, once you know what to look for, they show up just about everywhere, so understanding how they work is essential.

CHAPTER 21 Options and Corporate Finance

> **option**
> a contract that gives its owner the right to buy or sell some asset at a fixed price on or before a given date.

Options are a part of everyday life. 'Keep your options open' is sound business advice and 'We're out of options' is a sure sign of trouble. In Chapter 20, we showed that an **option** is an arrangement that gives its owner the right to buy or sell an asset at a fixed price any time on or before a given date. The most familiar options are equity options. These are options to buy and sell shares of equity, and we shall discuss them in some detail in the following pages.

Of course, equity options are not the only options. In fact, at their root, many different kinds of financial decisions amount to evaluating options. We shall show how understanding options adds several important details to the NPV analysis covered in earlier chapters.

Also, virtually all corporate securities have implicit or explicit option features, and the use of such features is growing. As a result, understanding securities that possess option features requires a general knowledge of the factors determining an option's value.

This chapter starts with a description of different types of option. We identify and discuss the general factors that determine option values and show how ordinary debt and equity have option-like characteristics. We then examine employee share options and the important role of options in capital budgeting. We conclude by illustrating how option features are incorporated into corporate securities by discussing warrants, convertible bonds and other option-like securities.[1]

21.1 OPTIONS: THE BASICS

> **exercising the option**
> the act of buying or selling the underlying asset via the option contract.
>
> **strike price**
> the fixed price in the option contract at which the holder can buy or sell the underlying asset. Also, the *exercise price* or *striking price*.
>
> **expiration date**
> the last day on which an option may be exercised.
>
> **American option**
> an option that may be exercised at any time until its expiration date.
>
> **European option**
> an option that may be exercised only on the expiration date.

An option is a contract giving its owner the right to buy or sell an asset at a fixed price on or before a given date. For example, an option on a building might give the buyer the right to buy the building for €1 million on or any time before the Saturday before the third Wednesday in January 2020. Options are a unique type of financial contract because they give the buyer the right, but not the obligation, to do something. The buyer uses the option only if it is advantageous to do so; otherwise, the option can be thrown away.

There is a special vocabulary associated with options. Here are some important definitions:

1. **Exercising the option**: The act of buying or selling the underlying asset via the option contract.
2. **Strike or exercise price**: The fixed price in the option contract at which the holder can buy or sell the underlying asset.
3. **Expiration date**: The maturity date of the option; after this date, the option is dead.
4. **American** and **European option**: An American option may be exercised at any time up to the expiration date. A European option differs from an American option in that it can be exercised only on the expiration date.

PUTS AND CALLS

Options come in two basic types: puts and calls. A call option gives the owner the right to *buy* an asset at a fixed price during a particular time period. It may help you remember that a call option gives you the right to 'call in' an asset.

A put option is essentially the opposite of a call option. Instead of giving the holder the right to buy some asset, it gives the holder the right to *sell* that asset for a fixed exercise price. If you buy a put option, you can force the seller of the option to buy the asset from you for a fixed price and thereby 'put it to them'.

What about an investor who *sells* a call option? The seller receives money up front and has an *obligation* to sell the asset at the exercise price if the option holder wants it. Similarly, an investor who *sells* a put option receives cash upfront and is then obligated to buy the asset at the exercise price if the option holder demands it.

The asset involved in an option can be anything. The options that are most widely bought and sold, however, are equity options. These are options to buy and sell shares of equity. Because these are the best-known types of option, we shall study them first. As we discuss equity options, keep in mind that the general principles apply to options involving any asset, not just shares of equity.

OPTION QUOTATIONS

Now that we understand the definitions for calls and puts, let's see how these options are quoted. Table 21.1 presents information, obtained from the NYSE Euronext website (www.euronext.com), about Air France-KLM options expiring in March 2021. At the time of these quotes Air France-KLM was selling for €4.92.

Each option contract relates to purchasing 100 shares. Notice that for every exercise price, there are two options: puts (P) and calls (C). Notice how the option premiums increase as the option becomes more 'in the money'; that is, when the pay-off on the option, Max[0, S-X], is higher.

TABLE 21.1

Option information for Air France-KLM Corporation

MARCH 2021 PRICES – 22/02/21

SETTL	LAST	BID	ASK		STRIKE		BID	ASK	LAST	SETTL.
0.59	-	0.57	0.64	C	4.40	P	0.06	0.12	0.09	0.09
0.52	-	0.49	0.56	C	4.50	P	0.08	0.14	-	0.11
0.44	-	0.42	0.48	C	4.60	P	0.11	0.16	-	0.14
0.38	-	0.35	0.41	C	4.70	P	0.14	0.20	-	0.18
0.32	-	0.29	0.35	C	4.80	P	0.18	0.23	-	0.22
0.27	-	0.23	0.29	C	4.90	P	0.22	0.28	-	0.27
0.22	-	0.19	0.22	C	5.00	P	0.28	0.33	-	0.33
0.15	0.15	0.11	0.16	C	5.20	P	0.40	0.46	-	0.45
0.09	-	0.06	0.12	C	5.40	P	0.55	0.62	-	0.59
0.07	-	0.05	0.10	C	5.50	P	0.64	0.70	-	0.67
0.02	-	-	0.05	C	6.00	P	-	1.16	-	1.12

Source: Data from NYSE Euronext.

OPTION PAY-OFFS

Suppose you buy 50 Iberdrola April €8.00 call option contracts. Today is 8 March, Iberdrola is selling for €7.69, and the option closed at €0.10. You wish to buy, so the contracts cost €10 each (a call contract is for 100 shares). You spend a total of 50 × €10 = €500. You wait a while, and the expiration date rolls around.

Now what? You have the right to buy Iberdrola shares for €8.00 each. If Iberdrola is selling for less than €8.00 a share, then this option isn't worth anything, and you throw it away. In this case, we say the option has expired 'out of the money' because the share price is less than the exercise price. Your €500 is, alas, a complete loss.

If Iberdrola is selling for more than €8.00 per share, you need to exercise your option. In this case, the option is 'in the money' because the share price exceeds the exercise price.

Suppose Iberdrola has risen to, say, €10 per share. Because you have the right to buy Iberdrola at €8, you make a €2 profit on each share upon exercise. Each contract involves 100 shares, so you make €2 per share × 100 shares per contract = €200 per contract. Finally, you own 50 contracts, so the value of your options is a handsome €10,000. Notice that because you invested €500, your net profit is €9,500.

As our example indicates, the gains and losses from buying call options can be quite large. To illustrate further, suppose you purchase the equity with the €500 instead of buying call options. In this case, you will have about €500/€7.69 = 65.02 shares. We can now compare what you have when the option expires for different share prices:

TABLE 21.2

Call option pay-off profile

Ending share price	Option value (50 contracts) (€)	Net profit/loss (50 contracts) (€)	Share value (65.02 shares) (€)	Net profit/loss (65.02 shares) (€)
4	0	−500	260.08	−239.92
6	0	−500	390.12	−109.88
7.69	0	−500	500	0
8	0	−500	520.16	20.16
10	10,000	9,500	650.20	150.20
12	20,000	19,500	780.24	280.24
14	30,000	29,500	910.28	410.28

The option position clearly magnifies the gains and losses on the equity by a substantial amount. The reason is that the pay-off on your 50 option contracts is based on 50 × 100 = 5,000 shares of equity instead of just 65.02.

In our example, notice that if the share price ends up below the exercise price, then you lose all €500 with the option. With the equity, you still have about what you started with. Also, notice that the option can never be worth less than zero because you can always throw it away. As a result, you can never lose more than your original investment (the €500 in our example).

It is important to recognize that equity options are a zero-sum game. By this, we mean that whatever the buyer of an equity option makes, the seller loses, and vice versa. To illustrate, suppose, in our example just preceding, you *sell* 50 option contracts. You receive €500 upfront, and you will be obligated to sell the equity for €8.00 if the buyer of the option wishes to exercise it. In this situation, if the share price ends up below €8.00, you will be €500 ahead. If the share price ends up above €8.00, you will have to sell something for less than it is worth to lose the difference. For example, if the share price is €10.00, you will have to sell 50 × 100 = 5,000 shares at €10.00 per share so that you will be out €10.00 − 8.00 = €2 per share, or €10,000 total. Because you received €500 upfront, your net loss is €9,500. We can summarize some other possibilities as follows:

Ending share price(€)	Net profit to option seller(€)
4	500
6	500
7.69	500
8	500
10	−9,500
12	−19,500
14	−29,500

Notice that the option buyer's net profit (calculated previously) is just the opposite of these amounts.

EXAMPLE 21.1

PUT PAY-OFFS

Suppose you buy 10 Iberdrola April €7.60 put contracts for €0.17. How much does this cost (ignoring commissions)? Just before the option expires, Iberdrola is selling for €7 per share. Is this good news or bad news? What is your net profit?

The option is quoted at €0.17, so one contract costs 100 × €0.17 = €17. Your 10 contracts total €170. You now have the right to sell 1,000 shares of Iberdrola for €7.60 per share. If the share price is currently €7, then this is most definitely good news. You can buy 1,000 shares at €7 and sell them for €7.60. Your puts are thus worth €7.60 − €7 = €0.60 per share, or €0.60 × 1,000 = €600 in all. Because you paid €170, your net profit is €600 − €170 = €430.

CONCEPT QUESTIONS

21.1a What is a call option? A put option?
21.1b If you thought an equity would drop sharply in value, how might you use equity options to profit from the decline?

21.2 PUT-CALL PARITY

Recall that the purchaser of a call option pays for the right, but not the obligation, to buy an asset for a fixed time at a fixed price. The purchaser of a put option pays for the right to sell an asset for a fixed time at a fixed price. The fixed price is called the *exercise* or *strike* price.

PROTECTIVE PUTS

Consider the following investment strategy. Today, you buy one share of Vodafone for £110. At the same time, you also buy one put option with a £105 strike price. The put option has a life of one year, and the premium is £5. Your total investment is £115, and you plan to hold this investment for one year and then sell out.

What have you accomplished here? To answer, we created Table 21.3, which shows your gains and losses one year from now for different share prices. In the table, notice that the worst thing that ever happens is that the value of your investment falls to £105. The reason is that if Vodafone's share price is below £105 per share one year from now, you will exercise your put option and sell your equity for the strike price of £105: so that is the least you can receive.

TABLE 21.3

Gains and losses in one year

Share price in one year (£)	Value of put option (strike price = £105) (£)	Combined value (£)	Total gain or loss (combined value less £115) (£)
125	0	125	10
120	0	120	5
115	0	115	0
110	0	110	−5
105	0	105	−10
100	5	105	−10
95	10	105	−10
80	25	105	−10

Note: Original investment: purchase one share at £110 plus a one-year put option with a strike price of £105 for £5. The total cost is £115.

protective put
the purchase of equity and a put option on the equity to limit the downside risk associated with the equity.

Thus, by purchasing the put option, you have limited your downside risk to a maximum potential loss of £10 (= £115 − £105). This particular strategy of buying an equity and simultaneously buying a put on the equity is called a **protective put** strategy because it protects you against losses beyond a certain point. Notice that the put option acts as a kind of insurance policy that pays off if an asset you own (the equity) declines in value.

In our example, we picked a strike price of £105. You could have picked a higher strike price and limited your downside risk to even less. Of course, a higher strike price would mean that you would have to pay more for the put option, so there is a trade-off between the amount of protection and the cost of that protection.

AN ALTERNATIVE STRATEGY

Now consider a different strategy. You take your £115 and purchase a one-year call option on Vodafone with a strike price of £105. The premium is £15. That leaves you with £100, which you decide to invest in a riskless asset such as a T-bill. The risk-free rate is 5 per cent.

What does this strategy accomplish? Once again, we shall create a table to illustrate your gains and losses. Notice that in Table 21.4, your £100 grows to £105 based on a 5 per cent interest rate. If you compare Table 21.4 with Table 21.3, you will make an interesting discovery. No matter what the share price is one year from now, the two strategies *always* have the same value in one year!

TABLE 21.4

Gains and losses in one year

Share price in one year (£)	Value of call option (strike price = £105) (£)	Value of risk-free asset (£)	Combined value (£)	Total gain or loss (combined value less £115) (£)
125	20	105	125	10
120	15	105	120	5
115	10	105	115	0
110	5	105	110	−5
105	0	105	105	−10
100	0	105	105	−10
95	0	105	105	−10
80	0	105	105	−10

Note: Original investment: purchase a one-year call option with a strike price of £105 for £15. Invest £100 in a risk-free asset paying 5 per cent. The total cost is £115.

The fact that the two strategies always have the same value in one year explains why they have the same cost today. If one of these strategies were cheaper than the other today, there would be an arbitrage opportunity to buy the cheaper one and simultaneously sell the more expensive one.

REAL WORLD INSIGHTS

When markets are volatile, options can be handy if you want to protect yourself against large movements in prices. You will have seen that when prices are expected to grow, call options are good investments. Similarly, when price falls are on the horizon, you should invest in put options. What happens if you don't know which way prices will go, only that they are definitely going to jump up or collapse? In this case, the straddle strategy is a good option. A straddle is an option portfolio of the same number of puts and calls, each having the same exercise price and expiration date.

> Consider a hypothetical pharmaceutical firm, CovidVac, that is researching a new vaccine to eliminate all coronavirus variants. CovidVac has a share price of €102, and there is no evidence either way on the outcome of the trials. If the trials show strong results in building immunity to the virus, you anticipate the company's share price will rise to €120, but if the trials are a failure, the share price will fall to €80. A similar example happened to many pharmaceutical firms in 2021 with Covid-19. Investors were uncertain of each vaccine's long-term efficacy, thereby increasing uncertainty in future share values for companies releasing vaccines.
>
> Returning to our hypothetical example, assume you create a straddle by investing in one put and one call with an exercise price of €102 and the same maturity of three months. After 90 days, CovidVac will be priced at either €120 or €80. Let's look at the value of your straddle portfolio in each case:
> Share price = €120. Pay-off to call = €18; Pay-off to put = €0; Total straddle pay-off = €18.
> Share price = €80. Pay-off to call = €0; Pay-off to put = €22; Total straddle pay-off = €22.
> In either case, your pay-off is positive.
>
> It is important to remember that each option incurs a cost when you purchase it. Assuming that the premium on both calls and puts is €5 for an exercise price of €102, your total cost will be €10, and the straddle will only be profitable if the share price falls or grows by more than €10. This means that CovidVac will need to fall below €92 or be above €112 before you can make any money. This is around 10 per cent within a three-month period, a very large movement in prices.

THE RESULT

Our example illustrates an important pricing relationship. It shows that a protective put strategy can be exactly duplicated by a combination of a call option (with the same strike price as the put option) and a riskless investment. In our example, notice that the investment in the riskless asset, £100, is exactly equal to the present value of the strike price on the option calculated at the risk-free rate: £105/1.05 = £100.

Putting it all together, what we have discovered is the *put-call parity (PCP) condition*. It says that:

$$\text{Price of underlying equity} + \text{Price of put} = \text{Price of call} + \text{Present value of strike price} \tag{21.1}$$

In symbols, we can write:

$$S + P = \text{PV}(E) + C \tag{21.1a}$$

where S is the share price, P is the put value, and $\text{PV}(E)$ and C are the present value of the exercise price and the value of the call option.

Because the present value of the exercise price is calculated using the risk-free rate, you can think of it as the price of a risk-free, pure discount instrument (such as a T-bill) with a face value equal to the strike price. In our experience, the easiest way to remember the PCP condition is to remember that 'share plus put equals T-bill plus call'.

The PCP condition is an algebraic expression, meaning that it can be rearranged. For example, suppose we know that the risk-free rate is 0.5 per cent per month. A call with a strike price of €40 sells for €4, and a put with the same strike price sells for €3. Both have a three-month maturity. What's the share price?

To answer, we use the PCP condition to solve for the share price:

$$\begin{aligned} S &= \text{PV}(E) + C - P \\ &= €40/1.005^3 + 4 - 3 \\ &= €40.41 \end{aligned}$$

The PCP condition really says that between a riskless asset (such as a T-bill), a call option, a put option and a share of equity, we can always figure out the price of any one of the four given the prices of the other three.

> **EXAMPLE 21.2**
>
> ### PUT-CALL PARITY
>
> Suppose a share of equity sells for £60. A six-month call option with a £70 strike price sells for £2. The risk-free rate is 0.4 per cent per month. What's the price of a six-month put option with a £70 strike?
>
> If we use the PCP condition to solve for the put price, we get:
>
> $$P = PV(E) + C - S = £70/1.004^6 + £2 - £60 = £10.34$$
>
> Notice that in this example, the put option is worth a lot more than the call. Why?

> **EXAMPLE 21.3**
>
> ### MORE PARITY
>
> Suppose a share of equity sells for €110. A one-year, at-the-money call option sells for €15. An at-the-money put with the same maturity sells for €5. Can you create a risk-free investment by combining these three instruments? How? What's the risk-free rate?
>
> Here, we can use the PCP condition to solve for the present value of the strike price:
>
> $$PV(E) = S + P - C = €110 + €5 - €15 = €100$$
>
> The present value of the strike price is thus €100. Notice that because the options are at the money, the strike is the same as the share price, €110. So, if you put €100 in a riskless investment today and receive €110 in one year, the implied risk-free rate is obviously 10 per cent.

> **CONCEPT QUESTIONS**
>
> **21.2a** What is a protective put strategy?
> **21.2b** What strategy exactly duplicates a protective put?

21.3 FUNDAMENTALS OF OPTION VALUATION

Now that we understand the basics of puts and calls, we can discuss what determines their values. We shall focus on call options in the discussion that follows, but the same type of analysis can be applied to put options.

VALUATION OF A CALL AT EXPIRATION

We have already described the pay-offs from call options for different share prices. In continuing this discussion, the following notation will be useful:

S_1 Share price at expiration (in one period)
S_0 Share price today
C_1 Value of the call option on the expiration date (in one period)

C_0 Value of the call option today

E Exercise price on the option

From our previous discussion, remember that if the share price (S_1) ends up below the exercise price (E) on the expiration date, then the call option (C_1) is worth zero. In other words:

$$C_1 = 0 \text{ if } S_1 \leq E$$

Or, equivalently:

$$C_1 = 0 \text{ if } S_1 - E \leq 0 \qquad (21.2)$$

This is the case in which the option is out of the money when it expires.

If the option finishes in the money, then $S_1 > E$ and the value of the option at expiration is equal to the difference:

$$C_1 = S_1 - E \text{ if } S_1 > E$$

Or, equivalently:

$$C_1 = S_1 - E \text{ if } S_1 - E > 0 \qquad (21.3)$$

For example, suppose we have a call option with an exercise price of £10. The option is about to expire. If the equity is selling for £8, then we have the right to pay £10 for something worth only £8. Thus, our option is worth exactly zero because the share price is less than the exercise price on the option ($S_1 \leq E$). If the equity is selling for £12, then the option has value. Because we can buy the equity for £10, the option is worth $S_1 - E = £12 - £10 = £2$.

Figure 21.1 plots the value of a call option at expiration against the share price. The result looks something like a hockey stick. Notice that for every share price less than E, the value of the option is zero. For every share price greater than E, the value of the call option is $S_1 - E$. Also, once the share price exceeds the exercise price, the option's value goes up in step with the share price.

FIGURE 21.1

Value of a call option at expiration for different share prices

As shown, the value of a call option at expiration is equal to zero if the share price is less than or equal to the exercise price. The value of the call is equal to the share price minus the exercise price ($S_1 - E$) if the share price exceeds the exercise price. The resulting 'hockey stick' shape is highlighted.

BOUNDING THE VALUE OF A CALL

Now that we know how to determine C_1, the value of the call at expiration, we turn to a somewhat more challenging question: how can we determine C_0, the value sometime *before* expiration? We shall be discussing this in the next several sections. For now, we shall establish the lower and upper for the value of a call option.

Lower Bound

Consider an American call that is in the money prior to expiration. For example, assume that the share price is £60 and the exercise price is £50. In this case, the option cannot sell below £10. To see this, note the following simple strategy if the option sells at, say, £9:

Date	Transaction	(£)
Today	1 Buy call.	−9
Today	2 Exercise call – that is, buy the underlying share at the exercise price.	−50
Today	3 Sell share at current market price.	+60
Arbitrage profit		+1

The type of profit that is described in this transaction is an arbitrage profit. Arbitrage profits come from transactions with no risk or cost and cannot occur regularly in normal, well-functioning financial markets. The excess demand for these options would quickly force the option price up to at least £10 (= £60 − £50).

Of course, the price of the option is likely to be above £10. Investors will rationally pay more than £10 because of the possibility that the equity will rise above £60 before expiration. For example, suppose the call actually sells for £12. In this case, we say that the option's intrinsic value is £10, meaning it must always be worth at least this much. The remaining £12 − £10 = £2 is sometimes called the *time premium*, and it represents the extra amount that investors are willing to pay because of the possibility that the share price will rise before the option expires. Given that the potential price is infinite at expiration, the £2 time premium represents the possibility of price increases over the time remaining.

Upper Bound

Is there an upper boundary for the option price as well? It turns out that the upper boundary is the price of the underlying share. That is, an option to buy equity cannot have a greater value than the equity itself. A call option can be used to buy equity with payment of the exercise price. It would be foolish to buy equity this way if the shares could be purchased directly at a lower price. The upper and lower bounds are represented in Figure 21.2.

THE FACTORS DETERMINING CALL OPTION VALUES

The previous discussion indicated that a call option's price must fall somewhere in the shaded region of Figure 21.2. We shall now determine more precisely where in the shaded region it should be. The factors that determine a call's value can be broken into two sets. The first set contains the features of the option contract. The two basic contractual features are the exercise price and the expiration date. The second set of factors affecting the call price concerns characteristics of the equity and the market.

Exercise Price

An increase in the exercise price reduces the value of the call. For example, imagine that there are two calls on an equity selling at £60. The first call has an exercise price of £50, and the second one has an exercise price of £40. Which call would you rather have? Clearly, you would rather have the call with an exercise price of £40, because that one is £20 (= £60 − £40) in the money. In other words, the call with an exercise price of £40 should sell for more than an otherwise identical call with an exercise price of £50.

Expiration Date

The value of an American call option must be at least as great as the value of an otherwise identical option with a shorter term to expiration. Consider two American calls: one has a maturity of nine months, and the other expires in six months. Obviously, the nine-month call has the same rights as the six-month call, and it also has an additional three months within which these rights can be exercised. It cannot be worth less and will generally be more valuable.

FIGURE 21.2 The upper and lower boundaries of call option values

Upper bound = Share price

Lower bound = Share price − Exercise price

Value of the call must lie in the shaded region.

The Risk-Free Rate

The higher the risk-free rate (R_f) is, the more the call is worth. This result is a little less obvious. Normally, we think of asset values as going down as rates rise. In this case, the exercise price is a *cash outflow*, a liability. The current value of that liability goes down as the discount rate goes up.

Share Price

Other things being equal, the higher the share price, the more valuable the call option will be. For example, if an equity is worth £80, a call with an exercise price of £100 isn't worth very much. If the share price soars to £120, the call becomes much more valuable.

Consider Figure 21.3, which shows the relationship between the call price and the share price prior to expiration. The curve indicates that the call price increases as the share price increases. Furthermore,

FIGURE 21.3 Value of a call option as a function of share price

it can be shown that the relationship is represented not by a straight line but by a convex curve. That is, the increase in the call price for a given change in the share price is greater when the share price is high than when the share price is low.

The Key Factor: The Variability of the Underlying Asset

The greater the variability of the underlying asset, the more valuable the call option will be. Consider the following example. Suppose that, just before the call expires, the share price will be either £100 with a probability of 0.5 or £80 with a probability of 0.5. What will be the value of a call with an exercise price of £110? Clearly, it will be worthless because no matter what happens to the equity, the share price will always be below the exercise price.

What happens if the share price is more variable? Suppose we add £20 to the best case and take £20 away from the worst case. Now the equity has a one-half chance of being worth £60 and a one-half chance of being worth £120. We have spread the equity returns, but of course, the expected value of the share has stayed the same:

$$(1/2 \times £80) + (1/2 \times £100) = £90 = (1/2 \times £60) + (1/2 \times £120)$$

Notice that the call option has value now because there is a one-half chance that the share price will be £120, or £10 above the exercise price of £110. This illustrates an important point. There is a fundamental distinction between holding an option on an underlying asset and holding the underlying asset. If investors in the marketplace are risk-averse, a rise in the variability of the equity will decrease its market value.

More generally, increasing the variance of the possible future prices on the underlying asset doesn't affect the option's value when the option finishes out of the money. The value is always zero in this case. On the other hand, increasing the variance increases the possible pay-offs when the option is in the money, so the net effect increases the option's value. Put another way, because the downside risk is always limited, the only effect is to increase the upside potential. In a later discussion, we shall use the usual symbol, σ^2, to stand for the variance of the return on the underlying asset.

SUMMARY

The most important thing to remember is that the value of an option depends on five factors. Table 21.5 summarizes these factors and the direction of their influence for both puts and calls. In Table 21.5, the sign in parentheses indicates the direction of the influence.

TABLE 21.5

Five factors that determine option values

Factor	Direction of influence	
	Calls	Puts
The current value of the underlying asset	(+)	(−)
The exercise price on the option	(−)	(+)
Time to expiration on the option	(+)	(+)
Risk-free rate	(+)	(−)
The variance of return on the underlying asset	(+)	(+)

In other words, the sign tells us whether the value of the option goes up or down when the value of a factor increases. For example, notice that increasing the exercise price reduces the value of a call option. Increasing any of the other four factors increases the value of the call. Notice also that the time to expiration and the variance of return act the same for puts and calls. The other three factors have opposite signs in the two cases.

CONCEPT QUESTIONS

21.3a What is the value of a call option at expiration?
21.3b What are the upper and lower bounds on the value of a call option any time before expiration?
21.3c Assuming that the share price is certain to be greater than the exercise price on a call option, what is the value of the call? Why?

21.4 AN OPTION PRICING MODEL

Option pricing can be a complex subject. Fortunately, as is often the case, many of the key insights can be illustrated with a simple example. Suppose we are looking at a call option with one year to expiration and an exercise price of £105. The equity currently sells for £100, and the risk-free rate, R_f, is 20 per cent. The value of the equity in one year is uncertain, of course. To keep things simple, suppose we know that the share price will be either £110 or £130. It is important to note that we *don't* know the odds associated with these two prices. In other words, we know the possible values for the equity but not the probabilities associated with those values.

Because the exercise price on the option is £105, we know that the option will be worth either £110 − 105 = £5 or £130 − 105 = £25; but, once again, we don't know which. We do know one thing, however: our call option is certain to finish in the money.

The Basic Approach

Here is the crucial observation: it is possible to duplicate the pay-offs on the equity exactly, using a combination of the option and the risk-free asset. How? Do the following: buy one call option and invest £87.50 in a risk-free asset (such as a T-bill).

What will you have in a year? Your risk-free asset will earn 20 per cent, so that it will be worth £87.50 × 1.20 = £105. Your option will be worth £5 or £25, so the total value will be either £110 or £130, just like the value of the equity:

Share price (£)	vs.	Risk-free asset value (£)	+	Call value (£)	=	Total value (£)
110		105		5		110
130		105		25		130

As illustrated, these two strategies – buying a share of equity or buying a call and investing in the risk-free asset – have exactly the same pay-offs in the future.

Because these two strategies have the same future pay-offs, they must have the same value today, or else there would be an arbitrage opportunity. The equity sells for £100 today, so the value of the call option today, C_0, is given by:

$$£100 = £87.50 + C_0$$
$$C_0 = £12.50$$

Where did we get the £87.50? This is just the present value of the exercise price on the option, calculated at the risk-free rate:

$$E/(1 + R_f) = £105/1.20 = £87.50$$

Given this, our example shows that the value of a call option in this simple case is given by:

$$S_0 = C_0 + \frac{E}{1 + R_f}$$
$$C_0 = S_0 - \frac{E}{1 + R_f}$$

(21.4)

In words, the value of the call option is equal to the share price minus the present value of the exercise price.

A More Complicated Example

From our previous example, we have an equity that currently sells for £100. It will be worth either £110 or £130 in a year, and we don't know which. The risk-free rate is 20 per cent. We are now looking at a different call option, however. This one has an exercise price of £120 instead of £105. What is the value of this call option?

This case is a little harder. If the equity ends up at £110, the option is out of the money and worth nothing. If the equity ends up at £130, the option is worth £130 − 120 = £10.

Our basic approach to determining the value of the call option will be the same. We shall show once again that it is possible to combine the call option and a risk-free investment in a way that exactly duplicates the pay-off from holding the equity. The only complication is that it's a little harder to determine how to do it.

For example, suppose we bought one call and invested the present value of the exercise price in a riskless asset as we did before. In one year, we would have £120 from the riskless investment, plus an option worth either zero or £10. The total value would be either £120 or £130. This is not the same as the equity value (£110 or £130), so the two strategies are not comparable.

Instead, consider investing the present value of £110 (the lower share price) in a riskless asset. This guarantees us a £110 pay-off. If the share price is £110, then any call options we own are worthless, and we have exactly £110 as desired.

When the equity is worth £130, the call option is worth £10. Our risk-free investment is worth £110, so we are £130 − 110 = £20 short. Because each call option is worth £10, we need to buy two of them to replicate the value of the equity.

Thus, in this case, investing the present value of the lower share price in a riskless asset and buying two call options exactly duplicates owning the equity. When the equity is worth £110, we have £110 from our risk-free investment. When the equity is worth £130, we have £110 from the risk-free investment plus two call options worth £10 each.

Because these two strategies have the same value in the future, they must have the same value today, or arbitrage would be possible:

$$\begin{aligned} S_0 &= £100 = 2 \times C_0 + £110/(1 + R_f) \\ 2 \times C_0 &= £100 - 110/1.2 \\ C_0 &= £4.17 \end{aligned}$$

Each call option is thus worth £4.17.

EXAMPLE 21.4

DON'T CALL US, WE'LL CALL YOU

We are looking at two call options on the same equity, one with an exercise price of €20 and one with an exercise price of €30. The equity currently sells for €35. Its future price will be either €25 or €50. If the risk-free rate is 10 per cent, what are the values of these call options?

The first case (with the €20 exercise price) is not difficult because the option is sure to finish in the money. We know that the value is equal to the share price less the present value of the exercise price:

$$\begin{aligned} C_0 &= S_0 - E/(1 + R_f) \\ &= £35 - 20/1.1 \\ &= £16.82 \end{aligned}$$

In the second case, the exercise price is €30, so the option can finish out of the money. At expiration, the option is worth €0 if the equity is worth €25. The option is worth €50 − 30 = €20 if it finishes in the money. As before, we start by investing the present value of the lowest share price in the risk-free asset. This costs €25/1.1 = €22.73. At expiration, we have €25 from this investment. If the share price is €50, we need an additional €25 to duplicate the equity pay-off. Because each option is worth €20 in this case, we need

€25/20 = 1.25 options. So, to prevent arbitrage, investing the present value of €25 in a risk-free asset and buying 1.25 call options must have the same value as the equity:

$$S_0 = 1.25 \times C_0 + €25/(1 + R_f)$$
$$€35 = 1.25 \times C_0 + €25/(1 + 0.1)$$
$$C_0 = €9.82$$

Notice that this second option had to be worth less because it has a higher exercise price.

A CLOSER LOOK

Before moving on, it will be useful to consider one last example. Suppose the share price is £100, and it will move either up or down by 20 per cent. The risk-free rate is 5 per cent. What is the value of a call option with a £90 exercise price?

The share price will be either £80 or £120. The option is worth zero when the equity is worth £80, and it is worth £120 − 90 = £30 when the equity is worth £120. Therefore, we shall invest the present value of £80 in the risk-free asset and buy some call options.

When the equity finishes at £120, our risk-free asset pays £80, leaving us £40 short. Each option is worth £30 in this case, so we need £40/30 = 4/3 options to match the pay-off on the equity. The option's value must thus be given by:

$$S_0 = £100 = 4/3 \times C_0 + £80/1.05$$
$$C_0 = (3/4) \times (£100 - 76.19)$$
$$= £17.86$$

To make our result a little bit more general, notice that the number of options that you need to buy to replicate the value of the equity is always equal to $\Delta S/\Delta C$, where ΔS is the difference in the possible share prices, and ΔC is the difference in the possible option values. In our current case, for example, ΔS would be £120 − 80 = £40 and ΔC would be £30 − 0 = £30, so $\Delta S/\Delta C$ would be £40/30 = 4/3, as we calculated.

Notice also that when the equity is certain to finish in the money, $\Delta S/\Delta C$ is always exactly equal to 1, so one call option is always needed. Otherwise, $\Delta S/\Delta C$ is greater than 1, so more than one call option is needed.

21.5 THE BLACK–SCHOLES OPTION PRICING MODEL

We're now in a position to discuss one of the most celebrated results in modern finance, the Black–Scholes Option Pricing Model (OPM). The OPM is a sufficiently important discovery that it was the basis for the Nobel Prize in Economics in 1997. The underlying development of the Black–Scholes OPM is fairly complex, so we shall focus only on the main result and how to use it.

BLACK–SCHOLES MODEL

$$C = S\,\text{N}(d_1) - Ee^{-Rt}\text{N}(d_2)$$

where

$$d_1 = \frac{\ln(S/E) + (R + \sigma^2/2)t}{\sqrt{\sigma^2 t}}$$
$$d_2 = d_1 - \sqrt{\sigma^2 t}$$

This formula for the value of a call, C, is one of the most complex in finance. However, it involves only five parameters:

1. S = Current share price
2. E = Exercise price of a call

3. R = Annual risk-free rate of return, continuously compounded
4. σ^2 = Variance (per year) of the continuous share price return
5. t = Time (in years) to the expiration date

In addition, there is this statistical concept:

$N(d)$ = Probability that a standardized, normally distributed, random variable will be less than or equal to d.

Rather than discuss the formula in its algebraic state, we illustrate the formula with an example.

EXAMPLE 21.5

BLACK-SCHOLES OPTION PRICING MODEL

Consider Private Equipment plc (PEP). On 4 October of year 0, the PEP 21 April call option (exercise price = £49) had a closing value of £4. The equity itself was selling at £50. On 4 October, the option had 199 days to expiration (maturity date = 21 April, year 1). The annual risk-free interest rate, continuously compounded, was 7 per cent.

This information determines three variables directly:

1. The share price, S, is £50.
2. The exercise price, E, is £49.
3. The risk-free rate, R, is 0.07.

In addition, the time to maturity, t, can be calculated quickly: the formula calls for t to be expressed in years.

4. We express the 199-day interval in years as $t = 199/365$.

In the real world, an options trader would know S and E exactly. Traders generally view government Treasury bills as riskless, so a current quote from newspapers, such as the *Financial Times* or a similar source, would be obtained for the interest rate. The trader would also know (or could count) the number of days to expiration exactly. Thus, the fraction of a year to expiration, t, could be calculated quickly.

The problem comes in determining the variance of the underlying equity's return. The formula calls for the variance between the purchase date of 4 October and the expiration date. Unfortunately, this represents the future, so the correct value for variance is not available. Instead, traders frequently estimate the variance from past data, and they may also use intuition to adjust their estimate. For example, if anticipation of an upcoming event is likely to increase share price volatility, the trader might adjust their estimate of variance upwards to reflect this.

The preceding discussion was intended to highlight the difficulties in variance estimation, not to present a solution. For our purposes, we assume that a trader has come up with an estimate of variance:

5. The variance of Private Equipment plc has been estimated to be 0.09 per year.

Using these five parameters, we calculate the Black-Scholes value of the PEP option in three steps.

Step 1: Calculate d_1 and d_2

These values can be determined by a straightforward, albeit tedious, insertion of our parameters into the basic formula. We have:

$$d_1 = \left[\ln\left(\frac{S}{E}\right) + (R + \sigma^2/2)t\right] \Big/ \sqrt{\sigma^2 t}$$

$$= \left[\ln\left(\frac{50}{49}\right) + (0.07 + 0.09/2) \times \frac{199}{365}\right] \Big/ \sqrt{0.09 \times \frac{199}{365}}$$

$$= (0.0202 + 0.0627)/0.2215 = 0.3742$$

$$d_2 = d_1 - \sqrt{\sigma^2 t}$$

$$= 0.1527$$

Step 2: Calculate $N(d_1)$ and $N(d_2)$

Perhaps the easiest way to determine $N(d_1)$ and $N(d_2)$ is from the Microsoft Excel function NORMSDIST. In our example NORMSDIST(0.3742) and NORMSDIST(0.1527) are 0.6459 and 0.5607, respectively.

We can also determine the cumulative probability from Table 21.6. For example, consider $d = 0.37$. This can be found in the table as 0.3 on the vertical and 0.07 on the horizontal. The value in the table for $d = 0.37$ is 0.1443. This value is not the cumulative probability of 0.37. We must first make an adjustment to determine cumulative probability. That is:

$$N(0.37) = 0.50 + 0.1443 = 0.6443$$
$$N(-0.37) = 0.50 - 0.1443 = 0.3557$$

$N(d)$ represents areas under the standard normal distribution function. Suppose that $d_1 = 0.24$. The table implies a cumulative probability of $0.5000 + 0.0948 = 0.5948$. If d_1 is equal to 0.2452, we must estimate the probability by interpolating between $N(0.25)$ and $N(0.24)$.

TABLE 21.6

Cumulative probabilities of the standard normal distribution function

d	0.00	0.01	0.02	0.03	0.04	0.05	0.06	0.07	0.08	0.09
0.0	0.0000	0.0040	0.0080	0.0120	0.0160	0.0199	0.0239	0.0279	0.0319	0.0359
0.1	0.0398	0.0438	0.0478	0.0517	0.0557	0.0596	0.0636	0.0675	0.0714	0.0753
0.2	0.0793	0.0832	0.0871	0.0910	0.0948	0.0987	0.1026	0.1064	0.1103	0.1141
0.3	0.1179	0.1217	0.1255	0.1293	0.1331	0.1368	0.1406	0.1443	0.1480	0.1517
0.4	0.1554	0.1591	0.1628	0.1664	0.1700	0.1736	0.1772	0.1808	0.1844	0.1879
0.5	0.1915	0.1950	0.1985	0.2019	0.2054	0.2088	0.2123	0.2157	0.2190	0.2224

Unfortunately, our table handles only two significant digits, whereas our value of 0.3742 has four significant digits. Hence we must interpolate to find $N(0.3742)$. Because $N(0.37) = 0.6443$ and $N(0.38) = 0.6480$, the difference between the two values is 0.0037 ($= 0.6480 - 0.6443$). Since 0.3742 is 42 per cent of the way between 0.37 and 0.38, we interpolate as:

$$N(0.3742) = 0.6443 + 0.42 \times 0.0037 = 0.6459$$

Step 3: Calculate C

We have:

$$C = S \times [N(d_1)] - Ee^{-Rt} \times [N(d_2)]$$
$$= £50 \times [N(d_1)] - £49 \times e^{-0.07 \times (199/365)} \times [N(d_2)]$$
$$= £50 \times 0.6459 - £49 \times 0.9626 \times 0.5607$$
$$= £32.295 - 26.447$$
$$= £5.85$$

The estimated price of £5.85 is greater than the £4 actual price, implying that the call option is underpriced. A trader believing in the Black-Scholes model would buy a call. Of course, the Black-Scholes model is fallible. Perhaps the disparity between the model's estimate and the market price reflects an error in the trader's estimate of variance.

It is no exaggeration to say that the Black–Scholes formula is among the most important contributions in finance. It allows anyone to calculate the value of an option, given a few parameters. The formula's attraction is that four of the parameters are observable: the current share price, S; the exercise price,

E; the interest rate, R; and the time to the expiration date, t. Only one of the parameters must be estimated: the variance of return, σ^2.

PUT OPTION VALUATION

Our examples thus far have focused only on call options. Just a little extra work is needed to value put options. Basically, we pretend that a put option is a call option and use the Black–Scholes formula to value it. We then use the continuously compounded version of the put-call parity (PCP) condition to solve for the put value. To see how this works, suppose we have the following:

$S = £40$
$E = £40$
$R = 4\%$ per year, continuously compounded
$\sigma = 80\%$ per year
$t = 4$ months

What's the value of a *put* option on the equity?

For practice, calculate the Black–Scholes call option price and see if you agree that a call option would be worth about £7.52. Now, recall the PCP condition:

$$S + P = \text{PV}(E) + C$$

The continuously compounded version of the above equation is:

$$S + P = Ee^{-Rt} + C$$

which we can rearrange to solve for the put price:

$$P = Ee^{-Rt} + C - S$$

Plugging in the relevant numbers, we get:

$$P = £40 \times e^{-0.04(1/3)} + 7.52 - 40$$
$$= £6.99$$

Thus the value of a put option is £6.99. So, once we know how to value call options, we also know how to value put options.

A CAUTIONARY NOTE

For practice, let's consider another put option value. Suppose we have the following:

$S = €70$
$E = €90$
$R = 8\%$ per year, continuously compounded
$\sigma = 20\%$ per year
$t = 12$ months

What's the value of a put option on the equity? For practice, calculate the call option's value and see if you get €1.65. Once again, we use PCP to solve for the put price:

$$P = Ee^{-Rt} + C - S$$

The put value we get is:

$$P = €90 \times e^{-0.08(1)} + 1.65 - 70$$
$$= €14.73$$

Does something about our put option value seem odd? The answer is yes. Because the share price is €70 and the strike price is €90, you could get €20 by exercising the put immediately, so it looks as though we have an arbitrage possibility. Unfortunately, we don't.

This example illustrates that we have to be careful with assumptions. The Black–Scholes formula is for European-style options (remember that European-style options can be exercised only on the final day, whereas American-style options can be exercised at any time). In fact, our PCP condition holds only for European-style options.

What our example shows is that an American-style put option is worth more than a European-style put. The reason is not hard to understand. Suppose you buy a put with a strike price of €80. The very best thing that can happen is for the share price to fall to zero. If the share price did fall to zero, no further gain on your option would be possible, so you would want to exercise it immediately rather than wait. If the option is American style, you can, but not if it is European style. More generally, it often pays to exercise a put option once it is well into the money because any additional potential gains are limited, so American-style exercise is valuable.

What about call options? Here the answer is a little more encouraging. As long as we stick to non-dividend-paying equities, it will never be optimal to exercise a call option early. Again, the reason is not complicated. A call option is worth more alive than dead, meaning you would always be better off selling the option than exercising it. In other words, for a call option, the exercise style is irrelevant.

Here is a challenge for the more mathematically inclined among you. We have a formula for a European-style put option. What about for an American-style put? Despite a great deal of effort, this problem has never been solved, so no formula is known. To be clear, we have numerical procedures for valuing put options but no explicit formula. Call us if you figure one out.

Now that we have shown how to value call and put options, we now consider their use in corporate finance.

SPREADSHEET STRATEGIES 21.1

The easiest way to find the value of an option is to use a spreadsheet. Consider an equity with a share price of £65 and an annual return standard deviation of 50 per cent. The riskless interest rate is 5 per cent. Calculate the call and put option values with a strike of £60 and a 3-month period to expiration.

	A	B	C	D	E
1	Share Price =	65		d1=	0.495171
2	Strike Price =	60		d2=	0.245171
3	Sigma =	0.5		N(d1) =	0.68976
4	Time =	0.25		N(d2) =	0.596838
5	Rate =	0.05			
6					
7	Call =	9.468982		Put =	3.72365
8					

Formula entered in E1 is =(LN(B1/B2)+(B5+0.5*B3^2)*B4)/(B3*SQRT(B4))
Formula entered in E2 is =E1−B3*SQRT(B4)
Formula entered in E3 is =NORMSDIST(E1)
Formula entered in E4 is =NORMSDIST(E2)
Formula entered in B7 is =B1*E3−B2*EXP(−B5*B4)*E4
Formula entered in E7 is =B2*EXP(−B5*B4)+B7−B1

CONCEPT QUESTIONS

21.5a What are the five factors that determine an option's value?
21.5b Which is worth more, an American-style put or a European-style put? Why?

21.6 OPTION APPLICATIONS: EMPLOYEE SHARE OPTIONS

Options are important in corporate finance in a lot of different ways. In this section, we begin to examine some of these by looking at executive (employee) share options, or ESOs. An ESO is, in essence, a call option that a firm gives to employees, giving them the right to buy shares of equity in the company. The practice of granting options to employees has become widespread. It is almost universal for upper management and sometimes given to other employees. Although ESOs have become a controversial topic of late (see opening vignette), an understanding of ESOs is important.

ESO FEATURES

Because ESOs are basically call options, we have already covered most of the important aspects. However, ESOs have a few features that make them different from regular share options. The details differ from company to company, but a typical ESO has a 10-year life, which is much longer than most ordinary options. Unlike traded options, ESOs cannot be sold. They also have what is known as a 'vesting' period. Often, for up to three years or so, an ESO cannot be exercised and must be forfeited if an employee leaves the company. After this period, the options 'vest', which means they can be exercised. Sometimes, employees who resign with vested options are given a limited time to exercise their options.

Why are ESOs granted? There are basically two reasons. First, going back to Chapter 2, the owners of a corporation (the shareholders) face the basic problem of aligning shareholder and management interests and providing incentives for employees to focus on corporate goals. ESOs are a powerful motivator because, as we have seen, the pay-offs on options can be huge. High-level executives, in particular, stand to gain enormous wealth if they are successful in creating value for shareholders.

The second reason why some companies rely heavily on ESOs is that an ESO has no immediate, up-front, out-of-pocket cost to the corporation. In smaller, possibly cash-strapped companies, ESOs are simply a substitute for ordinary wages. Employees are willing to accept them instead of cash, hoping for big pay-offs in the future. In fact, ESOs are a major recruiting tool, allowing businesses to attract talent that they otherwise could not afford.

At the same time, there are several significant criticisms of executive share options. The most notable criticism is that share options encourage managers to take on more risky projects to increase the size of their personal remuneration. Given the role of executive compensation in the banking sector, and the perverse incentives to maximize share price at the expense of bank risk, regulators worldwide have moved to limit top executive pay. However, this does not seem to have reduced the extremely high remuneration deals for executives.

VALUING EXECUTIVE COMPENSATION

In this section, we value executive share options. Not surprisingly, the complexity of the total compensation package often makes valuation a difficult task. The economic value of the options depends on factors such as the volatility of the underlying equity and the exact terms of the option grant.

Only a few countries fully disclose the details of executive pay, and in Example 21.6, we shall estimate the economic value of the options held by the chief executive of a hypothetical company. Example 21.6 is necessarily simplistic, but it illustrates how we can value executive share options. Simple matters such as requiring the executive to hold the option during the vesting period can significantly diminish the value of a standard option.

Equally important, the Black–Scholes formula has to be modified if the equity pays dividends, and it is no longer applicable if the volatility of the equity is changing randomly over time. These are not issues with the standard short-term equity options but are very important for long-term options such as ESOs. Intuitively, a call option on a dividend-paying equity is worth less than a call on an equity that pays no dividends: all other things being equal, the dividends will lower the share price. Nevertheless, let us see what we can do.

The value of the options we computed in Example 21.6 would be the economic value of the options if they were to trade in the market. The real question is this: whose value are we talking about? Are these the costs of the options to the company? Are they the values of the options to the executives?

The total value of €24 million for Ian Brown's options in Example 21.6 is the amount that the options would trade at in the financial markets and which traders and investors would be willing to pay for them.

> **EXAMPLE 21.6**
>
> ### OPTIONS AT SUNSHINE RAIN LTD
>
> Consider Ian Brown, the chief executive officer (CEO) of Sunshine Rain, who has been granted 2 million executive share options. The average share price at the time of the options grant was €39.71. We shall assume that his options are at the money. The risk-free rate is 5 per cent, and the options expire in 5 years. The preceding information implies that:
>
> 1. The share price (S) of €39.71 equals the exercise price (E).
> 2. The risk-free rate, $R = 0.05$.
> 3. The time interval, $t = 5$.
>
> In addition, the variance of Sunshine Rain is estimated to be $(0.2168)^2 = 0.0470$.
>
> This information allows us to value Ian Brown's options using the Black–Scholes model:
>
> $$C = SN(d_1) - Ee^{-Rt}N(d_2)$$
> $$d_1 = \left[(R + \sigma^2/2)t\right]/\sqrt{\sigma^2 t} = 0.758$$
> $$d_2 = d_1 - \sqrt{\sigma^2 t} = 0.273$$
> $$N(d_1) = 0.776$$
> $$N(d_2) = 0.608$$
> $$e^{-0.05 \times 5} = 0.7788$$
> $$C = €39.71 \times 0.776 - €39.71 \times (0.778 \times 0.608) = €12.03$$
>
> Thus the value of a call option on one share of Sunshine Rain equity is €12.03. Because Mr Brown was granted options on 2 million shares, the market value of his options, as estimated by the Black–Scholes formula, is about €24 million (= 2 million × €12.03).

If Sunshine Rain was very large, it would not be unreasonable to view this as the cost of granting the options to the CEO, Ian Brown. Of course, in return, the company would expect Mr Brown to improve the value of the company to its shareholders by more than this amount. As we have seen, perhaps the main purpose of options is to align the interests of management with those of the firm's shareholders. Under no circumstances, though, is the €24 million necessarily a fair measure of what the options are worth to Mr Brown.

As an illustration, suppose that the CEO of London Conversation plc has options on 1 million shares with an exercise price of €30 per share, and the current share price of London Conversation is €50. If the options were exercised today, they would be worth €20 million (underestimating their market value). Suppose, in addition, that the CEO owns €5 million in company equity and has €5 million in other assets. The CEO clearly has a very undiversified personal portfolio. By the standards of modern finance, having 25/30 or about 83 per cent of your personal wealth in one equity and its options is unnecessarily risky.

Although the CEO is wealthy by most standards, shifts in share price impact the CEO's economic wellbeing. If the price drops from €50 per share to €30 per share, the current exercise value of the options on 1 million shares drops from €20 million down to zero. Ignoring the fact that if the options had more time to mature they might not lose all of this value, we nevertheless have a rather startling decline in the CEO's net worth from about €30 million to €8 million (€5 million in other assets plus equity that is now worth €3 million). But that is the purpose of giving the options and the equity holdings to the CEO – namely, to make the CEO's fortunes rise and fall with those of the company. It is why the company requires the executive to hold the options for at least a vesting period rather than letting the executive sell them to realize their value.

The implication is that when options are a large portion of an executive's net worth, the total value of the position to the executive is less than market value. As a purely financial matter, an executive might be happier with €5 million in cash than €20 million in options. At least the executive could then diversify his personal portfolio. The shift in recent years from executive share options to restricted stock units suggests that, in practice, the effective minimum value of executive share options is not zero.

If companies systematically respond to deep out-of-the-money options by converting them to RSUs, they are exercising another option to exchange the share option for an RSU. As with any option, this has value to the holder, in this case, the senior executive.

REAL WORLD INSIGHTS

Executive compensation is usually made up of base salary plus some or all of the following elements:

1. Base salary.
2. Annual bonuses.
3. Long-term incentives, such as retirement contributions, options and restricted stock units.

When stock markets are on an upward trajectory, the final component of compensation, options, is by far the biggest part of total compensation for many top executives. In many parts of Europe, full disclosure of executive pay is not yet normal practice. However, this has not stopped politicians and the media from decrying the total pay of executives, whose share options are a major component of their total remuneration. The figure below presents a breakdown of chief executive pay in Europe between 2015 and 2019. Bonuses represent any payments paid for performance during the year, and long-term incentives include executive share options.

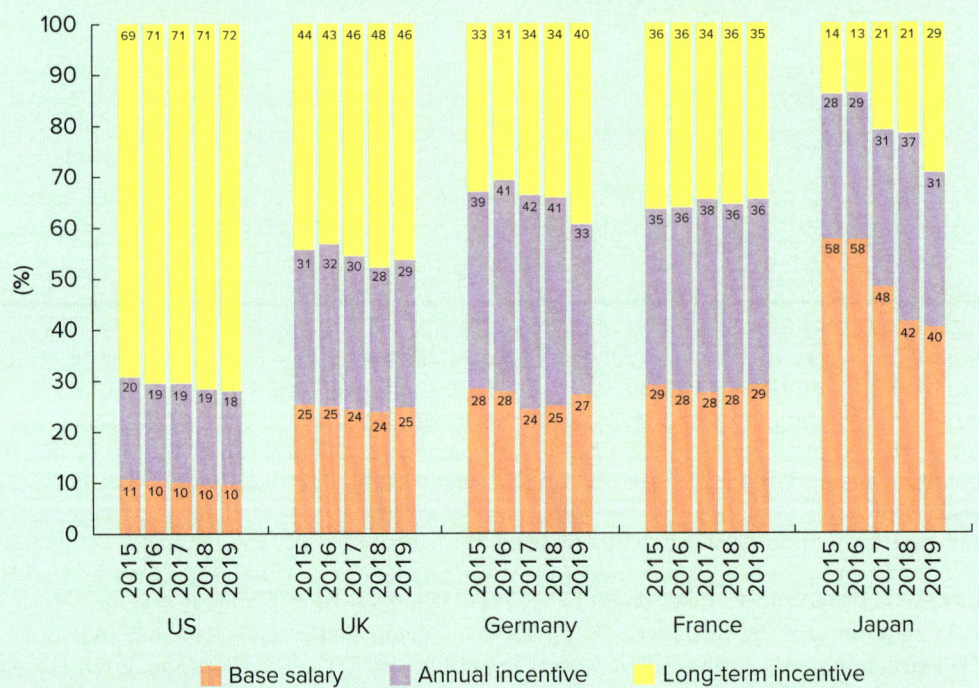

Source: Willis Towers Watson, CEO pay landscape in Japan, the US and Europe – 2020 analysis, December 2020.

As can be seen, performance-based remuneration (annual bonuses and long-term incentives) has been more popular in Europe and the US than in Japan.

CONCEPT QUESTIONS

21.6a What are the key differences between a traded share option and an ESO?
21.6b What are the benefits of ESOs? Why are ESOs controversial?
21.6c Why is the value of an ESO to the holder less than its market value?

21.7 OPTION APPLICATIONS: EQUITY AS A CALL OPTION ON THE FIRM'S ASSETS

One of the most important insights we gain from studying options is that the equity in a leveraged firm (one that has issued debt) is effectively a call option on the firm's assets. This is a remarkable observation, and we explore it next.

Looking at an example is the easiest way to get started. Suppose a firm has a single debt issue outstanding. The face value is £1,000, and the debt is coming due in a year. There are no coupon payments between now and then, so the debt is effectively a pure discount bond. In addition, the current market value of the firm's assets is £980, and the risk-free rate is 12.5 per cent.

In a year, the shareholders will have a choice. They can pay off the debt for £1,000 and thereby acquire the firm's assets free and clear, or they can default on the debt. If they default, the bondholders will own the assets of the firm.

In this situation, the shareholders essentially have a call option on the firm's assets, with an exercise price of £1,000. They can exercise the option by paying the £1,000 or choose not to exercise the option by defaulting. Whether or not they will choose to exercise obviously depends on the value of the firm's assets when the debt becomes due.

If the value of the firm's assets exceeds £1,000, then the option is in the money, and the shareholders will exercise by paying off the debt. If the value of the firm's assets is less than £1,000, then the option is out of the money, and the shareholders will optimally choose to default. We now illustrate that we can determine the debt and equity value using our option pricing results.

CASE I: THE DEBT IS RISK-FREE

Suppose that in one year, the firm's assets will be worth either £1,100 or £1,200. What is the value today of the equity in the firm? The value of the debt? What is the interest rate on the debt?

To answer these questions, we first recognize that the option (the firm's equity) is certain to finish in the money because the value of the firm's assets (£1,100 or £1,200) will always exceed the face value of the debt. In this case, from our discussion in previous sections, we know that the option value is simply the difference between the value of the underlying asset and the present value of the exercise price (calculated at the risk-free rate). The present value of £1,000 in one year at 12.5 per cent is £888.89. The firm's current value is £980, so the option (the firm's equity) is worth £980 − 888.89 = £91.11.

We see that the equity, which is effectively an option to purchase the firm's assets, must be worth £91.11. The debt must, therefore, actually be worth £888.89. In fact, we didn't really need to know about options to handle this example because the debt is risk-free. The reason is that the bondholders are certain to receive £1,000. Because the debt is risk-free, the appropriate discount rate (and the interest rate on the debt) is the risk-free rate, and we, therefore, know immediately that the current value of the debt is £1,000/1.125 = £888.89. The equity is thus worth £980 − 888.89 = £91.11, as we calculated.

CASE II: THE DEBT IS RISKY

Suppose now that the value of the firm's assets in one year will be either £800 or £1,200. This case is a little more difficult because the debt is no longer risk-free. If the assets' value turns out to be £800, then the shareholders will not exercise their option and thereby default. The equity is worth nothing in this case. If the assets are worth £1,200, the shareholders will exercise their option to pay off the debt and enjoy a profit of £1,200 − 1,000 = £200.

We see that the option (the equity in the firm) will be worth either zero or £200. The assets will be worth either £1,200 or £800. Based on our discussion in previous sections, a portfolio with the present value of £800 invested in a risk-free asset and (£1,200 − 800)/(200 − 0) = 2 call options exactly replicates the value of the assets of the firm.

The present value of £800 at the risk-free rate of 12.5 per cent is £800/1.125 = £711.11. This amount, plus the value of the two call options, is equal to £980, the current value of the firm:

$$£980 = 2 \times C_0 + £711.11$$
$$C_0 = £134.44$$

Because the call option, in this case, is actually the firm's equity, the value of the equity is £134.44. The value of the debt is thus £980 − 134.44 = £845.56. Finally, because the debt has a £1,000 face value and a current value of £845.56, the interest rate is (£1,000/845.56) − 1 = 18.27%. This exceeds the risk-free rate, of course, because the debt is now risky.

EXAMPLE 21.7

EQUITY AS A CALL OPTION

Swenson Software has a pure discount debt issue with a face value of €100. The issue is due in a year. At that time, the firm's assets will be worth either €55 or €160, depending on the sales success of Swenson's latest product. The assets of the firm are currently worth €110. If the risk-free rate is 10 per cent, what is the value of the equity in Swenson? The value of the debt? The interest rate on the debt?

To replicate the value of the assets of the firm, we first need to invest the present value of €55 in the risk-free asset. This costs €55/1.10 = €50. If the assets turn out to be worth €160, then the option is worth €160 − 100 = €60. Our risk-free asset will be worth €55, so we need (€160 − 55)/60 = 1.75 call options. Because the firm is currently worth €110, we have:

$$€110 = 1.75 \times C_0 + €50$$
$$C_0 = €34.29$$

Thus, the equity is worth €34.29; the debt is worth €110 − 34.29 = €75.71. The interest rate on the debt is about (€100/75.71) − 1 = 32.1%.

CONCEPT QUESTIONS

21.7a Why do we say that a leveraged firm's equity is effectively a call option on the firm's assets?

21.7b All other things being the same, would the firm's shareholders prefer to increase or decrease the volatility of the firm's return on assets? Why? What about the bondholders? Give an intuitive explanation.

21.8 OPTION APPLICATIONS: CAPITAL BUDGETING

real option
an option that involves real assets as opposed to financial assets such as shares of equity.

Most of the options we have discussed so far are financial options because they involve the right to buy or sell financial assets such as shares of equity. In contrast, **real options** involve real assets. As we shall discuss in this section, our understanding of capital budgeting can be greatly enhanced by recognizing that many corporate investment decisions really amount to the evaluation of real options.

To give a simple example of a real option, imagine that you are shopping for a used car. You find one that you like for £4,000, but you are not completely sure. You give the car owner £150 to hold the car for you for one week, meaning that you have one week to buy the car, or else you forfeit your £150. As you probably recognize, what you have done here is purchase a call option, giving you the right to buy the car at a fixed price for a fixed time. It's a real option because the underlying asset (the car) is a real asset.

The use of options such as the one in our car example is common in the business world. For example, property developers frequently need to purchase several smaller tracts of land from different owners to assemble a single larger tract. The development can't go forward unless all the smaller properties are obtained. In this case, the developer will often buy options on the individual properties but will exercise those options only if all the necessary pieces can be obtained.

These examples involve explicit options. As it turns out, almost all capital budgeting decisions contain numerous *implicit* options. We discuss the most important types of these next.

THE INVESTMENT TIMING DECISION

Consider a business that is examining a new project of some sort. What this normally means is that management must decide whether to make an investment outlay to acquire the new assets needed for the project. If you think about it, what management has is the right, but not the obligation, to pay some fixed amount (the initial investment) and thereby acquire a real asset (the project). In other words, essentially all proposed projects are real options!

Based on our discussion in previous chapters, you already know how to analyse proposed business investments. You would identify and analyse the relevant cash flows and assess the net present value (NPV) of the proposal. If the NPV is positive, you would recommend taking the project, where taking the project amounts to exercising the option.

There is an important qualification to this discussion that involves mutually exclusive investments. Remember that two (or more) investments are mutually exclusive if we can take only one of them. A standard example is a situation in which we own a piece of land that we wish to build on. We are considering building either a petrol station or an apartment building. We further think that both projects have positive NPVs, but of course, we can take only one. Which one do we take? The obvious answer is that we take the one with the larger NPV.

Here is the key point. Just because an investment has a positive NPV doesn't mean we should take it today. That sounds like a complete contradiction of what we have said all along, but it isn't. The reason is that if we take a project today, we can't take it later. Put differently, almost all projects compete with themselves in time. We can take a project now, a month from now, a year from now, and so on. We therefore have to compare the NPV of taking the project now with the NPV of taking it later. Deciding when to take a project is called the *investment timing decision*.

A simple example is useful to illustrate the investment timing decision. A project costs €100 and has a single future cash flow. If we take it today, the cash flow will be €120 in one year. If we wait one year, the project will still cost €100, but the cash flow the following year (two years from now) will be €130 because the potential market is bigger. If these are the only two options, and the relevant discount rate is 10 per cent, what should we do?

To answer this question, we need to compute the two NPVs. If we take it today, the NPV is:

$$NPV = -€100 + 120/1.1 = €9.09$$

If we wait one year, the NPV at that time would be:

$$NPV = -€100 + 130/1.1 = €18.18$$

This €18.18 is the NPV one year from now. We need the value today, so we discount back one period:

$$NPV = €18.18/1.1 = €16.53$$

So the choice is clear. If we wait, the NPV is €16.53 today compared with €9.09 if we start immediately, so the optimal time to begin the project is one year from now.

The fact that we do not have to take a project immediately is often called the *option to wait*. In our simple example, the value of the option to wait is the difference in NPVs: €16.53 − 9.09 = €7.44. This €7.44 is the extra value created by deferring the start of the project instead of taking it today.

As our example illustrates, the option to wait can be valuable. Just how valuable depends on the type of project. If we were thinking about a consumer product intended to capitalize on a current fashion or trend, then the option to wait is probably not valuable because the window of opportunity is probably short. In contrast, suppose the project in question is a proposal to replace an existing production facility with a new, higher-efficiency one. This type of investment can be made now or later. In this case, the option to wait may be valuable.

There is another important aspect of the option to wait. Just because a project has a negative NPV today doesn't mean that we should permanently reject it. For example, suppose an investment costs £120 and has a perpetual cash flow of £10 per year. If the discount rate is 10 per cent, then the NPV is £10/0.10 − 120 = −£20, so the project should not be taken.

> **EXAMPLE 21.8**
>
> ### THE INVESTMENT TIMING DECISION
>
> A project costs £200 and has a future cash flow of £42 per year forever. If we wait for one year, the project will cost £240 because of inflation, but the cash flows will be £48 per year forever. If these are the only two options, and the relevant discount rate is 12 per cent, what should we do? What is the value of the option to wait? In this case, the project is a simple perpetuity. If we take it today, the NPV is:
>
> $$NPV = -£200 + 42/0.12 = £150$$
>
> If we wait one year, the NPV at that time would be:
>
> $$NPV = -£240 + 48/0.12 = £160$$
>
> So £160 is the NPV one year from now, but we need to know the value today. Discounting back one period, we get:
>
> $$NPV = £160/1.12 = £142.86$$
>
> If we wait, the NPV is £142.86 today compared with £150 if we start immediately, so the optimal time to begin the project is now.
>
> What's the value of the option to wait? It is tempting to say that it is £142.86 − £150 = −£7.14, but that's wrong. Why? Because, as we discussed earlier, an option can never have a negative value. In this case, the option to wait has a zero value.

We should not just forget about this project forever, though. Suppose that next year, for some reason, the relevant discount rate fell to 5 per cent. Then the NPV would be £10/0.05 − 120 = £80, and we would take the project (assuming that further waiting wasn't even more valuable). More generally, as long as there is some possible future scenario under which a project has a positive NPV, then the option to wait is valuable, and we should shelve the project proposal for now.

MANAGERIAL OPTIONS

Once we decide the optimal time to launch a project, other real options come into play. Thus far, in our capital budgeting analysis, we have more or less ignored the impact of managerial actions that might occur *after* a project is launched. In effect, we assumed that, once a project is launched, its basic features cannot be changed.

In reality, depending on what actually happens in the future, there will always be opportunities to modify a project. These opportunities, which are an important type of real option, are often called *managerial options*. There are a great number of these options. How a product is priced, manufactured, advertised or produced can all be changed, and these are just a few of the possibilities.

Contingency Planning

The various what-if procedures, particularly the break-even measures we discussed in an earlier chapter, have a use beyond that of simply evaluating cash flow and NPV estimates. We can also view these procedures and measures as primitive ways of exploring the dynamics of a project and investigating managerial options. What we think about in this case are some of the possible futures that could come about and what actions we might take if they do.

For example, we might find that a project fails to break even when sales drop below 10,000 units. This is a fact that is interesting to know, but the more important thing is to go on then and ask: what actions are we going to take if this actually occurs? This is called *contingency planning*, and it amounts to an investigation of some of the managerial options implicit in a project.

There is no limit to the number of possible futures or contingencies we could investigate. However, there are some broad classes, and we consider these next.

The Option to Expand

One particularly important option we have not explicitly addressed is the option to expand. If we truly find a positive-NPV project, then there is an obvious consideration. Can we expand the project or repeat it to get an even larger NPV? Our static analysis implicitly assumes that the scale of the project is fixed.

For example, if the sales demand for a particular product exceeded expectations greatly, we might investigate increasing production. If this is not feasible for some reason, then we could always increase cash flow by raising the price. Either way, the potential cash flow is higher than we have indicated because we have implicitly assumed that no expansion or price increase is possible. Overall, because we ignore the option to expand in our analysis, we underestimate NPV (all other things being equal).

The Option to Abandon

At the other extreme, the option to scale back or even abandon a project is also quite valuable. For example, if a project does not break even on a cash flow basis, then it can't even cover its own expenses. We would be better off if we just abandoned it. Our DCF analysis implicitly assumes that we would keep operating even in this case.

If sales demand were significantly below expectations, we might be able to sell off some capacity or put it to another use. Maybe the product or service could be redesigned or otherwise improved. Regardless of the specifics, we once again *underestimate* NPV if we assume that the project must last for some fixed number of years, no matter what happens in the future.

The Option to Suspend or Contract Operations

An option that is closely related to the option to abandon is suspending operations. Frequently we see companies choosing to temporarily shut down an activity of some sort. For example, car manufacturers sometimes find themselves with too many vehicles of a particular type. In this case, production is often halted until the excess supply is worked off. At some point in the future, production resumes.

The option to suspend operations is particularly valuable in natural resource extraction. Suppose you own a gold mine. If gold prices fall dramatically, then your analysis might show that it costs more to extract an ounce of gold than you can sell the gold for, so you cease mining. The gold stays in the ground, however, and you can always resume operations if the price rises sufficiently. In fact, operations might be suspended and restarted many times over the life of the mine.

Companies also sometimes choose to scale back an activity permanently. If a new product does not sell as well as planned, production might be cut back and the excess capacity put to some other use. This case is really just the opposite of the option to expand, so we shall label it the option to contract.

Options in Capital Budgeting: An Example

Suppose we are examining a new project. To keep things relatively simple, let's say that we expect to sell 100 units per year at €1 net cash flow apiece into perpetuity. We thus expect that the cash flow will be €100 per year.

In one year, we shall know more about the project. In particular, we shall have a better idea of whether it is successful. If it looks like a long-term success, the expected sales will be revised to 150 units per year. If it does not, the expected sales will be revised downwards to 50 units per year. Success and failure are equally likely. Notice that because there is an even chance of selling 50 or 150 units, the expected sales are still 100 units, as we originally projected. The cost is €550, and the discount rate is 20 per cent. The project can be dismantled and sold in one year for €400 if we decide to abandon it. Should we take it?

A standard DCF analysis is not difficult. The expected cash flow is €100 per year forever, and the discount rate is 20 per cent. The PV of the cash flows is €100/0.20 = €500, so the NPV is €500 − 550 = − €50. We shouldn't take the project.

This analysis ignores valuable options, however. In one year, we can sell out for €400. How can we account for this? What we have to do is to decide what we are going to do one year from now. In this simple case, we need to evaluate only two contingencies – an upward revision and a downward revision – so the extra work is not great.

In one year, if the expected cash flows are revised to €50, then the PV of the cash flows is revised downwards to €50/0.20 = €250. We get €400 by abandoning the project, so that is what we shall do (the NPV of keeping the project in one year is €250 − 400 = −€150).

If the demand is revised upwards, then the PV of the future cash flows at year 1 is €150/0.20 = €750. This exceeds the €400 abandonment value, so we shall keep the project.

We now have a project that costs €550 today. In one year, we expect a cash flow of €100 from the project. In addition, this project will be worth either €400 (if we abandon it because it is a failure) or €750 (if we keep it because it succeeds). These outcomes are equally likely, so we expect the project to be worth (€400 + 750)/2, or €575.

Summing up, in one year, we expect to have €100 in cash plus a project worth €575, or €675 total. At a 20 per cent discount rate, this €675 is worth €562.50 today, so the NPV is €562.50 − 550 = €12.50. We should take the project.

The NPV of our project has increased by €62.50. Where did this come from? Our original analysis implicitly assumed we would keep the project, even if it were a failure. At year 1, however, we saw that we were €150 better off (€400 versus €250) if we abandoned. There was a 50 per cent chance of this happening, so the expected gain from abandoning is €75. The PV of this amount is the value of the option to abandon: €75/1.20 = €62.50.

Strategic Options

Companies sometimes undertake new projects to explore possibilities and evaluate potential future business strategies. This is a little like testing the water by sticking a toe in before diving. Such projects are difficult to analyse using conventional DCF methods because most of the benefits come in the form of *strategic options* – that is, options for future, related business moves. Projects that create such options may be very valuable, but that value is difficult to measure. Research and development, for example, is an important and valuable activity for many firms, precisely because it creates options for new products and procedures.

To give another example, a large manufacturer might open a retail outlet as a pilot study. The primary goal is to gain some market insight. Because of the high start-up costs, this one operation won't break even. However, using the sales experience gained from the pilot, the firm can then evaluate whether to open more outlets, to change the product mix, to enter new markets, and so on. The information gained and the resulting options for actions are all valuable, but coming up with a reliable cash figure is probably not feasible.

Conclusion

We have seen that incorporating options into capital budgeting analysis is not easy. What can we do about them in practice? The answer is that we need to keep them in mind as we work with the projected cash flows. We shall tend to underestimate NPV by ignoring options. The damage might be small for a highly structured, very specific proposal, but it might be great for an exploratory one.

> **CONCEPT QUESTIONS**
>
> **21.8a** Why do we say that almost every capital budgeting proposal involves mutually exclusive alternatives?
> **21.8b** What are the options to expand, abandon and suspend operations?
> **21.8c** What are strategic options?

SUMMARY AND CONCLUSIONS

This chapter has described the basics of option valuation and discussed option-like corporate securities:

1. Options are contracts giving the right, but not the obligation, to buy and sell underlying assets at a fixed price during a specified period. The most familiar options are puts and calls involving shares of equity. These options give the holder the right, but not the obligation, to sell (the put option) or buy (the call option) shares of equity at a given price.

As we discussed, the value of any option depends on only five factors:
   (a) The price of the underlying asset.
   (b) The exercise price.
   (c) The expiration date.
   (d) The interest rate on risk-free bonds.
   (e) The volatility of the underlying asset's value.
2. The put-call parity (PCP) condition tells us that among a call option, a put option, a risk-free investment such as a T-bill, and an underlying asset such as shares of equity, we can replicate any one using the other three.
3. The Black–Scholes Option Pricing Model (OPM) lets us explicitly value call options given values for the five relevant inputs, which are the price of the underlying asset, the strike price, the time to expiration, the risk-free rate, and the standard deviation of the return on the underlying asset.
4. Many companies use executive share options (ESOs). Such options are similar to call options and serve to motivate employees to boost share prices. ESOs are also an important form of compensation for many workers, particularly at more senior management levels.
5. Almost all capital budgeting proposals can be viewed as real options. Also, projects and operations contain implicit options, such as the option to expand, the option to abandon, and the option to suspend or contract operations.

CHAPTER REVIEW AND SELF-TEST PROBLEMS

21.1 Value of a Call Option Equity in REM plc is currently selling for £25 per share. In one year the price will be either £20 or £30. T-bills with one year to maturity are paying 10 per cent. What is the value of a call option with a £20 exercise price? A £6 exercise price?

21.2 Put-Call Parity An equity sells for €40 per share. The continuously compounded risk-free rate is 8 per cent per year. A call option with one month to expiration and a strike price of €45 sells for €1. What is the value of a put option with the same expiration and strike?

21.3 Black-Scholes An equity sells for €40 per share. The continuously compounded risk-free rate is 4 per cent. The standard deviation of the return on the equity is 80 per cent. What is the value of a put option with a strike of €45 and a three-month expiration?

SOLUTIONS

21.1 With a £20 exercise price, the option can't finish out of the money (it can finish 'at the money' if the share price is £20). We can replicate the value of the equity by investing the present value of £20 in T-bills and buying one call option. Buying the T-bill will cost £20/1.1 = £18.18.

If the share price ends up at £20, the call option will be worth zero, and the T-bill will pay £20. If the share price ends up at £30, the T-bill will again pay £20, and the option will be worth £30 − 20 = £10, so the package will be worth £30. Because the T-bill-call option combination duplicates the pay-off on the equity, it has to be worth £25, or arbitrage is possible. Using the notation from the chapter, we can calculate the value of the call option:

$$S_0 = C_0 + E/(1 + R_f)$$
$$£25 = C_0 + £18.18$$
$$C_0 = £6.82$$

With the £26 exercise price, we start by investing the present value of the lower share price in T-bills. This guarantees us £20 when the share price is £20. If the share price is £30, then the option is worth £30 − 26 = £4. We have £20 from our T-bill, so we need £10 from the options to match the equity. Because each option is worth £4 in this case, we need to buy

£10/4 = 2.5 call options. Notice that the difference in the possible share prices (S) is £10, and the difference in the possible option prices (C) is £4, so $S/C = 2.5$.

To complete the calculation, we note that the present value of the £20 plus 2.5 call options has to be £25 to prevent arbitrage, so:

$$£25 = 2.5 \times C_0 + £20/1.1$$
$$C_0 = 6.82/2.5$$
$$= £2.73$$

21.2 The PCP condition says that:

$$S + P = E \times e^{-Rt} + C$$

Filling in the relevant numbers and rearranging to solve for P, the put price, we get:

$$P = €45 \times e^{-0.08(1/12)} + 1 - 40$$
$$= 5.70$$

21.3 We shall do this one the long way and then check our answer using our options spreadsheet. We shall calculate the value of a call option and then convert it to a put using PCP. We first need d_1 and d_2.

$$d_1 = \left[\ln\left(\frac{S}{E}\right) + \left(R + \sigma^2/2\right)t\right] / \sqrt{\sigma^2 t}$$
$$= \left[\ln\left(\frac{40}{45}\right) + \left(0.04 + 0.8^2/2\right) \times \frac{1}{4}\right] / \sqrt{0.8^2 \times \frac{1}{4}}$$
$$= -0.07$$
$$d_2 = d_1 - \sqrt{\sigma^2 t}$$
$$= 0.47$$

Referring to Table 21.4, the values of $N(d_1)$ and $N(d_2)$ are 0.4721 and 0.3192, respectively. Notice that in both cases, we average two values. Plugging all the numbers in:

$$C = S \times [N(d_1)] - Ee^{-Rt} \times [N(d_2)]$$
$$= €40 \times 0.4721 - €45 \times e^{-0.04 \times (1/4)} \times 0.3192$$
$$= €4.66$$

Converting to a put as in our previous question:

$$P = Ee^{-Rt} + C - S$$

Plugging in the relevant numbers, we get:

$$P = €45 e^{-0.04(1/4)} + 4.66 - 40$$
$$= €9.21$$

Using our spreadsheet, we get the following:

	A	B	C	D	E
1	Share Price =	40		d1 =	-0.06946
2	Strike Price =	45		d2 =	-0.46946
3	Sigma =	0.8		N(d1) =	0.472313
4	Time =	0.25		N(d2) =	0.319371
5	Rate =	0.04			
6					
7	Call =	4.6638		Put =	9.216043

Our 'by hand' approach was pretty accurate in this case.

QUESTIONS AND PROBLEMS

Level of difficulty: Basic · Intermediate · Challenge

21.1 Calculating Option Values T-bills currently yield 2.1 per cent and the Man Group plc share price is £0.97. There is no possibility that the equity will be worth less than £0.50 per share in one year.

(a) What is the value of a call option with a £0.97 exercise price? What is the intrinsic value of a call option with a £0.97 exercise price?

(b) What is the value of a call option with a £0.70 exercise price? What is the intrinsic value of a call option with a £0.70 exercise price?

(c) What is the value of a call option with a £1.10 exercise price? What is the intrinsic value of a call option with a £1.10 exercise price?

21.2 Understanding Option Quotes Use the option quote information from Euronext Liffe shown here for Aegon NV to answer the questions that follow. The equity is currently selling for €4.02.

TABLE 21.7

26 February 2021 Prices – 22/02/21

SETTL	LAST	BID	ASK		STRIKE		BID	ASK	LAST	SETTL.
0.44	–	0.45	0.60	C	3.50	P	–	0.15	–	0.01
0.34	–	0.35	0.50	C	3.60	P	–	0.15	–	0.01
0.25	–	0.27	0.38	C	3.70	P	–	0.15	–	0.01
0.16	–	0.16	0.27	C	3.80	P	–	0.03	–	0.03
0.08	0.14	0.10	0.20	C	3.90	P	–	0.04	0.05	0.05
0.05	–	0.04	0.08	C	4.00	P	0.02	0.07	0.09	0.11
0.02	0.03	0.01	0.06	C	4.10	P	0.07	0.15	–	0.18
0.01	–	–	0.15	C	4.20	P	–	0.27	–	0.27
–	–	–	–	C	4.30	P	–	–	–	–
0.01	–	–	0.15	C	4.40	P	–	0.46	–	0.47

(a) Are the call options in the money? What is the intrinsic value of an Aegon NV call option?

(b) Are the put options in the money? What is the intrinsic value of an Aegon NV put option?

21.3 Calculating Pay-offs Use the option quote information on Bayer AG from Euronext Liffe shown here to answer the questions that follow. Assume lot size per contract is 100 shares and the share price is €53.63.

TABLE 21.8

March 2021 Prices – 22/02/21

SETTL	LAST	BID	ASK		STRIKE		BID	ASK	LAST	SETTL.
4.07	–	3.73	3.97	C	51.00	P	1.32	1.48	-	1.18
3.74	–	3.41	3.67	C	51.50	P	1.50	1.66	-	1.35
3.42	–	3.10	3.33	C	52.00	P	1.69	1.85	1.60	1.53
3.11	–	–	–	C	52.50	P	-	–	–	1.72
2.83	–	2.54	2.73	C	53.00	P	2.13	2.29	2.09	1.95

SETTL	LAST	BID	ASK		STRIKE		BID	ASK	LAST	SETTL.
2.57	–	–	–	C	53.50	P	–	–	–	2.18
2.31	2.00	2.04	2.19	C	54.00	P	2.63	5.05	–	2.43
2.09	–	–	–	C	54.50	P	–	–	–	2.71
1.87	1.79	1.64	1.80	C	55.00	P	3.15	3.39	–	2.99
1.68	–	–	–	C	55.50	P	–	–	–	3.29
1.50	1.39	1.30	1.46	C	56.00	P	3.75	4.04	–	3.62

(a) Suppose you buy 10 contracts of the March €53.50 call option. How much will you pay, ignoring commissions?

(b) In part (a), suppose that Bayer equity is selling for €51 per share on the expiration date. How much is your options investment worth? What if the terminal share price is €56? Explain.

(c) Suppose you buy 10 contracts of the March €53.50 put option. What is your maximum gain? On the expiration date, Bayer is selling for €51 per share. How much is your options investment worth? What is your net gain?

(d) In part (c), suppose you *sell* 10 of the March €53.50 put contracts. What is your net gain or loss if Bayer is selling for €51 at expiration? For €56? What is the break-even price – that is, the terminal share price that results in a zero profit?

21.4 Calculating Option Values The price of ABC plc will be either £2 or £1.50 at the end of the year. Call options are available with one year to expiration. UK government bond yields are currently at 3 per cent.

(a) Suppose the current share price of ABC plc is £1.74. What is the value of the call option if the exercise price is £1.75 per share?

(b) Suppose the exercise price is £1.90 in part (a). What is the value of the call option now?

21.5 Equity as an Option Rackin Pinion NV's assets are currently worth €1,050. In one year they will be worth either €1,000 or €1,270. The risk-free interest rate is 7 per cent. Suppose Rackin Pinion has an outstanding debt issue with a face value of €1,000.

(a) What is the value of the equity?

(b) What is the value of the debt? The interest rate on the debt?

(c) Would the value of the equity go up or down if the risk-free rate were 20 per cent? Why? What does your answer illustrate?

21.6 Put-Call Parity BP plc shares are currently selling for £4.29 per share. A put option with an exercise price of £4.40 sells for £0.25 and expires in three months. If the risk-free rate of interest is 2.6 per cent per year, compounded continuously, what is the price of a call option with the same exercise price?

21.7 Put-Call Parity A Capgemini put option and a call option with an exercise price of €1 and three months to expiration sell for €0.28 and €0.11, respectively. If the risk-free rate is 0.5 per cent per year, compounded continuously, what is the current share price?

21.8 Put-Call Parity Danone call and put options with an exercise price of €17 expire in four months and sell for €2.07 and €2.03, respectively. If the equity is currently priced at €17.03, what is the annual continuously compounded rate of interest?

21.9 Black-Scholes The spot price of XYZ plc is 394.5p, with a standard deviation of 20 per cent. A call option on the stock expires in 219 days, and it has a strike price of 400p, with a quoted price of 18p. The risk-free rate is 1 per cent.

(a) Find the Black-Scholes value of the call.

(b) Why does the Black-Scholes value not match the quoted price of the call?

21.10 Black-Scholes and Asset Value Coal mining is becoming more popular because of the demand for energy in Asia. Assume that you have the rights to a coal mine and the most recent valuation of the mine was £6.7 million. Because of increasing demand from Asia, the price of similar mines has grown by 15 per cent per annum, with an annual standard deviation of 20 per cent. A buyer has recently approached you and wants an option to buy the mine in the next 12 months for £7 million. The risk-free rate of interest is 3 per cent per year, compounded continuously. How much should you charge for the option?

21.11 Abandonment Value We are examining a new project. We expect to sell 7,500 units per year at £68 net cash flow apiece for the next 10 years. In other words, the annual operating cash flow is projected to be £68 × 7,500 = £510,000. The relevant discount rate is 14 per cent, and the initial investment required is £2,300,000.

(a) What is the base-case NPV?

(b) After the first year, the project can be dismantled and sold for £1,500,000. If expected sales are revised, based on the first year's performance, when would it make sense to abandon the investment? In other words, at what level of expected sales would it make sense to abandon the project?

(c) Explain how the £1,500,000 abandonment value can be viewed as the opportunity cost of keeping the project in one year.

21.12 Abandonment In the previous problem, suppose you think it is likely that expected sales will be revised upwards to 9,500 units if the first year is a success, and revised downwards to 4,000 units if the first year is not a success.

(a) If success and failure are equally likely, what is the NPV of the project? Consider the possibility of abandonment in answering.

(b) What is the value of the option to abandon?

21.13 Abandonment and Expansion In the previous problem, suppose the scale of the project can be doubled in one year, in the sense that twice as many units can be produced and sold. Naturally, expansion will be desirable only if the project is a success. This implies that if the project is a success, projected sales after expansion will be 19,000. Again assuming that success and failure are equally likely, what is the NPV of the project? Note that abandonment is still an option if the project is a failure. What is the value of the option to expand?

21.14 Abandonment Decisions Top Products is considering a new product launch for its products. The firm expects to have annual operating cash flow of €18 million for the next eight years. Top Products uses a discount rate of 14 per cent for new product launches. The initial investment is €75 million. Assume that the project has no salvage value at the end of its economic life.

(a) What is the NPV of the new product?

(b) After the first year, the project can be dismantled and sold for €30 million. If the estimates of remaining cash flows are revised, based on the first year's experience, at what level of expected cash flows does it make sense to abandon the project?

21.15 Black-Scholes A call option matures in six months. The underlying share price is £85, and the share's return has a standard deviation of 20 per cent per year. The risk-free rate is 4 per cent per year, compounded continuously. If the exercise price is £0, what is the price of the call option?

21.16 Black-Scholes Bayer AG is currently priced at €53.63. A call option with an expiration of six months has an exercise price of €52. The risk-free rate is 1 per cent per year, compounded continuously, and the standard deviation of the equity's return is infinitely large. What is the price of the call option?

21.17 Abandonment Decisions Consider the following project of Hand Clapper SA. The company is considering a four-year project to manufacture clap-command garage door openers. This project requires an initial investment of €12 million, which will be depreciated straight-line to zero over the project's life. An initial investment in net working capital of €900,000 is required to support spare parts inventory: this cost is fully recoverable whenever the project ends. The company believes it can generate €9.1 million in pre-tax revenues with €3.7 million in total pre-tax operating costs. The tax rate is 38 per cent and the discount rate is 13 per cent. The market value of the equipment over the life of the project is as follows:

Year	Market value (€ millions)
1	8.20
2	6.10
3	4.70
4	0.00

(a) Assuming Hand Clapper operates this project for four years, what is the NPV?

(b) Now compute the project NPV assuming the project is abandoned after only one year, after two years, and after three years. What economic life for this project maximizes its value to the firm? What does this problem tell you about not considering abandonment possibilities when evaluating projects?

21.18 Black-Scholes and Dividends In addition to the five factors discussed in the chapter, dividends also affect the price of an option. The Black–Scholes option pricing model with dividends is:

$$C = S \times e^{-dt} \times N(d_1) - E \times e^{-Rt} \times N(d_2)$$
$$d_1 = [\ln(S/E) + (R - d + \sigma^2/2) \times t]/(\sigma \times \sqrt{t})$$
$$d_2 = d_1 - \sigma \times \sqrt{t}$$

All of the variables are the same as in the Black–Scholes model without dividends except for the variable d, which is the continuously compounded dividend yield on the share.

(a) What effect do you think the dividend yield will have on the price of a call option? Explain.

(b) Genmab A/S is currently priced at 2.26 Danish kroner (DKr) per share, the standard deviation of its return is 50 per cent per year, and the risk-free rate is 5 per cent per year, compounded continuously. What is the price of a call option with a strike price of DKr2.00 and a maturity of six months if the share has a dividend yield of 2 per cent per year?

21.19 Put-Call Parity and Dividends The put–call parity condition is altered when dividends are paid. The dividend adjusted put–call parity formula is:

$$S \times e^{-dt} + P = E \times e^{-Rt} + C$$

where d is again the continuously compounded dividend yield. The Black–Scholes option pricing model with dividends is:

$$C = S \times e^{-dt} \times N(d_1) - E \times e^{-Rt} \times N(d_2)$$
$$d_1 = [\ln(S/E) + (R - d + \sigma^2/2) \times t]/(\sigma \times \sqrt{t})$$
$$d_2 = d_1 - \sigma \times \sqrt{t}$$

(a) What effect do you think the dividend yield will have on the price of a put option? Explain.

(b) Genmab A/S is currently priced at 2.26 Danish Kroner (DKr) per share, the standard deviation of its return is 50 per cent per year, and the risk-free rate is 5 per cent per year compounded continuously. What is the price of a put option with a strike price of DKr2.00 and a maturity of six months if the share has a dividend yield of 2 per cent per year?

21.20 Black–Scholes An equity is currently priced at £50. The share will never pay a dividend. The risk-free rate is 12 per cent per year, compounded continuously, and the standard deviation of the share's return is 60 per cent. A European call option on the share has a strike price of £100 and no expiration date, meaning that it has an infinite life. Based on Black–Scholes, what is the value of the call option? What do you know about the relative prices of the put and call if share price and exercise price are the same? Do you see a paradox here? Do you see a way out of the paradox?

MINI CASE

EXOTIC CUISINES EMPLOYEE SHARE OPTIONS

As a new university graduate, you've taken a management position with Exotic Cuisines plc, a restaurant chain that just went public last year. The company's restaurants specialize in exotic main dishes, using ingredients such as wild boar, crocodile and pheasant. A concern you had going in was that the restaurant business is very risky. However, after some due diligence, you discovered a common misperception about the restaurant industry. It is widely thought that 90 per cent of new restaurants close within three years; however, recent evidence suggests the failure rate is closer to 60 per cent over three years. So it is a risky business, although not as risky as you originally thought.

During your interview process, one of the benefits mentioned was employee share options. Upon signing your employment contract, you received options with a strike price of £50 for 10,000 shares of company equity. As is fairly common, your share options have a three-year vesting period and a 10-year expiration, meaning that you cannot exercise the options for three years, and you lose them if you leave before they vest. After the three-year vesting period you can exercise the options at any time. Thus the employee share options are European (and subject to forfeit) for the first three years and American afterwards. Of course, you cannot sell the options, nor can you enter into any sort of hedging agreement. If you leave the company after the options vest, you must exercise within 90 days or forfeit.

Exotic Cuisines equity is currently trading at £24.38 per share, a slight increase from the initial offering price last year. There are no market-traded options on the company's equity. Because the company has been traded for only about a year, you are reluctant to use the historical returns to estimate the standard deviation of the equity's return. However, you have estimated that the average annual standard deviation for restaurant company shares is about 55 per cent. Because Exotic Cuisines is a newer restaurant chain, you decide to use a 60 per cent standard deviation in your calculations. The company is relatively young, and you expect that all earnings will be reinvested back into the company for the near future. Therefore you expect no dividends will be paid for at least the next 10 years. A three-year Treasury note currently has a yield of 3.8 per cent, and a 10-year Treasury note has a yield of 4.4 per cent.

QUESTIONS

1. You're trying to value your options. What minimum value would you assign? What is the maximum value you would assign?
2. Suppose that in three years the company's equity is trading at £60. At that time, should you keep the options or exercise them immediately? What are some of the important determinants in making such a decision?
3. Your options, like most employee share options, are not transferable or tradable. Does this have a significant effect on the value of the options? Why?
4. Why do you suppose employee share options usually have a vesting provision? Why must they be exercised shortly after you depart the company even after they vest?
5. As we have seen, much of the volatility in a company's share price is due to systematic or market-wide risks. Such risks are beyond the control of a company and its employees. What are the implications for employee share options? In the light of your answer, can you recommend an improvement over traditional employee share options?

ADDITIONAL READING

A very rich empirical and theoretical research field considers option pricing dynamics. The reference list below focuses on options as they relate to corporate finance.

1. Amram, M., Li, F., & Perkins, C.A. (2006). How Kimberly-Clark uses real options'. *Journal of Applied Corporate Finance*, *18*(2), 40–47.
2. Giaccotto, C., Goldberg, G.M., & Hegde, S.P. (2007). The value of embedded real options: Evidence from consumer automobile lease contracts. *Journal of Finance*, *62*(1), 411–445.
3. Granadier, S.R., & Malenko, A. (2011). Real options signaling games with applications to corporate finance. *Review of Financial Studies*, *24*(2), 3993–4036.
4. Lambrecht, B.M., & Pawlina, G. (2010). Corporate finance and the (in)efficient exercise of real options. *Multinational Finance Journal*, *14*(1/2), 129–156.
5. McDonald, R.L. (2006). The role of real options in capital budgeting: Theory and practice. *Journal of Applied Corporate Finance*, *18*(2), 28–39.

Endnote

1. For further in-depth discussion on this topic, please refer to Hillier et al., *Corporate Finance*, 4th edn.

CHAPTER 22
MERGERS AND ACQUISITIONS

LEARNING OBJECTIVES
After studying this chapter, you should understand:

LO1 The different types of merger and acquisition, why they should (or shouldn't) occur, and the terminology associated with them.

LO2 How accountants construct the combined balance sheet of the new company.

LO3 The gains from a merger or acquisition and how to value the transaction.

KEY NOTATIONS
EPS	Earnings per share
NPV	Net present value
V	Value of a firm

THE COVID-19 PANDEMIC THAT DISRUPTED ECONOMIES also had an important side effect. Technology firms, such as Zoom, were able to take advantage of the new, digital focused, business environment and suddenly experienced substantially higher valuations than pre-lockdown estimates. This led to a wave of merger and acquisition activity in the technology sector, as companies consolidated their operations to take advantage of the new opportunities arising at pace. In 2020, global technology mergers and acquisitions deals amounted to over $600 billion, an increase of over 95 per cent on the previous year.

This chapter explores the reasons why corporate restructurings, such as acquisitions, should take place. Just as important, it also presents reasons why they should not.

There is no more dramatic or controversial activity in corporate finance than the acquisition of one firm by another or the merger of two firms. It is the stuff of headlines in the financial press, and it is occasionally an embarrassing source of scandal.

The acquisition of one firm by another is, of course, an investment made under uncertainty, and the basic principles of valuation apply. One firm should acquire another only if doing so generates a positive net present value for the acquiring firm's shareholders. However, because the NPV of an acquisition candidate can be difficult to determine, mergers and acquisitions, or M&A activities, are interesting topics in their own right.

Some of the special problems that come up in this area of finance include the following:

- The benefits from acquisitions can depend on such things as strategic fits. Strategic fits are difficult to define precisely, and it is not easy to estimate the value of strategic fits using discounted cash flow techniques.
- There can be complex accounting, tax and legal effects that must be taken into account when one firm is acquired by another.
- Acquisitions are an important control device for shareholders. Some acquisitions result from an underlying conflict between the interests of existing managers and those of shareholders. Agreeing to be acquired by another firm is one way in which shareholders can remove existing managers.
- Mergers and acquisitions sometimes involve 'unfriendly' transactions. In such cases, when one firm attempts to acquire another, the activity does not always confine itself to quiet, genteel negotiations. The sought-after firm often resists takeover and may resort to defensive tactics with exotic names such as poison pills, greenmail and white knights.

We discuss these and other issues associated with mergers in the sections that follow. We begin by introducing the basic legal, accounting and tax aspects of acquisitions.

22.1 THE LEGAL FORMS OF ACQUISITION

There are three basic legal procedures that one firm can use to acquire another firm:

1. Merger or consolidation
2. Acquisition of shares
3. Acquisition of assets

Although these forms are different from a legal standpoint, the financial press frequently does not distinguish between them. The term *merger* is often used regardless of the actual form of the acquisition.

In our discussion, we shall frequently refer to the acquiring firm as the bidder. This is a company that offers to pay cash or securities to obtain another company's equity or assets. The firm that is sought (and perhaps acquired) is often called the *target* firm. The cash or securities offered to the target firm are the *consideration* in the acquisition.

MERGER OR CONSOLIDATION

merger
the complete absorption of one company by another, wherein the acquiring firm retains its identity and the acquired firm ceases to exist as a separate entity.

consolidation
a merger in which an entirely new firm is created, and both the acquired and acquiring firms cease to exist.

A **merger** is the complete absorption of one firm by another. The acquiring firm retains its name and identity, and it acquires all the assets and liabilities of the acquired firm. After a merger, the acquired firm ceases to exist as a separate business entity.

A **consolidation** is the same as a merger, except that an entirely new firm is created. In a consolidation, both the acquiring and acquired firms terminate their previous legal existence and become part of a new firm. For this reason, the distinction between the acquiring and the acquired firm is not as important in a consolidation as it is in a merger.

The rules for mergers and consolidations are basically the same. Acquisition by merger or consolidation results in a combination of the assets and liabilities of acquired and acquiring firms; the only difference lies in whether a new firm is created. We shall henceforth use the term *merger* to refer generically to both mergers and consolidations.

There are some advantages and some disadvantages of using a merger to acquire a firm:

- A primary advantage is that a merger is legally simple and does not cost as much as other forms of acquisition. The reason is that the firms agree to combine their entire operations. Thus, there is no need to transfer title in individual assets of the acquired firm to the acquiring firm.
- A primary disadvantage is that a merger must be approved by a vote of each firm's shareholders.

Typically, two-thirds (or even more) of the share votes are required for approval. Obtaining the necessary votes can be time-consuming and difficult. Furthermore, as we discuss in greater detail a bit later, the co-operation of the target firm's existing management is almost necessary for a merger. This co-operation may not be easily or cheaply obtained.

ACQUISITION OF SHARES

A second way to acquire another firm is to purchase the firm's voting shares with an exchange of cash, shares of equity or other securities. This process will often start as a private offer from the management of one firm to that of another.

Regardless of how it starts, at some point, the offer is taken directly to the target firm's shareholders. This can be accomplished by a **tender offer**. A tender offer is a public offer to buy shares. It is made by one firm directly to the shareholders of another firm.

> **tender offer**
> a public offer by one firm to directly buy the shares of another firm.

Those shareholders who choose to accept the offer tender their shares by exchanging them for cash or securities (or both), depending on the offer. A tender offer is frequently contingent on the bidder's obtaining some percentage of the total voting shares. If not enough shares are tendered, then the offer might be withdrawn or reformulated.

The tender offer is communicated to the target firm's shareholders by public announcements such as those made in newspaper advertisements. Sometimes, a general mailing is used in a tender offer. However, this is not common because a general mailing requires the names and addresses of the shareholders of record. Obtaining such a list without the target firm's co-operation is not easy.

The following are some factors involved in choosing between an acquisition of shares and a merger:

- No shareholder meetings have to be held in an acquisition of shares, and no vote is required. If the target firm's shareholders don't like the offer, they are not required to accept it and need not tender their shares.
- In an acquisition of shares, the bidding firm can deal directly with the target firm's shareholders by using a tender offer. The target firm's management and board of directors can be bypassed.
- An acquisition is occasionally unfriendly. In such cases, an acquisition of shares is used to circumvent the target firm's management, which is usually actively resisting acquisition. Resistance by the target firm's management often makes the cost of acquiring shares higher than the cost of a merger.
- Frequently, a significant minority of shareholders will hold out in a tender offer. The target firm cannot be completely absorbed when this happens, and this may delay the realization of merger benefits or be costly in some other way.
- Complete absorption of one firm by another requires a merger. Many acquisitions by shares are followed up with a formal merger later.

ACQUISITION OF ASSETS

A firm can effectively acquire another firm by buying most or all of its assets. This accomplishes the same thing as buying the company. In this case, however, the target firm will not necessarily cease to exist; it will have just sold off its assets. The 'shell' will still exist unless its shareholders choose to dissolve it.

This type of acquisition requires a formal vote of the shareholders of the selling firm. One advantage of this approach is that there is no problem with minority shareholders holding out. However, the acquisition of assets may involve transferring titles in individual assets. The legal process of transferring assets can be costly.

ACQUISITION CLASSIFICATION

Financial analysts typically classify acquisitions into three types:

1. *Horizontal acquisition:* This is an acquisition of a firm in the same industry as the bidder. The firms compete with each other in their product markets. Lloyds TSB's merger with HBOS is an example of a horizontal merger in the banking industry.
2. *Vertical acquisition:* A vertical acquisition involves firms at different steps of the production process. The acquisition by an airline company of a travel agency would be a vertical acquisition.
3. *Conglomerate acquisition:* When the bidder and the target firm are in unrelated business lines, the merger is called a conglomerate acquisition. The acquisition of a food products firm by a computer firm would be considered a conglomerate acquisition.

A NOTE ABOUT TAKEOVERS

A *takeover* is a general and imprecise term referring to the transfer of control of a firm from one group of shareholders to another. A takeover thus occurs whenever one group takes control from another.

This can occur through any one of three means: acquisitions, proxy contests or going-private transactions. Thus takeovers encompass a broader set of activities than just acquisitions. These activities are depicted in Figure 22.1.

As we have already mentioned, a takeover achieved by acquisition will occur by merger, tender offer or purchase of assets. In mergers and tender offers, the bidder buys the voting equity of the target firm.

Takeovers can also occur with **proxy contests**. These occur when a group attempts to control seats on the board of directors by voting in new directors. A proxy is the right to cast someone else's votes. In a proxy contest, proxies are solicited by an unhappy group of shareholders from the rest of the shareholders.

In **going-private transactions**, all the equity shares of a public firm are purchased by a small group of investors. Usually, the group includes members of incumbent management and some outside investors. Such transactions have come to be known generically as **leveraged buyouts (LBOs)** because a large percentage of the money needed to buy up the equity is usually borrowed. Such transactions are also termed *management buyouts* (MBOs) when existing management is heavily involved. The firm's shares are delisted from stock exchanges and can no longer be purchased in the open market.

ALTERNATIVES TO MERGER

Firms don't have to merge to combine their efforts. At a minimum, two (or more) firms can simply agree to work together. They can sell each other's products, perhaps under different brand names, or jointly develop a new product or technology. Firms will frequently

---

proxy contest
an attempt to gain control of a firm by soliciting a sufficient number of shareholder votes to replace existing management.

going-private transactions
transactions in which all publicly owned equity in a firm is replaced with complete equity ownership by a private group.

leveraged buyouts (LBOs)
going-private transactions in which a large percentage of the money used to buy the equity is borrowed. Often incumbent management is involved.

FIGURE 22.1 The various forms of takeover

Takeovers
- Acquisition
  - Merger or consolidation
  - Acquisition of shares
  - Acquisition of assets
- Proxy contest
- Going private

establish a **strategic alliance**, which is usually a formal agreement to co-operate in pursuit of a joint goal. An even more formal arrangement is a **joint venture** which commonly involves two firms putting up the money to establish a new firm. For example, Verizon Wireless is a joint venture between Verizon Communications and Vodafone.

> **strategic alliance** agreement between firms to co-operate in pursuit of a joint goal.
>
> **joint venture** typically an agreement between firms to create a separate, co-owned entity established to pursue a joint goal.

> **CONCEPT QUESTIONS**
>
> **22.1a** What is a merger? How does a merger differ from other acquisition forms?
> **22.1b** What is a takeover?

22.2 ACCOUNTING AND TAX CONSIDERATIONS

Many mergers involve companies in two different countries, and because of inconsistent accounting and tax rules, this presents difficulties in assessing the value of acquisitions. There has been a concerted effort by accounting standard setters and regulatory authorities to streamline the administrative and bureaucratic challenges that face merging firms. In the subsequent discussion, we shall try to be as generic as possible about the accounting and tax considerations without losing the necessary detail. However, given the heterogeneity of regulations across countries, it is impossible to specify every regulation in place regarding mergers.

In Europe and many other countries (but not the USA), International Financial Reporting Standards govern how companies account for transactions. To improve the efficiency of the accounting treatment of cross-border mergers, the International Accounting Standards Board (IASB) and the US Financial Accounting Standards Board (FASB) have been working together to converge the standards of the two systems. This is an ongoing project, and developments will continue in the future.

In a similar fashion to accounting standards, governments have also attempted to integrate country-level tax laws. The taxation of mergers and acquisitions across national borders can be complex and prohibitive in cost, and this deters many corporations from pursuing cross-border mergers. Every national tax system is different, but in recent years there have been several treaties to smooth out these differences.

In Europe, the main treaty is the Cross-Border Merger Directive. As Chapter 2 attests, governance systems across Europe are quite varied, and employee participation is stronger in some countries (e.g. Germany, France and Belgium) than in others. The EU Merger Directive presents a cohesive framework that allows European national taxation systems to operate fully within a broader international context. Because of Brexit, the UK is no longer able to take advantage of the Cross-Border Merger Directive, and corporate restructurings between British and European Union firms require more bureaucracy to complete. It is unclear at the time of writing whether this will have an impact on the frequency of mergers between UK and European firms.

> **CONCEPT QUESTIONS**
>
> **22.2a** Why is taxation important in mergers and acquisitions?
> **22.2b** Why are accounting rules important in mergers and acquisitions?

22.3 GAINS FROM ACQUISITIONS

To determine the gains from an acquisition, we first need to identify the relevant incremental cash flows or, more generally, the source of value. In the broadest sense, acquiring another firm makes sense only if there is some concrete reason to believe that the target firm will somehow be worth more in our hands than it is worth now. As we shall see, there are a number of reasons why this might be so.

SYNERGY

Suppose Firm A is contemplating acquiring Firm B. The acquisition will be beneficial if the combined firm has a greater value than the sum of the individual firm values. If we let V stand for the value of the merged firm, then the merger makes sense only if:

$$V_{AB} > V_A + V_B$$

where V_A and V_B are the individual firm values. A successful merger thus requires that the value of the whole exceeds the sum of the parts.

The difference between the value of the combined firm and the sum of the values of the firms as separate entities is the incremental net gain from the acquisition:

$$\Delta V = V_{AB} - (V_A + V_B) \qquad (22.1)$$

When ΔV is positive, the acquisition is said to generate **synergy**.

If Firm A buys Firm B, it gets a company worth V_B plus the incremental gain, ΔV. The value of Firm B to Firm A (VB*) is thus:

$$\text{Value of Firm B to Firm A} = V_B^*$$
$$= \Delta V + V_B$$

We place an asterisk (*) on VB* to emphasize that we are referring to the value of Firm B to Firm A, not the value of Firm B as a separate entity.

VB* can be determined in two steps: (1) estimating V_B; and (2) estimating ΔV. If B is a public company, its market value as an independent firm under existing management (V_B) can be observed directly. If Firm B is not publicly owned, its value will have to be estimated based on similar publicly owned companies. Either way, the problem of determining a value for VB* requires the determination of a value for ΔV.

To determine the incremental value of an acquisition, we need to know the incremental cash flows. These are the cash flows for the combined firm, less what A and B could generate separately. In other words, the incremental cash flow for evaluating a merger is the difference between the cash flow of the combined company and the sum of the cash flows for the two companies considered separately. We shall label this incremental cash flow ΔCF.

> **synergy**
> the positive incremental net gain associated with the combination of two firms through a merger or acquisition.

EXAMPLE 22.1

SYNERGY

Firms A and B are competitors with very similar assets and business risks. Both are all-equity firms with after-tax cash flows of £10 per year forever, and both have an overall cost of capital of 10 per cent. Firm A is thinking of buying Firm B. The after-tax cash flow from the merged firm would be £21 per year. Does the merger generate synergy? What is VB*? What is ΔV?

The merger does generate synergy because the cash flow from the merged firm is $\Delta CF = £1$ greater than the sum of the individual cash flows (£21 versus £20). Assuming the risks stay the same, the merged firm's value is £21 / 0.10 = £210. Firms A and B are each worth £10/0.10 = £100, for a total of £200. The incremental gain from the merger, ΔV, is thus £210 − 200 = £10. The total value of Firm B to Firm A, VB*, is £100 (the value of B as a separate company) plus £10 (the incremental gain), or £110.

From our discussions in earlier chapters, we know that the incremental cash flow, ΔCF, can be broken down into four parts:

$$\Delta CF = \Delta EBIT + \Delta Depreciation - \Delta Tax - \Delta Capital\ requirements$$
$$= \Delta Revenue\ \Delta Cost\ \Delta Tax\ \Delta Capital\ requirements$$

where $\Delta Revenue$ is the difference in revenues, $\Delta Cost$ is the difference in costs, ΔTax is the difference in taxes, and $\Delta Capital\ requirements$ is the change in new non-current assets and net working capital.

Based on this breakdown, the merger will make sense only if one or more of these cash flow components are beneficially affected by the merger. The possible cash flow benefits of mergers and acquisitions thus fall into four basic categories: revenue enhancement, cost reductions, lower taxes and reductions in capital needs.

How Are the Synergistic Gains Shared?

In general, the acquiring firm pays a premium for the acquired, or target, firm. For example, if the equity of the target is selling for €50, the acquirer might need to pay €60 a share, implying a premium of €10, or 20 per cent. The gain to the target in this example is €10. Suppose that the synergy from the merger is €30. The gain to the acquiring firm, or bidder, would be €20 (= €30 − €10). The bidder would actually lose if the synergy were less than the premium of €10.

REVENUE ENHANCEMENT

One important reason for an acquisition is that the combined firm may generate greater revenues than two separate firms. Revenue increases may come from marketing gains, strategic benefits or increases in market power.

Marketing Gains

It is frequently claimed that mergers and acquisitions can produce greater operating revenues from improved marketing. For example, improvements might be made in the following areas:

1. Previously ineffective media programming and advertising efforts
2. A weak existing distribution network
3. An unbalanced product mix

Strategic Benefits

Some acquisitions promise a strategic advantage. This is an opportunity to take advantage of the competitive environment if certain things occur or, more generally, to enhance management flexibility with regard to the company's future operations. In this latter sense, a strategic benefit is more like an option than a standard investment opportunity.

For example, suppose a computer manufacturer can use its technology to enter other businesses. The electronics and software technology from the computer manufacturer can provide opportunities to begin manufacturing other types of consumer electronics (think Apple).

One example is Procter & Gamble's initial acquisition of the Charmin Paper Company as a strategic investment, which allowed Procter & Gamble to develop a highly interrelated cluster of paper products – disposable nappies, paper towels, feminine hygiene products, and bathroom tissue.

Market Power

One firm may acquire another to increase its market share and market power. In such mergers, profits can be enhanced through higher prices and reduced competition for customers. Of course, mergers that substantially reduce competition in the market may be challenged by the governments to avoid a monopoly situation that is too powerful.

SUSTAINABILITY IN FINANCE

Sustainability and environment risks are important in cross-border mergers and acquisitions because of potential hidden liabilities from past operations in different regulatory regimes. This is why intensive due diligence is required before bid completion to ensure there are no nasty surprises once both parties have signed up to an acquisition or merger deal.

The Due Diligence report will cover three broad areas: Environment, People and Governance. Environmental risks include damage to the environment from past operations and exposure to future litigation or regulatory scrutiny. Future climate risks will also be investigated. People risks consider the potential risks of legal action taken by past or current employees concerning health and safety violations. Finally, Governance risks are concerned with any aspect of corporate regulatory compliance and current standards of health, safety and cybersecurity.

With an increase in the risk of legal liability regarding environmental damage from a firm's operations, the G20 Task Force on Climate-Related Financial Disclosures has argued for more climate-related corporate disclosure. Among the Task Force's recommendations are:

1. All climate-related risks (short, medium and long term) should be identified, and their impact on the organization's operations, strategy and financial planning should be disclosed.
2. The process for identifying, assessing and managing climate-related risks should be recorded and become part of the company's overall risk management framework.
3. Climate target and metrics, together with performance against those targets, should be clearly communicated to all stakeholders.

COST REDUCTIONS

One of the most basic reasons to merge is that a combined firm may operate more efficiently than two separate firms. A firm can achieve greater operating efficiency in several different ways through a merger or an acquisition.

Economies of Scale

Economies of scale relate to the average cost per unit of producing goods and services. If the per-unit cost of production falls as the production level increases, then an economy of scale exists (see Figure 22.2).

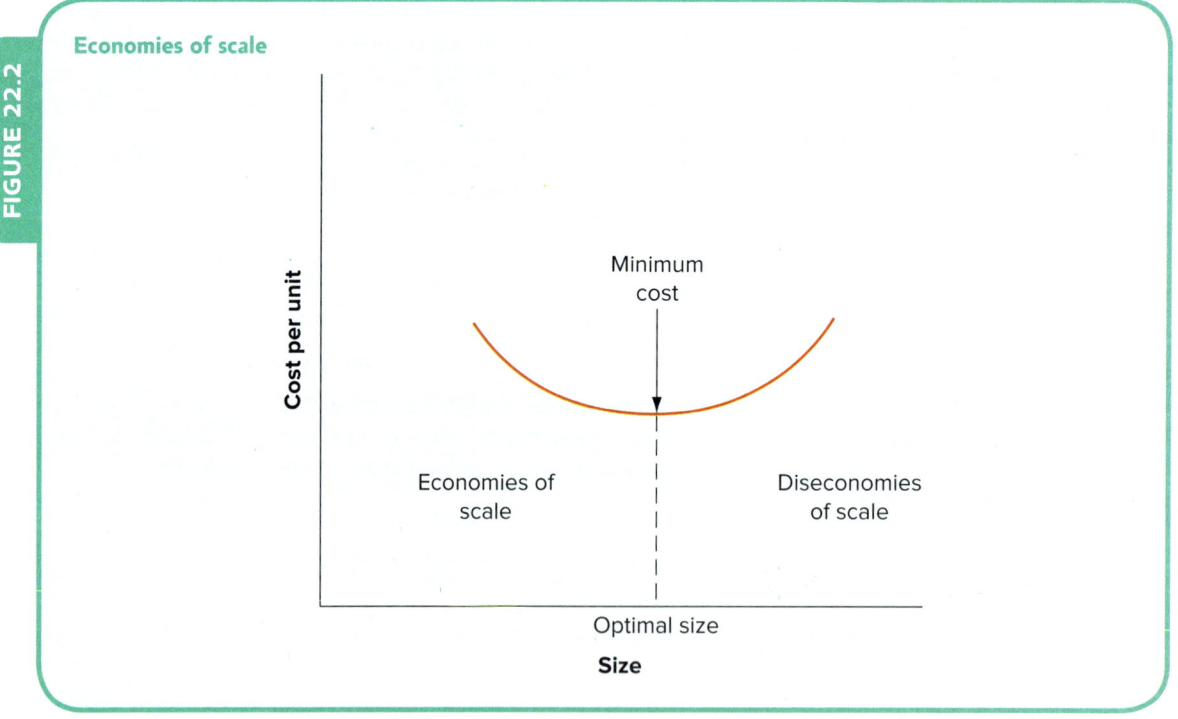

FIGURE 22.2 Economies of scale

Frequently, the phrase *spreading overhead* is used in connection with economies of scale. This expression refers to sharing central facilities such as corporate headquarters, top management, and computer services. For example, when Lloyds TSB and HBOS announced their merger agreement in 2008, this was one of the main reasons given for the action.

Economies of Vertical Integration

Operating economies can be gained from vertical combinations as well as from horizontal combinations. The main purpose of vertical acquisitions is to make it easier to co-ordinate closely related operating activities. Benefits from vertical integration are probably why most forest product firms that cut timber also own sawmills and hauling equipment. Economies of vertical integration may explain why some airline companies have purchased hotels and car rental companies.

Technology transfers are another reason for vertical integration. A company will often decide that the cheapest – and fastest – way to acquire another firm's technological skills is to buy the firm. For obvious reasons, this rationale is particularly common in high-tech industries.

Complementary Resources

Some firms acquire others to make better use of existing resources or provide the missing ingredient for success. Think of a ski equipment shop that could merge with a tennis equipment shop to produce more even sales over the winter and summer seasons, thereby improving shop capacity.

LOWER TAXES

Tax gains are a powerful incentive for some acquisitions. The possible tax gains from an acquisition include the following:

- The use of tax losses
- The use of unused debt capacity
- The use of surplus funds
- The ability to write up the value of depreciable assets.

Net Operating Losses

Firms that lose money on a pre-tax basis will not pay taxes. Such firms can end up with tax losses they cannot use. These tax losses are referred to as *net operating losses* (NOL).

A firm with net operating losses may be an attractive merger partner for a firm with significant tax liabilities. In the absence of any other effects, the combined firm will have a lower tax bill than the two firms considered separately. This is a good example of how a firm can be more valuable merged than standing alone.

There are two qualifications to our NOL discussion:

1. Many countries' tax laws permit firms that experience periods of profit and loss to even things out through loss carry-back and carry-forward provisions. For example, a firm that has been profitable in the past but has a loss in the current year may get refunds of income taxes paid in the past 3 years. After that, losses could, for example, be carried forward for up to 20 years. A merger to exploit unused tax shields must offer tax savings over and above what can be accomplished by firms via carry-overs.
2. Tax authorities may disallow an acquisition if the acquisition's principal purpose is to avoid paying tax by acquiring a deduction or credit that would not otherwise be available.

Unused Debt Capacity

Some firms do not use as much debt as they are able to. This makes them potential acquisition candidates. Adding debt can provide important tax savings, and many acquisitions are financed with debt. The acquiring company can deduct interest payments on the newly created debt and reduce taxes.

Surplus Funds

Another quirk in the tax laws involves surplus funds. Consider a firm with free cash flow: cash flow available after all taxes have been paid, and after all positive net present value projects have been financed. In such a situation, aside from purchasing fixed-income securities, the firm has several ways to spend the free cash flow, including:

- Paying dividends
- Buying back its own shares
- Acquiring shares in another firm.

We discussed the first two options in an earlier chapter. We saw that an extra dividend would increase the income tax paid by some investors. A share repurchase will reduce the taxes paid by shareholders compared with paying dividends, but this is not a legal option if the sole purpose is to avoid taxes that shareholders would have otherwise paid.

To avoid these problems, the firm can buy another firm. By doing this, the firm avoids the tax problem associated with paying a dividend. Also, the dividends received from the purchased firm are not taxed in a merger.

Asset Write-Ups

We have previously observed that, in a taxable acquisition, the acquired firm's assets can be revalued. If the assets' value increases, tax deductions for depreciation will be a benefit, but this benefit will usually be more than offset by taxes due on the write-up.

> **REAL WORLD INSIGHTS**
>
> In recent years, there have been many prominent technology firm mergers and acquisitions. To illustrate, in a single month of 2021 (January), Workday acquired the Danish firm, Peakon, for $700 million; the German software firm, SAP, bought another German firm Signavio for $400 million; Citrix purchased Wrike for $2.25 billion; Cisco paid $4.5 billion for Acacia; and Qualcomm acquired Nuvia for $1.4 billion.
>
> Valuing tech companies is similar to valuing any business. The characteristics of every valuation are the same, in that future cash flows and company risk have to be estimated. The difference for technology firms is that information regarding future cash flows is difficult to forecast, and corporate risk is a challenge to estimate because technology firms rarely have peer companies to compare against. Another issue for technology firms is that valuation metrics are not as closely linked to profits, cash or sales, as is the case when valuing other firms. Relevant metrics for technology firms include the number of users, the number of players of a game or even the number of followers of the company on social media. Bitcoin exchanges and other cryptocurrencies add a further dimension to valuation because of the lack of information regarding the underlying corporate fundamentals.
>
> A key factor in tech company valuation is subscriber or user growth. The more users, the larger the customer population, and it is more likely for cash to be generated from the users through subscriptions or payments. Forecasting subscriber growth is therefore fundamental to any valuation. This is the greatest challenge facing valuation efforts because past subscriber growth does not necessarily translate into future subscriber growth.
>
> Many technology firms use advertising revenues to drive profits and so, in addition to subscriber growth, analysts must also forecast advertising demand and the effectiveness of advertising on technology platforms. Arguably, Twitter and WhatsApp have been unsuccessful in converting users into revenue because they have been ineffective in leveraging their popularity for revenue generation. Techniques such as sensitivity analysis, scenario analysis and simulation (see Chapter 10) are regularly used in valuing technology firms because they capture the inherent uncertainty in the company operations both today and the future. Sensitivity analysis and Monte Carlo simulation allow the modelling of the company's fundamentals, and scenario analysis can assess the impact of external events, such as new government regulation. Real options valuation permits assessing opportunities that arise from using the core technology in other industries or geographical locations. Common examples include scale-up, diversification and abandonment opportunities.

REDUCTIONS IN CAPITAL NEEDS

All firms must invest in working capital and fixed assets to sustain an efficient level of operating activity. A merger may reduce the combined investments needed by the two firms. For example, Firm A may need to expand its manufacturing facilities, whereas Firm B may have significant excess capacity. It may be much cheaper for Firm A to buy Firm B than to build from scratch.

In addition, acquiring firms may see ways of managing existing assets more effectively. This can occur with a reduction in working capital resulting from more efficient handling of cash, trade receivables or inventory. Finally, the acquiring firm may also sell off certain assets that are not needed in the combined firm.

Firms will often cite many reasons for merging. Typically, when firms agree to merge, they generate a list of the economic benefits shareholders can expect from the merger.

AVOIDING MISTAKES

Evaluating the benefit of a potential acquisition is more difficult than a standard capital budgeting analysis because so much of the value can come from benefits that are intangible or otherwise difficult to quantify. Consequently, there is a great deal of room for error. Here are some general rules that should be remembered:

- **Do not ignore market values:** There is no point to, and little gain from, estimating the value of a publicly traded firm when that value can be directly observed. The current market value represents investors' consensus opinion concerning the firm's value (under existing management). Use this value as a starting point. If the firm is not publicly held, then the place to start is with similar publicly held firms.
- **Estimate only incremental cash flows:** It is important to estimate the incremental cash flows that will result from the acquisition. Only incremental cash flows from an acquisition will add value to the acquiring firm. Acquisition analysis should thus focus only on the newly created and incremental cash flows from the proposed acquisition.
- **Use the correct discount rate:** The discount rate should be the required rate of return for the incremental cash flows associated with the acquisition. It should reflect the risk associated with the use of funds, not the source. In particular, if Firm A is acquiring Firm B, then Firm A's cost of capital is not particularly relevant. Firm B's cost of capital is a much more appropriate discount rate because it reflects the risk of Firm B's cash flows.
- **Be aware of transaction costs:** An acquisition may involve substantial (and sometimes astounding) transaction costs. These will include fees to investment bankers, legal fees and disclosure requirements.

A NOTE ABOUT INEFFICIENT MANAGEMENT

There are firms whose value could be increased with a change in management. These are poorly run firms that do not efficiently use their assets to create shareholder value. Mergers are a means of replacing management in such cases.

That a firm might benefit from a change in management does not necessarily mean that existing management is dishonest, incompetent or negligent. Instead, just as some athletes are better than others, some management teams might be better at running a business. This can be particularly true during times of technological change or other periods when innovations in business practice are occurring. In any case, to the extent that corporate 'raiders' can identify poorly run firms or firms that, for other reasons, will benefit from a change in management, these raiders provide a valuable service to target firm shareholders and society in general.

> **CONCEPT QUESTIONS**
>
> **22.3a** What are the relevant incremental cash flows for evaluating a merger candidate?
> **22.3b** What are some different sources of gain from acquisitions?

22.4 SOME FINANCIAL SIDE-EFFECTS OF ACQUISITIONS

In addition to the various possibilities we have discussed thus far, mergers can have some purely financial side-effects – that is, things that occur regardless of whether the merger makes economic sense or not. Two such effects are particularly worth mentioning: EPS growth and diversification.

EPS GROWTH

An acquisition can create the appearance of growth in earnings per share, or EPS. This may fool investors into thinking that the firm is doing better than it really is. What happens is easiest to see with an example.

Suppose Global Resources Ltd acquires Regional Enterprises. The financial positions of Global and Regional before the acquisition are shown in Table 22.1. We assume that the merger creates no additional value. Hence, the combined firm (Global Resources after acquiring Regional) has a value that is equal to the sum of the values of the two firms before the merger.

TABLE 22.1

Financial positions of Global Resources (GR) and Regional Enterprises (RE). Exchange ratio: 1 share in GR for 2.5 shares in RE

	GR before merger	RE before merger	GR after merger: market is smart	GR after merger: market is fooled
Earnings per share (£)	1	1	1.43	1.43
Share price (£)	25	10	25	35.71
Price–earnings ratio	25	10	17.5	25
Number of shares	100	100	140	140
Total earnings (£)	100	100	200	200
Total value (£)	2,500	1,000	3,500	5,000

Before the merger, both Global and Regional have 100 shares outstanding. However, Global sells for £25 per share, compared with £10 per share for Regional. Global, therefore, acquires Regional by exchanging 1 of its shares for every 2.5 Regional shares. Because there are 100 shares in Regional, this will take 100 / 2.5 = 40 shares in all.

After the merger, Global will have 140 shares outstanding, and several things will happen (see the third column of Table 22.1):

1. The market value of the combined firm is £3,500. This is equal to the sum of the values of the separate firms before the merger. If the market is 'smart', it will realize that the combined firm is worth the sum of the values of the separate firms.

2. The earnings per share of the merged firm are £1.43. The acquisition enables Global to increase its earnings per share from £1 to £1.43, which is an increase of 43 per cent.

3. Because the share price of Global after the merger is the same as that before the merger, the price–earnings ratio must fall. This is true as long as the market is smart and recognizes that the merger has not altered the total market value.

If the market is 'fooled', it might mistake the 43 per cent increase in earnings per share for true growth. In this case, the price–earnings ratio of Global may not fall after the merger. Suppose the price–earnings ratio of Global remains equal to 25. Because the combined firm has earnings of £200, the total value of the combined firm will increase to £5,000 (= 25 × £200). The per-share value for Global will increase to £35.71 (£5,000 / 140).

This is earnings growth magic. Like all good magic, it is just an illusion. For it to work, the shareholders of Global and Regional must receive something for nothing. This, of course, is unlikely with so simple a trick.

DIVERSIFICATION

Diversification is commonly mentioned as a benefit of a merger. The problem is that diversification *per se* probably does not create value. Going back to Chapter 12, recall that diversification reduces unsystematic risk. We also saw that an asset's value depends on its systematic risk, and systematic risk is not directly affected by diversification. Because the unsystematic risk is not especially important, there is no particular benefit from reducing it.

Shareholders can get all the diversification they want by buying equities in different companies. As a result, they won't pay a premium for a merged company just to benefit from diversification.

> **CONCEPT QUESTIONS**
>
> **22.4a** Why can a merger create the appearance of earnings growth?
> **22.4b** Why is diversification by itself not a good reason for a merger?

22.5 THE COST OF AN ACQUISITION

We've discussed some of the benefits of an acquisition. We now need to discuss the cost of a merger. We learned earlier that the net incremental gain from a merger is:

$$\Delta V = V_{AB} - (V_A + V_B)$$

Also, the total value of Firm B to Firm A, V_B^*, is:

$$V_B^* = V_B + \Delta V \qquad (22.2)$$

The NPV of the merger is:

$$\text{NPV} = V_B^* - \text{Cost to Firm A of acquisition} \qquad (22.3)$$

To illustrate, suppose we have the following pre-merger information for Firm A and Firm B:

	Firm A	Firm B
Share price (€)	20	10
Number of shares	25	10
Total market value (€)	500	100

Both of these firms are 100 per cent equity. You estimate that the incremental value of the acquisition, ΔV, is €100.

The board of Firm B has indicated that it will agree to a sale if the price is €150, payable in cash or shares. This price for Firm B has two parts. Firm B is worth €100 as a stand-alone, so this is the minimum value that we could assign to Firm B. The second part, €50, is called the *merger premium*, and it represents the amount paid above the stand-alone value.

Should Firm A acquire Firm B? Should it pay in cash or shares? To answer, we need to determine the NPV of the acquisition under both alternatives. We can start by noting that the value of Firm B to Firm A is:

$$\begin{aligned} V_B^* &= \Delta V + V_B \\ &= €100 + 100 \\ &= €200 \end{aligned}$$

The total value received by A as a result of buying Firm B is thus €200. The question then is: how much does Firm A have to give up? The answer depends on whether cash or equity is used as the means of payment.

CASE I: CASH ACQUISITION

The cost of an acquisition when cash is used is just the cash itself. So, if Firm A pays €150 in cash to purchase all of Firm B's shares, the cost of acquiring Firm B is €150.

The NPV of a cash acquisition is:

$$\begin{aligned} \text{NPV} &= V_B^* - \text{Cost} \\ &= €200 - 150 \\ &= €50 \end{aligned}$$

The acquisition is, therefore, profitable.

After the merger, Firm AB will still have 25 shares outstanding. The value of Firm A after the merger is:

$$V_{AB} = V_A + (V_B^* - \text{Cost})$$
$$= €500 + 200 - 150$$
$$= €550$$

This is just the pre-merger value of €500 plus the €50 NPV. The price per share after the merger is €550 / 25 = €22, representing a gain of €2 per share.

CASE II: EQUITY ACQUISITION

Things are somewhat more complicated when shares are the means of payment. In a cash merger, the shareholders in B receive cash for their equity. The cost of the acquisition, in this case, is the amount of cash needed to pay off B's shareholders. In a share merger, no cash actually changes hands. Instead, the shareholders of Firm B come in as new shareholders in the merged firm. The value of the merged firm, in this case, will be equal to the pre-merger values of Firms A and B plus the incremental gain from the merger, V:

$$V_{AB} = V_A + V_B + \Delta V$$
$$= €500 + 100 + 100$$
$$= €700$$

To give €150 worth of shares for Firm B, Firm A will have to give up €150 / 20 = 7.5 shares. After the merger, there will be 25 + 7.5 = 32.5 shares outstanding, and the per-share value will be €700 / 32.5 = €21.54.

Notice that the per-share price after the merger is lower under the share purchase option. The reason has to do with the fact that B's shareholders own equity in the new firm.

It appears that Firm A paid €150 for Firm B. However, it actually paid more than that. When all is said and done, B's shareholders own 7.5 shares of equity in the merged firm. After the merger, each of these shares is worth €21.54. The total value of the consideration received by B's shareholders is thus 7.5 × €21.54 = €161.55.

This €161.55 is the true cost of the acquisition because it is what the sellers actually receive. The NPV of the merger to Firm A is:

$$\text{NPV} = V_B^* - \text{Cost}$$
$$= €200 - 161.55$$
$$= €38.45$$

We can check this by noting that A started with 25 shares worth €20 each. The gain to A of €38.45 works out to be €38.45 / 25 = €1.54 per share. The value of the equity has increased to €21.54, as we calculated.

When we compare the cash acquisition with the stock acquisition, we see that the cash acquisition is better because Firm A gets to keep all the NPV if it pays in cash. If it pays in equity, Firm B's shareholders share in the NPV by becoming new shareholders in A.

CASH VERSUS SHARES

The distinction between cash and equity financing in a merger is an important one. If cash is used, the cost of an acquisition is not dependent on the acquisition gains. All other things being the same, if equity is used, the cost is higher because Firm A's shareholders must share the acquisition gains with Firm B's shareholders. However, if the NPV of the acquisition is negative, then the loss will be shared between the two firms.

Whether a firm should finance an acquisition with cash or with shares of equity depends on several factors, including the following:

1. **Sharing gains:** If cash is used to finance the acquisition, the selling firm's shareholders will not participate in the potential gains from the merger. Of course, if the acquisition is not a success, the losses will not be shared, and the acquiring firm's shareholders will be worse off than if equity had been used.
2. **Taxes:** Acquisition by paying cash usually results in a taxable transaction. Acquisition by exchanging equity is generally tax-free.
3. **Control:** Acquisition by paying cash does not affect the control of the acquiring firm. Acquisition with voting shares may have implications for control of the merged firm.

In a typical year, in terms of the total number of deals, cash financing is much more common than equity financing. The same is usually true based on the total cash values, although the difference is smaller. The reason is that equity financing becomes more common if we look at very large deals.

> **CONCEPT QUESTIONS**
>
> **22.5a** Why does the true cost of a stock acquisition depend on the gain from the merger?
> **22.5b** What are some important factors in deciding whether to use equity or cash in an acquisition?

22.6 VALUATION OF MERGERS IN PRACTICE

In practice, merger valuation is a highly complex and subjective task. Mergers and acquisitions have two distinct differences from the typical investment project that a firm will undertake. First, the size of a merger will be significantly larger, which means that the risks of misevaluation are substantially higher, especially if the target or bidder firm is privately held.

The second difference is that if the target company is listed on a stock exchange, the share price can be used as an indicator of the value of the target's equity. While this makes things intuitively easier, because of the run-up in target valuations when takeover bids are rumoured, share price valuations may be too high if the current share price is used.

When considering a potential target for acquisition or merger, both firms should evaluate various post-merger valuation scenarios.

STAGE 1: VALUE THE TARGET AS A STAND-ALONE FIRM

First, consider the target as a stand-alone entity. This is the base case valuation upon which a merger can be assessed. To value a company requires estimates of future cash flows and the appropriate rates for discounting the cash flows. The initial valuation should then be compared to the current share price of the target, if available, to form an initial opinion of the merger.

STAGE 2: CALIBRATE THE VALUATION

It is unlikely your initial valuation of the target firm will be equal to its share price, and any differential in valuations needs to be explained. To make matters more challenging, an observed price may reflect takeover probabilities and potential takeover premiums and/or it may not incorporate private information gained as a result of your in-depth analysis. For example, private information could be provided by the target firm's management if the merger is friendly and fully supported by the target's board. Alternatively, new information may have been discovered in the course of your investigations. Because the effort in this phase is so great and the analysis so extensive, your valuation may be better than that of the market. This is especially true if the target firm is listed on a small exchange or emerging market where valuations may not be accurate.

If you do not have more information than the market, and there is still a difference between your valuation and the share price, your valuation is probably incorrect. In other words, your estimates of future cash flows and discount rates will be different from those of the market. At this point, it is strongly recommended you revisit your assumptions to see if any input can be improved. It is imperative your assumptions are close to reality because they are the building blocks for the rest of your analysis.

STAGE 3: VALUE THE SYNERGIES

Whereas stages 1 and 2 focus on your initial valuation of the target, stage 3 concerns your assessment of the benefits of a possible merger or acquisition. To do this, you must value the synergies associated with combining the target and the acquirer. In the same way as you initially valued the target firm, you value synergies by estimating the incremental cash flows generated by the new firm along with an appropriate discount rate. Some synergies are easier to predict, while others are considerably more difficult.

For example, synergies from tax savings or reductions in fixed costs are easier to predict than increased sales or reductions in variable costs.

The future cash flows and the discount rate used in the base case valuation are likely to be used in valuing risky synergies. For example, you may believe that the proposed merger will lead to a 10 per cent increase in the target's cash flows in the five years after the merger. Valuing this synergy will require both the pre-acquisition discount rate and the cash flows of the target. In addition, valuing synergies may require an estimate of the acquiring firm's cost of capital and expected cash flows. Hence, the acquiring firm will want to use the procedures outlined in stages 1 and 2 to value its own equity and calibrate its cost of capital and cash flows.

When synergies are valued, it is important to discount cash flows arising from the synergy using the weighted average of both firms' cost of capital. For example, as a result of the declining population in Japan and an increasingly competitive global whisky industry, Suntory (the Japanese alcoholic spirits firm) acquired the US whisky firm, Beam Inc. Assume that, as a result of the acquisition, both companies will increase their pre-tax profits by 10 per cent per year. Given that the gain in each year is proportional to the pre-acquisition cash flows of both firms, the appropriate discount rate would be an equally weighted average of the two firms' costs of capital.

The Suntory–Beam example illustrates a case where synergies affect both parties to the merger equally. However, this will not always be the case. If the acquisition were expected to result in a proportional increase in Suntory's profits but not Beam's, you would use Suntory's cost of capital to value the synergy.

STAGE 4: VALUE THE MERGER

The final part of the analysis is to add the base case valuation of the target to the value of the synergies from the merger or acquisition. The merger should go ahead if the costs, which include the bid premium and all transaction costs, are lower than the combined incremental value of the merger.

22.7 DEFENSIVE TACTICS

Target firm managers frequently resist takeover attempts. Resistance usually starts with press releases and mailings to shareholders that present management's viewpoint. It can eventually lead to legal action and solicitation of competing bids. Managerial action to defeat a takeover attempt may make target firm shareholders better off if it elicits a higher offer premium from the bidding firm or another firm.

Of course, management resistance may simply reflect the pursuit of self-interest at the expense of shareholders. This is a controversial subject. At times, management resistance has greatly increased the amount ultimately received by shareholders. At other times, management resistance appears to have defeated all takeover attempts, to the detriment of shareholders.

In this section, we describe various defensive tactics that have been used by target firms' management to resist unfriendly attempts. The law surrounding these defences is not settled, and some of these manoeuvres may ultimately be deemed illegal or otherwise unsuitable.

THE CORPORATE CHARTER

The corporate charter consists of the articles of incorporation and corporate by-laws that establish the firm's governance rules. The corporate charter establishes the conditions that allow for a takeover. Firms frequently amend corporate charters to make acquisitions more difficult. For example, usually, two-thirds (67 per cent) of the shareholders of record must approve a merger. Firms can make it more difficult to be acquired by changing this required percentage to 80 per cent or so. Such a change is called a *supermajority amendment*.

Another device is to stagger the election of the board members. This makes it more difficult to elect a new board of directors quickly. Such a board is sometimes called a *classified board*.

REPURCHASE AND STANDSTILL AGREEMENTS

Managers of target firms may attempt to negotiate *standstill agreements*. These are contracts wherein the bidding firm agrees to limit its holdings in the target firm. These agreements usually lead to the end of a takeover attempt.

Standstill agreements often occur at the same time that a *targeted repurchase* is arranged. In a targeted repurchase, a firm buys a certain amount of its own equity from an individual investor, usually at a substantial premium. These premiums can be thought of as payments to potential bidders to eliminate unfriendly takeover attempts. Critics of such payments view them as bribes and label them *greenmail*.

POISON PILLS AND SHARE RIGHTS PLANS

Illegal in Europe but common in the USA, a *poison pill* is a tactic designed to repel would-be suitors. The term comes from the world of espionage. Agents are supposed to bite a pill of cyanide rather than permit capture. Presumably, this prevents enemy interrogators from learning important secrets.

In the equally colourful world of corporate finance, a poison pill is a financial device designed to make it impossible for a firm to be acquired without management's consent – unless the buyer is willing to commit financial suicide.

Poison pill provisions of one form or another are often called *share rights plans* (SRPs) or something similar. SRPs differ quite a bit in detail from company to company; we shall describe a kind of generic approach here. In general, when a company adopts an SRP, it distributes equity rights to its existing shareholders.

These rights allow shareholders to buy shares of equity (or preference shares) at some fixed price. The rights issued with an SRP have some unusual features. First, the exercise, or subscription, price on the right is usually set high enough that the rights are well out of the money, meaning that the purchase price is much higher than the current share price. The rights will often be good for 10 years, and the purchase, or exercise, price is usually a reasonable estimate of what the equity will be worth at the end of that time.

In addition, unlike ordinary equity rights, these rights can't be exercised immediately, and they can't be bought or sold separately from the ordinary shares. Also, they can essentially be cancelled by management at any time; often, they can be redeemed (repurchased) for a penny or some similarly trivial amount.

Things get interesting when, under certain circumstances, the rights are 'triggered'. This means that the rights become exercisable, they can be bought and sold separately from the equity, and they are not easily cancelled or redeemed. Typically, the rights will be triggered when someone acquires 20 per cent of the ordinary equity or announces a tender offer.

When the rights are triggered, they can be exercised. Because they are out of the money, this fact is not especially important. Certain other features come into play, however. The most important is the *flip-in provision*.

The flip-in provision is the 'poison' in the pill. In the event of an unfriendly takeover attempt, the holder of a right can pay the exercise price and receive equity in the target firm worth twice the exercise price. In other words, holders of the rights can buy shares in the target firm at half price. Simultaneously, the rights owned by the raider (the acquirer) are voided. The goal of the flip-in provision is to massively dilute the raider's ownership position.

The rights issued in connection with an SRP are poison pills because anyone trying to force a merger will trigger the rights. When this happens, all the target firm's shareholders can effectively buy shares in the merged firm at half price. This greatly increases the cost of the merger to the bidder because the target firm's shareholders end up with a much larger percentage of the merged firm.

Notice that the flip-in provision doesn't prevent someone from acquiring control of a firm by purchasing a majority interest. It just acts to vastly increase the cost of doing so.

A poison pill intends to force a bidder to negotiate with management. Frequently, merger offers are made with the contingency that the target firm will cancel the rights.

Some new varieties of poison pill have appeared on the scene in recent years. For example, a 'chewable' pill, common in Canada but not in the United States, is a pill that is installed by shareholder vote and can be redeemed by shareholder vote. Then there's the 'deadhand pill', which explicitly gives the directors who installed the pill, or their handpicked successors, the authority to remove the pill. This type of pill is controversial because it makes it virtually impossible for new directors elected by shareholders to remove an existing poison pill.

Recently, a method of circumventing poison pills has grown in popularity. Hedge funds or other large investors, all of whom have the same agenda, such as removing the company's management or changing the way the company operates, band together and purchase a large block of equity. They then vote to remove the board of directors and company management without triggering the poison pill provision.

Since poison pills are illegal in many countries, including all of Europe, this has led to a higher frequency of hostile takeovers, especially by hedge funds looking to take over a company quickly and sell it on at a profit. Outlawing poison pills has also led to some criticism because acquiring firms can quickly take control of a target firm before other, possibly better, bids are being prepared by rival bidders.

GOING PRIVATE AND LEVERAGED BUYOUTS

As we have previously discussed, going private is what happens when the publicly owned shares in a firm are replaced by complete equity ownership of a private group, which may include elements of existing management. Consequently, the firm's equity is taken off the market (if it is exchange-traded equity, it is delisted) and is no longer traded.

One result of going private is that takeovers via tender offer can no longer occur because there are no publicly held shares. In this sense, an LBO (or, more specifically, an MBO) can be a takeover defence. However, it's a defence only for management. From the shareholders' point of view, an LBO is a takeover because they are bought out.

OTHER DEVICES AND JARGON OF CORPORATE TAKEOVERS

As corporate takeovers have become more common, a new vocabulary has developed. The terms are colourful, and, in no particular order, some of them are listed below.

- **Golden parachute:** Some target firms provide compensation to top-level managers if a takeover occurs. Golden parachutes are very controversial in economic downturns, as there is nothing the media like more than to splash an incredibly generous severance package all over the front pages when the company is in financial distress. A good example concerns the shareholder and media backlash concerning a $78 million parachute payment for the outgoing Novartis (Swiss pharmaceutical firm) chairman in 2013. The payment was for a consulting and non-compete agreement, otherwise known as a 'golden gag'. As a result of the torrent of criticism, the firm had to scrap the payment completely. The opposite of a golden parachute is a 'golden handcuff', which is an incentive package designed to get executives to stay on board once the acquisition is completed. Depending on your perspective and the amounts involved, golden parachutes can be viewed as a payment to management to make it less concerned for its own welfare and more interested in shareholders when considering a takeover bid.
- **Poison put:** A poison put is a variation on the poison pill we described earlier. A poison put forces the firm to repurchase securities at some set price.
- **Crown jewel:** Firms often sell or threaten to sell major assets – crown jewels – when faced with a takeover threat. This is sometimes referred to as the *scorched earth strategy*. This tactic often involves a lock-up, which we discuss shortly.
- **White knight:** A firm facing an unfriendly merger offer might arrange to be acquired by a different, friendly firm. The firm is thereby rescued by a white knight. Alternatively, the firm may arrange for a friendly entity to acquire a large block of equity. So-called *white squires* or *big brothers* are individuals, firms, or even mutual funds involved in these types of friendly transactions. Sometimes white knights or others are granted exceptional terms or otherwise compensated. Inevitably, it seems, this has been called *whitemail*.
- **Lock-up:** A lock-up is an option granted to a friendly suitor (a white knight, perhaps), giving it the right to purchase equity or some of the assets (the crown jewels, possibly) of a target firm at a fixed price in the event of an unfriendly takeover.
- **Shark repellent:** A shark repellent is any tactic (a poison pill, for example) designed to discourage unwanted merger offers.
- **Bear hug:** A bear hug is an unfriendly takeover offer designed to be so attractive that the target firm's management has little choice but to accept it. For example, in 2020, Gardaworld launched an unsuccessful bear hug of G4S, which was 68 per cent higher than the existing share price.
- **Fair price provision:** A fair price provision requires that all selling shareholders receive the same price from a bidder. The provision prevents a 'two-tier' offer, where a bidder offers a premium to buy only enough shares to gain control of the firm and a lower price for the remaining shares. Such an offer can set off a stampede among shareholders as they rush to get the better price.

- **Dual-class capitalization:** In an earlier chapter, we noted that some firms, such as Alphabet, have more than one class of equity and that voting power is typically concentrated in a class of shares not held by the public. Such a capital structure means that an unfriendly bidder will not succeed in gaining control.
- **Countertender offer:** Better known as the 'Pac-man' defence, the target responds to an unfriendly overture by offering to buy the bidder! This tactic is rarely used, in part because target firms are usually too small to realistically purchase the bidder.

CASE STUDY: TAKEDA AND SHIRE

Now that we have discussed the various strategies an acquirer and target may use, it is insightful to examine a case study of what actually happens in a merger or acquisition.

In March 2018, global pharmaceuticals firm Takeda announced a potential bid for London Stock Exchange-listed Irish pharmaceutical firm Shire plc. This was the start of a rollercoaster 10-month period for Takeda and Shire that involved shareholder revolts, share price collapses and the downgrading of Takeda's creditworthiness.

With so many bad events, it is surprising the takeover was successful at all. Many bidding companies would probably have backed off long before the actual completion in January 2019. Let's take a look at the main events that unfolded in the timeline.

Takeda Announces Its Intention to Bid for Shire

Around 24 March 2018, rumours spread across the financial markets that Takeda was interested in buying Shire. Takeda announced that it was considering a bid for Shire for several reasons: to advance Takeda's stated Vision 2025, build on its current strong momentum, and create a truly global, value-based Japanese biopharmaceutical leader. The statement also said the bid was at a very preliminary and exploratory stage. The Takeda share price tumbled on the announcement. In contrast, Shire's share price rocketed by more than 20 per cent.

Shire Rejects Four Bids from Takeda

Following the initial announcement, Takeda made four formal bids to the Shire board, starting at £41 billion, all of which were rejected. Another pharmaceutical giant, Alergen, also announced it was interested in buying Shire. Like Takeda, Alergen's price fell on its own announcement, and, as a result, Alergen pulled back its interest. As each bid was made, the premium grew higher, and Shire's share price grew so that, by 19 April, it was more than 20 per cent above its price at the beginning of March. On the other hand, Takeda continued to fall and was 20 per cent below its starting March price.

Shire Accepts the Fifth Takeda Bid

Between 20 and 25 April, both companies continued to negotiate over the terms of the bid before arriving at a final deal: Takeda would pay £27.26 in Takeda stock and £21.75 in cash, valuing Shire at approximately £46 billion. The market responded savagely, with a 7 per cent fall in Takeda's share price, taking it to a 17-month low.

Takeda Shareholders in Revolt

Once the bid was accepted by Shire, Takeda had to persuade its own shareholders to accept the deal. A group of 130 anonymous founding shareholders and ex-employees released a statement stating, 'We are not opposed to acquisitions. We fully realise that Takeda needs to strengthen its pipeline, but we want [Takeda] to protect Takeda's 230-year tradition and manage the company in a sustainable and stable manner... You are plunging headlong into a massive financial commitment that could threaten the very future of the company. The members of our group fear for the future of our beloved Takeda.'

Although the 130 shareholders held a little over 1 per cent of the company, their opposition captured the Japanese media's attention. To successfully get the bid accepted by Takeda's shareholders, at least 67 per cent of shareholders had to agree at a special meeting. For the meeting itself to be quorate, 33 per cent of the company's total votes had to be represented.

The meeting took place on 28 June, and around 90 per cent of Takeda's shareholders supported the firm's proposal to buy Shire.

Over May and June, the Shire share price continued to trend up and ended June over 30 per above its value on 1 March. Takeda was unable to regain its value over the same period. However, after Takeda's shareholders formally authorized the bid, both companies' share prices jumped on the announcement as uncertainty regarding the deal was eroded.

Takeda Completes Its Purchase of Shire

It took 7 months for Takeda to complete the acquisition of Shire. Acquisitions are an expensive activity, and the final £46 billion price included more than $1 billion in lawyer and investment banking fees.

In documents disclosed by the company, the costs were detailed: $648 million to be paid to investment advisers and underwriters for the acquisition; $105 million to be paid to lawyers; $26 million to accountants; $10 million to public relations advisers; and $156.7 million in other costs and expenses.

Looking at the remaining share price movements for both companies before the acquisition, it is clear that Takeda's value did not improve over the intervening months. On the other hand, Shire shareholders did exceptionally well with a 45 per cent premium on the March 2018 share price. Unfortunately, Takeda shares were trading at a 40 per cent discount on their March 2018 price.

Figure 22.3 presents the full evolution of Shire and Takeda share prices over the course of the acquisition.

FIGURE 22.3 Shire and Takeda share price indices, March 2018–January 2019

Note: Prices are converted into indices with a base date of 1 March 2018 to show the relative performance of each firm's shares over the acquisition period.

CONCEPT QUESTIONS

22.7a What can a firm do to make a takeover less likely?
22.7b What is a share rights plan? Explain how the rights work.

22.8 SOME EVIDENCE ON RESTRUCTURINGS: DO M&A PAY?

One of the most controversial issues surrounding our subject is whether mergers and acquisitions benefit shareholders. Many studies have attempted to estimate the effect of mergers and takeovers on share prices of the bidding and target firms. These studies have examined the gains and losses in equity value around the time of merger announcements.

One conclusion that clearly emerges is that M&A pay for target firm shareholders. There is no mystery here. The premium typically paid by bidders represents an immediate, relatively large gain, often of the order of 20 per cent or more.

Matters become much murkier when we look at bidders, and different studies reach different conclusions. One thing is clear, however. Shareholders in bidder firms seem to neither win nor lose very much, at least on average. This finding is a bit of a puzzle, and there are a variety of explanations:

- Anticipated merger gains may not be completely achieved, and shareholders thus experience losses. This can happen if managers of bidding firms tend to overestimate the gains from an acquisition.
- The bidding firms are usually much larger than the target firms. Thus, even though cash gains to the bidder may be similar to cash gains earned by the target firm's shareholders, the percentage gains will be much lower.
- Another possible explanation for the low returns to bidding firms' shareholders is that management may not be acting in the interest of shareholders. Perhaps the bid attempt is to increase the firm's size, even if this reduces its value per share.
- The market for takeovers may be sufficiently competitive that the NPV of acquiring is zero because the prices paid in acquisitions fully reflect the acquired firms' value. In other words, the target firm's shareholders capture all of the gains.
- Finally, the takeover announcement may not convey much new information to the market about the bidding firm. This can occur because firms frequently announce intentions to engage in merger 'programmes' long before they announce specific acquisitions. In this case, the share price for the bidding firm may already reflect anticipated gains from mergers.

CONCEPT QUESTIONS

22.8a What does the evidence say about the benefits of mergers and acquisitions to target company shareholders?

22.8b What does the evidence say about the benefits of mergers and acquisitions to acquiring company shareholders?

22.9 DIVESTITURES AND RESTRUCTURINGS

In contrast to a merger or acquisition, a **divestiture** occurs when a firm sells assets, operations, divisions and/or segments to a third party. Note that divestitures are an important part of M&A activity. After all, one company's acquisition is usually another's divestiture. Also, following a merger, it is common for certain assets or divisions to be sold. Monopolies or competition regulations may require such sales; they may be needed to raise cash to help pay for a deal; or the divested units may simply be unwanted by the acquirer.

Divestitures also occur when a company decides to sell off a part of itself for reasons unrelated to mergers and acquisitions. This can happen when a particular unit is unprofitable or not a good strategic fit. Or a firm may decide to cash out of a very profitable operation. Finally, a cash-strapped firm may have to sell assets to raise capital (this commonly occurs in bankruptcy).

A divestiture usually occurs like any other sale. A company lets it be known that it has assets for sale and seeks offers. If a suitable offer is forthcoming, a sale occurs.

In some cases, particularly when the desired divestiture is a relatively large operating unit, companies will elect to do an **equity carve-out**. To do a carve-out, a parent company first creates a completely separate company, of which the parent is the sole shareholder. Next, the parent company arranges an initial public offering (IPO) in which a fraction, perhaps 20 per cent or so, of the parent's equity is sold to the public, thus creating a publicly held company.

divestiture
the sale of assets, operations, divisions and/or segments of a business to a third party.

equity carve-out
the sale of equity in a wholly owned subsidiary via an IPO.

spin-off
the distribution of shares in a subsidiary to existing parent company shareholders.

split-up
the splitting up of a company into two or more companies.

Instead of a carve-out, a company can elect to do a **spin-off**. In a spin-off, the company simply distributes shares in the subsidiary to its existing shareholders on a *pro-rata* basis. Shareholders can either keep the shares or sell them as they see fit. Very commonly, a company will first do an equity carve-out to create an active market for the shares and then subsequently do a spin-off of the remaining shares at a later date.

In a less common, but more drastic, move a company can elect to do (or be forced to do) a **split-up**. A split-up is just what the name suggests: a company splits itself into two or more new companies. Shareholders have their shares in the old company swapped for shares in the new companies.

CONCEPT QUESTIONS

22.9a What is an equity carve-out? Why might a firm wish to do one?
22.9b What is a split-up? Why might a firm choose to do one?

SUMMARY AND CONCLUSIONS

This chapter has introduced you to the field of mergers and acquisitions. We mentioned several issues:

1. **Forms of merger:** One firm can acquire another in several different ways. The three legal forms of acquisition are merger or consolidation, acquisition of shares and acquisition of assets.
2. **Tax issues:** Mergers and acquisitions can be taxable or tax-free transactions. The primary issue is whether the target firm's shareholders sell or exchange their shares. Generally, a cash purchase will be a taxable merger, whereas an exchange of shares will not be taxable. In a taxable merger, there are capital gains effects and asset write-up effects to consider. In an exchange of shares, the target firm's shareholders become shareholders in the merged firm.
3. **Merger valuation:** If Firm A is acquiring Firm B, the benefits (ΔV) from the acquisition are defined as the value of the combined firm (V_{AB}) less the value of the firms as separate entities (V_A and V_B):

$$\Delta V = V_{AB} - (V_A + V_B)$$

The gain to Firm A from acquiring Firm B is the increased value of the acquired firm, ΔV, plus the value of B as a separate firm, V_B. The total value of Firm B to Firm A, V_B^*, is thus:

$$V_B^* = \Delta V + V_B$$

An acquisition will benefit the acquiring firm's shareholders if this value is greater than the cost of the acquisition. The cost of an acquisition can be defined in general terms as the price paid to the target firm's shareholders. The cost frequently includes a merger premium paid to the shareholders of the acquired firm. Moreover, the cost depends on the form of payment – that is, the choice between paying with cash or paying with equity.
4. **Benefits:** The possible benefits of an acquisition come from several sources, including the following:
   (a) revenue enhancement
   (b) cost reductions
   (c) lower taxes
   (d) reductions in capital needs.
5. **Defensive tactics:** Some of the most colourful language of finance comes from defensive tactics used in acquisition battles. Poison pills, golden parachutes, crown jewels and greenmail, are some of the terms that describe various anti-takeover tactics.

6. **Effect on shareholders:** Mergers and acquisitions have been extensively studied. The basic conclusions are that, on average, the shareholders of target firms do well, whereas the shareholders of bidding firms do not appear to gain much.
7. **Divestitures:** For a variety of reasons, companies often wish to sell assets or operating units. For relatively large divestitures involving operating units, firms sometimes elect to do carve-outs, spin-offs, or split-ups.

CHAPTER REVIEW AND SELF-TEST PROBLEMS

22.1 Merger Value and Cost Consider the following information for two all-equity firms, A and B:

	Firm A	Firm B
Shares outstanding	2,000	6,000
Share price (£)	40	30

Firm A estimates that the value of the synergistic benefit from acquiring Firm B is £6,000. Firm B has indicated that it would accept a cash purchase offer of £35 per share. Should Firm A proceed?

22.2 Mergers and EPS Consider the following information for two all-equity firms, A and B:

	Firm A	Firm B
Total earnings (€)	3,000	1,000
Shares outstanding	600	400
Share price (€)	70	15

Firm A is acquiring Firm B by exchanging 100 of its shares for all the shares in B. What is the cost of the merger if the merged firm is worth €63,000? What will happen to Firm A's EPS? To its P/E ratio?

SOLUTIONS

22.1 The total value of Firm B to Firm A is the pre-merger value of B plus the £6,000 gain from the merger. The pre-merger value of B is £30 × 6,000 = £180,000, so the total value is £186,000. At £35 per share, A is paying £35 × 6,000 = £210,000: the merger therefore has a negative NPV of £186,000 − 210,000 = −£24,000. At £35 per share, B is not an attractive merger partner.

22.2 After the merger, the firm will have 700 shares outstanding. Because the total value is €63,000, the share price is €63,000 / 700 = €90, up from €70. Because Firm B's shareholders end up with 100 shares in the merged firm, the cost of the merger is 100 × €90 = €9,000, not 100 × €70 = €7,000.

Also, the combined firm will have €3,000 + 1,000 = €4,000 in earnings, so EPS will be €4,000 / 700 = €5.71, up from €3,000 / 600 = €5. The old P/E ratio was €70 / 5 = 14.00. The new one is €90 / 5.71 = 15.76.

QUESTIONS AND PROBLEMS

22.1 **Calculating Synergy** Assume that ABC plc is planning to offer £30 billion cash for all of the equity in XYZ plc. Based on recent market information, XYZ is worth £20 billion as an independent operation. If the merger makes economic sense for ABC, what is the minimum estimated value of the synergistic benefits of the merger?

22.2 **Balance Sheets for Mergers** Consider the following pre-merger information about firm X and firm Y:

	Firm X	Firm Y
Total earnings (£)	74,000	35,000
Shares outstanding	21,000	10,000
Per-share values:		
Market (£)	25	28
Book (£)	20	7

Assume that firm X acquires firm Y by paying cash for all the shares outstanding at a merger premium of £5 per share. Assuming that neither firm has any debt before or after the merger, construct the post-merger balance sheet for firm X.

22.3 **Balance Sheets for Mergers** Assume that the following balance sheets are stated at book value. Construct a post-merger balance sheet assuming that Reflection plc purchases Lhanger plc, and both sets of accounts are presented according to International Financial Reporting Standards.

Reflection plc			
	£		£
Current assets	12,000	Current liabilities	2,100
Non-current assets	17,000	Non-current liabilities	5,900
		Equity	21,000
Total	29,000	Total	29,000

Lhanger plc			
	£		£
Current assets	6,400	Current liabilities	1,600
Non-current assets	2,600	Non-current liabilities	2,900
		Equity	4,500
Total	9,000	Total	9,000

The fair market value of Lhanger's non-current assets is £10,000, compared with the £2,600 book value shown. Reflection pays £18,000 for Lhanger, and raises the needed funds through an issue of long-term debt. Construct the post-merger balance sheet, assuming that the acquisition method of accounting is used.

22.4 **Balance Sheets for Mergers** Solar Power plc has acquired Wind Power plc in a merger transaction. Construct the balance sheet for the new corporation. The following balance sheets represent the pre-merger book values for both firms:

Solar Power plc			
	£		£
Current assets	6,600	Current liabilities	4,800
Goodwill	800	Non-current liabilities	5,900
Net non-current assets	7,900	Equity	4,600
Total	15,300	Total	15,300

Wind Power plc			
	£		£
Current assets	1,100	Current liabilities	900
Goodwill	350	Non-current liabilities	0
Non-current assets	2,800	Equity	3,350
Total	4,250	Total	4,250

The market value of Wind Power's non-current assets (excluding goodwill) is £5,800; the market values for current assets and goodwill are the same as the book values. Assume that Solar Power plc issues £8,400 in new long-term debt to finance the acquisition. Construct the balance sheet for the new corporation.

22.5 **Cash versus Equity Payment** Fresnillo plc, the silver and gold mining firm, is analysing the possible acquisition of Weir Group plc, the Scottish-based engineering firm. Assume both firms have no debt. Fresnillo believes the acquisition will increase its total after-tax annual cash flows by £183 million indefinitely. The current market value of Weir Group is £1.3 billion and that of Fresnillo is £2.9 billion. The appropriate discount rate for the incremental cash flows is 12 per cent. Fresnillo is trying to decide whether it should offer 50 per cent of its equity or £1.6 billion in cash to Weir Group's shareholders.

(a) What is the cost of each alternative?

(b) What is the NPV of each alternative?

(c) Which alternative should Fresnillo choose?

22.6 **EPS, P/E and Mergers** The shareholders of Flannery SA have voted in favour of a buyout offer from Stultz Corporation. Information about each firm is given here:

	Flannery	Stultz
Price-earnings ratio	5.25	21
Shares outstanding	60,000	180,000
Earnings (€)	300,000	675,000

Flannery's shareholders will receive one share of Stultz equity for every three shares they hold in Flannery.

(a) What will the EPS of Stultz be after the merger? What will the P/E ratio be if the NPV of the acquisition is zero?

(b) What must Stultz feel is the value of the synergy between these two firms? Explain how your answer can be reconciled with the decision to go ahead with the takeover.

22.7 **Cash versus Equity as Payment** Consider the following pre-merger information about a bidding firm (Firm B) and a target firm (Firm T). Assume that both firms have no debt outstanding.

	Firm B	Firm T
Shares outstanding	3,000	10,000
Price per share (£)	50	10

Firm B has estimated that the value of the synergistic benefits from acquiring firm T is £30,000.

(a) If firm T is willing to be acquired for £12 per share in cash, what is the NPV of the merger?

(b) What will the price per share of the merged firm be, assuming the conditions in (a)?

(c) In part (a), what is the merger premium?

(d) Suppose firm T is agreeable to a merger by an exchange of equity. If B offers one of its shares for every three of T's shares, what will the price per share of the merged firm be?

(e) What is the NPV of the merger assuming the conditions in (d)?

22.8 **Cash versus Equity as Payment** In Problem 22.7, are the shareholders of firm T better off with the cash offer or the equity offer? At what exchange ratio of B shares to T shares would the shareholders in T be indifferent between the two offers?

22.9 **Effects of a Share Exchange** Consider the following pre-merger information about firm A and firm B:

	Firm A	Firm B
Total earnings (DKr)	900	600
Shares outstanding	550	220
Price per share (DKr)	40	15

Assume that firm A acquires firm B via an exchange of equity at a price of DKr20 for each share of B's equity. Neither A nor B has any debt outstanding.

(a) What will the earnings per share, EPS, of firm A be after the merger?

(b) What will firm A's price per share be after the merger if the market incorrectly analyses this reported earnings growth (that is, the price–earnings ratio does not change)?

(c) What will the price–earnings ratio of the post-merger firm be if the market analyses the transaction correctly?

(d) If there are no synergy gains, what will the share price of A be after the merger? What will the price–earnings ratio be? What does your answer for the share price tell you about the amount A bid for B? Was it too high? Too low? Explain.

22.10 **Merger NPV** Show that the NPV of a merger can be expressed as the value of the synergistic benefits, ΔV, less the merger premium.

22.11 **Merger NPV** Youthspark is analysing the possible acquisition of AdultSkills. Neither firm has debt. The forecasts of Youthspark show that the purchase would increase its annual after-tax cash flow by €2 million indefinitely. The current market value of AdultSkills is €50 million. The current market value of Youthspark is €150 million. The appropriate discount rate for the incremental cash flows is 8 per cent. Youthspark is trying to decide whether it would offer 40 per cent of its equity or €70 million in cash to AdultSkills.

(a) What is the synergy from the merger?

(b) What is the value of AdultSkills to Youthspark?

(c) What is the cost to Youthspark of each alternative?

(d) What is the NPV to Youthspark of each alternative?

(e) Which alternative should Youthspark use?

22.12 **Merger NPV** Farrods PLC has a market value of £800 million and 35 million shares outstanding. Redridge department store has a market value of £300 million and 25 million shares outstanding. Farrods is contemplating acquiring Redridge. Farrods' CFO concludes that the combined firm with synergy will be worth £1.5 billion, and Redridge can be acquired at a premium of £200 million.

(a) If Farrods offers 20 million shares of its equity in exchange for the 25 million shares of Redridge, what will the equity price of Farrods be after the acquisition?

(b) What exchange ratio between the two equities would make the value of equity offer equivalent to a cash offer of £350 million?

22.13 Calculating NPV Gentley plc and Rolls Manufacturing are considering a merger. The possible states of the economy and each company's value in that state are shown here:

State	Probability	Gentley	Rolls
Boom	0.45	£300,000	£260,000
Recession	0.55	£110,000	£80,000

Gentley currently has a bond issue outstanding with a face value of £140,000. Rolls is an all-equity company.

(a) What is the value of each company before the merger?

(b) What are the value of each company's debt and equity before the merger?

(c) If the companies continue to operate separately, what are the total value of the companies? The equity? The debt?

(d) What would be the value of the merged company? What about the value of the merged company's debt and equity?

(e) Is there a transfer of wealth in this case? Why?

(f) Suppose that the face value of Gentley's debt was £100,000. Would this affect the transfer of wealth?

22.14 Economies of Scale Iberdrola, the Spanish electricity giant, has in recent years pursued an aggressive acquisition strategy throughout the world. Companies that have been acquired by the firm include Scottish Power (UK, 2006), Energy East (US, 2008) and Elektro (Brazil, 2011). During peak times each firm operates at 100 per cent capacity and during off-peak times, the average usage of electricity amounts to about 60 per cent of total capacity per firm. The peak periods begin at 9:00 a.m. and 5:00 p.m. local time and last about 45 minutes. Explain why Iberdrola's acquisition strategy may make sense.

22.15 Bid Offers In 2012 a consortium of investors put forward a bid for the Rangers Football Club plc. The bid details were as follows: £5,000,000 in cash; cancellation of an existing Rangers debt worth £8,000,000; an additional sum of £500,000 payable for the shares of the major owner; the assumption of the football debts (up to a maximum of aggregate amount of £1,000,000) owed by the company to Scottish football clubs; Rangers Football Club successfully qualifying for the group stages of the UEFA Champions League competition to be held in seasons 2012/13 and/or 2013/14, an additional £500,000; and on Rangers Football Club successfully qualifying for the quarter-final stages of either of the UEFA Champions League competition to be held in seasons 2012/13 or 2013/14, an additional £1,000,000. How much cash was actually offered?

22.16 Merger Profit In Problem 22.15, why do you think the bid was structured in this way? What are the benefits to the bidders? What are the benefits to the sellers?

MINI CASE

THE RURAL WIRELESS SERVICES–NUVOLA SA MERGER

Rural Wireless Services (RWS) has been in merger talks with Nuvola SA for the past six months. After several rounds of negotiations, the offer under discussion is a cash offer of €550 million for Nuvola. Both companies provide wireless and cloud computing services to under-represented communities, particularly in rural regions. The management of each firm believes a merger will result in significant synergies resulting from economies of scale in manufacturing and significant savings in general and administrative expenses.

The management has prepared the following pro forma financial statements for Nuvola, assuming the merger takes place. The financial statements include all synergistic benefits from the merger:

	2022	2023	2024	2025	2026
Sales (€)	800,000,000	900,000,000	1,000,000,000	1,125,000,000	1,250,000,000
Production costs (€)	562,000,000	630,000,000	700,000,000	790,000,000	875,000,000
Depreciation (€)	75,000,000	80,000,000	82,000,000	83,000,000	83,000,000
Other expenses (€)	80,000,000	90,000,000	100,000,000	113,000,000	125,000,000
EBIT (€)	83,000,000	100,000,000	118,000,000	139,000,000	167,000,000
Interest (€)	19,000,000	22,000,000	24,000,000	25,000,000	27,000,000
Taxable income (€)	64,000,000	78,000,000	94,000,000	114,000,000	140,000,000
Taxes (40%) (€)	25,600,000	31,200,000	37,600,000	45,600,000	56,000,000
Net income (€)	38,400,000	46,800,000	56,400,000	68,400,000	84,000,000

It has been agreed that Nuvola will require investments each year for continuing operations, along with sources of financing. The following table outlines the required investments and sources of financing:

	2022	2023	2024	2025	2026
Investments:					
Net working capital (€)	20,000,000	25,000,000	25,000,000	30,000,000	30,000,000
Non-current assets (€)	15,000,000	25,000,000	18,000,000	12,000,000	7,000,000
Total (€)	35,000,000	50,000,000	43,000,000	42,000,000	37,000,000
Sources of financing:					
New debt (€)	35,000,000	16,000,000	16,000,000	15,000,000	12,000,000
Profit retention (€)	0	34,000,000	27,000,000	27,000,000	25,000,000
Total (€)	35,000,000	50,000,000	43,000,000	42,000,000	37,000,000

The RWS management team believe that the capital structure at Nuvola is not optimal. If the merger takes place, Nuvola will immediately increase its leverage with a €110 million debt issue, which would be followed by a €150 million dividend payment to RWS. This will increase Nuvola's debt-to-equity ratio from 0.50 to 1.00. RWS will also be able to use a €25 million tax loss carry-forward in 2020 and 2021 from Nuvola's previous operations. The total value of Nuvola is expected to be €900 million in five years, and the company will have €300 million in debt at that time.

Equity in RWS currently sells for €94 per share, and the company has 18 million shares of equity outstanding. Nuvola has 8 million shares of equity outstanding. Both companies can borrow at an 8 per cent interest rate. The risk-free rate is 1 per cent, and the expected return on the market is 6 per cent. The current cost of capital for RWS is 11 per cent. The beta for Nuvola equity at its current capital structure is 1.30.

You are to analyse the financial aspects of the potential merger. Specifically, answer the following questions:

QUESTIONS

1. Suppose Nuvola shareholders will agree to a merger price of €68.75 per share. Should RWS proceed with the merger?
2. What is the highest price per share that RWS should be willing to pay for Nuvola?
3. Suppose RWS is unwilling to pay cash for the merger but will consider an equity exchange. What exchange ratio would make the merger terms equivalent to the original merger price of €68.75 per share?
4. What is the highest exchange ratio RWS would be willing to pay and still undertake the merger?

ADDITIONAL READING

As the size of this chapter attests, the study of mergers, acquisitions and corporate restructuring is huge. Below is a list of recent papers in the area. Naturally, the categorization of papers is not mutually exclusive and papers do overlap categories. However, hopefully the groupings will aid the reading effort.

The Merger, Acquisition and Corporate Restructuring Process

1. Aktas, N., De Bodt, E., & Roll, R. (2013). MicroHoo: Deal failure, industry rivalry, and sources of overbidding. *Journal of Corporate Finance, 19*, 20–35.
2. Aktas, N., De Bodt, E., & Roll, R. (2013). Learning from repetitive acquisitions: Evidence from the time between deals. *Journal of Financial Economics, 108*(1), 99–117.
3. Alexandridis, G., Petmezas, D., & Travlos, N.G. (2010). Gains from mergers and acquisitions around the world: New evidence. *Financial Management, 39*(4), 1671–1695.
4. Antoniou, A., Arbour, P., & Zhao, H. (2008). How much is too much: Are merger premiums too high? *European Financial Management, 14*(2), 268–287.
5. Eckbo, B.E. (2009). Bidding strategies and takeover premiums: A review. *Journal of Corporate Finance, 15*(1),10–29.
6. Erel, I., Liao, R.C., & Weisbach, M.S. (2012). Determinants of cross-border mergers and acquisitions'. *Journal of Finance, 67*(3), 1045–1082.
7. Erel, I., Jang, Y., & Weisbach, M.S. (2015). Do acquisitions relieve target firms' financial constraints? *Journal of Finance, 70*(1), 289–328.
8. Faccio, M., & Masulis, R. (2005). The choice of payment method in european mergers and acquisitions. *Journal of Finance,* 60(3), 1345–1388.
9. Frésard, L., Hoberg, G., & Phillips, G.M. (2020). Innovation activities and integration through vertical acquisitions. *Review of Financial Studies, 33*(7), 2937–2976.
10. Hodgkinson, L., & Partington, G.H. (2008). The motivation for takeovers in the UK. *Journal of Business Finance and Accounting, 35*(1&2), 102–126.
11. Holmen, M., & Knopf, J. (2004). Minority shareholder protection and private benefits of control for Swedish mergers. *Journal of Financial and Quantitative Analysis, 39*, 167–191.
12. Martynova, M., & Renneboog, L. (2008). A century of corporate takeovers: What have we learned and where do we stand?'. *Journal of Banking and Finance, 32*(10), 2148–2177.
13. Pan, Y., Siegel, S., & Wang, T.Y. (2020). The cultural origin of CEOs' attitudes toward uncertainty: Evidence from corporate acquisitions. *Review of Financial Studies, 33*(7), 2977–3030.
14. Veld, C., & Veld-Merkoulova, Y.V. (2004). Do spin-offs really create value? The European case. *Journal of Banking and Finance, 28*(5), 1111–1135.

Pre-Restructuring

15. Field, L.C., & Karpoff, J.M. (2002). Takeover defenses of IPO firms. *Journal of Finance, 57*(5), 1857–1889.

Post-Restructuring

16. Devos, E., Kadapakkam, P., & Krishnamurthy, S. (2009). How do mergers create value? A comparison of taxes, market power, and efficiency improvements as explanations for synergies. *Review of Financial Studies, 22*(3), 1179–1211.
17. Draper, P., & Paudyal, K. (2008). Information asymmetry and bidders' gains. *Journal of Business Finance and Accounting, 35*(3&4), 376–405.
18. Masulis, R.W., Wang, C., & Xie, F. (2007). Corporate governance and acquirer returns. *Journal of Finance, 62*(4), 1851–1889.

APPENDIX A
MATHEMATICAL TABLES

Table A.1 Future value of £1 at the end of t periods $= (1 + r)^t$

Table A.2 Present value of £1 to be received after t periods $= \dfrac{1}{(1+r)^t}$

Table A.3 Present value of an annuity of £1 per period for t periods $= \dfrac{\left[1 - \dfrac{1}{(1+r)^t}\right]}{r}$

Table A.4 Future value of an annuity of £1 per period for t periods $= \dfrac{[(1+r)^t - 1]}{r}$

Table A.5 Cumulative normal distribution

TABLE A.1

Future value of £1 at the end of t periods = $(1 + r)^t$

Period	1%	2%	3%	4%	5%	6%	7%	8%	9%	10%	12%	14%	15%	16%	18%	20%	24%	28%	32%	36%
1	1.0100	1.0200	1.0300	1.0400	1.0500	1.0600	1.0700	1.0800	1.0900	1.1000	1.1200	1.1400	1.1500	1.1600	1.1800	1.2000	1.2400	1.2800	1.3200	1.3600
2	1.0201	1.0404	1.0609	1.0816	1.1025	1.1236	1.1449	1.1664	1.1881	1.2100	1.2544	1.2996	1.3225	1.3456	1.3924	1.4400	1.5376	1.6384	1.7424	1.8496
3	1.0303	1.0612	1.0927	1.1249	1.1576	1.1910	1.2250	1.2597	1.2950	1.3310	1.4049	1.4815	1.5209	1.5609	1.6430	1.7280	1.9066	2.0972	2.3000	2.5155
4	1.0406	1.0824	1.1255	1.1699	1.2155	1.2625	1.3108	1.3605	1.4116	1.4641	1.5735	1.6890	1.7490	1.8106	1.9388	2.0736	2.3642	2.6844	3.0360	3.4210
5	1.0510	1.1041	1.1593	1.2167	1.2763	1.3382	1.4026	1.4693	1.5386	1.6105	1.7623	1.9254	2.0114	2.1003	2.2878	2.4883	2.9316	3.4360	4.0075	4.6526
6	1.0615	1.1262	1.1941	1.2653	1.3401	1.4185	1.5007	1.5869	1.6771	1.7716	1.9738	2.1950	2.3131	2.4364	2.6996	2.9860	3.6352	4.3980	5.2899	6.3275
7	1.0721	1.1487	1.2299	1.3159	1.4071	1.5036	1.6058	1.7138	1.8280	1.9487	2.2107	2.5023	2.6600	2.8262	3.1855	3.5832	4.5077	5.6295	6.9826	8.6054
8	1.0829	1.1717	1.2668	1.3686	1.4775	1.5938	1.7182	1.8509	1.9926	2.1436	2.4760	2.8526	3.0590	3.2784	3.7589	4.2998	5.5895	7.2058	9.2170	11.703
9	1.0937	1.1951	1.3048	1.4233	1.5513	1.6895	1.8385	1.9990	2.1719	2.3579	2.7731	3.2519	3.5179	3.8030	4.4355	5.1598	6.9310	9.2234	12.166	15.917
10	1.1046	1.2190	1.3439	1.4802	1.6289	1.7908	1.9672	2.1589	2.3674	2.5937	3.1058	3.7072	4.0456	4.4114	5.2338	6.1917	8.5944	11.806	16.060	21.647
11	1.1157	1.2434	1.3842	1.5395	1.7103	1.8983	2.1049	2.3316	2.5804	2.8531	3.4785	4.2262	4.6524	5.1173	6.1759	7.4301	10.657	15.112	21.199	29.439
12	1.1268	1.2682	1.4258	1.6010	1.7959	2.0122	2.2522	2.5182	2.8127	3.1384	3.8960	4.8179	5.3503	5.9360	7.2876	8.9161	13.215	19.343	27.983	40.037
13	1.1381	1.2936	1.4685	1.6651	1.8856	2.1329	2.4098	2.7196	3.0658	3.4523	4.3635	5.4924	6.1528	6.8858	8.5994	10.699	16.386	24.759	36.937	54.451
14	1.1495	1.3195	1.5126	1.7317	1.9799	2.2609	2.5785	2.9372	3.3417	3.7975	4.8871	6.2613	7.0757	7.9875	10.147	12.839	20.319	31.691	48.757	74.053
15	1.1610	1.3459	1.5580	1.8009	2.0789	2.3966	2.7590	3.1722	3.6425	4.1772	5.4736	7.1379	8.1371	9.2655	11.974	15.407	25.196	40.565	64.359	100.71
16	1.1726	1.3728	1.6047	1.8730	2.1829	2.5404	2.9522	3.4259	3.9703	4.5950	6.1304	8.1372	9.3576	10.748	14.129	18.488	31.243	51.923	84.954	136.97
17	1.1843	1.4002	1.6528	1.9479	2.2920	2.6928	3.1588	3.7000	4.3276	5.0545	6.8660	9.2765	10.761	12.468	16.672	22.186	38.741	66.461	112.14	186.28
18	1.1961	1.4282	1.7024	2.0258	2.4066	2.8543	3.3799	3.9960	4.7171	5.5599	7.6900	10.575	12.375	14.463	19.673	26.623	48.039	85.071	148.02	253.34
19	1.2081	1.4568	1.7535	2.1068	2.5270	3.0256	3.6165	4.3157	5.1417	6.1159	8.6128	12.056	14.232	16.777	23.214	31.948	59.568	108.89	195.39	344.54
20	1.2202	1.4859	1.8061	2.1911	2.6533	3.2071	3.8697	4.6610	5.6044	6.7275	9.6463	13.743	16.367	19.461	27.393	38.338	73.864	139.38	257.92	468.57
21	1.2324	1.5157	1.8603	2.2788	2.7860	3.3996	4.1406	5.0338	6.1088	7.4002	10.804	15.668	18.822	22.574	32.324	46.005	91.592	178.41	340.45	637.26
22	1.2447	1.5460	1.9161	2.3699	2.9253	3.6035	4.4304	5.4365	6.6586	8.1403	12.100	17.861	21.645	26.186	38.142	55.206	113.57	228.36	449.39	866.67
23	1.2572	1.5769	1.9736	2.4647	3.0715	3.8197	4.7405	5.8715	7.2579	8.9543	13.552	20.362	24.891	30.376	45.008	66.247	140.83	292.30	593.20	1178.7
24	1.2697	1.6084	2.0328	2.5633	3.2251	4.0489	5.0724	6.3412	7.9111	9.8497	15.179	23.212	28.625	35.236	53.109	79.497	174.63	374.14	783.02	1603.0
25	1.2824	1.6406	2.0938	2.6658	3.3864	4.2919	5.4274	6.8485	8.6231	10.835	17.000	26.462	32.919	40.874	62.669	95.396	216.54	478.90	1033.6	2180.1
30	1.3478	1.8114	2.4273	3.2434	4.3219	5.7435	7.6123	10.063	13.268	17.449	29.960	50.950	66.212	85.850	143.37	237.38	634.82	1645.5	4142.1	10143.0
40	1.4889	2.2080	3.2620	4.8010	7.0400	10.286	14.974	21.725	31.409	45.259	93.051	188.88	267.86	378.72	750.38	1469.8	5455.9	19427.0	66521.0	*
50	1.6446	2.6916	4.3839	7.1067	11.467	18.420	29.457	46.902	74.358	117.39	289.00	700.23	1083.7	1670.7	3927.4	9100.4	46890.0	*	*	*
60	1.8167	3.2810	5.8916	10.5200	18.679	32.988	57.946	101.260	176.030	304.48	897.60	2595.90	4384.0	7370.2	20555.0	56348.0	*	*	*	*

*The factor is greater than 99,999.

TABLE A.2

Present value of £1 to be received after t periods $= \dfrac{1}{(1+r)^t}$

Period	1%	2%	3%	4%	5%	6%	7%	8%	9%	10%
1	.9901	.9804	.9709	.9615	.9524	.9434	.9346	.9259	.9174	.9091
2	.9803	.9612	.9426	.9246	.9070	.8900	.8734	.8573	.8417	.8264
3	.9706	.9423	.9151	.8890	.8638	.8396	.8163	.7938	.7722	.7513
4	.9610	.9238	.8885	.8548	.8227	.7921	.7629	.7350	.7084	.6830
5	.9515	.9057	.8626	.8219	.7835	.7473	.7130	.6806	.6499	.6209
6	.9420	.8880	.8375	.7903	.7462	.7050	.6663	.6302	.5963	.5645
7	.9327	.8706	.8131	.7599	.7107	.6651	.6227	.5835	.5470	.5132
8	.9235	.8535	.7894	.7307	.6768	.6274	.5820	.5403	.5019	.4665
9	.9143	.8368	.7664	.7026	.6446	.5919	.5439	.5002	.4604	.4241
10	.9053	.8203	.7441	.6756	.6139	.5584	.5083	.4632	.4224	.3855
11	.8963	.8043	.7224	.6496	.5847	.5268	.4751	.4289	.3875	.3505
12	.8874	.7885	.7014	.6246	.5568	.4970	.4440	.3971	.3555	.3186
13	.8787	.7730	.6810	.6006	.5303	.4688	.4150	.3677	.3262	.2897
14	.8700	.7579	.6611	.5775	.5051	.4423	.3878	.3405	.2992	.2633
15	.8613	.7430	.6419	.5553	.4810	.4173	.3624	.3152	.2745	.2394
16	.8528	.7284	.6232	.5339	.4581	.3936	.3387	.2919	.2519	.2176
17	.8444	.7142	.6050	.5134	.4363	.3714	.3166	.2703	.2311	.1978
18	.8360	.7002	.5874	.4936	.4155	.3503	.2959	.2502	.2120	.1799
19	.8277	.6864	.5703	.4746	.3957	.3305	.2765	.2317	.1945	.1635
20	.8195	.6730	.5537	.4564	.3769	.3118	.2584	.2145	.1784	.1486
21	.8114	.6598	.5375	.4388	.3589	.2942	.2415	.1987	.1637	.1351
22	.8034	.6468	.5219	.4220	.3418	.2775	.2257	.1839	.1502	.1228
23	.7954	.6342	.5067	.4057	.3256	.2618	.2109	.1703	.1378	.1117
24	.7876	.6217	.4919	.3901	.3101	.2470	.1971	.1577	.1264	.1015
25	.7798	.6095	.4776	.3751	.2953	.2330	.1842	.1460	.1160	.0923
30	.7419	.5521	.4120	.3083	.2314	.1741	.1314	.0994	.0754	.0573
40	.6717	.4529	.3066	.2083	.1420	.0972	.0668	.0460	.0318	.0221
50	.6080	.3715	.2281	.1407	.0872	.0543	.0339	.0213	.0134	.0085

APPENDIX A Mathematical Tables

Period	12%	14%	15%	16%	18%	20%	24%	28%	32%	36%
1	.8929	.8772	.8696	.8621	.8475	.8333	.8065	.7813	.7576	.7353
2	.7972	.7695	.7561	.7432	.7182	.6944	.6504	.6104	.5739	.5407
3	.7118	.6750	.6575	.6407	.6086	.5787	.5245	.4768	.4348	.3975
4	.6355	.5921	.5718	.5523	.5158	.4823	.4230	.3725	.3294	.2923
5	.5674	.5194	.4972	.4761	.4371	.4019	.3411	.2910	.2495	.2149
6	.5066	.4556	.4323	.4104	.3704	.3349	.2751	.2274	.1890	.1580
7	.4523	.3996	.3759	.3538	.3139	.2791	.2218	.1776	.1432	.1162
8	.4039	.3506	.3269	.3050	.2660	.2326	.1789	.1388	.1085	.0854
9	.3606	.3075	.2843	.2630	.2255	.1938	.1443	.1084	.0822	.0628
10	.3220	.2697	.2472	.2267	.1911	.1615	.1164	.0847	.0623	.0462
11	.2875	.2366	.2149	.1954	.1619	.1346	.0938	.0662	.0472	.0340
12	.2567	.2076	.1869	.1685	.1372	.1122	.0757	.0517	.0357	.0250
13	.2292	.1821	.1625	.1452	.1163	.0935	.0610	.0404	.0271	.0184
14	.2046	.1597	.1413	.1252	.0985	.0779	.0492	.0316	.0205	.0135
15	.1827	.1401	.1229	.1079	.0835	.0649	.0397	.0247	.0155	.0099
16	.1631	.1229	.1069	.0930	.0708	.0541	.0320	.0193	.0118	.0073
17	.1456	.1078	.0929	.0802	.0600	.0451	.0258	.0150	.0089	.0054
18	.1300	.0946	.0808	.0691	.0508	.0376	.0208	.0118	.0068	.0039
19	.1161	.0829	.0703	.0596	.0431	.0313	.0168	.0092	.0051	.0029
20	.1037	.0728	.0611	.0514	.0365	.0261	.0135	.0072	.0039	.0021
21	.0926	.0638	.0531	.0443	.0309	.0217	.0109	.0056	.0029	.0016
22	.0826	.0560	.0462	.0382	.0262	.0181	.0088	.0044	.0022	.0012
23	.0738	.0491	.0402	.0329	.0222	.0151	.0071	.0034	.0017	.0008
24	.0659	.0431	.0349	.0284	.0188	.0126	.0057	.0027	.0013	.0006
25	.0588	.0378	.0304	.0245	.0160	.0105	.0046	.0021	.0010	.0005
30	.0334	.0196	.0151	.0116	.0070	.0042	.0016	.0006	.0002	.0001
40	.0107	.0053	.0037	.0026	.0013	.0007	.0002	.0001	*	*
50	.0035	.0014	.0009	.0006	.0003	.0001	*	*	*	*

Interest rate

*The factor is zero to four decimal places.

TABLE A.3

Present value of an annuity of £1 per period for t periods $= \left[\dfrac{1 - \dfrac{1}{(1+r)^t}}{r}\right]$

Number of periods	1%	2%	3%	4%	5%	6%	7%	8%	9%	10%
1	.9901	.9804	.9709	.9615	.9524	.9434	.9346	.9259	.9174	.9091
2	1.9704	1.9416	1.9135	1.8861	1.8594	1.8334	1.8080	1.7833	1.7591	1.7355
3	2.9410	2.8839	2.8286	2.7751	2.7232	2.6730	2.6243	2.5771	2.5313	2.4869
4	3.9020	3.8077	3.7171	3.6299	3.5460	3.4651	3.3872	3.3121	3.2397	3.1699
5	4.8534	4.7135	4.5797	4.4518	4.3295	4.2124	4.1002	3.9927	3.8897	3.7908
6	5.7955	5.6014	5.4172	5.2421	5.0757	4.9173	4.7665	4.6229	4.4859	4.3553
7	6.7282	6.4720	6.2303	6.0021	5.7864	5.5824	5.3893	5.2064	5.0330	4.8684
8	7.6517	7.3255	7.0197	6.7327	6.4632	6.2098	5.9713	5.7466	5.5348	5.3349
9	8.5660	8.1622	7.7861	7.4353	7.1078	6.8017	6.5152	6.2469	5.9952	5.7590
10	9.4713	8.9826	8.5302	8.1109	7.7217	7.3601	7.0236	6.7101	6.4177	6.1446
11	10.3676	9.7868	9.2526	8.7605	8.3064	7.8869	7.4987	7.1390	6.8052	6.4951
12	11.2551	10.5753	9.9540	9.3851	8.8633	8.3838	7.9427	7.5361	7.1607	6.8137
13	12.1337	11.3484	10.6350	9.9856	9.3936	8.8527	8.3577	7.9038	7.4869	7.1034
14	13.0037	12.1062	11.2961	10.5631	9.8986	9.2950	8.7455	8.2442	7.7862	7.3667
15	13.8651	12.8493	11.9379	11.1184	10.3797	9.7122	9.1079	8.5595	8.0607	7.6061
16	14.7179	13.5777	12.5611	11.6523	10.8378	10.1059	9.4466	8.8514	8.3126	7.8237
17	15.5623	14.2919	13.1661	12.1657	11.2741	10.4773	9.7632	9.1216	8.5436	8.0216
18	16.3983	14.9920	13.7535	12.6593	11.6896	10.8276	10.0591	9.3719	8.7556	8.2014
19	17.2260	15.6785	14.3238	13.1339	12.0853	11.1581	10.3356	9.6036	8.9501	8.3649
20	18.0456	16.3514	14.8775	13.5903	12.4622	11.4699	10.5940	9.8181	9.1285	8.5136
21	18.8570	17.0112	15.4150	14.0292	12.8212	11.7641	10.8355	10.0168	9.2922	8.6487
22	19.6604	17.6580	15.9369	14.4511	13.1630	12.0416	11.0612	10.2007	9.4424	8.7715
23	20.4558	18.2922	16.4436	14.8568	13.4886	12.3034	11.2722	10.3741	9.5802	8.8832
24	21.2434	18.9139	16.9355	15.2470	13.7986	12.5504	11.4693	10.5288	9.7066	8.9847
25	22.0232	19.5235	17.4131	15.6221	14.0939	12.7834	11.6536	10.6748	9.8226	9.0770
30	25.8077	22.3965	19.6004	17.2920	15.3725	13.7648	12.4090	11.2578	10.2737	9.4269
40	32.8347	27.3555	23.1148	19.7928	17.1591	15.0463	13.3317	11.9246	10.7574	9.7791
50	39.1961	31.4236	25.7298	21.4822	18.2559	15.7619	13.8007	12.2335	10.9617	9.9148

APPENDIX A Mathematical Tables

Number of periods	\multicolumn{11}{c}{Interest rate}
	12%	14%	15%	16%	18%	20%	24%	28%	32%	36%
1	.8929	.8772	.8696	.8621	.8475	.8333	.8065	.7813	.7576	.7353
2	1.6901	1.6467	1.6257	1.6052	1.5656	1.5278	1.4568	1.3916	1.3315	1.2760
3	2.4018	2.3216	2.2832	2.2459	2.1743	2.1065	1.9813	1.8684	1.7663	1.6735
4	3.0373	2.9137	2.8550	2.7982	2.6901	2.5887	2.4043	2.2410	2.0957	1.9658
5	3.6048	3.4331	3.3522	3.2743	3.1272	2.9906	2.7454	2.5320	2.3452	2.1807
6	4.1114	3.8887	3.7845	3.6847	3.4976	3.3255	3.0205	2.7594	2.5342	2.3388
7	4.5638	4.2883	4.1604	4.0386	3.8115	3.6046	3.2423	2.9370	2.6775	2.4550
8	4.9676	4.6389	4.4873	4.3436	4.0776	3.8372	3.4212	3.0758	2.7860	2.5404
9	5.3282	4.9464	4.7716	4.6065	4.3030	4.0310	3.5655	3.1842	2.8681	2.6033
10	5.6502	5.2161	5.0188	4.8332	4.4941	4.1925	3.6819	3.2689	2.9304	2.6495
11	5.9377	5.4527	5.2337	5.0286	4.6560	4.3271	3.7757	3.3351	2.9776	2.6834
12	6.1944	5.6603	5.4206	5.1971	4.7932	4.4392	3.8514	3.3868	3.0133	2.7084
13	6.4235	5.8424	5.5831	5.3423	4.9095	4.5327	3.9124	3.4272	3.0404	2.7268
14	6.6282	6.0021	5.7245	5.4675	5.0081	4.6106	3.9616	3.4587	3.0609	2.7403
15	6.8109	6.1422	5.8474	5.5755	5.0916	4.6755	4.0013	3.4834	3.0764	2.7502
16	6.9740	6.2651	5.9542	5.6685	5.1624	4.7296	4.0333	3.5026	3.0882	2.7575
17	7.1196	6.3729	6.0472	5.7487	5.2223	4.7746	4.0591	3.5177	3.0971	2.7629
18	7.2497	6.4674	6.1280	5.8178	5.2732	4.8122	4.0799	3.5294	3.1039	2.7668
19	7.3658	6.5504	6.1982	5.8775	5.3162	4.8435	4.0967	3.5386	3.1090	2.7697
20	7.4694	6.6231	6.2593	5.9288	5.3527	4.8696	4.1103	3.5458	3.1129	2.7718
21	7.5620	6.6870	6.3125	5.9731	5.3837	4.8913	4.1212	3.5514	3.1158	2.7734
22	7.6446	6.7429	6.3587	6.0113	5.4099	4.9094	4.1300	3.5558	3.1180	2.7746
23	7.7184	6.7921	6.3988	6.0442	5.4321	4.9245	4.1371	3.5592	3.1197	2.7754
24	7.7843	6.8351	6.4338	6.0726	5.4509	4.9371	4.1428	3.5619	3.1210	2.7760
25	7.8431	6.8729	6.4641	6.0971	5.4669	4.9476	4.1474	3.5640	3.1220	2.7765
30	8.0552	7.0027	6.5660	6.1772	5.5168	4.9789	4.1601	3.5693	3.1242	2.7775
40	8.2438	7.1050	6.6418	6.2335	5.5482	4.9966	4.1659	3.5712	3.1250	2.7778
50	8.3045	7.1327	6.6605	6.2463	5.5541	4.9995	4.1666	3.5714	3.1250	2.7778

TABLE A.4

Future value of an annuity of £1 per period for t periods $= \dfrac{[(1+r)^t - 1]}{r}$

Number of periods	1%	2%	3%	4%	5%	6%	7%	8%	9%	10%
1	1.0000	1.0000	1.0000	1.0000	1.0000	1.0000	1.0000	1.0000	1.0000	1.0000
2	2.0100	2.0200	2.0300	2.0400	2.0500	2.0600	2.0700	2.0800	2.0900	2.1000
3	3.0301	3.0604	3.0909	3.1216	3.1525	3.1836	3.2149	3.2464	3.2781	3.3100
4	4.0604	4.1216	4.1836	4.2465	4.3101	4.3746	4.4399	4.5061	4.5731	4.6410
5	5.1010	5.2040	5.3091	5.4163	5.5256	5.6371	5.7507	5.8666	5.9847	6.1051
6	6.1520	6.3081	6.4684	6.6330	6.8019	6.9753	7.1533	7.3359	7.5233	7.7156
7	7.2135	7.4343	7.6625	7.8983	8.1420	8.3938	8.6540	8.9228	9.2004	9.4872
8	8.2857	8.5830	8.8932	9.2142	9.5491	9.8975	10.260	10.637	11.028	11.436
9	9.3685	9.7546	10.159	10.583	11.027	11.491	11.978	12.488	13.021	13.579
10	10.462	10.950	11.464	12.006	12.578	13.181	13.816	14.487	15.193	15.937
11	11.567	12.169	12.808	13.486	14.207	14.972	15.784	16.645	17.560	18.531
12	12.683	13.412	14.192	15.026	15.917	16.870	17.888	18.977	20.141	21.384
13	13.809	14.680	15.618	16.627	17.713	18.882	20.141	21.495	22.953	24.523
14	14.947	15.974	17.086	18.292	19.599	21.015	22.550	24.215	26.019	27.975
15	16.097	17.293	18.599	20.024	21.579	23.276	25.129	27.152	29.361	31.772
16	17.258	18.639	20.157	21.825	23.657	25.673	27.888	30.324	33.003	35.950
17	18.430	20.012	21.762	23.698	25.840	28.213	30.840	33.750	36.974	40.545
18	19.615	21.412	23.414	25.645	28.132	30.906	33.999	37.450	41.301	45.599
19	20.811	22.841	25.117	27.671	30.539	33.760	37.379	41.446	46.018	51.159
20	22.019	24.297	26.870	29.778	33.066	36.786	40.995	45.762	51.160	57.275
21	23.239	25.783	28.676	31.969	35.719	39.993	44.865	50.423	56.765	64.002
22	24.472	27.299	30.537	34.248	38.505	43.392	49.006	55.457	62.873	71.403
23	25.716	28.845	32.453	36.618	41.430	46.996	53.436	60.893	69.532	79.543
24	26.973	30.422	34.426	39.083	44.502	50.816	58.177	66.765	76.790	88.497
25	28.243	32.030	36.459	41.646	47.727	54.865	63.249	73.106	84.701	98.347
30	34.785	40.568	47.575	56.085	66.439	79.058	94.461	113.28	136.31	164.49
40	48.886	60.402	75.401	95.026	120.80	154.76	199.64	259.06	337.88	442.59
50	64.463	84.579	112.80	152.67	209.35	290.34	406.53	573.77	815.08	1163.9
60	81.670	114.050	163.05	237.99	353.58	533.13	813.52	1253.20	1944.80	3043.8

Interest rate

APPENDIX A **Mathematical Tables** 667

Number of periods	Interest rate										
	12%	14%	15%	16%	18%	20%	24%	28%	32%	36%
1	1.0000	1.0000	1.0000	1.0000	1.0000	1.0000	1.0000	1.0000	1.0000	1.0000
2	2.1200	2.1400	2.1500	2.1600	2.1800	2.2000	2.2400	2.2800	2.3200	2.3600
3	3.3744	3.4396	3.4725	3.5056	3.5724	3.6400	3.7776	3.9184	4.0624	4.2096
4	4.7793	4.9211	4.9934	5.0665	5.2154	5.3680	5.6842	6.0156	6.3624	6.7251
5	6.3528	6.6101	6.7424	6.8771	7.1542	7.4416	8.0484	8.6999	9.3983	10.146
6	8.1152	8.5355	8.7537	8.9775	9.4420	9.9299	10.980	12.136	13.406	14.799
7	10.089	10.730	11.067	11.414	12.142	12.916	14.615	16.534	18.696	21.126
8	12.300	13.233	13.727	14.240	15.327	16.499	19.123	22.163	25.678	29.732
9	14.776	16.085	16.786	17.519	19.086	20.799	24.712	29.369	34.895	41.435
10	17.549	19.337	20.304	21.321	23.521	25.959	31.643	38.593	47.062	57.352
11	20.655	23.045	24.349	25.733	28.755	32.150	40.238	50.398	63.122	78.998
12	24.133	27.271	29.002	30.850	34.931	39.581	50.895	65.510	84.320	108.44
13	28.029	32.089	34.352	36.786	42.219	48.497	64.110	84.853	112.30	148.47
14	32.393	37.581	40.505	43.672	50.818	59.196	80.496	109.61	149.24	202.93
15	37.280	43.842	47.580	51.660	60.965	72.035	100.82	141.30	198.00	276.98
16	42.753	50.980	55.717	60.925	72.939	87.442	126.01	181.87	262.36	377.69
17	48.884	59.118	65.075	71.673	87.068	105.93	157.25	233.79	347.31	514.66
18	55.750	68.394	75.836	84.141	103.74	128.12	195.99	300.25	459.45	700.94
19	63.440	78.969	88.212	98.603	123.41	154.74	244.03	385.32	607.47	954.28
20	72.052	91.025	102.44	115.38	146.63	186.69	303.60	494.21	802.86	1298.8
21	81.699	104.77	118.81	134.84	174.02	225.03	377.46	633.59	1060.8	1767.4
22	92.503	120.44	137.63	157.41	206.34	271.03	469.06	812.00	1401.2	2404.7
23	104.60	138.30	159.28	183.60	244.49	326.24	582.63	1040.4	1850.6	3271.3
24	118.16	158.66	184.17	213.98	289.49	392.48	723.46	1332.7	2443.8	4450.0
25	133.33	181.87	212.79	249.21	342.60	471.98	898.09	1706.8	3226.8	6053.0
30	241.33	356.79	434.75	530.31	790.95	1181.9	2640.9	5873.2	12941.0	28172.0
40	767.09	1342.0	1779.1	2360.8	4163.2	7343.9	22729.0	69377.0	*	*
50	2400.0	4994.5	7217.7	10436.0	21813.0	45497.0	*	*	*	*
60	7471.6	18535.0	29220.0	46058.0	*	*	*	*	*	*

*The factor is greater than 99,999.

TABLE A.5

Cumulative normal distribution

d	N(d)	d	N(d)	d	N(d)	d	N(d)	d	N(d)
-3.00	.0013	-1.58	.0571	-.76	.2236	.06	.5239	.86	.8051	1.66	.9515
-2.95	.0016	-1.56	.0594	-.74	.2297	.08	.5319	.88	.8106	1.68	.9535
-2.90	.0019	-1.54	.0618	-.72	.2358	.10	.5398	.90	.8159	1.70	.9554
-2.85	.0022	-1.52	.0643	-.70	.2420	.12	.5478	.92	.8212	1.72	.9573
-2.80	.0026	-1.50	.0668	-.68	.2483	.14	.5557	.94	.8264	1.74	.9591
-2.75	.0030	-1.48	.0694	-.66	.2546	.16	.5636	.96	.8315	1.76	.9608
-2.70	.0035	-1.46	.0721	-.64	.2611	.18	.5714	.98	.8365	1.78	.9625
-2.65	.0040	-1.44	.0749	-.62	.2676	.20	.5793	1.00	.8413	1.80	.9641
-2.60	.0047	-1.42	.0778	-.60	.2743	.22	.5871	1.02	.8461	1.82	.9656
-2.55	.0054	-1.40	.0808	-.58	.2810	.24	.5948	1.04	.8508	1.84	.9671
-2.50	.0062	-1.38	.0838	-.56	.2877	.26	.6026	1.06	.8554	1.86	.9686
-2.45	.0071	-1.36	.0869	-.54	.2946	.28	.6103	1.08	.8599	1.88	.9699
-2.40	.0082	-1.34	.0901	-.52	.3015	.30	.6179	1.10	.8643	1.90	.9713
-2.35	.0094	-1.32	.0934	-.50	.3085	.32	.6255	1.12	.8686	1.92	.9726
-2.30	.0107	-1.30	.0968	-.48	.3156	.34	.6331	1.14	.8729	1.94	.9738
-2.25	.0122	-1.28	.1003	-.46	.3228	.36	.6406	1.16	.8770	1.96	.9750
-2.20	.0139	-1.26	.1038	-.44	.3300	.38	.6480	1.18	.8810	1.98	.9761
-2.15	.0158	-1.24	.1075	-.42	.3372	.40	.6554	1.20	.8849	2.00	.9772
-2.10	.0179	-1.22	.1112	-.40	.3446	.42	.6628	1.22	.8888	2.05	.9798
-2.05	.0202	-1.20	.1151	-.38	.3520	.44	.6700	1.24	.8925	2.10	.9821
-2.00	.0228	-1.18	.1190	-.36	.3594	.46	.6772	1.26	.8962	2.15	.9842
-1.98	.0239	-1.16	.1230	-.34	.3669	.48	.6844	1.28	.8997	2.20	.9861
-1.96	.0250	-1.14	.1271	-.32	.3745	.50	.6915	1.30	.9032	2.25	.9878
-1.94	.0262	-1.12	.1314	-.30	.3821	.52	.6985	1.32	.9066	2.30	.9893
-1.92	.0274	-1.10	.1357	-.28	.3897	.54	.7054	1.34	.9099	2.35	.9906
-1.90	.0287	-1.08	.1401	-.26	.3974	.56	.7123	1.36	.9131	2.40	.9918
-1.88	.0301	-1.06	.1446	-.24	.4052	.58	.7190	1.38	.9162	2.45	.9929
-1.86	.0314	-1.04	.1492	-.22	.4129	.60	.7257	1.40	.9192	2.50	.9938
-1.84	.0329	-1.02	.1539	-.20	.4207	.62	.7324	1.42	.9222	2.55	.9946
-1.82	.0344	-1.00	.1587	-.18	.4286	.64	.7389	1.44	.9251	2.60	.9953
-1.80	.0359	-.98	.1635	-.16	.4364	.66	.7454	1.46	.9279	2.65	.9960
-1.78	.0375	-.96	.1685	-.14	.4443	.68	.7518	1.48	.9306	2.70	.9965
-1.76	.0392	-.94	.1736	-.12	.4522	.70	.7580	1.50	.9332	2.75	.9970
-1.74	.0409	-.92	.1788	-.10	.4602	.72	.7642	1.52	.9357	2.80	.9974

d	N(d)	d	N(d)	d	N(d)	d	N(d)	d	N(d)
-1.72	.0427	-.90	.1841	-.08	.4681	.74	.7704	1.54	.9382	2.85	.9978
-1.70	.0446	-.88	.1894	-.06	.4761	.76	.7764	1.56	.9406	2.90	.9981
-1.68	.0465	-.86	.1949	-.04	.4840	.78	.7823	1.58	.9429	2.95	.9984
-1.66	.0485	-.84	.2005	-.02	.4920	.80	.7881	1.60	.9452	3.00	.9987
-1.64	.0505	-.82	.2061	.00	.5000	.82	.7939	1.62	.9474	3.05	.9989
-1.62	.0526	-.80	.2119	.02	.5080	.84	.7995	1.64	.9495		
-1.60	.0548	-.78	.2177	.04	.5160						

This table shows the probability [N(d)] of observing a value less than or equal to d. For example, as illustrated, if d is –.24, then N(d) is .4052.

APPENDIX B
KEY EQUATIONS

Chapter 3

3.1: The balance sheet identity or equation

$$\text{Assets} = \text{Liabilities} + \text{Shareholder's equity}$$

3.2: The income statement equation

$$\text{Revenues} - \text{Expenses} = \text{Income}$$

3.3: The cash flow identity

$$\text{Cash flow from assets} = \text{Cash flow to creditors} + \text{Cash flow to shareholders}$$

3.4: The total cash flow

$$\text{Total cash flow} = \text{Cash flow from operating activities} + \text{Cash flow from investing activities} + \text{Cash flow from financing activities}$$

3.5: The current ratio

$$\text{Current ratio} = \frac{\text{Current assets}}{\text{Current liabilities}}$$

3.6: The quick or acid-test ratio

$$\text{Quick ratio} = \frac{\text{Current assets} - \text{Inventory}}{\text{Current liabilities}}$$

3.7: The total debt ratio

$$\text{Total debt ratio} = \frac{\text{Total assets} - \text{Total equity}}{\text{Total assets}}$$

3.8: The debt–equity ratio

$$\text{Debt–equity ratio} = \frac{\text{Total debt}}{\text{Total equity}}$$

3.9: The equity multiplier

$$\text{Equity multiplier} = \frac{\text{Total assets}}{\text{Total equity}}$$

3.10: The times interest earned ratio

$$\text{Times interest earned ratio} = \frac{\text{Operating profit}}{\text{Interest}}$$

3.11: The cash coverage ratio

$$\text{Cash coverage ratio} = \frac{\text{Operating profit} + \text{Non-cash deductions}}{\text{Interest}}$$

3.12: The inventory turnover

$$\text{Inventory turnover} = \frac{\text{Cost of goods sold}}{\text{Inventory}}$$

3.13: The days' sales in inventory

$$\text{Days' sales in inventory} = \frac{365 \text{ days}}{\text{Inventory turnover}}$$

3.14: The receivables turnover ratio

$$\text{Receivables turnover} = \frac{\text{Sales}}{\text{Trade receivables}}$$

3.15: The days' sales in receivables

$$\text{Days' sales in receivables} = \frac{365 \text{ days}}{\text{Receivables turnover}}$$

3.16: The payables turnover ratio

$$\text{Payables turnover} = \frac{\text{Credit purchases}}{\text{Trade payables}}$$

3.17: The days' purchases in payables

$$\text{Days' purchases in payables} = \frac{365 \text{ days}}{\text{Payables turnover}}$$

3.18: The net working capital (NWC) turnover ratio

$$\text{NWC turnover} = \frac{\text{Sales}}{\text{NWC}}$$

3.19: The property, plant and equipment (PPE) turnover ratio

$$\text{PPE turnover} = \frac{\text{Sales}}{\text{Property, plant and equipment}}$$

3.20: The total asset turnover

$$\text{Total asset turnover} = \frac{\text{Sales}}{\text{Total assets}}$$

3.21: Profit margin

$$\text{Profit margin} = \frac{\text{Net income}}{\text{Sales}}$$

3.22: Return on assets

$$\text{Return on assets} = \frac{\text{Net income}}{\text{Total assets}}$$

3.23: Return on equity

$$\text{Return on equity} = \frac{\text{Net income}}{\text{Total equity}}$$

3.24: Return on capital employed

$$\text{Return on capital employed} = \frac{\text{Profit before interest and taxes}}{\text{Total equity} + \text{non-current liabilities}}$$

3.25: The price-earnings (P/E) ratio

$$\text{P/E ratio} = \frac{\text{Price per share}}{\text{Earnings per share}}$$

3.26: The price-sales ratio

$$\text{Price-sales ratio} = \frac{\text{Price per share}}{\text{Sales per share}}$$

3.27: The market-to-book ratio

$$\text{Market-to-book ratio} = \frac{\text{Market value per share}}{\text{Book value per share}}$$

3.28: The Tobin's Q ratio

$$\text{Tobin's Q} = \frac{\text{Market value of firm's assets}}{\text{Replacement cost of firm's assets}}$$
$$= \frac{\text{Market value of firm's debt and equity}}{\text{Replacement cost of firm's assets}}$$

3.29: The Du Pont identity

$$\text{ROE} = \underbrace{\frac{\text{Net income}}{\text{Sales}} \times \frac{\text{Sales}}{\text{Assets}}}_{\text{Return on assets}} \times \frac{\text{Assets}}{\text{Total equity}}$$
$$= \text{Profit margin} \times \text{Total asset turnover} \times \text{Equity multiplier}$$

Chapter 4

4.1: The future value of £1 invested for t periods at rate of r per period

$$\text{Future value} = £1 \times (1 + r)^t$$

4.2: The present value of £1 to be received t periods in the future at a discount rate of r

$$PV = £1 \times \frac{1}{(1+r)^t}$$
$$= \frac{£1}{(1+r)^t}$$

4.3: The relationship between future value and present value (the basic present value equation)

$$PV \times (1+r)^t = FV_t$$
$$PV = \frac{FV_t}{(1+r)^t}$$
$$= \left[FV_t \times \frac{1}{(1+r)^t} \right]$$
$$= FV_t \times (1+r)^{-t}$$

Chapter 5

5.1: The present value of an annuity of C pounds per period for t periods when the rate of return or interest rate is r

$$\text{Annuity present value} = C \times \left[\frac{1 - \text{Present value factor}}{r} \right]$$
$$= C \times \left\{ \frac{1 - [1/(1+r)^t]}{r} \right\}$$
$$= C \times \left\{ \frac{1}{r} - \frac{1}{r(1+r)^t} \right\}$$

5.2: The future value factor for an annuity

$$\text{Annuity FV factor} = \frac{\text{Future value factor} - 1}{r}$$
$$= \frac{(1+r)^t - 1}{r}$$
$$= \frac{(1+r)^t}{r} - \frac{1}{r}$$

5.3: Present value for a perpetuity

$$\text{PV for a perpetuity} = C/r$$

APPENDIX B **Key Equations** 673

5.4: Growing annuity present value

$$\text{Growing annuity present value} = C \times \left[\frac{1 - \left(\frac{1-g}{1+r}\right)^t}{r-g} \right]$$

5.5: Growing perpetuity present value

$$\text{Growing perpetuity present value} = C \times \left[\frac{1}{r-g} \right] = \frac{C}{r-g}$$

5.6: Effective annual rate (EAR), where m is the number of times the interest is compounded during the year

$$\text{EAR} = [1 + (\text{Quoted rate}/m)]^m - 1$$

5.7: Present value of a series of cash flows C_i over t periods with a discount rate, APR.

$$PV = C_0 + \frac{C_1}{1 + APR} + \frac{C_2}{(1 + APR)^2} + \cdots + \frac{C_T}{(1 + APR)^T}$$
$$= C_0 + \sum_{i=1}^{T} \frac{C_i}{(1 + APR)^i}$$

5.8: Effective annual rate (EAR), where q stands for the continuously compounded quoted rate

$$\text{EAR} = e^q - 1$$

Chapter 6

6.1: Bond value if bond has (1) a face value of F paid at maturity, (2) a coupon of C paid per period, (3) t periods to maturity, and (4) a yield of r per period

$$\text{Bond value} = \underbrace{\frac{C \times 1 - 1/(1+r)^t - 1}{r}}_{\text{Present value of the coupons}} + \underbrace{\frac{F}{(1+r)^t}}_{\text{Present value of the face amount}}$$

6.2, 6.3: The Fisher effect

$$1 + R = (1 + r) \times (1 + h)$$
$$R = r + h + r \times h$$

6.4: Approximation of the Fisher effect

$$R \approx r + h$$

Chapter 7

7.1: Price of an equity that pays a dividend, D_1, next year, has a price, P_1, next year and a discount rate R.

$$P_0 = \frac{D_1 + P_1}{1 + R}$$

7.2: Per-share value

$$P_0 = D/R$$

7.3: The dividend growth model

$$P_0 = \frac{D_0 \times (1 + g)}{R - g} = \frac{D_1}{R - g}$$

7.4: The dividend growth model

$$P_t = \frac{D_t \times (1 + g)}{R - g} = \frac{D_{t+1}}{R - g}$$

7.5: Price of an equity today – Two Stage model

$$P_0 = \frac{D_1}{R - g_1} \times \left[1 - \left(\frac{1 + g_1}{1 + R} \right)^t \right] + \frac{P_t}{(1 + R)^t}$$

7.6: Price of an equity at time t – Two Stage model

$$P_t = \frac{D_{t+1}}{R - g_2} = \frac{D_0 \times (1 + g_1)^t \times (1 + g_2)}{R - g_2}$$

7.7: Total return to an equity investor

$$R - g = D_1/P_0$$
$$R = D_1/P_0 + g$$

7.8: $\text{FCFF} = \text{Cash flow from operations} + \text{Cash flow from investing activities}$

7.9: $\text{FCFF} = \text{Cash flow from operations} + \text{Cash flow from investing activities} + \text{Net interest payment} \times (1 - \text{Tax rate})$

Chapter 9

9.1: Bottom-up approach to operating cash flow (OCF) $\quad \text{OCF} = \text{Net income} + \text{Depreciation}$

9.2: Top-down approach to operating cash flow (OCF) $\quad \text{OCF} = \text{Sales} - \text{Costs} - \text{Taxes}$

9.3: Tax shield approach to operating cash flow (OCF) $\quad \text{OCF} = (\text{Sales} - \text{Costs}) \times (1 - T) + \text{Depreciation} \times T$

Chapter 10

10.1: Operating cash flow (OCF)
$$\text{OCF} = [(P - v) \times Q - FC - D] + D = (P - v) \times Q - FC$$

10.2: Relationship between operating cash flow (OCF) and sales volume
$$Q = \frac{FC + OCF}{P - v}$$

10.3: Degree of operating leverage (DOL)
$$\text{DOL} = 1 + FC/OCF$$

Chapter 11

11.1: Total cash return $\quad \text{Total cash return} = \text{Dividend income} + \text{Capital gain (or loss)}$

11.2: Total cash if equity is sold $\quad \text{Total cash if equity is sold} = \text{Initial investment} + \text{Total return}$

11.3: Historical variance $\quad \text{Var}(R) = \frac{1}{T-1}\left[(R_1 - \bar{R})^2 + \ldots + (R_T - \bar{R})^2\right]$

11.4: Geometric average return $\quad \text{Geometric average return} = [(1 + R_1) \times (1 + R_2) \times \ldots \times (1 + R_T)]^{1/T} - 1$

Chapter 12

12.1: Risk premium
$$\text{Risk premium} = \text{Expected return} - \text{Risk-free rate} = E(R_U) - R_f$$

12.2: Expected return on a portfolio $\quad E(R_P) = x_1 \times E(R_1) + x_2 \times E(R_2) + \ldots + x_n \times E(R_n)$

12.3: Total return
$$\text{Total return} = \text{Expected return} + \text{Unexpected return}$$
$$R = E(R) + U$$

12.4: Announcement $\quad \text{Announcement} = \text{Expected part} + \text{Surprise}$

12.5: Total risk $\quad \text{Total risk} = \text{Systematic risk} + \text{Unsystematic risk}$

12.6: The capital asset pricing model (CAPM) $\quad E(R_i) = R_f + [E(R_M) - R_f \times \beta_i]$

Chapter 13

13.1: Required return on equity, R_E (dividend growth model) $\quad R_E = D_1/P_0 + g$

13.2: Required return on equity, R_E (CAPM) $\quad R_E = R_f + \beta_E \times (R_M - R_f)$

13.3: Required return on preferred stock, R_P $\quad R_P = D/P_0$

13.4: Combined market value of the debt and equity $\quad V = E + D$

APPENDIX B **Key Equations** 675

Chapter 13

13.5: Percentages of the total capital represented by the debt and equity

$$100\% = E/V + D/V$$

13.6: Weighted average cost of capital (WACC)

$$WACC = (E/V) \times R_E + (D/V) \times R_D \times (1 - T_C)$$

13.7: Weighted average cost of capital (WACC) if a firm uses preference shares

$$WACC = (E/V) \times R_E + (P/V) \times R_P + (D/V) \times R_D \times (1 - T_C)$$

13.8: Weighted average flotation cost

$$f_A = (E/V) \times f_E + (D/V) \times f_D$$

Chapter 15

15.1: M&M Proposition II

$$R_E = R_A + (R_A - R_D) \times (D/E)$$

15.2: Present value of interest tax shield

$$\text{Present value of the interest tax shield} = \frac{T_C \times D \times R_D}{R_D} = T_C \times D$$

15.3: Value of a levered firm

$$V_L = V_U + T_C \times D$$

15.4: M&M Proposition II with corporate taxes

$$R_E = R_U + (R_U - R_D) \times (D/E) \times (1 - T_C)$$

Chapter 17

17.1: Average daily float

$$\text{Average daily float} = \frac{\text{Total float}}{\text{Total days}}$$

17.2: Opportunity costs (The Baumol-Allais-Tobin (BAT) model)

$$\text{Opportunity costs} = (C/2) \times R$$

17.3: Trading costs

$$\text{Trading costs} = (T/C) \times F$$

17.4: Total cost

$$\text{Total cost} = \text{Opportunity costs} + \text{Trading costs} = (C/2) \times R + (T/C) \times F$$

17.5: The optimal initial cash balance

$$C^* = \sqrt{(2T \times F)/R}$$

17.6: The optimal cash balance (The Miller-Orr model)

$$C^* = L + (3/4 \times F \times \sigma^2/R)^{1/3}$$

17.7: The upper limit

$$U^* = 3 \times C^* - 2 \times L$$

17.8: Average cash balance

$$\text{Average cash balance} = (4 \times C^* - L)/3$$

17.9: Trade receivables

$$\text{Trade receivables} = \text{Average daily sales} \times ACP$$

17.10: Cash flow with old policy

$$\text{Cash flow with old policy} = (P - v)Q$$

17.11: Cash flow with new policy

$$\text{Cash flow with new policy} = (P - v)Q'$$

17.12: The present value of the future incremental cash flows

$$PV = [(P - v)(Q' - Q)]/R$$

17.13: Cost of switching

$$\text{Cost of switching} = PQ + v(Q' - Q)$$

17.14: The net present value (NPV) of switching

$$\text{NPV of switching} = -[PQ + v(Q' - Q)] + [(P - v)(Q' - Q)]/R$$

17.15: Break-even analysis

$$NPV = 0 = -[PQ + v(Q' - Q)] + \frac{(P - v)(Q' - Q)}{R}$$

$$Q' - Q = \frac{PQ}{(P - v)/(R - v)}$$

17.16: The NPV of granting credit

$$NPV = -v + (1 - \pi)P/(1 + R)$$

17.17: The NPV of extending credit

$$NPV = -v + (1 - \pi)(P - v)/R$$

17.18: Total carrying costs	Total carrying costs	= Average inventory × Carrying costs per unit
		= $(Q/2) \times CC$
17.19: Total restocking cost	Total restocking cost	= Fixed cost per order × Number of orders
		= $F \times (T/Q)$
17.20: The total costs associated with holding inventory	Total costs	= Carrying costs × Restocking costs
		= $(Q/2) \times CC + F \times (T/Q)$
17.21: Carrying costs	Carrying costs = Restocking costs	
	$(Q^*/2) \times CC = F \times (T/Q^*)$	
17.22: Economic order quantity	$Q^* = \sqrt{\dfrac{2T \times F}{CC}}$	

Chapter 18

18.1: Relative purchasing power parity (PPP)	$\dfrac{E(S_1) - S_0}{S_0} = h_{FC} - h_{HC}$
18.2: Expected exchange rate at time 1	$E(S_1) = S_0 \times [1 + (h_{FC} - h_{HC})]$
18.3: Interest rate parity (IRP)	$\dfrac{F_1}{S_0} = \dfrac{1 + R_{FC}}{1 + R_{HC}}$
18.4: Interest rate parity (IRP)	$(F_1 - S_0)/S_0 = R_{FC} - R_{HC}$
18.5: Interest rate parity (IRP)	$F_1 = S_0 \times [1 + (R_{FC} - R_{HC})]$
18.6: IRP approximation	$F_t = S_0 \times [1 + (R_{FC} - R_{HC})]^t$
18.7: Uncovered interest parity (UIP)	UIP: $E(S_1) = S_0 \times [1 + (R_{FC} - R_{HC})]$
18.8: Uncovered interest parity (UIP)	$E(S_t) = S_0 \times [1 + (R_{FC} - R_{HC})]^t$
18.9: International Fisher effect (IFE)	IFE: $R_{HC} - h_{HC} = R_{FC} - h_{FC}$

Chapter 21

21.1: Put-call parity (PCP) condition	Price of underlying equity + Price of put = Price of call + Present value of strike price
21.1a: Put-call parity (PCP) condition	$S + P = PV(E) + C$
21.2: Call option payoff when the underlying asset price, S_1, is less than or equal to the exercise price, E.	$C_1 = 0$ if $S_1 - E \leq 0$
21.3: Call option payoff when the underlying asset price, S_1, is greater than the exercise price, E.	$C_1 = S_1 - E$ if $S_1 - E > 0$
21.4: Value of a call option	$S_0 = C_0 + \dfrac{E}{1 + R_f}$
	$C_0 = S_0 - \dfrac{E}{1 + R_f}$

Chapter 22

22.1: Value gain from an acquisition	$\Delta V = V_{AB} - (V_A + V_B)$
22.2: The value of firm B to an acquirer	$V_B^* = V_B + \Delta V$
22.3: NPV of a merger	NPV $= V_B^*$ − Cost to Firm A of acquisition

APPENDIX 3A
FINANCIAL PLANNING

> **LEARNING OBJECTIVE**
> **LOA1** How to undertake long-term financial planning using financial statements.

IN THIS APPENDIX, we consider the role of corporate financial planning in the context of financial statement analysis. There are definitely other ways to estimate growth and plan for the future, but the techniques introduced in this appendix can be justified on the back of audited financial reports. We also consider the components of a financial plan and link corporate growth rates to its financing needs.

It is also important to emphasize that estimated growth rates and other assumptions which go into corporate financial planning can be very subjective. The methods in this appendix may give the impression that financial planning is a mechanical process, but it is far from it. Analysts should treat the approaches given here as the first steps and not the end.

3A.1 FINANCIAL PLANNING

A lack of effective long-range planning is a commonly cited reason for financial distress and failure. As we discuss in this section, long-range planning means systematically thinking about the future and anticipating possible problems before they arrive. There are no magic mirrors, of course, so the best we can hope for is a logical and organized procedure for exploring the unknown. Financial planning establishes guidelines for change and growth in a firm. It normally focuses on the big picture. This means it is concerned with the major elements of a firm's financial and investment policies without examining the individual components in detail.

Financial planning formulates how financial goals are to be achieved. A financial plan is thus a statement of what is to be done in the future. Many decisions have long lead times, which means they take a long time to implement. In an uncertain world, this requires that decisions be made far in advance of their implementation. If a firm wants to build a factory in 2025, it might have to begin lining up contractors and financing in 2022 or earlier.

GROWTH AS A FINANCIAL MANAGEMENT GOAL

Because the subject of growth is discussed in various places in this chapter, we need to start with an important warning: growth, by itself, is not an appropriate goal for the financial manager. As we discussed in Chapter 1, the appropriate goal is to increase the market value of the owners' equity. Of course, if a firm is successful in doing this, then growth will usually result. Growth may thus be a desirable consequence of good decision-making, but it is not an end unto itself. We discuss growth simply because growth rates are so commonly used in the planning process. As we shall see, growth is a convenient means of summarizing various aspects of a firm's financial and investment policies. Also, if we think of growth as growth in the firm's market value, then goals of growth and increasing the market value of the firm's equity are not all that different.

WHAT CAN PLANNING ACCOMPLISH?

Because a company is likely to spend a lot of time examining the different scenarios that will become the basis for its financial plan, it seems reasonable to ask what the planning process will accomplish.

Examining Interactions

As we discuss in greater detail in the following pages, the financial plan must make explicit the linkages between investment proposals for the firm's different operating activities and its available financing choices. In other words, if the firm is planning on expanding and undertaking new investments and projects, where will the financing be obtained to pay for this activity?

Exploring Options

The financial plan allows the firm to develop, analyse, and consistently compare many different scenarios. Various investment and financing options can be explored, and their impact on the firm's shareholders can be evaluated. Questions concerning the firm's future lines of business and optimal financing arrangements are addressed. Options such as marketing new products or closing plants might be evaluated.

Avoiding Surprises

Financial planning should identify what may happen to the firm if different events take place. It should particularly address what actions the firm will take if things go seriously wrong or, more generally, if assumptions made today about the future are seriously in error. As physicist Niels Bohr once observed, 'Prediction is very difficult, particularly when it concerns the future.' Thus one purpose of financial planning is to avoid surprises and develop contingency plans.

Ensuring Feasibility and Internal Consistency

Beyond a general goal of creating value, a firm will normally have many specific goals. Such goals might be couched in terms of market share, return on equity, financial leverage, and so on. At times, the linkages between different goals and aspects of a firm's business are difficult to see. Not only does a financial plan make these linkages explicit, it also imposes a unified structure for reconciling goals and objectives.

In other words, financial planning is a way of verifying that the goals and plans made for specific areas of a firm's operations are feasible and internally consistent. Conflicting goals will often exist. To generate a coherent plan, goals and objectives will have to be modified, and priorities will have to be established.

For example, one goal a firm might have would be 12 per cent growth in unit sales per year. Another goal might be to reduce the firm's total debt ratio from 40 to 20 per cent. Are these two goals compatible? Can they be accomplished simultaneously? Maybe yes, maybe no. As we shall discuss, financial planning is a way of finding out just what is possible – and, by implication, what is not possible.

Conclusion

The most important result of the planning process is that it forces managers to think about goals and establish priorities. In fact, conventional business wisdom holds that financial plans don't work, but financial planning does. Since the future is inherently unknown, we can establish the direction we want to travel and make some educated guesses about what we shall find along the way. If we do a good job, we won't be caught off guard when the future rolls around.

> **CONCEPT QUESTIONS**
>
> **3A.1a** What are the two dimensions of the financial planning process?
> **3A.1b** Why should firms draw up financial plans?

3A.2 FINANCIAL PLANNING MODELS: A FIRST LOOK

Just as companies differ in size and products, the financial planning process will differ from firm to firm. This section discusses some common elements in financial plans and develops a basic model to illustrate these elements. What follows is just a quick overview; later sections will take up the various topics in more detail.

We can begin our discussion of long-term planning models with a relatively simple example. Chute SA's financial statements from the most recent year are as follows:

Chute SA Financial statements					
Income statement		**Statement of financial position**			
	€		€		€
Sales	1,000	Assets	500	Debt	250
Costs	800			Equity	250
Net profit	200	Total	500	Total	500

Unless otherwise stated, the financial planners at Chute assume that all variables are tied directly to sales and current relationships are optimal. This means that all items will grow at the same rate as sales. This is obviously oversimplified; we use this assumption only to make a point.

Suppose sales increase by 20 per cent, rising from €1,000 to €1,200. Planners would then also forecast a 20 per cent increase in costs, from £800 to £800 × 1.2 = £960. The pro forma income statement would thus be:

Pro forma income statement	
	€
Sales	1,200
Costs	960
Net profit	240

The assumption that all variables will grow by 20 per cent lets us easily construct the pro forma statement of financial position as well:

Pro forma Statement of financial position			
	€		€
Assets	600 (+100)	Debt	300 (+50)
		Equity	300 (+50)
Total	600 (+100)	Total	600 (+100)

Notice that we have simply increased every item by 20 per cent. The numbers in parentheses are the euro changes for the different items.

Now we have to reconcile these two pro formas. How, for example, can net profit be equal to €240 and equity increase by only €50? The answer is that Chute must have paid out the difference of €240 − 50 = €190, possibly as a cash dividend. In this case, dividends are the plug variable.

Suppose Chute does not pay out the €190. In this case, the addition to retained earnings is the full €240. Chute's equity will thus grow to €250 (the starting amount) plus €240 (net income), or €490, and debt must be retired to keep total assets equal to €600.

With €600 in total assets and €490 in equity, debt will have to be €600 − 490 = €110. Because we started with €250 in debt, Chute will have to retire €250 − 110 = €140 in debt. The resulting pro forma statement of financial position would look like this:

Pro forma statement of financial position			
	€		€
Assets	600 (+100)	Debt	110 (−140)
		Equity	490 (+240)
Total	600 (+100)	Total	600 (+100)

In this case, debt is the plug variable used to balance projected total assets and liabilities.

This example shows the interaction between sales growth and financial policy. As sales increase, so do total assets. This occurs because the firm must invest in net working capital and non-current assets (such as property, plant and equipment) to support higher sales levels. Because assets are growing, total liabilities and equity (the right side of the statement of financial position) will grow as well.

The thing to notice from our simple example is that the way the liabilities and owners' equity change depends on the firm's financing policy and its dividend policy. The growth in assets requires that the firm decides on how to finance that growth. This is strictly a managerial decision. Note that, in our example, the firm needed no outside funds.

In the Chute SA example, we described a simple planning model in which every item increased at the same rate as sales. This may be a reasonable assumption for some elements. For others, such as long-term borrowing, it probably is not: the amount of long-term borrowing is something set by management, and it does not necessarily relate directly to the level of sales.

We now describe an extended version of our simple model. The basic idea is to separate the income statement and statement of financial position into two groups – those that vary directly with sales and those that do not. Given a sales forecast, we shall then calculate how much financing the firm will need to support the predicted sales level.

> **percentage of sales approach**
> a financial planning method in which accounts are varied depending on a firm's predicted sales level.

The financial planning model we describe next is based on the **percentage of sales approach**. Our goal here is to develop a quick and practical way of generating pro forma statements. We defer discussion of some 'bells and whistles' to a later section.

THE INCOME STATEMENT

We start with the most recent income statement for Bogle plc, as shown in Table 3A.1. Notice that we have simplified things by including costs, depreciation and interest in a single cost figure.

TABLE 3A.1

Bogle plc Statement of Comprehensive Income

	£	£
Sales		1,000
Costs		800
Profit before taxes		200
Taxes (28%)		56
Profit attributable to shareholders		144
Dividends	48	
Addition to retained earnings	96	

Bogle has projected a 25 per cent increase in sales for the coming year, so we anticipate sales of £1,000 × 1.25 = £1,250. To generate a pro forma income statement, we assume that total costs will continue to run at £800/1,000 = 80 per cent of sales. With this assumption, Bogle's pro forma income statement is shown in Table 3A.2. The effect here of assuming that costs are a constant percentage of sales is to assume that the profit margin is constant. To check this, notice that the profit margin was £144 / 1,000 = 14.4 per cent. In our pro forma, the profit margin is £180 / 1,250 = 14.4 per cent: so it is unchanged.

TABLE 3A.2

Bogle plc Statement of Comprehensive Income

	£	£
Sales		1,250
Costs		1000
Profit before taxes		250
Taxes (28%)		70
Profit attributable to shareholders		180
Dividends	60	
Addition to retained earnings	120	

Next, we need to project the dividend payment. This amount is up to Bogle's management. We shall assume Bogle has a policy of paying out a constant fraction of net income in the form of a cash dividend. For the most recent year, the **dividend payout ratio** was this:

$$\text{Dividend payout ratio} = \text{Cash dividend/Net income} = £48/144 = 1/3 \quad (3A.1)$$

We can also calculate the ratio of the addition to retained earnings to net income:

$$\text{Addition to retained earnings/Net income} = £96/144 = 2/3$$

This ratio is called the **retention ratio** or *plowback ratio*, and it is equal to 1 minus the dividend payout ratio because everything not paid out is retained. Assuming that the payout ratio is constant, here are the projected dividends and addition to retained earnings:

Projected dividends paid to shareholders = £180 × 1/3 = £ 60
Projected addition to retained earnings = £180 × 2/3 = £120
£180

dividend payout ratio
the amount of cash paid out to shareholders divided by net income.

retention ratio
the addition to retained earnings divided by net income. Also called the *plowback ratio*.

THE STATEMENT OF FINANCIAL POSITION

To generate a pro forma statement of financial position, we start with the most recent statement, as shown in Table 3A.3.

TABLE 3A.3

Bogle plc Statement of Financial Position

Assets	£	Percentage of sales	Liabilities and owners' equity	£	Percentage of sales
Current assets			**Current liabilities**		
Cash	160	16	Trade payables	300	30
Trade receivables	440	44	Notes payable	100	n/a
Inventory	600	60			
Total	1,200	120	Total	400	n/a
Non-current assets			**Long-term debt**	800	n/a
Property, plant and equipment	1,800	180	**Owners' equity**		
			Ordinary shares and paid-in surplus	800	n/a
			Retained earnings	1,000	n/a
			Total	1,800	n/a
Total assets	3,000	300	**Total liabilities and owners' equity**	3,000	n/a

On our statement of financial position, we assume that some items vary directly with sales and others do not. For items that vary with sales, we express each as a percentage of sales for the year just completed. When an item does not vary directly with sales, we write 'n/a' for 'not applicable'.

For example, on the asset side, inventory is equal to 60 per cent of sales (= £600/1,000) for the year just ended. We assume this percentage applies to the coming year, so for each £1 increase in sales, inventory will rise by £0.60. More generally, the ratio of total assets to sales for the year just ended is £3,000/1,000 = 3, or 300 per cent. This ratio of total assets to sales is sometimes called the **capital intensity ratio**. It tells us the amount of assets needed to generate £1 in sales; so the higher the ratio, the more capital-intensive the firm. Notice also that this ratio is just the reciprocal of the total asset turnover ratio we defined in the last chapter.

For Bogle, assuming that this ratio is constant, it takes £3 in total assets to generate £1 in sales (apparently, Bogle is in a relatively capital-intensive business). Therefore, if sales increase by £100, Bogle will have to increase total assets by three times this amount, or £300.

On the liability side of the statement of financial position, we show trade payables varying with sales. The reason is that we expect to place more orders with our suppliers as sales volume increases, so payables will change 'spontaneously' with sales. Notes payable, on the other hand, represent short-term debt such as bank borrowing. This item will not vary unless we take specific actions to change the amount, so we mark it as 'n/'.

Similarly, we use 'n/a' for long-term debt because it won't automatically change with sales. The same is true for ordinary shares and paid-in surplus. The last item on the right side, retained earnings, will vary with sales, but it won't be a simple percentage of sales. Instead, we shall explicitly calculate the change in retained earnings based on our projected net income and dividends.

We can now construct a partial pro forma statement of financial position for Bogle. We do this by using the percentages we have just calculated wherever possible to calculate the projected amounts. For example, property, plant and equipment are 180 per cent of sales: so, with a new sales level of £1,250, the

> **capital intensity ratio**
> a firm's total assets divided by its sales, or the amount of assets needed to generate £1 in sales.

property, plant and equipment amount will be 1.80 × £1,250 = £2,250, representing an increase of £2,250 − 1,800 = £450. It is important to note that we initially assume no change for items that don't vary directly with sales and simply write in the original amounts. The result is shown in Table 3A.4. Notice that the change in retained earnings is equal to the £110 addition to retained earnings we calculated earlier.

TABLE 3A.4

Bogle plc Partial Pro Forma Statement of Financial Position

Assets	Projected (£)	Change from previous year (£)	Liabilities and owners' equity	Projected (£)	Change from previous year (£)
Current assets			**Current liabilities**		
Cash	200	40	Trade payables	375	75
Trade receivables	550	110	Notes payable	100	0
Inventory	750	150			
Total	1,500	300	Total	475	75
Non-current assets			**Long-term debt**	800	0
Property, plant and equipment	2,250	450	**Owners' equity**		
			Ordinary shares and paid-in surplus	800	0
			Retained earnings	1,120	120
			Total	1,920	120
Total assets	3,750	750	**Total liabilities and owners' equity**	3,195	195
			External financing needed	555	555

Inspecting our pro forma statement of financial position, we notice that assets are projected to increase by £750. However, without additional financing, liabilities and equity will increase by only £195, leaving a shortfall of £750 − 185 = £555. We label this amount, *external financing needed (EFN)*.

A PARTICULAR SCENARIO

Our financial planning model now reminds us of one of those good news-bad news jokes. The good news is we're projecting a 25 per cent increase in sales. The bad news is that this isn't going to happen unless Bogle can somehow raise £555 in new financing.

This is a good example of how the planning process can point out problems and potential conflicts. If, for example, Bogle has a goal of not borrowing any additional funds and not selling any new equity, then a 25 per cent increase in sales is probably not feasible.

If we take the need for £555 in new financing as given, we know that Bogle has three possible sources: short-term borrowing, long-term borrowing and new equity. The choice of some combination of these three is up to management; we shall illustrate only one of the many possibilities.

Suppose Bogle decides to borrow the needed funds. In this case, the firm might choose to borrow some over the short term and some over the long term. For example, current assets increased by £300, whereas current liabilities rose by only £75. Bogle could borrow £300 − 75 = £225 in short-term notes payable and leave total net working capital unchanged. With £555 needed, the remaining £555 − 225 = £330 would have to come from long-term debt. Table 3A.5 shows the completed pro forma statement of financial position for Bogle.

TABLE 3A.5

Bogle plc Pro Forma Statement of Financial Position

Assets	Projected (£)	Change from previous year (£)	Liabilities and owners' equity	Projected (£)	Change from previous year (£)
Current assets			**Current liabilities**		
Cash	200	40	Trade payables	375	75
Trade receivables	550	110	Notes payable	325	225
Inventory	750	150	Total	700	300
Total	1,500	300	**Long-term debt**		
Non-current assets			Owners' equity	1,300	330
			Ordinary shares and paid-in surplus	800	0
Property, plant and equipment	2,250	450	Retained earnings	1,120	120
			Total	1,920	120
Total assets	3,750	750	**Total liabilities and owners' equity**	3,750	750

We have used a combination of short-term and long-term debt as the plug here, but we emphasize that this is just one possible strategy; it is not necessarily the best one by any means. There are many other scenarios we could (and should) investigate. The various ratios we discussed earlier in the chapter come in handy here. For example, we would surely want to examine the current ratio and total debt ratio to see whether we were comfortable with the previous scenario's new projected debt levels.

Now that we have finished our statement of financial position, we have all of the projected sources and uses of cash. We could finish off our pro formas by drawing up the projected statement of cash flows along the lines discussed earlier. We shall leave this as an exercise and instead investigate an important alternative scenario.

AN ALTERNATIVE SCENARIO

The assumption that assets are a fixed percentage of sales is convenient, but it may not be suitable in many cases. In particular, note that we effectively assumed that Bogle was using its non-current assets (property, plant and equipment) at 100 per cent of capacity because any increase in sales led to an increase in fixed assets. For most businesses, there would be some slack or excess capacity, and production could be increased by perhaps running an extra shift. For example, according to the European Commission, the overall capacity utilization for European manufacturing companies in the first quarter of 2013 ranged between 53 per cent (Cyprus) to 84 per cent (Austria).

Assume that Bogle is operating at only 71.4 per cent of capacity, so the need for external funds will be quite different. When we say '71.4 per cent of capacity', we mean that the current sales level is 71.4 per cent of the full-capacity sales level:

$$\text{Current sales} = £1,000 = 0.714 \times \text{Full-capacity sales}$$
$$\text{Full-capacity sales} = £1,000/0.714 = £1,401$$

This tells us that sales could increase by more than 40 per cent – from £1,000 to £1,401 – before any new fixed assets would be needed.

We assumed it would be necessary to add £450 in property, plant and equipment in our previous scenario. No spending on net fixed assets is needed in the current scenario because sales are projected to rise only to £1,250, which is substantially less than the £1,401 full-capacity level.

As a result, our original estimate of £555 in external funds needed is too high. We estimated that £450 in new property, plant and equipment would be needed. Instead, no spending on new net fixed assets is necessary. Thus, if we are currently operating at 71.4 per cent capacity, we need only £555 − 450 = £105 in external funds. The excess capacity thus makes a considerable difference in our projections.

These alternative scenarios show that it is inappropriate to manipulate financial statement information in the planning process blindly. The results depend critically on the assumptions made about the relationships between sales and asset needs. We return to this point a little later.

One thing should be clear by now. Projected growth rates play an important role in the planning process. They are also important to outside analysts and potential investors.

> **CONCEPT QUESTIONS**
>
> **3A.2a** What is the basic idea behind the percentage of sales approach?
> **3A.2b** Unless it is modified, what does the percentage of sales approach assume about fixed asset capacity usage.

3A.3 EXTERNAL FINANCING AND GROWTH

External financing needed (EFN) and growth are obviously related. All other things staying the same, the higher the rate of growth in sales or assets, the greater will be the need for external financing. In the previous section, we took a growth rate as given, and then we determined the amount of external financing needed to support that growth. In this section, we turn things around a bit. We shall take the firm's financial policy as given and then examine the relationship between that financial policy and the firm's ability to finance new investments and thereby grow.

Once again, we emphasize that we are focusing on growth not because growth is an appropriate goal; instead, for our purposes, growth is simply a convenient means of examining the interactions between investment and financing decisions.

EFN AND GROWTH

The first thing we need to do is establish the relationship between EFN and growth. To do this, we introduce the simplified income statement and balance sheet (statement of financial position) for Hoffman AG in Table 3A.6. Notice that we have simplified the statement of financial position by combining short-term and long-term debt into a single total debt figure. Effectively, we are assuming that none of the current liabilities varies spontaneously with sales. This assumption isn't as restrictive as it sounds. If any current liabilities (such as trade payables) vary with sales, we can assume that any such accounts have been netted out in current assets. Also, we continue to combine depreciation, interest and costs on the income statement.

Suppose Hoffman is forecasting next year's sales level at €600, a €100 increase. Notice that the percentage increase in sales is €100/500 = 20%. Using the percentage of sales approach and the figures in Table 3A.6, we can prepare a pro forma income statement and balance sheet as in Table 3A.7. As Table 3A.8 illustrates, at a 20 per cent growth rate, Hoffman needs €100 in new assets (assuming full capacity). The projected addition to retained earnings is €52.8, so the external financing needed is €100 − 52.8 = €47.2.

Notice that Hoffman's debt–equity ratio was originally (from Table 3A.6) equal to €250/250 = 1.0. We shall assume Hoffman does not wish to sell new equity. In this case, the €47.2 in EFN will have to be borrowed. What will the new debt–equity ratio be? From Table 3A.7, we know that total owners' equity–is projected at €302.8. The new total debt will be the original €250 plus €47.2 in new borrowing, which equals €297.2. The debt–equity ratio thus falls slightly from 1.0 to €297.2/302.8 = 0.98.

Table 3A.8 shows EFN for several different growth rates. The projected addition to retained earnings and the projected debt–equity ratio for each scenario are also given (you should probably calculate a few of these for practice). In determining the debt–equity ratios, we assumed that any needed funds were borrowed, and we also assumed that any surplus funds were used to pay off debt. Thus, for the zero growth case, debt falls by €44, from €250 to €206. In Table 3A.8, notice that the

TABLE 3A.6

Hoffman AG Income Statement and Statement of Financial Position

Income Statement		
	€	€
Sales		500
Costs		400
Profit before taxes		100
Taxes (34%)		34
Profit attributable to shareholders		66
Dividends	22	
Addition to retained earnings	44	

Statement of Financial Position					
Assets			Liabilities and owners' equity		
	€	Percentage of sales		€	Percentage of sales
Current assets	200	40	Total liabilities	250	n/a
Non-current assets	300	60	Owners' equity	250	n/a
Total assets	500	100	Total liabilities and owners' equity	500	n/a

TABLE 3A.7

Hoffman AG Income Statement and Statement of Financial Position

Income Statement		
	€	€
Sales (projected)		600.0
Costs (80% of sales)		480.0
Profit before taxes		120.0
Taxes (34%)		40.8
Profit attributable to shareholders		79.2
Dividends	26.4	
Addition to retained earnings	52.8	

Statement of Financial Position					
Assets	Liabilities and owners' equity				
	€	Percentage of sales		€	Percentage of sales
Current assets	240.0	40	Total liabilities	250.0	n/a
Non-current assets	360.0	60	Owners' equity	302.8	n/a
Total assets	600.0	100	Total liabilities and owners' equity	552.8	n/a
			External financing needed	47.2	n/a

TABLE 3A.8

Growth and projected EFN for Hoffman AG

Projected sales growth (%)	Increase in assets required (€)	Addition to retained earnings (€)	External financing needed, EFN (€)	Projected debt–equity ratio
0	0	44.0	−44.0	0.70
5	25	46.2	−21.2	0.77
10	50	48.4	1.6	0.84
15	75	50.6	24.4	0.91
20	100	52.8	47.2	0.98
25	125	55.0	70.0	1.05

increase in assets required is simply equal to the original assets of €500 multiplied by the growth rate. Similarly, the addition to retained earnings is equal to the original €44 plus €44 times the growth rate.

Table 3A.8 shows that Hoffman will run a surplus for relatively low growth rates, and its debt–equity ratio will decline. Once the growth rate increases to about 10 per cent, however, the surplus becomes a deficit. Furthermore, as the growth rate exceeds approximately 20 per cent, the debt–equity ratio passes its original value of 1.0.

Figure 3A.1 illustrates the connection between growth in sales and external financing needed in more detail by plotting asset needs and additions to retained earnings from Table 3A.8 against the growth rates. As shown, the need for new assets grows faster than the addition to retained earnings, so the internal financing provided by the addition to retained earnings rapidly disappears.

FIGURE 3A.1 Growth and related financing needed for Hoffman AG.

FINANCIAL POLICY AND GROWTH

Based on our preceding discussion, we see a direct link between growth and external financing. In this section, we discuss two growth rates that are particularly useful in long-range planning.

The Internal Growth Rate

The first growth rate of interest is the maximum growth rate that can be achieved with no external financing of any kind. We shall call this the **internal growth rate** because this is the rate the firm can maintain with internal financing only. In Figure 3A.1 this internal growth rate is represented by the point where the two lines cross. At this point, the required increase in assets is exactly equal to the addition to retained earnings, and EFN is therefore zero. We have seen that this happens when the growth rate is slightly less than 10 per cent. With a little algebra, we can define this growth rate more precisely:

> **internal growth rate**
> the maximum growth rate a firm can achieve without external financing of any kind.

$$\text{Internal growth rate} = \frac{\text{ROA} \times b}{1 - \text{ROA} \times b} \quad (3A.2)$$

Here ROA is the return on assets, and b is the plowback, or retention, ratio defined earlier in this chapter.

For Hoffman AG, net income was €66 and total assets were €500. ROA is thus €66/500 = 13.2 per cent. Of the €66 net income, €44 was retained, so the plowback ratio, b, is €44/66 = 2/3. With these numbers, we can calculate the internal growth rate:

$$\begin{aligned}\text{Internal growth rate} &= \frac{\text{ROA} \times b}{1 - \text{ROA} \times b}\\ &= \frac{0.132 \times (2/3)}{1 - 0.132 \times (2/3)}\\ &= 9.65\%\end{aligned}$$

Thus Hoffman AG can expand at a maximum rate of 9.65 per cent per year without external financing.

The Sustainable Growth Rate

We have seen that if Hoffman AG wishes to grow more rapidly than at a rate of 9.65 per cent per year, external financing must be arranged. The second growth rate of interest is the maximum growth rate a firm can achieve with no external equity financing while maintaining a constant debt–equity ratio. This rate is commonly called the **sustainable growth rate** because it is the maximum growth rate a firm can maintain without increasing its financial leverage.

> **sustainable growth rate**
> the maximum growth rate a firm can achieve without external equity financing while maintaining a constant debt–equity ratio.

There are various reasons why a firm might wish to avoid equity sales. For example, as we discuss in Chapter 14, new equity sales can be expensive. Alternatively, the current owners may not wish to bring in new owners or contribute additional equity. Why a firm might view a particular debt–equity ratio as optimal is discussed in Chapters 13 and 15; for now, we shall take it as given.

Based on Table 3A.8, Hoffman's sustainable growth rate is approximately 20 per cent because the debt–equity ratio is near 1.0 at that growth rate. The precise value can be calculated:

$$\text{Sustainable growth rate} = \frac{\text{ROE} \times b}{1 - \text{ROE} \times b} \quad (3A.3)$$

This is identical to the internal growth rate except that ROE, return on equity, is used instead of ROA.

For Hoffman AG, net income was €66 and total equity was €250; ROE is thus €66/250 = 26.4 per cent. The plowback ratio, b, is still 2/3, so we can calculate the sustainable growth rate as follows:

$$\begin{aligned}\text{Sustainable growth rate} &= \frac{\text{ROE} \times b}{1 - \text{ROE} \times b}\\ &= \frac{0.264 \times (2/3)}{1 - 0.264 \times (2/3)}\\ &= 21.36\%\end{aligned}$$

Thus Hoffman AG can expand at a maximum rate of 21.36 per cent per year without external equity financing.

Determinants of Growth

We have seen that the return on equity, ROE, could be decomposed into its various components using the Du Pont identity. Because ROE appears so prominently in the determination of the sustainable growth rate, it is obvious that the factors important in determining ROE are also important determinants of growth. We know that ROE can be written as the product of three factors:

$$\text{ROE} = \text{Profit margin} \times \text{Total asset turnover} \times \text{Equity multiplier}$$

If we examine our expression for the sustainable growth rate, we see that anything that increases ROE will increase the sustainable growth rate by making the top bigger and the bottom smaller. Increasing the plowback ratio will have the same effect.

Putting it all together, what we have is that a firm's ability to sustain growth depends explicitly on the following four factors:

1. **Profit margin:** An increase in profit margin will increase the firm's ability to generate funds internally and increase its sustainable growth.
2. **Dividend policy:** A decrease in the percentage of profit attributable to shareholders (net income) paid out as dividends will increase the retention ratio. This increases internally generated equity and thus increases sustainable growth.
3. **Financial policy:** An increase in the debt–equity ratio increases the firm's financial leverage. Because this makes additional debt financing available, it increases the sustainable growth rate.
4. **Total asset turnover:** An increase in the firm's total asset turnover increases the sales generated for each pound or euro in assets. This decreases the firm's need for new assets as sales grow and thereby increases the sustainable growth rate. Notice that increasing total asset turnover is the same thing as decreasing capital intensity.

The sustainable growth rate is a handy planning number. What it illustrates is the explicit relationship between the firm's four major areas of concern: its operating efficiency as measured by profit margin, its asset use efficiency as measured by total asset turnover, its dividend policy as measured by the retention ratio, and its financial policy as measured by the debt–equity ratio.

Given values for all four of these, there is only one growth rate that can be achieved. This is an important point, so it bears restating:

> If a firm does not wish to sell new equity and its profit margin, dividend policy, financial policy, and total asset turnover (or capital intensity) are all fixed, there is only one possible growth rate.

As we described early in this chapter, one of the primary benefits of financial planning is that it ensures internal consistency among the firm's various goals. The concept of the sustainable growth rate captures this element nicely. We now see how a financial planning model can be used to test the feasibility of a planned growth rate. If sales are to grow at a rate higher than the sustainable growth rate, the firm must increase profit margins, increase total asset turnover, increase financial leverage, increase earnings retention, or sell new shares.

> **CONCEPT QUESTIONS**
>
> **3A.3a** How is a firm's sustainable growth related to its accounting return on equity (ROE)?
> **3A.3b** What are the determinants of growth?

3A.4 SOME CAVEATS REGARDING FINANCIAL PLANNING MODELS

Financial planning models do not always ask the right questions. A primary reason is that they tend to rely on accounting relationships and not financial relationships. In particular, the three basic elements of firm value tend to get left out – namely cash flow size, risk and timing.

Because of this, financial planning models sometimes do not produce meaningful clues about what strategies will lead to increases in value. Instead, they divert the user's attention to questions concerning the association of, say, the debt–equity ratio and firm growth.

The financial model we used for Hoffman AG was simple – in fact, too simple. Our model, like many in use today, is really an accounting statement generator at heart. Such models are useful for pointing out inconsistencies and reminding us of financial needs, but they offer little guidance concerning what to do about these problems.

In closing our discussion, we should add that financial planning is an iterative process. Plans are created, examined and modified over and over. The final plan will be a result negotiated between all the different parties to the process. Upper-level managers have a goal in mind, and it is up to the planning staff to rework and ultimately deliver a feasible plan that meets that goal.

Therefore, the final plan will implicitly contain different goals in different areas and satisfy many constraints. For this reason, such a plan need not be a dispassionate assessment of what we think the future will bring; it may instead be a means of reconciling the planned activities of different groups and a way of setting common goals for the future.

> **CONCEPT QUESTIONS**
>
> **3A.4a** What are some important elements that are often missing in financial planning models?
> **3A.4b** Why do we say planning is an iterative process?

SUMMARY AND CONCLUSIONS

This appendix has introduced some of the basics of financial planning. Financial planning forces the firm to think about the future. We have examined a number of features of the planning process. We described what financial planning can accomplish, and the components of a financial model. We went on to develop the relationship between growth and financing needs, and we discussed how a financial planning model is useful in exploring that relationship.

Corporate financial planning should not become a purely mechanical activity. If it does, it will probably focus on the wrong things. In particular, plans all too often are formulated in terms of a growth target, with no explicit linkage to value creation, and they frequently are overly concerned with accounting statements. Nevertheless, the alternative to financial planning is stumbling into the future.

APPENDIX REVIEW AND SELF-TEST PROBLEMS

3A.1 Financial Ratios Consider the statement of financial position for Wiggat Dylan Group.

	December			December
	£m			£m
Current assets			**Current liabilities**	
Cash	761.3		Accounts payable	855.5
Short-term investments	390.8		Accrued expenses	809.6
Trade receivables	347.1		Notes payable/short-term debt	188.1
Notes receivable: short term	19.9		Current port. of LT debt/capital leases	524.8
Receivables: other	131.6		Other current liabilities	1,370.4

	December		December
	£m		£m
Current assets		**Current liabilities**	
Total inventory	24.2	Total current liabilities	3,748.4
Other current assets	404.8		
Total current assets	2,079.7	**Non-current liabilities**	
		Long-term debt	711.3
Non-current assets		Deferred income tax	97.8
Property/plant/equipment	897.6	Minority interest	12.7
Intangible assets	3,432.4	Other liabilities, total	451.7
Long-term investments	143.4	**Total non-current liabilities**	1,273.5
Notes receivable: long term	126.4		
Other long-term assets	338.9	**Total liabilities**	**5,021.9**
Total non-current assets	4,938.7	Ordinary share capital	59.8
		Additional paid-in capital	8.9
		Retained earnings (accumulated deficit)	1,726.0
		Other equity, total	201.8
		Total equity	**1,996.5**
Total assets	**7,018.4**	**Total liabilities and shareholders' equity**	**7,018.4**

Based on the statement of financial position, calculate the following ratios:

Current ratio _____
Quick ratio _____
Cash ratio _____
Inventory turnover _____
Receivables turnover _____
Days' sales in inventory _____
Days' sales in receivables _____
Total debt ratio _____
Long-term debt ratio _____
Times interest earned ratio _____
Cash coverage ratio _____

3A.2 ROE and the Du Pont Identity Calculate the ROE for Wiggat Dylan Group, and then break down your answer into its component parts using the Du Pont identity.

3A.3 Calculating EFN Based on the following information, what is EFN if sales are predicted to grow by 15 per cent? Use the percentage of sales approach, and assume the company is operating at full capacity. The payout ratio is constant.

Income statement		Statement of financial position			
	£m	Assets	£m	Liabilities and owners' equity	£m
Sales	31,601	Current assets	16,152	Current liabilities	13,320
Costs	22,920	Non-current assets	30,632	Non-current liabilities	17,552
Profit before taxes	8,861			Owners' equity	15,912
Taxes (29.39%)	2,551				
Net income	6,130	Total assets	46,784	Total liabilities and owners' equity	46,784
Dividends	2,971				
Addition to retained earnings	3,159				

3A.4 EFN and Capacity Use Based on the information in Problem 3A.3, what is EFN, assuming 60 per cent capacity usage for non-current assets? What is it, assuming 95 per cent capacity?

3A.5 Sustainable Growth Based on the information in Problem 3A.3, what growth rate can the firm maintain if no external financing is used? What is the sustainable growth rate?

SOLUTIONS

3A.1 We've calculated the following ratios based on the ending figures.

Current ratio	£2,079.70/£3,748.40	= 0.55 times
Quick ratio	£2,055.50/£3,748.40	= 0.55 times
Cash ratio	£761.30/£3,748.40	= 0.20 times
Inventory turnover	£6,282.50/£24.20	= 259.61 times
Receivables turnover	£8,167.10/£347.10	= 23.52 times
Days' sales in inventory	365/259.61	= 1.41 days
Days' sales in receivables	365/23.52	= 15.51 days
Total debt ratio	£5,021.90/£7,018.40	= 71.55%
Long-term debt ratio	£711.30/£2,707.80	= 26.27%
Times interest earned ratio	£109/£114	= 0.96 times
Cash coverage ratio	£236.60/£114	= 2.08 times

3A.2 The return on equity is the ratio of net income to total equity. This is £44.7/£1,996.6 = 2.2 per cent.

Given the Du Pont identity, ROE can be written as follows:

$$\text{ROE} = \text{Profit margin} \times \text{Total asset turnover} \times \text{Equity multiplier}$$
$$= £44.7/£8,167.1 \times £8,167.1/£7,018.4 \times £7,018.4/£1,996.5$$
$$= 0.55\% \times 1.16 \times 3.52$$
$$= 2.2\%$$

Notice that return on assets, ROA, is £44.7/£7,018.4 = 0.64 per cent.

3A.3 We can calculate EFN by preparing the pro forma statements using the percentage of sales approach. Note that sales are forecast to be £31,601 × 1.10 = £34,761.

Pro forma financial statements		
Income statement (£m)		
Sales	36,341	Forecast
Costs	26,358	72.53% of sales
Profit before taxes	9,983	
Taxes (29.39%)	2,934	
Net income	7,050	
Dividends	3,417	48.47% of net income
Addition to retained earnings	3,633	

Statement of financial position					
Assets			**Liabilities and owners' equity**		
	£m	%		£m	%
Current assets	18,575	51.11	Current liabilities	15,318	42.15
Non-current assets	35,227	96.93	Non-current liabilities	17,552	n/a
			Owners' equity	19,545	n/a
Total assets	53,802	148.05	Total liabilities and owners' equity	52,415	n/a
			EFN	1,387	n/a

3A.4 Full-capacity sales are equal to current sales divided by the capacity utilization. At 60 per cent of capacity:

$$£31,601 = 0.60 \times \text{Full-capacity sales}$$
$$£52,668 = \text{Full-capacity sales}$$

With a sales level of £36,341, no new non-current assets will be needed, so our earlier estimate is too high. We estimated an increase in non-current assets of £35,227 − 30,632 = £4,595. The new EFN will thus be £1,387 − 4,595 = −£3,208, a surplus. No external financing is needed in this case.

At 95 per cent capacity, full-capacity sales are £33,264. The ratio of non-current assets to full-capacity sales is thus £30,632/33,264 = 92.08 per cent. At a sales level of £36,341, we shall thus need £36,341 × 0.9208 = £33,465 in non-current assets, an increase of £2,833. This is £4,595 − 2,833 = £1,762 less than we originally predicted, so the EFN is now £1,387 − 1,762 = −£375, a surplus. No additional financing is needed.

3A.5 The firm retains $b = 1 - 0.4847 = 51.53$ per cent of net income. Return on assets is £6,130/46,784 = 13.10 per cent. The internal growth rate is thus:

$$\frac{\text{ROA} \times b}{1 - (\text{ROA} \times b)} = \frac{0.1310 \times 0.5153}{1 - (0-1310 \times 0.05153)}$$
$$= 7.24\%$$

Return on equity is £6,130/15,912 = 38.52%, so we can calculate the sustainable growth rate as follows:

$$\frac{\text{ROE} \times b}{1 - (\text{ROE} \times b)} = \frac{0.3852 \times 0.5153}{1 - (0-3852 \times 0.05153)}$$
$$= 24.77\%$$

Level of difficulty: Basic | Intermediate | Challenge

QUESTIONS AND PROBLEMS

3A.1 Pro Forma Statements Consider the following financial statements (ignoring taxes):

Income statement			Statement of financial position		
	€m			€m	€m
Sales	50,710	Assets	39,582	Debt	23,072
Costs	45,740			Equity	16,510
Net profit	4,970	Total	39,582	Total	39,582

Sales and every item on the statement of financial position are expected to increase by 15 per cent. Create the pro forma statements, and reconcile them. What is the plug variable here?

3A.2 Pro Forma Statements and EFN In the previous question, assume the firm pays out half of net profit in the form of a cash dividend. Costs and assets vary with sales, but debt and equity do not. Prepare the pro forma statements and determine the external financing needed.

3A.3 **EFN** Consider the following financial statements:

Income statement			Statement of financial position		
	€m			€m	€m
Sales	7,477	Current assets	11,108	Current liabilities	12,136
Costs	6,730	Non-current assets	13,355	Non-current liabilities	6,565
Profit before taxes	747			Total liabilities	18,701
Tax	233 31.19%			Equity	5,762
Net profit	514	Total assets	24,463	Total	24,463

Assets, costs and current liabilities are proportional to sales. Non-current liabilities and equity are not. The company maintains a constant 40 per cent dividend payout ratio. As with every other firm in its industry, next year's sales are projected to increase by exactly 15 per cent. What is the external financing needed?

3A.4 **Calculating Internal Growth** Consider the following financial statements:

Income statement			Statement of financial position		
	€m			€m	€m
Sales	76,651	Current assets	44,129	Current liabilities	37,005
Costs	72,760	Non-current assets	50,797	Non-current liabilities	31,275
Profit before taxes	3,891			Total liabilities	68,280
Tax	1,434 36.85%			Equity	26,646
Net profit	2,457	Total assets	94,926	Total	94,926

Assets and costs are proportional to sales. Debt and equity are not. The company maintains a constant 30 per cent dividend payout ratio. No external equity financing is possible. What is the internal growth rate?

3A.5 **Calculating Sustainable Growth** For the company in the previous problem, what is the sustainable growth rate?

3A.6 **Internal Growth** If the Football Shoppe has an 8 per cent ROA and a 20 per cent payout ratio, what is its internal growth rate?

3A.7 **Sustainable Growth** If Garnett Ltd has a 15 per cent ROE and a 25 per cent payout ratio, what is its sustainable growth rate?

3A.8 **Full-Capacity Sales** Seaweed Manufacturing is currently operating at only 95 per cent of non-current asset capacity. Current sales are £600,000. How fast can sales grow before any new non-current assets are needed?

3A.9 **Non-Current Assets and Capacity Usage** For the company in the previous problem, suppose non-current assets are £440,000 and sales are projected to grow to £830,000. How much in new non-current assets is required to support this growth in sales? Assume the company maintains its current operating capacity.

3A.10 **Growth and Assets** A firm wishes to maintain an internal growth rate of 8 per cent and a dividend payout ratio of 25 per cent. The current profit margin is 5 per cent, and the firm uses no external financing sources. What must total asset turnover be?

3A.11 **Sustainable Growth Rate** Coheed plc had equity of £135,000 at the beginning of the year. At the end of the year the company had total assets of £250,000. During the year the company sold no new equity. Net income for the year was £19,000, and dividends were £3,500. What is the sustainable growth rate for the company? What is the sustainable growth rate if you use the formula ROE × b and beginning of period equity? What is the sustainable growth rate if you use end of period equity in this formula? Is this number too high or too low? Why?

3A.12 Internal Growth Rates Calculate the internal growth rate for the company in the previous problem. Now calculate the internal growth rate using ROA × b for both beginning of period and end of period total assets. What do you observe?

3A.13 Constraints on Growth Nearside NV wishes to maintain a growth rate of 10 per cent per year and a debt–equity ratio of 0.50. Profit margin is 6.70 per cent, and the ratio of total assets to sales is constant at 1.35. Is this growth rate possible? To answer, determine what the dividend payout ratio must be. How do you interpret the result?

3A.14 EFN Define the following:

S = Previous year's sales

A = Total assets

D = Total debt

E = Total equity

g = Projected growth in sales

PM = Profit margin

b = Retention (plowback) ratio

Show that EFN can be written as follows:

$$\text{EFN} = -\text{PM}(S)b + [A - \text{PM}(S)b] \times g$$

Hint: Asset needs will equal $A \times g$. The addition to retained earnings will equal $\text{PM}(S)b \times (1 + g)$.

3A.15 Growth Rates Based on the result in Problem 3A.14, show that the internal and sustainable growth rates are as given in the chapter. *Hint:* For the internal growth rate, set EFN equal to zero and solve for g.

3A.16 Sustainable Growth Rate In the chapter, we discussed the two versions of the sustainable growth rate formula. Derive the formula ROE × b from the formula given in the chapter, where ROE is based on beginning of period equity. Also, derive the formula ROA × b from the internal growth rate formula.

APPENDIX 6A

THE TERM STRUCTURE OF INTEREST RATES, SPOT RATES AND YIELD TO MATURITY

IN THE MAIN BODY OF CHAPTER 6, we showed that yields could be different for various bond maturities and provided several reasons why this should be the case. This appendix focuses on some practical implications resulting from that discussion.

Consider two zero-coupon bonds. Bond A is a one-year bond and bond B is a two-year bond. Both have face values of €1,000. The one-year interest rate, r_1, is 8 per cent. The two-year interest rate, r_2, is 10 per cent. These two rates of interest are examples of *spot rates*. Perhaps this inequality in interest rates occurs because inflation is expected to be higher over the second year than over the first. The two bonds are depicted in the following time chart:

```
    0           Year 1        1         Year 2         2
    |----------------------|----------------------|
Bond A  ←——— 8% ———→  €1,000
Bond B  ←——————————— 10% ———————————→  €1,000
```

We can easily calculate the present value for bond A and bond B as follows:

$$PV_A = \frac{€1,000}{1.08} = €925.93$$

$$PV_B = \frac{€1,000}{(1.10)^2} = €826.45$$

Of course, if PV_A and PV_B were observable and the spot rates were not, we could determine the spot rates using the PV formula because

$$PV_A = €925.93 = \frac{€1,000}{1 + r_1} \rightarrow r_1 = 8\%$$

and

$$PV_B = €826.45 = \frac{€1,000}{(1 + r_2)^2} \rightarrow r_2 = 10\%$$

Now we can see how the prices of more complicated bonds are determined. Try to do the next example. It illustrates the difference between spot rates and yields to maturity.

> **EXAMPLE 6A.1**
>
> ## ON THE SPOT
>
> Given that the spot rate r_1 equals 8 per cent and r_2 equals 10 per cent, what should a 5 per cent coupon, two-year bond cost? The cash flows C_1 and C_2 are illustrated in the following time chart:
>
> ```
> 0            Year 1            1            Year 2            2
> |--------------------------------|--------------------------------|
> Bond A  ←———— 8% ————→ €1,000
> Bond B  ←———————————— 10% ————————————→ €1,000
> ```
>
> The bond can be viewed as a portfolio of zero-coupon bonds with one- and two-year maturities. Therefore:
>
> $$PV = \frac{€50}{1 + 0.08} + \frac{€1{,}050}{(1 + 0.10)^2} = €914.06 \quad \text{(6A.1)}$$
>
> We now want to calculate a single rate for the bond. We do this by solving for y in the following equation:
>
> $$€914.06 = \frac{€50}{1 + y} + \frac{€1{,}050}{(1 + y)^2} \quad \text{(6A.2)}$$
>
> In Equation (6A.2), y equals 9.95 per cent. As mentioned in the chapter, we call y the *yield to maturity* on the bond. Solving for y for a multi-year bond is generally done using trial and error.[1] Although this can take much time with paper and pencil, it is virtually instantaneous on a handheld calculator.
>
> It is worthwhile to contrast Equations (6A.1) and (6A.2). In (6A.1), we use the market-wide spot rates to determine the price of the bond. Once we get the bond price, we use (6A.2) to calculate its yield to maturity. Because Equation (6A.1) employs two spot rates, whereas only one appears in (6A.2), we can think of yield to maturity as some sort of average of the two spot rates.[2]
>
> Using these spot rates, the yield to maturity of a two-year coupon bond whose coupon rate is 12 per cent and PV equals €1,036.73 can be determined by:
>
> $$€1{,}036.73 = \frac{€120}{1 + r} + \frac{€1{,}120}{(1 + r)^2} \rightarrow r = 9.89\%$$
>
> As these calculations show, two bonds with the same maturity will usually have different yields to maturity if the coupons differ.

Graphing the Term Structure

Remember that the *term structure of interest rates* can only be calculated when default-free (i.e. government), zero-coupon bonds are available. Governments issue coupon bonds in most countries, so an approximation of the term structure must be calculated, called the *yield curve*. Figure 6A.1 graphs a particular term structure. Figure 6A.1 shows that the spot rates are increasing with longer maturities: $r_3 > r_2 > r_1$. As discussed, graphing the term structure is easy if we can observe spot rates, and default-free, zero-coupon bonds are available.

FIGURE 6A.1

The term structure of interest rates

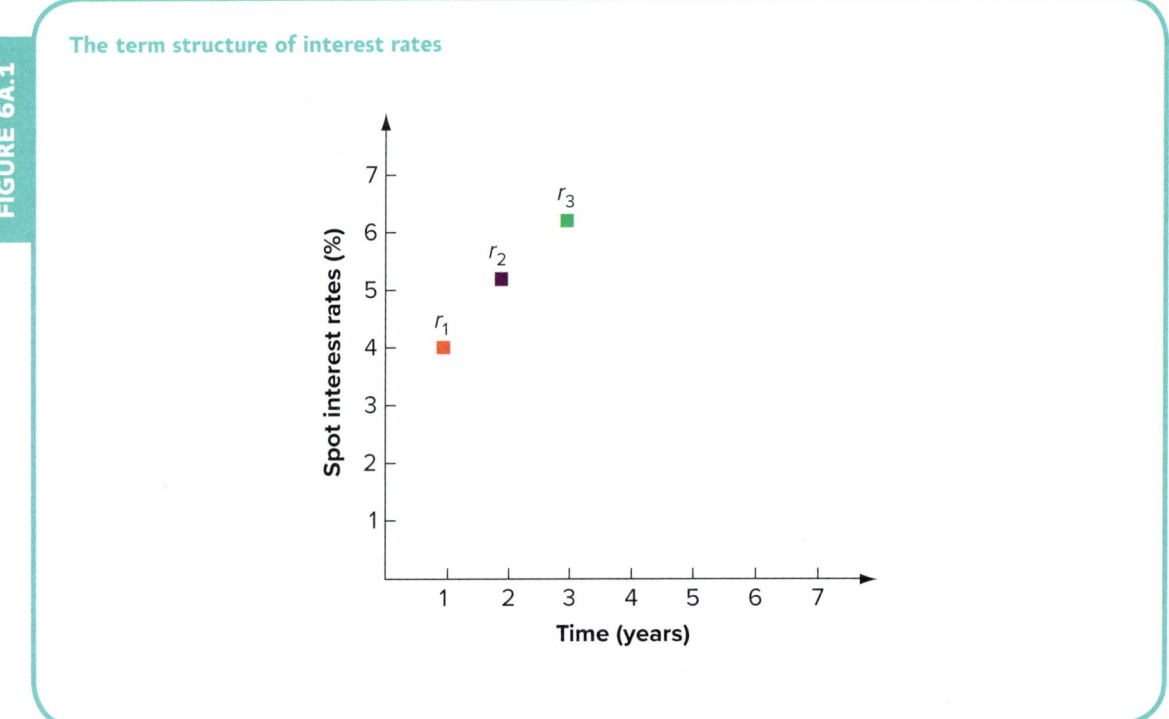

A given term structure, such as that in Figure. 6A.1, exists for only a moment in time – say 10:00 a.m., 30 December 2010. Interest rates are likely to change in the next minute so that a different (though quite similar) term structure would exist at 10:01 a.m.

EXPLANATIONS OF THE TERM STRUCTURE

Figure 6A.1 showed one of the many possible relationships between the spot rate and maturity. We now want to explore the relationship in more detail. We begin by defining a new term, the forward rate. Next, we relate this forward rate to future interest rates. Finally, we consider alternative theories of the term structure.

Definition of Forward Rate

Earlier in this appendix, we developed a two-year example where the spot rate over the first year was 8 per cent and the spot rate over the two years was 10 per cent. Here, an individual investing €1 in a two-year zero-coupon bond would have €1 × (1.10)2 in two years.

To pursue our discussion, it is worthwhile to rewrite:[3]

$$€1 \times (1.10)^2 = €1 \times 1.08 \times 1.1204 \qquad (6A.3)$$

Equation (6A.3) tells us something important about the relationship between one- and two-year rates. When an individual invests in a two-year zero-coupon bond yielding 10 per cent, his wealth at the end of two years is the same as if he received an 8 per cent return over the first year and a 12.04 per cent return over the second year. This hypothetical rate over the second year, 12.04 per cent, is called the *forward rate*. Thus we can think of an investor with a two-year zero-coupon bond as getting the one-year spot rate of 8 per cent and *locking in* 12.04 per cent over the second year. This relationship is presented in Figure 6A.2.

APPENDIX 6A The Term Structure of Interest Rates, Spot Rates and Yield to Maturity

FIGURE 6A.2

Breakdown of a two-year spot rate into a one-year spot rate and forward rate over the second year

With a two-year spot rate of 10 per cent, an investor in a two-year bond receives €1.21 at date 2.
This is the same return *as if* the investor received the spot rate of 8 per cent over the first year and a 12.04 per cent return over the second year.

€1 ——— 8% ——— €1.08 ——— 12.04% ——— €1 × 1.08 × 1.1204 = €1.21

Because both the one-year spot rate and the two-year spot rate are known at date 0, the forward rate over the second year can be calculated at date 0.

More generally, if we are given spot rates r_1 and r_2, we can always determine the forward rate, f_2, such that:

$$(1 + r_2)^2 = (1 + r_1) \times (1 + f_2) \tag{6A.4}$$

We solve for f_2, yielding:

$$f_2 = \frac{(1 + r_2)^2}{1 + r_1} - 1 \tag{6A.5}$$

EXAMPLE 6A.2

LOOKING FORWARD

If the one-year spot rate is 7 per cent and the two-year spot rate is 12 per cent, what is f_2?
We plug in Equation (6A.5), yielding:

$$f_2 = \frac{(1.12)^2}{1.07} - 1 = 17.23\%$$

Consider an individual investing in a two-year zero-coupon bond yielding 12 per cent. We say it is as if he receives 7 per cent over the first year and simultaneously locks in 17.23 per cent over the second year. Note that both the one-year spot rate and the two-year spot rate are known at date 0. Because the forward rate is calculated from the one-year and two-year spot rates, it can be calculated at date 0.

Forward rates can be calculated over later years as well. The general formula is:

$$f_n = \frac{(1 + r_n)^n}{(1 + r_{n-1})^{n-1}} - 1 \tag{6A.6}$$

where f_n is the forward rate over the nth year, r_n is the n-year spot rate, and r_{n-1} is the spot rate for $n - 1$ years.

EXAMPLE 6A.3

FORWARD RATES

Assume the following set of rates:

Year	Spot rate (%)
1	5
2	6
3	7
4	6

What are the forward rates over each of the four years?
The forward rate over the first year is, *by definition*, equal to the one-year spot rate. Thus we do not generally speak of the forward rate over the first year. The forward rates over the later years are:

$$f_2 = \frac{(1.06)^2}{1.05} - 1 = 7.01\%$$

$$f_3 = \frac{(1.07)^3}{(1.06)^2} - 1 = 9.03\%$$

$$f_4 = \frac{(1.06)^4}{(1.07)^3} - 1 = 3.06\%$$

An individual investing £1 in the two-year zero-coupon bond receives £1.1236 [£1 × (1.06)²] at date 2. They can be viewed as receiving the one-year spot rate of 5 per cent over the first year and receiving a forward rate of 7.01 per cent over the second year. An individual investing £1 in a three-year zero coupon bond receives £1.2250 [£1 × (1.07)³] on date 3. They can be viewed as receiving the two-year spot rate of 6 per cent over the first two years and receiving a forward rate of 9.03 per cent over the third year.

An individual investing £1 in a four-year zero-coupon bond receives £1.2625 [£1 × (1.06)⁴] on date 4. They can be viewed as receiving the three-year spot rate of 7 per cent over the first three years and receiving a forward rate of 3.06 per cent over the fourth year.

Note that all of the four spot rates in this problem are known at date 0. Because the forward rates are calculated from the spot rates, they can be determined at date 0.

The material in this appendix is likely to be difficult for a student exposed to term structure for the first time. It helps to state what the student should know at this point. Given Equations (6A.5) and (6A.6), a student should be able to calculate a set of forward rates, given a set of spot rates. This can simply be viewed as a mechanical computation. In addition to the calculations, a student should understand the intuition of Figure 6A.2.

We now turn to the relationship between the forward rate and the expected spot rates in the future.

Estimating the Price of a Bond at a Future Date

In the example from the body of this chapter, we considered zero-coupon bonds paying €1,000 at maturity and selling at a discount before maturity. We now wish to change the example slightly. Now each bond initially sells at par, so that payment at maturity is above €1,000.[4] Keeping the spot rates at 8 per cent and 10 per cent, we have the following:

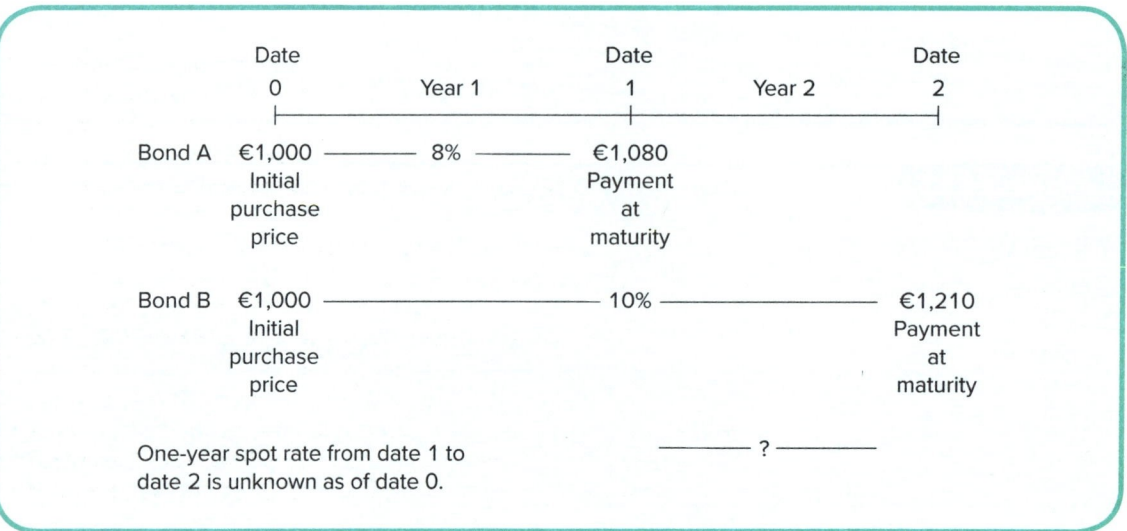

The payments at maturity are €1,080 and €1,210 for the one- and two-year zero-coupon bonds, respectively. The initial purchase price of €1,000 for each bond is determined as follows:

$$€1,000 = \frac{€1,080}{1.08}$$
$$€1,000 = \frac{€1,210}{(1.10)^2}$$

We refer to the one-year bond as bond A and the two-year bond as bond B.

There will be a different one-year spot rate when date 1 arrives. This will be the spot rate from date 1 to date 2. We can also call it the spot rate over year 2. This spot rate is not known as of date 0. For example, should the inflation rate rise between date 0 and date 1, the spot rate over year 2 is likely to be high. Should the inflation rate fall between date 0 and date 1, the spot rate over year 2 is likely to be low.

Now that we have determined each bond's price at date 0, we want to determine what the price of each bond will be on date 1. The price of the one-year bond (bond A) must be €1,080 at date 1 because the payment at maturity is made then. The hard part is determining what the price of the two-year bond (bond B) will be at that time.

Suppose we find that, on date 1, the one-year spot rate from date 1 to date 2 is 6 per cent. We state that this is the one-year spot rate *over* year 2. This means that you can invest €1,000 at date 1 and receive €1,060 (€1,000 × 1.06) on date 2. Because one year has already passed for bond B, the bond has only one year left. Because bond B pays €1,210 on date 2, its value at date 1 is:

$$€1,141.51 = \frac{€1,210}{1.06} \tag{6A.7}$$

Note that no one *knew* ahead of time the price that bond B would sell for on date 1 because no one knew that the one-year spot rate over year 2 would be 6 per cent.

Suppose the one-year spot rate beginning at date 1 turned out to be not 6 per cent, but 7 per cent instead. This means that you can invest €1,000 at date 1 and receive €1,070 (€1,000 × 1.07) at date 2. In this case, the value of bond B at date 1 would be:

$$€1,130.84 = \frac{€1,210}{1.07} \tag{6A.8}$$

Finally, suppose that the one-year spot rate at date 1 turned out to be neither 6 per cent nor 7 per cent, but 14 per cent instead. This means that you can invest €1,000 at date 1 and receive €1,140 (€1,000 × 1.14) on date 2. In this case, the value of bond B at date 1 would be:

$$€1,061.40 = \frac{€1,210}{1.14}$$

The price that bond B will sell for on date 1 is unknown before date 1 because the one-year spot rate prevailing over year 2 is unknown until date 1.

It is important to re-emphasize that although the forward rate is known at date 0, the one-year spot rate beginning at date 1 is unknown ahead of time. Thus the price of bond B at date 1 is unknown ahead of time. Before date 1, we can speak only of the amount that bond B is *expected* to sell for on date 1. We write this as follows:[5]

The amount that bond B is expected to sell for on date 1:

$$\frac{€1,210}{1 + \text{Spot rate expected over year 2}} \tag{6A.9}$$

It is worthwhile making two points now. First, because each individual is different, the expected value of bond B differs across individuals. Later we shall speak of a consensus expected value across investors. Second, Equation (6A.9) represents one's forecast of the price that the bond will be selling for on date 1. The forecast is made ahead of time – that is, on date 0.

THE RELATIONSHIP BETWEEN FORWARD RATE OVER SECOND YEAR AND SPOT RATE EXPECTED OVER SECOND YEAR

Given a forecast of bond B's price, an investor can choose one of two strategies at date 0:

1. Buy a one-year bond. Proceeds at date 1 would be:

$$€1,080 = €1,000 \times 1.08 \qquad \text{(6A.10)}$$

2. Buy a two-year bond but sell at date 1. *Expected* proceeds would be:

$$\frac{€1,000 \times (1.10)^2}{1 + \text{Spot rate expected over year 2}} \qquad \text{(6A.11)}$$

Given our discussion of forward rates, we can rewrite Equation (6A.11) as:

$$\frac{€1,000 \times 1.08 \times 1.1204}{1 + \text{Spot rate expected over year 2}} \qquad \text{(6A.12)}$$

(Remember that 12.04 per cent was the forward rate over year 2: that is, $f_2 = 12.04\%$.)

Under what condition will the return from strategy 1 equal the expected return from strategy 2? In other words, under what condition will Equation (6A.10) equal Equation (6A.12)?

The two strategies will yield the same expected return only when:

$$12.04\% = \text{Spot rate expected over year 2} \qquad \text{(6A.13)}$$

In other words, if the forward rate equals the expected spot rate, one would expect to earn the same return over the first year, whether one:

- Invested in a one-year bond
- Invested in a two-year bond but sold after one year.

THE EXPECTATIONS HYPOTHESIS

Equation (6A.13) seems fairly reasonable. It is reasonable that investors would set interest rates so that the forward rate would equal the spot rate expected by the marketplace a year from now.[6] For example, imagine that individuals in the marketplace do not concern themselves with risk. If the forward rate, f_2, is less than the spot rate expected over year 2, individuals desiring to invest for one year would always buy a one-year bond. That is, our work shows that individuals investing in a two-year bond but planning to sell at the end of one year would expect to earn less than if they simply bought a one-year bond.

Equation (6A.13) was stated for the specific case where the forward rate was 12.04 per cent. We can generalize this as follows:

Expectations hypothesis:

$$f_2 = \text{Spot rate expected over year 2} \qquad \text{(6A.14)}$$

Equation (6A.14) says that the forward rate over the second year is set to the spot rate that people expect to prevail over the second year. This is called the *expectations hypothesis*. It states that investors will set interest rates such that the forward rate over the second year is equal to the one-year spot rate expected over the second year.

LIQUIDITY PREFERENCE HYPOTHESIS

At this point, many students think that Equation (6A.14) *must* hold. However, note that we developed Equation (6A.14) by assuming that investors were risk-neutral. Suppose, alternatively, that investors are averse to risk.

Which strategy would appear riskier for an individual who wants to invest for one year?

1. Invest in a one-year bond.
2. Invest in a two-year bond but sell at the end of one year.

Strategy 1 has no risk because the investor knows that the rate of return must be r_1. Conversely, strategy 2 has much risk: the final return is dependent on what happens to interest rates.

Because strategy 2 has more risk than strategy 1, no risk-averse investor will choose strategy 2 if both strategies have the same expected return. Risk-averse investors can have no preference for one strategy over the other only when the expected return on strategy 2 is *above* the return on strategy 1. Because the two strategies have the same expected return when f_2 equals the spot rate expected over year 2, strategy 2 can have a higher rate of return only when the following condition holds:

Liquidity preference hypothesis:

$$f_2 > \text{Spot rate expected over year 2} \quad (6A.15)$$

That is, to induce investors to hold the riskier two-year bonds, the market sets the forward rate over the second year to be above the spot rate expected over the second year. Equation (6A.15) is called the *liquidity preference hypothesis*.

We developed the entire discussion by assuming that individuals are planning to invest over one year. We pointed out that a two-year bond has extra risk for these types of individuals because it must be sold prematurely. What about individuals who want to invest for two years? (We call these people investors with a two-year *time horizon*.)

They could choose one of the following strategies:

3. Buy a two-year zero-coupon bond.
4. Buy a one-year bond. When the bond matures, immediately buy another one-year bond.

Strategy 3 has no risk for an investor with a two-year time horizon because the proceeds to be received at date 2 are known as of date 0. However, strategy 4 has risk because the spot rate over year 2 is unknown at date 0. It can be shown that risk-averse investors will prefer neither strategy 3 nor strategy 4 over the other when:

$$f_2 < \text{Spot rate expected over year 2} \quad (6A.16)$$

Note that the assumption of risk aversion gives contrary predictions. Relationship (6A.15) holds for a market dominated by investors with a one-year time horizon. Relationship (6A.16) holds for a market dominated by investors with a two-year time horizon. Financial economists have generally argued that the typical investor's time horizon is generally much shorter than the maturity of typical bonds in the marketplace. Thus economists view (6A.15) as the best depiction of equilibrium in the bond market with *risk-averse* investors.

However, do we have a market of risk-neutral or risk-averse investors? In other words, can the expectations hypothesis of Equation (6A.14) or the liquidity preference hypothesis of Equation (6A.15) be expected to hold? As we shall learn later in this book, economists view investors as being risk-averse for the most part. Yet economists are never satisfied with a casual examination of a theory's assumptions. To them, empirical evidence of a theory's predictions must be the final arbiter.

There has been a great deal of empirical evidence about the term structure of interest rates. Unfortunately (perhaps fortunately for some students), we shall not present the evidence in any detail. Suffice it to say that, in our opinion, the evidence supports the liquidity preference hypothesis over the expectations hypothesis. One simple result might give students the flavour of this research. Consider an individual choosing between one of the following strategies:

1. Invest in a one-year bond.
2. Invest in a 2-year bond but sell at the end of one year.
3. Invest in a 20-year bond but sell at the end of one year.

(Strategy 3 is identical to strategy 2, except that a 20-year bond is substituted for a two-year bond.)

The expectations hypothesis states that the expected returns on all three strategies are identical. The liquidity preference hypothesis states that the expected return on strategy 3 should be above the expected return on strategies 1 and 2, and strategy 2 should be above strategy 1. Though no one knows what returns are actually expected over a particular time period, actual returns from the past may infer expectations. The results from January 1926 to December 1999 for the US are illuminating. The average yearly return on strategy 1 is 3.8 per cent, and on strategy 3, 5.5 per cent over this time period.[7,8] This evidence is generally considered consistent with the liquidity preference hypothesis and inconsistent with the expectations hypothesis.

APPENDIX 6A The Term Structure of Interest Rates, Spot Rates and Yield to Maturity

QUESTIONS AND PROBLEMS

6A.1 **Bond Pricing** The one-year spot rate is 8 per cent and the two-year spot rate is 10 per cent.

(a) What is the price of a two-year bond that pays an annual coupon of 6 per cent?

(b) What is the yield to maturity of this bond?

6A.2 **Bond Pricing** The one-year spot rate is 11 per cent and the two-year spot rate is 8 per cent. What is the price of a two-year bond that pays an annual coupon of 5 per cent?

6A.3 **Forward Rates** If the one-year spot rate is 7 per cent and the two-year spot rate is 8.5 per cent, what is the one-year forward rate over the second year?

6A.4 **Forward Rates** Assume the following spot rates:

Year	Spot rate (%)
1	4.0
2	5.5
3	6.5

(a) Calculate the one-year forward rate over the second year.

(b) Calculate the one-year forward rate over the third year.

6A.5 **Term Structure** Assume the following forward rates:

Maturity	Forward rates (%)
1	4.5
2	6.0

Compute the spot rates for years 1 and 2.

6A.6 **Term Structure** Given the following two scenarios, for what range of spot rates expected over year 2 would you be better off adopting strategy 1? Explain.

Strategy 1: Buy a two-year bond and then sell it in year 1.

Strategy 2: Buy a one-year bond.

Endnotes

1. The quadratic formula may be used to solve for y for a two-year bond. However, formulae generally do not apply for bonds with more than four payment dates.
2. Yield to maturity is not a simple average of r_1 and r_2. Rather, financial economists speak of it as a time-weighted average of r_1 and r_2.
3. 12.04 per cent is equal to

$$\frac{(1.10)^2}{(1.08)} = 1$$

when rounding is performed after four digits.
4. This change in assumptions simplifies our presentation, but does not alter any of our conclusions.

5. Technically, Equation (6A.9) is only an approximation, because of Jensen's inequality. That is, expected values are:

$$\frac{€1,210}{1 + \text{Spot rate}} > \frac{€1,210}{1 + \text{Spot rate expected over year 2}}$$

However, we ignore this very minor issue in the rest of the analysis.

6. Of course, each individual will have different expectations, so Equation (6A.13) cannot hold for all individuals. However, financial economists generally speak of a consensus expectation. This is the expectation of the market as a whole.

7. Taken from *Stocks, Bonds, Bills and Inflation 2000 Yearbook* (Chicago: Ibbotson Associates, Inc.). Ibbotson Associates annually updates work by Roger G. Ibbotson and Rex A. Sinquefield.

8. It is important to note that strategy 2 does not involve buying a 20-year bond and holding it to maturity. Rather, it consists in buying a 20-year bond and selling it one year later – that is, when it has become a 19-year bond. This round-trip transaction occurs 74 times in the 74-year sample from January 1926 to December 1999.

INDEX

Abandonment, option for 621
Absolute priority rule (APR) 444
Absolute purchasing power parity (PPP) 527–9
Abu Dhabi
   equity risk premiums in (April 2020) 297
   First Abu Dhabi Bank (FAB) 545
Acacia, acquisition by Cisco 640
Accounting break-even 269–74
   calculation of break-even level 271
   cash break-even 273
   cash flow and 271
   cash flow and, base case 271
   financial break-even 273–4
   payback and break-even 271
   revisit to 273
   uses for 270
Accounting insolvency 443
Acid-test ratio 53
Acquisition
   acquisition classification 634
   of assets 633
   legal forms of 632–5
   merger or, factors involved in choice 633
   of shares 633
Acquisition costs
   cash acquisition 643–4
   cash vs shares 644–5
   control 644–5
   equity acquisition 644
   sharing gains 644
Adidas, beta coefficient for 332
Administration of bankruptcy 444–5
AdMob 13
Advent International 384
Advisory services 482
Affect heuristic 558–9
After-tax cash flow 227
Ageing schedule, monitoring receivables and 505
Agency cost 24
Agency problem, control of corporation and 24–31
Agency relationships
   type I 24
   type II 29–30
Agency theory 35
Air France/KLM, option information for 597
Almeida, H., Fos, V. and Kronlund, M. 465
Alphabet Inc 13, 25, 28, 440

corporate finance in action 13–14
Amazon 226
Ambiguity aversion 560
American depositary receipt (ADR) 521
American option 596
Amortization schedule 112
Amortized loans 111–14
   partial amortization, example of balloon payments and 113
   spreadsheet strategy, loan amortization 114
Amsterdam SE All Shares Index 294
Anadarko 178
Anchoring, adjustment and 560
Anglo American Plc 159
Announcements
   news and 326
   surprises, expected returns and 325–6
Annual percentage rate (APR) 108–9
Annual portfolio returns, standard deviations of 328
Annual reports 43–52
Annual returns (2010-20), capital market history and 295
Annuities 98
   annuities due, note about 103
   annuity due vs ordinary annuity, example of 103
   annuity tables 99–100
   calculations for, summary of 104
   funding payments for 100–101
   interest rate for, finding the rate 102
   ordinary annuity form 98
   present value interest factor for annuities (PVIFA) 99
Apple 27, 168, 226, 303, 405, 637
   iPhone 261
Appraisal techniques, use of 210–11
Arbitrage 562
   limits of 562–5
Arithmetic or geometric average return 306
Arithmetic vs geometric averages 304
Articles of incorporation 20–21
Assets
   acquisition of 633
   asset-specific risks 327, 331

management of 54–6
management ratios 58
turnover ratios 55–6
utilization ratios 54
write-ups of 640
AstraZenica 60
AT&T 186
Auction markets 10–11
Australia
   bank vs market-based financial systems 33
   bills and bonds in, equity risk premiums relative to (1900-2010) 298
   capital budgeting techniques, use in 211
   corporate tax rates in 49
   corporation types in 22
   currency symbol for 523
   debt to equity, estimated ratio in 442
   initial IPO returns for 393
   risk premiums relative to bonds in (1900-2019) 305
Austria
   bank vs market-based financial systems 33
   corporate tax rates in 49
   corporation types in 22
   Corruption Perceptions Index (TI 2018) for 32
   Corruption Perceptions Index (TI 2019) for 540
   debt to equity, estimated ratio in 442
   derivative usage around world (% of firms) 589
   equity risk premiums in (April 2020) 297
   initial IPO returns for 393
   international business angel networks in 386
   ownership structures of companies in 34
   small and medium-sized enterprises (SMEs) in 19
Automatic dividend reinvestment plans (ADRs or DRIPs) 457
Autoveloce SpA 417–18, 419, 420–21
Avagnought SA 84
Availability bias 561
Average accounting return (AAR) 197–8, 212
   advantages and disadvantages of 198
   average accounting return rule 198

   projected yearly revenue and costs for 197
Average annual returns (2011-20) 296
Average collection period 495
Average cost vs marginal cost, example of 268
Average returns 296–9, 303–6
   arithmetic average return or geometric average return 306
   arithmetic vs geometric averages 304
   average annual returns (2011-20) 296
   calculation of 296
   calculation of geometric averages 304–5
   equity and country risk premiums (April 2020) 297
   excess return on a risky asset 297
   geometric averages, examples of 306
   historical record on 296
   real world insight, 'spoofing' prices in stock markets 298–9
   risk-free returns 297
   risk premiums and 297–8
   Treasury bills 297
   world annualized equity risk premium relative to bonds and bills (1900-2010) 298
Average vs marginal tax rates 49–50

Babcock International 398, 399–400, 400–401
Bahrain
   bank vs market-based financial systems 33
   corporate tax rates in 49
   Corruption Perceptions Index (TI 2018) for 32
   Corruption Perceptions Index (TI 2019) for 540
   Economist Big Mac index 528
   equity risk premiums in (April 2020) 297
   exchange rate quotations (January 2021) 524
   ownership structures of companies in 34
Balance sheet 43–7

Index

Bank loans 405–6
  line of credit 406
  loan commitment 406
  non-revolving loan commitment 406
  as percentage of external financing 405
  revolver 406
  types of 406
Bank overdrafts 483
  short-term loans vs 484
Bank vs market-based financial systems 33
Banker's acceptances 486
Bankruptcy
  absolute priority rule (APR) 444
  accounting insolvency 443
  administration of 444–5
  business failure and 443
  claims, priority of 444
  company voluntary agreement (CVA) 444
  European Union (EU), bankruptcy laws in 445
  financial distress costs 431–2
  France, bankruptcy laws in 445
  law of 443–5
  legal bankruptcy 443
  liquidation 444
  milking the property, selfish strategy three 433
  process of 443–5
  real world case
    financial distress costs 432
    Lehman Brothers bankruptcy 431
  reorganization 443
  risk taking in excess, selfish strategy three 432
  Scotland, bankruptcy laws in 444–5
  selfish strategies, summary of 433
  South Africa, bankruptcy laws in 445
  technical insolvency 443
  underinvestment, selfish strategy three 432–3
  United States, bankruptcy laws in 445
Bankruptcy costs 430–33
  agency costs 432–3
  direct costs 431
  indirect costs 431–2
Barings Bank 556
Barter exchanges 494
BASF 353
Baumol-Allais-Tobin (BAT) model
  example of (Vulcan SA) 491
  implications of 493
  opportunity costs 489
  optimal balance 490–91
  total cost 490
  trading costs 489–90

Beam Inc, acquisition by Suntory 646
Bear hug 648
Behavioural finance 552–70
  affect heuristic 558–9
  ambiguity aversion 560
  anchoring, adjustment and 560
  arbitrage 562
    limits of 562–5
  availability bias 561
  behavioural finance 553
  biases 553–5
  Bitcoin bubble 552, 565
  bubbles 565–6
  capital market history, lessons from 309
  Celtic Tiger (1995-2007) 566
  clustering illusion 559
  cognitive errors 553
  confirmation bias 554
  crashes 565–6
  cryptocurrencies 552
  false consensus 561
  firm-specific risk 562
  framing effects 555–8
    debt avoidance 557
    disposition effect 557
    endowment effect 558
    frame dependence 556
    house money 557–8
    loss aversion 556–7
    mental accounting 557
    money illusion 558
    myopic loss aversion 558
    playing with house money 557
    regret aversion 558
  gambler's fallacy 560–61
  global credit crunch 566
  heuristics 558–61
  high dividends, rationale for 461
  hot hands effect 559
  implementation costs 563
  independent deviations from rationality 562
  investor rationality 561
  learning objectives 552
  market efficiency 561–7
    foundations of 561–2
  mini case, Supercold Skis 570
  noise trader risk 563
  over-optimism bias 554
  overconfidence bias 553
  planning fallacy 555
  Property Bubble (2006-present) 566
  questions and problems 568–9
  randomness and representativeness 559
  rationality, independent deviations from 562
  reading suggestions 570
  real world insight
    Hersh Shefrin on behavioural finance 567

  over-confidence and pride 560
  recency bias 560
  representativeness heuristic 559
  review of issues 568
  Roaring Twenties (1920-29) 566
  Royal Dutch Shell price ratio 563–5
  self-attribution bias 554–5
  self-test problems 568
  small numbers, law of 560
  South-East Asian Bubble (1997) 566
  South Sea Bubble (1720) 566
  summary and conclusions 567
  3Com/Palm mispricing 563, 564
  Tulpenmanie (1633-37) 566
Bel-20 Index 294
Belgium
  average annual returns of companies in (2011-2020) 296
  bank vs market-based financial systems 33
  bills and bonds in, equity risk premiums relative to (1900-2010) 298
  corporate tax rates in 49
  corporation types in 22
  Corruption Perceptions Index (TI 2018) for 32
  Corruption Perceptions Index (TI 2019) for 540
  debt to equity, estimated ratio in 442
  derivative usage around world (% of firms) 589
  equity risk premiums in (April 2020) 297
  initial IPO returns for 394
  international business angel networks in 386
  ownership structures of companies in 34
  risk premiums relative to bonds in (1900-2019) 305
  small and medium-sized enterprises (SMEs) in 19
  stock market index levels (2010-2020) 294
Berkshire Hathaway 464, 470
Beta (β) coefficient 331–2
  risk premium and 334–7
Biases 553–5
Bid and offer rates 523–4
Bid-ask spread 524
Bid price setting 242–4
Big brothers 648
Bitcoin bubble 552, 565
Bitcoin exchanges 640
Black-Scholes option pricing model
  cautionary note 612–13
  example of implementation 610–11
  put option valuation 612

Blackstone 383
BME Spanish Exchanges 11
BMW 537, 562
Bohr, Niels 678
Bond valuation 126–58
  bond at future date, estimation of price of 700–701
  bond buying and selling 143–4
  bond cash flows 128
  bond current yield, example of calculation of 132
  bond features 134–9
    prices and 127
  bond markets 143–5
  bond price quotations 145
  bond price reporting 144
  bond ratings 139–41
  bond types 141–3
  bond values and yields 127–30
  bond yields
    determinants of 148–52
    examples of 133
    yield curve and 150–52
  bonds and bond valuation 127–34
  borrowers 134
  catastrophe bonds 142
  clean price bonds 145
  CoCo bonds 143
  convertible bonds 143
  coupon rate 127
  coupons 127
  credit ratings, determinants of 141
  creditors 134
  current yield 132
  debentures 136
    secured obligation in UK 138
    unsecured obligation in US 138
  debt securities 134, 136, 137
  debtors 134
  default-free bonds 148
  default risk premium 151
  determinants of bond yields 148–52
  dirty price bonds 145
  discount bond 129
  equity securities 134
  European Union (EU), Eurozone yield curve for 151
  face value 127
  Fisher effect 146–7
  floating-rate bonds 142
  government bonds 131, 141
  income bonds 143
  indentures 136–9
    bearer form 137
    blanket mortgage 137
    call premium 138
    call-protected bond 138
    call provision 138
    collateral 137

Bond valuation—*Cont.*
   deferred call
      provision 138
   mortgage securities 137
   mortgage trust
      indenture 137
   negative covenant 139
   note 137–8
   positive covenant 139
   principal value 137
   protective covenants 139
   real world insight,
      negative and
      positive (gearing)
      covenants 139
   registered form 137
   repayment 138
   security 137–8
   seniority 138
   sinking fund 138
   subordinated debt 138
   terms of bond 137
   trust deed 137
   unsecured bond 137–8
   inflation
      inflation premium 149
      interest rates and 145–8
      present values and 147
   interest rate risk 130–31
   interest rate risk
      premium 149
   interest rate term structure
      148–50
   irredeemable bonds 127
   learning objectives 126
   lenders 134
   liquidity premium 151
   London Stock Exchange
      (LSE) bond issue
      features 136
   long-term debt, basics 136
   maturity 127
   mini case, financing
      expansion with bond
      issue 157
   mortgage-backed security
      (MBS) 126
   municipal notes 141
   nominal interest rates
      145–6, 148
   NoNo bonds 143
   notations 126
   notes 136
   premium bond 129
   present values, inflation
      and 147
   privately placed debt 136
   public-issue bonds 136
   pure discount bonds 142, 148
   put bonds 143
   questions and
      problems 153–7
   reading suggestions 157
   real vs nominal interest
      rates 145–6
   real world insight,
      Pandemic Emergency
      Financing Bonds 143
   redeemable bonds 127
   review of issues 152–3
   securities, debt or equity?
      134–5
   self-test problems 152–3
   semi-annual coupons,
      example of 130
   short-term debt 136
   spreadsheet strategy,
      bond prices and yields,
      calculation of 133–4
   summary and
      conclusions 152
   taxability premium 151
   time to maturity, interest
      rate risk and 131
   Treasury issues 141
   Treasury yield curve 150–51
   unfunded debt 136
   United Kingdom
      government bond yields
      (March 2020) 148
      yield curve for 150
   warrants 142
   yield to maturity
      (YTM) 127–8
      trial and error in finding
      132–4
   zero bond coupons 142
Book value vs market value,
   dilution and 402–4
Borrowers 134
   borrowing costs, example
      of calculation of 99
Bounding value of a call 604
   upper and lower bounds
      604, 605
BP (British Petroleum) 19, 371
Brazil
   corporate tax rates in 49
   Corruption Perceptions
      Index (TI 2019) for 540
   debt to equity, estimated
      ratio in 442
Break-even analysis 265–70
   accounting break-
      even 269–74
      uses for 270
   average cost vs marginal
      cost, example of 268
   break-even measures,
      summary of 274
   cash flow, accounting and
      financial break-even
      points 272–4
   contribution margin per
      unit 269
   fixed costs 267
   incremental cost 267
   incremental revenue 268
   marginal cost 267
   marginal revenue 268
   operating leverage and
      276–7
   total costs 267–8
      output level and 268
   variable costs 266–7
      example of 267
      output level and 266
Brexit 257, 545
   free movement 545
   goods, trade in 545
   impact on corporate
      finance 545
   services, trade in 545
Brin, Sergey 13, 28
Bristol Plc 456–7
Brounen, D., De Jong, A. and
   Koedijk, K. 443
BT Group 330
Bubbles 565–6
Buffett, Warren 464
Bulgaria
   corporation types in 22
   initial IPO returns for 394
Business and financial
   risk 424–5
Business angel networks 386
Business failure
   bankruptcy and 443
   failure in financial planning
      and 479–80
Business foundation idea 13
Business organization, forms
   of 19–23
Buy low, sell high 337–8
Buyout financing 387

CAC 40 Index 294
Call option values, factors
   determining 604–6
   exercise price 604
   expiration date 604
   risk-free rate 605
   share price 605–6
   variability of underlying
      asset, key factor 606
Calls 596–7
   call at expiration, valuation
      of 602–3
Canada
   bills and bonds in, equity
      risk premiums relative to
      (1900-2010) 298
   corporate tax rates in 49
   currency symbol for 523
   debt to equity, estimated
      ratio in 442
   initial IPO returns for 394
   risk premiums relative to
      bonds in (1900-2019) 305
Capital
   capital gains yield 169
   capital intensity ratio 682
   capital needs, reductions
      in 640
   capital rationing 277–8
   divisional cost of 368–9
   dual-class capitalization 649
   growth capital 387
   later stage capital 387
   observed capital
      structures 441–3
   reductions in capital
      needs 640
   unlevered cost of
      capital 427
   working capital 5
   see also Capital investment
      decisions; Raising
      capital; Venture
      capital (VC)
Capital asset pricing model
   (CAPM) 338–9, 340
   criticisms of 341
   empirical tests of 341
Capital budgeting
   abandonment, option
      for 621
   appraisal techniques, use
      of 210–11
   contingency planning 620
   contraction of operations,
      option for 621
   corporate finance and 4–5
   decision on 187
   expansion, option for 621
   firms using 211
   implicit options 619
   investment timing decision
      619–20
   managerial options 620–22
   options, corporate finance
      and 618–22
   options in, example of 621–2
   practice of 210–13
   problems of, solution to 365
   real options 618
   strategic options 622
   suspension, option for 621
Capital investment
   decisions 223–56
   after-tax cash flow 227
   bid price setting 242–4
   cost-cutting proposals,
      evaluation of 240–42
   buy or not buy question,
      example of 241–2
   depreciation 232–8
      annual depreciation 235
      book value vs market
        value 233
      capital spending 236
      depreciation tax shield 240
      example of 234
      net working capital
        (NWC) change to 236
      operating cash flows 235
      projected cash flows 237
      projected income
        statements 235
      projected revenues 235
      projected total cash
        flows 237
      reducing-balance
        depreciation 232–3
      example of 234
      total cash flow and value
        236–7
   discounted cash flow
      analysis, special cases
      of 240–46
   equipment with different
      lives, evaluating options
      for 244–5
   equivalent annual cost
      (EAC) 246–7
   erosion 226
   financing costs 227
   incremental cash
      flows 224, 225–7
   learning objectives 223

Index

mini case, Conchbit by Conch Republic (Part 1) 254–5
net working capital 226–7
  cash collections and cost, example of 232
  cash revenues, determination of 231
  closer look at 230–32
notations 223
operating cash flow
  bottom-up approach 239
  tax shield approach 239–40
  top-down approach 239
operating cash flow (OCF), alternative definitions of 238–40
opportunity costs 225
pro forma financial statements 228–9
  project cash flows and 227–30
project cash flows 224, 229, 230–38
  pro forma financial statements and 227–30
  project net working capital and capital spending 229
  project operating cash flow 229
projected capital requirements, example of 228
projected income statement, example of 228
projected total cash flow
  example of 230
  value and 229–30
questions and problems 249–54
reading suggestions 255
real world insight
  cost-cutting proposals 242
  investment appraisal 225–6
relevant cash flows 224
review of issues 246–9
self-test problems 246–9
side effects 226
stand-alone principle 224
summary and conclusions 246
sunk costs 225
winner's curse 243
Capital market efficiency 306–10
  efficient market hypothesis 307–8
    common misconceptions about 308–9
  forms of market efficiency 309
  price behaviour in an efficient market 307
Capital market history, lessons from 289–316
  annual returns (2010-20) 295
  average returns 296–9, 303–6

arithmetic average return or geometric average return 306
arithmetic vs geometric averages 304
average annual returns (2011-20) 296
calculation of 296
calculation of geometric averages 304–5
equity and country risk premiums (April 2020) 297
excess return on a risky asset 297
geometric averages, examples of 306
historical record on 296
real world insight, 'spoofing' prices in stock markets 298–9
risk-free returns 297
risk premiums and 297–8
Treasury bills 297
world annualized equity risk premium relative to bonds and bills (1900-2010) 298
behavioural finance 309
calculation of returns, example of 293
capital market efficiency 306–10
  efficient market hypothesis 307–8
  efficient market hypothesis, common misconceptions about 308–9
  forms of market efficiency 309
  price behaviour in an efficient market 307
capital market history, use of 305
cash returns 290–92
delayed reaction 308
efficient and inefficient markers, share price reaction to new information in 308
efficient market reaction 308
first lesson, returns 298
historical record 294–6
income component of return 290
learning objectives 289
mini case, Holdon Sustainable Investment Fund 315–16
normal distribution usefulness of 302
notations 289
over- reaction 308
questions and problems 312–14
reading suggestions 316

real world insight, market movements, driving forces 303
returns 290–94
review of issues 310–11
second lesson, variability of returns 302–3
self-test problems 310–11
semi-strong-form efficient markets 309
standard deviation 299, 300
  calculation of 300–301
stock market index levels (2010-20) 294
strong-form efficient markets 309
summary and conclusions 310
United Kingdom, histogram of returns on equities (1926-2019) 301
variability of returns 299–303
  historical record 301
  historical variance and standard deviation 299–301
  normal distribution 302
  return variability 299
variance 299–300
  calculation of 300–301
weak-form efficient markets 309
worldwide risk premiums relative to bonds (1900-2010) 305
year-by-year stock market index levels (2010-20) 295
Capital rationing 277–8
  hard rationing 278
  soft rationing 277–8
Capital structure
  capital structure weights 362
  corporate finance and 5
  cost of capital and 416
  cost of equity capital and 421–5
  decisions about 415
  question concerning 415–16
Carillon 432
Carlyle Group 383
Carnival Cruise Line 303
Cash coverage 54
Cash discounts 499
Cash dividends 453
  dividend payment and 453–6
  repurchase vs 463–4
Cash flows
  accounting and financial break-even points 272–4
  cash flow hedging, cautionary note on 576
  cash flow identity 50
  equity valuation and 160–62
  from financing activities 51
  to and from firms 9–10
  from investing activities 51
  from operating activities 50–51
  timing of, note about 97–8

Cash holding, reasons for 480–81
Cash management vs liquidity management 481
Cash returns 290–92
Catastrophe bonds 142
Catering theory of dividends 462
CBOE Holdings 581
Celtic Tiger (1995-2007) 566
CEO remuneration STOXX Europe 600 (2018) 26
Certificates of deposit (CD) 485
Chemical Venture Capital Corporation 386
Chevron 371
Chief financial officer (CFO) 3
Chile, debt to equity, estimated ratio in 442
China
  average annual returns of companies in (2011-2020) 296
  bank loans as % of external financing 405
  bank vs market-based financial systems 33
  capital budgeting techniques, use in 211
  corporate tax rates in 49
  corporation types in 22
  Corruption Perceptions Index (TI 2018) for 32
  Corruption Perceptions Index (TI 2019) for 540
  currency symbol for 523
  debt to equity, estimated ratio in 442
  derivative usage around world (% of firms) 589
  Economist Big Mac index 528
  equity risk premiums in (April 2020) 297
  exchange rate quotations (January 2021) 524
  initial IPO returns for 394
  ownership structures of companies in 34
  stock market index levels (2010-2020) 294
  underpricing of IPOs in, determinants of 395
Cinven 384
Cisco, acquisition of Acacia 640
Citicorp Venture Capital 386
Citrix, acquisition of Wrike 640
Claims in bankruptcy, priority of 444
Classes of shares 28
Clean price bonds 145
Clientele effect 461–2
Clustering illusion 559
CoCo bonds 143
Codes of corporate governance 37
Cognitive errors 553
Collection effort 505
Collection policy 505
Commercial paper 486

Commodity price volatility 573
Common Consolidated Corporate Tax Base (CCCTB) 233
Company voluntary agreement (CVA) 444
Compensating balances 481
Competition, goal of beating 6
Complementary resources 639
Compound growth, note about 76
Compound interest 72, 74
  compounding over long horizons, example of 76
  example of 75
Compounding
  comparing rates, effect of 105–10
  continuous compounding, note about 109–10
  valuation, time value of money and 72
Confirmation bias 554
Conglomerate acquisition 634
Connected stakeholders 30–31
ConocoPhillips 178
Consolidation 632–3
Consols 103–4
Constant growth, case of 162–5
Contingency planning, capital budgeting and 620
Continuous compounding, note about 109–10
Contraction of operations, option for 621
Contribution margin per unit 269
Control of firms 27
Convertible bonds 143
Core values, example of 8
Corporate borrowing, homemade leverage and 420–21
Corporate charter 646
Corporate finance 2–17
  Alphabet Inc., corporate finance in action 13–14
  auction markets 10–11
  Authority for Financial Markets (Netherlands) 10
  beginning a business 13
  BME Spanish Exchanges 11
  business foundation idea 13
  capital budgeting 4–5
  capital structure 5
  cash flows to and from firms 9–10
  chief financial officer (CFO) 3
  competition, goal of beating 6
  core values, example of 8
  corporate finance outlined 3
  corporate securities, trading in 11
  cost minimization, goal of 6
  current share value, goal of maximization of 7
  dealer vs auction markets 10–11
  Deutsche Börse 11
  distress and bankruptcy, goal of avoidance of 6
  earnings growth, goal of maintenance of 6
  economic environment 12
  environmental positivity, goal of 6
  equity 5
  European Central Bank (ECB) 12
  European Monetary Union (EMU) 12
  exchange rate policy 12
  finance director (FD) 3
  Financial Conduct Authority (UK) 10
  financial management decisions concerning 4–5
  goal appropriateness 7
  potential goals 6
  real world insights 6–7
  financial manager 3–5
  financial markets
    cash flows between economy, firms and 10
    corporations and 9–11
    integrated nature of 2
  financial technologies 2
  fiscal policy 12
  foreign trade policy 12
  goal of financial management 6–9
  Google becoming Alphabet 13
  Google share issue 13
  International Accounting Standards (IAS) 3
  learning objectives 2
  listing 11
  London Stock Exchange (LSE) 11
  long-term debt 5
  macroeconomic policy 12
  market share, goal of maximization of 6
  mini case, web information 16
  monetary policy 12
  NASDAQ 11
  not-for-profit sector, goal appropriateness 7
  NYSE Euronext 11
  organizational chart 4
  over-the-counter (OTC) markets 11
  peer-to-peer trading platforms 11
  people, objectives concerning 8–9
  planet, objectives concerning 8–9
  primary vs secondary markets 10–11
  profit, objectives concerning 8–9
  profit maximization, goal of 6
  questions and problems 15–16
  reading suggestions 16–17
  real world insight, primary vs secondary markets 11
  review of issues 14–15
  sales maximization, goal of 6
  secondary markets 10
  self-test problems 14–15
  SIX Swiss Exchange 11
  societal improvement, goal of 6
  summary and conclusions 14
  survival, goal of 6
  sustainability in finance 8–9
  Tokyo Stock Exchange 11
  triple bottom line 8–9
  what is it about? 14
  working capital 5
  working capital management 5
Corporate governance 18–41
  agency cost 24
  agency problem, control of corporation and 24–31
  agency relationships
    type I 24
    type II 29–30
  agency theory 35
  articles of incorporation 20–21
  bank vs market-based financial systems 33
  business organization, forms of 19–23
  CEO remuneration STOXX Europe 600 (2018) 26
  classes of shares 28
  codes of corporate governance 37
  connected stakeholders 30–31
  control of firms 27
  corporation 20–21
  culture, corporate governance and 35
  cumulative voting, effect of 27
  example of 28
  dividends 29
  double taxation 21
  ethics, corporate governance and 35–6
  European Union (EU), small and medium-sized enterprises (SMEs) in 19
  external stakeholders 30–31
  financial system, bank-based and market-based countries 33
  framework for, importance of strength of 36
  general partnerships 20
  internal stakeholders 30–31
  international corporate governance 31–6
  international corporations 22
  investor protection, legal environment 31–3
  joint-stock companies 21
  learning objectives 18
  legal systems 32
  limited liability companies 21
  limited liability partnership (LLP) 20
  limited partnerships 20
  management goals 24–5
  managerial compensation 25–7
  memorandum of association 20–21
  micro-enterprises 19
  mini case, Glyndebourne Wines Ltd 40
  optimal allocation of resources 35
  ownership structure 34
  partnerships 20
  pay mix targets (CEOs, 2018) 26
  proxy voting 28
  public limited companies 21
  questions and problems 39–49
  reading suggestions 41
  real world insights
    controlling shareholders 30
    shareholder activism 25
  related party transactions 29
  review of issues 38–9
  self-test problems 38–9
  shareholder interests, managers' acting in 25–9
  shareholder rights 27
    general rights 28–9
    pre-emptive right 29
  shares, classes of 28
  single-tier boards 21
  sole traders 19–20
  stakeholders 30–31
  stewardship theory 35
  straight voting, effect of 27
  summary and conclusions 37–8
  sustainability in finance 23
  Transparency International Corruption Perceptions Index (2018) 32
  trustees 23
  two-tier boards 21
  UN Sustainable Development Goals 36
  unlimited liability 19
Corporate tax rates 49
Corporations smooth dividends 465
Cost-cutting proposals, evaluation of 240–42
  buy or not buy question, example of 241–2
Cost effects 499
Cost minimization, goal of 6
Cost of an acquisition 643–5
Cost of capital 353–82
  appropriate discount rate 354
  capital, divisional cost of 368–9
  capital budgeting problems, solution to 365
  capital structure and 416

Index

capital structure weights 362
cost of equity
  cost of capital, estimation in practice of 358–9
  dividend growth model approach 355–7
  example of 358
  security market line (SML) approach 357–8
debt, cost of 359–60, 366
  bank loans 360
  floating rate bonds 360
  redeemable and irredeemable debt, example of cost of 359–60
debt and preference shares, costs of 359–61
dependence on use of funds primarily, not source 354
dividend growth model approach to cost of equity
  advantages and disadvantages of 357
  estimation of growth rate (g) 356–7
  implantation of approach 355–6
divisional and project costs of capital 367–71
  divisional cost of capital 368–9
  pure play approach 369
  subjective approach 369–70
economic value added (EVA) 367
equity, cost of 355–9, 366
financial policy and cost of capital 355
flotation costs and weighted average cost of capital (WACC)
  basic approach 371–2
  calculation of weighted average flotation cost, example of 372
  internal equity, flotation costs and 373
  net present value (NPV), flotation costs and 372–3
learning objectives 353
market value added (MVA) 367
mini case, cost of capital for Pavegen 380–81
net present value (NPV) 354
notations 353
preference shares, cost of 360
  example of 360
preliminary concerns 354–5
questions and problems 376–80
reading suggestions 381
real world insight, weighted average cost of capital (WACC) 370–71

required return 354
  cost of capital vs 354
review of issues 374–5
RWE AG in Germany
  debt, cost of 364
  equity, cost of 364
  weighted average cost of capital (WACC) 365
security market line (SML) approach to cost of equity, advantages and disadvantages of 357–8
approach to cost of equity, implementation of approach 357
subjective approach to costs of capital and 370
weighted average cost of capital (WACC) and 368
self-test problems 374–5
summary and conclusions 374
sustainability of finance 361–2
taxes and weighted average cost of capital (WACC) 362–3
warehouse problem, solution to 365
weighted average cost of capital (WACC) 353, 354, 361–7
  calculation for RWE AG in Germany 364–5
  calculation of 363
  flotation costs and 371–3
  performance evaluation with 367
  return on invested capital (ROIC) in oil and gas and 371
  security market line (SML) and 367–8
  using the WACC 366–7
Cost of debt 499
Cost of equity
  cost of capital, estimation in practice of 358–9
  dividend growth model approach 355–7
  example of 358
  security market line (SML) approach 357–8
  value of firm and 429–30
Cost reductions, mergers, acquisitions and 638–9
Costs of holding cash 481
Costs of issuing securities 397–8
Countertender offer 649
Coupons
  bond valuation and 127
  coupon rate 127
Covered interest arbitrage 531–2
Covid-19 pandemic 2, 12, 126, 142, 257, 317, 414, 464

business model disruption by 452
  economic shock of, lockdowns and 160
  economies disrupted by 242, 631
  FTSE 100 Index volatility resulting from 289
  valuation of bonds and equities during disruption of 135
Crashes 565–6
Credit analysis 503–4
  credit, granting of 503–4
  one-time sale 503–4
  repeat business 504
Credit and receivables 494–5
Credit management 481
Credit policy
  analysis of 499–501
  break-even application 501
  collection policy 495
  components of 494–5
  credit analysis 495
  credit policy effects 499
  evaluation of a proposal for 499–501
  switching policies, net present value (NPV) of 499–500
  terms of sale 494–5
Credit ratings, determinants of 141
Creditors 134
Croatia, small and medium-sized enterprises (SMEs) in 19
Cross-rates
  international corporate finance and 521
  triangle arbitrage and 524–5
Crown jewel mergers 648
Cryptocurrencies 640
  behavioural finance and 552
Culture, corporate governance and 35
Cumulative voting, effect of 27
  example of 28
Current income, desire for 459
Current ratio 53
Current share value, goal of maximization of 7
Current yield 132
CVC Capital Partners 384
Cyclical activities 482
Cyprus
  initial IPO returns for 394
  small and medium-sized enterprises (SMEs) in 19
Czech Republic, small and medium-sized enterprises (SMEs) in 19

Daimler, beta coefficient for 332
DAX 30 Index 294
Days' payables in receivables, payables turnover and 55
Days' sales in inventory, inventory turnover and 54
Days' sales in receivables

receivables turnover and 54–5
short-term financial planning and 495
Dealer vs auction markets 10–11
Debentures 136, 138
Debt, cost of 359–60, 366
  bank loans 360
  floating rate bonds 360
  redeemable and irredeemable debt, example of cost of 359–60
Short-term financial planning and management 499
Debt and preference shares, costs of 359–61
Debt securities 134, 136, 137
Debtors 134
Deceptive advertising, example of 79
Default-free bonds 148
Default risk premium 151
Defensive tactics 646–50
DeJager, David 362
Delayed reaction 308
Dell 405
Denmark
  average annual returns of companies in (2011-2020) 296
  bank vs market-based financial systems 33
  bills and bonds in, equity risk premiums relative to (1900-2010) 298
  corporate tax rates in 49
  corporation types in 22
  Corruption Perceptions Index (TI 2018) for 32
  Corruption Perceptions Index (TI 2019) for 540
  currency symbol for 523
  debt to equity, estimated ratio in 442
  derivative usage around world (% of firms) 589
  Economist Big Mac index 528
  equity risk premiums in (April 2020) 297
  exchange rate quotations (January 2021) 524
  initial IPO returns for 394
  international business angel networks in 386
  ownership structures of companies in 34
  risk premiums relative to bonds in (1900-2019) 305
  small and medium-sized enterprises (SMEs) in 19
  stock market index levels (2010-2020) 294
Depreciation 232–8
  annual depreciation 235
  book value vs market value 233

Depreciation—Cont.
  capital spending 236
  depreciation tax shield 240
  example of 234
  net working capital (NWC) change to 236
  operating cash flows 235
  projected cash flows 237
  projected income statements 235
  projected revenues 235
  projected total cash flows 237
  reducing-balance depreciation 232–3
  reducing-balance depreciation, example of 234
  total cash flow and value 236–7
Derivations of selected formulae 124–5
  annuity, present value of an 124–5
  perpetuity, present value of an 124
Derivative instruments 486
Derivative securities 572
Derivative usage around world (% of firms) 589
Descartes, René 203–4
Determinants of bond yields 148–52
Determinants of growth 689
Deutsche Börse 135, 143, 173, 337
  corporate finance and 11
DiaCare Project 361–2
Dilution 402–4
  correct arguments 403–4
  misconception on (market-to-book ratio less than 1) 403
  new issues and 402–3
Dirty price bonds 145
Discount bonds 129
Discount rate 78–9
  determination of 82–4
Discounted cash flow (DCF) analysis, special cases of 240–46
Discounted cash flow (DCF) valuation 79, 91–125
  amortization schedule 112
  amortized loans 111–14
    partial amortization, example of balloon payments and 113
    spreadsheet strategy, loan amortization 114
  annual percentage rate (APR) 108–9
  annuities 98
    annuity due vs ordinary annuity, example of 103
    annuity tables 99–100
    calculations for, summary of 104
    funding payments for 100–101

  interest rate for, finding the rate 102
  ordinary annuity form 98
  present value interest factor for annuities (PVIFA) 99
  annuities due, note about 103
  borrowing costs, example of calculation of 99
  cash flow timing, note about 97–8
  comparing rates, effect of compounding 105–10
  consols 103–4
  continuous compounding, note about 109–10
  derivations of selected formulae 124–5
    annuity, present value of an 124–5
    perpetuity, present value of an 124
  effective annual percentage rate (EAR) 106–7, 109–10
    example of 107
    quoting a rate, example of 107–8
  effective annual percentage rates and compounding 106
  effective annual rates, calculation and comparison of 106–8
  fixed rate mortgage 115
  future value calculations 93–4
  future value for annuities 102
  future value with multiple cash flows 92–4
  growing annuities and perpetuities 105
  interest-only loans 111
  investments, value calculations for, examples of 96
  learning objectives 91
  loan types and loan amortization 110–15
  mini case, MBA decision 123–4
  multiple cash flows, future and present values of 92–8
  nominal interest rate 106
  notations 91
  offset mortgage 115
  perpetuities 103–4
    calculations for, summary of 104
  preference shares, example of 104
  present value calculations 95–6
  present value for annuity cash flows 98–102
  present value with multiple cash flows 94–7
  pure discount loans 110–11
  questions and problems 118–23

  real world insights
    borrowing costs 109
    corporate valuation 98
    mortgage choices 115
  review of issues 116–18
  saving, future value calculation, example of 94
  self-test problems 116–18
  spreadsheet strategies
    annuity payments 101
    annuity present values 100
    calculation of present values with multiple future cash flows 97
    loan amortization 114
  suggested reading 124
  summary and conclusions 115
  time lines 92–3
  total charge for credit (TCC) 108
  treasury bills, example of 111
  valuing level cash flows, annuities and perpetuities 98–105
Discounted payback 194–7
  calculation of, example of 196
  discounted payback period 194–5, 212
  discounted payback rule 194
  discounted payback rule, advantages and disadvantages of 196
  future value of projected cash flows 195
  ordinary and discounted payback 195
Discounts
  discount factor, valuation and 78–9
  discount instruments 486 selling at 526
  valuation and 77
Disney+ 226
Distress and bankruptcy, goal of avoidance of 6
Distribution of dividends 453, 466
Diversification
  diversifiable risk 330–31
  effect of 340
  market history and effect of 328–9
  mergers, acquisitions and 642
  portfolio risk and 328–31
  principle of 329–30
  systematic risk and 330–31
  unsystematic risk and 330
Divestitures and restructurings 651–2
Dividend growth model
  approach to cost of equity
  advantages and disadvantages of 357
  estimation of growth rate (g) 356–7

  implantation of approach 355–6
Dividend payouts
  chronology of 454
  declaration date 454
  dividend payout ratio 681
  ex-dividend date 454, 455
  payment, date of 454
  procedure for, example of 454
  record, date of 454
Dividend policy 453
  dividends and, true-false test questions about 457–8
  dividends set equal to cash flow (current policy) 456
  does it matter? 456–8
  growth and 689
  initial dividend greater than cash flow (alternative policy) 456–7
  irrelevance of, illustration of 456–7
Dividends
  corporate governance and 29
  dividend cuts 460
  dividend discount model 164
  dividend growth, examples of 76, 163
  dividend growth model 164
    example of 164–5
  dividend yield, equity valuation and 169
  extra cash dividend 453
  homemade dividends 457
  liquidating dividend 453
  paying dividends, pros and cons of 467
  payout policies and, what we know and don't know about 465–8
  regular cash dividend 453
  survey evidence on 467–8
Dividends and payout policy 452–77
  automatic dividend reinvestment plans (ADRs or DRIPs) 457
  behavioural finance rationale for high dividends 461
  cash dividends 453
    dividend payment and 453–6
    repurchase vs 463–4
  catering theory of dividends 462
  clientele effect 461–2
  corporations smooth dividends 465
  current income, desire for 459
  distribution 453, 466
  dividend and payout policies, what we know and don't know about 465–8
  dividend cuts 460
  dividend decisions, survey responses on 468

Index

dividend market, clientele effect and 462
dividend payout
  chronology of 454
  declaration date 454
  ex-dividend date 454, 455
  payment, date of 454
  procedure for, example of 454
  record, date of 454
dividend policy 453
  dividends and, true-false test questions about 457–8
  dividends set equal to cash flow (current policy) 456
  does it matter? 456–8
  initial dividend greater than cash flow (alternative policy) 456–7
  irrelevance of, illustration of 456–7
dividend restrictions 458
dividend yield 454
dividends 453
  dividend payers and 465
  dividend policy and, observations concerning 466–7
  survey evidence on 467–8
dividends per share 454
earnings per share and share repurchases 465
effective tax rate 458
ex-dividend date, price behaviour around 455
extra cash dividend 453
flotation costs 458
high-dividend payout, real-world factors favouring 459–60
high intensity interval training (HIIT) 461
homemade dividends 457
information content effect 461
information content of dividends 460–61
International Financial Reporting Standards (IFRS) 469
learning objectives 452
liquidating dividend 453
low-dividend payout, real-world factors favouring 458–9
mini case, Homeware Sustainables (HS) 475–6
notations 452
odd-lots 469
open market purchases of shares 463
paying dividends, pros and cons of 467
price behaviour around ex-dividend date 455
questions and problems 472–5

reading suggestions 476–7
real world insights
  dividends in practice, importance of 457
  recessions and crises, repurchasing activity during 464
regular cash dividend 453
repurchase
  cash dividends vs 463–4
  real world considerations in 464
  of shares 462
  resolution of real-world factors? 460–62
  review of issues 471
round lots 469
self-control by investors 461
self-test problems 471
share repurchases 462
  alternative to cash dividends 462–5
  earnings per share and 465
special dividend 453
standard method of cash dividend payout 453–4
stock dividends, large and small 469
stock dividends and stock splits 468–70
  benchmark case 469
  details about 469
  reverse splits 470
  trading range 469–70
  value of 469–70
stock splits 469–70
summary and conclusions 470–71
targeted repurchase 463
tax and other benefits from higher dividends 459
  tax-exempt investors 459
taxes and 458
tender offers 463
Divisional and project costs of capital 367–71
  divisional cost of capital 368–9
  pure play approach 369
  subjective approach 369–70
Double taxation 21
DoubleClick 13
Du Pont identity 59–60
Dual-class capitalization 649

Early-stage financing and venture capital 384–8
Earnings before interest, taxes, depreciation and amortization (EBITDA) 54
Earnings before interest and taxes (EBIT) 54
Earnings growth, goal of maintenance of 6
Earnings per share (EPS)
  EPS growth 641–2
  share repurchases and 465
EasyJet Plc
  best and worst case scenarios 265

  external competition 264
  fuel price 264–5
  macroeconomic environment 264
  sensitivity analysis 264
Ecofys 361–2
Economic value added (EVA) 367
Economies of scale 638
Economist Big Mac index 528–9
Economy
  economic environment, corporate finance and 12
  economic exposure, risk management and 576
  equity returns and states of 318–19
  states of economy, equity returns and 318–19
Effective annual percentage rate (EAR) 106–7, 109–10
  example of 107
  quoting a rate, example of 107–8
Effective annual rates, calculation and comparison of 106–8
Effective tax rate 458
Efficient and inefficient markers, share price reaction to new information in 308
Efficient market reaction 308
EGL Group 191
Egypt, initial IPO returns for 394
Elringklinger GB 55
Employee share options (ESOs) 613–16
  example of 615
  executive compensation, valuation of 614–16
  features of 614
  real world insight, executive compensation and 616
Energy Breakthrough Corporation 388
Eni SpA 178
Environmental positivity, goal of 6
EQT 384
Equations 670–76
  announcement 674
  annuity present value growth 673
  average cash balance 675
  average daily float 675
  balance sheet identity 671, 672
  bond value if bond has (1) face value of F paid at maturity, (2) coupon of C paid per period, (3) t periods of maturity, and (4) yield of r per period 673
  bottom-up approach to OCF 674
  break-even analysis 675

call option payoff when underlying asset price, $S1$, is greater than exercise price, E. 676
capital asset pricing model (CAPM) 674
carrying costs 675
cash coverage ratio 671
cash flow identity 671
cash flow with new policy 675
cash flow with old policy 675
combined market value of debt and equity 674
cost of switching 675
current ratio 671
days' purchases in payables 671
days' sales in inventory 671
days' sales in receivables 671
debt-equity ratio 671
degree of operating leverage (DOL) 674
dividend growth model 673
Du Pont identity 672
economic order quantity 675
effective annual rate (EAR) where m is number of times interest compounded in year 673
effective annual rate (EAR) where q stands for continuously compounded quoted rate 673
equity multiplier 671
expected exchange rate at time I 676
expected return on portfolio 674
extending credit, NPV of 675
Fisher effect 673
  approximation of 673
future value 672
future value factor of an annuity 672
future value of £1 invested for t periods at rate of r per period 672
geometric average return 674
granting credit, NPV of 675
historical variance 674
income statement equation 671
interest rate parity (IRP) 676
  approximation 676
international Fisher effect (IFE) 676
inventory holding, total costs associated with 675
inventory turnover 671
market-to-book ratio 672
M&M Proposition II 675
M&M Proposition II with corporate taxes 675
net present value (NPV) of switching 675
net working capital (NWC) turnover ratio 671

Equations—Cont.

NPV of a merger 676
operating cash flow (OCF) 674
opportunity costs (Baumol-Allais-Tobin [BAT] model) 675
optimal cash balance (Miller-Orr model) 675
optimal initial cash balance 675
payables turnover ratio 671
per-share value 673
percentages of total capital represented by debt and equity 674
perpetuity present value growth 673
present value for a perpetuity 672
present value of £1 to be received t periods in the future at discount rate of r 672
present value of an annuity of C pounds per period for t periods when rate of return is r 672
present value of future incremental cash flows 675
present value of interest tax shield 675
present value of series of cash flows G over t periods with discount rate, APR 673
price-earnings (P/E) ratio 672
price of an equity that pays a dividend, $D1$, next year, has price $P1$ next year and discount rate R 673
price of equity at time t, two stage model 673
price of equity today, two stage model 673
price-sales ratio 672
profit margin 671
property, plant and equipment (PPE) turnover ratio 671
put-call parity (PCP) condition 676
quick or acid-test ratio 671
receivables turnover ratio 671
relationship between future and present value (basic present value equation) 672
relationship between OCF and sales volume 674
relative purchasing power parity (PPP) 676
required return on equity R^E (CAPM) 674
required return on equity R^E (dividend growth model) 674
required return on preferred stock R^P 674
return on assets 672
return on equity 672
risk premium 674
tax shield approach to OCF 674
times interest earned ratio 671
Tobin's Q ratio 672
top-down approach to OCF 674
total asset turnover 671
total carrying costs 675
total cash flow 671
total cash if equity sold 674
total cash return 674
total cost 675
total debt ratio 671
total restocking cost 675
total return 674
total return to equity investor 673
total risk 674
trade receivables 675
trading costs 675
uncovered interest parity (UIP) 676
upper limit 675
value gain from an acquisition 676
value of call option 676
value of firm B to an acquirer 676
value of levered firm 675
weighted average cost of capital (WACC) 674
weighted average cost of capital (WACC) if firm uses preference shares 674
weighted average flotation cost 674

Equinor 178
Equipment with different lives, evaluating options for 244–5
Equity
 corporate finance and 5
 cost of 355–9, 366
 country risk premiums (April 2020) and 297
 equity carve-out 651
 equity securities 134
 unlevering of, example of 421
Equity as call option on firm's assets 617–18
 example of 618
 risk-free debt and 617
 risky debt and 617–18
Equity valuation 159–84
 capital gains yield 169
 cash flows 160–62
 constant growth, case of 162–5
 dividend discount model 164
 dividend growth, example of 163
 dividend growth model 164
 example of 164–5
 dividend yield 169
 firm valuation 174–8
  cash flow valuation, example of 177
  common valuation multiples 177
  FCFF valuation, example of 175–6
  financing activities, cash flow from 175
  free cash flow to the firm (FCFF) 175
  International Accounting Standards (IAS) 175
  market multiples valuation 177–8
  operations, cash flow from 175
  present value of the firm 176
  real world insight, market multiples valuation 178
  valuation of firm's cash flows 176–7
 growing perpetuities 163
 growth stocks, example of 162
 learning objectives 159
 mini case, share valuation at Ecorenewable Energy 183–4
 non-constant growth, case of 165–7
 notations 159
 ordinary equity features 172
 ordinary shares, features of 172–3
 preference shares
  are preference shares debt? 173
  cumulative dividends 172
  features of 172–3
  Financial Instruments: Presentation (IAS) 173
  International Accounting Standards (IAS) 173
  non-cumulative dividends 172
  stated value 172
 price-earnings (P/E) ratio 171
 questions and problems 180–83
 reading suggestions 184
 real world insight, equity and bond valuation 160
 required return, components of 169–70
 review of issues 178–80
 self-test problems 178–80
 share valuation 160–72
 stock markets 173–4
  ask prices 173
  bid prices 173
  brokers 173–4
  dealers 173–4
  primary market 173
  secondary market 173
  stock market reporting 174
 subnormal growth, example of 167
 summary and conclusions 178
 summary of cases 170
 two-stage growth case of 168–9
 example of 168
 United Kingdom, equity data for selected industries in 171
 zero growth, case of 162
Equivalent annual cost (EAC) 246–7
Erosion 226
ESG 587
Estonia, small and medium-sized enterprises (SMEs) in 19
Ethics, corporate governance and 35–6
Eurex 581, 587
EURIBOR 584
Euro Disney 226
Euro Overnight Index Average (EONIA) 360
Eurobond 521–2
Eurocurrency 522
Euronext see NYSE Euronext
Europe
 bills and bonds in, equity risk premiums relative to (1900-2010) 298
 Brent spot oil price in (2010-21) 573
 derivative usage around world (% of firms) 589
 dividends and dividend payers in 465
 European option 596
 industry debt ratios in 442
 private equity investments into 387
 risk premiums relative to bonds in (1900-2019) 305
European Central Bank (ECB) 12, 141
European Commission 19–20, 233, 684
European Monetary Union (EMU) 12, 141
 international corporate finance and 520–21
European Union (EU) 223, 232, 233, 361–2
 annual percentage rate (APR) in 109
 bankruptcy laws in 445
 corporation types in 22
 Eurozone yield curve for 151
 International corporate finance 521
 share repurchase activity in 462
 small and medium-sized enterprises (SMEs) in 19

Eurotunnel 261
Eurozone
  currency symbol for 523
  Economist Big Mac index 528
  exchange rate quotations (January 2021) 524
Evaluation of investments, example of 81
Evaluation of NPV estimates
  basic problem 258
  estimation risk 258–9
  forecasting risk 258–9
  projected vs actual cash flows 258
  sources of value 259
Ex-dividend date, price behaviour around 455
Examples
  annual percentage rate (APR) 108–9
  annuity due vs ordinary annuity 103
  average cost vs marginal cost 268
  Bai' al-Inah agreements 544
  Bai Salam contracts 541
  BAT model 491
  Black-Scholes option pricing model 610–11
  bond yields 133
  book value vs market value 46–7
  borrowing costs 99
  break-even EBIT 419
  buying decision, operating cash flow and 241–2
  capital budgeting appraisal techniques, evaluation of projects with 210–11
  carrying costs 510
  cash collections and cost 232
  cash flow valuation 177
  Comic Collectibles as investments 83
  compound interest 75
  compounding, Manhattan Island and effect of 76
  core values 8
  cost of equity 358
  cost of equity capital 423
  crossover rate, calculation of 205–6
  current events, bond yields and 132
  deceptive advertising? 79
  discounted payback calculation 196
  dividend day 455
  dividend growth 76, 163
  dividend growth, value of equity and 164–5
  earnings per share, calculation of 47
  economic order quantity (EOQ) 510–11
  effective annual rate (EAR) 107

election buying 28
equity as call option 618
equivalent annual costs 245–6
evaluation of investments 81
exercise prices, call options and 608–9
Fisher effect 146–7
forward rates 699–700
forward trading currency 526
free cash flow to the firm (FCFF) 175
free cash flow to the firm (FCFF) valuation 175–6
geometric average return, calculation of 304–5
geometric averages 306
growth stocks 162
Ijarah Thumma al Bai' contracts 543
inflation and exchanging currency 530
interest on interest 72
interest rate swaps 584
internal rate of return (IRR) 203
internal rate of return (IRR), calculation of 201
internal rate of return (IRR), finding all possible rates 203–4
investment timing decision 620
investment value 96
irredeemable debt, cost of 359–60
market value vs book value 46–7
Murabahah transactions 542
net present value (NPV) rule, use of 190–90
operating leverage 276
option application 615
parity checking exchange rates 532
partial amortization, example of balloon payments and 113
payback calculation 192
payments to pay of debt, finding number of 101
portfolio expected return 323
portfolio variance and standard deviation 324–5
Pound for Euros exchange 526
preference shares 104
preference shares, cost of 360
put-call parity 602
put pay-offs 598–9
quoting a rate 107–8
redeemable debt, cost of 359–60
reducing-balance depreciation 234
repurchase price of a repo, calculation of 486
restocking costs 510

retirement, saving for 84
return for single-period investment 82
risk and return 340
risk-free investments 602
risk-to-reward ratio, 'buy low, sell high' and 337–8
saving for university 83
saving up 78, 94
semi-annual coupons 130
single period present value (PV) 77
spot rates 697
standard deviation, calculation of 300–301
statement of financial position, development of 44–5
supernormal growth 167
switching policies, net present value (NPV) and 501
synergy 636
time value of money 85
total risk vs beta 332
Treasury bills 111
two-stage growth 168
unequal probabilities 319–20, 321
unleveraging the equity 421
variable costs 267
variance, calculation of 300–301
weighted average cost of capital (WACC), use of 366–7
weighted average flotation cost, calculation of 372
Yen for Euros exchange 524
Excess return on a risky asset 297
Exchange rate policy 12
Exchange rate quotations 523, 524
Exchange rate risk 536–9
  cash payment and receipt management 539
  home currency invoicing 538–9
  International Accounting Standards Board (IASB) Standard 21 (IAS21) 538
  long-run exposure 537
  receipt and payment matching 539
  short-run exposure 536–7
  translation exposure 537–8
Exchange rate volatility 573
Exchange rates 523–7
Executive Agency for Small and Medium Enterprises (EASME) 361
Exercising options 596
Expansion, option for 621
Expectations hypothesis 702, 703
Expected and unexpected returns 325
Expected returns 318–20

announcements, surprises and 325–6
calculation of 319, 320
systematic risk and 337
variances and 318–22
Expected risk premium 319
Expiration date of options 596
External financing and growth 685–9
External financing needed (EFN) 683, 685
External stakeholders 30–31
Extra cash dividend 453
Exxon Mobil 371

Face value 127
Fair price provision 648
False consensus 561
Feasibility, confirmation of 678–9
Finance director (FD) 3
Financial Conduct Authority (UK) 10
Financial distress costs 431–2
Financial engineering 572
Financial Executives International (FEI) 567
Financial flows as % of GDP 405
Financial leases 484
Financial leverage, capital structure policy and 414–51
  bankruptcy
    absolute priority rule (APR) 444
    accounting insolvency 443
    administration of 444–5
    business failure and 443
    claims, priority of 444
    company voluntary agreement (CVA) 444
    European Union (EU), bankruptcy laws in 445
    financial distress costs 431–2
    France, bankruptcy laws in 445
    legal bankruptcy 443
    liquidation 444
    milking the property, selfish strategy three 433
    real world case financial distress costs 432
    Lehman Brothers bankruptcy 431
    reorganization 443
    risk taking in excess, selfish strategy three 432
    Scotland, bankruptcy laws in 444–5
    selfish strategies, summary of 433
    South Africa, bankruptcy laws in 445
    technical insolvency 443

Financial leverage, capital structure policy and—*Cont.*
  underinvestment, selfish strategy three 432–3
  United States, bankruptcy laws in 445
bankruptcy costs 430–33
  agency costs 432–3
  direct costs 431
  indirect costs 431–2
bankruptcy law 443–5
bankruptcy process 443–5
business and financial risk 424–5
capital structure
  cost of capital and 416
  cost of equity capital and 421–5
  decisions about 415
  question concerning 415–16
corporate borrowing, homemade leverage and 420–21
cost of capital, capital structure and 416
cost of equity, value of firm and 429–30
equity, unlevering of, example of 421
Europe, industry debt ratios in 442
financial leverage 416–17
  basics of 417–19
  break-even EBIT, example of 419
  effect of 416–21
  EPS and ROE and, example of 417–18
  EPS vs EBIT 418–19
  unlevering the equity, example of 421
financial risk 425
firm values
  equity value and, an example 415–16
  no debt vs debt plus dividend 415
homemade leverage
  corporate borrowing and 420–21
  proposed capital structure vs original capital structure with 420
interest tax shield 426
learning objectives 414
liquidation and reorganization 443
mini case, Sustainable Lakes, recapitalization for 450
M&M Proposition I
  with corporate taxes 425–30
  cost of equity and financial leverage 422–3
  cost of equity and WACC with no taxes 423

no-tax case 429
Pie Model 421–2
  extended Pie Model 437–8
  marketed claims vs non-marketed claims 438–9
  tax case 429
  taxes and 426–7
M&M Proposition II
  with corporate taxes 425–30
  cost of equity and WACC with no taxes 423
  no-tax case 429
  tax case 429
  taxes, WACC and 427–8
notations 414
observed capital structures 441–3
optimal capital structure 433–7
  capital structure question 436
  cost of capital and 434–5
  financial distress and capital structure 437
  managerial recommendations on capital structure 437
  recap on 435–7
  static theory of capital structure 433–4, 435
  taxes and capital structure 437
payoffs to shareholders, debt plus dividend 416
pecking-order theory 440–41
  implications of pecking-order 441
  internal finance, pecking-order and 440–41
pie model 437–9
questions and problems 447–9
reading suggestions 451
real world insight, capital structure, M&M 30 years later 424–5
restructurings 415
review of issues 446
self-test problems 446
shareholders, debt plus dividend payoffs to 416
signalling 439–40
summary and conclusions 445
unlevered cost of capital 427
value of firm, cost of equity and 429–30
weighted average cost of capital (WACC) 416
Financial management
  decisions about 4–5
  goal appropriateness 7
  potential goals 6
  real world insights 6–7
Financial manager 3–5
Financial markets

cash flows between economy, firms and 10
corporations and 9–11
integrated nature of 2
Financial planning 677–95
  accomplishments with 678–9
  alternative scenario dealing with 684–5
  capital intensity ratio 682
  determinants of growth 689
  dividend payout ratio 681
  dividend policy, growth and 689
  external financing and growth 685–9
  external financing needed (EFN) 683, 685
  feasibility, confirmation of 678–9
  financial planning 678–9
  financial policy, growth and 689
  financial position statement 682–3
  financial statement information, problems with manipulation of 684–5
  growth and EFN 685–7
  growth and financial policy 688–9
  growth as financial management goal 678
  growth determinants 689
  income statement 680–81
  interactions, examination of 678
  internal consistency, confirmation of 678–9
  internal growth rate 688
  iterative process 690
  learning objectives 677
  models for
    caveats regarding 689–90
    first look 679–85
  options, exploration of 678
  percentage of sales approach 680–81
  plowback ratio 681
  priorities and goals, thinking about 678
  pro forma statements 679–80, 683, 684
  problems and potential conflicts, scenario dealing with 683–4
  profit margin, growth and 689
  projected growth rates, importance of 684–5
  questions and problems 693–5
  retention ratio 681
  review of issues 690–93
  self-test problems 690–93
  summary and conclusions 690
  surprises, avoidance of 678
  sustainable growth rate 688
  total asset turnover, growth and 689

Financial policy and cost of capital 355
Financial ratios 52, 58
  grouping of 52
Financial risk
  management 571–94
  cash flow hedging, cautionary note on 576
  commodity price volatility 573
  derivative securities 572
  derivative usage around world (% of firms) 589
  economic exposure 576
  Europe, Brent spot oil price in (2010-21) 573
  exchange rate volatility 573
  financial engineering 572
  financial risk, management of 573–7
  forward contracts 577
  forward contracts, hedging with 577–80
    basics about forward contracts 577
    buyers of forward contracts 577
    caveat about 579
    credit risk and 579–80
    cross-hedging 582
    forward contracts in practice 580
    forwards and hedging 579–80
    pay-off profile 577–8
    risk profile of oil buyer 578
    sellers of forward contracts 577
    settlement date 577
  futures contracts 580
  futures contracts, hedging with 580–82
  futures and hedging 582
  futures exchanges 581–2
  trading in futures 580
  hedging 572
  price volatility and 572–3
  immunization 572
  interest rate risk, hedging with options
    captions 588
    compound options 588
    interest rate caps 588
    preliminary notice 588
    swaptions 588
  interest rate volatility 572
  learning objectives 571
  long-term exposure hedging 576–7
  market to market resettlement 580
  mini case, McAfee Mortgages Ltd 593
  oil buyer, risk profile of 578
  option contracts 585
  option contracts, hedging with 585–90
    call options 585, 588
    call price 588

Index

commodity price risk,
  hedging with
  options 587
exchange rate risk,
  hedging with
  options 587
exercise price 585
expiration date 585
floor 588
futures options 587
interest rate risk,
  hedging with
  options 588
option hedging 586–7
option pay-off
  profiles 585–6
option premiums 585
option terminology 585
options vs forwards 585
put options 585, 588
strike price 585
practice of 588–90
questions and
  problems 591–2
reading suggestions 593
real world insight
  cryptocurrencies,
    futures contracts
    in 580
  sustainability 587
review of issues 590–91
risk exposure reduction 575
risk profile 574
self-test problems 590–91
short-run exposure
  hedging 576
summary and
  conclusions 590
swap contracts, hedging
  with 582–5
  commodity swaps 583
  currency swaps 583
  interest rate swaps 583
  interest rate swaps,
    example of 584
  matched (balanced)
    books 584
  swap books 584
  swap dealers 583–4
transactions exposure 576
transitory changes 576
United Kingdom, changes in
  10-year government bond
  yields (2010-21) 572
wheat buyer, risk profile
  of 575
wheat grower, risk
  profile of 574
Financial side-effects of
  acquisitions 641–3
Financial statement
  analysis 42–68
  acid-test ratio 53
  annual report 43–52
  asset management 54–6
  asset management ratios 58
  asset turnover ratios 55–6
  asset utilization ratios 54
  average vs marginal tax
    rates 49–50

balance sheet 43–7
cash coverage 54
cash flow from financing
  activities 51
cash flow from investing
  activities 51
cash flow from operating
  activities 50–51
cash flow identity 50
corporate tax rates 49
current ratio 53
days' payables in
  receivables, payables
  turnover and 55
days' sales in inventory,
  inventory turnover
  and 54
days' sales in receivables,
  receivables turnover
  and 54–5
Du Pont identity 59–60
earnings before interest,
  taxes, depreciation and
  amortization (EBITDA) 54
earnings before interest
  and taxes (EBIT) 54
financial ratios 52, 58
  grouping of 52
financial statement
  evaluation
  aspirant group 61
  benchmark choice 61
  external uses 60–61
  internal uses 60
  International Accounting
    Standards (IAS) and 61
  peer group analysis 61
  problems with statement
    analysis 61–2
  rationale for 60–61
  time trend analysis 61
financing activities, cash
  flow from 51
flat rate tax 50
income statement 47–8
  earnings per share
    (EPS) 47
  earnings per share (EPS),
    calculation of 47
  International Accounting
    Standards (IAS) and
    47, 48
  Leonardi SpA Statement
    of Cash Flows (2018)
    48, 51
  Leonardi SpA Statement
    of Comprehensive
    Income (2018) 47
  matching principle 48
  net income 47
  non-cash items 48
  recognition (or realization)
    principle 48
inventory turnover 54
investing activities, cash
  flow from 51
learning objectives 42
liquidity measures 52–3
long-term solvency
  measures 53–4

marginal tax rates 49–50
market-to-book ratio 57
market value measures 56–7
market value ratios 58
mini case, Friday Quantum
  Solutions (FQS) 67–8
net cash flow 51–2
net working capital (NWC)
  turnover 55
notations 42
operating cash flow
  (OCF) 50–51
  calculation of 51
  International Accounting
    Standards (IAS)
    and 51
payables turnover 55
price-earnings (P/E) ratio 57
price-sales ratio 57
profit margin 56
profitability measures 56
profitability ratios 58
property, plant and
  equipment (PPE)
  turnover 55
questions and
  problems 64–7
quick (acid-test) ratio 53
ratio analysis 52–9
reading suggestions 68
real world insight
  return on equity for
    AstraZenica 60
  sustainability in
    finance 62
receivables turnover 54–5
return on assets (ROA) 56
return on book assets
  (or equity) 56
return on capital employed
  (ROCE) 56
return on equity (ROE) 56
  closer look at 59–60
return on investment
  (ROI) 56
review of issues 63–4
self-test problems 63–4
short-term solvency (or
  liquidity) measures 52–3
statement of cash
  flows 50–52
statement of financial
  position 43–7
  assets (left side) 43
  balance sheet identity 44
  bonds and bondholders 43
  book value 46–7
  building, example of 44–5
  current assets 43
  current liabilities 43–4
  fair value amount 46
  fixed assets 45
  historical cost model 46
  intangible assets 43
  International Accounting
    Standards (IAS) and 46
  Leonardo SpA (2018) 45
  liabilities (right side) 43–4
  long-tern debt 45
  market value 46

  market value vs book
    value 46–7
  net working capital 44–5
  non-current assets 43
  non-current liabilities 43–4
  ordinary equity 43–4
  owners' equity 44
  owners' equity
    (right side) 43–4
  revaluation model 46
  shareholders'
    equity 43–4
  tangible assets 43
summary and
  conclusions 62
taxes 48–50
times interest earned
  (TIE) 54
Tobin's Q ratio 57
total debt ratio 53
turnover measures 54–6
turnover ratios 58
using financial statement
  information 60–62
Financial statement
  information, problems with
  manipulation of 684–5
Financial system, bank-based
  and market-based
  countries 33
Financial technologies 2
Financial Times 150, 174
  Commodities and
    Agriculture Data Archive
    (February 2021) 581
Financing activities, cash
  flow from 51
Financing costs 227
Financing life cycle of a
  firm 384–8
Financing stages 387
Finland
  bank vs market-based
    financial systems 33
  bills and bonds in, equity
    risk premiums relative to
    (1900-2010) 298
  capital budgeting
    techniques, use in 211
  corporate tax rates in 49
  corporation types in 22
  Corruption Perceptions
    Index (TI 2018) for 32
  Corruption Perceptions
    Index (TI 2019) for 540
  debt to equity, estimated
    ratio in 442
  derivative usage around
    world (% of firms) 589
  equity risk premiums in
    (April 2020) 297
  initial IPO returns for 394
  international business
    angel networks in 386
  ownership structures of
    companies in 34
  risk premiums relative to
    bonds in (1900-2019) 305
  small and medium-sized
    enterprises (SMEs) in 19

Index

Firm-specific risk 562
Firm valuation 174–8
  cash flow valuation, example of 177
  common valuation multiples 177
  FCFF valuation, example of 175–6
  financing activities, cash flow from 175
  free cash flow to the firm (FCFF) 175
  International Accounting Standards (IAS) 175
  market multiples valuation 177–8
  operations, cash flow from 175
  present value of the firm 176
  real world insight, market multiples valuation 178
  valuation of firm's cash flows 176–7
Firm values
  equity value and, an example 415–16
  no debt vs debt plus dividend 415
First Abu Dhabi Bank (FAB) 545
Fiscal policy, corporate finance and 12
Fisher, Irving 146
Fisher effect 146–7
Fitch Ratings 139–40
Fixed costs, break-even analysis and 267
Fixed rate mortgages 115
Flat rate tax 50
Flip-in provision 647
Floating-rate bonds 142
Flotation costs 458
  weighted average cost of capital (WACC) and basic approach 371–2
  calculation of weighted average flotation cost, example of 372
  internal equity, flotation costs and 373
  net present value (NPV), flotation costs and 372–3
Flutter Entertainment Plc 330
Foreign bonds 522
Foreign exchange market 522–3
  exchange rates and 522–7
Foreign trade policy 12
Forward contracts 577
  hedging with 577–80
    basics about forward contracts 577
    buyers of forward contracts 577
    caveat about 579
    credit risk and 579–80
    cross-hedging 582
    forward contracts in practice 580
    forwards and hedging 579–80
    pay-off profile 577–8
    risk profile of oil buyer 578
    sellers of forward contracts 577
    settlement date 577
Forward exchange rate 526–7
  definition of 698–9
  example of 526
  examples of calculation of 699–700
  future spot rates and 533
  over 2nd year and spot rate expected, relationship between 702
Forward trade 526
Forwards, financial planning and 486
Framing effects 555–8
  debt avoidance 557
  disposition effect 557
  endowment effect 558
  frame dependence 556
  house money 557–8
  loss aversion 556–7
  mental accounting 557
  money illusion 558
  myopic loss aversion 558
  playing with house money 557
  regret aversion 558
France
  average annual returns of companies in (2011-2020) 296
  bank loans as % of external financing 405
  bank vs market-based financial systems 33
  bankruptcy laws in 445
  bills and bonds in, equity risk premiums relative to (1900-2010) 298
  capital budgeting techniques, use in 211
  corporate tax rates in 49
  corporation types in 22
  Corruption Perceptions Index (TI 2018) for 32
  Corruption Perceptions Index (TI 2019) for 540
  debt to equity, estimated ratio in 442
  derivative usage around world (% of firms) 589
  equity risk premiums in (April 2020) 297
  initial IPO returns for 394
  international business angel networks in 386
  ownership structures of companies in 34
  risk premiums relative to bonds in (1900-2019) 305
  small and medium-sized enterprises (SMEs) in 19
  stock market index levels (2010-2020) 294
  underpricing of IPOs in, determinants of 395
FTSE 100 Index 289, 294, 330
FTSE 250 Midcap Index 294
Future spot rates 533
Future value 72–6, 80–86
  for annuities 102
  calculations of 93–4
  compounding and 71–7
  future value interest factor (FVIF) 72, 75, 78–9
  with multiple cash flows 92–4
  problems with 73–6
Futures, financial planning and 486
Futures contracts 580
  hedging with 580–82
    futures and hedging 582
    futures exchanges 581–2
    trading in futures 580

G20 Task Force on Climate-Related Financial Disclosures 638
Gains from acquisitions 635–41
Gambler's fallacy 560–61
Gates, Bill and Melinda 388
General cash offer 389
General Electric (GE) 223
General Milk Plc 225
General Motors (GM) 142
General partnerships 20
General Theory of Employment, Interest and Money (Keynes, J,M.) 480
Geometric averages, examples of 306
Germany
  average annual returns of companies in (2011-2020) 296
  bank loans as % of external financing 405
  bank vs market-based financial systems 33
  bills and bonds in, equity risk premiums relative to (1900-2010) 298
  capital budgeting techniques, use in 211
  corporate tax rates in 49
  Corruption Perceptions Index (TI 2018) for 32
  Corruption Perceptions Index (TI 2019) for 540
  debt to equity, estimated ratio in 442
  derivative usage around world (% of firms) 589
  equity risk premiums in (April 2020) 297
  initial IPO returns for 394
  international business angel networks in 386
  ownership structures of companies in 34
  Partnerschaftsgesellschaft (PartG) in 20
  risk premiums relative to bonds in (1900-2019) 305
  small and medium-sized enterprises (SMEs) in 19
  stock market index levels (2010-2020) 294
  underpricing of IPOs in, determinants of 395
Giacometti, Alberto 83
GIGO (garbage in, garbage out) system 258
Gilts 522
GlaxoSmith Kline (GSK) 144, 457
Global credit crunch 566
Globalization 521
Goal of financial management 6–9
Going-private
  leveraged buyouts and 648
  transactions 634
Golden parachute 648
Google 25
  becoming Alphabet 13
  share issue 13
Government bonds 131, 141
Granting credit, costs of 502
Graphing term structure 697–8
Greece
  bank vs market-based financial systems 33
  corporate tax rates in 49
  Corruption Perceptions Index (TI 2018) for 32
  Corruption Perceptions Index (TI 2019) for 540
  debt to equity, estimated ratio in 442
  derivative usage around world (% of firms) 589
  equity risk premiums in (April 2020) 297
  initial IPO returns for 394
  international business angel networks in 386
  ownership structures of companies in 34
  small and medium-sized enterprises (SMEs) in 19
Greenmail 647
Growth
  determinants of, financial planning and 689
  external financing needed (EFN) and 685–7
  as financial management goal 678
  financial policy and 688–9
  growing annuities 105
  growing perpetuities 105, 163
  growth stocks, example of 162
Growth capital 387

Halma 330
Harvard Business Review 9
HBOS, merger with Lloyds TSB 634, 638
Heathrow Airport 225
Hedging 572
  price volatility and 572–3
  see also Financial risk management

Helsinki Stock Exchange 174
Heuristics 558–61
Hewlett-Packard 226, 405
High-dividend payout, real-world factors favouring 459–60
High intensity interval training (HIIT) 461
Historical record 294–6
  on average returns 296
H&M 303
Holding cash, costs of 481
Homemade dividends 457
Homemade leverage
  corporate borrowing and 420–21
  proposed capital structure vs original capital structure with 420
Honda 537
Hong Kong
  corporate tax rates in 49
  debt to equity, estimated ratio in 442
  initial IPO returns for 394
  ownership structures of companies in 34
Horizontal acquisition 634
Hot hands effect 559
HS2 Rail 225–6
Hungary, small and medium-sized enterprises (SMEs) in 19

Iberdrola 598
IBM 582
Iceland, Corruption Perceptions Index (TI 2019) for 540
IDEM Italy 581
Immunization 572
Imperial Brands Plc 159, 330
Implementation costs 563
Implicit options 619
Income bonds 143
Income component of return 290
Income statements
  financial planning and 680–81
  financial statement analysis and 47–8
  earnings per share (EPS) 47
  earnings per share (EPS), calculation of 47
  International Accounting Standards (IAS) and 47, 48
  Leonardi SpA Statement of Cash Flows (2018) 48, 51
  Leonardi SpA Statement of Comprehensive Income (2018) 47
  matching principle 48
  net income 47
  non-cash items 48
  recognition (or realization) principle 48

Incremental cash flows 224, 225–7
Incremental cost, break-even analysis and 267
Incremental revenue, break-even analysis and 268
Indentures 136–9
  bearer form 137
  blanket mortgage 137
  call premium 138
  call-protected bond 138
  call provision 138
  collateral 137
  deferred call provision 138
  mortgage securities 137
  mortgage trust indenture 137
  negative covenant 139
  note 137–8
  positive covenant 139
  principal value 137
  protective covenants 139
  real world insight, negative and positive (gearing) covenants 139
  registered form 137
  repayment 138
  security 137–8
  seniority 138
  sinking fund 138
  subordinated debt 138
  terms of bond 137
  trust deed 137
  unsecured bond 137–8
India
  average annual returns of companies in (2011-2020) 296
  bank vs market-based financial systems 33
  capital budgeting techniques, use in 211
  corporate tax rates in 49
  Corruption Perceptions Index (TI 2018) for 32
  Corruption Perceptions Index (TI 2019) for 540
  currency symbol for 523
  debt to equity, estimated ratio in 442
  derivative usage around world (% of firms) 589
  Economist Big Mac index 528
  equity risk premiums in (April 2020) 297
  exchange rate quotations (January 2021) 524
  initial IPO returns for 394
  National Stock Exchange in 581
  ownership structures of companies in 34
  stock market index levels (2010-2020) 294
  underpricing of IPOs in, determinants of 395
Indonesia
  debt to equity, estimated ratio in 442
  initial IPO returns for 394

Inefficient management, note about 641
Inflation
  inflation premium 149
  interest rates and 145–8
  present values and 147
Information content effect 461
Information content of dividends 460–61
Initial public offerings (IPOs) 389
  underpricing and 393–6
    average first-day sales for IPOs (1980-2019) 395
    determinants of underpricing 395
    initial IPO returns, equal weighted averages for 393–4
    underpricing, reasons for existence of 394–6
    'winner's curse' and 396
Innovation or surprise 326
Interactions, examination of 678
Intercontinental Exchange (ICE) 581
Interest-breaking instruments 485
Interest on interest 72
Interest-only loans 111
Interest rate parity (IRP)
  international corporate finance and 532
  unbiased forward rates and 530–34
Interest rate risk
  bond valuation and 130–31
  hedging with options
    captions 588
    compound options 588
    interest rate caps 588
    preliminary notice 588
    swaptions 588
  interest rate risk premium 149
Interest rate term structure 148–50
Interest rate volatility 572
Interest rates, term structure, spot rates and yield to maturity 696–705
  bond at future date, estimation of price of 700–701
  expectations hypothesis 702, 703
  explanations of term structure 698–701
  forward rate
    definition of 698–9
    examples of calculation of 699–700
    over 2nd year and spot rate expected, relationship between 702
  graphing term structure 697–8
  liquidity preference hypothesis 702–3

price of bond at future date, estimation of 700–701
  spot rates 696
  yields to maturity and, example of difference between 697
  term structure graphing 697–8
  time horizon, liquidity preference hypothesis and 703
  yields to maturity and spot rates, example of difference between 697
Interest tax shield 426
Internal consistency, confirmation of 678–9
Internal growth rate 688
Internal rate of return (IRR) 198–209, 212
  advantages and disadvantages of 207
  calculation of, example of 201
  identification of, example of 203
  internal rate of return rule 199
  internalrate of return rule 199
  investing or financing? 206–7
  MIRR or, which is better? 208–9
  modified internal rate of return (MIRR) 207–9, 212
  multiple rates of return 202
    example of 203–4
  mutually exclusive investments and 204–6
  net present value (NPV) and 199–212
  non-conventional cash flows and 202
  problems with 202–7
  redeeming qualities of 207
  spreadsheet strategy, calculation of IRRs 201
Internal stakeholders 30–31
International Accounting Standards Board (IASB) 635
International Accounting Standards (IAS) 3
International capital budgeting 534–6
  foreign currency approach 534, 535–6
  home currency approach 534, 535
  unremitted cash flows 536
International Consolidated Airlines 330
International corporate finance 520–51
  absolute purchasing power parity (PPP) 527–9
  American depositary receipt (ADR) 521
  bid and offer rates 523–4

International corporate finance—*Cont.*
  bid-ask spread 524
  Brexit and 545
    free movement 545
    goods, trade in 545
    impact on corporate finance 545
    services, trade in 545
  covered interest arbitrage 531–2
  cross-rate 521
  cross-rates, triangle arbitrage and 524–5
  discount, selling at 526
  Economist Big Mac index 528–9
  eurobond 521–2
  Eurocurrency 522
  European Monetary Union (EMU) 520–21
  European Union (EU) 521
  exchange rate quotations 523, 524
  exchange rate risk 536–9
    cash payment and receipt management 539
    home currency invoicing 538–9
    International Accounting Standards Board (IASB) Standard 21 (IAS21) 538
    long-run exposure 537
    receipt and payment matching 539
    short-run exposure 536–7
    translation exposure 537–8
  exchange rates 523–7
  foreign bonds 522
  foreign exchange markets 522–3
    exchange rates and 522–7
  forward exchange rate 526–7
  forward rates of exchange, example of 526
  future spot rates and 533
  forward trade 526
  future spot rates 533
  gilts 522
  globalization 521
  interest rate parity (IRP) 532
    unbiased forward rates and 530–34
  international capital budgeting 534–6
    foreign currency approach 534, 535–6
    home currency approach 534, 535
    unremitted cash flows 536
  international currency symbols 523
  International Fisher Effect (IFE) 533–4
  international supply chains 520–21

Islamic corporate finance 541–5
  advanced payment sale 541
  Bai' al-Inah, example of 544
  Bai Salam, example of 541
  goodwill loan 542
  hire purchase 542
  ijarah susuk, structuring of 544
  Ijarah Thumma al Bai', example of 543
  Islamic bonds 544
  joint venture 542–3
  leasing 543
  Murabahah, example of 542
  profit-sharing 543
  real world insight, *susuk* bond issue by First Abu Dhabi Bank (FAB) 545
  safekeeping 543
  sale and buyback 543–4
  stated cost plus profit 542
  susuk bonds 544
  types of 541–4
learning objectives 520
London Interbank Offer Rate (LIBOR) 522
mini case, West Coast Electronics goes carbon neutral 550
multinationals 521
net present value (NPV), foreign investments and 521
notations 520
political risk 539–41
Pounds for Euros exchange, example of 526
premium, selling at 526
purchasing power parity 527–30
questions and problems 547–50
reading suggestions 550–51
real world insights
  Europe, risks facing companies in 539
  Transparency International Corruption Perceptions Index 540–41
  relative purchasing power parity (PPP) 529–30
  appreciation of currency 530
  basic idea 528
  depreciation of currency 530
  inflation and exchange, example of 530
  result 528–30
review of issues 546–7
Secured Overnight Financing Rate (SOFR) 522
self-test problems 546–7

spot exchange rate 526
spot trade 526
Sterling Overnight Index Average (SONIA) 522
summary and conclusions 545–6
swaps 522
terminology 521–2
transaction types 526–7
triangle arbitrage 524–5
unbiased forward rates (UFR) 533
uncovered interest parity (UIP) 533
Yen for Euros exchange, example of 524
International corporate governance 31–6
International corporations 22
International currency symbols 523
International Financial Reporting Standards (IFRS) 635
  dividends and payout policy 469
  raising capital 408
International Fisher Effect (IFE) 533–4
International supply chains 520–21
Inventory management 481, 506
  ABC approach to 507
  ABC inventory analysis 507
  carrying costs 506, 508
  carrying costs, example of 510
  derived-demand inventories, management of 511–13
  economic order quantity (EOQ) model 507–11
    extensions to 511
  financial manager and 505
  finished goods 506
  holding inventory, costs of 508
  inventory costs 505
  inventory depletion 508
  inventory policy, financial manager and 505
  inventory types 505
  just-in-time (JIT) inventory 511–13
  kanban systems 513
  keiretsu groups 513
  materials requirements planning (MRP) 511
  raw materials 506
  real world insight, inventory control in oil and gas 513
  reorder points 511, 512
  restocking costs, example of 510
  restocking quantity 508
  safety stocks 511, 512
  shortage costs 506, 509
  techniques for 507–13
  total costs 509

Inventory turnover 54
Invest Europe 383
investing activities, cash flow from 51
Investments
  comic collectibles as 83
  criteria for, summary of 212
  evaluation of, example of 81
  of idle cash 485–6
  investment timing decision 619–20
  for more than one period 72–6
  in receivables 495
  for a single period 71
  value calculations for, examples of 96
Investor protection, legal environment 31–3
Investor rationality 561
Iran
  Corruption Perceptions Index (TI 2019) for 540
  currency symbol for 523
  initial IPO returns for 394
Iraq, Corruption Perceptions Index (TI 2019) for 540
Ireland
  bank vs market-based financial systems 33
  bills and bonds in, equity risk premiums relative to (1900-2010) 298
  Celtic Tiger (1995-2007) 566
  corporate tax rates in 49
  Corruption Perceptions Index (TI 2018) for 32
  Corruption Perceptions Index (TI 2019) for 540
  debt to equity, estimated ratio in 442
  derivative usage around world (% of firms) 589
  equity risk premiums in (April 2020) 297
  initial IPO returns for 394
  international business angel networks in 386
  ownership structures of companies in 34
  risk premiums relative to bonds in (1900-2019) 305
  small and medium-sized enterprises (SMEs) in 19
Irredeemable bonds 127
Islamic corporate finance 541–5
  advanced payment sale 541
  Bai' al-Inah, example of 544
  Bai Salam, example of 541
  goodwill loan 542
  hire purchase 542
  ijarah susuk, structuring of 544
  Ijarah Thumma al Bai', example of 543
  Islamic bonds 544
  joint venture 542–3

Index 721

leasing 543
Murabahah, example of 542
profit-sharing 543
real world insight, *susuk* bond issue by First Abu Dhabi Bank (FAB) 545
safekeeping 543
sale and buyback 543–4
stated cost plus profit 542
susuk bonds 544
types of 541–4
Israel
  debt to equity, estimated ratio in 442
  initial IPO returns for 394
Issuing securities, costs of 397–8
Italy
  bank loans as % of external financing 405
  bank vs market-based financial systems 33
  bills and bonds in, equity risk premiums relative to (1900-2010) 298
  corporate tax rates in 49
  corporation types in 22
  Corruption Perceptions Index (TI 2018) for 32
  Corruption Perceptions Index (TI 2019) for 540
  debt to equity, estimated ratio in 442
  derivative usage around world (% of firms) 589
  equity risk premiums in (April 2020) 297
  initial IPO returns for 394
  international business angel networks in 386
  ownership structures of companies in 34
  risk premiums relative to bonds in (1900-2019) 305
  small and medium-sized enterprises (SMEs) in 19
Iterative process in financial planning 690

Japan
  bills and bonds in, equity risk premiums relative to (1900-2010) 298
  corporate tax rates in 49
  currency symbol for 523
  debt to equity, estimated ratio in 442
  just-in-time system in 512–13
  risk premiums relative to bonds in (1900-2019) 305
J.J. Sprint Plc 415
Jobs, Steve 27
Johnson & Johnson 457
Joint-stock companies 21
Joint ventures 635
Jordan, Corruption Perceptions Index (TI 2019) for 540

Keynes, John Maynard 6, 480, 563
KKR 383

Korea
  debt to equity, estimated ratio in 442
  initial IPO returns for 394
KPMG UK 226
Kunst en Ambacht (K&A) NV 463
Kuwait, currency symbol for 523

Later stage capital 387
Latvia, small and medium-sized enterprises (SMEs) in 19
Law of bankruptcy 443–5
Learning objectives
  behavioural finance 552
  bond valuation 126
  capital investment decisions 223
  capital market history, lessons from 289
  corporate finance 2
  corporate governance 18
  cost of capital 353
  discounted cash flow valuation 91
  dividends and payout policy 452
  equity valuation 159
  financial leverage, capital structure policy and 414
  financial planning 677
  financial risk management 571
  financial statement analysis 42
  international corporate finance 520
  mergers and acquisitions 631
  net present value and other investment criteria 186
  options and corporate finance 595
  project analysis and evaluation 257
  raising capital 383
  return, risk and security market line 317
  short-term financial planning and management 479
  valuation, time value of money 70
Lease financing 406–9
  accounting for leases 408–9
  buying vs leasing 407
  financial leases 407–8
  leveraged leases 408
  operating leases 407
  sale and leaseback 408
Leeson, Nicholas 556
Legal bankruptcy 443
Legal forms of acquisition 632–5
Legal systems 32
LEGO Group 62
Lehman Brothers 431
Lenders 134
Leonard Green and Partners 384
Leveraged buyouts (LBOs) 634
  going-private and 648

Limited liability companies (Ltd companies) 21
Limited liability partnership (LLP) 20
Limited partnerships 20
Lindt 470
Liquidation
  bankruptcy and 444
  liquidating dividend 453
  reorganization and 443
Liquidity management 481
  cash management vs 481
Liquidity measures 52–3
Liquidity preference hypothesis 702–3
Liquidity premium 151
Listing 11
Lithuania, small and medium-sized enterprises (SMEs) in 19
Liverpool FC 414
Lloyds TSB, merger with HBOS 634, 638
LME London Exchange 581
Loan types and loan amortization 110–15
Lock-up 648
London Interbank Offer Rate (LIBOR) 522
London Stock Exchange (LSE) 143, 173, 263, 294, 307, 337
  bond issue features 136
  corporate finance and 11
Long-term debt 5
  basics of 136
  issuing of 404
Long-term exposure hedging 576–7
Long-term solvency measures 53–4
L'Oréal, beta coefficient for 332, 333
Low-dividend payout, real-world factors favouring 458–9
Lower taxes 639–40
Luxembourg
  corporation types in 22
  Corruption Perceptions Index (TI 2018) for 32
  Corruption Perceptions Index (TI 2019) for 540
  small and medium-sized enterprises (SMEs) in 19

Macroeconomic policy 12
Malaysia
  bank loans as % of external financing 405
  capital budgeting techniques, use in 211
  corporate tax rates in 49
  Corruption Perceptions Index (TI 2018) for 32
  Corruption Perceptions Index (TI 2019) for 540
  debt to equity, estimated ratio in 442
  derivative usage around world (% of firms) 589

Economist Big Mac index 528
  equity risk premiums in (April 2020) 297
  exchange rate quotations (January 2021) 524
  initial IPO returns for 394
  underpricing of IPOs in, determinants of 395
Malta, small and medium-sized enterprises (SMEs) in 19
Management buy-outs (MBOs) 634
Management goals 24–5
Managerial compensation 25–7
Managerial options in capital budgeting 620–22
Manchester United FC 414
Manhattan Island 76
Manufacturers Hanover Venture Capital Corp 386
Marginal cost, break-even analysis and 267
Marginal revenue, break-even analysis and 268
Marginal tax rates 49–50
Market efficiency
  behavioural finance and 561–7
  foundations of 561–2
Market portfolios, security market line (SLM) and 338
Market risk premium 338
Market risks 327, 331
Market share, goal of maximization of 6
Market-to-book ratio 57
Market to market resettlement 580
Market value added (MVA) 367
Market value measures 56–7
Market value ratios 58
Marvel Comics 83
Mathematical tables 660–69
  cumulative normal distribution 668–9
  future value of £1 at end of t periods 661
  future value of annuity of £1 per period for t periods 666–7
  present value of £1 to be received after t periods 662–3
  present value of annuity of £1 per period for t periods 664–5
Maturity 127
MEFF Spain 581
Memorandum of association 20–21
Mercedes-Benz 438, 537
Mergers and acquisitions 631–59
  accounting, tax considerations and 635
  acquisition
    of assets 633
    classification of 634
    legal forms of 632–5

Index

Mergers and acquisitions—Cont.
  acquisition costs
    cash acquisition 643–4
    cash vs shares 644–5
    control 644–5
    equity acquisition 644
    sharing gains 644
    taxes 644
  acquisition of shares 633
    merger or, factors involved in choice 633
  assets
    acquisition of 633
    asset write-ups 640
  avoidance of mistakes 641
  bear hug 648
  big brothers 648
  capital needs, reductions in 640
  complementary resources 639
  conglomerate acquisition 634
  consolidation 632–3
  corporate charter 646
  cost of an acquisition 643–5
  cost reductions 638–9
  countertender offer 649
  crown jewel 648
  defensive tactics 646–50
  diversification 642
  divestitures and restructurings 651–2
  dual-class capitalization 649
  earnings per share (EPS) growth 641–2
  economies of scale 638
  equity carve-out 651
  fair price provision 648
  financial side-effects of acquisitions 641–3
  flip-in provision 647
  G20 Task Force on Climate-Related Financial Disclosures 638
  gains from acquisitions 635–41
  going-private
    leveraged buyouts and 648
    transactions 634
  golden parachute 648
  greenmail 647
  horizontal acquisition 634
  inefficient management, note about 641
  International Accounting Standards Board (IASB) 635
  International Financial Reporting Standards 635
  joint venture 635
  learning objectives 631
  legal forms of acquisition 632–5
  leveraged buyouts (LBOs) 634
    going-private and 648
  lock-up 648
  lower taxes 639–40
  management buy-outs (MBOs) 634
  merger
    alternatives to 634–5
    consolidation or 632–3
  mini case, Rural Wireless Services (RWS) - Nuvola SA merger 657–8
  mistakes, avoidance of 641
  net operating losses 639
  notations 631
  poison pills 647–8
  poison put 648
  problems special to 632
  proxy contest 634
  questions and problems 654–7
  reading suggestions 659
  real world insights
    sustainability and environmental risks in cross-border mergers 637–8
    technology mergers and acquisitions 640
  reductions in capital needs 640
  restructurings, do M&A pay? 650–51
  revenue enhancement 637
    market power 637
    marketing gains 637
    strategic benefits 637
  review of issues 653
  scorched earth strategy 648
  self-test problems 653
  share rights plans 647–8
  shares, acquisition of 633
  shark repellent 648
  spin-off 651
  split-up 651
  spreading overhead 638
  standstill agreement 646–7
  strategic alliance 635
  summary and conclusions 652–3
  supermajority amendment 646
  surplus funds 639–40
  synergy 636–7
    example of 636
    synergistic gains, sharing of 637
  Takeda and Shire, case study on 649–50
    bid intention, announcement of 649
    completion of purchase 650
    rejection of four bids by Shire 649
    revolt from Takeda shareholders 649–50
    share price indices (March 2018 - January 2019) 650
  takeovers
    forms of 634
    note about 634
  targeted repurchase 647
  tender offer 633
  United States, Financial Accounting Standards Board (FASB) 635
  unused debt capacity 639
  valuation of mergers in practice 645–6
    calibration of valuation 645
    merger value 646
    stand-alone firm, valuation of target as 645
    value of synergies 645–6
  vertical acquisition 634
  vertical integration, economies of 639
  white knight 648
  white squires 648
Metallgesellschaft AG 582
Mexico
  currency symbol for 523
  debt to equity, estimated ratio in 442
Micro-enterprises 19
Microsoft 388
Microsoft Excel™ 85
Milking the property, selfish strategy 433
Miller, Merton 421, 424–5, 429
Miller-Orr model
  basic idea 491–2
  implications of 493
  using the model 492–3
Mini cases
  behavioural finance 570
  capital investment decisions 254–5
  capital market history, lessons from 315–16
  corporate governance 40
  cost of capital for Pavegen 380–81
  credit policy for Schwarzwald AG 519
  discounted cash flow (DCF) valuation 123–4
  dividends and payout policy 475–6
  financial leverage, capital structure policy and 450
  financial risk management 593
  financial statement analysis 67–8
  financing expansion with bond issue 157
  international corporate finance 550
  MBA decision 123–4
  mergers and acquisitions 657–8
  net present value and other investment criteria 220–21
  options and corporate finance 629
  project analysis and evaluation 286–7
  raising capital 412
  return, risk and security market line 349–50
  share valuation at Ecorenewable Energy 183–4
  short-term financial planning and management 519
  valuation, time value of money 90
  web information 16
Minuit, Peter (and Manhattan Island purchase) 76
Mistakes, avoidance of 641
M&M Proposition I
  with corporate taxes 425–30
  cost of equity and financial leverage 422–3
  cost of equity and WACC with no taxes 423
  extended Pie Model 437–8
  marketed claims vs non-marketed claims 438–9
  no-tax case 429
  Pie Model 421–2
  tax case 429
  taxes and 426–7
M&M Proposition II
  with corporate taxes 425–30
  cost of equity and WACC with no taxes 423
  no-tax case 429
  tax case 429
  taxes, WACC and 427–8
Models for financial planning
  caveats regarding 689–90
  first look 679–85
Modified internal rate of return (MIRR) 207–9, 212
  combination approach 208
  discounting approach 208
  IRR or, which is better? 208–9
  reinvestment approach 208
Modigliani, Franco 421, 424–6, 429
Monetary policy 12
Money market deposits 485
Monitoring receivables 505
Monte Carlo simulation 640
Moody's 139–40
Mortgage-backed security (MBS) 126
Motorola Mobility 13
Multinationals 521
Multiple cash flows, future and present values of 92–8
Municipal notes 141
Musk, Elon 560
Mutually exclusive investments
  crossover rate, calculation of 205–6
  decisions about 204
  NPV profiles for 205

NASDAQ 11, 303
NB Private Equity Partners 383
Net cash flow 51–2
Net operating losses 639

Net present value and other
  investment criteria 186–222
 average accounting return
  (AAR) 197–8, 212
  advantages and
    disadvantages of 198
  average accounting
    return rule 198
  projected yearly revenue
    and costs for 197
 capital budgeting, practice
  of 210–13
  appraisal techniques, use
    of 210–11
  firms using 211
 capital budgeting
  decision 187
 discounted payback 194–7
  calculation of, example
    of 196
  discounted payback
    period 194–5, 212
  discounted payback
    rule 194
  discounted payback
    rule, advantages and
    disadvantages of 196
  future value of projected
    cash flows 195
  ordinary and discounted
    payback 195
 internal rate of return (IRR)
  198–209, 212
  advantages and
    disadvantages of 207
  calculation of, example
    of 201
  identification of,
    example of 203
  internal rate of return
    rule 199
  investing or financing?
    206–7
  MIRR or, which is better?
    208–9
  modified internal rate
    of return (MIRR)
    207–9, 212
  multiple rates of
    return 202
  example of 203–4
  mutually exclusive
    investments and 204–6
  net present value (NPV)
    and 199–212
  non-conventional cash
    flows and 202
  problems with 202–7
  redeeming qualities of 207
  spreadsheet strategy,
    calculation of IRRs 201
 investment criteria,
  summary of 212
 learning objectives 186
 mini case, Davies Gold
  Mining 220–21
 modified internal rate of
  return (MIRR) 207–9, 212
  combination approach 208
  discounting approach 208

IRR or, which is better?
  208–9
 reinvestment
  approach 208
 mutually exclusive
  investments
  crossover rate,
    calculation of 205–6
  decisions about 204
  NPV profiles for 205
 net present value (NPV)
  187–91, 212
  basic idea 187–8
  estimation of 188–90
  net present value
    profile 200
  net present value rule 189
  net present value rule,
    use of 189–90
  project cash flows 189
  spreadsheet strategy,
    calculation of NPVs 190
 notations 186
 payback rule 191–4
  analysis of 193
  calculation of payback,
    example of 192
  definition of 191–3
  expected cash flows for
    projects 192
  investment projected
    cash flows 193
  payback period 191, 212
  payback period rule
    191–2
  payback period rule,
    advantages and
    disadvantages of 194
  redeeming qualities
    of 193–4
  summary of 194
 profitability index (PI)
  209, 212
  advantages and
    disadvantages of 209
 questions and problems
  216–20
 reading suggestions 221
 review of issues 213–15
 self-test problems 213–15
 strategic asset allocation 187
 summary and
  conclusions 213
 sustainability in finance 191
Net present value (NPV)
 basic idea 187–8
 cost of capital and 354
 estimates of, evaluation of
  258–9
 estimation of 188–90
 foreign investments
  and 521
 net present value
  profile 200
 net present value rule 189
 net present value rule, use
  of 189–90
 project cash flows 189
 spreadsheet strategy,
  calculation of NPVs 190

Net working capital
  (NWC) 226–7
 cash collections and cost,
  example of 232
 cash revenues,
  determination of 231
 closer look at 230–32
 turnover and 55
Netflix 226, 303
Netherlands
 Authority for Financial
  Markets in 10
 average annual returns
  of companies in
  (2011-2020) 296
 bank vs market-based
  financial systems 33
 bills and bonds in, equity
  risk premiums relative to
  (1900-2010) 298
 capital budgeting
  techniques, use in 211
 corporate tax rates in 49
 corporation types in 22
 Corruption Perceptions
  Index (TI 2018) for 32
 Corruption Perceptions
  Index (TI 2019) for 540
 debt to equity, estimated
  ratio in 442
 derivative usage around
  world (% of firms) 589
 equity risk premiums in
  (April 2020) 297
 international business
  angel networks in 386
 risk premiums relative to
  bonds in (1900-2019) 305
 small and medium-sized
  enterprises (SMEs) in 19
 stock market index levels
  (2010-2020) 294
New equity sales and value of
  firm 396–7
New York Stock Exchange
  (NYSE) 597
 NYSE Euronext 11, 143,
  173, 307, 337, 597
 NYSE LIFFE 581–2
New Zealand
 bills and bonds in, equity
  risk premiums relative to
  (1900-2010) 298
 debt to equity, estimated
  ratio in 442
 risk premiums relative to
  bonds in (1900-2019) 305
News and announcements 326
Nigeria, Corruption
  Perceptions Index
  (TI 2019) for 540
Noise trader risk 563
Nokia 174
Nominal interest rates
 bond valuation 145–6, 148
 discounted cash flow
  valuation 106
Non-constant growth, case
  of 165–7
Non-diversifiable risk 331

Non-payment, probability
  of 499
Non-traditional cash offer 390
NoNo bonds 143
Normal distribution,
  usefulness of 302
North Country Manufacturing
  (NCM) 402–3
Norway
 bank vs market-based
  financial systems 33
 bills and bonds in, equity
  risk premiums relative to
  (1900-2010) 298
 corporation types in 22
 Corruption Perceptions
  Index (TI 2018) for 32
 Corruption Perceptions
  Index (TI 2019) for 540
 currency symbol for 523
 debt to equity, estimated
  ratio in 442
 derivative usage around
  world (% of firms) 589
 Economist Big Mac
  index 528
 exchange rate quotations
  (January 2021) 524
 international business
  angel networks in 386
 risk premiums relative to
  bonds in (1900-2019) 305
Not-for-profit sector, goal
  appropriateness 7
Notations
 bond valuation 126
 capital investment
  decisions 223
 capital market history,
  lessons from 289
 cost of capital 353
 discounted cash flow
  valuation 91
 dividends and payout
  policy 452
 equity valuation 159
 financial leverage, capital
  structure policy and 414
 financial statement
  analysis 42
 international corporate
  finance 520
 mergers and acquisitions 631
 net present value and other
  investment criteria 186
 options and corporate
  finance 595
 project analysis and
  evaluation 257
 raising capital 383
 return, risk and security
  market line 317
 short-term financial
  planning and
  management 479
 valuation, time value of
  money 70
Notes 136
Nuvia, acquisition by
  Qualcomm 640

724　Index

Obligation to sell 596
Observed capital structures 441–3
Ocado 303
Odd-lots 469
Offset mortgage 115
Oil buyer, risk profile of 578
Oman
　bank vs market-based financial systems 33
　Corruption Perceptions Index (TI 2018) for 32
　Corruption Perceptions Index (TI 2019) for 540
　Economist Big Mac index 528
　exchange rate quotations (January 2021) 524
OMS Stockholm 30 Index 294
OMX Copenhagen 20 Index 294
OMX (Nord and Baltic markets) 581
Open market purchases of shares 463
Operating activities, cash flow from 50–51
Operating cash flow (OCF)
　alternative definitions of 238–40
　bottom-up approach 239
　calculation of 51
　financial statement analysis 50–51
　International Accounting Standards (IAS) and 51
　sales volume and 272
　sales volume and break-even 270–75
　tax shield approach 239–40
　top-down approach 239
Operating leases 484
Operating leverage 275–7
　basic idea 275
　break-even and 276–7
　capital intensive projects 275
　degree of operating leverage (DOL) 275–6
　example of 276
　implications of 275
　measurement of 275–6
Operating leverage, break-even analysis and 276–7
Opportunity costs 225
Optimal allocation of resources 35
Optimal capital structure 433–7
　capital structure question 436
　cost of capital and 434–5
　financial distress and capital structure 437
　managerial recommendations on capital structure 437
　recap on 435–7
　static theory of capital structure 433–4, 435
　taxes and capital structure 437

Optimal credit policy 501–3
Option applications 613–16, 617–18, 618–22
　capital budgeting and 618–22
　employee share options (ESOs) 614–16
　equity as call option on firm's assets 617–18
Option contracts, hedging with 585–90
　call options 585, 588
　call price 588
　commodity price risk, hedging with options 587
　exchange rate risk, hedging with options 587
　exercise price 585
　expiration date 585
　floor 588
　futures options 587
　interest rate risk, hedging with options 588
　option hedging 586–7
　option pay-off profiles 585–6
　option premiums 585
　option terminology 585
　options vs forwards 585
　put options 585, 588
　strike price 585
Option pay-offs 597–8
Option pricing model 607–9
　basic approach 607
　call option choice, example of 608–9
　closer look 609
　more complicated example 608
Option quotations 597
Option valuation, fundamentals of 602–7
Options 596
　basics on 596–9
　corporate finance and 618–22
　exploration of 678
　short-term financial planning and management 486
Options and corporate finance 595–630
　American option 596
　Black-Scholes option pricing model
　　cautionary note 612–13
　　example of implementation 610–11
　　put option valuation 612
　bounding value of a call 604
　　upper and lower bounds 604, 605
　call at expiration, valuation of 602–3
　call option values, factors determining 604–6
　　exercise price 604
　　expiration date 604

　　risk-free rate 605
　　share price 605–6
　　variability of underlying asset, key factor 606
　calls 596–7
　capital budgeting and 618–22
　　abandonment, option for 621
　　contingency planning 620
　　contraction of operations, option for 621
　　expansion, option for 621
　　implicit options 619
　　investment timing decision 619–20
　　managerial options 620–22
　　options in, example of 621–2
　　real options 618
　　strategic options 622
　　suspension, option for 621
　employee share options (ESOs) 613–16
　　example of 615
　　executive compensation, valuation of 614–16
　　features of 614
　　real world insight, executive compensation and 616
　equity as call option on firm's assets 617–18
　　example of 618
　　risk-free debt and 617
　　risky debt and 617–18
　European option 596
　exercising the option 596
　expiration date 596
　learning objectives 595
　mini case, Exotic Cuisines employee share options 629
　notations 595
　obligation to sell 596
　option applications 613–16, 617–18, 618–22
　　capital budgeting and 618–22
　　employee share options (ESOs) 614–16
　　equity as call option on firm's assets 617–18
　option pay-offs 597–8
　option pricing model 607–9
　　basic approach 607
　　call option choice, example of 608–9
　　closer look 609
　　more complicated example 608
　option quotations 597
　option valuation, fundamentals of 602–7
　options 596
　options, basics on 596–9

　put-call parity (PCP) 599–602
　　alternative strategy 600
　　example of 602
　　exercise price 599
　　PCP condition 601
　　protective puts 599–600
　　real world insight, straddle payoff 600–601
　　strike price 599
　puts 596–7
　questions and problems 625–9
　reading suggestions 630
　restricted stock units (RSUs) 595
　review of issues 623–4
　self-test problems 623–4
　spreadsheet strategy 613
　strike price 596
　summary and conclusions 622–3
Options contracts 585
Options in capital budgeting, example of 621–2
Ordinary equity features 172
Ordinary shares, features of 172–3
Organizational chart, corporate finance 4
Over-optimism bias 554
Over-reaction 308
Over-the-counter (OTC) markets 11
Overconfidence bias 553
Overvalued securities 337–8
Ownership structure, corporate governance 34

Page, Larry 13, 28
Pakistan
　bank loans as % of external financing 405
　debt to equity, estimated ratio in 442
Partnerships 20
Pay mix targets (CEOs, 2018) 26
Payables turnover 55
Payback rule 191–4
　analysis of 193
　calculation of payback, example of 192
　definition of 191–3
　expected cash flows for projects 192
　investment projected cash flows 193
　payback period 191, 212
　payback period rule 191–2
　payback period rule, advantages and disadvantages of 194
　redeeming qualities of 193–4
　summary of 194
Paying dividends, pros and cons of 467

Index

Payoffs to shareholders, debt plus dividend 416
Peakon, acquisition by Workday 640
Pecking-order theory 440–41
  implications of pecking-order 441
  internal finance, pecking-order and 440–41
Peer-to-peer trading platforms 11
Pelaton 383
People, objectives concerning 8–9
Percentage of sales approach 680–81
Periods, finding number of 84–6
Perpetuities 103–4
Peru, debt to equity, estimated ratio in 442
Philippines, debt to equity, estimated ratio in 442
Philips 223
Planet, objectives concerning 8–9
Planned expenditures 482
Planning fallacy 555
Plowback ratio 681
Poison pills 647–8
Poison put 648
Poland
  bank loans as % of external financing 405
  bank vs market-based financial systems 33
  capital budgeting techniques, use in 211
  derivative usage around world (% of firms) 589
  international business angel networks in 386
  small and medium-sized enterprises (SMEs) in 19
Political risk 539–41
Portfolios 322–5
  diversification of 329
  expected returns on 322–3
    example of 323
  portfolio betas 333
    example of 333
  portfolio variance 323–5
    standard deviation and, example of 324–5
  portfolio weights 322
Portugal
  corporation types in 22
  debt to equity, estimated ratio in 442
  international business angel networks in 386
  small and medium-sized enterprises (SMEs) in 19
Possible expenditures 482
Pounds for Euros exchange, example of 526
Poverty Alleviation International Inc 177
Practice of capital budgeting 210–13
Practice of financial risk management 588–90

Precautionary motives 480
Preference shares
  are preference shares debt? 173
  cost of 360
    example of 360
  cumulative dividends 172
  example of 104
  features of 172–3
  Financial Instruments: Presentation (IAS) 173
  International Accounting Standards (IAS) 173
  non-cumulative dividends 172
  stated value 172
Preliminary concerns, cost of capital 354–5
Premium, selling at 526
Premium bonds 129
Present value (PV)
  for annuity cash flows 98–102
  calculations of 95–6
  inflation and 147
  with multiple cash flows 94–7
  present vs future value 81
  time value of money and 77–8
Price behaviour around ex-dividend date 455
Price-earnings (P/E) ratio
  equity valuation and 171
  financial statement analysis and 57
Price of bond at future date, estimation of 700–701
Price-sales ratio 57
Primary vs secondary markets 10–11
Prime Robotics Ltd 463
Priorities and goals, thinking about 678
Private equity firms 384–5
Private equity fundraisers 384–5
Private new security issues 390
Private placements 404
  privately placed debt 136
Privileged subscription 390, 398
Pro forma financial statements 228–9
  financial planning and 679–80, 683, 684
  project cash flows and 227–30
Problems of capital budgeting, solution to 365
Problems special to mergers and acquisitions 632
Process of bankruptcy 443–5
Process of raising capital 389
Procter & Gamble 160, 169–70
Profit, objectives concerning 8–9
Profit margin 56
  growth and 689
Profit maximization, goal of 6
Profitability index (PI) 209, 212

advantages and disadvantages of 209
Profitability measures 56
Profitability ratios 58
Project analysis and evaluation 257–87
  accounting break-even
    calculation of break-even level 271
    cash break-even 273
    cash flow and 271
    cash flow and, base case 271
    financial break-even 273–4
    payback and break-even 271
    revisit to 273
    uses for 270
  break-even analysis 265–70
    accounting break-even 269–74
    accounting break-even, uses for 270
    average cost vs marginal cost, example of 268
    cash flow, accounting and financial break-even points 272–4
    contribution margin per unit 269
    fixed costs 267
    incremental cost 267
    incremental revenue 268
    marginal cost 267
    marginal revenue 268
    operating leverage and 276–7
    total costs 267–8
    total costs, output level and 268
    variable costs 266–7
    variable costs, example of 267
    variable costs, output level and 266
  break-even measures, summary of 274
  capital rationing 277–8
    hard rationing 278
    soft rationing 277–8
  Easy Jet Plc
    best and worst case scenarios 265
    external competition 264
    fuel price 264–5
    macroeconomic environment 264
    sensitivity analysis 264
  evaluation of NPV estimates
    basic problem 258
    estimation risk 258–9
    forecasting risk 258–9
    projected vs actual cash flows 258
    sources of value 259
  learning objectives 257
  mini case, White Mountain Thyme Whisky Ltd 286–7

notations 257
NPV estimates, evaluation of 258–9
operating cash flow (OCF)
  sales volume and 272
  sales volume and break-even 270–75
operating leverage 275–7
  basic idea 275
  break-even and 276–7
  capital intensive projects 275
  degree of operating leverage (DOL) 275–6
  example of 276
  implications of 275
  measurement of 275–6
questions and problems 281–6
reading suggestions 287
review of issues 279–80
sales volume, operating cash flow and 272
scenario and other what-if analyses 259–65
  best case 261
  case study, EasyJet Plc 263–5
  getting started 259–60
  'paralysis of analysis' 261
  real world insight, internet of things 262
  scenario analysis 260–62
  sensitivity analysis 262–3
  sensitivity analysis for unit sales 263
  simulation analysis 265
  worst case 261
self-test problems 279–80
summary and conclusions 279
sustainability in finance 278
what-if analyses 259–65
Project cash flows 224, 229, 230–38
  pro forma financial statements and 227–30
  project net working capital and capital spending 229
  project operating cash flow 229
Projected capital requirements, example of 228
Projected growth rates, importance of 684–5
Projected income statement, example of 228
Projected risk premium 319
Projected total cash flows
  example of 230
  value and 229–30
Property, plant and equipment (PPE) turnover 55
Property Bubble (2006-present) 566
Proportionate ownership, dilution of 402
Proxy contests 634
Proxy voting 28

Public-issue bonds 136
Public limited companies (Plcs) 21
Public traditional negotiated cash offer 390
Purchasing power parity (PPP) 527–30
Pure discount bonds 142, 148
Pure discount loans 110–11
Put bonds 143
Put-call parity (PCP) 599–602
  alternative strategy 600
  example of 602
  exercise price 599
  PCP condition 601
  protective puts 599–600
  real world insight, straddle payoff 600–601
  strike price 599
Puts 596–7

Qualcomm, acquisition of Nuvia 640
Questions and problems
  behavioural finance 568–9
  bond valuation 153–7
  capital investment decisions 249–54
  capital market history, lessons from 312–14
  corporate finance 15–16
  corporate governance 39–49
  cost of capital 376–80
  discounted cash flow valuation 118–23
  dividends and payout policy 472–5
  equity valuation 180–83
  financial leverage, capital structure policy and 447–9
  financial planning 693–5
  financial risk management 591–2
  financial statement analysis 64–7
  international corporate finance 547–50
  mergers and acquisitions 654–7
  net present value and other investment criteria 216–20
  options and corporate finance 625–9
  project analysis and evaluation 281–6
  raising capital 410–12
  return, risk and security market line 346–9
  short-term financial planning and management 516–18
  valuation, time value of money 88–90
Quick (acid-test) ratio 53

Raising capital 383–413
  alternative issue methods 389–90

bank loans 405–6
  line of credit 406
  loan commitment 406
  non-revolving loan commitment 406
  as percentage of external financing 405
  revolver 406
  types of 406
book value vs market value, dilution and 402–4
business angel networks 386
buyout financing 387
costs of issuing securities 397–8
dilution 402–4
  correct arguments 403–4
  misconception on (market-to-book ratio less than 1) 403
  new issues and 402–3
early-stage financing and venture capital 384–8
Europe, private equity investments into 387
financial flows as % of GDP 405
financing life cycle of a firm 384–8
financing stages 387
general cash offer 389
growth capital 387
initial public offerings (IPOs) 389
  underpricing and 393–6
  average first-day sales for IPOs (1980-2019) 395
  determinants of underpricing 395
  initial IPO returns, equal weighted averages for 393–4
  underpricing, reasons for existence of 394–6
  'winner's curse' 396
International Financial Reporting Standards (IFRS) 408
later stage capital 387
learning objectives 383
lease financing 406–9
  accounting for leases 408–9
  buying vs leasing 407
  financial leases 407–8
  leveraged leases 408
  operating leases 407
  sale and leaseback 408
long-term debt issuing 404
mini case, financing expansion with bond issue 412
new equity sales and value of firm 396–7
non-traditional cash offer 390
notations 383
private equity firms 384–5
private equity fundraisers 384–5

private new security issue 390
private placements 404
privileged subscription 390, 398
process of 389
proportionate ownership, dilution of 402
public traditional negotiated cash offer 390
questions and problems 410–12
reading suggestions 412–13
replacement capital 387
review of issues 409
rights 398–402
  Babcock International, value to individual shareholder of rights in 400
  effect of rights offer on share price 399–400
  effects on shareholders 400–401
  mechanics of rights issues 398–401
  number of rights needed to purchase a share 399
  oversubscription privilege 401
  real world insight, Aveva Group rights issue 401
  standby fee 401
  standby underwriting 401
  subscription price 398–9
  underwriting arrangements 401
rights issue (or offering) 389, 398
seasoned equity offering (SEO) 389
  debt usage and 397
  issue costs and 397
  managerial information and 396
securities, methods of offering new securities 390
seed money 387
self-test problems 409
selling securities to public, basic procedure 388–9
selling stock to public, costs of 397–8
  abnormal returns 397
  direct expenses 397
  Green Shoe option 397
  gross spread 397
  indirect expenses 397
  underpricing 397
share warrants 398
summary and conclusions 409
sustainability in finance 388
term loans 404
underwriters 390–93
  aftermarket 392
  best efforts underwriting 391
  choice of 391

Dutch auction underwriting 391–2
firm commitment underwriting 391
Green Shoe provision 392
gross spread 391
lock-up agreements 392–3
quiet period 393
syndicates 391
types of 391–2
uniform price auction underwriting 391–2
value, dilution of 402–4
venture capital (VC) 384
  funding by sector, breakdown of 385
  realities 387–8
  suppliers of 385–6
Randomness and representativeness 559
Fooled by Randomness (Taleb, N.) 554–5
Rate of return 82
Ratio analysis 52–9
Rationality, independent deviations from 562
Reading suggestions
  behavioural finance 570
  bond valuation 157
  capital investment decisions 255
  capital market history, lessons from 316
  corporate finance 16–17
  corporate governance 41
  cost of capital 381
  discounted cash flow valuation 124
  dividends and payout policy 476–7
  equity valuation 184
  financial leverage, capital structure policy and 451
  financial risk management 593
  financial statement analysis 68
  international corporate finance 550–51
  mergers and acquisitions 659
  net present value and other investment criteria 221
  options and corporate finance 630
  project analysis and evaluation 287
  raising capital 412–13
  return, risk and security market line 350–51
  short-term financial planning and management 519
  valuation, time value of money 90
Real Madrid 97
Real options in capital budgeting 618

Index

Real vs nominal interest rates 145–6
Real world cases
  financial distress costs 432
  Lehman Brothers bankruptcy 431
Real world insights
  asset classes 329
  Aveva Group rights issue 401
  borrowing costs 109
  capital asset pricing model (CAPM) 340–41
  capital structure, M&M 30 years later 424–5
  controlling shareholders 30
  corporate valuation 98
  cost-cutting proposals 242
  cryptocurrencies, futures contracts in 580
  dividends in practice, importance of 457
  equity and bond valuation 160
  Europe, risks facing companies in 539
  executive compensation and 616
  Hersh Shefrin on behavioural finance 567
  internet of things 262
  inventory control in oil and gas 513
  investment appraisal 225–6
  market movements, driving forces 303
  market multiples valuation 178
  mortgage choices 115
  negative and positive (gearing) covenants 139
  over-confidence and pride 560
  Pandemic Emergency Financing Bonds 143
  primary vs secondary markets 11
  recessions and crises, repurchasing activity during 464
  return on equity for AstraZenica 60
  shareholder activism 25
  'spoofing' prices in stock markets 298–9
  straddle payoff 600–601
  sustainability and environmental risks in cross-border mergers 637–8
  sustainability in finance 62
  susteinability and risk management 587
  susuk bond issue by First Abu Dhabi Bank (FAB) 545
  technology mergers and acquisitions 640
  trade credit 494
  Transparency International Corruption Perceptions Index 540–41
  valuation of bonds 84
  valuation of companies 71
  weighted average cost of capital (WACC) 370–71
Receivables
  investment in 495
  monitoring of 505
  receivables period 495
  receivables turnover 54–5
Recency bias 560
Redeemable bonds 127
Reductions in capital needs 640
Regular cash dividend 453
Reinvesting interest 72
Related party transactions 29
Relative purchasing power parity (PPP) 529–30
  appreciation of currency 530
  basic idea 528
  depreciation of currency 530
  inflation and exchange, example of 530
  result 528–30
Relevant cash flows 224
Renault 19
  beta coefficient for 332
Reorganization, bankruptcy and 443
Replacement capital 387
Representativeness heuristic 559
Repsol 371
Repurchase
  cash dividends vs 463–4
  real world considerations in 464
  repurchase agreements (Repo) 485–6
  repurchase price, example of calculation of 486
  of shares 462
Required return 354
  components of 169–70
Resolution of real-world factors? 460–62
Restricted stock units (RSUs) 595
Restructurings
  do M&As pay? 650–51
  financial leverage and 415
Retention ratio 681
Retirement, example of saving for 84
Return, risk and security market line 317–51
  announcements news and 326
  surprises, expected returns and 325–6
  annual portfolio returns, standard deviations of 328
  asset-specific risks 327, 331
  beta (ß) and risk premium 334–7
  beta (ß) coefficient 331–2
  buy low, sell high example 337–8
  calculation of variance 320–21
  capital asset pricing model (CAPM) 338–9, 340
    criticisms of 341
    empirical tests of 341
  diversifiable risk 330–31
  diversification
    effect of 340
    market history and effect of 328–9
    portfolio risk and 328–31
    principle of 329–30
    systematic risk and 330–31
    unsystematic risk and 330
  economy, equity returns and states of 318–19
  expected and unexpected returns 325
  expected returns 318–20
    announcements, surprises and 325–6
    calculation of 319, 320
    systematic risk and 337
    variances and 318–22
  expected risk premium 319
  innovation or surprise 326
  learning objectives 317
  market portfolios, security market line (SLM) and 338
  market risk premium 338
  market risks 327, 331
  mini case, Beta for Ørsted A/S 349–50
  news and announcements 326
  non-diversifiable risk 331
  notations 317
  overvalued securities 337–8
  portfolio betas 333
    example of 333
  portfolio diversification 329
  portfolio expected returns 322–3
    example of 323
  portfolio variance 323–5
    standard deviation and, example of 324–5
  portfolio weights 322
  portfolios 322–5
  projected risk premium 319
  questions and problems 346–9
  reading suggestions 350–51
  real world insights
    asset classes 329
    capital asset pricing model (CAPM) 340–41
  returns, systematic and unsystematic components of 327–8
  review of issues 343–5
  reward-to-risk ratio 334–7
    basic argument 335–6
    fundamental result 336–7
  risk, systematic and unsystematic 327–8
  risk and return
    example of 340
    summary of 339–40
  risk premium 318
  risk-to-reward ratio 340
  security market line (SML) 318, 334–42
    cost of capital and 342
    basic idea 342
    cost of capital 342
  self-test problems 343–5
  share price volatility 317
  standard deviations of annual portfolio returns 328
  states of economy, equity returns and 318–19
  summary and conclusions 343
  surprise, innovation or 326
  systematic and unsystematic components of return 327–8
  risks 327, 339
  systematic risk
    beta and 331–3
    expected returns and 337
    measurement of 331–2
    principle of 331
    principle of, beta and 340
  total return 339
  total risk 339
  total risk vs beta, example of 332
  unequal probabilities, examples of 319–20, 321
  unique risks 327, 331
  unsystematic risk 330–31
  variance, calculation of 320–21
Return on assets (ROA) 56
Return on book assets (or equity) 56
Return on capital employed (ROCE) 56
Return on equity (ROE) 56
  closer look at 59–60
Return on investment (ROI) 56
return on your investment 290
Returns
  arithmetic or geometric average return 306
  capital market history, lessons from 290–94
  example of calculation of 293
  expected and unexpected returns 325
Revenue effects 499
Reviews of issues
  behavioural finance 568
  bond valuation 152–3
  capital investment decisions 246–9
  capital market history, lessons from 310–11
  corporate finance 14–15

728 Index

Reviews of issues—*Cont.*
  corporate governance 38–9
  discounted cash flow
      valuation 116–18
  dividends and payout
      policy 471
  equity valuation 178–80
  financial leverage, capital
      structure policy and 446
  financial planning 690–93
  financial risk
      management 590–91
  financial statement
      analysis 63–4
  international corporate
      finance 546–7
  mergers and
      acquisitions 653
  net present value and
      other investment
      criteria 213–15
  options and corporate
      finance 623–4
  project analysis and
      evaluation 279–80
  raising capital 409
  return, risk and security
      market line 343–5
  short-term financial
      planning and
      management 514–15
  valuation, time value of
      money 87
Reward-to-risk ratio 334–7
  basic argument 335–6
  fundamental result 336–7
Rights 398–402
  Babcock International, value
      to individual shareholder
      of rights in 400
  effect of rights offer on
      share price 399–400
  effects on shareholders
      400–401
  mechanics of rights
      issues 398–401
  number of rights needed to
      purchase a share 399
  oversubscription
      privilege 401
  real world insight, Aveva
      Group rights issue 401
  standby fee 401
  standby underwriting 401
  subscription price 398–9
  underwriting
      arrangements 401
Rights issue (or offering)
    389, 398
Risk
  exposure reduction 575
  management of 482
  and return
      example of 340
      summary of 339–40
  risk-free returns 297
  risk premium 297–8, 318
  risk profile 574
  risk taking in excess,
      selfish strategy 432

risk-to-reward ratio 340
systematic and
    unsystematic risk 327–8
Roaring Twenties (1920-29) 566
Roche Group 261
Rolls-Royce 330
Romania
  bank loans as % of external
      financing 405
  small and medium-sized
      enterprises (SMEs) in 19
Ronaldo, Christiano 97–8
Round lots 469
Royal Dutch Shell Plc 21,
    159, 371
  price ratio 563–5
Russia
  bank vs market-based
      financial systems 33
  corporation types in 22
  Corruption Perceptions
      Index (TI 2018) for 32
  Corruption Perceptions
      Index (TI 2019) for 540
  Economist Big Mac index 528
  international business
      angel networks in 386

Sales maximization, goal of 6
Sales volume, operating cash
    flow and 272
SAP
  acquisition of Signavio 640
  beta coefficient for 332
Saudi Arabia
  bank vs market-based
      financial systems 33
  Corruption Perceptions
      Index (TI 2018) for 32
  Corruption Perceptions
      Index (TI 2019) for 540
  currency symbol for 523
  Economist Big Mac
      index 528
  exchange rate quotations
      (January 2021) 524
Saudi Aramco 383
Saving, future value
    calculation, example of 94
Saving for purchases,
    example of calculation of
    time required 85
Saving for university,
    example of 83
Saving up, example of 78
Scenario and other what-if
    analyses 259–65
  best case 261
  case study, EasyJet
      Plc 263–5
  getting started 259–60
  'paralysis of analysis' 261
  real world insight, internet
      of things 262
  scenario analysis 260–62
  sensitivity analysis 262–3
  sensitivity analysis for unit
      sales 263
  simulation analysis 265
  worst case 261

Scorched earth strategy 648
Scotland, bankruptcy laws in
    444–5
Seasonal activities 482
Seasonal cash demands 482
Seasoned equity offering
    (SEO) 389
  debt usage and 397
  issue costs and 397
  managerial information
      and 396
Secondary markets 10
Secured Overnight Financing
    Rate (SOFR) 360
  international finance
      and 522
Securities
  debt or equity? 134–5
  methods of offering new
      securities 390
Security market line (SML)
    334–42
  basic idea 342
  cost of capital and 342
  return, risk and 318,
      338–9, 340
Seed money 387
Self-attribution bias 554–5
Self-control by
    investors 461
Self-test problems
  behavioural finance 568
  bond valuation 152–3
  capital investment
      decisions 246–9
  capital market history,
      lessons from 310–11
  corporate finance 14–15
  corporate governance 38–9
  discounted cash flow
      valuation 116–18
  dividends and payout
      policy 471
  equity valuation 178–80
  financial leverage, capital
      structure policy and 446
  financial planning 690–93
  financial risk management
      590–91
  financial statement
      analysis 63–4
  international corporate
      finance 546–7
  mergers and
      acquisitions 653
  net present value and
      other investment criteria
      213–15
  options and corporate
      finance 623–4
  project analysis and
      evaluation 279–80
  raising capital 409
  return, risk and security
      market line 343–5
  short-term financial
      planning and
      management 514–15
  valuation, time value of
      money 87

Selfish strategies, summary
    of 433
Selling securities to public,
    basic procedure 388–9
Selling stock to public,
    costs of 397–8
  abnormal returns 397
  direct expenses 397
  Green Shoe option 397
  gross spread 397
  indirect expenses 397
  underpricing 397
Semi-annual coupons,
    example of 130
Semi-strong-form efficient
    markets 309
Share acquisition 633
Share classes 28
Share price volatility 317
Share repurchases 462
  as alternative to cash
      dividends 462–5
  earnings per share and 465
Share rights plans 647–8
Share valuation 160–72
Share warrants 398
Shareholder rights 27
  general rights 28–9
  pre-emptive right 29
Shareholders
  debt plus dividend
      payoffs to 416
  interests of, managers'
      acting in 25–9
  payoffs to shareholders,
      debt plus dividend 416
Shark repellent 648
Shefrin, Hersh 567
Short-run exposure
    hedging 576
Short-term capital,
    management of 481–5
Short-term debt 136
Short-term financial planning
    and management 479–519
  advisory services 482
  ageing schedule,
      monitoring receivables
      and 505
  average collection period 495
  bank overdrafts 483
      short-term loans vs 484
  banker's acceptances 486
  barter exchanges 494
  Baumol-Allais-Tobin
      (BAT) model
      example of
          (Vulcan SA) 491
      implications of 493
      opportunity costs 489
      optimal balance 490–91
      total cost 490
      trading costs 489–90
  business failure and failure
      in 479–80
  cash discounts 499
  cash holding, reasons
      for 480–81
  cash management vs
      liquidity management 481

Index 729

certificates of deposit (CD) 485
collection effort 505
collection policy 505
commercial paper 486
compensating balances 481
cost effects 499
cost of debt 499
costs of holding cash 481
credit analysis 503–4
    credit, granting of 503–4
    one-time sale 503–4
    repeat business 504
credit and receivables 494–5
credit management 481
credit policy
    analysis of 499–501
    break-even application 501
    collection policy 495
    components of 494–5
    credit analysis 495
    credit policy effects 499
    evaluation of a proposal for 499–501
    switching policies, net present value (NPV) of 499–500
    terms of sale 494–5
cyclical activities 482
days' sales in receivables 495
debt, cost of 499
derivative instruments 486
discount instruments 486
financial leases 484
forwards 486
futures 486
granting credit, costs of 502
holding cash, costs of 481
interest-breaking instruments 485
inventory management 481, 506
    ABC approach to 507
    ABC inventory analysis 507
    carrying costs 506, 508
    carrying costs, example of 510
    derived-demand inventories, management of 511–13
    economic order quantity (EOQ) model 507–11
    extensions to 511
    financial manager and 505
    finished goods 506
    holding inventory, costs of 508
    inventory costs 505
    inventory depletion 508
    inventory policy, financial manager and 505
    inventory types 505
    just-in-time (JIT) inventory 511–13
    kanban systems 513
    keiretsu groups 513
    materials requirements planning (MRP) 511
    raw materials 506
    real world insight, inventory control in oil and gas 513
    reorder points 511, 512
    restocking costs, example of 510
    restocking quantity 508
    safety stocks 511, 512
    shortage costs 506, 509
    techniques for 507–13
    total costs 509
investing idle cash 485–6
investment in receivables 495
learning objectives 479
liquidity management 481
    cash management vs 481
Miller-Orr model
    basic idea 491–2
    implications of 493
    using the model 492–3
mini case, credit policy for Schwarzwald AG 519
money market deposits 485
monitoring receivables 505
non-payment, probability of 499
notations 479
operating leases 484
optimal credit policy 501–3
options 486
planned expenditures 482
possible expenditures 482
precautionary motives 480
questions and problems 516–18
reading suggestions 519
real world insight, trade credit 494
receivables
    investment in 495
    monitoring of 505
receivables period 495
repurchase agreements (Repo) 485–6
    repurchase price, example of calculation of 486
revenue effects 499
review of issues 514–15
risk management 482
seasonal activities 482
seasonal cash demands 482
self-test problems 514–15
short-term capital, management of 481–5
short-term finance, sources of 483
short-term leases 483–4
short-term loans 483
    bank overdrafts vs 484
speculative motives 480
summary and conclusions 513–14
target cash balance 487–94
    adjustment costs 487
    basic idea 487–8
    Baumol-Allais-Tobin (BAT) model 488–91, 493
    borrowing and 493–4
    determination of 487–94
    holding cash, opportunity costs of 494
    influences on 493–4
    Miller-Orr model 491–3
    trading costs and 494
temporary cash surpluses 482
terms of the sale 495–9
    account size, credit period and 497
    banker's acceptance 498
    basic form 495–6
    cash discounts 497–8
    cash discounts and average collection period (ACP) 498
    collateral value 497
    commercial drafts 498
    competition, credit period and 497
    consumer demand 497
    consumer type, credit period and 497
    cost, credit period and 497
    cost of credit, cash discounts and 497–8
    credit instruments 498
    credit period 496–7
    credit risk 497
    end of month (EOM) 496
    invoice date 496
    length of credit period 496–7
    middle of month (MOM) 496
    open accounts 498
    perishability, credit period and 497
    profitability, credit period and 497
    promissory notes 498
    receipt of goods (ROG) 496
    standardization 497
    time drafts 498
    trade acceptance 498
    trade discounts 498
total credit cost curve 501–3
trade credit 494
transaction motive 480
Treasury bills 486
Short-term solvency (or liquidity) measures 52–3
Side effects, investment decisions and 226
Siemens, beta coefficient for 332, 333
Signalling 439–40
Signavio, acquisition by SAP 640
Simple interest 72, 74
Singapore
    bank loans as % of external financing 405
    capital budgeting techniques, use in 211
    Corruption Perceptions Index (TI 2018) for 32
    Corruption Perceptions Index (TI 2019) for 540
    currency symbol for 523
    debt to equity, estimated ratio in 442
    derivative usage around world (% of firms) 589
    Economist Big Mac index 528
    exchange rate quotations (January 2021) 524
    underpricing of IPOs in, determinants of 395
Single-tier boards 21
SIX Swiss Exchange 11
Slack 383
Slovakia, small and medium-sized enterprises (SMEs) in 19
Slovenia, small and medium-sized enterprises (SMEs) in 19
Small numbers, law of 560
Societal improvement, goal of 6
Sole traders 19–20
Somalia
    Corruption Perceptions Index (TI 2018) for 32
    Corruption Perceptions Index (TI 2019) for 540
Sony Playstation 243
South Africa
    bank vs market-based financial systems 33
    bankruptcy laws in 445
    bills and bonds in, equity risk premiums relative to (1900-2010) 298
    capital budgeting techniques, use in 211
    corporation types in 22
    Corruption Perceptions Index (TI 2018) for 32
    Corruption Perceptions Index (TI 2019) for 540
    currency symbol for 523
    debt to equity, estimated ratio in 442
    derivative usage around world (% of firms) 589
    Economist Big Mac index 528
    exchange rate quotations (January 2021) 524
    risk premiums relative to bonds in (1900-2019) 305
South-East Asian Bubble (1997) 566
South Sea Bubble (1720) 566
South Sudan
    Corruption Perceptions Index (TI 2018) for 32
    Corruption Perceptions Index (TI 2019) for 540
Spain
    bank loans as % of external financing 405

Spain—*Cont.*
  bank vs market-based financial systems 33
  bills and bonds in, equity risk premiums relative to (1900-2010) 298
  BME Spanish Exchanges 11
  corporation types in 22
  Corruption Perceptions Index (TI 2018) for 32
  Corruption Perceptions Index (TI 2019) for 540
  debt to equity, estimated ratio in 442
  derivative usage around world (% of firms) 589
  international business angel networks in 386
  risk premiums relative to bonds in (1900-2019) 305
  small and medium-sized enterprises (SMEs) in 19
Special dividend 453
Speculative motives 480
Spin-off 651
Split-up 651
Spot exchange rates 526
  spot rates and yields to maturity 696
  yields to maturity and, example of difference between 697
Spot trade, corporate finance and 526
Spreading overhead 638
Spreadsheet strategies
  annuity payments 101
  annuity present values 100
  bond prices and yields, calculation of 133–4
  calculation of present values with multiple future cash flows 97
  loan amortization 114
  options and corporate finance 613
  time value of money calculations 85
SSE Composite Index 294
Stakeholders 30–31
Stand-alone principle 224
Standard & Poor's (S&P) 139–40
  BSE Sensex Index 294
  S&P 500 303
Standard deviation 299, 300
  of annual portfolio returns 328
  calculation of 300–301
Standard method of cash dividend payout 453–4
Standstill agreement 646–7
Statement of cash flows 50–52
Statement of financial position 43–7
  assets (left side) 43
  balance sheet identity 44
  bonds and bondholders 43
  book value 46–7
  building, example of 44–5

current assets 43
current liabilities 43–4
fair value amount 46
fixed assets 45
historical cost model 46
intangible assets 43
International Accounting Standards (IAS) and 46
Leonardo SpA (2018) 45
liabilities (right side) 43–4
long-tern debt 45
market value 46
market value vs book value 46–7
net working capital 44–5
non-current assets 43
non-current liabilities 43–4
ordinary equity 43–4
owners' equity 44
owners' equity (right side) 43–4
revaluation model 46
shareholders' equity 43–4
tangible assets 43
States of economy, equity returns and 318–19
Sterling Overnight Index Average (SONIA) 360
  international corporate finance and 522
Stewardship theory 35
Stock dividends, large and small 469
Stock dividends and stock splits 468–70
  benchmark case 469
  details about 469
  reverse splits 470
  trading range 469–70
  value of 469–70
Stock markets 173–4
  ask prices 173
  bid prices 173
  brokers 173–4
  dealers 173–4
  index levels (2010-20) 294
  primary market 173
  secondary market 173
  stock market reporting 174
Stock splits 469–70
Stockholm Stock Exchange 463
Straight voting, effect of 27
Strategic alliances 635
Strategic asset allocation 187
Strategic options in capital budgeting 622
Strike price 596
Strong-form efficient markets 309
Subnormal growth, example of 167
Summaries, conclusions and behavioural finance 567
  bond valuation 152
  capital investment decisions 246
  capital market history, lessons from 310
  corporate finance 14
  corporate governance 37–8

discounted cash flow valuation 115
dividends and payout policy 470–71
equity valuation 178
financial leverage, capital structure policy and 445
financial planning 690
financial risk management 590
financial statement analysis 62
international corporate finance 545–6
mergers and acquisitions 652–3
net present value and other investment criteria 213
options and corporate finance 622–3
project analysis and evaluation 279
raising capital 409
return, risk and security market line 343
short-term financial planning and management 513–14
valuation, time value of money 86
Sunk costs 225
Suntory, acquisition of Beam Inc 646
Supermajority amendment 646
Surplus funds 639–40
Surprises
  avoidance of 678
  innovation or 326
Survival, goal of 6
Suspension, option for 621
Sustainability in finance
  corporate finance 8–9
  corporate governance 23
  net present value and other investment criteria 191
  project analysis and evaluation 278
  raising capital 388
Sustainable growth rate, financial planning and 688
Swap contracts, hedging with 582–5
  commodity swaps 583
  currency swaps 583
  interest rate swaps 583
  interest rate swaps, example of 584
  matched (balanced) books 584
  swap books 584
  swap dealers 583–4
Swaps in international corporate finance 522
Sweden
  average annual returns of companies in (2011-2020) 296

bank loans as % of external financing 405
bank Vs market-based financial systems 33
bills and bonds in, equity risk premiums relative to (1900-2010) 298
capital budgeting techniques, use in 211
Corruption Perceptions Index (TI 2018) for 32
Corruption Perceptions Index (TI 2019) for 540
currency symbol for 523
debt to equity, estimated ratio in 442
derivative usage around world (% of firms) 589
Economist Big Mac index 528
exchange rate quotations (January 2021) 524
international business angel networks in 386
risk premiums relative to bonds in (1900-2019) 305
small and medium-sized enterprises (SMEs) in 19
stock market index levels (2010-2020) 294
Switzerland
  bank vs market-based financial systems 33
  bills and bonds in, equity risk premiums relative to (1900-2010) 298
  Corruption Perceptions Index (TI 2018) for 32
  Corruption Perceptions Index (TI 2019) for 540
  currency symbol for 523
  debt to equity, estimated ratio in 442
  derivative usage around world (% of firms) 589
  Economist Big Mac index 528
  exchange rate quotations (January 2021) 524
  international business angel networks in 386
  risk premiums relative to bonds in (1900-2019) 305
Synergy 636–7
  example of 636
  synergistic gains, sharing of 637
Syngenta Finance AG 70
Syria
  Corruption Perceptions Index (TI 2018) for 32
  Corruption Perceptions Index (TI 2019) for 540
Systematic and unsystematic components of return 327–8
Systematic and unsystematic risks 327
  security market line and 339
Systematic risk

Index

beta and 331–3
expected returns and 337
measurement of 331–2
principle of 331
principle of, beta and 340

Taiwan, debt to equity,
    estimated ratio in 442
Takeda and Shire, case study
    on 649–50
  bid intention,
    announcement of 649
  completion of purchase 650
  rejection of four bids by
    Shire 649
  revolt from Takeda
    shareholders 649–50
  share price indices (March
    2018 - January 2019) 650
Takeovers
  forms of 634
  note about 634
Taleb, Nassim 554–5
Target cash balance 487–94
  adjustment costs 487
  basic idea 487–8
  Baumol-Allais-Tobin (BAT)
    model 488–91, 493
  borrowing and 493–4
  determination of 487–94
  holding cash, opportunity
    costs of 494
  influences on 493–4
  Miller-Orr model 491–3
  trading costs and 494
Targeted repurchase
  dividends and payout
    policy 463
  mergers and
    acquisitions 647
Tax and other benefits from
    higher dividends 459
  tax-exempt investors 459
Taxes
  acquisition costs and 644
  after-tax cash flow 227
  average vs marginal tax
    rates 49–50
  capital structure and 437
  corporate tax rates 49
  depreciation tax shield 240
  dividends and payout
    policy 458
  double taxation 21
  earnings before interest,
    taxes, depreciation and
    amortization
    (EBITDA) 54
  earnings before interest
    and taxes (EBIT) 54
  effective tax rate 458
  financial statement
    analysis 48–50
  flat rate tax 50
  interest tax shield 426
  lower taxes 639–40
  marginal tax rates 49–50
  M&M Proposition I
    with corporate
      taxes 425–30

cost of equity and WACC
    with no taxes 423
  no-tax case 429
  tax case 429
  taxes and 426–7
M&M Proposition II
  with corporate taxes
    425–30
  cost of equity and WACC
    with no taxes 423
  no-tax case 429
  tax case 429
  taxes, WACC and 427–8
tax and other benefits from
    higher dividends 459
  tax-exempt investors 459
  taxability premium 151
Technical insolvency 443
Telefonica, beta coefficient
    for 332
Temporary cash surpluses 482
Tender offers 633
  dividends and payout
    policy 463
Term loans 404
Term structure
  explanations of 698–701
  graphing of 697–8
Terminology in international
    corporate finance 521–2
Terms of the sale 495–9
  account size, credit period
    and 497
  banker's acceptance 498
  basic form 495–6
  cash discounts 497–8
  cash discounts and average
    collection period (ACP)
    498
  collateral value 497
  commercial drafts 498
  competition, credit period
    and 497
  consumer demand 497
  consumer type, credit
    period and 497
  cost, credit period and 497
  cost of credit, cash
    discounts and 497–8
  credit instruments 498
  credit period 496–7
  credit risk 497
  end of month (EOM) 496
  invoice date 496
  length of credit
    period 496–7
  middle of month
    (MOM) 496
  open accounts 498
  perishability, credit period
    and 497
  profitability, credit period
    and 497
  promissory notes 498
  receipt of goods (ROG) 496
  standardization 497
  time drafts 498
  trade acceptance 498
  trade discounts 498
Tesco 61–2

Tesla Motors 303, 560, 561–2
Thailand, debt to equity,
    estimated ratio in 442
3Com/Palm mispricing
    563, 564
Time horizon, liquidity
    preference hypothesis
    and 703
Time lines 92–3
Time to maturity, interest rate
    risk and 131
Time value of money 71
  calculations of 84–6
Times interest earned (TIE) 54
T-Mobile/Sprint 186
Tobin's Q ratio 57
Tokyo Stock Exchange 11
Total asset turnover, growth
    and 689
Total charge for credit
    (TCC) 108
Total costs
  break-even analysis 267–8
  output level and 268
Total credit cost curve 501–3
Total debt ratio 53
Total return 339
Total risk 339
  beta vs, example of 332
Total SE 371
Toyota 537
  Landcruiser 233
TPG 383
Trade credit 494
Trainline 383
Trans-Anatolian Pipeline
    (TANAP) 191
Trans-Atlantic Pipeline
    (TAP) 191
Transaction motive 480
Transaction types 526–7
Transactions exposure 576
Transitory changes, risk
    management and 576
Transparency International
    (TI) Corruption Perceptions
    Index 32, 540
Treasury bills 486
  average returns 297
  example of 111
Treasury issues 141
Treasury yield curve 150–51
Triangle arbitrage 524–5
Triple bottom line 8–9
Trustees, corporate
    governance and 23
Tullow Oil Plc 30
Tulpenmanie (1633-37) 566
Turkey
  bank loans as % of external
    financing 405
  debt to equity, estimated
    ratio in 442
Turnover measures 54–6
Turnover ratios 58
Twitter 640
Two-stage growth
  case of 168–9
  example of 168
Two-tier boards 21

Uber 71, 383
Unbiased forward rates
    (UFR) 533
Uncovered interest parity
    (UIP) 533
Underinvestment, selfish
    strategy on 432–3
Underwriters 390–93
  aftermarket 392
  best efforts underwriting 391
  choice of 391
  Dutch auction
    underwriting 391–2
  firm commitment
    underwriting 391
  Green Shoe provision 392
  gross spread 391
  lock-up agreements 392–3
  quiet period 393
  syndicates 391
  types of 391–2
  uniform price auction
    underwriting 391–2
Unequal probabilities,
    examples of 319–20, 321
Unfunded debt 136
Unique risks 327, 331
United Arab Emirates (UAE)
  bank vs market-based
    financial systems 33
  Corruption Perceptions
    Index (TI 2018) for 32
  Corruption Perceptions
    Index (TI 2019) for 540
  Economist Big Mac
    index 528
  exchange rate quotations
    (January 2021) 524
United Kingdom
  average annual returns
    of companies in
    (2011-2020) 296
  bank loans as % of external
    financing 405
  bank vs market-based
    financial systems 33
  bills and bonds in, equity
    risk premiums relative to
    (1900-2010) 298
  capital budgeting
    techniques, use in 211
  changes in 10-year
    government bond yields
    (2010-21) 572
  Corruption Perceptions
    Index (TI 2018) for 32
  Corruption Perceptions
    Index (TI 2019) for 540
  currency symbol for 523
  debentures, secured
    obligation in 138
  debt to equity, estimated
    ratio in 442
  derivative usage around
    world (% of firms) 589
  Economist Big Mac index 528
  equity data for selected
    industries in 171
  exchange rate quotations
    (January 2021) 524

732 Index

United Kingdom—Cont.
  Financial Conduct
    Authority (FCA) 432
  government bond yields
    (March 2020) 148
  histogram of returns on
    equities (1926-2019) 301
  international business
    angel networks in 386
  risk premiums relative to
    bonds in (1900-2019) 305
  small and medium-sized
    enterprises (SMEs) in 19
  stock market index levels
    (2010-2020) 294
  underpricing of IPOs in,
    determinants of 395
  yield curve for 150
United Nations (UN)
  Sustainable Development
    Goals 36
United States
  annual percentage rate
    (APR) in 109
  bank loans as % of external
    financing 405
  bank vs market-based
    financial systems 33
  bankruptcy laws in 445
  bills and bonds in, equity
    risk premiums relative to
    (1900-2010) 298
  capital budgeting
    techniques, use in 211
  Chicago Mercantile
    Exchange 581
  corporation types in 22
  Corruption Perceptions
    Index (TI 2018) for 32
  Corruption Perceptions
    Index (TI 2019) for 540
  currency symbol for 523
  debentures, unsecured
    obligation in 138
  debt to equity, estimated
    ratio in 442
  derivative usage around
    world (% of firms) 589
  Economist Big Mac index 528
  Environmental Protection
    Agency 261–2
  exchange rate quotations
    (January 2021) 524
  Federal Reserve 303
  Financial Accounting
    Standards Board
    (FAS) 635
  risk premiums relative to
    bonds in (1900-2019) 305

underpricing of IPOs in,
  determinants of 395
Unlevered cost of capital 427
Unlimited liability 19
Unsystematic risk 330–31
Unused debt capacity 639

Valuation, time value of
  money 70–90
  compound growth, note
    about 76
  compound interest 72, 74
    compounding over
      long horizons,
      example of 76
  compounding 72
  deceptive advertising,
    example of 79
  discount 77
  discount factor 78–9
  discount rate 78–9
    determination of 82–4
  discounted cash flow
    (DCF) valuation 79
  dividend growth,
    example of 76
  evaluation of investments,
    example of 81
  finding number of
    periods 84–6
  future value 72–6, 80–86
    compounding and 71–7
    future value interest factor
      (FVIF) 72, 75, 78–9
    problems with 73–6
  interest on interest 72
  investing for a single
    period 71
  investing for more than
    one period 72–6
  investments
    comic collectibles as 83
    example of
      evaluation of 81
  learning objectives 70
  mini case, Hreon SA 90
  notations 70
  periods, finding number
    of 84–6
  present value (PV) 77–8, 80–86
    discounting and 77–80
    multiple periods, present
      values for 78–80
    present vs future value 81
    single period case 77–8
  questions and problems
    88–90
  rate of return 82

reading suggestions 90
real world insight
  valuation of bonds 84
  valuation of
    companies 71
  reinvesting interest 72
  retirement, example of
    saving for 84
  review of issues 87
  saving for purchases,
    example of calculation
    of time required 85
  saving for university,
    example of 83
  saving up example 78
  self-test problems 87
  simple interest 72, 74
  spreadsheet strategy,
    time value of money
    calculations 85
  summary and
    conclusions 86
  time value of money 71
    calculations of 84–6
Valuation of mergers in
  practice 645–6
  calibration of
    valuation 645
  merger value 646
  stand-alone firm, valuation
    of target as 645
  value of synergies 645–6
Value
  dilution of 402–4
  of firm, cost of equity
    and 429–30
  of level cash flows,
    annuities and
    perpetuities 98–105
Variability of returns 299–303
  historical record 301
  historical variance and
    standard deviation
    299–301
  normal distribution 302
  return variability 299
Variable costs
  break-even analysis
    and 266–7
  example of 267
  output level and 266
Variance 299–300
  calculation of 300–301,
    320–21
Venture capital (VC) 384
  funding by sector,
    breakdown of 385
  realities about 387–8
  suppliers of 385–6

Verizon Communications 635
Vertical acquisition 634
Vertical integration,
  economies of 639
Visa Equity Partners 384
Vodafone 19, 76, 135, 635
Volkswagen 261–2
  beta coefficient for 332

Wall Street Journal 309
Walt Disney Company 226
Warburg Pincus 383
Warrants 142
Weak-form efficient markets 309
Webster's New Millennium™
  Dictionary of English 13
Weighted average cost of
  capital (WACC) 416
Wellcome Trust 23
What-if analyses 259–65
  see also Scenario and other
    what-if analyses
WhatsApp 640
Wheat market
  buyer, risk profile of 575
  grower, risk profile of 574
White knight 648
White squires 648
Winner's curse 243
Workday, acquisition of
  Peakon 640
Working capital 5
Working capital management 5
World annualized equity risk
  premium relative to bonds
  and bills (1900-2010) 298
World Bank 143, 582
World Health Organization
  (WHO) 143
Worldwide risk premiums
  relative to bonds
  (1900-2010) 305
Wrike, acquisition by Citrix 640

Yahoo! Finance 174, 364
Year-by-year stock market
  index levels (2010-20) 295
Yen for Euros exchange,
  example of 524
Yield to maturity (YTM) 127–8
  spot rate and, example of
    difference between 697
  trial and error in
    finding 132–4
YouTube 13

Zero bond coupons 142
Zero growth, equity valuation
  and case of 162